The Spanish Civil War

THE SPANISH CIVIL WAR

Revolution and Counterrevolution

Burnett Bolloten

The University of North Carolina Press

Chapel Hill and London

Publication of this book was made possible in part by a grant
from the Program for Cultural Cooperation between Spain's
Ministry of Culture and United States Universities.

The paper in this book meets the guidelines for permanence
and durability of the Committee on Production Guidelines for
Book Longevity of the Council on Library Resources.

95 94 93 92 91   5 4 3 2 1

Library of Congress Cataloging-in-Publication Data

Bolloten, Burnett, 1909–1987.
    The Spanish Civil War : revolution and counterrevolution
/ by Burnett Bolloten.
        p.   cm.
    Includes bibliographical references (p.
    ISBN 0-8078-1906-9 (alk. paper)
    1. Spain—History—Civil War, 1936–1939.   2. Spain—
Politics and government—1931–1939.   3. Communism—
Spain—History.   4. Partido Comunista de España—History.
5. Negrín, Juan.   I. Title.
DP269.B6563   1990
946.081—dc20   89-77911
                                                    CIP

To Betty and Gregory

Contents

Part I: Civil War, Revolution, and the Collapse of the 1931–1936 Republic

Part II: The Rise of the Communists

Part III: Curbing the Revolution

Part IV: From the Revolutionary Militia to a Regular Army

Part V: The Communist Triumph

Part VI: The Reflux of the Revolution

Part VII: The Eclipse of Largo Caballero and Indalecio Prieto

Part VIII: Communist Influence Crests

Part IX: Doubts, Divisions, and Disasters Proliferate. Communist Influence Wanes.

Part X: The End of the Resistance Policy

Maps

Foreword

*T*he Spanish Revolution was the most unique of twentieth-century collectivist revolutions. It was the only sweeping and violent revolution to take place in a West European country and, despite the eventual growth of Communist hegemony, it was the only truly pluralist revolution, carried out by a variety of distinct, often mutually competitive and hostile, forces. It was also the only major revolution in a larger country that failed, being completely defeated and overthrown by adverse military power. For all these reasons, the Spanish Revolution has never received the attention from students of comparative revolutions that it should otherwise command. Another reason for its relative obscurity in the roster of twentieth-century revolutions is what Burnett Bolloten originally called "the grand camouflage," the fact that it took place within a multiparty Popular Front Republican political framework, broke out only after civil war had begun, and was systematically presented by its supporters and propagandists abroad as something quite different from what it was. Ultimately, the perceived international importance of the civil war and foreign military intervention came virtually to monopolize attention.

The revolution occurred in Spain, in the broadest perspective, because of the unique historical situation of that country in the early twentieth century. During the 1930s, as for the past hundred years, Spain was both the least modernized of the larger Western European countries and civically and culturally the most advanced of the economically backward Southern (and Eastern) European countries.

Though Marx predicted the inevitability of revolution at the climax of industrialization, history has shown that modernizing societies are much more prone to severe conflict during the early and early-to-medium phases of industrialization. The low wages and extreme economic pressures of the earlier stages of industrial development, together with the concentration of masses of alienated workers in new urban environments, created potentially explosive conditions that become attenuated in the later phases of industrialization. Social rebelliousness was heightened in Spain by the simultaneous emergence of the modern agrarian problem—the demographic expansion of a large class of landless laborers and dwarfholders, mainly in the southern half of the country, whose economic situation actually declined in some respects during the slow modernization of the nineteenth century and who lived in greater real or comparative immiseration by the early twentieth century than during the final phases of the old regime.

The leftward trend of Spanish politics was at first unchecked by modern nationalism, the major mobilizing force of the right in some other countries but almost unknown in Spain save in the special regions of centrifugal micronationalism, where it only compounded social and political cleavage. Spain at first managed largely to avoid major international pressures on its domestic political development, staying out of the alliance system and not participating in World War I. It thus became a unique case, almost a special laboratory example, of the full range of modernization conflicts and potential sociopolitical rivalries found then and later in other countries, but in the Spanish case little influenced or distorted by foreign war, occupation, or overt foreign pressures of any kind.

Indirect foreign influence of a sort was nonetheless a factor in the final cleavage and breakdown of the Spanish polity. This came about not through direct pressure or intervention but simply through the mutual fear of the major Spanish political actors, as the internal polarization grew, that the worst examples of foreign political extremism were being imitated in Spain and that a Spanish version of either communism or fascism might soon triumph. This fear, which was palpable on the eve of the Civil War, served psychologically to justify the most dire measures to avoid falling prey to the equivalent of the worst foreign extremisms in Spanish guise, or so the militants of left and right came to believe. Thus, though not involved in international alliances and military conflict, Spain was in this way closely associated psychologically with the politics of the rest of Europe and fully prone to the worst political pressures of the period—indeed, because of the severity of internal division, prone to such pressures, even though of the Spaniards' own making, to an exaggerated degree.

If mass revolutionary movements came to Spain somewhat late by Russian standards, their growth was not at first contested by strong central nationalism and right reactionary forces, as in many parts of Central and Eastern Europe. That in turn led the revolutionaries to overestimate their strength, forgetting that underlying conservative social forces were nonetheless potentially stronger than in civically undeveloped Russia and that the international balance was quite different in Western Europe in the 1930s from what it had been in Eastern Europe in 1917–20. Both of these factors, the underlying strength of a partially quiescent Spanish right that was eventually mobilized by Franco and the weight of international forces, were ultimately decisive in the defeat of the Revolution.

The Spanish Civil War, within which the Revolution took place, was the most important political event in European and indeed Western affairs during the 1930s prior to the outbreak of World War II. Its importance to the world at large stemmed not so much from the domestic conflict in Spain as from the involvement and threatened involvement of major powers and equally from the manner in which the struggle was perceived in terms of the major political tensions in other countries. To supporters of the Republic, the war was normally cast as a contest between democracy and fascism, and indeed as the only forum in the Western world in which the advance of fascism was being contested at that time. Actual developments within the Republican zone were often little appreciated outside Spain. Almost as soon as the Civil War ended, attention was diverted to the general war developing in Europe, so that the Spanish conflict was viewed for years as little more than prelude or footnote to the European struggle.

Given the combination of cultural repression inside Spain during the generation that followed and the categorical lack of attention to Spanish domestic politics and history outside the country, virtually no serious study was directed toward the Spanish Civil War in the next two decades. Only after the beginning of the 1960s did a series of scholarly works appear that began to cast the Spanish struggle in accurate historical perspective and detail.

Of these new studies, the only one devoted to the politics of the Revolution in the Republican zone was Burnett Bolloten's *The Grand Camouflage*, distant ancestor of the present work, published by Hollis and Carter (London) in 1961. This constituted a major scholarly breakthrough, presenting for the first time detailed documentation on the political struggle among the major Republican forces during the first nine months of the Civil War. It lifted the events of July 1936 to April 1937 out of the realm of propaganda and party polemics onto the plane of fully documented history, providing a detailed account of the socioeconomic and political revolution of the Anarchosyndicalists, the POUM, and the revolutionary Socialists during the initial months of the Civil War, particularly in the regions of Catalonia, Aragon, and the Levante.

A second fundamental contribution of Bolloten's work was to document step-by-step the growth of Communist political and military power. This revealed the expansion of Communist power first in the Republican central zone and then progressively in certain others, with steadily mounting Communist influence in the army, the police, and political apparatus. If this was the dark side of Republican politics, it is all the more important that it be fully clarified. The cause of historical understanding of the Republic obviously could not have been served by any process that did not bring all major developments into the light of day, and the significance of Bolloten's contribution lay in the fact that it was he who pioneered the task. Reconstruction and understanding of the immediate past of Spain was not merely a pedantic exercise but in fact an absolute intellectual necessity or prerequisite for the effective and enduring reestablishment of democracy in Spain. It is no exaggeration to say that Bolloten's work was a noteworthy step in that lengthy but vital process. Thus Josep Tarradellas, first president of the restored democratic Generalitat of Catalonia, rightly called it "one of the most important books among the 15 or 20 thousand volumes that have been published on the war in Spain."

Yet, not altogether surprisingly, *The Grand Camouflage* often did not gain the welcome among historical and political commentators that it deserved. The book had in fact been completed in 1952, but because it opened up an entirely new perspective that contradicted much of standard opinion, it had been rejected by numerous American publishers, including five university presses. As Raymond Carr observed in his foreword to the 1979 edition of *The Spanish Revolution*, "Perhaps the title was unfortunate, in itself a camouflage which hid the fact that this was the work of a dedicated scholar who had combed every available source in order to reconstruct the confused politics of Republican Spain in the Civil War." Moreover, Hollis and Carter insisted on adding the subtitle "The Communist Conspiracy in the Spanish Civil War," giving the mistaken impression that the book was another anti-Communist tract.

Appearing in 1961, the book fell victim to the passions of the Cold War. Hailed by conservatives and anti-Communists as an exposure of Communist intrigue and domination, it was vociferously denounced not merely by Communists and pro-Communists but also by some other leftists and supporters of the Republic as an effort in some fashion to impugn or besmirch the Republican cause, even though that was very far from the intent of the author or the substance of the book. Bolloten's work in fact effectively refuted the rightist charge of a Communist plot to overthrow the Republic in 1936. It was nonetheless alleged that the author was an agent or employee of the CIA or some political force, and the book was cast in a totally misleading light in the pirated edition brought out in Barcelona by the Falangist publisher Luis de Caralt, with an introduction by Manuel Fraga Iribarne, three months after it had appeared in England. Despite Bolloten's every effort to block publication of what he called a "hurried and bowdlerized" translation, it was released in Spain before any action could be taken. (His repudiation of this edition first appeared in the *Boletín Informativo* of the Centro de Documentación y Estudios [Paris, June 1963].) The situation was rectified only with the appearance of an accurately translated and legally authorized Spanish edition under the title *La revolución española: Las izquierdas y la lucha por el poder* (Mexico City, 1962), with a subsequent edition published by the Institute of Hispanic-American Studies at Stanford two years later.

Withal, Burnett Bolloten was not a professional scholar by training or a university professor drawing a guaranteed salary. After his early years as a United Press correspondent, he lived an independent life as a freelancer and private businessman, eventually building a secure career in California real estate during the 1950s and 1960s. Though he taught briefly as a lecturer at Stanford University from 1962 to 1965, the need to earn a living on his own greatly diminished the time available to him for scholarly work. Not only did it delay the appearance of Bolloten's first book until 1961, but it also limited the scope of that work and made impossible its further development until after his retirement from business in the 1970s.

Only then did he have the opportunity to prepare an expanded study, which appeared in English and in Spanish in 1979 under the more appropriate title of *The Spanish Revolution*. This second book retained all the strengths of the first, especially its massive foundation of primary sources—which in fact has made it a reference work or source book for other historians—and its rigorous objectivity.

The Spanish Revolution provided much more complete treatment of the political struggle of the first ten months of the Civil War, including the climactic conflict in Barcelona during May 1937 and the ouster of Largo Caballero, not merely expanding the scope of the earlier study but including much new material. It thus became the standard and well-nigh definitive treatment of this whole crucial problem area.

Yet there remained the political history of the second half of the Civil War, on which Bolloten had been collecting massive documentation which he had never had leisure to prepare fully for publication. The 1980s were devoted to the final completion of this lifelong task, producing the present edition, which Bolloten finished only in the very last weeks of his long and remarkable life. The last third of the present work is totally new, dealing with the growth of Communist power—above all in the military and the police—during the balance of 1937 and well into 1938. The offensive against the POUM and other leftist dissidents (primarily *cenetistas*) is thoroughly treated, as are the two cabinet reorganizations of 1938. The peculiar and complex figure of Juan Negrín, ultimate wartime leader of the Republic, is more fully and carefully depicted here than in any other published work. Careful attention is given to the final phase of Republican politics, with its growth of defeatism and increasing revulsion against Communist domination. The concluding contribution of this magisterial work is to examine thoroughly the very last steps: the final controversial Communist reassignments in military commands, the role of Negrín and of the Communists in attempting a nominal policy of last-ditch resistance, and the development of the Casado conspiracy to overthrow them.

At the same time, extensive new documentation has been added to the main part of the book, made available since the broad opening and reorganization of Spanish archives. The product is thus not merely a longer and more complete work but in many respects a new and largely definitive account, the first truly thorough and accurate examination of the politics of the Spanish Revolution and the Republican zone in detail from beginning to end. It constitutes a monument of scholarship to which future students will be permanently indebted and is also a monument to the persistent endeavors of its author. Few have succeeded so well in so important and difficult an enterprise.

Equally important, Bolloten has bequeathed to future historians the enormous collection of primary and secondary material on the Spanish Civil War to which he devoted much of his life. The Bolloten Collection in the Hoover Institution at Stanford University contains 2,500 imprints (many of them rare items), 12,000 bound newspapers from the Civil War era, 10 large scrapbooks, about 125,000 frames of microfilm, over 67 boxes of manuscripts, and 2 large crates of assorted documents. This rich concentration of materials makes it one of the two or three most important sources in the world for the study of the Spanish Civil War. The legacy of Burnett Bolloten is truly an enduring one.

Stanley G. Payne

Preface

*B*urnett Bolloten died before he could put the finishing touches on this preface. Nevertheless, he left both written and oral instructions to be followed in completing his preliminary remarks. Rather than repeat in substance what has already been said in previous editions, I have chosen to include only the material that pertains to the present edition. This preface, then, is a faithful reconstruction of his notes (transcribed by his wife, Betty, and son, Gregory) and earlier drafts.

George Esenwein

In 1977, I began work on this present edition, which incorporates nearly fifty years of research and analytical study. Above all, this work reflects the extensive use I have made of Spanish Civil War newspapers and periodicals. Unlike those historians who do not appreciate the value of using newspapers as a primary source, I strongly believe that it is impossible to understand the passions, the emotions, and the real issues that touched the lives of Civil War participants without consulting the press. I have found that newspapers, more than any other source, reflect clearly the views and feelings of the numerous and diverse factions that were engaged in that terrible conflict. Over the years, close to five hundred different newspaper and periodical titles (some having as many as a thousand issues covering the Civil War) were consulted. In order to evoke the atmosphere of those troubled times, I have quoted directly from over two hundred different titles.

In the course of writing this edition, I have significantly enlarged the scope of my researches. I have amassed much new material in the form of newspapers, periodicals, books, pamphlets, microfilms, and photocopies of original documents. Most of these sources were obtained from research libraries and from public and private institutions located both in the United States and abroad.

For their stintless aid in providing me with materials and answering my inquiries, I should like to express my gratitude to all those persons, institutions, and publishers listed alphabetically in the Acknowledgments. But special mention must be made here of persons who have been of special assistance in completing this study.

I owe a debt of deep gratitude to Dr. George Esenwein, both for his friendship and for his valuable assistance over a period of eight years. He saved me countless hours of labor by hauling back and forth to my home hundreds of books and articles that he had found through interlibrary loan, the Stanford Green Library, and the Hoover Institution Library and Archives. This assistance enabled me to study the extensive range of publications from England, France, Germany, Italy, and the United States dealing with European diplomatic history during the thirties. As a result, I was able to elaborate upon a vitally important subject that was earlier developed in *The Grand Camouflage* and *The Spanish Revolution*. I greatly valued the long discussions I had with George and the friendly use I made of him as a sounding board. Among other things, these conferences helped me to solidify my thoughts and convictions on several intricate and extremely controversial topics. I am also indebted to him for the excerpts I used from his own writings and for the long footnotes he wrote expressly for me, which the reader will find in various chapters.

I am indebted to Professor Stanley G. Payne for his unwavering support and for his indispensable contributions to this edition. Apart from writing the foreword, he has generously given of his time in reviewing the manuscript. [Because the author was unable to complete the final chapter himself, Professor Payne was kind enough to write one section of the conclusion.]

Special thanks are due to my friend of twenty-seven years, Professor Ronald Hilton of Stanford University, now executive director of the California Institute of International Studies. Not only has Professor Hilton constantly encouraged me with his contagious drive and vitality, but he has also allowed me to draw upon his unparalleled knowledge of Spanish language and culture. Through the years Professor Hilton has been a powerful and effective advocate of my work, and for this I am most grateful.

For his unremitting moral support and help for the past twenty-five years, I want to thank Dr. David Wingeate Pike of the American College in Paris.

Hilja Kukk of the Hoover Institution has generously aided me over the years by ferreting out obscure materials from the library and archives and by painstakingly translating from key Soviet sources information that I have utilized in my investigations.

I should like to thank two Spaniards who have loyally assisted my efforts in publishing this and previous editions of my work in Spain. For nearly twenty-five years, Luciano Navas has provided me with the latest literature on the Civil War, and Pedro F. Grande has enthusiastically supported the publication and distribution of *The Grand Camouflage* and *The Spanish Revolution*.

Through her dedication and hard work between 1938 and 1952, Gladys Evie Bolloten helped to lay the foundation on which all my volumes on the Civil War are based.

In preparing the manuscript for publication I have greatly benefited from the work conscientiously performed by Mrs. Pauline B. Tooker (typescript), Mrs. Barbara Walker (bibliography), and Mrs. Myrna B. Rochester (index). Above all, Mrs. Tooker has been an outstanding editor and typist; her extraordinarily high standards as well as her deep concern and loyal support in seeing the manuscript through its final stages have been enormously helpful to me.

I should like to extend special thanks to the following people who kindly consented to read and make useful comments on a rather unwieldy manuscript of some two thousand pages: Professor Paul Avrich, Lewis Bateman (editor, North Carolina), Javier Pradera (editor, Madrid), Stephen Schwartz, Professor Paul Seabury, Professor Joan Connelly Ullman, and Ella Wolfe.

Betty and Gregory Bolloten have supported me to the utmost at every turn. They have assisted me in many ways and unselfishly devoted countless hours of work to the manuscript. It is largely thanks to their dedicated efforts that this edition has reached completion.

While the author acknowledges the contributions of the aforementioned persons and institutions, he alone bears the responsibility for the final conclusions expressed or implied in this work.

Author's Note

Libraries and Other Institutions Consulted

All data used in the preparation of this work can be found in books, correspondence, documents, interviews, newspapers, periodicals, microfilm, microfiche, and clippings held by one or more of the following libraries or institutions:

Archivo Histórico del Comite Central del Partido Comunista de España, Madrid
Archivo Histórico Nacional, Madrid
Archivo Histórico Nacional, Salamanca
Biblioteca Nacional, Madrid
Biblioteca Universitaria de Barcelona, Barcelona
Bibliothèque Nationale, Paris
Brandeis University, Waltham, Massachusetts
British Museum Newspaper Library, London
Centre d'Estudis d'Història Contemporània, Barcelona
Centre International de Recherches sur l'Anarchisme, Geneva
Centro de Documentación Histórico-Social, Barcelona
Centro de Estudios Históricos Internacionales, Facultad de Geografía e Historia
    (Salas Maurín-Nin)
Fundación Francisco Largo Caballero, Madrid
Fundación Pablo Iglesias, Madrid
Harvard College Library, Cambridge, Massachusetts
Hemeroteca Municipal de Madrid, Madrid
Hemeroteca Nacional, Madrid
Hoover Institution on War, Revolution and Peace, Stanford University, California
    (Bolloten Collection)
Institut Municipal d'Història de Barcelona, Barcelona
International Institute of Social History, Amsterdam
Library of Congress, Washington, D.C.
Ministerio de Cultura, Madrid (Centro de Información Documental de Archivos)
New York Public Library, New York
Public Records Office, Richmond, England
Servicio Histórico Militar, Madrid
Stanford University Library, Stanford

University of California Library, Berkeley
University of California Library, San Diego (Southworth Collection)
University of Michigan Library, Ann Arbor, Michigan (Labadie Collection)
University of Nevada, Reno, Basque Studies Program

Note References

As a general rule, when no more than one book or pamphlet by an author is listed in the Bibliography, only the name of the author is given after the first mention in each chapter. When more than one work by the same author is included in the Bibliography, the full title or an abbreviated one is given in the notes to ensure proper identification.

The place of publication of all newspapers and periodicals cited in the text or notes is given in the Bibliography. In the case of newspapers and periodicals having identical titles, the place of publication is also given in the notes for accurate identification.

The precise location of all documents cited, whether originals or copies, is given in the Bibliography.

Designation of Opposing Sides

I have referred to General Franco's forces first as "rebels" or "insurgents" and later as "Nationalists." The latter title was used by the supporters of the military uprising after they formed their own regime in October 1936.

On the other hand, I have used the terms "anti-Franco forces," "left-wing forces," and "Republicans" interchangeably throughout the book. Although the political accuracy of such labels as "Nationalist" and "Republican" may be questioned in view of the profound sociopolitical changes that occurred on both sides of the battle lines after 18 July 1936, this nomenclature has been used by most historians of the Civil War and has the advantage of simplicity.

Place Names

The following anglicized forms have been used:

Andalusia	(Andalucía)	Estremadura	(Extremadura)
Castile	(Castilla)	Navarre	(Navarra)
Catalonia	(Cataluña)	Saragossa	(Zaragoza)
Cordova	(Córdoba)	Seville	(Sevilla)

Accents on Spanish place names have been omitted in most instances to conform with English usage: for example, Aragon: Aragón; Cadiz: Cádiz; Malaga: Málaga.

Proper Names

The names of all Spaniards have been arranged in the index on the basis of the paternal name in accordance with Spanish usage. For example, references to

Francisco Largo Caballero will be found under Largo, the paternal name, and not under Caballero, the maternal name. However, he is frequently referred to by me and in quotations from Spanish sources as Caballero, which is the name both friends and opponents often used at the time.

Catalan Names

In most cases the Spanish equivalent of Catalan proper names has been used: for example, Juan Comorera: Joan Comorera; Luis Companys: Lluis Companys; Federico Escofet: Frederic Escofet; José Tarradellas: Josep Tarradellas. One notable exception is the Catalan name Generalitat, which has been used throughout the text.

Acronyms and Other Abbreviations

AHN	Archivo Histórico Nacional, Madrid and Salamanca
AIT	Asociación Internacional de Trabajadores (Anarchosyndicalist labor international)
BL	Bolshevik Leninists (Spanish section of Leon Trotsky's Fourth International)
BOC	Bloque Obrero y Campesino (merged with Izquierda Comunista in 1935 to form the POUM)
CADCI	Centre Autonomista de Dependents del Comerç i de la Industria (office workers' and retail clerks' labor union in Catalonia)
CEDA	Confederación Española de Derechas Autónomas (federation of right-wing Catholic parties)
CI	Communist or Third International (Comintern)
CLUEA	Consejo Levantino Unificado de la Exportación Agrícola (agricultural export organization in the Valencia region controlled by the CNT)
CNT	Confederación Nacional del Trabajo (Anarchosyndicalist labor federation, inspired ideologically by the FAI)
Comintern	Communist International or Third International (the world Communist organization, controlled by Moscow, uniting the national Communist parties or "sections" of the Comintern)
ERC	Esquerra Republicana de Catalunya (left Republican middle-class party in Catalonia)
FAI	Federación Anarquista Ibérica (Anarchist federation, ideological guide of the CNT)
FE	Falange Española (Fascist party)
FIJL	Federación Ibérica de Juventudes Libertarias (Anarchist youth federation)
FOUS	Federación Obrera de Unidad Sindical (POUM-controlled labor federation)

GEPCI	Federación Catalana de Gremios y Entidades de Pequeños Comerciantes e Industriales (Catalan federation of small businessmen, manufacturers, and handicraftsmen controlled by the PSUC)
GPU	Gosudarstvennoe Politicheskoe Upravlenie (State Political Administration, Soviet secret police, renamed NKVD)
GRU	Glavnoye Razvedyvatelnoye Upraveleniye (chief intelligence directorate of the Soviet general staff)
HI	Hoover Institution
IISH	International Institute of Social History, Amsterdam
JAP	Juventudes de Acción Popular (Catholic youth movement controlled by José María Gil Robles)
JCI	Juventud Comunista Ibérica (POUM youth organization)
JSU	Federación de Juventudes Socialistas Unificadas (Communist-controlled merger of the Socialist and Communist youth organizations)
ML	Movimiento Libertario (entire Anarchosyndicalist movement comprising the CNT, FAI, and FIJL)
NKVD	Narodnyi Komissariat Vnutrennikh Del (People's Commissariat of Internal Affairs, Soviet secret police, formerly OGPU or GPU)
OGPU or GPU	Ob' 'edinennoe Gosudarstvennoe Politicheskoe Upravlenie (Unified State Political Administration attached to the Sovnarkom, the Council of People's Commissars, Soviet secret police renamed NKVD)
PCE	Partido Comunista de España (Spanish Communist party)
Politburo	Political Buro or Political Bureau (the inner executive committee or controlling body of the Communist party)
POUM	Partido Obrero de Unificación Marxista (anti-Stalinist, revolutionary Marxist party)
PSOE	Partido Socialista Obrero Español (Socialist party)
PSUC	Partit Socialista Unificat de Catalunya (Communist-controlled merger of four Socialist and Communist parties of Catalonia)
SHM	Servicio Histórico Militar
SIM	Servicio de Investigación Militar (military intelligence service controlled by Communists)
SIPM	Servicio de Información y Policía Militar (Francoist)
UGT	Unión General de Trabajadores (Socialist trade-union federation)
UME	Unión Militar Española (right-wing military organization)
UMRA	Unión Militar Republicana Antifascista (left-wing military organization)
USC	Unió Socialista de Catalunya (Catalan Socialist party, merged with three smaller parties to form the PSUC)

Leading Participants

See index for these and other participants.

Abad de Santillán, Diego, leading CNT-FAI theoretician and militant

Adroher, Enrique ("Gironella"), propaganda secretary of POUM

Aiguadé, Artemio, councillor of internal security in the Catalan government, ERC member, pro-Communist

Aiguadé, Jaime, Esquerra member, minister in second Negrín government, resigned August 1938

Alcalá-Zamora, Niceto, liberal Catholic, leader of Derecha Liberal Republicana, first prime minister of the Republic, resigned October 1931, first president of the Republic December 1931, dislodged from presidency May 1936

Alvarez del Vayo, Julio, left-wing Socialist, Communist ally, foreign minister, general commissar of war

Andrade, Juan, radical member of POUM executive, former Trotskyist

Ansó, Mariano, left Republican minister of justice, November 1938, close friend of Negrín

Antón, Francisco, secretary of Madrid Communist party, inspector-commissar of central front, removed by Prieto

Antonov-Ovseenko, Vladimir A., Soviet consul general in Barcelona, disappeared in Stalin's purges

Araquistáin, Luis, left Socialist leader, close associate of Francisco Largo Caballero, ambassador to France

Arredondo, Lieutenant Colonel Manuel, Largo Caballero's aide-de-camp, removed because of Communist sympathies

Asensio, Colonel José (later general), Republican officer, Largo Caballero supporter, undersecretary of war, forced to resign under Communist pressure

Azaña, Manuel, left Republican, prime minister February–May 1936, president of the Republic May 1936–February 1939, member of Izquierda Republicana

Azcárate, Pablo de, Spanish ambassador to London, pro-Negrín

Baldwin, Stanley, British prime minister before Neville Chamberlain

Balius, Jaime, leader of radical Anarchist group "The Friends of Durruti"

Baráibar, Carlos de, left Socialist leader, succeeded Asensio as undersecretary of war

Barceló, Lieutenant Colonel Luis, Communist army officer

Belayev, Soviet NKVD operative

Berzin, General Ian K. ("Grishin"), principal Soviet military adviser 1936–37, disappeared in Stalin's purges

Besteiro, Julián, right-wing Socialist leader, joined Colonel Casado's National Council of Defense against Negrín

Bonnet, Georges, French foreign minister

Burillo, Ricardo, Communist, chief of police in Madrid, then Barcelona

Calvet, José, president of the Unió de Rabassaires, pro-PSUC

Calvo Sotelo, José, parliamentary leader of monarchist Renovación Española, assassinated before Civil War

"El Campesino." See González, Valentín

Cardona Rosell, Mariano, CNT national committee member

"Carlos, Comandante." See Vidali

Carrillo, Santiago, JSU secretary, PCE member from November 1936, PCE secretary after World War II

Carrillo, Wenceslao, left Socialist leader, father of Santiago Carrillo, director general of security until May 1937, joined Colonel Casado's National Council of Defense against Negrín

Casado, Colonel Segismundo, Republican army officer, operations chief of war ministry general staff, commander of central army, formed National Council of Defense against Negrín, March 1939

Casares Quiroga, Santiago, left Republican leader, succeeded Manuel Azaña in premiership and assumed control of war ministry, May 1936

Castro, Enrique, member of PCE central committee, first commander of Fifth Regiment, director of Institute of Agrarian Reform, subcommissar of organization in the General Commissariat of War, later (September 1938) secretary general of the commissariat, left Soviet Union and PCE after World War II

Checa, Pedro, leading member of the politburo of the PCE

Claudín, Fernando, Communist leader of JSU, broke with Santiago Carrillo after Civil War

Codovila, Vittorio ("Medina"), Comintern delegate

Comorera, Juan, PSUC secretary, former USC leader, member of the Catalan government

Companys, Luis, liberal Republican, President of Catalonia (Generalitat), ERC member

"Contreras, Carlos." See Vidali

Cordón, Colonel Antonio, leading Communist officer, head of technical secretariat undersecretaryship of war, Eastern army chief of staff, promoted to undersecretary of the army by Negrín

Daladier, Edouard, minister of defense, later premier of France

Díaz, José, PCE secretary

Díaz Tendero, Captain Eleuterio, left Socialist, pro-Communist, head of information and control department, appointed by Negrín to head personnel section of defense ministry

Domínguez, Edmundo, left Socialist, secretary of UGT National Federation of Building Workers, transferred allegiance to Communists, inspector-commissar of central front

"Douglas" ("Duglas"), General. See Smushkevich

Durán, Major Gustavo, pro-Communist, head of Madrid section of SIM, removed by Prieto

Durruti, Buenaventura, Anarchist leader

Escofet, Major Federico, Esquerra member, general commissioner of public order in Catalonia July 1936

Escribano, Antonio, JSU leader in Alicante province, opponent of the Communists, resigned from JSU national executive

Estrada, Major Manuel, Communist officer, chief of war ministry general staff, removed by Largo Caballero

Fernández Grandizo, Manuel. See "Munis"

Fernández Ossorio y Tafall, Bibiano, left Republican, director of *Política*, secretary of Izquierda Republicana, Communist ally, made general commissar of war by Negrín

Fischer, Louis, influential supporter of Moscow and PCE

Franco, General Francisco, military commander in Canary Islands at outbreak of Civil War, leader of military rebellion in Spanish Morocco, Nationalist generalissimo and head of state from October 1936

Galán, Francisco, PCE member, promoted to colonel by Negrín

Galán, Juan, PCE member, subchief of intelligence department, armed forces inspector

Galarza, Angel, left Socialist, minister of interior under Largo Caballero

Garcés Arroyo, Santiago, Socialist, Negrinista, promoted by Negrín to head SIM 1938

García Oliver, Juan, CNT-FAI leader, minister of justice November 1936–May 1937

García Pradas, José, director of CNT (Madrid), supported Casado's coup against Negrín March 1939

Gaykis, Leon, Soviet ambassador after Marcel Rosenberg, disappeared in Stalin's purges

Gerö, Ernö ("Pedro"), Comintern delegate in Catalonia, later minister in Soviet-controlled Hungarian government after World War II

Gil Robles, José María, leader of Catholic CEDA, escaped to Portugal

Giral, José, liberal Republican, prime minister July 1936–September 1936, Izquierda Republicana member

"Gironella." See Adroher

Goded, General Manuel, rebel general defeated in Barcelona

Gómez, Mariano, chief justice of supreme court

Gómez, Sáez, Paulino, moderate Socialist, supporter of Prieto, delegate of public order in Catalonia after May events, minister of interior April 1938

Gómez, Sócrates, opponent of Santiago Carrillo, attempted to re-create Socialist Youth Federation in 1938

Gómez, Trifón, right-wing Socialist, head of quartermaster corps, opponent of Negrín

González, Valentín ("El Campesino"), Communist militia leader, escaped from
    Soviet Union after World War II
González Marín, Manuel, CNT member of Madrid Junta de Defensa, joined
    National Council of Defense against Negrín March 1939
González Peña, Ramón, moderate Socialist, president of new UGT executive
    1937, supported Negrín against Prieto
Gorev, General Vladimir, Soviet officer, described as "savior of Madrid," ex-
    ecuted by Stalin
Gorkin, Julián, member of POUM executive, international secretary, director of
    La Batalla
"Grigorovich," General. See Shtern
"Grishin," General. See Berzin
Guarner, Colonel Vicente, police chief of Catalonia July 1936, ERC member
Halifax, Viscount, Lord Privy Seal, later foreign secretary and member of
    Neville Chamberlain's "Inner Cabinet"
Henderson, Sir Nevile, British ambassador to Berlin, supporter of Neville
    Chamberlain
Hernández, Jesús, member of PCE politburo, minister of education September
    1936–April 1938, chief political commissar of central-southern zone April
    1938–March 1939, expelled from PCE after World War II
Hernández Zancajo, Carlos, left Socialist leader, supporter of Largo Caballero
    throughout war
Hidalgo de Cisneros, General Ignacio, air force chief, moderate Socialist,
    joined PCE
Hoare, Sir Samuel (Viscount Templewood), member of Neville Chamberlain's
    "Inner Cabinet"
Ibárruri, Dolores ("La Pasionaria"), member of PCE politburo
Irujo, Manuel de, Basque Nationalist leader, minister of justice in Negrín gov-
    ernment, resigned December 1937, minister without portfolio until his res-
    ignation August 1938
Isgleas, Francisco, CNT councillor of defense in the Catalan government
Jurado, Lieutenant Colonel Enrique (later general), Republican officer, op-
    posed Negrín at end of war
Kandelaki, David, Stalin's trade envoy in Berlin
"Kléber, General Emilio" (Manfred Stern), Soviet general, commander No-
    vember 1936 of Eleventh International Brigade, disappeared in Stalin's
    purges
Koltzov, Mikhail, Pravda's representative, Stalin's personal agent, disappeared
    in Stalin's purges
Krivitsky, Walter, NKVD officer defected to West 1937
Kulik, General G. ("Kuper" or "Kupper"), Soviet officer, adviser to General
    Pozas
"Kuper" or "Kupper," General. See Kulik

Kuznetsov, Nicolai G., Soviet officer, naval adviser and chargé, entrusted with protection of Spanish gold on high seas

Lamoneda, Ramón, moderate Socialist, PSOE secretary, later supporter of Negrín and PCE

Largo Caballero, Francisco, left-wing Socialist leader, UGT secretary, prime minister and war minister September 1936–May 1937

Líster, Enrique, prominent Communist militia leader, commander of Fifth Regiment, promoted to colonel by Negrín

Lizarza Iribarren, Antonio de, commander of Carlist militia, visited Mussolini in 1934

Llopis, Rodolfo, left Socialist, undersecretary to Prime Minister Largo Caballero, remained loyal to Socialist leader

López, Juan, CNT leader, minister of commerce November 1936–May 1937

Maisky, Ivan, Soviet ambassador to London

"Malinó." See Malinovsky

Malinovsky, Rodion ("Malinó"), Soviet officer, survived purges, became Soviet defense minister with rank of marshal

Mantecón, José Ignacio, member of left Republican party, pro-Communist, appointed governor general of Aragon August 1937

Martí Feced, Carlos, liberal Republican, joined provisional Catalan government during May events, ERC member

Martín Blázquez, José, Republican officer in Largo Caballero's war ministry, defected to London 1937

Martínez Amutio, Justo, left-wing Socialist, leader of Valencia PSOE organization, governor of Albacete

Martínez Barrio, Diego, leader of moderate Unión Republicana, vice-president of the Republic, prime minister of stillborn government of conciliation 18–19 July 1936

Martínez Cabrera, General Toribio, Republican officer, anti-Communist, removed by Communists, placed on trial for loss of Malaga, exonerated

Marty, André, leading French Communist, Comintern delegate, International Brigades organizer

Más, Valerio, secretary of CNT regional committee, entered Catalan provisional government during May events

Maura, Miguel, leader of moderate Conservative Republican party, called for multiparty national Republican dictatorship before Civil War

Maurín, Joaquín, POUM leader, imprisoned by Nationalists at outbreak of Civil War

"Medina." See Codovila

Melchor, Federico, JSU leader, joined PCE November 1937

Méndez Aspe, Francisco, left Republican, pro-Negrín, involved in gold shipment to Russia 1936, finance minister April 1938–March 1939

Mera, Cipriano, Anarchist commander of CNT forces central front, supported Casado's coup against Negrín

Meretskov, K. A. ("Petrovich"), Soviet officer, adviser to Enrique Líster and Martínez Cabrera, survived purges, became Red Army chief of staff with rank of marshal

Miaja, General José, Republican officer, member of Diego Martínez Barrio's ill-starred government of conciliation 18–19 July 1936, president of Junta de Defensa de Madrid, PCE member, headed Casado's National Defense Council against Negrín

Mije, Antonio, member of PCE politburo, subcommissar in General Commissariat of War

Minev, Stefan. See "Stefanov"

Miravitlles, Jaime, member of Central Antifascist Militia Committee, ERC affiliate

Modesto, Colonel Juan, Communist militia leader, later Popular Army officer, promoted to general by Negrín, March 1939

Mola, General Emilio, Nationalist general, organizer of military rebellion on peninsula

Montseny, Federica, CNT-FAI leader, minister of health November 1936–May 1937

"Moreno." See "Stefanov"

Morón, Gabriel, moderate Socialist, succeeded Antonio Ortega as general security director

"Munis, G." (Manuel Fernández Grandizo), leader of Bolshevik Leninists (Spanish section of Trotsky's Fourth International)

Negrín, Juan, moderate Socialist, later pro-Communist, finance minister September 1936, prime minister May 1937, prime minister and defense minister April 1938–March 1939

Nelken, Margarita, left Socialist Cortes deputy, joined PCE

Nin, Andrés, POUM leader assassinated 1937 by NKVD

Núñez Maza, Carlos, PCE member, technical secretary in general direction of aviation, promoted to undersecretary of air by Negrín, April 1938

Orlov, Alexander, NKVD chief (Spain) from September 1936 until defection to United States, August 1938

Ortega, Lieutenant Colonel Antonio, PCE member, appointed director general of security by Negrín in place of Wenceslao Carrillo, forced to resign over Nin scandal

Ossorio y Gallardo, Angel, Republican jurist

Ossorio y Tafall, Bibiano. See Fernández Ossorio y Tafall

"Pablo," General. See Pavlov

Pascua, Marcelino, moderate Socialist, Negrinista, Spanish ambassador to Moscow

"La Pasionaria." See Ibárruri

Pavlov, General D. G. ("Pablo"), Soviet officer, commanded Soviet tank corps in Spain, perished in Stalin's purges

"Pedro." See Gerö

Peiró, Juan, CNT minister of industry November 1936–May 1937

Pérez Salas, Colonel Jesús, Republican officer, undersecretary of defense under Prieto

"Petrovich." See Meretskov

Pi Sunyer, Carlos, mayor of Barcelona, ERC member

Portela Valladares, Manuel, leader of Center party, resigned premiership February 1936

Pozas, General Sebastián, liberal Republican officer, commander of central front, made military commander of Catalonia and Eastern army during May events, PCE and PSUC member

Pretel, Felipe, left Socialist, UGT treasurer, secretary general of commissariat of war, transferred allegiance to PCE

Prieto, Horacio M., CNT national secretary until November 1936

Prieto, Indalecio, moderate Socialist, navy and air minister September 1936, defense minister May 1937–April 1938, forced out of office by Negrín

Ptukhin, E. S., Soviet air force officer, succeeded Smushkevich

Queipo de Llano, Gonzalo, rebel general, seized Seville

Ravines, Eudocio, Peruvian Communist, editorial staff member of *Frente Rojo* (Valencia)

Regler, Gustav, German Communist writer, political commissar of Twelfth International Brigade, left Communist party after war

Río, José del, Republican leader, joined Casado's National Council of Defense against Negrín

Rodríguez, Benigno, PCE member, Negrín's political secretary

Rodríguez Salas, Eusebio, PSUC member, general commissioner of public order in Catalonia

Rodríguez Vega, José, left Socialist, abandoned Largo Caballero for Negrín, became secretary of new UGT executive 1937

Rojo, Major Vicente (later lieutenant colonel, then general), chief of staff during defense of Madrid November 1936–May 1937, chief of central general staff May 1937–February 1939, pro-Negrín

Rosal, Amaro del, left Socialist, later pro-Communist, president of the bank employees' union (Federación Nacional de Banca), officially joined PCE 1948

Rosenberg, Marcel, Soviet ambassador September 1936–February 1937, succeeded by Gaykis, disappeared in Stalin's purges

Salgado, Manuel, CNT member, joined Casado's National Council of Defense against Negrín

San Andrés, Miguel, left Republican, joined Casado's National Council of Defense against Negrín

Sánchez Román, Felipe, leader of conservative National Republican party, joined Martínez Barrio's government of conciliation 18–19 July 1936

Sanjurjo, General José, monarchist officer in exile, leader of military rebellion, died in airplane accident on way to Spain July 1936

Serra Pàmies, Miguel, PSUC leader, left party after war

Shtern, Gregoriy M. ("Grigorovich"), chief Soviet military adviser from May 1937 after Berzin, perished in Stalin's purges

Silva, José, Communist, general secretary of Institute of Agrarian Reform

Simon, John, member of Neville Chamberlain's "Inner Cabinet"

Smushkevich, Yakov ("Douglas" or "Duglas"), commander Soviet air force units in Spain, perished in Stalin's purges

Stashevsky, Arthur, Soviet trade envoy, friend of Negrín, disappeared in Stalin's purges

"Stefanov, Boris" ("Moreno"), leading Bulgarian Communist, Comintern delegate, real name Stefan Minev

Stern, Manfred. See "Kléber"

Tarradellas, José, liberal Republican, premier of the Catalan government, ERC member

Togliatti, Palmiro ("Ercole Ercoli," "Alfredo"), leading Italian Communist, Comintern delegate

Uribe, Vicente, minister of agriculture, member of PCE politburo

Val, Eduardo, CNT member, joined Casado's National Council of Defense against Negrín

Valdéz, Miguel, PSUC leader, councillor in the Catalan government

Vanni, Ettore, Italian Communist, editor in chief of *Verdad* (Valencia)

Vansittart, Sir Robert, British permanent undersecretary of foreign affairs, opponent of appeasement, removed by Neville Chamberlain

Vázquez, Mariano R., regional committee secretary of Catalan CNT July 1936, national secretary of CNT November 1936 to 1939

Vidali, Vittorio ("Comandante Carlos," "Carlos Contreras," "Enea Sormenti"), Italian Communist, chief political commissar of Fifth Regiment, closely associated with NKVD

Vidarte, Juan-Simeón, moderate Socialist, undersecretary of interior May 1937, Negrín supporter

Vidiella, Rafael, member of PSUC executive, former leader of Catalan Federation of PSOE

Voronov, N., Soviet officer, in charge of Soviet artillery in Spain, survived purges, became president of Soviet Artillery Academy

Wilson, Sir Horace, Neville Chamberlain's intimate colleague and chief diplomatic adviser

Zabalza, Ricardo, left Socialist, secretary of UGT National Federation of Land Workers, opposed Communists

Zugazagoitia, Julián, moderate Socialist, director of *El Socialista* until May 1937, minister of interior May 1937–April 1938

The deepest tragedy for the intelligentsia involved in the Spanish struggle was that truths and lies were inextricably entangled, that the deceivers were also deceived.

It has been said that those who fought and died in Spain, with the bloom of their illusions untouched, were the lucky ones.

—Julian Symons,
The Thirties: A Dream Revolved

Part I

Civil War, Revolution, and the Collapse of the 1931–1936 Republic

Although the outbreak of the Spanish Civil War in July 1936 was followed by a far-reaching social revolution in the anti-Franco camp—more profound in some respects than the Bolshevik Revolution in its early stages—millions of discerning people outside Spain were kept in ignorance, not only of its depth and range but even of its existence, by virtue of a policy of duplicity and dissimulation of which there is no parallel in history.

—Burnett Bolloten,
The Grand Camouflage, *1961*

1

The Brewing Upheaval

The enmities that gave rise to the Civil War were not of sudden growth. They had been steadily developing since the fall of the Monarchy and the proclamation of the Republic in April 1931 and, with increasing intensity, since the victory of the Popular Front—the left coalition—in the February 1936 elections.

In the months between the elections and the Civil War, the Republic had experienced, both in town and country, a series of labor disturbances without precedent in its history, disturbances that were partly a reaction to the policies of the governments of the center-right that had ruled Spain from December 1933. In that two-year period—named *el bienio negro*, the black biennium, by the Spanish left—not only had the laws fixing wages and conditions of employment been revoked, modified, or allowed to lapse,[1] but much of the other work of the Republic had been undone. The labor courts, writes Salvador de Madariaga, a moderate Republican and onetime minister of justice, who, according to his own testimony, remained equidistant from both sides during the Civil War, assumed a different political complexion, and their awards were as injurious to the workers as they had previously been to the employers. "Simultaneously, the Institute of Agrarian Reform was deprived of funds. Viewed from the standpoint of the countryside and in terms of practical experience, of the bread on the peasant's table, these changes were disastrous. There were many, too many, landowners who had learned nothing and forgotten nothing and who behaved themselves in such an inhuman and outrageous fashion toward their working folk—perhaps out of revenge for the insults and injuries suffered during the period of left rule—that the situation became worse not only in a material but also in a moral sense. The wages of the land workers again fell to a starvation level; the guarantee of employment vanished, and the hope of receiving land disappeared altogether."[2]

Speaking in the Cortes, the Spanish parliament, on 23 July 1935, José Antonio Primo de Rivera, the leader of the Falange Española, the fascist party, founded in October 1933, described life in the countryside as "absolutely intolerable." "Yesterday," he declared, "I was in the province of Seville. In that province there is a village called Vadolatosa, where the women leave their homes at three in the morning to gather chick-peas. They end their work at noon, after a nine-hour day, which cannot be prolonged for technical reasons. And for this labor these women receive one peseta."[3]

Especially illuminating was the moderate Republican newspaper *El Sol*. "Since the advent of the Republic," it stated on 9 June 1936, "we have been oscillating dangerously between two extremes, particularly in the countryside. During the first biennium [1931–33] agriculture was burdened with a ridiculous working day, and the wave of idleness and indiscipline through which it passed ended by ruining it. The farm laborers received high wages and worked as little as possible.[4] . . . During the second biennium [1933–35] we fell into the other extreme. Within a few months wages declined sharply from ten and twelve pesetas a day to four, three, and even two. Property took revenge on labor, and did not realize that it was piling up fuel for the social bonfire of the near future. At the same time many landlords who had been forced on government orders to reduce rents devoted themselves to evicting tenant farmers. . . . These errors prepared the triumph of the Popular Front, a triumph that was due less to the real strength of the left, considerable though it was, than to the lack of political understanding of the right."[5]

And, under the influence of the mounting social ferment that followed the victory of the Popular Front, José María Gil Robles, leader of the Catholic Confederación Española de Derechas Autónomas—a loose federation of right-wing parties, known by its initials as the CEDA, whose nucleus was Acción Popular[6]—declared: "Without showing any indulgence of any kind we must give a social character to the CEDA. At first, certain groups will withdraw, but this does not bother me; it even makes me happy. The conservative classes in Spain must understand either that they make voluntary sacrifices by giving up a large part of what they have or that they will disappear for ever."[7]

On another occasion, he stated: "There are many, very many [employers and landowners] who know how to fulfill their obligations with justice and charity, but there are also many who, with suicidal egotism, as soon as the right entered the government, lowered wages, raised rents, tried to carry out unjust evictions, and forgot the sad experience of the years 1931–33. As a result, in many provinces the left increased its votes among the small cultivators and agricultural workers, who would have remained with us had a just social policy been followed."[8]

It was largely for the above-mentioned reasons that the victory of the Popular Front in February 1936 was followed by a grave crisis in the countryside that found expression in the strikes of land workers for higher wages and shorter hours; employers often replied by allowing the grain to burn or rot in the field. Two versions of this aspect of the agrarian crisis that complement rather than contradict each other were given by the Republican press: "Every day," said *El Sol* on 14 June 1936, "we receive letters telling us the same thing. The harvest is less than the average, but the laborers, without worrying about it, demand ridiculous conditions for reaping and threshing. In some villages, these conditions are such that the tenant farmers, landowners, small peasant proprietors, and *colonos* [peasants settled on the land under the Agrarian Reform Law] . . . affirm that they will have to let the grain rot or burn, because if they were to accede to the imperious and menacing demands of the unions they would have to sell every bushel at a price that would scandalize the purchasers. . . . Not only powerful landowners and comfortable absentee landlords cultivate the Spanish soil. There are hundreds of thousands of small proprietors and *colonos* for whom an equitable solution of the present agricultural strikes is a question of life and death."[9]

On the other hand, the left-wing Republican *La Libertad* stated on 26 June 1936: "In the countryside . . . there clearly exists a definite aim on the part of reactionary elements to boycott the regime, to drive the peasant masses to desperation, and place the government in a very difficult position. Otherwise, how can it be explained that there are entire provinces where employers intend leaving the harvest in the fields . . . , using it exclusively as fodder, whereas it would be far more profitable to pay the wages they should pay and gather the crop? How, too, can cases like that of Almendralejo be explained, where the employers swore not to offer a single day's work, threatening to kill any proprietor who did?"

The agrarian crisis also expressed itself in the rebellious mood of landless peasants, who had grown impatient of the Agrarian Reform Law of the Republic and of what they regarded as dilatoriness by government officials in the matter of land distribution. "Time is passing and the land remains in the hands of the political bosses," wrote a local peasant leader on 30 May in *El Obrero de la Tierra*, the organ of the left-wing Socialist Federación Nacional de los Trabajadores de la Tierra, the National Federation of Land Workers. "Disappointment is once again setting in, and we are on the same road as that of 1931. Is the Popular Front government going to destroy the illusions of the peasants? Are the peasants ready to see their hopes evaporate yet again? No. They want land, and those whose job it is to let them have it must not be surprised, should they fail to quicken their pace, if the peasants seize what the government does not give them and what they need so badly."[10]

On 11 April, José Díaz, secretary of the small but rapidly expanding Communist party, had demanded that the government accelerate the distribution of land. The number of settlements was insufficient. The big landowners should be expropriated and their lands distributed among the peasants without delay. The government, he continued, was not treating the matter seriously enough. "This is one of the fundamental conquests of the democratic revolution, and we should put forth every effort to achieve it."[11]

But in many villages patience had already evaporated, the peasants refusing to wait until the government—which was composed entirely of liberal and moderate Republicans—might satisfy their needs. On 7 March, *El Obrero de la Tierra* reported:

The peasants of Cenicientos in the province of Madrid have occupied in a body the pasture land called "Encinar de la Parra," covering an area of 1,317 hectares, and have begun to work it. When the occupation was completed, they sent the following letter to the minister of agriculture:

"In our village there is an extensive pasture land susceptible of cultivation, which in the past was actually cultivated, but which today is used for shooting and grazing. Our repeated requests to lease the land from the owner, who, together with two or three other landowners, possesses almost the entire municipal area—at one time communal property—have been in vain. As our hands and ploughs were idle and our children hungry, we had no course but to occupy the land. This we have done. With our labor it will yield what it did not yield before; our misery will end and the national wealth will increase. In doing this, we do not believe that we have prejudiced anyone, and the only thing we ask of Your Excellency is that you legalize this situation and grant us credits so that we can perform our labors in peace."

On 17 March, *La Libertad* reported from Manasalbas in Toledo province: "Two thousand hungry peasants of this locality have just seized the estate 'El Robledo' which [Count] Romanones appropriated to himself twenty years ago without giving anything to the people."

And an article in a Communist organ stated: "The agricultural workers of a small village near Madrid showed the way by taking over the land for themselves. Two weeks later the farm laborers of ninety villages in the province of Salamanca did the same thing.[12] A few days afterward this example was followed by the peasants of several villages in Toledo province; and at daybreak on 25 March, eighty thousand peasants of the provinces of Cáceres and Badajoz occupied the land and began to cultivate it. The revolutionary action of [these] peasants caused absolute panic in government circles. . . . [But] instead of using force, the government was obliged to send a large contingent of experts and officials from the Institute of Agrarian Reform to give an appearance of legality to the seizure of the land."[13]

A Spanish Communist wrote that the peasant leaders "calculate that the agrarian law plans fifty thousand settlements a year, which means that it will take twenty years to settle a million peasants and more than a century to give land to all. Realizing this, the peasants just occupy the land."[14]

The full extent of the social tension that gripped the Spanish countryside in the spring and early summer of 1936, writes Edward E. Malefakis, a leading authority on the agrarian situation before the Civil War, cannot be understood solely from a discussion of organized land seizures and strikes. "Just as the electoral victory of the center-right in 1933 had permitted the established classes to revenge themselves upon the workers in hundreds of small ways, most of them in defiance of the law, so, too, the victory of the Popular Front gave the workers license to impose their will with impunity. . . . Intimidation of all those who did not belong to the labor unions seems to have become the order of the day. Perhaps the most constant source of trouble was the gangs of workers who entered farms to force their managers to grant work. The stealing of animals and crops, and the cutting of trees for firewood or for lumber also became common." Referring to the province of Badajoz, Malefakis says: "Thousands of peasants wandered around the province in a futile search for jobs; farm managers of any importance continued to be subjected to repeated *alojamientos* [the forced hiring of extra workers], and small owners lived in constant fear that they, too, would become victims of the workers' aggression as the definition of the words 'bourgeois' and 'fascist' expanded to include property of every size." Malefakis observes that *El Sol*—"as objective a source as we have for these troubled times"—was deeply preoccupied by the fate of the small owners and tenants, whom it considered to have been more severely injured by the social and economic crisis than were the large holders.[15]

If the unrest in the countryside was a source of acute disquietude to the government, no less so were the labor disputes in the urban centers. From the end of May until the outbreak of the Civil War, the Republic had been convulsed by strikes affecting almost every trade and every province. Despite the censorship, the columns of the press abounded with reports of strikes in progress, of old strikes settled, of new strikes declared, and of others threatened, of partial strikes and general strikes, of sit-down strikes, and sympathetic strikes.[16] There were strikes not only for higher wages, shorter hours, and paid holidays, but for the enforcement of the decree of 29 February, compelling employers to reinstate and indemnify all workers who had been discharged on political grounds after 1 January 1934.[17] This measure was promised in Section I of the Popular Front program and was particularly resented by employers.[18] "We have had men pushed back on to our payroll for whom we have no economic work," reported Sir Auckland Geddes, chairman of the British-owned Rio Tinto Company, in April 1936, "and within the last few days we have had an irritating stoppage, the result of demands for compensation for what amount to accusations of wrongful dismissals of men who were in fact in prison for taking part in the revolutionary movement in October 1934 and to whom naturally we did not pay wages while they were in jail."[19]

The most serious of the stoppages that plagued the urban centers was the paralyzing strike of the Madrid construction workers. Although the Socialist trade-union federation, the Unión General de Trabajadores (UGT) accepted a settlement proposed by the government's arbitration board, the more radical Anarchosyndicalist labor union, the Confederación Nacional del Trabajo (CNT), rejected the award, seeking rather to transform the strike into a revolutionary confrontation with the employers and the state. In a sterile attempt to end the stoppage, which was punctuated by bloody and even lethal confrontations between members of the contending unions, the government arrested some of the Anarchosyndicalist leaders and closed their headquarters. Adding to the turmoil were the efforts of Falangist gunmen to crush the strike and the intransigence of the building contractors themselves, whose "rebelliousness," to quote from a statement issued by their national association after the outbreak of the Civil War, "contributed so much to the preparation of a favorable atmosphere for the crusade to reconquer immortal Spain. . . . It was we who gave the order on 10 June to close down all our workshops and buildings with a view to initiating this epic."[20]

The building contractors accepted the government's award on 3 July, but the CNT continued the strike in spite of the UGT's efforts to end it.[21]

A powerful psychological factor contributing to the prevailing turbulence was the memory of the repression that followed the left-wing rebellion in Asturias in October 1934. The rebellion had been triggered by President Niceto Alcalá-Zamora's decision to allow three members of the Catholic CEDA led by José María Gil Robles to join the cabinet formed on 4 October by Alejandro Lerroux, the leader of the Radical party. Since the victory of the center-right in the November 1933 elections, the Radical party had governed with the parliamentary support of the CEDA, but without its participation in the cabinet. The Socialists, who were the strongest opposition force, regarded the CEDA, whose avowed aim was the establishment of an authoritarian Catholic state, as the principal "fascist" threat and decided that if it were allowed to enter the government they would fight.

Because he distrusted Gil Robles and feared that the Socialists might revolt, President Alcalá-Zamora had avoided bringing the CEDA into the first government formed by Lerroux after the November elections, but since it was the largest parliamentary group and political organization, its democratic right to representation could not be forever denied. Although Gil Robles had never formally accepted the Republic because of its assault upon the church, he had nevertheless proclaimed his intention to respect the democratic method of attaining power and denounced fascism as a heresy. Still, his inconsistent and ambiguous statements alarmed the Socialists.[22]

"Clearly, the CEDA leadership did not regard itself as Fascist," writes Richard Robinson in his admirably dispassionate and meticulously documented study of the Spanish right, "but for Socialists the internal doctrinal niceties of the Right were unimportant. The negative critique of pure Fascism was for them irrelevant; the real question was, what were the positive intentions of Gil Robles? He had, in practice, accepted the Republic and constantly advocated the legal, democratic method of attaining power, the path of evolution; but in power, what would he do? . . . The ultimate goal of the CEDA was a State based on Catholic corporative principles. This State would be the result of a process of gradual transformation of the liberal-democratic structure by constitutional and democratic means. . . . The Socialists, however, were not inclined to draw a distinction between fascism and evolutionary Catholic corporativism, which, if it were attained would mean the end of Socialism just as the attainment of Socialism would mean suppression of political Catholicism."[23]

Although Gil Robles had ruled out violence and dissociated himself from fascism, he nevertheless alarmed the opposition when he declared in the heat of the 1933 election campaign: "We must proceed to a new State. . . . What does it matter if it costs us bloodshed! We need complete power. . . . Democracy is for us not an end, but a means for proceeding to the conquest of a new State. When the time comes Parliament either agrees or we make it disappear."[24]

"While it was inherent in [Gil Robles's] declared aims," writes Robinson, "that liberal-parliamentarism would be abolished some time, the bald manner in which he had now stated this conveyed the impression that it might be sooner rather than later. . . . Whether or not Gil Robles was clear in his mind about his intentions, his Socialist opponents were clear in theirs. . . . Largo Caballero [the left Socialist leader] told Socialists [in November 1933]: '. . . The enemies have already begun the war, and say through the mouth of Gil Robles that if Parliament does not serve their purpose they will go against it. All right. We reply: We are proceeding legally towards the evolution of society. But if you do not want this, we shall make the revolution violently. . . . If legality is of no use to us, if it hinders our advance, we shall bypass bourgeois democracy and proceed to the revolutionary conquest of power.' "[25]

When, on 4 October 1934, President Alcalá-Zamora yielded to the CEDA's demands for representation in the government, the Socialists declared a general strike. The strike failed everywhere except in the mining region of Asturias, where, supported by the Anarchists and Communists, it quickly developed into a struggle for power. After almost two weeks of fighting, this dress rehearsal in proletarian revolution and prelude to the Civil War was crushed with the aid of Moorish troops and Foreign Legionaries.[26]

The repression, writes a conservative Republican, a onetime Radical party deputy and an uncompromising opponent of the left, was savage and pitiless in its methods: "The accused were tortured in the jails; prisoners were executed without trial in the courtyards of the barracks, and eyes were closed to the persecutions and atrocities committed by the police during those sixteen months. Officially, there were only three executions. What clemency! But there were thousands of prisoners and hundreds of dead, tortured, and mutilated. Execrable cruelty! There we have the tragic balance-sheet of a repression that, had it been severe yet legal, clean and just in its methods, would have caused far less harm to the country."[27] And a liberal historian writes: "Every form of fanaticism and cruelty that was to characterize the Civil War [of 1936] occurred during the October [1934] revolution and its aftermath: utopian revolution marred by sporadic red terror; systematically bloody repression by the 'forces of order.' "[28]

As a result of the revengeful feelings that the repression engendered,[29] the animosity between workers and employers in the towns and rural areas, and, finally, the rooted antagonism between the forces of the left and right, the spring and early summer following the victory of the Popular Front in the February 1936 elections passed in a continual commotion heightened by provocations and retaliations on both sides. When, on 12 March, gunmen of José Antonio Primo de Rivera's Falange Española, which contributed its share to the swell of violence, attempted—in retaliation for the slaying on 6 March of several party members— to assassinate the famous jurist and moderate Socialist deputy, Luis Jiménez de Asúa,[30] the government proscribed the party and imprisoned its leaders.[31] But this measure was to no avail, for the Falange survived and even grew in clandestinity and, according to one right-wing historian, "served as a catalyst unifying the will to resist of certain segments in the country that were growing constantly."[32]

In fact, none of the measures adopted by the beleaguered government of

Premier Manuel Azaña, the leader of the liberal Izquierda Republicana, the Republican Left party, to calm the situation achieved their purpose and the State of Alarm—a milder form of security alert than martial law—that had been proclaimed on the morrow of the elections was prolonged month after month at the expense of civil liberties. Day after day and week after week there occurred fresh scenes of violence and effervescence: mass meetings and demonstrations, arson and destruction, including the burning of churches and Catholic schools, the closing of party and trade-union headquarters, seizures and attempted seizures of property, rioting and bloody clashes with the police, and assassinations and counterassassinations.[33] "Government censorship tried to suppress the news of strikes and assassinations because the ministers feared the contagion of violence," attests Frank E. Manual. "Copy for daily newspapers had to be rushed to the official press bureau for examination; the deleted sections appeared as blank space or with broken type. The Paris *Temps*, arriving a few days late in Madrid, was often more informative than the newspapers of the Spanish capital. Only when one gathered a batch of provincial papers and turned to the pages entitled Social Conflicts could one fully realize the scope of labor discontent for which there were no official statistics."[34]

"Everyone in his senses knew," writes a Republican army officer, "that Spain, far from being a happy and blissful country, was living on a volcano."[35]

In this turmoil, the military revolt—supported by a large section of the police, by monarchists and Falangists, by the powers of finance and business, by the majority of the Catholic clergy, by large landowners, by those medium and small holders, tenant farmers, sharecroppers, and *colonos* who chafed at the aggressive demands of their farm workers, and by the more prosperous segment of the urban middle class—broke out in Spanish Morocco on 17 July 1936, initiating the Civil War. Because of the extraordinary diversity of property relations among the small peasantry in the various regions in which they lived, the people of the countryside saw the Civil War not simply as a conflict between the landed aristocracy and landless peasants, as has been commonly supposed. As Edward Malefakis observes, "What is unusual about the Spanish case is that the peasantry instead of lending the bulk of its support to one side or the other remained so divided within itself that it is impossible to determine which side a majority of its members favored in the conflict. . . . [Other] civil wars . . . can be interpreted essentially as struggles by the peasantry against other social groups. In Spain, although this type of struggle was not lacking, the civil war was also to a very significant degree a fratricidal conflict of peasant against peasant."[36]

It must be stressed that the advocates of military rebellion did not wait for the psychic temperature to reach its peak before planning a coup d'etat. According to the testimony of one right-wing historian, directives for an insurrection were prepared at the end of February 1936, shortly after the elections, "should circumstances make it necessary as was easily imagined at the time."[37] The same historian reveals that the idea of a coup had been stirring in the minds of monarchist and army leaders ever since General José Sanjurjo's abortive revolt against the Republic in August 1932.[38] In a speech on 22 November 1937, Antonio Goicoechea, the leader of Renovación Española, the party of Alphonsine monarchists, declared that in March 1934, he and certain right-wing leaders had planned a coup d'etat backed by an insurrection of the army. He and other monarchists had visited Italy to secure the support of the Italian government in the event civil war should break out in Spain.[39] An eyewitness account of the meeting with Mussolini, attended by both Alphonsine and Carlist monarchists, and a reproduction of the resultant political and military accords—the originals of which are now among the captured Italian documents of World War II in the National Archives in Washington, D.C.—are given by Antonio de Lizarza Iribarren, commander of the Carlist militia.[40] According to this version, it was understood that no copy or record of the agreement would be taken back to Spain, but Goicoechea violated his promise to Mussolini by taking his own draft to Madrid, where it was discovered during the Civil War, much to the anxiety of Lizarza, the only conspirator who had not been able to flee the Republican zone. According to Lizarza, nothing came of the Rome agreement because the July 1936 rebellion was undertaken by officers not involved in the negotiations with Mussolini,[41] and the significance attached to the agreement is described by Ricardo de la Cierva, one of Spain's leading historians of the Civil War, as "grossly exaggerated."[42] But it is probably true, as Lizarza claims, that the accord helped to create in Rome "a climate favorable to the rebellion and therefore made it easier for Italy to decide to support the [Spanish] Army on 27 July 1936."[43]

Moreover, according to his biographer, General Sanjurjo, the leader of the abortive revolt of August 1932, had been urging that a coup d'etat be carried out just before the February 1936 elections.[44] Nothing came of this conspiracy, but the electoral triumph of the left coalition increased the resolve of rightist leaders to transmute their designs into practice.

Indeed, even as the results of the first-round voting were still coming in, together with reports of attempted jailbreaks, demonstrations, church burnings, and other outbursts of revolutionary exultation, *ABC*, the mouthpiece of Renovación Española, declared on 18 February that the revolution begun in 1931 would continue its violent course until it encountered an effective reaction in the form of "radical solutions without formulas for compromise and accommodation."[45]

At 4 A.M. on 17 February, immediately following the first round of the elections, Gil Robles awakened Manuel Portela Valladares, the interim premier and head of the recently formed Center party. "I described the situation to him in a few words: anarchy was already rampant in several provinces; civil governors were abandoning their posts; rioting mobs were seizing official documents.[46] If urgent measures were not applied with an iron hand, there was immense danger that the future of Spain would be enveloped in tragedy. . . . 'The strictest orders,' I said, 'must be given to the governors to act with the utmost vigor in those constituencies where new elections and run-offs will have to be held.' " Portela then telephoned Alcalá-Zamora. "I noticed that the President rejected outright

Señor Portela's proposal for the immediate declaration of martial law, although he authorized the proclamation of a state of alarm within a few hours. Fear of a military coup? I do not know. The fact is that a measure that might have averted so many painful events was not adopted. . . . [I] was dolefully convinced that in the summits of power there was neither the will nor the courage to avert the dangers threatening the heart of Spain."[47]

Later in the day, General Francisco Franco, then chief of the central general staff, apprehensive of the consequences of a leftist takeover, urged Portela to declare martial law rather than give power to the Popular Front. " 'I am old, I am old,' " replied the prime minister, according to the semiofficial Nationalist history of the Civil War. " 'The task you propose is greater than my strength. . . . It is for a man with greater energy. . . . Why not the Army?' 'The Army,' responded Franco, 'lacks the necessary moral unity at the present time to undertake the task. Your intervention is required, because you have authority over Pozas [General Sebastián Pozas, Inspector General of the Civil Guard] and you can still rely on the unlimited resources of the state with the police forces under your command in addition to my collaboration, which I promise you will not be lacking.' Portela was agitated and anxious. . . . 'Let me sleep on it,' he ended up saying."[48]

José Calvo Sotelo, the monarchist leader, then urged Portela to call upon General Franco "to save Spain," but to no avail. Fearing that the impatience of the left could not be controlled unless power were given to the Popular Front without delay, Portela, shunning further responsibility and in a mood of moral collapse, resigned on 19 February. President Alcalá-Zamora, who had recoiled from a declaration of martial law on the ground that he did not want to "provoke the revolutionaries," then appointed the liberal Republican Manuel Azaña as the new prime minister. Azaña hastily put together a cabinet of liberal and moderate Republicans to govern the country in the name of the Popular Front.[49]

It was not a moment too soon. Already local organizations of the Popular Front, according to José Díaz, the Communist leader, had overturned many city councils, "not by legal means, but by revolutionary means, placing them in the hands of Communists, Socialists, and left Republicans."[50]

To protect itself from the right, Azaña's government immediately adopted measures to secure key military posts. General Franco, who on 17 July was to head the rising in Morocco and later the entire insurrectionary movement, was relegated to the obscure post of military commander in the Canary Islands; General Emilio Mola, in charge of the vitally important Army of Africa, was posted to the provincial garrison at Pamplona in Navarre, the center of the Carlist monarchists or Traditionalists and their zealous militia, the *requetés*, where it was thought he would be isolated, but from where in fact he was able to direct unhindered the plans for the insurrection on the mainland and to conspire with the disaffected Navarrese;[51] while General Manuel Goded, inspector general in the war ministry, was transferred to the minor post of garrison commander in the Balearic Islands.[52]

"In wholesale changes on February 22 and 28 all the top positions were given to generals considered more or less friendly to the liberal Republic," writes Stanley G. Payne in his imposing study of the Spanish military. "In the spring of 1936, there were but 84 generals on the active list in the Spanish Army, for most of the 425 names in the *Anuario* [*Militar de España*] belonged to generals in various stages of retirement. Of the 84 men in command positions, the majority held moderate views on politics, and after the sifting and shifting of recent years few were monarchists or outright reactionaries. Almost all the major territorial commands and posts in the ministry of war were by March in the hands of generals known either for their pro-republicanism or for their sense of duty to the constitution."[53]

The measures taken by Azaña's government were so far-reaching and well-considered, writes Vicente Palacio Atard, a right-wing historian, that only one of the eight chiefs of the organic divisions into which Spain was territorially divided supported the rebellion. Moreover, none of the three inspectors general of the army rebelled, and the top positions in the Army of Africa were placed in the hands of persons of absolute trust. "The two most dangerous chiefs, Franco and Goded, on active service and with command positions, were confined to insular posts and were practically without mobility." Generals Joaquín Fanjul, José Enrique Varela, and Luis Orgaz who, with Franco and Goded, enjoyed great ascendancy in the army, were deprived of commands, and the last two were imprisoned. Thus assured of the control of the top positions in the army, Palacio Atard continues, the government assumed that it possessed "control of the army *from above*, the most effective method, based on the operation of hierarchical discipline in the armed forces." Other steps were taken to ensure control by the government. "If the changes in the military commands by executive order from the month of March to the very day of the rising are examined, there is evidence of unusual shifts in command positions, the meaning of which is very clear. To be sure, these changes did not disrupt the entire conspiratorial process, but caused confusion and agitated those who understood their significance."[54]

By mid-March the changes in command positions caused such unrest in military circles that Azaña's war minister, General Carlos Masquelet, issued the following communiqué to reassure leftist opinion: "Certain rumors, which would appear to be circulating insistently concerning the state of mind of officers and noncommissioned officers, have come to the knowledge of the minister of war. These rumors, which, of course, can be described as false and without foundation, tend indubitably to maintain public disquiet, sow animosities against the military, and undermine, if not destroy, discipline, which is the fundamental basis of the army. The minister of war has the honor of making public that all the officers and noncommissioned officers of the Spanish Army, from the highest to the most modest posts, maintain themselves within the limits of the strictest discipline, disposed at any moment to fulfill their duties scrupulously and—needless to say—to obey the orders of the legally constituted government."[55]

But the communiqué did nothing to allay leftist fears. *El Socialista*, the organ of the Socialist party executive, stated that its intelligence service had furnished it with "alarming news" and that to disregard the "ominous and threatening content" of leaflets circulating in the barracks, in the streets, and in political centers would be dangerous.[56]

Although the conspirators were concerned about the government's measures, they pursued their plans with undiminished vigor. That they might eventually rely upon the moral and material support of a large segment of the population seemed certain in view of the prevailing climate of apprehension and inasmuch as the parties of the right and center had received at least half the votes.[57]

The landed proprietors feared that the measures adopted by the center-right since December 1933 to undo the agrarian reform of the first two years of the Republic would be repealed. In fact, the abrogation of two of these measures was promised in Section III of the Popular Front program,[58] namely, the law providing for the return of their estates to landowners implicated in the Sanjurjo rising of August 1932[59] and the Law of Leases,[60] which had resulted in the expulsion of eighty thousand tenant farmers during the first two months.[61]

The employers of labor both large and small in the towns and rural areas feared that the laws establishing the system of labor arbitration and fixing wages and conditions of work, which had been rescinded, undermined, or allowed to lapse, would once more be revived. Indeed, Section VII of the Popular Front program stated that labor legislation would be restored "in all the purity of its principles."

The church feared that the anticlerical provisions of the Constitution, which had been disregarded, would once more be enforced, for Section VIII of the Popular Front program declared that "the Republic must regard the educational system as the indefeasible function of the State." Referring to the situation after the victory of the center-right in the 1933 elections, Salvador de Madariaga writes: "The Jesuits went on teaching: Azaña's plans for the substitution of lay for religious education in new institutions were shelved, and a law was passed granting the priests two-thirds of their salaries for the year 1934 as a gracious act of the Republic, politically wise, perhaps, but of doubtful fidelity to the Constitution."[62] Azaña's government, formed after the victory of the Popular Front, at first acted cautiously on this issue, for on 28 April only the Socialist and Communist deputies voted in favor of a motion to abolish stipends, and the motion was defeated.[63] But the new government formed on 19 May, with Francisco J. Barnés, a left Republican, as minister of public instruction, opened old wounds. "Azaña's government," writes Richard Robinson, "had on 28 February ordered inspectors to visit schools run by religious congregations. Apparently these inspectors often closed down schools on their own initiative. With the appointment of Barnés, however, it would seem that closure of schools run by the congregations and the illegal confiscation of private schools became, in effect, official policy. Cedista spokesmen [members of the CEDA] asked that no schools be closed unless there were places for their pupils in State schools. The minister replied that Catholics must now suffer for their sins of omission in failing to develop sufficiently the State system since 1933. On 4 June, the CEDA temporarily withdrew from the Cortes because the minister's insulting language as much as his policy gave 'intolerable offence to the Catholic conscience of the country.' Cedistas continued to complain of religious persecution, while the government went ahead with its laicising policies."[64]

Furthermore, right-wing and even moderate army officers, disquieted by the public displays of enmity toward the army since the victory of the Popular Front,[65] feared that their grievances against the military reforms of the Republic that had been instituted by Manuel Azaña, premier and war minister during the first biennium (1931–33), and had been partially redressed by the governments of the center-right, would now go unheeded.[66]

And, finally, all the forces of the center-right feared that although the liberal government formed by Azaña wished to remain within the framework of the Popular Front program—a program he promised to fulfill "without removing a period or a comma"[67]—broad sections of the working class and peasantry, spurred by their electoral triumph and apparently oblivious of the formidable power of the defeated, were determined to go beyond it, and that, judging from the revolutionary fervor that had gripped the country, the course of events could only be reversed by force, or, as one history favorable to the military rising expressed it, by "a surgical operation."[68]

Premier Manuel Azaña's inability to temper the revolutionary ebullience of the left soon became apparent. True, he had declared on assuming the headship of the government in February 1936 that he wished to govern "within the law and without dangerous experiments,"[69] and on 3 April in the Cortes he had condemned the acts of violence and the seizures of property that were embarrassing his government.[70] But, as *El Sol* pointed out on 28 March, his government was being subjected every day to greater pressure from the extreme left, which not only demanded, and obtained, the fulfillment of the basic points of the Popular Front program, but on many occasions hastened to carry out measures whose execution was being delayed. "This tactic," *El Sol* commented, "is in conflict with the sobriety of the prime minister. No one doubts this, but what can he do at the present time?"

It was clear from Azaña's speech in the Cortes on 15 April—three months before the Civil War—that he already discerned the approaching hecatomb: "I am fully aware that violence, rooted as it is in the Spanish character, cannot be proscribed by law, but it is my deepest wish that the hour may sound when Spaniards will cease shooting one another. Let no one take these words for incapacity or as an expression of a coward who is inhibited by or shrinks from the dangers that beset the regime that he has been entrusted to defend. No! We have not come here to preside over a civil war, but rather to avoid one."[71]

Despite this show of confidence, Azaña was in truth already an exhausted and demoralized man. "Intelligent and astute, Azaña—who would have governed wisely in a country not racked by a storm—lacked the vigor to handle the ordeal," testifies Claudio Sánchez-Albornoz, the famous intellectual and a member of Azaña's own party. "Once I saw him slumped in his armchair, exhausted, immobile. 'Albornoz, I can't take it anymore! What a country! What a situation!' "[72]

Azaña's inability to cope with the situation, writes Stanley G. Payne, was demonstrated. "The Prime Minister lacked the will to throttle extremists, perhaps because he was not certain that the Army would prove a reliable instrument of suppression. Azaña's reluctance or incapacity to use the forces of order to maintain order aroused great discontent among the military, the Civil Guard and even the Assault Guards. Young activists in the Officer Corps more nearly agreed with the disgruntled minority of ranking generals than they did with the majority of senior republican generals who tried to smile benignly at the dissolution of civic discipline."[73]

Under the aggressive directorship of José Calvo Sotelo, parliamentary leader of Renovación Española and the Bloque Nacional, the National Front, representing both the Alphonsine and Carlist branches of the Monarchy, the monarchists made what capital they could of the prevailing turbulence. "If a state does not know how to guarantee order, peace, and the rights of all its citizens," Calvo Sotelo declared in the Cortes on 15 April 1936, "then the representatives of the state should resign." Later in his speech he warned: "We look at Russia and Hungary, we read and review the pages of their recent history, and because we know that it was a tragedy, a short one for Hungary, a permanent one still for Russia, we want Spain to avoid that tragedy. And we tell the government that this task devolves upon it and that in order to fulfill that task it will certainly not lack the votes or support of those who are present. Ah! But if the government shows weakness, if it vacillates . . . we must stand up here and shout that we are ready to resist with every means, saying that the precedent of extermination, of tragic destruction that the bourgeois and conservative classes experienced in Russia will not be repeated in Spain."[74]

The right was becoming convinced, writes Richard Robinson in his detailed chronicle of this period, that the continued disorder and prevalence of strikes were part of a plan to bring economic collapse as the precondition for revolution. "On 11 June, the Cedista Carrascal stated that the Minister of the Interior had simply lost control of the country; [provincial] governors were acting independently of the ministry, mayors independently of the governors and the masses were doing as they pleased. A statement from the government the next day [publicly appealing to governors and mayors to put an end to the usurpation of authority by armed bands] suggests that Carrascal's claims were substantially true."[75]

Gil Robles, the dynamic and ambitious leader of the CEDA, had particular reason for alarm, inasmuch as a large number of his followers, disillusioned by the results of the elections and his advocacy of nonviolence, were either openly deserting him or, according to his own testimony, "were helping other parties [of the right] that advocated solutions of force, especially the Falange Española."[76] True, during the campaign prior to the November 1933 elections, he had threatened to abolish the Cortes if he could not conquer the state by democratic means, but after the electoral victory of the center-right he had defended evolutionary rather than dictatorial methods for achieving his Catholic corporative state despite monarchist criticism and increasing pressure for violent action from his youth movement, the JAP, the Juventudes de Acción Popular.[77] Ricardo de la Cierva, a supporter of the military rising, affirms: "Gil Robles is absolutely right when he described in [*Ya*, 17 Apr. 1968] the attitude of Luca de Tena [the owner of the Alphonsine monarchist newspaper *ABC*] in the following words, which are also applicable to the militant monarchists in general: 'He had no faith in legal methods; he regarded my efforts to get the right to live and govern under the Republic as causing serious damage to the Monarchy and believed in good faith that an appeal to force would better serve his ideals. . . . For this reason he always advocated insurrection, collaborated in its preparation as far as he could, gave maximum support to the [insurrectionary] movement in his newspaper.' "[78]

Even after becoming war minister in May 1935, Gil Robles had refused to seize power with the help of the military and the monarchists,[79] a refusal that in the years ahead they would not forgive. In 1936, faced by the mounting defection of his followers, particularly within his youth movement—which, according to a leader of the Falange, joined his party "almost en masse" between January and July[80]—and by the decision of the Derecha Regional Valenciana, one of the principal components of the CEDA, to prepare for violence,[81] Gil Robles declared forebodingly in the Cortes on 15 April: "Do not deceive yourselves, Señores Diputados! A substantial body of public opinion that represents at least half the nation will not resign itself to inevitable death, I assure you. If it cannot defend itself in one way, it will defend itself in another. Faced by the violence propounded by one side, the violence of the other will assert itself and the government will play the abject role of spectator in a civil strife, which will ruin the nation spiritually and materially. On the one hand, civil war is being fomented by the violence of those who wish to proceed to the conquest of power by means of revolution and, on the other, it is being nourished, supported, and encouraged by the apathy of a government that does not dare turn against its supporters who are making it pay such a heavy price for their help."[82]

Although aware, according to his own admission, that "fascism was sweeping ahead largely at the expense of the CEDA,"[83] Gil Robles nevertheless stuck to his nonviolent stand and declared in the Cortes on 19 May 1936: "Those of us who comprise the party, in whose name I speak, can feel neither enthusiasm for nor affinity with fascist ideology. You must understand that I do not say this in order to gain goodwill, which I know will by no means be granted to me; I say it because it conforms to a profound conviction both of myself and my party. Viewed from a purely national standpoint, a movement that carries a foreign label and is not in keeping with the characteristics and traditions of the Spanish people can have little appeal to us; if we look at the philosophical content of certain totalitarian doctrines regarding the state we cannot forget that they are saturated with a philosophical and political pantheism that is deeply opposed to our doctrinal convictions . . . ; if we consider the question of tactics we cannot, on any account, as believers, accept methods whose sole and exclusive aim is the conquest of power through violence."[84]

In response to his nonviolent stand, *No Importa*, the underground bulletin of

the Falange, declared on 6 June that it was "shameful to try to narcotize the people with the lure of peaceful solutions. *There are no longer any peaceful solutions*."[85] The Falange's aggressive self-confidence can undoubtedly be attributed not only to its mounting influence among civilians, but also to what Ricardo de la Cierva describes as its "increasingly preponderant role in the army, thanks to the growing number of [Falangist] members or sympathizers among the younger army chiefs and lesser officers." This, he points out, is another demonstration of the "youthful character of the uprising."[86] "It is most important to realize," he writes elsewhere, "that the average age of the military supporters of the rising was considerably lower than that of those loyal to the government."[87]

"The panorama was distressing," recalls Gil Robles in his memoirs. "I felt certain that it was necessary to do everything possible to divert the right from the path of violence . . . , but the truth is that the conviction was becoming rooted in everybody's mind that there was no other course but dictatorship to halt the anarchy that was draining our blood. Nobody sincerely believed any longer in the possibility of democratic normalcy."[88] And, on 15 July, after the assassination of the monarchist leader Calvo Sotelo, he declared before the Permanent Deputation of the Cortes, in what proved to be his last speech in Spain: "When the lives of our citizens are at the mercy of the first gunman, when the government is incapable of putting an end to this state of affairs, do not imagine that people can have faith either in legality or democracy. Rest assured that they will proceed further and further down the paths of violence and that those among us who are incapable of preaching violence or of profiting from it will be slowly displaced by others, more audacious and more violent, who will exploit this deep national feeling."[89]

Although Gil Robles argues in his memoirs that he wished to remain within the framework of legality, that he had never been a supporter of military coups, that, because of his opposition to violence, he was not kept apprised by the organizers of the insurrection of their preparations, that he did everything possible to avoid civil war, that neither the CEDA nor he personally participated "in any concrete way in the preparation of the rebellion, though some members collaborated in the initial work," that he rejected a proposal by General Mola, who was in charge of the rebel plans on the peninsula, for all rightist deputies to gather in Burgos on 17 July to declare the government and parliament unlawful, and that only after the insurrection occurred did the majority of his followers support it,[90] he himself offers ample evidence to suggest that he did more than straddle the fence, but was at times an active, if not enthusiastic, participant in the military conspiracy.

Rarely a day passed, he records in his memoirs, that some friend or provincial delegate of the party did not come to him for advice. "To all of them I gave the same instructions: to act individually according to their consciences without implicating the party; to establish direct contact with the military forces; not to form autonomous militias, but to wait for concrete orders when the rising occurred."[91] He acknowledges furthermore that at the beginning of July 1936 several party members requested him to turn over to General Mola part of what remained of the party's electoral fund and that he authorized the transfer of 500,000 pesetas to the general. "I was faced by a grave moral crisis," he confesses. "The donations to the party had been made solely for electoral purposes because at that time the struggle was confined to legal grounds. I am absolutely sure that, under the new circumstances, had the donors been consulted as to the employment of the funds, nearly all of them would have demanded that they be applied to what, unfortunately, was now the only way to prevent the triumph of anarchy."[92]

Moreover, in a document signed on 27 February 1942, while he was in exile in Portugal, but revealed many years later, Gil Robles stated that after the 1936 elections the use of force for the restoration of public order was legally justified. "No solution other than a military one could be envisaged, and the CEDA was prepared to give it all possible support. I cooperated with advice, with moral support, with secret orders for collaboration, and with financial aid in not insignificant amounts taken from the party's electoral funds."[93]

Nevertheless, he seems to have given this support only halfheartedly in the knowledge that the CEDA was disintegrating; and his refusal to comply with General Mola's suggestion that all rightist deputies convene in Burgos on 17 July to declare the government and parliament unlawful contributed to the "contempt," as one leading historian favorable to the uprising put it, in which he was held by the conspirators.[94] "My refusal obviously placed me in a very difficult position in relation to the insurgent military," Gil Robles affirms. "I deliberately attempted until the last moment to remain aloof from anything that would signify an incitement to violence. In view of the fact that I had advocated legal action for five years as the only form of public conduct, it would have been improper to attempt to ensure my political survival by any action that betrayed my clearly defined trajectory."[95]

Because of his indecisive stand and because after the outbreak of the Civil War the military preferred to dissociate themselves from the policies of the "old-time politicians,"[96] Gil Robles—whose organization in February 1936 held more seats in the Cortes than any other party—sank into oblivion only five months later. To be sure, his political eclipse appeared inevitable from the moment his policy of nonviolence resulted in mass defections to the Falange and in the growth of middle-class sentiment for violent and fascist solutions. The mounting support for fascist ideology and the spectacular change in the political panorama that had occurred since the February elections were noted on 12 June to "Gaziel," the pen name of Augustín Calvet, director of *La Vanguardia*, who was regarded as politically sympathetic to Manuel Azaña. Charging that the Popular Front had itself created the fascist menace, he asked:

How many votes were cast for the fascists in the last elections? Nothing to speak of: a ridiculous figure. If, after the victory of the Popular Front, we had had a good government in Spain concerned with the general interests of the country and capable of imposing its will on everyone, starting with its own supporters, that handful of fascists would have disappeared, pulverized by the force of reality. Today, on the contrary, travelers arrive from Spain saying, "Everyone there is becoming fascist." What has changed? What has happened? Is it perhaps possible that people have suddenly undertaken a profound study of political science and after extensive reading and numerous comparisons have come to the theoretical conclusion that the fascist regime is the best of all? No, man, no! . . . What is happening is simply that one cannot live there, that there is no government. Owing to the strikes and the conflicts, the state of uneasiness and the damage, and the thousand and one daily annoyances—not to mention the crimes and the attempted assassinations—many citizens are fed up and disgusted. In this situation they instinctively seek some relief and a way out, and since they cannot find them they begin little by little to hanker for a regime where these things at least appear possible. What is the type of political regime that radically suppresses these intolerable excesses? Dictatorship, fascism. Hence, without wanting it, almost without realizing it, the people "feel" themselves fascist. Of the inconveniences of a dictatorship they know nothing, as is natural. Of these they will learn later, when they have to put up with them, and then they will worry about them. But meanwhile they see in that form of strong government nothing more than an infallible means of shaking off the insufferable vexations of the existing lawlessness.[97]

2

Divisions and Deadlock on the Left

When viewed from the angle of social and political antagonisms that ravaged the country before the Civil War, the conflict was strictly Spanish in its origin. No foreign intervention was necessary to ignite the tinder of civil strife, although it is true that foreign powers used the war for their own purposes. Weeks before the outbreak of the military revolt, weeks before the first foreign airplane or tank reached Spain, the country was ripe for a conflagration. Only the failure of the revolt in the main cities of Madrid, Barcelona, Valencia, Malaga, and Bilbao, a failure that ruined all possibility of the decisive initial victory planned by the insurgents,[1] was necessary to precipitate a far-reaching social revolution that was more profound in some respects than the Bolshevik Revolution in its early stages. Instead of protecting the propertied classes from the incursions of the left, the military revolt—to use the phrase of Federica Montseny, a prominent member of the FAI, the Federación Anarquista Ibérica, the formidable Iberian Anarchist Federation, whose goal was the establishment of anarchist or libertarian communism—"hastened the revolution we all desired, but no one had expected so soon."[2]

She was addressing herself, of course, to the powerful Anarchosyndicalist or Anarchist-oriented labor federation, the CNT, over which the FAI strove to exercise a guiding influence and which had condemned the Popular Front program as a "profoundly conservative document"[3] out of harmony with the "revolutionary fever that Spain was sweating through her pores."[4]

But she in no way expressed the feelings of the substantial body of moderate opinion represented in the Popular Front coalition. Certainly a revolution was not desired by Premier Manuel Azaña, the leader of the Republican Left party, who became president of the Republic on 10 May. Nor was it desired by his party colleague and intimate associate, Santiago Casares Quiroga, who succeeded him in the premiership on 13 May and at the same time assumed control of the war ministry.[5]

Nor was a revolution desired by other leading politicians of the party, whose membership was mainly recruited from the civil service, liberal professions, small landowners and tenant farmers, and small traders and manufacturers. Nor was it desired by Diego Martínez Barrio, speaker of the Cortes, vice-president of the Republic, and grand master of the Spanish Grand Orient, whose party, the Unión Republicana, the Republican Union party—a split-off from Alejandro Lerroux's Radical party—formed the most moderate section of the Popular Front coalition, and had, together with Azaña's party, declared its opposition, in the Popular Front program itself, to working-class control of production as well as to the nationalization and free distribution of the land to the peasants.[6]

Nor, indeed, was a revolution desired by Julián Besteiro, the leader of the small right-wing faction of the Socialist party, or by Indalecio Prieto, the leader of the moderate or center faction, who controlled the executive committee and who, in distinction from the numerically stronger left-wing Socialists led by Francisco Largo Caballero, the secretary of the powerful labor federation, the UGT, had pursued a policy of restraint in the months preceding the rebellion and had denounced the strikes and disorders that had racked the country.[7]

"Two positions, equally disinterested and honest," writes Julián Zugazagoitia, a moderate Socialist and director before the Civil War of *El Socialista*, "confronted each other in the Socialist party: the majority, led by Largo Caballero, that regarded the coalition with the republicans as a thing of the past and advocated the formation of a united working-class front with a view to the total exercise of power . . . : the minority personified by Prieto, that took into account the realities of the Spanish scene, and considered, inasmuch as the conservative parties were fighting resolutely, that any dissociation from the Republic and the republicans would be extremely dangerous. . . . Largo Caballero and his principal collaborators, [Luis] Araquistáin and [Julio] Alvarez del Vayo, believed that a military coup would be condemned to inevitable defeat both by the opposition of the state and the action of the workers through a general strike. . . . [The] social symptoms of the period . . . , far from causing them the slightest anxiety, aroused in them a secret sense of satisfaction in view of the fact that the strikes, disputes, and bloody encounters represented the governmental failure of the republicans."[8]

Although Largo Caballero had signed the Popular Front program,[9] he did not regard the alliance with the liberal Republicans as more than a temporary coalition to achieve victory at the polls. On 12 January 1936, a few days before the publication of the program, he had made his future position sufficiently clear:

> [Our] duty is to establish socialism. And when I speak of socialism . . . I speak of Marxist socialism. . . . Our aspiration is the conquest of political power. By what means? Those we are able to use! . . . [Let] it be well understood that by going with the left republicans we are mortgaging absolutely nothing of our ideology and action. Nor do I believe that they demand this of us, because to do so would be the same as asking us to betray our ideas. It is an alliance, a circumstantial coalition, for which a program is being prepared that is certainly not going to satisfy us, but that I say here and now to all those present and to all those who can hear and read that . . . everyone, everyone united, must fight to defend. . . . Do not be dismayed, do not be disheartened, if you do not see things

in the program that are absolutely basic to our ideology. No! That must never be a reason for ceasing to work with complete faith and enthusiasm for victory. We must do so in spite of everything. That way, comrades, after victory, and freed of every kind of commitment, we shall be able to say to everyone, absolutely everyone, that we shall pursue our course without interruption, if possible, until the triumph of our ideals.[10]

A former stucco worker, a reformist for more than forty years, except for an occasional spurt of revolutionary activity, a labor delegate in General Primo de Rivera's Council of State during the dictatorship, Caballero, after two years of disillusionment as minister of labor during the Republican-Socialist coalition, had been fired in 1933 by revolutionary ideas and had become metamorphosed— at the age of sixty-four—into the exponent of the left wing of Spanish socialism.

This radical transformation had been brought about to a large extent by the apathy or indifference of the liberal Republicans led by Manuel Azaña toward the implementation of the Agrarian Reform Law enacted in September 1932. In truth, they were more concerned with their anticlericalism than with executing a serious program of land reform. The Republican parties, writes Malefakis, had been nurtured on anticlericalism, antimilitarism, and antimonarchism. "The deepest emotions of these heirs to the French Revolution were awakened by the anti-aristocratic implications of the agrarian reform rather than by the reform itself. Azaña perfectly typified these attitudes. . . . On agrarian matters he eloquently pleaded for reform in a number of speeches during the first enthusiastic months of the Republic but thereafter remained silent. Except in two instances, one searches in vain in the three volumes of his collected speeches for more than a passing reference to what was, after all, probably the most urgent question of the day."[11] In a subsequent passage, Malefakis affirms: "The Left Republicans were led to espouse agrarian reform partly to gain the support of the Socialists for their political and cultural reforms, partly because they considered it necessary for the maintenance of social order, and partly because the humanitarian instincts of their liberal philosophy dictated the freeing of the peasantry. None of these reasons was sufficient to sustain them once the tremendous cost of the reform, as well as its inevitable violation of the respect of the property rights and for individual economic opportunity which have constituted the core of the liberal philosophy, became apparent. As a result they began to hedge upon their commitment almost as soon as the Agrarian Reform Law was enacted."[12]

The refusal of the Republican parties to treat agrarian reform seriously, writes Gerald Brenan, in his classic work, *The Spanish Labyrinth*, lay at the root of the Socialists' disillusion with the Republic. "It was a feeling that welled up from below, affecting the young more than the old, the recently joined rather than the confirmed party men. . . . This feeling found a leader in Largo Caballero. As [secretary] of the UGT he was especially alive to the danger of losing ground to the Anarcho-Syndicalists. And he had also a personal grievance. First of all he had quarrelled with Azaña. Then as Minister of Labor he had been especially disgusted at the way in which much of the legislation drawn up by him had been sabotaged. . . . Thus it came about that already in February 1934 he was saying that 'the only hope of the masses is now in social revolution. It alone can save Spain from Fascism.' "[13]

Around him had gathered the mass of Socialist workers and the majority of members of the powerful Socialist youth movement, the Federación Nacional de Juventudes Socialistas, who, dissatisfied with the results of collaboration with the liberal Republicans and with the "reformist" tendencies within the Socialist party, the Partido Socialista Obrero Español (PSOE), wished to bring about the radicalization or "Bolshevization" of the party and the expulsion from its ranks of all reformist or centrist elements.[14] These goals were clearly enunciated in the clandestine but widely read pamphlet, *Octubre, segunda etapa*, which was drawn up in 1935 by the leaders of the Socialist youth federation then in jail for their part in the October 1934 uprising.[15] Largo Caballero was proclaimed "chief and initiator of this revolutionary resurgence,"[16] and shortly thereafter he was hailed by his followers as the "Spanish Lenin."[17] Although esteemed for his simplicity, personal integrity and incorruptibility by opponents inside and outside his own party,[18] Largo Caballero was on this occasion carried away by the enthusiasm of his own supporters and never repudiated the appellation, which only events would disavow. In fact, when interviewed in his cell in 1935, after the October uprising, he affirmed: "You see here behind bars the future master of Spain! Lenin declared Spain would be the second Soviet Republic in Europe. Lenin's prophecy will come true. I shall be the second Lenin who shall make it come true."[19]

In March 1936, four months before the Civil War, the influential Madrid Socialist organization, the Agrupación Socialista Madrileña, over which Largo Caballero presided, had drafted a new program for the Socialist party to be submitted to its next national congress, affirming that its "immediate aim" was "the conquest of political power by the working class by whatever means possible" and "the dictatorship of the proletariat organized as a working-class democracy." "The illusion that the proletarian Socialist revolution . . . can be achieved by reforming the existing state must be eliminated," ran the preamble. "There is no course but to destroy its roots. . . . Imperceptibly, the dictatorship of the proletariat or workers' democracy will be converted into a full democracy, without classes, from which the coercive state will gradually disappear. The instrument of the dictatorship will be the Socialist party, which will exercise this dictatorship during the period of transition from one society to another and as long as the surrounding capitalist states make a strong proletarian state necessary."[20]

Clearly, some of the language of the program enunciated by the Madrid Socialist organization was borrowed from the standard works of Lenin and Stalin, whose teachings the aging Caballero had studied and embraced only in recent years. In the succeeding months, aglow with his revolutionary faith, Caballero toured the provincial capitals, proclaiming before rapt audiences that the Popular

Front program could not solve the problems of Spain and that a working-class dictatorship was necessary.[21]

Caballero's revolutionary stance deepened the already irreconcilable divisions within the Socialist party. Julián Besteiro, the dignified, soft-spoken and once influential "academic" Marxist, representing the right wing of the party, who had urged his Socialist colleagues in 1933 to accept democracy and had remonstrated that "the illusion of the dictatorship of the proletariat is paid for too dearly,"[22] had retired into the background,[23] and the struggle for control of the Socialist movement between the revolutionary Caballero and the evolutionary Prieto—at once political and highly personal—had moved to center stage. To Prieto, Caballero was irresponsible: "He is a fool who wants to appear clever: He is a frigid bureaucrat who plays the role of a mad fanatic."[24] Prieto held that the Socialists were not strong enough to carry out a successful revolution and should solidify their alliance with the Republicans. To Caballero, Prieto's reformism was anathema, and he regarded his opponent as a "republicanoid" rather than a Socialist. "For me," he wrote in *Mis recuerdos*, his published memoirs, "Prieto was never a Socialist . . . either in his ideas or his actions." "[He] was envious, arrogant, and disdainful; he believed he was superior to everyone; he would tolerate no one who cast the slightest shadow in his path."[25]

Although Largo Caballero's adherents greatly outnumbered those of Prieto, the latter derived his strength from his control of the party's executive committee and its organ, *El Socialista*, as well as from his control of some of the local sections. Largo Caballero's strength, on the other hand, came from the UGT, from the vigorous Socialist youth movement, from most of the local sections of the party, particularly the Agrupación Socialista Madrileña, and from his mouthpiece *Claridad*. So bitter was the feuding between the two factions on the crucial issue of revolution or evolution that on one occasion, when Prieto and two famous Asturian miners' leaders, Ramón González Peña and Belarmino Tomás, were scheduled to speak at a mass meeting in Ecija, they were forced to flee under a hail of bullets.[26]

This infighting led Salvador de Madariaga, independent Republican and historian, to assert: "*What made the Spanish Civil War inevitable was the Civil War within the Socialist Party*. . . . No wonder Fascism grew. Let no one argue that it was Fascist violence that developed Socialist violence . . . ; it was not at the Fascists that Largo Caballero's gunmen shot but at their brother Socialists. . . . It was [Largo Caballero's] avowed, nay, his proclaimed policy to rush Spain on to the dictatorship of the proletariat. Thus pushed on the road to violence, the nation, always prone to it, became more violent than ever. This suited the Fascists admirably, for they are nothing if not lovers and adepts of violence."[27]

In the months before the Civil War, the official relations between Largo Caballero and the Communist party (PCE), a small if rapidly growing force, were on such a friendly footing that the left Socialist leader had encouraged the fusion of the Socialist and Communist trade-union federations[28] as well as the merging of the parties' youth organizations. Moreover, in March 1936, the Caballero-controlled Madrid section of the Socialist party had decided to propose at the next national congress the fusion of the Socialist and Communist parties,[29] a merger the Communists themselves also strongly advocated.[30] As Stanley G. Payne points out, the left-wing Socialists had "extraordinarily naïve and uncritical notions about affiliating with the Comintern and cooperating with the Communist party, and when they spoke of union with the latter they conceived of it as the eventual absorption of the Communists by the Socialist party."[31]

Largo Caballero had personally recommended this amalgamation in several public statements[32] and had replied favorably to a Communist proposal that a liaison committee representing both parties be formed with a program designed "to facilitate the development of the democratic revolution and to carry it to its final consequences."[33] This stand, in strident contrast to that of Indalecio Prieto, who was hostile through and through to the Communists, was warmly praised by José Díaz, the secretary of the PCE: "The masses of the Socialist party . . . see in the line of Largo Caballero the one that approaches most the revolutionary path, the path of the Communist party and the Communist International."[34]

But in spite of the smooth course of their official relations with Caballero, the Communists were disturbed by the left Socialist leader's agitation for an immediate social overturn, for they were then endeavoring to strengthen the Popular Front by reinforcing their contacts with the liberal Republicans in accordance with the Kremlin's foreign policy. In fact, José Díaz, while publicly urging the creation of workers' and peasants' alliances "as future organs of power"[35] and frankly acknowledging that the dictatorship of the proletariat was the party's ultimate goal,[36] declared in an oblique reference to Largo Caballero's ultra-revolutionary posture: "We must oppose every manifestation of exaggerated impatience and every attempt to break up the Popular Front prematurely. The Popular Front must continue. We have still a long way to travel with the Left Republicans."[37] In private, the Communists used such phrases as "infantile leftist"[38] and "senile leftist sickness"[39] to characterize Caballero's tendencies.[40] But they could not afford to press their differences with the left Socialist leader, for his popularity had reached its peak, and they valued his utility as a link between themselves and the masses that followed him.[41] Moreover, the idea of working-class unity had laid hold of his imagination, and this promised to facilitate the fusion of the PSOE and the PCE as it had already facilitated the merging of their respective trade-union organizations and youth movements. "The important point for the unity movement," affirmed José Díaz, "and for the whole advance of the revolution in Spain is that the line represented by Largo Caballero should gain the victory in the Socialist party."[42] Writing shortly after the fusion of the Union of Young Communists and the Socialist Youth Federation in April 1936, Santiago Carrillo, the leader of the united organization, the Federación de Juventudes Socialistas Unificadas, known as the JSU, stated in reference to conversations he and other representatives of the two youth movements had previously held in

Moscow: "As Manuilski, the old Bolshevik, told us . . . , the important thing now for the movement of unity and for the whole course of the Spanish Revolution is that the tendency represented by Largo Caballero should triumph in the Socialist party. If this victory does not occur, unity and the very future of the Revolution—I continue to quote Manuilski—would be compromised."[43]

The center faction of the PSOE led by Indalecio Prieto viewed the growing threat of Communist influence in the Socialist movement with unconcealed animosity. It condemned their campaign for the merging of the two parties as the "fraud of unification"[44] and the fusion of the two youth movements as the "absorption of the Socialist youth by the Communist party."[45] Indeed, with such distrust and revulsion did the center faction regard the Communists that it refused even to answer their proposal to establish a liaison or coordinating committee between the two parties. "The Communist party," wrote José Díaz, "has proposed to the Socialist party the formation of a liaison committee with a program designed to faciiitate the development of the democratic revolution and to carry it to its final consequences. This proposal has been left unanswered by the present reformist and centrist leadership. On the other hand, it has been welcomed by the left wing. The masses of the Socialist party repudiate the attitude of the present reformist executive and see in the line of Largo Caballero one that approaches most the revolutionary path, the path of the Communist party and the Communist International."[46]

Indalecio Prieto, the leading light and dominant force of the center faction, found Largo Caballero's collaboration with the Communists extremely dangerous. A masterful character of humble origins, minister of finance in the first government of the Republic in 1931, and the owner of *El Liberal* of Bilbao, an influential newspaper in the industrial North—in which he had once worked as a copywriter and later as editor—he enjoyed immense prestige among liberal and even conservative Republicans, with whom he had infinitely more in common than with the left-wing Socialists. In fact, the differences between the two factions in the spring of 1936 were so pronounced that he declared they would result in a schism at the next party congress.[47] An expert parliamentarian, an eloquent but sometimes frenzied speaker, he would pound his chest with such force that, as one Cortes deputy expressed it, "no one knows what to admire more: the strength of his fist or the resistance of his thorax."[48] "He beats his chest so violently," writes another witness, "shouts at the top of his lungs, and frequently injures himself, causing himself to bleed."[49] Skilled in maneuvers in governing circles and his own party—maneuvers that had been instrumental not only in dislodging Alcalá-Zamora from the presidency of the Republic and raising Manuel Azaña on 10 May to that high office,[50] but in ousting Caballero from the executive committee of the Socialist party[51]—Prieto was often cited as the most astute politician in the Republican regime. His ability was acknowledged by opponents as well as friends.[52]

In contrast to Caballero, Prieto had thrown all his influence before the Civil War on the side of moderation. "[What] no country can stand," he contended in his 1936 May Day speech, "is the constant blood-letting of public disorder without any immediate revolutionary goal; what no country can stand is the waste of its public authority and economic strength through continued disquiet, anxiety, and agitation. Some simple souls may argue that this disquiet, this anxiety, and this agitation can only harm the dominant classes. This is an error. . . . [The] working class itself will not be long in feeling the pernicious effects as a result of the damage to and possible collapse of our economy. . . . What we should do is to proceed intelligently to the destruction of privileges, to demolish the foundations on which these privileges rest; but this is not done through isolated, sporadic excesses, which leave in their wake as a sign of the people's efforts some scorched images, burnt altars, or church doors blackened by flames. That, I tell you, is not revolution . . . [If] a truly revolutionary organization, intelligently revolutionary, does not capture this wasted energy, if it does not control it, guide it into fruitful channels, then listen to me when I declare: this is collaborating with fascism." In this atmosphere, he continued, fascism would flourish because a terrified middle class, unable to discern on the horizon a solution for its salvation, would turn to fascism. "[Let] it not be said, to the discredit of democracy, that barren disorder is possible only when a democratic government is in power, because then the facts will cry out that only democracy permits disorders and that only the whip of dictatorship is capable of preventing them. . . . [Should] abuse and disorder become a permanent system, that will not be the way to socialism or to the consolidation of the democratic Republic, which I believe is our concern. . . . That way does not lead to socialism or to communism; it leads to a completely hopeless anarchy that is not even in keeping with libertarian [Anarchist] ideology; it leads to economic chaos that may finish off the country."[53]

On 4 May, Largo Caballero's organ, *Claridad*, issued a rebuke. "The working class wants the democratic Republic . . . not for its intrinsic virtues, not as an ideal form of government, but because within that regime the class struggle, which is stifled under despotic regimes, encounters greater freedom of action to achieve its immediate and short-range goals. If it were not for this, why would the workers want the Republic and democracy? To believe that the class struggle should cease so that only democracy and the Republic may exist is to disregard the forces that move history. It is putting the cart before the horse."[54]

In the midst of the disturbances that convulsed the country in the spring of 1936, a movement was set in motion—with which Prieto was not unconnected—to place him in the premiership. "Around his person," records a right-wing historian, "an atmosphere was being created—which Miguel Maura [leader of the moderate Conservative Republican party and one of the founders of the Republic in 1931] was trying to build up and diffuse—an atmosphere favorable to placing him in a position from which he would be able to curb as far as possible the disorders that were taking place. Prieto was the hope not only of the moderates of the Popular Front . . . but of many moderates of the right."[55] According to Maura, Prieto inspired him with "greater respect and deeper esteem" than any other politician with whom he had to deal.[56]

Yet, when President Azaña offered him the premiership, he dared not accept the post, not only because of the opposition of the executive committee of the UGT, controlled by Caballero,[57] but because a caucus of the Socialist deputies, the majority of them members of the left faction, had voted overwhelmingly not to share power with the Republicans.[58] "When entrusted with the task of forming the [government]," Prieto wrote after the war, "I declined, because the majority of the parliamentary socialist caucus was vehemently opposed to any coalition Cabinet, especially if I were to preside over it."[59] Thus Prieto was denied any hope of a viable government based on the parliamentary support of his own party. "What would have been said of me at that time," Prieto declared some years later, "if, ignoring the resolution of the parliamentary caucus, I had accepted the power Señor Azaña offered me? I should have appeared, with a certain degree of justification, as the only person responsible for the destruction of the Socialist party. Furthermore, if in parliament I had been denied the votes of the majority of the representatives of the Socialist party, I should have been compelled, in order to govern parliamentarily, to seek support among the right, as a result of which I should have covered myself with ignominy. . . . At that time I was branded a traitor. The fault . . . was not mine; the fault lay with those who prevented the solution."[60]

In the opinion of the Spanish historian Santos Juliá, Prieto erred when he directed the "Azaña operation" in taking it for granted that he would form the new government. "As a result, he ran the grave and futile risk at a time of acute social and political tensions of elevating Azaña to the presidency of the Republic without having in his hand all the cards necessary to guarantee a true Popular Front government. It was too dangerous a game to enter without being completely sure of success, and Prieto entered it and lost, which proves perhaps *a posteriori* that he was not the supposedly great statesman that he and his coreligionists believed he was. To blame the failure of the operation on the irresponsibility of Largo Caballero is to fall into the vicious circle of accusations, because the policy of Largo was precisely to prevent that operation. It was not up to him to make it succeed, but rather Prieto. The political responsibility of Largo lies not in his frustrating the policy of Prieto, but in not substituting it for any other, which is not the same thing."[61]

However this may be, one must not lose sight of the fact that Prieto lost his gamble because of the opposition of the left Socialists.

Behind the left Socialists' opposition to a government headed by Prieto and the support they gave a few days earlier to Premier Azaña's election to the presidency there lay, according to Luis Araquistáin, Caballero's most trusted aide, a sinister purpose. "I am inclined . . . to give considerable weight to the following statement made to me [after the war] by Luis Araquistáin shortly before his death in Paris," attests Juan Marichal, editor of Azaña's collected works. "According to Araquistáin, the extreme wing of the Socialist party—in which he was the most 'penetrating' thinker—wanted to eliminate Azaña from any executive function and at the same time prevent Prieto from becoming premier. This would place the government in hands utterly incapable of restraining the masses or of calming the right and would hasten the advent of a purely revolutionary government. The maneuver, according to Araquistáin, was very simple: Azaña was 'pushed' toward the presidency of the Republic and when, as was to be expected, he thought of Prieto as his successor in the premiership he encountered the outright veto of the Socialist party. 'In this way, we rendered both men useless,' the former Socialist leader told me, adding, 'Don't you think we went to extremes?' "[62]

Marichal's account is confirmed by Mariano Ansó, a cabinet minister during the Civil War, who, despite political differences, remained on cordial terms with Araquistáin. He claims that during a tête-à-tête with the Socialist leader several years later, he did not omit the slightest detail regarding the "large-scale maneuver conceived by him" and executed by the Largo Caballero wing. "I agree with Marichal," Ansó affirms, "that in Araquistáin's account there was a touch of horror and even remorse over the far-reaching consequences of his action."[63] In his published memoirs, Largo Caballero, although he stood at the epicenter of the political crisis, gave no hint of Araquistáin's political machinations. Indeed, it is curious, bearing in mind his prewar revolutionary stance, that he should claim that he regarded Azaña's elevation to the presidency as a "political error," since, as he puts it, the Republican Left party was the only party—because Azaña was its leader and also head of the Popular Front coalition—that offered any guarantee that the electoral program would be fulfilled. "If Azaña were elected president of the Republic," he claims to have thought at the time, "Spanish republicanism would become a flock without a shepherd; everyone would pull his own way; the Republic would lack a basic organ for its support and development. This fear of ours was confirmed later, unfortunately."[64] It is unlikely that this was Largo Caballero's thinking at the time or that of Araquistáin, his close adviser, in view of their identical prewar revolutionary positions. At the beginning of March 1936, Araquistáin had written:

There is no possibility of reconciliation with the classes who were defeated at the polls on 16 February. . . . As long as the landed nobility and the Church are not expropriated; as long as the banks and the capitalist press are not controlled; as long as the large industries are not nationalized . . . there will be neither peace nor prosperity.

The right wants to roll back the Spanish revolution, to keep all its privileges, and hopes that Azaña, from the center, will help it. Azaña would like to stabilize the revolution, to regulate it within the framework of capitalist society, and harbors the illusion that both the right and the left will help him in this mythical task of national conciliation. . . .

Peace and harmony are chimerical, and no less chimerical is a policy of conciliation. . . . There are only two choices: revolution or counterrevolution. . . . There is no middle road and he who dreams of centrist positions . . . risks being consumed by two fires.[65]

In a public statement made after the war, Araquistáin confessed: "Another factor that contributed to the fall of the Republic was probably the internecine struggle within our party. I believe that the fault lay with all of us. We all contributed, some in one way, some in another, to the state of internal decomposition that showed the enemy that we were weakened and that the moment for rebellion had arrived. I believe that if we had not been in that lamentable condition . . . the result would have been different." Had a Socialist been at the helm of government, he contended, he might have aborted the military conspiracy. "Some will say that all this is water under the bridge. Ah! But the future may offer similar situations, and a knowledge of history is never useless."[66]

Because the dissensions within the PSOE precluded any possibility of a viable government under Prieto, on 13 May—two months before the Civil War— President Azaña named Santiago Casares Quiroga, his close associate and a member of his party, to head the new administration, which, like the previous cabinet, was composed entirely of liberal and moderate Republicans. Although Prieto declared after the war that he would have covered himself with ignominy if, as premier, he had been compelled to seek support among the right, there is evidence that in reality he may not have been opposed to this approach. Gil Robles recounts that in April and May, conversations were held between Manuel Giménez Fernández, representing the liberal wing of the CEDA, and Miguel Maura and Julián Besteiro, with the knowledge of Prieto—"the central figure in these projects"—and Azaña, to discuss the idea of a government of national concentration. After Casares Quiroga had formed his cabinet on 15 May, Gil Robles received a visit from José Larraz—president of Editorial Católica, publishers of *El Debate*, the mouthpiece of the CEDA—who told Gil Robles that he had visited Prieto the previous day and that they had alluded to the "vague possibility of including the CEDA in a government presided by Prieto in order to counter the revolutionary solutions proposed by some elements of the Socialist party." Gil Robles replied that because Casares Quiroga had just formed his government, he judged Prieto's chances of success very problematical. "How could I under the circumstances have ventured to offer the participation of the CEDA in a hypothetical government that the majority of our deputies were not ready to support . . . ? I would simply have succeeded in destroying the only well-organized force of the Spanish right." He then suggested to Larraz that a coalition government comprising moderate Socialists, Republicans, and elements of the center and supported by the parliamentary votes of the CEDA would be "more reasonable," but that a government with direct participation of the CEDA would be unworkable. "Apart from the absolute discredit into which we would have fallen among our voters, it did not appear logical to suppose that the masses of the Popular Front would agree to our ministerial collaboration, in view of the fact that the entry of the CEDA in the government [in 1934] had provoked . . . the revolutionary movement of October."[67]

Nothing came of these backstage negotiations to avert the approaching cataclysm, not only because the Socialists were riven by discord, but because the

CEDA, undermined by defections to parties of the right that were bent on a violent settlement, was threatened with disintegration. Hence it fell to the hapless Casares Quiroga to preside during the next few weeks, as premier and war minister, over Spain's precipitous descent into civil war.

On 19 May he presented his new cabinet to the Cortes. In accordance with the policy of Azaña, he endeavored to maintain a balancing position between the right and left. To appease the left, he announced that he would accelerate the rhythm of the Popular Front program, that he would defend the Republic from its enemies, and that leniency no longer would be shown toward the foes of the Republic. "I tell you that wherever the enemy presents himself, whether he be open or concealed, we shall crush him." On the other hand, to appease the right he said that he would not be coerced from below, and he condemned the illegal political strikes, confiscations of property, and acts of violence. "The government cannot work in dignity under these conditions. I appeal to all of you to help me with your loyal and cordial cooperation."[68]

But, during his few short weeks in office, he did little to calm the social turbulence and, like Azaña, turned a deaf ear to every warning concerning the brewing military revolt.[69] A consumptive, who tried hard to present a tough and energetic exterior, Casares proved impetuous and ineffectual. His threats and invective against the right—rarely matched by equal vehemence against the left—angered his opponents but were little more than bluster. "The political climate required a man of greater energy," writes Zugazagoitia, director of the moderate *El Socialista*. "Persons of good judgment who had collaborated with him when he was minister of the interior [1931–33] advised me to distrust his energetic appearance. They maintained that his energy, like that of Don Manuel Azaña, was purely oral and that once the parliamentary debate had ended was without consequence."[70]

By mid-June, Casares Quiroga's government was adrift, and it was evident that his attempts to maintain the precarious social equilibrium were failing. Government authority had now declined to such a point that Miguel Maura, the liberal Catholic leader, was calling in *El Sol* for a multiparty national Republican dictatorship.[71] "[The] dictatorship that Spain needs today," he wrote on 23 June, "is a national dictatorship with a broad social base extending from the nonrevolutionary Socialist working class to the conservative middle class, which is now convinced that the hour of renunciation and sacrifice in the interest of genuine social justice has sounded. . . . The dictatorship would be directed by men of the Republic, by republicans of probity, who . . . place the supreme interests of Spain and the Republic above class or party objectives."

On 25 June he wrote:

National indiscipline is now unbearable. The government is powerless to control it. The warring sides—and there are more than two—abandon themselves to the barbaric sport of man hunting. Illegal strikes and employer violations of government orders germinate with tropical fertility. The irreparable ruin of the economy and the collapse of government finances are terrifyingly near. To the right and to the left of the regime the aligned forces, organized and armed, pressure the state to the point of asphyxiation, and proclaim their intention to attack and overthrow it. And all this is happening because the Popular Front, which was an excellent electoral tool, is not and cannot be an instrument of government. It is an amalgam, which in addition to being hybrid, is destructive of peace and of the wealth of the country. . . .

Today, the Republic is no more than the tool—unconscious I would like to believe—of the extreme, revolutionary segment of the working class, which, shielded by the liberal democratic system and the blindness of certain representatives of the republican parties, is preparing in minute detail an assault on the government and the extermination of capitalist and middle-class society. . . .

We republicans who eagerly made the greatest personal sacrifice to collaborate in the birth of the regime . . . are called fascists and, as such, merit extermination. . . .

If the Republic is to be this, it is inexorably condemned to imminent extinction at the hands of those who claim to be its only defenders, or, what is more probable, at the hands of a reaction from the opposite direction. . . .

[Either] all republicans—and I include in this denomination those on the left and right who wish to maintain the republican regime—decide to subordinate their party interests to the supreme interests of the regime . . . or they resign themselves to watching it die in the agonies of a bloody civil war, whose outcome will be either a fascist or a Red dictatorship. . . .

A regime that does not defend itself does not deserve to live. But a regime that surrenders itself passively and merrily to its declared enemies, in addition to deserving death, deserves the contempt of history. . . . The Republic knows that if, under the protection of its democratic laws . . . , either one side or the other prevails, the Republic in Spain, together with freedom and democracy, will die. The Republic knows that if this should happen Spain will be devastated by disasters heretofore unknown in its history, because none of its adversaries is equipped to establish a political and social regime that is humane and habitable.

On 27 June, Maura wrote wistfully: "I do not harbor the slightest hope that my reasoning will convince those who currently bear the weight of government responsibility in Spain."

3

Military Rebellion and Civil War

*I*f through their passivity Azaña and Casares Quiroga appeared supine or even impotent before the dangers closing in more menacingly every day upon the Republic from the left and right, this was partly because they were afraid to provoke the left to greater agitation and aggression and partly because they underrated the ability of the army dissidents to stage a successful insurrection.[1] This state of mind was characteristic of the entire cabinet. Indalecio Prieto testifies: "Señor Azaña was unsuccessful in selecting his advisers, because he formed a government that was too personal, . . . too domesticated. The key portfolios . . . were given to intimates. His will and his opinion completely dominated them. The devotion he inspired among his intimates frequently bordered on idolatry and the idolaters never disagree with the idol. For that reason, since Azaña did not believe that there would be a rebellion, neither did the government."[2] As Palacio Atard, a supporter of the military rising, points out, Azaña and Casares Quiroga were confident that their control of the top command positions guaranteed the "effective subordination" of the army and overlooked "the ability of the young officers to assure the success of the rebellion in many garrisons by overpowering their superiors."[3] Furthermore, to quote Juan Marichal, the reports of the conspiratorial activities in the army "did not play in Manuel Azaña's anguished mind the same role as the attitudes and actions of the extreme left."[4] This is confirmed by Zugazagoitia, who recounts that on his commenting in his newspaper upon certain subversive military activities, Manuel Azaña, then prime minister, personally reprimanded him on the ground that such comments did more harm than good. The truth of the matter was, he adds, that Azaña was annoyed at the time, not with the military, "who were carefully concealing their designs through the exercise of a perfect discipline," but with the voters, "who had ensured the victory of the Popular Front and were provoking a fabulous number of strikes and disturbances in the sphere of public order."[5] In a private talk with Gil Robles, after becoming president of the Republic, Azaña did not conceal his fears regarding the course of events. "I don't know where we will end up," he said. "Your friends should give me a margin of confidence. They should not make difficulties for me. I have enough problems on the other side."[6]

Because Azaña and Casares Quiroga feared the social ferment more than the conspiratorial activities reported to them day by day and because, as Richard Robinson puts it, the existence of an armed antirevolutionary force was for the left Republicans the only hope of preserving a certain independence of action vis-à-vis the workers' organizations, they took no determined action against the military.[7] They paid scant heed to the demands of the Communists, for example, that the government should remove "the fascist and monarchist chiefs in the army" and should carry out "an energetic and thorough purge of the state apparatus," cleansing the army, the secret police, the Civil Guard, the Assault Guard, and the courts of law of "all reactionary, fascist, and monarchist officers and elements who hold positions of authority."[8]

"The most that the government would do after receiving detailed reports of an intrigue in some garrison," writes Stanley G. Payne, "was to transfer a number of officers to another post. It hesitated to do even this much with generals such as Mola and Goded, though lesser lights in the UME [Unión Militar Española, the right-wing military organization] were rotated two or three times during the spring of 1936. . . . Azaña and Casares seem to have believed, just as the rightists did, that the main threat would come from Azaña's own allies of the revolutionary left."[9]

The occasional shifts in command positions and the continuing agitation by the extreme left against the army were nevertheless causing apprehension among rightist officers. On 23 June, from his remote garrison in the Canary Islands, General Franco wrote a warning letter to Casares Quiroga expressing the "grave state of anxiety" in the army. He protested against the substitution of officers "with a brilliant history" by men who, he claimed, were regarded by 90 percent of their comrades as "inferior in qualifications," and stressed the peril that this implied for army discipline. "Those who represent the army as disloyal to the Republic are not telling the truth," he asserted, and he urged that it be treated with "consideration, fairness, and justice."[10] This letter, affirms Manuel Aznar, a supporter of the general, was written so that he could "arm himself with every possible justification before God, history, and his own conscience" before making a final decision.[11]

Isolated in his command post far out in the Atlantic, General Franco was proceeding cautiously and did not finally commit himself to the insurrection until the end of June or the beginning of July,[12] a vacillation that infuriated some of the conspirators, who threatened to act without him.[13] "Franco's sphinx-like attitude may have simply been prompted by caution," Richard Robinson speculates. "On the other hand his conduct during the Republic suggests that he had a strong respect for legality, and therefore needed to be sure in his own mind whether or not rebellion was justified in the circumstances. His letter of 23 June to Casares Quiroga can be interpreted either as an attempt to effect a change in policy to avoid a rising, or as an effort to make the conspirators' task easier.[14] He had, it seems, good reason for delaying his pledge, for the conspiracy was not going well. In a confidential report dated 1 July to those involved in the "patriotic movement," General Emilio Mola, who was directing the conspiracy from his provincial garrison in Pamplona, stated that the enthusiasm for the cause had "not yet reached the degree of exultation necessary for a decisive victory. . . . An effort has been made to provoke a violent situation between two opposing political sectors so that, based on the violence created, we may proceed; but the fact is that up to now—notwithstanding the help given by some political elements—this has not happened, because there are still fools who believe that agreement is possible with the representatives of the masses under control of the Popular Front."[15] Furthermore, plans for the uprising were being hindered by political differences between the rival Alphonsine and Carlist monarchists as well as by disagreements between the Falange and the military conspirators.

The most valuable and fascinating account of the conspiratorial activities of military and political leaders and their difficulties in reaching agreement is given by Ricardo de la Cierva in his *Historia de la guerra civil española.*[16] Cierva, a leading historian favorable to the uprising, had access during the Franco regime to unpublished primary sources in the official Archivo de la Guerra de Liberación of the Servicio Histórico Militar de Madrid as well as to other unpublished materials made available to him by important participants in the conspiracy. In his work, Cierva effectively disposes of many of the inaccuracies and half-truths regarding the conspiracy that first appeared in official and semiofficial publications, such as Arrarás's *Historia de la cruzada española*, which, he asserts, deliberately obscures the role of General Mola in the preparation of the rising "in order to place in the forefront other military figures." The principal organizer and responsible figure, he affirms, was General Mola, who "on his own initiative, managed to fuse, although imperfectly, the diverse conspiracies and rebellious impulses against the Republic and the Popular Front."[17] Thus, Cierva implicitly contradicts a statement in the *Historia de la guerra de liberación, 1936–1939*, published by the Spanish Central General Staff in 1945, that credits General Franco with full responsibility and leadership of the rebellion.[18]

Although the rivalries and dissensions among the forces of the right were still simmering when Franco finally pledged himself to support the rebellion, a dramatic event soon occurred that coalesced the disputing forces.

On 13 July, José Calvo Sotelo, the monarchist parliamentary leader and one of the most important of the civilian conspirators, was slain by leftist members of the police as a reprisal for the murder of Lieutenant José Castillo, a left-wing member of the Republican Guardia de Asalto, the Assault Guard. Acting on their own initiative, Castillo's colleagues, accompanied by several Socialists, drove to Calvo Sotelo's residence in an official truck and announced that they had orders to arrest him. "Ignorant of the enormity that was about to be perpetrated against his person," writes a Socialist historian, "the prisoner descended resolutely with the republican officers. . . . As soon as they had left the city precincts Calvo Sotelo was killed and his corpse placed in the cemetery del Este. The ultimate barrier of disorder had been passed. Nothing more was required, after this incident, for the government and the reactionaries to lose, the former, what shreds of authority remained to it, the latter, what judgment they still possessed."[19]

"The principal monarchist support for the conspiracy," writes Ricardo de la Cierva, "was, of course, the enormous personality of José Calvo Sotelo, which was magnified by the eclipse of Gil Robles after the elections and aggrandized by his titanic struggle against the Republic and against the Popular Front, which he regarded as the logical degeneration of the Republic. . . . Calvo Sotelo was the mouthpiece of resistance, the herald of rebellion. . . . [His] death was the final call to military and civilian rebellion, the violent signal for civil war."[20]

In a later passage, Cierva writes: "Clearly the conspiracy had been under way long before 13 July. Its point of no return had already been passed, and the uprising would almost certainly have taken place even without the terrible news. But the terrible news, which spread throughout Spain from the early hours of the morning of the thirteenth, contributed decisively to erasing the difficulties and doubts of the conspirators."[21]

Fearing that the assassination would be used as a pretext to trigger the insurrection and hoping to restrain the conspirators, Prieto sounded a warning note: "If reaction dreams of a bloodless coup d'etat . . . it is utterly mistaken. If it supposes that it will find the regime defenseless, it deludes itself. To conquer, it will have to overcome the human barrier with which the proletarian masses will bar its way. There will be . . . a battle to the death, because each side knows that the adversary, if he triumphs, will give no quarter. Even if this were to happen, a decisive struggle would be preferable to this continuous bloodletting."[22]

The government of Casares Quiroga vigorously denounced the assassination. It promised not only to take immediate steps to guarantee "elementary respect for human life," but to expedite the judicial investigation of the crime and "to apply the law to all in order that the disruptive work of so many extremists may not triumph over the aims of the Republic."[23]

But the condemnation did nothing to mollify the right. As Zugazagoitia puts it: "The conservative and military forces, for a long time organized for insurrection, were deeply wounded. Calvo Sotelo was the civilian head of the movement. He had infused respect into all the men of the Monarchy because of his superior preparation and talent. His work in the ministry of finance, as collaborator of General Primo de Rivera, had given him experience as an administrator that could not be underestimated. . . . He had gained the confidence not only of the monarchists but also of more than half the deputies of the CEDA, whose devotion [to the party] had been chilled by the tactics of Gil Robles, whom they reproached for not using his control of the war ministry [in 1935] to bring down the regime . . . and for not instituting a dictatorship fashioned after that in Portugal."[24]

On 15 July, at a meeting of the Permanent Deputation of the Cortes two days before the Civil War began, Fernando Suárez de Tangil, the count of Vallellanos, speaking for the monarchists, charged: "This crime, without precedent in our political history, has been committed by the government's own agents. And this was possible thanks to the climate created by the incitements to violence and personal attack upon the deputies of the right uttered every day in parliament. . . . We cannot coexist with the protectors and moral accomplices of this deed a moment longer. We do not want to deceive the country and international opinion by accepting a role in a farce that pretends that a civilized and normal state exists, whereas, in reality, we have lived in complete anarchy since 16 February."[25]

And at the funeral of Calvo Sotelo, Antonio Goicoechea declared on behalf of Renovación Española: "Before this flag, placed like a cross over your breast, before God who hears us and sees us, we take a solemn oath to consecrate our lives to this triple work: to imitate your example, to avenge your death, and to save Spain."[26]

If there had remained up to this time even a glimmer of hope for compromise, it was at once extinguished. Positions were now being taken up for what Prieto had warned would be a battle to the death in which the adversaries would give no quarter. The Socialists and Communists, who in the past few months had been organizing their own militia,[27] were now feverishly mobilizing their forces, and the conspirators, both military and civilian, were putting the final touches to their plans for insurrection.

There can be no doubt that the moderates of the Popular Front were aghast at the assassination of the monarchist leader, but no one deplored it more than President Manuel Azaña, who was fully aware of its dire import. Essentially a man of temperate views, he had sought to hold Spain on a middle course. He had hoped for substantial reforms within the framework of the Republican Constitution, but not for a deluge that would submerge that Constitution. For this reason, when the rebellion broke out in Melilla in Spanish Morocco on 17 July—with a successful coup against the Republican commander, General Manuel Romerales, by his subordinates—and was spreading to the peninsula, Azaña still hoped for a solution that would save the Republic from being ground between the upper and nether millstones of the right and left. On the evening of 18 July, in a last-minute endeavor to prevent the country from plunging into civil war and revolution, he had the government of Casares Quiroga resign[28] and entrusted Diego Martínez Barrio—whose party, the Unión Republicana, it will be remembered, constituted the most moderate segment of the Popular Front coalition—with the formation of a new, somewhat conservative, cabinet in the expectation that this might encourage the insurgent army officers to negotiate.

"I have accepted this task," Martínez Barrio declared over the radio, "for two essential reasons: to spare my country the horrors of civil war and to protect the Constitution and the institutions of the Republic."[29] There was no time to lose, for the dangers to the Republic multiplied as garrison after garrison rose in revolt and as the left-wing organizations mobilized their members and ever more insistently demanded arms to combat the insurrection. For two days, Casares Quiroga had refused to arm the workers lest the power of state pass into their hands. "[His] ministry," an eyewitness said to Zugazagoitia, "is a madhouse, and the wildest inmate is the minister himself. He neither eats nor sleeps. He shouts and screams as though possessed. His appearance frightens you, and it would not surprise me if he were to drop dead during one of his frenzied outbursts. . . . He will hear nothing of arming the people and says in the most emphatic terms that anyone who takes it upon himself to do so will be shot."[30]

Casares Quiroga's orders were disregarded, for, prior to his resignation, five thousand rifles were handed out to the workers in Madrid on the sole authority of Lieutenant Colonel Rodrigo Gil, the chief of the Artillery Park and political associate for many years of Largo Caballero. This information, which has been amply confirmed, was given to me by Margarita Nelken, left Socialist deputy, who was sent to the Artillery Park by the Casa del Pueblo, headquarters of the Socialist UGT.[31] The version given by Lázaro Somoza Silva in his biography of General José Miaja[32] to the effect that the general, who was military commander of Madrid at the time, ordered the distribution not only lacks confirmation but conflicts with his presence a few hours later in Martínez Barrio's government which, as we shall see, was committed to the withholding of arms. In fact, when Carlos Núñez Maza, then technical secretary in the general direction of aviation, asked Miaja to give arms to the Casa del Pueblo, the general refused to do so, according to Ignacio Hidalgo de Cisneros,[33] second in command at that time of the general direction of aviation under General Miguel Núñez de Prado.

Even as Martínez Barrio was attempting to form a new government, the revolutionary workers—thanks in part to the distribution of arms by Lieutenant Colonel Rodrigo Gil—were beginning to assume police functions. "Groups of armed workers were patrolling the streets and beginning to stop automobiles," Martínez Barrio recalled. "Not a single soldier could be seen and, what is still more surprising, not a single guardian of public order. The absence of the coercive organs of the state was manifest."[34] And a Communist testifies: "At the stroke of midnight, all the exits from the Puerta del Sol, the approaches to the barracks, the working-class headquarters, the workers' districts, and the entrances to the city are being watched. The armed workers control motor traffic. Automobiles and streetcars are carefully searched. Flying patrols race through the different suburbs, carrying orders and inspecting sentry posts."[35]

Caught between the military rebellion and the counteraction of the left, Martínez Barrio was confronted by a double peril. To parry the danger, he would first have to withhold the distribution of arms for which workers were clamoring outside the ministry of the interior, a matter his talks with prospective members of his cabinet centered on. Felipe Sánchez Román, who became a member of Martínez Barrio's government and was the leader of the small, conservative National Republican party that had refused to join the Popular Front because of his opposition to Communist participation,[36] told me, when I interviewed him in Mexico shortly after the war, that, on arriving at the Presidential Palace, where he had been called by President Azaña before the formation of the new government, he was advised of a "serious development—the appearance of groups of workers demanding arms outside the ministry of the interior." Martínez Barrio, he said, was already there and had been insisting that arms be withheld. Asked by Martínez Barrio for his opinion, Sánchez Román replied that the distribution of arms would be "ineffective militarily and pregnant with inconceivable dangers politically."[37] Martínez Barrio has related that at a meeting of the Casares Quiroga government at 6 P.M. on Saturday, 18 July, attended by Indalecio Prieto, the moderate Socialist, and by Largo Caballero, the left-wing Socialist, everyone except himself remained silent in response to Caballero's "resolute opinion" that arms should be distributed, his own answer being that the people should be urged "to rally round the legitimate organs of government."[38] It is noteworthy that Indalecio Prieto, in an article written after the war commenting on Martínez Barrio's narration of the government crisis, neither confirms nor denies the assertion that he was among those who remained silent when Caballero proposed that arms be distributed.[39]

To avert the approaching cataclysm, Martínez Barrio would not only have to withhold the distribution of arms, but above all he would have to dissuade the military leaders from their drastic course. With this end in view, he held telephone conversations with various garrisons, in an attempt, according to his own testimony, to secure the adhesion of those army leaders who were still undecided and to deflect from their purpose those who had already revolted.[40] The most important of these conversations was with General Mola, commander of the Pamplona garrison in charge of the rebel plans on the peninsula. But Martínez Barrio strove in vain to obtain the general's support. "If you and I were to reach a compromise," Mola replied, "we should betray our ideals as well as our men. We should both deserve to be lynched."[41] According to Sánchez Román, who was with Martínez Barrio at the time of this conversation, the latter pleaded desperately with Mola: "At this very moment the Socialists are ready to arm the people. This will mean the end of the Republic and democracy. We should think of Spain. We must avoid civil war at all costs. I am willing to offer you, the military, the portfolios you want, on the terms you want."[42] In fact, *El Pensamiento Navarro*, published in Pamplona, Mola's headquarters, stated in its issue of 19 July 1936, which appeared a few hours after this conversation, that Martínez Barrio had offered Mola the ministry of war.[43] "We shall demand full responsibility for everything that has happened up to now," Martínez Barrio promised Mola, "and we shall redress the damage caused."[44] To this General Mola replied with finality: "What you propose is now impossible. The streets of Pamplona are filled with *requetés* [the right-wing Carlist militia]. From my balcony all I can see are their red berets. Everyone is preparing to fight. If I were to tell these men that I had reached an agreement with you my head would be the first to roll. And the same would happen to you in Madrid. Neither of us can now control our masses."[45] In his own version of this crucial dialogue, Martínez Barrio attributes to Mola the following reply: "I have a duty toward the valiant Navarrese who have placed themselves under my command. If I wanted to act differently they would kill me. Of course, it is not death that frightens me, but the ineffectiveness of this new move and my own conviction. It is late, too late."[46]

In spite of this response, Martínez Barrio proceeded with the formation of what he later called his government of conciliation.[47] If it possessed a distinctly moderate complexion, this was not so much from the presence of five members of the Unión Republicana all known for their comparatively conservative views, as from the inclusion of three members of the National Republican party—including its leader, Sánchez Román—who had declined to join the Popular Front.[48]

In his account of the government crisis, Martínez Barrio states that he invited Indalecio Prieto to join his cabinet, but that the executive committee of the Socialist party, controlled by the moderate wing, decided against participation, although it offered its "determined and loyal support."[49] This offer is inferentially confirmed by Julián Zugazagoitia, director at the time of *El Socialista*, organ of the executive committee, who states that when the director of another newspaper asked him what the attitude of his own paper would be toward the new government in view of the fact that Martínez Barrio would deny arms, as Casares Quiroga had done, he replied: "I shall confine myself to giving the news of the crisis and its solution. I do not think we should make any violent comment. We should do more harm than good. From now on, and as long as the war lasts, *El Socialista* will be an organ that adheres scrupulously to the government unless the party should decide otherwise."[50]

But the new government was ill-fated from the outset, for the control of events had already passed into the hands of men intent on a final reckoning between the left and right.

For nearly two days the plans of the insurgent army officers had been unfolding. Following their seizure of Spanish Morocco on Friday, 17 July, they had captured the Seville garrison on Saturday at 2 P.M. thanks to a daring coup by General Gonzalo Queipo de Llano. His coolheaded seizure of the Seville garrison from the Republican commander, General José Fernández de la Villa Abrile, is described by his biographers and supporters, Antonio Olmedo Delgado and Lieutenant General José Cuesta Monereo.[51] Queipo de Llano was inspector-general of the *carabineros*, or carabineers, a corps composed of customs and excise officials and guards. Under the pretense of inspecting customs posts, he was able to travel thousands of miles in conspiratorial activities without arousing suspicion.[52] Because he had enthusiastically welcomed the advent of the Republic in 1931 and was related by marriage to the first president of the Republic, Alcalá-Zamora, he was distrusted by the conspirators. But the removal by the Popular Front of Alcalá-Zamora from the presidency, which Queipo deeply resented,[53] helped to remove this distrust. Nevertheless, as the conservative historian Ricardo de la Cierva points out, the rebel generals did not have much faith in Queipo's "decision-making ability," so he was sent to what "in the last analysis" was certain defeat in Seville, a defeat that was "transformed into one of the most unexpected and decisive successes of the Civil War" thanks to the "suicidal courage" of the general.[54] But despite his initial success, not until a week later, with the aid of Moorish troops and Foreign Legionaries from Spanish Morocco, was Queipo de Llano able to subdue the working-class suburbs of Seville.[55] To quell strikes, he resorted to the threat of extreme measures. According to his biographers, he signed a proclamation declaring that all the leaders of any labor union on strike would "immediately be shot" as well as "an equal number of members selected discretionally."[56]

Shortly after Queipo de Llano's capture of the Seville garrison on Saturday, 18 July, at 2 P.M., the rebels struck in other provincial capitals. They rose in Cadiz at 4 P.M., in Malaga at 5 P.M., in Cordova at 6 P.M., in Valladolid on Sunday, 19 July, at 12:30 A.M., and in Burgos at 2 A.M. In two of these provincial capitals, Burgos and Valladolid, not only the Civil Guard—the gendarmerie created by the Monarchy—but also the Assault Guard—the police force created by the Republic—had joined the rebellion.

In Burgos, according to the *Diario de Burgos* of 20 July, "the assault and civil guards adhered to the movement from the first moment."[57] In Valladolid, according to *El Norte de Castilla* of 19 July, published in that city, the assault and civil guards "joined the movement unanimously."[58] However, in Seville, Cadiz, and Malaga, likewise according to insurgent sources, the assault guards, with few exceptions, supported the Popular Front.[59] In Cordova, on the other hand, there was only slight opposition to the rising on the part of the assault guards.[60]

It should be noted that the Assault Guard, which was created by the Republic in 1931, maintained order in the cities, whereas the Civil Guard, a survival of the Monarchy, confined its law enforcement largely to the countryside. Before the creation of the Assault Guard there had been no effective force for maintaining order in the urban areas. Stanley G. Payne writes:

> The minister of the interior in the provisional government [of the Republic], Miguel Maura, was one of the few responsible, farsighted leaders produced by the Republic. He realized that the problem of public order was fundamental to the future of the new regime. Urban violence had plagued the country intermittently for years, in part because of the absence of an effective police force. When such a disturbance became really alarming, the Army was usually called on to restore peace in the towns, while the Civil Guard kept order in the countryside. Neither institution was properly equipped or trained for urban police duties. . . . Untrained in effective methods of crowd dispersal, the guards often resorted to bloodshed, thus exciting more violence and resentment. To avoid recourse either to the Army or to the Civil Guard, Maura created a national republican police force, armed only with pistols and clubs; these "assault guards" were to be used for the suppression of demonstrations in the larger towns. As chief of the Assault Guards, the Director General of Security [Angel Galarza, the first attorney general of the Republic and Socialist minister of the interior in Largo Caballero's wartime government in 1936–37] selected Colonel Agustín Muñoz Grandes, who had won an impressive reputation as a leader and organizer for his work with the Regulares [Moorish troops in the service of the Spanish army].[61]

Although created by the Republic, the assault guards, according to the moderate Socialist Zugazagoitia, comprised many individuals hostile to the new regime who had entered the corps when it was under the control of Muñoz Grandes.[62] These were obviously not removed after the victory of the Popular Front in the 1936 elections; for, according to the official (Franco) history of the military rebellion, *Historia de la cruzada*, adversaries of the Republican regime abounded in the corps. "Lieutenant Colonel Agustín Muñoz Grandes," it continues, "who until the advent of the Popular Front had been commander of the corps, maintains contact with many of its officers, and is therefore aware of the excellent disposition of hundreds of guards to participate in a coup against the government."[63]

Even as Martínez Barrio was announcing to the press about 5 A.M. on Sunday, 19 July, the composition of his government,[64] events were moving faster than his words. In Saragossa, where assault guards had been carrying out arrests in trade-union and left-wing party headquarters shortly after midnight,[65] the troops under General Miguel Cabanellas had just declared martial law, and, in Huesca, General Gregorio de Benito had also risen, seconded by a small garrison of assault and civil guards. In Barcelona, where General Manuel Goded would arrive later in the day from the Balearics to assume command, the insurgents were leaving their barracks to occupy strategic posts, and in the south a force of Moorish troops that would play a decisive role in securing Cadiz for the rebel cause was nearing that vital port. Moreover, General Franco, who, in return for his pledge to support the insurrection, had been promised, according to Stanley Payne, the command of the Moorish troops and Foreign Legionaries in Morocco, "that is, of all the militarily significant units in the Spanish Army"[66]—a command that was to prove an important step toward his assumption of supreme power on the Nationalist side two months later, when he was named generalissimo and head of state by the rebel hierarchy[67]—was flying to the protectorate from the Canary Islands to take command of the Moroccan forces and at 7 A.M. would reach his destination.

It is interesting to record that the de Havilland Dragon Rapide, piloted by Captain Cecil Bebb, which flew General Franco secretly from the Canaries to Spanish Morocco on 18–19 July, was chartered on 9 July in Croydon, England, by Luis Bolín, the London correspondent of the Madrid monarchist daily *ABC* at the request of its publisher, the Marquess Juan Ignacio Luca de Tena.[68]

Before leaving the Canaries on his historic flight, General Franco declared martial law and issued the following proclamation:

Spaniards! To all those who feel the sacred love of Spain, . . . to all those who have sworn to defend it to the death against its enemies the Nation calls out for help. The situation in Spain is becoming more critical every day. Anarchy reigns in the majority of towns and villages. Officials appointed by the government preside over—if they do not actually foment—the social disorders. With revolvers and machine guns differences are settled between citizens who are cowardly and treacherously assassinated, while government authorities do nothing to impose peace and justice. Revolutionary strikes of all kinds paralyze the life of the Nation. . . . Can we cowardly and traitorously abandon Spain to the enemies of the Fatherland without resistance and without a fight? No! Traitors may do so, but

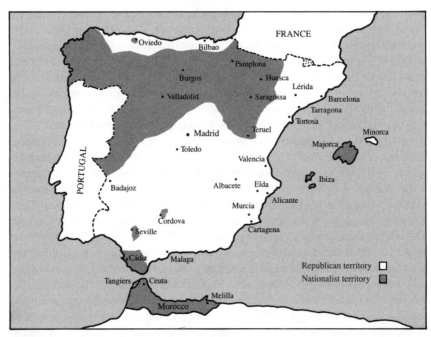

Map 1. Division of Spain, 20 July 1936

we who have sworn to defend the Nation shall not! . . . We offer you justice and
equality before the law; peace and love among Spaniards; liberty and fraternity
free from libertinism and tyranny! . . . Viva España![69]

The liberal Republic of 1931 had now run its course and would soon be
consumed by civil war, a war whose outcome for years to come could be only a
dictatorship of the left or right. It was for this reason that President Azaña, fearing
that Casares Quiroga could not withhold much longer the distribution of arms and
that such distribution would signify the end of the democratic regime, had in a
final throw appointed Martínez Barrio to form a new government to negotiate
with the rebel leaders.

But if Martínez Barrio's cabinet was rejected by the right, it was also rejected
by the left, which regarded it purely as a government of surrender. The moderate
wing of the Republican middle class "was confident that by breaking its ties with
the working class it could reach an agreement with the rebel generals and with
reaction," asseverates the official Communist history of the Civil War and Revolution. "The attitude of Martínez Barrio and those who supported him, in offering
ministries to the insurgent generals and in refusing at the same time to arm the
people so that they could defend the Republic, could not lead to an intermediate
path between capitulation and resistance but to the surrender of the Republic by
the Republican leaders." And why, it asks, did Casares Quiroga and Martínez

Barrio not give arms to the people? "The explanation lies in their class limitations. These Republican leaders preferred to reach an understanding with the rebels rather than give arms to the people because they feared that this would result in an increase in the influence and role of the working class in the leadership of the country."[70]

In working-class circles alarm and indignation were extreme when the list of the new cabinet became known,[71] for not a little distrust was attached to some of the ministers' names. *Claridad*, organ of the left Socialists, once said of Felipe Sánchez Román, a member of the new government, that, although a "republican of unquestionable sincerity," he was "one of the most reactionary figures discovered by the new [Republican] regime,"[72] and of Antonio Lara, another member of the government, it said that he was a "low political trickster."[73] As for Martínez Barrio, the Anarchosyndicalist *Solidaridad Obrera* stated a few months before the outbreak of the Civil War that he possessed intimate friends among the Andalusian landowners and that he had frequently been seen in the lobbies of the Cortes "conversing amicably with the fiercest enemies of the working class."[74] Some members of the middle-class Republican Left party were hostile to the government, despite the inclusion of four representatives. "In the headquarters of the Left Republicans," writes Marcelino Domingo, the president of the party, representing its right wing, and a minister in the new cabinet, "many colleagues of mine, on hearing of the formation of the government, destroyed their membership cards with shameful anger without stopping to consider that my participation at least should have been a reason for respect as well as a guarantee for them. Their understanding of duty and of the sacrifices that duty imposes was different from mine."[75] And President Azaña, the leader of the party, observed: "Some Republicans, more hotheaded than perceptive, even spoke of the 'treason' of the President of the Republic."[76]

In the streets the atmosphere was explosive as members of the left-wing organizations voiced their opposition. "Large demonstrations are formed spontaneously," wrote an eyewitness. "They move toward the ministry of the interior and toward the ministry of war like an avalanche. The people shout, 'Traitors, cowards!' Impromptu speakers harangue the masses, 'They have sold us out! We must begin by shooting them first.' "[77]

Faced by this storm of popular indignation and disappointed in his hopes of a peaceful settlement with the insurgent leaders, Martínez Barrio decided to resign. "Only Prieto made a last attempt to dissuade me," he writes. "But it was a vain attempt, shattered by my attitude. Within a few minutes the political demonstration had brought about the ruin of my government. It was senseless to ask me to combat the military rebellion with mere shadows, stripped of authority, and ludicrously retaining the name of ministers."[78]

"Two Spains, ready to fight without quarter until total victory or defeat, now confront each other," wrote a supporter of the military rebellion. "No other alternative is possible."[79]

4

The Revolution and the Rise of
the Third Republic

*R*ebuffed by the left and by the right, the cabinet of Martínez Barrio passed into oblivion even before the names of its members appeared in the official *Gaceta de Madrid* on that febrile day of 19 July. All thought of compromise with the insurgent generals had to be abandoned. A new government was formed that decided that to combat the rebellion, it must accede to the demands of the working-class organizations for the distribution of arms. "When I took charge of the government of the Republic," testifies its premier, José Giral, "I had to consider that the only way to combat the military rising was to hand to the people the few arms we had at our disposal."[1] Salvador Quemades, leader of the Left Republican party, attests: "Lacking the means of throttling the insurrection, the government had to yield the way to the political and trade-union organizations—the people—so that they could grapple with the rebel movement."[2] But it was a government in name only, swept along helplessly by the tide, a government that presided not over the preservation of the Republican regime of 1931, but over its rapid dissolution under the double impact of military rebellion and social revolution. In all the ministries, according to its premier, Popular Front committees were immediately established to assist and supervise the ministers,[3] expunging all semblance of real authority.

Such was the government of liberal Republicans formed by José Giral, confidant of Manuel Azaña, the president of the Republic. Its composition, as given in the official *Gaceta de Madrid* on 20 and 22 July, was as follows:

José Giral	Left Republican	Prime Minister
Augusto Barcia	Left Republican	Foreign Affairs
General Sebastián Pozas	Liberal Republican	Interior
General Luis Castelló	Liberal Republican	War

Plácido Alvarez Buylla	Republican Union	Industry and Commerce
Enrique Ramos y Ramos	Left Republican	Finance
Manual Blasco Garzón	Republican Union	Justice
Bernardo Giner de los Ríos	Republican Union	Communications and Merchant Marine
Mariano Ruiz Funes	Left Republican	Agriculture
Francisco Barnés	Left Republican	Education
Antonio Velao	Left Republican	Public Works
Juan Lluhí y Vallescá	Esquerra—Catalan Left Republican	Labor, Health, and Supplies

On 6 August, Lieutenant Colonel Juan Hernández Sarabia, an Azañista, succeeded Luis Castelló in the ministry of war.[4] "What is admirable," President Azaña told José Giral a year later, "is the calm courage with which you took command when no one wanted to obey and when everyone, from the most important to the most obscure, was preparing to flee."[5]

In town after town and city after city the state shivered into fragments as rebellious garrisons joined the insurrectionary movement or met with defeat at the hands of armed workers and forces loyal to the government. Because the revolt collapsed in Madrid, Barcelona, Valencia, Malaga, and Bilbao, as well as in some of the smaller towns and cities, the insurgents initially captured only a third of the national territory. Of the estimated 8,850 army chiefs and officers on active service—excluding Spanish Morocco, where practically the entire officer corps sided with the revolt—4,660 were located in the rebel camp on 20 July and the remainder in the left zone,[6] many of whom eventually escaped, as others had before them, into rebel territory. Although the number of regular army officers who served in the wartime Popular Army created by the left is given as 2,000 by Enrique Líster, one of its Communist leaders,[7] Julio Alvarez del Vayo, its commissar general, affirms that "barely five hundred officers remained in the service of the Republic" and that "practically nothing was left of the old army that could be put to any use."[8] Inasmuch as the officer corps in general was distrusted if not execrated by the left and that officers were often pushed aside, imprisoned, or executed if their loyalty were in question, the lower figure may be closer to the mark. In fact, it is corroborated by the highly reliable Republican army officer, Colonel Jesús Pérez Salas.[9] It is noteworthy that, contrary to common belief, far fewer generals on active service supported the rebellion than remained with the government. Ricardo de la Cierva, historian and supporter of the military uprising, stated that of the eighteen divisional generals or their equivalent in Spain on

17 July, only four joined the rebellion: Cabanellas, Queipo de Llano, Franco, and Manuel Goded.[10] According to Vicente Palacio Atard, also a supporter of the military uprising, of the fifty-six brigadier generals on active service "fourteen rebelled and not less than twenty-nine remained on the side of the government."[11] Nevertheless, Madariaga, historian and independent Republican, is no doubt correct when he asserts: "Of the officers who sided with the government, only a minority did so out of personal conviction. The majority would have joined their comrades had they been in a position to do so; they often tried and at times succeeded in crossing the line."[12]

The Civil Guard, the constabulary created by the Monarchy and preserved by the Republic as a rampart of the state, also crumbled.[13] Although, out of a total of 34,320 officers and men, 20,120 are estimated to have been located in the left camp on 20 July,[14] it is difficult to determine how many actually remained under the authority of the government, for while many discarded their uniforms and joined the proletarian militia, thousands of others deserted to the insurgents.[15] True, in November 1936, according to a Communist source, the corps numbered 15,000 officers and men in the left zone,[16] but this was after its reorganization as the National Republican Guard and the subsequent enlistment of thousands of new recruits.[17]

The secret police likewise dissolved, most of its agents siding with the insurrection.[18] Even the Assault Guard, the police corps created by the Republic in 1931 as a buttress for the new regime, comprising some 25,000 officers and men,[19] was shattered as a result of widespread defections to the rebel cause[20] and of the assumption of police functions, in those places where the revolt had foundered, by vigilance committees and militia units improvised by the labor unions and the parties of the left.[21]

"The state collapsed and the Republic was left without an army, without a police force, and with its administrative machinery decimated by desertions and sabotage," writes the left-wing Socialist Alvarez del Vayo, who became foreign minister a few weeks later.[22] "From the army leaders and the magistrates on the Supreme Tribunal down to the customs officials, we were obliged to replace the majority of the personnel who, until 18 July 1936, had been in charge of the machinery of the republican state. In the foreign ministry alone ninety per cent of the former diplomatic corps had deserted."[23] In the words of the famed Communist leader, La Pasionaria (Dolores Ibárruri), "the whole state apparatus was destroyed and state power lay in the street."[24] The moderate Socialist, Zugazagoitia, later minister of the interior, wrote: "The power of state lay in the street, pulverized, and a fragment of it lay in the hands and at the disposal of every antifascist citizen, who used it in the manner that best suited his temperament."[25] Indeed, so complete was the collapse that, to quote a Republican jurist, only "the dust of the state, the ashes of the state" remained.[26]

The control of ports and frontiers, a vital element of state power, formerly exercised by the *carabineros*, was undertaken by workmen's committees or by local bodies under the authority of the labor unions and left-wing parties. "The government could do absolutely nothing," recalled the moderate Socialist Dr. Juan Negrín, when premier in a later cabinet, "because neither our frontiers nor our ports were in its hands. They were in the hands of individuals, of local, district, or provincial bodies, and naturally the government could not make its authority felt."[27] "The control of the frontier [at Ripoll]," reported a Communist daily, "is strictly maintained by workers and customs officials, who take their orders only from the working-class organizations."[28] "In the customs room at Port-Bou," wrote an eyewitness, "there is no sign of the revolution that agitated all of us in Paris. The customs officials are still in their old uniforms and they go about their tasks listlessly as though something has shorn them even of this power. A door opens into the passport room. Here is the explanation for everything. At various points in the room, members of the antifascist militia stand guard. They wear blue overalls over which an ammunition belt is thrown. They are armed to the teeth with pistols and rifles. Behind a long table sit three workers with pistols at their sides. They are examining passports and credentials."[29]

In the navy, according to Bruno Alonso, its commissar general during the Civil War, and a moderate Socialist, 70 percent of the officers were killed by their men, and authority was exercised by sailors' committees. "The age-old oppression," he wrote, "to which the crews had been subjected and the traditional injustices and humiliations they had suffered had left sediments of rancor deep within them, which exploded when the uprising occurred and contributed in large measure to the overflowing of passions."[30] "The group of officers that survived the acts of violence," wrote Zugazagoitia, "was dependent on committees elected by the sailors, who did exactly as they pleased."[31]

The functions of municipalities and other local governing bodies in the left camp were also assumed by committees in which the Socialist and Anarchist-oriented labor unions were the ruling force.[32] "These organs of the Revolution," declared an Anarchosyndicalist leader a few weeks after the outbreak of the Civil War, "have resulted in the disappearance of government delegates in all the provinces we control, because they had no option but to obey the decisions of the committees. . . . The local organs of administration of the old bourgeois regime have become mere skeletons, because their life force has been replaced by the revolutionary vitality of the workers' unions."[33] "The committees," ran an article in a left Socialist review, "were the germ of proletarian power. All revolutionary segments were represented in them. . . . In the villages they assumed control of political and economic life. In the towns . . . they took into their hands the direction of all activities."[34] "In the atmosphere charged with electricity and powder . . . that followed immediately on 19 July," wrote Rafael Tasis i Marca, director general of prisons in the region of Catalonia, "the municipalities [in the Catalan Provinces] became lifeless, colorless. . . . The rubber stamps of the committees replaced . . . the signatures of the mayors."[35] "There is not a single place," said an Anarchosyndicalist paper, with reference to the province of Tarragona, "where a local antifascist militia committee has not been set up. These committees control the entire life of the community."[36] "The center of gravity of the war and of politics," writes Antonio Ramos Oliveira, a Socialist historian, "was the street. Power was in the hands of the people, the parties, the committees."[37]

The courts of law were supplanted by revolutionary tribunals, which dispensed justice in their own way. "Everybody created his own justice and administered it himself," declared Juan García Oliver, a leading Anarchist who became minister of justice in November 1936. "Some used to call this 'taking a person for a ride' [*paseo*] but I maintain that it was justice administered directly by the people in the complete absence of the regular judicial bodies."[38] In Madrid, according to Arturo Barea, a Socialist, each of the branches and groups of the trade unions and political parties set up "its own police, its own prison, its own executioners, and a special place for its executions."[39] Judges, magistrates, and district attorneys were relieved of office, some imprisoned and others executed,[40] while in many places judicial records were burned.[41]

In an attempt to curb the revolutionary terror, the government of José Giral set up "popular tribunals." These courts gave a semblance of constitutionality to the executions,[42] but did little to bring the terror under control. In fact, Indalecio Prieto, the moderate Socialist, recounts that when in September 1936 the Popular Tribunal of Madrid—comprising three professional judges and fourteen jurors belonging to the principal parties and labor organizations of the left[43]—notified the government of its verdict to condemn to death the former Radical minister Rafael Salazar Alonso, the cabinet's decision to commute the sentence to life imprisonment could not be implemented. Prieto, a minister at the time, had cast the deciding vote in favor of commutation on the ground that Salazar Alonso's participation in the military rebellion had not been proved, but shortly afterward Mariano Gómez, the president of the tribunal, a former magistrate in Valencia and later president of the Supreme Court, told him that he was sure that the government's decision would cause a "terrible mutiny" within the Popular Tribunal and that the prisoner would be shot anyway. "The government," he added, "lacking adequate means to enforce its decisions, will not be able to save his life and . . . its authority will crumble. But this will not be the worst: The Popular Tribunal, I am very sure, will refuse to continue functioning and, after Salazar Alonso, all the political prisoners—perhaps this very evening—will be riddled with bullets." On being told that more than one hundred prisoners might be shot, Prieto reversed his decision and cast his vote in favor of the death penalty.[44]

The banks were raided and their safe deposit boxes emptied.[45] Penitentiaries and jails were invaded, their records destroyed, their inmates liberated. "The jails were opened to release friendly political prisoners," writes a supporter of the Republic, "and the common-law criminals who came out with them acted on their own account."[46] There were, of course, singular episodes. "The judge of the Criminal Court," writes Madariaga, "suddenly found in his private apartment the thief and criminal whom he had recently sentenced to thirty years' hard labor transmogrified into a militiaman who, after demanding all the silver and gold objects of the household and tying them into a linen sheet, shot him dead in the presence of his wife and daughter."[47]

Hundreds of churches and convents were burned or put to secular uses.[48] "Catholic dens no longer exist," declared the Anarchosyndicalist organ, *Solidaridad Obrera*. "The torches of the people have reduced them to ashes."[49] "The oppressed people," said an article in an Anarchist youth journal, "put to the torch whatever dens of obscurantism and deception they found in their path. Churches, convents, centers of reaction, whatever smacked of incense and darkness, have been set ablaze."[50] "For the Revolution to be a fact," ran an Anarchist youth manifesto, "we must demolish the three pillars of reaction: the church, the army, and capitalism. The church has already been brought to account. The temples have been destroyed by fire and the ecclesiastical crows who were unable to escape have been taken care of by the people."[51] In the province of Tarragona, reported *Solidaridad Obrera*, "the churches in all the villages have been set ablaze. Only those buildings that could be used for the benefit of the people have been kept, but not those that were a serious danger after burning. Many churches have been converted into communal warehouses as well as into garages for the antifascist militia."[52] And so it was in countless towns and villages. Nevertheless, the Reverend Hewlett Johnson, known as the "Red" dean of Canterbury, asserted, when interviewed by me in the spring of 1937 in Valencia, that "not a single church" had been destroyed or desecrated. This is not surprising. As David Caute says, "this saintly looking cleric was one of the most perseverant fellow-travellers of his time."[53] In contrast to his assertion that not a single church had been desecrated or destroyed, the "Collective Letter of the Spanish Bishops," dated 1 July 1937, claimed that the number of churches and chapels "destroyed or completely sacked" was as high as twenty thousand.[54]

Paul Blanshard explains the phenomenon of the burning of church buildings in the following way: "During [the last one hundred years] the Church has again and again been humbled by its political opponents, its buildings burned by anticlerical mobs, and its leading religious orders expelled from the country. The nation which claims to be the most Catholic nation in the world has probably murdered more priests and nuns and burned more convents and schools than any other nation in the world. . . . The Church has been victimized because the Church has been regarded as part of the ruling structure of political power. For almost two hundred years the advocates of political democracy in Spain have been automatically anti-clerical, and the defenders of dictatorship have tended to be pro-Catholic."[55]

Thousands of members of the clergy and religious orders as well as of the propertied classes were killed,[56] but others, fearing arrest or execution, fled abroad, including many prominent liberal and moderate Republicans.[57] In a conversation in June 1937 with the Republican jurist Angel Ossorio y Gallardo regarding the large number of "outstanding and even eminent republicans" who had left Spain, President Azaña complained: "All of them left without my consent and without my advice. And some (I gave him their names) deceived me. Those who wanted to stay, here they are, and nothing has happened to them! Of the ministers who formed my government in February [1936] do you know how many remained in Spain? Two: Casares and Giral. If anyone at all was in danger, it was Casares. He is in Madrid. Of the "political" ambassadors I appointed, only one, on leaving his post, came to Valencia to greet [me] and to offer his services to the government: Díez-Cañedo. The others remained in France. . . . I raised many of them from nothing. I saved all of them from the wreck of 1933 and made them deputies, ministers, ambassadors, undersecretaries, etcetera, etcetera. They all had a duty to serve the Republic to the very end and to remain with me as long as I was in office. Two or three of them understood this, belatedly, and have returned."[58]

Thousands of persons fearing detention or summary execution took refuge in embassies and legations in Madrid. The number of such refugees has been variously estimated. Norman J. Padelford says that it was calculated to be in excess of 5,000.[59] Aurelio Núñez Morgada, Chilean ambassador and dean of the diplomatic corps in Madrid, affirms that it exceeded 15,000,[60] while Alvarez del Vayo, who as foreign minister conducted the negotiations for the evacuation of the refugees, gives it as 20,000.[61] On the other hand, Javier Rubio, after exhaustive investigation of diplomatic correspondence and other sources, arrives at the lower figure of 7,500, which he nonetheless describes as "unprecedented in the history of international relations."[62] The Norwegian legation, which was one of the smallest missions, housed 900 refugees, according to Felix Schlayer, its chargé d'affaires,[63] while the Mexican embassy gave asylum to over 800, according to Ambassador General Manuel Pérez Treviño.[64]

Hundreds, if not thousands, of lives were spared because of this sanctuary extended by foreign missions, for as the left Socialist Luis Araquistáin wrote privately to his wife on the fifth day of the Revolution, "The clean-up is going to be fearful. It is already. Not a single fascist will remain alive, especially the most important. No one can restrain the people."[65]

"We have confirmed something we only knew in theory," wrote Federica Montseny, a leading Anarchist, in the welter of these events, "namely, that the Revolution, in which uncontrolled and uncontrollable forces operate imperiously, is blind and destructive, grandiose, and cruel; that once the first step has been taken and the first dike broken, the people pour like a torrent through the breach, and that it is impossible to dam the flood. How much is wrecked in the heat of the struggle and in the blind fury of the storm! Men are as we have always known them, neither better nor worse. . . . They reveal their vices and their virtues, and while from the hearts of rogues there springs a latent honesty, from the depths of honest men there emerges a brutish appetite—a thirst for extermination, a desire for blood—that seemed inconceivable before."[66]

"We do not wish to deny," avowed Diego Abad de Santillán, a prominent Anarchist in the region of Catalonia, "that the nineteenth of July brought with it an overflowing of passions and abuses, a natural phenomenon of the transfer of power from the hands of the privileged to the hands of the people. It is possible that our victory resulted in the death by violence of four or five thousand inhabitants of Catalonia who were listed as rightists and were linked to political or ecclesiastical reaction. But this shedding of blood is the inevitable consequence of a revolution, which, in spite of all barriers, sweeps on like a flood and devastates everything in its path, until it gradually loses its momentum."[67]

And a Basque Nationalist, a Republican and Catholic, writes:

> Blood, a great deal of innocent blood was shed on both sides. . . . But the most radical difference as far as the Republican zone was concerned—which does not justify, but at least explains, the excesses—lies in the very fact of the [military] insurrection. The army, almost the entire secret police, the administration of justice, whatever police forces there were, whose duty it was to maintain order, revolted, leaving the legal government defenseless. The latter was compelled to arm the people, the jails were opened to release friendly political prisoners, and the common-law criminals who came out with them acted on their own account. Furthermore, with the stirring up of the lower depths of society, the malefactors that exist in every city, in every nation, came to the surface, and found an easy field for their work. In normal times, the police would have kept them under control, but the very insurrection deprived the government of coercive forces and helped the criminals to secure arms. Is it surprising that during the first few days of the revolt these uncontrolled elements did as they pleased? At the same time the extreme left-wing organizations dispensed justice in a rude and elementary fashion, the justice of men who had suffered and had been molded in an atmosphere of hatred. All this does not justify the crimes committed in the Republican zone, but it readily explains them.
>
> What cannot be explained, and even less justified, are the crimes, much greater in number and in sadism, that were committed precisely by that army, by that police force, by those educated young gentlemen who lacked for nothing and who boasted of their Catholicism.[68]

"The Revolution," wrote President Azaña sometime later, "commenced under a republican government that neither wished to support it nor could support it. The excesses began to unfold themselves before the astonished eyes of the ministers. Faced by the Revolution, the government had the choice either of upholding it or suppressing it. But even less than uphold it could the government suppress it. It is doubtful whether it had forces enough for this. I am sure it did not. Even so, their use would have kindled another civil war."[69]

Shorn of the repressive organs of the state, the liberal government of José Giral possessed nominal power, but not power itself,[70] for this was split into countless fragments and scattered in a thousand towns and villages among the revolutionary committees that had instituted control over post and telegraph offices,[71] radio stations,[72] and telephone exchanges,[73] organized police squads and tribunals, highway and frontier patrols, transport and supply services, and created militia units for the battlefronts. In short, nowhere in Spain did the cabinet of José Giral exercise any real authority, as prominent adherents of the anti-Franco camp have amply testified.[74]

The economic changes that followed the military insurrection were no less dramatic than the political.

In those provinces where the revolt had failed, the workers of the two trade-union federations, the Socialist UGT and the Anarchosyndicalist CNT,[75] took into their hands a vast portion of the economy.[76]

In spite of the massive and irrefragable evidence that a far-reaching social revolution shattered the Republican regime in July 1936, Herbert M. Matthews, *New York Times* correspondent in the left camp during the Civil War and recognized authority on Spain for four decades, whose books and articles had an appreciable impact on American opinion, made light of the revolutionary changes in his last book on the Civil War published in 1973. After quoting the liberal historian Gabriel Jackson as saying that the "most profound social revolution since the fifteenth century took place in much of the territory remaining in the hands of the Popular Front," he comments: "In more or less strong terms, nearly every historian of the Spanish Civil War makes the same point. I would say that there was a revolution of sorts, but it should not be exaggerated. In one basic sense, there was no revolution at all, since the republican government functioned much as it did before the war."[77]

This quotation exemplifies how some journalists friendly to the government later perpetuated through their writings the half-truths and distortions they had disseminated at the time of the Civil War.

Proof of the extent and depth of the Revolution is not lacking, even from Communist sources, despite the fact that the Communist International, following the directives of the Kremlin, tried for diplomatic reasons, as will be seen in a subsequent chapter, to screen from the outside world the far-reaching social revolution that had swept the country. "Are the big industrialists who rose against the people still owners of the plants?" asked José Díaz, general secretary of the Communist party. "No, they have disappeared and the plants . . . are in the hands of the workers, controlled by the unions."[78] "Today," declared Antonio Sesé, secretary of the Communist-controlled Catalan section of the UGT, "the workers have the plants, the workers have the banks, the workers have the land, and the workers have the arms."[79] Mikhail Koltzov, leading Soviet journalist and Stalin's personal agent in Spain, stated quite early in the war that, according to a rough estimate, approximately eighteen thousand industrial and commercial enterprises were taken over by the workers' unions and by the state, twenty-five hundred of them located in Madrid and three thousand in Barcelona.[80]

Landed properties were seized, some were collectivized, others divided among the peasants, and notarial archives as well as registers of property were burned in countless towns and villages, although the destruction of property records was not acknowledged in the official journal until more than a year later.[81] "In none of the provinces" of the anti-Franco camp, affirmed José Díaz, the Communist leader, "do big landowners exist."[82]

Hundreds of seizures made by the agricultural workers' unions affiliated with the UGT and CNT were subsequently registered with the Institute of Agrarian Reform, an agency of the ministry of agriculture, which issued frequent reports listing confiscated properties. The wording of these reports might indicate that the estates had been sequestered by the institute and then turned over to the agricultural workers' unions, but the fact is that, with very few exceptions, the institute merely recorded the expropriations. "I can affirm," writes Rafael Morayta Núñez, secretary general of the institute during the first months of the Revolution, "and this everyone knows, that it was not the government that handed the land to the peasants. The latter did not wait for a government decision, but appropriated the estates and cultivable lands themselves."[83] In the province of Ciudad Real, for example, according to an acute observer, "an overwhelming majority of all the larger estates have been expropriated and collectivized by their hands, and the business of the [Institute of Agrarian Reform] in the whole matter has only been to give a legal *placet*."[84] The unions saw an advantage in registering their confiscations with the institute, for this tended to legalize their action and rendered the sequestered estates eligible for technical and economic assistance from that agency.[85]

Railways, streetcars and buses, taxicabs and shipping, electric light and power companies, gasworks and waterworks, engineering and automobile assembly plants, mines and cement works, textile mills and paper factories, electrical and chemical concerns, glass bottle factories and perfumeries, food-processing plants and breweries, as well as a host of other enterprises, were confiscated or controlled by workmen's committees, either term possessing for the owners almost equal significance in practice. For example, in the region of Catalonia the telephone system belonging to the Compañía Telefónica Nacional de España, a subsidiary of the International Telephone and Telegraph Corporation, was placed under the control of a joint CNT-UGT committee, with the consequence—according to the testimony of the Anarchosyndicalists, who were the dominant influence on that body—that the management was left with practically no other function but to keep an account of income and expenses and was powerless to withdraw funds without the committee's consent.[86] Another example is that of the hydroelectric enterprise, Riegos y Fuerzas del Ebro, a subsidiary of the Barcelona Traction, Light, and Power Company, which was also controlled by a joint CNT-UGT committee. This committee took charge of the company's installations, bank accounts, and other assets with the result that the management, according to an official report, was unable to "exercise effective control over its business and its finances."[87]

Motion-picture theaters and legitimate theaters, newspapers and printing shops, department stores and hotels, deluxe restaurants and bars were likewise sequestered or controlled, as were the headquarters of business and professional associations and thousands of dwellings owned by the upper classes.[88]

But the economic changes in town and country, as will be seen in the ensuing chapters, were not confined to the property of the wealthy strata of society. With the collapse of the state, all barriers had fallen away, and it was too enticing a moment for the revolutionary masses not to attempt to remold the entire economy to their heart's desire.

"In the early days of radiant optimism," wrote Manuel Azaña after the conflict had ended, "the minds of nearly all Spaniards were fired by a messianic goal. If, in the Nationalist camp, it was Christian civilization in the West they were saving, in the Republican camp the prophets proclaimed the birth of a new civilization. Terrible hyperboles that easily inflame what is visionary in the Spanish soul!"[89]

5

The Revolution Hits the Small Bourgeoisie

To the dismay of thousands of handicraftsmen, small manufacturers, and tradesmen, their premises and their equipment were expropriated by the labor unions of the Anarchosyndicalist CNT and often by the somewhat less radical unions of the Socialist UGT.[1]

In Madrid, for instance, the unions not only took over the premises and equipment of shoemakers, cabinetmakers, and other small-scale producers, but collectivized all the beauty parlors and barber shops, establishing the same wages for the former owners as for their employees.[2] In Valencia, a city of over 350,000 inhabitants, nearly all plants, both large and small, were sequestered by the CNT and UGT,[3] as were those in the province of Alicante,[4] while in the region of Catalonia, where the Anarchosyndicalists were in almost unchecked ascendancy during the first months of the Revolution,[5] collectivization in many towns was carried out so thoroughly that it embraced not only the large factories but the least important branches of handicraft.[6] The collectivization movement also infringed upon another preserve of the middle classes. In Barcelona, the capital of Catalonia, with a population of nearly 1.2 million, the Anarchosyndicalist workers collectivized the wholesale business in eggs and fish[7] and set up a control committee in the slaughterhouse, from which they excluded all intermediaries;[8] they also collectivized the principal market for fruit and vegetables and suppressed all dealers and commission agents as such, permitting them, however, to join the collective as wage earners.[9] The milk trade in Barcelona was likewise collectivized. The Anarchosyndicalists eliminated as unhygienic over forty pasteurizing plants, pasteurized all the milk in the remaining nine, and proceeded to displace all dealers by establishing their own retail outlets.[10] Many of the retailers entered the collective, but some refused to do so: "They asked for a much higher wage than that paid to the workers . . . , claiming that they could not manage on the one allotted to them."[11] In Granollers, one of the principal market towns of Catalonia and a hive of middlemen before the war, all intermediaries were suppressed or crowded out of the channels of trade, the peasants having no alternative but to dispose of their produce through local supply committees set up by the CNT.[12] The same pattern occurred in countless other localities all over the

57

left camp.[13] In the region of Valencia, the center of the great orange industry, to take yet another example of the invasion by the unions of the field of private trade, the CNT set up an organization for purchasing, packing, and exporting the orange crop, with a network of 270 committees in different towns and villages, elbowing out of this important trade several thousand middlemen.[14] In short, the labor unions impinged upon the interests of the middle classes in almost every field. Retailers and wholesalers, hotel, café, and bar owners, opticians and doctors, barbers and bakers, shoemakers and cabinetmakers, dressmakers and tailors, brickmakers and building contractors, to cite but a few examples, were caught up relentlessly by the collectivization movement in numberless towns and villages.[15]

If some members of the middle classes accommodated themselves to their new situation as workers instead of employers in their former businesses, in the mute hope that the revolutionary fever would quickly burn itself out and that their property would be restored, they were soon to be disappointed; for, after the first few weeks of widespread and uncoordinated seizures, some of the unions began a systematic reorganization of entire trades, closing down hundreds of small plants and concentrating production in those with the best equipment. "Those small employers of labor who are a little enlightened," declared *Solidaridad Obrera*, the principal Anarchosyndicalist organ in Spain, "will easily understand that the system of producing goods in small plants is not efficient. Divided effort holds back production. Operating a tiny workshop with handicraft methods is not the same as operating a large plant that utilizes all the advances of technology. If our aim is to do away with the contingencies and insecurities of the capitalist regime, then we must direct production in a way that ensures the well-being of society."[16] In accordance with this outlook, the CNT workers, sweeping along with them those of the UGT, closed down more than seventy foundries in the region of Catalonia and concentrated their equipment and personnel in twenty-four.[17] "In these," a spokesman for the socialized industry declared, "we rectified the defects [in the foundries] of those small employers who did not concern themselves with technical matters, and whose plants were centers of tuberculosis."[18] In Barcelona, the CNT and UGT woodworkers' unions—which had already set up control committees in every shop and factory and used the former employers as technical managers at the standard wage for workers[19]—reorganized the entire industry by closing down hundreds of small workshops and concentrating production in the largest plants.[20] In the same city the CNT carried out equally radical changes in the tanning trade, reducing 71 plants to 40,[21] while in the glass industry, 100 plants and warehouses were cut down to 30.[22] Still more drastic was the CNT's reorganization of the barber shops and beauty parlors in Barcelona; 905 were closed, and their personnel and equipment were concentrated in 212 of the largest establishments, the dispossessed owners being given the same rights and duties as their former employees.[23] A similar reorganization, or socialization, as it was called, was effected in the dressmaking, tailoring, metal, carpentry, and leather goods trades in Valencia,[24] in the candy industry in Torrente, where 45 small plants were closed and production centralized in a new building housing several hundred workers,[25] in the shoemaking industry of Sitges,[26] the metal and textile industries of Alcoy,[27] the lumber trade of Cuenca,[28] the brickmaking industry of Granollers,[29] the tanning trade of Vich,[30] the baking industry of Barcelona,[31] and the cabinetmakers' trade of Madrid[32] and of Carcagente,[33] to give only a few examples. "In all the towns and villages of Catalonia, Aragon, the Levante, and Castile," wrote one observer who had traveled widely in these regions, "the small plants where work was carried on badly under uneconomic and unhygienic conditions were closed down as rapidly as possible. The machinery was gathered together in several workshops, sometimes in a single workshop. In this way, the regulation of production was simplified and coordination of effort was more effective."[34]

It is no wonder then that in the first shock of these revolutionary events the small-scale producers and businessmen looked on themselves as ruined; for even when the Anarchosyndicalists respected the small man's property, some among them made it clear that this was only a temporary indulgence while the war lasted. "Once this war has ended and the battle against fascism has been won," warned a prominent Anarchosyndicalist in Valencia, "we shall suppress every form of small property and in the way it suits us. We shall intensify collectivization and socialization, and make them complete."[35] To be sure, the Anarchosyndicalists claimed that the "accommodating and intelligent behavior of the workers captured the sympathy of many small businessmen and manufacturers who had no objection whatever to socializing their businesses and becoming workers with the same rights and duties as the others,"[36] but only in the most exceptional cases did members of the small bourgeoisie welcome the revolutionary changes,[37] and the goodwill they showed could not afford a real index of what they felt in their hearts. The working class was armed; it was virtual master of the situation, and the small bourgeoisie had no course but to defer to the power of events and to acquiesce in the loss of their property.

But material prosperity was not the only aspiration of the small bourgeoisie. As Albert Pérez-Baró, a former member of the CNT, who played a prominent role in the collectivization movement in Catalonia, later averred: "The ambition of the small bourgeoisie, which was very large in Catalonia, had always been to attain a measure of economic independence through small-scale production and trade. The small businessman, manufacturer or property owner often lived a more wretched life than a trained worker, . . . but they preferred a mediocre independent existence to a higher standard of living under the thumb of others."[38]

"Very often," recalled Juan Ferrer, secretary of the CNT commercial employees union, "the owner would address the assembly [of workers], practically bringing tears to everyone's eyes with the story of the sacrifices he had made to build up the firm—only now to see it threatened with collectivization. In these cases, I always suggested to the assembly that he be made the managing director, since the works council had to appoint one anyway."[39]

But, in general, the workers had little sympathy for the small tradesman and manufacturer. According to Pérez-Baró, thirty to forty years of revolutionary propaganda had made the employers appear in the eyes of innocent workers not as "class enemies," but as "personal enemies," which resulted in a series of abuses against them. "We alienated their sympathy, although this did not show itself until about a year later when the revolutionary movement had entered its descending phase."[40]

Nevertheless, the more radical workers did not rely entirely upon force or the threat of force to achieve their ends. Sometimes they tried persuasion: "You small shopkeepers who know nothing of social questions," ran an appeal issued by the Food Section of the Shop Assistants' Union of Barcelona, "are about to be absorbed by developments that will completely transform the present social structure into one more just and more noble, in which the exploitation of man by man will be a thing of the past.

"The groveling existence you have led until now, devoted exclusively to a business at which you work twelve to fourteen hours a day in order to sell four wretched cabbages, two kilos of rice, and three liters of oil, must end. . . . This food section calls upon you to educate yourselves every day with the help of our union, located on the mezzanine of 12, Plaza de Maciá, where, as a result of continual contact with our comrades, you will succeed in freeing yourselves socially and morally from the prejudices that have dominated you until today."[41]

But the middle classes had not schemed and saved for years and struggled to survive the competition of the larger concerns to see their hopes of independence ruined in a day. If they had expected anything from the Revolution, it was freedom from competition and a greater share of the social wealth, not expropriation and a worker's wage. Even before the collectivization movement had struck them with its full force, a profound disquietude had diffused itself among them, and the Anarchosyndicalists had tried in vain to allay their fears by painting the future in attractive colors. In the second month of the Revolution *Solidaridad Obrera* said:

> News that the small bourgeoisie is deeply alarmed has reached our ears. We were under the impression that the anxiety of the first few days had evaporated, but the uneasiness of the shopkeeper, the businessman, the small manufacturer, the artisan, and small peasant holder persists. They lack confidence in the leadership of the proletariat. . . .
>
> The small bourgeoisie will lose nothing by the disappearance of capitalism. It must not doubt that it will profit many times over. For example, take the daily anxiety of the majority of the shopkeepers and small manufacturers over the payment of bills, rents, and taxes. . . .
>
> When private property and freedom to trade in other people's goods have disappeared, we shall have saved from a nightmare many shopkeepers who live under the constant threat of eviction and distraint. . . .
>
> The small bourgeoisie must not worry. It must draw closer to the proletariat.

It can be quite sure that when private property and trade have been abolished a new mode of life will be introduced, a mode of life that will in no way injure those who may feel themselves affected by these social changes.

The small bourgeoisie should throw off its fears; for once fascism has been crushed, it can look to the future with greater optimism.[42]

6

The Revolution in the Countryside.
Libertarian Communism in
Theory and Practice.

*J*ust as the artisans, small manufacturers, and small businessmen were exercised by the collectivization movement, so, too, were the peasant owners, tenant farmers, and sharecroppers. While rural collectivization was applied almost without exception to the large estates on which landless peasants had worked as day laborers before the Revolution—a form of cultivation they spontaneously adopted—thousands of small and medium farmers were caught in the sweep of the collectivization movement in the first weeks of the Revolution. Even those who were not immediately affected apprehended in its rapid growth a mortal danger to themselves; for not only did the collective system of agriculture threaten to drain the rural labor market of wage workers and to create ruinous competition in the production and sale of farm produce, but it also presented a standing threat to the existing small holders as well as to those tenant farmers and sharecroppers who, having appropriated the land, felt that the Revolution had accomplished its mission.[1]

"It is impossible to determine exactly how much land was seized by working-class organizations in Republican Spain," writes Edward E. Malefakis, "because of the shifting lines of battle and because the seizures only gradually found their way into governmental statistics as they were retroactively legalized by the IRA [Institute of Agrarian Reform]. . . . In trying to reconcile the evidence available, I have come to the conclusion that approximately one-third of all lands and (since collectivization occurred mainly on arable land) between half and two-thirds of all cultivated land in Republican Spain were seized. By a cruel irony, the victims were predominately small and medium holders, since most of the latifundio districts had fallen to the Nationalists almost immediately after the outbreak of hostilities and consequently were not included in the IRA reports."[2]

In the Andalusian province of Jaén, for example, where the Socialists comprised the principal labor force and where medium and small proprietors held an appreciable portion of the land before the outbreak of the Civil War, collectivized agriculture soon established itself as the predominant form at the expense not only of the large landowners but also of the medium and small proprietors. "Fear of the revolution caused the large holders to flee, if they could, to other places where they were unknown," writes Garrido González in his study of the collective farm movement in Jaén. "On the other hand, the medium and small owners tried to spend several days unnoticed if they feared reprisals by the day laborers with whom they may have clashed in the past over questions of wages and work conditions. . . . The fact of the matter was that in those early days power was in the hands of the armed militiamen." The Socialists, the CNT, and the Communists knew, Garrido continues, that "the great moment had arrived, that the massive occupation of the land and its collective exploitation represented the revolution for which they had waited so long."[3]

If the individual farmer viewed with dismay the swift and widespread collectivization of agriculture, the farm workers of the Anarchosyndicalist CNT and the Socialist UGT saw it as the commencement of a new era. The Anarchosyndicalists, who were the classic revolutionaries of Spain and the main promoters of rural collectivization, regarded it as an essential feature of the Revolution. It was one of their prime objectives and held their minds with a powerful fascination. They believed not merely that it would result in an improvement in the standard of living of the peasant by the introduction of scientific agronomy and mechanical equipment,[4] not merely that it would protect him from the hazards of nature and from the abuses of intermediaries and usurers, but that it would uplift him morally. "Those peasants who are endowed with an understanding of the advantages of collectivization or with a clear revolutionary conscience and who have already begun to introduce [collective farming] should endeavor by all convincing means to prod the laggards," said *Tierra y Libertad*, the mouthpiece of the FAI, which exercised a strong ideological influence over the unions of the CNT. "We cannot consent to small holdings . . . because private property in land always creates a bourgeois mentality, calculating and egotistical, that we wish to uproot forever. We want to reconstruct Spain materially and morally. Our revolution will be both economic and ethical."[5]

Collective labor, said another publication of the FAI, banishes hate, envy, and egoism and opens the way for "mutual respect and solidarity because all those who live collectively treat one another as members of a large family."[6]

Collectivization was also a means of uplifting the peasant intellectually. "The greatest disadvantage of individual farming, which occupies all able-bodied members of the family: the father, the mother, the children," contended Diego Abad de Santillán, a leading theoretician and activist of the CNT and FAI, "is the excessive amount of labor. . . . There are no fixed hours of work, and the expenditure of physical energy is unlimited. . . . [The] peasant should not sacrifice himself or his children to the point of exaggeration. It is essential that he should have the time and energy to educate himself and his family, so that the light of civilization can illuminate life in the countryside.

"Work on collective farms is easier and enables members to read newspapers, magazines, and books, to cultivate their minds and open them to every progressive development."[7]

Similar views were held by the Socialist UGT,[8] but a still more powerful reason for the advocacy of collective farming and opposition to the breakup of the large estates lay in the fear that the small landowning peasant might one day become an obstacle and even a threat to the future development of the Revolution. "Collectivization," said a local secretary of the powerful National Federation of Land Workers, affiliated with the UGT, "is the only means of making headway. We must not even think of parcelation at this stage. The soil is not everywhere the same and some harvests . . . are better than others. If we were to divide up the land we should relapse into that old state of affairs when some hard-working peasants had no food while the lucky ones lived well, and once again we should have masters and servants."[9] "On no account," declared the executive committee of the federation, "shall we allow the land, equipment, and livestock to be divided up, because it is our intention to apply collectivization to all expropriated estates so that labor and the produce thereof are shared equally among the peasant families."[10]

"We Anarchosyndicalists," declared the organ of the youth movement of the CNT and FAI, "believed from the very beginning that individual farming would lead directly to large properties, to the domination of political bosses, to the exploitation of man by man, and finally to the reestablishment of the capitalist system.

"The CNT did not want this to happen and consequently fomented industrial and agricultural collectives."[11]

This fear that a new class of wealthy landed proprietors would eventually rise on the ruins of the old if individual tillage were encouraged was no doubt partly responsible for the determination of the more zealous collectivizers to secure the adherence of the small cultivator, whether willing or forced, to the collective system. It is, of course, true that the official policy of the CNT, as well as that of the less radical UGT, was, within certain limits, one of respect for the property of the small Republican farmer.[12] "I consider that voluntary membership should be the fundamental basis of any collective farm," said left-wing Socialist leader Ricardo Zabalza, general secretary of the National Federation of Land Workers. "I prefer a small, enthusiastic collective, formed by a group of active and honest workers, to a large collective set up by force and composed of peasants without enthusiasm, who would sabotage it until it failed. Voluntary collectivization may seem the longer course, but the example of the small, well-managed collective will attract the entire peasantry, who are profoundly realistic and practical, whereas forced collectivization would end by discrediting socialized agriculture."[13] However, although neither the UGT nor the CNT permitted the small Republican farmer to hold more land than he could cultivate without the aid of hired labor,[14] and in many instances he was unable to dispose freely of his surplus crops because he was compelled to deliver them to the local committee on the latter's terms,[15] he was often driven under various forms of pressure, as will be shown later in this chapter, to attach himself to the collective system. This was true particularly in villages where the Anarchosyndicalists were in the ascendant. Whereas the Socialist-led National Federation of Land Workers included in its ranks an appreciable number of smallholders and tenant farmers, who had little or no propensity for rural socialization and had joined the organization because of the protection it had afforded them against *caciques*, landlords, usurers, and middlemen,[16] the Anarchosyndicalist peasant unions were composed, at the outbreak of the war, almost entirely of laborers and indigent farmers who had been fired by the philosophy of anarchism. For these zealots, rural collectivization was the foundation stone of the new regime of anarchist, or libertarian communism, as it was called, that they had looked forward to establishing on the morrow of the Revolution. Libertarian communism would be a regime "of human brotherhood that would attempt to solve economic problems without the state and without politics in accordance with the well-known principle, 'from each according to his abilities, to each according to his needs,' "[17] a regime without classes, based on labor unions and self-governing communes, that would be united into a nationwide confederation, and in which the means of production and distribution would be held in common.[18]

"Libertarian communism," wrote Isaac Puente, a prominent Anarchist writer, "is the organization of society without the state and without private property. For that reason it is not necessary to invent anything or create any new form of organization. The nuclei around which our future economic life will revolve are already present in our society: the labor union and the free commune—the labor union, in which the workers of the factories and collectives gather together spontaneously, and the free commune, an assembly with an ancient tradition, in which the people in the villages and hamlets also gather together spontaneously and which offers a solution to all the community problems in the rural areas.

"These two bodies, obeying democratic and federative principles, . . . will make sovereign decisions and will not be controlled by any higher body. Their only obligation will be to unite into industrial federations that will take collective possession of all private property and will regulate production and consumption in each locality."[19]

Although the majority of CNT-FAI members regarded libertarian communism as the final goal of their movement, there were a few "individualist" Anarchists who, while opposed to the employment of hired labor, held that an anarchist society should not be limited to one particular system of production. "Anarchism," wrote one of the foremost Spanish libertarians, "must be made up of an infinite variety of systems and of individuals free from all fetters. It must be like an experimental field . . . for all types of human temperament."[20]

Although no hard and fast rules were observed in establishing libertarian communism, the procedure was more or less the same everywhere. A CNT-FAI committee was set up in each locality where the new regime was instituted. This committee not only exercised legislative and executive powers, but also administered justice. One of its first acts was to abolish private trade and to collectivize the soil of the rich, and often that of the poor, as well as farm buildings, machinery, livestock, and transport. Except in rare cases, barbers, bakers, carpenters, sandalmakers, doctors, dentists, teachers, blacksmiths, and tailors also came under the collective system. Stocks of food and clothing and other necessities were concentrated in a communal depot under the control of the local committee, and the church, if not rendered useless by fire, was converted into a storehouse, dining hall, café, workshop, school, garage, or barracks. In many communities money for internal use was abolished because the Anarchists believed that "money and power are diabolical philters that turn a man into a wolf, into a rabid enemy, instead of into a brother."[21] "Here in Fraga [a small town in Aragon], you can throw bank notes into the street," ran an article in a libertarian paper, "and no one will take any notice. Rockefeller, if you were to come to Fraga with your entire bank account you would not be able to buy a cup of coffee. Money, your God and your servant, has been abolished here, and the people are happy."[22] In libertarian communities where money was suppressed, wages were paid in coupons, the scale being determined by the size of the family. "The characteristic of the majority of the CNT collectives," wrote a foreign observer, "is the family wage. Wages are paid according to the needs of the members and not according to the labor performed by each worker."[23] Locally produced goods such as bread, wine, and olive oil were distributed freely if abundant, while other articles could be obtained with coupons at the communal depot. Surplus goods were exchanged with other Anarchist towns and villages; money was used only for transactions with communities that had not adopted the new system.[24]

Although a complete picture of life in all the libertarian towns and villages cannot be given here, a good impression can be gleaned from the following descriptions:

In Alcora, according to an eyewitness, money was no longer in circulation. Everybody can get what he needs. From whom? From the committee, of course. However, it is impossible to provision five thousand persons through a single center of distribution. Hence, there are stores where, as before, one can satisfy one's requirements, but these are mere centers of distribution. They belong to the entire village, and their former owners no longer make a profit. Payment is made not with money but with coupons. Even the barber shaves in exchange for coupons, which are issued by the committee. The principle whereby each inhabitant shall receive goods according to his needs is only imperfectly realized, for it is postulated that everyone has the same needs. . . .

Every family and every person living alone has received a card. This is punched daily at the place of work; hence no one can avoid working, [for] on the basis of these cards coupons are distributed. But the great flaw in the system is that owing to the lack of any other measure of value, it has once again been necessary to have recourse to money in order to put a value on the labor performed. Everyone—the worker, the businessman, the doctor—receives coupons to the value of five pesetas for each working day. One part of the coupon bears the inscription "bread," of which every coupon will purchase a kilo; another part represents a certain sum of money. However, these coupons cannot be regarded as banknotes, as they can be exchanged only for consumer goods, and this in a limited degree. Even if the amount of these coupons were larger, it would not be possible to acquire means of production and become a capitalist, were it only on the most modest scale, for they can be used solely for the purchase of consumer goods. All the means of production belong to the community.

The community is represented by the committee. . . . All the money of Alcora, about 100,000 pesetas, is in its hands. The committee exchanges the products of the community for other goods that are lacking, but what it cannot secure by exchange it purchases. Money, however, is retained only as a makeshift and will be valid as long as other communities have not followed Alcora's example.

The committee is the paterfamilias. It owns everything; it directs everything; it attends to everything. Every special desire must be submitted to it for consideration; it alone has the final say.

One may object that the members of the committee are in danger of becoming bureaucrats or even dictators. That possibility has not escaped the attention of the villagers. They have seen to it that the committee shall be renewed at short intervals so that each inhabitant will serve on it for a certain length of time.

All this has something touching in its naïveté. It would be a mistake to criticize it too harshly and to see in it more than an attempt on the part of the peasants to establish libertarian communism. Above all, one should not forget that the agricultural laborers and even the small tradesmen of such a community have had until now an extremely low standard of living. . . . Before the Revolution a piece of meat was a luxury, and only a few intellectuals had needs that went beyond the bare necessities of life.[25]

In a conversation with some of the peasants of Alcora, this acute observer goes on to furnish what may be regarded as a typical example of the minute control exercised by the committee of each libertarian village over the lives of its inhabitants:

"What happens if someone wants to go to town, for example?"

"That's very simple. He goes to the committee and exchanges his coupons for money."

"So he can exchange as many coupons as he likes?"

"No, of course not."

These good fellows are rather surprised at my difficulty in understanding.

"When is he entitled to money, then?"

"As often as he needs it. He only has to ask the committee."

"So the committee examines the reasons?"

"Of course."

I am somewhat alarmed. This regulation, it seems to me, must allow very little freedom under libertarian communism, and I try to find out on what grounds the committee of Alcora permits traveling. . . .

"If someone has a girl outside the village, can he get money to pay her a visit?"

The peasants assure me that he can.

"As often as he likes?"

"Good heavens, he can go every night from Alcora to see his girl if he wants to."

"But if someone wants to go into town to see a movie, can he also get money?"

"Yes."

"As often as he likes?"

The peasants begin to doubt my common sense.

"On holidays, of course, but there is no money for vice."[26]

Of the libertarian village of Castro, Franz Borkenau, an eyewitness, writes:

The salient point of the anarchist regime in Castro is the abolition of money. Exchange is suppressed; production has changed very little. . . . The committee took over the estates, and runs them. They have not even been merged, but are worked separately, each by the hands previously employed on its lands. Money wages, of course, have been abolished. It would be incorrect to say that they have been replaced by pay in kind. There is no pay whatever; the inhabitants are fed directly from the village stores.

Under this system, the provisioning of the village is of the poorest kind; poorer, I would venture to say, than it can possibly have been before, even in the wretched conditions in which the Andalusian *braceros* [farm laborers] are wont to live. The pueblo is fortunate in growing wheat, and not only olives, as many other pueblos of its kind; so there is at any rate bread. Moreover, the village owns large herds of sheep, expropriated with the estates, so there is some meat. And they still have a store of cigarettes. That's all. I tried in vain to get a drink, either of coffee or wine or lemonade. The village bar had been closed as nefarious commerce. I had a look at the stores. They were so low as to foretell approaching starvation. But the inhabitants seemed to be proud of this state of things. They were pleased, they told us, that coffee drinking had come to an end; they seemed to regard this abolition of useless things as a moral improvement. What few commodities they needed from outside, mainly clothes, they hoped to get by direct exchange of their surplus in olives. . . . Their hatred of the upper class was far less economic than moral. They did not want the good living of those they had expropriated, but to get rid of their luxuries, which to them seemed to be so many vices. Their conception of the new order which was to be brought about was thoroughly ascetic.[27]

Puritanism was a characteristic of the libertarian movement. According to George Esenwein, an authority on Spanish Anarchism, puritanism was "one of the several strands of anarchist ideology that can be traced from the beginnings of the movement in 1868 up to the Civil War. This tendency, which sprang from the recognition of a moral dichotomy between the proletariat and the middle classes, advocated above all a lifestyle unfettered by materialistic values. Thus excessive drinking, smoking and other practices that were perceived as middle-class attributes were nearly always censured."[28] In the libertarian village of Magdalena de Pulpis, for example, the abolition of alcohol and tobacco was hailed as a triumph.[29] In the village of Azuara, the collectivists closed the café because they regarded it as a "frivolous institution."[30] "An Anarchist should not smoke," the Anarchist periodical *Revista Blanca* once stated. "An Anarchist should never do anything that injures his health, least of all if it costs money." Nor should an Anarchist visit the brothel: "The man who frequents houses of ill fame is not an Anarchist. . . . If an Anarchist is not superior to other men, he cannot call himself an Anarchist. . . . He who buys a kiss puts himself on the level of the woman who sells it. Hence, an Anarchist must not purchase kisses. He should merit them."[31]

Because of the Anarchist belief in free love or the "Free Union," compromise with the other villagers was sometimes necessary. Gaston Leval, the well-known French Anarchist writer and activist, who visited Magdalena de Pulpis during the war, testifies:

> We asked for information about marriages. Our comrades of course believe in the free union, but a marriage is an event that the peaceful villages do not overlook willingly. On the other hand, to follow the official procedure would have meant violating one's principles. It was therefore necessary to find a way to marry people legally without doing so. This was the procedure:
>
> Four couples have been united since the beginning of the revolution. Accompanied by their families and their friends, they appeared before the secretary of the committee. Their first and last names, their ages and their desire to unite were recorded in a register. Custom was respected and the festivity was assured. At the same time, in order to respect libertarian principles, the secretary pulled out the page on which all these details were inscribed, tore it into tiny pieces while the couples were descending the stairway, and, when they were passing under the balcony, threw the pieces at them like confetti. Everyone was happy.
>
> I explained that it was necessary to preserve the memory of these marriages, births and deaths, if for no other reason than for social studies, which only those persons who do not study anything could disdain. They understood me and promised they would restore the register.[32]

In the Anarchist village of Graus, to judge from a Socialist, the standard of living was higher than before the war. "The land, the mills, livestock, business, transport, handicraft workshops, sandalmaking, poultry breeding, and the liberal professions all come under the collective system. The village is an economic unit in the service of the common good. There is work for all. There is well-being for all. Misery and slavery have been driven out. . . . A powerful siren regulates the life of the village: the hours of labor, refreshment, and rest. . . . Men over sixty years of age are exempted from work. . . . This is one of the first principles of the collective. . . . When a collectivist decides to marry, he is given a week's vacation with the usual income, a house is found for him—house property is also collectivized—and he is provided with furniture . . . which he pays off gradually without interest. All the services of the collective are at his disposal. From birth to death he is protected by the collective."[33]

Referring to the village of Membrilla, an Anarchist account records:

On 22 July, the big landowners were expropriated, small property was liquidated, and all the land passed into the hands of the commune. The smallholders understood these measures, which freed them from their debts and their worries regarding the payment of wages.

The local treasury was empty. Among private individuals the sum of thirty thousand pesetas in all was found and seized. All the food, the clothing, the tools, etc., were distributed equitably among the population. Money was abolished, labor was collectivized, property was taken over by the community, and the distribution of consumer goods was socialized. However, it was not the socialization of wealth but that of poverty. . . .

There is no longer any retail trade. Libertarian communism reigns. The drugstore is managed by its former owner, whose accounts are controlled by the commune. . . .

Three liters of wine are distributed to every person per week. Rent, electricity, water, medical attention, and medicines are free. The consultation of a specialist outside the commune, if it is necessary, is paid for by the committee. I was seated near the secretary when a woman came in to ask permission to go to Ciudad Real in order to consult a specialist about a stomach ailment. Without bureaucratic dilatoriness she immediately received the cost of her journey.[34]

Far less expeditious was the committee in the libertarian village of Albalate de Cinca, whose authority to hand out or withhold money gave it autocratic powers. "A woman wanted to go to Lerida to consult a specialist," wrote Agustín Souchy, a prominent foreign Anarchosyndicalist, who directed the CNT's Foreign Information department in Barcelona.

When she arrived at committee headquarters it was seven o'clock. . . . Its members work in the fields together with the labor groups, and in their spare time they attend to the affairs of the village as well as of the [CNT] organization.

"To obtain money for the journey you must first secure a doctor's certificate," the president explains.

This reply did not satisfy the old woman. She complained of rheumatism and tried unsuccessfully to induce the committee to give her the money without a doctor's certificate.

"There are some people," said the president, "who take advantage of the new possibilities that the collective offers. Many never went to town before. . . . Now that they can travel without cost, they exaggerate a little!"

Perhaps the explanation of the president was one-sided. The doctor could have given a more objective opinion on the matter.[35]

In his oral history, Fraser, who spoke with some survivors of the collectives many years later, makes the following telling comment: "With the abolition of money, the collective held the upper hand since anyone wishing to travel had to get 'republican' money from the committee. This meant justifying the trip. . . . In Mas de las Masas, the collective prided itself on sending people to Barcelona for specialist medical attention. . . . But for a person without a union card to leave the village, even on a short trip, it was necessary to get a pass, according to a right-winger. . . . Ill-health in Alloza was seen as a valid justification and the schoolmaster's father-in-law left to have a hernia operation, taking the opportunity not to return. . . . Conditions obviously varied from collective to collective and, as in many other aspects, generalization is impossible."[36]

And, in a later passage, Fraser states: "The utopian elements of the experiment, mainly the abolition of money, complicated matters. The arbitrariness of some committees indicated the limits of libertarian democracy which could only be overcome by elected and revocable delegates answerable to a general assembly. Thus as a form of war communism, collectivization suffered from serious defects."[37]

Describing other aspects of life in the libertarian villages he visited, Agustín Souchy said of Calaceite:

Here there used to be many small cultivators . . . as well as blacksmiths and carpenters, all of whom had their own little workshops, where they labored in a primitive way without machinery. The collectivist ideal showed them the path to communal labor. Now there is a large smithy in which ten men work; they have modern machinery, a healthy and bright place to produce in. All the carpenters of the village labor together in a big workshop. . . .

The able-bodied [agricultural] workers have been divided into twenty-four labor groups, each group comprising twenty members. According to prearranged rules, they till the village lands collectively. Formerly every man worked for himself; today he works for the community. . . .

The village has two drugstores and a doctor. They belong to the collective, not because they were forced to, but because they wished to. There was trouble with the bakers. They wanted neither to join the collective nor to work under the new conditions, so they left the village. Fresh bakers have not been called in. A temporary solution has been found: the women bake the bread as of old, but the village wants new bakers to come in.

Once the village was poor; today it is happy. Many people used to go hungry, but now they can eat.[38]

A report on the district of Valderrobres in the province of Teruel states: "Collectivization was nevertheless opposed by opponents on the right and adversaries on the left. If the eternally idle who had been expropriated had been asked what they thought of collectivization, some would have replied that it was robbery and others a dictatorship. But, for the elderly, the day workers, the tenant farmers and small proprietors who had always been under the thumb of the big landowners and heartless usurers, it appeared as a salvation."[39]

Of Calanda, Souchy wrote:

What was once the church is now a food warehouse. . . . The new meat market is in the annex, hygienic and elegant, such as the village has never known. No purchases are made with money. The women receive meat in exchange for coupons without paying anything or rendering any service. They belong to the collective and that is sufficient to entitle them to food. . . .

Collectivists and individualists live peacefully side by side. There are two cafés in the village. One for the individualists, and the other for the collectivists. They can permit themselves the luxury of taking coffee every night. . . .

A splendid expression of the collective spirit is the communal barber shop, where the service is free. The peasants never used to shave. Now nearly all faces are well groomed. Everyone can have a shave twice a week. . . .

Wine is served at the rate of five liters a week. Food is not lacking. . . .

Everything is collectivized with the exception of those small stores whose owners wished to maintain their independence. The drugstore belongs to the collective and so does the doctor, who receives no money. He is provided for like other members of the collective.[40]

With reference to the village of Maella, an article in *Tierra y Libertad* stated: "Money has disappeared. . . . In this village neither doctors nor teachers receive money. With complete unselfishness they have abandoned that ridiculous privilege. Nobody at all receives pay."[41]

In Muniesa, bread, meat, and oil were distributed freely, but in contrast to most libertarian villages some money was in circulation. "Every male worker," commented Souchy, "receives a peseta a day; women and girls receive seventy-five céntimos; and children under ten, fifty céntimos. This money should not be regarded as a wage. It is distributed together with vital necessities so that the population can purchase supplementary goods."[42]

Antireligious as well as anticlerical sentiments were deeply rooted in the Spanish working-class movement, particularly among the Anarchists. Ever since the 1870s, the forerunner of the modern FAI, the Alianza de la Democracia Socialista, had called for "the abolition of cults, the substitution of science for faith, and of human justice for divine justice."[43] Moreover, the Russian Anarchist Mikhail Bakunin, from whom the Spanish libertarians derived most of their theoretical arsenal, once declared that "the existence of a god is incompatible with the happiness, the dignity, the intelligence, the moral sense, and the liberty of men, because, if in fact there is a god, my intelligence, however great, my will, however strong, are nothing compared with the divine will and intelligence."[44] In *God and State*, he affirmed that there were three ways whereby the people could escape from their lot: two imaginary and one real. "The first are the tavern and the church, the debauchery of the body and the debauchery of the mind, the third is the social revolution."[45] The attitude of the Spanish Anarchists toward religion had not changed since the days of Bakunin and the Alianza: "Humanity," said an article in *Tierra y Libertad*, shortly before the outbreak of the Civil War, "will not enter a new world of justice and liberty as long as it kneels before God and submits humbly to the state."[46] And in the early days of the Revolution, *CNT*, the leading libertarian organ in Madrid, declared editorially: "Catholicism must be swept away implacably. We demand not that every church should be destroyed, but that no vestige of religion should remain in any of them and that the black spider of fanaticism should not be allowed to spin the viscous and dusty web in which our moral and material values have until now been caught like flies. In Spain, more than any other country, the Catholic church has been at the head of every retrograde aim, of every measure taken against the people, of every attack on liberty."[47]

"Catholic mysticism no longer exists [in the village of Mazaleón]," affirmed Souchy. "The priests have disappeared, and the Christian cult has ended. But the peasants did not want to destroy the Gothic building that majestically crowns the mountain. They turned it into a café and an observatory. . . . They broadened the windows of the church and constructed a large balcony where the altar was once located. The view embraces the southern spurs of the Aragonese mountains. It is a place for tranquillity and for reflection. Here the villagers sit on Sundays, taking coffee and enjoying the calm of the evening."[48]

In almost every region of the anti-Franco camp there were ardent spirits who, exhilarated by the initial progress of the collectivist movement in the villages, whether in the virtually all-embracing form of libertarian communism or in the restricted form of collectivized agriculture, continued to drive it forward with boiling energy. They had an apostolic belief in the justice and grandeur of their aims and were determined to bring them to fruition wherever they could and without procrastination. "We are in the thick of the Revolution," declared one zealous libertarian, "and we must destroy all the chains that subject us. If we do not break them now, when can we?

"We must carry out a total revolution. Expropriation must also be total. This is not the time for sleeping, but for rebuilding. When our comrades return from the front, what will they say if we have been idle? If the Spanish worker does not carve out his own liberty, the State will return and will reconstruct the authority of the government, destroying little by little the conquests made at the cost of a thousand sacrifices and a thousand acts of heroism.

"The rear should act energetically so that the blood of the Spanish proletariat is not shed in vain. . . . We must carry out our revolution, our own particular revolution, expropriating, expropriating, and expropriating the big landlords, as well as those who sabotage our aspirations."[49]

At a congress of the collective farms of Aragon, one delegate declared that collectivization should be carried out with the maximum intensity, avoiding the example of those villages where it had been only partially realized.[50] This statement exemplified the mood of thousands of fervent proponents of collective farming, who were unfettered by any fear of alienating those peasant holders and tenant farmers for whom individual cultivation was paramount. They had power in their hands, and they paid no heed to the much-reiterated warnings of the leaders, such as the one uttered during the congress of the CNT Peasants' Union of Catalonia that "to introduce wholesale collectivization would be to invite disaster because it would clash with the love and affection of the peasants for the land they have obtained at such great sacrifice."[51]

Although CNT-FAI publications cited numerous cases of peasant proprietors and tenant farmers who had adhered voluntarily to the collective system,[52] there can be no doubt that an incomparably larger number doggedly opposed it or accepted it only under extreme duress. This aversion to rural collectivization on the part of smallholders and tenant farmers was on occasions conceded by the Anarchosyndicalists, although they sometimes claimed that they had overcome it. "What we have been up against most," said the general secretary of the CNT Peasants' Federation of Castile, "is the backward mentality of the majority of small owners. Just imagine what it meant for the peasant proprietor, accustomed to his small plot of land, his donkey, his wretched hut, his petty harvest—modest possessions for which he had more affection than for his sons, his wife, and his mother—to have to give up this burden that he has carried with him from time immemorial, and say: 'Take them, comrades. My humble belongings are for everyone. We are all equal. A new life has begun for us.' Yet that is exactly what we have succeeded in getting the Castilian peasant to do. When a child dies in the countryside one no longer hears that heartrending saying once so common: 'Little angels go to heaven.' Under the capitalist system, the peasant used to get furious when his mule or his ass died, but remained quite calm when he lost a child. That was natural. His small property cost him endless sacrifices; not so his child. Often the death of his little children solved his economic problems."[53] Even in Aragon, whose debt-ridden peasants were strongly affected by the ideas of the CNT and FAI, a factor that gave a powerful spontaneous impetus to collective farming, the libertarians themselves have occasionally acknowledged the difficulty they encountered when collectivizing the soil. "It has been an arduous and complicated task," said one of them in reference to the village of Lécera. "More correctly, it still is. We want men to convince themselves, by their own experience, of the justice and the advantage of our ideas."[54]

While rural collectivization in Aragon embraced more than 70 percent of the population in the area under left-wing control[55] and many of the 450 collectives of the region[56] were largely voluntary, it must be emphasized that this singular development was in some measure due to the presence of militiamen from the neighboring region of Catalonia, the immense majority of whom were members of the CNT and FAI. It could not have been otherwise; for after the defeat of the military rising in Barcelona the militiamen had left for Aragon not only to prosecute the struggle against the rebel or Nationalist forces that occupied a substantial part of the region, but to spread the Revolution. "We are waging the war and making the Revolution at the same time," declared Buenaventura Durruti, one of the outstanding activists of the libertarian movement,[57] himself a commander of a CNT-FAI militia force on the Aragon front. "The revolutionary measures in the rear are not taken merely in Barcelona; they extend from there right up to the firing line. Every village we conquer begins to develop along revolutionary lines."[58] "We militiamen must awaken in these persons the spirit that has been numbed by political tyranny," said an article in a CNT newspaper, referring to the villagers of Farlete. "We must direct them along the path of the true life, and for that it is not sufficient to make an appearance in the village; we must proceed with the ideological conversion of these simple folk."[59] Of the village of Bujaraloz, another article in a CNT newspaper stated: "The change is radical. The initiative in carrying it into effect lay with the peasants, and it was confirmed some days later with the arrival of the first column of Catalan volunteers, that of Durruti, that passed through the village on its march toward Saragossa, giving a fresh impulse to the revolutionary atmosphere."[60]

As a consequence, the fate of the peasant owner and tenant farmer in the communities occupied by the CNT-FAI militia was determined from the outset; for although a meeting of the population was generally held to decide on the establishment of the collective system, the vote was always taken by acclamation, and the presence of armed militiamen never failed to impose respect and fear on all opponents. Even if the peasant proprietor and tenant farmer were not compelled to adhere to the collective system, life was made difficult for recalcitrants; not only were they prevented from employing hired labor and disposing freely of their crops, as has already been seen,[61] but they were often denied all benefits enjoyed by members.[62] In practice, this meant that in the villages where libertarian communism had been established they were not allowed to receive the services of the collectivized barber shops, to use the ovens of the communal bakery and the means of transport and agricultural equipment of the collective farms, or to obtain supplies of food from the communal warehouses and collectivized stores. Moreover, the tenant farmer, who had believed himself freed from the payment of rent by the execution or flight of the landowner or of his steward, was often compelled to continue such payment to the village committee.[63] All these factors combined to exert pressure almost as powerful as the butt of the rifle and eventually forced the small owners and tenant farmers in many villages to relinquish their land and other possessions to the collective farms. As Souchy put it: "Those instances in which the small owners gave up their property for idealistic reasons were few, although not altogether rare. In some cases fear of seizure by force was the reason for relinquishing their land in favor of the collectives.[64] But nearly always the reasons were economic.

"Isolated and left to his fate, the small owner was lost. He had neither means of transport nor machinery. On the other hand, the collectives had economic facilities that he could never afford. Not all the small owners realized this immediately. Many joined the collectives later on when they were convinced, through their own experience, of the advantages they offered."[65]

In rare instances, according to the French Anarchist writer, Gaston Leval, the small owner was given better land in exchange for his collectivized parcel. Referring to Carcagente, in the region of Valencia, he asserts: "After the flight of the big landowners, the cultivation of the land was totally reorganized . . . without any need to resort to force. Those peasants who had insisted on keeping their individual holdings and whose land lay in the middle of a collectivized area were offered better land than they possessed and they were also helped to reestablish themselves on condition that they did not exploit anyone. But there were few such cases."[66]

The fact is that many small owners and tenant farmers were forced to join the collective farms before they had had an opportunity to decide freely. Although the libertarian movement tended to minimize the factor of coercion in the development of collectivized agriculture or even to deny it altogether,[67] it was, on occasions, frankly admitted. "During the first few weeks of the Revolution," wrote Higinio Noja Ruiz, a prominent member of the CNT, "the partisans of collectivization acted according to their revolutionary opinions. They respected neither property nor persons. In some villages collectivization was only possible by imposing it on the minority. This necessarily occurs in every revolution. . . . The system, to be sure, is good, and satisfactory work has been done in many places; but it is painful to see antipathies created in other localities owing to a lack of tact on the part of the collectivizers."[68]

Referring to Catalonia, a rich and productive region, where the mass of peasants were small proprietors and leaseholders, known as rabassaires, the leading CNT newspaper, *Solidaridad Obrera*, commented: "Certain abuses have been committed that we consider counterproductive. We know that certain irresponsible elements have frightened the small peasants and that up to now a certain apathy has been noted in their daily labors."[69] Writing shortly afterward about the same region, Juan Peiró, one of the foremost leaders of the CNT, asked:

Does anyone believe . . . that through acts of violence an interest in or a desire for socialization can be awakened in the minds of our peasantry? Or perhaps that by terrorizing it in this fashion it can be won over to the revolutionary spirit prevailing in the towns and cities?

The gravity of the mischief that is being done compels me to speak clearly. Many revolutionaries from different parts of Catalonia . . . after conquering their respective towns have tried to conquer the countryside, the peasantry. Have they tried to achieve this by informing the peasantry that the hour of its emancipation from the social exploitation to which it has been subjected year after year has arrived? No! Or have they tried to accomplish this by carrying to the countryside, to the consciousness of the peasant, the spirit and the moral standards of the Revolution? No, they have not done that either. When they have gone into the countryside, carrying with them the torch of the Revolution, the first thing they have done has been to take away from the peasant all means of self-defense, . . . and, having achieved this, they have robbed him even of his shirt.

If today you should go to different parts of Catalonia to speak to the peasant of Revolution, he will tell you that he does not trust you, he will tell you that the standard-bearers of the Revolution have already passed through the countryside. In order to liberate it? In order to help it liberate itself? No, they have passed through the countryside in order to rob those who throughout the years and throughout the centuries have been robbed by the very persons who have just been defeated by the Revolution.[70]

To compel any person, by whatever means, to enter the collective system was, of course, contrary to the spirit of anarchism. Errico Malatesta, the Italian Anarchist whose writings had an important influence on the Spanish libertarian movement, once stated: "One may prefer communism, or individualism, or collectivism, or any other kind of system imaginable, and work by propaganda and example for the triumph of one's ideas, but it is necessary to beware, on pain of inevitable disaster, of affirming that one's own system is the only one, the infallible one, good for all men, in all places, and at all times, and that it should be made to triumph by other means than by persuasion based on the lessons of experience."[71] At another time, he stated: "The revolution has a purpose. It is necessary for destroying the violence of governments and of privileged persons; but a free society cannot be formed except by free evolution. And over this free evolution, which is constantly threatened as long as men exist with a thirst for domination and privilege, the Anarchists must watch."[72] But even this surveillance implied, in order to be effective, the existence of armed forces, of elements of authority and coercion. Indeed, in the first large-scale social revolution that occurred after these lines were written—the Spanish Revolution—the CNT and FAI created armed forces to protect the collective system and used them, moreover, to spread it. The fact that these forces were distasteful to some Anarchist leaders only emphasizes the cleavage between doctrine and practice.[73]

Theoretically, the Anarchists were opposed to the state dictatorship advocated by the Marxists. Rejecting the dictatorship of the proletariat, Bakunin, the Russian Anarchist, whose influence on the Spanish libertarian movement was deeprooted, wrote:

The Marxists . . . console themselves with the belief that this dictatorship will be provisional and short. They say that its only concern and its only aim will be that of educating and elevating the people, both economically and politically, and to such a level that all governments will soon become unnecessary. . . .

They say that the yoke of state dictatorship is a transitional means indispensable for achieving the complete emancipation of the people: anarchy or liberty is the objective, the state or dictatorship, the means. Hence, in order to emancipate the laboring masses, it is first of all necessary to enslave them. . . .

They affirm that only the dictatorship—their own undoubtedly—can represent the will of the people. But we reply: no dictatorship can have any other aim than that of its own perpetuation and it cannot produce and develop among the people who support it anything but slavery. Liberty can be created only by liberty, that is to say, by the rebellion of the people and by the free organization of the working masses from below upward.[74]

In 1920 Lenin wrote, defining and justifying the dictatorship of the proletariat: "The scientific concept, dictatorship, means neither more nor less than unlimited power resting directly on force, not limited by anything, not restrained by any laws or any absolute rules. Nothing else but that."[75] Commenting on this definition of the dictatorship of the proletariat, Bertram D. Wolfe once made the following observation: "This formulation is beautiful in its pedantic clarity, for the first giant step in the establishment of a totalitarian power is the destruction of all the restraints that, even in a nonrevolutionary autocracy, tend to limit power: the restraints of religion, morals, traditions, institutions, constitutions written or unwritten, laws, customs, private conscience, public opinion—in short, anything and everything that may place any limits on power and any restrictions upon an attempt to atomize and remake a people. The history of all totalitarian regimes has proved the rightness of Lenin's 'scientific' definition."[76]

If, theoretically, during the Spanish Revolution, the CNT and FAI were opposed to the state dictatorship advocated by the Marxists, they nevertheless established a form of parochial dictatorship in many localities, with the aid of vigilance groups and revolutionary tribunals. While these fell far short of the "scientific concept" of totalitarian dictatorship defined by Lenin, the CNT and FAI exercised their power in a naked form not only against priests and landowners, moneylenders and merchants, but in many cases against small tradesmen and farmers.[77]

But in spite of the cleavages between doctrine and practice that plagued the Spanish Anarchists whenever they collided with the realities of power, it cannot be overemphasized that notwithstanding the many instances of coercion and violence, the revolution of July 1936 distinguished itself from all others by the generally spontaneous and far-reaching character of its collectivist movement and by its promise of moral and spiritual renewal. Nothing like this spontaneous movement had ever occurred before. "The collectivist movement, like no other social movement in Europe's modern history," writes George Esenwein, "attempted on a grand scale to overcome not just the material but also the spiritual impoverishment that afflicted the lives of millions of people. Characteristic of most collectives, for example, was a strong sense of social solidarity: welfare programs were instituted which provided villages for the first time with medical care and maintenance for orphans, widows, the infirm and all others in dire need. There was also a strong commitment to education, one of the collectives' first activities being to establish schools, especially in remote hamlets where the people had for centuries been deprived of the basic right to education."[78]

Whatever we might think of the impracticality or ingenuousness of collectivization as a solution to the agrarian problems of Spain in the modern world,[79] the experience in its day must remain a unique experiment, which, in the words of George Woodcock, one of the major authorities on the history of Anarchism, "cannot be ignored in a final assessment of the Anarchist claims to have discovered a way to live in a free and peaceful community."[80]

It is essential at this stage to point out that in order to comprehend the complexities of the internecine strife that raged in the left camp during the Civil War, one must first of all recognize the depth and range of the social revolution and the fact that the Republic of 1931 ceased to exist not in April 1939, with the victory of General Franco, but in July 1936, when the military rebellion and social revolution reduced the regime to ashes.[81]

Part II

The Rise of the Communists

7

Hope for the Middle Classes

The foregoing chapters have made clear the pessimism, bordering on despair, that took possession of a large section of the urban and rural middle classes from the outset of the Revolution. Confronted by the brute facts, they found cold comfort in the words of the Republican jurist Angel Ossorio y Gallardo, that in view of the "immense social revolution" that had taken place, "the only thing we members of the middle classes can do is to place ourselves alongside the proletariat."[1] Nor could they take comfort in the promises held out by the revolutionaries of a new and better world once private property and trade had disappeared into the limbo of things past; for the immense majority of the small manufacturers, artisans, tradesmen, peasant proprietors, and tenant farmers placed their hopes of a better life, not in the abolition, but in the accumulation of private property. To develop as they wished, they needed freedom of trade, freedom from the competition of the large concerns now collectivized by the labor unions, freedom to produce goods for personal profit, freedom to cultivate as much land as they pleased, and to employ hired labor without restriction. To defend that freedom, they needed above all, a regime in their own image, based on their own police corps, their own courts of law, and their own army; a regime in which their own power would be unchallenged and undiluted by revolutionary committees. But now all hope of such a regime had gone, and the middle classes had no alternative but to withdraw into the background. They were far too prudent to swim against the tide, and they adapted their attire to suit the changed conditions. "The appearance of Madrid," observed a conservative Republican, "was incredible: the bourgeoisie giving the clenched-fist salute. . . . Men in overalls and rope sandals, imitating the uniform adopted by the [working-class] militia; women bareheaded; clothes, old and threadbare; an absolute invasion of ugliness and squalor, more apparent than real, of people who humbly begged permission to remain alive."[2] A Communist observer wrote of Barcelona: "The Ramblas lie sloping gradually upwards for more than a mile to the Plaza de Catalunya. From the other end you looked down on an unending harvest of heads. Today there is not a hat, a collar, or a tie to be seen among them; the sartorial symbols of the bourgeoisie are gone, a proletarian freedom has swarmed in along the Calle del Hospital and the

Calle del Carmen from the Paralelo."[3] "So long as no headgear is seen on the streets," declared *Solidaridad Obrera*, the CNT organ in Barcelona, "the Revolution is ours."[4]

In Malaga, recalls Gerald Brenan in his memoirs, "I ran into Sir Peter Chalmers-Mitchell getting off a tram. He was dressed in an immaculate white alpaca suit, complete with a bow tie—the only man in Malaga except the foreign consuls who dare to wear such a bourgeois symbol."[5]

Short of risking their liberty or their lives in openly opposing the Revolution, there was nothing the middle classes could do but to adjust themselves to the new regime in the hope that eventually the tide might change. Certainly they could not look for support to any of the right-wing parties that until the outbreak of the war had represented their more conservative layers, for those parties had perished in the flames of the Revolution. Nor could they turn to the liberal Republican parties, such as the Izquierda Republicana, the Unión Republicana, and the Esquerra Republicana de Catalunya, the Left Republican party of Catalonia, the strongest middle-class party in that region, for the majority of the leaders were either accommodating themselves to the radicalism of the situation or were characterized by inertia born of fear. "In twenty-four hours, minds that once appeared averse to change have evolved strikingly," wrote a famous Anarchist within a few days of the Revolution. "Displaying a remarkable ability to adapt themselves, men who were spiritually very far removed from us have accepted the new order of things without protest. Nobody in Catalonia is startled today to hear of socialization of industry and the disappearance of private property."[6]

Other Republican leaders, regarding everything as lost, had either left the country or were fleeing to the ports. Even Manuel Azaña, the president of the Republic, only yesterday the idol of the liberal segment of the middle classes, was paralyzed by pessimism and fear and had plummeted overnight from his summit of acclaimed leadership. From the very first moment, affirms Angel Ossorio y Gallardo, Manuel Azaña felt that the war was lost, and the excesses that had occurred in the early days revolted and demoralized him.[7] True, many of the leaders of the liberal republican parties would have been capable navigators in calm seas, but they were helpless in the midst of the storms that had buffeted the Republic before the Civil War and even more so now in face of the hurricane that had shattered the coercive organs of the state. "The slight resistance we offered to the assaults of other organizations, our silence and our aloofness in face of the daring advances of the audacious led many persons to believe that we no longer existed," declared Salvadar Quemades, president of the Left Republican party. "They could not understand the noble aim that impelled us to stifle our indignation. The prudence and sense of responsibility that others lacked had to distinguish our behavior, if the wall of resistance we had to erect with arms in our hands against the violent onset of the enemy were not to collapse."[8] But, floundering in the flood of the Revolution, the liberal as well as the conservative members of the middle classes were impressed at the time only by the manifest impotence of their parties and soon began to cast about for an organization that would serve as a breakwater to check the revolutionary tide set in motion by the Anarchosyndicalist and Socialist labor unions.

They did not have to search for long. Before many weeks had passed the organization that succeeded in focusing upon itself their immediate hopes was the Communist party.

A minor factor in Spanish politics before the Civil War, with only seventeen seats in the Cortes[9] and an officially estimated membership of 40,000 on 18 July 1936,[10] the Communist party was soon to mold decisively the course of events in the camp of the anti-Franco forces. Championing the interests of the urban and rural middle classes—a stand few Republicans dared to assume in that atmosphere of revolutionary emotionalism—the Communist party became within a few months the refuge, according to its own figures, of 76,700 peasant proprietors and tenant farmers and of 15,485 members of the urban middle classes.[11] "The Republican middle class," writes a Socialist, "surprised by the moderate tone of Communist propaganda and impressed by the unity and realism which prevailed in this party, flocked in great numbers to join its ranks."[12]

That the Communist party's influence among the middle classes went far beyond the aforementioned figures is indubitable, for thousands of members of the intermediate classes in both country and town placed themselves under its wing without actually becoming adherents of the party. From the very outset of the Revolution, the Communist party, like the PSUC, the Partit Socialista Unificat de Catalunya, the Communist-controlled United Socialist Party of Catalonia, took up the cause of the middle classes, who were being dragged into the vortex of the collectivization movement or were being crippled by the disruption of private trade, the lack of financial resources, and the requisitions carried out by the working-class militia.

"In a capitalist society, the small tradesmen and manufacturers," declared *Mundo Obrero*, the Communist organ in Madrid, "constitute a class that has many things in common with the proletariat. It is, of course, on the side of the democratic Republic, and it is as much opposed to the big capitalists and captains of powerful fascist enterprises as the workers. This being so, it is everybody's duty to respect the property of these small tradesmen and manufacturers.

"We therefore strongly urge the members of our party and the militia in general to demand, and, if need be, to enforce respect for these middle-class citizens, all of whom are workers, and who therefore should not be molested. Their modest interests should not be injured by requisitions and demands that are beyond their meager resources."[13]

Treball, the Communist organ in Catalonia, said:

> It would be unpardonable to forget the multitude of small commodity producers and businessmen of our region. Many of them, thinking only of creating what they had believed would be a position of independence for themselves, had succeeded in setting up their own businesses. Then came a change in the situation precipitated by the attempted coup d'état of the fascists. The immense majority

of small commodity producers and businessmen, who had lived completely on the margin of events, are now more confused than anyone because they feel that they are being harmed and that they are at an obvious disadvantage in comparison with the wage earners. They declare that nobody is concerned about their fate. They are elements who might tend to favor any reactionary movement because in their opinion anything would be better than the economic system that is being instituted in our region. . . .[14]

The distressing situation of many of these people is obvious. They cannot run their workshops and businesses because they have no reserve capital; they have hardly enough to eat, especially the small manufacturers, because the wages they have to pay to the few workers they employ prevent them from attending to their own daily needs. . . .

A moratorium must be granted to all those people who have placed themselves at the service of the antifascist militia, so that they do not have to bear the full weight of the requisitions imposed by the war. A moratorium must be granted and a credit should be opened so that their businesses do not go into liquidation.[15]

To protect the interests of the urban middle classes in this region the Communists organized eighteen thousand tradesmen, handicraftsmen, and small manufacturers into the Federación Catalana de Gremios y Entidades de Pequeños Comerciantes e Industriales, the Catalan federation of small businessmen (known as the GEPCI),[16] some of whose members were, in the phrase of *Solidaridad Obrera*, the CNT organ, "intransigent employers, ferociously antilabor," including Gurri, the former president of the Tailoring Trades Association.[17]

Lest the reader believe that the Communists' support of the middle classes was altruistic rather than pragmatic, that they were concerned more with the welfare of these classes than with the strengthening of their position vis-à-vis their Anarchosyndicalist and Socialist opponents, he should be reminded of Lenin's words that the enemy can be conquered only "by taking advantage of every, even the smallest opportunity of gaining a mass ally, even though this ally be only temporary, vacillating, unstable, unreliable and conditional. Those who do not understand this do not understand a particle of Marxism, or of scientific modern socialism in general."[18]

In the countryside the Communists undertook a spirited defense of the small and medium proprietor and tenant farmer against the collectivizing drive of the rural wage workers, against the policy of the labor unions prohibiting the farmer from holding more land than he could cultivate with his own hands, and against the practices of revolutionary committees that requisitioned harvests, interfered with private trade, and collected rents from tenant farmers.

The liberal Republicans, on the other hand, whose primary concern should have been the defense of the very classes whose interests the Communists were championing, remained cautious to the point of timidity. A consultation of their newspapers offers sufficient proof of this. In fact, they did not venture to raise their voices until April 1937, when the revolutionary tide was receding. "We are tired of remaining silent," declared Miguel San Andrés, the left Republican deputy. "The plundering of the small manufacturer, of the small farmer, and intellectual, of all those people who have been working year after year in order to save a little money cannot be tolerated. . . . We have seen our interests trampled underfoot, and have remained silent."[19]

Not so the Communists. From the outset of the Revolution they were vociferous in the defense not only of the small businessman but also of the small farmer and did their best to profit from any discontent in the countryside. "In the early days of the military rebellion," wrote Julio Mateu, a member of the central committee of the party, in reference to the province of Valencia, "when an endless chain of committees and more committees tried to make a clean sweep of the entire countryside by immediately converting all small proprietors into agricultural workers, by despoiling them of their land and harvests, there was a real danger of setting the peasants against the antifascist organizations. The modest agricultural producers, who for a long time had been oppressed by the political bosses and reactionary usurers, were once again maltreated, this time because of lack of understanding on the part of those who should have helped them in their development. The mistake of considering simple Catholic peasants as enemies prompted some organizations to commit such injustices as to collect from the tenant farmers the rents they formerly paid to the landowners. . . . We have passed through moments of real danger, having been within an ace of unleashing a civil war in the rear between the farmers and the agricultural workers. Fortunately, this has been averted, although at the cost of bursting our lungs in an intense campaign of political education in the villages aimed at securing respect for small property."[20]

Speaking at a public meeting, Vicente Uribe, a member of the PCE's central committee and minister of agriculture from September 1936, declared:

> The present policy of violence against the peasants has two dangers. The first is that it may estrange those who are on our side, on the antifascist side. The other is still more serious: it will endanger the future food supply of Spain. . . . It cannot be tolerated that while at the fronts the soldiers are giving their lives and their blood for the common cause, there are persons far behind the lines who use rifles belonging to the people in order to impose by force ideas that the people do not accept.
>
> But I tell you, peasants; I tell you, workers of the countryside, that despite the abuses some persons are committing, despite the barbarities they are perpetrating, your obligation is to work the land and extract the utmost from it, because you are protected by the government, by parties and by organizations, and because you have at your side the Communist party. . . . Even though violence is used, it is your duty as patriots, your duty as republicans, your duty as antifascists to call upon the government, to call upon the Communists, and you can be sure that, in order that you may cultivate the land peacefully, we shall be at your side armed with rifles."[21]

Speaking a few days later at another meeting, he stated, in reference to the establishment of libertarian communism by the Anarchosyndicalists in some of the villages of Valencia province: "We know that some committees have set up a certain type of regime, a regime in which everyone is subjected to the mercy of their will. We know that they confiscate harvests and commit other abuses, such as seizing small peasant farms, imposing fines, paying for goods with vouchers, in other words, a whole series of irregularities. You know perfectly well that these actions—and listen carefully to this—can never, never have the approval of the government nor even its connivance. . . . We say that the property of the small farmer is sacred and that those who attack or attempt to attack this property must be regarded as enemies of the regime."[22]

It was only natural that the Communists' defense of the interests of peasant owners and tenant farmers should have brought their party a broad wave of adherents. In their campaign they were most successful, of course, in areas where small and medium-sized farms predominated. In the rich orange- and rice-growing province of Valencia, for example, where the farmers were prosperous and had supported right-wing organizations before the Civil War, fifty thousand had by March 1937, according to official figures, joined the Peasant Federation,[23] which the PCE had set up for their protection in the first months of the Revolution. "The Communist party," complained a Socialist, "devotes itself to picking up in the villages the worst remnants of the former Partido Autonomista, who were not only reactionary, but also immoral, and organizes these small proprietors into a new peasant union by promising them the possession of their land."[24] And Pedro García, the Socialist secretary of the UGT agricultural workers in Valencia province, affiliated with the powerful National Federation of Land Workers (Federación Nacional de los Trabajadores de la Tierra), protested that the PCE was fostering the growth of a rival peasant organization in the province, "which sooner or later might be used for political purposes as a shock force in the villages against the UGT peasant unions."[25]

In addition to providing its members with fertilizers and seed and securing credits from the ministry of agriculture—likewise controlled by the PCE—the new Peasant Federation served as a potent instrument in checking the rural collectivization promoted by the agricultural workers of the CNT and UGT and in combating the CLUEA (Consejo Levantino Unificado de la Exportación Agrícola), which was set up by the unions (primarily the CNT) in order to control the purchase, packing, and exportation of the valuable orange crop formerly handled by a swarm of middlemen.[26] That the protection and promise of eventual change held forth by the Peasant Federation should have induced many of its members to apply for admission into the PCE is understandable. "Such is the sympathy for us in the Valencia countryside," Julio Mateu, general secretary of the federation, affirmed, "that hundreds and thousands of farmers would join our party if we were to let them. These farmers, many of whom believed in God—and still do— and prayed and in private beat their breasts, love our party like a sacred thing. When we tell them that they should not confuse the Peasant Federation with the party, and that even without a membership card it is possible to be a Communist by working for its political line, they are wont to reply, 'The Communist party is our party.' Comrades, what emotion the peasants display when they utter these words!"[27]

Because the PCE gave the urban and rural middle classes a powerful infusion of new hope and vitality, it is not surprising that a large part of the copious flow of new members into the party in the months following the Revolution came from these classes. It is almost superfluous to say that these new recruits were attracted, not by Communist principles, but by the hope of saving something from the ruins of the old social system. Furthermore, in addition to defending their property rights, the PCE defined the social overturn, not as a proletarian, but as a bourgeois democratic revolution. Within a few days of the outbreak of the war, politburo member Dolores Ibárruri, popularly known as La Pasionaria (the Passion Flower), declared in the name of the central committee:

> The revolution that is taking place in our country is the bourgeois democratic revolution that was achieved over a century ago in other countries, such as France, and we Communists are the front-line fighters in this struggle against the obscurantist forces of the past.
>
> Cease conjuring up the specter of communism, you generals, many times traitors, with the idea of isolating the Spanish people in its magnificent struggle against those who wish to turn Spain into a tragic, backward country, a country in which the military, the clergy, and the political bosses would be the absolute masters of life and property! We Communists are defending a regime of liberty and democracy, and side by side with Republicans, Socialists, and Anarchists we shall prevent Spain from retrogressing, cost what it may. . . .
>
> It is a lie to speak of chaos; a lie to say that a chaotic situation exists here, as do the reports given out by traitors to the Republic!
>
> In this historic hour the Communist party, faithful to its revolutionary principles and respecting the will of the people, places itself at the side of the government that expresses this will, at the side of the Republic, at the side of democracy. . . .
>
> The government of Spain is a government that emerged from the electoral triumph of 16 February, and we support it and we defend it because it is the legal representative of the people fighting for democracy and liberty. . . .
>
> Long live the struggle of the people against reaction and fascism! Long live the Democratic Republic![28]

Thus, from the outset, the Communist party appeared before the distraught middle classes not only as a defender of property, but as a champion of the Republic and of orderly processes of government. Not that these classes had complete confidence in its good faith, but they were ready to support it as long as it offered them protection and helped to restore to the government the power assumed by revolutionary committees. That their support was shot through with suspicion and fear was natural, for in the past the Communists had pursued an entirely different policy, as will be seen in the ensuing chapter.

8

The Popular Front

"*O*ur task is to win over the majority of the proletariat and to prepare it for the assumption of power," La Pasionaria had declared toward the end of 1933. "This means that we must bend all our efforts to organize workshop and peasant committees and to create soviets. . . . The development of the revolutionary movement is extremely favorable to us. We are advancing along the road that has been indicated to us by the Communist International and that leads to the establishment of a Soviet government in Spain, a government of workers and peasants."[1]

This policy was in strange contrast to the seemingly moderate goals pursued by the Communist party after the outbreak of the Civil War and Revolution in July 1936. The change that had occurred stemmed from the resolutions passed at the Seventh World Congress of the Communist International in 1935, officially adopting the Popular Front policy.

At the root of this new policy lay the deterioration in German-Soviet relations since Adolf Hitler's rise to power in January 1933 and Joseph Stalin's fear that Germany's revived military strength would ultimately be directed against the USSR. Suffering from the aftereffects of compulsory collectivization and bending every effort to strengthen her political and military system, the Soviet Union was careful not to offer any provocation that would draw her into permanent estrangement from the Nazi regime.

Isaac Deutscher writes:

> Hitler's bloody suppression of all domestic opposition and his racial persecutions affected diplomatic routine business between Moscow and Berlin as little as it affected similar business between Paris or London and Berlin. Stalin undoubtedly calculated on the strength of the Bismarckian tradition among the German diplomats, a tradition which demanded that the Reich should avoid embroilment with Russia. In the first year of Hitler's chancellorship [Stalin] did not utter in public a single word about the events in Germany, though his silence was excruciating to the bewildered followers of the Comintern.
>
> He broke that silence only at the seventeenth congress of the party, in January

1934. Even then he refrained from drawing the conclusions from events which had ended so disastrously for the European Left, and he vaguely fostered the illusion that fascism, "a symptom of capitalist weakness," would prove short-lived. But he also described the Nazi upheaval as a "triumph for the idea of revenge in Europe" and remarked that the anti-Russian trend in German policy had been prevailing over the older Bismarckian tradition. Even so, he was at pains to make it clear that Russia desired to remain on the same terms with the Third Reich as she had been with Weimar Germany.[2]

Indeed, *Izvestiia*, the organ of the Soviet government, declared within a few weeks of Hitler's appointment to the Reich chancellorship that the USSR was the only state that had "no hostile sentiments toward Germany, whatever the form and composition of that country's government."[3] But Russia's advances had been coldly received, and at the end of 1933, Vyacheslav Molotov, chairman of the Council of People's Commissars, complained that during the past year the ruling groups in Germany had made a number of attempts to revise relations with the Soviet Union.[4]

With a view to seeking safeguards against the menace of German expansion and to making her influence felt in the chancelleries of Western Europe, the Soviet Union reversed her attitude of hostility toward the League of Nations and joined that body in September 1934. "On entering the League of Nations," said the weekly bulletin of the Comintern, *International Press Correspondence*, "it will be possible for the U.S.S.R. to struggle still more effectively and practically against a counterrevolutionary war on the U.S.S.R."[5] But in spite of this move, uneasiness regarding German intentions continued unabated. "The direct threat of war has increased for the USSR," declared Molotov in January 1935. "We must not forget that there is now in Europe a ruling party that has proclaimed as its historical task the seizure of territory in the Soviet Union."[6]

As a further move to ward off the German threat to her security, Russia concluded a Pact of Mutual Assistance with France on 2 May 1935. This treaty was favored by the French mainly to remove any links that still remained between the USSR and Germany since the Russo-German rapprochement begun at Rapallo in 1922[7] and to end the opposition of the French Communist party to the national defense program;[8] in fact, it was never supplemented by any positive military agreement between the respective general staffs[9] and from the beginning elicited very little enthusiasm even from government circles.[10]

Some idea of what the French ministry of foreign affairs, even at the time of the French Popular Front government of Léon Blum, thought of the Franco-Soviet pact may be gathered from a memorandum by the acting state secretary of the German Foreign Office relating to a conversation on 1 September 1936 with the French ambassador, François-Poncet. Referring to the proposed meeting of the five Locarno Powers (Great Britain, France, Belgium, Italy, and Germany) to negotiate a new Western pact to take the place of the Locarno Agreement, the memorandum stated:

M. François-Poncet was particularly interested in hearing whether we were willing to go to the conference and negotiate on the first points on the agenda without bringing up the fifth point, or whether we wanted to force the French Government now, in advance, expressly to renounce the fifth point, that is, the ties in the east. In other words, did the German Government take the stand that it was possible to start out by negotiating on a Western Pact, leaving the eastern questions open? Or did it demand from the very first that France renounce her eastern ties, before Germany would enter into a discussion concerning a Western Pact? If Germany followed the first course, he believed he could say that the Franco-Russian ties would gradually cool, particularly since they had never been popular with a large sector of the French people; we would then attain our objective slowly but surely. If, on the other hand, we should apply pressure to the French Government now and demand that it give up the Russian alliance, the French Government could only refuse to do so. In a long discourse M. François-Poncet tried to convince me of the rightness of the one alternative and the wrongness of the other, emphasizing solemnly during the course of his statements that there were no special military ties between France and the Soviet Union.[11]

Moscow was fully alive to the possibility that the pact might eventually be disregarded, and it thus became a vital task for French Communists to ensure that France would honor her commitments.

"We can congratulate ourselves on the Franco-Soviet treaty," declared Vaillant Couturier, the French Communist leader, "but as we have no confidence that the French bourgeoisie and the fascist cadres of the French army will observe its clauses, *we shall act accordingly*. We know that whatever may be the interests that lead certain French political circles toward a rapprochement with the USSR, the champions of French imperialism hate the Soviet Union."[12]

The agonizing dilemma of French policymakers, which for diplomatic reasons they could not reveal publicly, was nevertheless frankly expressed by Pierre Taittinger, a rightist member of the Chamber of Deputies: "The very existence of France is at stake. By a policy of outright alliance with the USSR, we should immediately be drawn into a conflict with Germany. The outcome of this conflict would be terrifying for us. If Germany were defeated, our country would be contaminated very quickly by Bolshevism. If she were victorious, France would be wiped off the map."[13]

Powerful forces both in France and Britain opposed any hard and fast commitments in Eastern Europe that might entangle the West in a war with Germany, and these forces seemed ready to countenance the latter's expansionist aims at the expense of the Soviet Union.

In France, François le Grix, the royalist and editor of the *Revue Hébdomadaire*, declared on 6 April 1935 that the two essential conditions for preserving Western civilization were to avoid war and eliminate Pan-Germanism and Bolshevism by "leaving them grappling with each other" and that he hoped that Germany would beat Russia, in which case, "it is very possible that she will consider herself satisfied; at least Western Europe would have a respite to get organized."[14]

"In those prewar years," writes Sumner Welles, who became U.S. undersecretary of state in 1937, "great financial and commercial interests of the Western democracies, including many in the United States, were firm in the belief that war between the Soviet Union and Hitlerite Germany could only be favorable to their own interests. They maintained that Russia would necessarily be defeated, and with this defeat Communism would be destroyed; also that Germany would be so weakened as a result of the conflict that for many years thereafter she would be incapable of any real threat to the rest of the world."[15]

On 6 May 1935, William Dodd, U.S. ambassador to Berlin, made the following notation in his diary regarding a letter he had received from Lord Lothian, influential British statesman and diplomat: "He indicated clearly that he favors a coalition of the democracies to block any German move in their direction and to turn Germany's course eastwards."[16] And in an article in the *Daily Mail* entitled "Why Not a Franco-British Alliance?" Viscount Rothermere, one of the British press lords, wrote: "The new bond between France and Britain would have another effect of inestimable importance. It would turn Germany's territorial ambitions in the direction where they can do least harm and most good—towards the east of Europe."[17]

The influence and public acceptance of the *Daily Mail* in those prewar years should not be underrated. According to Franklin Reid Gannon's analysis of the British press and Germany, "[it] was the largest paper of the most complete newspaper combine in Great Britain. In 1937, its circulation was 1,580,000; it was the only popular daily paper which had a predominantly upper- and middle-class readership." And of Viscount Rothermere himself, he writes: "[He] was very near to being unbalanced on the issue of communism, and constantly importuned Ward Price [George Ward Price, the *Daily Mail*'s chief foreign correspondent] to write articles like that of 21 September 1936 in which he stated that Bolshevism was a greater threat to the British Empire than National Socialism and . . . that if Hitler did not exist, 'all Western Europe might soon be clamouring for such a champion.' "[18] But there was nothing bizarre in this thought. Even former Liberal prime minister David Lloyd George declared in Parliament a year later: "In a very short time, perhaps in a year, perhaps in two, the Conservative elements in this country will be looking to Germany as the bulwark against Communism in Europe. . . . [If] her defence breaks down against the Communists . . . , Europe will follow. . . . Do not let us be in a hurry to condemn Germany. We shall be welcoming Germany as our friend."[19]

Although at no time was the *Daily Mail* considered to be a mouthpiece of the Conservative governments of Stanley Baldwin and Neville Chamberlain, it nevertheless expressed the private concerns of a large and influential body of conservative opinion. According to General Baron Geyr von Schweppenburg, former military attaché to the German embassy in London, Major-General Sir John Dill at the War Office and those members of the British general staff who thought as he did "were convinced that another war between the British Empire and Germany would be a tragedy, not only for the Empire, but for the whole of Europe. They saw quite clearly that such a war would only forward the designs of Russia."[20] And in aviation circles, there was a strong pro-German element, whose most strident and vociferous exponent, according to Richard Griffiths, was C. G. Grey, the editor of *The Aeroplane*, which, on 19 April 1933, expressed the view that Germany was "the first line of defence of Western civilization against Eastern barbarism."[21]

Although in those prewar years cabinet ministers did not openly express their fears of Russia, Sir Samuel Hoare (later, Viscount Templewood), who held several key positions under Baldwin and Chamberlain, gave public utterances some years later to these concerns: "[We] had solid reasons for distrusting the Soviet. For more than twenty years, successive British Governments had suffered from Russian plots and intrigues. British party politics had been constantly poisoned by Russian propaganda. Russian secret agents were continuously exploiting any chance of stirring up trouble. Russian money was finding its way into the pockets of British agitators. . . . The attempts to incite mutinies in the fighting services and strikes in the ranks of labour went on unabated during the whole period between the two wars, and the Russian Embassy in London never ceased to be a centre of espionage and agitation. . . . [We] should not have been human if we had not been influenced by this long record of Russian duplicity and hostility."[22]

Whatever we may think of the policy of "appeasement" of Germany in the prewar years, it is impossible to understand the course of events in Europe, including the Spanish Civil War, unless we take into account this fear of Russia.

That the Western democracies were confronted with a fateful choice is indubitable. On the one hand, they could oppose and destroy the Nazi regime while it was still weak, leaving the Soviet Union free to develop its resources and become in time, with allied Communist parties, the greatest menace in the world. "I feel that if the Nazi regime in Germany is destroyed then the country will go communist," stated the Marquess of Londonderry, secretary of state for air from 1931 to 1935, in a letter to Winston Churchill on 9 May 1936, "and we shall find a lining-up of France, Germany, and Russia and the menace of communism as the most powerful policy in the world."[23]

This was not his only misgiving. In his book *Ourselves and Germany*, published in 1938, Londonderry expressed concern that unless Britain soon arrived at an Anglo-German understanding Germany would "strike out along a course of Weltpolitik frankly antagonistic to Great Britain and her many imperial and commercial interests. It is to avert such an unfortunate eventuality as this that I have made every effort to convince the people of this country of the value and importance of a friendly understanding between Britain and Germany." And in a later passage he wrote that he was "at a loss to understand why we could not make common ground in some form or other with Germany in opposition to Communism."[24]

No less explicit was Thierry Maulnier, who, in an article written after the sacrifice of Czechoslovakia to Nazi Germany at Munich in September 1938, expressed the views of the parties of the French right. "These parties," he wrote, "felt that in the event of war not only would the disaster be tremendous, not only would the defeat and devastation of France be within the bounds of possibility, but, even more, that Germany's defeat would mean the collapse of those authoritarian systems that form the principal bulwark against Communist revolution and that it would perhaps lead to the immediate bolshevization of Europe. In other words, a French defeat would indeed have been a defeat of France, while a French victory would have been less a victory for France than for the principles quite rightly regarded as leading directly to the ruin of France and of civilization itself. It is a pity that the men and parties in France who shared in that belief did not in general admit it, for there was nothing inavowable about it.[25] Indeed, in my opinion, it was one of the principal and well-founded reasons, if not the best-founded, for not going to war in September 1938."[26]

On the other hand, the Western democracies could, though not without opprobrium and extreme peril to themselves, allow the Nazi regime to overrun the nontotalitarian states in Central and Southeastern Europe lying west of Russia's border in the hope that it would in time come into collision with the rising power of the Soviet Union.

The view of the staunchest conservative opponent of any policy involving the sacrifice to Nazi Germany of the small states in Central and Southeastern Europe must be recorded here. Winston Churchill wrote to the Marquess of Londonderry in October 1937:

We all wish to live on friendly terms with Germany. We know the best Germans are ashamed of the Nazi excesses and recoil from the paganism on which they are based. We certainly do not want to pursue a policy inimical to the legitimate interests of Germany, but you must surely be aware that, when the German Government speaks of friendship with England, what they mean is, that we shall give them back their former colonies, and also agree to their having a free hand, as far as we are concerned, in Central and Southern Europe.

This means that they would devour Austria and Czechoslovakia as a preliminary to making a gigantic Middle-European bloc. It would certainly not be in our interest to connive at such policies of aggression. It would be wrong and cynical in the last degree to buy immunity for ourselves at the expense of smaller states in Central Europe.

It would be contrary to the whole tide of British and United States opinion for us to facilitate the spread of Nazi tyranny over countries which now have a considerable measure of democratic freedom. In my view, we should build up so strong a Federation of Regional Agreements under the League of Nations that

Germany will be content to live within her own bounds in a law-abiding manner, instead of seeking to invade her smaller neighbours, slay them and have their farms and homes for themselves.[27]

And speaking to Ivan Maisky, the Soviet ambassador to the United Kingdom, Churchill, in the spring of 1935, criticized some of the supporters of Western security: "These people," he said, according to Maisky's version of the conversation, "argue that . . . Germany has to fight somewhere, . . . so let her better carve out an empire for herself at the expense of the States in eastern and south-eastern Europe. . . . Such ideas are, of course, complete idiocy, but unfortunately they are still fairly popular in certain quarters of the Conservative Party. But I am firmly convinced that in the long run the victory will be not with the supporters of western security, but with those who, like [Sir Robert] Vansittart [permanent undersecretary at the Foreign Office from 1931 to 1938] or myself, consider that peace is indivisible, and that Britain, France and the U.S.S.R. must be the backbone of the defensive alliance which will keep Germany in a wholesome state of apprehension."[28]

On 7 November 1935, Vansittart wrote to Lord Wigram, private secretary to King George V: "Any attempt at giving Germany a free hand to annex other people's property in Central and Eastern Europe is both absolutely immoral and completely contrary to all the principles of the League [of Nations] which form the backbone of the policy of this country. Any British Government that attempted to do a deal would almost certainly be brought down in ignominy—and deservedly. . . . Any suggestion that a British Government contemplates leaving, let alone inviting Germany to satisfy her land-hunger at Russia's expense, would quite infallibly split the country from top to bottom."[29]

But in those prewar years there were more powerful voices than those of Winston Churchill and Robert Vansittart, who was removed from his post by Prime Minister Neville Chamberlain in 1938. How far British policy toward Germany was determined by the fear of Russia is illustrated by Lord Lloyd, a Conservative Peer and a leading British diplomat. In his pamphlet, *The British Case*, written shortly after the outbreak of war between Britain and Germany in September 1939 and given the stamp of official endorsement by the commendatory preface of Lord Halifax, then secretary of state for foreign affairs under Prime Minister Neville Chamberlain, Lord Lloyd wrote: "However abominable [Hitler's] methods, however deceitful his diplomacy, however intolerant he might show himself of the rights of other European peoples, he still claimed to stand ultimately for something which was a common European interest, and which therefore could conceivably provide some day a basis for understanding with other nations equally determined not to sacrifice their traditional institutions and habits on the blood-stained altars of the World Revolution."[30]

To prevent the Western democracies from compounding their differences with the Third Reich at the possible expense of Russia, to guarantee that the Franco-Soviet Pact of Mutual Assistance would not fall by the wayside, and, moreover, to conclude similar alliances with other countries, notably Great Britain, it was essential for the Soviet Union that governments hostile to German aims in Eastern Europe should be brought into office. With this end in view, the Popular Front line was formally adopted at the Seventh World Congress of the Comintern in August 1935. Thus a new era of wooing the Socialist and Liberal parties was officially inaugurated, ending the fissiparous policy of denouncing the Socialists as "social fascists" and as the "mainstay of the bourgeoisie, including that of the fascist countries,"[31] which so facilitated Hitler's rise to power. But it should not be forgotten that some sections of the Comintern had, in accordance with the new trend in Soviet foreign policy, been seeking cooperation with other parties even before 1935.[32] This attempt had been most successful in France.[33]

The foreign political goals of the Soviet Union should not obscure the fact that long before the formal adoption by the Comintern of the Popular Front line, in Spain most of the parties of the left saw a compelling domestic reason for a movement of unity, namely, the defeat of the left by the center-right in the November 1933 elections. The Communists claimed that they initiated the movement of unity in Spain, but the efforts of the liberal Republicans led by Manuel Azaña to forge a coalition of Republicans and Socialists with which to confront the center-right at the next elections should not be discounted.[34]

In its program, the Seventh World Congress of the Comintern decided that one of the immediate tasks of the Communists in all countries was to bring the peasantry and the small urban bourgeoisie into a "wide anti-fascist people's front." This was essential, it argued, because the "dominant circles of the British bourgeoisie support German armaments in order to weaken the hegemony of France on the European Continent . . . and to direct Germany's aggressiveness against the Soviet Union."[35] Certainly, British support of German rearmament in the first half of 1935 alone lent support to these charges.

On 6 February 1935, Sir John Simon, then secretary of state for foreign affairs, had stated in the House of Commons: "Germany's claim to equality of rights in the matter of armaments cannot be resisted, and ought not to be resisted."[36] On 18 June 1935, the Anglo-German Naval Agreement had been signed, giving the German navy 35 percent of British naval tonnage. Criticizing this agreement on 11 July 1935, Winston Churchill declared: "We have condoned, and even praised the German treaty-breaking in fleet building."[37] "In Russia," wrote Max Beloff, the British historian, "the [naval] pact was interpreted as a sign of Britain's weakness and of her desire to divert Germany from air preparations to naval building, where she felt stronger. It might also serve to divert Germany's attention eastward and to allow Britain to disengage herself from Europe, so as to salvage her menaced position in the Far East. A new field of activity would be open for British advocates of an entente with Germany. The Germans would not, the Russians argued, observe the agreement, and only welcomed it as a breach in the treaties. It was clear that the German command of the Baltic [the gateway to Russia] would be unassailable. [According to Maisky, "the British Government's desire to assure Germany supremacy in the Baltic against the U.S.S.R." was the most important motive for concluding the agreement.]³⁸ Nor does there seem any reason to doubt that it was the Baltic situation which Herr Hitler had chiefly in mind."³⁹ Furthermore, in the summer of 1935, Germany reintroduced conscription in violation of the Versailles Treaty. This, too, was condoned by Britain.⁴⁰

With the threat of growing German power undoubtedly in mind, the Seventh World Congress of the Comintern declared that the struggle for peace opened up the greatest opportunity for creating the broadest united front with the peasantry and the small urban bourgeoisie and that "all those interested in the preservation of peace should be drawn into this united front." This goal was to be achieved by mobilizing the people against "the plundering price policy of monopoly capital and the bourgeois governments" and against "increasing taxation and the high cost of living."⁴¹ Although the congress reaffirmed the aims of the Communist International, namely, the revolutionary overthrow of the rule of the bourgeoisie and the establishment of the dictatorship of the proletariat in the form of soviets,⁴² the policy of unity with the middle classes could not but lead sooner or later to an attempt on the part of the Comintern's various sections to deemphasize their revolutionary goals and to disarm the suspicion with which they were once regarded. "All revolutionary slogans, with reference to the class struggle and to the Dictatorship of the Proletariat," writes Arthur Koestler, who, in 1935, worked for the propaganda department of the Comintern, "were in one sweep relegated to the lumber room. They were replaced by a brand new façade, with geranium boxes in the windows, called 'Popular Front for Peace and against Fascism.' Its doors were wide open to all men of good will—Socialists, Catholics, Conservatives, Nationalists. The notion that we had ever advocated revolution and violence was to be ridiculed as a bogey refuted as a slander spread by reactionary war-mongers. We no longer referred to ourselves as 'Bolsheviks,' nor even as Communists—the public use of the word was now rather frowned at in the Party—we were just simple, honest, peace-loving anti-Fascists and defenders of democracy."⁴³

Did this mean that the Comintern had now abandoned its hegemonic aims? By no means. The congress made it clear that a Popular Front government "could become a special transitional form to proletarian rule."⁴⁴ "Fifteen years ago," declared Georgi Dimitrov, general secretary of the Comintern, in his main report to the congress, "Lenin called upon us to focus all our attention on 'searching out forms of *transition* or *approach* to the proletarian revolution.' It may be that in a number of countries the *united front government* will prove to be *one* of the most important transitional forms."⁴⁵

The result of this new policy was that in Spain, as one historian points out, the Communists "very carefully walked a fence between appealing to the revolutionary masses and the moderate republican [middle-class] elements, sometimes contradicting themselves."⁴⁶

9

Foreign Intervention

From the standpoint of Soviet foreign policy, the Popular Front line met with appreciable success. In the early months of 1936, both in France and Spain, the Communists participated in general elections on a broad basis and helped to bring liberal governments into office, uniting not only with the Socialists, their former foes, but also with the moderate parties.

That Germany should have viewed with alarm the success of a policy designed to establish an anti-German front by reinforcing and extending Russia's political and military ties with Western Europe is natural, but not until the outbreak of the military revolt in Spain in July 1936 did an opportunity arise to counter this threat to her own plans by direct intervention on the side of the rebellion. Contrary to the opinion widely held, no promises of German military aid were given to the organizers of the revolt prior to the outbreak of hostilities. According to the documents relating to Spain in the archives of the German foreign ministry, published in Washington by the Department of State in 1950, Hitler did not promise assistance until several days after the outbreak of the rebellion, when General Franco sent a German businessman resident in Spanish Morocco and the local Nazi leader to Germany to request planes and other support.[1] This request was quickly acceded to, for according to Nazi sources German airplanes were active on the side of General Franco in the first weeks of the war either in transporting Moorish troops and Foreign Legionaries from Spanish Morocco to the mainland or in bombing operations.[2]

At the Nuremberg trials in 1946, Hermann Goering, Hitler's air force chief, stated:

> When the civil war broke out in Spain, Franco sent a call for help to Germany and asked for support, particularly in the air. One should not forget that Franco with his troops was stationed in Africa and that he could not get the troops across, as the fleet was in the hands of the communists [the forces of the left]. . . . The decisive factor was, first of all, to get his troops over to Spain.
>
> The Führer thought the matter over. I urged him to give support under all circumstances, firstly, in order to prevent the further spread of communism in that

theater and, secondly, to test my young Luftwaffe at this opportunity in this or that technical aspect.

With the permission of the Führer, I sent a large part of my transport fleet and a number of experimental fighter units, bombers, and antiaircraft guns; and in that way I had an opportunity to ascertain, under combat conditions, whether the material was equal to the task. In order that the personnel, too, might gather a certain amount of experience, I saw to it that there was a continuous flow, that is, that new people were constantly being sent and others recalled.[3]

Although Germany did indeed use Spain as a training and testing ground for personnel and new weapons later in the war, it is most unlikely that Goering had this idea in mind during the first days of the conflict. As Angel Viñas points out in his valuable work *La Alemania nazi y el 18 de julio*, Hitler's initial assistance in July 1936 consisted of twenty Junker-52 transport planes flown by pilots of the *Lufthansa*.[4] "It is true that six Heinkel-51 fighters were dispatched, but only for purposes of protection . . . and their pilots were prohibited from entering combat except in self defense. . . . [The] decision to send aircraft in numbers dates from October 1936 and their transfer from November, in other words, at a much later time."[5]

In going to the aid of General Franco, Germany had a twofold objective. On the one hand, although fearful of the international complications that might arise from being drawn too deeply into the Spanish conflict[6] at a time when she was not yet ready for a large-scale war, she hoped to secure strategic advantages in preparation for the coming struggle in Western Europe. Quite early in the war Hitler himself revealed to party leaders and diplomats: "It is to our advantage that no Bolshevik State should exist [in Spain] forming a bridge by land between France and North Africa."[7] On another occasion, he affirmed that "his sole objective was to prevent Spanish foreign policy from being influenced after the war by Paris, London or Moscow. In this way, in the final confrontation over the reorganization of Europe, Spain will not be among the enemies of Germany, but, if possible, among her friends."[8]

In a communication to Wilhelmstrasse, dated 1 May 1937, the German ambassador to General Franco wrote: "There is no doubt that, [after] a war won because of our intervention, a Spain socially ordered and economically reconstructed with our help will in the future be not only a very important source of raw materials for us, but also a faithful friend for a long time to come."[9] On the other hand, Hitler no doubt hoped that the defeat of the Popular Front and the resurgence of the right in Spain would weaken the French Popular Front and strengthen those forces in France that were opposed to blocking German expansion eastward and regarded the Franco-Soviet Pact of Mutual Assistance as likely to entangle their country in a struggle that, in the event of a German defeat, would result in the enthronement of communism in Europe. "What Moscow wants," ran an article that was typical of an appreciable segment of French opinion, "is a war between French and German soldiers. At some time or another, on some pretext or another, Russia hopes that she will be able to force us to throw our troops against the [German] frontier and deal a double blow by weakening the dreaded German power and by delivering our country up to a foreign war that would ring in the hour of the Bolshevik Revolution."[10]

Russia was not blind to the dangers of German intervention in Spain. But, anxious not to give body and color to attacks that pictured her as the open patron of world revolution lest she antagonize the moderate parties in the West on whom she based her hopes of an anti-German front, she formally adhered on 23 August 1936 to the international Non-Intervention Agreement that had been proposed by France to prevent an extension of the conflict[11] and undertook, together with the other countries participating in the accord, not to send arms to Spain. "Had the Soviet Union not agreed to the French proposal for neutrality," commented a Communist newspaper, "it would have very seriously embarrassed the [French] Government, and considerably assisted fascists in France and England, as well as the governments of Germany and Italy, in their campaign against the Spanish people. . . . If the Soviet Government took any step which added further fuel to the present inflammable situation in Europe, it would be welcomed by the Fascists of all countries and would split the democratic forces, thus directly preparing the way for so-called 'preventive warfare' against Bolshevism as represented by the USSR."[12]

The Soviet Union's concern for Western democratic opinion ill accords with the charge put forward by rebel sources, based on the publication of "secret" Communist documents, that the Communists had been conspiring to set up a Soviet regime in Spain in the summer of 1936,[13] for it is obvious that had they attempted to set up such a regime they would have ruined the Kremlin's efforts to establish a firm alliance with the democratic powers. For this reason alone—to say nothing of the fact that they certainly did not have the necessary strength—the charge may be safely discounted. In fact, even José María Gil Robles, the leader of the right-wing Catholic CEDA, writes: "I never believed in the possibility at that time of a Communist uprising, much less in one directly involving the Comintern. . . . Confronted by the Hitlerite threat, Stalin favored a rapprochement with England and France. The Franco-Soviet pact and the resolutions of the Seventh Congress of the Third International [Comintern] testify that he subordinated revolution in Europe to the policy of containment of German imperialism. And nothing could have awakened greater hostility among the European democracies than an attempt to implant a Communist state in Spain. . . . The real danger lay not in a carefully organized Communist insurrection, but in the climate of anarchy that prevailed everywhere. The last time I spoke with Señor Azaña . . . he did not conceal from me his fear of being overwhelmed by the masses of the Popular Front."[14]

The "secret" documents that formed the basis for the charge that the Communists were conspiring to set up a Soviet regime in the summer of 1936 have not only been exposed conclusively as forgeries by Herbert R. Southworth, a partisan of the left,[15] but have been recognized as such by one of Spain's foremost historians of the Civil War, Ricardo de la Cierva, a supporter of the military uprising, who claims that they were written by the Spanish right-wing author Tomás Borrás. "Hence," he affirms, "the documents were born spurious . . . [but] they were utilized with tremendous effectiveness by Spanish and foreign propagandists." He cautions, however, that "to refute their authenticity" is not to deny the danger and the deep fear of communism that existed at the time.[16] Moreover, he produces evidence from Spanish Communist party sources showing that the party had not abandoned its revolutionary goals, and he argues that during the first half of 1936 it contributed "effectively to the intensification of the revolutionary dynamism of the proletariat."[17]

Still, in spite of this evidence, in spite of the seemingly revolutionary character of the language the Communists sometimes employed before the Civil War so as not to lose touch with the radical temper of the Anarchosyndicalists and left-wing Socialists, in spite of the fact that they publicly urged the creation of workers' and peasants' alliances as "future organs of power"[18] and acknowledged that the dictatorship of the proletariat was the party's ultimate goal,[19] and in spite of their warnings to the liberal government that the agricultural workers would divide up the estates of the big landed proprietors by force of arms if it did not carry out the agrarian reform more expeditiously,[20] they were careful to maintain their alliance with the moderates. "The Popular Front must continue," wrote José Díaz. "We have still a long way to travel with the Left Republicans."[21] Again, in spite of their demands for the purging of the army[22] and their threat just before the military insurrection that unless the government fulfilled the Popular Front program they would strive for the creation of a government of a "revolutionary popular character,"[23] this language was designed more to propitiate the prevailing revolutionary sentiment and to goad the government into action against the right than to encourage an immediate social overturn. Indeed, during the strike of the Madrid construction workers before the Civil War that seriously embarrassed the government and threatened to develop into a revolutionary confrontation with the employers and the state, the Communists did their best to induce the Anarchosyndicalists to terminate it.[24]

That the military insurrection and the far-reaching social revolution it spawned came at an awkward time for the Kremlin there can be no doubt. Furthermore, as Fernando Claudín, the former Spanish Communist leader, wrote many years later: "The outbreak of the Spanish revolution—the only revolution that occurred in Europe during the existence of the Communist International, except for the ephemeral Hungarian Soviet Republic of 1919—took the leaders of the 'world party' unawares."[25] Their dilemma could not have been more excruciating. How could they support the revolutionary movement in Spain and continue to appeal to moderate opinion abroad?

To resolve the dilemma, Stalin, while officially adhering to the Non-Intervention Agreement, decided on 28 August 1936, as we shall see shortly, to embark on a policy of cautious military intervention under cover of his proclamation of neutrality and to pursue a policy of moderation and restraint in face of the revolutionary upheaval.

His decision to intervene came late as compared with that of Adolf Hitler and, indeed, as compared with that of Benito Mussolini, for according to Fascist sources, Italian aircraft and naval ships were in operation at the beginning of August.[26] As in the case of Hitler, there is no record of any promise of aid having been given by Mussolini either to General Franco or to General Mola immediately before the outbreak of hostilities. True, in 1934, the Italian government had signed an agreement with Spanish monarchist leaders providing for military support in the event civil war should break out in Spain, but as Lizarza Iribarren, one of the conspirators, has pointed out, nothing came of the accord, because the July 1936 rebellion was undertaken by officers not involved in the negotiations with Mussolini. Nevertheless, the agreement helped to create in Rome "a climate favorable to the rebellion" and Mussolini, after some hesitation, decided to support it on 27 July. On the other hand, Count Galeazzo Ciano, the Italian foreign secretary, expressed his approval from the outset without first consulting his chief.

This was corroborated in 1967 by Luis Bolín, the London correspondent of the Madrid monarchist newspaper *ABC*, who chartered the de Havilland Dragon Rapide that flew General Franco from the Canary Islands to head the revolt in Spanish Morocco on 18–19 July. In his book *Spain: The Vital Years*, Bolín reproduces a hitherto unpublished document signed by General Franco (and countersigned by General Sanjurjo in Lisbon, the leader-designate of the rebellion, just before his ill-fated flight to Spain to head the revolt) authorizing Bolín to negotiate urgently in England, Germany, or Italy for the purchase of aircraft and supplies. Bolín flew to Rome on 21 July, where he was assisted by former king Alfonso's equerry, the Marqués de Viana. Their request for help, although sympathetically received by foreign minister Ciano, was at first denied by Mussolini, a fact confirmed by Roberto Cantalupo, the Italian ambassador to Franco.[27] Not until some days later did Mussolini agree to help, and, on 30 July, twelve Savoia-81 bombers were dispatched to Spanish Morocco, although only nine arrived safely at their destination.[28]

In 1968, José María Gil Robles published the following version of the purchase of the first Italian planes: "When the rising occurred and it became necessary to establish an aerial bridge for the passage of troops from Morocco to the peninsula, the Italian government gave notice that the contract for the purchase of the planes should be drawn up with one of the signatories of the [Rome] agreement of 1934. It was essential that señores Goicoechea [head of Renovación Española, who had participated in the accord], Sainz Rodríguez, and Zunzunegui leave urgently for Italy with concrete orders from [General] Mola. They conducted the first successful negotiations for the purchase of war material, almost at the very moment that Luis Antonio Bolín, commissioned by General Franco, was experiencing difficulties in his negotiations. During their interview in Rome with

Count Ciano on 25 July, the shipment of transport planes was agreed upon. By 1 August there had already arrived in Nador [the Spanish Moroccan airfield near Melilla] fourteen Italian Savoia-Marchetti military planes, and on 2 August, the number at the same airfield was twenty-four. Thus the pact of 1934 was fulfilled."[29] The official (pro-Franco) *Historia de la cruzada*, published in 1940, also claims that, because Bolín's negotiations were meeting with difficulty, General Mola, who was aware of the negotiations in 1934 conducted by Antonio Goicoechea, requested the latter to leave for the Italian capital to assist those who were already there. The Italian government, it added, had certain reservations up to this point about giving help because of lack of information regarding the significance of the rising. "The presence of Goicoechea in Rome, who, already in 1934 had agreed with Ciano on a possible counterrevolutionary movement, dissipated all doubts."[30]

Despite minor discrepancies in dates, the above evidence from four sources refutes the testimony of Pierre Cot, air minister in the French Popular Front government, to the effect that the shipment of Italian airplanes had been decided upon before 17 July, the date of the military uprising.[31] It also disproves the claim made by Yvon Delbos, the French foreign minister, to the United States chargé d'affaires in Paris on 6 August 1936 "that the Italian air corps personnel who manned the planes had been enrolled for this duty at least as early as 20 July."[32]

The following excerpt from a report dated 18 December 1936 by the German ambassador in Rome, Ulrich von Hassell, to the Wilhelmstrasse on the interests of Germany and Italy in the Spanish Civil War sheds light on the motives of Italian intervention in Spain. It also throws light on the advantages to Germany of Italy's involvement by perpetuating the estrangement between Mussolini and the Western democracies that had begun with the Italian invasion of Ethiopia in 1935 and by threatening the transit of French troops from North Africa in the event of a general European conflagration:

> The interests of Germany and Italy in the Spanish troubles coincide to the extent that both countries are seeking to prevent a victory of Bolshevism in Spain or Catalonia. However, while Germany is not pursuing any immediate diplomatic interests in Spain beyond this, the efforts of Rome undoubtedly extend towards having Spain fall in line with its Mediterranean policy, or at least towards preventing political cooperation between Spain on the one hand and France and/or England on the other. The means used for this purpose are: immediate support of Franco; a foothold on the Balearic Islands, which will presumably not be evacuated voluntarily unless a central Spanish government friendly to Italy is set up; political commitment of Franco to Italy; and a close tie between Fascism and the new system of government to be established in Spain. . . .
>
> In connection with the general policy indicated above, Germany has in my opinion every reason for being gratified if Italy continues to interest herself deeply in the Spanish affair. The role played by the Spanish conflict as regards Italy's relations with France and England could be similar to that of the Abyssin-

ian conflict, bringing out clearly the actual, opposing interests of the powers and thus preventing Italy from being drawn into the net of the Western powers and used for their machinations. The struggle for dominant political influence in Spain lays bare the natural opposition between Italy and France; at the same time the position of Italy as a power in the Western Mediterranean comes into competition with that of Britain. All the more clearly will Italy recognize the advisability of confronting the Western powers shoulder to shoulder with Germany—particularly when considering the desirability of a future general understanding between Western and Central Europe on the basis of complete equality. In my opinion the guiding principle for us arising out of this situation is that we should let Italy take the lead in her Spanish policy, but that we ought simultaneously to accompany this policy with so much active good will as to avoid a development which might be prejudicial to Germany's direct or indirect interests, whether it be in the form of a defeat for Nationalist Spain or in the nature of a direct Anglo-Italian understanding in case of further stagnation in the fighting. We surely have no reason for jealousy if Fascism takes the fore in the thorny task of creating a political and social content behind the hitherto purely military and negatively anti-Red label. . . . We must deem it desirable if there is created south of France a factor which, freed from Bolshevism and removed from the hegemony of the Western powers but on the other hand allied with Italy, makes the French and British stop to think—a factor opposing the transit of French troops from Africa and one which in the economic field takes our needs fully into consideration.[33]

Because of the advantages accruing to Germany as a result of Italy's involvement, Germany encouraged Italy to make a major military investment in Spain in the course of the Civil War. Even more important to Germany than the aforementioned benefits was the diversion of Italy's attention from Austria and Czechoslovakia, whose absorption was essential to the ultimate success of Hitler's designs in Eastern Europe. It is no coincidence that Austria, whose independence Mussolini had been ready to protect against a Nazi coup in 1934, was occupied by Hitler in March 1938 with Italian acquiescence. By that time, Italy had become so bogged down in the Spanish conflict that she could not extricate herself without German aid.

On the other hand, Hitler carefully restricted his involvement to a limited number of air force squadrons and artillery and tank units, ignoring proposals to send substantial ground forces to Spain. On 5 December 1936, Wilhelm Faupel, his ambassador to General Franco, recommended that "in order to prevent Bolshevism from taking hold first in half and later in all of Spain . . . one strong German and one strong Italian division would be required, [whose] superior training and leadership can still gain a quick and decisive victory, which may no longer be possible a few months later, even with stronger forces."[34] This proposal went unheeded. Hitler's policy in Spain was shrewd and farseeing. On the one hand, he was careful to avoid the expansion of the Civil War into a major European conflict at a time when he was not yet ready; on the other, he wished to prolong the war in order to keep the Western powers at loggerheads and bind Mussolini closer to Germany. As he disclosed at a secret meeting on 5 November 1937, outlining his war plans and recorded by his adjutant Colonel Friedrich Hossbach, a hundred percent victory for Franco was not desirable from the German point of view, but rather "a continuance of the war" and "the keeping up of the tension in the Mediterranean."[35] In short, as Gerhard L. Weinberg correctly states, "A prolonged war, not a quick victory by Franco, was what German interests—as Hitler defined them—called for. This could best be accomplished by sending assistance not in a flood but in driblets."[36]

While some historians have denied that Hitler deliberately prolonged the war,[37] André Brissaud, in his work on Admiral Canaris, Hitler's chief of German intelligence, makes German policy abundantly clear: "Canaris has no doubt in his mind about the orientation of Hitler's policy in Spain, which is to continue moderate aid to Franco—sufficient to ensure his gratitude (permitting the Germans to gain important economic advantages in the peninsula) and to prevent the republicans from winning—but not large enough to give the Caudillo a quick victory. On the other hand, Hitler's desire that the 'tension in the Mediterranean should continue' has a double purpose: the annexation of Austria and Czechoslovakia, while allowing Mussolini to get bogged down more and more in the war, causing him relentlessly to increase his stakes and to reduce his Continental forces to the point of forcing him to accept, without any possible reaction, the annexation by Germany, first of Austria, then of Czechoslovakia."[38]

While, at the outset of the Civil War, Hitler and Mussolini responded to General Franco's appeals for help after only slight hesitation, Stalin moved with extreme caution before committing himself. Walter Krivitsky, one of the top Soviet operatives in Western Europe, with headquarters in The Hague, who defected to the West at the end of 1937, testifies:

> It was late in August when three high officials of the Spanish Republic were finally received by Russia. They came to buy war supplies, and they offered in exchange huge sums of Spanish gold. . . . [To] conceal the operation Stalin issued, on Friday, August 28, 1936, through the Commissar of Trade a decree forbidding "the export, re-export, or transit to Spain of all kinds of arms, munitions, war materials, airplanes and warships." . . . The fellow travellers of the Comintern, and the public, roused by them, already privately dismayed at Stalin's failure to rush to the support of the Spanish Republic, now understood that he was joining Léon Blum's policy of non-intervention. Stalin was in reality sneaking to the support of the Spanish Republic. [At an extraordinary session of the politburo Stalin said] that neither France nor Britain would willingly allow Spain, which commands the entrance to the Mediterranean, to be controlled by Rome and Berlin. A friendly Spain was vital to Paris and London. Without public intervention, but by an adroit use of his position as the source of military supplies, Stalin believed it possible to create in Spain a regime controlled by him. That done he could command the respect of France and England, win from them the offer of a real

alliance, and either accept it or—with that as a bargaining point—arrive at his underlying steady aim and purpose, a compact with Germany.[39]

That was Stalin's central thought on Spanish intervention. He was also moved, however, by the need for some answer to the foreign friends of the Soviet Union who would be disaffected by the great purge and the shooting of his old Bolshevik colleagues. The Western world does not realize how tenuous at that time was Stalin's hold on power, and how essential it was to his survival as dictator that he should be defended in those bloody acts by foreign communists and eminent international idealists. It is not too much to say that their support was essential to him. And his failure to defend the Spanish Republic . . . might have cost him their support.[40]

Because Krivitsky was denounced as an impostor by Communists and Communist partisans[41] when he made his revelations in a series of articles in 1938 and 1939, and later in book form in 1939,[42] and inasmuch as he is cited many times in this volume, it is important to quote the following passage from an article by the renowned and widely respected scholar on Soviet affairs, Boris Nicolaevsky, written after Krivitsky's mysterious suicide in Washington, D.C., in 1941:[43] "[Krivitsky's] competence and intelligence were indeed exceptional. He worked intermittently [in France, Holland, and Italy] in responsible positions in the secret apparatus of the Comintern, in the military intelligence (the so-called Fourth Administration), and in the GPU [NKVD]. . . . There wasn't anybody whom he did not see nor a secret he did not hear during that time. . . . In the course of the last three years [before his defection] Krivitsky worked in the foreign department . . . of the GPU as one of the three responsible representatives of that fearsome organization in western Europe. About that department—its tasks and the nature of his work—there is only a faint notion abroad. He played a very important role in the apparatus of the GPU and exercised very great influence on the whole policy making of the Soviet Union."[44]

The campaign denouncing Krivitsky as an impostor succeeded in creating around him a suspect aura that partially explains the cautious manner in which some historians even many years later treated his evidence. Hugh Thomas, for example, found it necessary to caution his readers in the first edition of his history of the Spanish Civil War, published in 1961, that "Krivitsky's evidence must be regarded as tainted unless corroborated" and that "his book and articles in the *Saturday Evening Post* . . . were probably written by a well known American Sovietologist often thought to be helped . . . by the FBI,"[45] although in a revised edition, published four years later, he changed this to read, "Krivitsky's evidence can generally be accepted, though his details are sometimes wrong."[46]

Less flexible is the well-known historian Angel Viñas, an official of the Spanish ministry of foreign affairs, who stated in a letter to the Catalan writer Joan Llarch: "I earnestly beg you not to pay any attention to the assertions that still run wild to the effect that the conduct of Negrín, [his] shipment of gold [to Moscow], and [his handling] of Republican finances were inspired if not controlled by Stashevsky, the Soviet attaché. There are still gentlemen, like Bolloten, who refuse to discard that legend taken from Soviet defectors to the West who had no knowledge of events in Spain."[47]

Despite certain "errors and exaggerations" in Krivitsky's writings, alleged by Elizabeth Poretsky, the wife of the slain NKVD agent Ignace Reiss,[48] Krivitsky was, in fact, the first person to reveal the presence in Spain of General Ian K. Berzin, the principal Soviet military adviser; of Alexander Orlov, the chief NKVD (secret police) operative; of Arthur Stashevsky, the adviser to Juan Negrín, the minister of finance, and to reveal the true name of General Emilio Kléber, the charismatic leader of the International Brigades, as shown later in this volume. But more important still, he also asserted, as we have seen, that Stalin, while seeking an alliance with Britain and France during the Civil War, had in mind an alternative course—a compact with Germany. As early as December 1936, Krivitsky further claimed, Stalin had commissioned his trade envoy in Berlin, David Kandelaki, "to exert every effort toward making a secret deal with Hitler."[49] Although nothing came of the negotiations, Krivitsky's claim, while at variance with Russia's consistent and passionate support of collective security, was authenticated some years later. "These very secret negotiations," Leonard Shapiro, one of the leading Soviet scholars in Europe, wrote in 1960, "were first disclosed by Krivitsky. That they in fact took place is now confirmed in a personal dispatch from Neurath [German foreign minister] to Schacht [Reichsbank president], dated 11 February 1937, from which it is clear that Kandelaki, in the name of Stalin and Molotov, put out feelers for an agreement with Germany but was rebuffed by Hitler. The document is among the files of the German Foreign Ministry which fell into Allied hands during the Second World War."[50]

Hitler's reason for not wishing to enter into negotiations is explained by Neurath in the same dispatch: "As to the possibility of entering into conversations with the Russian Government I am, in agreement with the Führer, of the opinion that at the present time they could lead to no results whatever but that, on the contrary, they would at most be used by the Russians for the purpose of achieving the aim they are pursuing of obtaining a closer military alliance with France and also, if possible, of reaching a further *rapprochement* with Britain."[51]

The claim that Stalin was putting out feelers for a political agreement with Germany as early as 1936–37 was not acceptable to some historians in the early 1950s. "Many books published by émigrés from the USSR contain sensational stories about secret German-Soviet relations, especially in the nineteen-thirties," Edward Hallett Carr wrote in 1951, "but these frequently contradict one another and are still unsubstantiated by serious evidence."[52] It is therefore interesting to recall what the well-informed Krivitsky wrote as far back as March 1938, but to which little attention was paid at the time:

In the fall of 1935 . . . it seemed to Stalin that a favorable moment was approaching for successful negotiations. Stalin's optimism can be explained by the fact that at that time Germany had extended new credits on favorable terms to the

Soviet Union. And right away one could hear in the Politburo the much-flaunted phrase of Stalin: "Well, how can we expect Hitler to wage war against us if he gives us all these credits?" . . . That credits have been decided upon is a fact, but the rest of the matter remains unchanged. Nevertheless, Stalin is confident and will not give up. In the fall of 1936, it again seems to Stalin that Hitler will agree to negotiate. During the Politburo meeting all the preliminary data is carefully examined. . . . The work of preparing for the talks is given to the Soviet trade representative Kandelaki and to a resident [in Berlin] of the People's Commissariat of International Affairs. . . . In the spring of 1937, Kandelaki goes to Moscow together with the aforementioned resident of the PCIA. When they arrive there the mood in the Politburo is elevated; everybody is talking about the forthcoming great events that will change the course of our foreign policy by 180 degrees. . . . In Europe, a colossal game is being played by Hitler and Stalin. It is impossible to say at this time who in the end will deceive whom.[53]

But at the time nothing was known of these moves behind the scenes, and between 1934 and 1938 the Soviet Union became the main advocate of collective security and the League of Nations. Whether Stalin's ultimate goal, as Krivitsky suggests, was a pact with Hitler, or whether he held this option in reserve to be exercised only in the event collective security failed cannot be said with certainty. Collective security did fail, as we know, and the principal reason for its failure was not surprisingly its Soviet sponsorship, for the minds of European statesmen were by and large dominated by fear: fear that collective security might lead to war with Germany and that the collapse of the Nazi regime would result in the Bolshevization of Europe. It was this fear, as we shall see, that lay at the root of British and French policy toward the Spanish Civil War and other critical events that dominated the European scene before the outbreak of World War II.

Because of Stalin's caution in committing himself to the Spanish venture, the first Soviet artillery, tanks, and airplanes, together with pilots and tank operators, did not reach Spain until October 1936. In spite of all that has been said to the contrary, they did not arrive before then, as confirmed by such military men of high rank as Generals José Miaja, Sebastián Pozas, and Ignacio Hidalgo de Cisneros, with whom I was able to converse freely after the war. For example, Hidalgo de Cisneros, the chief of the air force, stated that the first Russian bombers, tanks, and artillery reached Spain in October and the first combat airplanes on 2 November. This information was later corroborated by Juan Modesto, a commander of the Communist-controlled Fifth Regiment, who wrote that the first Soviet tanks arrived late in October and that in November Soviet airplanes "put an end to the impunity with which German and Italian aircraft were bombing the capital of Spain."[54]

It was not until the 1970s that the USSR published total estimates of Soviet weaponry shipped to Spain. "The Soviet Union," said one Soviet source in 1974, "sent to the Spanish Government 806 military aircraft, mainly fighters, 362 tanks, 120 armored cars, 1,555 artillery pieces, about 500,000 rifles, 340 grenade launches, 15,113 machine-guns, more than 110,000 aerial bombs, about 3,400,000 rounds of ammunition, 500,000 grenades, 862 million cartridges, 1,500 tons of gunpowder, torpedo boats, air defense searchlight installations, motor vehicles, radio stations, torpedoes and fuel. Not all these war materials reached their destination because . . . some Soviet vessels and ships chartered from other countries were sunk by the Italians or forced into ports held by the insurgents."[55] Another source, also published in 1974, gave the following breakdown of Soviet weaponry (based on official figures furnished by the Institute of Military History of the Soviet Union) that the Soviet Union "managed to send" (*"udalos' napravit'"*) to Spain during the war: 648 airplanes, 347 tanks, 60 armored vehicles, 1,186 artillery pieces, 20,486 machine guns, and 497,813 rifles.[56]

As for other Soviet military aid to Spain, Segismundo Casado, operations chief on the general staff of the war ministry in the left zone, affirms that in the second half of September "there made their appearance at the ministry of war certain Generals and Chiefs of the Soviet Army who were supposed to be 'military technicians' and were known as 'friendly advisers,' " and that from that day onward light arms began to arrive.[57] On the other hand, Vicente Rojo, chief of staff during the defense of Madrid, who worked closely with Soviet military advisers, states that the "Soviet technicians, in the capacity of a military mission, arrived in October before the first shipment of arms."[58]

Although the Russians sent no Soviet infantrymen to Spain, the first units of the International Brigades—which were organized on the initiative of the Comintern[59] and whose leaders, according to Carlo Penchienati, a commander of the Garibaldi Brigade, were, with rare exceptions, all Communists[60]—went into action in the second week of November. Furthermore, the Italian Communist Luigi Longo, known by the name of Gallo—political commissar of the Twelfth International Brigade and in later years head of the Italian Communist party after the death of Palmiro Togliatti—states that the first 500 volunteers arrived in Albacete, their training base, on 14 October 1936.[61] According to a pro-Soviet estimate, as many as 42,000 anti-Fascists from 53 countries may have gone to Spain as volunteers.[62] Among them were a number of Russian emigrés, mainly living in France, who, according to the Soviet writer L. K. Shkarenkov, "made no secret of the fact that by taking part in the battles against fascists in Spain, they wanted to earn for themselves forgiveness and the right to return to their homeland."[63]

In supplying arms and some of his best foreign cadres, Stalin was careful not to become involved in a major conflict with Italy and Germany. Krivitsky attests that Stalin "doubly cautioned his commissars that Soviet aid to Spain must be unofficial and handled covertly, in order to eliminate any possibility of involving his government in war. His last phrase passed down by those at that politburo meeting as a command to all high officers of the service was: *Podalshe ot artillereiskovo ognia!* 'Stay out of range of the artillery fire!' "[64] Nevertheless, the Soviet Union, geographically so far removed from the scene of action, had serious logistical problems and ran grave risks in supplying arms to Spain. "Any vessel flying the Soviet or Republican flag was liable to be attacked by fascist submarines or aircraft and to be sunk or captured by Franco," says a Soviet source previously cited. "From the beginning of the war up to May 4, 1937, 86 attacks were made on Soviet ships. The *Komsomol*, *Timiryazev* and *Blagoyev* were sunk and the *Petrovsky*, *Vtoraya Pyatiletka*, *Soyuz Vodnyikov* and *Smidovich* were captured and taken into ports held by the insurgents. The fascists attacked and sank ships regardless of the flag they were flying, if they were suspected of carrying cargoes from Soviet ports to Republican Spain."[65]

There is some evidence that although Stalin would initially have preferred a rapid victory for the Republican forces, he eventually decided that there were advantages to be gained by a prolongation of the conflict. According to the former NKVD chief Alexander Orlov, a Soviet general who returned to Spain from Moscow in the summer of 1937 told him that the politburo had adopted a *new line* toward Spain. "Until then," Orlov writes, "the policy of the politburo was to assist the Spanish Republican Government to the utmost with armaments, Soviet pilots and tank detachments in order to secure for the Republicans a speedy victory over Franco. But now the politburo [had] come to the conclusion that it would be more advantageous to the Soviet Union if neither of the warring camps gained preponderant strength and if the war in Spain dragged on as long as possible and thus tied up Hitler there for a longer time. . . . [I] was shocked by the Machiavellian calculations of the politburo, which in its desire to gain time wanted the Spanish people to bleed as long as possible."[66]

Although it is difficult to imagine that so hardened and sophisticated an agent as Orlov could have been shocked by the Machiavellian calculations of the politburo, his assertion that Stalin decided to allow the war to drag on as long as possible corresponds with the Comintern's policy in Spain.

10

Camouflaging the Revolution

Because of her fear of involvement in a war with Italy and Germany, Russia limited her aid to bolstering the resistance of the anti-Franco forces until such time as Britain and France, faced by the threat to their interests in the Mediterranean of an Italo-German overlordship of Spain, might be induced to abandon the policy of nonintervention. Russia, moreover, was careful not to throw her influence on the side of the left wing of the Revolution or to identify herself with it. To have done otherwise would have revived throughout the world, among the very classes whose support the Comintern was seeking, fears and antipathies it was striving most anxiously to avoid. It would have given a deathblow to the French Popular Front—in which the cleavage of opinion was already running deep[1]—and rendered sterile of result every effort to establish a basis of agreement with the moderate parties in other countries, particularly in Britain, where the Communists' campaign for a Popular Front was already meeting with opposition from the Labour party.[2] "The People's Front in France," wrote a British Communist, "has driven back the fascist reaction and stands united with the Soviet Union for peace. If we could do the same in Britain, if the criminal opposition to unity could be overcome, if we could combine a corresponding Anglo-Soviet pact with the Franco-Soviet Pact, then we could build a front which could hold in check the fascist war offensive."[3] Indeed, it was for these reasons that, from the very inception of the war, the Comintern had sought to minimize and even conceal from the outside world the profound revolution that had taken place in Spain by defining the struggle against General Franco as one for the defense of the bourgeois democratic Republic.

Some forty years later, a left-wing opponent of the Spanish Communist party summed up the political predicament of the Comintern and its Spanish section in the following manner: "The Communist International and the Spanish Communist party could only resolve the dilemma by distorting reality. What was taking place in Republican Spain—the elimination of employers and priests, the expropriation of industry and land, workers' control, the creation of revolutionary committees, peasant collectives, workers' militia, and popular tribunals—was not social revolution; it was not a war to the bitter end between the bourgeoisie and the proletariat. It was a bourgeois democratic revolution, a war between bourgeois democracy and the vestiges of feudalism and obscurantism, it was a struggle of the legal government against the insurgent military, a struggle between the Spanish nation and the Nazi invaders."[4]

And Fernando Claudín, a former Communist and member of the party for thirty years, writes: "The problem [for Stalin] was that the Spanish proletariat had left these reasonable limits [the bourgeois democratic revolution] far behind. In the weeks after 19 July, the capitalist order practically ceased to exist in the Republican area: the means of production and political power in effect passed into the hands of the workers' organizations. All historians of the Spanish Civil War are in agreement on this point, except for those who do not aim for historical truth, but to justify the policy of Stalin and the Comintern. The latter 'historians' continue to proclaim that the content of the Spanish revolution never went beyond the 'bourgeois democratic stage,' because to say otherwise would be a recognition that Stalinist policy in Spain was to hold back the revolution."[5]

The Comintern, writes an authoritative student of the Spanish scene, was particularly anxious that its policy be well propagandized among the Western democracies. "Consequently, all Communist front organizations in the various countries and sympathetic observers of the Communist policies, such as Louis Fischer in the United States, stressed the bourgeois aspects of the new policy. Louis Fischer, in his pamphlet *War in Spain*, declared: '. . . Some have regarded the Communists' advocacy of democracy in Spain as a tactical maneuver to mislead foreign democracies and bourgeois liberals into supporting the Loyalists. This interpretation is wrong; such a trick would soon become too transparent for use. The democratic slogan means that the Communists have no desire to establish in Spain a dictatorship guided by one party as in Russia. Spanish conditions are different.' "[6]

Although the Western governments were fully apprised of the radical nature of the Revolution through diplomatic channels, through members of the foreign press and through businessmen and refugees who had fled the country, the Communists and their allies harped on the moderate character of the Revolution with passionate intensity.

"The working-class parties in Spain, and especially the Communist party," wrote André Marty, a member of the executive committee of the Comintern, in an article widely published in the world Communist press in August 1936, "have on several occasions clearly indicated what they are striving for. Our brother party has repeatedly proved that the present struggle in Spain is not between capitalism and socialism but between fascism and democracy. In a country like Spain, where feudal institutions and roots are still very deep, the working class and the entire people have the immediate and urgent task, *the only possible task*—and all recent appeals of the Communist party repeat and prove it—not to bring about the Socialist revolution, but to defend, consolidate, and develop the bourgeois democratic revolution.

"The only slogan of our party that was spread right across *Mundo Obrero*, its daily paper, on 18 July, was 'Long Live the Democratic Republic!'

"All this is well known. Only dishonest people can maintain the contrary. . . .

The few confiscations that have been made—for example, the offices and news-papers of the rebels—constitute sanctions against proven enemies and saboteurs of the regime and were made not as Socialist measures, but as measures for the defense of the Republic."[7]

"The Central Committee of the Spanish Communist party," ran a statement published by the Communist party of France on 3 August, "has asked us to make known to public opinion, as a reply to interested and fantastic reports in a certain press, that the Spanish people in their struggle against the rebels are not striving for the establishment of the dictatorship of the proletariat, but have only one aim: THE DEFENSE OF THE REPUBLICAN ORDER AND RESPECT FOR PROPERTY."[8] And a manifesto issued by the French Communist party on the same day declared:

"We speak for the Communist comrades, for the Socialists, and for all fighters for freedom in Spain, *when we declare that it is not a question of establishing socialism in Spain.*

"It is simply and solely a question of the defense of the democratic republic by the constitutional government, which, in face of the rebellion, has called upon the people to defend the republican regime."[9]

"The people of Spain," wrote Harry Pollitt, secretary of the British Commu-nist party, a few days later, "are not fighting to establish Soviets, or the proletar-ian dictatorship. Only downright lying scoundrels, or misguided self-styled 'Lefts' declare that they are—and both combine to help the aims of the fascist rebels."[10] And even seven months later, an article in the Communist *Labour Monthly*, published in London, declared: "To talk of bourgeois economy having 'disappeared' is just balderdash."[11]

"Really, people are sometimes surprising," wrote Franz Borkenau, an acute observer. "Representative members of the PSUC [the Communist-controlled United Socialist Party of Catalonia] express the opinion that there is no revolution at all in Spain, and these men with whom I had a fairly long discussion are not, as one would suppose, old Catalan Socialists, but foreign Communists. Spain, they explain, is faced with a unique situation: the Government is fighting against its own army. And that is all. I hinted at the fact that the workers were armed, that the administration had fallen into the hands of revolutionary committees, that people were being executed without trial in thousands, that both factories and estates were being expropriated and managed by their former hands. What was revolu-tion if it was not that? I was told that I was mistaken; all that had no political significance; these were only emergency measures without political bearing."[12]

On 7 August, in the third week of the raging social upheaval, Jesús Her-nández, the director of the Madrid Communist daily *Mundo Obrero* and a mem-ber of the politburo, made the following statement to the foreign press: "[I] can tell you truthfully that making a proletarian revolution does not enter either into the plans or minds of the workers. Our party has reiterated this many times during the past few days through our Secretary José Díaz, our comrade Pasionaria and *Mundo Obrero*. In other words, without ceasing to be Communists and while maintaining our revolutionary significance intact, we affirm that in order to reach the state where we can realize our maximum aspirations certain historical conditions have to exist that are not now present. For some time, we have been living through the bourgeois democratic revolution. The problem of the land and all the problems that characterize a democratic revolution have yet to be resolved. Consequently, until we have achieved this stage [of the revolution] we cannot, we should not and we shall not speak of proletarian revolution or, as the traitors to the Republic assert, establish Communism."[13]

Before many weeks had passed, the Communists took advantage of German and Italian intervention to tone down the class character of the war still further. "In the beginning," declared a Spanish Communist party manifesto, "it was possible to describe the struggle simply as one between democracy and fascism, between progress and reaction, between the past and the future. But now it has broken through these bounds and become transformed into a holy war, into a national war, into a defensive war of the people, who feel that they have been betrayed and that their deepest sentiments have been wounded."[14]

11

Largo Caballero Forms
a New Government

*T*hat the Communist party's policy of camouflaging or distorting the true nature and scope of the Revolution could have been initiated only with the acquiescence or active support of other organizations can be open to no doubt; nor can there be any doubt that to ensure the success of its policy it had to become the ruling party in the left camp. This could be accomplished only at the expense of other left-wing movements, especially the left Socialists, who controlled the UGT, the Socialist labor federation, and the influential Madrid section of the Socialist party, the Agrupación Socialista Madrileña. Despite the startling growth of the CNT, the Anarchosyndicalist labor federation, in the capital before the Civil War, the Socialists were in all likelihood still the most powerful force in Madrid and in Old and New Castile on the morrow of the Revolution.

It has already been seen that in the months before the Civil War the official relations between the left-wing Socialists and the Communists had been so cordial that Francisco Largo Caballero, the left Socialist leader, in the ingenuous belief that he could absorb the Communists, had given his support to the fusion of the Socialist and Communist labor federations as well as to the merging of the parties' youth organizations. Moreover, the Agrupación Socialista Madrileña, which he controlled, had decided in March 1936 to propose at the party's next national congress the fusion of the Socialist and Communist parties, a merger that the Communists themselves strongly advocated. But, in spite of the smooth course of official relations, the Communists were disturbed by the left Socialist leader's agitation in favor of an immediate social overturn and, in private, characterized his ultrarevolutionary tendencies as "infantile leftist."[1]

In view of the underlying differences between the Communists and the left-wing Socialists, it is not surprising that the outbreak of the Revolution in July 1936 should have thrown their disparate attitudes into sharp focus. "When the Communist party raised the necessity of defending the democratic Republic," declared José Díaz, its general secretary, in a report to the central committee in March 1937, "the Socialists, a large proportion of our Socialist comrades, took the stand that the democratic Republic had no longer any raison d'être and advocated the setting up of a Socialist republic. This would have divorced the working class from the democratic forces, from the petty bourgeois and popular layers in the country. It was natural that our policy of uniting all the democratic forces with the proletariat should have met with certain difficulties owing to the failure of some Socialist comrades to understand that . . . this was not the moment to speak of a Socialist republic, but of a democratic republic with a profound social content."[2]

Although there is no record that any leading Socialist made a public declaration, either oral or written, at the outbreak of the Revolution urging the establishment of a Socialist republic, such a proposal may conceivably have been made in backstage discussions with the Communists. Certainly it would have been entirely consistent with Largo Caballero's prewar revolutionary policy calling for a working-class dictatorship and with the aims of his most ardent supporters up to the very inception of the conflict, and it is significant that the Communist leader's assertion was never voluntarily challenged. Nor indeed did an assertion by André Marty, French Communist leader, member of the Comintern, and an organizer of the International Brigades in Spain, to the effect that the Socialists abandoned their proposal to establish a Socialist republic as a result of Communist influence elicit any spontaneous denial. "When from the first day of the rebellion," he affirmed in 1937, "the Communist party declared that the prime need was the defense of the democratic Republic, many top-ranking Socialist leaders held, on the contrary, that a *Socialist republic* should be immediately established. This would have immediately smashed the Popular Front and led to the victory of fascism. Today, thanks to our influence, many leaders of the Socialist party have changed their attitude and adopted the platform of the Communist party."[3]

And in a speech early in September 1936, Antonio Mije, a member of the politburo, affirmed: "Even those who used to speak of proletarian revolution without taking into account the present situation understand today the correctness of the Communist party line in defending the democratic Republic."[4]

Anxious no doubt to protect Largo Caballero from the stigma of bowing to Communist policy, his supporters avoided any public discussion of his sudden change in stance. In fact, only when questioned many years after the war, Luis Araquistáin, the Socialist leader's most intimate associate, dismissed José Díaz's and André Marty's assertions as "pure nonsense" and as a "Communist lie."[5]

By mid-August Largo Caballero had so tempered his earlier revolutionary language—at least to the outside world—as to declare in a letter to Ben Tillett, the British trade-union leader, that the Spanish Socialists were fighting only for the triumph of democracy and had no thought of establishing socialism.[6] Precisely what arguments the Communist leaders may have adduced to sway Largo Caballero were never disclosed, but if their assertions should be true, as would seem likely, they no doubt held that the setting up of a Socialist republic would antagonize the Western powers and destroy the advantages to be gained from keeping in office the cabinet of José Giral, which, in view of the policy generally

adopted by foreign powers in cases of insurrection against a legitimate government, could rightfully claim that it be allowed to purchase arms freely in the
markets of the world.[7]

The Communist effort to present to the Western democracies a moderate,
nonrevolutionary government, in total command of the situation, had a compelling logic. Witness, for example, the following minute written on 29 August 1936
by Sir Alexander Cadogan, deputy undersecretary of state under British foreign
secretary Anthony Eden, released by the Public Record Office years later: "In
more normal circumstances—i.e., if the 'existing [Spanish] Government' exercised real control and had any chance of surviving—I should say that, failing
international agreement, we should most scrupulously observe our regular and
normal policy of allowing or licensing shipments to the established Government
and not to the rebels. In the present state of Spain, or in the situation that is likely
rapidly to develop, the ordinary rule cannot be blindly followed. What is the
existing Government? How far do those in power in Barcelona recognise the
Madrid Authorities? How far, in effect, have the latter control of Madrid itself? . . . Apart from the international aspect of the matter and our desire to avoid
'alignments,' it may well be that in the near future it will become clearer, even to
our Labour people, that the 'existing Government' is becoming less and less
deserving of their sympathy."[8]

But however much Largo Caballero may have allowed himself in behind-the-
scenes discussions with the Communists to be influenced by their forceful argument that the government should present a moderate face to the Western powers,
it is clear from an editorial in his newspaper *Claridad* on 22 August 1936 that he
had reservations about Communist policy and was not ready to turn his back
completely upon the Revolution. "Some persons," declared the editorial, which
was undoubtedly written by Luis Araquistáin, the director of the left Socialist
daily and Largo Caballero's intimate adviser, "are saying: 'Let us crush fascism
first, let us finish the war victoriously, and then there will be time to speak of
revolution and to make it if necessary.' Those who express themselves in this way
have obviously not reflected maturely upon the formidable dialectical process
that is carrying us all along. The war and the Revolution are one and the same
thing. Not only do they not exclude or hinder each other but they complement and
support each other. The war needs the Revolution for its triumph in the same way
that the Revolution needed the war to bring it into being.

"The Revolution is the economic annihilation of fascism and is consequently
the first step toward its military annihilation. . . . The people are not fighting for
the Spain of 16 July, which was still dominated socially by hereditary castes, but
for a Spain from which those castes have been finally rooted out. The most
powerful auxiliary of the war is the complete economic extinction of fascism.
That is the revolution in the rear that will make more assured and more inspired
the victory on the battlefields."

A no less serious cause of discord between the Communists and the left
Socialists in the weeks immediately following the outbreak of the Civil War was

their disagreement over the liberal Republican government of José Giral. The Communists did what they could to shore up his shaky administration, for which even in retrospect they have only words of praise: "The historical merit of the Giral government," affirms the official Spanish Communist history of the Civil War, "is that it knew how to accept and acknowledge the new politicosocial realities that were emerging in Spain."[9]

In an unpublished memoir, politburo member Vicente Uribe writes: "Although the Giral government was more of a phantom than anything else, the party supported it with all its strength. . . . It could have collapsed of its own accord at any moment. It was the legal embodiment of the Republic and had to be maintained at all costs."[10]

The Communists' support of the Giral government contrasted sharply with the mistrust of Luis Araquistáin, Caballero's trusted counsellor, as revealed in a confidential letter he addressed to the left Socialist leader on 24 August 1936, shortly after the fall of Badajoz and Mérida, a loss that resulted in the linking up of General Franco's northern and southern forces. After stating tactfully that he was proud of the fact that on "fundamental issues, and nearly always without prior discussion, my thoughts have coincided with yours," he stated: ". . . the responsibility that now weighs upon us is so great, particularly upon me as director of our newspaper, that I do not venture to publish personal opinions about changes that appear necessary in the present political situation without knowing whether they are shared by you." He then continued:

The republican government is virtually dead. It has neither the authority, nor the competence, nor the will to wage the war seriously and ensure a complete and revolutionary victory. You who are better informed than anyone else as to what is happening know this better than I. The maintenance of this government in office is jeopardizing victory. . . . Every day that passes increases the possibility of international complications and of our alienating the sympathy of the world because of acts such as those committed the night before last in the Model Prison [the execution of political prisoners] due solely to the impotence of the government. For these reasons, I believe that this government should disappear as soon as possible. . . .

Another republican government would be purposeless. It would be as inept and inefficient as the present one. It is also unlikely that a government headed by Prieto composed exclusively of his friends [the centrists in the PSOE] and the Republicans would improve the situation very much. . . . [It] would inspire the combatants with even greater distrust than a Republican government from the point of view of the revolutionary process. This would increase the uneasiness of the militiamen and would perhaps discourage them from fighting for a cause whose political and social objectives would not appear clear to them.

If we reject Prieto or anyone else of his political inclination or close to it— [Julián] Besteiro, for example—there is no one left but you. There are two possibilities: a homogeneous government composed of our left wing or a mixed gov-

ernment. The former would encounter strong resistance from the republican parties, the centrists, and especially from Azaña, at least while the war lasts. . . .
On the other hand, I am convinced that he would not oppose a government headed by you . . . if the centrists and the republicans accept this solution. . . .
If they do not accept it, then it would be time to consider a violent seizure of power before the war is over. . . .

I know and share your objections to a coalition government with people who possess distinct and even antagonistic ideologies. . . . But I conceive the possibility of a coalition government that would not arouse alarm inside or outside the country and that could, in fact, be a great war government and, at the same time, without saying so, a great revolutionary government. Everything depends on the number and the character of the portfolios that are distributed. . . . The following is the projected government to which I allude:

Socialists (Group 1—left)
   Premiership
   War
   Interior
   Navy or Finance
   State [Foreign Affairs] or Agriculture

Socialists (Group 2—center)
   Finance or Navy
   Agriculture or State
   Industry and Commerce

Communists (Eventually, one member of the CNT)
   Public Works
   Labor

Republicans
   Communications (Izquierda Republicana)
   Public Instruction (Unión Republicana)
   Justice (Esquerra Republicana de Catalunya)

This distribution could undoubtedly be improved upon. But the important thing is to control the key portfolios of war and revolution and a sufficient number of them to be assured of a majority. . . . In this way, the real government, strictly speaking, would be the first group, namely, you. . . .

A coalition government, such as I have outlined, would either be effective or, if not, it could be changed so as to give it greater homogeneity in a leftward direction by eliminating lukewarm or counterrevolutionary elements. Once power is in your hands, Azaña would not be an obstacle to the progressive revolutionary transformation of the government. . . .

I don't expect you to reply in writing to this letter. You can give me your opinion about all this verbally in just one or two words.[11]

There is no record of Largo Caballero's reply to Araquistáin, but there is no doubt that he shared his views. Three days later, on 27 August, he was complaining to Mikhail Koltzov, Pravda's correspondent—whom Arthur Koestler, who knew him personally, describes as "the most brilliant and influential journalist in the Soviet Union" and as "a confidant of Stalin"[12]—about the Giral government's "complete ineptitude." "The ministers are incapable, stupid, and lazy," he fulminated. "Nobody listens to [the ministers]. None of them is at all concerned with what the other is doing. They don't have the slightest conception of responsibility or of the gravity of the situation. . . . Besides, whom do they represent? All the popular forces are united outside the framework of the government, around the Socialist and Anarchist labor unions. The working-class militia doesn't believe in the government. The masses hold out their hands to us; they ask us for governmental leadership, but we remain passive, we avoid responsibility, we remain inactive!"[13]

A former Cortes deputy offers the following version of the simmering crisis that, although lacking direct corroboration, has elements of credibility in view of Araquistáin's letter to Largo Caballero: At a meeting of his followers in Madrid after the fall of Badajoz, Largo Caballero decided to replace Giral's "impotent" administration by a working-class government and to set up a proletarian dictatorship. This plan was thwarted only by the timely intervention of the Soviet ambassador, who argued successfully that the war should be continued "under the banner of the democratic Republic," thus averting "the danger that the premature establishment of a working-class government and a proletarian dictatorship would have represented."[14] Although denying this version, the official Spanish Communist history of the Civil War virtually confirms it: "On the other hand, it is true that Largo Caballero increased his attacks on and sharpened his criticism of the Giral government, especially at the end of August, when the military situation of the Republic had deteriorated. Some of his closest correligionists, such as Araquistáin and [Carlos de] Baráibar, agitated more or less publicly in favor of the idea of eliminating the Republican ministers and giving the direction of the country to Caballero with a view to establishing a 'working-class dictatorship.' "[15]

That the government of José Giral would have been helpless without the backing of the Communists and moderate Socialists, who worked within the ministries in unofficial but vital capacities, is certain. Even Indalecio Prieto, the leader of the moderate or center faction of the Socialist party, who for weeks worked assiduously behind the scenes to bolster the government, scorned its impotence. "Indalecio Prieto," wrote Koltzov, who interviewed the Socialist leader on 26 August, "occupies no official position. Nevertheless, he has been given an enormous, luxurious office, as well as a secretarial staff in the ministry of the navy. . . . He is seated in his armchair, an enormous fleshy mass with a pale ironic face. His heavy eyelids are half-closed, but under those lids the most watchful eyes of Spain are peering. He has won the solid, everlasting reputation of a practical politician, very shrewd and even cunning. . . . I ask his opinion of the situation. In ten minutes he makes a careful analysis, penetrating and pessimistic. He derides the impotence of the government."[16]

And Pietro Nenni, International Brigade commissar, and, after World War II, head of the Italian Socialist party, wrote on 14 August 1936: "I have been observing Prieto for several days. More than a man, he is a prodigious machine in operation. He thinks of a hundred things at once. He knows everything. He sees everything. . . . In shirt sleeves, sweating and panting, Indalecio goes from person to person, gives orders, signs papers, takes notes, growls over the telephone, chides one person, smiles at another. He is nothing; he is not a minister; he is only a deputy of a parliament in recess. And yet he is everything; the animator and coordinator of government action."[17]

Despite Prieto's frenzied activity behind the scenes, the government was impotent and the moderate Socialist leader knew it. Although contemptuous of Largo Caballero and his radical policies, Prieto acknowledged that he was the only politician who could head a government at that time. "He is a fool who wants to appear clever," he told Mikhail Koltzov. "He is a frigid bureaucrat who plays the role of a mad fanatic, a disorganizer, a meddler who imagines he is a methodical bureaucrat. He is a man capable of ruining everything and everybody. Our political differences during the past few years lie at the heart of the struggle within the Socialist party. But, at least today, in spite of everything, he is the only man or, better still, his is the only name that can appropriately head a new government." Prieto then added that he was ready to join a government headed by Largo Caballero because "there is no other way out either for Spain or for me if I am to be useful to the country."[18]

The Communists, on the other hand, opposed any change in the administration, and for a few days José Giral's teetering government managed to survive. But, faced by the lightning advance of General Franco's forces toward Madrid[19] and tired of presiding over a government to which the power of state belonged on paper only and which lacked the support of the majority of the working class, José Giral, at the suggestion of President Azaña, according to a report in *Claridad*, proposed that the government be broadened to include other Popular Front organizations.[20] Although the report did not state whether Largo Caballero was to head a new cabinet or simply to participate in an expanded administration under Giral, the authoritative Koltzov clears up this dubiety. He noted in his diary on 3 September that at first the cabinet reorganization was to be modest. Two or three Socialists belonging to the Prieto and Caballero factions were to join it. But suddenly the "old man" demanded for himself the war ministry and, almost immediately thereafter, the premiership. This met with general opposition, except from Prieto. It was felt that Caballero's "bluntness, his unsociability, and his impatience" would make "normal cooperation impossible." Alvarez del Vayo—at that time Largo Caballero's trusted adviser but a Communist sympathizer—endeavored to convince the Socialist leader that he should take the war ministry and leave the premiership to Giral. Everyone then went over to the central committee of the Communist party so that it could mediate. The central committee also objected to Largo Caballero's becoming head of the government, but he insisted on "all or nothing." The general situation and the pressure of time,

Koltzov observed, favored Caballero, for rumors of the crisis were spreading and in wartime such a situation could not be prolonged a single day. "Prieto declared that notwithstanding his relationship with Caballero, which was well known to everyone, he would not oppose him and that he was ready to accept any post in a government headed by him. . . . It was very distressing for everyone to accept a government presided by the old man. . . . In spite of everything, Largo Caballero is, in fact, today, the most venerable and representative figure in the labor movement. . . . As for his leftist demagogic extremism, Vayo puts everyone at ease: this will disappear the very day he assumes responsibility for running the country." Feeling himself on firm ground, Koltzov continues, Caballero then presented another demand in the form of an ultimatum: that the Communists enter the cabinet. "The party was against this. It preferred to give the Popular Front government all its support while remaining on the outside; furthermore, it did not want to create unnecessary difficulties of an international nature lest the future government be called Bolshevik, Soviet. The old man stated that all this was nonsense, that he too would decline,[21] that everything could go to hell, and that the [Communist] party would be held accountable for whatever happened."[22] The party's opposition to entering the government is confirmed by César Falcón, editor during the first months of the war of *Mundo Obrero*, its organ in Madrid: "The Communist party maintained a position contrary to that of Caballero. Why change the government when for various reasons the national and international situation was not opportune for the participation of Socialists and Communists?"[23]

It is noteworthy that the *initial* reaction of Dr. Juan Negrín, the moderate Socialist (who was to become the most controversial figure of the Spanish Civil War) to the idea of a government headed by Largo Caballero, in which he was offered the ministry of finance, was similar to that of the Communists. "I do not know of a more senseless act from a national and international standpoint," he told a Socialist colleague. "Are we determined to lose the war? Do not count on my collaboration."[24]

In an unpublished memoir, politburo member Vicente Uribe writes: "On one occasion Largo Caballero proposed that we should go to the war ministry and throw out Giral. Of course, we flatly refused and explained our reason. The situation became tense and we left the meeting. Later, Caballero sent a representative to inquire whether we had broken off relations with him. We told him that we had not, but that he could not count on us to expel Giral forcibly, for we all had to regard one another as allies in a common cause."[25]

But, in face of Largo Caballero's inflexible attitude and new directives from Moscow that the Communist party should join the government—directives that were received with "no little astonishment," according to former politburo member Jesús Hernández[26]—the Spanish Communist leaders reversed their position, and a new cabinet was formed.

Confronted by Largo Caballero's obstinacy, the Kremlin and the Spanish politburo had no alternative but to yield. Comintern delegate Boris Stefanov makes this clear in a long report to Moscow now available in the Archivo

Histórico del Comité Central del PCE in Madrid. "The party," he states, "faced with the preparations by Caballero and the Socialist youth for carrying out the violent overthrow of the Giral Government, decided to join the [new] government so as to prevent this change from happening."[27]

Although in the course of the acrimonious consultations, Largo Caballero failed to put together the type of government Araquistáin had recommended, the new administration formed on 4 September was greeted with an extraordinary display of popular exuberance. Julián Zugazagoitia, a centrist and an opponent of Largo Caballero, recalls: "Things are going badly, very badly. The enemy is in Talavera de la Reina [on the main highway to Madrid]. The presence of Largo Caballero in the government is acclaimed with indescribable enthusiasm. The militiamen parade before him, cheering him and pledging themselves to die before retreating. The cabinet shakeup restores morale, which is at a low ebb."[28]

The members of the cabinet, the parties to which they belonged, and the portfolios they held, were as follows:[29]

Francisco Largo Caballero	Socialist (left)	Prime Minister and War
Julio Alvarez del Vayo	Socialist (left)	Foreign Affairs
Angel Galarza	Socialist (left)	Interior
Anastasio de Gracia	Socialist (moderate)	Industry and Commerce
Juan Negrín	Socialist (moderate)	Finance
Indalecio Prieto	Socialist (moderate)	Navy and Air
Jesús Hernández	Communist	Education and Fine Arts
Vicente Uribe	Communist	Agriculture
José Giral	Left Republican	Minister without portfolio
Mariano Ruiz Funes	Left Republican	Justice
Bernardo Giner de los Ríos	Republican Union	Communications
José Tomás y Piera	Left Republican party of Catalonia	Labor and Health

There is testimony by Largo Caballero's politicomilitary secretary, José María Aguirre, who accompanied the left Socialist leader to the National Palace for consultations with Azaña, that Caballero wished to make Araquistáin his minister of foreign affairs, but that Azaña vetoed the proposal. "Vayo is a Soviet agent," Caballero allegedly told Aguirre. "The Russians have exerted pressure on Azaña—as they have been doing on me—to entrust him with the ministry of foreign affairs. They will deny us arms if we refuse." Caballero then conveyed the news to Araquistáin, who later told Aguirre: "I advised [Caballero] to yield to Azaña and the Russians. Since Vayo is not very smart, we shall surround him. I am going to Paris [as ambassador]. We must do the impossible to avoid defeat."[30]

Later in the month Julio Just, a member of the Left Republican party, was made minister of public works,[31] and Manuel de Irujo, a member of the Basque Nationalist party, was appointed minister without portfolio.[32]

"The participation of the bourgeois parties in the Loyalist government is . . . a symbol," wrote Louis Fischer, a mouthpiece at that time of Soviet policy. "To capitalists in fascist Spain, and to the outside world, it is intended as an indication that the Republic has no plan now of setting up a Soviet State or a communist regime after victory in the civil war."[33]

The fact that the Catholic Basque Nationalist party, a middle-class organization, had opposed the military rebellion and had agreed to participate in the Largo Caballero government—on condition that the Basque country be granted autonomy[34]—was exploited to the full by the Communists and by fellow travelers in their domestic and foreign propaganda. The following excerpt from a letter reproduced in the Nationalist newspaper *Heraldo de Aragón* on 10 June 1937 and allegedly written by Alvarez del Vayo to another member of the government, whose identity was not given, is worth quoting in view of its credibility: "How many times I have remembered what you said four months ago in my presence! It was necessary, you said—and you will recall that I immediately assented—to give the outside world the impression of a bourgeois tendency [in the government]. Nothing has favored us so much abroad as unity with the Basque Nationalist party."

Communist praise of José Antonio Aguirre, who became premier of the autonomous Basque government, was at times so extravagant that it embarrassed him. "I must confess," he stated in a report to the central government, "that as far as I am concerned the eulogies and headlines of the newspapers, principally the Communist newspapers, were sometimes so exaggerated, the adjectives so friendly and laudatory, that instead of feeling flattered I blushed with shame. This old tactic has no place in the customs of the Basque people, who are forthright and not doublefaced."[35]

Referring to the composition of the Largo Caballero government, the official Spanish Communist history of the Civil War observes: "This was the first time that a Communist party had participated in a coalition government, together with a Socialist party and various middle-class parties. It was also the first time that Communists and Catholics formed part of the same government.[36] In the international arena there was no precedent for such a coalition government with these characteristics."[37] Of greater importance historically is the fact, as Stanley G. Payne points out, that this unprecedented coalition was "but one of the first of several major features by which the Popular Front governments of wartime Spain anticipated the coalition regimes and 'People's Democracies' that emerged from the wreck of the Second World War in Europe."[38]

12

The Communists Strive for Hegemony

Although the Communist party held only two portfolios in the new administration, its meager representation furnished no real index of its strength in the country, either at the time the cabinet was constituted, when the number of its adherents had swollen far beyond the prewar total of 40,000, or a few months later, when it became, with an officially estimated membership of nearly a quarter of a million, the strongest political party in the anti-Franco camp. The precise figure, according to José Díaz, its general secretary, in a report to the central committee in March 1937, was 249,140, of which 87,660 (35.2 percent) were industrial workers, 62,250 (25 percent) agricultural laborers, 76,700 (30.7 percent) peasants, that is, peasant owners and tenant farmers, 15,485 (6.2 percent) members of the urban middle classes, and 7,045 (2.9 percent) intellectuals and members of the professional classes.[1]

If a large number of the party's new adherents, such as peasant owners, tenant farmers, tradesmen, small manufacturers, civil servants, army and police officers, doctors, teachers, writers, artists, and other intellectuals, had been members of the liberal Republican parties or even right-wing sympathizers before the Civil War and had been attracted to the party by the hope either of rescuing something from the ruins of the old regime or of sharing in the Communists' growing power; if, moreover, an appreciable number had been members of the Socialist party or the UGT before the war, an even greater number had never cast their faith into any political mold and, like the converts from the Socialist movement, had been drawn to the Communist party by its proselytizing zeal, its immensely skillful propaganda, its vigor, its organizing capacity, in both the civilian and military fields, and the prestige it derived from Soviet arms and technicians.

Illustrative of the Communists' success in acquiring new members is the following testimony from a variety of sources:

"The Republican middle class, surprised by the moderate tone of Communist propaganda and impressed by the unity and realism which prevailed in this party, flocked in great number to join its ranks," writes the Socialist historian Antonio Ramos Oliveira. "Army officers and officials who had never turned the pages of a Marxist leaflet became Communists, some through calculation, others through moral weakness, others inspired by the enthusiasm which animated this organization."[2]

"Actually, bourgeois generals and politicians, and many peasants who approve the Communist party's policy of protecting small property holders, have joined its ranks," wrote Louis Fischer. "I think these people influence and are influenced. But essentially their new political affiliation reflects a despair of the old social system as well as a hope to salvage some of its remnants."[3]

"Whenever Poldi took us along to his many conversations with young officials of the various ministries," writes Arturo Barea, a Socialist, "I tried to assess them. It struck me that most of them were ambitious young men of the upper middle classes who now declared themselves Communists, not, as we had done in Madrid, because to us it meant the party of revolutionary workers, but because it meant joining the strongest group and having a share in its disciplined power. They had leaped over the step of humanist Socialism; they were efficient and ruthless."[4]

As for the intellectuals, another Socialist, F. Ferrándiz Alborz, affirms: "Traditional Spanish pride was transformed into humiliation in the hands of the intellectuals. Nearly all of them bowed to the will of the Communist party."[5] Indicative of the efforts made by the Communist party to capture the sympathy of the Spanish intellectuals and scientists were the elaborate measures taken by the Communist-controlled Fifth Regiment to evacuate them from Madrid in the early days of the siege, giving them every comfort and protection.[6]

Fernando Claudín, a former Communist and member of the party for three decades, writes:

> The Communist International and the Communist party of Spain understood from the first moment the decisive nature of the military problem. With the help of Soviet technicians and Communist cadres from other countries, the Communist Party of Spain concentrated all its energies on the solution of this problem. Its structure, its method of functioning, the training of its cadres, made it particularly adept for this task. . . . The semimilitary features of the Bolshevik model after which it had fashioned itself enabled the Communist Party of Spain to convert itself rapidly into the *military party* of the Republic, into the organizational nucleus of the army, that had to be created quickly and without which everything was condemned to death: libertarian experiments, the Republican state, parties, and labor unions. The most elementary common sense caused the masses, independently of their political and union predilections, to understand that without an army, without a single command, without discipline, without a war economy, with "iron" unity—as the Communist party put it—in the front and in the rear, without subordinating every other consideration to the urgent necessity of defeating the enemy forces that were advancing, there was no salvation. If the membership of the Communist party and of its great auxiliary the Unified Socialist Youth (JSU) grew very rapidly in the first months of the war as well as its political influence and authority, this was not due to the fact that the proletariat considered

the Communist Party of Spain "more revolutionary" than the *Caballeristas* and Anarchosyndicalists, but more clear-sighted and more capable of handling the crucial problem of the situation. The prestige that the Soviet Union acquired through its help to the Republic had undoubtedly no small influence on the growth of the Communist Party of Spain, but the principal factor is the one we have just indicated. It is significant that the membership and influence of the party increased relatively little within the unions of the UGT, without mentioning those of the CNT, in other words, within the organized working class. Numerous petty bourgeois elements joined the Communist party of Spain, attracted by the reputation the party had acquired as the defender of order, of legality, and of small property. And above all, a large number of young men not yet trained in the traditional unions and working-class organizations adhered to the party—or placed themselves under its leadership through the JSU—attracted by the military virtues of the party and by a simplified ideology in which revolution was identified with antifascism intermingled with patriotism.[7]

Hardly inferior to all these factors as a source of Communist strength was the relative weakness or even impotence of other organizations. From the inception of the conflict, the liberal Republicans, lacking influence among the masses and clearly out of their depth, had retired into the background—or, as one friend of the Spanish Republic put it, they "remained in a comatose state throughout the war"[8]—ceding to the Communists the delicate work of opposing the left wing of the Revolution and defending the interests of the middle classes. Symptomatic of the change was the favorable publicity given to the Communist party by *Política*, the organ of the Left Republican party. "The change in the attitude of the bourgeois Republicans is . . . very interesting," ran an article in *Pravda*. "Previously they tried not to notice the Communist party and spoke of it with animosity and disdain. Now some organs of the republican press devote whole laudatory articles to it."[9]

The left Republicans not only gave friendly publicity to the Communists, whose declared policy coincided with their own—for example, José Giral, himself a member of the Left Republican party, observed that the coincidence of views between his party and the Communists was almost identical[10]—but not a few, to quote Indalecio Prieto, the moderate Socialist leader, actually served the ambitions of the Soviet Union.[11]

Furthermore, because of their lack of centralized direction, the Anarchosyndicalists, in spite of their numerical strength, were an unequal match for the Communists with their monolithic organization, their cohesion, and, above all, their discipline. According to Ettore Vanni, the former Italian Communist and director of *Verdad*, the Communist newspaper in Valencia, Communist discipline was "accepted with a fanaticism that at once dehumanized us and constituted our strength. In face of the demands of the war, everything vanished: the family, the home, the individual. For us there was only one thing: the party—everywhere and always the party."[12]

In its discipline, unscrupulousness, and totalitarian nature lay the principal ingredients of the party's political success. Gerald Brenan writes:

[The Communists] were incapable of rational discussion. From every pore they exuded a rigid totalitarian spirit. Their appetite for power was insatiable and they were completely unscrupulous. To them winning the war meant winning it for the Communist party. . . . But perhaps more serious . . . was their lack of moral or political integrity. Their opportunism extended to everything. They seemed to have no program that could not be reversed if its reversal promised them any advantage, and they were just as ready to use the middle classes against the proletariat as the proletariat against the middle classes. No doubt the historical method of Marxism lends itself to a good deal of stretching; even so, their going back on so many of their past tenets recalled the feats of those Jesuit missionaries of the seventeenth century who, the better to convert the Chinese, suppressed the story of the Crucifixion. It is a comparison worth insisting on. By their devotion to an institution rather than to an idea, to a foreign Pope rather than to a national community, they were following the road laid down by Loyola. And their impact on Spain was very similar. Just as the Jesuits from the time of Lainez had turned their backs on the great ascetic and mystical movements of their age and had worked to reduce everything to a dead level of obedience and devotion, so the Communists showed that the great release of feeling that accompanies a revolution was distasteful to them. They frowned on all its impulses, both its cruel and its creative ones, and applied a severely practical spirit to its various manifestations.[13]

Lacking centralized direction, the Anarchosyndicalists could not compete with the monolithic organization of the Communist party, guided and bolstered as it was by some of the best brains from the Communist cadres of other countries. "In defense of the libertarians," writes the libertarian historian César M. Lorenzo, "it should be stated clearly that the cultural level of the Socialists, Communists, and members of other parties was scarcely higher. Not only did illiteracy weigh heavily on political life, but also the archaism of an education that offered little in the way of scientific disciplines and had always been monopolized by the Church (in spite of the efforts of a Francisco Giner de los Ríos among the middle classes and a Francisco Ferrer among the proletariat) blunted the faculties of educated persons."[14] Even if it is true, as Lorenzo contends, that during the first weeks of the Civil War the CNT played the dominant role in Madrid, this dominance—which is by no means certain—did not last for long.[15] Having no plan for the conquest of power, he affirms, lacking the undisputed hegemony it possessed in Catalonia, Aragon, or Malaga, the CNT could not centralize the conduct of military operations and the organization of the police and judiciary or transform the structure of the economy. "As a result, Madrid was delivered up to indescribable disorder. Each ideological sector formed a state within a state, each had its own militia, its own tribunals, its 'chekas,' its prisons, its own private buildings, its own food and munitions depots; each waged war in its own way and occupied itself solely with its needs. . . . [The] government was incapable of performing the task of unification. Since the Socialists proved too sluggish to assume this responsibility, since the libertarians, because of their doctrines, their extreme antiauthoritarianism, could not or would not assume the responsibility, it was logical that someone else would take their place. This was the Communist party.

"From the very beginning the Stalinists had created a military structure. Their disciplined troops, with their hierarchical makeup, endowed with perfect auxiliary services, soon showed their superiority over all other militia forces. . . . In the months of September and October, they seized the ascendancy from the libertarians, carried other parties along in their wake, and appeared as the best defenders of the capital."[16]

In a later passage, Lorenzo argues that a libertarian revolution in Spain would have been possible only if 90 percent of the population had been favorable to the ideas disseminated by the CNT and FAI, but all social and political groups hostile to the Anarchosyndicalists, he confesses, far exceeded in numbers the adherents of the CNT and FAI.

> Hence to establish Libertarian Communism it would have been necessary to coerce a large number of people, to stop them from sabotaging, from calumniating, from provoking disorders: it would have been necessary to arrest their leaders, dissolve their organizations, muzzle their press. In other words, to establish Libertarian Communism it would have meant instituting a Libertarian Communist dictatorship; it would have meant negating . . . that very Communism that is the antithesis of all political power, of all oppression, of the police and the army. It would have meant reconstructing the state, transforming organized Anarchism into a kind of ruling caste overseeing the rest of the population, a caste that would become more and more tyrannical and privileged. (Bakunin, Kropotkin, and Malatesta had clearly shown the danger of power and had explained the genesis of the state.)
>
> But if the Spanish libertarians had not been held back by these theoretical considerations and by their devotion to their ideology, could they actually have taken power? It is very doubtful. . . . Taking power was only possible by a party that wielded iron discipline, a party organized militarily with a revolutionary general staff, with a centralized and hierarchical apparatus, an implacable ideological line, and combat groups possessing unquestioned leaders. Within the CNT everyone had his own opinion, everyone acted according to his own judgment, the leaders were ceaselessly criticized and challenged, the autonomy of the regional federations was inviolable, just as the autonomy of the local federations and unions was inviolable within the regional federations. To get a decision accepted . . . a militant had to exhaust himself making speeches, personal contacts, moving from place to place. Among the libertarians the ballot was repugnant; the unanimity they sought required interminable debates. How, under these conditions, could the CNT have taken power even if its "leaders" had desired it?[17]

At the outbreak of the Revolution, the Socialists—despite Anarchosyndicalist claims to the contrary—were in all probability still the strongest force in the capital and in Old and New Castile. They were soon undermined by open and secret defections to the Communist party, for which their own passivity was in some degree responsible. A leading left-wing Socialist, at one time very much influenced by the Communist party, confesses that the "dynamic quality of the Communists was very congenial to me as compared with the extreme sluggishness of many Socialists."[18] Another left-wing Socialist writes: "I had lost all confidence in the Socialist party's power of assuming responsibility and authority in a difficult situation, and my companion, Torres, an old member of the Socialist Youth Organization, had recently joined the Communists."[19] On 9 March 1937 the moderate Socialist organ, *El Socialista*, referred editorially to a letter from a group of Socialists stating that they were joining the Communist party because their own party showed no sign of life at the fronts.[20]

The Socialists were entangled in factional strife. In the hands of the centrists led by Indalecio Prieto, the executive committee of the party was in a state of irreconcilable belligerence with local units sympathetic to Largo Caballero. "Each provincial federation and division acted on its own initiative," attests Wenceslao Carrillo, one of the leading Caballero Socialists in the Agrupación Socialista Madrileña, controlled by the left wing. "Only the Madrid division maintained contact with a number of federations and sections, which asked it for directives."[21] "The life of the Socialist movement," writes Gabriel Morón, a prominent centrist, "was reduced to a faint breath, manifesting itself in internal dissensions. . . . In the rear, as at the front, the boldest, the most zealous and unscrupulous imposed their views, made their influence felt, and asserted their personality." Later he attests: "There were no individuals with these moral and temperamental traits left in the Socialist party. On the other hand, the Communist party was filled with them to the point of congestion."[22]

The Communists took full advantage of the divisions within the Socialist party. Referring some years after the war to the dissensions among the leaders of the Socialist party, Jesús Hernández, former politburo member and one of the two Communist ministers in the government, wrote: "We managed to exploit their suicidal antagonisms for our own ends. One day we supported one side against the other. The next day we reversed our position and supported the opposite side. And today, the next day, and every day we incited one side against the other so that they would destroy one another, a game we played in full view and not without success."[23]

The drive that the Communists initiated to engulf the Socialist movement began under the most promising auspices. That the successes they rapidly achieved, particularly at the expense of its predominant left wing, should have irked Largo Caballero was, of course, inevitable; for when, before the war, he had advocated fusion with the Communists, he may have believed, as he later contended, that he could absorb them,[24] but never had he anticipated the absorption of his own following. His resentment was acute when, within a few days of the inception of the war, the Catalan federation of the PSOE led by Rafael Vidiella, hitherto a stout supporter, merged with the Catalan section of the PCE and two other organizations to form the PSUC, the United Socialist party of Catalonia, which accepted the discipline of the Comintern or Third International[25] and brought the local organization of the UGT under its dominion.[26] But in other parts of the left zone, particularly in Madrid, the stronghold of the left-wing Socialists, the danger to Largo Caballero's influence revealed itself in its full stature. Lacking directives from their own party, which was racked and torn by internal discord, a large number of left Socialist workers, swayed by the dynamism and proselytizing methods of the Communists,[27] were ebbing away and embracing the rival movement. To make matters worse, some of Largo Caballero's most trusted aides, both in the PSOE and the UGT, had transferred their attachment to the Communists, either in secrecy or without disguise. These included Julio Alvarez del Vayo, foreign minister and vice-president of the Madrid section of the Socialist party; Edmundo Domínguez, secretary of the UGT National Federation of Building Workers, the Federación Nacional de la Edificación; Amaro del Rosal, the president of the UGT bank employees' union, the Federación Nacional de Banca, and a member of the UGT executive committee; Felipe Pretel, the treasurer of the Socialist labor union;[28] and the two well-known Cortes deputies and intellectuals, Margarita Nelken[29] and Francisco Montiel, both members of the PSOE.

Addressing the plenary session of the central committee of the Communist party in March 1937, Montiel stated: "It is wonderful, for those of us who were outside the Communist party until a few weeks ago, to contemplate how, in the very midst of the revolutionary struggle, one organization that was for many years a powerful political force and had almost a monopoly of the political leadership of the Spanish proletariat was disintegrating, ruined by its mistakes, and how another organization, composed in the early days of little more than a handful of men, but guided to perfection by Marxism and Leninism, could become after 18 July the real force in the struggle against fascism and the real directing force of the Spanish masses."[30]

A still more important development that told on Largo Caballero's political influence was the loss of his authority over the JSU,[31] which was formed three months before the outbreak of the Civil War as a result of the amalgamation of the Union of Young Communists and the Socialist Youth Federation, whose representatives had met in Moscow with the executive committee of the Young Communist International to draw up plans for the fusion of the two organizations.[32] Santiago Carrillo, general secretary of the JSU, claimed in 1937 that its membership, which (according to his figures) had been 40,000 at the time of the fusion, had risen to 150,000 just before the outbreak of the Civil War[33] and to 300,000 in April 1937.[34]

The preparatory operations for this merger, recounts Luis Araquistáin, Largo Caballero's close collaborator and adviser, or "eminence grise," as his opponents described him, were conducted in the home of his brother-in-law, Julio Alvarez del Vayo.[35] "I lived in Madrid, one floor above him, and witnessed the daily visits paid to him by young Socialist leaders for the purpose of interviewing the Comintern agent then prominent in Spain, a certain [Vittorio] Codovila,[36] who used the false name of Medina, and spoke Spanish with a strong South American accent. . . . It was there that a voyage to the Muscovite Mecca was organized for them; it was there that it was agreed to deliver the Socialist youth, the new working-class generation of Spain, to Communism."[37] Although Araquistáin undoubtedly approved of the negotiations at the time, he never publicly acknowledged his acquiescence after the outbreak of the Civil War.

It should be kept in mind that both Araquistáin and Largo Caballero had maintained cordial relations with representatives of the Communist International long before the Civil War. According to Amaro del Rosal, a former Caballerista and member of the UGT executive, who supported the Communists during and after the war, Caballero was frequently visited in jail after the 1934 rebellion by Comintern delegates. "The relations with the Communist party," he writes, "had entered a cordial phase and the sympathy toward the Soviet Union manifested itself on all occasions. Delegates of the Third [Communist] International maintained friendly relations with the most well-known Caballeristas, such as Araquistáin, Alvarez del Vayo and others. Caballero—although he forgets to say so in *Mis recuerdos* [his published memoirs]—frequently received in jail [after the rebellion of October 1934] delegates of the International, among them Medina (Vittorio Codovila), who were always accompanied by Araquistáin or by Alvarez del Vayo. Before 1934, he received them in his offices of the UGT. . . . After he was freed, the interviews were resumed at the same place."[38]

As for the fusion of the two youth organizations, which took place in April 1936, Largo Caballero had, in spite of everything that has since been said to the contrary, encouraged the merger,[39] although it is true that in a joint statement issued in March 1936, before the merger had taken place, it was agreed that until a national congress of unification had determined democratically the principles, program, and definitive structure of the united organization and elected a directive body, the fusion would be effected on the basis of the entry of the Young Communists into the Socialist Youth Federation.[40] But stimulated by Largo Caballero's policy of uniting the working-class movements, the fusion of the two organizations took place precipitately, and no congress of unification was held.[41] Largo Caballero had not opposed the merger because the Union of Young Communists was incomparably smaller than his own Socialist Youth Federation—only three thousand members in contrast with fifty thousand, according to one estimate[42]—and because he had believed that through his supporters he would be able to control the united movement. However, in the sequel he was rudely deceived; for within a few months of the inception of the Civil War, Santiago Carrillo, general secretary of the JSU and hitherto a sedulous admirer[43]—known as the *niño mimado* (spoilt child) of the Socialist leader, who would address him endearingly as "Santiaguito,"[44]—quietly joined the Communist party together with other former leaders of the Socialist Youth Federation.[45] Some of them, including Carrillo (who became secretary of the party in exile and returned to Spain in that capacity after the death of General Franco in 1975) later became members of its central committee[46] (Carrillo being appointed deputy member of the politburo) and transformed the JSU into one of the main props for Communist policy.

When a group of Socialist youth leaders headed by Carrillo broke the news of their defection to Largo Caballero, he was shattered. Carrillo himself testifies: ". . . after listening to us, he said with tears in his eyes: 'From now on, I can no longer believe in the Spanish revolution.' That was because we, the youth, were its real strength. This force was leaving him. He was sincere, because he believed that it was his task to lead the Spanish revolution. But he did not reproach us. He simply showed his sorrow."[47] However, at a later date, Largo Caballero told a close collaborator: "He was more than a son to me. I shall never forgive the Communists for having taken him from me."[48] In his unpublished memoirs, he also expressed his bitterness: "In the Socialist Youth, Judases like Santiago Carrillo and others were not lacking who managed to simulate a fusion they called the JSU. Later, they revealed their treachery when they joined the Communist International."[49]

Commenting on this defection, Carlos de Baráibar, the left Socialist leader, who, according to his own confession, was very much influenced by the Communists early in the war, recalls: "A group of leaders of the Unified Socialist Youth [JSU] visited me to inform me that they had decided to join the Communist party en masse. . . . I considered it monstrous that such a thing could have happened . . . with no one's knowledge other than that of Alvarez del Vayo who, as I learned later, was informed of every step taken. And all of them were advised by the person whom we used to call the 'eye of Moscow,' the secret representative of the Comintern [Vittorio Codovila]."[50]

Many years later, Carrillo acknowledged Codovila's influence upon him even before the outbreak of the Civil War. "I already knew him," he told Régis Debray and Max Gallo. ". . . I must say that at that time Codovilla [sic] worked very well with me. I am partly indebted to him for having become a Communist."[51]

Carrillo joined the Communist party on 7 November 1936.[52] His onetime close associate, Fernando Claudín, a leader of the JSU during the war and an authority on the subject, writes: "As he explained to us at the time, [Carrillo joined the party] because, during the critical days of the defense of Madrid, when the enemy had reached its vulnerable defenses, the Socialist party appeared inoperative. Its national and local leaders had abandoned the capital for Valencia and Barcelona. . . . The top leaders of the Communist party remained there, setting an example." And, in a later passage, he adds: "[As] leader of the JSU, Santiago Carrillo became an outstanding personality, but his position of deputy member of the Politburo was practically ignored. . . . He rarely attended [its meetings], being simply the man charged with the implementation of party policy. He did not belong to the inner circles, where important questions were decided, attended by the delegates of the Communist International . . . , the top

Soviet representatives (diplomatic, military and secret service) and the most prominent leaders of the Spanish Communist party."[53]

In order fully to understand the future course of events, it is essential at this point to emphasize the power that Moscow's foreign representatives—the Comintern "delegates" or "instructors," as they were called[54]—exercised at that time over the Spanish Communist leaders. Vittorio Codovila, an Argentinian, was, in the words of onetime central committee member Enrique Castro, "the real head of the party."[55] Furthermore, according to Eudocio Ravines, a former Peruvian Communist who knew Codovila personally and who worked on the staff of the Communist organ *Frente Rojo* in Valencia, Codovila had "liquidated politically" the Spanish party leadership before the Civil War and replaced it with "elements subordinate to his will."[56] According to the same knowledgeable source, Boris Stefanov, a Bulgarian, "one of the few friends of Lenin who had survived the purges" and one of Stalin's closest friends, was also in Spain, using the alias Moreno, and is described by Ravines, who knew him personally, as "the maximum director of the Revolution, the war, the feints, and maneuvers of the Communist party. His word was taken as though it were personally inspired by Stalin."[57] Equally important was the fact that Palmiro Togliatti, the Italian Communist and, like Stefanov, a member of the executive committee of the Comintern, who had escaped from Mussolini's Italy in 1925 and became head of the Italian Communist party after World War II, was also active in Spain, especially after the departure of Codovila in the summer of 1937. At that time Togliatti became the virtual head of the party, directing strategy and writing many of the speeches of José Díaz and La Pasionaria.[58] Using the aliases Ercole Ercoli and Alfredo, Togliatti remained in Spain with Stefanov until the end of the Civil War.

That Togliatti was the de facto leader of the party is confirmed by Enrique Líster, an unwavering supporter of the Kremlin: "He was the delegate in Spain of the Communist International, whom the entire Politburo obeyed without a murmur."[59]

In his testimony before the U.S. Senate Subcommittee on Internal Security in February 1957, Alexander Orlov, chief NKVD (Soviet secret police) official in Spain from September 1936 until his defection in July 1938, stated: "Palmiro Togliatti was also in Spain . . . with me, and he had been a good friend of mine at that time. He directed the Spanish Communist party and the Spanish Communist military forces on behalf of Moscow. . . . [At] the head of the Italian Communist party [today] stands the most able man in the Communist movement—that means Palmiro Togliatti."[60] Furthermore, in the opinion of the American Communist John Gates, head commissar in 1938 of the Fifteenth Brigade, "Togliatti was the most powerful Communist figure in Spain. His responsibility was the whole policy of the Spanish Communists. . . . The enormous growth of the Spanish Communist party after the fascist revolt must be attributed in large part to his advice and leadership. . . . Togliatti was a brilliant tactician, probably the most able in the Communist world."[61]

Tribute to Togliatti also comes from Santiago Carrillo, who wrote in 1971, when secretary of the party in exile: "[He] was an invaluable counsellor and, for many of us, who were very young and inexperienced, a veritable maestro."[62] "He was an extraordinary person," he told Régis Debray and Max Gallo in 1974. "I believe he was the most cultured, the most intelligent leader in the Communist movement."[63]

The most interesting testimony is given by Justo Martínez Amutio, the Socialist governor of Albacete, the headquarters of the International Brigades, who had personal dealings with him: "He was the most skillful of all the [political] agents sent by Stalin and the real director of Communist party policy until the end of the war. I considered him . . . superior in intelligence and ability to Stefanov. . . . The entire political orientation of the Comintern within the International Brigades was directed by this man, who together with Stefanov planned the domestic and military policies of the Communist party. . . . He was in the habit of asking questions courteously, insisting on details and learning through various channels about the personality of the most prominent political and military figures, wheedling out of his interlocutors their views. But, as far as he was concerned, no one could judge either from his gestures or facial expressions . . . what he was thinking or feeling."[64]

"El Campesino" describes Togliatti as "cold, cynical, without nerves and without scruples,"[65] a description exemplified by Enrique Castro in his account of a meeting of Spanish Communist leaders in Moscow after the war: "Togliatti finishes cleaning his glasses. He examines them at length in the light, then looks at us one after the other. He crosses his legs and assumes the immobility of a rock. . . . I am reminded of the words of his secretary in Spain: 'He is the type of man that would make love to me just as coldly as he would have given orders to shoot me!' "[66]

Given the monolithic character of the Comintern apparatus, it is not surprising that Codovila, Stefanov, and, later, Togliatti, with their vast political experience in the world Communist movement and wielding power that flowed directly from the Kremlin, had little difficulty dominating the meetings of the Spanish politburo, which directed the policy of the party and the JSU. "Spain had no Lenin," writes Fernando Claudín. "There was instead an abundance of Comintern advisers. Genuine revolutionaries and organizers like José Díaz and Pedro Checa, and popular orators of the stature of Dolores Ibárruri, did not possess the necessary theoretical basis to oppose the Popular Front schemes of the Comintern."[67] According to an inveterate opponent of the Communists, their leaders were "intellectually mediocre, weak and accustomed to submission."[68]

However this may be, thanks to the power and influence of Vittorio Codovila and to the help of Santiago Carrillo and other Socialist youth leaders, who had joined the Communist party, the JSU quickly became an important instrument of Comintern policy. Shortly after the defection, the Communists consolidated their hold still further. Instead of holding the projected national congress of unification that was to determine democratically the principles, program, and definitive structure of the united organization and to elect a directive body, Santiago Carrillo convened in Valencia, in January 1937, a national conference. To this he appointed as delegates not only the representatives of the local sections of the JSU, but a large number of young Communists from the fronts and factories, a stratagem that enabled him to control the conference from start to finish and to secure the election of a national committee and an executive packed with Communist party nominees. "Instead of holding a congress," wrote Antonio Escribano, the delegate from Alicante province, "the Communists convened that 'hoax,' the Conference of Valencia. They gave it the full weight of a 'democratic' congress of unification, but the truth is quite the opposite."[69]

"Could we," asked Santiago Carrillo, defending his action a few months later, "could we, in wartime, and considering the changes that have taken place in our country and in our own organization, hold a congress attended exclusively by the representatives of the local sections? Could we, with our youth at the fronts, hold the same type of congress that we should have held before 18 July, when our youth was not yet defending its liberty with arms? No, we could not have held such a congress. We had to adapt ourselves to the situation. And the situation made it compulsory that our congress, our national conference, should be attended not only by the representatives of the local sections, but also by those young men who were striving with great sacrifice to increase war production in the factories and by those who were giving their blood for our liberty on land, on sea, and in the air; in other words, by that part of our youth, the best part—not in the local sections, but at the front—that has a legitimate right to direct and control the life of its federation."[70]

The following excerpt from a letter sent to me some years after the war by Antonio Escribano is of interest: "I remember when the national committee of the JSU was elected. . . . Several veterans of the youth movement met with Carrillo and his associates and elected representatives for each province. Later they read the 'election' of the national committee which everyone approved by acclamation because instructions had been given to agree to everything proposed by the leadership."[71]

In this coup Carrillo had undoubtedly been aided by his liberal praise of Largo Caballero. "It is necessary to say here and now," he had declared in his speech at the conference, "that as ever, and even more than ever, Largo Caballero enjoys the support of the Spanish youth in the factories and at the fronts. I must also add that Comrade Largo Caballero is for us the same as he was before: the man who helped our unification. He is the man from whom we are expecting much useful advice so that, in the interests of the common cause we are defending, the unity of the Spanish youth may be a reality."[72]

Carrillo also undoubtedly had been aided not only by the fact that few of the young Socialist delegates were aware at the time that he had joined the Communist party, believing that he and other leaders of the JSU were acting in full accord with Largo Caballero and his supporters in the Socialist party, but also by the fact that all debate had been avoided. Antonio Escribano recalls:

> Nothing at all was debated [at the conference]. Those who did speak confined themselves to making a report or address, but no discussion followed. A certain Carrasco spoke on behalf of the antitankists on how to destroy tanks; a sailor spoke on his own subject, an aviator likewise, and so on and so forth. The fact is that nothing regarding the unification of the two organizations was debated. On the contrary, everything that had happened was taken for granted. Those of us who were loyal to Caballero did not raise any objections at the conference for two reasons, both fairly ingenuous when I look back on them today, although justifiable at the time. These reasons were: 1. 90 percent of the young Socialists who attended the conference did not know that Carrillo, Lain, Melchor, Cabello, Aurora Arnaiz, etc., had gone over outright to the Communist party. We believed that they were still young Socialists and that, strange as it seemed to us, they were acting in agreement with Caballero and the Socialist party. Had we known that this group of recreants had betrayed us, I can assure you that an entirely different situation would have arisen. But we were taken off our guard. That is the truth of the matter, which, for my part I am not ashamed to confess. 2. The atmosphere and the manner in which the conference was conducted took us by surprise, and when we wished to react the assembly had already come to an end. We members of the Socialist Youth Federation had been accustomed to discuss the agendas of our congresses and assemblies democratically and exhaustively, and had firmly believed that the conference in Valencia would be conducted in the same way. . . . Nothing of the kind occurred. When we realized what had happened, it was too late. The conference had ended.[73]

In fact, not until some time later, when the struggle between Largo Caballero and the Communists had entered an acute phase and the full import of the PCE's victory at the Conference of Valencia was fully understood, did the first cleft appear. This occurred when a number of prominent Caballeristas, including Sócrates Gómez, Tundidor López, and Leoncio Pérez, publicly protested the coup[74] and when open letters to Santiago Carrillo from José Gregori Martínez, general secretary of the provincial committee of the Valencia JSU, and Rafael Fernández, general secretary of the JSU of Asturias, were published, declining the seats on the national committee to which they had been elected at the conference on the ground that their local sections had not been consulted.[75] "[Anyone] who protested—as I did at the Communist party's domination of the JSU—was slandered, blackened and sometimes physically eliminated," recalled Sócrates Gómez, who toward the end of the war led the Socialist opposition movement to the Communists inside the JSU. "The Communist party never attempted to take account, calmly and coolly, of differences of political opinion; they launched instead into insults, slanders, defamations."[76]

If, in conjunction with all these developments, the skill of the Communists in using artifice and subterfuge, in playing one hostile faction against another, in packing pivotal positions with secret party members or with fellow travelers, in bestowing patronage and exerting pressure upon anyone who joined their ranks or served their interests, is taken into consideration, their early emergence as the real power in the anti-Franco camp should be readily appreciated.

13

Dr. Juan Negrín and
Julio Alvarez del Vayo

The two ministries the Communist party held in the government furnished no real index of its strength in the country nor did they afford a true indication of the influence it wielded in its councils. The real weight of the Communists in the government lay less in the two portfolios they held than in the influence they enjoyed over Dr. Juan Negrín, the minister of finance, and over Julio Alvarez del Vayo, the foreign minister, at that time Largo Caballero's man of confidence.

Though vice-president of the Madrid section of the Socialist party and officially a member of its left wing, Alvarez del Vayo soon came to be regarded by the leading figures in his party as a Communist at heart. "He called himself a Socialist," affirmed Largo Caballero, "but was unreservedly in the service of the Communist party and promoted all their machinations."[1] A few days before the end of the war, the Madrid section decided to suspend him and to propose to the national executive his expulsion from the Socialist party because of his pro-Communist activity.[2] A supporter of the Soviet Union and of Comintern policy before the Civil War,[3] he had played an important part, as we have seen, in bringing about the fusion of the Socialist and Communist youth movements, and during the war he endorsed the Communists' campaign for the fusion of the Socialist and Communist parties.[4] However, some years later, after emigrating to the United States and becoming a member of the editorial staff of the *Nation*,[5] he denied that he had ever advocated a merger of the two parties.[6]

As Largo Caballero's trusted adviser during the early months of the Civil War, he not only possessed his ear on matters of foreign policy, but was appointed by him to head the vital General Commissariat of War that directed the political orientation of the armed forces. In this body, according to Pedro Checa, a member of the politburo and head of the party's central committee, he served the Communist party "scrupulously."[7] Yet, in spite of his many services, there is evidence that in the inner circles of the party he commanded little or no respect. "He is an idiot, but is more or less useful," was the party's opinion, according to a former central committee member.[8] Nevertheless, according to some, he had other qualities. Louis Fischer, a champion of the Soviet regime for almost twenty years, portrays him "as a gorgeous human being,"[9] while Ovadii Savich, the Tass representative in Spain between 1937 and 1939, describes him as "the most likeable person in the government."[10]

In his capacity as foreign minister, Alvarez del Vayo was in charge of appointments not only to the foreign press bureau—which censured the dispatches of correspondents with an eye to opinion abroad—but also to the propaganda department of the ministry.[11] "During the three months that I was director of propaganda for the United States and England under Alvarez del Vayo," wrote Liston Oak, "I was instructed not to send out one word about this revolution in the economic system of loyalist Spain. Nor are any foreign correspondents in Valencia [the provisional seat of government from November 1936] permitted to write freely of the revolution that has taken place."[12] Del Vayo also appointed the Czech Communist Otto Katz, alias André Simone, as director of the foreign propaganda bureau in Paris, the Agencia Española,[13] who, together with his assistant Arthur Koestler, received directives from Willi Muenzenberg, the Comintern's master propagandist in Western Europe.[14] In London, the foreign propaganda bureau, known as the Spanish News Agency, was run by Geoffrey Bing, a member of the British Communist party.[15]

But valuable as were Alvarez del Vayo's services to the Communists in helping them to implement their strategy of infiltration and domination in the early stages of the Civil War, the main instrument in bringing their plans to fruition in its final stages was Dr. Juan Negrín, who even after fifty years remains the most controversial figure of the war. Son of a wealthy businessman, a professor of physiology at the Madrid School of Medicine, a Cortes deputy for the Canary Islands and an adherent before the war of Indalecio Prieto's anti-Communist center faction of the PSOE,[16] minister of finance in Largo Caballero's government, prime minister from May 1937 to April 1938, and premier and defense minister from April 1938 until the end of the war in March 1939, he was more responsible than any other Spaniard for the later success of Communist policy. Whether or not he surrendered himself "body and soul" to the Communist party, as charged by Largo Caballero,[17] can only be determined by a painstaking evaluation of all the evidence.

A detailed account of his services to the Communists and of his vast contribution to the success of their policy, especially as premier and defense minister during the last year of the war, will be given later in this work. However, since some well-known writers and historians have in recent years attempted to attenuate the criticisms of Negrín's role by attributing them to "postwar recriminations of the exile world"[18] or to reject them altogether[19] and have also tried to "resituate" Negrín historically by discounting or ignoring critical accounts and crucial evidence that reveal the true forces behind him,[20] it is important at this early stage to take into consideration the following countervailing information in order to place him in his true historical context even before he became what his admirers have termed "the incarnation of the Republic."

For example, one individual who exercised an extraordinary but little-known influence over Negrín was Benigno Rodríguez, a party member, one of the founders of the famous Communist Fifth Regiment, its propaganda chief, and editor of its organ, *Milicia popular*. According to Jorge Semprún, for many years an intimate associate in exile of Santiago Carrillo, Benigno Rodríguez was made political secretary of Negrín "on party orders" and "knew everything about everything." "Benigno was a stupendous individual, almost unbelievable, self-taught, with a vast and solid culture, and endowed with a keen political and human intuition, but who possessed a Stalinist superego that constantly repressed his deepest emotions."[21]

Enrique Castro, a former member of the PCE's central committee, affirms that Negrín was controlled directly by the party and by two of his closest collaborators: by Benigno Rodríguez and Manuel Sánchez Arcas, the latter "a good architect, marvellous person, blindly obedient to the party, who occupied [in 1938] the undersecretaryship of propaganda."[22] Benigno Rodríguez remained at Negrín's side up to the end of the Civil War and drafted, together with Togliatti, the prime minister's last speech on Spanish soil.[23]

Negrín did not take Rodríguez's support and companionship for granted. In the words of Antonio Cordón, his undersecretary of the army in April 1938 and a prominent member of the Communist party—who like all supporters and apologists of Negrín made much of his political independence and who affirms that it was his "correct ideas" that earned him the backing of the party[24]—"Negrín appreciated Benigno's great merit, his talent, his enormous capacity for work, his unshakeable enthusiasm and always showed him, even after the war, great affection and consideration."[25] Jacinto Toryho, former director of the CNT organ, *Solidaridad Obrera*, describes Benigno Rodríguez as Negrín's "principal adviser" and as the "Black Pope" during his premiership—a characterization to which I personally subscribe with the qualification that Negrín did not always follow the proffered advice. "His office," attests Toryho, "was next to the premier's, who never made a decision without consulting him. He was put there so that Negrín would know where to go to *orient himself.*"[26]

Like Alvarez del Vayo, Negrín was suspended toward the end of the war from the Madrid section of the Socialist party because of his political conduct.[27] Although he was Prieto's own man and recommended by him to head the ministry of finance in Largo Caballero's government in September 1936,[28] Negrín freed himself long before the war had run its course, at first secretly and then openly, from the personal and political bonds that tied him to the moderate Socialist leader. Never a member of the Communist party, he provided a convenient façade for its hegemonic aims.

Too many people, anxious not to hurt the cause of the Republic, have appeared blind to Negrín's services to the Communist party.[29] Claude Bowers, for example, the U.S. ambassador to Spain during the Civil War, claimed that Negrín was "as remote from Communism as it is possible to be."[30] Since one does not have to be a Communist to serve the interests of the party and can serve its ends—

whether wittingly or unwittingly—even more effectively outside the party, there can be no doubt that Bowers's political ingenuousness and sympathy for the Republican cause obscured his judgment. According to the famous Spanish writer Ramón Sender, a onetime sympathizer of the Communist party: "Mr. Bowers was our friend—an honest man so impressed by the strength of our arguments that he refused to see the shadows being cast over us by Moscow's sinister Machiavellianism. Most of us Spaniards did not see them either."[31] It is to Bowers's credit that he later confessed to Sender that he had changed his mind about Negrín.[32]

"Negrín," writes Frank Sedwick, "was to open the doors wide to Communist domination of the government and the armed forces. . . . Undeniably he was a strong leader, an indefatigable worker, and a fighter to the end. His courage, self-confidence, resourcefulness, and vigorous personality won him the perpetual praise of Herbert Matthews [of the *New York Times*] and certain other correspondents whose personal involvement with the Loyalist [Republican] cause may have taken a measure of objectivity from their writing."[33]

It is curious that thirty-four years after the Civil War, notwithstanding all the available evidence corroborating Negrín's support of the Communists, Herbert Matthews still denied Negrín's extraordinary services to the Communist cause and remained until Negrín's death in 1956 his principal apologist in the vast bibliography on the Spanish conflict. In 1957, he wrote: "Those, like myself, who had watched him closely during the Civil War and who retained a deep admiration and affection for him in the after years, will have no doubts about the verdict of time. He lost, but he made a mark on Spanish history of which future generations will have a reason to be proud."[34] In his final work on Spain, published in 1973, he wrote: "Mistaken beliefs about Negrín have colored and distorted a great many histories, especially perhaps those of the most scrupulous postwar scholars, hardly any of whom had the opportunity of knowing Dr. Negrín. He was the key figure on the Republican side. Get his character and motives wrong and the history being written will be wrong. Even a scholar as discerning and shrewd as Hugh Thomas, whose portrayal of Dr. Negrín is quite fair and sympathetic, could not allow himself to believe that certain charges against Don Juan—that he yielded to Communist demands for instance—were completely false. In his book *The Spanish Revolution*, Professor Payne is wrong in saying: 'That [Negrín] was dedicated to the cause of a leftist victory irrespective of tactics or consequences seems without question.' Dr. Negrín used and worked with the Communists simply for practical reasons which had nothing to do with 'leftism' or any ideology. He had no political coloration or preference for any political party or movement as such."[35]

In spite of Matthews's mild criticism of Thomas, both writers have expressed similar misleading views regarding the supposed independence of Negrín. "It is true that few politicians have successfully used a Communist party, and not been later swallowed by it," Thomas wrote in 1965. "But in the 1930s and in Spain the possibility did not seem so far-fetched. Negrín's personal self-confidence and his reserved secret nature perhaps led him to think that he could slough off the

Communist connection when necessary. . . . It would in fact be ludicrous to suppose that so tough and independent-minded an intellectual, with so bad a temper, could ever be subservient to anyone.[36] Though he was on excellent terms with the Russian economic adviser, [Arthur] Stashevsky, on one occasion (when Minister of Finance) he had told another Russian not to try and dictate the internal affairs of Spain. Otherwise, added Negrín, 'there is the door.' "[37] The source of this anecdote which Thomas omitted from the 1977 edition of his book[38] was Pablo de Azcárate, the Republican ambassador in London, who was a perfervid admirer of Negrín's[39] and who, in the words of his former friend and colleague at the League of Nations, Salvador de Madariaga, later "abandoned the strict path of truth for the putrid intellectual bog of Communism."[40]

Although Thomas omitted the anecdote, he retained substantially the following assertion: "Negrín had no close relations with the leaders of the Spanish Communist party and had a strong dislike for La Pasionaria." In order to bolster his thesis that Negrín remained by and large independent of the Communists, he quotes the former politburo member, Jesús Hernández, in both editions, as acknowledging that "a time would have come when it would have been necessary to 'liquidate' Negrín."[41] But what Hernández really stated supports the opposite thesis: "To destroy Francisco Largo Caballero we relied principally on Negrín and, to a certain extent, on Prieto. To get rid of Prieto we utilized Negrín and other prominent Socialists, and had the war lasted we would not have hesitated to ally ourselves with the devil in order to exterminate Negrín *if he had obstructed us.*"[42] The fact is that at no time, as will be seen in the course of this work, did Negrín obstruct Communist policy to the point that it became necessary to eliminate him. Furthermore, contrary to Thomas's assertion, Negrín not only maintained close relations with significant Spanish Communists, such as Benigno Rodríguez and Sánchez Arcas, and with others, as we shall see later, but also with Arthur Stashevsky, the Soviet trade envoy, his unofficial economic adviser, to whom Stalin, according to Walter Krivitsky, one of the top Soviet intelligence operatives in Western Europe, had assigned the task of "manipulating the political and financial reins of loyalist Spain."[43]

Another well-known apologist of Negrín, Professor Juan Marichal of Harvard University, has stated: "Negrín cannot be regarded as an automatic follower of Soviet policy. . . . I believe that I am not being dogmatic when I affirm . . . that few men in European history during the last century and a half have displayed such a combination of intelligence and character, of moral integrity and intellectual capacity."[44] In contrast, Krivitsky asserts that Stashevsky discovered in Negrín "a willing collaborator of his financial schemes."[45] Although we have only Krivitsky's word for this allegation, four knowledgeable supporters of Negrín have confirmed the close relationship between the two men. Louis Fischer—who was personally acquainted with most of the leading Russians in Spain, and who, Indalecio Prieto claims, was Negrín's "principal propaganda agent" abroad and "probable financial director" of that propaganda to judge from the "large sums" he received from Negrín[46]—affirms that Stashevsky "not only arranged Spanish purchases of Russian arms but was Negrín's friendly adviser on many economic problems."[47] Alvarez del Vayo, an unwavering supporter of Negrín's, acknowledges that the Russian with whom Negrín had the most contact was Stashevsky and that they formed a "real friendship."[48] Mariano Ansó, a minister under Negrín, observes that his "talent and irresistible charm made a deep impression" on the Soviet trade envoy;[49] and Santiago Garcés Arroyo, appointed by Negrín to head the Servicio de Investigación (SIM), says that Negrín "got along very well" with Stashevsky and that "they ate together every day."[50] On the other hand, Angel Viñas, a staunch defender of Negrín and an authority on Republican finances and Spanish gold reserves—who describes him as "one of the most clearsighted and extraordinary politicians" of the entire Republican era and the "great statesman of the Republic"[51]—while confirming that Stashevsky was a "key man in implementing the initial aid for Republican Spain" and was directly involved with Negrín in major financial operations relating to the purchase of arms in the Soviet Union,[52] casts doubt on the manipulative role that Stalin, according to Krivitsky, assigned to the Soviet trade envoy.[53]

Krivitsky also asserts that Stashevsky offered to ship the enormous Spanish gold reserves—estimated at that time as the third largest in the world—to the Soviet Union and to supply Madrid with arms and munitions in exchange. "Through Negrín," Krivitsky alleged, "he made the deal with Caballero's government."[54] On the other hand, Alexander Orlov, who was head of the Soviet secret police in Spain from 1936 until his defection to the United States in 1938[55] and who, as will be seen, was entrusted by Stalin with the arrangements for the actual shipment, affirms that Negrín, "aware of the deteriorating [military] situation," sounded out Stashevsky about storing the gold in Russia. "The envoy cabled Moscow," Orlov adds, "and Stalin leaped to the opportunity."[56]

Two letters from Premier Largo Caballero to Marcel Rosenberg, the Soviet ambassador, formally requesting his government's approval of the shipment, appear, on the surface at least, to rule out the intervention of Stashevsky. The letters were published thirty-four years later by Marcelino Pascua, Spain's wartime ambassador to Moscow and a longstanding friend of Negrín's,[57] who carried them personally to the Soviet capital.[58] In his first letter, dated 15 October 1936, Largo Caballero stated that in his capacity as prime minister he had decided to request the Soviet ambassador to ask "your government if it will kindly agree to the deposit of approximately 500 metric tons of gold, the exact weight to be determined at the time of delivery,"[59] and in the second letter, dated 17 October, acknowledging Russia's acceptance of the proposal, Largo Caballero stated that "we plan to arrange for the payment of certain orders placed abroad . . . and for transfers of foreign currency to be charged against the gold that your government has agreed to accept on deposit."[60]

Much as these official letters—both of which, according to Pascua, were drafted by Negrín[61]—appear to call in question Stashevsky's role, they do not exclude the possibility that they were simply the result of preliminary discussions between the Soviet trade envoy and the finance minister and that they were subsequently approved and signed by Premier Largo Caballero. The carefully phrased language of the letters—the first requesting and the second acknowledging Russia's *approval* of the proposed shipment—may well have been used, at Stashevsky's suggestion, to disguise Stalin's special interest in acquiring the Spanish treasure.

14

Spanish Gold Shipped to Moscow

Because of the threat to Madrid,[1] the question of moving the gold reserves from the capital to safer keeping was first discussed by the Giral cabinet,[2] although the idea was not acted upon until Largo Caballero formed his administration on 4 September with Dr. Juan Negrín as finance minister.

On 13 September by a *decreto reservado*—a confidential decree—countersigned by President Azaña, Negrín obtained authority from the cabinet to transfer the gold and silver stocks as well as the paper currency held by the Bank of Spain "to a place that offers in his opinion the maximum security." Article 2 stated that the decree would be submitted "in due course" to the Cortes, but it never was.[3] Within a few days, ten thousand cases of gold coins and ingots were transferred to a large cave at Cartagena.[4]

That Cartagena should have been selected is not surprising. "It was a large naval base," writes Angel Viñas, "adequately armed and defended, somewhat removed from the theater of operations and from which it would be possible, if necessary, to ship the reserves to another place. . . . Perhaps the cabinet may not have anticipated their ultimate destination," he comments. "In fact, immediately after their arrival at Cartagena, it was decided to increase the volume of shipments to France."[5]

Obviously, the purpose of the transfer to Cartagena was not simply to protect the gold reserves from capture by enemy forces, but to accelerate their conversion into foreign exchange for the purchase of urgently needed war material. As Viñas points out—quoting Gordón Ordás, a conservative Republican, who was one of several government representatives entrusted with the purchase of arms abroad—the Non-Intervention Agreement rendered the purchase of arms difficult unless there were available "sufficient money on deposit to effect cash payments, since any attempt to buy on credit was fruitless."[6]

To meet this problem, both the Giral and Largo Caballero governments made a number of gold shipments to the Bank of France for conversion into foreign currency, such shipments aggregating about 200 metric tons as compared with a total in gold reserves of approximately 710 metric tons.[7] Most of the shipments to France were made after the transfer to Cartagena.[8] Nevertheless, according to

Luis Araquistáin, one of the arms purchasers and largest recipients of funds,[9] grave problems arose because of partial and irregular shipments and because of delays in obtaining authorizations from the Bank of France for the release of the necessary funds, with the result that on some occasions weeks went by without a single purchase being made.[10] Gordón Ordás records that these delays were responsible for the collapse of important transactions and that British banks tried to "delay as long as possible the release of funds to a destination that did not appear desirable to them."[11]

Hardly less disturbing was the angry reaction of the rebel or Nationalist junta in Burgos, which was accurately apprised of the gold shipments through its agents and friends in Spain and France.[12] By means of official communiqués, radio broadcasts, telegrams, and letters of protest addressed to Western governments, to the Bank of France, and to other central banks, as well as by threats of legal suits, Burgos did what it could to obstruct the sale of the gold, charging that the acceptance of the reserves used by the Bank of Spain to guarantee its currency was "a monstrous complicity with the Marxist gang," that their sale was an act of "pillage" and a violation of the basic banking law, the Ley de Ordenación Bancaria, governing the gold reserves that "form part of the national patrimony just like the territory of the nation."[13]

Although Viñas does not examine in detail the juridical aspects of the depletion of the gold reserves, whose essential purpose was to serve as a backing for the paper currency in circulation, he states that the financing of the war made it essential "to circumvent the strict provisions of the Ley de Ordenación Bancaria, which necessarily precluded the alienation and application of the reserves for such purposes as the purchase of weapons and war materials."[14] On the other hand, Alvarez del Vayo skates over the massive gold shipment to Russia with the bland remark that it "took place strictly in accordance with the Ley de Ordenación Bancaria."[15]

The emotional atmosphere created by the Nationalists' campaign over the gold shipments to France undoubtedly caused misgivings in the minds of Negrín and Largo Caballero and led them to fear that France might eventually block the use of the gold reserves. This apprehension must also have contributed to their decision, whether inspired by Stashevsky or not, to ship the bulk of the reserves to Russia, where they could be used for the purchase not only of Soviet arms and supplies, but also of foreign exchange necessary for the acquisition of arms and supplies in other countries. The principal channel for these transactions in Western and Central Europe was the Soviet-controlled Banque Commerciale pour l'Europe du Nord in Paris (the Eurobank) that was (and still is) under Soviet control, and whose operations were shrouded in absolute secrecy, an undoubted advantage in the prevailing climate,[16] but one that now leaves the bank's accounting open to the charge of possible manipulation[17] since it has never published any records relating to its transactions on behalf of the Republican government.[18]

Nor have the foreign exchange accounts of the Spanish ministry of finance, under Negrín's control during this crucial period, come to light. Marcelino

Pascua, who was a protégé of Negrín's[19] and Spain's wartime ambassador to Moscow, asserts that "only Juan Negrín possessed the pertinent records."[20] Viñas lays great stress on this absence of documentation: *"As long as the relevant documentation of the Republican ministry of finance and the Eurobank cannot be found . . . there is no possibility of reconstructing, even partially, the foreign financing of the Republic or of determining the destination of the foreign exchange generated by the sale of the Spanish gold in Moscow.* This distressing conclusion . . . must be made perfectly clear."[21]

Equally obscure are the transactions on behalf of the ministry of finance conducted by the Moscow Narodny Bank in London. Viñas writes: "The participation [of this bank] in the network of international transactions of the Republic is an unexplored theme and we fear that the difficulty of gaining access to the relevant documentation is even greater than in the case of the Eurobank. The two banks collaborated closely and the Republican funds in foreign exchange must have flowed in abundance to the Soviet bank in London, if only because the Republic chartered mainly English ships."[22]

On 20 October 1936, three days after Largo Caballero had written his letter acknowledging Russia's agreement to accept the gold reserves on deposit, NKVD chief Alexander Orlov received the following coded telegram from Joseph Stalin:

"Together with Ambassador Rosenberg, arrange with the head of the Spanish Government, Caballero, for the shipment of the gold reserves of Spain to the Soviet Union. . . . This operation must be carried out with the utmost secrecy.

"If the Spaniards demand from you a receipt for the cargo, refuse. I repeat, refuse to sign anything, and say that a formal receipt will be issued in Moscow by the State Bank."[23]

Stalin's instructions made good business sense and should not be misinterpreted. The following observation by the pro-Communist Amaro del Rosal, who was the president of the UGT bank employees' union, the Federación Nacional de Banca, is, I believe, accurate: "The refusal to give a receipt had nothing extraordinary about it. Because of the very nature of the shipment, it could not be insured by any insurance company, for that would have meant revealing the secret to the enemy. On the other hand, the Soviet State Bank could not take any risk. The shipment might fall into enemy hands and the ships might be sunk in an act of war. The guarantee for the Spanish state lay in the fact that in each ship there would be a representative of the Bank of Spain who would oversee the loading and supervise the expedition until its destination. . . . The receipt would be given at the end of the journey after the preparation of an inventory in which the representatives of the Bank of Spain would participate. Drawing up the inventory was a detailed job that lasted three months."[24]

The official receipt for 7,800 of the original 10,000 cases of ingots and coins transferred from Madrid to Cartagena (the balance of 2,200 went to France and Valencia between September 1936 and February 1937[25]) was issued on 5 February 1937, bearing the signatures of Marcelino Pascua, the Spanish ambassador, G. F. Grinko, people's commissar of finance, and N. N. Krestinski, deputy people's commissar for foreign affairs.[26] The work of opening the 7,800 cases and of counting and weighing the contents of each case was done, the receipt indicated, "in the presence and with the participation of one of the following persons: Arturo Candela, Abelardo Padin, José Gonzalec [*sic*] and José Velasco." The weight of the shipment was given as 510,079,529.13 grams or 510.08 metric tons, with a value at that time of $518 million, based on an estimated pure gold content of 460.52 metric tons.[27]

Almost twenty years later—long after Negrín's relations with the Soviet Union had begun to cool—a copy of the receipt and a large number of other documents in Negrín's possession relating to the gold deposited in Moscow were turned over to the Franco authorities by his son Rómulo as a result of negotiations initiated at Negrín's request, shortly before his death in France on 12 November 1956, by his close friend and former justice minister, Mariano Ansó. The documents, Negrín had told Ansó, were the property of the Spanish state regardless of the form of government in power. Shortly after his death, his son Rómulo, "wishing to carry out the will of his father," turned the papers over to the Spanish consulate general in Paris.[28]

In an accompanying document dated 14 December 1956 that was drafted and signed by Ansó and countersigned by Negrín's son, acknowledging that it reflected faithfully the feelings of his father, Ansó expressed Negrín's "deep concern with the interests of Spain as opposed to those of the USSR" and his fear that "without documentation to support her rights" Spain would be left "defenseless in a necessary settlement of accounts arising from what was perhaps the largest and most important transaction carried out between two countries."

After listing a number of other matters that "weighed on Negrín's mind"—including the retention by the USSR of "important and numerous units of the Spanish merchant fleet"—Ansó affirmed that in any financial settlement of accounts between Spain and Russia, Negrín felt that it was "his duty as a Spaniard to give his unconditional support to the interests of the nation."[29]

These, we must assume, were the thoughts and concerns of a man seasoned in later years by gradual disillusionment with the Soviet Union,[30] a man vastly different from the vaguely idealistic professor of physiology and newcomer to government with whom Alexander Orlov arranged for the shipment, on 22 October 1936, of the bulk of the Spanish gold reserves to the Soviet Union. "The finance minister seemed the very prototype of the intellectual—opposed to communism in theory, yet vaguely sympathetic to the 'great experiment' in Russia," Alexander Orlov wrote some years later. "This political naïveté helps to explain his impulse to export the gold to that country. Besides, with Hitler and Mussolini supporting the Nationalists and the democracies standing aloof, Russia was an ally, the one great power helping the Spanish Republicans. 'Where are the gold reserves, now?' I asked. 'At Cartagena,' Negrín replied, 'in one of the old caves used by the Navy to store munitions.' Stalin's luck again, I thought excitedly. My problem was immensely simplified by the fact that the cargo was already in Cartagena. That capacious harbor was where Soviet ships were unloading arms and supplies. So not only the ships but also trustworthy Soviet manpower were within easy reach."[31]

Whatever we may think of Orlov's use of the term "political naïveté" with regard to Negrín—especially in the light of Martínez Amutio's portrait of him as a man of "inordinate ambitions" and "of great intelligence devoted almost completely to the fulfillment of his passions and aspirations"[32]—there can be no doubt that in view of the attitude of the Western powers the gold could not have been mobilized successfully for the war effort had it not been shipped to Russia. Orlov told Negrín that he would carry out the operation with the Soviet tank soldiers who had recently arrived in Spain. "I wish to stress that, at that time, the Spanish Government . . . was not in full control," he informed the U.S. Senate subcommittee. "I frankly told the finance minister Negrín that if somebody got wind of it, if the Anarchists intercepted my men, Russians, with truckloads of Spanish gold, they would kill my men, and it would be a tremendous political scandal all over the world, and it might even create an internal revolution. So . . . I asked him whether the Spanish government could issue to me credentials under some fictitious name . . . as a representative of the Bank of England or the Bank of America, because then . . . I would be able to say that the gold was being taken for safekeeping to America. . . . Negrín did not object. He thought it was a fine idea. I spoke more or less decent English, and I could pass for a foreigner. So he issued to me the credentials of a man named Blackstone, and I became the representative of the Bank of America."[33] In a book written eight years earlier, Alvarez del Vayo mentions this incident, but either did not know or did not wish to reveal the true identity of Blackstone. "On the Russian side," he wrote, "there took part in the operation only an attaché from the Embassy chosen by Ambassador Rosenberg, of whom all we knew was that he was to be called Blackstone. Negrín jocularly baptized him with that name when he was introduced by the Ambassador."[34]

Orlov's fears about the Anarchists were not unfounded. They had already shown a keen interest in transferring the gold reserves to Barcelona, the stronghold of the CNT and FAI, not only for safekeeping, but for the purchase of war material. Diego Abad de Santillán, the prominent FAI leader, refers to a meeting with Prime Minister Giral in August 1936: "We explained to him that if he helped us to obtain the financial resources we needed, we could crush the enemy by ourselves. We deplored the fact that the central government—because of an insensate hatred of Catalonia and a fear of the popular revolution . . .— could obstruct our work upon which the victory and salvation of everyone depended. . . . We spoke at length about the gold in the Bank of Spain that was in danger and recommended its immediate transfer [to Barcelona]. Shortly afterwards the Giral government fell."[35]

Subsequently, Santillán made plans to raid the vaults of the Bank of Spain and seize at least a portion of the gold. "We knew in advance," he attests, "that force would have to be used. We had approximately three thousand men of confidence in Madrid and had prepared all the details for the transfer of the gold in special trains. . . . Before the government could have taken any action, we would have left for Catalonia. . . . We informed the National Committee of the CNT and some of the better known comrades [of the FAI] of our intentions. The plan caused chills of terror among our friends. Their principal argument against the project . . . was that it would only have increased the hostility to Catalonia."[36]

There is additional evidence that some of the Anarchists did indeed have a plan to raid the Bank of Spain. Juan-Simeón Vidarte, the moderate Socialist leader, claims that Luis Companys, the president of the semiautonomous region of Catalonia, informed Largo Caballero that the FAI was preparing "an assault on the vaults of the Bank of Spain in order to seize the gold and take it to a safer place in Barcelona," and urged him to take "every kind of precaution."[37] Also, President Azaña states that in September 1936 Santillán told him that there were four thousand men of the CNT "ready to come to Madrid to take possession of the gold."[38]

Although nothing came of the Anarchist plan, there can be little doubt that Orlov's fears that there would have been a tremendous political scandal if the Anarchists had intercepted his men were justified.

After being dubbed by Negrín with the name of Blackstone, Orlov left for Cartagena and asked for sixty Spanish sailors to load the gold onto the Soviet ships. Next he arranged to transport the gold from the cave to the piers. "A Soviet tank brigade had disembarked in Cartagena two weeks earlier," he wrote, "and was now stationed in Archena [north of Murcia], forty miles away. It was commanded by Colonel S. Krivoshein, known to the Spanish as Melé. Krivoshein assigned to me twenty of his army trucks and as many of his best tank drivers. . . . The sixty Spanish sailors had been sent to the cave an hour or two in advance. . . . And so, on October 22, in the expiring twilight, I drove to the munitions dump, the cavalcade of trucks behind me." Stacked against the walls were thousands of identical wooden boxes. "The crates held gold ingots and coins—hundreds of millions of dollars' worth! Here was the treasure of an ancient nation, accumulated through the centuries!"[39] The loading took three nights, from 7 P.M. to dawn. On the second or third day, Orlov testified before the U.S. Senate subcommittee, there was a tremendous bombardment and somebody mentioned that if a bomb hit the neighboring cave where thousands of pounds of dynamite were stored they would all be blown to bits. "The health of [Francisco] Méndez Aspe [head of the treasury and Negrín's man of confidence] was a very serious thing. He was a very nervous man. He told us we must discontinue loading or we [would] perish. I told him we could not do it, because the Germans would continue to bombard the harbor and the ship [would] be sunk, that we must go on with it. So he fled and left just one assistant, a very nice Spanish fellow, who did the counting of the gold [boxes] for them."[40]

On 25 October, seventy-eight hundred cases of gold were shipped to Odessa in four Soviet vessels[41] and were delivered to the Precious Metals Department of the People's Commissariat of Finance in Moscow between 6 and 10 November.[42] The extraordinary scene at the Russian port was described to Krivitsky by one of his associates: "The entire vicinity of the pier was cleared and surrounded by cordons of special troops. Across this cleared and empty space from dock to railroad track, the highest OGPU [NKVD] officials carried the boxes of gold on their backs.[43] For days and days they carried this burden of gold, loading it onto freight cars, and then taking it to Moscow under armed convoys. He attempted to give me an estimate of the amount of gold they had unloaded in Odessa. We were walking across the huge Red Square. He pointed to the several open acres surrounding us, and said: 'If all the boxes of gold that we piled up in Odessa yards were laid side by side here in the Red Square, they would cover it from end to end.' "[44]

But even more impressive than this imagery is the fact, as the receipt shows, that of the 7,800 cases only 13 contained ingots, while 7,787 contained coins, millions upon millions of gold pieces—American dollars, Argentinian, Chilean, and Mexican pesos, Austrian, Belgian, French, and Swiss francs, Dutch florins, English sovereigns, German marks, Italian lira, Portuguese escudos, Russian rubles, and Spanish pesetas—some of them antique, others rare enough to possess a numismatic value in excess of their weight in fine gold, coins that, if we borrow the above imagery, would have carpeted the Red Square from end to end.

The Spanish treasury was never credited with the numismatic value of the rare and antique coins. Yet extraordinary care was taken in listing coins that were false, defective, or contained less than the legal amount of gold.[45] On the other hand, the rare and antique coins, whose numismatic value was far greater than their gold content, have never been accounted for by the Russians. It is most unlikely that all the coins were melted down, especially the antique Portuguese pieces, weighing 318,603.3 grams and specifically listed as such in the official Soviet receipt, whose numismatic value obviously far exceeded their estimated fine gold content of 286,743 grams.[46] As for the rest of the coins, how many rare pieces were among them may never be known.

Roger Bland of the Department of Coins and Metals at the British Museum, who estimates that the total number of coins was over 60 million, expressed the opinion in a letter to me that "it is very doubtful whether it would have been worthwhile to sort through them all *just to see whether there were any coins of numismatic value*" and that "the coin market, which was much smaller than it is today would have been swamped by even a tiny fraction."[47] He was undoubtedly correct on both points, but he was not aware that the Russians did, in fact, sort through all the coins in their search for false and defective pieces.[48] Hence, the following question may legitimately be asked: Is it not possible that simultaneously they set aside all the numismatic coins with the idea of disposing of them gradually on the international market?

Herbert Matthews claimed that Negrín discovered to his dismay some months later that the Russians were not only melting the coins into bars but charging an exorbitant price for doing so.[49] "Since coins are worth more per weight than bars, he stopped that process, and protested the charge that the Russians were demanding."[50] But there is no substantiating evidence that he ever protested or even informed any of the cabinet members of his alleged concern. Nor is there any evidence that the Russians ever reimbursed the Spanish treasury for any excess charge or that the treasury was paid for any rare and antique coins on the basis of their numismatic value. Since Negrín, as finance minister, was necessarily aware that the gold reserves contained numismatic coins, the question must be asked: Why, before agreeing to the transfer to Russia, did he not insist that the Spanish treasury be given appropriate credit for them? The documents discovered in the Bank of Spain, upon which Angel Viñas based his research, reveal that instead of receiving credit for the rare and antique coins the Spanish treasury was credited, as its orders for the sale of the gold were executed, only with the fine gold value of whatever quantities the precious metals department of the People's Commissariat of Finance claimed it had melted down and refined.[51] Furthermore, there is no record in the documents of any instructions to the Russians to stop the melting and refining. On the contrary, Viñas, a champion of Negrín, shows that the fifteen orders given by the Spanish treasury in 1937, involving the sale of 358.5 tons of fine gold (over 70 percent of the total), were all executed with Negrín's approval.[52]

The Russians never revealed what became of the antique Portuguese coins. Nor have they revealed how many rarities were found among the 60 million coins they examined so carefully. There is no evidence other than Matthews's assertion twenty years later that Negrín ever discussed the issue with them. Moreover, there were no independent witnesses to the melting and refining; hence it is not unreasonable to speculate that the Russians may even have retained the numismatic coins they found and substituted their own reserves to execute the Spanish orders. In the absence of Soviet documents, this possibility cannot be entirely discounted. Increasing the uncertainty regarding the fate of the numismatic coins is the fact that even the four Spaniards from the Bank of Spain who accompanied the shipment to Odessa and who were present at the counting and weighing did not, as far as can be determined, witness the melting and refining. In any case, they were not allowed to return to Spain. "It is possible," writes Viñas, "that Negrín and Méndez Aspe decided that they should remain in Moscow so that no rumors regarding the destination of the gold would leak out."[53] He describes their plight in the Soviet capital: They were totally unprepared for a long stay and were very worried about their families in Spain and other personal matters. Eventually, their families joined them in Moscow, but their constant desire was to return to Spain.[54] In the course of his extensive research in the Bank of Spain, Viñas was shown "a moving letter" from Arturo Candela, one of the four bank employees who had accompanied the gold to Moscow, addressed to Julio Carabias, vice-governor of the bank, urging him "in a disguised way," to "get them out of here."[55] "In the summer of 1938," testifies Viñas, "Negrín and Méndez Aspe decided to take Pascua's advice and permitted them to leave the USSR.[56] . . . The Soviet government insisted that the strictest silence be maintained, but allowed them to go. For their part, the Republicans suggested that they be assigned to Spanish agencies in Stockholm, the U.S.A., Mexico, and Buenos Aires. On 27 October 1938, they left Moscow."[57]

As for the high-ranking Soviet officials who intervened in the gold operation, there is evidence that at least two were shot, although there is no way of knowing whether their deaths were associated directly or indirectly with the gold shipment. According to the authoritative *Who Was Who in the USSR*, G. F. Grinko, people's commissar of finance, and N. N. Krestinski, deputy people's commissar for foreign affairs (both of whom signed the official receipt), were executed on 15 March 1938 on charges of alleged membership in the anti-Soviet "rightist Trotskyite Bloc." Grinko, ironically, was also accused of "efforts to undermine the financial might of the USSR."[58] In addition, there is evidence that Stashevsky, Negrín's economic adviser, who was involved in the gold shipment, also vanished in the purges.

Although Angel Viñas arrives at the conclusion that the gold deposit was virtually exhausted less than a year before the end of the Civil War,[59] an important question must be asked. Were the massive amounts of foreign exchange generated by the sale of the gold to the Soviet State Bank and transferred to the Soviet-controlled Banque Commerciale de l'Europe du Nord in Paris, where they were credited to the accounts of the ministry of finance, also used up? Inasmuch as the operations of the Banque Commerciale were shrouded in absolute secrecy and its records of the accounts held by the ministry of finance have never been published, and inasmuch as the pertinent documents of the ministry itself have not been located, this question must be left unanswered, as Viñas himself has concluded. In a talk at the Spanish Institute in New York in April 1980, Viñas summarized the problem in the following words: "We know nothing about the Soviet bank in France and we do not know what happened to the foreign currencies owned by the Republic."[60]

Any complete study of the financial transactions between Spain and the USSR must take into account the question of Soviet credits extended to the Negrín government. So far, such a study has been attempted only by Viñas. On the basis of Republican documents, he shows that Negrín's strategy was to secure long-term credits from the Soviet Union, so as to retain as much of the remaining gold deposit as possible. This strategy was unsuccessful. In the fall of 1937, Negrín instructed Pascua to request a credit of $150 million, but, on 29 October, the ambassador replied: "I am continuing to press for credits. However, you have no idea how difficult it is to get a quick decision. They [the Russians] are extremely calculating, procrastinating, and at times not absolutely dependable." The Russians responded, Viñas continues, with an offer of $20 million to be used exclusively for nonmilitary supplies, and insisted that orders for war material be paid for as hitherto by the sale of the gold on deposit, "because, in order to fill them, the USSR must import raw materials, as a result of which it must drain its foreign exchange reserves." Not until March 1938, Viñas reveals, did Stalin grant a credit of $70 million, but only on the most stringent terms: $35 million was to be secured by an equivalent amount in gold and repaid in two years, while the unsecured balance was to be repaid in four years.[61] As the gold deposit, according to Soviet sources, was exhausted by the summer of 1938, other credits had presumably to be extended to pay for the arms shipments sent to Spain toward the end of the year, but no records have been found. Viñas, who had access to all the available documents, says simply: "It should not be excluded that the final Soviet shipments were made on credit."[62] And, in an article in *European Studies Review*, he affirmed: "On 13 July 1938, Pascua [then Spanish ambassador in Paris] met with the Soviet leaders [in Moscow] who accepted the proposal of Negrín for a total loan of $60,000,000. . . . Pascua now returned to Paris, and thereafter Negrín himself was personally to handle with Soviet representatives in Spain details concerning the credit operation. No documents on the results of such contacts have come to light."[63]

Martínez Amutio, who does not mention the source of his information, states that Negrín secured the credit he requested, but did not tell anyone where it was deposited. "No explanation, not a single piece of information that could help to clarify this unresolved question."[64] Pascua, a friend of Negrín's, says: "I do not know for sure how this transaction ended, for Negrín adopted toward me the same coldly calculated tactic of complete silence or evasiveness that he occasionally employed."[65]

Nineteen years later, on 5 April 1957, a few months after the death of Negrín, *Pravda* reported not only that the gold deposit was totally depleted—in proof of which it referred to a letter dated 8 August 1938 signed by Negrín and Méndez Aspe requesting the sale of the balance of the gold—but that the Spanish government still owed $50 million out of a Soviet credit of $85. "Negrín was well aware of this," the article added, "because his signature is on all the orders relating to the use of the gold and the credit."

The figure of $50 million may seem reasonable enough if we take into account the arms shipments made toward the end of 1938, but totally disregard the following items not included in Soviet calculations: the value of the antique and rare coins, the unknown quantities of foreign exchange held for the account of the Spanish treasury by the Soviet bank in Paris, the shipment to the USSR of Spanish raw materials and manufactured products,[66] the possible return to the Soviet Union of arms that arrived in France too late to be used in the defense of Catalonia in 1939,[67] the possible nonpayment of merchant ships purchased from the Spanish government at the end of the war, and the alleged transfer of plant machinery to the USSR.[68] The failure of the Soviet-controlled bank in Paris to publish any records of its wartime operations with the ministry of finance, as confirmed by the evidence of Angel Viñas quoted earlier in this chapter, and the fifty-year "non-appearance" of Negrín's personal records on the subject render impossible any exact accounting not only relative to the foreign exchange generated by the massive gold shipment in October 1936, as Viñas indicates, but also relative to other financial and economic transactions with the USSR, which even today are shrouded in suspicion and conjecture.

With regard to *Pravda*'s claim that the gold deposit was exhausted, Indalecio

Prieto was not convinced and responded vehemently: "We are dealing here with a colossal embezzlement. Regardless of my opinion of Juan Negrín, I declare him incapable of perpetrating the macabre hoax before his death of arranging . . . to turn over to Franco a document [the official receipt for the gold] with no material value." After listing various ways in which he claims that Spanish funds were used for the benefit of the French Communist party, including subsidies to the newspaper *Ce Soir* and the purchase of a dozen steamships by France-Navigation, a company secretly owned by the French Communist party,[69] Prieto continued: "Even though all those expenses were charged to the gold deposit in Russia, its total depletion is impossible. I repeat: We are dealing with a monumental embezzlement. To protect herself, Russia will forge whatever substantiating documents she considers necessary. . . . From his grave, Negrín will not be able to deny the authenticity of signatures imitated by expert forgers."[70]

One final question remains. Was the cabinet consulted before the gold was shipped to Russia? Both Negrín and Alvarez del Vayo claimed that it was.[71] Navy minister Prieto, however, said that it was not. "Señor Negrín, as minister of finance," he wrote, "obtained the consent of the government and the signature of the president of the Republic for a decree [the *decreto reservado* of 13 September] empowering him to take whatever measures he deemed necessary to safeguard the gold of the Bank of Spain. As a member of that government I accept my share of responsibility for the decree, although neither I nor the other ministers knew of the aim pursued. I do not know whether Largo Caballero, who was then head of the government, was aware of it.[72] The loading was surrounded with great secrecy. I found out about it by pure chance just when the gold was being loaded under the direction of Negrín and Méndez Aspe, having arrived at Cartagena to attend to matters connected with my department."[73] It is hard to believe that Prieto knew nothing about the planned shipment until his arrival in Cartagena, and his claim, as will be seen shortly, is contradicted by Orlov.

Prieto also asserted that Negrín could not disguise his "annoyance" when he saw him in Cartagena. "He undoubtedly assumed that I had gone there to nose around. He didn't give me any reason for his presence. I knew the motive because the chief of the Naval Base had told me that the finance minister had asked him for sailors to load the gold . . . and that he had consented. I approved the permit and that was the extent of my participation in the matter."[74]

Orlov gives supportive evidence that Prieto was initially unaware of the plan to ship the gold reserves to Russia. In his testimony before the U.S. Senate subcommittee, he stated that before the gold was loaded onto Soviet ships he decided to ask the Spanish government for an order to spread warships along the route in the Mediterranean. "I knew that such an order could not be issued without Prieto, . . . *who did not know anything about the whole plan of the gold operation.* So, I called up the Soviet ambassador. [I] asked him to take it up with Prime Minister Caballero and arrange that the navy minister, Prieto, should issue orders to the Spanish warships. . . . In a few days, the Spanish finance minister, Negrín, and . . . Prieto came to Cartagena. The orders were issued."[75]

Alvarez del Vayo also states that Prieto arranged for the necessary naval protection, although he unwittingly contradicts his assertion that Negrín transferred the gold to Russia "only after getting the consent of the whole government."[76] "As it was necessary to assure and protect the transportation by sea," he wrote, "Indalecio Prieto . . . was made *a co-partner in the secret*. He also received the news with gratification, and directly and personally took charge, arranging that a squadron should accompany the convoy nearly to Tunis."[77] Prieto, however, claims not only that he was initially unaware of the plan to ship the gold to the Soviet Union, but that he was not asked to furnish a naval escort and did not offer to provide one.[78] He adduced as evidence a letter from the commander of the destroyer fleet in Cartagena, Vicente Ramírez de Togores, who asserted that not a single Spanish warship escorted the Soviet merchant ships.[79] Mariano Ansó, Negrín's close friend, suggests that this letter may have been written just to oblige Prieto.[80] At all events, the assertion runs directly counter to the testimony of Nicolai G. Kuznetsov, the Soviet naval attaché and adviser, who was charged with the protection of the gold on the high seas and who makes it clear that a naval escort, including the cruiser *Libertad*, accompanied the Soviet ships as far as North Africa.[81]

Prieto also dismissed as a "lie" an assertion by Alvarez del Vayo that "Negrín insisted that President Azaña should be fully informed" and that the president was "pleasantly surprised by the plan."[82] Azaña "knew absolutely nothing about it," Prieto replied. "Largo Caballero and Negrín had acted in the same way toward the head of state as they had toward the ministers, concealing everything from them, even after it was a fait accompli. Azaña was enraged. . . . He told me he was going to resign immediately. Although sympathizing with him I tried to calm him. 'Your resignation,' I told him, 'would mean the collapse of the Republic because it would be used by the other nations to end [diplomatic] recognition in view of the fact that a substitute for the presidency, under existing circumstances, would be constitutionally impossible.' "[83]

From this welter of conflicting statements, the following reasonably safe conclusions can be drawn: (1) Although Negrín obtained the consent of the cabinet and the signature of President Azaña for the decree of 13 September, empowering him to transfer the gold reserves to a place that offered the maximum security, his decision a month later to ship the gold to Russia was made without conferring with the cabinet and without consulting either Prieto or Azaña. (2) Prieto was made a "co-partner in the secret," as Alvarez del Vayo claims, but only after Negrín and Caballero had decided to transfer the gold to Moscow. (3) Having signed the permit for the Spanish sailors to load the gold onto the Soviet ships, Prieto must have been asked to provide a naval escort, or even offered to provide one, since it would be chimerical to suppose that so important a mission could have been undertaken without his knowledge and consent. Indeed, Marcelino Pascua states that the friendship between Negrín and Prieto was at that time "close, even intimate, one might say," and that Negrín told him that he used to consult Prieto "frequently on various matters not only because he appreciated his greater political experience but because of their mutual confidence and attachment."[84]

Why, then, did Prieto deny his share of responsibility for the shipment? The answer is that his denial was first made in 1940 when his postwar enmity with Negrín had reached its peak. And why, one may ask, did Prieto, always distrustful of Moscow, cooperate? Because his thinking in October 1936 could not have been different from that of Largo Caballero who, although sharing Prieto's distrust of Moscow, felt that the attitude of the Western powers left no choice but to ship the gold to Russia.

Largo Caballero has made his own position very clear: it undoubtedly was the same as that of Prieto and of others privy to the shipment. "As the rebels were at the gates of Madrid," he wrote after the Civil War, "[Negrín] asked the government for authority to transfer the gold from the Bank of Spain to a safe place without stating where. This was a natural thing to do in order to prevent the treasure, through misadventure, from falling into the hands of the rebels; for without gold with which to purchase arms the defeat of the Republic would have been inevitable. . . . The first step taken by Negrín was to transfer the gold to [the naval base of] Cartagena. Later, fearing a landing, he decided to send it abroad. Where? England and France were the very soul of 'nonintervention.' . . . Could we have had any faith in them? No. Then, where else could we have sent it? There was no other place but Russia, the country that was helping us with arms and food. . . . With this gold we paid Russia for the war material she was sending us. . . . Also we used what gold we needed for other purchases."[85]

Yet, despite the undoubted military and financial advantages of shipping the gold to Moscow, there was one inescapable drawback: this important transfer, worth at the time over $500 million, approximately $7.6 billion at today's price of gold (1987), was to make the cabinet dependent in a large measure on the goodwill of Moscow. In his first book on Spanish gold published in 1976, Angel Viñas, the recognized authority on this subject, acknowledged that "the Republic lost negotiating leverage" when it shipped the bulk of the reserves to Moscow and that the transfer favored "the growing Soviet influence on the decisions of certain leaders of the Republic."[86] But three years later, in an extraordinary volte-face, he stated that to assert that the shipment placed the Republic in a position of dependency was an "idiotic argument used by people . . . with an enormous anti-Communist bias" who did not understand that since the Republic was *necessarily* dependent on the Soviet Union for the supply of arms, the transfer did not increase "qualitatively" the degree of its dependence.[87]

On the other hand, Dominique Grisoni and Gilles Hertzog, in their unique work on France-Navigation, argue that the transfer enabled Moscow to control not only the supply of Soviet arms to Spain, but also any purchases made *outside* the Soviet Union, because the payment for these transactions had to be made through the Soviet-controlled Banque Commerciale pour l'Europe de Nord in Paris. Furthermore, they affirm, the arms monopoly by the Soviet Union enabled it to control the political "evolution" of the Republic.[88]

Since the gold shipment placed the Spanish government in a position of financial dependency on Moscow, depriving it of bargaining power and of the ability to negotiate with other countries in the event of a lifting of the arms embargo—which was the principal aim of its foreign policy—one may wonder why Negrín and Largo Caballero did not attempt to preserve even a modicum of financial independence by making smaller shipments of gold, as needed, to pay for the purchase of arms and foreign exchange. Largo Caballero's argument that Negrín feared a landing of enemy forces in Cartagena is vitiated by the fact that, as Viñas has pointed out, this large naval base was "adequately armed and defended, somewhat removed from the theater of operations." The Nationalists knew that it would be futile to attempt to take Cartagena by assault, since they lacked the naval power, and indeed never made any attempt to do so. Hence, one must question not only the good judgment of those responsible for the gold shipment to Moscow, but also the degree of their resistance to Soviet cajolery and manipulation. One must also question their judgment in accepting Soviet accounting without any serious attempt at investigation or scrutiny. If such an attempt were ever made, there is no record of it in any of the documents turned over to the government of General Franco upon Negrín's death or in those found by Viñas in the Bank of Spain.

That Stalin was delighted over the safe arrival of the gold reserves there can be no doubt, for he had already begun shipping arms to Spain and only by the physical possession of the gold could he be assured of payment and of the political leverage it gave him. According to Alexander Orlov—who claims that he and Ambassador Rosenberg "were flabbergasted when . . . told that the Spanish Government was willing to trust Stalin with all the savings of the Spanish nation"—Stalin celebrated the arrival of the gold with a banquet attended by members of the politburo, at which he said, "The Spaniards will never see their gold again, as they don't see their ears," an expression based on a Russian proverb.[89]

In January 1937—two months after the arrival of the shipment—Orlov, according to his own account, received "a very warm letter" from Paul Alliluev, Stalin's brother-in-law, congratulating him on having received "the highest decoration of the Soviet Union, the Order of Lenin." Although Orlov did not give the reason for the award, it was in all probability connected with the gold shipment.[90]

15

Soviet Influence, Political Dissimulation, and the Plight of President Azaña

*I*n addition to the political and economic leverage that Moscow secured by the acquisition of Spanish gold, an equally significant development weighed heavily in favor of Soviet influence in the affairs of government. This was the arrival in September and October 1936 of military advisers and political agents, who exercised, in fact if not in form, the authority of ministers in several departments.

"As time went on," writes Colonel Segismundo Casado, operations chief on the general staff in the early months of the war, "Russian influence was increased at the War Ministry. [The Russian military advisers] looked over the plans of the General Staff and through the minister they rejected many technical proposals and imposed others."[1] In a later passage he says: "These 'friendly advisers' exercised authority just as much in the Air Force and in the Tank Corps."[2] Of Russian influence in high places, Luis Araquistáin writes: "The Air Force, directed by the Russians, operated when and where they pleased, without any coordination with the land and sea forces. The navy and air minister, Indalecio Prieto, meek and cynical, made fun of his office to anyone who visited him, declaring that he was neither a minister nor anything else because he received absolutely no obedience from the Air Force. The real air minister was the Russian General Duglas [Yakov Smushkevich]."[3] Later on, he adds: "Behind [the Russian officers] were innumerable political agents who were disguised as commercial agents and were in real control of Spanish politics. . . . They directed the Russian officers, the Communist party and Rosenberg himself [the Soviet ambassador], who in reality was only an ambassador of straw. The real ambassadors were those mysterious men who entered Spain under false names and were working under direct orders from the Kremlin and the Russian police."[4]

The influence of the Russians cannot be explained on the ground that the Soviet forces in Spain were strong enough to coerce the government by mere numbers. "I am sure," affirms Indalecio Prieto, "that at no time did the Russians in our territory aggregate more than five hundred, including aviators, industrial technicians, military advisers, naval men, interpreters, and secret agents.[5] Most of them were aviators, who, like the Germans and Italians, were relieved after short periods.[6] . . . Russia could not exercise any coercion because of the military forces she sent to Spain. Her ability to do so stemmed from the fact that she was, owing to the attitude of the other powers, our sole purveyor of war material and that her coercive instrument was the Spanish Communist party, the Communists, and the communistoids enrolled in other political organizations, principally in the Socialist party."[7]

In addition, the position of the Communists in the government was greatly strengthened by the fact that they could rely for support in major issues of domestic and foreign policy on the Republican and moderate Socialist representatives. José Giral, premier of the government formed on 19 July and minister without portfolio in Largo Caballero's administration, representing the Left Republican party, declared in a speech in March 1937, it will be recalled, that the coincidence of views between his party and the Communists was almost identical. "We have to take into account the attitude of the states that surround us," said *El Socialista*, which expressed the opinions of Prieto, the moderate Socialist leader. "We still hope that the estimate of Spanish events made by certain democracies will be changed, and it would be a pity, perhaps a tragedy, to compromise these possibilities by an irrepressible desire to accelerate the Revolution."[8] Furthermore, in spite of Russian pressure and the ravages on his following, Largo Caballero maintained tolerable relations with the Communist party during the first months of his incumbency; for, however provoked he may secretly have been, a large measure of agreement still existed between them. In fact, from the day his government was formed, he adopted the Communist viewpoint that it should impress the outside world with its moderation. Not that he or the other non-Communist members of his cabinet were concerned with the broader aims of Russian policy. They simply hoped that by proclaiming respect for legal forms, Britain and France, fearful of an Italo-German vassalage of Spain, would finally raise the arms embargo. It was necessary, Largo Caballero declared, during a private conversation shortly after taking office, "to sacrifice revolutionary language to win the friendship of the democratic Powers."[9] In this respect he was not remiss. "The Spanish Government is not fighting for socialism but for democracy and constitutional rule," he stated to a delegation of British members of Parliament.[10] And in a communiqué to the foreign press he said: "The Government of the Spanish Republic is not aiming at setting up a Soviet regime in Spain in spite of what has been alleged in some quarters abroad. The government's essential aim is to maintain the parliamentary regime of the Republic as it was set up by the Constitution which the Spanish people freely assumed."[11] No less instructive was the moderate tone of his speech when, as premier, he appeared before the rump Cortes on 1 February 1937: "When I assumed this post I renounced nothing, absolutely nothing in my political thinking. I say this before you and before the entire country. . . . But, in view of the danger that confronts our country as a result of the military uprising, I felt it my duty to assume the responsibilities that naturally devolve upon me because of my office by laying aside for a short time the immediate aspirations inherent in the ideology I have always defended."[12]

Illustrative of his cabinet's regard for foreign opinion was the declaration it issued after its first session. Avoiding all reference to the profound revolutionary changes that had taken place or to any social program, it stated:

1. In view of its composition, the government considers itself the direct representative of all those political forces that are fighting at the fronts *for the maintenance of the democratic Republic*, against which the rebels have taken up arms. . . .

2. The program of the government consists essentially of the firm intention to accelerate victory over the rebellion, coordinating the forces of the people by the necessary unity of action. . . . To this end all other political interests are subordinated, ideological differences being set aside. . . .

4. The government affirms the feelings of friendship of Spain toward all nations and its most devoted adherence to the covenant of the League of Nations, hoping that, in just return, our country will receive from others the same consideration it will give to them. . . .

6. The government greets with the utmost enthusiasm the land, sea, and air forces, as well as the People's Militia *who are defending the Republican Constitution*. Its highest aim is to be worthy of such heroic fighters, whose legitimate desires for social betterment will find in it a determined champion.[13]

Because it was essential for the sake of foreign opinion that legal forms be observed, the Cortes met on 1 October, as stipulated in the Constitution. The director of the Communist organ, *Mundo Obrero*, commented:

"The deputies of the nation, the legal representatives of the people, the deputies elected by the free will of the people on 16 February, have assembled this morning. The government has appeared before the Congress in accordance with the Republican Constitution.

"In the midst of civil war, while the struggle to impose Republican legality and the will of the people is proceeding at the fronts, the government is ratified by the chamber. Constituted as the genuine representative of the people, it has functioned as such until today. The head of the state gave it his confidence, and today it reinforces its legal origin . . . with the confidence of parliament. . . . On the one side is the Republic, with its legal organs. . . . On the other are the military traitors, the fascist blackguards, the adventurers of all classes in Spain and abroad. . . . The civilized world has now been able to judge; it is on our side in its entirety. To help the legal authorities of Spain is a duty imposed by international law; to help the rebels is a crime against civilization and against humanity."[14]

After the next session of the Cortes in December, the organ of the Left Republican party declared in language that paralleled that of the Communists:

Legality has only one medium of expression. This is what yesterday's session of the parliament of the Republic demonstrated. . . . *It was also the most eloquent demonstration of the continuity of the democratic Republican regime* and of the unshakable determination of the country not to allow the legality of its public life to disappear in the whirlwind of passions and appetites unleashed by this bloody Civil War.

At this time, . . . when the world is contemplating the unique struggle of the people of Madrid and of the Spanish people as a whole, *the Republic maintains a rich and vigorous constitutional life.* All its basic institutions, allowing for the exigencies of the times and the particular circumstances of a country at war, function normally. *Not one has been supplanted. . . .*[15]

The session of the Cortes of the Republic that took place yesterday once again destroys the specious arguments of those who, particularly outside Spain, take delight in stridently censuring a people fighting to defend rights that are so legitimate that in countries with an older democratic tradition they are not even mentioned because they are taken for granted. *Spain is today waging a struggle for republican and democratic consolidation such as other countries experienced many years ago.*

Would it be too much to ask those governments that are tolerating the international crime being committed in Spain by German and Italian intervention to appreciate what this signifies? Face to face with the enemy at home, the Spanish people, victorious in the February elections, would have triumphed over the barbarous rebellion within a few days. But face to face with the military apparatus of Germany and Italy, it has no course but to appeal frankly and sincerely to world opinion.

The same government, or rather a legal continuation of that government, the same Parliament, the same president of the Republic, the same institutions with which every country in the world had maintained friendly and cordial relations until 17 July exercise today, more than four months after the outbreak of the rebellion that is striving to put an end to the legal Constitution of Spain, the same powers and the same functions. Does this mean nothing at all? Or, in face of the inexcusable aggression of which these institutions have been the object, has the world lost all feeling?[16]

After the war the Communists, Republicans, and Socialists in exile, still hoping to influence world opinion in favor of the Spanish Republican cause, did what they could to conceal the depth of the 1936 Revolution. Some, in fact, even maintained that the Republican Constitution had remained inviolate during the Civil War. For example, Pablo de Azcárate, former Spanish ambassador in London and a fervent Negrín supporter, affirmed that "from 16 July 1936 to 5 March 1939 [the date of the overthrow of the Negrín government by a coalition of left-wing organizations] the constitution was in force, *in fact* and *in law*, throughout the territory under the legitimate authority of the Republic, and *in law only* in that ruled by the rebels."[17] It was undoubtedly this sort of political distortion and dishonesty that caused Salvador de Madariaga, who before the Civil War had been Azcárate's friend and colleague at the League of Nations and an admirer of his "capacity, integrity, and intellectual clarity," to become a pungent critic, when Azcárate—to quote once again the words of Madariaga—"abandoned the strict path of truth for the putrid intellectual bog of Communism."[18]

To ensure that the Western democracies would continue to recognize the government as the legally constituted authority, it was essential that Manuel Azaña, the president of the Republic, should remain in office to sanction its decrees and perform the diverse functions laid down in the Constitution. Whether he could be persuaded to do so indefinitely was open to grave doubt, not only because his hostility to the Revolution and the concomitant violence was a matter of common knowledge, but because of his conviction that the war was lost. In a letter written after the war, he frankly acknowledged his pessimism: "Everybody knows that I did everything possible from September 1936 to influence policy in favor of a compromise solution, because the idea of defeating the enemy was an illusion."[19] In the summer of 1937, Claudio Sánchez-Albornoz, famous Republican intellectual and member of the conservative flank of Izquierda Republicana, Azaña's own party, records the following conversation with the president: " 'The war is lost, totally lost,' Azaña said, 'but, if by some miracle, it should be won, we Republicans [i.e. members of the Republican parties] would have to embark on the first boat to leave Spain, if we are allowed to do so.' I agreed with him and added: 'If you believe . . . that the war is lost and that the fate of the Republicans is sealed, why don't you make peace?' 'Because I cannot,' he quickly replied. I could easily see in his eyes the anguish his impotence was causing him."[20]

It was because of Azaña's firm conviction that the war was lost that on 19 October 1936—three weeks before the government's transfer to Valencia as a result of the enemy's threatening advance upon the capital—he had decided to move to Barcelona, from where, it was feared, he might cross the border into France and there resign the presidency. "It was arranged with the president," recalls Largo Caballero, "that we should all go to Valencia. . . . First to leave was Señor Azaña. . . . Instead of staying in Valencia, as agreed, he went to Barcelona. It was a means of getting closer to the frontier. He did not consult with us or say a word to anyone."[21]

This criticism may not be entirely fair. Josefina Carabias, who had been Azaña's confidant for many years, writes: "It has been said that some ministers raised an outcry when the president informed them that he intended to leave Madrid that very afternoon with or without their permission. 'That is absolutely unconstitutional,' one of them told him. 'Undoubtedly, opening the jails and distributing rifles to the inmates is more in keeping with the constitution [Azaña replied]. Besides, what I intend to do today is exactly what you will be doing in a few days.' " Carabias denies a charge that, but for the vigilance of the FAI, Azaña would have escaped from Barcelona. "No doubt, he thought of resigning many times and on some occasions decided that he would do so, but he never thought of escaping. . . . He believed that it was his duty to remain at his post, above all because he knew that on the other side many persons were in jail or had suffered death simply because they had been accused of being his friends or supporters."[22]

But, in truth, if Azaña did not resign the presidency this was due to the pressure that was brought to bear upon him by Republicans and particularly by Indalecio Prieto, with whom he was always in close contact. Relating after the war how Azaña informed him in April 1938 of his intention to resign because of his inability to settle a government crisis in accordance with his own wishes, Prieto records his reply as follows: "You cannot resign . . . [because] your resignation would bring down everything and because you personify the Republic, which to a certain degree the countries not allied to Franco respect. If you were to resign, that respect, thanks to which we are still able to exist, would disappear."[23] Prieto, it will be recalled, had used a similar argument to dissuade Azaña from resigning the presidency when he learned about the gold shipment to Russia.

When Azaña left Madrid in October 1936, records Frank Sedwick in his biography of the president, the press announced that he was to make a tour of the eastern and Catalonian fronts. "Much has been written of his failure to visit the fronts and of his 'cowardice' in leaving Madrid, although few Republicans at that time thought Madrid could hold out.[24] Everything seemed to be disintegrating, and the rest of the government followed Azaña within three weeks. Little was left of the original diplomatic corps; many founders of the Republic and intellectuals like [Gregorio] Marañón, [Ramón] Pérez de Ayala, [José] Ortega y Gasset, and Madariaga either had left Spain already or were soon to make their exit. . . . On leaving Madrid, Azaña went to Barcelona. His enemies say he chose Barcelona so that he could be close to the French border in case of a Republican military collapse; his friends say he went to reside there in order, by his presence, to help keep Catalonia in tow."[25]

But few, least of all Azaña, harbored any illusions about the authority of his presidential office or his power or desire to check the Revolution in the Anarcho-syndicalist-dominated region of Catalonia. "From the beginning of the war," attests Juan Marichal, the compiler of Azaña's *Obras Completas*, "he saw that his only possible role was the very limited one of representing a symbolic brake on the revolutionary violence."[26]

Like the Republicans and Prieto, the Communists and their allies were especially troubled over Azaña's pessimism and the danger that he might at any time resign the presidency. "Reports reaching us regarding the attitude of Señor Azaña . . . were by no means reassuring," testifies Alvarez del Vayo. "We feared that his habitual pessimism, exacerbated by isolation, might lead him to make some irrevocable decision."[27]

According to Azaña's critics, physical fear as well as pessimism influenced his wartime conduct. Largo Caballero recalls that whenever he had official business to transact with Azaña in Madrid, the president would ask him when the government planned to leave. "Is it going to wait until the last moment when there will be no escape? I warn you. I have no desire to be dragged through the streets with a rope around my neck."[28]

"Fear that he might fall into the hands of the fascists," writes Ignacio Hidalgo de Cisneros, the Communist chief of the air force, "was a real obsession."[29] And Miguel Maura, the leader of the Conservative Republican party, who was minister of the interior in the first two governments of the Republic in 1931 but remained on the sidelines during the war, while attesting to Azaña's "extraordinary intelligence and august qualities," confirms this fear. "[He] was afflicted with overwhelming physical fear. . . . It was stronger than he and he did the unimaginable to disguise it."[30]

On the other hand, Cipriano Rivas-Cherif, Azaña's intimate and brother-in-law, depicts a more courageous figure[31] as does Mariano Ansó, a onetime Cortes deputy and member of Azaña's party. "Little by little," Ansó writes, "the myth of his cowardice was insidiously fostered . . . and by some who called themselves his friends. . . . [I] shared countless threats with him [before the Civil War], but I never saw him lose his self-control or dignity. . . . In the guardrooms and sacristies, in the summits of the aristocratic and banking world, they called for his head. For many people only his physical disappearance could have returned things to what they were."[32]

Whatever the truth regarding Azaña's inner fortitude, there can be no doubt that the thought of resignation weighed continually on his mind. As Claudio Sánchez-Albornoz puts it, Azaña was a bourgeois liberal who would have made an excellent head of government in France during the Third Republic, but who, "after 18 July 1936, was a prisoner of a combination of political forces—Socialism, Anarchism, Communism—in which the Republicans—bourgeois, democrats and liberals—counted for nothing. During the social upheaval that followed the military rising, he was forced to witness the acts of violence that stained the Republic in blood. One does not have to know him too well to understand . . . his torment over his inability to end them. . . . His well-known words after the crimes committed in the Model Prison in Madrid, 'I do not want to preside over a Republic of assassins,' honor him because no one in the enemy camp condemned similar crimes."[33]

Rivas-Cherif, who observed his brother-in-law's anguish, attests that Angel Ossorio y Gallardo managed to dissuade him from resigning.[34] On other critical occasions, writes Sedwick, both during and after the summer of 1936, it was Indalecio Prieto and the sincere moderates on the one hand who importuned Azaña to consider himself and his office as the necessary personification of the Republic abroad, while on the other hand it was those who received from Moscow their orders that the façade of a democratic Spain had to be maintained. "Knowingly or unknowingly, Azaña thus became the essential tool of both factions. Brave with the pen, a paper expert in military matters, a classic type of constitutionalist, that sensitive and fastidious intellectual never wanted any role in an actual war, particularly a civil war whose outcome could portend but little hope for his aspirations of a democracy in Spain. Yet he remained at his post."[35]

The pessimism of President Azaña and of many other Republican leaders was well known to the Kremlin. On 21 December 1936, Stalin, demonstrating how much he valued their diplomatic utility, gave Largo Caballero the following advice: "The Spanish Revolution," he stated in a letter that also bore the signatures of Vyacheslav Molotov, the chairman of the council of people's commissars, and Kliment Voroshilov, the commissar for defense, "traces its own course, different in many respects from that followed by Russia. This is determined by the difference in the social, historic, and geographic conditions, and *from the necessities of the international situation. . . . It is very possible that in Spain the parliamentary way will prove to be a more effective means of revolutionary development than in Russia. . . .* The Republican leaders must not be rejected, but, on the contrary, they must be attracted and drawn closer to the government. It is above all necessary to secure for the government the support of Azaña and his group, doing everything possible to help them to overcome their vacillations. *This is necessary in order to prevent the enemies of Spain from regarding her as a Communist Republic, and, in this way, to avoid their open intervention, which constitutes the greatest danger to Republican Spain.*"

The letter also contained other recommendations: (1) "The peasants, who are of great importance in an agrarian country like Spain must be taken into account. It would be advisable to issue decrees relating to agrarian questions and to the question of taxes, which are in the forefront of peasant interests." (2) "It is necessary to attract to the side of the Government the small and middle urban bourgeoisie or, in any case, to offer them the possibility of adopting a position of neutrality favorable to the Government by protecting them against attempts at confiscation and by assuring them, as far as possible, freedom of trade; otherwise these groups will embrace fascism."[36]

"This document," wrote the pro-Communist Amaro del Rosal, who, as we have seen, abandoned Largo Caballero quite early in the war, "was irrefutable proof of the affection for the Spanish people that three Communist leaders, genuine Socialists, expressed for another Socialist who enjoyed international political prestige in the revolutionary working-class movement."[37]

In his reply on 12 January 1937 Largo Caballero stated: "You are right in pointing out that there exist appreciable differences between the development of the Russian Revolution and our Revolution. Indeed, as you yourselves point out, the circumstances are different. . . . But, in response to your allusion [to the parliamentary method] it is advisable to point out that, whatever the future may hold for the parliamentary institution, it does not possess among us, or even among the Republicans, enthusiastic supporters. . . . I absolutely agree with what you say regarding the Republican political parties. We have endeavored, at all times, to bring them into the work of the government and into the war effort. They participate to a large extent in all organs of administration, local, provincial, and national. What is happening is that they themselves are doing hardly anything to assert their own political personality."[38]

Nevertheless, the Republican leaders, subdued and impotent, played a useful role in providing a moderate cover for the Revolution. Even President Azaña, whose isolation from public life and whose pessimism and dismay were common knowledge, decided, after six months of silence, to give public support to the official version of the Civil War which was directed at democratic opinion abroad and defined the struggle not as a conflict among classes but as a struggle by all Spaniards for national independence against foreign invaders and their traitorous Spanish allies. Enunciating the principles for which, he claimed, the Republican regime was fighting, Azaña conveyed no hint of the far-reaching social, economic and political upheaval that had ground the Constitution of 1931 into dust. Nor did he give any inkling of the ideological and political battles within the left camp that would determine the future course of the Revolution. "[We] are all fighting," he declared, "the worker and the intellectual, the teacher and the bourgeois—yes, there are also members of the bourgeoisie who are fighting—the unions and the political parties, and all Spaniards who are united under the Republican flag, we are all fighting for the independence of Spain and for the liberty of the Spanish people and our country."[39]

16

Spain in the Web of
the East-West Diplomatic Conflict

Stalin undoubtedly saw great advantages in the continued recognition of the Spanish government as the legally constituted authority. He knew that as long as it was recognized as such by Britain and France, it would not only be in a position to bring the question of Italo-German intervention before the League of Nations, but could demand that, in accordance with the generally accepted rules of international law in cases of insurrection against a legitimate government, it be permitted to purchase arms freely in the markets of the world. He knew, moreover, that if Britain and France were to abandon their policy of neutrality, Nazi ambitions in Central and Eastern Europe foreshadowed in Hitler's *Mein Kampf* in 1925—"[We] direct our gaze towards the lands in the east [and] think primarily only of Russia and its vassal border states"—might temporarily be thwarted and the dreaded attack on the Soviet Union deferred. Following a conversation with Ivan Maisky, the Soviet ambassador in London, on 3 November 1936, British foreign secretary Anthony Eden wrote to Viscount Chilston, British ambassador to Moscow, that the Soviet government was convinced that if General Franco were to win, "the encouragement given to Germany and Italy would be such as to bring nearer the day when another active aggression would be committed—this time perhaps in Central or Eastern Europe. That was a state of affairs that Russia wished at all costs to avoid and that was her main reason for wishing the Spanish Government to win in this civil strife."[1]

Furthermore, the thought had undoubtedly entered Stalin's strategic calculations that the civil war in Spain, inasmuch as Italo-German intervention posed a potential threat to France on her southern border and to British and French interests in the Mediterranean, might ultimately develop into a large-scale conflict in Western Europe, from which he could remain virtually aloof until the warring parties had fought to the point of mutual exhaustion and from which the Soviet Union would emerge master of the European continent.

Already in 1925, Stalin had enunciated his strategy in the event a general war should ravage Europe. In a speech at a plenary session of the central committee of the Soviet Communist party, published for the first time in 1947, he declared: "If war should begin it would not suit us to sit with folded arms. We should have to come out, but we should be the last to do so. And we should come out in order to throw the decisive weight into the scales, the weight that should tip the scales."[2]

According to Gustav Hilger, the counselor of the German embassy in Moscow in the 1930s: "It had always been the Kremlin's firm conviction that, sooner or later, war would break out between the capitalist powers. If the Soviet Union could be kept out of such an armed conflict, she could be expected to reap great benefit from it, since the capitalist powers would be weakened, and the balance of power would be shifted in favor of Soviet Russia. . . . Moreover, in Stalin's eyes the conclusion of a non-aggression pact with Hitler meant the removal of the danger of a German attack on the Soviet Union. This danger had weighed on the Soviet government and people like an evil nightmare ever since 1933 [the advent of Hitler to power]. . . . Thus he hoped to gain valuable time to push the Soviet armaments program at an accelerated pace. And then he would watch further developments. At a propitious moment, when the warring nations would be weakened sufficiently, he would be in a position to throw the power of the Soviet Union into the scales of world politics."[3] And the eminent British historian Arnold J. Toynbee, director of studies in the Royal Institute of International Affairs, writing in *Survey of International Affairs 1936*, stated: "If there was to be another war with Germany sooner or later, it was clearly in Russia's interest that the conflict should arise over an issue in which the Western Powers were directly concerned not over an issue which might throw the brunt of the conflict upon the USSR."

Foreign intervention against the new Soviet state in 1918–20—only sixteen years before the Spanish Civil War—and the Comintern's unremitting efforts to undermine the bourgeois world had created a chasm between the two systems, which diplomatic recognition a few years later had failed to bridge. "Ever since the Revolution of November 1917," wrote Sir John W. Wheeler-Bennett, the distinguished British historian, "the Bolsheviks had stood in fear and suspicion of the Western World. Both Lenin and Stalin knew well enough that by their actions and their policies they had declared an ideological war upon the rest of the world; a war which was deathless; a war which, though there might be long periods of truce, could not be concluded until one side or the other had gone down to irrevocable defeat."[4]

It is almost otiose to say that in British and French governing circles there existed profound distrust of the Soviet Union, for they perceived it not so much as an immediate military threat but as the fountainhead of a new, dynamic ideology which, in the event of war with Germany, would spread throughout Western Europe and could only benefit from an exhausting conflict among the capitalist powers. Neville Chamberlain, British prime minister from 1937 to 1940, suspected that the "Bolshies"—to use his own language—were "chiefly concerned to see the 'capitalist' Powers tear each other to pieces whilst they stay out themselves."[5] Highly significant is the following statement made by Sir Horace Wilson, Chamberlain's chief foreign policy adviser, to Theodor Kordt, the German chargé d'affaires in London, on 23 August 1938, which undoubtedly reflected the views of the prime minister: "Great Britain and Germany were in fact the two countries in which the greatest order reigned and which were the best governed. Both were built up on the national principle . . . the only working principle of human relationship. The reverse of this, Bolshevism, meant anarchy and barbarism. It would be the height of folly, if these two leading white races were to exterminate each other in war. Bolshevism would be the only gainer thereby."[6]

Fears of a war in Western Europe, first sparked by Hitler's remilitarization of the Rhineland in March 1936, were heightened by the outbreak of the Spanish conflict in July. On 25 November, the U.S. ambassador William Bullitt, who believed that "only the Russians had a vested interest in another war which would end with a 'general revolution' and the final victory of 'Stalin and Company,' "[7] reported to the State Department: "The French government [headed at that time by the Socialist leader Léon Blum] is convinced that the Soviet government desires to push the conflict to the bitter end on the theory that even though, in the first instance the Soviet government would suffer defeat through the over-throwing of the Madrid and Barcelona governments [that is, the central administration and the semiautonomous government of the region of Catalonia] by Italian and German troops enlisted in Franco's army, the final result would be an attempt by the Germans to establish a new status in Spanish Morocco and an attempt by the Italians to maintain possession of the Balearic Islands which would result in war between Germany and Italy on one side and France and England on the other. This the Soviet government anticipates would lead to eventual Bolshevization of the whole of Europe."[8]

Similar feelings of distrust of Soviet aims in Europe were expressed in a secret report by the British Chiefs of Staff Sub-Committee of the Committee of Imperial Defense, dated 22 February 1937, seven months after the outbreak of the Civil War. Without specifically referring to the Spanish conflict, the report affirmed that "the Soviet Government would have no fundamental objection to a war between the capitalist Powers of Europe, so long as the U.S.S.R. were not involved," that "in certain circumstances she might hope that such a war would give an opportunity to Communism to establish itself in Europe generally," and that there was no reason to suppose that she had abandoned "the ultimate hope of world revolution."[9]

Fears of a general European conflict, from which it was felt Russia alone would benefit, increased steadily during the Civil War and reached a peak during the crisis over Czechoslovakia. At a meeting of the British cabinet on 17 September 1938, Sir Thomas Inskip, Chamberlain's minister for coordination of defense, stated that while a war might destroy Hitler "it might almost certainly destroy a great deal more. The result might be changes in the state of Europe which might be satisfactory to no one except Moscow and the Bolsheviks."[10] At the same meeting, Lord Zetland, the secretary of state for India, referred to the "appalling results which would follow from a world war. This would bring about the destruction of the present world order and the emergence of something which might approximate to the ideals of those who controlled the destiny of Russia."[11] On 17 March 1937, Sir Alexander Cadogan, the permanent undersecretary for foreign affairs, had minuted: "The Russian object [of collective security] is to precipitate confusion and war in Europe: they will not participate usefully themselves; they will hope for the world revolution as a result (and a very likely one too)."[12]

And in a cable to the British ambassador to Germany, Sir Nevile Henderson, dated 23 May 1938, Lord Halifax, then foreign secretary, urged the ambassador to inform Von Ribbentrop, the German foreign minister, "with all [the] earnestness you can command" that if from any precipitate action there should start a European conflagration "only those will benefit from such a catastrophe who wish to see [the] destruction of European civilization."[13]

This disquietude was not confined to political circles. According to General Baron Geyr von Schweppenburg, military attaché to the German embassy in London, Sir John Dill at the War Office and those members of the general staff who shared his thoughts were convinced that another war between the British Empire and Germany would be a tragedy, not only for the empire, but for the whole of Europe. "They saw quite clearly that such a war would only forward the designs of Russia and in this they showed a great deal more foresight than many of their compatriots."[14]

While these apprehensions relate directly to the Czech crisis in September 1938, there can be no doubt that they plagued the British government during the Spanish Civil War and lay at the root of the policy of nonintervention and of British resolve to avoid a military confrontation with Germany over Spain. In the opinion of this author, they also lay at the root of the British government's pro-German policy in Central and Eastern Europe that soon became known as appeasement. That the French government of Edouard Daladier, comprising members of the moderate Radical Socialist party, secretly harbored the same forebodings is clear from the private conversations with the German ambassador in Paris, Count von Welczeck, published after World War II. Georges Bonnet, the foreign minister, told the ambassador in May 1938, five months before the Munich settlement, that "any arrangement" was better than war, "in the event of which all Europe would perish and both victor and vanquished would fall victims to world Communism."[15] Paul Reynaud, the minister of justice, was no less explicit. He told Welczeck that war would be a catastrophe from which Europe would never recover "with the exception of Russia, remote and already living under Communism," and that "everything must be done to avert the destruction of the civilized old world."[16] As for Premier Daladier he expressed himself to the ambassador in apocalyptic terms: "[The] catastrophic frightfulness of a modern war would surpass all that humanity had ever seen, and would mean the utter destruction of European civilization. Into the battle zones, devastated and denuded of men, Cossack and Mongol hordes would then pour, bringing to Europe a new 'Culture.' This must be prevented, even if it entailed great sacrifices."[17] And in a talk with German chargé d'affaires Bräuer a few months later, Daladier "stressed particularly the terrible and calamitous consequences of a European war." "Soviet Russia," he added, "would not let the opportunity pass of bringing world revolution to our lands, after the weakening of the European Continent."[18]

The Germans were not backward in encouraging the fears of the French leaders. "When Germany and France are exhausted," the military attaché in Paris, General Kühlenthal, told General Gamelin, the chief of the French general staff, "Russia, which will have bided her time, will intervene and that will mean world revolution."[19] For obvious diplomatic reasons the fears of the French leaders were never openly expressed, if only because of the Pact of Mutual Assistance with Russia, but they were publicly expressed by such writers as Thierry Maulnier, a partisan of the French right, who argued, as we have seen, that "Germany's defeat would mean the collapse of those authoritarian systems which form the principal bulwark against Communist revolution and that it would perhaps lead to the immediate Bolshevization of Europe." It was a pity, he added, that "the men and parties in France who share in that belief did not in general admit it, for there was nothing inavowable about it."

Any assessment of British and French diplomacy would be flawed if it failed to take into account the fear that a general European conflict would inure only to the advantage of the Soviet Union, yet so addled is the state of British historiography of the period that only rarely do the recognized authorities touch on this issue and, then, only superficially. An exception must be made of Sir John W. Wheeler-Bennett, who included in his classic work *Munich: Prologue to Tragedy* the following candid passage: "In Conservative circles, both in Britain and France, there was a deep-seated conviction that Russia wished to precipitate a European war, from which she would remain aloof, and which would result in the destruction or collapse of the capitalist system. On the rubble and ruins of the bourgeois-capitalism, Moscow would erect a Dictatorship of the Proletariat which, though differing from that of [German] National Socialism, would be no better and indeed prove worse. . . . [There] emerged the hope that if only German expansion could be directed toward the East it would cease to threaten Western civilization and the Russian trick might be turned against themselves. The on-march of German penetration would sooner or later dissipate its force on the steppes of Russia in a struggle which would exhaust both combatants for many years to come."[20]

From the diaries and letters of Sir Harold Nicolson, a supporter of Winston Churchill and a National Labor member of Parliament, professional diplomatist and famous writer, we glean some of the most illuminating insights into the fears and anxieties that beset many of the politicians of the day and determined British policy toward Germany and later toward the events in Spain. Writing shortly before the German march into the Rhineland on 7 March 1936, in violation of the Versailles and Locarno treaties, a violation that Britain and France, acting in concert, could have opposed successfully had they wished to fight, Nicolson penetrates the core of British and French unwillingness to intervene: "Naturally we shall win and enter Berlin. But what is the good of that? It would only mean communism in Germany and France, and that is why the Russians are so keen on it."[21] Of Henry and Honor Channon (Henry was a Conservative M.P.), Nicolson wrote on 20 September 1936: "[They think] we should let gallant little Germany glut her fill of the reds in the East and keep decadent France quiet while she does so. Otherwise we shall have not only reds in the West but bombs in London, Kelvedon [the Channons' country house], and Southend."[22] The following year, on 18 September 1937, Nicolson recorded in his diary: "Tory opinion is almost entirely on the run and would willingly let Germany take Russia and over-run the Near East so long as she leaves us alone."[23] On 6 June 1938, he recorded: "We have lost our will-power since our will-power is divided. People of the governing classes think only of their own fortunes, which means hatred of the Reds. This creates a perfectly artificial but at present most effective secret bond between ourselves and Hitler."[24] And, on 11 September 1938, at the time of the crisis over Czechoslovakia, Oliver Stanley, who held many prominent offices in prewar and wartime Conservative governments, told Sir Harold: " 'You see, whether we win or lose, it will be the end of everything we stand for.' By 'we' he means obviously the capitalist classes."[25]

Equally edifying is the following entry, on 18 November 1938, in the diplomatic diaries of Oliver Harvey, Foreign Secretary Anthony Eden's private secretary from January 1936 until February 1938 and subsequently private secretary to Lord Halifax until December 1939: "Any war will bring vast and unknown social changes—win or lose—and no war is a solution—vide 1914. Therefore play for time and avoid fighting at all costs except on a first-class vital British interest. . . . [The] rich classes in the [Conservative] Party . . . believe the Nazis on the whole are more conservative than Communists and Socialists: any war, whether we win or not, would destroy the rich idle classes and so they are for peace at any price."[26]

During the interwar years Hitler lost no opportunity to convince British statesmen and high level personalities that he was the protector of Western civilization and potential crusader against communism and that he desired peace and amity with Britain. In this he was ably assisted by his emissary in London, Joachim von Ribbentrop. "For some time Ribbentrop had been busy in London seeking to create a friendly atmosphere towards the Reich," writes John Evelyn Wrench, the biographer of Geoffrey Dawson, the influential editor of the semiofficial *Times* and a resolute believer in appeasement. "His propaganda had been carefully thought out. Nazi Germany undoubtedly stood as a wedge between Russian Communism and the West, and this was a fact of which Geoffrey was fully cognizant."[27] As we have already seen, Lord Lloyd, noted statesman and Conservative peer, stated in his pamphlet *The British Case*, written shortly after the outbreak of World War II and officially endorsed by Lord Halifax, then secretary of state for foreign affairs, that in spite of Hitler's "abominable methods" and disregard for the rights of other European peoples, "he still claimed to stand ultimately for something which was a common European interest, and which therefore could conceivably provide some day a basis for understanding with other nations equally determined not to sacrifice their traditional institutions and habits on the blood-stained altars of the World Revolution."

When Lord Lothian, influential statesman and diplomat, visited Hitler on 29 January 1935, the Nazi leader made it clear that "he knew what he was talking about, when it was a question of Communism. No one knew this question better than he: he had seen its ravages in Germany and fought it for many years. Communism was not an idea that would disappear in 10 or 20 years. . . . It was a world conquering idea, something that could be compared to the founding of a great religion. . . . It must be fought by another philosophy."[28] From that time on, Lord Lothian became, according to the British historian A. L. Rowse, who knew him personally, "the outstanding propagandist of 'better understanding' with Hitler, and more dangerous than most, because of his charm, his contacts and friendships at the top of English political society—he belonged to the inner circle—and because of his ability to write, such as not all of them had."[29]

Also, when Sir John Simon, foreign secretary in 1935, talked with the Nazi leader on 25 March of that year, he minuted: "Hitler made it perfectly plain that he would never agree to enter a pact of 'mutual assistance' with Russia. Communism, he declared, is the plague: unlike Nazi Socialism, which he claims seeks only to embrace Germans, it is a contagious infection which might spread over all Europe and all Asia. He has stamped it out of Germany and Germany is the barrier to prevent the pestilence coming westward. So he claims that we ought to be grateful. No eastern pact for him. The practical result of our Berlin visit is to establish that Germany greatly desires a good understanding with Britain."[30]

Hitler had no difficulty in convincing his many visitors of his sincerity. Some might arrive in a skeptical frame of mind, as British historian Martin Gilbert suggests, but they left "convinced that their fears were unjustified, that Hitler was a sincere believer in European peace, and that if he had hatreds, they were towards Communism, not Britain."[31] Others, however, were converted before they arrived. For example, when Lord Halifax, shortly before becoming foreign secretary, visited Hitler on 19 November 1937 at the request of Prime Minister Neville Chamberlain, he said, according to the German record of the conversation, that the great services the führer had rendered in rebuilding Germany were fully and completely recognized, and if British public opinion sometimes took up a critical attitude toward certain German problems, the reason might be in part that people in England were not fully informed of the motives and circumstances that underlay certain German measures. "In spite of these difficulties he *and other members of the British Government* were fully aware that the Führer had not only achieved a great deal inside Germany herself, but that, by destroying Communism in his country, he had barred its road to Western Europe, *and that Germany therefore could rightly be regarded as a bulwark of the West against Bolshevism.*"[32]

A year earlier, Thomas Jones, who moved widely in high-level political circles and was a close friend, adviser, and confidant of Prime Minister Stanley Baldwin—whose "inertia" was a cause of concern to those favoring Anglo-German friendship—emphasized with a decided note of urgency the need for an understanding between Great Britain and Germany. In a letter to a friend sent from Chequers, the prime minister's weekend retreat, on 23 May 1936, a few days after he had flown to meet Adolf Hitler, Jones wrote: "We have to choose between Russia and Germany and choose soon. . . . [Hitler] is asking for an alliance with us to form a bulwark against the spread of Communism. Our P.M. [prime minister] is not indisposed to attempt this as a final effort before he resigns after the Coronation next year to make way for Neville Chamberlain."[33]

But this attempt was never made by the indecisive, wavering Baldwin, who was loath to involve himself with foreign affairs,[34] and the effort to reach an understanding with Germany was left to his more resolute successor, Neville Chamberlain. Nevertheless, Baldwin was sufficiently stirred by the outbreak of the civil war in Spain and the fear of Soviet involvement to tell Anthony Eden, his foreign secretary, on 26 July, "that on no account, French or other, must he bring us in to fight on the side of the Russians."[35]

This too was the reaction to the Spanish conflict of Sir Samuel Hoare, the first lord of the admiralty in Baldwin's cabinet and later a member of the "inner group" in the government of Neville Chamberlain. Advocating "strict neutrality," he minuted on 5 August: "On no account must we do anything to bolster up Communism in Spain, particularly when it is remembered that Communism in Portugal, to which it would probably spread and particularly in Lisbon, would be a grave danger to the British Empire."[36]

Equally important was the view of Sir Maurice Hankey, who for twenty-five years presided over the inner machinery of the British cabinet and Committee of Imperial Defense: "In the present state of Europe," he affirmed on 20 July 1936, "with France and Spain menaced by Bolshevism, it is not inconceivable that before long it might pay us to throw in our lot with Germany and Italy, and the greater our detachment the better."[37]

According to Lawrence A. Pratt, who consulted the private papers of Lord Chatfield, the first sea lord, he and his staff had the same idea as Hankey and there is evidence that Admiral Roger Backhouse, commander of the Home Fleet and Chatfield's successor, proposed in 1936 that Britain associate herself with Germany and Italy in "crushing revolution in Spain."[38]

Sufficient evidence has by now been adduced, both in this and earlier chapters, to substantiate the claim that powerful forces in Britain and France looked upon Germany as the rampart of Western Europe against communism and did not wish to be drawn into a general European war from which Russia alone might emerge triumphant. Obviously, J. L. Garvin, the editor of the London *Observer*, an influential conveyer of Conservative opinion, was expressing more than a personal opinion when he wrote: "In no case whatever can it be to the interest of Britain and the British Empire that Germany should be overthrown to exalt still further and beyond restraint the Soviet Power of the future, and make Communism supreme, whether in Europe or Asia."[39] Similar views, as we have seen, were held by the French right and entertained, though not publicly expressed, by members of the moderate Radical Socialist party. Hence, it cannot be over-stressed that in spite of the risks involved to themselves of a Spain under possible bondage to Italy and Germany, Britain and France were not to be diverted from their policy of nonintervention and no attempt by the Communists and their allies to alter the character of the Spanish Revolution, either in form or in substance, could induce the British and French governments to challenge Germany in Spain.

Although Léon Blum, the Socialist premier of the Popular Front government in France, is alleged to have adopted a neutral stand under strong British pres-sure,[40] Blum himself consistently denied these allegations and accepted full responsibility.[41] Nevertheless, at the outbreak of the Civil War, in response to an appeal by José Giral, the Spanish prime minister, he was at first ready to supply the Spanish government with war material[42] but changed his mind after a visit to London to attend a conference on the status of the Locarno treaty following the German occupation of the Rhineland. Although the subject of Spain was not on the agenda, it came up indirectly. Joel Colton writes in his well-documented biography of Léon Blum: "Various members of the [British] cabinet expressed what Blum later described as 'great apprehension' over a policy of aiding Repub-lican Spain. 'It would be exaggerated,' he said later in recalling the talks, 'to speak of opposition. But counsels of prudence were dispensed and sharp fears expressed.'[43] In a luncheon conversation some Conservatives spoke in favor of a war between fascists and Bolsheviks in which the extremists would exterminate themselves; Spain, it was implied, could be the scene of such a felicitous Arma-geddon.[44] Blum, Delbos [Yvon Delbos, French foreign minister], and Léger [Alexis Saint-Léger Léger, secretary general of the ministry of foreign affairs] were clearly made to understand the negative attitude of the British Conserva-tives, who did not wish to take sides in the 'faction fight' in Spain; they hoped that the Spanish Civil War could be prevented from turning into a European conflagration.[45] Yet, by Blum's own testimony, no direct pressure was exerted upon him during his stay in London to adopt a policy of non-intervention."

Nevertheless, British pressure was strong even if indirect. "It was typical of Blum that he would not admit to such pressure and that he would later insist on assuming the entire blame himself. There is no doubt that he left London much disturbed over the official British climate of opinion and shaken in his determina-tion to aid Spain even if he was not yet prepared to abandon his original intention. It was in Paris that he encountered the decisive opposition."[46] This is undoubtedly correct, for it was there that he was subject to direct pressure from some of the Radical party ministers in his cabinet, from the president of the Republic,[47] from the combined forces of the French right, and from the powerful Radical party,[48] which represented within the Popular Front alliance a large segment of the middle classes, who, according to Jean Lacouture, Léon Blum's French biographer, "fearfully refused the slightest risk in foreign affairs."[49]

Equally indicative of the opposition of influential quarters in both Britain and

France to any military commitment that might involve them in a war with Germany was their hostility to the Franco-Soviet Pact of Mutual Assistance. If this hostility was undisguised by an important section of French opinion, to say nothing of the antipathy in official quarters,[50] it was no less patent in authoritative British newspapers. "British opinion," said the *Times*, the unofficial mouthpiece of the government, "is not prepared to accept . . . the leadership of France over the whole field of foreign politics, or to admit responsibility for all the liabilities which she had been accumulating . . . in the shape of alliances on the farther side of Germany. . . . The Franco-Soviet Pact is not regarded here as a helpful diplomatic achievement."[51]

"France," wrote "Scrutator" in the *Sunday Times*, "has made alliances in Eastern Europe for power—its motive is still power, even if there is no idea of aggression but only self-defense. Rightly or wrongly—wrongly, as some of us think—she convinced herself that the benefits to herself of an alliance with Russia and the Little Entente outweighed the risk of entanglements in disputes not really her own. In this regard, France's policy is not ours."[52]

"These pacts [the Franco-Soviet and Czech-Soviet treaties]," wrote J. L. Garvin in the *Observer*, "mean war and can mean nothing else. If we support them they mean war between Britain and Germany and can mean nothing else. If Britain is to give countenance or patronage to those fatal instruments; if we are to have any lot or part in them whatever; if we are to stand behind France and Czechoslovakia as the potential allies of Russia and Communism against Germany—then the situation becomes inherently deadly to peace, and it is no use talking of anything else. We cannot have it both ways. If we are to interfere with Germany in the East she must ultimately strike us in the West. Nothing else is possible."[53]

If such forthright expressions of opinion by these highly influential and quality newspapers were never matched by any official declaration, there can be no doubt that they corresponded closely to the position of the British government. This is plain from the minutes of the foreign affairs committee on 18 March 1938, released after World War II, which "reviewed at length the dangers of a situation in which France [through her commitments in Central and Eastern Europe] might drag Britain into a war, because, as [Prime Minister Chamberlain] pointed out, 'we could not afford to see France destroyed.' "[54]

Equally concerned were the British chiefs of staff, who reported in 1937: "If France becomes involved by decisions in which we should have no part, we are in danger of being drawn into a general European war, even though at that moment it might be highly dangerous for us."[55] "The underlying principle," writes Keith Middlemas, the British historian, "hedged about though it was with qualifications and restrictions, was never actually denied and the Chiefs of Staff enunciated it shortly before the fall of Austria [March 1938]. If France was 'in great danger . . . we cannot afford to allow [her] to be overrun and aerodromes established on French soil. Over the centuries the British people have fought to prevent the Low Countries [Holland and Belgium] falling to the possession of a hostile power.' "

As Middlemas points out, the Chamberlain cabinet reluctantly accepted that it was an overriding British interest not to see France defeated by Germany. Hitler might sweep eastward almost at will in 1938, but the balance of power in Western Europe should not, in the last resort, be overthrown.[56] Hence, it is not surprising that Chamberlain expressed himself at the foreign affairs committee as being "most uneasy at a situation in which French Ministers could decide whether Britain went to war or not."[57]

The vital question, then, as the British government perceived it, was to prevent a war in Western Europe arising not only as a result of the continuing threat presented by the Spanish conflict and possible French involvement, but from France's commitments in Eastern Europe. War in the West, it was felt, could be averted only by France disencumbering herself of her eastern entanglements and by an Anglo-German political agreement that would guarantee the status quo in Western Europe and allow German hegemony in the East as a bulwark against the Soviet Union.

Although British historians have on the whole avoided coming to grips with the thesis that Britain's aim was to turn Nazi aggression eastward, where the two totalitarian powers would exhaust themselves—a thesis which, in view of the fear of communism, has at least the merit of logicality—and have stressed other reasons for the policy of appeasement, the evidence is overwhelming, despite the supervised release and even disappearance of official documents from the records, that there were powerful currents in high level political and social circles that hoped that Germany would at least serve as a counterweight to Russia against the spread of communism. That these currents had existed since the early years of the Nazi regime has already been amply demonstrated, and the evidence is no less convincing that they continued to survive until the Nazis upset the balance of power in the spring of 1940 by invading Western Europe.

If it has been necessary to dwell at length on the principal motive force behind the appeasement policy, it is because the state of British historiography of the 1930s is so unsatisfactory. Unless the mainspring of appeasement can be incontrovertibly established, it is impossible not only to make sense of prewar European history and British policy, which otherwise appears as a succession of absurd blunders, but to understand Stalin's "moderate" course during the Spanish Civil War and Revolution. Nor is it possible to understand why his efforts to induce the democracies to end their policy of nonintervention by distorting the nature of the Revolution and to challenge Germany in Spain could never have met with the success he hoped.

Yet, while the majority of British historians have avoided or skated over the principal motive force behind the policy of appeasement and sought refuge in other explanations, there are, to be sure, notable exceptions. No less an authority than Arnold J. Toynbee—who at one time, according to Thomas Jones (who knew him personally) was "convinced of [Hitler's] sincerity in desiring peace in Europe and close friendship with England"[58]—stated in 1937 as clearly as might be expected: "The suggestion that a Western Pact should be concluded and that

Herr Hitler should be tacitly left free to do as he liked in the East commended itself to those British circles in which an Anglo-German *rapprochement* was regarded as highly desirable (either from fear of Germany's growing strength or from dislike of Russia or from other motives); and it was also likely to receive consideration in circles which were strongly opposed to any concession to Germany's claim for the return of her pre-war colonies. . . . [There] was little doubt that a considerable proportion of the British public, including some of the Government's supporters in the House of Commons, would deem it to be in the interests of the British Empire to abandon Eastern Europe to its fate, if by that means the question of a redistribution of colonial territory could be shelved."[59]

Then there is the testimony of Basil Henry Liddell Hart, military tactician and historian, who was an adviser to Leslie Hore-Belisha, war minister in the Chamberlain cabinet, who claims that in "Government circles I had long listened to calculating arguments for allowing Germany to expand eastwards, for evading our obligations under the League Covenant, and for leaving other countries to bear the brunt of any early stand against aggression."[60]

Even more explicit is Sir John W. Wheeler-Bennett: "This willingness to see Hitler dominant in Central and Eastern Europe was not, however, merely a by-product of the general trend of British diplomacy. It was of far greater significance than that, and represented one of the prime factors in the whole situation. Behind the general desire for peace and for an 'accommodation' with Hitler there lay, if not in the mind of Mr. Chamberlain himself at any rate in the minds of some of his advisers, the secret hope that, if German expansion could be directed towards the East, it would in time come into collision with the rival totalitarian imperialism of Soviet Russia. In the conflict which would ensue both the forces of National Socialism and Communism would be exhausted and, since it was believed by those who held these opinions that Bolshevik Russia was of greater danger to Britain than Nazi Germany, the prospect of Hitler defeating Stalin and greatly weakening himself in the process was not unwelcome."[61]

17

Wooing Britain and France

*I*t should now be clear that France's military commitments in Central and Eastern Europe ran counter to the aims of British foreign policy. It is also clear from German documents that even in French official circles the Franco-Soviet pact was regarded by some as an impediment to an eventual accommodation with Germany. Of this the Kremlin was fully conscious. Indeed, the fear that both Britain and France might arrive at some agreement with Germany at the expense of Eastern Europe was deeply grounded in Moscow. In a conversation with Joseph E. Davies, U.S. ambassador to Russia, in February 1937, Maxim Litvinov, Soviet commissar for foreign affairs, did not conceal this disquietude: "He could not understand," Davies informed the secretary of state, "why Great Britain could not see that once Hitler dominated Europe he would swallow the British Isles also. He seemed to be very much stirred about this and apprehensive lest there should be some composition of differences between France, England, and Germany."[1]

It was undoubtedly the fear that the impetus of German militarism might ultimately be directed against the East rather than against the West—augmented by the disappointment over the continued neutrality of Britain and France with regard to the Spanish conflict despite increasing Italo-German intervention,[2] over the failure of the French government to supplement the Franco-Soviet pact by any positive military agreement, and over the rejection of a Popular Front by the British Labor party[3]—that prompted the Kremlin to redouble its efforts in Spain with a view to enticing Britain and France from their neutrality.

At the end of January 1937, Juan Comorera, the leader of the PSUC, told the central committee of his party in words that reflected discussions that had taken place with Ernö Gerö, a top-ranking Comintern agent in Spain known as "Pedro," who had just returned from Moscow,[4] that "the essential thing at this time is to seek the collaboration of the European democracies, particularly that of England."[5]

"In the democratic bloc of powers," Comorera declared two days later at a public meeting, "the decisive factor is not France; it is England. It is essential for all party comrades to realize this so as to moderate [their] slogans at the present time. . . . England is not a country like France. England is a country governed by the Conservative party. England is a country of slow evolution, which is constantly preoccupied with imperial interests. England is a country of plutocrats, a country with a profoundly conservative middle class that reacts with great difficulty. . . . Some persons say that England could never on any account agree to the triumph of Germany over Spain because that would signify a danger to her own vital interests. But we should realize that the big capitalists in England are capable of coming to an understanding at any time with Italian and German capitalists if they should reach the conclusion that they have no other choice with regard to Spain.

"[Therefore] we must win, cost what it may, the benevolent neutrality of that country, if not its direct aid."[6]

That this was to be achieved not merely by accentuating the moderate tendencies initiated by the Communists at the outbreak of the Revolution, but by more tangible means, was evident from a note sent by Alvarez del Vayo, the philo-Communist foreign minister, in February 1937 to the British and French governments offering to transfer Spanish Morocco to these two powers in return for the adoption of measures designed to prevent further Italo-German intervention.[7]

It is significant that during the discussions that "Pedro" held with the PSUC leaders at the end of January upon his return from Moscow approximately two weeks before the offer was made, he spoke of the advisability of offering Spanish Morocco and the Canary Islands, also in the hands of General Franco, to Britain and France in order to win the support of these two powers. During her revolution, he argued, Russia had also been compelled to make territorial sacrifices.[8]

Jesús Hernández, politburo member and minister of education, affirmed, after he had ceased to belong to the Communist party, that "Litvinov [Soviet foreign minister] in Geneva and Rosenberg [Soviet ambassador] in Spain persuaded Alvarez del Vayo . . . to make 'certain offers' favorable to Great Britain and France with regard to Spanish Morocco in exchange for the help of both powers to the Republic."[9] On the other hand, Pablo de Azcárate, the philo-Communist Spanish ambassador in London, claims that the memorandum was inspired and drafted by him with the approval of Alvarez del Vayo.[10] In view of the pro-Soviet attitudes of both men and their frequent contact with the two Soviet diplomats, this version is not substantially different from that given by Hernández. Because Spanish Morocco was in the hands of General Franco, and there had recently been insistent reports that Germany was fortifying the coast opposite Gibraltar,[11] it must have been obvious to Moscow that no such assignment could have been made in favor of Britain and France and accepted by them without the risk of precipitating an international conflict. In fact, Hernández affirms that if these two countries, "which had more than ample motives for anxiety over the prospect of a violent change of the status quo in Morocco, had been lured by the seductive offer, the friction between the democratic powers and Germany and Italy would have reached white heat, creating favorable conditions for Soviet plans to push the two blocs into a war far removed from Russia's borders."[12]

It is doubtful, however, whether more than a few of the members of the Republican government were aware of the wider objectives of Soviet policy in Spain or even of the Moroccan proposal at the time it was made. Indalecio Prieto asserts that no proposal relating to Morocco was ever submitted to the cabinet and that if it had been, he would have "opposed any step in favor of such an impractical idea." He also asserts that he never heard of the proposal while serving as a cabinet minister.[13] This is true, for, according to Azcárate, Alvarez del Vayo informed him that only Azaña, Largo Caballero, and he had any knowledge of the secret memorandum. "The other members of the cabinet," he added, "were not to be informed for the time being."[14] This is confirmed in a letter dated 7 February 1937 addressed to Luis Araquistáin, the Spanish ambassador in Paris, by Alvarez del Vayo, who also stated that because of the "growing pessimism" of Prieto and his "contagious oratory," nothing could be achieved "if every move in foreign policy were subject to a majority vote."[15]

In spite of the secrecy, a copy of the memorandum fell into the hands of General Franco's administration[16] and was published in full in the enemy press.[17] In succeeding days, excerpts or summaries appeared in the major newspapers of Britain and France. "[There] is someone in our embassies who is in touch with the rebels," Vayo wrote Araquistáin on 18 March. "Otherwise it cannot be explained how they gained cognizance of the memorandum, . . . [but] I do not mind if the matter gets excessive publicity, for it shows that our international policy is aimed at close collaboration with the western democracies [and is] in the service of collective security and peace."[18]

And, in a second letter to Araquistáin on 9 April, Vayo stated: "We must win over London at all costs. . . . We already know that the British government . . . is exasperating in its stupidity and its inertia apart from the fact that the majority of the cabinet is fundamentally hostile to us. But we must win it over. How? On the one hand, by shaking up public opinion in all spheres (in this respect the visit of the British ecclesiastical delegation [to Republican Spain] has been an unsurpassable success) and, on the other hand, by constantly appealing to the crude self-interest and egotism of the British Empire."[19]

Signed by Alvarez del Vayo, the memorandum stated in part:

I

1. The Spanish government wishes Spain's future foreign policy, as far as Western Europe is concerned, to assume the form of active collaboration with France and the United Kingdom.

2. To this end, Spain would be ready to take into consideration, both in the matter of economic reconstruction and in her military, naval, and air relations, the interests of these two powers, insofar as this is compatible with her interests.

3. In the same manner, Spain would be ready to examine, in conjunction with these powers, the advisability or otherwise of modifying the present status of North Africa (Spanish Morocco) on condition that such modification is not made in favor of any power other than Great Britain and France. . . .

II

If these proposals, which are made in a spirit of full international collaboration, are appreciated at their true worth by the British and French governments, these governments would henceforth be responsible for the adoption of any measures within their power designed to prevent further Italo-German intervention in Spanish affairs, in view of the fact that the interests of peace, which are synonymous with the national interests of the Western democracies, demand the effective prosecution of this aim.

If the sacrifices the Spanish government is willing to make prove insufficient to prevent the further supplying of men and material to the rebels by Italy and Germany, and if, in consequence, the Republican government is compelled to fight the rebel generals, aided by two foreign powers, until victory is attained, then the proposals made in the first part of this note will be considered null and void, in view of the fact that their essential aim, which is to spare the Spanish people further suffering, would be frustrated.[20]

"The Spanish memorandum," wrote Alvarez del Vayo after the war, "gave the most conclusive proof of the Republic's desire for an understanding with Great Britain and France. Though it could not, in view of the existing circumstances, take the form of a pact of mutual assistance or an alliance, it was to all intents and purposes the same."[21] In a later passage, he says:

Neither of the two governments received the Republican initiative favorably,[22] and the international "leakage" by which the text of the Spanish memorandum was made known to the public gave evidence of an active hand behind the scenes which was doing everything possible to frustrate attempts to help the cause of the Spanish government. . . .

Although the February memorandum was an official statement of the Republic's foreign policy during the war, it must not be thought that it represented the extent of our efforts to persuade Great Britain and France to adopt an attitude more in keeping with their own interests. By every relevant argument, by communicating reports on Italo-German activity to both governments, by the submission of concrete proposals for combating the Italian menace in Majorca—by every means in our power we endeavored to bring about a change of attitude in London and Paris.[23]

We were not crying for the moon. We made no request for armed assistance. We only asked that in strict accordance with the policy of non-intervention—which Great Britain and France had imposed on us and should for that very reason have enforced—"Spain should be left to the Spaniards"; and that if those two democracies did not feel able to prevent Germany and Italy from continuing to intervene in Spain, they should make honorable recognition of the failure of their policy and reestablish in full the right to freedom of trade. In a word, we asked that international law should be respected.

The way in which the British and French governments ignored our warnings, suggestions, and requests was truly heartbreaking.[24]

Notwithstanding these disappointments, Russia continued to bolster the resistance of the anti-Franco forces in the stubborn belief that Britain and France could not permit an Italo-German vassalage of Spain and would sooner or later be forced to intervene in defense of their own interests, undermining or destroying Germany's military power before she had time to prepare for war in Eastern Europe.

"[Moscow]," affirmed Boris Stefanov, the Comintern delegate, "will try by every means to avoid being isolated, to force the Western democracies to fight Hitler, if there is no other course but war."[25]

"We want [the democratic states] to help us," declared José Díaz, the general secretary of the Spanish Communist party, "and believe that in this way they will be defending their own interests. We try to make them understand this and to enlist their help. . . . We know full well that the fascist aggressors find bourgeois groups in every country to support them, such as the Conservatives in England and the rightists in France, but fascist aggression is going forward at such a pace that national interests, in a country like France, for instance, must convince all men who desire the liberty and independence of their country of the necessity of standing up to this aggression. And today there is no more effective way of doing this than by giving concrete help to the Spanish people."[26]

"Moscow tried to do for France and England what they should have done for themselves," Juan Negrín, prime minister during the last two years of the war, declared after the end of the conflict. "The promise of Soviet aid to the Spanish Republic was that ultimately Paris and London would awake to the risks involved to themselves in an Italo-German victory in Spain and join the USSR in supporting us."[27]

But neither Britain nor France wished to risk a European conflict or even weaken the Nazi regime by challenging Germany in Spain. German intervention might indeed represent a future threat to British and French interests in the Mediterranean as well as to France on her southern border, but should not be allowed to interfere with the long-term strategy of securing peace in Western Europe by appeasing Germany in the East and using her as a countervailing force against the Soviet Union.

In Britain, the advocates of appeasement were greatly strengthened in May 1937, when Neville Chamberlain succeeded Stanley Baldwin as premier. To be sure, Baldwin had favored appeasement and a political settlement with Germany, but he was not a man of action. His tendency, as the Earl of Birkenhead attests, was "to dream and drift in the hope that matters would somehow sort themselves out."[28] On the other hand, Chamberlain, whose "remarkable gifts," according to Birkenhead, "were not those demanded by this particular moment of history," was "in every respect a man of action," "an administrator of a high order, and a debater of uncompromising skill and severity," with a "streak of ruthlessness which reminded many of his father, Joseph Chamberlain, and an autocratic tendency which led him to exercise an iron control over his Cabinet." His idea of a fair basis of discussion, Birkenhead adds, was that "the Germans should be told that we would not forcibly oppose them in obtaining their objects in Austria and Czechoslovakia, provided they did so by peaceful means."[29]

The qualification "by peaceful means" was a fundamental element of Chamberlain's policy, for although he and his supporters were ready to allow Germany a predominant position in Eastern Europe by absorbing Czechoslovakia and even, as will be seen in a later chapter, by disembarrassing themselves of the military commitment given to Poland on 31 March 1939, they knew that if Hitler were to use force to attain his ends, Britain might well be drawn into a war in Western Europe either through pressure of the parliamentary opposition and the press or through French entanglements in Central and Eastern Europe. For these reasons, any territorial changes west of Russia's borders were to be achieved "only by way of negotiation and a *gradual* revision of British policy."[30]

As for the fate that Chamberlain foresaw for Russia in his strategy of appeasement, no evidence has been uncovered in British documents to prove that he sought a military confrontation between the two totalitarian powers. Nor can we expect to see Chamberlain's strategy spelled out in any official document; for, as one British historian has observed in a general statement regarding the formulation of British policy, "it was often decided without Minutes, in the Prime Minister's Gothic-styled office in Parliament, during a walk in St. James's Park, in a West End club or in a country house"[31]—and, we should add, in the private confines of Sir Horace Wilson's office at 10 Downing Street.[32]

Although the British archives covering the years preceding World War II were opened under the Public Records Act of 1967, it is most unlikely that any cabinet papers, memoranda, or minutes will ever be found providing concrete evidence of a grand strategy relating to Eastern Europe, for such a politically explosive matter could have been discussed only in secrecy by Chamberlain's trusted associates. Indeed, the cabinet records so far released provide no inkling of any discussions on the subject. Furthermore, even if the precise aims of British policy were committed to paper, it should be borne in mind that the discretionary power of the lord chancellor—the cabinet officer responsible for all state papers—to exclude certain documents on security grounds from becoming available to the historian for "a hundred years or indeed in perpetuity"[33] limits the available material. This power may explain why Chamberlain's secret proposals to Germany regarding Poland, as we shall see in a later chapter, have, in the words of the British historian A. J. P. Taylor, "not surprisingly . . . disappeared from the British records,"[34] and why the volumes on British foreign policy give "very few letters and even fewer minutes."[35] It may also explain why certain "clandestine messages" by Neville Chamberlain to Adolf Hitler were not published, according to the British historian David Irving, in the volumes of official documents.[36]

But even though documentary proof of Chamberlain's strategy may never be found, there is no lack of evidence that he perceived the Soviet Union as the *major* threat to British interests and that he harbored the most profound distrust of Russian aims. It is not surprising that in his private diary he expressed, according to British historian Keith Middlemas, "a willing fatalism about the likelihood of conflict between the fascist and communist ideologies and complete indifference to the security arrangements of Eastern Europe."[37] Some years later, Lord Douglas-Home, who had been Chamberlain's private parliamentary secretary (known at the time as Lord Dunglass) and a supporter of his policy, exposed more clearly than perhaps any British historian the wellspring of appeasement: "I think the main thing is that Chamberlain, like many others, saw Communism as the major long-term danger. He hated Hitler and German Fascism, but he felt that Europe in general and Britain in particular were in even greater danger from Communism. Hitler was an evil man but in the short term one should—and possibly could—do a deal with him, and after that he could be controlled."[38] As for Chamberlain's distrust of Russia, the reader will recall his suspicion that the "Bolshies" were "chiefly concerned to see the 'capitalist' Powers tear each other to pieces whilst they stay out themselves." His biographer Keith Feiling points out that he distrusted "the purity of [Russia's] motives," that "Spain accentuated that distrust," and that Russia would not weep to see the Western powers and Germany involved in a deadly war.[39] In a letter to one of his sisters, dated 20 March 1938, he spoke of the Russians "stealthily and cunningly pulling all the strings behind the scenes to get us involved in a war with Germany."[40] And in another family letter, he stated: "I must confess to the most profound distrust of Russia. . . . I distrust her motives, which seem to me to have little connection with our ideas of liberty, and to be concerned only with getting everyone else by the ears."[41]

In assessing British foreign policy from the advent to power of Adolf Hitler in 1933 up to the outbreak of war in 1939, it is essential to understand the distrust and fear of Russia, exacerbated by the revolutionary events in Spain, that existed among the political elite. If we ignore or even underrate this apprehension, as so many histories of the period, memoirs, and biographies have done, then Britain's acquiescence in German rearmament and hegemony in Central and Eastern Europe becomes unintelligible and the politicians who conducted her foreign policy appear as naive and gullible men totally ignorant of European affairs. Indeed, according to the British historian A. L. Rowse, Chamberlain was a "vain old fool" and his "whole approach was that of a rather simple-minded businessman."[42]

Hardly less misleading is the judgment of the Earl of Birkenhead that "Chamberlain's misfortune, and that of the country, was that his knowledge of the world was narrow, and that his political and business training had ill-equipped him at sixty-eight [when he took office in 1937] to comprehend the larger issues of foreign policy."[43] These characterizations are contradicted by the well-known professor of international history, W. N. Medlicott, who states that "Mr. Chamberlain had been a *close student of foreign policy for many years*, with a powerful influence on cabinet decisions in such related fields as rearmament, sanctions, and supply."[44] Moreover, they overlook what Winston Churchill, scarcely a friendly witness, described as Chamberlain's "toughness of fibre," his "precision of mind" and "remarkable mental faculties."[45] Above all, the misleading assessments of Chamberlain's abilities disregard the fact that two of Chamberlain's closest supporters, Sir Samuel Hoare and Sir John Simon, were former foreign secretaries with extensive experience in European affairs. It is impossible to believe that these three men—who together with Lord Halifax, foreign secretary from 1938, comprised the "Inner Cabinet" that excluded the full cabinet from the "central decisions" of foreign policy[46]—had no strategy for the defense of British interests and no notion as to where their support of German aims in Eastern Europe might ultimately lead. Nor is it possible to believe that all the statesmen and politicians in Britain and France who supported German appeasement were naive men who had no idea what might happen when Germany became the predominant force in Eastern Europe and established a common border with Russia.

All the scattered evidence laboriously gathered from public statements, from official, once-confidential or secret documents that have up to now been released and from the diaries and autobiographies of diplomats, politicians, and civil servants, when pieced together in a comprehensible and logical form, as the author has done in this and other chapters, prove beyond a peradventure that powerful forces in Britain and France hoped to use Germany as a counterpoise to Russia and purchase immunity for the West from the devastation of war and revolution by supporting German hegemony in Eastern Europe against the threat of Communism. The reasons why so many British historians have ignored the most important component of the appeasement policy are discussed later in this volume.

The attitude, then, of the controlling forces in Britain and France toward the Spanish Civil War was determined not merely by their hostility to the revolutionary changes, of which they were fully apprised in spite of the efforts to conceal them behind the facade of a "democratic Republic," but by the whole field of foreign politics. Hence, it cannot be overemphasized that no attempt at dissimulation and persuasion on the part of successive Spanish governments, prompted mainly by the Communists at the behest of Moscow, and that no attempt even at curbing the Revolution, could have altered Anglo-French policy with regard to the Spanish conflict.

Nevertheless, despite the doubts that may occasionally have assailed them, the Spanish Communist leaders executed the directives of the Kremlin without apparent hesitation even though these directives meant antagonizing irreversibly other parties of the left and eventually undermining the war effort and the will to fight. "Those of us who 'directed' the Spanish Communist party," declared Jesús Hernández in a speech delivered some years after he had been expelled from the party, "acted more like Soviet subjects than sons of the Spanish people. It may seem absurd, incredible, but our education under Soviet tutelage had deformed us to such an extent that we were completely denationalized; our national soul was torn out of us and replaced by a rabidly chauvinistic internationalism that began and ended with the towers of the Kremlin."[47]

Yet the leaders of the Spanish Communist party did not necessarily understand the Kremlin's purely pragmatic aims in rendering aid to the anti-Franco zone. "I sincerely believed," writes Valentín González, more commonly known as "El Campesino," a much-publicized Communist militia leader and somewhat charismatic figure during the war, "that the Kremlin sent us its arms, its military and political advisers, and the International Brigades under its control as a proof of its revolutionary solidarity. . . . Only later did I realize that the Kremlin does not serve the people, but uses them to serve its own interests; that, with a treachery and hypocrisy without parallel, it makes use of the international working class as a pawn in its political maneuvers, and that in the name of world revolution, it tries to consolidate its own totalitarian counterrevolution and to prepare for world domination."[48]

Part III

Curbing the Revolution

18

Anarchist Philosophy and Government

*T*he efforts of the Communists from the outset of the Civil War to gain the support of Great Britain and France and to ensure the continued recognition first of the Giral and later of the Largo Caballero government as the legally constituted authority necessarily had an important effect on the course of the Revolution. If these two countries were to be influenced even in the smallest measure, the government would have to reconstruct the shattered machinery of state not upon revolutionary lines but in the image of the deceased Republic. Moreover, if the Caballero administration were to be a government in essence rather than in name, it would have to assume control of all the elements of state power appropriated by the revolutionary committees in the first days of the Civil War.[1] On this point all members of the cabinet were of one mind, and there can be little doubt that they would have been so irrespective of the need to impress foreign opinion.

But the work of reconstructing state power could not be achieved, or at least would be extremely difficult to achieve, without the participation in the government of the extreme wing of the Revolution, the powerful Anarchosyndicalist or libertarian movement, as it was more frequently called, represented by the Anarchist-oriented CNT and by the FAI, its ideological guide, whose mission it was to protect the CNT from deviationist tendencies[2] and to lead the trade-union federation to the Anarchist goal of libertarian communism. Formed in 1927 as a clandestine organization from the scattered Anarchist groups throughout the country, the FAI's initial purpose was to aid in the struggle against Miguel Primo de Rivera's military dictatorship (1923–30) inasmuch as the CNT, formed in 1910[3] and outlawed by Primo, had virtually ceased to function. César M. Lorenzo writes:

> It was only at the beginning of 1929, when the CNT was partially reconstructed, that [the FAI] started to become known. . . . Organized very loosely on the basis of autonomous groups [known as "affinity" groups because of their common place of work or residence, as in the case of Communist cells] and comprising on the average about ten men, it had a peninsular committee . . . that served as a connecting organ. . . . [The] FAI's real cohesion derived from the ideological in-

transigence of its members, who were ferocious enemies of authority, hierarchy, politics, the state, legal action, and compromise. The "Faistas" undertook the conquest of the CNT, imposing themselves by their radicalism, their violent language, their ceaseless criticism, forever predicting that the social revolution would arrive the very next day. . . . The FAI, it should be stressed, was in reality only a faction, in prodigious expansion, of the CNT; it was not an alien force attempting to control it, like the Communist party, for example, which failed very quickly in its efforts of penetration, but an appendix, an outgrowth of the CNT itself, formed by the latter's own militants already organized in the unions. Its true epicenter was Catalonia, the cradle and ever-turbulent seat of the libertarian movement. It was not long before it became a "state within a state" inside the CNT.[4]

"[What] is clear and beyond question," Federica Montseny, a leading member of both the CNT and the FAI, wrote many years after the war, "is that the CNT was founded by the most devoted and most dynamic segment of the Anarchists and attracted the working class to itself precisely because of this dynamism and devotion. . . . And one other thing that no one should forget is that, if the CNT saved itself on various occasions from falling into the hands of other political organizations, it was precisely because of the . . . unfailing vigilance and activity of the [Anarchist] comrades within its ranks. In this way, it protected itself from the influx of Marxists in the years that followed the Russian Revolution."[5]

The FAI attempted to accomplish its directive mission by virtue of the fact that its members, with few exceptions, belonged to the CNT and held many positions of trust. It was an established principle that any person belonging to a political party should not occupy any official position in the trade-union organization.[6] The FAI, moreover, kept a close and constant supervision over the unions of the CNT, often threatening to use force to prevent deviationist trends when argument failed. To be sure, this domination—or at least attempted domination—by the FAI was not always openly acknowledged by the CNT and FAI and indeed was at times emphatically denied,[7] but it was frankly admitted after the Civil War by other leaders of the CNT.[8] It is true, however, as José Peirats, the libertarian historian, points out that while the FAI exerted considerable influence over the CNT—"watching closely for heresies of CNT leaders who were not FAI members"—the CNT in turn exerted a powerful influence over the FAI.[9] Nevertheless, his assertion that the FAI was "in reality" directed by the CNT runs counter to other testimony.[10]

Although views were divided in the cabinet as to the advisability, from the standpoint of foreign opinion, of allowing the libertarians to participate in the government,[11] the advantages of having them share responsibility for its measures were indubitable. "The entry of representatives of the CNT into the present Council of Ministers would certainly endow the directive organ of the nation with fresh energy and authority," said *Claridad*, Largo Caballero's mouthpiece, on 25 October 1936, "in view of the fact that a considerable segment of the working class, now absent from its deliberations, would feel bound by its measures and its authority." But would the Anarchosyndicalists wish to become ministers in the central government and join in the reconstruction of the state? This was questionable even though quite recently they had, in violation of venerable principles, joined the Catalan regional government.

Rootedly opposed to the state, which they regarded as "the supreme expression of authority of man over man, the most powerful instrument for the enslavement of the people,"[12] the libertarians were equally opposed to every government whether of the right or left, including the Soviet government that had destroyed the Anarchist movement in the first years of the Russian Revolution. "The entire dialectic of the officials of the Russian government," said *Tierra y Libertad* of Barcelona, the FAI organ, two weeks before the outbreak of the Civil War, "cannot erase one palpable, one evident fact regarding the Russian experiment: that the route of the State is the route of the counterrevolution. We have always maintained that this is so, and the study of the last nineteen years of Russian events has provided a most eloquent demonstration of the correctness of our view. In proportion as the Soviet State became stronger the revolution perished in the iron grip of decrees, bureaucrats, repressive machinery, and taxation. The revolution is a thing of the people, a popular creation; the counterrevolution is a thing of the State. It has always been so, and will always be so, whether in Russia, Spain, or China."[13]

After the Civil War, a former leading Spanish Communist wrote: "The evolution of the Soviet State, the fate of Anarchism under it and the downgrading of the Soviet trade unions into a mere bureaucratic appendage contributed significantly to the hardening of the apolitical and antistate views of the Spanish Anarchosyndicalist masses and especially of its leading cadres."[14]

Anarchist opposition to all forms of government found vehement expression in polemics during the latter half of the nineteenth century between Bakunin, the great Russian Anarchist, whose writings had a far-reaching influence on the Spanish working-class movement, and Karl Marx. In the words of Bakunin, the "people's government" proposed by Marx would simply be the rule of a privileged minority over the huge majority of the working masses. "But this minority, the Marxists argue, would consist of workers. Yes, I dare say, of *former* workers, but as soon as they become rulers and representatives of the people they would cease to be proletarians and would look down upon all workers from their political summit. They would no longer represent the people; they would represent only themselves. . . . He who doubts this must be absolutely ignorant of human nature."[15] And the Italian Anarchist Errico Malatesta, whose influence on the Spanish libertarian movement was appreciable, stated: "The primary concern of every government is to ensure its continuance in power irrespective of the men who form it. If they are bad, they want to remain in power in order to enrich themselves and to satisfy their lust for authority; and if they are honest and sincere they believe that it is their duty to remain in power for the benefit of the people. . . . The Anarchists . . . could never, even if they were strong enough, form a government without contradicting themselves and repudiating their entire doctrine; and, should they do so, it would be no different from any other government; perhaps it would be even worse."[16]

Writing in 1930, six years before the Revolution, the Spanish Anarchist leader, Diego Abad de Santillán, stressed that "the transition from statism to Anarchism demands a new man, a new type of individual, morally superior," and that it was the Anarchists' mission to create him. "We shall only know the Promised Land of Anarchism if we succeed in creating men worthy of living in it. And we cannot create them if we ourselves are not already spiritually on the way to demonstrating that bosses and tyrants are unnecessary and that we know how to live like free men deserving of liberty."[17]

The establishment of the democratic Spanish Republic in 1931, following the fall of the Monarchy and the Berenguer dictatorship, did not cause the libertarians to modify their basic tenets: "All governments are detestable, and it is our mission to destroy them."[18] "All governments without exception are equally bad, equally contemptible."[19] "All governments are destroyers of liberty."[20] "Under the Monarchy and the Dictatorship," wrote an Anarchist at the time of the Republican-Socialist coalition in 1933, "the workers suffered hunger and a thousand privations, and they continue to do so today under the Republic. Yesterday it was impossible to satisfy their most urgent needs, and today conditions are the same. We Anarchists say this without fear that any worker will contradict us, and we say more. We say that at all times, under whatever type of government, the workers have been tyrannized and have had to wage bitter struggles so that their right to live and enjoy themselves after exhausting hours of labor would be respected."[21] Just as the libertarians made no distinction between governments of the left and governments of the right, they made no distinction between individual politicians: "For us, all politicians are equal—in electoral demagogy, in filching the rights from the people, in their desire for fame, in their opportunism, in their ability to criticize when in the opposition, and in their cynicism when justifying themselves once in power."[22]

In contrast to other working-class organizations, the CNT and FAI shunned parliamentary activity.[23] They held no seats in central or local governments, refrained from nominating candidates for parliament, and, in the crucial November 1933 elections that brought the parties of the right to power, they had enjoined their members to abstain from voting. "Our revolution is not made in Parliament, but in the street," *Tierra y Libertad* had declared a month before the elections.[24] "We are not interested in changing governments," Isaac Puente, an influential Anarchosyndicalist, had written at the time. "What we want is to suppress them. . . . Whatever side wins, whether the right or the left, will be our enemy, our jailer, our executioner, and will have at its disposal the truncheons of the assault guards, the bullying of the secret police, the rifles of the civil guard, and the outlook of prison wardens. The working class will have just what it has today: somber jails, spies, hunger, welts, and lacerations."[25] And a few days before the elections, *Tierra y Libertad* declared:

Workers! Do not vote! The vote is a negation of your personality. Turn your backs on those who ask you to vote for them. They are your enemies. They hope to rise to power by taking advantage of your trustfulness. Urge your parents, your children, your brothers and sisters, your relatives, and your friends not to vote for any of the candidates. As far as we are concerned they are all the same; all politicians are our enemies whether they be Republicans, Monarchists, Communists, or Socialists. Honorio Maura is just as shameless as Rodrigo Soriano and [Herrán] Barriobero. Largo Caballero and Prieto are just as cynical and despicable as Balbotín and his associates. . . . We need neither a State nor a government. The bourgeoisie needs them in order to defend its interests. Our interests lie solely in our working conditions, and to defend them we require no parliament. No one should vote. . . . Do not be concerned whether the rightists or the leftists emerge triumphant from this farce. They are all diehard rightists. The only left-wing organization that is genuinely revolutionary is the CNT, and because this is so, it is not interested in Parliament, which is a filthy house of prostitution toying with the interests of the country and the people. Destroy the ballots! Destroy the ballot boxes! Crack the heads of the ballot supervisers as well as those of the candidates![26]

In the February 1936 elections, however, the CNT and FAI changed their posture; for, while opposing the Popular Front program—which they regarded as a "profoundly conservative document" out of harmony with "the revolutionary fever that Spain was sweating through her pores"[27]—they decided not to urge their members to abstain from voting, not only because the left coalition promised a broad amnesty for thousands of political prisoners in the event of victory,[28] but because a repetition of the abstentionist policy of 1933 would have meant as great a defeat for the libertarian movement as for the parties that adhered to the Popular Front coalition.[29] This change of posture ensured the victory of the Popular Front coalition,[30] but did not imply any fundamental change of doctrine. The Anarcho-syndicalists' impressive background of hostility to all governments and to all politicians makes it hard to conceive that they would join the cabinet of Largo Caballero, especially as, for many years before the outbreak of the Civil War, they had been at sword's point with the Socialist leader and his rival trade-union organization, the UGT.

19

The Anarchosyndicalists Enter
the Government

As leader of the Socialist UGT, Largo Caballero's relations with the Anarcho-syndicalists in the years before the Civil War had been marked by constant enmity. During the dictatorship, or Military Directory, as it was officially called, of General Primo de Rivera (1923–30), Caballero had served as labor delegate on Primo's council of state, partly with the object of protecting and strengthening his own organization and partly in the hope of gaining ground from the Anarchosyn-dicalists, whose unions had been proscribed by the dictator. During the preceding years, writes Gerald Brenan in his classic work, the CNT had been increasing its numbers very rapidly. "With the aid of its *sindicato único* and the prestige of its great strikes it had not only swept away all the recent gains of its rival in the Andalusian campo, but it had invaded the Socialist preserve of the center and north. Here it had seized half the builders' union in Madrid, which was one of the first strongholds of the UGT, had drawn off many of the railwaymen and planted itself firmly in the Asturias, in the port of Gijón and in the great iron foundries of Sama and La Felguera.

"To Caballero, who had the whole organization of the UGT in his hands, this was a serious matter: the fear of losing ground to the CNT was almost an obsession with him. As a Marxist he felt the supreme importance of the unifica-tion of the proletariat. He sensed therefore in the Dictatorship a good opportunity for making some progress in this direction. Possibly the UGT would be able to absorb the CNT altogether. This hope was not fulfilled."

By using the arbitration boards of the dictatorship as a starting point, Brenan continues, the UGT greatly increased its strength in the country districts, espe-cially in Estremadura, Granada, Aragon, and New Castile, but it failed com-pletely in Catalonia and made no progress among the industrial proletariat. "The Anarchosyndicalists preferred to enter the reactionary *sindicato libre*, which they knew would break up with the fall of the Dictatorship."[1]

The UGT's collaboration with the Military Directory gave rise to what Largo Caballero described as "a campaign of insults and calumnies such as has seldom been experienced."[2] The Socialists did what they could to combat the onslaught. "[Their] participation in the various organs of the state," said an official announcement published in *El Socialista* on 25 October 1924, "is subject to the decisions of the congresses and assemblies of the Socialist party and the UGT. It has not involved nor does it involve political collaboration or agreement with the government's work."[3] And, in a statement issued on 10 December 1924, which referred to Largo Caballero's appointment to the post of councillor of state, the national committee of the Socialist party unanimously approved his conduct as "absolutely correct" and "scrupulous," since he had simply "limited himself" to accepting an assignment offered by his organization.[4]

Although the UGT made no conspicuous inroads into the ranks of the CNT, there can be little doubt that the Military Directory benefited from the backing it received from the Socialist trade-union organization. This is apparent from a report, dated 29 January 1930, by the director general of security to General Dámaso Berenguer, Primo de Rivera's successor; "Socialist behavior during the past six years has been frankly supportive of the government. The labor legislation and especially the arbitration boards have been the main reason why the Socialist workers, in spite of the labor crisis, have resisted the alluring appeals and proposals [of the Anarchosyndicalists] and why their leaders have refused to take part in the political agitation and rebellious movements they have been urged to join." The general directorate of security, the report concluded, considered that the active intervention of the Socialists in political and social problems represented "no danger to public order at the present time" but rather a "guarantee" that order would be maintained.[5]

If it is true that Largo Caballero believed it possible for the UGT to absorb the CNT, it is no less true that at one time the CNT likewise hoped to monopolize the entire trade-union movement. At an Anarchosyndicalist congress held in 1919, a resolution was passed giving the workers of Spain a period of three months in which to enter the CNT, failing which they would be denounced as scabs.[6] But nothing came of this attempt to absorb the rival movement.

When, a few years later, Largo Caballero served on Primo's council of state and used the arbitration boards to increase the strength of the UGT, he became the object of the CNT's unsparing criticism. Nor did relations between them improve with the advent of the Republic in 1931, when Caballero became minister of labor; for he again used his powers to augment the influence of the UGT at the expense of the rival organization and clashed with the CNT over his defense of state interference in labor disputes. Brenan writes:

> The Minister of Labor, Largo Caballero, had introduced a series of laws regulating the rights of the working classes in their dealings with capital. The most important of these, the law of December 24, 1931, laid down the conditions which all contracts between workers and employers must fulfill in order to be valid. A special tribunal was set up to decide alleged infractions. Another law, the *Ley de Jurados Mixtos*, established tribunals at which labor disputes were to

be compulsorily settled. . . . Another law required eight days notice to be given of every strike. Apart from the fact that these laws ran contrary to the Anarchosyndicalist principles of negotiating directly with the employers and interfered with the practice of lightning strikes, it was clear that they represented an immense increase in the power of the State in industrial matters. A whole army of Government officials, mostly Socialists, made their appearance to enforce the new laws and saw to it that, whenever possible, they should be used to extend the influence of the UGT at the expense of the CNT. This had of course been the intention of those who drew them up. In fact the UGT was rapidly becoming an organ of the State itself and was using its new powers to reduce its rival. The Anarchosyndicalists could have no illusions as to what could happen to them if a purely Socialist Government should come into power.[7]

Unlike the UGT, the CNT rejected the labor courts, or *jurados mixtos*, of the Republic, not only because they increased the power of the state in disputes between labor and management, but because their purpose, in the opinion of a prominent CNT-FAI member, was "to castrate the Spanish proletariat in the interests of 'class conciliation.' "[8] Not conciliation, but continual and implacable war between labor and management was what the CNT wanted, and direct action was its method: violent strikes, sabotage, and boycott.[9] This was not simply a means of improving the standard of living of the workers; above all, it was a method of agitation, of stimulating and keeping alive a spirit of revolt in preparation for the day of insurrection. "Direct action," declared the International Workingmen's Association (AIT) with which the CNT was affiliated, "finds its highest expression in the general strike, which should be a prelude to the social revolution."[10] Famed for their frequent uprisings in the years before the military rebellion, the Anarchosyndicalists were the classic force of Spanish insurrection. It mattered little whether these uprisings, invariably confined to a few localities, failed for lack of support elsewhere; what was important was that they should rouse the revolutionary temper of the working class. Today they might fail, but tomorrow they would be victorious. "If yesterday ten villages revolted," wrote Isaac Puente, "one thousand villages must rise tomorrow, even if we have to fill the holds of a hundred [prison] ships like the *Buenos Aires*. Defeat is not always failure. The future does not always belong to those who triumph. We never play our last card."[11]

The sharp divergence between the CNT and UGT was not in any way lessened by Largo Caballero's leftward swerve in 1933, for the Anarchosyndicalists continued to regard him with unrelenting animosity. Nor did his advocacy of the dictatorship of the proletariat, through the instrumentality of the Socialist party and of the unification of the CNT and UGT[12] a few months before the outbreak of the Civil War, temper this animosity; for they held that Largo Caballero was a "dictator in embryo," who favored "the absolute hegemony of the Socialist party on the morrow of the triumphant insurrection of the working class,"[13] and that under the cover of unification his "crooked aim" was to absorb the CNT in localities where the UGT was stronger.[14] No practical discussions to bring about the fusion ever took place, and the somewhat more cautious attitude adopted by the leadership of the UGT toward the developing strike movement, just before the military insurrection,[15] tended to increase still further the hostility of the CNT, which was sweeping the rank and file of the UGT along with it in several places. "The mass of workers were desperate," wrote an acute observer, "and were prepared to follow the most ardent leaders."[16] "In Madrid," *El Sol* reported, "we are witnessing the amazing spectacle of the CNT . . . declaring general strikes, continually organizing partial strikes, and inspiring intransigent and rigid attitudes that cause the government to despair."[17]

Then came the Civil War and the Revolution, creating fresh points of friction between the two trade-union federations.[18]

Yet, in spite of this discord, in spite of the traditional antigovernment stand of the Anarchosyndicalists and of their distrust of him personally, Largo Caballero tried, when forming his cabinet at the beginning of September 1936, to secure their participation in the belief, as his organ *Claridad* later put it, that they "would feel themselves bound by its measures and its authority."[19] But much as he needed them to share the responsibilities of office in order to forestall any criticism of his government's decrees, he offered them only a single seat without portfolio,[20] a meager reward for what would have entailed a flagrant breach of principle. That offer, commented the Madrid Anarchosyndicalist organ, *CNT*, some weeks later, was "neither generous nor enticing" and was "absolutely disproportionate to the strength and influence of the CNT in the country."[21]

To be sure, the CNT, if smaller than the UGT in Madrid province, yielded nothing to it in the majority of provinces within the left zone, such as Albacete, Guadalajara, Jaen, and Toledo (to mention but a few where the two federations had approximately the same number of adherents), and, in addition to being more powerful in the regions of Aragon, Catalonia, and Valencia, had, in all probability, more members than its Socialist rival in the total area controlled by the left-wing forces.[22]

Nevertheless, the national committee of the CNT accepted Largo Caballero's offer, subject, however, to ratification by the regional federations.[23] A national plenum of regional federations met on 3 September, but the delegates rejected the offer.[24] Two days later, after Caballero had already formed his cabinet, *CNT* in Madrid declared: "Perhaps many wonder how it is that the CNT, one of the principal forces preparing for the victory of the people at the front and in the rear . . . does not form part of this government. Undoubtedly, if the CNT were inspired by political ideas, the number of its seats in this government would have to be at least as large as that of the UGT and the Socialists." In other words, the CNT would have required the same number of seats as both the Largo Caballero faction of the Socialist party, which the paper identified with the UGT because of its control of the trade-union executive, and the Prieto faction, which controlled the party executive. "However," the article continued, "the CNT once again affirms its unshakable adhesion to its antiauthoritarian postulates and believes that the libertarian transformation of society can take place only as a result of the abolition of the State and the control of the economy by the working class."[25]

Although the delegates to the CNT national plenum rejected Largo Caballero's offer of a single seat—some of them even opposing collaboration with the Socialist leader altogether—they adopted, after "long and tumultuous debates," a compromise resolution accepting government participation in principle and providing for the restructuring of the government and the state.[26]

According to the resolution, "auxiliary commissions" were to be set up in each ministry comprising two representatives of the CNT, two of the UGT, two of the Popular Front parties, and one government delegate.[27] This project would have spared the CNT the embarrassment of direct participation in the cabinet, but would nonetheless have given it representation in every branch of government. According to Lorenzo, its rejection by Caballero was hardly surprising, for the commissions would have been "veritable organs of power," and the ministers would have been reduced to "simple executors" of the will of the two trade-union federations.[28]

In his unpublished memoirs, Largo Caballero writes: "In order to enter the government, [the Anarchosyndicalists] went so far as to try to impose a state structure based on extragovernmental bodies, which, in effect, would have caused the government, the President of the Republic and the parliament—in other words, the Republican state—to disappear. They wanted the Prime Minister [i.e., Largo Caballero] to become president of this Anarchosyndicalist State. He replied that he had accepted power in order to do everything possible to win the war and save the Republic, but not to betray it."[29] His attitude undoubtedly convinced the Anarchosyndicalist leaders of the futility of their aspirations.

Although the libertarian movement could not join the cabinet without striking at the very roots of official doctrine, some of its leaders were loath to leave the affairs of government entirely in the hands of rival organizations. Among the most resolute of these advocates of intervention in the government was the secretary of the national committee of the CNT, Horacio M. Prieto, a pragmatic libertarian, who, viewing as "unrealistic" the resolution of 3 September and feeling that "time was pressing ruthlessly," demanded that the CNT enter the government "with several ministers openly and without shame."[30] The CNT, he observed some years later, "should not have declined [to enter the government] in view of the important role we were playing in the war . . . , but fear of violating the ideological principles of the movement, respect for its ideas, for its tenets, and fear of shouldering this responsibility acted as a brake on initiative with the result that indecision prevailed."[31]

Because of this indecision, because of the fear of violating doctrinal scruples, but feeling that they could not leave the central government entirely in the hands of rival organizations, the delegates of the regional committees of the CNT tried a novel approach. At a plenary assembly held on 15 September they decided that the government should be replaced by a national council of defense composed of five members of their own organization, five of the UGT, and four members of the Republican parties.[32] The national council of defense, of course, would have been a government in everything but name, although the title would have been less offensive to the libertarian movement.

The Anarchosyndicalists certainly wanted to enter the government, wrote one libertarian after the war, "but they demanded that it should change its name to national council of defense. The purpose of this purely nominal change was to reconcile their fervent desire to enter the government with their antistate doctrine. What childishness! A movement that had cured itself of all prejudices and had always scoffed at mere appearances tried to conceal its abjuration of fundamental principles by changing a name. . . . This behavior is as childish as that of an unfortunate woman, who, having entered a house of ill fame and wishing to preserve a veneer of morality, asks to be called a hetera instead of a whore."[33]

As César M. Lorenzo, the son of Horacio M. Prieto, the secretary of the CNT national committee, observes: "The CNT had entered the Catalan government and fervently wished to enter the Basque government. Then why differentiate between a regional and a national government? . . . A municipal councillor, a judge, or a policeman was just as much an element, a part of the State, as a minister. Exercising authority in a village was neither more nor less antianarchist than exercising it in a nation. A vast territory can be administered very democratically, whereas a locality can be subjected to tyranny."[34]

Foreign Anarchists, who later criticized the Spanish libertarians for entering the government,[35] had previously approved of the idea of a national council of defense. "It is a curious thing," wrote Helmut Ruediger, representative in Spain of the International Workingmen's Association, with which the CNT was affiliated, and director of the German-language papers, *CNT-FAI-AIT Informationsdienst* and *Soziale Revolution*, both published in Barcelona, "that nearly all the dissenting comrades [abroad] accepted the program providing for the direction of the antifascist movement by a national council of defense. . . . Let us be frank. *This was also a program for the exercise of power*, the only difference being that the *name* was a little more pleasant to our Anarchist comrades in other countries."[36]

In the hope of avoiding any resistance to the proposed council on the part of Communists, Socialists, and Republicans because of possible repercussions in moderate circles abroad, the delegates of the CNT regional committees to the plenary assembly held on 15 September proposed that Manuel Azaña continue as president of the Republic.[37] "Our position abroad," declared *Solidaridad Obrera*, the leading newspaper of the CNT, "cannot deteriorate as a result of the new structure we propose; for it must be borne in mind that the decorative figures that characterize a petty-bourgeois regime would be retained so as not to frighten foreign capitalists."[38]

Nevertheless, the CNT's campaign in favor of a national council of defense elicited no support from any of the parties in the government and, on 28 September, at another plenary assembly of the regional committees of the CNT, the national committee secretary, Horacio Prieto, assailed the project as a waste of time since it was unacceptable to the political parties and, in his opinion, "evidenced a total lack of realism, taking into account foreign powers and the international aspect of the war." He hammered away at his arguments in favor of government participation "pure and simple," demanded that the delegates "put an end to so many scruples, moral and political prejudices, so many denials of reality, and so much semantic fuss," pleading that "it was necessary to act quickly, that every day that passed aggravated the position of the CNT."[39]

Although shaken by Prieto's words, the delegates still clung to their proposed solution. For several weeks the CNT waged a ceaseless campaign in favor of the national council of defense,[40] but its efforts were unavailing. Largo Caballero was adamant in his opposition. His attitude, which was identical with that of the Communists and Republicans,[41] found expression in the following passage taken from an editorial in his mouthpiece, *Claridad*: "A radical transformation of the organs of the State would occasion at the present time a loss of continuity, which would be fatal to us. Furthermore, we are waging a battle in Geneva [at the League of Nations], which, in the event of victory, could have far-reaching consequences for us because the scales would be tipped in our favor in view of the fact that we [would] obtain the material elements indispensable for winning the war. What would be the repercussions of the leap outside the bounds of the Constitution peremptorily demanded by the comrades of the CNT? We fear that it would put things just where our enemies want them."[42] A month later, another editorial in *Claridad* declared: "Quite as important as attending to the purely military needs of the Civil War—perhaps even more so—is to give to the institutions of the regime a form that will awaken the least suspicion in foreign countries."[43] That these editorials reflected the personal views of Largo Caballero was confirmed by Mariano Cardona Rosell, who became a member of the national committee of the CNT at the end of September 1936 and was one of the members of that body who conducted the negotiations with the premier.[44]

"Look, if we were to agree to what you propose," Largo Caballero allegedly told a group of CNT leaders, "we would, in effect, be putting ourselves on the same level as the Junta de Burgos [the rebel junta]. We would lose our trump card: the existence of the legal government of the Republic, proclaimed and legitimized by the people in various elections. Forget your priestly scruples and appoint your representatives in the government and I promise you that we shall do everything possible to help the collectives and to see that there is an equitable distribution of arms, so that the Communists, who are your great fear, do not begin to monopolize everything with the blackmail of Russian aid."[45]

Faced by Largo Caballero's unbending attitude and by opposition from other quarters, Horacio Prieto decided to "put an end to the last remnants of opposition" within the CNT and convoked a plenary session of the regional federations for 18 October. This time his arguments prevailed. The plenum accorded him full powers to conduct negotiations "in his own way" in order to bring the CNT into the government. "I was convinced," he wrote after the war, "of the necessity of collaboration, and I smothered my own ideological and conscientious scruples."[46]

Explaining the libertarian movement's new line, *CNT* declared: "We are taking into consideration the scruples that the members of the government may have concerning the international situation, . . . and for this reason the CNT is ready to make the maximum concession compatible with its antiauthoritarian spirit: that of entering the government. This does not imply renouncing its intention of fully realizing its ideals in the future; it simply means that . . . in order to win the war and to save our people and the world, it is ready to collaborate with anyone in a directive organ, whether this organ be called a council or a government."[47] In their negotiations with Caballero, the CNT representatives asked for five ministries, including war and finance, but he rejected their demand.[48] Finally, on 3 November, they accepted four: justice, industry, commerce, and health, none of which, however, was vital; moreover, the portfolios of industry and commerce had previously been held by a single minister.

The composition of the reorganized government was as follows:

Francisco Largo Caballero	Socialist	Prime Minister and War
Julio Alvarez del Vayo	Socialist	Foreign Affairs
Angel Galarza	Socialist	Interior
Anastasio de Gracia	Socialist	Labor
Juan Negrín	Socialist	Finance
Indalecio Prieto	Socialist	Navy and Air
Jesús Hernández	Communist	Education and Fine Arts
Vicente Uribe	Communist	Agriculture
Juan García Oliver	CNT	Justice
Juan López	CNT	Commerce
Federica Montseny	CNT	Health and Public Assistance
Juan Peiró	CNT	Industry
Carlos Esplá	Left Republican	Propaganda
José Giral	Left Republican	Minister without portfolio
Julio Just	Left Republican	Public Works
Bernardo Giner de los Ríos	Republican Union	Communications
Jaime Aiguadé	Left Republican party of Catalonia	Minister without portfolio
Manuel de Irujo	Basque Nationalist	Minister without portfolio[49]

It was not without foreboding that the CNT representatives crossed the unfamiliar threshold of ministerial responsibility. Indeed, according to one libertarian writer, they knew, when they took possession of their departments, that they could not influence the Revolution.[50] To be sure, Largo Caballero's decision to give the CNT four portfolios instead of one was an act neither of sympathy nor of generosity. There is evidence that he was motivated partly by his desire to invest his government with greater authority[51] at a time when he was planning to transfer his government to Valencia in the belief that at any moment Franco's forces might seize the capital. "[The] moment had arrived," he wrote later, "to leave the capital. The enemy had concentrated large forces and might make a surprise attack any night and enter Madrid."[52] He also feared, whether with grounds or not, that if the cabinet should leave Madrid without first admitting representatives of the libertarian movement, the CNT and FAI might set up an independent administration. "In Madrid's critical situation," writes Alvarez del Vayo, "had the Anarchists not been allowed to share the government's responsibility, it is more than likely that they would have seized the opportunity afforded by the government's departure for Valencia to try to set up a local junta of their own. This would have only produced confusion and disaster throughout the loyal territory."[53]

Whether warranted or not, this concern does not appear to have been an issue with President Azaña who, after his flight from Madrid two weeks earlier, was now installed in Barcelona with his presidential guard, conveniently close to the French border. Still savoring his presidential powers that, in the final analysis, he now derived not from the rule of law, as embodied in the Constitution, but from his tenuous role as constitutional cover for the Revolution, he refused at first to sanction the decrees appointing the libertarian ministers. He did not see, writes Largo Caballero, the effect that the revision of Spanish Anarchism would have upon the future. "From terrorism and direct action, it had moved to collaboration and to sharing the responsibilities of power. . . . It was a unique event in the world and would not be sterile. I told him that if he did not sign the decrees I would resign. He signed them, although with reservations."[54]

Azaña, records Alvarez del Vayo, raised serious objections to the appointment of two of the four candidates proposed for the ministerial posts—Federica Montseny and Juan García Oliver, both members of the FAI. "In different circumstances the natural course would have been to yield to the will of the President or to give him time to change his mind. But in those dark days through which Madrid was passing, any indecision would have been fatal. Already the prospective ministers, two of whom had come expressly from Barcelona, had begun to suspect that their entry into the government was not well considered in high places, and were talking about returning to Catalonia and breaking off relations between the CNT and the government. Twice I had to leave the Prime Minister's study in order to quiet and reassure them. A telephone conversation between the President of the Republic and the Prime Minister, not lacking in a certain dramatic quality, put an end to an embarrassing situation. Although we were unable to hear his voice, the rest of us could almost feel the exasperation of Señor Azaña coming over the wires. Within a few moments, however, Señor Largo Caballero was given authorization to send to the official gazette the notice of the appointment of the four CNT members, duly sanctioned by the President."[55]

Mindful of posterity, Azaña wrote in his memoirs some six months later: "Not only against my judgment, but against my most angry protest, was the cabinet reorganization of November incorporating the CNT and the Anarchists into the government—which the Republicans themselves considered inevitable and useful—forced upon me."[56]

In connection with this episode, the then mayor of Barcelona, Carlos Pi Sunyer, a member of the Catalan Esquerra and confidant of Azaña, relates in his memoirs that the president telephoned him one evening, saying that he wished to speak to him. "I went there immediately. I found him shattered, his morale in ruins. Even his intelligence, so brilliant, appeared dull, half-extinguished. He told me he wanted to go away, to leave Spain, to resign the presidency of the Republic. . . . What had happened? Largo Caballero had telephoned him to say that he was going to form a government with four CNT ministers. Azaña had objected, but, in spite of his objection, the decrees appointing them had appeared under his name in the official gazette. But he did not wish to ratify the appointments. . . . We spoke for a long time. When, finally, I left him, very late, he seemed to have resigned himself to remaining in the office to which destiny had tied him."[57]

Shortly after the names of the CNT ministers appeared in the *Gaceta de Madrid* of 5 November, Largo Caballero raised the question of transferring the seat of government to Valencia. Indalecio Prieto, the moderate Socialist and navy and air minister, who according to one of his own supporters was convinced like Largo Caballero that within three to six days the enemy would seize Madrid,[58] testifies: "Francisco Largo Caballero assembled his ministers in order to propose that the government should leave Madrid . . . without a moment's delay. Weeks before I had proposed that the government should leave, but with publicity. . . . I didn't want the transfer to take place at the last moment unexpectedly, which would give the impression of a flight. It was advisable, I felt, that the people of Madrid should be psychologically prepared so that they would find the measure justifiable and would bid us farewell with affection rather than vilify us as fugitives if we did not advise them in advance. But the premier disregarded my proposal.

"The subsequent debate on his proposal was most dramatic. The four members of the National Confederation of Labor who had just joined the government considered that they were victims of a deception. Believing that they had been made ministers solely in order to implicate them in this grave decision, they refused to approve it."[59]

In his unpublished memoirs, Largo Caballero writes: "The CNT ministers . . . at first maintained that none of the ministers should leave even if the enemy should capture all of them. 'It would be neither fair nor loyal,' they said, 'if the

government were to save itself and the rest of the populace were to be sacrificed.'
. . . They insinuated that it would be useless to try to leave, because the people
would prevent them. This was regarded as a veiled threat."[60]

Indalecio Prieto continues:

> After considerable discussion, [the CNT ministers] suggested that we should all
> leave except the four who would remain in Madrid. I joined in the debate, vigor-
> ously opposing that formula. "Either we all leave," I said, "or no one leaves. It
> would be unacceptable if some were to be branded as cowards and others hailed
> as heroes. Either we are all cowards or all heroes. . . ."
>
> The CNT ministers requested permission to discuss the matter among them-
> selves and left the conference room. . . . After considerable delay they returned
> to say that they would approve the proposal. Largo Caballero announced that the
> new residence would be Valencia and not Barcelona as had been expected, where
> the president of the Republic had moved. He demanded secrecy of everyone and
> stated that anyone could leave whenever he wished. I could count on two passen-
> ger planes that were to undertake the flight at dawn and were capable of carrying
> all those ministers who wished to fly. No one accepted my invitation at the time.
> Some believed it was too long to wait.
>
> No sooner had the cabinet meeting ended [on 6 November] than Largo Ca-
> ballero took to the highway and passed through the town of Tarancón that lay
> across the direct route to Valencia. Tarancón was occupied by the Rosal Column,
> composed of Anarchists and convicts from the San Miguel de los Reyes Peniten-
> tiary in Valencia, who had been freed at the outset of the rebellion. When news
> of the government's agreement reached Colonel Rosal he decided that no one
> should proceed to [Valencia]. Julio Alvarez del Vayo, the foreign minister, was
> the object of gross abuse.[61] Juan Peiró and Juan López, the CNT ministers, were
> turned back. They presented themselves at my house in the middle of the night,
> and I took them with me by plane.[62]

Also turned back was Pedro Rico, the rotund mayor of Madrid. Upon his
return to Madrid, writes Indalecio Prieto, instead of rejoining the city council, he
took refuge in the Mexican embassy. "His stay in the embassy, where all the
refugees with the exception of himself were rightists, was most disturbing to
Pedro Rico. He could not return to the City Hall, where his attempt to flee had
been condemned. Fearing reprisals, he did not dare sleep at home, even less walk
the streets. . . . [The] prospect of again confronting the militiamen at Tarancón
terrified him. I suggested that he should travel in the trunk of an automobile as I
and several Socialists had done in 1934 when we had [escaped] to France. . . . It
required the help of God to stuff him into the trunk. His fatness, greater than
mine, and his awkwardness made it very difficult to pack him in. This provided
an enjoyable spectacle to all those Franco supporters who witnessed the operation
in the patio of the Mexican embassy."[63]

Indalecio Prieto's account of the government's furtive departure from Madrid
is fully confirmed in all essentials by the famous Anarchist militia leader,

Cipriano Mera, later commander of the Fourteenth Division and the Fourth Army Corps, who hastened to Tarancón to protest the government's flight. There he found ministers, undersecretaries, and other government officials, as well as top military men, all detained by the Rosal Column. Horacio M. Prieto, the secretary of the CNT national committee, soon arrived, also on his way to Valencia with the other members. He defended the committee's departure on the grounds that it had to be close to the government "in order to be fully informed of events and to determine its policy accordingly"; Mera replied that the national committee of the CNT should not abandon Madrid, especially when everyone was fleeing. "Its presence in Madrid," he argued, "can be of great moral value to the people and can help to change the situation in our favor. . . . The departure of the government . . . is a shameful flight, because hardly eight hours ago it told the people of Madrid that it would share its fate."

But the decision to leave Madrid had been made, and Mera, declaring that he would organize a thousand men to defend the capital—"to show these people that, while they flee, we shall defend what they have abandoned"—returned to Madrid without shaking the hand of the national secretary "because I regarded him as a weakling and unworthy of the important post he held in a revolutionary organization such as ours."[64]

The decision of the Anarchosyndicalist ministers to leave Madrid had immediate reverberations in the libertarian movement. When they arrived in Madrid to take up their posts, writes César M. Lorenzo, the CNT leaders asked his father, Horacio M. Prieto, to instruct them how to act as ministers. Prieto replied that they had had sufficient experience as militants to know what to do in the interests of the CNT. A libertarian, even a national secretary, he told them, ought not to give orders to other libertarians or subject them to any special kind of discipline. The CNT was not the Communist party. They should act according to their good conscience. The latitude Prieto gave them, Lorenzo adds, was soon to turn against him, for when the question of the government's transfer to Valencia was debated, the ministers agreed without consulting the national committee. "Horacio Prieto could not . . . demand the resignation of the four ministers . . . and thus provoke a government crisis. The departure of the government for Valencia, which entailed the departure of the national committee,[65] provoked the anger of the militants of the CNT. They held Horacio Prieto responsible, accusing him of cowardice and calling him a 'liquidator.' " As a result, on 18 November, Horacio Prieto, at a special national plenum, tendered his "irrevocable resignation" as secretary of the national committee[66] and was succeeded by Mariano R. Vázquez, the secretary of the powerful regional committee of Catalonia.

But more important than the CNT ministers' departure from Madrid and the resignation of Horacio Prieto was the profound stir created in the libertarian movement by the decision of its leaders to enter the central government. Not only did this decision represent a complete negation of the basic tenets of Anarchism, shaking the whole structure of libertarian theory to the core, but, in violation of democratic principle, it had been taken without consulting the rank and file.[67]

From the day the cabinet was reorganized, the leading Anarchosyndicalist newspaper, *Solidaridad Obrera*, in an attempt to overcome the scruples of the purists, sought to justify the decision by minimizing the divergence between theory and practice.

"The entry of the CNT into the central government is one of the most important events in the political history of our country. Both as a matter of principle and by conviction, the CNT has been antistatist and an enemy of every form of government.

"But circumstances . . . have transformed the nature of the Spanish government and the Spanish State.

"At the present time, the government, as the instrument that controls the organs of the State, has ceased to be a force of oppression against the working class, just as the State no longer represents a body that divides society into classes. And both will oppress the people even less now that members of the CNT have intervened."[68]

In subsequent months, as the friction between the "collaborationist" and "abstentionist" tendencies in the libertarian movement increased, some supporters of government collaboration argued that the entry of the CNT into the cabinet had marked no recantation of Anarchist ideals and tactics,[69] while others frankly acknowledged the violation of doctrine and contended that it should yield to reality. "[The] philosophicosocial conceptions of Anarchism are excellent, wonderful, in theory," wrote Manuel Mascarell, a member of the national committee of the CNT, "but they are impractical when confronted with the tragic reality of a war like ours. The conduct of Anarchists and Anarchosyndicalists should be inspired by and should be in harmony with our Anarchist ideology, but when circumstances, when particular events demand a modification of tactics, Anarchists should not confine themselves to the limited framework of what, theoretically, in normal times, was held to be their line of action, because to cling obstinately to principles, to follow a rigid line without departing one iota from what is laid down in Anarchist textbooks and declarations is the most comfortable attitude one can adopt in order to justify doing nothing or risking nothing."[70]

As for the opponents of government collaboration, one libertarian historian writes: "I believe . . . that there was tacit consent on the part of many militants, enemies of collaboration, who uttered pious cries of wrath, but who allowed the others to have their way."[71]

Whatever the varied reactions within the libertarian movement, the CNT-FAI leaders had not entered the government without an inner struggle with conscience and principle. Not all of them admitted this conflict, but the confession of Federica Montseny, the minister of health and a member of the peninsular committee of the FAI—who, to use her own colorful language, had sucked Anarchist milk at her mother's breast[72]—gave unerring expression to the doubts and misgivings that had assailed a large segment of the libertarian movement. At a meeting of the CNT after she had ceased to belong to the cabinet she declared:

As the daughter of veteran Anarchists,[73] as the descendant, I might say, of a whole dynasty of antiauthoritarians, with an achievement, with a record, with a life of struggle in continual defense of the ideas I inherited from my parents, I regarded my entry into the government, my acceptance of the post to which the CNT assigned me, as having more significance than the mere appointment of a minister. Other parties, other organizations, other sectors cannot appreciate the struggle inside the movement and in the very consciences of its members, both then and now, as a result of the CNT's participation in the government. They cannot appreciate it, but the people can, and if they cannot then they should be informed. They should be told that for us—who had fought incessantly against the State, who had always affirmed that through the State nothing at all could be achieved, that the words "government" and "authority" signified the negation of every possibility of freedom for men and for nations—our intervention in the government as an organization and as individuals signified either an act of historical audacity of fundamental importance, or a rectification of a whole work, of a whole past, in the field of theory and tactics.

We do not know what it signified. We only know that we were caught in a dilemma. . . .

When I was appointed by the CNT to represent it in the government, I was in the Regional Committee of Catalonia; I had lived through the whole epic from 19 July to November without a stain. . . .

What inhibitions, what doubts, what anguish I had personally to overcome in order to accept that post! For others it could have meant their goal, the satisfaction of their inordinate ambitions. But for me it implied a break with my life's work, with a whole past linked to the ideals of my parents. It meant a tremendous effort, an effort made at the cost of many tears. But I accepted the post. I accepted it, conquering myself. I accepted it, ready to clear myself of responsibility before my own eyes for what I considered to be a rupture with everything I had been, on condition that I would always remain loyal, upright, honest, always faithful to the ideals of my parents and of my whole life. And that is how I entered the government.[74]

In a letter to me after the war, Severino Campos, who was secretary of the Catalan regional committee of the FAI and was present at the meeting of CNT-FAI leaders at which the entry of the CNT into the government was decided upon, said that Federica Montseny at first vigorously opposed her appointment as one of the four ministers, but finally yielded to pressure. The other appointees, he said, were not present at the meeting.[75] After the war, Montseny wrote to me stating that the four persons designated to represent the CNT in the government were selected by Horacio Prieto, secretary of the national committee. Juan Peiró and Juan López, she pointed out, represented the right wing and Juan García Oliver and herself the left. "[Horacio Prieto]," she added, "hoped that I would check the opposition of the puritans."[76]

In an article written several years after the war, Montseny affirmed that she personally "never had any illusions" as to the possibility of achieving anything in the government. "I knew, we all knew," she averred, "that in spite of the fact that the government was not at that time a real government, that power was in the street, in the hands of the combatants and producers, [governmental] *power would once again be coordinated and consolidated* and, what is worse, with our complicity and our help, and that it would ruin many of us morally."[77]

Such a complete departure by the CNT and FAI from their antigovernment creed could have been determined only by very powerful motives. Of these motives, the following given by leading members of the CNT were undoubtedly among the most important:

"We were compelled by circumstances," Montseny herself declared shortly after entering the cabinet, "to join the government of the Republic in order to avoid the fate of Anarchist movements in other countries that, through lack of foresight, resolution, and mental agility, were dislodged from the Revolution and saw other parties take control of it."[78]

"At that time," she affirmed at a later date, "we only saw the reality of the situation created for us: the Communists in the government and ourselves outside, the manifold possibilities, and all our conquests endangered."[79]

"Were we going to entrust the interests of the workers . . . exclusively to the political parties?" asked Juan López, CNT minister of commerce. "On no account!"[80]

"The CNT," wrote Manuel Villar, director of *Fragua Social*, the CNT newspaper in Valencia, "was compelled to participate in the government for the specific purpose of . . . preventing an attack on the conquests of the workers and peasants . . . , of preventing the war from being conducted in a sectarian manner and the army from being transformed into an instrument of a single party, of eliminating the danger of dictatorship, and of preventing totalitarian tendencies in every aspect of our economic and social life."[81]

Another reason was given by García Oliver, CNT-FAI minister of justice. To secure military aid from the "international bourgeoisie," he asserted, after he had left the cabinet, it was necessary "to give the impression that not the revolutionary committees were in control but rather the legal government."[82]

And, finally, according to Juan López, the minister of commerce, one of the CNT's fundamental objectives in entering the government was to regulate the political life of Spain by giving legal validity to the revolutionary committees that had sprung up in the first months of the Civil War.[83]

But the diverse explanations given by representatives of the libertarian movement as the rationale of the CNT's entry into the government would be incomplete if they did not include those adduced by Horacio M. Prieto, the principal advocate of collaboration. His son, César M. Lorenzo, writes:

> The reasons that made the participation of the CNT in the central government necessary were presented by Horacio Prieto in numerous speeches, lectures, de-

bates, and discussions. They can be summarized as follows: "The libertarians were not equipped psychologically or materially to impose their will in the Republican zone, even less to win the war against fascism. Even in the most unlikely event that they were to triumph over the fascists and the other antifascists, the Revolution would be suppressed by the economic blockade and armed intervention of foreign powers. Furthermore, the Republican government was leading the loyalists to disaster through its political blindness and military incapacity and was also devoting its efforts to combating the working class, its militia, and its revolutionary work. Hence, it was necessary, within the framework of an advanced democratic state, to save the gains of socialization, to centralize the conduct of [military] operations, and neutralize the pressure of the great powers. Finally, the de facto politicalization of the libertarians from the first days of the Civil War, through their participation in all local or regional organs of administration, and the desire of the popular masses to see created a true union of antifascists, had to be consummated in the sharing of supreme responsibility."[84]

20

Against the Revolutionary Committees

While the Anarchosyndicalist leaders fostered the hope that the libertarian movement's participation in the cabinet would enable it more successfully to defend its revolutionary conquests, the Communist leaders, on the other hand, their eyes turned toward the Western democracies, hoped that this participation, by enhancing the government's authority among the rank and file of the CNT and FAI, would facilitate the reconstruction of the shattered machinery of state, and would enable them, under cover of a democratic superstructure, to gather into their hands all the elements of state power appropriated by the revolutionary committees at the outbreak of the Civil War. They further hoped that the CNT's entry into the government would hasten the supplanting of these committees—which, in addition to assuming powers of state, had superseded the normal functions of the municipalities and of other local governing bodies—by regular organs of administration that had either been thrust into the shade or had ceased to function from the first day of the Revolution.

This policy represented a radical change for the Communists, who, at the time of the left-wing rising in Asturias in 1934, had called for the substitution of the Republican state by revolutionary organs of power.[1] It also contrasted with the policy pursued by the Russian Bolsheviks in 1917; for whereas the latter had directed their efforts during the first months of the Revolution to supplanting the old governing bodies by the Soviets, in the Spanish Revolution the Communists strove to replace the revolutionary committees by regular organs of administration. "An epidemic of exclusivist committees of the most varied shades and performing the most unexpected functions has broken out," complained the Communist organ, *Mundo Obrero*, early in the war. "We declare that each and every one of us should be interested in the defense of the democratic Republic, and for this reason all bodies should reflect accurately the composition of the Largo [Caballero] government as well as the aims that inspire it, aims we have all undertaken to support and defend. This is a prerequisite for winning the war, imposed by numerous factors, both of a national and international character, and to which we must adapt our step."[2]

The Communist view—shared by Socialists and Republicans—was that the committees, which in most cases were dominated by the more radical members of the CNT and UGT and whose authority was practically unlimited in their respective localities, should give way to regular organs of administration, in which all the parties forming the government would be represented and whose powers would be circumscribed by the laws of the state. The Anarchosyndicalists contended that these revolutionary bodies should, on the contrary, become the foundation stones of the new society. "The committees," declared *CNT*, the principal libertarian newspaper in Madrid, "are organs created by the people to oppose the fascist insurrection. . . . Without these committees, which replaced the municipal and provincial administrations as well as many other organs of bourgeois democracy, it would have been impossible to resist fascism. They are revolutionary committees that the people created in order to make the Revolution. . . . By this we do not mean to say that Spain should be split up by the work of hundreds of scattered committees. We want the reconstruction of Spanish society . . . to be based on the organs that have sprung up from the people, and we should like them to work in agreement with one another. Our prime motive in defending them is to prevent the resurgence of those bourgeois organs and norms that were shipwrecked so pitifully on 19 July."[3]

Inside the cabinet, however, the CNT-FAI ministers yielded step by step to their opponents, who applied constant pressure to end the power of the committees on the ground of placating foreign opinion and enhancing the government's prospects of securing arms from the Western powers. Writes Federica Montseny, one of the four Anarchosyndicalists in the cabinet: "The arguments of the Communists, Socialists, and Republicans were always the same: It was essential to give an appearance of legality to the Spanish Republic, to calm the fears of the British, French, and Americans. As a consequence, the State recovered the positions it had lost, while we revolutionaries, who formed part of the State, helped it to do so. That was why we were brought into the government. Although we did not enter it with that intention, we were in it, and therefore had no alternative but to remain imprisoned in the vicious circle. But I can state positively that, although we lost in the end, we defended our ground inch by inch and never voted for anything that curbed the conquests of the Revolution without first being authorized by the national committee of the CNT, on which there was a permanent representative of the FAI."[4]

In February 1937, Juan Peiró, CNT minister of industry, acknowledged his fear that Britain and France would not reverse their stand on the matter of supplying arms to the government but stated that victory depended on these two powers, "on condition that we prosecute the war and not the Revolution." This, he added, did not imply renouncing the Revolution. "The road to follow is this: We must wage the war, and, while waging it, limit ourselves to preparing for the Revolution by means of a conscientious and discreet control of the factories, for this is equivalent to taking up revolutionary positions and equipping ourselves in a practical way for the final assault on capitalist society after the end of the war."[5] A prominent member of the left wing of the libertarian movement wrote: "It was feared that we would lack the 'help' of the 'democratic' nations, if they were to see us driving ahead with the Revolution, and with this argument the politicians succeeded in causing the promoters of the movement for liberty in Spain to hesitate."[6]

As a result, the government, with the acquiescence of the CNT members, approved decrees that, far from giving legal validity to the committees as the CNT had hoped on entering the cabinet,[7] provided for their dissolution and replacement by regular provincial and municipal councils, in which all the parties adhering to the Popular Front as well as the trade-union organizations were to be represented.[8] In addition, a decree was published providing for the suppression of all controls on highways and at the entrance to villages set up by local committees and by parties or trade-union organizations and for the taking over of their functions by the police forces under the ministry of the interior.[9] All of these measures, of course, which threatened the predominant position of the Anarcho-syndicalists in numberless towns and villages and actually resulted in their exclusion from village councils in certain instances,[10] threw the more extreme spirits into a position of antagonism to the leadership of the CNT and FAI.

That Largo Caballero, despite his revolutionary stand before the war and the fact that the UGT, which he controlled, held a dominant position on the committees in many towns and villages, should have found common ground with the Communists and other members of the government on the matter of their dissolution is understandable, if only because of his concern for foreign opinion. When, shortly after taking office, he had declared that it was necessary to sacrifice revolutionary language in order to win the friendship of the democratic powers, he must have realized that his efforts to secure Anglo-French aid could not be confined solely to verbal adhesions to the Republican Constitution and that it would be necessary to dissolve the revolutionary organs that had assumed state functions.

"The pressure of the Communists . . . and the fear of provoking England and France convinced Largo Caballero of the need to respect Republican legality," argues one historian of the left, "[and] in the end he accepted the thesis of the Spanish Communist party: first let us win the war, then the revolution. Although he firmly maintained his revolutionary convictions, he believed that the moment was not opportune for taking power and that it should be postponed until after the war. . . . But the Communists, the reformist Socialists and the Republicans wanted to go further. [They wanted] to recapture the power lost by the small bourgeoisie in July and to crush the Revolution."[11]

Apart from the question of foreign opinion, Largo Caballero and most members of the cabinet had other cogent motives for opposing the committees, chiefly the fact that many of them were controlled by the CNT and FAI and that they impinged on the government's authority and obstructed its work in almost every sphere.[12] "At the present time," commented *Claridad*, the mouthpiece of Largo Caballero, "these organs can only serve as impediments to a function that belongs solely and exclusively to the Popular Front government, in which all parties and labor organizations in the country participate with full responsibility."[13] And the

Communist *Mundo Obrero* declared: "There may be some doubt as to whether or not the numerous bodies created at the beginning of the Civil War in the towns and villages of loyalist Spain were necessary. But there can be no doubt that at the present time they . . . greatly hinder the work of the government."[14] Criticism of the committees on this score came not only from the Communists and Socialists; even Juan Peiró, the Anarchosyndicalist minister of industry, avowed that they interfered with government functions. "The government issues an order," he declared at a public meeting of the CNT a few weeks before the promulgation of the aforementioned decrees, "but the local committees interpose their directives. While it tries to put order into things, they disorganize everything. (Murmurs from the audience.) Either the government is superfluous or the committees. (Cries of 'Yes!') What do these interjections mean? That the committees are superfluous? (More cries of 'Yes!' 'No!' 'Yes!') . . . The committees are not superfluous, but they must become auxiliary bodies of the government."[15]

Because of the cleavage in the libertarian movement on the question of dissolving the committees, it was a far cry from the promulgation of the decrees to their actual implementation, and in a large number of localities, where the Anarchosyndicalists were in undisputed ascendancy, and even in some where the less radical UGT was dominant, the committees subsisted in the teeth of government opposition.

It should be noted, however, that according to the Anarchosyndicalists, the delay in setting up the new municipal councils in some places was due to the efforts of the Popular Front parties to secure a representation out of proportion to their strength. "In spite of the time that has elapsed since the promulgation of the decree providing for the formation of the new municipal councils," wrote the FAI organ *Castilla Libre*, with regard to the province of Ciudad Libre (previously Ciudad Real), "they have been set up in only three or four localities. The Popular Front, which represents no one, wants to appropriate the majority of posts. We want proportional representation."[16]

"Those who defend the existence of a network of committees of all kinds," the Communists remonstrated, "forget one important thing: that at the present time nothing can be more prejudicial to us than the division of power. We know that the comrades who uphold the committees do not want Spain to be atomized by the scattered efforts of hundreds of these committees. On the other hand, they consider that the democratic organs [of the Republic] are useless at the present time. This is an error. As we have to defend the democratic structure of the State because it conforms to the present period of the Revolution and because it is a vital requisite for winning the war, it is inexplicable that anyone should think of converting that structure and the organs that give it life into a mere decoration."[17]

But persuasion alone could not ensure the enforcement of the decrees. Only by reconstructing the security forces of the Republic could the government impose its will and centralize in its hands all elements of state power assumed by the revolutionary committees. And of this the cabinet of Largo Caballero had long been conscious, as will now be seen.

21

The Security Forces

*E*arly in this volume it was shown that the police power of the Republic crumbled under the impact of the military rebellion and the social revolution. The Civil Guard, the Assault Guard, and the secret police disintegrated as a result of wholesale desertions to the rebel cause and the taking over of police functions by vigilance committees and militia units improvised by the left-wing organizations.[1] These forces, declared Angel Galarza, minister of the interior in the Largo Caballero government, "either well or badly, efficiently or inefficiently, some in absolute good faith, others driven by base ambitions and evil instincts, performed a function in the rear . . . , [and] were the only forces that at one time could be used against the fascists in the towns and villages."[2] "Fascism in the rear areas," wrote *Política*, the organ of the Left Republican party, "has been put down principally as a result of the intelligent and skillful work of the militia."[3]

With only the bare remnants of the Republican police corps at its disposal, the liberal government formed by José Giral on 19 July 1936 was impotent in the face of the revolutionary terror exercised by the working-class organizations, whose police squads and patrols carried out searches, arrests, and summary executions. In Madrid, according to Arturo Barea, a Socialist, each of the branches and groups of the trade unions and political parties set up "its own police, its own prison, its own executioners, and a special place for its executions."[4]

Nor could the Giral cabinet or any government that succeeded it hope to curb this terror and establish its authority in the eyes of the Western world without reconstructing and expanding the security forces under its control. On this point the Communists, Socialists, and Republicans were of one mind, although each had its own view as to who should ultimately control the reorganized police corps.

The first significant step in the reconstruction of the regular security forces was taken on 31 August 1936, when the Giral cabinet promulgated a decree providing for the purging and reorganizing of the Civil Guard, henceforth to be known as the National Republican Guard.[5] Under the Largo Caballero government, thousands of new members were recruited for this corps; the same was true of the Assault Guard, whose numbers increased by twenty-eight thousand at the beginning of December, according to Angel Galarza, the left-wing Socialist minister of the interior.[6] No less important was the growth of the *carabineros*, or carabineers, a corps composed of customs and excise officials and guards dependent on the ministry of finance, which, like the assault and civil guards, had fallen to pieces under the blow of the military insurrection and the Revolution. Although the Giral government planned to reorganize and use the corps as a force of public order against the left wing of the Revolution, its reconstruction and expansion were not seriously undertaken for this purpose until Dr. Juan Negrín—regarded at the time as a protégé and supporter of Indalecio Prieto—assumed control of the ministry of finance in September 1936 and began transforming it into an elite corps under the exclusive control of the moderate Socialists. Although, before the war, the carabineers had numbered approximately fifteen thousand in the entire country,[7] they were reported in April 1937 to total forty thousand in the left camp alone, that is, in about half the area of Spain.[8] True, some of them served in special carabineer units at the front, but the majority were kept in the rear.[9] It was common knowledge that Prieto and the moderate Socialists had encouraged the growth of the corps in order to strengthen their position vis-à-vis the Caballero Socialists, but it was evident that they regarded it primarily as a counterpoise to the extreme wing of the Revolution. Hugh Thomas is correct when he records that the Anarchosyndicalists accused Negrín of "building up the carabineers as a private army under the ministry of finance," but his argument that this was done by Negrín "to ensure that the government received proper customs dues"[10] is unacceptable in view of the fact that the territory under the control of the Republican government had been reduced, as already noted, by April 1937 to half its prewar size and that the number of carabineers had been increased from an approximate total of fifteen thousand to forty thousand.

In a speech addressed to the carabineers in December 1936, Jerónimo Bugeda, a moderate Socialist and Negrín's undersecretary, made clear the future role of the carabineers when he declared menacingly: "You are the guardians of the State that Spain wishes to create for herself. Those visionaries who believe that a chaotic situation of social indiscipline and licentiousness is permissible are utterly mistaken because the army of the people, as well as you carabineers, who are a glorious part of that army, will know how to prevent it."[11]

The Anarchists did not conceal their fears that the carabineers would eventually be used against them.[12] In a dispatch from Valencia published in the *New York Herald Tribune*, James Minifie reported: "A reliable police force is being built up, quietly but surely. The Valencia government discovered an ideal instrument for this purpose in the *carabineros*. . . . The Anarchists have already noticed and complained about the increased strength of this force 'at a time when we all know there's little enough traffic coming over the frontiers, land or sea.' They realize that it will be used against them."[13]

From a force of 40,000 in April 1937, the carabineers increased, according to a Communist source, to 60,000 at the beginning of 1938[14] and later in the year to 100,000, according to the Anarchists, who dubbed the corps "Negrín's 100,000 sons."[15] Whether or not this number was ever reached cannot be said with certainty, but throughout 1938 efforts continued to augment the size of the corps, first by lowering the age limit from 18 to 17 and then by raising it from 40 to 45.[16] Negrín had a predilection for the carabineers. He had a son in the corps, was waited on at table by them, and they guarded his house in Naquera, a small town near Valencia.[17] After he became defense minister in April 1938, he appointed a captain of the carabineers to head the SIM, the notorious Servicio de Investigación Militar, and, at the end of the war, according to Carlos Contreras (Vittorio Vidali), "stupidly" entrusted the shipment to Mexico of the fabulous Vita treasure to Enrique Puente, a Socialist and colonel of the carabineers, who betrayed him and turned the treasure over to Prieto, at that time Negrín's archenemy.[18]

Due to their special privileges, the carabineers were unpopular among the men and officers of the Popular Army and were called *la peste verde*, the green plague, after their green uniforms. Occasionally, some units served at the front, where, according to chief of the general staff, Vicente Rojo, "their presence was usually a source of displeasure owing to the privileges they enjoyed."[19] They earned 15 pesetas a day as against 10 for the Popular Army soldiers, were better fed and armed,[20] had their own factories and workshops, as well as transportation, which was often superior to that of the army. Later, as we shall see, when Negrín broke with Indalecio Prieto, he was hampered by the very force he had created.[21]

Concurrently with the reconstruction of the security forces, the government of Largo Caballero took steps to bring the independent squads and patrols of the working-class organizations under its control. Shortly after taking office, it published a decree providing for their incorporation into a Vigilance Militia, under the authority of the ministry of the interior, to collaborate with the official police forces in the maintenance of internal order.[22] All militiamen performing police functions who did not belong to the new corps were to be regarded as "disaffected elements," while the members were given priority if they wished to enroll in the regular security services.[23] The decree soon proved to be but a preparatory step toward the incorporation of the squads and patrols of the working-class organizations into the armed forces of the state.[24] Members of the Communist, Socialist, and Republican parties were quick to avail themselves of the opportunity to enter the official police corps, but the Anarchosyndicalists held back and in many places clung tenaciously to their own police squads and patrols in defiance of the government. Far from acquiescing in the absorption of their own militia by the state, some of the more resolute elements demanded that the government police corps should be dissolved and their members be incorporated into the militia of the working-class organizations.[25] But it was a vain demand; for the government, strengthened by the reorganized security forces and by the absence of any apparent protest by the CNT-FAI ministers, was beginning to disarm and arrest recalcitrants and take over the administration of public order in one locality after another, where the Anarchosyndicalists had been in control since the first days of the Civil War.[26] Some of the measures taken by the police in different localities were in accordance with instructions issued by the minister of the interior to local authorities under his jurisdiction to collect arms in the possession of all persons not belonging to official bodies under the control of the ministries of finance, interior, justice, and war.[27]

Parallel with the reconstruction of the government security services, important changes were taking place in the field of justice. The revolutionary tribunals set up by the working-class organizations in the early days of the war were gradually being displaced by a legalized form of tribunal composed of three members of the judiciary and fourteen members of the Popular Front parties and trade-union federations, two representing each organization.[28] Although decrees providing for the creation of the new courts were promulgated by the Giral government at the end of August 1936, they did not begin to function in all the provinces of the left camp until several weeks after the CNT had entered the Caballero government in November.[29]

While the reorganization of the regular police corps was gradually taking place, the Communists were making full use of their growing power and their skill in proselytism, defamation, and infiltration to secure for themselves a position of predominance.[30] Together with Soviet agents, they exerted what pressure they could on the civil governors of various provinces, as Justo Martínez Amutio, the civil governor of Albacete, testifies.[31] Moreover, aided by both overt and covert supporters in high places, by the timidity if not the complaisance of leading Socialists and Republicans, they secured for themselves pivotal positions in the reconstructed police apparatus. For instance, in November 1936, Santiago Carrillo, the councillor of public order in the Junta de Defensa de Madrid (which was set up when the Largo Caballero government moved to Valencia), and his successor, José Cazorla, both converts to the PCE, succeeded in taking control of the new security forces in the capital;[32] Luis Omaña Díaz and Loreto Apellániz, also party members, were appointed by Angel Galarza, the left Socialist minister of the interior, to the posts of general commissar and police inspector in Valencia, the new seat of government;[33] the Communists Justiniano García and Juan Galán were made chief and subchief of the Servicios Especiales, the intelligence department of the ministry of the interior, while two other Communists, Fernando Torrijos and a certain Adám, were appointed to vital posts in the police administration. Torrijos was made commissar general in the Department of Security, in charge of the appointment, transfer, and discipline of the police, and Adám was appointed head of the training center of the Secret Police School, the Escuela de Policía, that formed the cadres of the new secret police corps.[34]

From the time of its creation, this corps, ultimately more important than any of the uniformed forces of public order, became a mere arm of the Soviet secret police, which, because of the paramount position Spain now occupied in Soviet diplomacy, had established itself in the left camp quite early in the war. According to Walter Krivitsky, an emergency conference was held in Moscow on 14 September 1936 at which Abram Sloutski, head of the foreign division of the Soviet secret police,[35] was present. "From Sloutski," he adds, "I learned that at this conference a veteran officer of his department was detailed to establish the OGPU [NKVD][36] in Loyalist Spain. He was Nikolsky, alias Schwed, alias Lyova, alias [Alexander] Orlov."[37] The fact that these aliases were revealed by Krivitsky in 1939, long before they were published elsewhere, is proof of his inside knowledge of the NKVD, a knowledge already confirmed by two men of high integrity—Boris Nicolaevsky and Paul Wohl—who knew him intimately. Nikolsky was Orlov's party name, according to *The Legacy of Alexander Orlov*, which was prepared by the U.S. Senate Subcommittee on Internal Security after his death in the United States in 1973,[38] where he had resided since his defection in 1938; Schwed was the "code name," as Orlov himself confirmed in 1966, that Stalin employed to communicate with him regarding the shipment of Spanish gold to Russia,[39] and Lyova was corroborated by Louis Fischer, who met him in Madrid in mid-September 1936 and revealed this information in 1941.[40]

In reply to a questionnaire prepared by Stanley G. Payne,[41] Orlov stated on 1 April 1968 that he was appointed by the Soviet politburo on 26 August 1936 and that the date given by Krivitsky of 14 September is false. The discrepancy is not important; indeed, what is important is Krivitsky's knowledge of this top-secret appointment, considering the massive campaign against him as an impostor. Orlov also stated, in response to the same questionnaire, that Krivitsky had never held a high office in the Soviet secret police, but served only as an NKVD "letter drop" in The Hague—"the lowliest denomination on the operative scale." This statement can be dismissed as a belated attempt to denigrate Krivitsky, who exposed, as we shall see, the repressive role of Orlov's apparatus in Republican Spain, for in none of his books, articles, or testimony before the U.S. Senate subcommittee did Orlov make this charge. Nor could anyone supposedly so low on the scale of command have had such far-ranging and accurate inside knowledge as did Krivitsky.[42]

Within a few months of Orlov's appointment, the Soviet secret police, operating in intimate association with Spanish and foreign Communists, with crypto-Communists in the ranks of Socialists and Republicans, and with the Communist-controlled Spanish secret police, became a key factor in determining the course of events in the anti-Franco camp.[43] "The Stalinist secret services," writes the former Communist leader, Fernando Claudín, "behaved, in effect, within the Republic as though it were the Republic of Outer Mongolia."[44]

In reference to my book *The Grand Camouflage*, Herbert L. Matthews, former *New York Times* correspondent in the left-wing zone and an influential molder of public opinion, wrote on page 113 of his last work on Spain, *Half of Spain Died*: "Bolloten claims that the secret police in Spain became 'a mere arm' of the Soviet secret police apparatus and that the Russian OGPU quickly 'became the decisive force in determining the course of events in the anti-Franco camp.' This is a wild exaggeration. Governmental power at no time got out of the hands of Spanish republican leaders." Yet, on page 110, he observes: "As early as September 1936 the Communists, under the direction of the Russian NKVD representative, Alexander Orlov, began filling prisons with hundreds of *their*—not necessarily the Republican government's—enemies, torturing and killing many of them. There was not, as Burnett Bolloten, the former United Press correspondent on the Franco side [actually I was on the left-wing side from 18 July 1936], claimed, 'an independent Russian police system' dominating all of Loyalist Spain throughout the war. There were many police organizations (Hugh Thomas counted nine) including *some legitimate ones*."[45] It is, of course, true, as I have already pointed out earlier both in this volume and in *The Grand Camouflage*, that in the first months of the war police powers were exercised by a multiplicity of police squads, militia units, and patrols belonging to the various trade-union and political organizations. If, in fact, as Matthews concedes, there were many such units, including "some legitimate ones"—implying that there were many that escaped the authority of the government—if, moreover, as he allows, the Communists under the direction of the NKVD began filling prisons with "hundreds of their enemies . . . torturing and killing many of them," it is difficult to reconcile these statements with his assertion that "governmental power at no time got out of the hands of the Spanish republican leaders."

The following quotation on page 120 from the same work by Herbert Matthews should suffice to point out the incongruity of this assertion: "On November 6 and the night of November 7–8, 1936, when the fate of Madrid hung in the balance, about a thousand prisoners were taken from the Model Prison and massacred in Madrid and surrounding villages. . . . I believe, myself, that the orders came from the Comintern agents in Madrid because I know that the sinister Vittorio Vidali [alias Carlos Contreras in Spain, alias Enea Sormenti in the United States] spent the night in a prison briefly interrogating prisoners brought before him and, when he decided, as he almost always did, that they were fifth columnists, he would shoot them in the back of their heads with his revolver."

Since Vittorio Vidali was part of the NKVD apparatus in Spain, Alexander Orlov's responsibility for these assassinations cannot be gainsaid. Yet, in all his written and oral testimony, Orlov invariably describes his functions in Spain somewhat inoffensively as those of "chief Soviet adviser to the Republican government on intelligence, counter-intelligence, and guerrilla warfare"[46] and avoids any reference to his secret police functions and repressive role in the internal affairs of the left camp, whether against alleged rightists or anti-Stalinists. One the other hand, Louis Fischer describes Orlov as "chief of the GPU [NKVD] agents in Loyalist territory,"[47] a simple and unadorned title that expresses more bluntly the power he exercised over the lives of Spanish citizens. "The Ogpu [NKVD]," Krivitsky affirmed, "had its own special prisons. [This fact was confirmed by Santiago Carrillo in 1974 when he was secretary of the Spanish Communist party in exile.[48]] Its units carried out assassinations and kidnappings. It filled hidden dungeons and made flying raids. It functioned, of course, independently of the Loyalist government. The ministry of justice had no authority over the Ogpu, which was an empire within an empire. It was a power before which even some of the highest officers in the Largo Caballero government trembled. The Soviet Union seemed to have a grip on Loyalist Spain, as if it were already a Soviet possession."[49]

22

Nationalization versus Socialization

*I*f, in order to impose the will of the government, it was necessary to reconstruct the regular police corps and dissolve the revolutionary committees that had assumed functions formerly belonging to the state, the Communists, Socialists, and Republicans believed it was also necessary to weaken the power of the revolutionary committees in the factories by bringing the collectivized enterprises, particularly in the basic industries, under the control of the government.

A preliminary step in this direction was taken at the outset of the Revolution by José Giral's liberal Republican government. With a view to strengthening its position vis-à-vis the committees and to giving an aura of legality to their expropriations, it approved a decree on 2 August, proposed by the Republican minister of industry and commerce, Plácido Alvarez Buylla, providing for the sequestration by the state of industrial and commercial enterprises whose owners or managers had abandoned them—in other words, had escaped abroad, gone into hiding, or been imprisoned or executed at the outset of the Civil War. If the owners and managers, the decree stipulated, failed to present themselves for work within forty-eight hours of the publication of the decree, the state would proceed with the sequestration of their firms in order to guarantee their continued operation.[1]

Although government intervention during the early months was very limited and did not extend beyond the appointment of a representative of one of the Popular Front parties to each of certain officially designated industrial and commercial enterprises in Madrid that had been taken over by workers' committees,[2] the decree was nevertheless the first significant step taken by the central government with a view to controlling industry and trade.

Other decrees followed shortly afterward.

"By the decrees of 14 and 20 August and 1 September 1936," reads the official Communist history of the Civil War and Revolution, "the Giral government appointed a series of state advisers to various electric power companies and formed a Consejo General de Electricidad, Board of Electricity, with powers to intervene in technical and administrative questions in these companies. The executive committee of this council had a Popular Front composition: the Republican Elfidio Alonso; the Socialist Amador Fernández, the Communist Luis Cabo Giorla; the UGTista Manuel Lois, etc.

"There arose in the Spanish economy a very special kind of state capitalism. It was not the kind of state capitalism utilized or manipulated by the financial oligarchy. It was a state capitalism in which control was exercised through the representatives of the Popular Front parties, which assured no small influence to the working class. The Giral government, despite its limitations, carried out revolutionary measures that until that time no bourgeois government in Spain had undertaken. And one can only speak of it with respect and admiration."[3]

State capitalism or nationalization, the Communists knew, would eventually enable the central authority not only to organize the manufacturing capacity of the anti-Franco camp in accordance with the needs of the war and to control the output and allocation of war material, often assigned by the labor unions to their own locals or militia units,[4] but also to weaken the left wing of the Revolution at one of the principal sources of its power. They did not, of course, openly acknowledge the political advantages of nationalization and defended it solely on military and economic grounds.[5] In their campaign they were aided by the fact that collectivization suffered from palpable defects. In the first place, the collectivized enterprises appeared unconcerned with the problems of provisioning and distributing skilled labor, raw materials, and machinery in accordance with a single and rational plan of production for military needs. "We have been satisfied with throwing out the proprietors from the factories and putting ourselves in them as committees of control," declared Diego Abad de Santillán, CNT-FAI leader in the semiautonomous region of Catalonia. "There has been no attempt at connection, there has been no coordination of economy in due form. We have worked without plans and without real knowledge of what we were doing."[6] Furthermore, nonessential civilian goods and even luxury items were being produced simply because they yielded a high profit, with the resultant waste of raw materials and human effort.[7] According to Michael Seidman, in his study of the economic revolution in Barcelona, based in large measure on original trade-union sources, although the unions and factory committees standardized and modernized production, bought new machinery, improved working conditions and tried to eliminate a number of the most glaring deficiencies, they "often ran into the resistance of the workers themselves who continued to demand more pay, to fake illnesses, to sabotage production, and to reject the control and the discipline of the factory system."[8]

Albert Pérez-Baró, a CNT militant and a leading participant in the collectivist movement in Catalonia, describes the initial economic confusion: "After the first few days of euphoria, the workers returned to work and found themselves without responsible management. This resulted in the creation of workers' committees in factories, workshops and warehouses, which tried to resume production with all the problems that a transformation of this kind entailed. Owing to inadequate training and the sabotage of some of the technicians who remained—many others had fled with the owners—the workers' committees and other bodies that were improvised had to rely on the guidance of the unions. . . . Lacking training in economic matters, the union leaders, with more good will than success, began to issue directives that spread confusion in the factory committees and enormous chaos in production. This was aggravated by the fact that each union . . . gave different and often contradictory instruction."[9]

In order to overcome these problems and to give legal status to the collectives, which have been described by non-Anarchist historians as "the greatest experiment in workers' self-management,"[10] a decree on "Collectivization and Workers' Control" was approved on 24 October 1936 by the Generalitat, the semiautonomous government of Catalonia. The measure was sponsored by the CNT and signed by its representative in the government, Juan P. Fàbregas, the councillor of economy.[11] Under article 2, all firms employing more than one hundred workers were automatically collectivized and those employing less than one hundred could decide on collectivization provided that the majority of the personnel agreed. Although this part of the decree did little more than legalize the existing situation, the law, in the words of Pérez-Baró, "attempted to coordinate, codify and unite in a single practice what previously had been open to the interpretation of every trade union or workers' committee."[12] In addition, with the approval of the workers, a representative of the Generalitat was appointed by the CNT councillor of economy to each of the collectivized enterprises, which were grouped into large concentrations called general industrial councils. Each council was, in turn, represented in the Economic Council of Catalonia, a central planning and coordinating agency.[13] Not all Anarchosyndicalists approved of the decree. Diego Abad de Santillán, one of the FAI's leading ideologues, who succeeded Fàbregas as councillor of economy, wrote subsequently: "When I became councillor, I had no intention of taking into account or carrying out the decree; I intended to allow our great people to carry on the task as they best saw fit, according to their own inspiration."[14] The decree, he said, on another occasion, deprived "the working people of the initiative in an area where it did not require the advice of experts of any kind."[15] It is no wonder then that the decree was never vigorously enforced, that there were numerous violations, and that an important provision to form a bank of industrial and commercial credit to finance the collectivized enterprises was never implemented. Nor is it any wonder that when the workers in some of the collectivized plants asked José Tarradellas, the left Republican councillor of finance in the regional government, for financial assistance, he attempted, according to his own testimony, "to use their predicament to capture control of the collectives."[16]

Outside Catalonia, finance minister Juan Negrín, a centralist and a strong advocate of nationalization, also hoped to exploit the economic dislocation. "When the war broke out," he told Louis Fischer, "working-men's committees, often Anarchist, took over the factories. . . . They paid themselves in wages everything they took from sales. Now they have no money. They are coming to me for running expenses and for raw materials. We will take advantage of their plight to gain control of the factories."[17]

Although the Communists had cogent arguments in favor of nationalization, the Anarchosyndicalists, contrary to common belief, were not without their own plans for the nationwide control and rationalization of production. Rootedly opposed to state control or nationalization,[18] they advocated centralization—or socialization, as they called it—under trade-union management of entire branches of production.[19] "If nationalization were carried out in Spain as the Socialists and Communists desire," said one Anarchist newspaper, "we should be on the way to a dictatorship, because by nationalizing everything the government would become the master, the chief, the absolute boss of everyone and everything."[20]

In the opinion of the Anarchosyndicalists, socialization would eliminate the dangers of government control by placing production in the hands of the unions. This was the libertarian conception of socialization, without state intervention, that was to eliminate the wastes of competition and duplication, render possible industrywide planning for both civilian and military needs, and halt the growth of selfish actions among the workers of the more prosperous collectives by using their profits to raise the standard of living of the workers in the less favored enterprises.[21] According to Daniel Guérin, an authority on the Spanish Anarchist movement, "it appeared . . . that workers' self-management might lead to a kind of egotistical particularism, each enterprise being concerned solely with its own interests. This was remedied [in Barcelona] by the creation of a central equalization fund. . . . As a result, the excess revenues of the bus company were used to support the street cars, which were less profitable."[22] But, in actuality, there were many cases of inequality that could not be so easily resolved.

Already in the early months of the war, the leaders of some of the local unions of the CNT both in Catalonia and the rest of Spain had introduced limited forms of socializaton, confined to one branch of industry in a single locality, such as the cabinetmakers' trade in Madrid, Barcelona, and Carcagente, the dressmaking, tailoring, metal, and leather goods trades in Valencia, the shoemaking industry in Sitges, the metal and textile industries of Alcoy, the lumber trade of Cuenca, the brickmaking industry of Granollers, the tanning trade of Barcelona and Vich, and the shoemaking industry in the province of Alicante, to mention but a few examples.[23] These partial socializations were not regarded as ends in themselves but rather as transitional stages in the integration on a national scale of atomized branches of production into a socialist (that is, a libertarian) economy under trade-union control.

This work of socialization, however, could not go forward as rapidly as the libertarian planners desired. They encountered the opposition of many concerns in a privileged position, controlled by workers of the UGT as well as by those of the CNT, who did not wish to sacrifice their profits to help the less successful collectives.[24] In addition, the leadership of the PSOE and the Socialist UGT, like the Communist party, advocated government ownership and control of the basic industries[25] and opposed the collectivization of the property of the small bourgeoisie, on which complete Socialist planning, in accordance with the ideas of the CNT leaders, depended.

"The divergence of outlook between the CNT and UGT on economic matters was constant," testifies Mariano Cardona Rosell, a member of the national committee of the CNT, "owing to the fact that while the CNT advocated a more and more effective socialization it met with lack of cooperation on the part of the national, regional, and local leaders of the UGT, who paid little or no attention to this vital problem. As a result, the rank and file of the UGT followed the directives of the CNT in many localities."[26] These divergent attitudes rendered the establishment of a centrally coordinated industry impossible, either through libertarian socialization or nationalization, and partly explain why the elaborate plans for the socialization of industry under trade-union control propounded at the Enlarged National Economic Plenum of the CNT in January 1938 remained on paper.[27]

Another obstacle to the integration of industry into a libertarian economy lay in the fact that a large number of firms controlled by the CNT were in a state of insolvency or semi-insolvency and were compelled to seek government intervention to secure financial aid. They did not in general have recourse to the banks, for these were controlled by the UGT bank employees' union, the Federación Nacional de Banca, a fief of Amaro del Rosal, the president of the union and a Communist supporter. Because of their contempt for money, the CNT and FAI had never attempted to organize the bank employees and gave the UGT free rein, much to their regret during the Civil War.

In Catalonia, one of the peculiarities of the economic situation was that whereas the CNT had taken over the majority of industrial and business enterprises, the rival UGT had assumed control of the banks and other credit institutions under the general supervision of a banking commission on which the UGT and the Generalitat government were represented. Since, for both political and ideological reasons, the CNT enterprises refused to deposit their funds in the established banking institutions and conducted their transactions in cash, the profitable concerns amassed huge sums of money on their premises.[28] This hoarding created a serious currency shortage and restricted the basis of credit, which otherwise could have been used to finance the less successful enterprises. Hoping to remedy the situation, Councillor of Finance Tarradellas decreed that all sums in excess of one thousand pesetas were to be paid by check,[29] but the measure went unheeded. "[The] immobilization of large amounts of money," wrote *La Batalla*, the organ of the POUM, the dissident Marxist party, "is due to ideological reasons and cannot be resolved so long as two labor unions exist and nearly all the means of production are controlled by one union and the means of credit by the other."[30] As the CNT declined to use the financial institutions and inasmuch as it required funds for its socialization projects, a CNT congress held in February 1937 proposed that the organization create its own bank,[31] but nothing came of the project.[32]

Both in Catalonia and the rest of Republican Spain, this situation created grave economic problems for the CNT collectives. So desperately did some of them require funds that Juan Peiró, the Anarchosyndicalist minister of industry, openly recommended intervention by the central government,[33] having received in his department eleven thousand requests for funds in January 1937 alone.[34] According to the official Communist history, the CNT ministers of industry and commerce "tried by every means to legalize and consolidate the dominion of the CNT over the greater part of the economy, utilizing state funds to finance the 'syndicalized' [i.e., collectivized] enterprises in a state of bankruptcy."[35]

But the efforts of the CNT to obtain government aid to salvage these enterprises and to extend the collective system were unsuccessful. José Peirats, the Anarchosyndicalist historian, attests that Juan Peiró tried to draft a decree providing for the collectivization of all industries, but Largo Caballero made him desist, warning him that England, France, and Belgium, which owned substantial economic interests in Spain, would withdraw diplomatic recognition from the Republican government. Peiró then redrafted his decree, but the cabinet opposed it and made certain changes. From the cabinet the decree went to a ministerial commission that, according to Peirats, converted it into a skeleton. "But the calvary is not over. To put the decree into effect money is necessary, that is, a credit must be granted by the minister of finance [Juan Negrín]. He haggles like a usurer and finally grants an insignificant sum. . . . Finally, the Industrial Bank intervenes, which reduces the amount still further." The outcome, concludes Peirats, was that the government crisis of May 1937—discussed later in this volume—occurred before the minister of industry could put into effect this "eminently conservative" decree and that the first act of the new government, in which the CNT was not represented, was to "rescind the decree purely and simply."[36]

The Communists took advantage of the economic problems to further their campaign in favor of government control of industry and finance. "Economic power must be in the hands of a single entity," declared Pere Ardiaca, a leader of the Communist-controlled PSUC.[37] And PCE secretary Jose Díaz, referring to the "premature experiments in collectivization and socialization," declared: "If, in the beginning these experiments were justified by the fact that the big industrialists and landlords had abandoned their factories and estates and that it was necessary to continue production, later on they were not. . . . At first it was understandable that the workers should take possession of the abandoned factories in order to continue production at all costs. . . . I repeat that this was understandable, and we are not going to censure it. . . . [But] today when there is a government of the Popular Front, in which all the forces engaged in the fight against fascism are represented, such things are not only inadvisable, but they have the opposite effect from that intended. Today we must coordinate production rapidly and intensify it under a single direction so as to provision the front and the rear with everything they need. . . . To rush into these premature experiments in 'collectivization' and 'socialization' when the war is still undecided and at a time when the internal enemy, aided by foreign fascism, is violently attacking our positions and endangering the future of our country, is absurd and is tantamount to aiding the enemy."[38]

23

A Democratic and Parliamentary Republic of a New Type

At the root of the Communist party's opposition to the CNT's plans for the libertarian socialization of industry lay the fact that socialization was a threat to its own program of nationalization, and also that, to be effective, it must impinge on the property of the middle classes, whose support the Kremlin needed for the success of its foreign policy. To counter this danger, the Spanish Communists argued that the attempts to further the revolution at the expense of the middle classes were due to the workers' lack of political understanding. "In the first days of the rebellion," declared a Communist leader, referring to Valencia, "many workers fell into a mania of confiscating and socializing because they believed that we were in the midst of a social revolution. Nearly all industries were socialized. . . . This fever of 'socialization' not only laid hold of factories and workshops abandoned by bosses who supported the rebellion but even encroached on the small property of liberal and republican employers. . . . Why have the workers fallen into these errors? Mainly owing to a lack of understanding of the present political situation that leads them to believe that we are in the midst of a social revolution."[1]

Federico Melchor, a member of the executive committee of the JSU, the Communist-oriented Unified Socialist Youth Federation, affirmed: "We are not making a social revolution today; we are developing a democratic revolution, and in a democratic revolution, the economy . . . cannot be launched into Socialist channels. If we are developing a democratic revolution and say we are fighting for a democratic Republic, how can we attempt in the economic field to introduce methods of a totalitarian Socialist type? . . . Comrade Alvarez del Vayo said the other day, 'In order to triumph, a correct political line is necessary.' To that we should add: a correct political line based on a clear economic line, on a correct economic line, is necessary. These economic aberrations, these economic trends, these experiments that are carried out in our country, are not due to any accident; they stem from a whole ideology, from the ideological deformation of a broad section of the working-class movement that is trying to carry forward the economic development of our country without adapting itself to the stages that this economic development requires."[2]

These arguments of course conformed in all respects to the line laid down by the Communist International and to the requirements of Stalin's foreign policy. Palmiro Togliatti stated in November 1936 that "the task confronting the Spanish people was to carry out the bourgeois-democratic revolution," thus distorting the proletarian nature of the revolution that had exploded four months earlier.[3]

To argue along these lines in the prevailing state of revolutionary exultation was for the Communists a heavy task; for they had to contend not only with the libertarian movement, but also with the more radical members of the UGT, of the Socialist party, and of the JSU. From this task they did not shrink. "At a time of the greatest revolutionary effervescence," recalled Antonio Mije, a member of the politburo, "we Communists did not blush on the platforms of Madrid and the rest of Spain, when we came out in defense of the democratic Republic. Whereas some people were afraid even to mention the democratic Republic, we Communists had no objection to explaining to impatient elements, who did not understand the situation, that politically it was advisable to defend it against fascism."[4]

"We are fighting for the democratic Republic, and we are not ashamed to say so," affirmed Santiago Carrillo, the secretary of the JSU, in a speech at the national conference in January 1937 in which he outlined, for the first time since the fusion of the Socialist and Communist youth movements, the policy of the united organization. "Confronted by fascism and the foreign invaders, we are not fighting at the present time for the Socialist revolution."

(At this point, before proceeding with this citation, we must intercalate a statement that Carrillo made years later, which suggests what he and other Communist leaders may have really felt about their own asseverations. In an interview published in 1974, when he was secretary of the Communist party in exile, he said: "At that time, we called it a popular revolution. All of us knew that it was the establishment of socialism in Spain. That was clear. Where were the big capitalists, the large landowners, and the apparatus of the bourgeois State? They had all disappeared. Hence, the entire discussion appeared absurd and byzantine to me."[5])

But at the national conference, Carrillo expressed different thoughts: "There are," he continued, "some who say that at this stage we should fight for the Socialist revolution, and there are others who even say that we are practicing a deception, that we are maneuvering to conceal our real policy when we declare that we are defending the democratic Republic. Nevertheless, comrades, we are fighting for a democratic Republic, and, furthermore, for a democratic and parliamentary Republic. This is not a stratagem to deceive Spanish democratic opinion, nor to deceive democratic opinion abroad. We are fighting sincerely for the democratic Republic because we know that if we should commit the mistake of fighting at this time for the Socialist revolution in our country—and even for some considerable time after victory—we should see in our fatherland not only the fascist invaders but side by side with them the bourgeois democratic governments of the world that have already stated explicitly that in the present European situation they would not tolerate a dictatorship of the proletariat in our country."[6]

Failure to protect foreign capital, affirmed Federico Melchor, the JSU leader quoted earlier in this chapter, "would be an error in international relations because then England would decisively intervene against Spain not on our side but with Franco, because England has economic interests in our country to defend."[7]

Although there is no record that any democratic government ever threatened to intervene, the fear of incurring the open hostility of the democratic powers no doubt carried considerable weight among the rank and file of the JSU. Nevertheless, dissatisfaction with the policy adumbrated at the conference was not long in manifesting itself; for, within a few weeks, it was denounced by Rafael Fernández, general secretary of the JSU of the Asturias, as "anything but Marxist."[8] This was more than a personal opinion. It was the opinion of a substantial number of Socialists in the JSU, who felt themselves betrayed by what they regarded as a rightward swing, and their mood is accurately reflected in the following protest sent from the battlefront:

"I have read several times in different newspapers the speeches made by Carrillo . . . to the effect THAT THE UNIFIED SOCIALIST YOUTH IS FIGHTING FOR A DEMOCRATIC AND PARLIAMENTARY REPUBLIC. I believe that Carrillo is completely mistaken. As a young Socialist and revolutionary I am fighting for the collectivization of the land, of the factories, of the entire wealth of Spain, for the benefit of everyone, for the benefit of humanity.

"Do Carrillo and the others who aim at leading us along that prejudicial and counterrevolutionary road believe that the militants of the JSU are sheep? No, we are not sheep; we are revolutionaries!

"What would our comrades who have perished on the battlefields do if they could raise their heads and see that the JSU had been an accomplice in betraying the Revolution for which they gave their lives? They would do only one thing. They would spit in the face of the culprits."[9]

If it was difficult for the Communists to convince the radical members of the JSU of the correctness of their policy, it was still more difficult to convince the libertarian movement. Yet, the success of that policy depended on the compliance, if not the wholehearted approval, of this powerful movement. With this end in view, Soviet diplomatic representatives, according to Federica Montseny, Anarchosyndicalist minister of health, held frequent conversations with CNT-FAI leaders. "The advice they gave us," she wrote, "was always the same: it was necessary to establish in Spain a 'controlled democracy' (euphemistic term for a dictatorship); it was not advisable to create the impression abroad that a profound revolution was being carried out; we should avoid awakening the suspicion of the democratic powers." The behavior of the Russians, she adds, was very courteous. "I never heard them utter a threatening word. . . . When I went to Geneva in January and February of 1937 to attend the Congress of Hygiene, Rosenberg [the Soviet ambassador] urged me to go to Russia, saying, 'Comrade Stalin would be very happy to meet you. Go there, Federica! You will be received like a little queen.' [The Russians] never made any concrete offer that would have forced me to break relations with them. They were too subtle for that. But on various occasions, Rosenberg suggested that I send my daughter to Valencia to live with his wife and children in a villa they occupied on the outskirts. When I heard these suggestions the blood froze in my veins."[10]

If the CNT-FAI ministers felt compelled to make political concessions to Soviet policy at the expense of the Revolution in the hope of influencing the democracies, they did not adhere undeviatingly to the Communist slogan of the democratic Republic.[11] If, on entering the government, they had agreed to adopt the slogan, they did so, according to Juan López, CNT minister of commerce, "in order to produce an impression beyond the frontiers, but never to strangle the legitimate revolutionary conquests of the working class."[12]

That the libertarian movement as a whole accepted the Communist slogan of the democratic Republic with even less enthusiasm than did the CNT-FAI ministers was clearly reflected in its press:

"The thousands of proletarian combatants at the battle fronts," declared the *Boletín de Información*, "are not fighting for the 'democratic Republic.' They are proletarian revolutionaries, who have taken up arms in order to make the Revolution. To postpone the triumph of the latter until after we win the war would weaken considerably the fighting spirit of the working class. . . . If we wish to raise the enthusiasm of our fighters and inject the antifascist masses with revolutionary zeal, we must drive the Revolution forward with determination, liquidate the last vestiges of bourgeois democracy, socialize industry and agriculture, and create the directing organs of the new society in accordance with the revolutionary aims of the proletariat.

"It should be clearly understood that we are not fighting for the democratic Republic. We are fighting for the triumph of the proletarian revolution. The Revolution and the war are inseparable. Everything that is said to the contrary is *reformist counterrevolution*."[13]

CNT exclaimed: " 'Democratic revolution.' 'Parliamentary republic.' 'This is not the moment for carrying out the social revolution.' Here are a few slogans worthy of the political program of the Republican parties but degrading to the working-class organizations. . . . [If] the Socialist and Communist parties as well as their youth movement had honored their Socialist principles 'the entire apparatus of the old bourgeois state' (Marx) and the structure of capitalist economy would have been destroyed. In the *Communist Manifesto* Marx and Engels never referred to a transitional period of a 'democratic and parliamentary republic.' . . . For this reason, the Marxism of all the Spanish Marxist parties is a Marxism that has nothing in common with revolutionary Marxism but much with social-democratic reformism, against which Lenin directed his revolutionary theories outlined in *State and Revolution*."[14]

To counter the embarrassing denunciations of their policy in the CNT and FAI press, the Communists—who, at the beginning of the Civil War, as has already been seen, had likened the revolution taking place in Spain to the bourgeois

democratic revolution that had been achieved over a century before in France—
were compelled, for the purposes of home consumption, to modify their language. "What do the comrades of *CNT* accuse us of?" asked *Mundo Obrero* in
reply to the Anarchosyndicalist organ.

According to them, we have diverged from the path of revolutionary Marxism.
Why? Because we defend the democratic Republic. . . . [We] should like to de-
fine the character of the Republic in our country at the present time. . . . First,
the working class, the peasants, and the small bourgeoisie have *all the arms*; second, the peasants have the land: the agricultural laborers are working the former
large estates collectively or individually, and the tenant farmers now possess their
own land; third, working-class control has been established in all factories;
fourth, the big landowners, the bankers, the large industrialists and the big political bosses who joined the military rising have been expropriated and therefore
deprived of their social and political power; fifth, the greatest influence, the principal directing influence in the development of the democratic revolution is in the
hands of the entire working class; sixth, the former army of oppression has been
destroyed and we have a new army of the people. Hence, our Republic is a special type; it is a democratic and parliamentary republic with a social content that
has never existed before. And this republic . . . cannot be considered in the same
light [as those republics] where democracy is a fiction, a democracy based on the
absolute hegemony of the exploiters. This point having been established, we
must inform the comrades of *CNT* that by defending democracy and the Republic
we do not abjure or contradict the doctrines of revolutionary Marxism. It was Lenin who taught us that to be revolutionary one should not jump into space. It was
Lenin who taught us that to be revolutionary one should always bear in mind the
concrete situation of a given country so as to apply to it the most suitable revolutionary tactics.[15]

At a plenary session of the central committee of the Communist party in
March 1937, José Díaz declared:

We are fighting for the democratic Republic, for a democratic and parliamentary
Republic of a new type and with a profound social content. The struggle taking
place in Spain is not aimed at the establishment of a democratic Republic like
that of France or of any other capitalist country. No. The democratic Republic for
which we are fighting is different. We are fighting to destroy the material foundations on which reaction and fascism rest; for without their destruction no true political democracy can exist. . . .

And now I ask: To what extent have [they] been destroyed? In every province
we control big landowners no longer exist. The church, as a dominant power, has
likewise ceased to exist. Militarism has also disappeared, never to return. Nor
are there any big bankers and industrialists. That is the reality of the situation.
And the guarantee that these conquests will never be lost lies in the fact that the
arms are in the hands of the people, of the genuine antifascist people, of the

workers, the peasants, the intellectuals, and the small bourgeoisie, who were always the slaves of those castes. That is the best guarantee that the past will never return. And precisely for that reason, because we have a guarantee that our conquests will not be lost, we should not lose our heads and forget reality by attempting experiments in "libertarian communism" and "socialization" in whatever factory or village it may be. The present stage of political development in Spain is that of the democratic revolution, the victory of which depends on the participation of all the antifascist forces, and these experiments can only serve to drive them away and estrange them.[16]

But the efforts of the Communists to convince their critics were unavailing; for the adherents of the libertarian movement, particularly of its extreme wing, the Libertarian Youth (the Federación Ibérica de Juventudes Libertarias [FIJL]), were in their immense majority immovably hostile to Communist slogans and, in distinction from the leadership of the CNT and FAI, were becoming more and more skeptical as to whether any advantage could be gained by making concessions to foreign opinion. Some hint of the temper of the movement may be gleaned from the following quotations. In an attack on the Communist-led JSU that in January 1937 had officially espoused the cause of the democratic Republic, *Juventud Libre*, the leading organ of the Libertarian Youth, declared:

> The strongest argument that the Unified Socialist Youth can put forward in order to defend the democratic and parliamentary Republic is that we should desist from speaking of revolution so as not to make our position with regard to the European democracies more difficult. Childish argument! The European democracies know only too well who we are and where we are inevitably going; they know, just as the fascist countries know, that in Spain practically all the soldiers who are fighting against fascism are revolutionaries and will not permit this magnificent occasion for making the Revolution . . . to be snatched from them. Whether we speak either of the democratic and parliamentary Republic or of the Revolution, the European democracies will help us only if it suits them. . . .
>
> To deceive our soldiers, who are dying heroically on the battlefields, to deceive our peasants and workers, who are laboring in the rear areas, with a democratic and parliamentary Republic, is to betray the Spanish Revolution. . . .
>
> The economic wealth of the country as well as the arms are in our hands. Everything belongs to us. . . . We are defending everything we have against the international fascist criminals. The traitors who try to steal what belongs to us should be denounced as fascists and shot without mercy.[17]

"Anyone who comes to us at this time, when we have the possibility of transforming Spain socially, with the story that this transformation would not be approved of by the international bourgeoisie, is a joker," declared José García Pradas, director of *CNT*. "From the very moment that he aspires to make a revolution with the license of the international bourgeoisie, he has no authority to tell us what to do.

"If we have to refrain from making the Revolution in order to prevent the international bourgeoisie from clashing with us, if we have to conceal our every aim, if we have to renounce our every aim, then why are our comrades fighting? Why are we all fighting? Why have we thrown ourselves into this struggle, into this war without mercy against Spanish and foreign fascism?"[18]

And *Fragua Social*, the CNT organ, stated: "[At] the very moment when our country is being lashed by a tempest, by a real social revolution that has changed everything, the Communist party comes out with the demand for a parliamentary Republic, a republic that has already been left far behind by the march of events. Paradoxically, this results in a situation where the Communists form the extreme right wing of Loyalist Spain, the last hope of the small bourgeoisie, which sees its world going under. However strange it may appear, the Communists are the nerve center of a policy and of a campaign of propaganda aimed at pushing us back to the first years of the bourgeois Republic, a policy that ignores the existence of a triumphant and regenerating 19 July."[19]

It was, of course, incorrect to ascribe to the Communists the intention of rolling back the Revolution to before 19 July. It would be more accurate to say that under the veil of democratic institutions it planned to convert the popular revolution into a totalitarian one-party police state. This was undoubtedly what Stalin had in mind when he told Largo Caballero that "the parliamentary way" might prove a more effective means of revolutionary development than in Russia, and when he pressed him to support the fusion of the Socialist and Communist parties. It would also be more accurate to state, as two well-known Spanish Communists averred after the Civil War, that the "democratic and parliamentary Republic of a new type" was the forerunner of the "people's democracies"—in the first stage of their development—that emerged in Europe after World War II.[20]

While paving the way toward their own hegemony, the Communists needed everyone they could muster to defeat General Franco. "[This] should be called the hour of *all comrades*," ruminated former central committee member Enrique Castro according to his frank exposé of his cynical thinking at that time. "After the defeat of Franco, everyone will be correctly labelled: The Republicans, lackeys of the bourgeoisie, neither more nor less; the Socialists, lackeys of the bourgeoisie, but a little more so than the Republicans, the Anarchists, a threat to our revolution. This will give us sufficient reason to annihilate them after we have annihilated Franco. Until then, we'll call them comrades and give them a few pats on the back. To be sure, our humanity is something new in history. We shall treat them well during the period of the 'holy alliance.' Afterwards, we shall kill them quickly so that they don't suffer too much or too long."[21]

Despite the CNT's charges that the PCE wished to roll back the revolution to before 19 July, they could not return to the bourgeois Republic of 1931 without restoring the property of the big landowners and industrialists, in other words, without giving them a share in the affairs of state. This would have been incompatible with the party's long-term aims and with the Kremlin's purpose in Spain, which, under cover of a democratic superstructure, was to control her domestic and foreign policy in conformity with its own diplomatic needs. By curbing the Revolution, the PCE aimed not at restoring the property of the big landowners and industrialists but at finding a backing for itself among the middle layers of the population and at using them, as long as it suited its purpose, to offset the power of the revolutionary segment of the anti-Franco camp and to assure its own hegemony. This was its policy in the field of industry and trade and also in the field of agriculture, as will be seen in the succeeding chapter.

24

Balancing the Class Forces

Aided by the ministry of agriculture that they controlled, the Communists were able to influence substantially the course of events in the countryside. By far the most resounding of the decrees issued by Vicente Uribe, the Communist minister, was that of 7 October 1936, by which all rural properties belonging to persons who had intervened either directly or indirectly in the military insurrection were confiscated without indemnity and in favor of the state.[1] "This decree," commented *Mundo Obrero*, the Communist party organ, "breaks the foundation of the semifeudal power of the big landlords who, in order to maintain their brutal caste privileges and to perpetuate salaries of two pesetas a day and labor from dawn to dusk, have unleashed the bloody war that is devastating Spain."[2] Under the terms of the decree, the estates that had been cultivated directly by the owners or by their stewards or had been leased to large tenant farmers were given in perpetual usufruct to organizations of peasants and agricultural workers to be cultivated individually or collectively in accordance with the wishes of the majority of beneficiaries. Small cultivators who had leased estates were promised the permanent use of their holdings, not to exceed thirty hectares in dry sections, five in irrigated districts, and three in fruit-growing areas.[3] The decree of 7 October, affirmed the Communist organ *Frente Rojo*, "is the most profoundly revolutionary measure that has been taken since the military uprising. . . . It has abolished more than 40 percent of private property in the countryside."[4]

Although the language of the decree gave the impression that the government had taken the initiative in confiscating the properties of supporters of the military insurrection, in point of fact the measure merely set the seal of legality on expropriations already carried out by agricultural laborers and tenant farmers. The Communists, however, frequently represented the measure as having been instrumental in giving the land to the peasants. "In Communist newspapers," wrote Ricardo Zabalza, left-wing Socialist and general secretary of the powerful National Federation of Land Workers, the Federación Nacional de los Trabajadores de la Tierra, affiliated with the Socialist UGT, "we have read such things as this: 'Thanks to the decree of 7 October, a measure of a Communist minister, the peasants have the land today.' . . . Such statements no doubt make very effective propaganda among the ignorant, but they cannot convince anyone who is half-acquainted with the facts. . . . Before any Communist minister was in the government, the peasant organizations, on instructions from our federation, had already confiscated de facto all the land belonging to the rebels."[5] And, in an article published after he had ceased to belong to the Communist party, Rafael Morayta Núñez, the Communist secretary general of the Institute of Agrarian Reform in 1936 and 1937,[6] wrote: "I can state positively, and this everyone knows, that it was not the government that handed the land to the peasants. The latter did not wait for a government decision, but appropriated the estates and cultivable lands themselves. . . . Hence the much-vaunted decree of 7 October, which a certain political party practically claims to be exclusively its own creation, did not give those estates to the peasants or to anyone else; for the peasants were already working them several months before, and the only thing the decree accomplished—a decree that was, of course, approved by the government—was to give legal status to those expropriations."[7]

Years later the Communists continued to claim that the peasants had received the land due to their initiative. "The Spanish agricultural workers and peasants," wrote two prominent members of the party in exile, "did not receive the land from the hands of the bourgeoisie, but from the hands of the working class—on the initiative of the Communists."[8]

Because the decree applied only to the estates of persons charged with participating directly or indirectly in the military revolt and thereby exempted from legal confiscation the properties belonging to Republicans and other landowners who had not identified themselves with General Franco's cause, the Anarchosyndicalists considered that it was inadequate to the situation. *CNT* commented:

> The minister of agriculture has just promulgated a decree confiscating in favor of the State all rural properties whose owners intervened directly or indirectly in the fascist insurrection of 19 July. As usual, of course, the State arrives late. The peasants did not wait for such a vital problem to be settled by decree: they acted in advance of the government, and from the very beginning . . . they seized the property of the landowners, making the revolution from below. With a real understanding of the land problem, they were more expeditious than the State. They expropriated without making any distinction between owners who had intervened and owners who had not intervened in the rebel conspiracy. . . . The expropriation as a punishment, only of those who have intervened directly or have helped the fascists, leaves the supreme problem of the Spanish Revolution unsolved.
>
> Our authorities should understand once and for all that the nineteenth of July destroyed the regime of unjust privileges and that a new life is springing up all over Spain. As long as they do not understand this, as long as they cling to institutions and methods that became obsolete on 19 July they will always lag behind the conquests of the people.[9]

Criticisms of the limitations of the decree came also from the National Federation of Land Workers, controlled by the left-wing Socialists. At a national conference held in June 1937, the federation demanded that the decree should be amended so as to include within its scope not only persons implicated in the military uprising, but also those who had been regarded as enemies of the working class for having violated labor contracts, discharged workers unjustly because of their ideas, denounced them to the police without good reason, and encouraged strike breaking.[10]

But the Communist party could not countenance such an amendment. Seeking support among the propertied classes in the anti-Franco camp, it could not afford to repel the small and medium proprietors who had been hostile to the working-class movement before the Civil War, and, indeed, through the ministry of agriculture and the Institute of Agrarian Reform, which it controlled, it seconded, on the basis of the limitations of the decree of 7 October, many of their demands for the restitution of their land. "I can tell you about the Castilian countryside," declared a leader of FIJL, the libertarian youth movement, "because I am in daily contact with all the agricultural districts of Castile, districts to which the delegates of the Ministry of Agriculture go . . . with the object of returning to the bourgeoisie, to the fascists, to the landowners, the property they once possessed. The minister of agriculture claims that these are small proprietors. Small proprietors, with a splendid number of acres! Are the political bosses of the villages and those who used to conspire against the workers small proprietors? Are those who have twenty or twenty-five workers and three or four pairs of bullocks small proprietors? I must ask where the policy of the minister of agriculture is leading and just what is the limit to the term 'small proprietor.' "[11]

The protection the Communist party gave even to farmers who had belonged to right-wing parties before the Civil War—particularly in the province of Valencia, where it organized them into the Peasant Federation—irrevocably antagonized a large segment of the rural population. "The Communist party," complained a Socialist, referring to the Peasant Federation, "devotes itself to picking up in the villages the worst remnants of the former Partido Autonomista, who were not only reactionary, but also immoral, and organizes these small proprietors into a new peasant union by promising them the possession of their land."[12]

There can be no doubt that the Communist party's championship of the small, to say nothing of the medium proprietor, irrespective of his political antecedents, was one of the many important reasons for the bitter strife that soon developed between itself and the left wing of the Socialist party, which, as we have seen, controlled the National Federation of Land Workers.[13] The Communists demanded that collectivization be entirely voluntary,[14] thereby implying that the property of the right-wing as well as of the Republican farmer should be respected. The left-wing Socialists, while against the compulsory collectivization of the land of the small Republican farmer, were opposed to sacrificing the growth of the collective farm movement to the small owner who had been in open conflict with the rural wage worker before the Civil War. "The loyal small proprietor," declared the left Socialist paper, *Claridad*, the mouthpiece of the UGT, "should not be forced to enter the collective farms, but generous technical, economic, and moral aid should be given to every spontaneous initiative in favor of collectivization. When we say 'loyal small proprietor' we deliberately exclude both the small owners, who were brazen enemies of the working class, and the venomous and petty political bosses, who are now sniveling and trying to keep in the background and who constitute a real Fifth Column in the rural areas. As for these, we must draw their teeth and claws. It would be a veritable catastrophe if, on the basis of these elements, an attempt were made to create an organization of kulaks, while ignoring the courageous peasant fighters who have suffered imprisonment, torture, and misery."[15]

The former Communist leader and central committee member, Enrique Castro, who became director of the Institute of Agrarian Reform in September 1936, attests in *Hombres made in Moscú* that his main objectives in the institute were to "destroy the Socialists in the countryside" and to win the support of the peasants.[16] In this introspective memoir, he unveils his inner thoughts, which were clearly those of the party. "We need all these people who have an insane ambition to possess their own land," he mused. "We need them now and we shall need them for a long time to come—as long as it takes us to assume power and to consolidate ourselves in power. Afterwards, we'll talk about it! Afterwards, we'll clarify matters! Afterwards, we shall be able to say who is the real owner of the land! But until then, we must proclaim every day that the land is theirs, that the party gave it to them, that we gave them money, seed, equipment, and advice. Only if they feel that they are the owners of 'their' property will they fight to protect it."[17]

In their efforts to win the support of the middle layers of the rural population, both right-wing and Republican, the Communists were forced to restrain the collectivist tendencies not only among the left Socialists and Anarchosyndicalists, but even within their own youth movement. "Not only have we seen certain organizations advocate collectivization," said Santiago Carrillo, general secretary of the JSU, "but in the beginning we also saw our own youth defending it through failure to understand the character of the present struggle. However, the comrades of Badajoz and other peasant provinces know very well that when the [JSU] told them they were pursuing the wrong policy and that when they started to follow the correct one the situation in the countryside began to change. . . . It is hardly necessary for us to point out how the only country in the world that has made the revolution, the Soviet Union, began to collectivize the land after nine years of proletarian power. How, then, in a democratic Republic are we going to do what the Soviet Union did after nine years of workers' power? We declare that, as long as the situation in our country does not permit any other course, our line for a long time to come will be the defense of the small peasant, the defense of the legitimate interests of the small proprietor of the countryside."[18]

The policy of the Communists, as expressed by the minister of agriculture's decree of 7 October and by its practical application, was criticized for other reasons than those given in the foregoing pages. Ricardo Zabalza, general secretary of the National Federation of Land Workers that enrolled small tenant farmers as well as farmhands, affirmed, when interviewed about conditions in the province of Albacete: "There are many landowners whose properties have not been confiscated, either because they are adherents of the left or because they have passed themselves off as such. Their tenants are compelled by law to continue the payment of rent, and this is an injustice because the tenants of rebel landowners are freed from such payment."[19] Zabalza also criticized the decree on the ground that it prevented a distribution of land in favor of the village poor. This criticism was based on the fact that the tenant farmers and sharecroppers who benefited from the decree were legally entitled to retain all the land they had cultivated before the Revolution, provided that it did not exceed the specified limits, and were therefore unwilling to cede any portion of their holdings to the rural wage workers. "As a result," Zabalza argued, "the wage workers remain without land in many places or have to content themselves with the worst soil or with that farthest from the villages because the rest of the land, or nearly all of it, is in the hands of small owners and tenant farmers. This makes friction inevitable, for it is impossible to accept the galling injustice of a situation whereby the sycophants of the former political bosses still enjoy a privileged position at the expense of those persons who were unable to rent even the smallest parcel of land because they were revolutionaries."[20]

But more important still as a source of friction in the countryside was the fact that the Communists used the decree to stimulate the personal interest of those tenant farmers and sharecroppers who, before its publication, had been caught up by the collective farm movement or had agreed to a redistribution of land in favor of the agricultural laborers.

"Then came the decree of 7 October," declared the National Federation of Land Workers, "offering tenant farmers the possibility of retaining in perpetual usufruct all the land they formerly cultivated, provided that it did not exceed thirty hectares in dry sections, five in irrigated districts, and three in fruit-growing areas. This represented . . . a guarantee that no lessee, provided that he was not an open supporter of the rebellion, could be dispossessed of his land. . . . And the practical effect of this decree has been to create, among the tenant farmers and sharecroppers who had accepted the new order of things, a desire to recover their former parcels."[21]

Encouraged by the support they received from the Communists, many right-wing tenant farmers and sharecroppers who had accepted collectivization in the first months of the Revolution demanded the return of their former holdings. At the peak of the offensive against the collective farms, Ricardo Zabalza declared: "Our most fervent aim today is to guarantee the conquests of the Revolution, especially the collective farms that were organized by the different branches of our federation and against which a world of enemies is rising up, namely, the reactionaries of yesterday and those who held land on lease because they were lackeys of the political bosses, whereas our members were either denied land or evicted from their wretched holdings. Today these reactionaries protected by the famous decree of 7 October, and enjoying unheard-of official aid, are endeavoring to take by assault the collectivized estates with the object of dividing them up, distributing their livestock, their olive trees, their vineyards, and their harvests, and of putting an end to the agrarian revolution. . . . And in order to do this they are taking advantage of the absence of our best comrades, who are at the front and who would weep with rage if they should find on their return that their efforts and sacrifices had served only to enthrone their eternal enemies, who, to increase the mockery, are now protected by membership cards of a working-class organization."[22]

In their campaign against the collective farms, the Communists also endeavored to mobilize the agricultural laborers. Early in April 1937, Mariano Vázquez, who in November 1936 had succeeded Horacio Prieto as secretary of the national committee of the CNT, accused them of going to areas where the CNT and UGT had established collective farms by mutual agreement and of "stirring up egotistic impulses . . . by promising personal advantages to the laborers and inciting them to divide up the land that they were working collectively."[23] Nor did the Communists limit themselves to this procedure; for Vázquez also charged that they had assassinated dozens of Anarchosyndicalists in the province of Toledo,[24] and, a few months later, the general secretary of the CNT Peasants' Federation of Castile declared: "We have fought terrible battles with the Communists, especially with brigades and divisions under their control that have assassinated our best peasant militants and savagely destroyed our collective farms and our harvests, obtained at the cost of infinite sacrifice."[25]

The attacks on the agricultural collectives occurred at this time mainly in New Castile, the central region, where the Communist military units were predominant, and where, according to the CNT historian and militant, Juan Gómez Casas, some three hundred "model" collective farms had been established by the CNT and UGT.[26] José García Pradas, the director of the Anarchosyndicalist daily in Madrid, *CNT*, claims that Enrique Líster, the Communist commander of the Eleventh Division, was responsible for the assassination of a large number of Castilian peasants accused of being "uncontrollables" and "fascists." As many as sixty, he claims, were executed in Mora de Toledo.[27] Líster never denied that he had committed these assassinations. In that region, he affirmed years later, the Anarchists had established "a veritable terrorist dictatorship, as a result of which every day peasants from the villages . . . passed over to the enemy." He put an end to all that, he stated. "It was necessary to create a tribunal in Mora de Toledo and to take very strong, very severe measures. Later, I was accused of having shot such and such a person. I replied that I had, that I had carried out executions, and that I was ready to do so as many times as necessary, because—as I said in reply to the accusations—I am not fighting the war to protect bandits nor to exploit the peasants. I am fighting the war so that people will be free."[28]

It was inevitable that the attacks on the collectives should have had an unfavorable effect upon rural economy and upon morale, for while in some areas collectivization was anathema to the majority of peasants, in others collective farms were organized spontaneously by the bulk of the peasant population. Ralph Bates, noted author, assistant commissar of the Fifteenth International Brigade, and an authority on Spain and the Spanish Revolution, wrote to me after he had severed his ties with the Communist party: "The C.P. drive against collectivization was absolutely wrong, for while there were plenty of abuses, forced collectivization, etc., there were plenty of good collectives, i.e., voluntary ones."[29] In Toledo province, for example, where even before the war rural collectives existed,[30] 83 percent of the peasants, according to a source friendly to the Communists, decided in favor of the collective cultivation of the soil.[31]

As the campaign against the collective farms reached its height just before the summer harvest—a period of the year when even the more successful farms were beset with economic difficulties—a pall of dismay and apprehension descended upon the agricultural laborers. Work in the fields was abandoned in many places or carried on apathetically, and there was danger that a substantial portion of the harvest, vital for the war effort, would be left to rot.

The Communists then suddenly changed their policy.

The first intimation of this about-face came early in June 1937, when the minister of agriculture issued a decree promising various forms of aid to the collectives so that they could carry out "as satisfactorily and as speedily as possible the agricultural labors appropriate to the season."[32] This did not mean that no assistance had been given in the past. According to the Communist organ *Frente Rojo*, the Institute of Agrarian Reform—which was controlled by the minister of agriculture, and, under the decree of 7 October, had been charged with the task of apportioning aid to the beneficiaries—had since that date provided collective farms with 50 million pesetas in credits, farm implements, seeds, and fertilizers.[33] This is not unlikely. But this assistance must have gone solely to collectives that accepted the intervention of the institute; for the CNT, which rejected state intervention because it threatened the autonomy of its collectives, charged that the latter were denied all help from the minister of agriculture.[34] On the other hand, according to Mariano Cardona Rosell, a member of the national committee of the CNT and its representative on the executive commission of the National Service of Agricultural Credit, although the Institute of Agrarian Reform was not empowered to extend credits and assistance to collectives outside its jurisdiction, such collectives could apply for aid from the national service without any danger of control other than that arising from the credit transactions involved.[35] But this service, which operated under the auspices of the ministry of agriculture, and on whose executive commission there were representatives of the CNT and UGT as well as officials of that department,[36] did not begin to function properly until late in the summer of 1937. Moreover, although, according to Cardona Rosell, it extended very substantial credits to collective farms that applied for assistance, some CNT collectives did not take advantage of it for a long time owing to their suspicion of official bodies and the fear that these might curb their independence.[37]

The preamble to the minister of agriculture's decree of June 1937, previously mentioned, promising various forms of aid to the collectives, stated that help was necessary to avoid "economic failures that might chill the faith of the land workers in the collective form of cultivation they chose freely when they confiscated the land of the rebel exploiters." Said article 1 of the decree: "For the purposes of assistance by the Institute of Agrarian Reform, all collective farms set up since 19 July 1936 are considered legally constituted *during the current agricultural year*,[38] and no claim will be handled by the subsidiary departments of the Institute of Agrarian Reform for the return of land occupied by the said collectives . . . even in cases where it is alleged that errors have been made of a legal character or in defining the political status of the former owner or beneficiary of the collectivized land." "This means," commented *Frente Rojo*, the Communist organ, "that the only thing that counts in guaranteeing the legality of the collectives is the very act, the revolutionary act of having formed them, and that they are thus saved from any legal or political stratagem that might be devised against them." It did not mention the fact that the status of legality had been conceded only temporarily. "[The decree]," it asserted, "grants to the agricultural collectives formed since 19 July 1936 an indestructible legal position. . . . What began as a spontaneous impulse among a large section of the agricultural workers has now been converted by virtue of the decree into a legal form of agricultural labor."[39] Nevertheless, many months later, in a program of common action, the CNT and UGT found it necessary to demand that the collective farms be legalized.[40] This did not change matters, for toward the end of the Civil War *CNT*, the Anarchosyndicalist organ in Madrid, was still insisting that they be legalized.[41] In fact, Vicente Uribe, who remained in charge of the ministry of agriculture until the end of the conflict, never granted a permanent status of legality to the collectives.[42]

Although the decree of June 1937 offered no guarantee of legality beyond the current agricultural year, it produced a sense of relief in the countryside during the vital period of the harvest, and in that respect achieved its purpose.

But no sooner had the crops been gathered than apprehension again set in. On 11 August, the central government—which in May had been reorganized without the participation of the CNT—dissolved the Anarchist-dominated Regional Defense Council of Aragon that had been formed early in the war to control the Revolution in that part of Aragon occupied by the anti-Franco forces, predominantly libertarian. After the Communists had helped to prepare the way for its dissolution by a short though fierce campaign at the beginning of August,[43] the Eleventh Division under the command of Enrique Líster, acting on instructions from Indalecio Prieto, then defense minister, and with the full knowledge and approval of the cabinet, moved into the region and dissolved the council.[44] So as not to arouse suspicion, the division had been instructed to proceed to Aragon to "rest and reorganize" after the battle of Brunete on the central front, and a dissolution decree, secretly approved by the central government, was published only after the council had been dissolved.[45] "Hated by the people, the Council of Aragon collapsed without the firing of a single shot," writes Líster. "And when the next day the dissolution decree appeared in the *Gaceta* the council had ceased to exist."[46] Commenting on the decree, *Adelante*, mouthpiece at that time of the moderate Socialists in the government, said: "Perhaps the change that took place yesterday in Aragonese territory may not have extraordinary repercussions abroad. No matter. It deserves to have them because by this action the government offers the firmest testimony of its authority."[47]

Concurrently with the publication of the decree, José Ignacio Mantecón, a member of the Left Republican party, but a Communist sympathizer, who after the Civil War joined the party,[48] was appointed governor general of the region. "From the first day," writes Líster, "we understood each other perfectly and we gave him all our collaboration and help in his difficult task."[49] Backed by the military power of the Eleventh Division, Mantecón ordered the breakup of the collective farms and the arrest of militants of the CNT.[50] According to a report of the Aragon CNT, the land, farm implements, horses, and cattle confiscated from right-wing supporters were returned to their former owners or to their families; new buildings erected by the collectives, such as stables and hen coops, were destroyed, and in some villages the farms were deprived even of the seed necessary for sowing, while six hundred members of the CNT were arrested.[51]

Of this repression the tenant farmers and small owners who had entered the collective farms in the early weeks of the Revolution, when the power of the CNT and FAI in Aragon was undisputed, took full advantage. They divided up the land as well as the crops and farm implements, and, with the aid of the assault guards and Communist military forces, even raided those collectives that had been established in accordance with the wishes of their members. The situation became so serious that the Communists, although evading personal responsibility, later acknowledged that a dangerous policy had been adopted.

To redress the situation the party again changed its policy, and some of the dismantled collectives were restored. "The recognition of the rights of the collectives," wrote José Silva, the Communist general secretary of the Institute of Agrarian Reform,[52] "and the decision to return what had been unjustly taken away from them, together with the efforts of the governor general of Aragon in this direction, brought things back to normal. Tranquillity returned, and enthusiasm was revived among the peasants, who gave the necessary labor for sowing the abandoned land."[53]

After the destruction of the collective farms in Aragon, the Communist party was compelled to support collectives in other regions against former owners who sought the return of confiscated land.[54] This change was caused not only by the damage inflicted on rural economy and on morale at the front and in the rear by its previous policy, but by another important factor: much as the Communist party needed the backing of the small and medium tenant farmer and proprietor in the anti-Franco camp, it could not allow them to become too strong, lest, under the leadership of the liberal Republicans and moderate Socialists, they should, in conjunction with the urban middle classes, endeavor to take the affairs of state into their own hands. In order to guide domestic and foreign policy in accordance with Russia's diplomatic needs, the Communists had to be supreme. This they could be only by a careful interplay of the pieces on the board; for their influence rested not only on the inherent strength of their own party, powerful though it was, but on a careful balancing of class forces which, because of their mutual antagonisms, could not combine against the arbiter that stood between. Hence, if in the beginning it was essential for the Communists to destroy the power of the extreme left by an alliance with the middle strata of the population, it was no less important at a later stage to prevent these layers from acquiring too much strength and threatening the supremacy of their party.

But no attempt on the part of the Communists to balance one class against another could succeed for long unless they could gain control of the armed forces, both at the front and in the rear, unless they could incorporate the independent revolutionary militia into a regular army under the command of a staff of officers and political commissars amenable to their wishes. This necessity they recognized from the first days of the Revolution.

Part IV

*From the Revolutionary Militia
to a Regular Army*

25

The Revolutionary Militia

*T*he reader will remember that the government of liberal Republicans formed by José Giral at the outset of the Civil War inherited an officer corps whose cohesion had been shattered by the military insurrection and social revolution.

In an attempt to counter the rebellion, the government issued a decree releasing the enlisted men from all oaths of service and obedience to their officers. But the decree, wrote President Azaña, was not heeded in cities that were controlled by the military. On the other hand, it was observed in the garrisons of Madrid, Barcelona, Cartagena, Valencia, and other cities, where the rebellion had been thwarted:

> The men left their barracks and nearly all of them went home. An appreciable number joined the volunteer units that, under improvised leadership and with limited weapons, went to fight at the fronts. The few units that could be kept in their barracks were virtually useless. The rebellion had undermined discipline everywhere. The professional officers were suspect, and the ranks, composed mainly of workingmen, preferred to listen to the directives of their unions or parties than to those of their commanders. In Madrid, whose garrison consisted of thirteen regiments, it was a hard job, during the first few days, to organize four to six infantry units and a battalion of engineers for service in the Sierra.
>
> The Republican government gave arms to the people in order to defend the approaches to the capital. Several thousand rifles were handed out. But in Madrid, and especially in Barcelona, Valencia, and other places, the masses stormed the barracks and carried off the arms. In Barcelona they occupied all the military establishments. War material, which was already scarce, disappeared. They burned the draft records; they burned the horses' saddles. In Valencia the horses of a cavalry regiment were sold to the gypsies for five or ten pesetas each. At the beginning of a war that threatened to be terrible the deluded masses destroyed the last remnants of the military machine, a machine that was going to be so badly needed. These deeds, and others that were no less deplorable, were due to the following reasons: few people gauged the importance of the rebellion and the gravity of the situation. Many welcomed it as a favorable event.[1]

Because the government lacked the necessary forces with which to combat the military insurrection, the weight of the struggle at the fronts fell upon the labor unions and proletarian parties that organized militia forces under commanders appointed or elected from among the most resolute and respected of their men. These militia units, or "columns," as they were generally called, to which army officers were attached under the watchful eye of party or union representatives, were controlled exclusively by the organizations that had created them, the officers assigned by the war minister possessing little or no authority.[2]

"When, out of absolute necessity, [the working-class organizations] had to make use of us," complained a Republican army officer, "they employed only the minimum of loyal officers strictly indispensable to their needs; these were kept under constant vigilance and were, in addition, menaced because of their alleged fascist sympathies."[3]

In order to create a counterpoise to the revolutionary militia, no less than to organize additional armed units for service at the front, the liberal Republican government of José Giral decided, during the last days of July, to call up two years of conscripts,[4] a measure that met with trifling response, not only because many of the men were already in the militia, but also because the government lacked any coercive machinery for enforcing the draft.

In addition, during the first few days of August, the government published a decree providing for the creation of "volunteer battalions,"[5] and two weeks later, in a still more significant move, it issued a series of decrees aimed at the formation of a "volunteer army" that was to be raised from among men in the first-line reserve, with cadres composed of retired officers and of noncommissioned officers not then on active service, whose loyalty had been attested by a Popular Front organization.[6]

But the effect of these measures, too, was negligible because, as President Azaña testifies, "thousands upon thousands of volunteers preferred to enlist in the popular militia organized spontaneously by the unions and parties."[7] Hence, the volunteer army, as a professional officer testifies, remained on paper. "As for the combatants who had already enlisted in the militia, they preferred to remain in their own units with their friends and comrades-in-arms rather than join the new [volunteer] battalions."[8] Moreover, the idea of an army under the control of the government—a government whose premier, José Giral, and war minister, Hernández Sarabia, were both stalwart supporters of the moderate-minded Azaña—was viewed with alarm not only by the Anarchosyndicalists of the CNT but also by the left-wing Socialists of the UGT, whose secretary, Largo Caballero, had several violent interviews with José Giral on this account.[9] In an editorial published two days after the promulgation of the decrees, *Claridad*, the mouthpiece of Largo Caballero, declared that the measures could not be justified either on the ground that the militia forces were not large enough numerically to carry on the war or on the ground that they lacked efficiency; that the number of men incorporated in them or who desired to join them could be considered "virtually unlimited"; and that as far as their military efficiency was concerned, "it could not be greater and we doubt whether it could be surpassed by any other armed organiza-tion." Furthermore, *Claridad* affirmed, the reserve soldiers who had not yet volunteered for service in any other force were "not animated, however great their loyalty to the Republic, by the same political and combative ardor that had induced the militiamen to enlist," and the preferential right—granted them under the terms of one of the decrees—to enroll in the regular army units to be organized after the war would not stimulate the fighting zeal of the militia. Having disposed of the military arguments in favor of the volunteer army, the editorial continued:

"The new army, if there must be one, should have as its foundation the men who are fighting today and not merely those who have not yet fought in this war. It must be an army that is in keeping with the Revolution . . . to which the future State will have to adjust itself. To think of replacing the present combatants by another type of army that, to a certain extent, would control their revolutionary action, is to think in a counterrevolutionary way. That is what Lenin said (*State and Revolution*): 'Every revolution, after destroying the state apparatus, shows us how the governing class attempts to reestablish special bodies of armed men at "its" service, and how the oppressed class tries to create a new organization of this type capable of serving not the exploiters but the exploited.' "[10]

Unlike the left-wing Socialists, the Communists entertained no misgivings about the projected army, and, indeed, aided the Giral cabinet in implementing its decrees.[11] Yet, if as has already been shown, their championship of this govern-ment sprang from the need to keep it in office as a democratic veil to influence the Western world, if, in particular, their support of the military decrees was inspired by the need to create a centralized force of greater combat efficiency than the militia, the Communists also had a more subtle motive; for they not only regarded the decrees as a step toward a permanently organized army of the state, over which they hoped, in the course of time, by systematic and adroit penetration, to establish their supremacy, but they knew that as long as the unions and parties possessed their own armed units and as long as these units had not been merged into a regular army whose pivotal positions they themselves controlled, their own party could never be master of the anti-Franco camp.

In their endeavors to quiet the fears of the Caballero Socialists with regard to the creation of the volunteer army, the Communists were careful to conceal the political motive of their support under the sole and powerful argument of military efficiency and to refrain, as yet, from calling for the fusion of the militia into a government-controlled army, a demand that was soon to become an important item in their declared program.

Their central organ, *Mundo Obrero*, wrote:

We believe that all the parties and organizations belonging to the Popular Front will agree with us on the necessity of creating in the shortest possible time an army with all the technical efficiency required by a modern war. There can be no doubt that the cornerstone of our army is our heroic popular militia. But it is not enough to romance about its self-sacrifice and heroism. We must give thought to the measures that should be put into effect immediately with a view to increasing the efficiency of the people in arms. . . .

Some comrades have wished to see in the creation of the new volunteer army something like a detraction from the role of the militia, possibly because the decree lacks sufficient clarification. Undoubtedly the militia should enjoy all the advantages conceded to the volunteer army, and we do not entertain the least doubt that the government will say so immediately because no one under present circumstances could think of creating anything that runs counter to our glorious popular militia. Actually, the aim of the decree is to complement and reinforce the popular army, to give it greater efficiency, and to end the war as soon as possible.[12]

But the issuance of a further decree granting militiamen the same preferential right as conceded to members of the volunteer army[13] did nothing to remove the uneasiness that the government's project had created in the minds of the left-wing Socialists. The appointment of Diego Martínez Barrio—who had formed the ill-starred cabinet of conciliation on the morning of 19 July, and whose party, the Unión Republicana, stood on the right flank of the Popular Front coalition—to head the commission charged with the organization of this army[14] only tended to deepen their suspicion of the government's intentions. It was this suspicion, superimposed upon the imminent threat to Madrid consequent upon the rapid advance of General Franco's forces—an advance that had carried them more than 230 miles in twenty days after their capture of Badajoz on 14 August—that impelled José Giral, weary of presiding over a government that had power on paper only and lacked the support of the majority of the working class, to propose that the government be broadened to include other Popular Front organizations.

It was in these circumstances, as has already been shown, that a new government was formed on 4 September, with Largo Caballero as premier and war minister.

Whether Largo Caballero would carry out the thoroughgoing military reorganization that the Communists envisioned was by no means certain in view of his antipathy to the entire concept of militarization expressed not only in the above-quoted editorial in *Claridad*, but in the following interview given to Mikhail Koltzov, Stalin's unofficial envoy, on 27 August, one week before he entered the war ministry. Koltzov noted in his diary:

Largo Caballero himself is dressed in workman's overalls, a revolver in his belt. He is tanned by the sun and wind, very vigorous and hearty for someone who is nearly seventy years of age. Alvarez del Vayo has set up the appointment and acts as interpreter. . . . Without preliminary remarks of any kind, Largo Caballero fulminates against the government. . . . The working-class militia doesn't believe in the government, it doesn't believe in the war ministry, because the ministry makes use of the services of shady people, of former reactionary Monarchist generals, of career officers, who are obvious traitors. . . . To the question why there is such a delay in converting the militia units into a regular army and whose fault it is, he gives no precise answer and renews his attack on the government. He regards as dangerous the recently published decree laying the foundations for the volunteer army. . . . [He] sees in the decree a contempt for the working-class combatants and a bestowal of special privileges on career soldiers: "The military caste is being resuscitated"!

I try to make him see the value of reserves for the army, especially in a country like Spain, without military training, that has done hardly any fighting. He predicts that the regular army will wrest from the people the arms that have cost them so dearly.

A long and lively discussion ensues regarding the advantages of the army and the militia. . . . Largo Caballero cites passages from *State and Revolution* by Lenin regarding the people in arms. I remind him that it was Lenin himself who created the workers' and peasants' army, granting it absolute priority over the heterogeneous militia groups, columns, and detachments. The fusion of the best elements among the lesser officers, carefully selected, with the advanced revolutionary workers, comprises the alloy from which a powerful antifascist popular army can be forged. Whenever units of the army and detachments of militia or guerrillas exist side by side with equal rights, sooner or later a contradiction emerges that later degenerates into a conflict, and the army, being on a much higher level, always wins. Then why prolong this period of contradictions? The fusion of all the antifascist armed forces into a single military organism must be accelerated.

Again he offers no direct objections, but he censures the Communists for wanting "to organize everything, to place leaders everywhere, to give everything a title, a label, a number." He attributes this to the youthfulness of their leaders, to the party's self-confidence, which is based not on its own successes and its own experiences but on those of the Russian Communists. He says that by helping the [Giral] government the Communists are doing harm, that they are inviting catastrophe, and are increasing popular discontent. The working-class parties must sweep away the functionaries, the bureaucrats, the whole ministerial system of operation and adopt new, revolutionary forms of leadership. . . .

All this gushes from Largo Caballero with vehemence and irritation, with the stubborn force of conviction. It is difficult to comprehend the source of this belated radicalism, this maximalism, in a man who, for decades, defended the most conciliatory and reformist positions within the working-class movement, who entered into agreements and even coalitions with extreme right-wing bourgeois governments, including the reactionary Monarchist dictatorship of Primo de Rivera. But Alvarez del Vayo and many others affirm that the "old man" has in fact changed enormously deep down within himself, that the struggle in Asturias [in 1934] and [the experiences] of the entire subsequent period have caused him to revise his political course. . . .

We speak for another hour and a half. Caballero refers several times to the incapacity and lack of loyalty of the Republican generals, personal friends of

Azaña, all those Sarabias [a reference to Hernández Sarabia, minister of war]. Later, when we are alone, Alvarez del Vayo and I . . . enter a small bar. He is very pleased with the interview and the conversation. He is confident that the "old man" is now in complete agreement with the need for a regular people's army. "He did not tell you this frankly; that's his way, but you will see; he will come out in favor of the army. The old man is favorably disposed toward the Soviet Union and the experience of the Russian Revolution."[15]

But only time would tell how far Largo Caballero, in his new capacity as war minister, would travel with the Communists and their Russian aides in creating the type of army they had in mind.

The first major problems that confronted him in his new capacity were undoubtedly the defects of the militia system; for, in spite of *Claridad*'s claim that the efficiency of the militia could not be greater, these defects were indubitably among the principal reasons for General Franco's swift advance up the Tagus Valley toward the Spanish capital. True, they did not spring from any lack of combativity, for in street fighting or in small battles against a localized enemy, the militiamen showed great courage; they sprang rather from lack of training and discipline, from the absence of any effective unity, either of conception or of action, among the militia units, and from the rivalry existing between the various organizations.

President Azaña recalls:

There were Republican, Socialist, Communist, CNT, UGT, FAI, and other battalions and brigades, as well as units formed by workers belonging to the same trade, without any plan, each one leaving happily for the front, with commanders selected by the militiamen, and with political and strategic objectives of their own creation. No one was subject to military discipline. . . . The war ministry [under Hernández Sarabia] tried to put order into all this confusion. It officially recognized the militia units, tried to arm them, gave them professional leadership, when they were willing to accept it, and assigned tactical and strategic missions to them in accordance with the most urgent needs. Whether these missions were carried out or not depended on the mood of the men, the whims of the subordinate officers, or the directives of the political organizations. The personnel reports prepared by the war ministry every day . . . reveal the incredible heterogeneity of that army and the varied composition, in number and quality, of its units. . . . At any rate, the commander of each sector of the front was a professional officer appointed by the war ministry. There were other professional officers in subaltern command posts. . . . They were all in a difficult position. Their authority was not always respected. They had to convince their subordinates that orders should be obeyed and take care that they did not arouse any suspicion of disloyalty. If the men retreated in disorder, if they disobeyed, or fulfilled an order badly, the commander could not deal harshly with them.[16]

The militias' distrust of professional officers, their inexperience under fire, the paucity of heavy arms and the total absence of effective military leadership gave the enemy forces an advantage that far outweighed their inferior numbers. On the Andalusion front, for example, a career officer, a Major Menéndez, who had been assigned by the war ministry to assume command of a militia column on the Montoro sector, telephoned Madrid on 1 October 1936 to report that the enemy had attacked Alcalá la Real and occupied it without any resistance. The morale of the militia, he said, was terrible. There were two groups: "One doesn't obey anybody. All they can say is that they should shoot their officers. The other group, which does obey, flees on the slightest pretext. Fortunately, we had a few carabineers, men in their fifties, who were able to avert a real catastrophe. As for weapons, the situation is also very bad, because the column doesn't have a single cannon or machine gun. . . . I must tell you once again that there is no way to get the militiamen to obey."[17]

"It is hardly necessary to say," wrote a left-wing observer, "that these troops made every mistake that can be made. Night attacks were launched with *vivas* for the Revolution; artillery was often placed on the same line as the infantry. Sometimes there were really grotesque incidents. One day a militiaman told me that after lunch a whole detachment went into a neighboring field to eat grapes; when it returned its position was occupied by the enemy."[18] Referring to the offensives launched by Catalan militia forces against the besieged town of Huesca, in the region of Aragon, Manuel Aznar, a supporter of General Franco, writes: "In the early days, the attacks of the Catalan columns, nearly all of which were made up of Anarchist militia, were so completely uncoordinated and so divorced from the norms of military technique that their movements resembled the arbitrary efforts of disintegrated hordes rather than genuine military operations. As a result, Nationalist headquarters gained two to three months in which to assemble reinforcements, to learn from their own weaknesses, to concentrate war material, and to prepare for the transition from an elastic to a rigid defense. Furthermore, it could be seen from the concentration of artillery fire, the disposition of machine guns, the preparation of assaults, the bad organization of the troops, the irresolution of the subaltern commanders, and from the weakness of the offensives that the besieging army lacked the most essential psychological and technical elements for war."[19]

On the same front, according to Jesús Pérez Salas, a professional officer and a loyal Republican who commanded the Macià-Companys column in the early months of the war, it was impossible to carry out a combined operation involving different units.

Whenever the staff decided upon an operation of this kind, . . . it was obliged to call the [militia] commanders to headquarters and explain to all of them the fundamental objective of the operation and the role that each column was to play. Thereupon, a debate was initiated, during which the militia commanders expressed their agreement or disagreement, often forcing a change in the original plan by their vetoes. After a great struggle, an agreement was reached but always with respect to an operation on a reduced scale and of much smaller scope. Even so, it was never carried out, because when the time came for undertaking the operation there was always somebody who acted tardily, upsetting that coordination which is the key to success.

This was due to the fact that orders, even within each sector, were never carried out precisely, and that, as forces of very distinct ideology existed on the front, each one of them looked upon the failure of the others with a certain degree of satisfaction. The CNT, which formed the bulk of the forces, wished for the defeat of its political enemies of the POUM and the PSUC with all its heart. These, in their turn, held the men of the CNT in abomination.[20]

"Sectarianism, differences in outlook, and proselytizing zeal," wrote a prominent member of the CNT and FAI, "resulted not only in the militia units being indifferent to one another's existence and forgetting that they had a common foe, but also, on many occasions, in really dangerous situations arising among them."[21]

"Party pride seemed stronger than the feeling of common defense," affirms the Socialist writer Arturo Barea, who was in frequent contact with militiamen returning from the Madrid front. "A victory of an Anarchist battalion was paraded in the face of the Communists; a victory of a Communist unit was secretly lamented by the others. The defeat of a battalion was turned into ridicule for the political group to which it belonged. This strengthened the fighting spirit of the individual units, but also created a hotbed of mutual resentment damaging the military operations as a whole, and circumventing a unified command."[22]

But the most striking overall account that may be regarded as typical of the situation obtaining on most of the fronts in the early months of the Civil War is given by the Republican officer Major Aberri, who was sent from Barcelona to assist in the reorganization of the Aragon front:

On approaching Sariñena [headquarters of the militia forces], I came across a truck halted on the other side of the highway, and, at the request of a group of soldiers, I stopped my car. Their truck had broken down, but they did not know what was wrong with it. . . .

"Where are you going?" I asked them with surprise.

"To Barcelona, to spend the Sunday there."

"But aren't you supposed to be at the front?"

"Sure, but as there's nothing doing we are going to Barcelona."

"Have you been given leave?"

"No. Can't you see we are militiamen?"

They did not understand my question because it was the most natural thing in the world for them to leave the front when it was quiet. They knew nothing of discipline, and it was clear that nobody had bothered to instruct them on the subject. After a forty-hour week at the front they got bored and left it. . . .

Once [in Sariñena] I reported to the commander of the [Aragon] front [a professional officer] and informed him of my assignment. I told him what plans I had in mind, what I thought it necessary to do. He looked at me pityingly, and then replied:

"We shall see. We shall see. Things are not what they used to be, and you have to be pretty smart to get along with these fellows. At any rate I am having a conference with the heads of the [militia] columns very soon, and you will have an opportunity to judge for yourself. Meanwhile, stay and have lunch with me. . . ." We spoke at length during the meal and he told me about his tragedy; he had no authority and could not make himself obeyed by anybody. The leaders of the columns were demigods who accepted neither orders, advice, nor suggestions.

"You will see for yourself! The war cannot be waged in this way. I have no supplies; war material is distributed by the parties and trade unions; arms are not sent where they are most needed, but where [these organizations] decide. . . ."

The leaders of some of the columns arrived. . . . The majority of them had never served in the army. Some were accompanied by professional officers, who were called technicians, but who unfortunately were without authority. Their role was an auxiliary one, and their advice was to no purpose. Also to no purpose were the mortifications we officers had to suffer in spite of the fact that we had been loyal to our oath and had risked our all. Nobody had any confidence in us: any Tom, Dick, or Harry thought he had a right to spy on us and ignore our suggestions. . . .

The commander of the Aragon front recommended that a decisive operation be launched against Huesca. Everything pointed to the fact that this historic Aragonese town was almost without protection, and that with an intelligent and well-coordinated attack it would have fallen into the hands of the Republic. . . . Those present listened to his plan, which was discussed in detail, but unfortunately they finally decided to consult their respective trade-union organizations before accepting anything. In the end the discussion took a very regrettable turn because the commander's request that some of the columns should hand over to other units the additional material they needed was rejected out of hand. In other words, the commander of the front had absolutely no authority to decide on the disposition of men and arms.

I point these things out, even though briefly, since they accurately reflect the predicament of a people who, because of a lamentable indiscipline and a tremendous lack of equipment, had to perform prodigies of heroism in order to resist a regular army. . . . What could they not have achieved with good leaders, with sufficient war material, and with military discipline? I saw this later when I visited the different sectors of the front. There were no fortifications at that time. A position was taken by sheer courage, but since nobody bothered to fortify it, it was lost during the next enemy counterattack. The employment of war material was equally absurd. I was once in a position where there were several 10.5 guns, but there were no munitions. These were in the possession of a nearby column, which refused to part with them although it had no artillery itself. . . .

The system of trenches was also in keeping with the situation. At some points parapets had been thrown up with an eye to a neighboring column that belonged to a different political organization. There was a certain amount of satisfaction when a rival got a beating from the enemy. . . .

During my mission on the Huesca front, I had to pass a night very near the enemy lines. I was tired and I lay down to sleep, but shortly after wrapping myself up in my blanket, I heard someone singing at the top of his lungs. I got up and found a sentinel singing a jota for all he was worth.

"Listen," I said. "Don't you know that a sentinel should keep quiet?"

"Who the hell cares? That's what things were like in the past."

"No, man, no! They should be the same now. Don't you realize that they could spot you and plug a bullet into you from the other side?"

"Nuts! We have agreed not to plug one another. Besides, if I don't sing, I'll fall asleep."

In face of such reasoning I retired to my improvised "dormitory"—a blanket, the earth, and the grass—ready to sleep when this yokel of a guard had finished his repertoire. But no sooner had he stopped singing than I heard him speaking with a loud voice, as though carrying on a discussion with someone at a distance. I got up from my nook again and saw with amazement—afterward nothing amazed me—that our sentinel was talking to the sentinel on the fascist side of the lines, who was asking him what he had eaten for dinner. Our man, laying it on thick, gave him a pantagruellian menu. Lucullan had eaten at his own table.

"You've eaten all that!" retorted the other. "You've only had potatoes and you've had to be thankful for them!"

"You mean that potatoes are all *you've* eaten, and things are going to get even worse for you. We have everything we want here. Come over and you'll soon see."

Turning down this offer, the other fellow replied with an invitation to a certain member of his enemy's family, whom he qualified in not very academic language [your whore of a mother][23] to come over to his own lines, adding, "And shut up, you starving rat!"

"Starving rat!" exclaimed our sentinel. "Just to show you that we have more food here than we need, here's a sausage for you."

And without further ado, he flung a hand grenade over the parapet. The result was inevitable. Within a few seconds the firing became general along the entire front. Hand grenades, rifles, and machine guns performed their fantastic symphony for a good quarter of an hour.

Then silence fell, but only after several thousand cartridges had been wasted stupidly.[24]

In addition to all the aforementioned defects, the militia system had other notable shortcomings. There was, for example, no central general staff in the proper sense of the word. José Martín Blázquez, an officer in the war ministry, first under Hernández Sarabia and then under Largo Caballero, writes: "There was, of course, no general staff, but its functions were partly fulfilled by the intelligence department, which received all cables and [radio] messages. . . . Most of the other departments of the general staff were not created until after . . . Largo Caballero became minister of war."[25] It is worthy of remark that the war ministry under Hernández Sarabia had to rely upon the working-class organizations for much of its information. "In the offices of the UGT in Madrid," writes Alvarez del Vayo, "a permanent information bureau was set up, and this for some time was the war ministry's finest news agency. From every province, from every village where a representative of this organization was installed, the slightest movement of rebel troops was telephoned immediately to the central office."[26]

Still, there was no central military body that could review the situation on all the battlefronts, formulate a common plan of action, and decide on the allocation of available supplies of men, munitions, arms, and motor vehicles in such a way as to produce the best results on the most promising front. Nor could such central control be expected in the early days of spontaneous activity and individual initiative. "We all remember," writes a Republican sympathizer, "how we began to wage the war. A few friends got together, jumped into a truck or car that they owned or confiscated, one with a rifle, another with a revolver and a few cartridges and took to the highway to look for fascists. When we reached a point where we encountered resistance, we fought and, when munitions were exhausted, we generally retreated not to a defensive position . . . but to our point of departure."[27]

In the first months of the Revolution the war ministry exercised hardly any authority in the field of transportation and had to rely upon a National Committee of Road Transport, dominated by representatives of the CNT and UGT.[28] Not only did the committee pay scant heed to the demands of the war ministry,[29] but its own orders were for the most part disregarded by militia units, committees, trade-union branches, and local party headquarters that retained what vehicles they could for their own use without regard to general requirements.[30]

To make matters worse, each party and labor union had its own military headquarters that, in most cases, attended to the requirements of its own militia without any knowledge of or regard to the needs or military plans of other units on the same or neighboring sector, least of all on distant fronts,[31] and, frequently, supplies of one unit were stolen by another.[32] Alejandro Garcia Val, a commander at one time of the Communist party's Fifth Regiment, acknowledged after the war that the regiment often stole vehicles from the CNT to compensate for its own deficiency.[33]

Whereas the strength of General Franco's forces during the first few months of the war lay largely in the Moors and Foreign Legionaries with their stern discipline, training, and professional cadres[34] and in the modern aircraft that had been arriving from Italy and Germany since the first weeks of the war, the militia units, with few exceptions, had no staff of officers they would trust to lead them into the field; were, for the most part, ignorant of the organization of war, of cooperation between sections and companies, of the use of cover and camouflage, of the digging of trenches; were subject to the orders of no central military authority; had little or no discipline; and had no modern aircraft to protect them until the adversary reached the very gates of Madrid at the beginning of November.[35] In such circumstances, despite their numerical superiority, they were not only incapable of any sustained offensive action in the first months of the war, and at many points wasted month after month in fruitless sieges,[36] but they often crumbled under the onset of the enemy. "It is a phenomenon of this war," declared García Oliver, the Anarchist leader, "that when towns held by the fascists are attacked they hold out for a long time and that [when we are attacked] we do not resist at all. They surround a small town, and after a couple of days it is taken; but when we surround one we spend our entire life there."[37]

26

Discipline and the Anarchosyndicalist Militia

Of the manifold defects of the militia system that General Franco's victories forced to the front during the first weeks of the war, none was more hotly debated or called for more urgent correction than the lack of discipline. Although this problem beset all the militia units, whatever their ideology, its solution encountered a philosophical impediment only in those formed by the libertarian movement, for the liberty of the individual is the very core of Anarchism, and nothing is so antipodal to its nature as submission to authority. "Discipline is obedience to authority; Anarchism recognizes no authority," said *La Revista Blanca*, a leading Anarchist journal, in an issue published before the Civil War.[1]

The CNT-FAI militia reflected the ideals of equality, individual liberty, and freedom from obligatory discipline integral to the Anarchist doctrine. There was no officers' hierarchy, no saluting, no regimentation. "A CNT member will never be a disciplined militiaman togged up in a braided uniform, strutting with martial gait through the streets of Madrid, and rhythmically swinging his arms and legs," said an article in *CNT*.[2] And a resolution approved at a regional congress of the Valencia CNT stated: "When a comrade enters the CNT barracks, he must understand that the word barracks does not signify subjection to odious military regulations consisting of salutes, parades, and other trivialities of the kind, completely theatrical and negating every revolutionary ideal."[3] If there was no discipline in the CNT-FAI militia units in the early days of the Civil War, there were also no military titles, badges, or distinctions in the way of food, clothing, and quarters, and the few professional military men whose services were accepted acted only in an advisory capacity.[4] The basic unit was the group, composed generally of ten men;[5] each group elected a delegate, whose functions were somewhat akin to those of a noncommissioned officer of the lowest rank, but without the equivalent authority. The groups formed a century that elected its own delegate, and any number of centuries made up a *columna*, or "column,"[6] at whose head stood a committee of war.[7] This committee was likewise elective and was divided into various sections in accordance with the needs of the column.[8] The gradation into group and century delegates and a committee of war did not imply the existence of any permanent staff with special privileges since all delegates could be removed as soon as they failed to reflect the wishes of the men who had elected them.[9] "The first impression one gets," ran a CNT-FAI account, "is the total absence of hierarchy. . . . There is no one giving orders by authority."[10] Nevertheless, duties had to be assigned, and in such a way as to avoid friction. In the Anarchist Iron Column, for example, lots were drawn by the militiamen to decide who should stand guard at night and who in the early morning.[11]

The few professional officers who were nominally placed in charge of libertarian units were dismayed by the absence of discipline and hierarchical command. On one occasion, Captain Alberto Bayo, who led an attempt to take the island of Majorca, complained to the committee of war in Barcelona, headed by the famous Anarchist Juan García Oliver, that discipline was unknown and that it was essential to introduce a hierarchical structure with responsibility of command. To achieve this, he argued, an iron fist was necessary, and he requested permission from the committee to shoot the first man who got out of hand.

"So, whom do you propose to shoot," García Oliver asked me.

"The first man who gets unruly," I retorted, "the first who creates indiscipline among the men and does not obey orders, the man who appropriates to himself what belongs to the community, the thief, the criminal."

"You'll soon get rid of those ideas," he said, cutting me short. "Those are the ideas of the old society. In our regime, no unfortunate comrade is shot. He is corrected, but he is not deprived of life. . . . You'll free yourself pretty soon of those criminal ideas, because if you were to commit such a crime your head would roll right after his."

"It is absolutely imperative to set an example. One cannot lead these men unless the commander has coercive power over them, because speeches and harangues are useless at a time when thousands of men are overwhelmed." . . .

"Forget such measures of coercion and punishment! If a comrade errs, he should be corrected with affection and made to understand his mistake, but he should never be deprived of his life. The worker has entered a revolutionary period in which he is lord and master instead of slave. He can no longer be treated as he was in the past and you army officers had better convince yourselves of that!"[12]

But so serious were the drawbacks of this antiauthoritarian system, particularly in the field of battle, that a widespread call for discipline soon arose. "On repeated occasions we have stated that we do not believe in the discipline of the convent or of the barracks," declared *Solidaridad Obrera*, "but that in actions in which a large number of persons participate a precise coincidence of views and a perfect coordination of effort are indispensable.

"In the course of the last few days we have witnessed certain things that have broken our hearts and made us somewhat pessimistic. Our comrades act independently and in a great number of cases ignore the slogans issued by the [directing] committees [of the CNT].

"The Revolution will escape from our hands; we shall be massacred from lack of coordination if we do not make up our minds to give the word discipline its real meaning.

"To accept discipline means that the decisions made by comrades assigned to any particular task, whether administrative or military, should be executed without any obstruction in the name of liberty, a liberty that in many cases degenerates into wantonness."[13]

Gaston Leval, the well-known French Anarchist writer, who was active in Spain during the Civil War, maintained that it was incongruous to try to wage war on the basis of Anarchist ideas because "war and Anarchism are two conditions of humanity that are mutually repugnant; one is destruction and extermination, the other is creation and harmony; one implies the triumph of violence, the other the triumph of love." There were in the rear, he said, a large number of comrades who at first had rejected discipline altogether and then had accepted self-discipline, but "if self-discipline results in an effectual collective discipline in a particular column, this does not justify dangerous generalizations, because this is not the case in the majority of militia forces, and, to avoid disasters, a discipline imposed from without is essential."[14]

The following anecdote appeared in an Anarchosyndicalist refugee periodical about Buenaventura Durruti—the most revered of the Anarchist leaders and regarded as a purist in matters of doctrine—who organized the first of the militia columns that left Barcelona in July 1936 for Aragon in the hope of conquering Saragossa and who was killed on the Madrid front in November shortly after he and his men arrived to help in the defense of the threatened capital: While he was still in Aragon, a group of young militiamen left the front in panic with the object of returning to Barcelona. Apprised of their intention, Durruti hastened to intercept them. "Springing out of his car, and brandishing his revolver, he cowed them and made them face the wall. Meanwhile, a militiaman from the locality arrived on the scene and asked him for a pair of shoes, to which he replied vigorously, 'Look at the shoes these fellows are wearing; if they are all right you can have the pair you like. There's no need for the shoes to rot in the soil!' It was very far from Durruti's mind to shoot those youngsters because he was accustomed to say: 'Here no one is under compulsion. Those who are afraid to remain at the front can return to the rear.' But he was so convincing that all of them asked to return to the front, where they fought with unexampled heroism."[15]

In spite of the persuasiveness of the CNT's widespread call for discipline, it was no easy task to secure the acceptance of ideas that slashed at the roots of Anarchist doctrine, and not a little ingenuity was at times necessary. In an article that appeared in the organ of the peninsular committee of the FAI, a leading Anarchist argued: "If the war is being prolonged, this is due not only to the material help the rebels receive from the fascist countries, but also to the lack of cohesion, discipline, and obedience of our militia. Some comrades will object, 'We Anarchists cannot accept the command of anyone.' To these we should reply that Anarchists also cannot accept any declaration of war, yet we have all accepted the declaration of war against fascism because it is a question of life and death and involves the triumph of the proletarian revolution.

"If we accept war, we must also accept discipline and authority because without them it is impossible to win any war." Then, criticizing a statement made by a delegate at a recent FAI congress to the effect that Anarchists had always been enemies of discipline and that they should so continue, he said: "The Tarragona delegate starts from a fundamental error. We Anarchists have encouraged indiscipline against the institution and power of the bourgeoisie, not against our own movement nor against our own cause and our own interests. To lack discipline where the general interests of our antifascist movement are concerned is to condemn ourselves wittingly to failure and defeat."[16]

On static fronts the idea of obligatory discipline was slow in taking root among the CNT-FAI militia. But on the fluid central front, where the advantages of General Franco's superior military organization were presented in dramatic terms, the breakdown of traditional Anarchist principles had gone so far by the beginning of October that the CNT defense committee of Madrid, which was in charge of the Madrid CNT-FAI militia, was able to introduce regulations that included the following articles: "Every militiaman shall fulfill the regulations issued by battalion committees and century and group delegates.

"He shall not act on his own account in matters of war and will accept without discussion any post and any place to which he is assigned, both at the front and in the rear.

"Any militiaman not obeying the regulations issued by battalion committees and century and group delegates will be punished by his group, if the offense is slight, and by the battalion committee, if the offense is serious.

"Every militiaman must understand that, although he joined the militia voluntarily, he now forms part of it as a soldier of the Revolution and that his duty is to take orders and to execute them."[17]

Ricardo Sanz, a prominent CNT militia leader, wrote some years later: "The militiamen managed to understand that war is a school in which something is learned every day. As a result, things changed without the need to impose a draconian discipline on combatants, all of them volunteers, who could have abandoned the front without being called to account."[18]

Although many libertarians yielded to the idea of discipline as "one of the great sacrifices that the victory of redemptive ideals imposes,"[19] others saw in the acceptance of the concept of authority by the libertarian movement a blow so deadly to Anarchist principles, a threat so real to the future course of the Revolution, that they could not conceal their anxiety. "We know," stated a propaganda committee of the Anarchist youth movement, "that present circumstances have compelled us, for the time being, to forget some of our dearest principles . . . but do not let us forget that the basic tenet of Anarchism is antiauthoritarianism, and that if we sail along with the authoritarian current by which some comrades have already been carried away nothing will remain of Anarchist ideas. Let us remember that other revolutions were arrested in their ascending movement and were brought to disaster when they were warped by the authoritarian disease that every revolution breeds. . . . No, comrades, for the sake of the ideals that animate us all, for the sake of the Revolution, the Anarchist youth begs of you not to follow this path. The authoritarian germ will lead to hatred, and we must not forget that hatred in our midst is the worst enemy of the Revolution."[20]

27

The Fifth Regiment

*F*or the Marxist organizations, particularly for the Communist party, whose members were indoctrinated with the principles of leadership and control, the problem of military discipline caused no heart searching. This is not to suggest that indiscipline did not exist in the ranks of the Communist militia;[1] rather, no conscientious scruples had to be overcome, no ethical principles had to be laid aside, as in the case of the Anarchosyndicalists, before the problem could be solved. The Civil War had been in progress but a few days when *Mundo Obrero*, the Communist organ, affirmed that every militiaman should get used to the idea that he belonged to a militarized corps. "Discipline, Hierarchy, and Organization," it demanded. "Every man must obey his group, each group the body directly above it, and so on and so forth. In this way our victory will be assured."[2] The Communists saw in military discipline and organization the central problem of the war. They lost no time in vesting the commanders of their militia with adequate powers to enforce discipline, and they undertook, through their Fifth Regiment, the training of military cadres and the formation of units with technical staffs and specialized departments.

The Fifth Regiment was their outstanding military achievement and by far the most renowned military unit of the Civil War. Its extraordinarily rapid growth was aided by the fact that the Communist party had already set up before the war a quasi-military organization, known as the Milicias Antifascistas Obreras y Campesinas (MAOC), the Antifascist Militia of Workers and Peasants, which, though small in numbers, became the foundation stone of the new regiment. According to Juan Modesto, the national leader of the MAOC, later one of the most publicized Communist militia leaders, the MAOC was an organization of "popular self-defense"—a consequence of the "exacerbation of the struggle provoked by reaction, whose goal was to transform the Republic gradually into a fascist regime." The mission of the MAOC, he affirmed, was to defend the workers and their organizations, their press, locals, meetings, and demonstrations. Immediately after the failure of the military insurrection in Madrid, he added, the party ordered him "to concentrate all the militiamen . . . in the old Salesian Convent, where the MAOC of the working-class district of Cuatro Caminos had already established itself." It was in this convent that the Fifth Regiment was born.[3]

Enrique Líster, who became commander in chief of the regiment in September 1936 and who, like Modesto, received his military training in Moscow,[4] writes: "One of the questions most frequently asked is why the Regiment was called the Fifth and not the First, Fourth or Sixth. . . . On 17 July [the day of the military rising in Spanish Morocco] . . . we began to form five volunteer battalions, using the MAOC as a foundation. The Fifth Battalion had its recruiting and organizational center in Cuatro Caminos. . . . On 20 July, after taking part in the assault on the Montaña barracks, the Fifth Battalion . . . decided to occupy the Salesian Convent . . . and to transform itself into the Fifth Regiment of the People's Militia."[5]

The Italian Communist Vittorio Vidali—known in Spain as Carlos Contreras or Comandante Carlos—was one of the principal organizers of the regiment and its chief political commissar. Claud Cockburn (alias Frank Pitcairn), a reporter for the London *Daily Worker*, portrays him as a "husky, bull-necked man, who combined almost superhuman driving power with an unbreakable gaiety."[6] Enrique Castro, the regiment's first commander in chief, describes him as "an insurrectionary type of orator" helped by his head and gestures that somewhat resembled those of Mussolini,[7] while Antonio Cordón, a professional officer and a Communist, characterizes him as the "incarnation of revolutionary dynamism."[8] He undoubtedly embodied all these features, but behind his gaiety and congeniality, to which I can personally testify, there lay one of the most sinister and ruthless figures of the Communist movement. Justo Martínez Amutio, the left-wing Socialist and governor of Albacete, who knew Vidali well, offers the following vignette: "[Trained] in Moscow as an activist and agitator, [he was] sent by the Comintern and the GPU to Latin America . . . to assist [Medina] Codovila. . . . [He] was a combination of spy, agitator, and gangster, tough and implacable toward anyone whom he regarded as an obstacle to Moscow's policy. . . . He arrived in Spain hand and hand with Codovila at the end of 1934. His ostensible assignment . . . was to assist the International Red Aid. . . . From the first day [of the war] he threw himself into the great social turbulence. He knew the street well and was in his element among the unfettered and violent masses. . . . He formed and instructed the first patrols and execution squads, set up locals and barracks and organized the 'clean-up' of those whom he called fascist, using the methods of the NKVD." Prostitutes, pimps, common criminals, Martínez Amutio claims—"the entire riffraff of the lower depths of Madrid that Carlos knew perfectly"—were used by him "for the benefit of the party."[9]

In 1937, Vidali described to Anna Louisa Strong, associate editor of the *Moscow Daily News*, the formation of the Fifth Regiment:

> We had to create an army and staff at once, for most of the armed forces were with the rebels. We had at first just groups of comrades, old and young, men and

women, many of whom did not even know how to use a rifle. . . . We had only enthusiastic, determined people, seizing any weapons they could find, following any leaders that arose, rushing to any front which they heard it was necessary to seize from the enemy.

In those days we took anyone who knew anything and made him an officer. Sometimes it was enough just to look into a face and see that the eyes were intelligent and determined, and say to the man: "You are a captain. Organize and lead these men."

After two days we occupied the Salesian Convent—six hundred of us, of whom two hundred were Communists. We decided to organize and the war department said: "You will be the Fifth Battalion; already we have four other applications."

"No," we said, "we shall be the Fifth Regiment, for we shall get at least a thousand men."

Well, those first four battalions remained on paper, but the fifth had six thousand men in less than ten days. During this time the [Giral] government wrote us: "Comrades of the Fifth Battalion," and we answered back: "We of the Fifth Regiment." After we got six thousand men they admitted that we were a regiment. . . .

We decided to create a special company which should give an example of discipline. We called it the "Steel Company." . . . For this company we established special slogans designed to create an iron unity. "Never leave a comrade wounded or dead, in the hands of the enemy" was one of these. "If my comrade advances or retreats without orders, I have the right to shoot him" was another.

How Madrid laughed at that. The Spaniard is such an individualist that nobody will accept such discipline, they said. Then our first Steel Company— mostly Communists and metalworkers—paraded through the city; it made a sensation.[10] After that we created twenty-eight such companies of picked men, besides the ordinary muster of our regular Fifth Regiment militia.[11]

According to the official Communist history of the Civil War, "the oath of the militiamen of the Fifth Regiment was their moral code":

I, a son of the people and a citizen of the Spanish Republic, freely accept my role as a militiaman in the people's army.

I pledge myself before the Spanish people and the Government of the Republic . . . to defend with my life democratic liberties, the cause of progress and peace, and to carry the title of militiaman with honor.

I pledge myself to maintain discipline and to help to maintain discipline by carrying out to the letter the orders of my commanders.

I pledge myself to abstain from dishonorable acts and to prevent my comrades from committing them by making every effort to conduct myself correctly at all times with my mind focused on the high ideal of the democratic Republic.

I pledge myself to aid in the defense of the Spanish democratic Republic at the first call of the government. . . . If I should fail to fulfil this solemn pledge, let the contempt of my comrades fall upon me and let me be punished by the implacable hand of the law.[12]

So successful was the Fifth Regiment in its recruiting of Communists, Socialists, and Republicans, and of nonparty workers and peasants, that at the peak of its development in December 1936 it claimed that it had 60,000 men serving on different fronts.[13] Although Enrique Líster claimed during the war that it comprised 130,000 men,[14] his book, published many years after the war, names the more sober figure of 69,600.[15] On the other hand, Ramón Salas Larrazábal, a supporter of the right, who has produced in his four-volume history of the Popular Army the most complete study of this subject, claims that the total number of men enrolled in the regiment including the units trained in its induction and training centers in Albacete, Alicante, Almería, and Guadix, as well as in Madrid, never exceeded 30,000. "To reach the figure of 60,000 claimed by the Communists," he contends, "it would be necessary to include in the Fifth Regiment the International Brigades, which initially used the seal of the regiment's headquarters."[16]

According to Enrique Castro, the regiment quickly became metamorphosed into "a great center of political and military education."[17] Out of this center, which supervised every aspect of the volunteers' lives, political and spiritual, as well as economic and domestic, there flowed a large number of units possessing uniformity of method and organization. "They were parts of a building set," wrote Ralph Bates, assistant commissar of the Fifteenth International Brigade, "which could be rebuilt into an army when the time came. Their officers had precise rank and their orders received the backing of a disciplinary code which the volunteers accepted on enlistment. At the same time the political enthusiasm of the combatants was watched over and fostered by the political commissars."[18]

One of the great assets of the Fifth Regiment was the collaboration not only of professional military men who had been Communist party members before the war—such as Lieutenant Colonel Luis Barceló, a commander of the regiment[19] and head of the Inspección General de Milicias, the Office of the Inspector General of Militias, to which the militia units were required to apply for whatever arms and funds they needed from the war ministry[20]—but also of other professional officers, who, though far removed from Communist ideology, were attracted to the party because of its moderate propaganda,[21] superior discipline, and organization and because it alone seemed capable of building an army that could carry the war through to victory.[22]

In the prevailing wartime atmosphere, the discipline of the Communist party was undoubtedly one of its principal assets:

"The Communist party must be granted the credit of having set the example in accepting discipline," wrote a non-Communist professional officer. "By doing so it enormously increased not only its prestige, but its numbers. Innumerable men who wished to enlist and fight for their country joined the Communist party.

"It often happened that, when I came across a man who was just leaving for the front, I asked him:

" 'But why did you join the Communist party? You were never a Communist, were you? You were always a Republican.'

" 'I joined the Communists because they are disciplined and do their job better than anybody else,' was the answer."[23]

The party's discipline and the adherence of professional officers, as well as the collaboration of the foreign Communists with military experience, who were associated with the regiment for varying periods before helping to organize the International Brigades, were an undoubted advantage.[24] Most important was the preferential treatment the regiment received, as compared with other units, in the distribution of Soviet arms. Referring to the light arms that began to arrive in September, Segismundo Casado, operations chief on the war ministry general staff when Largo Caballero became minister of war, writes: "I noticed that these were not being given out in equal quantities, but that there was a marked preference for the units which made up the so-called Fifth Regiment."[25] Enrique Líster boasted in January 1937, at the time of the regiment's dissolution and fusion into the regular army, that it had thousands of machine guns and hundreds of pieces of artillery.[26] Although these figures were undoubtedly inflated for wartime propaganda purposes—to judge from the incomparably smaller number of machine guns estimated by Líster himself thirty years later[27]—it is nevertheless true, as Ralph Bates stated, that the units of the Fifth Regiment received "the cream of the weapons."[28] Because of this preferential treatment, because of the opportunity given to a large number of men of the regiment to train in Russia as tank operators,[29] and the attraction of the Communists' discipline and efficiency, the regiment was able to recruit heavily from non-Communist sources.

The influx of many Socialists and Republicans would appear to support the Communists' contention that the Fifth Regiment was not a Communist force but a force that belonged to the Popular Front as a whole. "We did not organize the Fifth Regiment in order to have an army of the Communist party," said José Díaz, the general secretary. "The Communist party does not need its own army. What the party wants is a strong, very strong army, a single army that can win the war and consolidate victory afterwards, an army of the people that will watch over the interests of the workers and peasants, of all antifascists."[30]

Nevertheless, as the Communist *International Press Correspondence* attested: "From the beginning, the Fifth Regiment was recruited and politically influenced by the Communist party."[31] In truth, it was under the rigid and all-embracing control of the party and was to all intents and purposes the principal element of its armed power during the first six months of the Civil War and would soon become the cornerstone of the Popular Army, the new regular army of the state that La Pasionaria herself acknowledged after the Civil War was "designed to play a decisive role in determining the future political structure of Spain."[32]

This frank admission gives added credence to the testimony of Enrique Castro, who after he had left the party[33] published the following excerpt from a speech he made to fellow Communists in the Fifth Regiment at a time when he was its first commander: "Comrades," he declared, "we have entered into a war that I believe will be terribly long. Only by winning this war shall we achieve the revolution, establish Socialism and become another Soviet Republic in an area of great importance for Communism in the entire world. You all know, comrades, that to wage a war an army is needed. . . . We are going to become the organizers of that army. . . . That army will be our army—listen carefully—our army. But we alone know this. For everyone else that army will be an army of the Popular Front. We shall direct it, but, above all, we must appear to others as combatants of the Popular Front. Is that clear?"[34]

There is really nothing strange about the candor of this speech, for it would be hard to imagine that there was a single sophisticated member of the party who did not believe that the Popular Front alliance was merely a transitory coalition, whose purpose was to advance the aims of the Comintern and the party, and that "an army of the Popular Front" would be a determining factor in shaping the present and future course of the Revolution.

28

The Popular Army

*I*mportant though the Fifth Regiment was to the Communist party as an element of armed power, there were potent political as well as military reasons why the Communists soon proposed that the independent party and trade-union militia should be incorporated into a government-controlled force. They knew that the war could not be carried through to victory without a single command that could decide on the disposition and manner of employment of all the fighting forces—in default of which there could be neither an organized army nor any planned strategy. They knew, too, that as long as the parties and labor unions possessed their own militia under the control of their own leaders and these forces were not fused into a regular army consolidated by the power of discipline and authority—an army of whose levers of command they aimed to secure control—they could never be the ruling force in the anti-Franco zone, determining, behind the curtain of democratic institutions, domestic and foreign policies.

During the life of the Giral cabinet, it will be recalled, the Communists had refrained from calling for the merging of the militia into a government-controlled army because of the Caballero Socialists' distrust of that cabinet's intentions, but once Largo Caballero himself was at the helm and in charge of the war ministry, they could do so without equivocation.[1] Indeed, the insistence of the two Communist ministers and the Soviet military advisers who, in urging their demands, made full use of the succession of defeats on the central front—highlighted on 27 September by the capture of Toledo, fifty-one miles from the capital—caused measures to be promulgated providing for the militarization of the militia and the creation of a military force, or Popular Army, as it was called, on a conscripted basis and under the supreme command of the war minister.[2] "Largo Caballero," writes Louis Fischer, whose personal contact with most of the leading Russians in Spain gives his testimony particular authority, "long resisted the idea of a regular army, and it was only with difficulty that his Soviet military advisers persuaded him to abandon the popular but inefficient form of party armies."[3]

"The Communist ministers Uribe and Hernández, the politburo, the Russian military and diplomatic advisers," attests Enrique Castro, who, it will be recalled, was the first commander in chief of the Fifth Regiment, "closed in on Largo

Caballero more and more. 'We must form the Popular Army!' 'We must form the Popular Army!' While supporting this slogan of the Communist party, the Fifth Regiment prepared . . . to convert its units into [brigades] of the new army, retaining its commanders, its commissars and its political hegemony in the new units. But, of this operation—the most secret and subtle of the entire war—only the Communists were aware. But not all of them, only the élite."[4]

But it was a long way, as events will show, from the publication of the military measures approved by Largo Caballero to their thoroughgoing execution, and, in succeeding months, the Communists, in barracks and trenches, in public harangues, and in the cabinet itself, pressed unremittingly for their enforcement.[5] Although the other militia forces resisted, Castro was not worried. "They will have to join the regular Popular Army. They have no alternative," he told members of the Fifth Regiment. "But when they do so it will already be rather late. The first units will all be in our hands, both militarily and politically, as well as many posts vital to the interests of the party."[6]

To set an example or, as the official Communist history of the Civil War put it, to demonstrate "the sincerity of its intentions,"[7] the Communist party progressively broke up the Fifth Regiment,[8] whose battalions, together with other forces, were welded into the "mixed brigades"[9] of the embryonic regular army. The Communist Enrique Líster, head of the regiment at the time, was made commander (with a Soviet officer at his side)[10] of the First Brigade.[11] Because they took the lead in disbanding their own militia, the Communists, according to Carlos Contreras (Vittorio Vidali), the regiment's chief political commissar, secured for themselves the control of five of the first six brigades, the majority of whose members had received their baptism of fire with the regiment.[12] Enrique Castro stated some years later that, in addition to Enrique Líster of the First Brigade, José María Galán, commander of the Third, and Miguel Gallo, commander of the Sixth (not to be confused with Luigi Gallo, or Longo, of the International Brigades) were party members,[13] and that José Martínez de Aragón and Arturo Arellano, commanders of the Second and Fourth Brigades, respectively, were Socialists with close ties to the Communists. Fernando Sabio, the commander of the Fifth Brigade, was described by Castro as a Socialist, but he did not indicate to what degree, if at all, he was under the influence of the Communist party.[14] Líster gives the names of all the commanders, but does not mention their political affiliation, except that of Martínez de Aragón, whom he describes simply as a "republican." He points out, however, that all were professional officers who had served either with the army or with the *carabineros* before the war.[15]

While they were thus gathering into their hands the control of the first units of the Popular Army, the Communists were not neglecting its commanding summits. Indeed, during the early weeks of Largo Caballero's tenure of the war ministry, they had already secured a promising foothold. This they were able to do partly because their relations with the war minister, notwithstanding his many grievances, were still of a tolerable nature (as a result, two of their adherents,

Antonio Cordón and Alejandro García Val, were appointed to the operations section of the general staff[16]), but mainly because in key positions in the war ministry they possessed men of supposedly unquestioned loyalty to Largo Caballero. These included such professional officers as Lieutenant Colonel Manuel Arredondo, his aide-de-camp, Captain Eleuterio Díaz Tendero, the head of the vital information and control department[17]—who in the months before the Civil War was the principal organizer of the UMRA, the left-wing Unión Militar Republicana Antifascista, which the Communists claim was an amplification of their Unión Militar Antifascista formed in 1934[18]—and Major Manuel Estrada, the chief of the war ministry general staff,[19] who, unknown to Largo Caballero, were being drawn or had already been drawn into the Communist orbit.[20]

By the same open and disguised occupation of directing posts, the Communists became firmly embedded in the vital general commissariat of war, set up for the purpose of exercising politicosocial control over the armed forces through the medium of political commissars or delegate commissars, as they were officially called.[21] The custom of installing commissars in the militia units had been adopted by the different parties and labor organizations at the outbreak of the Civil War with the object of keeping a constant vigil over the morale of the militiamen and the reliability of the professional officers. "Many of the militia battalions," attests Lieutenant Colonel Esteban Rovira, chief of the Forty-second Brigade, "were led by commanders who, conniving with the enemy, deserted at the first opportunity. This resulted in a natural distrust on the part of the men for their officers and made it necessary for them to have their own delegate in the military command in order to guarantee the loyal conduct of the officers. These delegates were the first political commissars."[22] In October 1936, in accordance with the general tendency toward centralization, a government body was created to regularize this practice. While the commissar was still expected to guard against disloyalty on the part of professional officers,[23] he was also expected to establish concord between the officers and men of the new regular army and to uphold the former's prestige and authority.[24] In addition to these duties and to the tasks of enforcing discipline[25] and watching over the morale of the soldiers,[26] the commissar had other responsibilities. "The commissar is the soul of the combat unit, its educator, its agitator, its propagandist," said Carlos Contreras. "He is always, or should be always, the best, the most intelligent, the most capable. He should occupy himself with everything and know about everything. He should interest himself in the stomach, in the heart, and in the brain of the soldier of the people. He should accompany him from the moment he enlists and receives his training until he leaves for the front and returns from it; he should interest himself in how he eats, how he sleeps, how he educates himself, and how he fights. He must see that his political, economic, cultural, and artistic needs are satisfied."[27] To be sure, not all commissars conducted themselves as they were expected to. "There are political commissars," affirmed Contreras, "who do not maintain close contact with the mass of the soldiers, who are not with them in the trenches, and who only want to be near the commanding officer."[28]

Because of the influence the commissar could exert upon the ranks, to say nothing of the opportunity his position gave him to sway the minds and hearts of the officers—he should engage in "political agitation among the officers and infuse them with the same spirit that animates the men," said the Communist leader Antonio Mije, a member of the politburo[29]—it is not strange that predominance in the commissariat of war was for the Communist party a vital factor in its bid for control of the regular army. It was well assured of this predominance to some extent because Mije occupied the subcommissariat of organization—the most important of the four subcommissariats created[30]—but principally because Felipe Pretel, the secretary general, and Julio Alvarez del Vayo, the commissar general, both of whom Largo Caballero had nominated because they possessed his unstinted confidence, secretly promoted the interests of the Communist party.[31] Before long, the party increased its influence still further owing to the appointment of José Laín, a JSU leader and recent Communist convert, as director of the school of commissars[32] and to the illness of Angel Pestaña, the leader of the Syndicalist party[33] who had occupied one of the four subcommissariats and who was replaced by Gabriel García Maroto, a friend of Alvarez del Vayo's and a left-wing Socialist with pronounced Communist leanings. Although critical of some of the Communists' methods, he eventually joined the party.[34] As Largo Caballero was not apprised until some months later of the defection of Alvarez del Vayo and Felipe Pretel and of the consequent extent of Communist penetration of the commissariat of war, the Communist party and its allies were able to exploit their privileged position without hindrance by appointing an overwhelmingly large number of Communist commissars at the expense of and to the extreme displeasure of other organizations. For example, García Maroto stated that, at the beginning of 1937, on the central front, Socialist battalions frequently complained to him that Communist commissars had been appointed to them and that they found this intolerable. He also said that Alberto Fernández Ballesteros, a Caballero Socialist, who held the position of inspector-commissar on the southern front, had protested that Antonio Mije, in appointing thirty commissars for that front, had selected only Communists.[35]

Because of the Communist party's control of the commissariat of war, such complaints could not reach Largo Caballero through the commissariat itself and did so, eventually, only through independent channels.[36]

Since the precise functions and powers of the political commissar were not strictly delimited by law, he possessed a broad measure of independence, which the Communist commissar—who was instructed to be "the organizer of the party in his unit, boldly and systematically recruiting the best elements from among the best fighters and recommending them for positions of responsibility"[37]—used to the full in helping to extend his party's dominion over the Popular Army. Even before the creation of the general commissariat of the war, the Communists had not neglected party activity at the front. "Teams of agitators must be created to inform militiamen of the attitude of the party with regard to all problems. . . . The Communists should take upon themselves the task of recruiting for the party the best fighters at the front."[38]

Jesús Hernández, Communist minister in the Largo Caballero government, declared, in a speech delivered some years later, after he had ceased to belong to the party:

> Dozens, hundreds of party and JSU "organizers" invaded the fronts and military units, and our officers were given categoric instructions to promote the maximum number of Communists to higher ranks, thus reducing the proportion of promotions open to members of other organizations. But it is my duty to state that while this reckless policy was being carried out the Communists did not cease fighting the enemy, and their resolution and discipline at the fronts showed them to be better than the best, a fact that facilitated the proselytizing work we had undertaken. . . . The zeal of some Communist officers and commissars was so unbridled and so undiplomatic that it went to the unspeakable extreme of removing officers and of sending men to the front line for refusing to become members of the Communist party or of the JSU.
>
> By this procedure the strength of the party was "reinforced" at the fronts by thousands of new adherents, but, as in the rear, the party destroyed unity, spread discord, and inflamed rivalry among military units of a different political complexion.
>
> That was the practical result of the policy we were ordered to carry out and were stupid enough to follow.[39]

Indalecio Prieto, the moderate Socialist leader, alleges that the Communists actually assassinated at the front Socialists who refused to join their party.[40] Jesús Pérez Salas, a professional officer and a loyal Republican, writes: "In accordance with their usual tactics and with the slogans they received, the Communist commissars, who formed the majority, endeavored to increase their party membership by ceaseless propaganda among the men in their units who did not share their ideas. They employed every means at their disposal, from the promise of future promotions to the threat of execution for offenses that had not been committed. This could not be viewed favorably by the other parties, inasmuch as they observed a continual reduction in the number of their members, who were compelled to change their party cards in order to avoid victimization. As a result of all this, a contest ensued between commissars representing different political views, with consequent prejudice to the armed forces."[41] And Colonel Segismundo Casado, the chief of operations on the war ministry general staff and an opponent of the Communists, affirms: "The commissariat [of war] was scarcely formed before it had started very active propaganda in the ranks of the Army, by arrangement with the directions which it received from the General Commissar. These directions could be summarised as intense proselytising work in the ranks, the persecution of anyone not affiliated to the party (secret and lying information being accepted as sufficient grounds for this); the actual elimination of those considered dangerous, for which monstrous responsibility the justification could be used that such persons had been killed for trying to go over to the enemy or for being traitors."[42]

The atmosphere created by the conduct of the Communist political commissars was certainly the very opposite from what Largo Caballero had hoped would be encouraged when the commissariat of war was formed. "When at the battle fronts or in the barracks and other places where the troops are billeted," ran a circular order signed by him, "disagreements or conflicts arise between soldiers or militiamen belonging to different trade-union organizations, delegate commissars shall act with perfect equanimity and in such a way that brotherly acts shall efface all divergences of opinion between the combatants as well as all selfish aims of individuals or groups."[43]

In addition to the work of the Communist political commissars and officers and to the help of crypto-Communists and philo-Communist Socialists in promoting the influence of the party in the Popular Army, yet another factor of greater consequence militated in its favor: this was the arrival, first of Soviet officers, then of Soviet arms.

"Shortly after [Largo Caballero's] government had been formed in September 1936," writes Luis Araquistáin, friend and political associate of the premier for many years, "the Russian ambassador presented to it a serving Soviet general [Vladimir Gorev], stating that he was military attaché of the embassy and offering his professional services. Later on fresh 'auxiliaries' sprang up spontaneously without being requested, and they introduced themselves *motu proprio* into the military staff and army corps, where they gave orders at will."[44] It would be incorrect, however, to infer that the principal Soviet military advisers arrived in Spain without the approval or at least the knowledge of the war minister. In point of fact—to judge from the exchange of letters between Soviet leaders and Largo Caballero, referred to in a later chapter—the war minister himself, through the Soviet ambassador, Marcel Rosenberg, actually requested the aid of Russian military advisers. On the other hand, it appears that not infrequently the advisers acted on their own accord without the consent of the war ministry, disregarding its views and conducting themselves independently and highhandedly. Colonel Segismundo Casado affirms that "their influence reached such a point as to control every project of the general staff and often entirely to reverse technical plans, replacing them with their own. These generally contained some political end; in questions of organization, appointing commanders; in news, in making propaganda in a party sense; in operations, putting on one side incontrovertible tactical and strategical considerations in order to impose their policy."[45] And the war minister himself testifies: "The Spanish government, and in particular the minister responsible for the conduct of operations, as well as the commanding officers, especially at headquarters, were not able to act with absolute independence because they were obliged to submit, against their will, to irresponsible foreign interference, without being able to free themselves from it under pain of endangering the assistance that we were receiving from Russia through the sale of war material. Sometimes, on the pretext that their orders were not being carried out as punctually as they desired, the Russian embassy and the Russian generals took the liberty of expressing to me their displeasure, stating that if we did not consider their cooperation necessary and fitting, we should tell them so plainly so that they could inform their government and take their departure."[46] On the other hand, Vicente Rojo, chief of the central general staff from May 1937 until February 1939, who enjoyed the support of the Communists and the Russians throughout the war, as will be seen in subsequent chapters, vehemently asserts that such charges were "false, absolutely false," and that "the directives for planning operations and the orders to execute them were *always* conceived and drafted by the chiefs of the republican general staff."[47]

This, to be sure, is not the impression one derives from the testimony of the Soviet general, N. Voronov, known in Spain as "Volter," who says of Rojo: "He liked to speak face to face [with us], openly exchanging opinions and taking down our proposals and good advice in his large notebook. When he was promoted to chief of the central general staff, our practical collaboration continued and I always wanted to help this renowned republican officer to the utmost of my ability."[48]

The relationship between the Spanish officers and the Soviet military advisers, according to Rojo, was one of cordiality and mutual respect: "[If] I can say anything about the Russian military commanders who were at the side of Spanish officers (not at mine), it is that they were excellent professional comrades, who helped me to overcome discretely enormous difficulties and that whenever they were given cause to overstep their functions they had the delicacy not to do so."[49]

On the other hand, K. A. Meretskov, the Soviet military adviser at one time to the chief of the general staff, General Toribio Martínez Cabrera, states in his memoirs published in Moscow in 1968 that "the mutual relations of the [Soviet] advisers with the military leaders of the Republic came up for discussion every day and somehow this complicated question could not be resolved in a pleasant manner."[50]

In spite of Rojo's denial of any intrusion by Soviet officers, Angel Lamas Arroyo, a colleague, who later escaped to the Nationalist side, affirms: "From Rojo himself I heard more than one complaint from which I inferred that the Russians considered their plans and directives superior to those of the Spanish general staff, [which] could not undertake anything on its own account without the final approval of the Russians."[51]

The behavior of the Russian civilians, to say nothing of the NKVD, was no less imperious than that of the military, if I may generalize from my own personal knowledge of Mirova, the Tass news agency representative in Valencia, and from the conduct of the Soviet ambassador—dealt with in a later chapter—as well as from that of Mikhail Koltzov, leading Soviet newspaper correspondent, who was influential in the Kremlin. Toward the end of 1936, Koltzov established himself in the Madrid commissariat of war, where, according to the Socialist Arturo Barea, then in charge of censoring the reports of foreign newsmen—a function that Koltzov placed arbitrarily under the control of the commissariat—he "intervened in most of the discussions on the authority of his vitality and arrogant will."[52]

In his last work on Spain, *Half of Spáin Died*, to which reference has been made on several occasions, Herbert Matthews, the *New York Times* correspondent during the Civil War and widely accepted authority on Spain for more than three decades, deliberately ignores the above-quoted testimony of Largo Caballero that appeared in my book *The Grand Camouflage*[53] and asserts: "Burnett Bolloten wrote of 'the minatory and imperious behavior of the Russian officers' and even of civilians like Mikhail Koltzov, the *Pravda* correspondent, who seemed to have the equivalent of a 'hot line' to Stalin. If so, this was behind the scenes and it never reached the stage of being high-handed with men like premiers Largo Caballero and Juan Negrín."[54] Matthews also ignored the fact that on one memorable occasion, described in *The Grand Camouflage*, and later in this volume, Largo Caballero, incensed by the Soviet ambassador's demands, expelled him from his office.[55]

29

General José Asensio.
Largo Caballero Defies the Communists.
The Government Leaves Madrid.

*T*here can be no doubt that the minatory and imperious behavior of the Soviet officers accelerated the deterioration of Largo Caballero's relations with the Communists that had already set in as a result of their absorption of the Socialist movement in Catalonia, of the JSU, and of many of his followers in the UGT and the Socialist party. While, for a time, these relations showed no manifest impairment, a significant crack in the smooth surface appeared when he appointed General José Asensio to the undersecretaryship of war on 22 October 1936.

As a commander during the first weeks of the war of the militia forces in the Sierra de Guadarrama, defending the northwestern approaches to Madrid, Asensio, at that time a colonel, had so inspired the confidence of the Socialist leader that when Largo Caballero became premier and war minister in September, he had made him a general and placed him in charge of the threatened central front in command of the Army of the Center. The Communists, who had already been striving to win Asensio's adherence to their party, acclaimed his promotion and new assignment, praised the military accomplishments of "this hero of the democratic Republic"[1] under whose direction their steel companies in the Sierra had "won victory after victory,"[2] and made him an honorary commander of their Fifth Regiment.[3] All these attentions, a prominent Communist acknowledged later, were designed to wean Asensio from Largo Caballero.[4] In the succeeding weeks, when Asensio showed no inclination to yield to the courtship of the Communists, and even evinced for them a profound antipathy, they demanded his removal from the command of the central front.[5]

The tactics they employed toward Asensio were their standard practice. Colonel Segismundo Casado writes:

> I may as well point out here what tactics the Communist party usually followed in their relationships with the commanders of the People's Army. They treated as

subordinate those commanders who were affiliated to their party, demanding simply that their orders should be carried out in whatever way best served their party ends, often in contradiction to their duty as soldiers. These officers generally obeyed blindly, paying more attention to the orders of the party than to those of the military high command. Other commanders on many occasions opposed their plans and rejected suggestions which sounded more like orders, or refused to take part in activities which would not have left them with a clear conscience. [The Communists] pretended to show the greatest consideration to those, but only for a short time, and in a wholly superficial way. They asked them to dine, they told them of the great admiration they had for them, for their intelligence or bravery. In a word, they attempted to stir their private ambitions, but when they were convinced that it was not possible to captivate them by such means, they started an insidious campaign of libel against them, so that the high command was obliged to relieve them. More than one commander lost his life or his freedom through simply doing his duty.[6]

"The commander who accepted Communist party membership without hesitation," wrote the organ of the moderate Socialists as the war was nearing its end, "soon acquired, in the Communist press, military qualities superior to those of Napoleon and Alexander, while those who dared to reject a membership that they had not requested were obliquely or openly criticized."[7]

The Communists' demand that Asensio be ousted from the command of the central front was aided by the military disasters that brought General Franco's forces close to the gates of Madrid during the month of October 1936. Yet, in spite of these defeats, it is generally agreed by Communists and non-Communists alike that Asensio possessed great military capabilities and exceptional mental gifts[8] and that the debacle was inevitable in view of the defects of the militia system and the lack of tanks, artillery, and aircraft.[9] These did not arrive from Russia until the end of October, while the International Brigades under Communist leadership that were to play a cardinal role in the defense of Madrid entered the field only in the second week of November, as will be seen in the following chapter.

Alvarez del Vayo, the pro-Communist foreign minister and commissar general of war, approved the rough draft of a letter written by Louis Fischer to Largo Caballero on 12 October questioning the loyalty of Asensio,[10] at the very time when the Communists were demanding his removal from the central front. Although del Vayo later voted in the cabinet for Asensio's dismissal from the undersecretaryship of war,[11] he contends that the general was "unquestionably one of the most capable and intelligent officers in the Republican army" and that he could "have become the greatest military genius."[12] It is noteworthy that the day before he approved Fischer's letter to Largo Caballero, Alvarez del Vayo had written the following lines in a note to Asensio: "I am aware of the very important operation due to begin at dawn. To know that you will be there personally directing it adds very much to my hopes. Owing to recent bitter experiences, we can only trust in your skill. For that reason I have decided to send you these intimate lines, which under all circumstances should remain between us."[13]

Although for a time Largo Caballero refused to remove Asensio, he finally yielded. But while propitiating the Communists with one hand, he diminished their victory with the other by elevating him to the undersecretaryship of war[14] in place of the pro-Communist Lieutenant Colonel Rodrigo Gil,[15] a former political associate. His determination to pursue an independent course found practical expression in two further moves some weeks later. He reinstated Segismundo Casado, whom he had dismissed from his post as chief of operations at the pressing instance of the Communists. Casado attributes his dismissal to the fact that he had warned the high command that the marked preference with which Russian arms were being distributed to the Fifth Regiment would cause suspicion and jealousy among the men and would soon bring about the accession to power of the Communist party. "This party," he adds, "observing what my opinion was, with the underhandedness which characterized it, started a campaign of discredit against me and convinced the minister of war that I was not the most suitable person to fill the office of operations chief because I had the faults of violence and pessimism."[16]

In addition to defying the Communists by reinstating Segismundo Casado, Largo Caballero removed Manuel Estrada, the chief of the war ministry general staff—who had recently joined the Communist party[17]—and replaced him by General Toribio Martínez Cabrera, a friend of Asensio's. In the whirl of events, these shifts passed almost unnoticed by the general public, but they gave the Communists cause for disquiet and convinced them of the rough weather ahead with Largo Caballero.

But while strengthening Largo Caballero's authority within the war ministry, the shifts did nothing in the long run to curtail the influence of the Communists on the vital central front. General Sebastián Pozas, a liberal Republican, whom Largo Caballero appointed to succeed Asensio as commander of the Army of the Center,[18] soon succumbed to their advances, as will be seen shortly, and on the evening of 6 November, with the enemy already in the outskirts of the capital, the cabinet hastily abandoned the imperiled city.

That same evening Mikhail Koltzov visited the deserted ministries. In his diary, he noted:

I made my way to the war ministry, to the [general] commissariat of war. . . . Hardly anyone was there. . . . I went to the offices of the prime minister. The building was locked. I went to the ministry of foreign affairs. It was deserted. . . . In the foreign press censorship an official . . . told me that the government, two hours earlier, had recognized that the situation of Madrid was hopeless . . . and had already left. Largo Caballero had forbidden the publication of any news about the evacuation "in order to avoid panic." . . . I went to the ministry of the interior. . . . The building was nearly empty. . . . I went to the central committee of the Communist party. A plenary meeting of the politburo was being held. . . . They told me that this very day Largo Caballero had suddenly decided to evacuate. His decision had been approved by the majority of the cabinet. . . . The Communist ministers wanted to remain, but it was made clear to them that such a step would discredit the government and that they were obliged to leave like all the others. . . . Not even the most prominent leaders of the various organizations, nor the departments and agencies of the state, had been informed of the government's departure. Only at the last moment had the minister told the chief of the central general staff that the government was leaving. . . . The minister of the interior, Galarza, and his aide, the director of security Muñoz, had left the capital before anyone else. . . . The staff of General Pozas, the commander of the central front, had scurried off. . . . Once again I went to the war ministry. . . . I climbed the stairs to the lobby. Not a soul! On the landing . . . two old employees are seated, like wax figures, wearing livery and neatly shaven . . . , waiting to be called by the minister at the sound of his bell. It would be just the same if the minister were the previous one or a new one. Rows of offices! All the doors are wide open. . . . I enter the war minister's office. . . . Not a soul! Further down, a row of offices—the central general staff, with its sections; the general staff, with its sections; the general staff of the central front, with its sections; the quartermaster corps, with its sections; the personnel department, with its sections. All the doors wide open. The ceiling lamps shine brightly. On the desks there are abandoned maps, documents, communiqués, pencils, pads filled with notes. Not a soul![19]

There can be little doubt that the government's precipitate and furtive departure—a departure that both Indalecio Prieto and the Communist ministers had urged the premier to organize and publicize ahead of time so as to avoid the "impression of a flight"[20]—did much to tarnish Caballero's reputation and to enhance the prestige of the Communist party. The latter, aided by its Fifth Regiment, by the presence of Soviet arms and military advisers, and by the arrival on 8 November of the Communist-controlled Eleventh International Brigade, the first of the International Brigades to enter the field, took the lead in defending the beleaguered city.

On the morning of 7 November, while the machinery of government, with its functionaries and files, was still en route to Valencia, *Mundo Obrero*, the Madrid Communist daily, declared: "[Thousands] upon thousands of men, of workers, whose future depends upon their courage, have rushed to the city's defense. The [locals of the] labor unions and of all the antifascist and working-class organizations are crammed with men ready to fight."[21] And *Milicia Popular*, the widely circulated organ of the Fifth Regiment, declared: "The fate of Madrid will be determined in a matter of hours. Thousands of militiamen are fighting the Moors and Foreign Legionaries, whose aim is to crush the people of Madrid. This is the historic hour, the hour of the decisive battle. It has been said again and again for many days that Madrid will be the tomb of fascism, and now the moment has arrived to turn those words into a reality. . . . The guns are thundering at our gates. Every Madrileño should be on his feet, ready to win, regardless of the price."[22]

During the first days of the defense of Madrid, *Milicia Popular* set aside its moderate, strictly "antifascist," language and evoked memories of the Russian Revolution in order to fire the revolutionary consciousness of the workers. In a front-page appeal, Carlos Contreras, the chief political commissar of the regiment, declared: "Madrid cannot fall. . . . Men and women, young and old are rushing to the trenches to defend their city, their lives and their future. . . . Long live the Spanish Revolution! . . . Today is the anniversary of the Russian Revolution. Our Russian brothers, surrounded by millions of enemies, starving, without planes and without tanks, and besieged on all sides, won their battle, because they had faith and confidence in the future. . . . We too have faith . . . and for that reason we shall conquer."[23]

The French historians Pierre Broué and Emile Témime are undoubtedly correct in stressing the underlying revolutionary faith that must have inspired many of the combatants: "For a large number of Spanish militants and 'Internationals' the defense of the capital was a revolutionary epic, whose purely antifascist emblem was only provisional. . . . Many of them believed that [the Communists' opposition to the revolution] was only a temporary tactical retreat and that the antifascist struggle would end in world revolution."[24]

Before leaving for Valencia on the evening of 6 November, General Asensio, the undersecretary of war, handed sealed orders, approved by Largo Caballero, to General Pozas, the commander of the Army of the Center, and to General José Miaja, who had just been appointed commander of the Madrid military district, inscribed: "Very confidential. Not to be opened until 6 A.M." Both generals decided not to wait until the designated hour to read their instructions. Had they done so, they contended, twelve precious hours would have been wasted.[25] Moreover, on opening their envelopes they found that they had been addressed incorrectly and that each had been given the other's assignment, a mistake that, in the opinion of Major Vicente Rojo, Miaja's chief of staff, might have "multiplied the probabilities of defeat" had it not been discovered in time.[26]

Pozas was given orders regarding the tactical movement of his battered forces and the establishment of new headquarters,[27] while Miaja was instructed to set up a Junta de Defensa or Defense Council, with himself as president, comprising members of all parties in proportion to their representation in the government, and to defend Madrid "at all costs." If all efforts to save the city should fail he was to retreat toward Cuenca "to establish a line of defense at a place indicated by [General Pozas], the commander of the Army of the Center."[28]

"No one in the government," affirmed Zugazagoitia, the director of *El Socialista* and a close associate of navy and air minister Indalecio Prieto, "believed that Madrid could be defended, the prime minister even less than the ministers, for he was only too well aware of the state of military confusion and disintegration. . . ."[29] Reluctantly, the war minister left Madrid convinced like Prieto that within three to six days it would be taken by the enemy."[30]

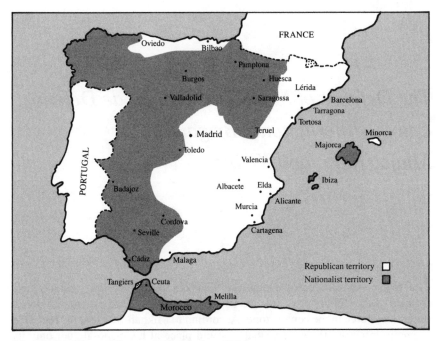

Map 2. Division of Spain, 7 November 1936

The battlefront was virtually nonexistent, writes Vicente Rojo. "The columns that had been containing the enemy on the Toledo and Estremadura highways were destroyed. Of the 3,500 men comprising one column, barely 300 could be found."[31]

That Miaja should have resented General Asensio's and Largo Caballero's action in giving him a task that in those days of peril to the capital seemed to augur only a fatal end is understandable and, according to Zugazagoitia, he realized immediately that he had been selected as a scapegoat.[32] In fact, General Pozas asserted that when Miaja learned of his assignment he nearly wept with rage at what he regarded as a deliberate attempt to sacrifice him to General Franco.[33]

Against this background of seemingly impending doom, this aging, easygoing, and undistinguished general—to whom nothing on that fateful day of 6 November 1936 could have appeared more enticing than a peaceful retirement—became a legendary figure almost overnight both in Spain and throughout the world, much to Largo Caballero's mortification, thanks to the unexpected resistance of Madrid. Miaja felt no sense of gratitude to the war minister for his sudden rise to fame and thenceforth their relationship was one of mutual enmity.

30

The Defense of Madrid, the Junta de Defensa, and the International Brigades. Miaja, Rojo, and Kléber.

*L*eft to his own resources, General José Miaja did the obvious thing: he accepted the help of the Communist party and its Fifth Regiment,[1] the best organized and disciplined force in the central zone. According to Mikhail Koltzov, the regiment promptly informed the general that it would place at his disposal "not only its units, its reserves, and its munitions, but also its entire general staff, as well as its commanders and commissars."[2]

Although Madrid's defenders were in the main poorly armed and organized, the militiamen had one great psychological advantage over their better equipped and more experienced opponents. "Our militiamen," recalls Víctor de Frutos, the Communist commander of the First of May Battalion, which defended the working-class suburb of Carabanchel,

> harbored the feeling more intensely than at any time during the previous four months that they were defending something of their own. It was clear that the proximity of their homes made them realize that they could yield no more. It was as if . . . they had barricaded themselves behind their doors . . . knowing that this was their last chance to save their lives, their property and their loved ones. . . . Simultaneously, a formidable barrier faced the enemy: Madrid would have to be conquered house by house. Every door was a barricade; every window a parapet for the defenders with homemade hand grenades. Yes, primitive hand grenades, but powerful enough to punish an enemy patrol. The streets were the entrance to Madrid. . . . Either the enemy advanced through them or he could not take the capital. And, to advance, he had to confront an army of militiamen whose ingenuity and courage were more important than all the tactics learned from military training. The housetops were observation posts. . . . This allowed us to take defensive measures at any time. . . . Many people maintain that the enemy forces did not advance toward the heart of Madrid for lack of decision. I

can state positively that they did not take Madrid because a psychological phenomenon unknown until then occurred among our militiamen due to the emotional reasons noted previously.[3]

Among the Socialist and Communist militiamen, Carlos Contreras (Vittorio Vidali), the chief political commissar of the Fifth Regiment, was a rousing figure. He was the "political soul" of the defense of Madrid, said Alvaro Menéndez, a fellow Communist, himself a participant in the fighting in the Casa de Campo. Running wildly from place to place, with eyes swollen from lack of sleep, "Comandante Carlos," as he was popularly called, exhorted the men to hold their ground. "It is better to die defending our country and our honor," he declared, "than to be stood up against a wall and shot." The International Brigade, he promised, was on its way to defend the threatened capital.[4]

The British author Vincent Brome gives the following account of that historic event:

The battle of Madrid, which began on 7 November 1936, pitted an ill-armed, unorganized but numerically far superior mass of Madrileños against an army of Moroccans and legionaries, fully trained, properly equipped and numbering roughly 20,000. The Madrileños had some Russian tanks and aircraft in support and Franco's troops were supplemented by German and Italian men and equipment. . . .

Now, as the grey, uncertain dawn broke on 7 November, the ancient city of Madrid heard the thunderous beginning of an artillery bombardment such as it had never encountered before . . . , but to everyone's surprise, as the shells burst, houses collapsed, men, women and children were buried beneath the debris and a great film of dust rose above the city like a ghost presence, there were very few scenes of real panic. The propagandists within the city had done their work well. Flaming speeches, powerfully written pamphlets, moving exhortations on the radio and a number of poems charged with stirring imagery had created an atmosphere in Madrid where heroism came naturally in the least expected person. . . . Workers of all kinds answered the radio call for recruits and moved towards the front lines, some completely unarmed but fanatically prepared to take up the arms of the killed and wounded. Women and children toiled all day building barricades and a group of women presently demanded and began to organize a women's fighting battalion. . . .

And then, on the misty morning of 8 November, a strange new band of fighters, disciplined men they seemed to the Madrileños wearing corduroy and steel helmets, came marching, in good order, along the Gran Vía towards the front.[5]

This was the Eleventh International Brigade—the "International Column" as it was first called by the Spanish press—under the electrifying leadership of the Soviet General "Emilio Kléber."

An eyewitness—the CNT journalist Eduardo de Gúzman, later editor in chief (in January 1937) of the Anarchist newspaper *Castilla Libre*—records:

Midmorning, the Edgar André and Paris Commune Battalions—1,700 German, French, Polish and Italian antifascists—march through the Puerta del Sol, the Plaza de Callao and along the Gran Vía toward the battlegrounds. . . . People gather to applaud them enthusiastically. In different languages, the men sing revolutionary songs. . . . They enter the Casa de Campo, where the enemy has already taken the Garabitas and Cerro del Aguila heights. . . . At the same time, the CNT militia cross Madrid in their trucks. . . . Singing a revolutionary hymn and with black and red kerchiefs flying, they proceed through the Paseo de San Vicente and the Dehesa de la Villa, cross the Manzanares River and enter the Casa de Campo, where soon more than half of them would die. . . . The "internationals" fight with courage. The Spaniards—libertarians, Communists, Socialists, Republicans and liberals—fight at their side with equal determination. . . . The battle continues without letup through the 8th and 9th, while enemy airplanes try to intimidate the civilian population with massive bombardments of the working-class districts and Argüelles. But the civilian population holds out stoically and the combatants do not yield a single step.[6]

In his dramatic account of the entrance of the International Brigades onto the stage of history, Hugh Thomas writes:

By the evening of 8 November the brigade was in position. The Edgar André and the Commune de Paris battalions were sent to the Casa de Campo. The Dombrowsky battalion went to join Líster and the Fifth Regiment at Villaverde. Kléber took command of all the Republican forces in the University City and the Casa de Campo. He immediately startled the Spanish commanders with his efficiency. . . . It has often been argued that the International Brigade saved Madrid. This XIth International Brigade, however, probably comprised only about 1,900 men.[7] The XIIth International Brigade, which eventually arrived at the Madrid front on about 12 November, comprised about 1,550.[8] This force was too small to have turned the day by numbers alone. Furthermore, the militia and workers had checked Varela [Colonel José Enrique Varela, the enemy commander] on 7 November, before the arrival of the Brigade. The victory was that of the populace of Madrid. The bravery and experience of the Brigades was, however, crucial in several later battles. The example of the International Brigades fired the militiamen to continue to resist, while giving to the Madrileños the feeling that they were not alone. . . . [On 9 November] Valera, checked in the Casa de Campo, mounted a new attack . . . in the Carabanchel sector. But the street-fighting baffled the Moroccans, who made no progress. In the Casa de Campo, Kléber assembled the whole of the International Brigade. In the misty evening they launched an attack. "For the Revolution and Liberty—forward!" Among the ilex and gum trees, the battle lasted all night and into the morning of 10 November. By then, only Mount Garabitas in the Casa de Campo was left to the Nationalists. But one third of the International Brigade was dead.[9]

Robert Colodny, in his account of this epic, is more emphatic than Thomas on the importance of the role played by the Eleventh International Brigade. "Madrid was saved," he writes, "when the three battalions of the Eleventh International Brigade, the Edgar André, the Commune de Paris and the Dombrowski, under the command of General Kléber, deployed in the Casa de Campo, and with the support of Soviet tanks and planes,[10] halted the charge of Varela's veterans. The appearance of the foreign volunteers stiffened the resistance of the militia and won the time necessary to organize, train and equip the Republican brigades."[11] And a Spanish historian writes: "The arrival of [the Eleventh International Brigade] is spectacular and the militiamen are fired with enthusiasm when they see these experienced soldiers . . . fighting with them side by side. In the ranks of the defenders of Madrid, the optimism is contagious. Now there are Russian fighter planes and Russian tanks and these Germans, Poles, Frenchmen and Hungarians ready to defend the Manzanares River and the Casa de Campo! Who said all is lost?"[12]

Why did these hardcore revolutionaries from all over Europe and America, mainly Communist idealists, go to fight and die in Spain? What noble cause inspired them to shed their blood in torrents in the battles of Madrid, the Jarama, Brunete, and the Ebro, the worst battles of the war? Was their great crusade simply to defend the democratic Republic of 1931, as some of their survivors insist even to this day? Not so, according to Sandor Voros, a political commissar in the Fifteenth Brigade. He went to Spain "to fight under the leadership of the Comintern, the giants of the revolution; to fight and die, yes, die if necessary on the side on the legendary Communist leaders who had defied prison, torture, consumed by but one ambition—to free the masses from oppression. . . . I was 'the hard-tempered steel blade of the class struggle, a Communist.' I was 'the expression of international solidarity forged into the armed fist of the revolutionary working class by the Comintern.' "[13] And William Herrick, the author of *Hermanos!* who also fought in the Fifteenth Brigade, stated in two letters to me: "When I went to Spain I had absolutely no belief in bourgeois democracy; to me the party line about democracy was only a tactic, a ploy, which in the end, I, we, hoped would bring the Communist party to power. Everyone I knew among the American volunteers, except possibly one or two, believed as I did that the popular front, the slogan for democracy, was merely a strategy to help the Communist party seize power. . . . The Veterans of the Abraham Lincoln Brigade have been lying about this for nearly fifty years. . . . It goes without saying that we of the International Brigades were also moved by antifascism. . . . It was while we were in Perpignan [close to the Spanish border] that our political commissar . . . told us that we were to answer that *we were antifascists, not to say we were Communists when asked the question in Spain.*"[14]

In Madrid, meanwhile, Major Vicente Rojo, whom Largo Caballero had appointed as Miaja's chief of staff just before his departure on 6 November, had put together a general staff to defend Madrid, composed, in accordance with his instructions, of members of the "available personnel" of the war ministry general staff,[15] whose chief, General Toribio Martínez Cabrera, with other senior officers had, like the war minister, abandoned the capital for Valencia. According to Captain Antonio López Fernández, Miaja's aide, Rojo's staff was formed of men whom the war ministry had not deemed sufficiently important to take to Valencia, but who were "officers of the highest order who until then had vegetated, almost ignored, in posts of the lowest category in the general staff."[16] Among these neglected officers was Major Rojo himself, who, in the words of one authority, had been "widely recognized as the best military strategist in the Army."[17] According to the Nationalist historian Ramón Salas Larrazábal, in his monumental four-volume study of the Popular army, Rojo enjoyed "great prestige," was regarded as "one of the most competent members" of the Spanish army, and was "liked and esteemed by all his comrades in arms." During the war, he adds, even though he may have lost the affection of many of his comrades, "he retained the respect of all."[18]

On 10 November, the fourth day of the battle for Madrid, the ubiquitous and influential Mikhail Koltzov, who was better acquainted with the military situation than any other journalist in Spain, wrote in his diary: "Miaja is very little involved in operational details; he even knows little about them. These are matters he leaves to his chief of staff and to the commanders of columns and sectors. Rojo wins the confidence of the men by his modesty, which conceals his great practical knowledge and an unusual capacity for work. This is the fourth day that he has remained bent over the map of Madrid. In an endless chain, commanders and commissars come to see him, and to all of them, in a low calm voice, patiently, as though in a railroad information office, sometimes repeating himself twenty times, he explains, teaches, indicates, annotates papers, and frequently draws sketches."[19]

Nevertheless, it was General Miaja, the president of the newly formed Junta de Defensa or Defense Council, who made the headlines. Of Vicente Rojo, his chief of staff, the press said nothing. On 20 December, Koltzov noted in his diary: "For some reason not a line about Vicente Rojo has appeared in a single newspaper in Madrid or in any other newspaper in Spain. The reporters go into raptures in their descriptions and portrayals of commanders and commissars, of quartermasters and medical corpsmen. They publish enormous portraits of singers and dancers who work in hospitals, but of the man who, in fact, directs the entire defense of Madrid they write not a word. I imagine this is not due to enmity or antipathy, but simply to the fact that 'it hasn't occurred to them.' Here at times the most obvious things do not occur to one. It is difficult not to notice Vicente Rojo. Without exaggeration . . . he is accessible twenty-four hours a day. . . . As chief of the general staff of the defense of Madrid [he] holds in his hands all the threads of the complex web of units, groups, batteries, isolated barricades, sapper crews, and air force squadrons. Without resting, without sleeping, he follows carefully every movement of the enemy in every single one of the myriad sectors into which the battle line is divided."[20]

Not until 16 January 1937 did Koltzov note in his diary that the silence of the press had been broken. "Now they mention him. He is cited in second place in the list of leaders and heroes in the defense of Madrid. I cannot help but rejoice at having contributed to this by speaking of Rojo in the press before anyone else. *El*

Socialista says in an editorial article: 'We are grateful to Mikhail Koltzov for the discovery he has made, for having shown us a man who in the seclusion of his modest office devotes all his powers to saving Madrid.' "[21] "With his journalistic vision," writes Alvarez del Vayo, Koltzov "discovered on General Miaja's staff a modest but extraordinarily competent officer, Vicente Rojo. . . . Koltzov called Rojo to the attention of the journalists of the Madrid press and his name began to be mentioned. Koltzov was alert to everything."[22]

Because of the conspicuous role played by General Miaja, the president of the Junta de Defensa, and the vital though less conspicuous part played by Vicente Rojo, his chief of staff, it is of special interest to record that in the convulsive months before the Civil War, when political loyalties were shifting rapidly, they had secretly joined the UME, the right-wing Unión Militar Española. A documentary work published by General Franco's government states:

> In order to appreciate the lack of sincerity in the conduct of these two officers, who were caught at the time of the [insurrectionary] movement in territory dominated by the Red Government, it is sufficient to bear in mind that both were enrolled in the Unión Militar Española (UME), which had been formed . . . with the patriotic aim of throwing up, at the opportune moment, a dike capable of protecting Spain from the Communist tide. But once this moment had arrived and the Nationalist rising in Madrid had failed, General Miaja and Major Rojo—who had seen the fate that had befallen so many generals and lesser officers of the army, a large number having been assassinated precisely because they had belonged to the UME—instead of siding with their comrades, hastened to offer their services to the Popular Front. But, as their consciences were not clear, and inasmuch as they believed that, by doing away with the file cards recording their membership in this organization, all trace of their previous conduct would disappear, General Miaja . . . went, on 18 July 1937 to the [police department in charge of political records] and demanded that both his card and that of Vicente Rojo . . . be shown to him. Once in his possession, he put them away in his pocket.[23]

A photostatic copy of a document signed by officials of the Republican police department, testifying to the incident, is published in appendix 10 of the same work. The authenticity of the document was confirmed by the highly reliable republican army officer Colonel Jesús Pérez Salas.[24] Miaja's and Rojo's membership in the UME is attested by Largo Caballero, who saw the official list of members that was found during a search of the UME's headquarters in Madrid.[25]

Although there is no evidence that either Miaja or Rojo was involved in any way in the military conspiracy, their precautionary adherence to the UME before the war, in the midst of the internecine turmoil, and the rumors of an impending army coup would explain why, at the inception of the conflict, Rojo, who had been highly esteemed by the army chiefs,[26] offered his services to the government only after being warned by a friend that if he failed to do so he might be shot,[27] and why Miaja, then commander of the Madrid military district, entered Martínez

Barrio's "government of conciliation" as war minister, in the belief that it would capitulate to the demands of the insurgent generals.[28] This indeed was also the assessment of the left, to judge from its violent reaction. Miaja's precautionary step in joining the UME before the war would also explain why, after the collapse of Martínez Barrio's government, he refused to join the cabinet of José Giral as war minister because he believed, as he confessed, that the victory of the insurrection was inevitable.[29] It is noteworthy that when interviewed by me after the war, he stated that he refused to join the government because it had neither an army nor a police force with which to combat the rebellion.[30]

This was only the beginning of Miaja's checkered Civil War career. Shortly after the collapse of Martínez Barrio's government, he was placed in charge of the Cordova front, where, at the head of a large heterogeneous force of militiamen, former regular army soldiers, and civil and assault guards, he failed to capture the ancient Moorish capital, raising some doubts among the militiamen about his loyalty—the lot of many a professional officer during the war. Francisco Moreno Gómez, in his *Historia de la guerra civil an Córdoba, 1936–1939*, ascribes Miaja's failure to his "characteristic sluggishness in operations and his lack of audacity at decisive moments."[31] But, in addition, misfortune stalked him from the outset, when hundreds of guards and other members of his column deserted, taking refuge with their families (a total of twelve hundred to fifteen hundred persons, six hundred of whom were combatants)[32] in the ancient Santuario de la Virgen de la Cabeza, where they held out until 1 May 1937 in one of the most heroic exploits of the war.[33]

In mid-August 1936, Miaja was recalled from the Cordova front and made military commander of Valencia.[34] He then disappeared mysteriously and the war ministry instructed a certain judge of Lola of the army juridical corps to investigate his case, but within a few days he reappeared and the case was dropped.[35] Finally, on 22 October, as the enemy was speeding toward the capital, he was reappointed military commander of the Madrid district,[36] which adds substance to the view that even before he was named president of the Defense Council on 6 November and ordered to defend the capital at all costs, he had been chosen as a scapegoat.[37]

Yet, in spite of his unheroic past, a singular twist of fortune and a well-directed campaign of propaganda by the Communist party that needed a front behind which it could maneuver freely, made Miaja the most glorified figure in the defense of Madrid. As Gustav Regler, the former German Communist and political commissar of the Twelfth International Brigade put it, "Republican propaganda needed a hero to put on a pedestal. . . . As a matter of policy, as well as from a sense of tact, we endorsed this glowing picture when talking to the foreign correspondents and even to the Spanish people."[38]

"Thanks to his great prestige as a result of his achievement," wrote Pedro Martínez Cartón, a lesser member of the politburo of the Communist party, "General Miaja became the best loved general in Spain."[39] Miaja quickly became intoxicated by his new-found popularity. "When I am in my car," he told Julián

Zugazagoitia, "women call out to me, 'Miaja!' 'Miaja!' And they scream to each other, 'There goes Miaja! There goes Miaja!' . . . I greet them and they greet me. They are happy and so am I."[40] And Colonel Segismundo Casado attests: "I managed to apply a cold douche to lower the fever which he had caught from the people, the press, and above all, the clique which surrounded him and which brought him to a state of actual danger. More than once he told me that the popular enthusiasm had reached such a pitch that women even kissed him in the streets."[41]

But after the war, when Miaja had parted company with the Communist party following his participation in the National Council of Defense, which revolted against the Communists and the Negrín government in March 1939, the party in exile did what it could to explode the myth it had diligently created. "In order to distort the true situation regarding the defense of Madrid," wrote Antonio Mije, a member of the politburo, "there have been and there still are persons interested in attributing it to the traitor Miaja. Those who have made and continue to make such propaganda know nothing of what happened, nor of the military 'fruits' Miaja is capable of giving. He never knew more than what he was told as to what was going on in Madrid. He never felt the terrible and difficult situation in its full intensity. The tragedy of those days in Madrid could not penetrate the skull of a dull-witted general, lacking any knowledge of the people."[42]

No less acerbic is the postwar criticism by Enrique Líster, the Communist commander of the Fifth Regiment, who was in constant touch with the general. "The way we used Miaja during the first months of the war was one hundred percent right. His rank of general, in the service of the Republic, impressed a large number of people. His total inability to lead the forces under his command was unknown to the public at large. He understood nothing of the character of our war, nor of the kind of army we needed, but his role in the defense of Madrid, where he was unaware of what was going on, was positive for this very reason. We needed a general and he was a general. Although he knew little about military affairs, all of us tried to create an aura of prestige around him that he damn well didn't deserve. But we were right in acting the way we did. We were simply doing our duty, since it was in the interest of our struggle."[43]

And, according to Antonio Cordón, a faithful member of the party to the end, General José Asensio, who, as we have seen, had instructed Miaja on 6 November to set up the Junta de Defensa, could not understand how Miaja came to personify "all the energy, the heroism and tenacity of the people, and all the intelligence of its political leaders." "The people," Cordón added, "raised to their own level a mediocre general and presented him to the rest of the world as the embodiment of its own virtues and heroic deeds. This is how the myth of Miaja was created."[44]

Nor has Miaja's image fared much better over the years at the hands of Soviet Communists who knew him personally. Ilya Ehrenburg, noted writer and *Izvestiia*'s correspondent during the Civil War, describes the general in his memoirs as a "sick old man, overburdened by events" and as a figurehead.[45] Rodion Malinovsky, later the famous Marshal Malinovsky and Soviet defense minister, known in Spain as Colonel Malinó, affirms that Miaja had nothing at all to do with Madrid's defense.[46]

Still, during the war, when the Communists needed a malleable and self-indulgent figure behind whom they could operate at will, they not only glorified the general in their press, but pampered him and pandered to his vanity. Among those who served the party assiduously in this task through blatant flattery and attention, to judge from the reminiscences of Enrique Castro, a witness and a member at that time of the party's central committee, was María Teresa León—the wife of the famous Communist poet Rafael Alberti—who became "the almost constant companion of the general, whom she dazzled and distracted, thus helping the others to do what had to be done without the old soldier getting in their way."[47] And Herbert L. Matthews, the *New York Times* correspondent in Madrid, says of Miaja: "The picture of the loyal, dogged, courageous defender of the Republic—a picture built up from the first days of the siege of Madrid—was a myth. He was weak, unintelligent, unprincipled."[48]

For his part, Miaja needed the Communists as a protective shield—"Other men had been bumped off at the beginning of the war for much less [than membership in the UME]," Caballero acidly observed some years later.[49] Prodded by Francisco Antón, the secretary of the Madrid Communist party organization and inspector-commissar of the central front, his principal activator and mentor,[50] Miaja soon entered the Communist fold. "General Miaja," wrote the well-informed Louis Fischer, an active supporter of the party during the war, "carried a Communist party card though he probably knew as much about communism as Francisco Franco. Communist propaganda had inflated him into a myth."[51] Juan-Simeón Vidarte, moderate Socialist and admirer of Miaja's "good nature and camaraderie," once asked him if it were true that he had become a Communist. He attests: "Miaja began to laugh with his characteristic joviality. Unbuttoning his jacket, he took out a red card showing his Communist affiliation."[52]

Because Miaja's allegiance to the Communist party has recently been disputed, it is noteworthy that shortly after the war, Ignacio Hidalgo de Cisneros, the Communist chief of the air force, assured me that Miaja was a member of the party. Furthermore, Vicente Rojo, Miaja's chief of staff and later chief of the central general staff, who throughout the war remained on excellent terms with the party and never criticized it in any of his postwar writings, describes Miaja in *¡Alerta los pueblos!* as a Communist,[53] while Largo Caballero, in his unpublished memoirs, states that he was informed by the secret service of the general staff that Miaja was "an affiliate of the party with card number 28,695."[54]

Actually, Miaja's espousal of the Communist cause was no secret at the time. Even the Comintern organ, *International Press Correspondence*, on 6 February 1937 stated in an article by its correspondent in Madrid, Hugh Slater, that he was a member of the party, while Jesús Hernández, the Communist minister of education, declared publicly on 28 May 1937 that Miaja was "impregnated with Communist policy."[55]

President Manuel Azaña noted in his diary in May 1937: "Miaja has succumbed to the temptation of 'converting' to communism. The idea is laughable. From where did Miaja get his communism? Four years ago when I was war minister he told me that he was a staunch Republican, but that he could not compromise with the Socialists and they should be shot! It is most likely that he has embraced the Communists as a precautionary measure to gain the support and protection of a political party. Nothing more disagreeable could have happened to Largo, who is at daggers drawn with the Communists and who rages against them and their Russian mentors and inspirers. According to Largo, the result of Miaja's 'communism' is that all the important military posts in Madrid are given to Communists and that the units they command get all they ask for, whereas supplies to other units are curtailed."[56]

Just as important to the Communist party as its influence over General Miaja, the president of the Defense Council—which because of the exodus of many of the outstanding political figures was composed, according to Vicente Rojo, mainly of "young men who had voluntarily decided to remain in the city ready to participate actively in its defense"[57]—was the party's control of most of the council's key posts. Its composition and the affiliation of its members, as published in *Mundo Obrero*, the Communist party organ,[58] were as follows, the true political allegiance of its members, however, if different from the given affiliation, being indicated in brackets:

General José Miaja	[Communist]	President[59]
Fernando Frade	Socialist [Communist]	Secretary[60]
Antonio Mije	Communist	War
Santiago Carrillo	JSU [Communist]	Public Order[61] (Police)
Amor Nuño	CNT	War Industries
Pablo Yagüe	UGT [Communist]	Supplies[62]
José Carreño	Left Republican	Communications and Transport
Enrique Jiménez	Republican Union	Finance
Francisco Caminero	Syndicalist	Civil Evacuation
Mariano García	JJ.LL. (Anarchist Youth Federation)	Information and Liaison

On 1 December 1936, the junta was restructured and renamed the Junta Delegada de Defensa de Madrid or *Delegate* Defense Council in compliance with an order issued by Largo Caballero on 25 November,[63] which was designed to enhance the authority of the government. "The aim of the Delegate Defense Council," said its official bulletin, "is to fulfil the orders issued by the Government of the Republic, the genuine representative of the will of the Spanish people freely expressed in the elections held last February."[64] Henceforth, the members of the junta were called delegates instead of councillors. After several modifica-

tions, the makeup of the reorganized council, on 15 January 1937, until its dissolution on 23 April 1937, was as follows:[65]

General José Miaja	[Communist]	President
Máximo de Dios	Socialist	Secretary[66]
José Cazorla	JSU [Communist]	Public Order[67] (Police)
Francisco Caminero	Syndicalist party	Front Services
Enrique Jiménez	Republican Union	Evacuation
Isidoro Diéguez	Communist	Militias
Manuel González Marín	CNT	Transport
Lorenzo Iñigo	JJ.LL. (Anarchist Youth Federation)	War Industries
Luis Nieto	UGT [Communist]	Supplies[68]
José Carreño	Left Republican	Propaganda and Press

In addition to occupying the majority of key posts, the Communists were also influential in the propaganda and press department, where the left Republican José Carreño was in charge. Here, they controlled the official radio station, *Radio Madrid*, whose director was the German Communist Kurt Hager, alias Félix Albin.[69]

General Miaja played a twofold role: as president of the junta, which filled the political vacuum left by the departure of the government, and as head of the Madrid military command, which was in charge of the planning and execution of military operations. Despite the compelling evidence of his political allegiance, much of which was included in my book *La revolución española*, published in 1980, the Spanish historians Julio Aróstegui and Jesús A. Martínez ignore this evidence in their work, *La junta de defensa de Madrid*, which appeared in 1984. They also pass over the important testimony of Largo Caballero in his unpublished memoirs—giving Miaja's Communist party membership number—although they studied the memoirs with critical attention.[70] This neglect of bothersome evidence enables them to make the startling claim that the alleged Communist affiliation of Miaja is "simply ridiculous."[71] However, they do acknowledge that the Communists became "his first political counsellors"[72] and that he "rarely dissented from them."[73]

The authors' denial of the general's political allegiance is clearly designed to bolster their impassioned thesis that the PCE and its appendage, the JSU, were not the dominant force in the junta as I and others have claimed. Enrique Castro, for instance, who for a short time was himself a Communist member of the junta, writes: "The Communist party, like an invisible god, dominated everything: the city and the people; Miaja, the Junta de Defensa, everyone!"[74] It is true that the Communists did not occupy the majority of seats, but they did hold the majority of key posts: presidency, war (later, militias), public order, and supplies. They also occupied twice as many seats in the council as any other ideological group, which was in obvious violation of the instructions given to General Miaja that the junta should comprise members of all parties *in proportion to their representation in the government*.[75] But equally important in assessing their true influence in the junta were the external factors that favored the party: the prestige of their Fifth Regiment, the dramatic arrival of the International Brigades, and the presence of Soviet advisers, planes, and tanks, a presence that elicited the unqualified gratitude of most of the organizations of the left. In this propitious atmosphere, it was not difficult for the Communists to gain acceptance of certain measures that might otherwise have been the subject of acrimonious debate.

Although *La junta de defensa de Madrid* is a valuable contribution to the historiography of the Civil War, since it makes available for the first time, in their entirety, the minutes of the Defense Council, discusses its crucial role in the defense of Madrid, the friction between General Miaja and Largo Caballero and the volcanic eruptions between the Communists and Anarchosyndicalists, and provides a wealth of data hitherto unknown, its petulant denial of Miaja's political allegiance and its overzealous attempt to minimize the true weight of the Communists in the junta—even to the point of downplaying as "exaggerated" the Communists' own accounts of their leading role[76]—vitiates its objectivity.

Before citing a few examples of the dominant position held by the Communists in the Defense Council, it is necessary to digress briefly to record that the well-known pro-Communist historian, Manuel Tuñón de Lara (described by an opposing leftist writer as "a progressive catholic 'historian,' who since 1936 has always played the Communists' game")[77] uses his preface in *La junta de defensa de Madrid*—whose theme, despite its importance, covers only a tiny area in a vast canvas—to condemn my entire work, *La revolución española*, in which forty years of research were invested. "[The] rigorous study of a concrete event such as the Junta," he writes, "is an indirect contribution to the destruction of one of the myths of the historiography of the Civil War that comes from abroad, specifically, from the United States: the 'Bolloten myth,' a myth created by a work whose accumulation of sources and testimony is truly impressive, but which places its entire scholarship in the service of an a priori outlook that he tries to substantiate. Curiously enough, the author underwent this process of a priori 'ideologization' after he had already begun his work."[78]

It is true that when I first began to write about the Civil War and Revolution in 1936, as a British correspondent for the United Press, I was very much influenced by the wartime propaganda of the Communist party, as indeed were many other journalists who supported the Republic, and that it took several years to cast off the slough of distortions and lies that encumbered my thinking. Evidently, Tuñón de Lara would have had no complaint had I not challenged the many myths about the Civil War and Revolution created by the Spanish Communist party and by its domestic and foreign friends.

The following examples based largely on data in *La junta de defensa de Madrid* illustrate to what degree that Communists, because of their dominant position—due in some measure to the passivity or acquiescence of other organizations—were able to get their way within the council on three fundamental issues:

The first example is the exclusion from the junta of the anti-Stalinist POUM, which, as will be seen in a later chapter, was targeted for liquidation by the NKVD. Even Aróstegui and Martínez point out that this exclusion was "imposed" by the Communist party[79] and without "the slightest gesture of disagreement" by the other organizations.[80] Not even González Marín, the Anarchosyndicalist representative in the junta, who should have seen in this exclusion a possible danger to the CNT, defended the POUM. Aróstegui and Martínez confirm that the Soviet ambassador, Marcel Rosenberg, was involved in this exclusion[81] and they quote, without rebuttal, the following statement apparently made to the local POUM leader Enrique Rodríguez by Manuel Albar, a member of the Socialist party executive: "Ambassador Rosenberg vetoed your admission. It is of course unfair, but you should understand that the U.S.S.R. is powerful and that between Soviet help and support of the POUM there is only one possible choice."[82] On 29 November, *La Batalla*, the POUM organ, declared that the opposition to the party's representation in the junta came not only from the PCE and the JSU but also from "higher up—from the Soviet Embassy that, together with the Soviet Consulate in Barcelona, is inspiring the campaign of insults and calumnies against us. . . . It is intolerable from every point of view that on the basis of the help that is being given us an effort is being made . . . to meddle in and even to direct Spanish politics."

On 29 January, the junta, on the proposal of the Communist delegate, Isidoro Diéguez, approved without a dissenting voice the seizure of the POUM's newspaper *El Combatiente Rojo* and its radio station in Madrid, for having, in his words, devoted themselves "solely and exclusively to combating the government and the Popular Front."[83] Thereupon, José Cazorla, the Communist delegate of public order, announced that as the POUM was "illegal" he would seize all its buildings and its cars.[84] Again, there was not a dissenting voice, not even from the highly articulate and fiery González Marín, who was present at the session.[85] Although the exclusion of the POUM from the Defense Council was a prime example of the junta's deference to Communist and Soviet demands, Aróstegui and Martínez claim that this matter involved the Spanish Communist party and probably Soviet and Comintern agents, *"but not the Defense Council."*[86]

The second example of Communist ascendency was the party's manipulation of the Junta de Defensa after the fall of Malaga in February 1937, when, as will be seen in a subsequent chapter, it unleashed a vigorous campaign for the purging of all commanding military posts, a campaign that although directed against officers who were suspect or incompetent was aimed essentially at those appointees of Largo Caballero who were opposed to its efforts to control the army. It was no coincidence that in a letter addressed to Largo Caballero on behalf of the junta on 13 February—urging the enforcement of conscription and a single command—the Communist delegate, Diéguez, included a demand for the removal of "doubtful and suspect elements and of all those who through incompetence or passivity serve the enemy's plans."[87] That this demand was directed against Largo Caballero's undersecretary, General José Asensio, the party's bête noir, was evident three days later when the Communist organ *Mundo Obrero* denounced him as the "organizer of defeats" who deserved "the maximum penalty."[88] Although the campaign for the purging of the commanding military posts, as Enrique Castro—who was chief of the operations section in the junta's war council in November 1936—observed years later, was "one more step toward the attainment of hegemony" by the party,[89] no one in the junta appears to have perceived the danger and the letter was approved for personal delivery to Caballero by a special commission composed of Diéguez, Máximo de Dios, and González Marín, and for publication in the press.[90] In this way, the junta served the machinations of the Communist party against the premier who, under simultaneous and irresistible pressure from his opponents in the cabinet, was forced, as will be seen in a subsequent chapter, to remove Asensio. Clearly, the Communists' ability to manipulate the junta was an important element in their offensive against the left Socialist leader. It is therefore untrue, as Aróstegui and Martínez contend, that "the great offensive against Largo Caballero was waged *outside* [*al margen de*] the Junta."[91]

The third and final example of the Communists' dominant role in the Junta de Defensa was the immediate action taken by Santiago Carrillo, the councillor of public order, and later by his successor, José Cazorla, to monopolize police functions in Madrid. No sooner had the council been formed than Carrillo appointed five of his most trusted associates—Alfredo Cabello, Fernando Claudín, Federico Melchor, Luis Rodríguez Cuesta, and Segundo Serrano Poncela—to the top positions in his department,[92] all of whom had just entered or would soon enter the Communist party.[93] According to Aróstegui and Martínez, the security services were "completely professionalized," the independent political and trade-union police squads disappeared, and the Communist party succeeded in taking control of the new security forces, on which it imposed "the predominance" of its followers.[94] This centralization of police functions under the aegis of a single party would not have been so easily achieved had the Socialist and Republican councillors opposed it. But they did not oppose it, and their failure to do so clearly reflected the real power relations existing at the time within the junta and the dominant role of the Communist party. This was a prime example of Communist hegemony by default. It was not until April 1937, when the deep-rooted antagonism between Cazorla and González Marín finally surfaced in a fierce confrontation over the CNT's denunciations of Communist killings and clandestine jails,[95] that the Socialist and Republican representatives in the junta evinced the first faint signs of apprehension[96] and that, according to Aróstegui and Martínez, "an anticommunist front of Socialists, Anarchists, and Republicans appeared to be forming . . . as a result, particularly, of the excesses of a certain 'antianarchist terror.' "[97] While it is impossible to say how far this nascent realignment of forces would have gone if Largo Caballero had not dissolved the junta as a consequence of the formation of a new city council in Madrid on 23 April,[98] there can be little doubt that the dominant influence of the Communists within that body had enabled them to reorganize and centralize under their control the bulk of the security services in Madrid.

In the military field, where the Communists possessed the best apparatus, their party was assured not only of the political allegiance of General Miaja, the commander of the Madrid military district, but of the active support of Major Vicente Rojo, his chief of staff. Although there is no evidence that Rojo ever joined the party, his constant and intimate association with the Communist military leaders in Madrid and with General Vladimir Gorev, the Soviet adviser—officially the Soviet military attaché—in organizing the defense of Madrid, enabled him to live down an ambiguous past and to establish himself in Russian favor. This is evidenced not only by Mikhail Koltzov's praise of him during the war itself,[99] but by that of other Soviet participants many years after the war had ended.[100] It is also evidenced by the place reserved for him in the Spanish Communist party's official history of the Civil War, published in Moscow in 1966. "Vicente Rojo," it states, "enjoyed great prestige in the army owing to his extensive knowledge of military science. A man of profound religious convictions, he dedicated himself with exemplary loyalty to the cause of the people and the Republic. Through his sangfroid and courage, through his capabilities as a strategist and organizer, he very soon won general respect."[101]

Rojo first emerged as a public figure in the scenario of the Civil War in September 1936, when he brought terms of surrender to Colonel José Moscardó, the defender of the besieged Alcázar in Toledo, Spain's prestigious Infantry Academy, where, before the war, he had been highly regarded as a professor of military history and where, during the first days of the rebellion, approximately eighteen hundred men, women, and children had taken refuge. According to Cecil Eby's dramatic chronicle of the siege, based on extensive oral and printed evidence,[102] Rojo's position was ambiguous. After Moscardó had rejected the conditions of surrender, someone asked Rojo why he did not remain with the defenders. "Rojo became pensive. 'If I did, this very night my wife and children in Madrid would be killed,' he said. Not until afterwards did anyone note that Rojo had avoided telling them whether he wanted to stay with them or not. Before being blindfolded again [prior to being escorted from the fortress], Rojo dumped the contents of his tobacco pouch on the desk and said, 'This is the best memento I can give you.' As the bandage was tightened around his eyes, he suddenly cried out, '*Viva España!*' as a soldier might do if he were facing a republican firing squad. Though this was a monarchist cheer, it was ambiguous—which Spain was Major Rojo alluding to?" Again, on the matter of the mines that were being dug in order to destroy the fortress, Rojo muttered as he was leaving the building, " 'For the love of God, keep hunting for the entrance to the mines.' "[103]

Whatever may have been the real political sympathies of Vicente Rojo, the truth lies buried with him in Spain, where he was allowed to return many years after the Civil War had ended and where he died in June 1966.[104] Even Carlos

Contreras, who, as chief political commissar of the Communist Fifth Regiment, knew him well, acknowledged that the Communist party was never absolutely sure of his true allegiance.[105] Koltzov, too, while zealous in his praise of Rojo's military talents, expressed certain doubts about his politics. "It is said of Vicente Rojo," he wrote in his diary on 20 December 1936, "that he is too reserved, that he says little about political matters, that he remains silent on burning issues, that perhaps he is keeping something to himself. I would like to think that this is not true. For the moment the defense of Madrid is to a very large extent his accomplishment. This carries more weight than the resounding and frequently empty utterances of revolutionary upstarts who come from the old aristocratic army. Rojo teaches the men, he creates cadres of officers from the people. . . . New books will be written on the new military art of the Spanish people in their struggle for liberty. Vicente Rojo will write them. Books will also be written about him."[106] Whatever may have been Rojo's private political beliefs, there can be no doubt that his outstanding military ability, his total dedication to his work, and, above all, his readiness to cooperate with the Spanish Communists in securing positions of control in the army, especially as the war advanced, overrode all other considerations. From the rank of major, he was soon promoted to lieutenant colonel, then to colonel, and finally to general in October 1937.[107] In May 1937, he became chief of the central general staff,[108] in which post, according to the testimony of one professional colleague whose word is beyond question, he did what he could to promote Communist predominance in the army.[109] He remained in this post until after the fall of Catalonia in February 1939 and the flight of the left-wing forces across the border into France. Convinced that the war was lost, he refused to accompany the Communist-dominated Negrín government to the central zone. This was his only major disagreement with Communist policies during more than two years of quiet but close collaboration.

In assessing Rojo's political posture during the war, the evidence of Santiago Garcés Arroyo, who was appointed by Negrín to head the Military Investigation Service in April 1938 and who at the time served the interests of the Communist party, cannot be disregarded.[110] In an interview given to the Spanish historian Heleno Saña, in 1974, he said: "There is no doubt that Rojo played the game of the Communists. He identified himself totally with them to the point that he wished to join the party. Negrín, whom he consulted, prevented him from doing so. He told him in the fall of 1938: 'You cannot become a Communist at the very moment when we are negotiating with the English for assistance.'"[111]

A factor that may have caused some historians to overlook Rojo's pro-Communist stance during the war[112] was his Catholic faith, which he openly avowed despite great danger to himself.[113] Moreover, José Martín Blázquez, a professional officer, who knew Rojo personally before the war, says that he had no liking for Azaña and that "his political views were obviously far removed from the left."[114]

His unusual case is explained in part by Enrique Castro, a former member, as we have seen, of the Communist party's central committee and onetime commander in chief of the Fifth Regiment: "Politically Rojo could never have been with the party. He accepted the party because he understood that it was not only a political force but also a military force; he accepted it because he knew that as long as he acted correctly the party would defend him against everyone and everything. But he was not a Communist nor could he ever have been. He believed blindly in God, and he was a man of such faith, with such a sense of dignity, that he did not conceal his faith in spite of the fact that being a militant Catholic placed him at that time in mortal danger."[115]

While it is no doubt true that Rojo never joined the Communist party, it is no less true that a man can often serve its interests better without an identifying label. When, early in the war, as commander in chief of the Fifth Regiment, Castro ordered a militiaman to take care of Rojo, he added, " 'We need him. He can be very useful to the party.' 'But . . . he is a Catholic,' the militiaman objected. 'For that reason perhaps,' " was Castro's telling answer.[116]

In a penetrating essay on Vicente Rojo, M. Teresa Suero Roca writes:

> One question comes to mind: Why did Rojo, who was so unlike the Communists, succumb to them? Some say he was *accommodative*. This answer seems too fa-cile. We have already referred to versions alleging that he was a virtual "pris-oner" of the side on which he fought. . . . If it is true that the Communists pro-posed that he be made chief of staff in the defense of Madrid and, later, chief of the central general staff, what were their reasons? They were always interested in maintaining the appearance of a democratic government for the sake of domestic and particularly foreign opinion. . . . Were they not also interested [for the same reasons] in having an officer who was apolitical, a practising Catholic, and a conservative occupy the highest post in the army? . . . All this helped them to present a democratic façade, while taking into their hands all the levers of power. It is possible that Rojo or, more likely, his family was subjected to pressure and that this pressure forced him to submit. As we have seen, Rojo belonged to the UME. Others had been shot for this very reason. Under the circumstances, he may have felt compelled to yield, thus giving the Communists an opportunity to exploit his personal characteristics as well as his talents.[117]

Rojo's immense contribution to the defense of Madrid was overshadowed not only by the publicity given to Miaja, but also by the dramatic entrance upon the scene of the charismatic General Emilio Kléber at the head of the Eleventh International Brigade.

Kléber's real name, according to an article in the Soviet newspaper *Soviet-skaia Bukovina*, of 10 February 1965,[118] was Manfred Zalmanovich Stern, his nom de guerre being derived from that of the famous general of the French Revolution, Jean Baptiste Kléber. This, apparently, was the first time in almost thirty years of official Soviet silence that his full name was ever revealed by any Soviet source, although in 1939 the Soviet defector Walter Krivitsky correctly gave Kléber's last name as Stern.[119] It is now clear, as we shall see later, that he was not, as some historians have erroneously believed,[120] the General Gregoriy

M. Shtern or Stern, who served as the chief Soviet military adviser in Spain from May 1937 under the assumed name of General Grigorovich.

According to Carlos Contreras,[121] chief political commissar of the Fifth Regiment, who knew Kléber well, the general arrived in Spain from Russia in September 1936, worked with the regiment for a while, then proceeded to Albacete, where he helped to organize the first of the International Brigades (the Eleventh and Twelfth), and arrived in Madrid on 8 November. There he was assigned to the most seriously threatened sectors of the front—the University City and Casa de Campo. Within a few days his popularity surpassed Miaja's. Gustav Regler, the German Communist and political commissar of the Twelfth International Brigade, attests that Kléber was "the real defender of Madrid" and created the legend of the invincibility of the International Brigades, that he "risked his life a hundred times [and] had the charm that was necessary for the Spanish character."[122] "The Madrileño, who found his face attractive," writes Julián Zugazagoitia, the director of *El Socialista* of Madrid, "learned his name without any phonetic difficulty. As he pronounced it, he endowed him, by autosuggestion, with the maximum virtue and the maximum ability. His name effaced all others."[123] On arriving in Madrid a few days after Kléber, Ludwig Renn, the German Communist writer and commander of the Thaelmann Battalion of the Twelfth International Brigade, found that the newspapers "were full of the Eleventh Brigade and General Kléber who, unknown a week before, was now the most popular man in Spain. He had driven back Franco's best troops, the Moors and Foreign Legionaries."[124] The foreign press was also unstinting in its praise. "He was the man of the hour then," recalls Herbert Matthews, "and we all played him up sensationally—as he deserved."[125]

Walter Krivitsky wrote:

Kléber was presented to the world, in interviews and sketches, as the strong man of the hour, fated to play a momentous role in the history of Spain and the world. His physical appearance lent color to the legends. He was big in stature, his features were heavy and his shock of grey hair belied his forty-one years. Kléber was introduced to the world as a soldier of fortune, a naturalized Canadian, a native of Austria, who, as an Austrian war prisoner in Russia, had joined the White Guards in their fight against the Bolsheviks, only to become converted finally to communism. . . . I had known Kléber and his wife and children and brother for many years. His real name was Stern. He was a native of Bukovina. . . . During the World War he served as an officer, was taken prisoner by the Czar's troops, and sent to a camp at Krasnoyarsk, Siberia. After the Soviet revolution he joined the Bolshevik Party and the Red army. . . . Then he attended the Frunze Military Academy, from which he was graduated in 1924. For a while we worked together in the Intelligence Department of the General Staff. In 1927 Kléber was assigned to the military section of the Comintern. . . . He went to China for the Comintern on confidential missions. Kléber had never been to Canada and never associated with the White Guards. This bit of fiction was used to cover up the fact of his being a staff officer of the Red Army. It made his role as leader of the International Brigade more plausible. In reality, despite the dramatic part assigned to him, he was without power in the Soviet machine.[126]

According to Contreras, Kléber's rise to fame in the defense of Madrid immediately aroused Miaja's and Caballero's jealousy. "It was his popularity among the people that killed him," Contreras told me.[127] What he did not disclose, however, was that Spanish Communist leaders, as the evidence will show, also resented Kléber's popularity and in all probability were equally responsible for his fall. And in this resentment, shared by all those Spaniards who saw their place in history dimmed by Kléber's sudden radiance, not only personal jealousy but national pride was a powerful ingredient. "[The] national pride of the Spanish Republicans," writes Verle Johnston in his history of the International Brigades, "soared with the successful defense of Madrid, and Miaja and the General Staff did not appreciate the spotlight being focused with such intensity upon a foreigner. It seems to have been for this reason that the Political Commissariat of the International Brigades, either on the request or at least with the concurrence of the Spanish Communist Party, removed Kléber from Madrid very suddenly early in January [1937]."[128] On the other hand, Contreras claimed that General Gorev, the Soviet military adviser to Miaja and Rojo, proposed that Kléber be removed.[129] The two versions are by no means incompatible inasmuch as the decision may have been arrived at by Gorev, in deference to Spanish pride, in agreement with the Spanish Communist party and the political commissariat of the International Brigades. It is noteworthy that the chief political commissar of the brigades, André Marty, the French Communist deputy, known as "the butcher" of Albacete, their headquarters,[130] was, according to Louis Fischer—then quartermaster of the brigades—"at daggers drawn" with General Kléber.[131]

It is now known that the offensive against Kléber was initiated, though not necessarily inspired, by Vicente Rojo who, to judge from his own guarded testimony, seems to have enjoyed the quiet support of Gorev in the Kléber incident,[132] and who, until Koltzov brought him into public view in January 1937, had remained unnoticed by the Spanish press. This omission must have been extremely painful to a man who had contributed so much to the organization of Madrid's defense and explains why he totally ignores Kléber in his book *España heroica*, published in 1942, which nevertheless names the Spanish commanders on the various sectors of the Madrid front.[133] Rojo, of course, could not have forgotten Kléber. Indeed, in a letter to General Miaja dated 26 November 1936—only eighteen days after Kléber's arrival in Madrid, but published for the first time in 1967 in his book *Así fué la defensa de Madrid*, thirty-one years later—he condemned the "exaggerated" publicity given to Kléber, his "artificial" popularity, and "false" gifts of leadership. "His men," he contended, "are fighting well, but nothing more, and this many others are doing who are not commanded by Kléber." In addition, he accused Kléber of making false reports on the military situation, of insubordination and political ambitions, and warned Miaja against "an underhanded maneuver that may oust you from the functions that, as all your subordinates can see, you are performing with enthusiasm."[134]

Whether Rojo acted on his own initiative or with the foreknowledge and even at the prompting of Spanish Communist leaders may never be proved, but it is significant that Spanish Communist memoirs and histories barely mention Kléber's important contribution to the defense of Madrid. In fact, neither Enrique Líster, the most publicized Communist militia commander on the Madrid front, nor Dolores Ibárruri (La Pasionaria), the famed Communist leader, so much as mention him in their memoirs, although they devote considerable space to the capital's defense.[135] Even the official Spanish Communist history of the Civil War, published in 1967, thirty-one years after the event, which is generous in its praise of Rojo, devotes only a few noncommittal lines to Kléber.[136] All this evidence lends support to the suspicion that Spanish Communist leaders had more to do with his removal than has hitherto been supposed. Hence, it is not easy to subscribe to the version by Franz Borkenau, written in 1937[137] and echoed many years later by several historians without due credit or substantiating evidence,[138] that Kléber's downfall was due to a coalition of Largo Caballero, Miaja, and the Anarchists, who suspected that he was planning a Communist coup d'etat with the backing of the International Brigades. The idea that this comparatively small body of men might leave the front to stage a coup against the government—at the very time when Stalin was counseling Largo Caballero in his letter of December 1936 to do everything possible "to prevent the enemies of Spain from considering her as a Communist republic"—simply does not jibe with the Communists' more subtle designs in Spain for controlling the reins of government. Even Borkenau, who gives no sources, seems to question the validity of his own version.[139]

After his removal from Madrid, Kléber went into temporary retirement in Valencia, was later offered a minor post by Largo Caballero on the rapidly disintegrating Malaga front—which he refused[140]—then appeared in the summer of 1937 on the Aragon front, without the previous publicity, at the head of the Forty-fifth Division, from which he was soon removed by Rojo, then chief of the central general staff. According to Carlos Contreras, "Rojo found some reason to remove Kléber. He did not want to leave, was very upset and wept."[141] Shortly thereafter he was recalled to the Soviet Union. Although it was rumored that he was shot,[142] it was not until the publication of the above-mentioned article in *Sovietskaia Bukovina*, twenty-eight years later, that his liquidation was confirmed by any source behind the Iron Curtain. "His fate was tragic," said the article. "During the period of the Stalin cult he was unjustly accused and convicted. He died in a [labor] camp and was [posthumously] rehabilitated."

31

Soviet Officers, Journalists, and Diplomats

*N*either General Emilio Kléber's evanescent glory in the most difficult days of Madrid's defense nor Major Vicente Rojo's invaluable organizational work behind the lines should obscure the role of General Vladimir Gorev, the Soviet military adviser, who controlled the Russian artillery, tank, and air force units on the central front. According to Louis Fischer, who had easy access to the Soviet officers in Spain,[1] Gorev was the real hero of Madrid. "On November 5 [1936]," he wrote after the war, "I went to the War Office to see General Gorev who had taken command of the military situation. . . . He had organized the defense of Madrid. More than any one man he was the savior of Madrid."[2] This, too, was the view of Carlos Contreras.[3] On the other hand, Koltzov's diary, from which all reference to Gorev, whether open or disguised, was either excluded by the author or excised by Soviet censors—no doubt because at the time of its publication in 1938 the general had disappeared in Stalin's purges[4]—gives generous recognition to Rojo.[5] By contrast, Ilya Ehrenburg, *Izvestiia*'s correspondent, in his memoirs published in 1963, ten years after Stalin's death, makes only passing reference to Rojo but reserves a conspicuous place in history for Gorev. "Vladimir Yefimovich Gorev," he writes, "seldom looked in at the cellars of the [war] ministry; he spent most of his time at the front. He was under forty but had great military experience. Intelligent, reserved, and at the same time passionate—I could even call him poetical—he won everybody's esteem. To say that the people had faith in him would be an understatement: they believed in his lucky star. Six months later the Spaniards had learned how to wage war, they had talented commanders—Modesto, Líster and others less well known. But in the autumn of 1936, with the possible exception of chief of staff Rojo, there were few men of vigor and military knowledge among the commanders of the Republican army. In the November days Gorev played a tremendous role, helping the Spaniards halt the Fascists in the suburbs of Madrid."[6] Even Rojo, who emphatically denies that Gorev "or any other foreigner" was in charge of the defense of Madrid, acknowledges that the general "cooperated efficaciously," was in "close contact" with him "a large part of the time," and was a "very valuable auxiliary in the difficult hours of the battle for Madrid when Soviet matériel began to arrive quite heavily."[7]

Thus it seems clear from the evidence available that credit for the organization of Madrid's defense—without detracting from Kléber's vital contribution in the field of battle—belongs both to Rojo and Gorev, working together in close cooperation.

Because many years of Soviet silence has frequently led to the confusion of Gorev with General Ian K. Berzin, the principal Soviet military adviser in Spain[8]—known during the war as General Grishin[9]—it is important to note that their separate identities have now been positively established as a result of a number of books published in the Soviet Union between 1965 and 1971 that show that Gorev was both military attaché at the Soviet embassy in Madrid and adviser to General Miaja, and hence to Vicente Rojo, whereas Berzin was the overall senior Soviet military adviser.[10]

According to sovietologist David Dallin, Berzin was the first chief and head for fifteen years of the chief intelligence directorate of the Soviet general staff, i.e., the GRU (Glavnoye Razvedyvatelnoye Upraveleniye).[11] The fact that he occupied this cardinal position and was appointed to head the Soviet military mission in Spain gives a measure of the importance that Stalin attached to the Spanish conflict at that time. Known by his friends as Starik (the Old Man),[12] Berzin was, according to Whittaker Chambers, who worked for Soviet intelligence, his "international chief" and was known by that nickname in the Soviet spy ring operating in the United States.[13]

In the defense of Madrid, Gorev was assisted by a group of high-ranking Soviet officers: G. I. Kulik, his immediate superior, known in Spain as General Kuper or Kupper, and adviser to General Pozas, commander of the central front;[14] D. G. Pavlov, who, under the pseudonym of General Pablo, commanded the Soviet tank corps;[15] N. Voronov, known as Volter, who was in charge of Soviet artillery;[16] and Yakov Smushkevich, known as General Duglas or Douglas,[17] commander of the Soviet air force units and adviser to Major (later General) Ignacio Hidalgo de Cisneros, who was named chief of the air force by navy and air minister Indalecio Prieto on 7 September 1936. A moderate Socialist and personal friend of Prieto's, Cisneros was the son of an aristocratic family from the province of Alava. Together with his wife Constancia de la Mora, a granddaughter of the famous conservative prime minister, Antonio Maura, he joined the Communist party, as did many other Socialists, quite early in the war because of its discipline and efficiency and the help received from the USSR.[18]

Referring to the important battle of the Jarama in February 1937, the Communist commander Enrique Líster says of Pavlov: "From the sixth to the thirteenth he was the real organizer of republican resistance. General Pablo was a man of great energy, was intelligent, courageous, and quick in his decisions; he enjoyed great prestige among those of us who knew him. A valuable collaborator of the general was Captain Antonio, his interpreter-adjutant-secretary and I don't know what else besides, whom I had known at the Lenin School, where he was called Pintos, and who in his own country after the war, under the real name of Kravchenkov, won the high award of Hero of the Soviet Union."[19] And of Yakov

Smushkevich, Major General of Aviation G. Prokofiev writes, "[He] was the soul of the organization of the massive actions of the republican aviation."[20]

Berzin, Gorev, Pavlov, Smushkevich, and E. S. Ptukhin, who succeeded Smushkevich in May 1937,[21] as well as Gregoriy M. Shtern or Stern, known in Spain as General Grigorovich,[22] who succeeded Berzin on the same date, perished in Stalin's purges between 1937 and 1941. "During this time," declared Nikita Khrushchev, secretary of the Soviet Communist party, in his famous denunciatory speech against Stalin in February 1956, "the cadre of leaders who had gained military experience in Spain and in the Far East was almost completely liquidated."[23] According to Ilya Ehrenburg, who managed to survive the purges, many of the Soviet commanders in Spain "fell victim to the abuses of power in later years."[24] Louis Fischer attributes their execution to the "long history of angry rivalry" between the NKVD and the Red Army, which resented "being spied upon by unknown members of their units who collected information or misinformation and purveyed it to headquarters for misuse. . . . This situation long antedated the Spanish civil war but was exacerbated by it. Soviet army officers in Spain told me they were being 'pushed around' and 'spied upon' by the NKVD. They carried their complaints to Stalin and they were executed."[25]

The fate of Soviet journalists in Spain was no better. Of the three outstanding journalists who covered the Spanish Civil War—Ehrenburg of *Izvestiia*, Mirova of the Tass news agency, and Koltzov of *Pravda*, all of whom were Jews—only Ehrenburg survived. Mirova was arrested upon her return to Moscow in 1937[26] and was not heard from again. As for Koltzov, both a brilliant journalist and a literary figure and Stalin's personal representative in Spain, who discussed the Spanish situation with the Soviet dictator once or twice daily on the telephone from Madrid,[27] he was, according to the authoritative *Who Was Who in the USSR*, arrested in 1938, died in imprisonment on 4 April 1942, and was posthumously rehabilitated.[28] It is of special interest that although a biography of Koltzov is included in the *Bolshaia sovetskaia entsiklopediia*, the Great Soviet Encyclopedia, volume 33, published in 1938, his name was left out of the second edition, volume 22, prepared before Stalin's death in 1953. His collected works appeared between 1933 and 1936, when he was still in high favor, but were not republished until 1957, four years after the dictator's death. In a biography of Koltzov in *Sovetskie pisateli* (Soviet Writers), volume 1, published in Moscow in 1959 during the Khrushchev "de-Stalinization" era, his brother, B. E. Efimov, says that he "perished by the foul hand of the concealed enemies of the people."[29] *Russkie sovetskie pisateli-prozaiki* (Soviet Russian Prose Writers), published in Leningrad between 1959 and 1966, is more explicit: "Koltzov's literary and social activity," it states, "was suddenly brought to an end in December 1938, when he became a victim of the tyranny that reigned in the years of Stalin's personal cult."[30] However, the third edition of the Great Soviet Encyclopedia, volume 12, published in 1973, while reinstating Koltzov, makes no reference to his death, reflecting the softer attitude toward Stalin during the post-Khrushchev era.

Koltzov was not arrested immediately upon his return to the Soviet Union in 1938, for he visited Louis Fischer in May. "He was still 'all right,' " Fischer wrote in 1941. "That is why he dared to come. He was purged the same year [1938]. His articles and books are no longer published and most of his friends think he has been shot. Next to Radek he was probably the most influential Soviet journalist. Koltzov, incidentally, is the 'Karkov' of Ernest Hemingway's *For Whom the Bell Tolls*. Koltzov was very emotional about Spain. But when talking to strangers he wrapped himself in a smoke-screen, which consisted of equal parts of brittle *Pravda*—editorial prose and literary spoofing. That made him seem pompous and cynical."[31] Claud Cockburn, the British writer, alias Frank Pitcairn, who was a reporter of the London *Daily Worker*, the organ of the British Communist party, during the Spanish Civil War, drew the following portrait of Koltzov in his autobiography, written after he had left the party:

I spent a great deal of my time in the company of Mikhail Koltzov, who then was editor of *Pravda* and, more importantly still, was at that period the confidant and mouthpiece and direct agent of Stalin himself. He was a stocky little Jew . . . with a huge head and one of the most expressive faces of any man I ever met. What his face principally expressed was a kind of enthusiastically gleeful amusement—and a lively hope that you and everyone else would, however depressing the circumstances, do your best to make things more amusing still. He had a savagely satirical tongue [he had once been the editor of *Krokodil*, the Moscow satirical weekly][32] and an attitude of entire ruthlessness toward people he thought either incompetent or even just pompous. People who did not know him well—particularly non-Russians—thought his conversation, his sharply pointed Jewish jokes, his derisive comments on all kinds of Sacred Cows unbearably cynical. . . . To myself it never seemed that anyone who had such a powerful enthusiasm for life . . . could possibly be described properly as "cynical." Realistic is perhaps the word—but that is not quite correct either, because it implies, or might imply, a dry practicality which was quite lacking from his nature. . . . As the Spanish war ground its way to its gruesome conclusion and all over Europe people who had supported the Republic became truly cynical,[33] despairing, without faith or enthusiasm for anything, I found myself looking forward more and more eagerly to conversations with Koltzov. . . . He was a man who could see the defeat for what it really was, could assume that half the big slogans were empty and a lot of the big heroes stuffed or charlatans, and yet not let that bother him at all or sap his energy and enthusiasm. . . . Koltzov had appointed me London correspondent of *Pravda*. This position I held only for a short time because very soon after that came the news of his disappearance. As his personal appointee, I had to be quietly dropped. I do not know to this day what Koltzov had done or was supposed to have done in Moscow. His fall—and, one presumes, execution—came at the height of his power there, and a lot of people when they heard of it could not believe it. They spread stories that he had been sent to China as a top secret agent under another name. A lot of his friends went on believing that for years, as a kind of wishful thinking to soften their grief. Others were thrown into total disarray by the news, became despairing and totally cynical.[34]

Of the top-ranking Soviet officers who served in Spain between 1936 and 1937 in the highest advisory capacities, only Berzin and Gorev—both of whom were recalled to the Soviet Union in 1937—perished during the war itself. Others perished later.

According to *Who Was Who in the USSR*, Berzin was arrested by the NKVD in late 1937 and died that year in imprisonment.[35] However, both the *Sovetskaia voennaia entsiklopediia* (Soviet Military Encyclopedia)[36] and the *Bol'shaia sovetskaia entsiklopediia*[37] give the date of his death as 29 July 1938. Although his liquidation was not confirmed by Soviet sources until many years later—by Ilya Ehrenburg in 1963,[38] by *Komsomolskaya Pravda* of 13 November 1964,[39] and by the Soviet-published work *Bortsy Latvii v Ispanii, 1936–1939* in 1970[40]—Walter Krivitsky had announced his disappearance as far back as 1939.[41] In the light of what is now known of the unchecked power of the NKVD and of Krivitsky's extraordinary knowledge of the Soviet secret police, his disclosures—which, it will be recalled, were denounced at the time as lies because of the Communist campaign against him as an imposter—have unassailable credibility today. Indeed, they offer the most likely explanation thus far for Ian Berzin's liquidation and for that of Arthur Stashevsky, Juan Negrín's adviser on financial matters, who, it seems, shared Berzin's opposition to the NKVD's activities in Spain. Krivitsky wrote:

General Berzin had served for fifteen years as chief of the Military Intelligence of the Red Army. A native of Latvia, he led, at the age of sixteen, a guerrilla band in the revolutionary struggle against the Czar. . . . Berzin joined the Red Army under Trotsky and rose to a powerful position in the high command. Large-framed, already grey-haired, given to few words, crafty, Berzin was selected by Stalin to organize and direct the Loyalist Army [in Spain].

Stalin's chief political commissar in Spain was Arthur Stashevsky. He was of Polish extraction. Short and stocky, he looked like a business man, and nominally he was the Soviet trade envoy in Barcelona. But Stashevsky, too, had served in the Red Army. He resigned from the military service to take up the task of reorganizing the Russian fur industry. . . . His success was brilliant. . . . Stalin now assigned to him the job of manipulating the political and financial reins of Loyalist Spain. . . .

In March 1937, I read a confidential report from General Berzin to the Commissar of War, Voroshilov. It was also read by Yezhov [chief of the NKVD]. . . . He stated that our OGPU [NKVD][42] agents were compromising the Soviet authority in Spain by their unwarranted interference and espionage in government quarters. He concluded with a demand that [Alexander] Orlov, [chief NKVD operative in Spain] be recalled from Spain at once. "Berzin is absolutely right," was Sloutski's comment to me, after I had read the report. Sloutski, chief of the Foreign Division of the OGPU, went on to say that our men were behaving in Spain as if they were in a colony, treating even Spanish leaders as colonists handle natives. When I asked him if anything would be done about Orlov, Sloutski said it was up to Yezhov.

Yezhov, grand marshal of the great purge then under way, himself looked upon Spain as a Russian province. Moreover, Berzin's associates in the Red Army were already being seized all over the Soviet Union, and Berzin's own life was no safer than any. With so many of his comrades in the nets of the OGPU, any report from him would be viewed with suspicion at the Kremlin.

In April, Stashevsky arrived in Moscow to report to Stalin personally on the Spanish situation. Though a rock-ribbed Stalinist, a rigidly orthodox party man, Stashevsky also felt that the conduct of the OGPU in the Loyalist areas was an error. Like General Berzin, he opposed the high-handed colonial methods used by Russians on Spanish soil.

Stashevsky had no use for dissenters or "Trotskyists" in Russia, and approved the OGPU method of dealing with them, but he thought that the OGPU should respect the regular Spanish political parties. Cautiously he intimated that Stalin might perhaps change the Spanish policy of the OGPU. The "Big Boss" pretended to agree with him, and Stashevky left the Kremlin quite elated.[43]

A few months later both Stashevsky and Berzin were recalled to Moscow and disappeared in Stalin's purges. Krivitsky gives the date of their recall as July 1937 and states that Stashevsky's wife, who was in Paris at the time, informed him that her husband and General Berzin "had come through, but had stopped only between trains, proceeding to Moscow in great haste." "The execution of the leading commanders of the Red Army," Krivitsky adds, "portended ill for Berzin. Like Stashevsky, he had been intimately associated with the purged commissars and generals since the beginning of the Soviet revolution, nearly twenty years before. Against that fact his achievements in Spain and his strict and obedient loyalty would count for nothing."[44] Although Krivitsky appears to link Berzin's and Stashevsky's fate, at least partially, to their criticism of the NKVD's methods in Spain, it is perhaps significant that Orlov, who had undoubtedly read Krivitsky's charges against him after his defection to the United States in 1938, avoids any reference to the accusations in his book *The Secret History of Stalin's Crimes*, although it will be remembered that he made a special point of denigrating Krivitsky in his reply to the questionnaire presented to him by Stanley Payne in 1968.[45]

As for General Gorev, Ehrenburg discovered his "fate" when he arrived in Moscow in December 1937,[46] while Nikcolai G. Kuznetsov, the Soviet naval attaché and adviser to the Spanish Republican fleet in 1936–37, known as Kolya,[47] states in his book published in Moscow in 1966 that Gorev was "suppressed," but gives no date.[48] "It is interesting to note," writes Orlov, "that General Gorev was arrested only two days after Kalinin, the President of the Soviet Union and member of the politburo, had presented him with the Order of Lenin in a special ceremony in the Kremlin for his outstanding services in the Spanish Civil War. This episode showed that even the members of the politburo did not know who was on the death list, and that the matters of executions were being decided by two men only: by Stalin and Yezhov [chief of the NKVD]." In addition to confirming the arrest and execution without trial of Gorev and Berzin,

Orlov gives the names of brigade commanders Kolev and Valua who, he says, "helped the Spanish government create the Republican Army" and were among the "many Soviet commanders" in Spain who were recalled to Moscow in 1937 and executed.[49]

With the exception of Berzin and Gorev, who were purged in 1937—and with the further exception of Voronov who occupied high positions in the ministry of defense including that of president of the Academy of Artillery Science,[50] of Kulik who survived until 1950,[51] and Kuznetsov, who became commander in chief of the naval forces of the USSR and first deputy minister of the navy[52]— most of the other top-ranking officers who served in Spain between 1936 and 1937 were liquidated in 1941, the year of Germany's invasion of Russia and two years after the Spanish Civil War. According to *Who Was Who in the USSR*, Shtern and Smushkevich died in imprisonment in October, while Ptukhin was executed in June.[53] The same source states that all three were posthumously rehabilitated.

In a book published in Moscow in 1972, Alexander Yakovlev, the famous Soviet airplane designer, makes the following observations about Soviet aircraft during the Civil War that throw some light on Smushkevich's liquidation. "Despite their high manoeuverability our fighters proved to be inferior to the German machines in regard to speed and especially in regard to the caliber and range of their weapons. Our SB bombers could not fly without fighter escort, but our fighters, being weaker than the German, could not provide effective cover. However great the heroism of the republican fliers, what counted in the long run was the quality of combat materiel. What happened came as an unpleasant, one might even say an inexplicable surprise, especially coming as it did after the dazzling string of records in aviation. Yet there it was: we were definitely lagging behind Hitler Germany, our potential adversary. . . . Stalin took our reverses in Spain very much to heart. And he vented his displeasure and wrath on those who were only quite recently looked upon as heroes and were enjoying the honors they fully deserved. The first victims were Smushkevich and Rychagov, both twice Heroes of the Soviet Union, and undeservedly as it turned out subsequently."[54]

Although it is true that Smushkevich was eventually shot by Stalin, it is by no means certain that events in Spain were even partially responsible, for upon his recall to Moscow in 1937 he was named deputy chief of the air force and in 1940 was promoted to the position of inspector general. It was not until 28 October 1941—at the time of the serious reverses on the Russian front during World War II—that he was executed.[55]

Also in 1941, General Pavlov, the commander of the Soviet tank forces in Spain, was purged, joining the ranks of those who, to use the words of Ehrenburg, "were destroyed for no reason at all by their own people."[56]

As for the lesser officers who served in Spain in different advisory and technical capacities, how many perished in Stalin's purges is unknown, but some attained high rank and even eminence in the Soviet Union years later. For example, P. Batov, I. Eremenko, M. Iakushin, S. Krivoshein, A. Novak, G.

Prokofiev, and A. Rodimtsev became general officers of various grades,[57] while R. Malinovsky and K. A. Meretskov attained the rank of marshal, Malinovsky becoming Soviet defense minister and Meretskov Red Army chief of staff.[58]

Meretskov arrived in Madrid in October 1936 and returned to Moscow in June 1937. He served as adviser to Enrique Líster in the First Mixed Brigade for a brief period, then as adviser to General Martínez Cabrera, the chief of the war ministry general staff, at which time he was known as Petrovich, and finally as adviser, for a short time, to General José Miaja.[59]

Another of the lower-ranking officers who survived the purges was the guerrilla war specialist Mamsurov Judji-Umar, known in Spain as Hajji or Ksanti, who later became a general. "At Gaylord's, a Madrid hotel, Hemingway met our army men," recalls Ilya Ehrenburg. "He liked Hajji, a man of reckless courage, who used to penetrate behind the enemy lines (he was a native of the Caucasus and could easily pass himself off as a Spaniard). Much of what Hemingway says about the activity of guerrillas in his book *For Whom the Bell Tolls* he heard from Hajji.[60] (What a good thing that at least Hajji survived. I met him once later and was overjoyed.)"[61]

Not all the lesser officers were as fortunate. The former German Communist Gustav Regler, well-known author and political commissar of the Twelfth International Brigade, who had fought in the German army during World War I, tells of a party he attended in February 1937 at the invitation of Koltzov, where officers of the Russian delegation were assembled:[62]

> Gorkin, an engineer, was the first to greet me. He had set up searchlight installations for us, the only defense we possessed against night air attacks—the A.A. guns had still to be bought abroad. Now he had been recalled to Russia, and this was his farewell party. He was beaming with satisfaction. His work had been approved of, and in Moscow he would get his reward. . . .
>
> The next day Koltzov visited Arganda. He found me on the balcony of the staff building. Pointing to the searchlight beside me, he asked, "What's that?"
>
> "A legacy from Gorkin," I replied. . . .
>
> He laughed cuttingly and said: "A legacy? That's the literal truth!"
>
> "Has something happened to him on his journey?" I asked.
>
> "No," said Koltzov. . . . "But something will happen to him when he arrives. . . . He'll be arrested when he reaches Odessa."
>
> For some moments I was dumbfounded. Then I asked:
>
> "How do you know? Is it something political?"
>
> "Yes," said Koltzov and it was as though another world was speaking as he went on: "Why are you so surprised? Because of the farewell party? We knew all about it. In fact, that's why we gave him a party. . . . The French give a man rum before they lead him out to the guillotine. . . . In these days we give him champagne."
>
> "I'm going into the line," I said. "I don't feel well."
>
> "It's not easy for a European to get used to Asiatic customs," said Koltzov.

"I prefer American customs," I said. "I'm going to join Hemingway [who had just arrived in Spain and was visiting the front]. . . . One can breathe more freely in his neighborhood, if you'll forgive me for saying so."

"I'll come with you," said Koltzov. . . . "Perhaps I need a breath of western democracy too!"

(I assume that it was this humanity which . . . caused his death in a Stalin gaol.)[63]

It is worth adding here the following incident recounted by Regler to Ernest Hemingway that resulted in the two becoming friends: two volunteers had lost their heads in an engagement near the Escorial, seeing enemies everywhere in the mist, and had shouted to the others to run.

I had them arrested and brought to headquarters. . . . I decided to send them to a sanatorium, and I reported this to Marty [political commissar of the International Brigades]. He replied promptly that he knew of a suitable place, near Alcalá de Henares. They were taken there, and two days ago I had heard that they had been shot in the castle by a Russian execution squad. "Swine!" said Hemingway, and spat on the ground. The gesture made me his friend, and thereafter I lost no opportunity of proving the fact. I told him the inside stories of operations and crises which I had witnessed earlier. I let him know our losses and gave him advance information whenever I could, feeling certain that he really understood what it was all about. I gave him secret material relating to the Party which he respected, because it was fighting more actively than any other body, although he despised its Martys. He used my material later in *For Whom the Bell Tolls*, and countless readers learned from the brutal interpolations in a work of romantic fiction about things that they would not listen to in real life. He depicted the spy-disease, that Russian syphilis, in all its shameful, murderously stupid workings, writing with hatred of the huntsman for the poacher.[64]

In spite of the liquidation of an undetermined number of Soviet officers of various ranks after their return from Spain, the Soviet general staff derived what knowledge it could from the Spanish conflict as did its German counterpart. Indeed, a book published by the Red Army high command in 1939 on the Spanish experience referred to "several crucial matters vital from a practical standpoint in preparing the Red Army for action."[65] But it should not be overlooked that while the Civil War allowed the USSR to test new weapons and techniques in the field of battle, it also served as a testing ground for new weapons and techniques in the field of politics. As Julián Gorkin, a left-wing opponent of Soviet policy in Spain, wrote: "It has been repeatedly said that the Spanish Civil War was a general rehearsal for the Second World War; what is not clearly understood is that it was also the first testing ground for 'popular democracy,' perfected forms of which we have been obliged to witness in a dozen countries during the postwar period. The men and methods used to convert these countries into Kremlin satellites were tested in Spain. For this reason, among many, the Spanish experience had and continues to have historical and universal significance."[66]

As the official Soviet *Kommunisticheskii internatsional: kratkii istoricheskii ocherk* (Outline History of the Communist International) puts it: "The course of events in Spain revealed a fact of paramount importance, namely, that the popular front, the new democracy, was a connecting link between the defensive antifascist struggle and the ultimate aim—the struggle for socialism [i.e., Communist ascendancy]. The significance of the Spanish experience for an understanding of the means of approach to the socialist stage of the revolution was fully grasped and appreciated by the Comintern."[67]

Although the Comintern delegates and NKVD agents who executed Soviet policies in Spain arrived without the approval of Largo Caballero, the same cannot be said of the principal Soviet military advisers. In fact, the letter sent by Stalin, Molotov, and Voroshilov in December 1936 to Largo Caballero—from which a passage has already been quoted in this volume—stresses that the advisers were sent to Spain as a result of his "repeated requests" transmitted through Marcel Rosenberg, the Soviet ambassador. Furthermore, in his reply of 12 January 1937, Largo Caballero refers to the comrades "requested by us," acknowledging that they were rendering a "great service" and were "discharging their duties with real enthusiasm and extraordinary courage."[68]

Still, in spite of this seemingly friendly exchange of correspondence and Stalin's assurance to Largo Caballero that the advisers had been "categorically ordered not to lose sight of the fact that . . . a Soviet comrade, being a foreigner in Spain, can only be really useful if he adheres strictly to the functions of an adviser and an adviser only,"[69] the power that the Soviet officers necessarily wielded eventually exasperated the war minister and explains his later censure of "irresponsible foreign interference."

Some idea of the friction that soon arose between Largo Caballero and Miaja as a result of the latter's virtual dependence on the Russians may be gained from a telegram sent by the war minister to the general on 17 November 1936, reminding him that the only orders he should obey were those issued by the government, and from Miaja's reply, in which, after taking cognizance of the fact that Largo Caballero had found it necessary to remind him of the most elementary principle of discipline and subordination, which, in his long military career he had never forgotten, he asked to be relieved by someone worthy of Largo Caballero's confidence.[70] Because of the prestige he had acquired, Miaja no doubt anticipated that the war minister would not act upon his request. And he was right.

That the Soviet advisers operated to all intents and purposes independently of the war and air ministries has been confirmed by the Spanish chief of the air force, Hidalgo de Cisneros, a Communist party member,[71] by Luis Araquistáin, Largo Caballero's close political associate, and by the war minister himself. Furthermore, Colonel Segismundo Casado, chief of operations on the war ministry general staff, affirms: "I can state clearly that during the whole war neither the air force nor the tank corps was controlled by the minister of national defense, nor in consequence by the central general staff. The minister and his staff were not even aware of the quantity and types of their machines and only knew the situation of those which were used in actual operations. In the same way the minister and his staff were not aware of the situation, and even of the existence of a great number of unknown [airfields] maintained in secret by the 'friendly advisers' and certain of the aviation chiefs who were entirely in their confidence."[72]

Perhaps even more galling to Largo Caballero than the autonomy of the Soviet advisory staff was the growth of Communist influence in the armed forces, particularly in the central zone. Here the presence of Soviet officers, the marked favoritism shown to the Communists in the distribution of arms and supplies from Russia,[73] the intrepid role of the International Brigades, their superior efficiency, as well as that of the Spanish Communist units,[74] all helped to swell the influence of the party and to attract into its orbit an imposing number of regular army officers.

Although some Spanish opponents of the Communists have underrated the importance of the efficiency of the International Brigades as a model for Spanish units,[75] it has nonetheless received ample recognition. *Claridad*, for example, stated on 11 November 1936: "Our proletarian and peasant masses, weighed down by centuries of oppression and ignorance—the work of social castes that have demonstrated their absolute incapacity for organization—must make superhuman efforts to equal these comrades from other nations. Intelligence is sharpened in school. The militiamen of the International Column have had opportunities of cultivating their intelligence during their childhood and youth. Our masses, on the other hand, have had no such opportunities. But when we triumph, we shall have them, and our children shall have even more. For this we are fighting; for this we are dying."[76]

"An indication—and a very important one—of the effectiveness of the Communist party's war work," wrote the correspondent in Spain of the London *Daily Worker*, "is offered by the fact that today the majority of the loyal generals, not to mention the younger loyal officers, have applied for and received membership in the Communist party."[77] And the Socialist historian Antonio Ramos Oliveira, a supporter of Juan Negrín, wrote: "Army officers and officials who had never turned the pages of a Marxist leaflet, became communists, some through calculation, others through moral weakness, others inspired by the enthusiasm which animated this organization."[78]

Among the high-ranking officers who joined the party, General José Miaja, the president of the Defense Council, figured prominently, as did the liberal and aging General Sebastián Pozas, the commander of the Army of the Center, whose Soviet adviser was General Kulik, later Marshal Kulik, known in Spain as Kuper. To Jesús Hernández, former politburo member, Kulik was "coarse but congenial," "impressively strong and tall who reminded one of a polar bear."[79] To Enrique Castro he was "large and crude. . . . His shaven head and enormous brutal face were impressive. But even more so were his shouts and hands, which moved as though they were the sails of a La Mancha windmill. His staff stood in dread of him."[80] By contrast, the aging Pozas was phlegmatic, nay, effete. No match for the overpowering Kulik, he was quite content to let the Russian general run the show and never bothered to adjust his peacetime schedule to meet the exigencies of a relentless war. "It wasn't until late in the morning that he would be roused from his sleep," recalls General Kulik's aide, Rodion Malinovsky, a future marshal of the Soviet Union and defense minister whose ashes are now immured in the Kremlin walls.[81] "His toilet and breakfast occupied several hours. Later on he would receive his chief of staff, a colonel, who was as old as he. They would exchange pleasantries, after which the audience would end. Out of respect for the truth it must be said that in his convictions he was absolutely loyal to the republicans, a matter of far-reaching importance. But the traditions of the old military routine weighed heavily upon him."[82]

After the February 1936 elections, Pozas had been appointed inspector general of the Civil Guard and had incurred the hostility of the right-wing army chiefs because of his efforts to ensure the loyalty of this corps to the Republic.[83] At the outbreak of the Civil War he became minister of the interior in the Giral cabinet and urged the arming of the people.[84] After assuming command of the Army of the Center in October 1936, he discreetly joined the Communist party,[85] and, in May 1937, when in command of the eastern army, he also joined the PSUC, the Communist-controlled United Socialist party of Catalonia.[86] But despite his membership he was simply a name with propaganda value without a shred of influence in the inner circles of the party.

Whereas a large number of officers joined the party, influenced by all the factors enumerated previously as well as by the knowledge that membership would enable them to secure for their units supplies of Russian war material,[87] others were swayed by its moderate propaganda. Colonel Jesús Pérez Salas, a professional officer with genuine Republican sympathies, writes:

> It cannot be denied that the Communists were masters in the art of propaganda, as a result of which they managed to deceive everybody. This propaganda consisted principally in affirming that their only aim was to defeat Franco and put into effect once again the laws of the Republic. All their leaders, especially La Pasionaria, made loud protestations of loyalty to the regime and to the Constitution, which they claimed they were endeavoring to reestablish. To achieve this end it was necessary, they said, to organize an efficient and disciplined army that would replace the undisciplined militia of the CNT. So well did they carry out that slogan that they managed to deceive everybody. Some professional military men fell into the snare, and not a few, out of enthusiasm for Communist propaganda, thoughtlessly joined the party.
>
> As for myself, who had no other desire than that of winning the war, I believed that the Communists' seemingly fine aims were necessarily a step in that direction. Unfortunately, this was not so. By their propaganda, they aimed only at gaining supremacy in the army in order to use it for their own personal advantage, subordinating to the latter the war against Franco. This was the reason that impelled me to oppose them.[88]

Some officers, particularly those without political affiliation before the war, were drawn to the party for strictly personal motives.

"There were," writes Bruno Alonso, a moderate Socialist and chief political commissar of the Republican fleet, "few, very few professional military leaders, without party affiliation before 18 July, but loyal to the Republic, who did not bow to the predominant political influence, some from inclination, others out of weakness of will, and many out of fear lest their lack of political antecedents should result in some arbitrary and irreparable act against them."[89]

"Let me remind you," the Communist Antonio Cordón warned a fellow officer in the war ministry, "that we are living in strange times, when people are killed for nothing at all. I seriously advise you to join the Communist party. It needs you, and you need it."[90]

While most foreign journalists and writers who covered the Republican side were ignorant of the Communists' hegemonic aims within the Popular Army or preferred not to speak of them for fear of providing fuel for enemy propaganda, John Dos Passos wrote candidly about what he perceived was happening. In July 1937, he said: "In Spain the working class has defended itself with a magnificent heroism that will remain one of the bloodstirring episodes of European history. Meanwhile, behind the lines a struggle as violent almost as the war has been going on between the Marxist concept of the totalitarian state, and the Anarchist concept of individual liberty. More and more, as the day-to-day needs of the army become paramount over the turbulent effort of the working class in revolt against oppression, the Communist Party forges ahead as the organizer of victory. The Anarchists and the Socialists with their ideas of individual and local freedom and self-government have given way step by step before this tremendously efficient and ruthless machine for power. . . . The question which cannot be answered now is whether the Spanish people will have paid too high a price for the fine new army they have organized, and whether the Communist Party . . . won't turn out to be only one more magnificent instrument for power, which means a magnificent instrument for oppression."[91]

Dos Passos had visited Spain early in 1937 to investigate the disappearance of his old friend José Robles, who had "been put out of the war" by the Russians.[92] Although deeply disturbed, he had conscientious scruples about telling all he knew. Reflecting some years later on his dilemma, he wrote: "How to tell about it? You didn't want to help the enemy. . . . At the same time you wanted to tell the truth. . . . There were things you suspected you couldn't yet be sure of. Just describe what happens, I told myself. Through surface events give what hints you truthfully can of the great forces working underneath. . . . What I was seeing, I know now, was the taking over of the dying liberal republic by an outpost of international communism."[93]

If the growth of Communist influence at all levels in the army finally told upon the patience of the war minister, still more provoking, especially to a man of Largo Caballero's temperament—who even in dealings with his own colleagues was obstinate and irascible, and who, according to General Asensio, his undersecretary, wished to direct and control everything personally[94]—was the importunity of his opponents. Time and again the obduracy with which he withstood the pressure to which he was constantly submitted led to fierce clashes with the Russian generals[95] and with the Soviet ambassador, Marcel Rosenberg.

"More than as an ambassador," testifies Luis Araquistáin, intimate of Largo Caballero, "[Rosenberg] acted like a Russian viceroy in Spain. He paid daily visits to Largo Caballero, sometimes accompanied by Russians of high rank, military or civilian. During the visits, which lasted for hours on end, Rosenberg tried to give the head of the Spanish government instructions as to what he should do in order to direct the war successfully. His suggestions, which were practically orders, related mainly to army officers. Such and such generals and colonels should be dismissed and others appointed in their place. These recommendations were based, not on the competence of the officers, but on their political affiliations and on the degree of their amenability to the Communists."[96]

"[Rosenberg]," writes Ginés Ganga, a left-wing Socialist Cortes deputy, "used to carry in his pocket a collection of notes couched in the following or similar terms: 'It would be expedient to dismiss X, chief of such and such a division, and replace him by Z'; 'A, employee of such and such a ministry, does not fulfill his duty. It would be advisable to replace him by B'; 'It is necessary to imprison M and bring him to trial for disloyalty,' and so on, ceaselessly."[97]

It is most likely that among the Soviet officials of high rank who, according to Araquistáin, sometimes accompanied Rosenberg on his daily visits to Largo Caballero, was Alexander Orlov, who undoubtedly kept the attitudes of top-ranking Soviet diplomats under careful scrutiny, a task greatly simplified by the fact that his own headquarters were located in the Soviet embassy. Hence, it may be assumed that if Rosenberg failed to execute Soviet policy with sufficient vigor or ventured to criticize NKVD methods in Spain, as Krivitsky stated that General Berzin and Arthur Stashevsky had done, his aberrant behavior was immediately reported to Moscow. This may explain why Orlov made no reference whatsoever in his book *The Secret History of Stalin's Crimes*, or in any other written or oral testimony, during the thirty-five years he lived in exile in the United States, to the recall to Moscow of Rosenberg, of Stashevsky, or of Leon Gaykis, Rosenberg's successor in February 1937, all of whom mysteriously vanished without a trace. The only reference I have been able to find in Soviet sources to any of these three men is in Ehrenburg's *Eve of War, 1933–41*, which says that he learned of Rosenberg's "fate" when he arrived in Moscow in December 1937.[98] As for Stashevsky and Gaykis, President Azaña noted in his diary on 29 July 1937 that Negrín had read telegrams to him that day from Marcelino Pascua, the Spanish ambassador in Moscow, stating that he was unaware of Gaykis's "situation" or of that of "another important person who was involved in commercial and financial matters" [an obvious reference to Stashevsky].[99] On 6 August, Azaña wrote: "There is still no knowledge of the whereabouts of Gaykis . . . who went to his country on a leave of absence."[100] Nineteen years later, Vittorio Vidali was informed by an "old Bolshevik" in Moscow that Gaykis "was still alive and had been 'rehabilitated.' "[101] Beyond this brief reference, no other information on Gaykis has come to light.

Orlov's complete silence on the fate of these top-ranking officials, with whom he was in frequent if not daily contact, must of necessity raise two questions. Why did he not consider their recall to Moscow and ultimate disappearance important enough even to mention? Was he perhaps directly responsible for their recall and, hence, indirectly, for their disappearance?

Whatever Rosenberg's private thoughts may have been on the attitude of the NKVD in Spain, he appears, on the surface at least, to have executed Soviet policy as vigorously as his conscience permitted. Although we do not know, of course, what the innermost thoughts of this cultured and apparently sensitive diplomat[102] may have been regarding the policy pursued by Stalin and by his chief NKVD agent in Spain, his encounters with Largo Caballero were matched in ferocity only by Largo Caballero's encounters with the Communist ministers.

According to Indalecio Prieto, who, as a member of the government, must be regarded as an important witness, "a situation of unbelievable tension" arose between the two ministers and the premier. "Very violent scenes occurred during cabinet meetings, and, in addition, Largo Caballero had tumultuous discussions with the ambassador of the USSR, Señor Rosenberg. I cannot make out whether the attitude of Señor Rosenberg was a reflection of the anger of the Communist ministers or whether the anger of the latter was a reflection of the attitude of the Russian ambassador. What I do know . . . is that the action of Russian diplomacy on the premier, or better still, against the premier, and the pressure of the Communist ministers were simultaneous and alike."[103]

In this situation of mounting conflict with the Russians and their Spanish aides, Largo Caballero, faced by the depredations on his following, by the traditional enmity of the moderate wing of his own party, and by the silent animosity of the liberal Republicans, looked to the Anarchosyndicalists for support against his tenacious adversaries. About this time, rumors were circulating that he was planning to form a "trade-union government" composed solely of representatives of the UGT and CNT. The rumors were fueled by a brief report in the UGT organ *Claridad* on 3 March, stating that the UGT executive (of which Caballero was secretary) and the CNT national committee were holding "frequent meetings" and that "while confusion and chaos increase in the realm of politics, the foundations are being laid in the trade-union field for a rapid and definitive solution to the present situation." The rumors were further fueled by optimistic reports in the CNT press that the leadership of the two rival unions were on the verge of reaching a historic alliance that would resolve fundamental problems.[104] Although Largo Caballero may have given fleeting thought to the idea of a trade-union government as a means of political survival, nothing came of the alleged project, which was severely censured by Communist party secretary José Díaz during the plenum of the central committee at the beginning of March. "[A] trade-union government," he warned, ". . . would mean the destruction of the Popular Front and of the unity of the Spanish people. . . . [Anyone] who attempts to break this unity will be branded by our brave combatants as an enemy of our cause."[105]

Although it does not appear that the two unions seriously discussed the idea of forming a trade-union government, a brief rapprochement between Largo Caballero and the Anarchosyndicalist leaders definitely occurred. The novel relationship thus established was a potent factor in disposing the Socialist leader to a policy of conciliation toward his former adversaries. In particular, it deterred him from carrying out, at the pressing instance of the Communists, a thoroughgoing militarization of a regular army, an army to which he himself had never been especially partial and which he knew was anathema to the libertarian movement.

32

The Libertarian Movement and
the Regular Army

"We do not want a national army," cried *Frente Libertario*, the newspaper of the Anarchosyndicalist militia on the central front. "We want the popular militia, which incarnates the will of the masses, and is the only force that can defend the liberty and the free social order of the Spanish people. As before the Civil War, we now cry, 'Down with chains.' The army is enslavement, the symbol of tyranny. Away with the army."[1] Juan López, the CNT leader, declared shortly before entering the cabinet of Largo Caballero, "We do not want a uniformed and disciplined militia organized into military units."[2]

The Anarchosyndicalists could not accept a regular army without violating their antiauthoritarian principles. True, the exigencies of an implacable struggle had forced them to recognize that their militia units needed some measure of restraint on individualism, but that was entirely different from accepting an out-and-out militarization involving the rigorous subordination of these units to government control, the restoration of rank and privilege, the appointment of officers by the war ministry, the introduction of differential pay rates, heavy disciplinary punishments, and the compulsory salute. "When this word [militarization] is uttered—why not admit the fact?—we feel uneasy, disturbed; we shudder because it calls to mind the constant assaults on dignity and the human personality," avowed *Nosotros*, the Anarchist organ in the region of Valencia. "Until yesterday, to militarize implied—and for many people it still implies—regimenting men in such a way as to destroy their wills by breaking their personality in the mechanism of the barracks."[3]

But if the CNT and FAI had ethical motives for their hostility to militarization and the regular army, they had powerful political motives as well. At a congress of the CNT two months before the outbreak of the Civil War, a resolution was approved to the effect that a standing army—and by this was meant any standing army organized after the overthrow of the old regime—would constitute the greatest threat to the Revolution, "because under its influence a dictatorship would be forged that would necessarily deal it a mortal blow." Drafted by a commission composed of some of the outstanding leaders of the libertarian movement, the resolution stated that the greatest guarantee for the defense of the Revolution would be the armed people. "There are thousands of workers," it added, "who have passed through the barracks and have a knowledge of modern military technique. Every commune will have its arms and [other] elements of defense, for they will not be destroyed and transformed into instruments of labor until the Revolution had been finally consolidated. We urged the necessity of holding onto airplanes, tanks, armored cars, machine guns, and antiaircraft guns because it is from the air that the real danger of foreign invasion exists. If that invasion should occur the people will mobilize themselves rapidly in order to oppose the enemy and will return to their work as soon as they have accomplished their defensive mission."[4]

It is no wonder, therefore, that the attempt of José Giral's moderate government in the first weeks of the war to create volunteer battalions and, later, a volunteer army under its control should have been viewed with suspicion by the libertarian movement. *Solidaridad Obrera*, the leading CNT newspaper in Spain, declared with regard to the first of these two measures that even before the military rebellion had been defeated the middle classes were thinking of the regime to be established on the day of victory. But, it affirmed, the workers would not rest on their laurels and would not allow their triumph to be snatched from them.[5] García Pradas, director of the principal Anarchosyndicalist organ in the central zone, *CNT*, declared that no one should enlist in the volunteer army because such an army would result in the creation of a new caste that would try to settle accounts after the victory over fascism. The people, he added, had shown that they did not need to join an army in order to win the war and should therefore not allow themselves to be deceived.[6]

Hence, it is not at all surprising that when, a few weeks after entering the war ministry, Largo Caballero promulgated measures providing for the militarization of the militia and the creation of a regular army, anxiety grew in the movement and mounted into alarm when the Communists made manifest progress in penetrating the military apparatus.

In an effort to still the fears of the FIJL, the libertarian youth organization, as to the Communists' intentions regarding the army, Santiago Carrillo, the general secretary of the Communist-run Unified Socialist Youth, declared: "I know . . . there are comrades of the Unified Socialist Youth who desire unity with the young libertarians in order to win the war, but that they believe in their heart of hearts that, when the war is over and the armies return from the front, we are going to use these armies to crush, to destroy, to liquidate our brothers, the young libertarians. . . . But I tell you, comrades, that such ideas must be discarded because they are mistaken, because when we call for unity with the young libertarians we do so sincerely. We know that our libertarian comrades are a force necessary for victory, and we are also convinced that after victory they will collaborate with us in building up a strong, free, and democratic Spain. That is our belief, and all we ask of them is that on their part they should abandon their sectarian prejudices, that they should not regard us as passing friends of today and enemies of tomorrow, but as friends today, tomorrow, and always."[7]

Neither the Anarchist youth organizations nor the libertarian movement as a whole, however, was under any illusions as to the nature of the threat presented by the Communists, if only because of the annihilation of the Russian Anarchists by the Bolsheviks. The CNT-FAI leaders had proposed in September 1936 that a "war militia" be created on the basis of compulsory service and under the joint control of the CNT and UGT partly in the hope of parrying the Communist danger.[8] But neither of these two proposals had evoked a responsive echo, and with the Communist threat still uppermost in their minds, the Anarchosyndicalist leaders had finally decided to solicit representation in the cabinet and thus secure for the libertarian movement some measure of influence in the military machine. This, to be sure, had meant jettisoning not only their antigovernment creed, but also their antimilitarist principles, which, in the opinion of Manuel Villar, director, from December 1936, of the CNT newspaper in Valencia, *Fragua Social*, had proved inimical to the libertarian movement. For, he contended, whereas many Anarchosyndicalists had regarded the holding of commanding posts with repugnance, the Communists had embarked on an unbridled drive to occupy all they could.[9] "Were we in a position to be squeamish about doctrines?" he asked. "If the CNT had allowed the levers of revolutionary action to escape from its hands, the Revolution itself would have suffered from the lessening of our influence. And as the Revolution was the objective, and the CNT one of its most powerful determining factors, the most revolutionary course was to take those steps that would keep us in the political, military, and economic center of gravity."[10]

But the role the CNT-FAI ministers were able to play in the counsels of the cabinet, particularly in regard to military matters, fell far short of their expectations; for they found, to use the words of Juan Peiró, the Anarchosyndicalist minister of industry, that they had no rights or responsibilities regarding the direction of the war.[11] Hoping to remedy this situation, they proposed that a kind of inner cabinet be created to handle military affairs, in which the CNT would be given representation.[12] This proposal—supported by the Communists no doubt in the belief that the new body would enable them to subject Caballero's actions to closer scrutiny and control[13]—materialized in the decree of 9 November, establishing a Higher War Council that was empowered to "harmonize and unify everything related to the war and its direction."[14] The council was composed of Largo Caballero, the war minister; Indalecio Prieto, the moderate Socialist leader and minister of air and navy; Vicente Uribe, the Communist minister of agriculture; Julio Just, the left Republican minister of public works; García Oliver, the CNT-FAI minister of justice; and Alvarez del Vayo, the philo-Communist minister of foreign affairs and general commissar of war.[15]

In spite of its official aim, this new body was condemned to futility from the outset owing to the dissensions between Largo Caballero and the Communists as well as to the rivalry between the premier and Indalecio Prieto that deprived it of any unanimity and also of the most relevant military information essential to the proper discharge of its functions. The Communists soon had grounds for open dissatisfaction since the Higher War Council met only on rare occasions owing to the resolve of the war minister not to relinquish to his opponents what remained of his authority,[16] while the Anarchosyndicalists, who had hoped that it would serve to augment their influence in military affairs, found that their voice had scant effect amid the strength of their opponents.

As a result, the libertarian movement was unable to use its participation in the government to increase its say in the military field or even curb the progress of the Communists, but rather was obliged in the end to circumscribe its efforts to maintaining control of its own militia units and securing arms from the war ministry. This was no easy task, for the latter had decided that weapons would be withheld from militia forces that were unwilling to transform themselves into regular units with the prescribed cadres. At the regional congress of the Valencia CNT, held in November 1936, the representative of the Alcoy paperworkers declared: "[There] is the case of a [CNT] column organized in Alcoy with more than one thousand militiamen, which the government does not arm because it has no officers; on the other hand, the Socialists, who are less in number, have been able to organize a column and obtain the necessary arms because they conform to the government's conditions."[17]

To circumvent these stipulations, the Anarchosyndicalists decided that their units should simulate acquiescence by adopting military names, an expedient that was employed by most of the CNT-FAI units, including those on the central front, in which, to quote the director of the Anarchist *Castilla Libre*, "everything save the nomenclature remained unchanged."[18] At the CNT regional congress, the Alcoy delegate declared that rather than be left without arms it would be better to meet the government's demands by introducing officer rank and insignia. "But," he added meaningfully, "as far as we are concerned, a century delegate is nothing more than a century delegate."[19] This stratagem did not help the libertarian units to secure the arms they needed, and, in the long run, they were forced to yield to the concept of militarization.

It was not only the need for military supplies that finally induced the libertarian movement to bow to the concept of militarization: it was also—and this was no doubt the most important consideration—the need to overcome the defects of the militia system.

One of the most serious of these defects is adequately illustrated by the following excerpt from an unpublished article written by a regular army corporal, who was posted to a CNT-FAI column on the Madrid front: "In the column we found a professional army captain . . . who secretly advised Ricardo Sanz [its Anarchosyndicalist leader] on everything he thought should be done. Sanz, who had common sense, always accepted his counsel; but every time a decision had to be taken he had to convene a general assembly of the militiamen and make the captain's advice appear as if it were his own, cleverly inculcating it into the assembly so that it would look like the fruit of debate."[20]

Captain Alberto Bayo, the titular head of the invasion of the Balearic Islands by Catalan militia, records the following conversation he had with the members of the Anarchist militia committee when giving them orders for the invasion of Majorca:

" 'Now, just a minute,' one of the big chiefs replied. . . . 'We only take orders from the leaders of the CNT and we cannot carry out your orders without their approval.'

" 'Nevertheless, they will have to be carried out without their knowledge,' I retorted energetically, 'because they are in Barcelona and the landing is a military secret that I cannot risk sending by cable, radio, or even by code, and it must be undertaken tomorrow morning without vacillation and without delay.'

" 'We are very sorry,' they replied, 'but we cannot participate if it is to be carried out tomorrow. We risk our men only when ordered by our leaders.' . . .

"Over and over again I held my patience; I reasoned with them, I ordered them angrily, I beseeched them. . . . Finally they agreed to discuss among themselves whether they would carry out the landing the next day or wait until they received orders from their central committee."[21] The disadvantages of this democratic, antimilitaristic procedure soon made themselves apparent. "Those in charge would order an operation," declared Federica Montseny at a public meeting, "and the militiamen would meet to discuss it. Five, six, and seven hours were lost in deliberation, and when the operation was finally launched the enemy had already attained his objective. Such things make one laugh, and they also make one weep."[22]

But they did something else as well; they caused the Anarchosyndicalist militia leaders, especially on the central front, where the pressure of the enemy was unremitting, to turn their backs on their traditional attitude toward militarization. "It was [after the capture of Aravaca and Pozuelo outside Madrid] that all my ideas regarding discipline and militarization were shattered," Cipriano Mera, the CNT militia leader—who eventually became commander of the Fourteenth Division and then of the Fourth Army Corps—confessed some months later. "The blood of my brothers shed in the struggle made me change my views. I understood that if we were not to be definitely defeated, we had to construct our own army, an army as powerful as that of the enemy, a disciplined and capable army, organized for the defense of the workers. Henceforth I did not hesitate to urge upon all combatants the necessity of submitting to new military principles."[23]

And, in his memoir, *Guerra, exilio y cárcel de un anarcosindicalista*, Mera writes: "It was no longer a matter of street fighting or simple skirmishes, in which enthusiasm could compensate for lack of training. . . . This was a real war. Hence, we needed militarized units with officers capable of planning operations and opposing the enemy with the fewest possible losses in men and material. . . . I always believed . . . that there was nothing stronger than self-discipline in free men and that a common commitment to a single ideal was superior to any other factor. I noticed in the midst of battle that convictions and great ideas could inspire great gestures and heroic deeds . . . , but these were insufficient to give us the cohesion we needed on the battle fronts. . . . We had paid for our improvisation and whims with the lives of too many comrades. To reduce the bloodletting, it was necessary to change our conduct radically, if not our ideas. . . . When one has defended an ideal all one's life, it is sad to have to recognize the fact that, if we really wanted to win the war, we had to create an army with the necessary discipline. . . . I was horrified at the thought of wearing a military uniform, but saw no alternative."[24]

That this was not idle rhetoric is attested by Vicente Rojo, General Miaja's pro-Communist chief of staff. Referring to the night of 6–7 November, when General Franco's army had reached the outskirts of Madrid, Rojo—who identifies Mera only by the initial M—recalls that at 2 A.M. a leader of one of the militia units that "had fought most vigorously and had suffered the greatest number of casualties" came to his headquarters.

" 'I have come to ask you to give me a rank, any rank,' said Mera. 'Make me a sergeant. . . . I want to command like an officer so that my orders are strictly obeyed. I no longer wish to be M, "the man in charge." I want to be sergeant M, so that what happened today will not be repeated.'

" 'What happened today was a success for you and a triumph for your unit,' Rojo replied.

" 'Yes, but at what a cost in casualties.' . . .

"The inexorable imperatives of military tactics had removed the scales from the eyes of this fighter, a fighter who was as passionate and stubborn in the defense of his political and syndicalist convictions as he was courageous and tenacious in the field of battle."

Fifteen days later, Mera's unit, reorganized and retrained, became, according to Rojo, "one of our most brilliant shock units, and its leader, hewn from the same raw material as the guerrilla leaders of our War of Independence of 1808, became one of the most outstanding commanders in the cadres that emerged from the early militia army."[25]

Just as the CNT-FAI units on the Madrid front had, under the spur of necessity, introduced a modicum of discipline, so, under the same impulsion, they began to substitute a military for a militia structure and to urge the creation of cadres. *Frente Libertario*, the organ of the Madrid Anarchosyndicalist militia, declared that all prejudices should be laid aside and that the CNT should send to the military training academies a large number of comrades, who should begin to see that the military profession was as honorable and as essential as the trades that had calloused their hands. "The Popular Army now in formation," it added, "requires military technicians, and this need, which is of a national character, is felt especially by our organization, which must watch over the constant development of its power."[26] The Madrid Anarchosyndicalist militia was influenced not only by political considerations and by the rigor of the struggle around Madrid, but also by the example of the International Brigades, whose more efficient military organization soon asserted its superiority over the militia system. Little by little, affirms the director of the Anarchist *Castilla Libre*, the change that at first had been purely nominal went deeper. "The International Brigades have been

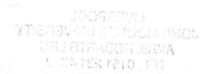

observed fighting, and it has been proved that, given the same heroism and expenditure of energy, organization results in greater efficiency. In our militia, cadres appear formed in accordance with the regulations of the war ministry. The battalion leaders become majors; the century delegates become captains, the first corporals and sergeants make their appearance."[27]

That this was not altogether a titular change was clear from statements made by many of the leading figures in the libertarian movement, who, having done with their antiauthoritarian past, became assiduous promoters of militarization. Cipriano Mera, for example, considered military discipline so important that he decided "to discuss matters only with generals, officers, and sergeants."[28] "One of the things that has done us most harm in the army," he declared at a later date, "is the excessive familiarity between officers and men who once belonged to the militia."[29] And Juan García Oliver, who before becoming minister of justice had been regarded as a pure Anarchist, now enjoined the students of one of the officers' training schools, with whose organization and administration he had been entrusted, to bear in mind that enlisted men "should cease to be your comrades and become the cogwheels of our military machine."[30]

García Oliver's assignment as chief organizer and administrator of the officers' training schools—an assignment sought by the CNT-FAI ministers upon entering the government in the hope of preventing the Communists from gaining control of the schools and impeding the graduation of officers sympathetic to the CNT and FAI[31]—had been given to the Anarchist leader by the Higher War Council because its members, owing to the enmity between Largo Caballero and his rivals, had been unable to agree upon any other candidate. In a speech in May 1937, when he was no longer a member of the council, García Oliver affirmed that he had received the genuine collaboration of the war minister and that the degree of confidence the latter had placed in him was due to the fact that he had not used his assignment for the benefit of his own organization.[32] Undoubtedly, one of the principal reasons for Caballero's support of the Anarchist leader was his desire to keep the officers' training schools out of the hands of the Communists. Nevertheless, the assignment did little to help the CNT and FAI, for the Anarchosyndicalists who enrolled in the schools were in a minority owing to the resistance by the rank and file of the libertarian movement to the creation of a regular army.[33] "This resulted in my bringing the matter up seriously before the national committee of the CNT," testifies García Oliver, "and in an agreement being reached and carried into practice whereby all the [CNT] Regional Committees of Defense were to pay special attention to the recruiting of students for the training schools." Referring to the existing hostility to officer rank, he attests: "When we sent lieutenants to assist the leaders of our CNT militia, who at that time were still opposed to militarization, they were made to dig trenches with pick and shovel in order to humiliate them." But he adds, "After the fall of Largo Caballero, when the CNT was no longer in the government, and when militarization was carried forward, those very comrades who had previously humiliated the lieutenants showed a very keen interest in attaining the upper ranks of the Republican army."[34]

As head organizer and administrator of the officers' training schools, García Oliver earned the admiration even of his ideological opponents. "[Antonio] Cordón and I," writes José Martín Blázquez, a professional officer in the war ministry, "made contact with him, but all we were left to do was to carry out his instructions. Quarters, instructors, equipment, and all other requirements were immediately supplied. Oliver was indefatigable. He arranged and supervised everything himself. He went into the smallest details, and saw to it that they were properly provided for. He even took an interest in the students' timetables and the kitchen arrangements. But above all he insisted that the new officers should be trained in the strictest discipline.

"I, who do not believe in improvisation, was astonished at the organizing capacity shown by this Catalan Anarchist. Observing the ability and assurance of all his actions, I realized that he was an extraordinary man, and could not but deplore that so much talent had been wasted in destructive activity."[35]

The startling about-face by some of the most prominent members of the libertarian movement was mirrored in the CNT press. Military bearing was commended,[36] and Anarchosyndicalist commissars were urged by the movement to impose "condign punishment, even the heaviest and most drastic," on men guilty of offenses.[37] On 12 February 1937—in the midst of the crucial battle of the Jarama, south of Madrid—an editorial in *CNT* had declared that militiamen should obey the orders of their commanders on pain of death.[38]

But it was not easy to secure general acceptance of the new rules by men who had been taught by their leaders to look upon all armies as the symbol of tyranny, who believed themselves emancipated for all time from the will of autocratic officers, and who had not only introduced the elective principle into their units, but had also lived on terms of equality with group and century delegates. Referring to the above-quoted statement by García Oliver urging the cadets to bear in mind that enlisted men "should cease to be your comrades and become the cogwheels of our military machine," a CNT-FAI member wrote: "When ideas of emancipation, when libertarian conceptions and revolutionary thoughts are seething within us, . . . we cannot understand how our comrade ministers can express themselves in such terms."[39] And writing about the militarization of the militia in Asturias, Solano Palacio, a prominent Anarchosyndicalist, avers: "What revolted the militiamen more than anything else was the fact that they were compelled to salute their officers, whom they had hitherto regarded as comrades."[40] The misgivings created among the men on the question of differential pay rates were reflected even in an Anarchosyndicalist newspaper that accepted militarization: "Economic differences create classes, and there should not be any in the Popular Army. In this army, everyone, from the militiamen to the generals, has the same needs and the same right to satisfy them. Differences will bring about an estrangement between those who command and those who obey, and the class feelings they engender will have repercussions contrary to the interests of the people. As we are fighting against all privileges, we cannot tolerate the existence of any in the army."[41]

"I should be guilty of insincerity if I were to say that resistance did not have to

be overcome," writes Miguel González Inestal, a member of the peninsular committee of the FAI. "In the libertarian camp every single militant had his share of scruples to conquer, of convictions to be adapted—and why not admit it?—of illusions to be buried. This was so not only because of our respect for a traditional attitude, consecrated by experience, but also because we feared, quite reasonably, that the resurrection either in part or in whole of the old army would bring about caste privileges, the deformation of youth, the resurgence of the past, the suppression of all social rights, and, above all, that it might end in that army's becoming the devourer of the Revolution, the instrument of a party."[42]

It was because the CNT and FAI feared the latter contingency and because they had no project, as did the Communists, for honeycombing the entire military edifice, that they were determined to maintain the integrity and homogeneous character of their armed units. Thus, although they had decided to convert these units into brigades of uniform military structure and merge them into the regular army under their own commanders, they were opposed to diluting them with nonlibertarian forces by forming mixed brigades under the control of officers appointed by the war ministry, a plan that was mainly of Russian provenance[43] and of which one of the important political aims was undoubtedly to nullify or at least dilute Anarchist influence in the armed forces. In fact, Martín Blázquez, the professional officer in the war ministry already quoted, once remarked to General José Asensio, the undersecretary of war, that "as soon as we have created our mixed brigades [Anarchist] influence will vanish."[44]

Although Largo Caballero, for political and technical reasons, had approved the militarization of the militia on the basis of mixed brigades,[45] his present desire for easy relations with the CNT, stemming from his growing antipathy to the Communists, inhibited him from attempting seriously to enforce the measure. As a result, the Anarchosyndicalist units, while submitting to the general staff for the purpose of military operations, remained under the exclusive control of the CNT and were composed of men and officers belonging to that organization.

In a report dated 8 May 1937, Helmut Ruediger, representative in Spain of the International Workingmen's Association (AIT), with which the CNT was affiliated, stated: "There is now in the central zone a CNT army of thirty-three thousand men perfectly armed, well-organized, and with membership cards of the CNT from the first to the last man, under the control of officers also belonging to the CNT. Furthermore, there are many comrades in mixed units, but the CNT aims at concentrating them all in CNT units."[46] On a later occasion, he wrote: "The CNT understood that it should undertake its own militarization. This was an excellent means of organizing a strong CNT army that would not only prosecute the war against Fascism, but would safeguard the Revolution later on."[47]

The homogeneous character of the Anarchosyndicalist units at this stage of the war has been amply confirmed to me by some of the leading figures in the libertarian movement, including Mariano Cardona Rosell, a member of the national committee of the CNT, and José García Pradas, director of the Anarchosyndicalist daily, *CNT*, and member of the Anarchosyndicalist Defense

Committee of Madrid that controlled the CNT-FAI armed forces on the central front.[48] García Pradas testifies:

> When the militarization of the militia was decreed, our forces in the central zone agreed to it only on the condition that they maintained a certain independence, a condition that included the retention of their own commanders. The government of Largo Caballero and succeeding ones, as well as the Defense Council of Madrid, were not willing to assent to this condition, but they were obliged to "swallow" it, because we would have preferred rebellion to submission. As time went on, we had to admit ordinary recruits into our units. These were never compelled to become members of the CNT, but we always refused to concede to the government the absolute right to appoint commanders on its own account. In general, what happened was that the [CNT] defense committee proposed to the ministry of war the names of persons it considered suitable, giving the requisite information, and the ministry, with this information in its possession, approved the recommendations and published the appointments. It was advisable to act in this way for various reasons, one of which was to obtain the high pay allowed to commanders. Our commanders in the central zone, after collecting their pay, turned over the greater part of it to the defense committee, which consequently had millions of pesetas at its disposal for aiding agricultural collectives. There were times when, with the acquiescence of our national committee in Valencia or Barcelona, the government wanted to impose certain commanders on us, but neither Eduardo Val, nor Manuel Salgado, nor myself—for a long time in charge of the defense committee—agreed to such a thing, and thanks to our attitude it was possible for us to maintain until the very end those forces with which we were able to crush the Communist party [in Madrid] in March 1939.

That Largo Caballero had assented to and had not simply connived at the evasion of the rigorous form of militarization agreed upon with the Russians is proved by the fact that General Toribio Martínez Cabrera, the chief of the war ministry general staff, who enjoyed his entire confidence, authorized the committee of war of the Anarchist Maroto Column in February 1937 to organize a brigade composed entirely of that column's members. That this was done either without the knowledge or in defiance of K. A. Meretzkov, Martínez Cabrera's Soviet adviser, a future marshal of the Soviet Union and Red Army chief of staff, can be open to little doubt. In a report to the general commissariat of war dated 12 March 1937, Alberto Fernández Ballesteros, inspector-commissar of the southern front and a left-wing Socialist Cortes deputy, stated that the committee of war of the Maroto Column alleged that it possessed written instructions from Martínez Cabrera to form a brigade out of members of the column and that both "the commander of the Granada sector, Colonel [Eutiquiano] Arellano, and Lieutenant Colonel Salazar certify having read said orders."[49]

The same dispensation to organize a brigade consisting entirely of CNT-FAI members was granted to the Anarchist Iron Column, as will be seen in the next chapter. Significant, too, is the fact that the following interview on the question of militarization and the mixed brigades, given by Mariano Vázquez, the secretary of the national committee of the CNT, to *Nosotros*, the unofficial mouthpiece of the Iron Column,[50] was published without a dissenting comment from the war ministry:

Nosotros: Will our columns disappear?

Vázquez: Yes, they will disappear. It is necessary that they disappear. [The national committee has already decided] that our columns, like all the others, should be transformed into brigades. . . . Now this transformation does not imply—although it might appear otherwise—any fundamental change because those who were previously in command of the columns will now command the brigades. This means that our comrades, who feel affection for the men in charge of operations, can be sure that they will not be compelled through capricious appointments to accept men whose ideology and, consequently, whose personal treatment they dislike. Furthermore, the political commissars, who are the real chiefs—don't let the word frighten you—of the brigades, will be appointed by the CNT to whom they will be answerable at all times. . . .

Nosotros: It has been said—and this is another point that worries our men—that these brigades will be mixed, that is to say that they will be composed of regular Marxist and CNT battalions. Is it true?

Vázquez: There is some truth in it, for that is one of the proposals in connection with the formation of the brigades. However, we have our own proposal: the future brigades, which logically it is for us to form, must be composed of comrades belonging to the CNT and FAI and also be under the control of these two organizations, although subject to orders—another word unpleasant to our ears—from the unified command, which all the forces accept voluntarily.[51]

Although the attenuated form of militarization accepted by the CNT-FAI leadership enabled the Anarchosyndicalist units to maintain a large measure of independence, it was nevertheless stubbornly resisted by the more extreme spirits of the libertarian movement, who clung passionately to their Anarchist beliefs. No account of this dramatic struggle between principle and practice, between the rank and file and the leadership, is complete unless it includes the story of the famed Columna de Hierro or Iron Column.

33

The Iron Column

"*T*here are some comrades who believe that militarization settles everything, but we maintain that it settles nothing. As against corporals, sergeants, and officers, graduated from the academies, and completely useless in matters of war, we have our own organization, and we do not accept a military structure." Thus spoke a delegate of the Iron Column at a CNT congress in November 1936.[1]

No column was more thoroughly representative of the spirit of Anarchism, no column dissented more vehemently from the libertarian movement's inconsistencies of theory and practice and exhibited a more glowing enmity for the state than the Iron Column,[2] which occupied a sector of the Teruel front during the first seven months of the war. "[Our] entire conduct must not aim at strengthening the State, we must gradually destroy it, and render the government absolutely useless," declared the above-quoted delegate. "We accept nothing that runs counter to our Anarchist ideas, ideas that must become a reality, because you cannot preach one thing and practice another."[3] Nor, in carrying out the social revolution, did any Anarchist militia unit inspire more fear among middle and small peasants, among landowners, merchants, and shopkeepers. Mainly recruited from among the more fiery elements of the libertarian movement in the region of Valencia, its three thousand members[4] included several hundred convicts from the San Miguel de los Reyes Penitentiary. "[The prisoners] had to be set free and someone had to face the responsibility of taking them to the front," ran a report issued by the column's committee of war. "We, who have always held society responsible for its own defects, regarded them as brothers. They joined us and risked their lives, fighting at our side for liberty. Imprisonment had earned them the contempt of society, but we gave them their freedom and the opportunity to rehabilitate themselves. We wanted them to help us, and at the same time we wished to offer them the possibility of social regeneration."[5] But these former convicts soon brought opprobrium upon the Iron Column; for, although some of them had been moved to embrace Anarchist ideals in the course of their internment, the immense majority were hardened criminals who had undergone no change of heart and had entered the column for what they could get out of it, adopting the Anarchist label as a camouflage.[6]

The notoriety that these malefactors visited upon the Iron Column created considerable friction between its committee of war and the regional committee of the Valencia CNT.[7] But a more important reason for discord lay in the fact that, whereas the regional committee supported the policy adopted by the national leaders of the CNT and FAI, the Iron Column criticized that policy on the grounds that the entry of the libertarian movement into the cabinet had helped to revive the authority of the state and had given added weight to the government's decrees. In fact, no sooner had the column received word that the four CNT-FAI leaders had entered the government than *Linea de Fuego*, its official mouthpiece, virulently censured the Anarchosyndicalist ministers. The state persists, it declared, "and all in the name of an organization that calls itself libertarian."[8] Such censure—accompanied on occasions by the threat of force if the column's views on certain matters were not adopted[9]—was mortifying to the regional committee and explains in large measure why it did little or nothing to assist the column in securing either men or supplies.

This boycott was a serious matter for the Iron Column. In the early months of the war it had been able to rely upon its own recruiting campaigns and upon confiscations carried out with the aid of Anarchist-controlled committees in villages and towns behind the lines.

"[During] our stay in Valencia," ran a manifesto issued by the column, "we noticed that, whereas our negotiations for the purchase of arms had failed, because of the lack of hard cash, in many shops there was a large quantity of gold and other precious metals, and it was this consideration that induced us to seize the gold, silver, and platinum in several jewelers' shops."[10] "Around October [1936]," recounts one historian, "the column abandoned the front . . . and went on an expedition to Valencia spreading panic in its path. Its goal was to 'cleanse the rear of all parasitic elements that endangered the interests of the revolution.' In Valencia, it stormed hotels and restaurants, terrifying the city. In a raid on jewelry stores, it seized all the gold and silver it could find."[11]

In the town of Castellón, according to an Anarchosyndicalist daily, the Iron Column performed "the task of redressing injustices and orienting consciences. In purifying bonfires, it burned accusations, depositions, indictments, and criminal lawsuits against the poor in spirit, the weak, and the humble, who had to pay for their rash actions, their frailties, and their misfortunes—in reality, the crimes of the others—with odious corporal punishment and humiliating deprivation of rights, whereas the big criminals who swindled, robbed, and assassinated were exonerated. . . . Amidst the crackle of the flames that destroyed those mountains of paper . . . a bureaucratic machine that belonged to the middle ages was reduced to ashes."[12]

But the forays of the Iron Column into the towns and villages of the Valencia region soon ended with the reestablishment of governmental authority. According to a Communist historian, "the thorough trouncing" that the column—"famous for its nocturnal 'combativity' in the rear"—received from trained government forces had "a decisive effect" on the restoration of authority in Valencia.[13] A report in *Linea de Fuego*, the Iron Column's daily newspaper, stated that a clash had occurred after the Guardia Popular Antifascista (a Communist and Socialist police unit in Valencia) had shot and killed an unarmed member of the column. "This crime," ran the report, "caused unanimous indignation" among the CNT-FAI columns on the Teruel front. "[We] agreed to go to Valencia the next day to attend the funeral of our fallen comrade and to demand accountability." The cortege was proceeding "quietly and silently," the report alleged, but was machinegunned after passing Communist party headquarters, resulting in 148 casualties among the militiamen. "[As] our sense of responsibility is greater than theirs, . . . we stifled our feelings. . . . We did not want to take reprisals or continue fighting. . . . But everyone should know that our conduct does not mean that we are afraid or have forgotten. Although we have now returned to the front to finish off the fascists, a day will come when we shall remember the events and those responsible will get what they deserve."[14]

Because of a decline in revolutionary fervor and the discredit into which the column had fallen in libertarian circles since the early days of the Civil War, its appeals for volunteers were no longer capable of furnishing it with an adequate supply of fresh recruits for the relief of the men at the front. Furthermore, the committees were being supplanted by regular organs of administration, in which the more revolutionary elements were no longer the preponderant force. Even more serious was the fact that the war ministry had not only decided to withhold arms from all militia units declining to reorganize themselves along the prescribed lines, but had decreed, although in carefully selected language, that the pay of all combatants—which in the case of the militia had previously been handed to each column in a lump sum without supervision and irrespective of its structure—would henceforth be distributed through regular paymasters stationed only in battalions. As the decree made no mention of paymasters in units that had not adopted a military framework, it was clear that if the Iron Column were to hold fast to its militia structure the time would soon arrive when all pay would be suspended.

The decree in question was submitted to the government by Largo Caballero and, after approval, was published in the *Gaceta de la Republica* on 31 December 1936. Although its language was discreet, its aims were clear. In this connection, José Martín Blázquez made the following statement to General Asensio, when he suggested to him that such a measure be adopted: "I now propose that we decree that those who decline to transform themselves from militiamen into soldiers should get no pay. If we give every battalion a paymaster who will only pay men who obey orders, and if the paymasters of every mixed brigade are subordinate to the quartermaster attached to every brigade command, the brigades, and consequently the whole army, can obviously be organized at once. At the same time it will do away with abuses such as take place in the 'Iron Column,' which numbers barely three thousand men, but receives pay for six thousand every month."[15] In connection with these abuses, according to information given to Alberto Fernández Ballesteros, left-wing Socialist Cortes deputy and inspector-commissar of the southern front, the CNT-FAI militia forces in Malaga inflated their payrolls to such an extent that in a single fortnight they obtained 400,000 pesetas more than they were entitled.[16] But it should not be supposed from the foregoing that the padding of payrolls was limited to the CNT-FAI militia, for the Communists, who exaggerated the size of their Fifth Regiment, indulged in the same practice.[17]

In spite of the Iron Column's earlier intransigence with regard to militarization, the committee of war, better informed than the rank and file of the column's plight, now realized that an uncompromising stand was no longer expedient. They knew that the column could not hold out against the pressure of the government and the hostility of the CNT-FAI leadership and that it would either have to assent to the limited form of militarization advocated by the national committee of the CNT or be left without the material support essential to its existence. But could the column be brought to heel? Unrest and demoralization were spreading, and there were already murmurings and threats among the more rebellious spirits that they would leave the front if militarization, even in the mildest form, were introduced. On 22 December alone, ninety-seven men had abandoned the front and were denounced as deserters by the committee of war.[18]

At this crucial juncture, at the end of January 1937, when dangers pressed in upon the column from every side, the committee of war issued a significant report to its members:

[In the beginning], the State was a phantom to which nobody paid any attention. The working-class organizations of the UGT and CNT represented the only guarantee for the Spanish people, . . . [but] almost without noticing it our own dear CNT itself became a sapless and lifeless phantom, having injected into the State its own power and prestige. It is now just another appurtenance of the State and another extinguisher of the flames of the revolution.

Once strengthened, the government began the work of reorganization, and at the moment it has at its disposal an army, like any other state army, as well as several coercive bodies of the old kind. Just as formerly, the police now take action against those workers who attempt to do anything useful from a social point of view. The people's militia has disappeared, and, in a word, the social revolution has been strangled.

If we had the help of the government and also of our organization—we refer to the responsible committees—we should have had more war material and more men for the relief of our comrades. But things turned out differently, and we had to allow our men to wear themselves out month after month behind their parapets. Such self-sacrifice is unknown, nor can it be expected of anyone, and every day tremendous problems arise. . . . We admit the internal problems of the column are difficult to solve, and before anything serious should occur, before demoralization and fatigue should spread and deal a violent blow at what has been conquered and maintained at the cost of unparalleled sacrifice, before all this should happen, we repeat, a formula satisfactory to everyone must be found. . . . If all the Anarchosyndicalist columns are militarized, and we stand out in opposition to the decision of the CNT and FAI as the only column that does not accept militarization, we shall be deprived of help not only from the government, but also from our own organization. With the necessary aid, our column could maintain intact the revolutionary principles that are in keeping with our character, but owing to the absence of that help we must acknowledge that our method of warfare has failed.

We know that the overwhelming majority of our comrades will be furious with those responsible for this, but we should like to point out that their protests will be suffocated violently by the State. There is no longer any possibility of organizing anything against its wishes, for it is sufficiently strong to crush whatever stands in its way. Furthermore, these days of utmost gravity impel us to silence our indignation. Once more we must imitate Christ.

We know the disadvantages of militarization. It conforms neither to our temperament nor to that of others who have always had a fine conception of liberty. But we are also aware of the inconveniences of remaining outside the orbit of the ministry of war. Sad indeed it is to admit that only two courses are now open to us: the dissolution of the column or its militarization. Any other course would be futile.[19]

At the end of the report the committee of war had expressed the hope that the question of militarization would be discussed at an assembly of the column then in progress. But, although the matter was debated, no decision was reached. It was therefore no accident that *Nosotros* published about this time the interview with the secretary of the national committee of the CNT, quoted in the last chapter, in which he was at pains to show that the transformation of the militia columns into mixed brigades along the lines agreed upon by the national committee would not involve any fundamental change. But even this assurance did not modify the intractability of the more zealous opponents of militarization, who constituted the majority of the members of the column.

At the beginning of March, however, matters were suddenly jolted into a climax.

In a ministerial order aimed particularly at accelerating the militarization of the Iron Column and undoubtedly issued after consultation with his CNT-FAI colleagues in the cabinet, Largo Caballero announced that the militia on the Teruel front would be made subordinate to the war ministry from 1 April and appointed José Benedito, commander of the Anarchosyndicalist Torres-Benedito Column, to the organizational section of the general staff for the purpose of effecting the necessary changes.[20] At the same time the Iron Column was notified, according to Martín Blázquez, that the decree of 30 December, providing for the distribution of pay through battalion paymasters subordinate to the paymaster general, would be enforced.[21]

Whatever the committee of war's private opinion may have been with regard to these developments, it was submerged by the indignation that swept the column. In a general assembly the men refused to submit to military reorganization and to the new financial regulations, and a large number decided to leave the front in protest.

Of this, Martín Blázquez, who claims to have inspired the decree, writes: "A part of the Anarchist 'Iron Column' before Teruel revolted against the imposition of my decree concerning the financial organization of the army. They maintained that the government was turning into a counterrevolutionary government and that it was organizing an army of mercenaries to deprive the people of its conquests of July 1936, when the army and the police forces had disappeared. They demanded that the money for the whole column should be paid *en bloc* as before, and refused to submit either to the organization of battalions or to the new financial arrangements."[22]

On their way to the rear, several centuries of the column became embroiled in an armed struggle between assault guards and Anarchists in the village of Vilanesa. "When the small incident was settled," ran a report issued a few days later by the left-wing Socialist minister of the interior, Angel Galarza, "the police, for some inexplicable reason . . . were attacked and had to be reinforced. Without instructions from the responsible elements [of the CNT and FAI], members of a certain organization ordered a kind of general mobilization, which occurred in several villages of the province, an attempt being made to cut communications and to impede the circulation of traffic as well as the entry into the villages of the police forces."[23] After a battle that cost both sides a number of dead and wounded, more than two hundred Anarchists were taken prisoner, of whom ninety-two, according to *Nosotros*, were members of the Iron Column.[24]

Fearful lest this defiance might give the war ministry an excuse for drafting the members of the column for service in the regular army or lest the Valencia CNT might try to incorporate them into other units of the libertarian movement, the committee of war issued the following guarded notice: "The Iron Column has neither been dissolved nor does it contemplate dissolution nor has it been militarized; in accordance with the resolution approved by all its members, it has asked to be relieved so as to rest and reorganize itself. That is what is now happening. At the present moment only about three centuries remain to be relieved. When this has been effected, an assembly of the whole column will be convened, wherein, with our customary seriousness and sense of responsibility, the position of the column and the road to be followed will be decided upon. Hence, until then, comrades must not enlist in other organized units . . . , for, as they belong to a column that at the present moment is resting, no one can compel them to do so."[25]

Nevertheless, the Iron Column was now in a state of virtual disintegration. The Communists would no doubt have had Largo Caballero draft its members forthwith into units of the regular army. "It is necessary to put an end to what remains of party and trade-union militia and autonomous columns, and to create a single army," said a manifesto issued by the party's central committee.[26] But Largo Caballero shunned a step that would have been regarded by the CNT-FAI leaders as a precedent dangerous to the independence of other libertarian units. In this way, the committee of war was given a breathing spell in the days before the proposed assembly that was to determine the column's future in which to win support among the men for the restricted form of militarization approved by the national committee of the CNT. While matters were in this posture, it is significant that the following article, written by a member of the column, appeared in the Anarchist newspaper, *Nosotros*.[27]

I am an escaped convict from San Miguel de los Reyes, that sinister penitentiary which the Monarchy set up in order to bury alive those who, because they weren't cowards, would never submit to the infamous laws dictated by the powerful against the oppressed. I was taken there, like so many others, to wipe out an offense; namely, for revolting against the humiliations to which an entire village had been subjected; in short, for killing a political boss.

I was young and am still young because I entered the penitentiary when I was twenty-three and was released, thanks to the Anarchist comrades who opened the gates, when I was thirty-four. For eleven years I was subjected to the torment of not being a man, of being merely a thing, a number!

Many prisoners, who had suffered as I had from bad treatment received since birth, were released with me. Some of them, once in the streets, went their own way; others, like myself, joined our liberators, who treated us like friends and loved us like brothers. With them we gradually formed the Iron Column; with them, at a mounting tempo, we stormed barracks and disarmed ferocious [civil] guards; and with them we rudely drove the fascists to the peaks of the Sierra, where they are now held. . . .

Hardly a soul has ever bothered about us. The stupefaction of the bourgeoisie when we left the penitentiary is still being shared by everyone; and instead of our being attended to, instead of our being aided and supported, we have been treated like outlaws and accused of being uncontrollable because we did not subordinate the rhythm of our lives, which we desired and still desire to be free, to the stupid whims of those who, occupying a seat in some ministry or on some committee, sottishly and arrogantly regarded themselves as the masters of men, and also because, after expropriating the fascists, we changed the mode of life in the villages through which we passed, annihilating the brutal political bosses who had robbed and tormented the peasants, and placing their wealth in the hands of the only ones who knew how to create it: the workers. . . . The bourgeoisie—there are many kinds of bourgeois individuals and they are in many places—wove ceaselessly with the threads of calumny the evil slanders with which we have been regaled because they, and they alone, have been injured and can be injured by our activities, by our rebelliousness, and by the wildly irrepressible desires we carry in our hearts to be free like the eagles on the highest mountain peaks, like the lions in the jungle.

Even our brothers, who suffered with us in the fields and factories and were vilely exploited by the bourgeoisie, echoed the latter's terrible fears and began to believe, because they were so informed by persons who wish to be regarded as leaders, that the men fighting in the Iron Column were merciless bandits. . . .

On some nights, on those dark nights when armed and alert I would try to penetrate the obscurity of the fields and the mystery of things, I would rise from behind my parapet as if in a dream . . . , gripping my rifle with a frenzied desire to fire, not merely at the enemy sheltered barely a hundred yards away, but at the other concealed at my side, the one who called me comrade. . . . And I would feel a desire to laugh and to weep and to run through the fields, shouting and tearing throats open with my iron fingers, just as I had torn open the throat of that filthy political boss, and to smash this wretched world into smithereens, a world in which it is hard to find a loving hand to wipe away one's sweat and to stop the blood flowing from one's wounds on returning from the battlefield tired and wounded. . . .

One day—a day that was mournful and overcast—the news that we must be militarized descended on the crests of the Sierra like an icy wind that penetrates the flesh. It pierced my body like a dagger. . . .

I have lived in barracks, and there I learned to hate. I have been in the penitentiary, and it was there, strangely enough, in the midst of tears and torment, I learned to love, to love intensely. In the barracks, I was on the verge of losing my personality, so severe was the treatment and the stupid discipline they tried to impose upon me. In prison, after a great struggle, I recovered that personality, for every punishment made me more rebellious. There I learned to hate every kind of hierarchy from top to bottom; and, in the midst of the most agonizing suffering, to love my unfortunate brothers. . . .

As a result of this experience . . . when, in the distance, I heard murmurs of the militarization order, I felt my body become limp, for I could see clearly that the guerrilla fearlessness I had derived from the Revolution would perish . . . and that I would fall once again into the abyss of obedience, into the animal-like stupor to which both barrack and prison discipline lead. . . .

There was never any relief for us, and worse still there was never a kind word. Everyone, fascists and antifascists, and even members of our own movement—what shame we have felt!—have treated us with aversion. We have never been understood . . . [because] during the war itself, we wished to lead a life based on libertarian principles, while others, both to their own misfortune and to ours, have remained yoked to the chariot of state. . . .

History, which records the good and the evil that men do, will one day speak, and it will say that the Iron Column was perhaps the only column in Spain that had a clear vision of what our Revolution ought to be. It will also say that of all columns, ours offered the greatest resistance to militarization, and that there were times when, because of that resistance, it was completely abandoned to its fate. . . .

Our past opposition to militarization was founded on what we knew about officers. Our present opposition is founded on what we know about them now. . . . I have seen . . . an officer tremble with rage or disgust when I spoke to him familiarly, and I know cases today of battalions that call themselves proletarian, whose officers, having forgotten their humble origin, do not permit the militiamen on pain of terrible punishment to address them as "thou."[28]

We used to live happily in the trenches . . . [because] none of us was superior to the other, all of us were friends, all comrades, all guerrillas of the Revolution. The delegate of a group or century was not imposed upon us; he was elected by us. He did not regard himself as a lieutenant or as a captain, but as a comrade. Nor were the delegates of the committees of the column colonels or generals; they were comrades. We used to eat, fight, laugh, and swear together. . . .

I don't know how we shall live now. I don't know whether we shall be able to accustom ourselves to abuse from corporals, from sergeants, and from lieutenants. I do not know whether, after having felt ourselves to be men in the fullest sense of the word, we shall get used to being domestic animals, for that is what discipline leads to and what militarization implies. . . .

But the hour is grave. We have been caught . . . in a trap and we must get out of it; we must escape from it as best we can. . . . The militarists, all the militarists—there are fanatical ones in our own camp—have surrounded us. Yesterday we were masters; today they are. The popular army, which has nothing popular about it except that the people form it, . . . does not belong to the people but to the government and it is the government that commands, it is the government that gives orders. . . .

Caught as we are in the militarists' net, there are only two possible roads. The first road leads . . . to the dissolution of the Iron Column, the second to its militarization. . . .

[But] the column, that Iron Column that caused the bourgeoisie and the fascists to tremble from Valencia to Teruel must not be dissolved; it must continue to the end. . . .

If we were to break up the column, if we were to disband and were later drafted, we should have to march, not with those whom we choose, but with those with whom we are ordered to march. . . .

Whatever we be called, column, battalion, or division, the Revolution, our Anarchist and proletarian Revolution, to which we have contributed glorious pages from the very first day, bids us not to surrender our arms and not to abandon the compact body we have constituted until now.

Sunday, 21 March, the day fixed for the holding of the assembly that was to vote on the future of the Iron Column, was a portentous one for all its members. In the past weeks the committee of war had been urging the acceptance of militarization as the only alternative to dissolution, and now that passions had spent their force and disintegration was upon the column, it was obvious that the proponents of militarization were certain to have their way. The arguments used by the committee during the assembly in favor of converting the column into a brigade—that the men belonged to age groups then being drafted by the government; that, even should they decide to disband, they would be inducted shortly afterward into the regular units organized by the state; that the war ministry had agreed to all of the four battalions of the proposed brigade being formed of members of the column and that only the artillery would be in the hands of professional officers[29]—were sufficiently powerful to ensure the favorable vote of the assembly.

A few days later, the committee of war announced to the members of the column that the unit would become the Eighty-third Brigade of the regular army.[30] The fact is that some of the members of the column were enrolled in other Anarchosyndicalist brigades. The famous Mexican artist David Alfaro Siqueiros, a member of the Mexican Communist party, who was given the command of the Eighty-second Brigade, testifies: "Because I was a Mexican officer,[31] I was given the command of units comprising Anarchists from the former Iron Column and Rosal Column, which because of their Anarchist creed were romantically opposed to the whole concept of military discipline. Other Mexican officers [among them the Communist, Colonel Juan B. Gómez] were also given the command of units with the same beliefs, because the Anarchists' love for Mexico, in contrast to their hatred of the Soviet Union, facilitated our organizational work."[32]

34

Largo Caballero Breaks with Moscow

*F*or all its seriousness, the episode of the Iron Column added but a ripple to the whirlpool of discord that for weeks had been swirling in Valencia, the seat of government.

Early in February 1937, enmities had acquired fresh malignancy with the fall of the strategic port of Malaga, from where the loosely organized and inadequately equipped militia columns, divided by dissensions and mutual suspicions, had been rolled back in precipitous confusion for more than eighty miles along the coast by an overwhelmingly superior enemy force composed of Spanish and Italian units. Copies of two important documents dealing with the loss of Malaga have been preserved.[1] No one wishing to apportion responsibility fairly can afford to ignore them, for they form, together with the valuable data in General José Asensio's book, *El General Asensio: Su lealtad a la república*, in Ramón Salas Larrazábal's *Historia del ejército popular de la república*,[2] and in José Manuel Martínez Bande's *La campaña de Andalucía*,[3] the basis of any serious study of this subject. One is a detailed account of the disaster given on 12 February 1937 to members of the Higher War Council by Colonel José Villalba, a professional officer with no party ties, in charge of the Malaga sector of the southern front; the other is a report dated 18 February 1937 to the commissariat of war by the left-wing Socialist Alberto Fernández Ballesteros, inspector-commissar of the southern front. These documents refer to the absence of military discipline and organization on the Malaga sector; the muddle and disorder in the rear; the irresponsibility of professional officers and militia leaders; the struggle between the different factions to the prejudice of military operations; the proselytizing efforts of the Communist party; the appointment of an excessive number of Communist political commissars by Cayetano Bolívar, chief political commissar of the Malaga sector; the wanton neglect of defensive works; the treachery of the two commanders in charge of fortifications, Romero and Conejo, who deserted to the enemy; the inadequate supplies of rifles, guns, and ammunition; the lack of assistance from the fleet and air force; and, finally, the failure of the war ministry to respond to the reiterated appeals of Colonel Villalba and other leaders for reinforcements and supplies. One of the most unlucky figures in the disaster was

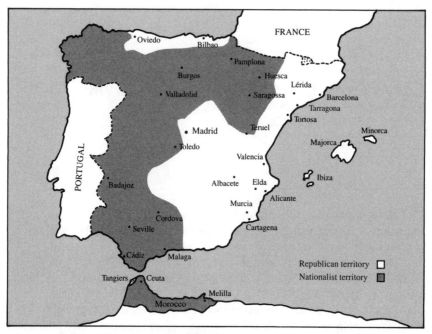

Map 3. Division of Spain, 8 February 1937

Villalba himself, who was assigned to the Malaga sector after enemy forces had pierced the eastern defenses at Estepona and when everything was fusing into disaster.

"Don't worry. He'll never return from there!" General Asensio, the undersecretary of war, is alleged to have told Antonio Cordón, the head of his technical secretariat, when signing the appointment.[4] Undoubtedly selected by the war ministry as a scapegoat, Villalba was later arrested and imprisoned.[5] After more than a year's internment, however, he was exculpated from any blame for the disaster and rehabilitated.[6]

A transcript of shorthand notes taken by a telephone operator shortly after midnight on 8 February of a heated exchange between Villalba and Asensio can be found in the pro-Nationalist work *Málaga: Sangre y fuego*, by Angel Gollonet and José Morales. Although this book, which was written during the war, is propagandist in nature, the following excerpt from the transcript, when viewed in the light of several interviews I had with Villalba in Valencia immediately after his return from Malaga, appears genuine:

> Villalba: Listen, Pepe, I have received orders from the ministry to return to Malaga and—
> Asensio: You should not have left Malaga.
> Villalba: The fascists have already entered Malaga and anybody who denies it is lying. . . .

Asensio: You should not have left Malaga alive. You should have remained there as instructed by the minister.

Villalba: You don't know what is happening in Malaga. So, I should go back to Malaga? I see, you want me to give myself up to Franco?

Asensio: You must return to Malaga. You should not have left it.

Villalba: Obviously, so that Queipo [the Nationalist General Gonzalo Queipo de Llano] can catch me! So that's what you want!

Asensio: You have received orders to return to Malaga and you must return with the troops.

Villalba: With what troops? I no longer have any troops, they are just a rabble. I warn you that not only Malaga but Motril will be lost if you do not provide help in time. But, look, how can I return to Malaga if the fascists are already there?

Asensio: The fascists are not there. . . .

Villalba: What you are saying is that I should give myself up to Franco. It's easy to talk from where you are. You should not have left Navalcarnero alive [the telephone operator indicates that the name of the location was "somewhat similar" to Navalcarnero]. Anyhow, I'll try to enter Malaga; I shall return there, but, remember, this is another dirty trick you are playing on me.

Asensio: In the Army, there are no dirty tricks; there are just orders![7]

Of the Malaga debacle the Communists made what use they could to advance their military policy. Day after day and week after week they had been urging that the military measures adopted by the government during the first months of its existence be put into effect,[8] and now the loss of Malaga gave dramatic import to their words. To be sure, the agitation upon which they throve was not without self-interest, for they saw in the rigid implementation of those measures a means, not only of bringing the war to a successful issue, but also of creating a military machine that, if harnessed to their party, would ensure their ascendancy in the affairs of state. They were therefore impatient of Largo Caballero's indulgence toward the Anarchosyndicalist militia and particularly of his dilatoriness on the matter of conscription, especially as voluntary recruiting had fallen off and a continuous stream of fresh men was needed to replace losses. They were also impatient of his laggard record regarding other matters and of his ingrained prewar habits. "Papers of the utmost military importance accumulate in enormous stacks unattended to, unexamined," Koltzov noted in his diary. "Regardless of what is happening Caballero retires at nine P.M. and no one dares to awaken the old man. Even if Madrid should fall in the middle of the night, the head of the government would learn of it only in the morning."[9] There was no power nor circumstance, writes Kirill A. Meretskov, onetime Soviet adviser to the chief of the central general staff, General Toribio Martínez Cabrera, that would make Caballero change his long-established routine. "Whenever he went to sleep all contact with the outside world was severed and all access to him was cut off."[10]

There is no doubt an element of exaggeration in these Soviet observations, for even the staunch Spanish Communist Antonio Cordón, who was the head of the technical secretariat of the undersecretaryship of war under Caballero, acknowledged that the war minister established a "rational work schedule" in the ministry. "He kept rigidly to his own schedule, which began at 8 A.M. sharp . . . and ended at 8 P.M., with a very brief interval for food. At 8 o'clock, he retired, and no one was allowed to disturb him unless the matter was very serious and urgent."[11]

Still, whatever Caballero's habits, the Communists and their Soviet allies could have lived with them, as they managed to live with those of such other prominent Spaniards as General Sebastián Pozas and Juan Negrín, who were more amenable to their wishes. But, as Cordón observes, "I soon found out that the firmness of character of the Socialist leader, which so many used to admire, including myself, was based on obstinacy, and was frequently transformed . . . by an exaggerated opinion of his own importance and qualifications into a negative trait."[12] With such men, to be sure, the Communists found it hard to deal. Moreover, as Koltzov observes in his diary, Largo Caballero had "crude ways." "From time to time he shouts; he does not permit objections. As minister of war, he resolves military problems personally."[13]

As far back as September 1936 the government had decided, largely as a result of Communist pressure, to call up the 1932 and 1933 classes,[14] but this decision had remained on paper, partly because Largo Caballero, as we have seen, believed in the superior morale and greater combat efficiency of volunteers,[15] and partly because he knew that the Anarchosyndicalists, whose support he needed, were opposed to the enrollment of their members in government units.

Although a CNT national congress decided to agree to the mobilization of the two classes announced by the government, it did so on the understanding that all men with Anarchosyndicalist membership cards should be drafted by the CNT for service in its own militia units. In Catalonia, the regional committee of the CNT stated with reference to this decision: "As it would be very childish to hand over our forces to the absolute control of the government . . . the national congress has decided that all persons in the [two mobilized] classes who belong to our trade-union organization should present themselves immediately to the CNT barracks or, in the absence thereof, to the trade-union or [CNT] defense committees [of their locality], which will take note of their affiliation, their age, their employment, the class to which they belong, their address, and all the necessary facts. A report will be sent to the Regional Committee of Defense, Nicolás Salmerón, 10. This committee will issue militia cards that will be sent to the inscribed comrades, who, of course, will henceforth be at the disposal of the Regional Committee, which will assign them to the column or front selected."[16]

When taken to task in February 1937, shortly after the fall of Malaga, by a delegation of the Communist-dominated Defense Council of Madrid for not enforcing the draft, Largo Caballero retorted that the government had neither barracks in which to house the conscripts nor money and arms with which to pay and drill them.[17] Moreover, a few days earlier, in response to Communist demands for the implementation of the draft, he had declared somewhat disingenuously, in reference to the decree of 29 October 1936 that rendered all able-bodied men between the ages of twenty and forty-five liable to conscription,[18] that compulsory military service was in force "de jure and de facto." "What the government and the war minister demanded," he continued, "is that organizations and unions of all kinds should impose on their members the discipline this measure requires so that when the military authorities deem it necessary to employ the services of men of military age they will encounter no obstacles. It is in this way, the minister considers, that those who wish to cooperate in the defense of national territory against the foreign invasion should carry on their propaganda and not by making demands on the government in connection with problems that have already been made the subject of legal measures, such as the decree of 29 October 1936."[19]

But, in truth, this was evasive sophistry designed to conceal the nonenforcement of the draft, and a few days later the Communist ministers, backed by the Republican and moderate Socialist representatives in the cabinet, compelled Caballero not only to repeat the call-up of the 1932 and 1933 conscripts but to include in the same draft the 1934 to 1936 classes.[20] This, however, did not change matters substantially for the libertarian movement. At the beginning of March, the regional committee of the CNT of Aragon, while taking cognizance of the government's mobilization orders, urged the workers in that region to present themselves at the recruiting depots of the CNT for enlistment in Anarchosyndicalist units.[21] On 15 March, the day when several of the mobilized classes were to present themselves at their induction centers,[22] the national committee of the CNT, the peninsular committee of the FAI, and the peninsular committee of the Libertarian Youth issued a joint manifesto enjoining the workers to "form themselves into brigades" and place themselves at the disposal of the "bodies directing the war"[23]—a reference, of course, to the defense committees of the CNT and FAI. In view of all this, it is hardly surprising that *Frente Rojo*, the Communist organ, should have affirmed a few weeks later that in several villages in the region of Estremadura it had been able to prove that men who should have enlisted in the regular army in compliance with the government's mobilization orders had been urged not to do so, and were being formed into battalions of a "certain political or trade-union character."[24]

Meanwhile, the PCE strove to utilize the Malaga debacle in another way: it demanded the purging of all positions of command. Although directed ostensibly against members of the officer corps who were suspect or incompetent,[25] this demand soon proved to be aimed specifically at those appointees of Largo Caballero who were opposing its permeation of the armed forces. In the words of Enrique Castro, the former member of the party's central committee, frequently quoted in this work, "Malaga was more than a military defeat; it was the grand pretext for the party to begin its most difficult political battle for 'hegemony'— the struggle for the overthrow of Largo Caballero."[26]

That the Communists' first target should have been General José Asensio is natural; for, as undersecretary of war, he held the most important position in the war ministry next to Largo Caballero, a position to which, it will be recalled, the minister, in a defiant gesture, had elevated him in reply to their demand that he be removed from the central front. The offensive against General Asensio was "unspeakable," wrote Largo Caballero some years later. "I had already been forced to relieve him of his command of the Army of the Center. . . . Now [the Communists] were determined to oust him from the ministry. 'Why?' I asked them. 'Because he is a traitor!' 'Give me proof, evidence!' . . . , but they never produced any. At every session of the cabinet the [Communist] ministers raised the same issue: the undersecretary must be dismissed from office; he is a danger in the ministry. I asked them for proof; they offered to furnish it, but they never did. Innocent oversight! . . . When they became convinced that by accusing him of being a traitor they got nowhere, they accused him of being a drunkard and a philanderer. I replied that I had never seen him drunk and that I was surprised they should denounce a Spanish general because he liked women, whereas I knew for certain that they had enrolled *homosexuals* in their party."[27]

But the Communists were undaunted by Caballero's obstinacy. Asensio had now become such an impediment to their plans for hegemony that the Russian ambassador, Marcel Rosenberg, personally demanded his dismissal. To this demand, Largo Caballero, afire with indignation, replied by expelling the Soviet diplomat from his office.

This signal event, confirmed by several colleagues of the premier and by Largo Caballero himself in both his published and unpublished memoirs,[28] is colorfully recorded by the left-wing Socialist Cortes deputy, Ginés Ganga, who affirms that Rosenberg threatened to withdraw Soviet aid unless the demand for the removal of the undersecretary of war were heeded. He writes:

> Those of us who used to frequent the ministry of war were at first struck by the daily visit, to which we finally became accustomed, of his Excellency, the Soviet ambassador, who spent several hours every day in the office of Largo Caballero, premier and war minister. . . . Rosenberg was usually accompanied by an interpreter, but what an interpreter! Not a secretary of the embassy, but the minister of foreign affairs of the Republic, Don Julio Alvarez del Vayo! . . .
>
> One morning the visit behind closed doors had already lasted two hours when suddenly "old man" Caballero was heard shouting. The secretaries gathered around the door of the office, not venturing to open it out of respect. Caballero's shouting increased in intensity. Then, all of a sudden, the door opened, and the aged premier of Spain, standing in front of his table, his arms outstretched and his shaking finger pointing to the door, was heard saying in a voice tremulous with emotion: "Get out! Get out! You will have to learn, Señor Ambassador, that although we Spaniards are very poor and need help from abroad very much, we are too proud to let a foreign ambassador attempt to impose his will on the head of the government of Spain! And as for you, Vayo, it would be better to remember that you are a Spaniard and minister of foreign affairs of the Republic and that you should not combine with a foreign diplomat in putting pressure on your prime minister."[29]

In his own version of this stormy incident, Largo Caballero affirms that he refused to put up with the interference by Moscow, which was "treating Spain like a Soviet colony." After two and a half hours of "insolence and audacity," during which the ambassador and Alvarez del Vayo claimed that Russia's counterespionage service had discovered proof of the disloyalty of General Asensio, Largo Caballero stood up, pounded on his marble desk and told the ambassador never again to raise the matter. "Such was [my] annoyance that not much more would have been needed [for me] to have pushed him out of the office."[30]

After expelling the Soviet ambassador, Largo Caballero remained alone with Alvarez del Vayo. "I rebuked him for playing the Communist game," he recalls. "All he could reply was that since people were saying, even if unjustly, [that Asensio was a traitor] he should be removed from office. A fine argument! But who were the people who were saying this? The Communists and no one else!"[31]

In a totally simplistic and lopsided interpretation of Largo Caballero's attitude toward the Soviet ambassador, the pro-Communist Amaro del Rosal, a member of the UGT executive during the war and former partisan of Largo Caballero, says that when the first personal clash with Rosenberg occurred "Caballero was in a permanent state of irritability." On previous occasions, he tells us, everything had transpired normally "in keeping with good diplomatic relations, especially relations between an ambassador of the first Socialist state and an old Socialist militant enveloped in popularity and revolutionary prestige." The ambassador, he claims, was the same as ever, but Caballero had changed. "His annoyance with the ambassador had no foundation; it was a reaction of personal irritability resulting from a new frame of mind, from a political evolution or, better still, from a political poisoning. . . . Rosenberg was a great friend of Caballero's, an effective and loyal adviser, the representative of the only country that was helping the Spanish Republic. How could the premier develop an attitude of hostility, of violence, toward that country and its representative? As long as Caballero was loyal to the Caballero of 1936 everything went smoothly; but to the degree that he began to divorce himself from the political line that had brought him to power, he began to bog down in his own contradictions."[32]

It is indeed curious that in the same work Amaro del Rosal states that "the campaign against Asensio was unfair," that it was "motivated by selfish professional ambitions," and that Asensio was a "great military figure, a fact that disturbed other military men,"[33] for this is an obvious reference to the Communist Antonio Cordón, who, as he himself avows, was frequently at odds with Asensio.[34] While personal intrigue and ambition no doubt played a role in Asensio's downfall, and although Cordón's fellow Communists must have used this ambitious young officer, who a year later became undersecretary of the army under Juan Negrín, to undo Asensio, it goes without saying that the campaign against the general—in which, it will be recalled, the Communists in the Defense Council of Madrid also exerted what pressure they could against Largo Caballero—served first and foremost the political ends of the party rather than Cordón's personal ambitions in the war ministry.

The Asensio episode illustrates to what degree the relations between Largo Caballero and the Soviet ambassador had deteriorated. In reply to the question posed by Stalin, Molotov, and Voroshilov in their letter of December 1936—"Is the Spanish government satisfied with [Rosenberg] or is it necessary to replace him with another representative?"—Largo Caballero had answered reassuringly as recently as 12 January 1937, just a few weeks before ejecting the ambassador from his office, "We are satisfied with his behavior and activity. Everyone here likes him. He is working hard, excessively, at the expense of his enfeebled health."[35]

Perhaps because of this friendly response or because they may have hoped that Largo Caballero's stormy scene with the ambassador was just a passing incident, Moscow and the PCE did not entirely despair of manipulating the Socialist leader. Indeed, they still hoped that they could use his influence to facilitate the fusion of the Socialist and Communist parties, as it had facilitated the unification of the two youth movements. "The Russian plan, passionately adhered to throughout the war, was to fuse the two parties," testified Luis Araquistáin, the left Socialist leader, whose intimate relations with Caballero invest his words with special authority, and who, like Caballero, had personally supported the fusion before the war.[36] "The new party would be called the Unified Socialist party, as in Catalonia, but in reality it would be a Communist party, controlled and directed by the Communist International and the Soviet authorities. The name would deceive the Spanish workers, and it was hoped that it would not alarm the Western powers. Stalin fervently desired that Largo Caballero should use his power in the government and his enormous authority in the Socialist party to impose the absorption of the latter by the Communist party."[37]

Who can doubt that the achievement of this goal would have been a giant step toward the absolute hegemony of the Communist party and the establishment of a single party state?

But although the influential Madrid section of the PSOE, the Agrupación Socialista Madrileña, which Caballero controlled and to which Araquistáin belonged, had advocated the merging of the two parties before the war,[38] his experiences had stamped out the last spark of his enthusiasm for amalgamation. After he had been maneuvered out of office in May 1937, Caballero gave another reason for his changed attitude toward the question of fusion. "The only thing I ask," he declared at a public meeting, "is that those who at one time wished to carry out this fusion should keep to the same program that we had, namely, that it should be realized on the basis of a revolutionary program. I remember very well that when we used to speak of this question the Communist party posed as a condition—because it had been so agreed in Moscow—that we should break relations with all the bourgeois parties." (This remark was a reference to a letter addressed before the war to the PSOE executive by the central committee of the PCE, proposing the fusion of the two organizations. Written during the early phase of the Popular Front period and couched in language designed to appeal more to the radicalism of the numerically superior left Socialists headed by Largo

Caballero than to the moderate Socialists led by Indalecio Prieto, who controlled the executive committee, the letter posed, inter alia, the following conditions: "Complete independence with regard to the bourgeoisie"; "complete rupture of the social democratic bloc with the bourgeoisie"; "recognition of the need for the revolutionary overthrow of bourgeois domination and for the establishment of the dictatorship of the proletariat in the form of soviets."[39]) "Do the [Communists] insist now, as they once did," Largo Caballero continued, "that we should break relations with all the bourgeois parties? No, on the contrary. The slogan they now have is that we should return to the days before 18 July."[40]

Whatever may have been the real weight of this issue in determining the changed attitude of Caballero and of other left Socialist leaders toward the fusion of the two parties, there can be no doubt that it was not so much their dislike of the moderate tone of the Communist party's present policy as its depredations of the Socialist movement and the fear that it would eventually absorb the Socialists that put the matter entirely out of court. This is suggested by the following account, given by Rodolfo Llopis, undersecretary to the premier, of a conversation among a group of leading left-wing Socialists that took place in January 1937.

> The conversation turned to what was, for all genuine Socialists, one of the most dramatic of subjects, namely, the disloyalty of the Communists. Someone present drew a picture that was only too familiar to all of us: the campaigns waged by the Communists at the front and in the rear; their drive to remove the Socialists from various organizations; . . . their barefaced proselytism, in which they unscrupulously employed the most reprehensible of methods; their constant disloyalty toward us. He spoke of the behavior of the Socialist youth leaders who had gone over to the Communist party, and of the "conquest" that the communists had made of the two Socialist deputies, Nelken and Montiel. . . . Meanwhile, he added, our party gave no sign of life; the executive committee [controlled by the moderate Socialists] remained silent. . . .
>
> Several other comrades spoke. Caballero likewise. He said just a few words, but they were clear and emphatic. "What is this about absorption?" he asked. "Nobody will ever absorb me. The party has a tradition as well as potentialities that cannot be thrown overboard. . . . The party cannot die. As long as I live there will be a [Socialist] party!"[41]

Even before the outbreak of the Civil War, when he had briefly harbored the illusion that through the fusion of the two parties he could absorb the Communists, Largo Caballero had grown wary of the idea of amalgamation, and no enticement laid before him by the Spanish politburo and the Comintern, not even a promise that he could head the united party,[42] could induce him to yield to their importunity. "[The Communist International]," he writes, referring to the prewar period, "wanted to fuse the Communist and Socialist parties and put them in its bag, but it encountered one great difficulty: the Communist party did not have men of authority and prestige for such an important task. . . . Unfortunately, they focused their attention upon me. In the Communist press, I was the only Marxist

Socialist, a revolutionary, the legitimate representative of the Spanish proletariat, the devoted friend of the workers, the only hope of the future, the Spanish Lenin! My photograph was displayed in newspapers, in movie theaters, in store windows, in Spain and abroad, even in Russia. They wanted to awaken in me those evil instincts that always dwell in the hearts of men: vanity and ambition, but those emotions were fast asleep in the very depths of my being. They didn't know me, otherwise they would not have thought of such stupidities." Vittorio Codovila, the Comintern delegate, known in Spain as Medina, visited Largo Caballero, pressing him for the fusion of the two parties: "I would be the head of the new party and hence the master of Spain because once fusion had been achieved all the workers would join the party and it would become an invincible force." Caballero did not yield: "[I] had already acquired too much experience to allow myself to be influenced by those siren calls." After he became premier in September 1936, pressure was resumed. "[I] replied courteously in the negative." Undeterred, Codovila again visited Largo Caballero. "My visitor told me that this was the psychological moment to carry out the fusion of the two parties; that all the workers were demanding the *Single Party*; that since I occupied the premiership, it would be a success, and that it was advisable to achieve it as soon as possible because in that way the war would be won. In short, he insinuated that I could and should carry out a coup d'etat. Restraining my indignation I replied that it was not true that all the workers were asking for fusion, and that, even if they were, I would not lend myself to the maneuver. I requested him not to mention the matter again. If anyone wanted the union of the workers all he had to do was to join the UGT and the Socialist party. . . . [I] was not ready to stain my modest political and trade-union history with the treachery he proposed. . . . Looking as red as a pomegranate, Medina withdrew. . . . I had placed the premiership, the war ministry, all the posts I held as well as my future tranquillity, in jeopardy." In spite of this rebuff, a final effort was made to persuade the left Socialist leader. Marcelino Pascua, the Spanish ambassador to Moscow, arrived unexpectedly in Valencia with an urgent request. "[He] asked me *on behalf of Stalin* if the fusion of the parties would be carried out. My reply to him was 'No!' "[43]

This unequivocal expression of Caballero's intractability just a few days after he had expelled the Soviet ambassador from his office finally convinced the Russians of the futility of further attempts to knead the Socialist leader to their purpose and became the signal for the launching of a whispering campaign to undermine what remained of his authority. Insidiously, the words "stupidity," "ineptitude," "vanity," and "senility" were bandied from mouth to mouth,[44] presaging the greatest political battle of the war, a battle that would eventuate in the political demise of the man who had been the most influential and popular of the left-wing leaders at the start of the fighting. Observing, as a Communist, the gradual development of this historic battle against the party's former allies, "against the oldest working-class party in the country, against its unquestioned leader Francisco Largo Caballero," Enrique Castro, then a member of the party's central committee, confesses that he "smiled and rubbed his hands with satisfaction," as the following thoughts occupied his mind:

"We shall win the battle. We shall win the battle against the Socialist party and against Largo Caballero. With the help of the masses, with the help of the other parties and organizations! And with the help of the Socialist party itself! Ha . . . Ha. Marvelous! Absolutely marvelous! What does it matter that idiots accuse us of disloyalty to our allies? Isn't the party doing what it is supposed to do? Is a proletarian revolution possible without a powerful Communist party in control? The imbeciles should not be astonished! What we are doing to conquer the masses, to achieve the true revolution, the Socialist revolution, is nothing new. Here are the texts of Lenin and Stalin! Texts that are within the reach of anyone who wants to know what they contain, of anyone who wants to know our aim, our method, our tactics and strategy. There is nothing new, nothing new! What is happening is that you, all of you, have been so dumb that you have not bothered to learn who we are and what we are. But that is not our fault. The fault is yours! . . . The political stupidity of our allies is without a doubt one of our best allies."[45]

He adds: "Spain had never witnessed a great political funeral. Now it would. And before very long. Largo Caballero, the politician, had entered his death agony. He was unaware of this, just as he was unaware of many important things during his lifetime. . . . [But] it made his political death the more terrible, a death that would come brutally and by surprise and in an atmosphere of almost complete political isolation."[46]

Now, more than ever, Largo Caballero needed the advice and support of men in whose political judgment he had total confidence in order to combat his ruthless adversaries, but there were no such men. Luis Araquistáin, his close associate and mentor for several years, was now ambassador in Paris far removed from the day-to-day intrigues in Valencia and, in any case, although a brilliant polemicist, was a political strategist of dubious ability. Moreover, once faithful supporters like Alvarez del Vayo, Santiago Carrillo, Margarita Nelken, Felipe Pretel, and Amaro del Rosal had transferred their allegiance to the Communists. To make matters worse, his immediate political entourage consisted of only three men in whom he could place his trust, none of whom was a match for the Communists, aided, as they were, by foreign advisers trained to perfection in the Leninist art of splitting rival organizations and destroying political opponents. Firstly, there was Rodolfo Llopis, the undersecretary to the premiership, a devoted follower and well-known educationalist (at one point president of the Socialist-controlled teachers' federation) who possessed neither the requisite vigor[47] nor political acumen; secondly, a political nonentity by the name of "Alfageme" (Eustaquio Aparicio); and, finally, the young upstart, the arrogant and inexperienced José María Aguirre, a former messenger for the Socialist deputies in the Cortes, who had managed to ingratiate himself in the good graces of the prime minister and had been more than bountifully rewarded with the title of politicomilitary secretary and the rank of captain.[48]

It is no wonder that during the campaign against Largo Caballero, Aguirre felt beyond his depth and regretted the absence of Araquistáin. In a private communication, Aguirre wrote to the ambassador on 28 February: "If only you could join us! . . . I have great faith in our chief. But, he is so alone! There is no one, or hardly anyone, who can help him to carry out effectively what has to be done."[49]

The question must necessarily arise why Araquistáin, who was undoubtedly aware of his chief's perilous position, never offered to return to Valencia to assist him.

The campaign against Largo Caballero was now gathering greater force.

"Why was this campaign waged [against me]? Do you know why?" Largo Caballero asked his audience at a public meeting some months after he had left the government.

> Because Largo Caballero did not want to be an agent of certain elements in our country, and because Largo Caballero defended national sovereignty in the military field, in the political field, and in the social field. And when these elements learned, very late, to be sure, that Largo Caballero could never become an agent of theirs, the line changed and the campaign against me started. But I can affirm that until shortly before this campaign commenced, I was offered everything that could be offered to a man with ambition and vanity: I could have been the head of the unified Socialist party; I could have been *the* political figure of Spain; I would have had the support of those who approached me; but only on the condition that I carried out their policy. And I replied that I would not do so on any account.
>
> As I was saying, they got to know me very late. They should have understood from the very first moment that Largo Caballero has neither the temperament nor the substance of a traitor. I categorically refused [to carry out their policy], with the result that on one occasion . . . I had a very violent scene with official representatives of a certain country whose duty it was to be more discreet, but who did not fulfill that duty. And I told them—in the presence of one of their agents, an agent, however, who held a ministerial portfolio [a reference to foreign minister Alvarez del Vayo]—that Largo Caballero would not tolerate any kind of interference in the political life of our country.[50]

35

Pressure on Largo Caballero Mounts

*I*ndependently of the effort by the Soviet ambassador to secure the dismissal of General José Asensio from the undersecretaryship of war, the Communists applied pressure from other directions. On 13 February, the Junta de Defensa de Madrid, it will be recalled, demanded, on the initiative of the Communist representative, Isidoro Diéguez, the removal from the army of "doubtful and suspect elements," a demand that was followed by a virulent denunciation of Asensio in *Mundo Obrero* as "the organizer of defeats" who deserved the "maximum penalty." At a cabinet meeting held a few days later, the Communist ministers formally demanded Asensio's ouster. Foreign minister Alvarez del Vayo, despite his personal conviction that the general was "unquestionably one of the most capable and intelligent officers in the republican army,"[1] gave the demand strong support. "Having decided that the fundamental factor was not one's own personal trust in the general," he explains, "but the suspicion which he inspired in a large section of the troops, I was one of the cabinet ministers who stood out most firmly for his dismissal. . . . The fight waged by Caballero against what he thought was an injustice done to his undersecretary had a certain greatness. He deeply resented the fact that I, for the first time, took a position different from his, and from that day, to my great regret, I ceased to be his most trusted minister."[2] In spite of Largo Caballero's bold defense of General Asensio, he was defeated by a broad opposition spanning the political spectrum from the Anarchosyndicalist to the left Republican ministers. This was confirmed by Federica Montseny in a letter to me after the war. Her honesty is particularly appreciated because of the reluctance of several of her former cabinet colleagues to furnish me with serviceable information regarding their respective attitudes.[3] The stand of the left Republican ministers during the debate was reflected in a derogatory allusion to Asensio in large type on the front page of *Política*, the national organ of their party,[4] the same day that Asensio's resignation was published in the official gazette.[5]

If Alvarez del Vayo had done much to undermine Largo Caballero's position in this crisis, the hostile attitude of the CNT and FAI toward the general, both in cabinet meetings and in their press, was also important.[6] A strict disciplinarian who had employed stern measures against retreating militiamen when in command of the central front and had ordered the execution, according to one authority, of several militia leaders who had refused to obey his orders to attack,[7] Asensio had long been distrusted in libertarian circles, where in the early days opposition to professional officers and to militarism in all its forms had been an article of faith. Hence, the CNT and FAI had been easily sucked into the campaign against the general as they had in the Junta de Defensa de Madrid and, without consciously desiring it, had thereby facilitated the workings of the Communists against Largo Caballero. In the above-mentioned letter to me regarding Asensio, Federica Montseny avowed that she later considered that the libertarian movement's opposition to the general was a mistake, not only because of his exceptional ability, but because it helped to weaken Largo Caballero in relation to the Communists.

But Largo Caballero was not to be easily divested of a collaborator in whose technical ability he had the maximum confidence and, with the object of using him in some capacity in the war ministry, instructed him to remain in Valencia under his direct orders.[8] At the same time, provoked by the struggle over Asensio, he took vigorous action against Communist influence in the war ministry. He assigned Lieutenant Colonel Antonio Cordón, a member of the Communist party and head of the technical secretariat of the undersecretaryship of war, to the Cordova front;[9] dismissed his aide-de-camp, Lieutenant Colonel Manuel Arredondo, on account of his sympathy for the party;[10] and posted him, along with Captain Eleuterio Díaz Tendero—the philo-Communist chief of the vital information and control department and chief organizer before the war of the left-wing officer organization, the UMRA—to the Basque front.[11]

Referring to these and other dismissals from the war ministry, Martín Blázquez, who at the time was Antonio Cordón's assistant in the technical secretariat, writes: "Whether because my services were regarded as more essential, or because I was believed to be less of a sympathizer with the Communist party, I was not dismissed from the ministry as so many others were. . . . Some of my colleagues, including Caballero's aide-de-camp Arredondo and Díaz-Tendero, were sent to the Army of the North at Bilbao. I confess I was alarmed at the prospect of being vindictively sent there myself. I was very pessimistic about the prospects on that front. I had made frequent requests for supplies for Bilbao, but they had all been rejected. 'We shall send nothing to the Army of the North,' I had been told. 'Let the Basques look after themselves! What have they got an independent Republic for?' In view of this shortsighted policy, being sent to the Army of the North obviously meant a very good chance of ending up before a fascist firing-squad."[12]

In this purge the Communists' greatest loss was undoubtedly that of Díaz-Tendero, the head of the information and control department that investigated the political antecedents of every man before he could enter the army.[13] Without actually being a member of the PCE, Díaz-Tendero, to quote Margarita Nelken, the left Socialist Cortes deputy, who knew him personally and switched her own allegiance to the Communists in December 1936, "did wonderful things for the party."[14] His ability to advance the interests of the Communists was undoubtedly enhanced by the central role he played in a special officer classification committee, whose task it was—so Stanley G. Payne attests—to categorize all available officers according to their political reliability.[15] "Particularly helpful to him," writes M. Teresa Suero Roca, "was the card index compiled before the war of all the army commanders as well as that portion of the records of the UME [the rightist Unión Militar Española] of which he had managed to take possession."[16] Thus he wielded considerable discretionary power, and his removal by Largo Caballero dealt a severe blow to the hegemonic designs of the PCE, the more so as, according to Asensio, it had previously proposed, with the support of representatives of other organizations, that Díaz-Tendero succeed him in his high office.[17]

In addition to the dismissal of Díaz-Tendero and the other officers from their key posts, Largo Caballero—in a move that seemed to offer an even greater threat to Communist plans for control of the armed forces—appointed six inspectors, all of them trusted left-wing Socialists,[18] to scrutinize the work of generals, of the lesser officers and noncommissioned officers, of the top officials in the commissariat of war,[19] and of political commissars of every rank.[20]

Cowed momentarily into discretion by this vehement reaction, the Communists ventured a mild criticism only of the latter measure[21] and refrained from condemning in their press the removal of their men from key positions in the war ministry, lest they exacerbate Caballero's anger still further. Through the ingenuity of Díaz-Tendero they contrived a means of denouncing these dismissals and of preventing Caballero from retaining Asensio in any capacity in the war ministry. As head of the information and control department, Díaz-Tendero had been in contact with all organizations, and was able—because his allegiance to the Communists was barely known outside the war ministry—to use the columns of *Nosotros*, the mouthpiece of the Iron Column.[22] This newspaper's dislike for Largo Caballero was untempered by the political considerations that restrained the language of the less extreme libertarian organs, which, in spite of their attacks on Asensio and their hostility to the Socialist leader before the war, were now conscious of his present value as an ally against the PCE. On 25 February, *Nosotros*, inspired and documented by Díaz-Tendero, published, under the caption "How the purging of the army is being carried out," an article containing one list of "sincere republican officers" dismissed from their posts and another of officers appointed in their stead, who had "never been known for their republican sympathies" and were "either disloyal or just indifferent." The first list included the above-mentioned Communist and pro-Communist officers—Antonio Cordón, Manuel Arredondo, and Díaz-Tendero—who had been removed from the war ministry, and the second included the name of Lieutenant Colonel Fernández, who had succeeded Díaz-Tendero in charge of the information and control department and who was, according to *Nosotros*, a great friend of Asensio's. But more interesting than all these facts, the paper affirmed, was that although the impression had been created that General Asensio had been removed, he had, in reality, been relieved of all responsibility and placed behind the scenes as technical adviser to the minister and the new undersecretary. "Moreover, his appointment has been made by a simple ministerial order, whereas assignments and appointments of generals, whatever their status, should be made by decree on the proposal of the government and with the signature of the head of state."

Although there is no corroborative evidence that such a ministerial order was ever issued by Largo Caballero—and, indeed, Asensio himself later denied its existence[23]—the war minister certainly did hope to use the general's services, as the latter himself has conceded.[24] Nevertheless, no formal appointment of the kind suggested was made, and it may be safely assumed that the allegation was designed to forestall any attempt to revive Asensio's authority in the war ministry.

In addition to the article inspired by Díaz-Tendero, *Nosotros* came out with the following invective against the war minister:

"Largo Caballero . . . is old, too old, and does not possess the mental agility necessary for solving certain problems upon which our own lives as well as the lives and liberty of the whole people depend.

"When the newspapers, all the newspapers—with the exception of those inspired by the war minister himself—accuse one man; when in the trenches, in the barracks, in the committees, in the streets, and in the ministries themselves, it is whispered or openly stated that General Asensio either through ineptitude or treachery has gone . . . from defeat to defeat; when it is common knowledge that on the very night the news of Malaga's fall was received, the general, now adviser to Largo Caballero, got drunk in a cabaret just like any individual who thinks only of wallowing in the mire and debasing himself, the minister should not . . . send letters to the press and adopt tragic airs with the idea of silencing such things." (This was a reference to two open letters written by Largo Caballero, one to Carlos Esplá, the left Republican minister, the other to the national executive of the Left Republican party, protesting the following allusion to Asensio's successor, Carlos de Baráibar, on the front page of the party organ, *Política*, of 21 February: "If in the dismissals we can discern victory, do not let us invite defeat as a result of the appointments." In the first of these letters Largo Caballero asked Esplá whether *Política* was about to begin "a new campaign of a disruptive character such as the one that has compelled me to deprive myself of an able collaborator" and urged him to use all his influence to stop it from developing.[25] In his letter to the national executive, he declared that he was not prepared to tolerate the initiation of a campaign by an official organ of a Popular Front party that might create "disagreeable situations" for his trusted collaborators.[26] In reply, *Política* contended somewhat meekly that the words to which Largo Caballero objected had been set up in type before the name of Asensio's successor was known,[27] while the national executive—no less sheepishly—affirmed that it did not see in them any attack on Carlos de Baráibar.[28])

"With hostile eyes the people see that they are being fooled," *Nosotros*'s invective against Caballero continued. "The resignation of Asensio is a trick because behind their backs he is extolled, having been elevated to a position of greater confidence at the side of the minister. . . . The minister of war, comrade Largo Caballero, should bear in mind that he is old, and, what is more, that he is becoming senile and that senile men should neither govern nor be allowed to govern."[29]

Angered by this abusive language and by the allegation regarding Asensio's appointment—an allegation that compelled him to abandon all idea of using his services, even unofficially, in the war ministry, lest he be accused of flouting public opinion and the will of the cabinet—Largo Caballero had Angel Galarza, left-wing Socialist minister of the interior, suspend the publication of *Nosotros*.[30] That same day the minister announced—without mentioning Díaz-Tendero by name—that a regular army officer suspected of inspiring several articles had been arrested, and that about two hundred copies of *Nosotros* had been found in his home.[31]

It is noteworthy that *Nosotros*'s attack on Largo Caballero had been embarrassing to the national leaders of the CNT. This was clear when, a few days later at the extraordinary congress of the Catalan CNT, the secretary of the national committee opposed and succeeded in defeating a motion of the Catalan organization that a protest should be made against the suspension of the paper.[32] Some months later, in reference to the attacks on Largo Caballero that had appeared in other libertarian newspapers, Helmut Ruediger, representative in Barcelona of the AIT with which the CNT was affiliated, wrote: "We all knew Caballero's past, but not all the editors of the CNT provincial papers knew that several months ago Caballero had become an opponent of Communist influence and that, consequently, to demand his removal was to do the work of the Communist party."[33]

A few months after the fall of Largo Caballero in May 1937, when the PCE had strengthened its position still further, Asensio was indicted for neglecting to supply the Malaga front with the necessary arms and munitions and was imprisoned pending trial.[34] In May 1938, he was released and rehabilitated, partly because of the intervention of influential friends, including Diego Martínez Barrio, the vice-president of the Republic, and of Vicente Rojo, then chief of the general staff, who was personally convinced of his innocence;[35] partly because he could have made a powerful case against his chief accusers; and partly because of the problem—having regard to the Communists' desire at that time to avoid widening still further the gulf between themselves and the left Socialists—of placing him on trial without impeaching his chief, Largo Caballero, to whose orders he was, as undersecretary of war, directly subordinate.

The *Nosotros* incident was the crowning indignity and injury that Largo Caballero had suffered at the hands of the Communists. For months he had watched their stealthy permeation of the Socialist movement and of the armed forces that had resulted in the loss of a substantial part of his own following, including many intimate associates. But no doubt fearing to forfeit Soviet supplies and also fearing to reveal to the outside world—particularly to Britain and France, which he still hoped might be enticed to raise the arms embargo—the depth of Communist penetration behind the Republican façade,[36] he had been inhibited from making any public statement against his tireless adversaries. In fact, it was not until October 1937, five months after the fall of his government, that he ventured any open criticism. He claimed that he waited so long because he did not wish it to be said that he had made any statement that had adversely affected Spain's position at Geneva or had demoralized the soldiers at the front. "I can assure you," he added, "that one of the greatest sacrifices I have ever made in my life was to keep silent during these past five months. But I am not worried, for, although the calumniators have thrust tooth and nail into my flesh, my conscience is satisfied that my silence was in the interests of Spain and in the interests of the war."[37] These considerations, apparently, also explain his forbearance during his incumbency.

Nevertheless, incensed by the *Nosotros* incident, he could no longer suppress his anger. Issuing from his silence on 26 February, he hit back with a public declaration, in which his diatribes against "fascist agents" were unmistakable allusions to the Communists.

On Sunday, 14 February, he stated, large contingents representing antifascist Spain marched through the streets of Valencia affirming their adhesion to the government and to the Republican Constitution. (This referred to a demonstration in his support organized after the fall of Malaga by the provincial secretariat of the Valencia UGT, which was controlled by the left-wing Socialists. In a notice inviting all the trade-union, political, and cultural organizations in Valencia province to participate, the secretariat stated that it wanted the government to see by the demonstration that it had the support of the working people. The Communists accepted the invitation and, at a gathering of the leaders of the local organizations, succeeded, thanks to the propitious atmosphere created by the fall of Malaga, in securing the adoption of a proposal that a ten-point petition be presented to Largo Caballero on the day of the demonstration embodying, among other things, the following demands: compulsory military service and the cleansing of all responsible military posts. That the Largo Caballero Socialists resented the petition is clear from the following lines in an editorial published in their newspaper the day before the demonstration: "We should not ask for compulsory military service, but should present ourselves when we are called up. . . . We should not ask for anything, but should give everything."[38] Owing to the participation of the Communists and to the petition, with which great play was made, the left-wing Socialists were unable to use the demonstration, as they had intended, to bolster Largo Caballero's authority. On the contrary, the Communists succeeded in using it very much to their own advantage.)

Largo Caballero's statement continued:

While [the demonstrators] were expressing their willingness to give the government unqualified support, and while as a result of this clamorous demonstration the position of Republican Spain and its legal government was strengthened in the eyes of the world, fascist agents redoubled their efforts to such an extent that they found in the midst of traditionally republican and working-class organizations a certain response and even help for their aims and intrigues. Disguised among us, and favored by our proletarian and republican kindness, they sowed confusion, stirred up passions, and encouraged indiscipline in our ranks. . . . The authorities know that fascist agents, with membership cards of the republican parties, the Socialist party, the Communist party, and the UGT and the CNT, have been operating freely in loyalist Spain and that their criminal acts have succeeded in disorienting many republican soldiers and even civilians, whose clear and self-sacrificing past certify to their good faith and loyalty. . . . A section of the press and of the antifascist parties and organizations, responsible members of those bodies, and well-intentioned yet thoughtless people, have become involved in the enemy's dark plot and facilitate his work. So well organized is espionage among us that I affirm in all sincerity that intrigues and passions are coiled around our feet like reptiles. . . .

A whole apparatus has wedged itself between the people and the government, perverting the consciences of many individuals and encouraging the darkest appetites, an apparatus that works consciously or unconsciously—in both ways I believe—against our cause, with the result, as I have already stated, that around the feet of those who should march, and are ready to march at the head of the democratic and working people, serpents of treason, disloyalty, and espionage are coiled.

I am not prepared to tolerate this state of things an hour longer.[39]

Although the Communists publicly described this veiled assault upon themselves as the "toads and snakes" manifesto in a denunciatory speech by politburo member Jesús Hernández, they did so on 28 May 1937, three months later, after the fall of the left Socialist leader.[40] When Largo Caballero issued his statement at the end of February, they were careful not to identify themselves publicly as the object of the assault and gave the statement a discreet reception in their press.[41] They also joined with other organizations at a meeting called by the premier in assuring him publicly of their support.[42]

Nevertheless, at the beginning of March, according to Hernández, in his book *Yo fui un ministro de Stalin*, written some years after he had left the party, a politburo meeting of "far-reaching importance" was held in Valencia, attended by the Moscow delegation comprising Stefanov, Codovila, Gerö, and Togliatti, and by Marty, organizer of the International Brigades. Also present were Orlov, head of the NKVD in Spain, and Gaykis, the Soviet chargé d'affaires, who, Hernández points out, were attending a Spanish politburo meeting for the first time. "In short," he says acridly, "more foreigners than Spaniards." At the meeting, he claims, the overthrow of Largo Caballero was presented by Togliatti as the primary short-term objective. His account of this meeting has been ignored by the official history of the Civil War prepared under the auspices of La Pasionaria,[43] herself a member of the politburo, but was vigorously assailed by Orlov and contains at least one serious inaccuracy.[44] An account is given here, since it offers the only testimony we have of purported behind-the-scenes disagreement with the

Moscow delegation over the proposed removal of Largo Caballero. It is true that Fernando Claudín, a party member at the time and a leader of the JSU, confirms this disagreement,[45] but neither he nor his close associate Santiago Carrillo (a deputy member of the politburo) was present at this historic meeting.

Hernández states that at the beginning of the meeting José Díaz, the party secretary, gave his reasons why the Communists should not destroy Largo Caballero: they would incur the enmity of the majority of the Socialist party, would be accused of striving for political and military hegemony, and would isolate themselves from other antifascists. "I saw my comrades beset by doubts," Hernández comments, "filled with vacillation and fear . . . panic-stricken by the thought of having to wage a political struggle—for the first time!—against the representatives of Moscow." Hernández claims that he supported José Díaz, arguing that Caballero had behaved loyally toward the Communists, that he had helped them gain predominance in the army, that he had not hindered them from receiving the best arms, that thanks to him they had been able to organize the Popular Front and unite the Socialist and Communist youth, that he had been "docile" to the Soviet advisers, and that he was the Communists' main support for the fusion of the Socialist and Communist parties. To break with Caballero, he added, would be the greatest victory they could hand to General Franco.

"Uribe, Checa, Pasionaria, and Mije [Pedro Martínez Cartón, the other full member of the politburo, was at the front] were petrified. They were waiting to hear the voice of Moscow before venturing an opinion." Then Stefanov spoke. Díaz and Hernández, he said, were defending a bad cause. It was not Moscow but "history" that condemned Caballero. Marty complained that Caballero rationed gasoline for the International Brigades and did not provide enough automobiles for his headquarters. " 'The trouble with you,' retorted Díaz, 'is that you have too large a bureaucratic machine.' 'I'm no bureaucrat!' Marty bellowed, thumping his chest with his fist. 'I'm a revolutionary, yes sir, a revolutionary!' 'So are we all,' replied Díaz. 'That remains to be seen,' answered Marty. 'You are a boor,' Hernández interposed, 'and neither your age nor your past history permit you to treat us with disrespect.' 'And you are a lump of shit,' Marty responded. Rising from his seat Díaz shouted, 'You are a guest at this meeting. If you are dissatisfied, there's the door!' "

Uproar followed. "Some were speechless . . . others incensed and rabid. Orlov, imperturbable, smoked in his armchair. Togliatti, cold and impenetrable, contemplated the scene with feigned serenity. Codovila . . . tried to calm Marty. Gueré [Gerö], open-mouthed, looked from one to the other with astonishment. Gaikins [Gaykis] ran a comb through his hair as though unaffected. Pasionaria, nervous and beside herself, shrieked 'Comrades! Comrades!' like a cracked record."

Gaykis spoke: " 'Caballero is withdrawing himself from Soviet influence. A few days ago he practically threw Rosenberg out of his office.' " Then came the turn of those members of the politburo who had not yet expressed themselves. " 'It won't make any difference,' " Hernández thought. " 'They'll sit where the sun is warmest.' . . . One after the other they rose . . . to condemn Largo Caballero and signify their agreement with the Soviet delegation. 'I can see,' Díaz said sarcastically, 'that the majority of the politburo agrees with the line expressed by the delegation, which I shall accept only out of discipline, putting on record my dissenting opinion.' " Togliatti, whom Hernández describes as the "heavy artillery" of the delegation, then spoke. "As could be expected his words were not designed to argue or convince. They were orders, devoid of tact or euphemism. . . . 'I propose that the campaign to soften up the position of Largo Caballero start at once. We shall begin with a large meeting in Valencia, at which Comrade Hernández will be the speaker.' " Hernández says that at first he objected but, prompted by Díaz, yielded to party discipline. Concluding the meeting, Togliatti stated: " 'As for Largo Caballero's successor . . . I believe we should proceed by a process of elimination. Prieto? Vayo? Negrín? Of the three, Negrín may be the most suitable. He is not anti-Communist like Prieto, nor stupid like Vayo.' "[46]

There is a baffling flaw in Hernández's account of this meeting that cannot be ignored. He claims that Orlov was present. This is most unlikely, not because Orlov himself has denied his presence,[47] but because Hernández's description of him as a man "almost two meters tall, elegant, and polished,"[48] is totally inaccurate. Bertram D. Wolfe, the famous sovietologist, who met Orlov personally many years after his defection to the United States, wrote: "This zeal to give verisimilitude by an exact description betrays a forgery. Two meters would be six feet, six and three-quarters inches. But Alexander Orlov, whom I have interviewed a number of times, is more than a foot shorter than that, much shorter than Hernández, broadshouldered and somewhat corpulent. He is neither elegant nor distinguished looking."[49]

In *The Spanish Revolution*, published in 1979, I attempted to explain this false portrayal by a personal experience that led me to believe that Hernández was referring not to Orlov but to a certain Belayev. I met Orlov and another high-ranking operative of the NKVD—who, in *The Spanish Revolution*, I assumed was Belayev—in the spring of 1937, when I was a United Press correspondent in Valencia. I do not recall the names by which they were introduced but discovered Orlov's identity many years later when, after Orlov's death in 1973, the U.S. Government Printing Office published *The Legacy of Alexander Orlov* containing transcripts of his testimony before the U.S. Senate Subcommittee on Internal Security together with his photograph taken in 1933. Thanks to this photograph and to my clear recollection of the man, I can state beyond peradventure that, far from being "almost two meters tall, elegant, and polished," Orlov was short, thickset, and inconspicuous and could have passed unnoticed in virtually any crowd. The physical appearance of the man, who I assumed was Belayev, matched so closely the one Hernández attributed to Orlov that I was persuaded Belayev was the person Hernández had in mind. This assumption, it now appears, was incorrect, for Enrique Castro, who met Belayev in Moscow, describes him as "heavy, rugged, and of medium height."[50]

Hence, we may be forced to conclude that Hernández never knew Orlov, at least by that name, and that the tall, elegant individual whom he frequently addressed as Orlov—witness the long dialogue in his book between himself and the supposed Orlov, in which he uses the latter's name more than a dozen times[51]—was neither Orlov nor Belayev but another NKVD agent. On the other hand, we may be compelled to conclude that his references to Orlov are pure fabrication.

In any event, there can be little doubt—to judge from Hernández's false description—that Orlov was not present at the Spanish politburo meeting called to discuss the overthrow of Largo Caballero. Orlov himself, as we have seen, has denied his presence. He also denied that Togliatti, the Comintern delegate, was there: "Hernández committed still another factual error, which completely demolishes his story. According to his narrative, this meeting [took place] in March 1937. . . . However, from the biography of Palmiro Togliatti by Marcella and Maurizio Ferrara [the Italian Communist writers],[52] we know that Palmiro Togliatti . . . arrived in Spain to take up his duties as representative of the Comintern in June 1937 [actually, July, according to the biography], i.e., *after* Largo Caballero had already resigned from the government. . . . Therefore, Togliatti could not have been at the meeting described and argued that Caballero must go. With Togliatti out, the imaginary meeting, with all of Hernández's fantastic trimmings, collapses."[53]

This part of Orlov's rebuttal, however, does not rest on solid ground, for, according to the Spanish Communist writer Adolfo Sánchez Vázquez, Togliatti was in Spain as a Comintern delegate during "practically" the entire conflict "from 1936 to 1939."[54] Hernández gives details regarding two important meetings held as early as August and November 1936, in which Togliatti participated, as well as another in Madrid, just before the fall of Largo Caballero in May 1937, during which a large-scale offensive in Estremadura was discussed.[55] Furthermore, Justo Martínez Amutio, who was governor of Albacete, the headquarters of the International Brigades, affirms that Togliatti was in Spain from September 1936 and records a conversation with him in December, during which Togliatti tried to gain his cooperation in the "purging" of the brigades of "spies and undesirables."[56] More important still is the testimony of Julián Gorkin, the POUM leader, who has researched this matter more thoroughly than any other person: "With regard to the date of Palmiro Togliatti's arrival in Spain and his personal and direct intervention at the head of the Communist apparatus, a polemic began, principally in Italy, that has not yet ended. . . . His official biographers, Marcella and Maurizio Ferrara, . . . assert that he did not arrive in Spain until July 1937. . . . On the basis of numerous depositions, of which I have preserved only those of former Spanish Communist leaders and agents of Moscow, who collaborated with him, I can prove the following: a) As head of the Latin section of the Comintern, Togliatti intervened in the affairs of Spain even before the proclamation of the Republic. . . . b) Togliatti belonged to the commission appointed in Prague, on 26 July 1936, to direct Spanish activities. . . . c)

[It was Togliatti] and Duclos [the French Comintern representative] who imposed in Madrid (in September 1936) the line the Spanish Communist party was to follow. d) In Spain or during frequent trips to Paris and Moscow, Togliatti was delegate number one of the Comintern and, as such, intervened directly in all important decisions."[57]

In a letter to me, Gorkin affirms: "Palmiro Togliatti had his friends, the Ferrara couple, write that biography after I had denounced him at a meeting in Rome for his role in Spain and had the important daily newspaper, *Il Messagero*, publish long extracts from the book by Jesús Hernández." The significance of the attempt by Togliatti's biographers to deny his presence in Spain until after the fall of Largo Caballero in May 1937 is clear when we bear in mind the following excerpt from Günther Nollau's *International Communism and World Revolution*, in which he discusses Togliatti's effort to gloss over his role in Spain when responding to questions in *Nuovi Argomenti* on 16 June 1956: "The undisputed fact that Togliatti was in Spain in his capacity as a Comintern functionary helps to give the lie to his recent assertion that the political decisions and practical measures taken by the national [Communist] parties between 1934 and 1939—for example in Spain—were entirely the product of their own initiative."[58]

With regard to the date of Togliatti's arrival in Spain, one point should be clarified. In a letter addressed to the Comintern on 15 September 1937, he stated that he had been in Spain "for more than a month."[59] This undoubtedly refers to his appointment as head of the Comintern delegation at the end of July but does not invalidate the claims that he was in Spain on several occasions before then. In any case, with respect to the alleged independence of the PCE, there is no dispute that both Stefanov and Codovila, the two other Comintern delegates, to whom the party was subordinate, were present at the historic meeting of the politburo at which the fate of Largo Caballero was decided.

Although Hernández does not give the exact date of the meeting, he does say that it took place a few days before the plenum of the central committee of the Communist party.[60] This was held in Valencia on 5–8 March 1937.[61] The public meeting at which he spoke was not a special meeting in the Tirys movie theater, as he seems to imply,[62] but a public session of the plenum held in that location on 7 March, which I personally attended as a representative of the United Press.[63]

Just before addressing the crowd, he claims that José Díaz said to him, "Pluck up your courage. The decision to destroy Caballero has been made. If you don't comply, it could mean your political downfall. And that should not happen on any account."[64]

"Both inside and outside the government," Hernández writes, "I served as a battering ram against Largo Caballero and against the undersecretary of defense, General Asensio, his man of confidence in military affairs. My name inspired odium. No one could perceive my personal drama, silent and disguised. And naturally I was judged on the basis of my conduct. This was neither the first nor the last time that I was compelled to stifle my personal feelings in order to obey Moscow. . . . The conflict between my conscience and my public actions was a silent, painful, and hidden duel. The party flattered me, and our followers acclaimed me as a hard-hitting orator, as the 'strong man' of the party leadership. The more my popularity grew, the more I saw myself sinking inexorably into the quagmire of the policy we were ordered to follow . . . and did follow. The fact that I was fully aware of what I was doing converted my duplicity into a moral torment."[65]

Although the overthrow of Largo Caballero was now Moscow's primary short-range objective, it was not until two months later that a suitable opportunity arose to oust him from the premiership. Meanwhile, the Communists continued to press their efforts to strip the military summits of all officers who were an impediment to their plans for hegemony. In this they were aided by an offensive launched on 8 March by General Franco's Italian allies on the Guadalajara sector of the Madrid front.

On the fifth day of the enemy's advance, when it seemed that nothing could arrest his triumphant progress, the two Communist ministers, Hernández and Uribe, supported by the majority of the cabinet, demanded that the chief of the central general staff, General Toribio Martínez Cabrera—whom Largo Caballero had recently appointed in place of the Communist Manuel Estrada—resign and that the Higher War Council be immediately convened to decide on his successor.[66]

Although *Mundo Obrero*, the Communist organ, had urged some days earlier, with Martínez Cabrera and other officers in mind, that the council should meet regularly to discuss all questions pertaining to the war, such as "the appointment and control of officers and the cleansing of the army of all hostile and incompetent elements,"[67] no action had been taken by Caballero. But now the demand of the Communist ministers could not be denied. Under the chairmanship of Caballero, the council met and, on the proposal of Julio Alvarez del Vayo, with the backing of Vicente Uribe, voted that Martínez Cabrera should be succeeded by José Miaja's chief of staff, Lieutenant Colonel Vicente Rojo.[68] Although Rojo, with the support of General Miaja—who stated in a letter to the war ministry that he could not dispense with Rojo, because of the Italian offensive, and that he "should have been consulted before the decision was made"—declined to accept the post,[69] and even though a dramatic counteroffensive soon transformed the Italian advance into a confused flight, Martínez Cabrera was not suffered to continue in office.[70]

In his published memoirs, Largo Caballero alleges that the Communist sponsorship of Rojo, as chief of the central general staff, and his refusal, backed by General Miaja, to accept the post were simply a maneuver to oust Martínez Cabrera.[71] This would explain why Rojo, according to his own testimony, incurred the war minister's enmity when he declined the post.[72] The Communists did not claim credit at the time for the removal of Martínez Cabrera, but Jesús Hernández publicly declared after the fall of Largo Caballero's government that his party had been instrumental in removing him.[73]

"What was the reason for depriving me of men who could be useful to me in the war ministry?" Largo Caballero asked. The reason, he said, was threefold. (1) They had refused to fall into line and enter the Communist party as Miaja had done. (2) The Communists wanted to fill the vacant posts with their own supporters "in order to know in detail what was going on in the war ministry." (3) The Communists wanted him to "get bored and to relinquish the portfolio of war."[74]

The removal of Martínez Cabrera was swiftly followed by another victory over Largo Caballero; for no sooner had the general been ousted than the Communist ministers and their allies in the cabinet secured the appointment of Vicente Uribe, the Communist minister of agriculture, and of Alvarez del Vayo, the pro-Soviet foreign minister, as government representatives on the central general staff.

"Experience has proved to us," stated *Mundo Obrero* on 18 March, "that the subordination of the highest military body to the minister of war is insufficient. Infinitely more just is the direct representation of the government in all the deliberations of the general staff. In this way, the officers who form the latter have at all times the help and advice of the government itself. . . . On the other hand, the arduous task of the holder of the portfolio of war requires this direct help of the two ministers. Our sincere congratulations to the government on this magnificent agreement."

36

Largo Caballero Hits Back

While the PCE was registering triumphs in the cabinet and in the Higher War Council, Soviet representatives in Spain were endeavoring to undermine Caballero's influence still further by winning the unconditional adhesion of Carlos de Baráibar, who had succeeded General Asensio in the undersecretaryship of war. A left-wing Socialist belonging to Caballero's intimate circle, Baráibar had been deprived, owing to serious illness, of a firsthand knowledge of the events that had recently extinguished Caballero's enthusiasm for the unification of the Socialists and Communists. The information he had received was derived, according to his own account, solely from pro-Communist sources, Largo Caballero himself having confined his conversations with Baráibar to the latter's state of health and refrained from troubling him with political developments.[1] As a result, Baráibar affirms, he took up his new post inclined to work for the fusion of the two parties. "I frankly avow," he writes, "that there was a moment when I, of all the left-wing Socialists, was the most influenced by the Communists—allowing for the unsurpassable exception of Alvarez del Vayo—and that I understood my resumption of work should distinguish itself by a continual and positive labor in favor of the immediate fusion of the two parties in order to rescue our own from the catastrophe into which its inefficiency was plunging it and at the same time to demonstrate the superiority of Communist methods."[2] In another article, he acknowledges that the "dynamic quality" of the Communists was "very congenial" to him as "compared with the extreme sluggishness of many Socialists."[3]

Notwithstanding the accusations Baráibar heard from the lips of Socialist colleagues when he was about to resume work that "on the very fronts, even in the field hospitals, the Socialists, just because they were Socialist, were receiving disgraceful treatment, whereas the Communists were favored in everything and even monopolized glory for themselves," and that a Socialist or an Anarchist battalion could be seen "barefooted and in tatters at the side of another battalion of the same brigade, but of Communist affiliation, that was equipped as if for a military parade," he was disposed to make allowance for exaggeration.

"The impression I received was so shocking," he writes, "that I honestly believed that there had been considerable exaggeration in all I had heard. Furthermore, the extremely artful replies made in various speeches by Socialists, such as Vayo, who, as we learned later, had long been in the service of the Communist party, appeared so impregnated with revolutionary Marxist fervor, so inspired by the great ideal of unification, so ardently desirous of eradicating whatever might be true in those accusations by means of a far-reaching policy, through which the Socialists and Communists, united more closely every day, would devote themselves to winning the war, that although I no longer lived in the state of ingenuousness that I did when I was cut off from active politics, I nevertheless believed that the evil could not be as great as it appeared, so heinous did it seem to me. For this reason, I felt inclined to continue working for that broad policy of unification, together with men who were incapable of committing such injustices—injustices that conformed to a carefully prepared plan."[4]

But once in the undersecretaryship of war, Baráibar changed his mind. "In that observatory . . . the impression I received was the most disagreeable of my life and shattered the dearest illusions I had cherished during my illness. I gradually discovered to what degree I had been credulous and had run the risk of letting myself be seduced by rose-colored spectacles that were as odious as they were distorting. In the short period during which I held that post, it was necessary to change the administration of the health and transport services and prepare for changes in the quartermaster corps."[5] As the control of this corps was in Communist hands, Baráibar testifies elsewhere, "this terrible weapon of corruption and proselytism was employed unscrupulously in the commission of abuses ranging from the petty fraud of giving a friend a special voucher to the enormous infamy of granting or not granting, as the case may be, food and clothing to an entire unit, depending on its political coloring or that of its commander."[6]

"I learned that on some fronts," writes Largo Caballero, "an annoying preference was shown for the Communists; they were given shoes, clothing, tobacco, and food. The others were treated as step-children—that is, when they were not shot in the back. I likewise learned that in some hospitals—just as the priests and nuns had once acted toward noncommunicants—non-Communists were not taken care of. They were neither treated properly nor fed properly; all the attention was given to Communist party members and future converts."[7] "It is a lamentable thing to have to acknowledge the fact that in order to get rope sandals a soldier must be a Communist," declared the left Socialist Cortes deputy for Madrid, Carlos Rubiera, early in the war. "In the [military] hospitals the same thing goes on as in the days of the nuns, when, in order to get a stew or chicken, or whatever there was, you had to wear and venerate the scapular or the cross. Now you need the hammer and sickle."[8] And even the moderate Socialists, who were cooperating with the Communist party as closely as they dared against Largo Caballero, their common enemy, condemned the privileged position enjoyed by the Communists at the front.[9]

"Without any desire to offend those persons who occupied positions of maximum responsibility," Baráibar testifies, "I must declare that all the levers on which they relied—the exceptions are so few that they are not worth mentioning—were in the hands of Stalinists who ran the services of the army with the utmost unscrupulousness and profited from its funds and perquisites of office, concerned only with the growth of the Communist party, with the reinforcement of its power, and, in some cases, only with personal gain. And what happened in the departments of the undersecretaryship of the war ministry also occurred in the different sections of the general staff. By means of a fantastic web of intrigue and in spite of the honesty of many persons who held technical posts of the greatest responsibility, and who were not members of any political party, . . . the Communists cornered all the commanding positions, and, protected by them, waged a campaign of proselytism as barefaced as it was menacing."[10]

A few weeks after the fall of Largo Caballero, *CNT* declared, "The Communist party orders officers who are subject to its control to use military discipline in order to make converts, with the result that we find thousands of cases where a military commander employs his prerogatives and the military code not in order to fight fascism, but to annihilate revolutionary organizations and weaken the power of other antifascist bodies."[11]

From the moment he entered the undersecretaryship, Baráibar was regaled by the Russians in the Hotel Metropol, Soviet headquarters in Valencia, and received regular visits from them at the war ministry, during which they endeavored to seduce him from his allegiance to Largo Caballero.[12] Although he does not refer in detail to these occasions, he nevertheless reveals: "I received all manner of flattery and was conceded the honor of being the only Socialist—next to Alvarez del Vayo, of course—capable of appreciating the urgent need . . . for the fusion of the working class. In short, I was being tenderly cultivated for the role of traitor to Largo Caballero."[13] But Baráibar refused to forsake the Socialist leader, and from the day he gave the Soviet ambassador to understand that he would not assume the role the Russians and the Spanish aides expected of him, he ceased to be the object of their cajolery.[14] His rebuff came as a rude surprise, for his recent support of the idea of Socialist-Communist unification, particularly at a time when its luster had begun to tarnish before the eyes of many of his own colleagues, had encouraged the Communists to believe that he would advance their interests in the war ministry. Far from fulfilling these expectations, Baráibar became a prop for Caballero's policy and, in the succeeding weeks, helped the war minister to carry out his most rigorous assault on Communist positions in the armed forces. By the end of March this assault had acquired such amplitude as to elicit a public denunciation by the politburo: "The unity of all antifascists necessary for winning the war is being hindered by a whole series of acts, especially during the last few days, such as the transfer or removal from commanding positions of officers and commissars—*just because they are Communists*—who have given repeated proofs of their abilities and talents."[15]

Largo Caballero's anger had undoubtedly been inflamed by the Communists' behavior in the war ministry and by the practices of their political commissars now being brought to his attention. These practices ranged from the withholding of non-Communist newspapers from the front[16] to the coercing of soldiers to join their party.[17] He had also recently learned of the sectarian conduct of the General Commissariat of War, which, it will be remembered, had been set up in October 1936 to regularize the appointment of commissars and had passed under the control of the Communists owing to the defection of Alvarez del Vayo and Felipe Pretel, whom the war minister had selected because they enjoyed his highest confidence. On 25 November he had issued instructions whereby all commissars were to be appointed by him on the proposal of Alvarez del Vayo, the general commissar, whose recommendations were to be submitted through Felipe Pretel, the secretary general.[18] Although these instructions gave no authority to the commissariat to permit candidates to take up their proposed assignments before formal ratification by the war minister, the candidates recommended by Alvarez del Vayo and Pretel, as well as by Mije, the Communist head of the subcommissariat of organization, to whom Alvarez del Vayo frequently delegated his powers, had been allowed to assume their duties "provisionally," a procedure that had greatly benefited the Communist party.[19]

"One of those most responsible," writes Largo Caballero, "was Alvarez del Vayo . . . , who until then had professed to be my trustworthy friend. He labeled himself a Socialist, but was unconditionally in the service of the Communist party and abetted all its maneuvers. . . . I summoned [him]; reprimanded him for his conduct and for appointing more than two hundred Communists without my knowledge and signature. He turned pale as he listened to me and with an absolutely deadpan expression replied that the appointments were of company commissars and that he had made them because he thought he had the authority. With the law in my hand I showed him that there were no exceptions whatsoever."[20]

Shortly after the war Alvarez del Vayo gave the following explanation: "When [the commissariat of war] was formed in Spain, the Communists . . . took a greater interest in its development and expansion than the other political parties. The latter, for whom it had no particular meaning and who looked on it at first as something rather exotic and unnecessary, contented themselves with presenting lists of candidates drawn up with no special care. The Communists, on the other hand, sent their most active members right from the day of its inception. This inequality grew during the critical period of the defense of Madrid. The situation on that front during the months of November and December 1936 made it necessary to increase the number of commissars. Hundreds of provisional nominations were made, and these only served to increase the existing disproportion."[21]

More than thirty years later, Alvarez del Vayo affirms that the most painful attacks upon him were those that pictured him as having "betrayed" Largo Caballero. "I had loved Don Francisco," he protests, "like no other of my chiefs. I was unquestionably one of the Socialists in whom he confided most at the start of the war. I was already his Foreign Minister and when the time came to create a War Commissariat he insisted that I become the general commissar. . . . Largo Caballero filled me with immense respect. He was an exemplary Socialist,

completely at harmony with the working class, from which he had come. . . .
With a noble face and youthful blue eyes, Largo Caballero easily won the affection of the masses, among whom, at the start of the war, he was much more
popular and beloved than any other leader. I was completely devoted to him. . . .
I appointed [the political commissars] without paying any attention to their
political affiliation. . . . Their party or political affiliation made no difference to
me. In the end it turned out that the Communists were greater in number than the
commissars who belonged to other parties. Largo Caballero was immediately
informed by the Socialists who surrounded him (and some of them owed their
posts to me) that I had delivered the War Commissariat to the Communists."[22]

Feeling himself cheated in the trust he had placed in Alvarez del Vayo and
realizing how very greatly the commissar general was under the spell of Communist influence, Largo Caballero decided to apprise Manuel Azaña, but although
the president of the Republic authorized Alvarez del Vayo's dismissal from the
cabinet, Caballero, oddly enough, retained him in office.

"One day in 1937," testifies Indalecio Prieto, the moderate Socialist minister,
who was in constant and intimate communication with Azaña during the war,
"the premier—Largo Caballero—telephones from Valencia to Barcelona, asking
President Azaña for an urgent interview, which is held halfway in Benicarló.
Largo Caballero loses no time in declaring: 'I have asked for this conference
because I must tell you, and I could not do so by telephone, that one of my
ministers is betraying me.' Azaña is surprised. Largo Caballero continues: 'The
minister belongs to my own party; he is a Socialist, the foreign minister.' The
prime minister then informs the president of the Republic of the disloyal conduct
of Julio Alvarez del Vayo. . . . Azaña authorizes Largo Caballero to discard
Alvarez del Vayo, but the prime minister does not use the authority granted him,
just as a few weeks earlier he did not take advantage of an opportunity I gave him
to get rid of that Communist puppet when, in the very midst of a cabinet meeting,
I told Alvarez del Vayo that his conduct was more befitting a Soviet official than
of a Spaniard who was a minister in the government. Annoyed by my words,
Alvarez del Vayo resigned,[23] . . . but Largo Caballero, far from accepting his
resignation, retained him in office. There are some men with a reputation for
firmness who are given to absurd weaknesses."[24]

The element of inconsistency in Caballero's action in all likelihood derived
partly from his hesitation to disrupt Alvarez del Vayo's work and diplomatic
connections at the League of Nations and partly from his fear of how Russia, the
sole purveyor of arms, might react to Alvarez del Vayo's removal. But his action
must also have stemmed in some measure from a knowledge of the frailness of his
position should the dismissal of his foreign minister provoke a cabinet crisis. For,
while it is certain that Caballero and his followers could rely upon the CNT in the
event of a government shake-up, divided though they were by differences of
principle and practice, it is no less certain that the Communists and their allies,
the moderate Socialists and Republicans, whatever the differences between them,
were united as one man in their hostility to the left Socialist leader. Thus, rather
than risk ejecting Alvarez del Vayo from the government or even from the

commissariat of war, Largo Caballero signed, in 14 April, a sensational executive order curbing the powers of that influential body. Not only did he subordinate it to himself in the matter of orientation, but all nominations, removals, and promotions were henceforth to be decided directly by him, while any commissar whose appointment and rank had not been confirmed by 15 May was to consider himself dismissed from the corps of commissars.[25]

This order provoked a hurricane of protest from the Communist party. "It is quite clear," objected *Frente Rojo*, "that the political commissar does not have everybody's sympathy and appreciation. . . . Who are those persons who are attempting to restrict his functions and who would even suppress them, were that possible? They are men with antiquated ideas who are still among us, men who counteract the creative work of our people with the foul practices of the old school. These are the enemies of the political commissars. . . . Far from restricting the work of the commissars and giving them a one-sided orientation, it is necessary for our army that their sphere of activity be broadened and that they be given ample means, as well as the necessary stimulus, for accomplishing their tasks."[26] The following day it asked: "Who can feel hostile to this corps of heroes? Who can feel antagonistic to the forgers of the people's army? Only the declared enemies of the people; only those who are irreconcilably opposed to the antifascist army; only the blind or the insensate who are driven by a torrent of passion to commit the worst infamies. Our commissars are the pride of our army! We must defend them as we would our own children!"[27]

"There are some persons," affirmed La Pasionaria, "who want to kill the commissar's initiative by subjecting him to bureaucratic regulations that will tend to render his magnificent work ineffective and to transform him into a man without enterprise, fearful of any bold action on which the commanding officer may frown.

"But this must not be allowed. The commissar cannot on any account be deprived of his distinguishing characteristics, he cannot be placed in subjection and politically castrated without inflicting grave damage on the organization and the discipline of our Popular Army.

"That would nullify all the constructive work, all the cleaning up that was effected in order to create the Popular Army, the genuine army of the people.

"It would mean leaving our soldiers at the mercy of officers who could at a given moment disfigure the character of our army by returning to the old days of barrack discipline.

"Commissars, stick to your posts!"[28]

"The war minister's recent order concerning the commissariat," retorted Caballero's mouthpiece, *Adelante*, "in no way restricts its functions. On the contrary, it invigorates them and places them within the bounds of the commissariat's aim, which is not to practice political sectarianism . . . but to create the moral atmosphere and sense of responsibility that will carry our army to victory under the supreme control of the man who, at this historic hour, is undertaking the tremendous and glorious task of directing the destinies of Spain."[29]

In its rejoinder, *Frente Rojo* declared: "The war minister can give the commissariat whatever orders he likes, but control must rest in the hands of the commissariat itself. If that is not so, why was it created? For the purpose of making another department of the war ministry? In that case the commissariat would be superfluous."[30]

Adelante contended:

> Nobody, least of all the minister of war . . . seeks to diminish the prestige of the [commissariat]. We have already pointed out the aim [of the order], an aim that, of course, will be carried out, namely, that the commissariat of war shall not be used by any party belonging to the Popular Front government coalition for the purposes of propaganda. It is essential that we all act with honesty and with loyalty. On behalf of the Socialist party, we declare that certain commissars belonging to the Communist party have misused their posts in order to make political converts. . . . We affirm that individuals of scant ideological stability and frivolous political behavior, who should have entered the corps of commissars as Socialists, Republicans, or Anarchists, have, contrary to their intimate convictions, submitted to pressure from commissars of a higher rank belonging to the Communist party and have asked to become members of that organization. And because pressure and coercion, if these did not have the desired results, were followed by a crescendo of defamation and threats, [the premier and war minister] decided . . . to put an end to a state of affairs that would necessarily have led to disaster, to an unbridgeable chasm of distrust and sectarianism being created between the soldiers belonging to different political and trade-union organizations.[31]

On 22 April, Alvarez del Vayo, seemingly oblivious of his own share of responsibility for the crisis, informed Luis Araquistáin in Paris of the flaring press polemics: "The controversy has already lasted three days and shows no signs of ending. It is truly regrettable. On other occasions I have managed to restrain the Communists, but in this case it is difficult, because they are convinced that Caballero's decree is designed to remove the Communist commissars—who in their immense majority have conducted themselves admirably—and they won't put up with that. I spoke to Gaikis [the new Soviet ambassador] last night. He is very worried. He foresees a rapid worsening of the political situation. . . . As you can see, instead of proceeding along the path of unity we are heading for a collision."[32]

Largo Caballero's decree had, of course, the unqualified support not only of the left-wing Socialists but also of the Anarchosyndicalists, who had long been exercised by the activities of the Communist political commissars. Back in December, *Frente Libertario*, organ of the CNT armed forces on the Madrid front, had stated that the editors had received countless letters complaining that in many units composed of members of different organizations the noncommissioned officers and commissars were devoting themselves to making political converts and were using coercive measures to this end.[33] And now *CNT*, the Madrid Anarchosyndicalist organ, declared: "The war minister, adopting a firm and just attitude that we all praise, has cut short the maneuvers through which the Communist party was planning to secure the political control of the entire Popular Army, maneuvers that included the appointment of a number of commissars utterly out of proportion to the size of its forces at the front. We all laud . . . the mission of the General Commissariat of War, but no one can allow this body, which was to guarantee the revolutionary character of our army, to bring to the battle fronts not only the same frenzied partisanship that the Communist party practices behind the lines, but also its intolerable plans for hegemony."[34]

The polemic that had raged in the press between the Communists and left-wing Socialists over the commissariat of war assumed a more rancorous character every day as mutual recrimination was stimulated by the presence of other barbed issues in the military field. These included the creation of reserves, which the Communists considered were being organized at too leisurely a pace;[35] the removal from the army of alleged traitors; a decree of Largo Caballero (16 February 1937) limiting the highest rank to which civilian militia leaders could rise to that of major,[36] regarded by the Communists as a hindrance to their plans to gain control of the regular army through the cadres trained in their Fifth Regiment;[37] a subsequent decree issued by Caballero denying admission to the officers' training schools of anyone lacking a recommendation from the CNT or UGT, viewed by the Communists as an attempt to "depoliticalize" the army and convert it into "a monopoly of the two labor federations";[38] and finally, the designation by the Higher War Council, over Largo Caballero's objections, of the Communist ministers of education and agriculture, Jesús Hernández and Vicente Uribe, to discharge missions of military significance in Madrid and the Basque country. With regard to this matter, in mid-March the council had appointed Jesús Hernández and Julio Just, left Republican minister of public works, to represent the government in Madrid. Their object was to establish closer relations with the Junta de Defensa and to study the needs of the central front. When the appointments came up for ratification by the government, Largo Caballero, fearing the additional influence that the Communists might gain from the presence of one of their ministers in Madrid, took exception to a proposal that the mission of the two ministers should be permanent. Owing to disagreement, the cabinet never defined the precise duties of the two ministers or settled the length of their stay in the capital, and when they returned temporarily to Valencia, *Adelante*, Largo Caballero's mouthpiece, declared that their mission had terminated.[39] Debate was still gyrating around this issue when the Higher War Council designated Vicente Uribe, its Communist representative, to undertake an investigation into the situation in the north, where a large-scale offensive had been opened on 1 April by General Franco's forces and his German and Italian allies. The war minister viewed this assignment with no less hostility than that given to Hernández, particularly as Uribe was accompanied by Gorev, the Soviet general.

But though important in themselves, these issues were for the most part only symptomatic of the fundamental cleavage between the two factions.

Adelante wrote:

For some time we have been consuming our reserves of patience in face of the sly insinuations and the malevolent criticisms that the newspapers and agitators of the Communist party have been directing . . . against members of the Spanish Socialist party and especially against the work of its most prominent figure. . . .

The Communist organ [*Frente Rojo*] inclines toward a monstrous abuse of criticism. Everywhere it sees defects, shortcomings, and lack of foresight. The time has come to silence these irresponsible statements by asking whether or not the inspirers, who see so many motes in the eyes of others, do not have a beam in their own. And on this matter, what can be said of the activities of the Communist party representatives in the government? The activity of the minister of agriculture is certainly not in all respects the most adequate to our national requirements. Nor is the behavior of the minister of education, as far as the functions entrusted to him by the government are concerned, the kind circumstances demand. In the whole of loyalist Spain the problems of agricultural production and distribution are still without a solution capable of guaranteeing the tranquillity of the rear. Thousands upon thousands of children are left without proper care by the minister of education.

Reserves? . . . Thousands of young Spaniards in the barracks are integrated into the war machine. The fundamental reserves, however, are based on the regulation of agricultural production and distribution. That is the matter that lies within the competence of the minister of agriculture!

Reserves? The most important reserves of the Spanish people are the children, the younger generation. What care are they receiving? What attention is being paid to them?

It is advisable to remind every member of the government that he has precise functions limited to the problems affecting his ministry. It is stupid, for instance, for a minister of education and fine arts, or for a minister of agriculture, to attempt to solve war problems. The ministers should confine themselves to their specific tasks and not meddle in business foreign to their own departments—except at cabinet meetings. They have enough to do solving their own problems. . . . We are not prepared to tolerate any further attempt to disturb the rear by negative criticisms and hypocritical assertions aimed at a systematic disparagement of those who are facing the rigors of the war with that silent and modest heroism with which great deeds are accomplished.

Enough silly talk! An end to high-sounding slogans that are not carried out and to appeals for cordiality, unity, and fraternity that are put into effect with mental reservations and with a view to personal advantage! . . . We Socialists raise above everything else the banner of the Spanish Revolution, a revolution that, thanks to the sacrifice of our martyrs and heroes and to our Spanish slogans and leaders, has been achieved in a Spanish way.[40]

Frente Rojo argued:

Do the comrades of *Adelante* really believe that the ministers are mere trade-union secretaries who should concern themselves only with the "business" of their respective unions? The Communist ministers represent their respective organizations in the government, as do the Socialist, Republican, and Anarchist ministers, and are, and should be, as much concerned as anyone else about the problems and situations created by the war. Or does *Adelante* believe that the war is being waged only by the war minister and that the question of victory or defeat affects him alone? The war and the administration of the country are conducted by the Popular Front, by all the parties and organizations comprising the Popular Front, and the men who represent them in the government have the same right and obligation to concern themselves with questions affecting the entire country as well as the lives and future of all Spaniards. From where does *Adelante* get its absolutist conceptions?

Our ministers intervened in the north and in Madrid at a very serious moment . . . and the results of their work inspire confidence. We do not say that they alone have solved the difficulties; they have contributed to their solution in a large degree, and their efforts, all the things they have accomplished, have the frank and full support of our party. . . .

Adelante demands that Hernández organize child reserves. It is true that the children have to be prepared for life as well as for the kind of society that will stem from our victory, but first we have to equip our army with the necessary reserves for attaining that victory. . . .

The comrades of *Adelante* should let us know whether they want a Popular Front policy or a policy based on a personal dictatorship.

Finally, is it not strange, having regard to the fact that the whole people—Anarchists, Socialists, Communists, and Republicans—have been demanding for months and months the cleansing of the commanding army posts, that this cleansing should begin with the political commissars? How many commissars have passed over to the enemy, we should like to know? How many officers have deserted and are still deserting? Here is a concrete task for the person concerned with the fate of our army. . . .

We do not quite understand the reiteration of the adjective "Spanish" in *Adelante*'s article. What is it insinuating? No one is more Spanish, profoundly and fervently Spanish, than the Communist party and its leaders, and it was precisely our party that characterized the present war as a war of national independence, as a war for the maintenance of Spanish sovereignty.[41]

Adelante declared:

The Communist party says it is supporting a Popular Front policy, but avails itself of every seasonable opportunity to pursue its own policy and to spread propaganda that must of necessity irritate non-Communists. In this way it only succeeds in achieving something quite distinct from what it brags about every day; in other words, it sows suspicion and sectarianism among the workers, rendering difficult the organic unity of the proletariat for which the Socialist party has been fighting for so long, and especially Largo Caballero, against whom the rage of four or five petty, resentful leaders is now concentrated . . . , leaders who are incapable of understanding that a man who is all self-sacrifice and determination can work modestly for seven long months while heaps of nonsensical slogans are spread about the rear with no better result than that of creating confusion. Where are the wits of those who disparage the leader of the Spanish working class? Do they think it is such an easy matter to destroy his prestige by a blustering political campaign? Do they not realize that Largo Caballero is not a political boss as *Frente Rojo* insinuated the night before last, nor an apprentice in dictatorship, nor even a potential dictator. He is the incarnation of a whole revolutionary movement. He is the personification of the history of the Spanish working class and the Marxist movement in Spain. He is the embodiment of forty years of exemplary conduct in our trade-union and revolutionary struggles.[42]

Part V

The Communist Triumph

37

The PCE Cultivates the Moderate Socialists

*T*hwarted by Largo Caballero's opposition to their plans for military hegemony and by his refusal to promote the political supremacy of their party through the fusion of the Socialist and Communist parties, the Communists now decided to ally themselves openly with the moderate or so-called center faction of the PSOE and to exploit its internal rivalries in order to undo the left Socialist leader.

Before the Civil War, the center faction, which controlled the executive committee of the party, had been intensely hostile to the Communists. It had condemned their campaign for the fusion of the two parties as the "fraud of unification"[1] and had denounced the coalescence of the two youth movements—which had been achieved thanks to the support of Largo Caballero—as the "absorption of the Socialist youth by the Communist party."[2] Indeed, the executive committee had viewed the Communists with such suspicion and dislike that it had refused to answer a proposal they had made to set up a liaison committee between the two parties. "The Communist party," wrote general secretary José Díaz in April 1936, "has proposed to the Socialist party the formation of a contact committee with a program designed to facilitate the development of the democratic Revolution and to carry it to its final consequences. This proposal has been left unanswered by the present reformist and centrist leadership. On the other hand, it has been welcomed by the left wing. The masses of the Socialist party repudiate the attitude of the present reformist executive and see in the line of Largo Caballero one that approaches most the revolutionary path, the path of the Communist party and the Communist International."[3]

While publicly extolling Largo Caballero, the leader of the left wing, the Communists excoriated Indalecio Prieto, the leader of the center faction. A masterful character, who enjoyed immense prestige in moderate circles, Prieto had infinitely more in common with the liberal and even conservative Republicans than with the left wing of his own party. Thus, when he declared to *L'Intransigeant* of Paris in the spring of 1936 that Spanish individualism could not conform to the "methods of Moscow" and that he favored Socialist collaboration in the Republican government, the Communist organ *Mundo Obrero* suggested that inasmuch as he had repudiated not only the "violent struggle for power" but the "essence of Marxism" by advocating "old-style working-class collaboration with the bourgeois Republic," he should "voluntarily resign from the Socialist party and join any of the Republican parties."[4] Yet, despite this taunt, in the spring of 1936 the Communists were secretly more in sympathy with Prieto's moderate stance than with Largo Caballero's ultrarevolutionary posture, which they obliquely or privately censured, but they knew that they had much to gain from publicly associating themselves with the powerful left wing of the PSOE as long as their friendship with Largo Caballero lasted.

Although collaboration between the PCE and the center faction of the PSOE had not been feasible before the Civil War, it now appeared practicable not only because of their common hostility toward Largo Caballero and their resolve to remove him from the premiership and war ministry but because of the softening of the attitude of a few leading centrists toward an eventual merger of the two parties. Furthermore, the support for unification in some of the local units controlled by the Prieto faction had made such headway that toward the end of 1936 the executive commission of the PSOE, according to its secretary Ramón Lamoneda (in a speech before the national committee a few months later), was faced with the possibility that "fusion might have taken place on the local, provincial and regional levels without any control by the party." But organic fusion from below presented too great a threat to the national leadership and Lamoneda, whose political allegiance had oscillated since 1921 between the PSOE and the PCE and who at this time was discreetly supporting the Communists,[5] was careful not to arouse the fears of the more cautious leaders of his party by encouraging local initiatives in favor of immediate fusion. "It seemed to us," he added, "that the most intelligent position . . . was to welcome this sentiment [in favor of unification] and to channel it by initiating discussions with the Communist party." In this way, the executive would be able to "impose its authority on [local units] and stop them from taking any initiative in favor of partial fusion without our knowledge."[6]

As a result, at the end of December 1936, the Socialist executive proposed to the politburo that a national committee be formed to coordinate the activity of the two parties.[7] "The leaders of the Caballero faction," records the official Communist history of the Civil War, "became alarmed over the new path taken by the executive committee. . . . Under the circumstances, the Communist party proposed that the PSOE executive should invite two representatives of the UGT [whose executive was controlled by Largo Caballero] to participate in the discussions. . . . Although the Caballero leadership agreed to the proposal . . . it showed neither haste nor desire to accelerate working-class unity. With all kinds of delays and the most hollow pretexts, the representatives of the UGT executive sabotaged the talks for almost three months."[8]

It was during this period that Largo Caballero administered his blunt rebuff to Stalin in refusing to agree to the fusion of the two parties. But, despite his animosity, the Communists found grounds for encouragement in Indalecio Prieto's unexpected friendliness toward Marcel Rosenberg, the Soviet ambassador,[9] and toward General Smushkevich, alias Duglas, the head of the Russian air force units in Spain, to whom he offered every facility in his capacity as navy and air minister. "Prieto was at first on excellent terms with the Russians," testified General Hidalgo de Cisneros, the Spanish chief of the air force, at one time an intimate of Prieto's,[10] who joined the Communist party quite early in the war. "He said that we should do everything we could to encourage them to help us. He urged the Russians to send us war material. He made two or three speeches to the Russian pilots, one of which he made in Albacete, thanking them for coming to Spain and saying that their country was the only one that had helped the Republic. He spoke like a Communist. He was on excellent terms with Duglas and Rosenberg."[11]

In the same uncharacteristic spirit of cooperation with the Communists, Prieto assured Vittorio Codovila ("Medina"), the Comintern delegate, of his readiness to work for the fusion of the PSOE and the PCE,[12] an intention he also conveyed to Pietro Nenni, International Brigade commissar and later head of the Italian Socialist party, during a conversation on 3 March 1937.[13]

Although Prieto's expression of friendly intentions was in strident contradiction with his past, he undoubtedly had inner reservations, to judge from his vigorous resistance to the Communists shortly after he became defense minister in May 1937. The following episode, recounted by Prieto, which occurred after he replaced Largo Caballero in the war ministry in May 1937, is worth recording: "One night, at an unaccustomed hour, Gaisky [Leon Gaykis, the Soviet ambassador, who succeeded Marcel Rosenberg in mid-March 1937] brought me some welcome news: an important shipment of war material that I felt might be decisive was about to leave Russian ports. The ambassador showed pleasure at my display of satisfaction. Two days later he came back to see me and asked me to support the fusion of the Socialist and Communist parties. I refused, and he repeated his demands almost threateningly. He insisted with tenacity, hinting that he was carrying out orders from Moscow and that I would be rewarded or punished according to the attitude I adopted. He did not sway me. During a third visit, but without referring in any way to our earlier conversation [Gaykis] informed me that the much-needed war material that had been offered would not be shipped. That was the punishment I received."[14]

But in the spring of 1937, Prieto still needed the Communists, as they did him, to compass the ruin of Caballero. Prieto had not forgiven his opponent for preventing him from assuming the premiership in May 1936. In fact, the relations between Prieto and Caballero even before that date had been so strained by mutual rivalry and antagonism that they barely spoke to each other. Largo Caballero testifies: "On one of the occasions when I was summoned by Señor Azaña and was talking with him and other ministers, Prieto entered. He greeted everyone, shook hands . . . but made an exception of me. I realized that my presence would be annoying and withdrew."[15] According to General Hidalgo de Cisneros, although Prieto and Largo Caballero formed part of the same cabinet, they avoided each other as much as possible and used intermediaries to discuss affairs jointly affecting their respective ministries.[16]

Like the Communists, Prieto was animated by hostility to the left wing of the

Revolution[17] and by the hope that a reflux of the far-reaching revolution that had swept the country in July 1936 would induce Britain and France to abandon their policy of neutrality. On 4 October 1936, *El Socialista*, which expressed Prieto's viewpoint, had stated: "We have to take into account the attitude of the states that surround us. . . . We still hope that the estimate of Spanish events made by certain democracies will be changed, and it would be a pity, a tragedy, to compromise these possibilities by accelerating the Revolution, which does not lead to any positive solution at the present time."[18] But between Prieto and the Comintern, which directed Spanish Communist policy, there was a profound divergence of aim; for whereas the Comintern was concerned first and foremost with the advantages that Russia's strategic position would derive from the raising of the arms embargo, Prieto—like President Azaña and other liberal Republicans who looked to the moderate Socialist politician for leadership—was interested solely in the Spanish scene. To his mind, Anglo-French aid would counteract the mounting influence of Russia, which he attributed largely to their neutrality: "The Western democracies," he declared after the war, "fearful of communism, did not realize that this movement grew in Spain as a result of their own lack of assis-tance. To the extent that these countries denied us help, popular sympathy went openly to Russia when it was learned that she was supplying us with the means of defense."[19]

Yet, because he now needed the Communists in order to oust Largo Caballero and little realized that, like the left Socialist leader, he too would eventually become their victim, Prieto did not allow the misgivings their growth and prosely-tizing methods were causing him[20] to interfere with the close association they were establishing with the executive committee of his party, over which he still preserved a directing influence through its president, Ramón González Peña, and other steadfast supporters, such as Manuel Albar, Manuel Cordero, Anastasio de Gracia, and Francisco Cruz Salido. Nor did the Communists allow their past distrust of Prieto to impede their courtship of the moderate Socialist leader and his center faction. As Boris Stefanov, the Comintern delegate, told Eudocio Ravines, the Peruvian Communist, in reference to Prieto, whose candidacy, as successor to Largo Caballero, he appears at one time to have endorsed: "For us, as you well know, there are neither friends nor enemies; there are persons who serve and persons who do not."[21]

In a statement reflecting the rapprochement between the PCE and the center faction, as well as the breach with Largo Caballero, the politburo declared at the end of March:

"Having regard to the fact that the relations between the Communists and Socialists are becoming closer every day owing to a correct understanding of the policy of the Popular Front, and that the hostility to the Communist party is not due to the opposition of the Socialist party itself, but to a few isolated individuals who do not interpret the correct feelings of the masses, the politburo considers it necessary to strengthen its ties with the Socialist party. It therefore invites the executive committee to hold a joint meeting with a view to examining the present situation and establishing on a permanent basis closer relations than have existed until now by the setting up of coordinating committees of a local and national character that will facilitate the discussion and adoption of measures leading to unity of action and AS QUICKLY AS POSSIBLE TO THE FUSION OF THE SOCIALIST AND COMMUNIST PARTIES INTO A GREAT SINGLE PARTY of the Spanish working class.

"With this aim in view, the politburo has appointed a delegation to establish relations immediately with the leadership of the Socialist party."[22]

As a result of the negotiations that took place during the month of April, a national coordinating committee was formed, in which Ramón Lamoneda represented the PSOE and José Díaz the PCE. Its first action was the issuance of instructions to all units of the two organizations to set up similar liaison committees in their respective localities.[23] In the succeeding months the idea of fusing the two parties was extolled, theoretically and rhetorically, with only slightly less enthusiasm by the Prieto Socialists[24] than by the Communists, but it never became a reality because of the apprehensions of the majority of the members of the Socialist executive. Nevertheless, all was not lost. "When it transpired that some of the Socialists were not yet ready for such unification," reveals the official *Kommunisticheskii internatsional: Kratkii istoricheskii ocherk* (Outline History of the Communist International), published in Moscow in 1969, "the Communist party and the ECCI [Executive Committee of the Communist International] came to the conclusion that the Communists 'should not force amalgamation of the Communist party with the Socialist party. . . .' It was recommended that those Socialists who were already prepared to join the Communist party should be persuaded that it would be more beneficial to continue to work within the Socialist party to strengthen unity of action and prepare the amalgamation of the workers' parties."[25]

But, in the volatile political situation of April 1937, the close relations that the Communists and Prieto Socialists had now established were of more immediate importance than organic fusion and were destined to exercise a fateful influence on the course of events during the decisive days ahead; for, behind the public agreement to work for the amalgamation of the PSOE and the PCE, there lay, as events will show, a secret compact to oust Largo Caballero from the premiership and war ministry.

38

Catalonia: The Military Insurrection and Social Revolution

Strengthened by their agreement with the moderate Socialists to oust Largo Caballero—an agreement to which some of the left Republican leaders were also privy—the Communists required but a suitable opportunity to bring the conflict with Largo Caballero to a head. This opportunity came with the eruption on 3 May 1937 of an armed conflict in Barcelona, the capital of the autonomous region of Catalonia and the largest industrial center on the peninsula.

Tensions in Barcelona had been mounting ever since the defeat of the military insurrection on 19–20 July 1936, when the CNT, the Anarchist-oriented labor federation, and its ideological guide, the FAI, which were by far the most powerful of the working-class organizations in Catalonia, had emerged virtual masters of the region and the driving force of the Revolution.

The Anarchosyndicalists and Anarchists of the CNT and FAI have consistently claimed most of the credit for the defeat of the military in Barcelona. Juan García Oliver, one of the principal actors in the drama, affirms that the forces of the CNT and FAI "almost exclusively" defeated the insurrection during the two memorable days of fighting and that more than four hundred of their men lost their lives, including the prominent militant Francisco Ascaso, who was killed during an assault on the Ataranzanas barracks.[1] On the other hand, Major Federico Escofet, a Catalan autonomist and moderate Republican, who was *comisario general de ordén público*, or general commissioner of public order, at the time of the insurrection, claims that although the contribution of the CNT and FAI was "substantial," these organizations could not have prevented the Barcelona garrison from seizing the city without the "heroic effort of the forces of public order,"[2] namely, the Assault and Civil guards—the latter commanded by General José Aranguren and Colonel Antonio Escobar, both loyal Republicans.[3]

Whatever their respective contributions to the defeat of the military, it was the decisive intervention of the CNT and FAI in the fighting[4]—despite Federico Escofet's refusal to provide them with arms[5]—that transmogrified the political complexion of Barcelona and the entire region immediately after the surrender of General Manuel Goded, who had assumed command of the insurgent garrison.[6]

With regard to Escofet's refusal to give arms to the Anarchosyndicalists, Diego Abad de Santillán, the CNT-FAI leader, testifies that around 3 A.M. on 19 July, one hour before the military insurrection in Barcelona, García Oliver went to police headquarters to request arms. Major Escofet, he says, replied that he had faith in his men and could not part with any weapons. A few hours earlier, the assault guards had received orders to recover some rifles that the Anarchosyndicalists had found in ships anchored in the port and had carried off to the CNT transport union. "A massacre might have occurred at the union . . . but for the intervention of Buenaventura Durruti [the famous Anarchist leader], who persuaded the men to hand over some of the weapons that were visibly worn. As a result, a confrontation was averted at a critical moment when the insurgent barracks were already on a war footing."[7]

Vicente Guarner, a Catalan and moderate Republican, who as chief of police was at Escofet's side during the military insurrection, describes the revolutionary effervescence that followed the defeat of the rebellion:

> Thousands of persons of both sexes, the majority of whom had not been involved in the fighting, poured into the streets armed with the weapons they had looted. . . . It was impossible to restore order. Nor could we keep discipline in our own forces, including the Civil Guard, which, intoxicated with enthusiasm, had been caught up by the atmosphere, and, in shirt sleeves, manned the trucks decorated with flags and with the initials of the various organizations, among which the inscription CNT-FAI predominated. As always in the history of Catalonia, the crowds began to burn churches and convents, the homes of well-known rightists and other private buildings. . . . We issued orders to the police stations and to the units of assault and security guards to collect fire arms . . . , but it was not humanly possible to get back the rifles, the revolvers and all the weaponry that the masses had seized and that until then had been denied to them out of fear that they would never be recovered. The soldiers and recruits of the garrison who had been released [from all oaths of service and obedience to their officers] by a strange decree issued by the Madrid government[8] . . . joined the popular masses or tried to return to their villages by any available means of transportation. The utter disorder for which we could find no solution was one of the many misfortunes created by the military insurrection. The police forces and the Catalan political authorities appeared to be holding up, but in reality it was the proletariat, which had seized large quantities of war material and exhibited certain gifts of organization, that assumed political leadership.[9]

Carlos Pi Sunyer, the left Republican mayor of Barcelona and an opponent of the CNT and FAI, writes: "When the outcome [of the fighting] was not yet certain, the Anarchosyndicalists . . . busied themselves above all with seizing the weapons that the defeated troops had abandoned in the streets and barracks. This was the decisive factor in the period of horrors that followed. . . . But the major responsibility . . . lay with the military [who did not foresee] that their possible defeat would mean that the weapons they had received to guarantee order would serve as instruments of terror and disorder."[10]

Following the defeat of the military insurrection, the workers of the CNT and FAI seized post offices and telephone exchanges, formed police squads and militia units in Barcelona and in other towns and villages of Catalonia, and through their factory, transport, and food committees established their dominion over most of the economic life of the region.[11] In Barcelona, their red and black flag, flying over the former headquarters of the employers' association, the Fomento Nacional del Trabajo—renamed Casa CNT-FAI—bore testimony to their power and to the triumph of the Revolution.

The Cambridge-educated British Communist and poet John Cornford, who was killed while fighting in Spain, was inspired by what he saw. "In Barcelona," he wrote, "one can understand physically what the dictatorship of the proletariat means. . . . The real rule is in the hands of the militia committees. . . . Everywhere in the streets are armed workers and militiamen, and sitting in the cafes which used to belong to the bourgeoisie. The huge Hotel Colon overlooking the main square is occupied by the United Socialist Party of Catalonia. Further down, in a huge block opposite the Bank of Spain, is the Anarchist headquarters. . . . It's as if in London the armed workers were dominating the streets. . . . It is genuinely a dictatorship of the majority, supported by the overwhelming majority."[12] "Capitalism no longer exists in our region," affirmed Jaime Miravitlles, a prominent member of the middle-class party, the Esquerra Republicana de Catalunya. "It is the labor unions that . . . control the large metallurgical and textile plants and public utility corporations."[13] The Anarchosyndicalists also controlled most of the Franco-Spanish border, one of the many prerogatives reserved to the central government. Madrid had been empowered by article 9 of the Statute of Catalan Autonomy of September 1932 to take control of internal order if the interests of the state were threatened, but, itself a prey to revolution, it had neither the will nor the strength to exert authority.

Just as the Republican Constitution of 1931 had become an empty formula as a result of the Revolution, so, too, had the Catalan statute. Not since the War of the Spanish Succession had Catalonia been so completely free from Madrid; but this freedom was hardly satisfying to the middle classes, the principal advocates of Catalan autonomy, for while the Revolution had destroyed the coercive power of Madrid, it had also shattered the political structure upon which the free enterprise system and the security of private property reposed. The statute had given Catalonia a parliament and an executive council—the government of the Generalitat—in which the Esquerra Republicana de Catalunya (ERC), the Republican Left of Catalonia, the strongest party of the Catalan middle and lower middle classes, was dominant, but the practical significance of these two bodies had all but disappeared in the whirlwind of the Revolution.

On 20 July, immediately after the defeat of the military insurrection, Luis

Companys, president of the autonomous region and head of the ERC, made the following conciliatory statement to a group of triumphant Anarchosyndicalist leaders that included García Oliver: "Today you are the masters of the city and of Catalonia . . . and I hope you will not take it amiss if I remind you that you have not lacked the help of the loyal men of my party whatever their number, as well as that of the guards and Mozos [Mozos de Escuadra, a special defense corps of the government of the Generalitat].[14] . . . You have conquered and everything is in your power. If you do not need me or do not want me as President of Catalonia, tell me now, and I shall become just another soldier in the struggle against fascism. If, on the other hand, you believe in this post . . . I and the men of my party. . . can be useful in this struggle. . . . You can count on me and my loyalty, both as a man and as a politician, who is convinced that today a shameful past has ended, and who sincerely desires that Catalonia shall march at the head of the most socially advanced countries."[15] Although the authenticity of President Companys's statement has been challenged by Major Escofet, who, as we have seen, was general commissioner of public order in Catalonia at the time of the events,[16] it has been accepted without question by Angel Ossorio y Gallardo, the Republican jurist, in his laudatory biography of Companys; by the Communist writer Manuel Benavides; and by Carlos Pi Sunyer, the mayor of Barcelona and close political associate of the president.[17]

The Anarchosyndicalist leaders had gone to the Generalitat Palace in response to a request by President Companys. "We were armed to the teeth with rifles, machine guns, and revolvers," recalled García Oliver. "Companys received us standing, visibly moved. . . . The formalities were brief. We sat down with rifles between our legs."[18] "During the interview," testifies Abad de Santillán, who was also present, "some of the members of the government of the autonomous region were pale and trembling."[19]

This was by no means Companys's first encounter with the leaders of the CNT and FAI. In the days of the Monarchy he had won prominence as their defense lawyer. He had little in common with them, for in all essential characteristics they were worlds apart, as indicated by his abandonment of his legal profession to organize politically the Catalan middle and lower middle classes. As one of the founders of the ERC and of the Unió de Rabassaires, he represented the small manufacturers, artisans, and businessmen, as well as the tenant farmers and sharecroppers of the region. This did not endear him to the CNT and FAI, and a remark in 1933 by *Solidaridad Obrera*, the Anarchosyndicalist organ, that he was "cut from the same cloth as other politicians,"[20] epitomized their feelings toward him. Their relations did not improve when in 1934 he was elected president of the Generalitat of Catalonia, and his government, faced with a critical period of social unrest, closed down the headquarters of the CNT and FAI and proscribed their press. "*Solidaridad Obrera*," wrote Abad de Santillán, "was unable to appear for more than a few months in 1934 notwithstanding the fact that it had the second largest circulation in the region. The trade-union activities of the CNT were carried on in complete clandestinity. Our locals, our clubs, and cultural centers were not opened throughout 1934, and the sole concern of the Generalitat government was the destruction of the CNT and the extermination of the FAI."[21]

But now the Anarchosyndicalists were at the helm.

"The most dramatic scene took place," recalls the Mayor of Barcelona, "when [Buenaventura] Durruti, [Mariano] Vázquez [secretary of the CNT regional committee] and García Oliver went to speak to the President of the Generalitat and when Companys appeared to resign himself to the fact that they were masters of the city. . . . [The] reason he behaved the way he did was his fear that, if he were to break with the CNT and FAI, they would take complete control of the city and that this would be followed inevitably by the worst horrors or by chaos and by the collapse of the common front of those who had fought together, leading to a fierce repression by the military and the *falangistas*. As long as this had not happened, the situation might gradually improve and the government might reestablish its authority."[22] In short, as Vicente Guarner, the chief of police, put it: "There was no alternative but to maintain 'the political façade' of the Catalan government and try to recover little by little the reins of power."[23]

In his propitiatory statement to the CNT-FAI leaders, Companys, to use the words of García Oliver, was "flexible" and "realistic." "[He] employed the language that circumstances dictated and rose to the very difficult occasion with a unique gesture of dignity and understanding . . . as a Catalan who realized that the great hour of his country had struck and as a very advanced liberal who had no fear of the boldest social changes."[24]

No doubt the legal assistance that Companys had given the Anarchosyndicalists in the past now helped to predispose them in his favor. No doubt, too, their revived confidence was reinforced by his later statements. "The militant workers," he declared at a public meeting in October, "are, of course, those who must pay the greatest attention to the work of the Revolution. We, the representatives of the small bourgeoisie who must be respected and heard, should ease the way for the workers. We must either go along with them or behind them, but in the long run, it is they who must dictate the law. It would be useless to try to avoid the future of the workers by stratagem or by force."[25]

A supple politician with a reputation for maudlin demagoguery, yet with a touch of genuine compassion for the underdog, he was quick to adapt himself to the prevailing mood. "There were few republicans," writes Abad de Santillán, "who had acquired such a perfect understanding of the situation created on 19 July, and there were few who expressed themselves with such clarity and with such force in favor of the new social regime controlled by the workers."[26] Clearly, Companys was too shrewd a politician to oppose the CNT and FAI at a time when they were in the full tide of victory. He knew that resistance would be perilous and that his party must choose between going under or being borne alone by the storm until it might reassert its sway. But loyalty to his followers and a humane impulse to protect even persons suspected of being sympathetic to General Franco prevented him from suffering in silence the violent forces set in motion by the Revolution. Indeed, pleas for restraint and censures of violence marked most of his public statements,[27] and his personal intervention enabled many persons whose lives were threatened to leave the country. "When, after July 1936, [Luis Companys] was overwhelmed by the Revolution," a Catalan scientist told Angel Ossorio, "and all of us had to run to the Generalitat to protect friends and institutions, I saw that he did everything possible to save all those he could, although at times without success. I know that many of our right-wing politicians . . . , such as Abadal, Ventosa y Calvell, Puig y Cadafalch, Count Montseny, high dignitaries of the church, innumerable priests, and many industrialists, who were able to escape, saved their lives thanks to the intervention of [Ventura] Gassol [councillor of culture in the Catalan government] and [José María] España [councillor of the interior], who acted at the request of and in full agreement with Companys."[28]

Yet Companys was careful to censure excesses and disorder in the name of the Revolution and refrained from criticizing the changes it had wrought. This, too, was the attitude during the first few months of the Civil War of other leaders of the Esquerra[29] as well as of *La Humanitat*, their party organ,[30] and if they ventured to criticize the Revolution they did so by innuendo rather than by frank dissent.

"In twenty-four hours, minds that once appeared averse to change have evolved strikingly," wrote Federica Montseny. "Displaying a remarkable ability to adapt themselves, men who were spiritually very far removed from us have accepted the new order of things without protest."[31]

"We could have been supreme, imposed an absolute dictatorship, declared the Generalitat government a thing of the past, and instituted in its place the real power of the people," wrote Diego Abad de Santillán, one of the leading theoreticians and militants of the Spanish libertarian movement and regarded by some as a purist. "But we did not believe in dictatorship when it was exercised against us, nor did we wish to exercise a dictatorship ourselves at the expense of others. [We decided that] the Generalitat government should remain at its post with President Companys at its head."[32] On another occasion, he wrote: "It is said too lightly that given a choice of dictatorships ours would have been preferable. Yes, it would have been preferable for those who assumed the role of dictators, but not for the working people. . . . An Anarchist dictatorship would be just as nefarious for Spain as a fascist or Communist dictatorship apart from the fact that we would become the negation of what we are and what we stand for."[33] And García Oliver, who, in violation of his antigovernment, antistate principles, became minister of justice in Largo Caballero's government a few months later, affirmed: "The fate of Spain . . . was being decided in Catalonia between libertarian communism, which would have been equivalent to an Anarchist dictatorship, and democracy, which signifies collaboration. . . . The CNT and FAI decided in favor of collaboration and democracy, renouncing the revolutionary totalitarianism that would of necessity have led to the throttling of the Revolution by an Anarchist and Anarchosyndicalist dictatorship."[34]

The decision to reject a totalitarian solution was taken at an extraordinary assembly of the Catalan CNT called after the defeat of the military insurrection.[35]

García Oliver, regarded at one time as an "anarcho-bolshevik," claims that he proposed that the CNT should "take the principal government buildings by assault," but that Buenaventura Durruti replied that a coup should not be carried out until after the capture of Saragossa, a CNT stronghold and capital of the neighboring region of Aragon. The capture, he said, was "a matter of no more than ten days." To this García Oliver responded that the revolution should not be left "in the middle of the street while waiting for the capture of this or that city."[36] Nevertheless, according to an official report by the CNT, the assembly unanimously rejected "totalitarian solutions," because a dictatorship would have led to the elimination of all those who had collaborated on 19–20 July in the victory over the rebel forces and because it would have been "crushed" by foreign intervention.[37]

Although opposition to dictatorship and the threat of foreign invasion were the arguments most frequently used by the Anarchosyndicalists to explain their decision not to impose their will in Barcelona,[38] they often established in the rural areas a form of parochial dictatorship with the aid of militia groups and revolutionary tribunals. Yet, while they did not balk at the use of force in instituting collectivized agriculture and libertarian communism in certain villages, they had no program, as did the Marxists, for concentrating the power of government in their own hands. Writing on this subject a year before the Civil War, Federico Urales, the veteran Spanish Anarchist and father of Federica Montseny, stated: "[Although] we do not desire power or dictatorship, we have not solved the problem of what force will be required between the time when the social revolution occurs and a libertarian regime based on economic equality and equal rights for all is established."[39]

The dilemma of the CNT on the day of the revolution is explained by Major Escofet, the moderate Republican commissioner of public order. When on 20 July, he recalls, the CNT in Barcelona found itself "virtually in control of the streets, the arms, and transportation, in other words, with power in its hands, its leaders, who were bold and energetic and experienced fighters, were disoriented. They had no plan, no clear doctrine, no idea what they should do or what they should allow others to do. The CNT concept of libertarian communism was devoid of realism and was silent as to the road it should follow in a revolutionary period."[40]

The dilemma of the CNT was acknowledged by Helmut Ruediger, representative in Barcelona of the International Workingmen's Association (AIT), with which the CNT was affiliated. In response to criticism by foreign Anarchists, he wrote: "Those who say that the CNT should have established its own dictatorship in 1936 do not know what they are demanding. . . . The CNT would have needed *a government program, a program for exercising power; [it would have needed] training in the exercise of power, an economic plan centrally directed, and experience in the use of the state apparatus.* . . . The CNT had none of these. Nor do those who believe that the CNT should have implanted its own dictatorship have such a program, either for their own country or for Spain. Do not let us delude ourselves! Furthermore, had it possessed such a program before 19 July *the CNT would not have been the CNT; it would have been a bolshevik party*, and, had it applied such methods to the Revolution, it would have dealt Anarchism a mortal blow."[41]

Lacking a program of their own for the seizure of governmental power, the CNT-FAI leaders (although antistatists and against all governments) decided to allow the Generalitat government to remain standing. But the war and revolution in Catalonia could not be directed by a government without influence over the largest and most radical segment of the working class. Nor could the Anarchosyndicalist leaders reinvigorate the government with their own authority without violating their antistate and antigovernment principles. Hence a Central Anti-Fascist Militia Committee was created, in which the CNT and FAI appropriated the key departments of war, public order, and transportation.[42] According to García Oliver, the committee was created at the suggestion of President Companys.[43] This is most likely, for no one could have realized more clearly than Companys that if the war were to be waged successfully, that if some of the values and institutions of the Republican regime were to be saved from the hurricane of the Revolution and the revolutionary terror subjected to even a modicum of control, some kind of central governing body was necessary—a government in essence if not in name, in which the CNT-FAI leaders could participate without loss of face and which could prosecute the war until such time as the nominal government might regain the essential elements of real power. If his conciliatory statement to the Anarchosyndicalist leaders was but a first step in this direction, then, far from representing a surrender to the FAI, it was, as Angel Ossorio y Gallardo, Republican jurist and biographer of the president, put it, an act of "supreme dexterity" designed to make the FAI surrender to Companys. "It should not be assumed," he added, "that he wished to deceive the FAI. The fact is that there is no greater dexterity than sincerity. What the president undoubtedly wanted to say was this: 'Practically speaking, I have only the nominal power. The real power is in your hands. . . . But don't you agree that your efforts require a directive body? If you do not have one you will easily fall into disorder and impotence. Use me then in a governing and leadership capacity.' "[44]

Although President Companys may have conceived of the role of the Central Anti-Fascist Militia Committee as that of an auxiliary body of the Generalitat government, the committee immediately became the de facto executive body in the region. Its power rested not on the shattered machinery of state but on the revolutionary militia and police squads and upon the multitudinous committees that sprang up in the region during the first days of the Revolution. The work of the militia committee, attests Abad de Santillán, himself a member, included the establishment of revolutionary order in the rear, the creation of militia units for the front, the organization of the economy, and legislative and judicial action. In sum: "The militia committee was everything; it attended to everything."[45] "The Central Anti-Fascist Militia Committee," he wrote on another occasion, "became the real and only power, the absolute, revolutionary power."[46]

To represent the Catalan government and the Esquerra on the militia committee, President Companys appointed the shrewd and extremely able politician José Tarradellas, whose "double objective," according to his biographer, was "to organize the war effort with the cooperation of all the antifascist forces" and "to achieve the total transfer of power from the Anarchists to the Generalitat government." To end the division of power would be no easy task even for a man as astute as Tarradellas, but, as his biographer points out, his friendship with the Anarchosyndicalists, which was due to "his ability to understand their noble and utopian aims," was "a decisive factor in his political activity."[47]

Although Tarradellas affirms that the Central Anti-Fascist Militia Committee was "powerfully influenced by the gigantic figure of President Companys,"[48] he also states that the Generalitat government was "more symbolic than real."[49] This is not to say that the government was destitute of power, for it could rely upon the remnants of the regular police corps—the Assault and Civil guards—and upon the militia organized by the political parties, although it is true that these were vastly outnumbered by the armed forces of the CNT and FAI. The council of finance of the Catalan government shared with the UGT bank employees' union control over the banking system of the region[50]—a source of power neglected by the CNT and FAI, partly because they represented predominantly the blue-collar workers of the region and partly because they had always advocated the abolition of money and credit—but the council served mainly as a rubber stamp for the Revolution, since one of its principal functions was to meet the financial needs of the militia committee. To be sure, the Generalitat government appeared to issue decrees or executive orders like a sovereign power, but most of those published in its official journal, the *Butlletí Oficial*,[51] were simply measures previously approved by the committee or were legislative acknowledgments of accomplished facts. True, as Companys gradually recovered his self-confidence, he resisted some of the committee's more extreme proposals, such as the abolition of the Catalan Parliament—which the revolutionaries regarded as an outmoded institution—and threatened to resign if they were put into effect. On one occasion, according to Miguel Serra Pàmies, a founder-member of the Communist-controlled PSUC, Companys told the committee members, "You can dispense with me if you like, you can dispense with the Generalitat government, you can arrest me, but tomorrow the whole world will know that the legal authority has been supplanted!"[52]

Companys was prone to theatrics. "He would throw a fit," attested Serra Pàmies, who knew him well, "pull his hair, toss things around, take off his jacket, tear off his tie, open his shirt. This behavior was typical."[53] But during the early days of the revolution, Companys exhibited more restraint and circumspection, and his government played a largely passive role as a rubber stamp for the Central Anti-Fascist Militia Committee. As Abad de Santillán, one of the committee's CNT-FAI members, affirms, "Everything had to be resolved or validated by the committee."[54] This is true. Witness, for example, the decree suspending the Catalan municipal councillors belonging to parties that opposed the Popular

Front;[55] the decrees establishing the forty-hour week and raising wages 15 percent;[56] the decree suspending eviction proceedings against militiamen;[57] the decree confiscating the property of the church and of persons implicated in the rising;[58] the executive order making compulsory the reinstatement of workers discharged on political grounds;[59] and the executive orders issued by the councillor of labor relating to the new working conditions established by the unions in various branches of industry.[60] "On 24 July 1936," wrote *Luz y Fuerza*, a CNT trade journal, "the workers of the Sociedad General de Aguas de Barcelona and of the Empresa Concesionaria de Aguas Subterráneas del Rio Llobregat confiscated both concerns and took over administrative and technical control. . . . The following day, the government of the Generalitat recognized the validity of the confiscation, and a government comptroller or *interventor* joined the committee of control."[61] "The government of the Generalitat," said a CNT-FAI report on the sequestration of the Metro Transversal subway by the Anarchosyndicalists, "has appointed a comptroller who has been accepted, in principle, by the workers, but whose function is entirely passive. Effective control is in the hands of the revolutionary committee of the enterprise."[62]

Obviously, the urban middle and lower middle classes were not satisfied with the inferior position of the Catalan government in the division of power or with the ability of the Anarchosyndicalists to collectivize at will,[63] nor were the tenant farmers and sharecroppers of the Unió de Rabassaires, which represented the majority of the peasant population in the region. Having seized the land, they felt that the Revolution had accomplished its mission. Not so the extreme spirits. In those villages where Anarchosyndicalist laborers were predominant, or where the influx of CNT-FAI militiamen weighted the scales in their favor, individual cultivation was abolished, often at the expense of rural production. "Certain abuses have been committed, which we consider counterproductive," confessed *Solidaridad Obrera*, the leading CNT newspaper. "We know that certain irresponsible elements have frightened the small peasants and that the latter are showing a lack of interest in their daily labors."[64] On another occasion it stated: "News that the small bourgeoisie is deeply alarmed has reached our ears. We were under the impression that the anxiety of the first few days had evaporated, but the uneasiness of the shopkeeper, the businessman, the small manufacturer, the artisan, and small peasant holder persists. They lack confidence in the leadership of the proletariat."[65] And referring to Hospitalet, a town of thirty thousand inhabitants outside Barcelona, a left-wing critic of the zealots of the collectivization movement stated: "All the small places of business have been taken over, such as food stores, meat markets, grain stores, small electric plants, etc. As a result, it is now said that the place in Catalonia where there are more fascists is Hospitalet, because the revolution has been discredited and discontent is growing."[66]

Seeing their world going under, it is no wonder that the urban rural middle classes sought desperately for help against the swell of the collectivization movement.

39

The Rise of the PSUC.
Dissolution of the Militia Committee.

*N*either in the towns nor in the villages of Catalonia could the intermediate classes turn for support to the Esquerra, hitherto their unfailing defender, for most of its leaders, like those of the other middle-class parties, Acció Catalana and Estat Català, were timorous to the point of self-effacement. In contrast, the Catalan Communists, who controlled the PSUC, the Partit Socialista Unificat de Catalunya, boldly defended—in consonance with the policy of the Spanish Communist party—the interests of those classes that were being dragged into the whirlwind of the collectivization movement or threatened with extinction by the disruption of trade, by the lack of financial resources, and by the requisitions carried out by the CNT and FAI. "It would be unpardonable," said *Treball*, the PSUC organ in Barcelona, "to forget the multitude of small commodity producers and businessmen in our region. . . . They declare that nobody is concerned about their fate. They are elements who tend to favor any reactionary movement because it seems to them that anything would be better than the economic system that is being instituted in our region. . . . The distressing situation of many of these people is obvious. They cannot run their workshops and businesses because they have no reserve capital; they have hardly enough to eat, especially the small manufacturers, because the wages they have to pay to the few workers they employ prevent them from attending to their own daily needs."[1]

And a PSUC manifesto declared: "We demand an economy freed from naive experiments and the ingenious plans of individuals who are operating today on the bleeding body of Catalonia with the recklessness and irresponsibility of a madman in a laboratory encircled by flames. We demand an economy freed from the influence or pressure of so many committees that have sprung up everywhere . . . [and] that sap the magnificent vitality of Catalonia."[2]

It was the PSUC, not the middle-class Esquerra, that opposed the revolutionaries of the CNT and FAI, defended the interests of the rabassaires and fearlessly organized eighteen thousand tradesmen, artisans, and small manufacturers into the GEPCI (Gremis i Entitats de Petits Comerciants i Industrials), the Catalan

Federation of Small Businessmen and Manufacturers. Because the PSUC allowed the GEPCI, many of whose members were employers of labor, to enter the Catalan UGT, which it controlled,[3] it was criticized by Juan J. Doménech, the CNT leader, who charged that, to increase its size, the UGT in Catalonia did not object to enrolling speculators, shopkeepers, and merchants or to their exploiting the workers.[4]

In the beginning, writes Albert Pérez-Baró, who played a leading role in the collectivization movement in Catalonia, the GEPCI began to function "at first timidly, then boldly." "For its part, the Esquerra Republicana de Catalunya, which had been regarded as the political organization most suited to the defense of the small bourgeoisie and which had relinquished its political leadership to the CNT because of prevailing circumstances, could not look favorably on the capture of its clientele by the PSUC and organized the Unió de Menestrals [artisans' union], which on occasions functioned alongside the GEPCI and on others against it."[5]

A small party at the outset of the Civil War, the PSUC was the result of the fusion of four minuscule organizations aggregating approximately 2,500 members: the Unió Socialista de Catalunya (USC), the largest component, which appealed strongly to Catalan nationalist sentiments; the Federació Catalana del PSOE; the Partit Comunista de Catalunya; and the Partit Català Proletaria. From information furnished me by Miguel Serra Pàmies, secretary before the war of the USC and subsequently a member of the PSUC's executive committee,[6] and from data provided by other sources, I arrive at the following numerical breakdown: USC, between 1,200 and 1,500 members; Federació Catalana del PSOE, between 600 and 700 members; Partit Comunista de Catalunya, less than 400 members; Partit Català Proletaria, approximately 80 members. Miguel Valdés, the PSUC leader, put the initial membership of the united party at around 3,000.[7] On the other hand, Luis Cabo Giorla, a member of the central committee of the PCE, gave the figure of 5,000.[8]

The above figures differ from those of the Soviet historian L. V. Ponamariova, who gives the membership of the USC at the time of unification in July 1936 as 2,000, that of the Federació Catalana del PSOE as 1,500, the Partit Comunista de Catalunya as 2,000, and the Partit Català Proletaria as 500, making a total initial membership of 6,000.[9] Whatever the true figures, it is obvious that the PSUC was only a diminutive organization at the outset of the Civil War.

According to USC secretary Serra Pàmies, the negotiations for the fusion of the four groups had been proceeding inconclusively before the war partly as a result of the insistence of the Communists that the united party be linked to the Communist International through the PCE and the demand by the Federació Catalana del PSOE that it affiliate with the Labor and Socialist International. The prospects of breaking the deadlock, affirmed Serra Pàmies, were not improved by the attitude of Juan Comorera, the president of the USC, who at first opposed any connection with either international, *particularly the Communist.*[10] Comorera is alleged to have told members of the executive committee of his party that it was essential to prevent the Communists from capturing the new organization.[11] But under the impact of the Revolution these differences melted away. The leaders of the four parties knew that the emergence of the CNT and FAI as masters of the situation left them scant hope of survival unless they united their forces. After a heated debate, Juan Comorera and Rafael Vidiella (president of the Federació Catalana del PSOE and at one time a loyal supporter of Caballero)[12] withdrew their objections to adherence to the Communist International,[13] and the PSUC was formed on 23 July.

Juan Comorera became the general secretary of the new party. His position during the long negotiations initiated in November 1935 appears ambiguous and is troubling to historians, for he stated in an interview published in *Justicia Social*, the organ of the USC, on 28 March 1936, that he favored affiliation with the Comintern. He also signed a document in June 1936, drafted by the liaison committee representing the four parties, which stated that the new party would recognize "the Communist International as the only International that interprets the desires of the world proletariat."[14] A plausible explanation for this ambiguity is that behind Comorera's public support of the Comintern lay his ambition to head the united party and his reluctance to burn his bridges with the Communists. Víctor Alba, an authority on left-wing Catalan politics, may indeed be right when he states that Comorera's support "was no doubt the price he had to pay for the post of general secretary, because [he] was among the most moderate members of the moderate USC . . . , and had no ideological reason for wishing that the new party should belong to the Third rather than to the Second International."[15] He could certainly not have forgotten the ultrarevolutionary language of the Catalan Communists before the advent of the Popular Front. Reporting on their first party congress in 1934, Vicente Uribe, the Spanish Communist leader, stated that the Catalan party "with the assistance and under the leadership of the Communist Party of Spain and its Central Committee [must] win the majority of the proletariat of Catalonia and the advanced masses in the rural districts *for Communism, for the Soviets, for the workers' and peasants' government and make Catalonia the unshakeable bulwark of the victory of the Soviet revolution in Spain.*"[16]

There is evidence that Comorera, in addition to once opposing affiliation with the Comintern, even resisted the fusion of the four parties. His opposition is recorded by Joaquín Almendros, the Barcelona secretary of the Federació Catalana del PSOE, who became a member of the executive committee of the united party. It is curious that his important testimony is not mentioned by Miquel Caminal in his well-documented, three-volume biography of Comorera or by Josep Lluís Martín i Ramos in his work on the origins of the PSUC. According to Almendros, it was Comorera who "put up the greatest resistance to unification." Comorera, he affirms, was a "true *Catalanista*," who believed that his organization should not become involved with the national parties and that "his natural allies" were the Catalan organizations: the Esquerra Republicana de Catalunya (with which the USC associated itself in elections), Acció Catalana, Estat Català and the Unió de Rabassaires. But, Almendros continues, the situation became critical after the defeat of the military insurrection. "Comorera had no course but to change his point of view," for he understood that only by fusion could the four parties confront "the destructive power of the Anarchists."[17]

According to Soviet historian Ponamariova, under pressure of the Civil War and the danger that the CNT leaders wished to direct the revolution "along the path of so-called 'libertarian communism,' " the four parties decided to merge into "a single party of the Catalan proletariat" and to adhere "to the Communist International through the Communist Party of Spain."[18]

By March 1937, only nine months after its formation, the PSUC claimed fifty thousand adherents. "Fifty thousand militants in Catalonia is a sort of miracle," declared Comorera. "In Catalonia there is no Marxist tradition. Forces diametrically opposed to Marxism have been and still are active, namely, the great mass of the peasantry, the segment of the working class that is Anarchist by tradition, and the other segment also linked by tradition and by its slow development to the petty bourgeois Republican parties. . . . To have created a party of fifty thousand militants in an atmosphere without any [Marxist] tradition, faced as we are by powerful adversaries who have done everything they could to hinder us, is a great triumph."[19] The figure of fifty thousand, which, according to Ponamariova, rose to sixty thousand in July 1937 and to ninety thousand before the end of the war,[20] does not appear to be greatly exaggerated. The recruits that flocked to the party came from many sources: manual and white-collar workers from the Catalan section of the UGT, government officials, police, teachers, tradesmen, artisans, small manufacturers as well as small and medium-sized farmers, tenant farmers, and sharecroppers, many of whom had formerly held Esquerra membership cards. "The PSUC," said Severino Campos, a prominent CNT-FAI militant, "devotes itself to making converts of persons who are not inspired by the slightest Marxist or, least of all, revolutionary sentiment."[21] However, speaking in July 1937, one year after its formation, at a time when the PSUC was at pains to deemphasize its middle-class composition, Comorera claimed that 60 percent of its members were industrial workers and 20 percent agricultural laborers. "If to these percentages," he continued, "we add those of officials, clerks, teachers, and of all other salaried workers, we can affirm that 97 percent of our party is composed of wage earners." The balance, he stated, was made up of "comrades in the liberal professions and of a negligible, an insignificant number of elements of the small bourgeoisie."[22] As no mention was made of the rabassaires, many of whom, according to Víctor Colomer, the agrarian secretary of the PSUC, joined the party,[23] it must be assumed that these tenant farmers and sharecroppers were classified somewhat loosely as agricultural laborers.

As noted earlier, from the time of the fusion, the PSUC adhered to the Communist International through the PCE. Shortly thereafter the leaders of the Catalan Communist party became the ruling nucleus. In addition to controlling the PSUC's organizational work, its press, and trade-union activities, they were in charge of internal vigilance. All records were in the hands of Joaquín Olaso, the head of the party's control commission, who exercised a constant surveillance over the PSUC leaders and monitored their telephone calls. This task was greatly simplified by the fact that most of the members of the central committee and local committee of Barcelona had been urged to live with their families in the *Pedrera*, a large apartment building seized by the party at the outbreak of the Civil War.[24]

"Pedro"—the Comintern delegate whose real name was Ernö Gerö and who, after World War II, held several high positions in the Soviet-controlled Hungarian government[25]—was placed at Juan Comorera's elbow, and Spanish Communist leaders were sent regularly to Barcelona, with directives. Within a few months, both Comorera and Rafael Vidiella, the former Caballero Socialist, reinforced their ties with the PCE, when they were made members of its central committee.[26]

The PSUC was directed behind the scenes by Pedro with extraordinary energy, tact, and efficiency. He had been a militant supporter of the Hungarian Soviet Republic in 1918 and personal secretary to its leader Bela Kún at the Comintern in 1934.[27] In addition, he is said to have been closely associated with the Soviet secret police during the purges and aided in the elimination of most "old Hungarian Communists," then living in the Soviet Union.[28] During the Civil War, he watched over *Treball*, the PSUC daily, occasionally wrote its editorials, and, aided by his knowledge of Catalan acquired as Comintern representative in Catalonia in the early thirties, smoothed over differences in the inner circle of the party resulting from the Catalan nationalism of some of its leaders and their reluctance to accept the centralizing aims of the Spanish Communists. One of Pedro's principal accomplishments was his success in subordinating Comorera's Catalanist tendencies to the PCE. The tactical skill of the Soviet delegate Pedro, writes Almendros, and of some members of the Spanish Communist party was illustrated by the way they fed Comorera's ambitions. "They managed to convince him that he might occupy the post of secretary general of the [Spanish] Communist party, a post that was in the hands of José Díaz and was shaky at the time. Because of this prospect, he began to forget the peculiarities of Catalonia and, consequently, of the new Catalan party. His surrender to the directives of the PCE and the Soviet delegate was complete. The PSUC became the blind and obedient servant of the [politburo]. As a result, during the weekly sessions of the party, Comorera acted as though he were directed by the orders and slogans issued by Moscow."[29]

Several times in the course of the war, the friction created by the Nationalist sentiments of some of the PSUC's leaders and by the centralizing tendencies of the Spanish Communist party threatened to erupt into open conflict, and only the tremendous tact and personal authority of Pedro succeeded in bringing the Catalanistas to heel.[30] After the war the Spanish Communist party in exile gave the following version of the friction within the PSUC: "From the moment the PSUC was formed all the healthy and loyal elements who had come from the four parties . . . with Comrade Juan Comorera at the head, looked for support and help to the [Spanish] Communist party. But, from the very first moment, some elements also came to the PSUC to begin an undeclared struggle against the line of the Communist International. . . . These wretched elements . . . fought against the Communist orientation of the party from the day of fusion, using their positions in both the central and executive committees to this end."[31]

In addition to keeping the recalcitrants in line, Pedro dominated the meetings of the party's executive committee, personally inspected the smallest units of the party, and, in short, exercised a close and constant supervision over almost every detail.[32] High in the confidence of Moscow, he even monitored the activities of Vladimir A. Antonov-Ovseenko, the Soviet consul general in Barcelona.[33]

Less than two weeks after the defeat of the military insurrection on 20 July and in the thick of the revolutionary ferment, the PSUC joined with the Esquerra in a maneuver to undermine the ascendancy of the Central Anti-Fascist Militia Committee. According to the official Communist history of the Civil War, *Guerra y revolución en España, 1936–1939*, the party attempted to "counteract the influence of the FAI" by accepting a proposal of the Esquerra to enter the government. On 31 July, a new administration was formed by the ERC leader Juan Casanovas with three PSUC representatives,[34] but the FAI "reacted violently" and sent a delegation to President Companys demanding "the immediate dissolution" of the government. According to Serra Pàmies, the delegation threatened to seize the Generalitat Palace, the seat of the Catalan government, unless Companys yielded. "Fearful of an open clash with the Anarchists," the official Communist history continues, "the Esquerra representatives decided that the PSUC ministers should withdraw. . . . Hoping to please the Anarchists, Casanovas even presented the list of candidates in his new government—excluding the PSUC—to Mariano Vázquez, secretary at that time of the Regional committee of the Catalan CNT. Only when Vázquez gave the list his approval did Casanovas dare to make it public."[35] The Anarchosyndicalist historian César M. Lorenzo records an event that illustrates to what degree the libertarians in Catalonia were at that time able "to lay down the law": Vidiella, one of the three PSUC representatives who had entered the government, and a member of the militia committee, was expelled from the latter "without ceremony" for not apprising the other members of his intentions.[36]

But this setback did not diminish the resolve of President Companys to concentrate the levers of power in the hands of the Generalitat government. A few weeks later, he called a meeting of the CNT-FAI representatives in the Central Anti-Fascist Militia Committee. "I recognize that you are the masters of the situation," he told them. "I am ready to go along with you as far as necessary. Everything is in a state of flux and I realize that it is the people who must reshape society. *If you wish, I shall quit,* but I feel I can be useful to you. The democracies—France in particular—know me. For this reason I am sure that we can secure weapons to conquer the fascists, which is something they will not provide the CNT and FAI. *We must save appearances.* Therefore, I suggest that we form a government of the Generalitat representing my party and the CNT, in which I shall be the prime minister. *After you have squeezed me dry, you may cast me aside as unusable. My only desire is to serve the revolution.*"[37]

In his efforts to breathe new life into the Generalitat government by superseding the militia committee, Companys was aided by pressure from the central government, which discountenanced a revolutionary body that exposed to the world at large that its authority in Catalonia was ineffectual. "We were told time and again," affirms Diego Abad de Santillán, "that as long as we persisted in maintaining [the militia committee] . . . arms would not reach Catalonia, that we would not be given foreign currency with which to purchase them abroad or raw materials for our industry." There was, therefore, no course, he asserted, if they were not to lose the war, but to dissolve the committee and join the Catalan government. "For the first time in the history of the modern labor movement, we Anarchists joined a government . . . , not because we had forgotten our doctrines or the nature of government. Circumstances beyond our control led us to situations and methods that were repugnant to us but unavoidable."[38]

Federica Montseny explained the historic decision differently. In Russia, she declared, in a speech on 14 October 1936, the Anarchists had tried to carry out their ideas in regions like the Ukraine where libertarian communism was established, but by not participating in all aspects of public life they found themselves removed from the direction of affairs and persecuted with "blood and fire." For that reason, she added, in Catalonia "we have participated in everything and established ourselves everywhere. . . . Thus, even in politics, we have made a revolution. There is no violation of principles, only a recognition of what history has taught us."[39]

Who made the historic decision to enter the Generalitat government? None of the leading Anarchosyndicalist spokesmen makes this clear, although there is some evidence that it was taken during the national plenum of regional committees of the CNT that began in the third week of September.[40]

In the new administration, formed on 28 September by José Tarradellas—who has been described by a supporter as a man "of great political foresight and extraordinary skill"[41]—the Anarchosyndicalists held only three out of twelve portfolios. In July, it will be recalled, Companys had appointed Tarradellas (who, forty-one years later, in 1977, was to become the first president of the Generalitat after the death of General Franco) to serve as government representative on the militia committee, and now, in accordance with his powers under the Catalan constitution, he delegated to him his executive functions by naming him first councillor or premier in the Generalitat government representing the Esquerra. The twelve seats in the government were apportioned among the various organizations as follows:

José Tarradellas	ERC	First Councillor (Premier) and Councillor of Finance
Artemio Aiguadé	ERC	Internal Security
Ventura Gassol	ERC	Culture

Juan P. Fábregas	CNT	Economy
Antonio García Birlan	CNT	Health and Public Assistance
Juan J. Domenech	CNT	Supplies
Juan Comorera	PSUC	Public Services
Miguel Valdés	PSUC	Labor and Public Works
Andrés Nin	POUM	Justice
Lieutenant Colonel Felipe Díaz Sandino	Independent (liberal Republican)	Defense
José Calvet	Unió de Rabassaires	Agriculture
Rafael Closas	Acció Catalana Republicana	Councillor without portfolio

Although the dissolution of the militia committee strengthened the authority of the Generalitat government, it did not end the division of power in the region; for the revolutionaries maintained their own police squads—the *patrullas de control* or patrols—under the authority of the CNT-dominated Junta de Seguridad and their armed militia under the authority of the CNT-controlled Secretariado de Defensa, as well as a vast network of defense, transport, and food committees that covered the length and breadth of the region. On the other hand, the Generalitat government, through Artemio Aiguadé, the councillor of internal security, and Martín Rouret, his *comisario general de orden público*, or police commissioner, could rely on the Assault and Republican guards as well as on the militia of the moderate parties.[42]

To end the division of power became the principal goal of the PSUC and the ERC councillors in the new government during the coming months. The first step in this direction was the decree of 9 October 1936 providing for the dissolution of the revolutionary committees that had emerged in the wake of the military uprising and for their replacement by regular municipal councils, in which the different organizations were to be seated in proportion to their representation in the government.[43] Since the majority of these committees were dominated by the CNT and FAI, the approval of the decree by the CNT councillors must have surprised the Esquerra, which, despite the resistance of the more radical members of the libertarian movement, managed to recover some of its lost power in the towns and villages of the region.

In the impassioned political struggle that was waged during the next few months to end the duality of police and military power, a distinction should be made between the policies of the Esquerra and those of the PSUC. On the one hand, Companys and Tarradellas hoped to end the dichotomy by subtle manipulation of the CNT and FAI and by turning to account their political artlessness and inexperience, thus avoiding encroachment by the central government and by the

Spanish Communist party on Catalan autonomy.[44] On the other hand, the PSUC—despite the Catalanist sentiments of many of its leaders—looked to the central government and the Spanish Communists for help despite the risk of impingement on the autonomy of the region, as will be seen in the succeeding chapters.

40

The POUM and the Trotskyists

The political arena in Catalonia was complicated by the presence of the POUM, the Partido Obrero de Unificación Marxista (the Workers' Party of Marxist Unification), formed in September 1935 through the fusion of Andrés Nin's Izquierda Comunista (Communist Left) with Joaquín Maurín's Bloque Obrero y Campesino (Worker and Peasant Bloc).[1] According to Nin, the membership of the POUM rose from six thousand in July 1936 to thirty thousand in December.[2] Although small by Anarchosyndicalist standards and possessing little more than a skeleton organization outside Catalonia, it was nonetheless a force to be reckoned with in the region.

A vigorous advocate of Socialist revolution and the dictatorship of the proletariat, an unrelenting critic of the Popular Front and of Stalin's trials and purges, the POUM was denounced as "Trotskyist." Although some of its leaders, including Andrés Nin and Juan Andrade, had once been disciples of Leon Trotsky and after the outbreak of the Civil War had favored giving him political asylum in Catalonia,[3] the POUM was not a Trotskyist party, and it frantically attempted to prove that it was not in numerous articles and speeches.[4] Nevertheless, in accordance with the tactic used by Stalin at the Moscow trials of amalgamating all opponents under a single label, the Communists denounced the dissidents of the POUM as Trotskyist agents of Franco, Hitler, and Mussolini.[5]

At the outbreak of the Civil War, Joaquín Maurín, general secretary of the party, was trapped in rebel territory and was arrested under an assumed name when trying to reach the Republican side. Released from Jaca prison in September 1937, he was reincarcerated a few days later when his true identity was discovered, and he was not freed until October 1946.[6] "Although Maurín himself never participated in the war," writes the Civil War scholar George Esenwein, "his legacy as the chief theoretical architect and organizer of the POUM undeniably left its stamp on the party's policies. While one cannot assess precisely the impact of his absence, there can be no doubt that it created profound problems for the POUM during the war. This is illustrated by the fact that when Nin took over the leadership, he lacked the ascendancy that Maurín had enjoyed; for, as Ignacio Iglesias, a good friend of Nin's and a POUMist, later wrote to Víctor Alba [historian and onetime member of the party]: 'Maurín was [for the majority of the POUM] something more than the "máximo" leader (dirigente máximo): He was, purely and simply, the leader, the only leader.' "[7] Maurín's ascendancy was also enhanced by the fact that his followers outnumbered Nin's by at least twenty-three to one at the time of the fusion.[8] The strong feeling for Maurín was evident at the first meeting of the central committee of the party held after the outbreak of the Civil War, when, according to Alba, Nin was named not general secretary—"a post and title reserved for Maurín"—but political secretary.[9]

Although the POUM was denounced by the Communists as Trotskyist, the truth is that Trotsky had profound differences with the POUM from its founding,[10] and within a few months of the outbreak of hostilities, a handful of orthodox followers, the Bolshevik Leninists, organized the exiguous Spanish section of his Fourth International.[11] "The POUM was never Trotskyist, i.e., a Bolshevik party," declared *Unser Wort*, a German-language organ of Trotsky's Fourth International. "The POUM leaders defended themselves desperately against the 'accusation' of Trotskyism and did not shrink even from the most contemptible means. Not only did they expel Trotskyists from their ranks, but, what is more, the POUM published these expulsions in the most provocative way."[12]

Bertram D. Wolfe, a leader at the time of the Communist party of the U.S.A. (Opposition), which was associated with the POUM through the International Bureau for Revolutionary Socialist Unity, wrote:

> The simple facts in the case are:
>
> 1. The P.O.U.M. is not Trotskyist. Its membership and leadership come predominantly from the Communist Party, the Catalonian section of which was expelled in bloc during the ultra-left wave of 1929, for rejecting union-splitting, for advocating the tactics of the united front, for opposing the stupid theory that the rest of the working class was "social fascist", for objecting to the mechanical transference of tactics to Spain which had no connection with Spanish realities. Its outstanding leader was Joaquín Maurín, repeatedly and bitterly attacked by Trotsky as "centrist", "opportunist", "petty-bourgeois", "main misleader of the Spanish proletariat", "Menshevik traitor" and similar choice epithets. . . . In his gentler moods, Trotsky pronounced "Maurinism . . . a mixture of petty bourgeois prejudices, ignorance, provincial science and petty politics", and concluded that ". . . the first step on the road to a revolutionary party in Spain must be to denounce the political vulgarity of Maurinism. In this, we must have no mercy. . . ."
>
> 2. Two of the leaders of the P.O.U.M., Andrés Nin and Juan Andrade, were former followers of Trotsky. They broke with him almost five years ago when they rejected his instructions to enter the Second International. . . . Since then, Trotsky has variously honored them as "a mere tail of the 'left' bourgeoisie", "the traitors Nin and Andrade" . . . and has declared that "in Spain, genuine revolutionists will no doubt be found who will mercilessly expose the betrayal of

Maurín, Nin, Andrade and Co., and lay the foundation for the Spanish Section of the Fourth International."

3. The Trotskyites are not members of the P.O.U.M. The P.O.U.M. has a standing order for the expulsion of all Trotskyites. *La Batalla* [the party organ] has carried a number of articles polemizing against Trotskyism, not in the "merciless", arrogant and insulting tone with which only Russians like Stalin and Trotsky can write of even their best political elements if they do not happen to serve their factional purposes in the party feud in the Soviet Union, but in a factual and theoretical form which both Trotskyites and Stalinites alike have long given up or forgotten.[13]

The Trotskyists inveighed against the POUM for entering the Catalan government, in which Andrés Nin occupied the post of councillor of justice. "Any form of coalition government on the basis of a common program with the bourgeoisie and the reformists is outright treason to the revolutionary program," they declared. "The essential task is the total destruction of the bourgeois state and its substitution by a government of workers, namely, committees or soviets."[14] And M. Casanova, a foreign Trotskyist volunteer in Barcelona, wrote: "The representative of our international organization in Barcelona [Jean Roux] foresaw and explained in August 1936 . . . the tragic consequences for the POUM and the Spanish revolution of the liquidation of the dual power [as a result of] the dissolution of the Central Antifascist Militia Committee. The leaders of the POUM did not listen to us. They preferred the 'practical' route of collaboration with the Generalitat government to the 'sectarian' voice of the Fourth International."[15]

In reply, the POUM argued that its presence in the Catalan government was a transitional step toward complete working-class power and that its slogan had always been and continued to be "a workers' government, committees of workers, peasants and combatants, and a Constituent Assembly."[16] The Trotskyists rejoined that this slogan was inconsistent with the POUM's participation in a government that, shortly after its formation, decreed the dissolution of the workers' committees and their replacement by local councils, giving representation both to middle-class and working-class parties. "Not on a single occasion during the Civil War did the POUM propose the seizure of power by the committees," wrote G. Munis (Manuel Fernández Grandizo), a former activist and factionalist in Nin's Izquierda Comunista and now the leader of the tiny group of Bolshevik Leninists.[17] The Trotskyists also censured the POUM for merging its trade-union organization, the FOUS, the Federación Obrera de Unidad Sindical,[18] with the PSUC-controlled Catalan UGT instead of with the revolutionary CNT, alleging that the POUM's purpose was to avoid friction with the Anarchosyndicalist leaders.[19] The POUM argued that it had made this move in the hope of giving the UGT a "revolutionary injection," thus making the fusion with the CNT more practicable.[20] Andrés Nin, the POUM leader, for his part, claimed that if the FOUS had entered the CNT it would have been only a small minority, whereas in the UGT (a negligible force in Catalonia as compared with the CNT)[21] it hoped to make its opinions prevail.[22] These hopes were quickly disappointed, for the UGT leadership prevented any free expression of opinion by refusing to hold general assemblies and expelled POUM members from prominent positions.[23] These expulsions, alleged *La Batalla*, the party organ, were "demanded for the most part by those petty bourgeois elements in the UGT who before the war had clashed with the revolutionary workers in the chambers of commerce and employers' associations."[24]

The Communists ignored the dissensions between the Trotskyites and the POUM, for they were both equally caustic in their criticisms of the USSR. They both condemned the Soviet government for initially adhering to the nonintervention agreement, and both claimed that the subsequent shipment of arms to Spain was due to Soviet self-interest. "This correction of a mistake," declared *La Batalla*, "is not due to any desire to advance the cause of the Spanish Revolution—Lenin would not have declared himself neutral for a single moment—but to self-preservation. . . . What really interests Stalin is not the fate of the Spanish or world proletariat, but the defense of the Soviet government."[25]

"There are people," declared PSUC secretary Juan Comorera at a public meeting, "who have the effrontery to assert that Russia is only defending her own interests, that she is on our side only because our defeat would mean her defeat." This was not true, he affirmed, because Russia was powerful enough to repel any aggression upon her own soil. "The fact is that the USSR is a workers' state and that the law of a workers' state is not self-interest but solidarity. . . . Our comrades in the USSR understand that our defeat would prolong the martyrdom of our comrades in Germany, Austria, Hungary, and Portugal by many years and would place the liberty of the workers of all of Eastern Europe and possibly all of Western Europe in imminent danger. . . . It is true that the USSR is powerful, but, comrades, the power of the Russian proletariat is not enough. The USSR is far away and between us lie too many miles and too much water. . . . In order to defeat international fascism it is imperative that democratic Europe be on our side."[26]

On 27 August, the POUM protested the execution of Grigorii E. Zinoviev and Lev B. Kamenev and of other old Bolsheviks by Stalin.[27] "The CNT, Socialists and Republicans did not understand the significance of what was happening in Moscow," writes Víctor Alba. "They gave little information and made no comment. The CNT, which should have seen in the trials a warning, treated them as though they were just a family quarrel."[28] The Trotskyists accused the POUM of "minimizing or hiding as far as possible the news about Stalin's trials and assassinations."[29] This was only partially true because, although there was a strong current of opinion in the POUM that feared to exasperate the Communists by denouncing the trials, this fear did not prevail.[30]

The opening of the new Moscow treason trial in January 1937 added fresh acerbity to the press polemics between the POUM and the Communists, when the POUM declared that the accused were innocent. Replied *Frente Rojo*, the Communist organ: "*La Batalla*, the organ of the band of counterrevolutionaries and *provocateurs* who direct the POUM, has at last exposed itself. The occasion for throwing off the mask is the trial in Moscow of the second gang of Trotskyist terrorists, spies, and assassins, accomplices of the Gestapo, who are directed, like the POUM, by Trotsky himself."[31] To this *La Batalla* retorted: "Stalin knows perfectly well that, with the exception of one or two of the accused, the others are not Trotskyists. . . . We also are accused of being Trotskyists. We are not. . . . The defendants in Moscow are also accused of several other things: They are agents of the Gestapo, they are in the service of fascism and foreign espionage. The same is said of us. . . . Fortunately Spain is not Russia, but an attempt is being made to put Spain under Russian tutelage and control, which, of course, we oppose with the utmost vigor. And that is what Stalin and his domestic and foreign bureaucrats do not forgive us. They do not forgive us for raising high the banner of Marx and Lenin, which they have abandoned and betrayed. They do not forgive us for proclaiming the truth about their domestic and foreign politics. They do not forgive us for fighting in Spain for the Socialist revolution, while they try to imprison us within the framework of the bourgeois and parliamentary republic."[32]

During the following months the polemics raged with increasing virulence. On 25 April *Treball*, the PSUC organ, declared: "The Trotskyists . . . know that they are definitely discredited among the masses; they know that the masses now recognize them as the most obvious enemies of the working class; they know that everyone realizes that they are not only assassins—this is proved by the case of Kirov [the Russian Communist leader, whose assassination was officially laid to a Trotskyist conspiracy]—but saboteurs and warmongers. They have seen that the workers reject them, that they spit in their faces, denounce them as the most disgusting of their enemies. Naturally, they dare not show their true face, but instead camouflage and disguise themselves. The Trotskyist Gorkin [Julián Gorkin, international secretary of the POUM, a member of its executive committee, director and principal editorial writer of *La Batalla*][33] uses the same method. But his explanations prove at least one thing: that the Catalan masses flee from Trotskyism as from the plague and that the POUM leaders are anxious to deny what they really are."

From the outset, the POUM had excoriated the Communists and Socialists for supporting the "democratic Republic": the international bourgeoisie, wrote *La Batalla*, was fully aware "that the issue in Spain is one of revolution or counterrevolution, of socialism or fascism. The Socialists and the Communists in their efforts to deceive the republican bourgeoisie at home and abroad only deceive the working class."[34]

To this type of criticism Santiago Carrillo, the secretary of the Communist-controlled Unified Socialist Youth, responded: "There are some who say that . . . we are practicing a deception . . . when we declare that we are defending the democratic Republic. . . . This is not a stratagem to deceive Spanish democratic opinion nor to deceive democratic opinion abroad, . . . because we know that if we should commit the mistake of fighting at this time for the Socialist revolution . . . we should see in our fatherland not only the fascist invaders, but side by side with them the bourgeois democratic governments of the world. . . . [The] Trotskyist elements know full well that if we were to call for social revolution as an immediate goal, we would be playing the game of Franco and Mola, [which] is to represent the legal government as a government of reds, as a government of Communists."[35]

On 18 November 1936, *La Batalla* declared that the leaders of the Communist International did not want a proletarian revolution in Spain. "A new victorious proletarian revolution in Europe, not under the sole auspices of the Third International, would mean the transfer of the center of gravity of the international working-class movement from Moscow to where that revolution was being carried out. For that reason . . . the Stalinist leaders in Spain must liquidate the organizations that do not submit blindly to their discipline. That applies to us as well as to the CNT and FAI. They consider that we are more difficult to destroy in the theoretical field and wish to destroy us first. As for the Anarchists they think they can destroy them afterward."

On 24 November, in a document presented to the CNT councillors, the PSUC proposed the exclusion of the POUM (i.e., of Andrés Nin, the councillor of justice) from the cabinet and the formation of a new government "with plenary powers."[36] The Anarchosyndicalists refused to countenance these proposals. On 8 December, President Companys, without publicly defining his position on the question of the POUM, declared that "a strong government with plenary powers capable of imposing its authority on everyone" was necessary.[37] To this the CNT replied that "a 'strong government' would simply be a dictatorship."[38] The Esquerra organ, *La Humanitat*, hitherto extremely circumspect,[39] ventured to object that the CNT's reaction was "inexplicable." "We cannot see what advantages a 'weak government' could offer in this hour of war and revolution because war and revolution are waged and won exclusively on the basis of iron discipline, of unity and action, . . . which are only feasible with a strong government . . . that imposes its authority inexorably. On everyone. Absolutely everyone."[40]

No headway was made in resolving the differences between the opposing sides, and on 12 December, Premier Tarradellas officially announced that the cabinet was in a state of crisis. That morning, Juan Andrade, a former supporter of Leon Trotsky and regarded by some as the most radical member of the POUM executive,[41] wrote in his "Nota Política Diaria" in *La Batalla*: "The dilemma facing the CNT is whether to decide in favor of the present policy of collaboration, which, in effect, is counterrevolutionary complicity, or in favor of an alliance with the revolutionary Marxist POUM. The issue before the working class is the creation of a Revolutionary Workers' Front, which . . . would block the advance of the counterrevolution and raise the question of proletarian power through committees of workers, peasants, and combatants."[42] The same day, Juan Comorera, PSUC leader and councillor in the outgoing cabinet, publicly demanded the ouster of the POUM, charging that it had been disloyal to the government—its leaders having attacked the government's decrees—and that it had waged an anti-Soviet campaign at a time when the Soviet Union "had placed itself on the side of our people and given us tremendous help." In addition, he demanded the suppression of the CNT-dominated Secretariado de Defensa and the Junta de Seguridad that controlled the revolutionary militia and the patrols, so as to give "plenary powers" to the councillors and to establish "an iron discipline within the government apparatus."[43] There were juntas and committees, he said later, that "govern more than the government itself."[44] On the other hand, the POUM, which had its own patrols and militia, argued that the junta and *secretariado*, in both of which it was represented, were "organs of revolutionary expression" that prevented the state "as presently constituted" from being turned into "a police state against the proletariat."[45] "Can the revolutionary working class in Catalonia," it asked, "allow these levers [of control] to be snatched from it? Not on any account. To agree to that would be to take a very dangerous step backward on the road of the Revolution."[46]

The Anarchosyndicalist leaders at first opposed the removal of the POUM from the government, but not apprehending any threat to their own organization or feeling any sympathy toward the POUM because of its Marxist ideology, its attempts to penetrate the CNT before the war,[47] and its frequent censure of the collectivizing ardor that had disaffected a large segment of the urban and rural middle classes,[48] they finally acquiesced in its exclusion in mid-December. In exchange, the PSUC dropped its demand for the suppression of the junta and the *secretariado* and agreed to give the portfolio of defense to the CNT in return for the portfolio of justice held by the POUM. It was clear from the manner in which the crisis was resolved that the PSUC's immediate concern had been the exclusion of the POUM from the government. Not so clear at the time, however, was the role of the Soviet consul general, Vladimir A. Antonov-Ovseenko, who, according to Miguel Serra Pàmies, the former PSUC leader and intimate of Juan Comorera, went to President Companys in December "to insist that the POUM not be allowed to remain in the government." "He used every argument," Serra Pàmies personally informed me some years later. "Soviet arms, the foreign situation, raw materials [for Spanish industry], and food shipments."[49]

Whether the CNT also received this warning either from Companys or directly from Antonov-Ovseenko cannot be said with certainty, but it is significant that Rudolf Rocker, the famous German Anarchist, who was in close touch with the CNT-FAI leaders, wrote in 1938 that the "Soviet ambassador" [*sic*] had threatened to deny further military aid unless the POUM was ousted.[50] At all events, it was apparent that the CNT's opposition to the removal of the POUM had begun to weaken on 13 December, when *Solidaridad Obrera* simply dismissed the crisis as a product of the rivalry between the two Marxist parties. To this, Juan Andrade rejoined that it was not just a conflict between two organizations. What was at stake, he warned, was "the whole future course of the revolution."[51]

The POUM was dismayed over its exclusion from the cabinet but decided to put a bold face on matters. "IT IS NOT POSSIBLE TO GOVERN WITHOUT THE POUM

AND STILL LESS AGAINST IT," declared *La Batalla* on 17 December in banner headlines. The POUM, it asserted, had emerged from the crisis clearly strengthened. "It has become the only genuine opposition force in Catalonia. Its revolutionary political positions are stronger than ever and thanks to them it will win over the working class."

Despite its declared optimism, the POUM was apprehensive. "Now that the [PSUC] has obtained its immediate goal, does anyone believe that it will renounce its aims? . . . With our elimination it has won its preliminary objective. For the moment it does not feel strong enough to go any further."[52]

To help the CNT to rationalize its sacrifice of the POUM, the PSUC agreed to withdraw officially from the cabinet. But this was only a nominal concession, for the PSUC representatives, Comorera, Valdés, and Vidiella simply appeared in the new government with UGT labels, although they were well-known members of the PSUC executive and within a few weeks were to become members of the central committee of the Spanish Communist party.[53]

The composition of the new government formed on 16 December 1936 was as follows:

José Tarradellas	ERC	First Councillor (Premier) and Councillor of Finance
Antonio María Sbert	ERC	Culture
Artemio Aiguadé	ERC	Internal Security
José Calvet	Unió de Rabassaires	Agriculture
Juan Comorera	UGT [PSUC]	Supplies
Miguel Valdés	UGT [PSUC]	Labor and Public Works
Rafael Vidiella	UGT [PSUC]	Justice
Francisco Isgleas	CNT	Defense
Diego Abad de Santillán	CNT	Economy[54]
Juan José Doménech	CNT	Public Services
Pedro Herrera	CNT	Health and Public Assistance

Solidaridad Obrera hailed what appeared to be the preponderant trade-union character of the new government as a victory for its syndical ideas and a defeat for the political parties as represented by the PSUC and the POUM. "With this solution of the crisis," it continued, "we feel that no one has cause for complaint or reproach of any kind. The two antagonists, the POUM and the PSUC, whose conflict has brought us to our present pass, have been excluded from the council of the Generalitat. Both are represented in the UGT . . . ; both stem from the same ideological branch, although slight differences of attitude and tactics separate them. In our opinion, neither has the right to cry out in protest."[55] The POUM was angry over this simplistic explanation of the crisis. "Our elimination has been carried out," said Juan Andrade, "not because of the casuistic claim that we are represented in the UGT, but because we hold intransigently revolutionary positions. . . . Anarchosyndicalism has always been guilty of paying more attention to form than to content. . . . The CNT leadership has opted for a course that is extremely dangerous. . . . It has preferred to yield to the antirevolutionary tendencies that desire our elimination . . . rather than maintain the uncompromising revolutionary line of the rank and file."[56]

The POUM did not disguise its belief that it had been forced out of the government by Soviet pressure. Jordi Arquer, the chief political commissar of the POUM militia, stated: "We have been defeated MOMENTARILY not by the PSUC-UGT but by a power that lies behind these organizations and is responsible for the maneuver raising before those who oppose its will the specter of abandoning us and leaving us without arms and munitions in face of the criminal hordes of Franco."[57] And *La Batalla* affirmed that there was a well-thought-out plan, imported from abroad, to liquidate the POUM. The plan, it said, comprised three stages: (1) the preparation of the political and psychological atmosphere, (2) the removal of the party from the Generalitat government in order to isolate it politically, and (3) the application of measures to annihilate it physically. "We are not afraid of fighting," it threatened. "We are not provoking anyone, but we are ready to respond with dignity to all provocations."[58]

Finally, Andrés Nin, the party leader, declared at a public meeting: "By using certain asiatic methods, it is hoped to curb the revolution and to sweep aside the CNT and the POUM. No one should harbor any illusions. Our party cannot be destroyed, because it is the very flesh and blood of the working class. . . . Our proletariat will not be restrained. It does not intend to fall under the tutelage of anyone. It is advancing unfalteringly and resolutely toward the Socialist revolution, and no obstacles, however great, will stop it."[59]

41

Moving toward Open Warfare in Catalonia

A notable consequence of the December crisis was the weakening of the CNT's position in the government. The POUM, the CNT's only possible ally, was alarmed at the passivity with which the Anarchosyndicalists had accepted its expulsion and at their failure to perceive that the victory of the PSUC represented an obvious menace to themselves. Not surprisingly, the POUM organ, *La Batalla*, reprinted, as proof of the growing danger, the following excerpt from a news release by the Transocean Agency, dated Moscow, 17 December 1936, which appeared in the Mexican newspaper *Universal Gráfico*: "The Soviet press expresses the hope that the cleaning up of the Spanish Anarchists and Trotskyists in Catalonia will be carried out with the same energy as in the USSR."[1] Although the Soviet consulate general in Barcelona denounced the statement as false—and indeed no such statement ever appeared either in *Izvestiia* or *Pravda*[2]—it undoubtedly served to impress upon the CNT the growing peril to itself.

Apart from the deterioration of the CNT's position in the government, another important consequence of the December crisis was the growth in self-confidence and pugnacity of the leaders of the ERC, the largest of the middle-class Republican parties in Catalonia. Their renewed self-assurance prompted *La Batalla* to declare disdainfully on 28 January: "For five months the Republicans remained subdued. They raised the clenched fist and listened solemnly to the 'International.' At times they appeared more revolutionary than the true revolutionaries. . . . [But] now the bourgeois Republicans are beginning to feel strong again."

Although the leaders of the ERC refrained from publicly gloating over the ouster of the POUM, there can be little doubt that they perceived in its removal a significant setback for the entire revolutionary movement. This was evident at a public meeting of their party held on 28 December 1936. So aggressive were their speeches, so suffused with veiled and even open threats to the future of the Revolution,[3] that President Luis Companys, who still believed that the collaboration of the CNT and FAI in the cabinet was essential if the libertarian movement were to be "domesticated" and gradually divested of its armed power, felt impelled to inject a note of caution. While criticizing the "confused network of committees and juntas," urging the centralization of all administrative authority in the hands of the government, and warning that "a revolution that does not have a disciplined, energetic, and responsible government is condemned to failure," he offered the following pacifier to the CNT and FAI: "Some republicans believe, even dream, that in the future a political and social system will be established equal to or similar to the one that existed before 19 July. This simply demonstrates their blindness and lack of loyalty because this is not possible. Nor would it be right or legitimate. I have said and I say it again that the time has come for political power to pass into the hands of the working classes. For this reason they should be the most interested in watching over the purity, the honor, the effectiveness, and wisdom of the work of government."[4] These words seemed to placate the libertarian leaders, who firmly believed in Companys's early commitment to the Revolution. Said *Solidaridad Obrera*: "Luis Companys is in agreement at the present time with the proletarian organizations . . . especially with the CNT, and reveals a political vision that is more perceptive, more sincere, and more loyal than that of some of his correligionists."[5]

But no amount of subtle statecraft or artful treatment of the CNT and FAI by President Companys or Premier José Tarradellas, the main architect of the policy of conciliation, could appease the more impatient members of the middle and lower middle classes, who were faced with immediate or gradual economic ruin. They longed for a rapid end to Anarchist power and saw in the dynamic leadership and aggressive policies of the PSUC the only hope of salvaging some of their possessions from the wreckage of the Revolution. No wonder that they continued to flock to the rival party in growing numbers. Tarradellas, on the other hand, undoubtedly believed, as one admirer capsulized his thinking, that "the time of the Esquerra would come when Anarchosyndicalism, through political immaturity, would collapse of its own accord" and that it was far wiser, at least for the time being, to pursue a policy of accommodation with its leaders than to force them into intransigent positions.[6]

For this reason, Tarradellas, while urging the centralization of all administrative authority in the Generalitat government and the enforcement of the government's decrees, frequently defended the CNT and FAI from Communist attack. On one occasion, for example, when an armed clash threatened to erupt in the town of Granollers, he endeavored to prevent the dispatch of government reinforcements.[7] On another, he sided with the CNT when the PSUC criticized the Anarchist-dominated commission of war industries, over which he presided,[8] and, on yet another, he vigorously defended the CNT councillor of defense, Francisco Isgleas, and his undersecretary, Juan Manuel Molina, against Communist charges of procrastination in implementing the government's decrees.[9] For his frequent defense of the libertarians, Tarradellas received their glowing praise.[10] Not surprisingly, he soon found himself at odds with the more truculent leaders of his party, such as Artemio Aiguadé, the councillor of internal security, who favored the fearless audacity and head-on tactics of the PSUC. "[I] knew," Tarradellas averred some years later, "that important people in the Esquerra were colluding to some degree with the Communists in order to put an end to the problem of the CNT, that there were people who believed that the matter could be resolved in one afternoon and that nothing would happen. I never held that view. It was not loyal, not by any means."[11]

His cautious policy, backed initially by Companys and by some of the other leaders of the Esquerra and Acció Republicana, a small Catalan middle-class party, irked the PSUC, but not until after the war did the party criticize the premier openly. "The bourgeois leaders," ran a PSUC document, specifically referring to Tarradellas, "collaborated directly and indirectly with the counter-revolutionary policy of Anarchism in the secret hope of precipitating its ideological collapse and then taking into their hands the political and economic power of the [region]."[12]

To the dismay of many of the Esquerra leaders, the PSUC was able to exploit Tarradellas's prudent tactics to attract to itself not only the more restless segment of the urban middle classes but also large numbers of sharecroppers and tenant farmers of the Unió de Rabassaires and adherents of the CADCI, the Centre Autonomista de Dependents del Comerç i de la Industria (union of office workers and retail clerks), both of which organizations had been inviolable preserves of the Esquerra before the outbreak of the Civil War.[13] It has now been revealed in the biography of PSUC secretary Juan Comorera, published in 1984, that José Calvet, the president of the Unió de Rabassaires and councillor of agriculture in every wartime cabinet of the Generalitat, not only "collaborated closely with Comorera" but was an active member of the PSUC.[14] Hence, the real strength of the PSUC in the various Catalan administrations was greater than appeared from their official composition.

No sooner had the PSUC achieved its goal during the cabinet reshuffle in December than it turned its attention to the committees that had assumed control of the wholesale food trades at the outset of the Revolution. In an attempt to weaken the power of the CNT in this vital area and to reestablish freedom of trade, Juan Comorera, the PSUC secretary and councillor of supplies in the new cabinet, decreed the dissolution of the committees. These committees, he alleged, shortly before issuing his decree, had replaced the middlemen, "to the prejudice of society," and were responsible for the enormous increase in the cost of food.[15] Although the Anarchosyndicalists argued that the committees prevented the rich from speculating at the expense of the workers, it is clear from the CNT and POUM press that the committees "in the name of 'Liberty and the Revolution'" were also guilty of "a thousand and one abuses"[16] and "in most cases perpetuate the vices of the bosses and speculate just like them."[17] Nevertheless, the real point at issue was not so much the question of the abuses as the economic power of the committees. The policy of the PSUC, affirmed POUM secretary Andrés Nin, was aimed at "the reestablishment of freedom of trade and the destruction of the entire revolutionary work of Comrade Doménech, the former [CNT] councillor of supplies, against the speculators."[18]

But it was a far cry from the publication of Comorera's decree to its enforcement as long as the armed power of the revolutionaries remained intact. To undermine their position, the PSUC applied unremitting pressure after the December crisis to end the duality of police power in the region. This was divided, as we have seen, between the patrols, on the one hand, under the authority of the CNT-dominated Junta de Seguridad, and the Assault and National Republican guards, on the other, under the control of the Esquerra councillor of internal security, Artemio Aiguadé. One important by-product of the crisis was the appointment by the pro-Communist Aiguadé[19] of Eusebio Rodríguez Salas, a PSUC member, as *comisario general de orden público*, or police commissioner, in place of the less aggressive, yet anarchophobic, Martí Rouret, a member of the Esquerra. Next to Comorera, Rodríguez Salas soon became the libertarians' principal object of execration. A former Anarchist, he had long before the war abjured his libertarian creed, joined Maurín's Bloque Obrero y Campesino, and finally allied himself with the small Catalan Communist party, bringing to the PSUC the fearlessness and daring that had characterized his activity as an Anarchist.[20]

Shortly after the December crisis, the Catalan UGT, which represented the PSUC in the government,[21] proposed that all the forces of public order—patrols as well as Assault and National Republican guards—be dissolved and their members incorporated into a single internal security corps.[22] The CNT rejected the proposal. "The patrols should not only be maintained; they should be increased," said *Solidaridad Obrera*. "All those attacks directed against them are directed at the very heart of our revolution."[23] And the executive committee of the POUM declared: "The proposal must not be approved. To approve it would be equivalent to delivering ourselves bound hand and foot to the bourgeoisie and assisting in the creation of armed forces designed to crush us. PUBLIC ORDER MUST REMAIN IN THE HANDS OF THE WORKING CLASS. To achieve this a security corps must be created that is based on the patrols. . . . Only in this way will revolutionary order be guaranteed."[24] Nevertheless, with the backing of the UGT-PSUC and Esquerra councillors, the government approved a series of decrees providing for the dissolution of the various forces of public order, including the revolutionary Workers' and Soldiers' Councils, and their reorganization into a single internal security corps, in which, significantly, the positions of command were to be held by the officers of the dissolved Assault and National Republican guards.[25]

As the libertarian movement—whose representatives in the government had approved some of the provisions or had been outvoted on others[26] but had nonetheless observed the principle of cabinet solidarity—did not denounce the decrees, the POUM declared: "If other organizations have not perceived clearly the trend of events and have not reacted as the situation demands, they will make themselves responsible before history. . . . The fate of the Revolution is in the balance. That is what these organizations that express their loyalty to the Revolution day by day do not appear to understand. . . . Their policy, which tends to maintain a unity that in no way benefits the Revolution, profits only reformism. . . . Our party has only one mission with regard to these decrees: to denounce them publicly and tirelessly, to work unremittingly and indefatigably for their abrogation, and to see that the working class imposes its own order and its own police forces."[27]

To this attack *Solidaridad Obrera* responded: "We state frankly in plain language and without beating about the bush that the decree relating to public order does not satisfy us. Our representatives in the council of the Generalitat have done the impossible, trying to polish it by removing all those features of a reactionary character. They have only partially succeeded. Although, as a disciplined organization, we respect the legislation, this does not mean that we renounce our efforts to substitute it for a new legal instrument reflecting more closely the true revolutionary political situation in our region. . . . We regard the creation of that single security corps, [which is] completely alien to the struggles and aspirations of the working people, as a mistake."[28]

During the next few days, open and furtive agitation against the decrees reached such intensity that, on 16 March, the regional committee of the CNT, to assuage the fears of the rank and file, announced that the government had agreed to postpone discussion of the decrees.[29] This confounded Tarradellas. There was "certainly some misunderstanding," he said, "as the decrees in question, which were undoubtedly well received by public opinion, were approved by the government and published in the *Diari Oficial* on 4 March." What had actually happened, he explained, was that the government had agreed to postpone the appointments to the key positions in the new corps.[30] This was true. In fact, because of the agitation, the appointments, which were to have been confined mainly to members of the Assault and National Republican guards, were never made, and the legislation died on the pages of the *Diari Oficial*, leaving the duality of police powers in the region unchanged.

Meanwhile, the PSUC was agitating for the implementation of other measures. "We have said repeatedly that without a regular army, without a single command, without discipline and without revolutionary order, there is no possibility of victory," declared the party's central committee.[31] Although the Catalan government had approved the mobilization of the 1934–35 classes in October,[32] the measure had remained unheeded, for the CNT held that it would be "very childish to hand over our forces to the absolute control of the government" and that its members should be drafted only by the CNT for service in libertarian units.[33] Even after the CNT took over the defense council in December, the Anarchosyndicalists continued to oppose the draft and strove to maintain the integrity and homogeneous character of their armed forces under the control of their own revolutionary leaders. Thus, while the PSUC pressed for the fusion of the militia into a regular army "in the service of the republican government,"[34] the CNT urged that the militia be organized into an army "in the service of the Revolution"[35] and that all positions of command from the war ministry down should be "CONTROLLED RIGIDLY BY THE REVOLUTIONARY TRADE-UNION ORGANIZATIONS."[36] There, in a nutshell, lay the irreconcilable conflict between the opposing sides.

In this dispute, the position of the POUM, which had its own militia forces, was clear: "The only guarantee that the working class can have as to the fate of the Revolution is its own army. And the army of the working class can be no other than . . . an army recruited from the militia. . . . It is absolutely necessary that control be maintained by the revolutionary organizations. . . . In short, our party declares itself resolutely in favor of a regular army, but of a regular army that is the living expression of the Revolution."[37]

Intensifying its agitation for a regular army under government control, the PSUC set up a Committee for the Popular Army comprising all parties and organizations with the exception of the CNT, FAI, and POUM. On 27 February, the committee published proposals for the immediate transformation of the militia into units of the regular army, for the mobilization of the 1934–35 classes, for the publication of their induction centers, for the dissolution of all military committees not possessing official government status, and for the appointment of political commissars "by the competent authorities" to all units of the Popular Army.[38]

On 28 February, the committee held an impressive demonstration and a military parade through the streets of Barcelona. To the CNT, this show of power was a grave challenge. On the ground that the committee usurped his authority, the CNT defense councillor Francisco Isgleas threatened to resign. To avert a cabinet crisis, the Esquerra, prompted by the conciliatory Tarradellas, urged that the activities of the committee be suspended despite "every good intention," inasmuch as they might constitute a "usurpation of functions and initiatives properly belonging to the Generalitat council."[39] A compromise was reached: the Committee for the Popular Army was officially constituted as an auxiliary body of the defense council, with Isgleas as vice-president and Companys as president.[40] This was nonetheless a victory for the PSUC. Through the machinery of the committee, now recognized as an official body, it was able to increase its agitation and to exert even greater pressure on the defense councillor. Mirroring the consternation of the libertarian movement, *Tierra y Libertad*, the leading mouthpiece of the FAI, declared that behind the PSUC's campaign for a regular army there lay "a policy of aggression against Anarchism."[41]

Simultaneously, Isgleas was under mounting pressure from the central government, which had long opposed the independence of the Catalan militia on the neighboring Aragon front and the military independence acquired by Catalonia as a result of the Revolution. But not until the beginning of March did the Generalitat government, hungry for arms and funds, agree to submit to Valencia's military decrees and to subordinate the Catalan militia to the war ministry.[42] As a result, on 18 March, Isgleas—who, with Tarradellas, had negotiated the financial and military accords on behalf of the Catalan government—was compelled to set firm dates for the call-up not only of the 1934–35 classes but also for the 1932–33 conscripts.[43]

On 23 March, *La Batalla* published the following article by Enrique Adroher (Gironella), the propaganda secretary of the POUM and delegate on the CNT-controlled defense council headed by Isgleas, denouncing Valencia's military policy toward Catalonia:

Valencia categorically refused economic help to Catalonia so as to force us to capitulate militarily. Valencia refused arms and ammunition for the Aragon front in order to prevent our proletarian forces from being victorious[44] and stimulating the revolutionary will of the Spanish workers. . . . While the Catalan Generalitat was obliged to beg for money from the central government to pay ten pesetas to the militiamen after one and a half to two months delay, Valencia bought over the officers, promoted them regularly and paid their salaries promptly. . . . From now on all the expenses of the Catalan army will be met by Valencia, including those of the military commands, of the People's School of War, and of military operations. Catalonia has lost her military independence. The Catalan proletariat has lost its army. . . . How can those who call themselves nationalists and even separatists [a reference to the Esquerra autonomists and the separatists of the small Estat Català party] face the Catalan people? How can the CNT councillors face their comrades fighting on the battlefields of Aragon? How can they all justify this shameful capitulation to the central government. . . . The attitude of the Catalan Left Republicans and of the PSUC reformists is understandable and logical. That they should prefer a thousand times more to see the army in the hands of the Valencia government than in the hands of the revolutionary Catalan proletariat is natural. But the capitulation of the CNT councillors is incomprehensible. It is incredible that the Anarchist comrades, who would rather allow themselves to be killed than permit a revolver to be taken away from them, should quietly agree to surrender the army, which, in the last analysis, is the real weapon of the working class. We have handed over to Valencia, to the partisans of the democratic republic, to the partisans of the strangulation of the revolution, the army of our social emancipation.[45]

Not all the Anarchists had "quietly" submitted to the demands of Valencia, as the POUM article stated; for early in March—as in the case of the Iron Column already discussed in this volume—nearly one thousand militiamen stationed in Gelsa on the Aragon front left in protest against the militarization decrees, fearing that these measures would transform the militia into an instrument of the state under the rigid control of the government. In Barcelona, they set up The Friends of Durruti (Los Amigos de Durruti)—named after the famous Anarchist, Buenaventura Durruti, killed in November on the Madrid front—to combat the "counterrevolutionary" policy of the leadership of the CNT and FAI. Officially constituted in March 1937 with Félix Martínez and Jaime Balius (the latter, director or editor-in-chief at the time of the CNT newspaper *La Noche*) as secretary and vice-secretary, respectively,[46] the organization increased its membership, according to Balius, to between four thousand and five thousand by the beginning of May.[47] None of its adherents, Balius affirmed, belonged to the Bolshevik Leninists, despite numerous claims to the contrary—for example, by Frank Jellinek, the *Manchester Guardian* correspondent in Spain, who alleged, as did the Communists, that the organization was "penetrated and controlled" by Trotskyists.[48] However, G. Munis (Manuel Fernández Grandizo), the leader of the minuscule group of Spanish Bolshevik Leninists, acknowledges a comradely relationship: "Not only did we work fraternally with the workers of the Friends of Durruti, but they helped us in the sale and distribution of our newspaper."[49]

Whether the withdrawal from the front of so large a group of militiamen had any effect on the Anarchosyndicalist leadership cannot be said with certainty, but it is noteworthy that only a day after the first draftees were due to present themselves at their induction centers, in compliance with the military decrees, the CNT councillors, led by Francisco Isgleas, walked out of the Generalitat government, provoking a cabinet crisis.[50]

The PSUC and CNT were now deadlocked over every crucial issue. The libertarian movement had tried to protect the independence of its armed forces by temporizing or by feigning acceptance of the government's decrees; but the pretense could not be continued, and an open split in the cabinet was inevitable. As a condition for resolving the crisis, the libertarians demanded that the legislation on public order "undergo such a fundamental change that only the title remain" and that the defense council should be authorized to prevent "by every means at its disposal military parades and demonstrations and whatever prejudices or undermines revolutionary morale and the will to fight."[51] The PSUC, on the other hand, declared that it had not provoked the crisis and had done everything possible to avoid it. "A government must be formed that will not allow any segment or group constantly to obstruct [its] work in favor of the war. A government must be formed that will honor its commitments and implement the decrees that have been approved unanimously but have not yet been put into effect."[52] Furthermore, it insisted that the Anarchosyndicalists sign a pledge that the military and public order decrees approved by the previous government would be executed "without modification" and that all the measures of the new government would be fulfilled.[53] But the CNT was not about to set its signature to any document that might later be used against it and that, in its opinion, "ran counter not only to the ideological principles that inspire our organization but to the very essence of the Revolution and to the conquests achieved by the working masses since 19 July."[54]

The crisis was now entering its second week with no solution in prospect. On 3 April, President Companys put together, as a last resort, a makeshift cabinet comprising six councillors:

José Tarradellas	ERC	First Councillor (Premier) and Councillor of Finance and Education
Artemio Aiguadé	ERC	Internal Security
Juan Comorera	PSUC	Public Works, Labor, and Justice

José Calvet	Unió de Rabassaires	Agriculture and Supplies
Francisco Isgleas	CNT	Defense
Juan J. Doménech	CNT	Economy, Public Services, and Health

No one regarded the new government as anything but a stopgap, least of all Companys, who, expressing his growing impatience with the CNT at the outset of the crisis, had called for a "government that can govern and can impose its will on those who obstruct its work."[55]

It was now becoming increasingly apparent that Companys was losing sympathy with the prudent tactics of Tarradellas, who hoped to maintain his policy of accommodation with the CNT until such time as it might nullify itself by its ideological contradictions and political naïveté. As Miquel Caminal, a Comorera admirer and a keen expositor of the Catalan political drama, observes, such important men in the Esquerra as Companys and Aiguadé were "closer to the positions of Comorera than to those of Tarradellas." While Tarradellas, he affirms, was ready to make formal but not substantive concessions to the CNT in the belief that an open breach of governmental unity would be fraught with "unforeseeable consequences," Comorera, on the other hand, believed that formal collaboration without substance would simply diminish the authority of the government and would have "even more dramatic consequences." The divergence of opinion, he adds, revolved around the question of "unity or authority."[56] Obviously, the PSUC's answer was "authority."

On 7 April, the PSUC and UGT launched a "Victory Plan" for Catalonia. "The whole problem at the present time," ran the preamble, "hinges on the question of power, on the question of authority. Without authority there can be no army. Without authority there can be no war industry. . . . Without authority there can be no victory." Its main points were: (1) the rapid creation of a regular Popular Army of Catalonia as an integral part of the Republican army, (2) immediate organization of five divisions on the basis of the 1932–36 classes, (3) nationalization of the basic war industries and the militarization of transport, (4) rapid creation of the single internal security corps in compliance with the decrees approved by the previous government of Catalonia, and (5) concentration of all arms in the hands of the government.[57]

The entire plan was in conflict with the revolutionary aims of the CNT. "We have already made too many [concessions]," warned *Solidaridad Obrera*, "and believe that the time has come to turn off the spigot."[58]

Andrés Nin, the POUM leader, welcomed this stand: "On 19 July the working class had power in its hands. . . . It allowed the opportunity to pass. . . . The proletariat still holds in its hands important positions. . . . If today we do not take advantage of the situation to take power peacefully, tomorrow we shall have to resort to a violent struggle to put an end to the bourgeoisie and the reformists. . . . With great anxiety we have watched the vacillations and doubts of the

CNT leadership. Too many concessions have been made to the counterrevolution. . . . For this reason we welcome with pleasure the CNT's present stand. . . . The CNT has declared: 'Here we stop! Not a single step backward!' "[59]

On 10 April, *Tierra y Libertad*, the FAI organ, reflecting the mood of the more radical spirits, declared: "CRUSH THE COUNTERREVOLUTION, COMRADES! That is your mandate. Our duty is to make it a reality." Despite this mandate, the CNT leaders continued their negotiations with the PSUC and Esquerra representatives in the Generalitat Palace in search of a modus vivendi that might stave off open warfare between the opposing camps. But the streets outside seemed paved with dynamite as sporadic clashes proliferated and the danger of civil war loomed more ominously with every passing hour. "No one could be sure of his physical safety," writes Miquel Caminal in his biography of Juan Comorera, "and the best proof of this were the spectacular bodyguards that always escorted some political leaders. Because of his political activity, Comorera held many lottery tickets and his official car was always accompanied by another with men armed to the teeth."[60]

On 16 April, President Companys set up another stopgap government to tide things over. A few weeks later he recorded:

> For a long time the councillor of [internal] security Aiguadé had been demanding additional forces [from the central government]; those of the Generalitat were insufficient [to meet the needs of the situation]: Only two thousand armed assault guards, six hundred others unarmed, and few national guards. The policy of unity and tact had to go hand in hand with an effort to increase the authority of the government by taking action in specific cases involving so-called uncontrolled [i.e., CNT-FAI] groups and coercive measures directed against the government's orders. This I had been demanding with insistence not only because of the pressure of public opinion, but also because of the very demands of the Ministry of the Interior and other authorities of Madrid, and the comments in the foreign press regarding the frontier, etc., etc. The complexity of the situation made reinforcements necessary, because even with the utmost tact it was anticipated that a clash might occur. The government of the Generalitat was exhausting its resources for resolving the situation and public opinion was pressing. The power of the government was growing constantly, but the majority of the people in Catalonia were irritated to such a degree that there was a danger that the government might lost public confidence and that the forces of public order in the service of the Generalitat might become demoralized.[61]

The new cabinet set up by Companys on 16 April possessed the same political composition as the one formed on 16 December, although with a few minor changes:

José Tarradellas	ERC	First Councillor (Premier) and Councillor of Finance

Antonio María Sbert	ERC	Culture
Artemio Aiguadé	ERC	Internal Security
José Calvet	Unió de Rabassaires	Agriculture
José Miret	UGT [PSUC]	Supplies
Rafael Vidiella	UGT [PSUC]	Labor and Public Works
Juan Comorera	UGT [PSUC]	Justice
Francisco Isgleas	CNT	Defense
Andrés Capdevila	CNT	Economy
Juan Doménech	CNT	Public Services
Aurelio Fernández	CNT	Health and Public Assistance

Like the makeshift cabinet formed on 3 April, the new government was stillborn. Its members could not agree on a common program, and the festering problems of military and police control remained in all their intractable complexity.

The POUM characterized the patched-up crisis as a mockery—"a mockery that is all the more intolerable because three weeks have passed—exactly three weeks—and then things are left exactly as they were." Again it criticized the CNT. "The comrades of the National Confederation of Labor did not know what attitude to adopt [at the outset of the war] toward the problem of power. . . . [Instead] of urging the working class to seize power completely, they preferred to regard it as a simple question of collaboration. . . . We are certain that the mass of CNT workers will view the solution of the present crisis with the same disfavor as we do. . . . [This] solution is no solution . . . because it has resolved nothing. . . . The problems of the Revolution . . . will be posed again in the future sooner than many believe. . . . The reformists will not abandon their aims. If the comrades of the CNT do not realize this, so much the worse for them and so much the worse for all of us. Because what is at stake is not the future of this or that organization, but the future of the Revolution."[62]

The next day the Barcelona committee of the POUM declared: "The government that has just been formed is an attempt to establish a truce, no matter how brief, in the struggle between the Revolution and the counterrevolution. The small bourgeoisie and the reformists will take advantage of this breathing spell that has been given them to gain and consolidate new positions. The working class has the historic duty to prepare itself for a definitive solution [of the crisis] . . . by instituting a Workers' and Peasants' Government."[63]

Although the CNT leadership had agreed to paper over the crisis, the real mood of the libertarian movement was reflected in its press. "The CNT," said *Solidaridad Obrera* on 17 April, "accepts the solution of the conflict on the understanding that the course followed by the previous council has been cut short and with the conviction that this course will be substituted by a just policy that respects and consolidates the revolutionary gains of the proletariat." "[The CNT]," ran another article in the same issue, "has on many occasions appeared flexible and accommodating in the extreme. But beware! Let no one mistake its meaning or think that the Spanish Anarchists will allow themselves to be trampled underfoot with impunity by their so-called comrades!"

The same day, *Ruta*, the organ of the FIJL, the Libertarian Youth, declared: "[The counterrevolution] is attempting to take possession of the state apparatus. Yesterday it asked for a large, single security corps. . . . Today it proposes a regular army devoid of revolutionary content. What is the aim of these rascally maneuvers? . . . To be able to rely on forces that will serve it without question, so that tomorrow it can drown the social gains of the proletariat in blood. How can this plan be frustrated? . . . By forging the military organization of the Revolution. . . . To [the young men in the rear] we make an ardent appeal: FORM THE CADRES OF THE REVOLUTIONARY YOUTH BATTALIONS!"

And another article in the same issue threatened: "The time has come to make the counterrevolution retreat. The FAI and the Libertarian Youth . . . have stated that . . . they will have to fight to put an end to those people who are incapable of being loyal and, even less, of feeling the cause of antifascism and the Revolution to the full. . . . [The] way to prevent the sacrifices of our comrades from being reduced to naught is . . . to create an army that will guarantee victory in the war and the Revolution and to remove from the public life of Catalonia, Comorera, Aiguadé, Rodríguez Salas, etc." And, finally, on the same day, *Tierra y Libertad* declared in banner headlines: "FOR CERTAIN POLITICAL PARTIES THE ESSENTIAL THING IS NOT THE DESTRUCTION OF FASCISM. WHAT OBSESSES THEM IS THE ANARCHIST MOVEMENT. WHAT CONSUMES THEIR BEST ENERGIES IS THEIR CAMPAIGN AGAINST THE CNT AND FAI. . . . IF THEY WANT TO REPEAT IN SPAIN WHAT THEY HAVE DONE IN OTHER COUNTRIES, THEY WILL FIND US ON A WAR FOOTING."

Meanwhile, the PSUC intensified its campaign for the integration of the Catalan militia columns on the Aragon front into the Popular Army and for the creation of a single internal security corps under the control of the Catalan government, but without success. It is true that certain structural changes, prompted by the military accords with Valencia, did in fact take place: the three Anarchosyndicalist units, Jubert, Durruti, and Ascaso, became the Twenty-fifth, Twenty-sixth, and Twenty-eighth divisions, respectively; the Barrio-Trueba Column of the PSUC, the Twenty-seventh; the POUM Column, the Twenty-ninth; and the Maciá-Companys Column of the Esquerra, the Thirtieth; but they all remained under the control of their respective organizations. As for the decrees on public order, they were consigned to all intents and purposes to the waste basket.[64]

In the midst of the heightening tension came an abortive attempt, on 24 April, on the life of the Communist police commissioner, Rodríguez Salas.[65] Then came the murder the next day of Roldán Cortada, leader and secretary to Rafael Vidiella, the PSUC councillor of labor and public works. A shiver of apprehension passed through the region. The assassination, which Rodríguez Salas attributed to "uncontrollables"[66]—a term now commonly used to characterize all refractory elements of the CNT, FAI, and FIJL (the Libertarian Youth) who were opposed to government collaboration and sought the adherence of the libertarian movement to its antistatist principles—added fresh heat to the simmering conflict. "AN END TO IMPUNITY!" cried *La Humanitat*, the Esquerra organ. "Public order must be organized rapidly and under the command of a single person, who must put an end, rapidly and relentlessly, to [these] criminal deeds that occur all too frequently. No longer can we permit groups of individuals who have been given the name of uncontrollables to impose by force their own will and their own law upon the majority of citizens."[67] "Isn't it a disgrace," asked the *Diari de Barcelona*, the mouthpiece of the separatist Estat Català, a small but militant middle-class nationalist party, "that there are still uncontrollables and *agents provocateurs*? . . . And the decrees on public order approved some time ago by the Generalitat, why have they not been implemented? What purpose do the authorities serve?"[68]

And a joint manifesto issued by the PSUC and UGT demanded: "An end to the assassination of militant workers! An end to provocations against antifascist and proletarian unity! War against *agents provocateurs* in the pay of national and international fascism! The people demand justice and are prepared to impose it at all costs."[69]

On 27 April, the day of Cortada's funeral, the PSUC organized a giant procession. "[It] was not merely a funeral; it was a plebiscite," said *Treball*, the party organ. "Thousands upon thousands of workers, of antifascists, marched through the streets of Barcelona . . . united fraternally in sorrow, but also in protest. . . . The grandiose funeral has demonstrated that the Catalan people are resolved to put an end to the murderers and nests of bandits who want to frustrate our victory over fascism. A plebiscite has been held. And the figures of the plebiscite tell us that what we have experienced up to now we cannot tolerate a day longer; that the antifascist masses must unite . . . against the enemy within, against those we call uncontrollables."[70]

While the CNT protested that it was "repugnant" to "make political capital out of a painful event that has cost the life of an antifascist comrade,"[71] the POUM declared that the funeral was a pretext for "a counterrevolutionary demonstration." "Through the unions large numbers of Catalan workers were mobilized . . . [moved by] sympathy for the death of a militant worker fallen in the struggle in the rear. . . . The essential political aim of demonstrations like that of yesterday is to create among the reactionary small bourgeoisie and among the most backward layers of the working class a POGROM atmosphere against the revolutionary vanguard of the Catalan proletariat: CNT, FAI, and POUM. A psychological climate is being created preparatory to actions of greater magnitude."[72]

Fast on the heels of Roldán Cortada's assassination came the slaying of Antonio Martín, the Anarchist president of the revolutionary committee in the border town of Puigcerdá, during an encounter with Assault and National Republican guards (Guardia Nacional Republicana, formerly the Civil Guard) in the neighboring village of Bellver.[73] Shortly thereafter truckloads of carabineers—a corps composed of customs and excise officials and guards—dispatched from Valencia by finance minister Juan Negrín, began seizing the frontier posts along the Franco-Spanish border hitherto controlled by revolutionary committees.[74] Two weeks earlier, on 16 April, an order issued by Negrín, assigning certain reorganized carabineer units for duty on the border,[75] had given advance warning of Valencia's intention to recapture this vital element of state power usurped by the revolutionaries and essential to the control of foreign trade and currency and to the flow of arms.[76]

Knowledge of the death of Martín, of the seizure of frontier posts by the carabineers, of attempted disarming by Assault and National Republican guards, and of raids by Rodríguez Salas, the Communist police commissioner, into the Anarchist stronghold of Hospitalet,[77] to flush out Roldán Cortada's alleged killers, caused the storm clouds gathering in Barcelona to darken and thicken perceptibly.

On 29 April, groups of armed men mobilized by the local committees of the CNT and FAI occupied the streets of the Catalan capital. All had rifles and some wore hand grenades around their waists. At 6 P.M. the government met but, after a brief session, announced that it would not continue its work under the pressure of groups who were "trying to impose their will by force and to compromise the war and revolution." "The government is therefore suspending its meeting and hopes that all persons not subject to its direct authority will immediately leave the streets so as to make it possible for the state of disquiet and alarm that Catalonia is presently experiencing to quickly disappear. At the same time the council of the Generalitat has taken the necessary steps to ensure the strict fulfillment of its orders."[78]

May Day was approaching. The negotiations that had been proceeding between the UGT and the CNT for a joint demonstration had to be abandoned.[79] The widening chasm between the opposing sides prevented any slogan from being found that was broad enough to bridge their differences even for a day. "[Under] the surface-aspect of the town," wrote George Orwell, an eyewitness, "under the luxury and growing poverty, under the seeming gaiety of the streets, with their propaganda-posters, and thronging crowds, there was an unmistakable and horrible feeling of political rivalry and hatred. People of all shades of opinion were saying forebodingly: 'There's going to be trouble before long.' The danger was quite simple and intelligible. It was the antagonism between those who wished the revolution to go forward and those who wished to check or prevent it—ultimately, between Anarchists and Communists."[80]

In the explosive atmosphere the new ultraradical Anarchist organization, the Friends of Durruti, became extremely active. In the last days of April, they plastered Barcelona with their slogans. "We accept their program," wrote Juan Andrade, commonly regarded as the most radical member of the POUM executive, "and are ready to agree to whatever proposals may be made to us.[81] There are two points in those slogans that are also the fundamental ones for us: All power to the working class, and democratic organs of the workers, peasants, and combatants, as an expression of proletarian power."[82]

On 1 May, the POUM executive declared:

> For two days, the workers have been standing guard. [They] . . . have been watching day and night over the fate of the Revolution. . . . They are neither uncontrollables or *provocateurs*. They are the same workers who fought in the streets on 19 July. . . .
>
> Bearing arms, they are keeping vigil because their patience is exhausted. They are tired of so much political capitulation, of paper governments based on impotent compromises. . . .
>
> We have no confidence in the members of the government. For this reason we keep watch in the streets. . . .
>
> We can no longer tolerate the real uncontrollables. We want control, but absolute control. At the front and in the rear. Control by the working class. . . .
>
> But our action must not degenerate into a sporadic movement, into a suicidal "putsch," that would jeopardize the triumphant march of the working class. No, not the action of groups only [but] the action of all the workers with a concrete program and a clear understanding of the needs and possibilities of the moment.
>
> And for this a Revolutionary Workers' Front [is needed] formed by the proletarian parties and organizations committed to winning the war and leading the Revolution to its final consequences.
>
> And a government [is needed] that is the expression of those who work and those who fight, a workers' and peasants' government, elected democratically by the workers and peasants and by the combatants.[83]

Meantime, the Assault and National Republican guards were increasing their efforts to disarm the Anarchosyndicalists in the streets. On 2 May, *Solidaridad Obrera* warned: "THE GUARANTEE OF THE REVOLUTION IS THE PROLETARIAT IN ARMS. TO ATTEMPT TO DISARM THE PEOPLE IS TO PLACE ONESELF ON THE WRONG SIDE OF THE BARRICADES. NO COUNCILLOR OR POLICE COMMISSIONER, NO MATTER WHO HE IS, CAN ORDER THE DISARMING OF THE WORKERS, WHO ARE FIGHTING FASCISM WITH MORE SELF-SACRIFICE THAN ALL THE POLITICIANS IN THE REAR, WHOSE INCAPACITY AND IMPOTENCE EVERYBODY KNOWS. DO NOT, ON ANY ACCOUNT, ALLOW YOURSELVES TO BE DISARMED!"

42

The May Events, Part 1

*T*he dynamics of the political conflict in Barcelona were now leading inexorably toward open warfare, toward that bloody episode and decisive turning point in the Spanish Revolution known as the May events.

No historical episode has been so diversely reported or defined. The Nationalist press almost uniformly described the events as an Anarchist revolt against the Catalan government,[1] although the *Diario de Burgos* also affirmed that the Anarchists had gone into the streets to destroy the Russians. "The Spanish people are not the Russian people," it added, "and the Reds, sometimes in spite of themselves, remember that they are Spaniards."[2] The *Pensamiento Navarro* declared that what had occurred was "a genuine Anarchist revolution," the "last stage of liberalism and democracy."[3] As for the foreign press, Hitler's *Voelkischer Beobachter*[4] and Mussolini's mouthpiece *Il Pòpolo d'Italia*[5] also spoke of an Anarchist uprising as did other prominent foreign newspapers of varying shades of opinion.[6]

But it was among the foreign supporters of the Republican camp and within the Republican camp itself that the versions of the May events differed sharply. *Pravda* defined the conflict as a "Trotskyist-Fascist putsch" ordered by "Franco and the Italo-German interventionists to distract the attention of Republican Spain from the front" and to "frighten bourgeois circles in England and France with the specter of 'anarchy.'"[7] For its part, *L'Humanité*, the organ of the French Communist party, characterized the events as a "Hitlerite putsch," whose ringleaders had adopted Anarchist slogans and "assured themselves of the assistance of irresponsible elements of the Iberian Anarchist Federation,"[8] while the *Daily Worker*, the organ of the American Communist party, reported that "monarchists, as well as fascist supporters of Franco, 'uncontrolled' anarchists and Trotskyists [had taken] part in the attempted uprising."[9] On the other hand, the Trotskyist Fourth International defined the events as "an attempt by the bourgeois governments of Valencia and Catalonia, under pressure from Anglo-French imperialism and the Soviet bureaucracy, to crush the revolutionary proletariat."[10]

Obfuscating the events still further was the statement by the Spanish embassy in Paris affirming that the "riots" were not exclusively Anarchist as "alleged by certain sources of propaganda seeking to spread confusion among world opinion" and that the old monarchist flag had appeared on several balconies in Barcelona "in the belief that the ringleaders were already masters of the situation."[11]

Inside Republican Spain, *Frente Rojo*, the leading Communist daily, characterized the disturbances as a putsch by "Trotskyist counter-revolutionary agents."[12] This view was opposed by the revolutionary left. According to the POUM, the conflict was "a spontaneous explosion of dissatisfaction of the majority of the working class," provoked by the Communists.[13] This too was the version of the CNT, although it also accused Catalan separatists of planning to make Catalonia an independent state in agreement with Mussolini.[14]

Few of these accounts were reconcilable, which partially explains why the May events, despite numerous attempts to clarify them, are still, after fifty years, shrouded in obscurity. One thing, however, is certain: the political temperature in Barcelona had by May 1937 reached flashpoint.

Seizing the initiative, Eusebio Rodríguez Salas, the PSUC police commissioner—acting in concert with Artemio Aiguadé, the Esquerra councillor of internal security, and in accordance with a prior decision by the PSUC's executive committee—made a daring move. At 3 P.M. on Monday, 3 May, accompanied by three truckloads of assault guards, he raided the *telefónica*, the central telephone exchange.[15] Strategically located in the Plaza de Cataluña, the CNT had taken possession of the building after the defeat of the military insurrection in July and regarded it as a "key position in the Revolution."[16] Swiftly entering the ten-story building, the assault guards occupied the ground floor but were stopped when they tried to reach the upper levels.[17] In response to an appeal for help by Rodríguez Salas, police reinforcements began to arrive and to "occupy the roofs of neighboring buildings and station themselves in the adjoining streets and avenues with a great show of force."[18] Within minutes, wrote an eyewitness, trucks carrying armed men of the CNT, FAI, and Libertarian Youth arrived. "They are ready to defend the conquests of the Revolution at all costs."[19]

In accordance with the Catalan government's decree on collectivization and workers' control of 24 October 1936 that legalized the sequestration or control of the larger commercial and industrial concerns seized by the unions during the first days of the Revolution,[20] the telephone exchange, owned by the Compañia Telefónica Nacional de España, a subsidiary of the International Telephone and Telegraph Corporation, was controlled by a committee of the CNT and UGT. On this body the Anarchosyndicalists were the dominant force, and their red and black flag, which had flown from the tower of the building ever since July, attested to their supremacy.

Although, in conformity with the decree, the committee was presided over by a government delegate, his presence merely created an illusion of official control where in reality none existed. "Serious things were going on there that the government had to end," declared Juan Comorera, the PSUC secretary. "All the interior controls of the telefónica were in the service, not of the community, but of one organization, and neither President Azaña nor President Companys, nor anyone else, could speak without an indiscreet controller overhearing."[21] This was no exaggeration. President Companys himself, in his notes on the May events, testifies that "all the telephone calls of the Generalitat authorities, of the President of Catalonia and of the President of the Republic were intercepted."[22] If this interception was not a prerogative bestowed by law, it was nonetheless, in the opinion of the CNT, an indefeasible right conferred by the Revolution. In its ability to interpose its veto, to intercept, as the CNT-FAI leader, Diego Abad de Santillán, puts it, "compromising messages and conversations" and to overhear persons "conspiring to whittle away the people's rights,"[23] the CNT possessed a vital element of real power, which neither the PSUC nor the Esquerra could permit for long if they were ever to be masters of the region.

Thus, when Rodríguez Salas raided the *telefónica* with an order signed by Aiguadé,[24] it is not unlikely that he had the tacit approval of most of the members of the government except those belonging to the CNT.[25] One other exception, however, was the shrewd and extremely circumspect premier, José Tarradellas. According to President Azaña—who, it will be recalled, had left Madrid for Barcelona in October 1936—Tarradellas told him on the first night of the fighting that he had learned of the raid only after the order had been given and that he considered the decision "hazardous" because the government lacked resources with which to subdue any resistance it might encounter.[26] "He criticized Aiguadé a lot," Azaña further testifies, "for having launched a battle without preparing for it, and Companys for talking so much about doing battle, as a result of which he had alarmed the Anarchists. He believed that ultimately everything would be settled through negotiation."[27]

On learning of the raid, the CNT councillors demanded the removal of both Rodríguez Salas and Aiguadé, but to no avail.[28] "The intransigence of the other parties," writes José Peirats, the Anarchosyndicalist historian, "and especially the opportunist attitude of the president of the Generalitat, who resolutely opposed this punishment, provoked a general strike followed by an outbreak of hostilities."[29]

In a retrospective account of the May events, Manuel Cruells, a staff reporter at the time on the *Diari de Barcelona*, the organ of Estat Català, representing the small separatist movement among the Catalan middle classes, states: "If Companys had adopted an energetic attitude by removing his councillor of the interior and the general commissioner of public order, as logically he should have done, there would have been no tragic week of May in Barcelona. . . . It is somewhat difficult to understand the attitude of President Companys under the particular circumstances. . . . Either he was badly informed and did not realize how grave the situation might become as a result of his refusal, or he was well informed and acquiesced in provoking the serious situation. . . . Why did the president not insist on the proposed resignations? Had he allowed himself to be carried away by the anti-FAI hysteria that had already begun to manifest itself in the streets? Did he wish to be loyal, as on other occasions, to certain friends in his own party? It is difficult to explain the real cause of the president's attitude, but we can affirm that it was decisive in sparking the conflict, suffused with hate, that Barcelona had to endure."[30]

As news of the raid on the telephone building became known, anger swept through the working-class districts, mainly Anarchosyndicalist. "Hundreds of comrades occupy the streets," wrote an Anarchist eyewitness. "They wish to go to the center of the city and make a CLEAN SWEEP of those who want to repeat the fascist provocation of 19 July. They are restrained with difficulty. The comrades . . . know what the aggressors are seeking. . . . What they want is to strangle the Revolution, destroy the conquests of the revolutionary workers, and simply reestablish the bourgeois democratic Republic. To achieve this goal it is necessary to provoke the Anarchists into a conflict, declare them enemies of the 'Popular Front' government, destroy their organizations, open the way to intervention by the democratic capitalist powers, and drown the onward march of the revolutionary Spanish workers in blood. The so-called 'workers' fatherland' is an accomplice in this executioners' job against the Revolution and is sacrificing the future liberty of the Spanish people for the help the democratic capitalist powers offer against the fascist threat to its existence."[31]

Hundreds of barricades were rapidly erected. "The building of these barricades was a strange and wonderful sight," wrote George Orwell, an eyewitness in the Ramblas, one of the main avenues. "With the kind of passionate energy that Spaniards display when they have definitely decided to begin upon any object of work, long lines of men, women, and quite small children were tearing up cobblestones, hauling them along in a handcart that had been found somewhere, and staggering to and fro under heavy sacks of sand."[32]

Before nightfall Barcelona was an armed camp. "Thousands upon thousands of workers have returned to the streets with arms in their hands," declared the POUM executive. "Plants, machine shops, warehouses have stopped work. The barricades of liberty have risen again in every part of town. The spirit of July has once more taken possession of Barcelona."[33] It is dubious whether those responsible for the assault on the *telefónica* had anticipated such a widespread popular reaction.

In a great ring around Barcelona extending from the working-class suburbs to the edge of the commercial and official section of the city, the Anarchosyndicalists were masters of the situation. Inside the business and political enclave of the Barrio Gótico, however, the opposing forces were fairly evenly matched. For example, in the Plaza de Cataluña, the central square, where the Anarchosyndicalists held the *telefónica*, the PSUC was entrenched in its headquarters, the Hotel Colón, which it had sequestered in July, and from whose windows almost the entire square could be swept by machine-gun fire.

In the working-class suburbs of Sarriá, Hostafrancs, and Sans, as well as the maritime quarter of Barceloneta, the Assault and National Republican guards were powerless.[34] Some surrendered without resistance, while others remained in their barracks, waiting to see how the crisis would run its course. "Instantaneously, nearly the whole of Barcelona was in the power of our armed groups," affirms Abad de Santillán. "They did not move from their posts, although they could have done so easily and overcome the small centers of resistance."[35] Had the CNT and FAI been interested in taking power, he asserted, their victory would have been complete, "but this did not interest us, for it would have been an act of folly contrary to our principles of unity and democracy."[36]

Near the Catalan parliament building not far from the port of Barcelona, where President Azaña had recently established his official residence, intermittent firing was going on. At 8 P.M. he instructed his general secretary, Cándido Bolívar, then in Valencia, to request Premier Largo Caballero for reinforcements to bolster his presidential guard. Caballero had already retired, and Bolívar brought the ruffled premier out of bed at 8:30 P.M. After urging him to dispatch additional forces without delay, Bolívar departed, little suspecting that his request would remain unheeded.[37] Shortly afterward interior minister Galarza informed Caballero that Aiguadé had asked for the "urgent dispatch of 1,500 guards, indispensable for suppressing the movement."[38]

At 11 P.M. Premier Tarradellas, acting on behalf of President Companys, visited Azaña to offer his apologies for the state of turbulence. The normally short trip of only a few minutes from the Generalitat Palace to the parliament building had taken an hour and a half. "He had been obliged to descend from his car at every barricade . . . to parley at length, and had been humiliated," Azaña notes in his diary. "When he began to make excuses [for the turmoil], stressing the fact that, as a Catalan, he felt ashamed, I interrupted him and repeated the remarks I had made to Bolívar to pass on to the prime minister. 'Don't make excuses! Suppress the insurrection! As far as I am concerned, guarantee my safety and my freedom of movement.' " Tarradellas then took leave of the president, who heard nothing more from the Catalan government during the rest of the fighting. "No one in the Generalitat asked about me, or tried to speak to me, or concerned himself with my position," Azaña remarks bitterly. "It was more than a scandalous discourtesy; it was an act of silent hostility."[39] Nor did Prime Minister Largo Caballero concern himself with the president's plight. "He neither called me nor sent me any message."[40]

"The whole night [3–4 May] the rebels were masters of the city," Azaña continues. "They raised barricades, occupied buildings and important points without anyone interfering with them. . . . I was not worried, but I was disturbed by the position they had put me in. I perceived vaguely that the conflict did not directly involve me, and I even thought that if things got worse it might help to achieve peace [in Spain]. What disgusted me and annoyed me was the scandal the rebellion would create abroad, the benefit the other rebels would derive from it, and its repercussions upon the war."[41]

That same night the executive committee of the POUM met with the regional committees of the CNT, FAI, and the Libertarian Youth. Julián Gorkin, a member of the executive, recalls: "We stated the problem in these precise terms: 'Neither of us has urged the masses of Barcelona to take this action. This is a spontaneous response to a Stalinist provocation. This is the decisive moment for the Revolution. Either we place ourselves at the head of the movement in order to destroy the internal enemy or else the movement will collapse and the enemy will destroy us. We must make our choice: revolution or counterrevolution.' [The regional committees] made no decision. Their maximum demand was the removal of the [police] commissioner who had provoked the movement. As though it were not the various forces behind him that had to be destroyed! Always the form instead of the substance! . . . Our party placed itself on the side of the movement, even though we knew it was condemned to failure."[42]

The following morning, Tuesday, 4 May, Aiguadé repeated his request for fifteen hundred assault guards, but interior minister Angel Galarza, acting on instructions from Largo Caballero, gave only a temporizing reply. "I have ordered the concentration of [police] forces in Castellón, Murcia, Alicante, and Valencia," he responded, "and, in case of necessity, should serious clashes occur in Catalonia . . . the necessary forces will be placed at your disposal. But the *premier and I agree that while everything should be prepared* the intervention of forces not stationed in Catalonia is undesirable, so long as those already there do not have to be employed to the full and have not been proved inadequate."[43] By temporizing, Largo Caballero hoped that the fighting would subside without government intervention. Waging a political battle for survival against the Communists, he was not inclined to antagonize the CNT and FAI or to strengthen the hand of his opponents in Catalonia by sending reinforcements to the region.

Meanwhile, the situation in Barcelona was deteriorating. The rattle of machine-gun fire, the explosion of hand grenades and dynamite, and the fire of mortars merged into a single roar. This "devilish noise," wrote Orwell, "echoing from thousands of stone buildings, went on and on and on, like a tropical rainstorm. Crack-crack, rattle-rattle, roar—sometimes it died away to a few shots, sometimes it quickened to a deafening fusillade, but it never stopped while daylight lasted."[44] Although isolated attempts were made to capture enemy strongholds, there was comparatively little fighting in the open. Most of the combatants remained in buildings or behind barricades and blazed away at their enemies opposite.[45]

"We realized that what was happening was that everybody's house was burning," declared Abad de Santillán some days later, "and that the only hope under the circumstances was to extinguish the flames and end the bloody slaughter."[46] A few months later, however, he had second thoughts: "Perhaps . . . we allowed ourselves to be guided much more by a sense of loyalty and generosity than by a precise understanding of the plot that had been hatched against us."[47]

At 2 P.M. the CNT and FAI appealed over the radio for a cease-fire: "Workers! . . . We are not responsible for what is happening. We are attacking no one. We are only defending ourselves. . . . Lay down your arms! Remember, we are brothers! . . . If we fight among ourselves we are doomed to defeat."[48]

But there were forces intent on stoking the conflict. Not only were Rodríguez Salas's men initiating new offensive actions, but the tiny Trotskyist group of Bolshevik Leninists and the dissident Anarchists of the Friends of Durruti, joined by some of the more militant members of the POUM, were extremely active.

The attitude of the POUM leaders, on the other hand, was pessimistic. "We did not feel ourselves spiritually or physically strong enough to take the lead in organizing the masses for resistance," a member of the executive acknowledged.[49] And George Orwell, a participant in the fighting and a POUM sympathizer, corroborates: "Those who were in personal touch with the POUM leaders at the time have told me that they were in reality dismayed by the whole business, but felt that they had got to associate themselves with it."[50]

"[As] the workers were already in the streets," declared the central committee of the POUM on 12 May, after the fighting had ended, "the party had to take a position. But what position? Isolate ourselves from the movement, condemn it, or make common cause with it? . . . We opted for the third position . . . , although we knew in advance that the movement could not triumph. To act in any other way would have been an unforgiveable betrayal. . . . It would have been possible to take power, but our party, a minority force within the working-class movement, could not assume the responsibility of issuing that slogan, particularly as the attitude of the CNT-FAI leaders, who were urgently calling upon the workers over the radio stations in Barcelona to abandon the struggle, created confusion and uncertainty among the combatants. To call upon the workers to take power would have meant leading them into a *putsch* that would have had fatal consequences for the working class. For this reason, it was necessary to issue limited slogans: to demand the removal of Rodríguez Salas and Aiguadé, the direct authors of the provocation, the rescission of the reactionary decrees on public order, and the creation of committees for the defense of the Revolution."[51]

The POUM leadership did not publicly display its pessimism and on the surface appeared combative despite its unsuccessful overtures to the regional committees of the libertarian movement on the night of 3 May for joint, aggressive action. The next morning, *La Batalla* urged the workers to remain in "a state of permanent mobilization" and to "prosecute and intensify the offensive that has been initiated as there is no better means of defense than attack. It is imperative to demand and obtain the resignation of the general commissioner of public order. . . . It is imperative to demand and obtain the abrogation of the decrees on public order adopted by reaction and reformism. To achieve all this and to continue the revolutionary action, broadening its scope every day and carrying it to its ultimate consequences, it is imperative that the working class, remaining in a state of mobilization and on the offensive, should form the Revolutionary Workers' Front and should proceed immediately with the organization of committees in defense of the Revolution."[52]

A few days later an article in *Pravda* declaimed: "On 4 May, the Trotskyist agents of Franco . . . through their organ, *La Batalla*, appealed to their followers . . . to remain 'in a permanent state of mobilization.' . . . Queipo de Llano, the well-known executioner in Seville, addressed the Catalan rebels by radio with the following words: 'We sympathize with you and we shall help you. Remain firm!' The appeals by the executioners of the Spanish people and by the Barcelona Trotskyists and 'left Anarchists' seem to be fresh proof of the ideological and organizational link between these enemies of the people. Spanish Trotskyism is exposed as the agent of international Fascism."[53]

Meanwhile, in Valencia (the seat of government), on Tuesday morning, 4 May, Premier Largo Caballero, fearing that the Communists might exploit the fighting to topple his government, summoned the CNT ministers. He told them that Aiguadé, the Esquerra councillor of internal security, had asked the minister of the interior to dispatch fifteen hundred assault guards.[54] "The government," Caballero argued, "could not do that because it would mean placing forces in the service of the person who may possibly have had something to do with the conflict. Before acceding, he would take over the administration of public order as provided in the Constitution."[55] He therefore suggested that representatives of the national committee of the CNT and of the executive committee of the UGT should leave for Barcelona immediately to try to end the hostilities.[56] A meeting of the national committee of the CNT was then summoned, at which it was decided to send representatives to Barcelona "so as to avoid the taking over of public order by the central government."[57] Mariano Vázquez, CNT secretary, and García Oliver, CNT minister of justice, were designated by the committee, while Carlos Hernández Zancajo and Mariano Muñoz Sánchez, both supporters of Largo Caballero, were appointed by the UGT executive.[58]

At 11 A.M. the central government met. Backed by Indalecio Prieto and by the left Republican ministers, the Communists pressed the premier to take immediate action, demanding not only that reinforcements be dispatched to Catalonia but that the government assume control of public order and of military affairs in the region. Succumbing to the threat of a cabinet crisis, Caballero reluctantly agreed to adopt these measures, but only if the situation did not improve by evening.

At 1:10 P.M. President Companys—who had undoubtedly instructed Aiguadé to request the fifteen hundred assault guards from Valencia—informed Largo Caballero that the situation was "very serious," that the police forces were "inadequate for rapid action and are becoming exhausted."[59] Caballero replied: "I deem it my duty to inform you that . . . all [the ministers] have decided that if the situation does not improve *by an early hour this evening*, the government will assume control of public order in accordance with the Statute [of Catalan Autonomy]. Tell me if you have any objection."[60] This was an extremely delicate question for President Companys—the chief custodian of regional autonomy—who certainly would have preferred the dispatch of reinforcements to the sacrifice of Catalan autonomy. But, fearful lest he be denied the much-needed forces unless he surrendered the control of public order, he responded: "*I believe that [the central government] should cooperate in strengthening the available forces* of the councillor of internal security." But, then, with resignation, he added, "In view of the danger that the [state of public order] may get worse the government of the Republic can adopt the measures it deems necessary."[61]

During a conversation with Azaña by teletype at 3 P.M., Prieto gave a slightly different version of this dialogue. The cabinet, he said, had decided that Caballero should suggest to the president of the Generalitat that, in accordance with the Statute of Catalan Autonomy, he should request the central government to assume control of public order. This procedure, the cabinet felt, was "preferable" to the other alternative under the statute, which empowered the central government to "intervene in the maintenance of internal order" in Catalonia "on its own initiative, when it considers that the general interests of the State or its security is in jeopardy."[62] After consulting with Companys, Caballero reported to the cabinet that the Catalan president "had not given him a concrete answer, but that he had gained the impression that the Generalitat acknowledged that it was powerless to subdue the movement."[63] Nevertheless, Prieto felt sufficiently sanguine to inform Azaña that he believed that when the cabinet met at 4:30 P.M. it would agree to "take over public order with or without the request of the Generalitat."[64]

The two versions are not inconsistent, and, in any case, there is no evidence that Companys offered any resistance to the assumption of public order by the central government.

In a written statement, signed on 9 August 1946 in the presence of several Catalan refugees, Jaime Antón Aiguadé, the nephew of Artemio Aiguadé, alleges that his uncle told him that President Companys surrendered the control of public order to Valencia without either consulting him or the Catalan government. He further alleges that, according to his uncle, Companys's pleas for reinforcements were inspired by Juan Comorera, the PSUC leader, who, "during those days did not move for a single moment from Companys's side, giving him advice and taking advantage of the moral depression of the president to propose solutions that suited the interests of the PSUC." It was Comorera, the document claims, who suggested to Companys that he "accept the solution proposed by the government of Valencia."[65]

However this may be, there can be little doubt that President Companys had the tacit if reluctant support of other leaders of the Esquerra, including that of Aiguadé himself, when he agreed to surrender the control of public order to Valencia, and that the document in question was a palpable attempt—during a period of postwar dissensions within the Esquerra—to lay the historic responsibility for the loss of Catalan autonomy solely at the door of Companys and the PSUC.

Despite Companys's go-ahead, Premier Largo Caballero was not yet willing to act. He was still hoping that his emissaries in Barcelona might end the bloodshed by mediation. But Indalecio Prieto, his Socialist rival and navy and air minister, wanted immediate action. An irreconcilable opponent of the CNT and FAI, he believed from the inception of the Revolution, according to his own account, that the most important task of the Republican government was to recover the reins of power.[66] At 12 noon on Tuesday, he notified Azaña by teletype that he had ordered the instant departure for Barcelona of two destroyers, whose commander had been given instructions "to place himself immediately at the service of your Excellency," and that the aviation in Lérida had been ordered to "fly low over Barcelona in a show of strength."[67]

As for the possibility of successful mediation by the CNT and FAI emissaries in Barcelona, Prieto was not optimistic. The head of the government, he informed Azaña at 3 P.M., was inclined to await the result of their negotiations before making a decision. "For my part, I stated that I had little confidence in that result . . . and that if we allowed time to pass and the city to be dominated by the rebels the task of taking over public order would be far more difficult."[68]

At 9:30 P.M., Prieto again teletyped Azaña. He told him that the destroyers *Lepanto* and *Sánchez Barcaiztegui* (which were to evacuate the president) had left Cartagena at 2 P.M. and that five companies of air force men would arrive in Valencia at 3 A.M. on route for Barcelona. "The spirit of the men and the ships' crews is magnificent," he assured Azaña. To this the president replied: "Here, in my residence [the Catalan parliament building], we continue without adequate means of defense. . . . Tell me, who will be in command as of tomorrow of the naval and air forces entrusted with the suppression of the uprising in Barcelona?" "The naval forces will be under the orders of the commander of the *Lepanto*," Prieto responded, "and the aviation will be commanded by the chief of the air force, Lieutenant Colonel Hidalgo de Cisneros. . . . I have already told you my opinion that this matter must be resolved within hours. . . . Clearly, my opinion is subject to that of the prime minister. The liaison [between the air force] and the ground forces is a simple matter, for all these forces have to do is to point out concrete targets to the aviation. Since there are no anti-aircraft defenses to impede low flights the targets will be hit easily. As for the ships, they have the very simple mission to secure free access to the port."[69]

Free access to the port from the parliament building was one of Azaña's main concerns, for under normal conditions it could be reached within minutes. Since the beginning of the conflict, Azaña had urged the government with "hysterical insistence"—as Constancia de la Mora, the wife of air force chief Hidalgo de Cisneros, put it—that steps be taken for his personal protection,[70] but only Prieto listened to his pleas.

"I have already stated," Azaña records in his diary, "that the prime minister did not attempt to communicate with me either directly or indirectly. Nor did he inform the ministers of my situation. Prieto got in touch with me by telegraph on Tuesday, mid-morning. He was aware of the tumult in Barcelona, but . . . he could not fully appreciate my position without seeing it. He told me that he was sending two destroyers to the port of Barcelona . . . to be placed at my disposal; that twenty airplanes would leave for Reus and Prat; that the ministries of the interior and war were sending two armed units, and that one thousand air force soldiers were being flown to Reus. He was very alarmed and ready to crush the rebellion."[71]

All day Tuesday the government in Valencia remained in continuous session. In the late afternoon Largo Caballero's opponents reminded him of the commitment he had made earlier in the day to assume control of public order and military affairs in Catalonia if the situation did not improve by the evening. During the entire day, the CNT and FAI in Barcelona had kept up their appeals for a cease-fire. At 3 P.M. they had exhorted over the radio: "Workers of the CNT, workers of the UGT! Do not put up with deceit and trickery. Above all let us unite. Lay down your arms! Heed only one slogan: Everyone back to work to defeat fascism!"[72]

Despite these appeals, wrote Agustín Souchy, the AIT representative in Casa CNT-FAI, Anarchosyndicalist headquarters, the hostilities could not be contained. "Rancor increased on all sides."[73]

While the cabinet debate in Valencia was still in progress, *Frente Rojo*, the Communist evening newspaper, declared: "For a long time we used to attribute anything that occurred to gangs euphemistically called 'uncontrollables.' Now we see that they are perfectly controlled; but by the enemy. This cannot be tolerated any longer. . . . There has been enough indulgence already. There is a limit to patience. When the existence of Spain as an independent nation is at stake, when the liberty of the Spanish people and the well-being and future of the popular masses is in jeopardy, we cannot allow ourselves to be stabbed in the back. . . . There can be no more discussion on these matters. We must act. And with the severity that circumstances demand. . . . All those who attempt, in one form or another, with some aim or another, to disturb [order] or break [discipline] should immediately feel the ruthless weight of popular authority, repression by the government, and punitive action by the popular masses."[74]

Inside the cabinet the debate assumed a rabid character. "Comrade Federica Montseny," said the CNT, "led the opposition for four hours against the Communists and Republicans who supported the taking over of public order and defense. It was a tumultuous debate, which we lost when the vote was taken."[75] It was decided, however, that the measures would not be put into effect until the last moment,[76] a condition wrung by Montseny and Caballero from their opponents in the belief that the CNT and UGT representatives now en route to Barcelona might negotiate a peaceful settlement. At 9:30 P.M., Prieto informed Azaña that the CNT ministers had "abstained from voting, because they felt that the taking over of public order should be postponed until the result of the negotiations were known."[77]

On their arrival in Barcelona, the emissaries from Valencia joined the Catalan leaders in the Generalitat Palace in appealing for a cease-fire. Mariano Vázquez, the CNT secretary, urged his embattled followers to remember the neighboring Aragon front, where "the fascists might attack at any moment."[78]

García Oliver, onetime organizer of revolutionary strikes, insurrections, and bank robberies, now minister of justice, declared: "Think of the pain, think of the anguish . . . of those antifascist workers in that part of Spain dominated by the whip of Hitler and Mussolini when they learn . . . that in [Catalonia] we are killing one another. . . . All of you should remain in your respective positions . . . but should cease firing, even though provoked by persons not interested in finding a solution to this conflict. . . . [I] declare that the guards who have died today are my brothers. I kneel before them and kiss them. . . . [All] those who have died today are my brothers."[79]

That some libertarians were incensed by their leaders' appeals for a cease-fire is confirmed by Anarchist sources. "When our representatives, who went to the Generalitat [Palace] to arrange a settlement," observed an eyewitness, "gave the order 'Cease Fire!' there were some comrades who felt, in their indignation, that it was a form of treachery to allow those assassins [a reference to the PSUC members and assault guards firing near Casa CNT-FAI] to escape without just punishment."[80]

There was also dissension among the leaders. Helmut Ruediger, vice-secretary of the AIT, who was active in Barcelona at the time of the May events, testifies:

> The problem as to whether the CNT should "go the whole way," taking into its own hands the reins of power, or should continue to collaborate was raised several times after the militants had decided in favor of collaboration on 19 July. The decision of 19 July was unanimous, although spontaneous. Not everyone realized what it signified. But it was during the May days, in particular, during the stormy meetings in Casa CNT-FAI in Barcelona, while the deafening noise of rifle and machine-gun fire could be heard on every side, that more than once the question—which finally received a negative response—was raised: "Should we or should we not *take power*?" It was in these terms that the representatives of the organization summed up the problem during those bloody days. But being *Anarchists*, what did they mean by "power"?
>
> Let us first agree as to what they definitely *did not* mean. Anarchism and revolutionary syndicalism have never seen in state power, in government, with its administrative and repressive machinery, the means of realizing the social changes they desire. Nor were they of the opinion that the basic condition of Socialist construction should be the erection of a new fascist-Stalinist style totalitarian superstate. They maintained that the social revolution should dispense with *both* the bourgeois state and the new totalitarian superstate, and that social reorganization, like the defense of the Revolution, should be concentrated in the hands of *working-class organizations*—whether labor unions or new organs of spontaneous creation, such as free councils, etc., which, as an expression of the will of the workers themselves, from *below up*, should construct the new social community, thus discarding all conventional forms of authoritarian "power" exercised from above.
>
> But in view of the fact that on 3 May the CNT, representing the majority of the Catalan industrial workers, was in open conflict with *all* organizations comprising the other social layers . . . (the small bourgeoisie, the intellectuals, the *immense mass* of the Catalan peasants, namely, the rabassaires [sharecroppers], white-collar workers, technicians, etc.) the question of "power" meant *whether the CNT at that time should crush them all, concentrate the leadership of public affairs in its own hands, and create its own repressive apparatus necessary to prevent the "crushed" from returning to public life*. The reply was "no," but the decisions of those tragic days later provoked a whirlwind of discussions, mutual recriminations, and struggles within the Spanish and international libertarian movement.[81]

At about 9:30 Tuesday night, shortly after the appeals for a cease-fire had been broadcast from the Generalitat Palace, the emissaries from Valencia met with members of the Catalan government under the chairmanship of Companys. "We proposed the formula that a provisional council [government] should be set up, composed of four representatives, [ERC, CNT, UGT, and Unió de Rabassaires] in which no one who had belonged to any of the previous governments should participate," said the CNT national committee. "In this way, we would remove Aiguadé and Rodríguez Salas, because we stipulated that the new councillor of internal security should assume absolute [that is, personal] control of public order." This proposal was accepted. But when the CNT suggested that the new government should be formed immediately "so that . . . public opinion would know that the conflict had been resolved," the PSUC leaders maintained that "it was first of all essential that the firing in the streets should cease." The CNT representatives tried to hold their ground. "We believed it was necessary to gain time to prevent the [central] government from having to assume control of public order, but no agreement was possible. Although the Esquerra and the Unió de Rabassaires did not join in the debate, they supported the Communist point of view. Finally, at 2 A.M. [Wednesday, 5 May], the meeting ended with a decision to announce over the radio . . . that we had reached agreement and that firing should cease completely in order to normalize the situation. . . . When the meeting was over we informed the [central] government that things were going well."[82]

Encouraged by this news, Largo Caballero announced before dawn that the government had approved "the necessary decrees for rapidly resolving the situation in Catalonia, but believes that their implementation will not now be necessary and that order will be restored in Barcelona today."[83] Vain hope! "During the remainder of the night," observed President Companys in his personal notes, "hard fighting continued in the streets, and the rapid dispatch of reinforcements was demanded by [the council of] internal security, by the Presidencia [the office of President Companys] and also by Vidiella [the PSUC leader]."[84]

The CNT leaders redoubled their efforts early Wednesday morning to quiet their following. "We threw into the balance all our influence, constantly sending delegations to the places where incidents were occurring."[85] But their efforts were not always well received. "I heard some comrades cry with rage over the telephone," recalls Abad de Santillán, "when they telephoned the [CNT-FAI] committees and the latter told them not to shoot, even though they were being attacked by machine-gun fire."[86]

Meanwhile, the Bolshevik Leninists and the Friends of Durruti did what they could to keep tempers afire and to give some direction to the fighting.[87] "Long live the revolutionary offensive! No compromise!" declared a leaflet distributed on the barricades by the Bolshevik Leninists. "This is the decisive moment. Next time it will be too late. . . . Only proletarian power can ensure military victory. Complete arming of the working class. Long live the unity of action of the CNT-FAI-POUM."[88] "A revolutionary junta!" demanded a leaflet signed by the Friends of Durruti. "Shoot the culprits. Disarm all the armed corps. . . . No surrender of the streets. The Revolution before everything. We salute our comrades of the

POUM who have fraternized with us on the streets, LONG LIVE THE SOCIAL REVOLUTION! DOWN WITH THE COUNTERREVOLUTION!"[89]

The next day, *La Batalla* printed the leaflet of the Friends of Durruti on its front page with the comment that it was of "really extraordinary interest" and that "we are very pleased to reproduce it."[90] But beyond this guarded comment, the POUM leadership kept a respectable distance between itself and the Friends of Durruti. Only the most radical elements of the party collaborated with it, but without the authority of the POUM executive. "On the third day of the fighting," writes George Esenwein, "the Friends of Durruti—according to the American Trotskyist Hugh Oehler, who was in Barcelona at the time—sent a delegation to the POUM headquarters inviting the executive to join in the setting up of a revolutionary junta, but failed to come to terms.[91] That there was a degree of cooperation between the Friends of Durruti and Marxist groups cannot be disputed. Yet, according to Clara and Paul Thalmann, who, along with other Bolshevik Leninists such as 'Moulin' (Hans Freund), briefly worked in close association with the Anarchist group, this amounted to little more than the distribution of one another's political leaflets. In no sense can the relationship of the Friends of Durruti with the POUM and the Trotskyists be described as a formal alliance."[92]

Although the executive of the POUM did not join other organizations in appealing over the radio for a cease-fire,[93] it did not dissociate itself publicly from the efforts at pacification of the CNT-FAI leadership. True, *La Batalla* had urged the workers in its issue of 4 May to remain in "a state of permanent mobilization" and to "prosecute and intensify the offensive that has been initiated," but these exhortations were not repeated in subsequent issues, for the POUM felt helpless in face of the passionate and repeated appeals for a cease-fire by the Anarchosyndicalist leadership.

"For four days," stated the *Spanish Revolution*, the English-language bulletin of the POUM, "the workers stood ready, vigilant and awaiting the CNT's order to attack. The order never came. . . . The National Confederation of Labor [CNT], held by the workers as the mass organization of the Revolution, recoiled before the question of workers' power. Caught up in the reins of the government, it tried to straddle the fence with a 'union' of the opposing forces. That is why the revolutionary workers' fight of May 3 to 7 was essentially *defensive* instead of *offensive*. The attitude of the CNT [leaders] did not fail to bring forth resistance and protests. The Friends of Durruti group brought the unanimous desire of the CNT masses to the surface, but it was not able to take the lead."[94]

According to Felix Morrow, the American Trotskyist, one of the most vitriolic critics of the leadership of the POUM and the CNT, this radical language was for "export purposes" only. "In general," he alleged, "*Spanish Revolution* has given English readers who could not follow the POUM's Spanish press, a distorted picture of the POUM's conduct; it has been a 'left face.' " "Instead [of putting itself at the head], the POUM leadership . . . put its fate in the hands of the CNT leadership *Not* public proposals to the CNT for joint action made before the masses, but a behind-the-scenes conference with the regional committee.[95]

Whatever the POUM proposals were, they were rejected. You don't agree? Then we shall say nothing about them. And the next morning . . . *La Batalla* had not a word to say about the POUM's proposals to the CNT, about the cowardly behavior of the CNT leaders, their refusal to organize the defense, etc."[96]

In the interest of objectivity, it is important at this stage to quote from "Senex," a defender of Anarchosyndicalist policy during the May events. In response to Felix Morrow's criticism of the CNT leadership in his book, *Revolution and Counter-Revolution in Spain*, he wrote:

It is often alleged by the revolutionary romantics of the Fourth International that had the Spanish workers struck out boldly for an uncompromising revolutionary line, they could have dispensed with Russian aid; the response of the international proletariat would have been so spontaneous, direct and overpowering in its effect that no government would dare to halt the flow of armaments to revolutionary Spain.

This point is brought out by Felix Morrow in his analysis of the May events in Barcelona in 1937. . . . The CNT, according to our author, should have taken up the challenge of the Stalinist and bourgeois forces and made the ensuing struggle the starting point not only of a thoroughgoing social revolution in Spain itself, but of a revolutionary world conflagration triumphantly sweeping the major countries of Europe. In other words, the CNT workers, upon whom rested the tremendous historic responsibility of holding the first line of defense against the fascists, should have thrown caution to the winds, indulged in a grandiloquent historic gesture, plunged recklessly into the adventure of breaking up the antifascist front, thus opening wide the gate to the fascist avalanche—and all in hope of immediately bringing about the world revolution. . . .

For—much to the astonishment of all of us—we are assured that the European revolution was so palpably near during the May events that it was only the reformist degeneracy of the Spanish anarchists that stopped it from proceeding along the "inevitable" stages of development envisioned by Felix Morrow and other revolutionary strategists.

It is interesting in this connection to trace the logical steps in the glib reasoning employed by the latter in order to conjure up the vision of a triumphant European revolution just waiting around the corner, ready to burst forth at the historic opportunity afforded by the May events, but hopelessly bungled up by the Catalonian anarchists.

Had the anarchist and POUM workers of Barcelona kept up their resistance against Stalinist aggression during the May days—Mr. Morrow assures us—entire loyalist Spain would have been swept by a triumphant social revolution.

"Any attempt by the bourgeois-Stalinist bloc to gather a proletarian force would have simply precipitated the extension of the workers' state to all Loyalist Spain." But—the reader will ask—what of the well-armed communist police and military units, the flying corps mainly controlled by the Stalinists, the assault guards, the carabineros, the civil guards, many of the socialist controlled military units, the bourgeois sectors, the navy controlled by the right socialist Prieto? Would they give up without any fight? Would all those units, many of whom were drilled and trained for the specific purpose of exercising a check upon the revolutionary workers, disintegrate at the first clash with the latter? And how about the International Brigades, the preponderant majority of whom were firmly controlled by the Stalinists?

That the workers supported by the CNT units stood a good chance of victory in the case of this new civil war, can be readily granted. But this would be a Pyrrhic victory at best, for it is clear that a civil war behind the front lines resulting in the demoralization of the front and the withdrawal of the troops for the participation in this new civil war would open wide the gates to the triumphant sweep of the fascists. . . .

No one with the least knowledge of the situation will say that . . . the French and British masses of people were ready to go to war for the sake of Spain. Nor will he readily concur with Felix Morrow that had the revolutionary forces of Catalonia ousted the bourgeois parties and socialist and Stalinist elements, "the French bourgeoisie would open its borders to Spain, not for intervention but for trade enabling the new regime to secure supplies—or face immediately a revolution at home." In order to do full justice to the profundity of such a statement, one has only to bear in mind that almost half of the French proletarian organizations are under the thumb of the Stalinists and the rest are swayed by the socialists. . . . How could a civil war waged against the socialists and the Stalinists of Spain, in the face of the terrific danger of a fascist break-through at that, fire the socialist- and communist-minded workers of France to the extent of having them lay down an ultimatum to [their] own bourgeoisie demanding arms for the anarchist workers of Catalonia? And, of course, the ultimatum would have to be laid down in the face of the frenzied opposition of the trade-union leadership (socialist and communist), of both parties who would use all powerful means at their disposal to slander, vilify, distort the nature of the struggle waged by the revolutionary forces of Spain.[97]

In the debate among the factions of the left that followed the May events, the view of Leon Trotsky himself cannot be excluded: "If the proletariat of Catalonia had taken power in May 1937," he wrote, "it would have found support in the whole of Spain. The bourgeois-Stalinist reactionaries would not even have been able to find two regiments with which to crush the Catalan workers. In the territory occupied by Franco not only the workers but also the peasants would have aligned themselves with the Catalan proletariat; they would have isolated the fascist army and started an irresistible process of disintegration inside it. Under these circumstances, it is doubtful whether a foreign government would have risked sending regiments to the flaming soil of Spain. Intervention would have become materially impossible, or, at least, extremely dangerous."[98]

No amount of debate on the May events will ever settle the disputes between the opposing factions. One week after the fighting had ended, a resolution of the

Paris-based secretariat of the Fourth International declared: "Owing to lack of serious revolutionary leadership the workers have been betrayed."[99] In June, the executive committee of the Spanish Bolshevik Leninists stated: "The POUM leadership was not even capable of an independent policy: it clung timidly to that of the CNT and slavishly repeated its defeatist slogans."[100] And, after the war, a foreign Trotskyist wrote: "Betrayed by their organizations, abandoned and handed over to the Stalinist scoundrels, the Barcelona workers made a last heroic attempt in May 1937 to defend the conquests of 19 July. . . . Once again, a revolutionary party had a magnificent opportunity to join the rising revolutionary movement, to drive it forward and lead it to victory. But while the leading Anarchists placed themselves right from the start on the other side of the barricades, the POUM joined the movement only to hold it back. In this manner, victory was presented to the Stalinist hangmen."[101]

The Communists and their supporters, on the other hand, both in Spain and abroad, in a synchronized campaign, represented the POUM's conduct differently. No sooner had the fighting ended than José Díaz, the Communist party secretary, declared that the "Trotskyists" of the POUM had inspired the "criminal putsch in Catalonia."[102] *Pravda*'s correspondent in Valencia sounded the same note, alleging that the Anarchist workers had been "deceived by the Trotskyist-fascist *agents provocateurs*,"[103] while the Communist John Langdon-Davies, writing in the liberal *News Chronicle* of London, stated: "This has not been an Anarchist uprising. It is a frustrated putsch by the 'Trotskyist' POUM working through their controlled organizations, 'Friends of Durruti,' and the Libertarian Youth."[104] For months the campaign continued unabated. In October 1937, the U.S. Communist Robert Minor, writing for the *Daily Worker*, described the fighting as a "fascist uprising led by Nin and Gorkin,"[105] while George Soria of the French Communist *L'Humanité*, in an article published in the Comintern organ, *International Press Correspondence*, in November, stated: "The POUM was anxious to maintain the state of disorder as long as possible, for this was the order [it] had received from General Franco." The POUM, he alleged, wanted to weaken the resistance of the people so that Catalonia could not go to the aid of the Basques, then under attack by Franco's German and Italian allies. "It was further hoped that it would be possible to organize widespread propaganda abroad against Republican Spain. And it actually happened that in those days the reactionary and fascist press abroad wrote about 'chaos' in Catalonia, and about a 'rebellion of the people against the Soviet dictatorship.' At the same time the insurgent radio transmitters in Salamanca and Saragossa broadcast unceasingly day and night orders couched in the same terms as those of the POUM: 'Hold your rifles ready, do not give up the fight at any price, combine with your brothers at the front, throw the Russian dictators out of your country.' "[106]

The Communist interpretation of the events was so well propagandized that, years later, the ingenuous Claude Bowers, U.S. ambassador to Spain, who during the Civil War was stationed in Hendaye, France, on the Franco-Spanish border, gave the following version: "In early May, the loyalist government moved against [the Anarchists] with cold steel. A crisis had been provoked by the anarchists and the POUM, which was composed of Trotsky communists. It was generally believed that many of these were Franco agents. In factories, they were urging the seizure of private property and strikes to slow down production in the midst of war."[107]

A memorandum by General Wilhelm von Faupel, German ambassador to Nationalist Spain, addressed to Adolf Hitler, on 11 May 1937 (but published several years after the war),[108] was used by the Communists as proof of the links between the "anarchotrotskyists" of the POUM and FAI and General Franco.[109] According to Faupel, Franco told him that one of his agents (who was obviously trying to take credit for the conflict) had succeeded in "having street shooting started by three or four persons." Since it was the raid by the Catalan Communist, Rodríguez Salas, on the telephone exchange that sparked the fighting, the Faupel document is a worthless piece of evidence. It was for this reason that I omitted any reference to it in the French revision of *The Grand Camouflage*, published in 1977.[110] In a letter to the *Times Literary Supplement*,[111] Herbert R. Southworth, a supporter of the Spanish Communist party line and of Juan Negrín during the Civil War, asked why I concealed "the very existence of the message." To this the distinguished British sovietologist Robert Conquest replied: "[Southworth] shows the cloven hoof so openly that few will be deceived when he attempts to revive the old [Stalinist] canard of Francoite inspiration in the May 1937 rising in Barcelona, a charge believed even at the time only by those who also believed that Trotsky was a German agent; indeed the slander on the POUM was part and parcel of the anti-Trotskyite falsification."[112]

43

The May Events, Part 2

*T*he continuance of heavy fighting on Wednesday, 5 May, brought the CNT leaders to the Generalitat Palace at an early hour. "The firing continues," wrote *Fragua Social*, the CNT organ in Valencia. "The streets of Barcelona are bathed in blood. The danger that our rear might crumble increases from hour to hour."[1]

"As the morning advanced," reported *Solidaridad Obrera*, "the fighting continued in various districts of the city and became general in the Plaza de Cataluña [where the telephone exchange was located], in the Calle de Claris, Layetana [renamed Vía Durruti, where Casa CNT-FAI and the General Commissariat of Public Order were uncomfortably close neighbors], and in the vicinity of the Generalitat Palace and the Avenida del 14 de Abril, increasing the number of wounded. . . . In several places . . . groups of individuals who could be described as *agents provocateurs* . . . devoted their time to firing their weapons and to arresting peaceful citizens, taking their union cards away from them. . . . One of the most lamentable activities of the *agents provocateurs* . . . [was sniping from housetops] in order to spread alarm in those districts where calm prevailed."[2]

On arriving at the Generalitat Palace the CNT leaders insisted that no time should be lost in forming the new government. They were aware that Caballero could not hold out much longer against his adversaries and that, failing a settlement through mediation, he would be forced to implement the measures he had approved the previous day. "Our efforts were unavailing," said a report issued by the CNT national committee, "for at 11:30 the session was adjourned. . . . When we reconvened, the Communists . . . argued that the [new government] should not be formed for three hours. We were [still] deliberating when we were informed that the central government had decided to take over public order and defense.[3] . . . We clearly observed the veiled satisfaction with which everyone welcomed the government's decision."[4]

At this juncture it is necessary to interpose a corrective observation. In spite of the CNT's accusation that "everyone welcomed the government's decision" to assume control of public order in the region, there is no hard evidence that any of the Esquerra or PSUC leaders actually *preferred* this extreme measure—which involved the loss of Catalan autonomy—to the simple dispatch of reinforcements as requested by Aiguadé at the outset of conflict. It is of course true that President Companys, under pressure from the central government and fear of the CNT and FAI, felt constrained to sacrifice Catalan autonomy rather than risk an Anarcho-syndicalist takeover of the region, but this is not to say that he welcomed the government's decision. It is also true, according to reliable testimony given to me after the war by the former PSUC executive committee member, Miguel Serra Pàmies, an intimate associate of Juan Comorera, that the latter informed the leaders of the party—who, in the words of Serra Pàmies, were "disoriented," "panic stricken," and "regarded the situation as lost"—that they should keep up the fight until the reinforcements from Valencia arrived to repress the CNT and FAI,[5] but there is no certainty that even this hardnosed politician *willingly* sacrificed the autonomy of the region. In contrast, the Spanish Communists, who were centralists at heart, were not concerned with the nationalist sentiments of the Catalans and had pressed hard, as we have seen, for the assumption of public order by the central government.

While the negotiations in the Generalitat Palace to form a new government in Barcelona were still in progress, the following teletyped exchange was taking place between Prieto and Azaña:

Prieto: A meeting of the cabinet has been called for 11 o'clock to hear García Oliver [who had now returned to Valencia]. Whatever he may report—and I anticipate that he will play down the situation—I shall defend the decree on public order and insist that it be put into effect. . . . I don't think your excellency should remain there. . . . The government urges you to move to Valencia.

Azaña: I doubt very much that the captain of the *Lepanto* [who had been given the command of the two destroyers sent by Prieto to evacuate the president] can reach me, because all access to the port is cut off. The airplanes have not yet made an appearance and the situation is unchanged. Firing continued throughout the night. It is confirmed that the insurrectionists have deployed artillery in the Paralelo in front of a movie theater occupied by the National Republican Guard. . . . Last night, elements of the CNT spoke to their comrades at the front by radio telling them to be ready to proceed to Barcelona when their help is needed. . . . The idea that I should move to Valencia is good, but absolutely unrealizable. This is one of the most serious aspects of the situation, because it is impossible to go beyond the railings of my residence. All over, machine guns and rifles are being fired and hand grenades exploded. I have been in this position since Monday afternoon. In this connection, I must tell you that the problem has two sides to it. One is that this is an Anarchist insurrection with all its grave consequences and deplorable effects, which I don't need to point out to you. The other is the inability of the Head of State to move freely and to exercise his functions. The first is in itself very serious and calls for the most urgent and forceful decisions. The second increases the gravity of the first and can have incalculable consequences. From Monday afternoon . . . I have been awaiting what I might reasonably expect, namely, that the government put together sufficient repressive forces to dominate the situation and free the President of the Republic from his captivity. . . . All these considerations impel me to notify you that I cannot put up with any further delay by the government in taking decisive steps to solve these problems. Since the President of the Republic cannot by himself suppress the insurrection with the sixty poorly armed soldiers of his guard, he will have to solve the other aspect of the question personally. You have more than enough political perspicacity and enough sensibility to understand that neither my personal respect, nor the dignity of my office, nor the scandal this situation is creating throughout the world can permit the Chief of State to continue another day in his present plight. . . . I shall try later to get in touch with the speaker of the Cortes [Diego Martínez Barrio, Azaña's successor in the event of his resignation], to whom I believe I owe an official and precise account of what is happening here, because of his high office.[6]

Prieto: [I] deplore the hours that have been lost. I consider that the government's fundamental duty is to guarantee the absolute freedom of movement of the Head of State at any cost. As for the arrival of rebellious forces from the front to join the insurrectionists, I guarantee that unless they move by night they will fail. . . . I do not believe that the liberty of the President of the Republic cannot be achieved. It is just a matter of resolve. We have sufficient means. I urge Your Excellency to be calm for a few hours. I am now going to attend the cabinet meeting and I shall let you know what happens.

Azaña's threat of resignation was not lost on Prieto, who undoubtedly conveyed it immediately to the cabinet. Nor, apparently, was it lost on Largo Caballero, for, on returning, Prieto stated: "The cabinet meeting lasted barely six minutes. . . . The prime minister said that there could be no further delays because of the very serious responsibility involved. He proposed that the decrees approved yesterday by published in a special issue of the *Gaceta [de la República]* and that the ministers of war, interior, and the navy adopt the necessary measures to restore order."

The president did not appear satisfied with this reassurance and repeated his threat to Prieto: "The situation is getting worse. As I have already told [you], the commander of the *Lepanto* has not yet been able to reach my residence. . . . In fact, since Monday afternoon the President of the Republic has been deprived of the necessary freedom to exercise his functions. Since I have already explained the reasons to the navy minister [Prieto], I shall simply remind him of them in case circumstances compel me to make irrevocable decisions. These can only be avoided if the government takes immediate and overpowering action."[7]

Azaña's threat of resignation was only one of several made during the war but never carried out largely because of the efforts of Prieto, who, although contemptuous of the president's faintheartedness, valued him as a constitutional cover for the Revolution. This was not the first time that Prieto had witnessed Azaña's faintheartedness. In October 1936, when the president was urging the government to leave Madrid owing to the mounting threat to the capital, he asked Prieto,

"Does the government want the fascists to catch me here?" Irritated by Azaña's hurry to depart and by his concern over his personal safety, Prieto remarked to air force chief Hidalgo de Cisneros, "That cowardly fairy is acting like an hysterical whore."[8] Known as one of the most eloquent orators of the Republic, Prieto also had a reputation for vulgar language in private conversation.

"Prieto was very alarmed, seriously concerned [about the events in Barcelona]," Azaña noted in his diary. "He did what he could to help me, but, even so, he did not quite understand the situation. The proof is that he told me that very morning that, in the government's opinion, *it was advisable that I leave for Valencia.* . . . 'The problem,' I said, 'is not that I am against going to Valencia, but that I cannot go into the street.' Martínez Barrio went to the telegraph and read the tape. It made such an impression upon him that, without waiting for the end of the conversation, he rushed off to see Caballero. He quickly returned, saying the government was going to do this, that, and the other, and I should be calm. I answered appropriately, and there was no further discussion."[9]

That Largo Caballero had now decided that he could no longer afford to temporize is clear from a teletyped message from Prieto to Azaña at 8 P.M.: "The prime minister has notified me of his interview with the representatives of the CNT. They went to ask him not to send reinforcements nor to use armed force." Caballero categorically refused to accede to these requests and told his visitors that they should let their coreligionists know that it was "folly to believe that they can conquer the State, because they will be crushed."[10]

Already at noon, immediately after the short cabinet meeting referred to by Prieto in his teletyped message to Azaña, a statement had been issued to the press promulgating the public order and military decrees approved the previous day[11] but not yet put into effect. Colonel Antonio Escobar of the National Republican Guard was named delegate of public order, while General Sebastián Pozas, a convert, as we have seen, to the Communist party, was made military commander of the region—officially the Fourth Organic Division—and of the so-called Eastern Army in neighboring Aragon, where the CNT and FAI were dominant. These appointments nullified the Catalan councils of defense and internal security and, along with them, the cherished autonomy of the region.

Although, at its party congress held in June 1937, the Esquerra criticized Valencia for not responding immediately to the Catalan government's requests for reinforcements and denounced the delay as a "maneuver" to force Catalonia to surrender her autonomy,[12] none of its leaders protested at the time. Indeed, the tone of the official announcement by the Generalitat Palace suggests that President Companys and the other Esquerra leaders accepted Valencia's decision with relief and that their fear of the CNT loomed larger momentarily than their devotion to the autonomy of the region. "[The] government of the Republic, on its own initiative, has taken charge of public order in Catalonia," ran the announcement. "With resources superior to those available to the Generalitat, the government of the Republic can meet the needs of the present situation. This is no time for comment. All we can recommend and should recommend, if we wish to serve the interests of the war against fascism, is loyal and determined collaboration with the government of the Republic. Long live the Republic! . . . We urge everyone to lay down his arms and to end the turmoil in the streets."[13]

To be sure, Companys—like Premier Tarradellas—would have preferred a gradual erosion of Anarchist power to any impingement on Catalan autonomy, but once the fighting had erupted and his requests for reinforcements had been denied, he bowed without protest to Valencia's decision to assume control of public order. Still, while acknowledging in his notes on the May events that it was the "mission" of the central government to proceed rapidly with the disarming of the frontier, he registered mild opposition to the taking over of public order.[14] Haunted by the fear that he would be held accountable before history for the surrender of Catalan autonomy—a fear that became an obsession in later months[15]—Companys made numerous attempts after the power of the CNT and FAI had been broken to regain control of public order, but always without success.[16]

Until the May events, the faith of the Anarchosyndicalist leadership in Companys had been virtually unquestioning. "In all his words and in all his actions," wrote Diego Abad de Santillán, "there was but a single attitude, a moral and spiritual purpose, that we shared almost completely. There were few Republicans who had acquired such a perfect understanding of the situation created on 19 July and there were few who expressed themselves with such clarity and such force in favor of a new social regime controlled by the workers. . . . The May events suddenly presented him to us in a different light. From that time on we began to doubt the sincerity of the president's past conduct. Was he or was he not implicated in the provocation of the bloody events? . . . While we played all our cards in an attempt to end that fratricidal bloodletting, we lacked the support of Companys for the first time since the July days. . . . Companys should explain to the Catalan working class, which supported him in very difficult times, if his role was that of an accomplice or of a prisoner in the May provocation and the subsequent invasion of the autonomous region."[17]

In accordance with the CNT's proposal of Tuesday night, a provisional government was finally set up on Wednesday, composed of four councillors: Carlos Martí Feced of the Esquerra; Valerio Más, the secretary of the CNT Regional Committee; Antonio Sesé, the secretary general of the PSUC-controlled Catalan UGT; and Joaquín Pou of the Unió de Rabassaires. Although the question of Artemio Aiguadé's removal from the council of internal security was automatically resolved as a result of the taking over of public order by the central government, Rodríguez Salas remained in charge of the general commissariat, pending the arrival of Antonio Escobar, the delegate of public order appointed by Valencia.

Fresh appeals were now broadcast from the Generalitat Palace. CNT secretary Mariano Vázquez again begged the workers to leave the streets. "We tell you that this situation must end. . . . We do not want this stigma to fall upon the Spanish Anarchists. . . . This is not the moment, in front of piled-up corpses, to discuss who is right. It is essential that you disappear with your weapons from the streets. . . . We must not wait for others to do so. We must do so ourselves. Afterward we shall talk. If you decide, when you discuss our conduct at our next assembly, that we deserve to be shot, then you may shoot us, but now you must obey our slogans."[18] But Vázquez's stentorian lungs could not prevail against the aroused rank and file, and the struggle continued unabated both in Barcelona and in some of the towns and villages of the region, such as Tarragona, Tortosa, and Mora La Nueva, where latent animosities surfaced in response to the news from the capital.[19]

Meanwhile, there was consternation among the militiamen on the Aragon front, some of whom were ready to march forthwith on Barcelona. Information is fragmentary and sometimes contradictory. According to a POUM source, the officers and political commissars of its Twenty-ninth Division were divided. Some were in favor of heading an expedition to Barcelona, others of consulting the party. Then news was received that troops in Lérida, on the main road to Barcelona, had laid siege to the locals of the POUM and CNT. José Rovira, the division commander, accompanied by a part of a shock battalion, left for Binéfar (twenty-six miles from Lérida). There he found one hundred men under Máximo Franco, the CNT commander of the 127th Mixed Brigade, on their way to Barcelona. The two men decided to proceed alone to Lérida to parley with civilian and military leaders. A compromise was reached: the militia returned to the front, and the soldiers outside the locals of the POUM and CNT withdrew.[20] In a somewhat different version, Julián Gorkin states that the POUM and the CNT sent emissaries from Barcelona with orders to the militiamen to return to the front and that these orders were obeyed "with absolute discipline."[21] For his part, Abad de Santillán affirms that the CNT undersecretary of defense, Juan Manuel Molina, fought "tooth and nail" to stop "a large motorized column" of the CNT from going to Barcelona. "We advised [Molina] to hand over the Capitanía General[22] and the command of our militia to General Pozas [the newly appointed commander of the Fourth Organic Division]. We could not rely on the leaders of our own organization for any decisive action against the Valencia decrees."[23] (This somewhat ambiguous statement by one of the most influential figures in the libertarian movement was evidently designed to throw responsibility on the other CNT-FAI leaders for the decision to relinquish control to Valencia, for there is no independent evidence that he personally opposed them at the time.) As for the Communist version of the movement of troops from the front, La Pasionaria states that two CNT battalions and one POUM battalion were halted on their way to Barcelona by Alfonso Reyes, the air force commander on the Aragon front, a PSUC member, who threatened to bomb the "deserters" unless they returned to the front. "The battalions," she affirms, "returned to their units and only a group of POUMists arrived in Barcelona."[24]

In Valencia, late Wednesday afternoon, a few hours after the government had announced the military and public order decrees, the Communist organ *Frente Rojo* published the following editorial:

Those who have provoked the disturbances in Catalonia are not our brothers. . . . They are neither Anarchists, nor Socialists, nor Communists, nor Republicans, nor are they antifascists of any kind. . . . They are our ferocious enemies. They are people without ideals, without hearts, in the service of the invaders. . . . What mercy can we show to those who, inspired by fascism, attempt to create a chaotic situation in the rear, a situation that may destroy the resistance of our army and may help the foreign interventionists? What mercy can we show to those who assassinate our workers, our soldiers, those heroic self-sacrificing defenders of the people? None, none whatsoever. . . .

There should not be a moment's vacillation. The government has assumed control of public order in Catalonia. . . . Those who provoked [the conflict] should suffer the consequences. But the decrees cannot remain a dead letter. We must act now with the utmost speed and with ruthless energy. Not many hours should be allowed to elapse before the situation in Catalonia is completely liquidated. . . . Whoever rises against the people, whoever collaborates bloodthirstily with the enemy, should be made to feel the force of the popular will. Everything, absolutely everything, must be done, so that another day does not pass before peace has been restored in Catalonia and all honest men and all sincere antifascists are once more working and fighting to win the war and carry the popular revolution forward.[25]

Meantime, in Barcelona, the fighting continued. Three serious incidents helped to envenom still further the political climate: Antonio Sesé, the newly designated PSUC-UGT councillor, was shot and killed when proceeding to the Generalitat Palace.[26] Who was responsible was never known, although accusations were plentiful. "It was alleged that he had been fired on from the [CNT] Public Entertainments Union," said the national committee of the CNT, "[but] it was subsequently proved that the bullet that cost him his life was not fired from the union building."[27] The Communists charged that he had been assassinated by "Trotskyist aggressors in the service of fascism,"[28] while Agustín Souchy, the CNT-FAI spokesman, declared that the shot had been fired "from a barricade belonging to Sesé's own party comrades."[29] That same day, Colonel Escobar, the newly appointed delegate of public order, was seriously wounded when shot at on his arrival in Barcelona to occupy his new post.[30] As a result, Valencia named Lieutenant Colonel Alberto Arrando as the new delegate of public order.[31] Then, sometime between Wednesday night and early Thursday morning, Camillo Berneri, a leading Italian Anarchist intellectual and militant, and his compatriot and coworker Francesco Barbieri were murdered by unknown assassins.[32]

Up to now the only armed forces to arrive in Barcelona from Valencia were the marines dispatched by Indalecio Prieto on board the destroyers *Lepanto* and *Sánchez Barcaiztegui* to evacuate the president, but they were unable to reach the Catalan parliament building.[33] To judge from Azaña's diary, the president was beside himself, furious over the "glacial indifference" and "insolent behavior" of Largo Caballero, and fearful of "perishing unjustly and tragically in Barcelona."[34] Although he claims in *La velada en Benicarló* that he diverted himself during the four days of fighting dictating the final draft,[35] there can be little doubt that he lived in dread of assassination. The Anarchosyndicalists, he knew, had not forgotten the horrendous massacre of Anarchist peasants during the rising of Casas Viejas in January 1933, and although there is no proof of the allegation that, as war minister, he had ordered the Assault and Civil guards to take neither wounded nor prisoners but to "shoot them in the belly,"[36] he bore the odium of this unsubstantiated accusation. Nor had the Anarchosyndicalists forgotten that in 1932 at the time of their uprising in the mining district of Alto Llobregat, Azaña, according to his own testimony before the Cortes, had given the general in command of the Fourth Organic Division "no more than fifteen minutes to extinguish [the rebellion] from the time of the arrival of his troops at the scene."[37] Hence, there was good reason for Azaña's agitation.

On Thursday morning, 6 May, during a break in the fighting, the commander of the *Lepanto*, accompanied by five or six marines, presented himself in the parliament building.[38] Azaña thought that any attempt to depart would be foolhardy. "Prieto continued to press me to take advantage of ten minutes of calm to leave for the port,"[39] but none of his suggestions appeared feasible to the president. "There was a faint smile of skepticism on Prieto's face," writes Julián Zugazagoitia, a Prieto intimate and later minister of the interior. "He was sure that with a little courage any of his suggestions could be carried out successfully, preferably evacuation by sea. The distance from the Catalan Parliament building to the port was very short, and the journey could have been made by car in four minutes. But Don Manuel preferred four days of fears and insecurity to four minutes of resolution."[40] Finally, according to Azaña, after another conversation with Prieto, "more pressing than ever, during which he expressed the thought that perhaps I was balking at taking the risk, I decided to go." But just as he was about to leave the parliament building, Azaña relates, the fighting resumed "with greater violence than ever," causing him to postpone his departure for Valencia until the following day.[41]

Meanwhile, it was clear from the heavy fighting on Wednesday that the calls for a cease-fire had not met with the unanimous approval of the rank and file. "Fighting had already been going on for three days," wrote Souchy, the AIT representative in the foreign information office of CNT-FAI headquarters, "and there was no sign of peace. . . . At about 5 P.M. the Regional Committee of the CNT made the following proposals: 'Hostilities to cease. Every party to keep its positions. The police and the civilians fighting on its side are asked to agree to a truce!' "[42] But these proposals passed unheeded.

The Friends of Durruti brought out a fresh leaflet that included the following demands: "Formation of a Revolutionary Junta." "Shooting of those guilty of attacking the working class." "Disarming of the armed [police] corps." This appears to have been the exact wording of the principal demands, according to an article published after the May events in *El Amigo del Pueblo*, the organ of the group. The article criticized a CNT-FAI pamphlet, *Los sucesos de Barcelona*, for its "lack of seriousness" and "scant documentation" in asserting that the leaflet had proclaimed that a revolutionary junta had already been formed and that the POUM had been invited to join it.[43] In any event, the regional committees of the CNT and FAI denounced the Friends of Durruti as agents provocateurs and declared that the leaflet was "absolutely intolerable and in conflict with the policy of the libertarian movement. . . . Everybody must fulfill the slogans of these committees. Now that the Council of the Generalitat has been formed, everybody must accept its decisions inasmuch as everybody is represented in it. All arms must leave the streets."[44]

The Friends of Durruti responded immediately to this denunciation with a manifesto distributed by hand on the barricades: "We knew beforehand that these committees could only hinder the forward march of the proletariat. . . . We, the Friends of Durruti, have sufficient moral authority to repudiate those individuals who, through incapacity and cowardice, have betrayed the workers and the revolution. . . . Their treachery is enormous. The two essential guarantees of the proletariat—internal security and defense—have been offered to our enemies on a platter. . . . Instead of planning a swift and bold offensive, time and munitions have been wasted by sniping. Intelligence and direction have been lacking. . . . Comrades! Remain on a war footing! Do not weaken! Long live the social revolution!"[45]

"One more terrible blow against the embattled workers," wrote Felix Morrow, the Trotskyist critic of the POUM already quoted. "The regional committee of the CNT gave to the entire press . . . a denunciation of the Friends of Durruti as *agents provocateurs*. . . . The POUM press did not defend the left-wing Anarchists against this foul slander."[46] The fact that the leaflet distributed by the Friends of Durruti had hailed the "Comrades of the POUM who have fraternized with us in the streets" was undoubtedly embarrassing to the POUM leadership, the more so as a rumor was in the air that the entire responsibility for the events was to be placed at the party's door. "I dimly foresaw," wrote George Orwell, "that when the fighting ended the entire blame would be laid upon the POUM, which was the weakest party and therefore the most suitable scapegoat."[47]

At about 8:30 Wednesday evening the provisional government appealed to all the workers and people of Catalonia to lay down their arms and to "forget their rancor and their enmities."[48] Other appeals were made. "Do not listen to the aggressors, to the Trotskyists who want the struggle to continue," the PSUC declared. "Let us unite around the government of the Generalitat."[49] Miguel Valdés, the PSUC leader, exhorted: "Workers of Barcelona, comrades of the CNT, we must not waste our energies a moment longer. We must put an end to the Trotskyist criminals, who in their newspapers continue inciting the antifascists of Catalonia to kill one another."[50]

Jacinto Toryho, the director of *Solidaridad Obrera*, an FAI member, also spoke. Referring to the "wave of collective insanity" that was destroying all the achievements of the first ten months of the Revolution as well as the "hope of the international proletariat," he stated: "This behavior, comrades of the CNT and

UGT, comrades of the PSUC and FAI, comrades of the assault and national guards, is unbelievable; it is despicable, despicable because it is degrading to all of us. . . . In Barcelona the workers are assassinating one another. . . . This state of insanity that has transformed the most sensible people into madmen must end. . . . Just think that there is a front nearby. Just think that this front may become demoralized if it should learn of this hecatomb. . . . Comrades of the police, return to your barracks! Comrades of the CNT, return to your locals! Comrades of the PSUC and UGT, return to your centers! Let peace return!"[51]

Throughout the evening, a joint appeal of the CNT and UGT was broadcast urging the workers to return to work. "It is necessary to return to normality. To continue this industrial inactivity at the present time when we are waging a war against fascism is equivalent to collaborating with our common enemy."[52]

As a result of these appeals, the fighting abated early Thursday morning, 6 May. Disconcerted by the attitude of their leaders, the Anarchosyndicalists' ardor had begun to wane and many of them abandoned the barricades. But, as the morning advanced, fighting flared up again. The national committee of the CNT said:

> The transport union ordered a return to work, but as the tracks were damaged, the repair cars had to be sent out before the streetcars could leave their depots. During the morning they had to return because they were fired upon. . . . The metro had to suspend its service because at some entrances the Communist police and members of Estat Català surrounded the passengers. . . . In some places large numbers of CNT cards were torn up. In others, our comrades were attacked. Our locals were besieged. . . . In the afternoon . . . the situation was more serious than ever. The comrades were ready to take matters into their own hands regardless of the consequences. [But] in spite of the many provocations . . . we could not close our eyes and wage the final battle. [It was perfectly clear] that we had played our enemies' game. They wanted us to go into the street; they wanted public order to pass into the hands of the [central] government. . . . We understood only too well the tragedy of those comrades who had been provoked and cornered and who had seen their comrades and friends fall. But, above all, it was necessary to prevent the entire struggle of the Spanish proletariat since 19 July from being suddenly reduced to naught.[53]

The POUM, feeling that further resistance was useless, instructed its followers to leave the barricades and presented the situation as optimistically as it could. "In view of the fact that the counterrevolutionary maneuver has been repulsed," declared the executive in a statement published in *La Batalla* on Thursday morning, 6 May, "the workers should withdraw from the struggle and return to work today, without fail and with discipline, to continue laboring with enthusiasm for the rapid defeat of fascism. The POUM orders all its armed militants to withdraw from the barricades and from the streets and to resume work, but to maintain a vigilant attitude." At the same time, *La Batalla* claimed that the proletariat had "obtained an important partial victory. . . . It has smashed the counterrevolutionary provocation. It has brought about the removal of those directly responsible for the provocation. It has dealt a serious blow to the bourgeoisie and the reformists. It could have achieved more, very much more, if the leaders of the predominant working-class organizations in Catalonia had risen to the occasion as did the workers. On the repeated orders of their leaders the masses have begun to withdraw from the struggle thus evidencing a great spirit of discipline. Nevertheless, the proletariat should remain vigilant. It should stand guard, bearing arms. It should keep watch over the activities of the bourgeoisie and the reformists and be ready to thwart their counterrevolutionary maneuvers." And, on 13 May, after the fighting had ended, *La Batalla* published the following summary of a long resolution adopted by the central committee of the party: "As the workers fighting in the streets lacked concrete aims and responsible leadership, the POUM had no alternative but to organize and direct a strategic retreat, . . . avoiding a desperate action that might have degenerated into a 'putsch' and resulted in the complete destruction of the most advanced section of the proletariat. The experience of the 'May days' shows unequivocally that the only progressive solution to the present problem lies in the seizure of power by the working class and that it is therefore essential to coordinate the revolutionary activity of the working masses through the formation of a revolutionary workers' front, uniting all organizations ready to fight for the total destruction of fascism. This can be accomplished only through military victory at the front and the victory of the revolution in the rear. The central committee considers that the policy pursued by the party during the events was absolutely correct and fully endorses the line of the executive committee, convinced that it has defended the interests of the Revolution and the broad working masses."[54]

On Thursday evening, 6 May, news was received in Casa CNT-FAI that fifteen hundred assault guards had reached the outskirts of Tortosa, 190 kilometers south of Barcelona. Both Federica Montseny, the CNT minister of health, who had arrived the previous day to help terminate the fighting, and Mariano Vázquez, the CNT secretary, hurried to the Generalitat Palace to communicate with Valencia. Not without reason were they apprehensive lest the assault guards en route to Barcelona might provoke every Anarchist-controlled community in their path to insurrection. It fell to García Oliver, the CNT minister of justice, now back in Valencia, and to Angel Galarza, Largo Caballero's minister of the interior, to persuade Vázquez and Montseny to facilitate the passage of the assault guards through Catalonia and to restore peace to the embattled city before the arrival of reinforcements. The secret discussions that took place by teletypewriter to put an end to the fighting form part of Companys's notes and documents on the May events,[55] the essential portions of which are reproduced here:

[García Oliver]: This is the ministry of the interior, Valencia. Is the minister of health there?

[Montseny]: Yes . . . Listen, García, Mariano is going to speak to you and then we shall talk to Galarza. . . .

[Vázquez]: This morning it looked as though the situation would soon clear up. . . . At midday, the situation began to deteriorate, because the police were preparing to attack union buildings. . . . The fact that Arrando [the new delegate of public order, who had replaced the wounded Escobar] has retained Rodríguez Salas as police commissioner has had a decisive influence on the situation. He is still in charge of the police and has no doubt instructed them to assume the attitude they are adopting. In many places the tearing up of CNT membership cards has been systematic. . . . Five comrades belonging to the bodyguard of Eroles [Dionisio Eroles, the Anarchist chief of services, in the General Commissariat of Public Order] have been taken from their homes and murdered. As a result of these and similar occurrences the comrades have taken steps to defend themselves. The atmosphere became more tense when news was received that 1,500 guards had arrived at Tortosa. It is impossible to foresee at this time what is going to happen. . . . [If] there is not a rapid change in the attitude of the police and in their leadership it will be impossible to avoid flareups in the villages through which they have to pass and where there has been no trouble up to now.

[García Oliver]: This is García Oliver. . . . The minister of the interior has ordered the immediate dismissal of Rodríguez Salas. He is ready to resolve the situation in Catalonia in the fairest possible way. It is imperative that the assault guards who are on their way to Barcelona reach their destination to relieve the police [who are] extremely exhausted, nervous and inflamed by the conflict. . . . You must understand this and make it clear to the committees and comrades. It is also imperative that you make it clear to the comrades and villages through which these impartial, absolutely impartial forces of appeasement have to pass. [The] government knows that without this strict impartiality the conflict, far from being resolved, would become worse, and would spread to the whole of Catalonia and the rest of Spain, and would result in the government's political and military downfall. . . . [The] minister of the interior [is considering] the advisability of dispatching these forces by other means than by road, which is too long and full of [potential] obstacles that may be spread in their path by all those aggressors interested in prolonging the present situation in Barcelona and bringing about the collapse of the government. As the administration of public order has now been taken over, I repeat that it is advisable that you immediately instruct the comrades in the villages not to place any obstacles in the way of these forces of appeasement. On the contrary, they should give them every kind of assistance and receive them with affection, because otherwise the danger exists . . . that if they are attacked en route they will become angered, as a result of which we should only have succeeded in transforming the problem of Catalonia into a national bonfire in which inevitably we would all be rapidly consumed. Above all, pay immediate attention to the province of Tarragona, where the POUM and the separatists [a reference to Estat Català] have many supporters, with the object of preventing them from mixing with [our] comrades and inciting them to armed resistance against the forces of public order. . . .

[Vázquez]: [Although we understand] the undeniable advantage of relieving the police in Barcelona, we should recognize that the problem here does not require the intervention of the police. The position is such that if they were merely to receive orders to return to their barracks for a few hours normality would return completely. It is imperative that the police should not attack or do anything at all for a period of three to four hours. This period would be sufficient to restore confidence as a result of which barricades would disappear and the police would abandon the buildings and places they occupy. . . .

[Galarza]: This is the minister of the interior. On learning at 7:30 P.M. that police commissioner Rodríguez Salas was still in command, I made the following statement [to Arrando], which I copy from the tape I have in front of me: "There should immediately be placed at the head of the administration of security a police commissioner, who is a member of the regular police corps, a man in whom you have more confidence; and the representatives of the unions and parties should stop intervening in public order." [Arrando] replied as follows: "I absolutely agree and shall obey your instructions immediately." . . . [Regarding] the time you require [to restore confidence], I have no objection to the following: At 10 P.M., the police will receive orders not to fire a single shot and to refrain from attacking any building. Only those forces necessary for vigilance will remain on the streets, but without searching for arms or making arrests for a period of three hours. You will undertake the responsibility of seeing that your people in the street and in [their] locals withdraw to their homes during this period and do not fire a single shot. I am going to issue these orders. Obviously, you understand that if they are not observed loyally by both sides nothing will be gained. The Premier is calling me. Wait a moment. . . . [Here] is García Oliver. . . .

[Montseny]: García, what Galarza says we can accept on condition that the truce is called tomorrow from 6 to 9 A.M., so as to give us time to organize a mass peace demonstration attended by the whole of Barcelona, and headed by the representatives of the organizations with their banners bound together. We shall suggest this to the UGT and are sure it will agree. . . .

[Galarza]: With regard to those three hours . . . I have no objection to their being between 6 and 9 A.M. As for the demonstration, provided there are no aggressors, it appears to me to be a very good idea, but I fear that these elements may take advantage of the general state of tension and that the demonstration may begin well but end badly. Perhaps it would be better to hold it on Sunday instead of tomorrow [Friday] and announce it in a joint statement of the two labor organizations. I am going to give orders to the police to observe the maximum prudence during the night. Leave it to me to see that after 9 A.M. tomorrow new and relaxed forces will be there with a person of my absolute confidence in command. [This was a reference to Lieutenant Colonel Emilio Torres Iglesias of the assault guards, who was appointed police chief of Barcelona].[56]

[Montseny]: Very well, Galarza. . . . The truce may prove to be a salvation, but bear in mind that I do not know up to what point your orders will be obeyed if the same persons remain in charge of public order. . . .

[Galarza]: Tomorrow, other officers will be there.[57] . . . But keep this absolutely to yourself lest there be someone interested in repeating the Escobar incident. Tell your people that some of them should try withdrawing to their homes after midnight, and if, as I hope, nothing prevents them from doing so and everyone else does the same, then three hours will not be necessary tomorrow for this operation. It will be very easy to make the test. However, this implies such responsibility for me that I hope not only that I can rely upon your help, but that you will understand that this is the last attempt I can make at this type of solution. Do not announce any of these agreements over the air, but give them to your men of confidence in writing and with your signature. Does this sound all right to you?

[Montseny]: We shall endeavor to make a test at night, although we cannot promise anything owing to the difficulty of getting around at night and orienting [our] people personally. . . . Mariano asks me to tell you that we should agree on 6 A.M. to 9 A.M., as this will give us time to work and will be much easier.

In accordance with their understanding with Galarza, Vázquez and Montseny worked feverishly throughout the night to arrange the truce. "We informed the Catalan organization of the agreements we had reached," said the national committee of the CNT, "and ordered the comrades to prepare to withdraw at 6 A.M."[58] Furthermore, directives were sent to the villages and towns on the main road to Barcelona to allow the assault guards to proceed without hindrance. In Tortosa, where fighting had erupted on Tuesday,[59] the local CNT was instructed not to offer any resistance to the assault guards. "Our comrades acted accordingly," said *Solidaridad Obrera*, "thereby displaying their discipline and respect for the directives of the organization."[60]

In Barcelona, several hours before dawn on Friday, 7 May, there were signs that the ardor of the revolutionaries had finally spent itself. A feeling that it would be futile to continue the struggle against the will of their leaders had overwhelmed them, and disillusionment was widespread. Many withdrew from the barricades and disappeared into the darkness. At dawn, the local committees of the CNT and UGT issued a joint appeal: "Comrades, everybody return to work!"[61]

That evening the assault guards from Valencia, accompanied by a force of carabineers sent by finance minister Juan Negrín, entered the city unopposed. "Shortly after 7 P.M. the first vehicles rolled into the city, carrying assault and security guards," reported *Solidaridad Obrera*, "and a quarter of an hour later the bulk of the forces arrived, entering via the Diagonal. They passed through the Paseo de Gracia, the Plaza de Cataluña, the Ronda, the Vía Durruti and the Paseo de Colón on their way to the Council of Internal Security. As they filed through the streets, the people of Catalonia welcomed them with tremendous enthusiasm and demonstrations of support, to which the guards replied with raised fists."[62] Reinforcements, equipped with the latest weapons, continued to arrive by land and sea, and within a few days the number in the region was estimated at twelve thousand.[63]

The predominance of the Anarchosyndicalists in Catalonia, the citadel of the Spanish libertarian movement, had now been broken. What would have appeared inconceivable a few months earlier, in the heyday of the CNT and FAI, had now become a reality and the most portentous victory of the Communists since the beginning of the Revolution.[64]

44

The Overthrow of Largo Caballero

*H*aving achieved their immediate objective in Catalonia, the Communists now brought their struggle with Largo Caballero to a head. Exploiting the upheaval, they demanded that the government suppress the POUM, which they held responsible for the bloodshed and whose leaders they had long been denouncing as Trotskyists and as a gang of spies and provocateurs in the service of international fascism.

At this point it is fitting to ask whether the Communists themselves believed in their own propaganda or whether they were merely following Moscow's directives compliantly. The answer to this question lies partly in an interview given in 1974 by Santiago Carrillo, then general secretary of the PCE, to Régis Debray and Max Gallo: "I had never regarded the Trotskyists as possible enemies until I went to the Soviet Union [in 1935]. . . . Although I did not really regard the Spanish Trotskyists as being fascist agents, I accepted what I had never acknowledged before. Later came the Moscow trials . . . with all those confessions, all those admissions of guilt. I must say that I was convinced at the time that the confessions were genuine. I could not imagine that they had been extorted. I had always believed that any revolutionary when confronted by the police should resist to the end. I could not conceive of that ideological element that determined those confessions: the monstrous proposition that a man could serve the party and the Revolution by admitting that he was their enemy even though it was not true. I am therefore among those who believed that those people were counterrevolutionaries, agents of the enemy."[1]

No sooner had the May fighting ended than the agitation of the PCE assumed a frenzied character as every instrument of propaganda at its disposal was set in motion to force acceptance of its will.

José Díaz declared at a public meeting on May 9:

> Our principal enemies are the fascists. However, the fascists have their agents who work for them. Of course, if these agents were to say, "We are fascists and we want to work among you in order to create difficulties," they would immediately be eliminated by us. For this reason they have to give themselves other

names. . . . Some call themselves Trotskyists, which is the name used by many disguised fascists who talk of revolution in order to spread disorder. I therefore ask: If everyone knows this, if the government knows it, why does it not treat them like fascists and exterminate them pitilessly? . . .

Every worker must know about the trial of the Trotskyists that has taken place in the USSR. . . . It was Trotsky himself who directed the gang of criminals that derailed trains in the Soviet Union, carried out acts of sabotage in the large factories, and did everything possible to discover military secrets with the object of handing them over to Hitler and the Japanese imperialists. And, in view of the fact that all this was revealed during the trial and that the Trotskyists declared that they had done these things under Trotsky's direction and in complicity with Hitler and the Japanese imperialists, I must ask: Is it not perfectly clear that the Trotskyists are not a political or social organization of a definite tendency like the Anarchists, Socialists, or Republicans, but a gang of spies and *provocateurs* in the service of international fascism? The Trotskyist *provocateurs* must be swept away!

That is why I stated in my speech at the recent plenary session of the central committee not only that this organization should be dissolved in Spain and its press suspended, but that Trotskyism should be swept out of all civilized countries, that is, if we really want to get rid of this vermin. . . .

In Spain itself, who but the Trotskyists inspired the criminal putsch in Catalonia? *La Batalla* in its 1 May edition was full of brazen incitements to revolt. . . . Well, this paper is still coming out in Catalonia. . . . Why? Because the government cannot make up its mind to seize it as every antifascist demands.

If, after ten months of war, a strong policy is not instituted to make the rear worthy of some of the fronts, I shall be forced to conclude, and I am sure every antifascist will be too, that unless this government imposes order in the rear another Popular Front government will have to do so.[2]

The riposte of Largo Caballero's mouthpiece *Adelante* was unequivocal. The measures of repression, it affirmed, advocated by the Spanish section of the Comintern represented a threat to the unity of the working class. "These measures would result in the most terrible disenchantment among the [leaders] of the CNT who are working zealously to get those workers who are influenced by Anarchist propaganda to participate in the tasks of government. A repressive action by the Popular Front government, which a Gil Robles or a Lerroux would endorse, would destroy . . . working-class unity. Perhaps it would end up pushing those who have resolutely renounced their former apolitical methods back to their old ways. If such a misfortune should occur, we would certainly lose the war and the revolution, because neither the war can be won nor the revolution achieved with half of the working class against us."[3]

Behind the scenes the PCE—which, it will be recalled, had recently established close relations with the Socialist party leadership—met with the Socialist executive in order to chart "a common course of action." "The two parties," affirms the official Communist history, "were in agreement regarding the gravity of the political situation and on the necessity of finding a solution to the simmering crisis."[4] That the Republicans were privy to these talks there can be no doubt. President Azaña, who, with Prieto's help, had been evacuated by air from Barcelona on 7 May,[5] states that the former premier and left Republican leader José Giral visited him in Valencia that same day on behalf of the Republican parties: "He told me that the Republicans as well as the Socialists and Communists had decided to do battle with Largo Caballero at the next cabinet meeting. . . . Giral added that the Republicans, Socialists, and Communists formed a bloc that would facilitate a solution. . . . Although [he] did not give any further explanation I understood that the conversations between the three parties were well advanced. The Communists, he told me, would take the initiative at the next cabinet meeting by demanding a change of policy and, if they were not successful, would resign from the government. The Socialists and Republicans would support their demand."[6]

Earlier in the day Largo Caballero had visited the president. Although Azaña was still enraged by the prime minister's "glacial indifference" to his plight in Barcelona,[7] he decided not to mention the matter. "[Caballero] arrived smiling and affable with a portfolio of decrees," he relates. "He did not say one word about Barcelona. . . . He began the conversation as though we had seen each other every day or I had just returned from a pleasure trip. . . . I had thought over very carefully what I should do during this first interview. My natural impulse was to ask him to explain his behavior. But upon reflection, I refrained from doing so and [decided] that if he did not speak of it, I, too, would say nothing. I was sure that if I were to raise the matter things would become so entangled that he would not be able to depart as prime minister. And I was determined . . . not to relieve him of his functions by a unilateral decision, especially as it might be regarded as an attempt to satisfy my justifiable anger. I remained silent."[8]

Thus, when the Republican, Socialist, and Communist leaders visited him on 7 and 8 May to voice their combined opposition to the government, Azaña—whose constitutional position, as Raymond Carr correctly states, gave him "for the first time since July 1936, a taste of power and an opportunity for revenge"[9]—was careful not to take sides openly in the dispute. "I listened to them all," he wrote, "but tried not to disclose my own opinion regarding the conduct of the government. On the other hand, of course, I could not approve it. In the first place, I told them that I considered their visits to be of an informative nature, but that on no account would I allow the inference to be drawn that I was giving them permission to mount an offensive against the government." He reminded them that contrary to his advice the Giral cabinet had resigned in September 1936 to make way for the Caballero government, "hailed as the government of victory," and that "the cabinet reorganization in November, involving the entry of the CNT and the Anarchists, which the Republicans themselves had deemed inevitable and useful," had been carried out "not only against my advice, but in face of my most angry protest." "Now, after a few months," he added, "the very people who had elevated Largo and admitted the FAI [into the government] could not abide them" and were turning to him to resolve the problem. He had not created the Largo Caballero "myth." If a change of policy was now considered necessary, this was because the parties had changed their attitude, "not because the President of the Republic has changed his opinion, which he has not."[10]

A few days later, on 13 May—just two days before the deadline when all political commissars whose appointment and rank had not been confirmed by Largo Caballero were to consider themselves dismissed from the corps of commissars—Jesús Hernández and Vicente Uribe, the two Communist ministers, demanded, at a tempestuous meeting of the cabinet, an immediate change in the premier's policy in the areas of war and public order. They also demanded the dissolution of the POUM in terms that left no room for compromise. The meeting, attests Azaña, who had been apprised of the proceedings by Giral and Prieto, was marked by "unusual violence and vulgarities. . . . Largo called the Communists 'liars and slanderers' and six hours were wasted in this way. The [moderate] Socialists, through Negrín, supported the arguments of the Communists, and the Republicans also said something."[11]

In the course of his acrimonious exchanges with the Communist ministers, Largo Caballero vehemently dissented from their view that the POUM was a fascist organization and declared that he would not dissolve the party, that he had not entered the government to serve the political interests of any of the factions represented in it, and that the courts of law would decide whether or not a particular organization should be dissolved.[12] In his unpublished "Notas Históricas sobre la Guerra de España," Largo Caballero states that he opposed the dissolution of the POUM "with the utmost energy" and "declared that as long as he presided over the government no political or trade-union organization would be dissolved, that if a crime were committed the courts would handle it, and that he was not going to play anybody's political game."[13] Failing to receive satisfaction, the Communist ministers rose and left the room.[14] "The Anarchist-POUM rising . . . in Barcelona," writes Jesús Hernández, "gave us . . . an excuse to provoke the crisis of the Largo Caballero government."[15]

"When the split in the cabinet occurred," testified Indalecio Prieto at a public meeting after the war, "Largo Caballero intended to continue the dispatch of routine matters. I was sitting next to him . . . and said: 'Look here, Caballero, something serious has happened. The ministerial coalition has been broken because one of the parties in the government has withdrawn from it. I therefore think it is your duty, without continuing this meeting, to tell the president of the Republic what has happened and resolve the situation with him.' "[16]

"The opinion expressed by Prieto," writes Julián Zugazagoitia, himself a moderate Socialist and minister of the interior in the succeeding government, "surprised Largo Caballero, who believed that the cabinet could nevertheless continue its deliberations. . . . Prieto's viewpoint, which was perfectly constitutional, was [later] condemned as part of the maneuver begun by the Communists to overthrow Largo Caballero."[17]

It was not until some years after the war that Prieto, reconciled with Caballero, publicly denied the charge that he had acted in secret agreement with the Communists. "Not until now," he declared, "have I bothered to contradict the mistaken assumption that I had dealings with the Communists in order to oust Largo Caballero. Apart from a rule that has guided my conduct toward them ever since the first unfortunate split in our party in 1921, a rule that has always kept me at a distance from them, I am incapable, because of my moral temper, of acting disloyally toward a coreligionist and a friend, who, as premier, was charged at that time with such delicate and complicated functions."[18] On the other hand, Vicente Uribe, one of the two Communist ministers who precipitated the crisis, declared in a speech in exile: "Prieto participated in the plan to remove Caballero from the leadership of the government, although without revealing himself openly. . . . [He] wanted to take revenge on Largo Caballero, whom he had not forgiven, among other things, for frustrating his ambition to become head of the government in May 1936."[19] Furthermore, Gabriel Morón, a onetime supporter of Indalecio Prieto and director general of security, also alleges that Prieto was in agreement with the Communists "to oust Largo Caballero."[20] But the most convincing evidence is that of Palmiro Togliatti, the Comintern delegate and de facto head of the party, who stated, in his report to Moscow on 30 August 1937, that "the centrists along with Prieto had played a very important role both in the preparation and the solution of the crisis."[21] In any event, the view expressed by Prieto that the withdrawal of the Communist ministers had broken the ministerial coalition was an important factor in shaping the course of events, for Caballero decided to suspend the cabinet meeting and to tender his resignation to the president.[22]

It is noteworthy, however, that according to Azaña, Caballero may have had no intention of resigning and was hoping that the president would "simply authorize him to replace the two Communist ministers."[23] "Largo," he recalls, "stressed to me the untimeliness of the crisis inasmuch as there were reasons of national interest that made it advisable for the government to continue to function in order to execute very important plans . . . whose suspension would be catastrophic."[24] The first of these was a plan to foment a rebellion in Spanish Morocco against General Franco, a plan conceived by Carlos de Baráibar, Caballero's undersecretary of war, and dismissed by Azaña as a "harebrained adventure."[25] The second was a large-scale offensive in the region of Estremadura, originally planned by Baráibar's predecessor, General José Asensio, and by General Martínez Cabrera, former chief of the war ministry general staff, both of whom, it will be recalled, had been forced out of office under Communist pressure.[26] "Largo told me," Azaña writes, "that he was thinking of going to Estremadura *to direct the operation in person*, so as to prevent the rivalries among the officers from ruining everything. I assumed that in reality he would direct nothing and that in fact he would restrict himself to signing the orders submitted by the general staff. There can be no question that he was very much sold on the project, from which he undoubtedly expected to derive the military advantages explained by his advisers and the political and personal advantage of appearing, in the eyes of the general public, as the director of a victorious operation."[27]

Largo Caballero's supporters have claimed that the operation might have been the turning point in the war had the Communists and their Soviet advisers not opposed it. "Its aim," writes Luis Araquistáin, the left Socialist leader and intimate of the premier and war minister, "was to cut the rebel army's lines of communication with the south, whence it received steady reinforcements of Italian and Moroccan troops. The success of that operation, by splitting the enemy into two unconnected parts and depriving him of the foreign troops and war material that were entering through the ports near the Strait of Gibraltar, could have changed the course of the war completely. The north [i.e., the Basque provinces against which General Franco was waging an all-out offensive] would have been saved; the whole of Andalusia would have been recovered. Probably the war itself would have been won. . . . At any rate, Franco's victory would have been neither so quick nor so decisive, and at least there would have been time and favorable circumstances for negotiating a diplomatic peace."[28]

The projected operation, placed under the overall command of Lieutenant Colonel Enrique Jurado, was, according to Ramón Salas Larrazábel, the Nationalist military historian, to involve a total of 100,000 men, the largest number yet deployed in a single operation.[29] On the other hand, he says, the Nationalists had available only six battalions, three *tabores* or Moroccan troops, eighteen Falangist *centurias*, ten cavalry squadrons, five batteries, and seven machine-gun companies. The only reserve force was a mixed Italo-Spanish brigade of Flechas Azules. In view of this disparity, he observes, the offensive would have achieved spectacular successes at least in the beginning. However, it was dubious whether the Republicans would have won a far-reaching victory, because of the Popular Army's known lack of an offensive capability. "Still, there can be no doubt that this was the opportune moment to try. The Nationalist aviation . . . was almost entirely in the north, hundreds of kilometers from the area selected for the offensive. The army reserves were either nonexistent or were also in the Basque provinces. . . . For this reason, the overwhelming initial superiority of the [Republican forces] could have been maintained for many days—for a longer period of time than was necessary for [them] to reach Badajoz and the Portuguese border. Whatever the time needed to transfer [Nationalist] reserves, the government forces were assured of absolute superiority in artillery, tanks, and men, and of a modest control of the air." A clear objective, he concludes, opened up before them: to cut off the bulk of the enemy's land forces from their bases in Andalusia and Africa and to place the Army of General Queipo de Llano in an "untenable position." At the very least, "the paralysis" of the offensive in the north would have been assured.[30]

Scheduled for the beginning of May, the launching of the offensive was delayed on various pretexts by General Miaja. Behind his dilatory maneuvers were the Spanish Communists and their Soviet allies, who feared the possible success of an operation that might delay their plans, now well advanced, for the overthrow of Largo Caballero.[31]

Miaja opposed the projected offensive from the very beginning, and when ordered to send several units from Madrid to the Estremadura sector, he at first refused.[32] "His disobedience," affirms Araquistáin, "was inspired by the Communists, who were then Miaja's real chiefs. . . . In the end Miaja had to abandon his insubordination in face of the energetic attitude of Largo Caballero and sent the troops that were required."[33]

This, however, was not the end of Communist resistance to the offensive. Colonel Segismundo Casado, chief of operations on the war ministry general staff, testifies: "[Miaja] realized that after the orders he had received he must proceed at once to move the forces under his command to the positions assigned to them. But during the afternoon of the same day a general, a 'friendly Russian adviser,' came to my office telling me that no aircraft could take part in the action against Mérida [Estremadura], because it was needed on other fronts. For several days past I had realized the possibility that the Communists were trying to hold up this action, and after listening to the 'friendly adviser' I was convinced that it could not be carried out."[34]

The highly regarded Nationalist military historian, José Manuel Martínez Bande, writes: "A great deal has been written about the reasons why this operation was not carried out. Strangely enough, the versions generally speaking coincide with the facts. Indeed, the projected offensive against Mérida was obstructed first by General Miaja and then by the Russian air force command. The documentation I consulted fully confirms this."[35]

According to Largo Caballero, the Russians had initially approved the project: "[They] proposed the names of brigade commanders, all of them Communists, to head the units that were to take part in the operation. But the general staff and I had already appointed men to these posts. . . . I gave orders to the effect that a memo be requested from the real chief of the air force [Soviet General Yakov Smushkevich or 'Douglas'] regarding the number of machines that could be assigned. He replied that we could count on ten airplanes. Ten airplanes for an offensive involving forty thousand men! I interpreted this as a reprisal for not having given the commanding posts to the Communists. We were tired of seeing the Communists assigned to places where they could receive all the laurels and the others where they received only the enemy's bullets."[36]

Jesús Hernández asserts that he personally argued in favor of the Estremadura offensive during a meeting at the headquarters of Soviet military adviser General G. Kulik, after instructions had been received from Moscow to oppose the "Asensio plan," and was accordingly rebuked by Comintern delegate Togliatti. Although he also affirms that Largo Caballero's resolve to carry out the offensive "finally collapsed" when the Russians informed him at the beginning of May that they would not provide him with the necessary aircraft,[37] it is clear from Caballero's conference with Azaña two weeks later, when he tendered his resignation, that he still hoped to execute the plan. Partly because Azaña felt that it would be impolitic to give the impression that he was eager to accept Largo Caballero's resignation and partly because the premier regarded the Estremadura offensive as a question of "national interest," Azaña told him that he would ponder the matter of his resignation overnight and give him a decision the next morning (14 May).[38]

The next day, Martínez Barrio, leader of Unión Republicana, visited the president. "[He] told me," Azaña relates, "that he considered the crisis very dangerous because of the attitude the unions might adopt in the event Caballero were removed. . . . In short, he favored postponing the crisis because it might mean a leap into the unknown. I did not share these fears entirely, save for the danger of a disturbance of public order by some unions and the Anarchists. Largo was credited with much greater power in the UGT than he actually had. And people, in general, were tired of abuses and incompetence. In any case, I had decided not to give Largo and his supporters the impression that I personally viewed his defeat as inescapable or that his inevitable fall and replacement were due to anger or antiproletarian bias on the part of the president. This point was of interest because already in March or April Largo had told me that he foresaw 'another expulsion of the workers from power as in 1933.' It was essential, in the public interest, that those who might feel that they had been 'expelled' from power should be expelled as a result of the well-known opposition of others [the Communists] who, because they wore the same labels, could speak in the name of the workers." After "carefully weighing the pros and cons" and concluding that "the fruit was not yet ripe enough" for him, Azaña told Caballero that he believed that the crisis should be postponed for a few days and that because the premier "had invoked reasons of national interest" he did not wish to hinder him from carrying out the Estremadura offensive. "It would not be hard to convince the Communists to rejoin the government," he added, "if [Caballero] were to explain to them the reason for the postponement. Should the Estremadura plan be successful . . . the situation would improve appreciably, and he would have a decisive argument with which to confound his critics. He agreed immediately."[39]

Largo Caballero gives a somewhat different version: "[The president] suggested that I should withdraw my resignation and proceed with the projected operation. If this turned out well, the political atmosphere would improve. Afterward we would talk about the matter again. I opposed the president's suggestion because I was convinced that the maneuvers against the government were at their height and that any postponement would be useless. He insisted, speaking to me of sacrifices and other things, and I reluctantly agreed to withdraw my resignation."[40]

To Azaña's surprise, Caballero made no attempt to bring the Communists back into the government or to inform them of the decision to postpone the crisis. "[Largo Caballero] must have thought that his omission . . . was very astute," Azaña writes. "But precisely because of this omission his Socialist opponents entered the scene to force his hand and to prevent him from using the postponement as a means of escape."[41] Azaña does not explain how they had learned of his agreement with Caballero, but Araquistáin suggests that it was "perhaps through Azaña himself, who used to be in constant touch with Indalecio Prieto."[42]

"We were preparing to leave that afternoon [for Estremadura]," Caballero

recalls, "when Lamoneda [secretary of the Socialist executive], Negrín, and de Gracia [two of the three moderate Socialist ministers] presented themselves in my office at the war ministry. Prieto did not go; he remained behind the scenes. They informed me that in view of the resignation of the Communists, the three Socialist ministers named by the party executive had resigned. I replied that their solidarity with the Communists was incomprehensible. . . . Negrín replied that it was a decision of the executive and they had to respect it."[43]

At a meeting of the national committee of the Socialist party in July 1937, Jerónimo Bugeda, a Prieto Socialist, confirmed that the executive committee had taken the view that the Socialists could not remain in the government after the Communists had withdrawn their collaboration.[44]

"The maneuver was clear," wrote Araquistáin. "The three ministers of the center [Prieto] faction joined hands with the Communists in order to oust Caballero. It was essential to prevent the Estremadura offensive from being carried out, lest it prove successful. This view was expressed by Juan-Simeón Vidarte, a Socialist deputy belonging to the Prieto faction, in the following frank and criminal words: 'If Caballero should succeed in this offensive, no one will be able to throw him out of the government.' "[45] In his memoirs, many years after the war, Vidarte did not reply to this accusation, but he did say the following about the Estremadura offensive: "I spoke to Prieto about Asensio's plan. He told me that the whole thing was nothing but an illusion harbored by Asensio and Caballero. Miaja had stated clearly that to provide eight or ten divisions would be to leave Madrid in grave danger. Prieto, as air minister, could not provide more than eight or ten airplanes. The operation . . . was unrealizable."[46]

It was because of the resignation of the moderate Socialist ministers, a resignation that could have been avoided had Indalecio Prieto so desired in view of the influence he still exercised over González Peña, the president of the Socialist executive, and other steadfast supporters, that the suspicion that he had acted in secret concert with the Communist ministers hardened into positive belief. Moreover, it had not been forgotten that Lamoneda had carried out, at Prieto's bidding, the subtle maneuver that had resulted in Caballero's removal from the executive before the outbreak of the Civil War.[47]

Upon learning of the resignation of the Socialist ministers, Largo Caballero visited President Azaña: "I told him what Lamoneda, Negrín, and de Gracia had said, and his reply was that he did not understand the attitude of these Socialists. As I insisted on resigning, he decided to begin consultations."[48] Azaña continued to hide his animosity: "I extended to him a few words of courtesy and personal consideration . . . ill-deserved, as they were, coming from me and after all that had happened."[49] This "polite affability," as he describes it,[50] served its purpose during the delicate negotiations that lay ahead, for Largo Caballero harbored only an occasional doubt with regard to the president's true attitude toward him.[51]

During the round of conferences that Azaña held on 15 May with a view to forming a new ministry, the concurrence of the Socialist executive and the Communist party was no less apparent than at the outset of the crisis. "The

Communists and the Socialists," attests Azaña, "lashed out at the incompetence of Largo, at his camarilla, at his lack of communication with the government and the Higher War Council, at his distrust of the Russians, etcetera, etcetera. The Communists told me that . . . they would agree to his retaining the premiership . . . but on no account the war ministry. . . . It was clear that the main point of contention would be the assignment of the portfolio of war and its separation from the premiership. . . . I called Largo Caballero and asked him to form a government. He appeared very pleased."[52]

On 17 May, Caballero submitted to the president his list of ministers. "In his proposal," writes Azaña, "the premier, that is to say, he personally, not only retained the portfolio of war, but he appropriated the portfolios of navy and air!" Considering that the crisis had arisen, Azaña observes, because Largo Caballero was not wanted in the war ministry, this "devouring" of defense portfolios could be construed as an attempt on his part to render a solution impossible and to leave the government. "But . . . on no account did Largo wish to withdraw from the government." It was one more step toward the "absorption of government functions" and "a way to exploit the crisis by throwing Prieto out of a leading ministry." " 'Are you going to dispense with Prieto?' " Azaña asked Caballero. " 'In spite of the services he has rendered and the prestige that he enjoys?' No, he was not going to dispense with him. He wanted to appoint him minister of agriculture, industry, and commerce! . . . It was obvious, without any further analysis of the proposal, that Largo would not be able to form a cabinet."[53]

Even before submitting his plan to President Azaña, Largo Caballero had been aware that it would encounter stern opposition from the Communists and Prieto Socialists, for although they had made no overt objection to his being premier, they had not concealed their determination to exclude him from the war ministry. For their part the Communists had publicly insisted that the prime minister in the new government should occupy himself exclusively with the affairs of his own office. Another condition that was equally significant—in view of the decree that was to have gone into effect on 15 May, whereby all political commissars whose appointment and rank had not been confirmed on that date were to consider themselves dismissed from the corps of commissars—was that the commissariat of war should enjoy autonomy in all matters connected with the appointment and political direction of the commissars.[54]

As for the Socialist executive, it demanded that Indalecio Prieto should head a new department known as the ministry of national defense,[55] a department that was to combine not only the navy and air ministry, which he had held in the outgoing government, but also the ministry of war. These demands were undoubtedly formulated in accordance with a prior agreement between the Communist and moderate Socialist leaders. After the war, Vicente Uribe, a member of the politburo, wrote: "Prieto was appointed minister of national defense by mutual agreement and on the understanding that he would correct the errors of Caballero, strengthen the unity of the people, and tighten the bonds between the Communists and the Socialists. I myself raised these matters with Prieto several times before he became defense minister, and he always told me that he was agreeable and would do nothing prejudicial to the unity of the Socialists and the Communists."[56]

Clearly, the demands of the Communists and Socialists were tantamount to rejecting Largo Caballero not only as war minister but also as premier, for the Prieto Socialists and the Communists understood well the psychology of the left Socialist leader; they knew that he would voluntarily relinquish no part of his authority, that in his heart there existed an indestructible pride, and that he would refuse to become an ornamental figure in a cabinet in which Prieto, his perennial adversary, would assume control of the most vital ministry. Indeed, even before they had publicly made known their views, the UGT executive, controlled by the left-wing Socialists, declared that it would give no support of any kind to a government in which both the premiership and the war ministry were not held by Largo Caballero.[57]

This statement had undoubtedly been inspired by Caballero himself, for it corresponded to his own position throughout the crisis. "With stubborn energy," recalls Azaña, "Largo had stated several times that he would not return to the government under any circumstances unless he personally held the ministry of war, because he considered that his presence in that office was in the national interest."[58] "You will remember," Caballero wrote to a Socialist colleague after the war, "that the Communists wanted to throw me out of the war ministry and to leave me as a figurehead in the premiership. . . . I declared at the time that, as a Socialist and as a Spaniard, it was my duty to remain in the war ministry, and that otherwise I would not accept the premiership; but I did not say that because I considered myself irreplaceable, nor anything of the kind, but because I had the firm intention of fighting it out with the Communist party and all its accomplices; this I could do only from the war ministry."[59] And on another occasion he wrote: "What was truly senseless was that the other parties united with the Communist party to oust me from the war ministry. Did they not see the danger to the war itself in that party's exclusivist conduct? . . . Moreover, were they so blind that they did not perceive the tremendous desire of the Communists to direct the policy of Spain?"[60]

In his efforts to retain both the war ministry and the premiership, Largo Caballero received the full backing of the CNT. While editorials in the Anarcho-syndicalist press declared that the working class wanted him to remain in office as a guarantee for the proletarian revolution,[61] that it saw in him "the most capable and honorable person for presiding over the government that must carry us to victory,"[62] and that his presence in the premiership and war ministry was "the most solid guarantee for the proletariat that the character of the struggle being waged against international reaction will not be distorted by anybody or any-thing,"[63] the national committee declared emphatically that it would not collabo-rate with any government in which he was not both premier and war minister.[64] Yet, in spite of this support, Caballero did not even bother to consult the Anarchosyndicalists when drafting his plan for a new government and, indeed, offered them only two seats, as compared with four in the previous cabinet.[65]

This treatment was intensely galling to the CNT, and, in reply, it declared that, although it did not aim at increasing its representation in the government, it could not accept fewer portfolios than before or agree on any pretext to parity with the Communist party, which had likewise been offered two seats, and which, it affirmed, had provoked the crisis and had not collaborated in the government with the same degree of loyalty as itself.[66]

If Largo Caballero had drafted his plan for a new government without regard for the views of the CNT, even less had he taken into account the opinion of the Communists. Far from heeding their demand that the premier should occupy himself exclusively with the affairs of his own office, he had defiantly claimed for himself not only the control of the land forces but also the control of the fleet and air force and of arms production.[67] One may wonder whether he really expected that the Communists and their allies would consent to this proposal. If so, his expectations were quickly disappointed; for while José Díaz replied that the plan revealed no inclination to take into account the wishes of the central committee, wishes that were those of the Spanish people as a whole, and that the Communists could not form part of the government on the proposed terms,[68] Ramón Lamoneda declared, in the name of the Socialist executive, that his party could not accept representation in the government because the plan neglected to take into consideration the executive's demands and also because the Communist party had replied in the negative.[69]

Likewise united with the Communists in opposition to Caballero's proposal was the Left Republican party, which echoed the Communist demand that the premier in the new government should concern himself solely with the affairs of his own office.[70]

For the sake of appearances, President Azaña attempted to iron out the differences between Caballero and the Communists and even admonished José Díaz for his intransigence.[71] But the Communist party remained adamant, as was to be expected, and the Prieto Socialists and the left Republicans stood behind the party. As a result, Caballero was forced to abandon his attempt to form a government.[72]

45

The Rise of Juan Negrín

As Largo Caballero had now been shunted aside, President Azaña charged a new man with the task of organizing a cabinet. This man was Juan Negrín, minister of finance in the outgoing government. Son of a wealthy middle-class family in the Canary Islands, a Cortes deputy representing Indalecio Prieto's center faction of the Socialist party, which he had joined in 1929, he was also a professor of physiology at the Madrid School of Medicine. "I decided to entrust Negrín with the formation of the government," wrote Azaña. "The public had expected that I would name Prieto. But it was better to have Prieto head the ministry combining the armed forces, for which there was no other possible candidate. In the premiership, his sudden changes of mood, his 'tantrums,' could be inconvenient. I felt that it would be preferable . . . to take advantage of the quiet energy of Negrín."[1] Prieto believed that Azaña had another reason for passing him over in favor of Negrín: "Azaña explained to me that he had not appointed me to head the cabinet because I was too much of an opponent of the Communists to preside over a coalition in which they were represented. I was very grateful for the explanation and even more grateful that I had been left out of [a post] in which I could not serve and did not want to serve."[2] Azaña's preference for Negrín is corroborated by José Giral, a loyal follower and confidant of the president, who told Prieto a few days later that he had decided to appoint Negrín because he was more "flexible" with the Communists. Inflexibility, he added, might create conflicts within the government.[3]

Just before Azaña appointed Negrín to form a new ministry, the Socialist executive told Prieto that it had decided to ask Azaña to entrust him with the premiership. "Anything but that," Prieto replied, according to Juan-Simeón Vidarte, a member of the executive. "I get along badly with the Communists and my relations with the CNT are not cordial. . . . [The Communists] are already broadcasting the name of Negrín in all directions as Caballero's successor. I believe that he has more support than I at the present time. He also has a calmer and more accommodating disposition. I definitely do not want to accept the premiership under these circumstances, not even if I could count on the benevolent support of Caballero, which I did not have [in May 1936] when I could have been premier and could possibly have averted the catastrophe. I commend the name of Negrín to you."[4]

Although Prieto eschewed the premiership, some believed that he hoped to control the government through Negrín, his intimate and votary, whom he had recommended to head the ministry of finance in September 1936. But those who believed that Prieto would become "the real head" of the government "deceive themselves," wrote Azaña, "not only because Prieto is too intelligent to overstep his role, but because the character of Negrín does not lend itself to that situation."[5] In any event, it is unlikely that Prieto realized, in May 1937, to what extent Negrín was harkening to the call of the Spanish Communists, for even Prieto, a vociferous anti-Communist before the Civil War, was finding it expedient to maintain friendly relations with Soviet and Comintern representatives.

Prieto and Negrín first met in 1931 in the Cortes, where Negrín represented the Canary Islands. In an intimate portrayal of Negrín, Prieto recalls:

> We became very friendly, but later we became political adversaries. The differences that gave rise to our enmity were due to the fact that, while head of the government, he allowed himself to become subservient to the Communists, a subservience that has been fully proved, although he insisted on denying it. . . .
>
> Juan Negrín was a man of very exceptional physical and intellectual vigor and possessed a cordiality and charm that were captivating. His capacity for work was as enormous as his disorganization. He was just as likely to work at his desk for twenty-four hours at a stretch as to leave it without a trace for a week. . . .
>
> At the League of Nations in Geneva, where he appeared in 1937, and where they must have thought that the government of the Republic was made up of ruffians, he sparkled with his winning manners, his culture, and command of foreign languages. But in a normal parliamentary regime, he could never have become a prime minister, nor even a minister, since he lacked oratorical gifts. His method of reading or reciting his speeches—they were written for him—was unsuitable to our Parliament, where very often it was essential to improvise.
>
> He ate and drank as much as four men, but to avoid witnesses to these excesses, he dined two or three times at different places. Many evenings he had his first dinner at my home, then a second in a restaurant, and later a third, if all went well, in some night club. Educated in Germany, he acquired certain habits redolent of Nero's Rome, such as emptying a full stomach, rinsing his mouth, and continuing to gorge himself with food and drink.
>
> At the end of 1936, the official in the finance ministry who audited small accounts questioned the superintendent closely because of the unbelievable sums expended on aspirin. The explanation of the superintendent was in absolute accord with the truth. The new minister would frequently ask for aspirin, open the container, put it to his lips, and swallow all the tablets in one gulp.[6]

Easygoing and a bon vivant, infinitely more pliable than the austere and stubborn Caballero, and presumed to be more acceptable to the Western democracies than the left Socialist leader because of his moderate background, Negrín had long been selected as Caballero's successor in the premiership by Arthur Stashevsky, the Soviet trade representative. "In my conversations with Stashevsky in Barcelona in November [1936]," wrote Walter Krivitsky, whose revelations on Soviet activities in Spain later proved, as we have seen, to be singularly accurate, "Stalin's next moves in Spain were already cropping out. Stashevsky made no secret to me of the fact that Juan Negrín would be the next head of the Madrid government. At that time, Caballero was universally regarded as the favorite of the Kremlin, but Stashevsky had already picked Negrín as his successor."[7]

Because Krivitsky was denounced as an impostor by the Communists and their supporters when he made his revelations in 1938 and 1939 and inasmuch as his credibility is still being assailed, it is essential to stress that Negrín's close association with Stashevsky is confirmed by four prominent devotees: Louis Fischer, who states that Stashevsky was Negrín's friendly adviser on many economic problems;[8] Alvarez del Vayo who affirms that Stashevsky and Negrín formed a "real friendship";[9] Mariano Ansó, a future minister under Negrín, who observes that his "talent and irresistible" charm made a deep impression on some of the men "with whom he dealt"—including Stashevsky[10] and Santiago Garcés Arroyo, a onetime Prietista, whom Negrín placed in charge of the Servicio de Investigación Militar (SIM) after forming his second government in April 1938. While blandly asserting that Negrín "ignored" the Communist party, Garcés acknowledges that "he got along very well with the Russians, especially with Arthur Stashevsky, . . . with whom he ate lunch every day."[11]

It is also noteworthy that Miguel Serra Pàmies, a member of the central committee of the PSUC, stated, when interviewed by me after the war, that in February 1937, three months before the overthrow of Largo Caballero, "Pedro," the Comintern agent in Catalonia, who had just returned from Moscow, had told him and other leaders of his party that Negrín was favored as Largo's successor.[12] Even as zealous an admirer of Negrín as Professor Juan Marichal of Harvard University—who asserts that "few men in European history during the last century and a half have displayed such a combination of intelligence and character, of moral integrity and intellectual capacity"[13]—acknowledges that he was "the candidate of the Soviet Union and the Spanish Communists."[14]

Juan Negrín, Krivitsky affirmed, had all the makings of a bureaucratic politician. "Though a professor, he was a man of affairs with the outlook of a businessman. He was just the type to suit Stalin's needs. . . . He would impress the outside world with the 'sanity' and 'propriety' of the Spanish Republican cause; he would frighten nobody by revolutionary remarks. . . . Doctor Negrín, of course, saw the only salvation of his country in close cooperation with the Soviet Union. It had become obvious that active support could come only from that source. He was ready to go along with Stalin in everything, sacrificing all other considerations to secure this aid."[15]

Whether Negrín was willing to abandon all moral and political scruples to secure Soviet aid as early as May 1937 is not entirely certain, although there is no doubt of his willingness to compromise his principles once he had become installed in the premiership and, in April 1938, in the defense ministry. Salvador de Madariaga may be right when he argues that it is not sure "whether at this early stage Negrín was aware" of the part for which he was being coached by the Communists nor even whether he would have acquiesced in it if he had. "It may still be found on closer scrutiny," he adds, "that in ousting Señor Largo Caballero, the Communists, both Russian and Spanish, were the only actors who knew the script of the whole play, while Don Indalecio Prieto and Dr. Negrín knew little more than some cues and the hard fact that they were getting rid of their rival in the Socialist party. That in the mind of Dr. Negrín the new Cabinet meant a move to the Right, to authority, order and centralization, was obvious."[16]

Especially important to Moscow was the fact that Negrín had no official ties with the Communist party. That Negrín himself must also have been aware that this public nonalignment was essential to his Communist promoters and that he would eventually be forced to choose between his loyalty to Prieto and Soviet demands is suggested by the following private and unauthenticated dialogue that allegedly occurred when, on behalf of the politburo, Jesús Hernández visited Negrín to offer his party's support:

"Doctor," I said, plunging into the purpose of the interview, "the politburo wishes to propose your candidacy for the premiership to the president of the Republic."

I observed Negrín. He did not show the slightest sign of surprise or emotion at this abrupt announcement of our intention. No doubt he knew more than I about what I was saying. . . .

"You realize that I am little known, least of all popular."

"Don't let that concern you. . . . Popularity is manufactured! If there is anything we Communists have that is well organized it is our agitprop section," I said, laughing.

"But I am not a Communist."

"That's an advantage. If you were a Communist we could not propose you for the premiership. We want a premier who is a *friend* of the Communists—nothing more, but nothing less," I said knowingly. . . .

"Many aspects of Communist policy seem appropriate and wise to me," said Negrín.

"You won't have much support within your own party if you replace Caballero. . . ."

"Little, very little."

"But you will be able to count on the power of the Communists," I affirmed.

"Only in that way shall I be able to govern," Negrín commented.

"Then you shall govern."

"I would not want you to interpret my acceptance as my consent to becoming your 'man of straw.' Don't expect that of me. Besides, I wouldn't be useful to your party, to myself, or to anyone else," Negrín commented, preoccupied.

"I understand and share your scruples, but I can assure you that our support will be as discreet as it will be staunch and respectful. But one thing cannot be avoided—you will be labeled a 'communistoid,'" I explained.

"That's inevitable. . . . Who do you plan to support as defense minister?" he inquired.

"We shall not object to Prieto."

"Prieto isn't much of a friend of yours," observed Negrín.

"True, but his personal prestige more than outweighs all the harm his anticommunism might do."

In making this statement about Prieto, I had in mind the tactic that we had decided to follow regarding the future defense minister. When the politburo discussed the pros and cons of accepting Prieto as head of the defense ministry, we took into account his great prestige in moderate political circles at home and abroad. In this respect Prieto was useful to us. We also took into consideration the negative side of his character. He was a pessimist; he had no faith in victory. To entrust him with the maximum responsibility for prosecuting the war was an anomaly. . . . The members of the politburo hesitated to support his candidacy. Togliatti [the Comintern delegate] gave us the following advice: "By supporting the candidacy of Prieto we shall bring him under our control. If he doesn't agree to serve us, we shall exploit his notorious and self-proclaimed pessimism to bring about his removal, whenever it is convenient for us. . . . [We] shall try to envelop him in such a heavy shroud of disrepute that he will be rendered useless as an outstanding Socialist leader. One enemy less."

"Personally, I hold [Prieto] in great esteem; but you will have problems with him," Negrín insisted.

"We shall try to 'neutralize' him," I replied, smiling.

"How?"

"The undersecretaryship is just as important as the ministry and, at times, more so, because of its technical aspects. When Prieto becomes minister we shall ask for the undersecretaryship of war and air. . . . The commissariat of war is virtually in our hands. And with your friendship. . . ."

"And that of the Russians," Negrín added, laughing.

"Agreed, Doctor?"

"Agreed."[17]

With the elevation of Juan Negrín to the premiership, Largo Caballero had been defeated, and the Communists had achieved their most resounding victory to date. During the incredibly short period of only ten months, the left Socialist leader, who had enjoyed at the outbreak of the Civil War more real influence and popularity than any politician in the Republican camp, had been nullified politically and virtually reduced to impotence. Not only had he lost control of the UGT of Catalonia and the federation of the Spanish Socialist party in the region, not only had he been despoiled of his authority in the JSU, the powerful Unified Socialist Youth Federation, but he had lost control to the Communists of *Clari-*

dad, his mouthpiece in Madrid,[18] and had been betrayed or forsaken by many of his closest collaborators as well as by countless supporters holding commanding positions in the UGT and in local Socialist units. And now, in a final agony, he had been ousted from the premiership and war ministry and soon would be assailed by the Communists as enemy number one of the working class. "From the moment I left the government," he recalled some years later in *Mis recuerdos*, his published memoirs, "Largo Caballero was no longer the same person. He had been transformed. He was no longer a Socialist and even less a Marxist. He was enemy number one of the working class. They called me arrogant, ambitious, intransigent, an Anarchist, and other idiotic names. [My] photographs disappeared from everywhere. The idol they had created, they themselves delighted in destroying."[19] And in "Notas Históricas," his unpublished memoirs,[20] he wrote:

> For a long time, in Russia, [Caballero] was the man of the hour. In all the cities, theaters, newspapers, international slogans, his name had been linked with everything that signified the emancipatory action of the working class. [The Communists] wanted to exploit for the benefit of Moscow the influence he had gained among the Spanish working class thanks to fifty years of sacrifice. They flattered him in every way: with articles, photographs, political proposals, invitations to visit Russia, etc. He was the savior of Spain and the proletariat. They thought he had the moral character of Alvarez del Vayo, that he would surrender to their policy and play their game. But when, in the government, he became convinced of the dishonest behavior of the Communists and began to adopt measures to impede their hegemony in the army, the commissariat of war, the general staff, the quartermaster corps, and medical corps, and when he told them that he would not betray the Socialist party or the UGT and that he would conduct foreign and domestic policy like a true Spaniard and a true Socialist, he ceased to be the leader of the [projected] united party and of everything that they had previously said he was.

On the other hand, the Communists, through the prestige derived from Soviet arms; through their own self-discipline, cohesion, and ruthless energy; and through their adroit permeation of almost the entire machinery of state, had risen within the same short period of only ten months from a position of relative insignificance to one where they virtually controlled the destinies of the anti-Franco camp.

But this power they themselves could never have achieved without the active support, the connivance, the unsuspecting good faith, and the obtuseness of others. As Valentín González, El Campesino, the former Spanish Communist, asked some years later, after he had left the PCE:

> With few exceptions, especially during the early part of the war, how many Spanish politicians and military men were there who did not welcome the Communist agents with open arms and refused to play their game? At least I was a convinced Communist, and my attitude had some logic to it; but what logic was there in the

attitude adopted by the others? Without the lack of understanding and the complicity that were almost general would it have been possible, in the course of a few months, for a party, as weak numerically as the Communist party, to penetrate—and nearly dominate—the whole governmental apparatus? . . .

I am not trying to excuse my mistakes, but I should like everyone else to confess his own. If we Spanish Communists were guilty of abuses and iniquities and established our rule completely or were on the point of doing so, it was because the others, with few exceptions, did not rise to the occasion. . . . The Communist parties [of the world] are strong in proportion as the other parties and trade-union organizations are weak and vacillating and play their game. That was the lesson of Spain and that, today, is the lesson of Europe and the world. If they understand this lesson, they will save themselves, but if they do not, then they are lost.[21]

Part VI

The Reflux of the Revolution

46

The Negrín Government and the Reaction of the Libertarian Movement

The period embracing the rise of Juan Negrín in May 1937 to the end of the Civil War falls into five stages. The first stage is distinguished by the efforts of the PCE and the Negrín government to tighten the reins of power and by the continuing descent of the Revolution; the second by the political eclipse of Largo Caballero, by the efforts of the new defense minister, Indalecio Prieto, to end the military predominance of the PCE, and by his ouster from the government in April 1938. The third stage is marked by the reorganization of the cabinet, by Negrín's assumption of both the premiership and defense ministry and by the high-water mark of Communist power; the fourth is identified by the growth of dissension and disillusion, by the failure of the government to secure Anglo-French support, and by overwhelming military defeats; and the fifth by the collapse of the PCE's power and influence and the overthrow in March 1939 of Negrín and his Communist allies through a coalition of left-wing and moderate forces, who vainly attempted to negotiate with General Franco a settlement without reprisals.

The composition of the Negrín cabinet formed on 17 May 1937 was as follows:[1]

Juan Negrín	Socialist	Premiership and Finance
Indalecio Prieto	Socialist	Defense
Julián Zugazagoitia	Socialist	Interior
Jesús Hernández	Communist	Education and Health
Vicente Uribe	Communist	Agriculture
José Giral	Left Republican	Foreign Affairs
Bernardo Giner de los Rios	Republican Union	Public Works
Manuel de Irujo	Basque Nationalist	Justice
Jaime Aiguadé	Esquerra	Labor and Social Welfare

Comprising only nine members as opposed to eighteen in the Largo Caballero government, and divested of left-wing Socialists and Anarchosyndicalists, the new cabinet increased the relative strength of the PCE. "Unlike Largo Caballero," recalls Ivan Maisky, the Soviet ambassador to the United Kingdom, "the new Premier understood the vital need to cooperate with the Communist party and did not grieve unduly that the Anarchosyndicalists refused to come into his cabinet. He boldly slashed the numbers of ministers from 18 to 9. This made the government more compact and functional, and, most important, the ratio of Communists within it was considerably higher."[2]

On the day of its formation, the government declared that it was the genuine representative of all the political parties, that it regretted that the efforts to bring the CNT and UGT into the cabinet had failed, and that it would not allow any organization regardless of its ideology to commit acts of violence.[3]

The reaction in libertarian circles was belligerent. The CNT and FAI press condemned the government as "counterrevolutionary,"[4] and on 25 May the national committee of the CNT characterized the PCE as "the party of the counterrevolution," which, in "close collaboration with the bourgeois republican parties and right-wing Socialists," had brought to fruition the "political maneuver" that had culminated in the "provocation in Barcelona" and the formation of the new government. It also accused the Communists of being "agents of a national and international conspiracy" and declared that it was essential that the people should take the party's guilt into account "on the day of reckoning." Nevertheless, it continued, "in spite of everyone and despite everything," the revolution would continue its course. "Here are the working masses ready to reaffirm their revolutionary will and their unshakeable opposition to the maneuvers prepared by the skilled hands of the new red jesuits."[5]

On 29 May, Mariano Vázquez, the national secretary, issued a report on the CNT plenum of regional committees that had just concluded its deliberations. The plenum had resolved, inter alia, not to collaborate "either directly or indirectly" with the government, to spread propaganda among the armed forces against "the government of the counterrevolution," and to reach an agreement with the UGT in order to conduct a joint campaign of opposition.[6]

But these bold resolutions were viewed by the opponents of the CNT as bluff and bluster; for only two days later representatives of the national committee, headed by Mariano Vázquez, visited Negrín "to discuss conditions for possible collaboration."[7] The reason for this volte-face was clear. The national committee of the UGT, controlled by moderate Socialists and Communists, had just repudiated the position adopted by the left Socialist executive during the cabinet crisis.[8] The executive, it will be recalled, had declared that it would support only a government in which Largo Caballero held both the premiership and war ministry, a posture that had received the full backing of the CNT. Fearing political isolation, the CNT decided to reverse its stand and solicited representation in the government. In a "minimum program," published on 8 June, the national committee proposed equal representation for the Marxist, Republican, and libertarian sectors in all matters relating to national defense, the economy, and public order. It also proposed the creation of "advisory committees" comprising an equal number of representatives of the CNT and UGT in several other areas.[9] But, in the existing circumstances, these "inordinate pretensions"[10]—as the official Communist history describes them—were totally unrealistic and, not surprisingly, came to nothing.

Just how far the FAI, once regarded as the ideological bastion of the CNT, was also willing to stray from its prewar commitment to *apoliticismo* and direct action as a result of the formation of the Negrín government was reflected in a resolution passed at an FAI plenum held in July 1937. It was agreed during the four-day meeting that the FAI would create a "new organic structure" and that the nerve centers of the FAI, the small affinity groups (*grupos de afinidad*), would be dissolved and replaced by local, district, and regional organizations (*agrupaciones*) consisting of a large number of members. In this way, the FAI would become a mass organization that would "extend to the public life of Spain" and "propel the Revolution from all the popularly based organs of power."[11] As Alejandro Gilabert, a leading *faísta* and secretary of the local federation of Anarchist groups in Barcelona, explained: "With the new structure, the FAI finds itself in circumstances whereby it can both orient and direct the revolution. The old organic structure, based on affinity groups, was very effective before the revolution, when organized anarchism existed clandestinely, on the fringes of legality, and against the law, when at times it was obliged to systematize violence in the struggle against the bourgeoisie and the State. Now, in face of a new situation that offers us the brightest prospects, it would be absurd for the FAI to maintain a position on the margin of present realities."[12]

What Gilabert did not mention was that in its new form the FAI would to all intents and purposes become a political party and that, in any case, the proposal would have to be put to a peninsular congress for ratification.[13] The proposed reorganization was acerbically criticized by those Anarchosyndicalists who were opposed to the politicalization of the libertarian movement. For example, Felipe Aláiz, a well-known member of the FAI, described this pillar of *apoliticismo* as "the new governmental party." In his judgment the decisive step was tantamount to rejecting everything that Anarchism stood for: "By constituting itself as a new political party [the FAI] is asserting that the people are incapable of directing their own destinies. These are the very people who made up the deficiencies of the State in the trenches and on the barricades in July [1936]. . . . [They are] the same people who cultivate the land, who transport the products, improve the soil and sacrifice themselves on the land, sea and in the air, but are now nothing more than a bunch of country bumpkins."[14]

Just how deep was the resistance within the FAI to the reorganization cannot be gauged accurately. To judge from the testimony of Alejandro Gilabert, opposition was considerable, so much so that "the differences reached the point of threatening a split."[15] In face of this "grave problem," a committee was nominated "to seek a formula of reconciliation that would unite the opposing views."

The committee decided that "the large opposition" would be free to continue as affinity groups "but that their resolutions of an organic nature will be taken into account only in proportion to the number of affiliates they represent."[16] However, as this compromise had to be put to a peninsular congress for ratification, the change was never formally sanctioned, since there is no record that a congress was held.[17]

Meanwhile, on 31 May, President Azaña—who a year later recorded woefully in his diary that Negrín was acting without consulting him and was always presenting him with accomplished facts[18]—made the following optimistic comment: "The new government has been received with general satisfaction. The people have heaved a sigh of relief. They expect energy, decision, the will to govern, the restoration of normal methods in the affairs of state, the crushing of indiscipline. Public anxiety . . . has been allayed by the belief that the government will soon put an end to the disorder in the rear. This is the most painful sore. The new premier has great confidence in his plans, in his authority. He affirms that the war will continue for a long time (another year!), and that he is preparing for this. Little known and still young, Negrín is intelligent, cultured, recognizes the problems and understands them. . . . One may agree or disagree with his personal views, but when I now speak to the head of the government I no longer have the impression that I am speaking to a corpse. After so many months this is a pleasant novelty for me."[19]

Despite the moderate complexion of the cabinet and the fact that the Communists held no more than the two seats they had occupied in the government of Largo Caballero, its composition was deceptive.

In the first place, although Julián Zugazagoitia, a Prietista, was made minister of the interior, the Communists not only retained all the pivotal positions in the police administration they had held previously, but Lieutenant Colonel Antonio Ortega, a party member,[20] was named director general of security in place of Wenceslao Carrillo, a supporter of Largo Caballero. At the request of Negrín, Juan-Simeón Vidarte, a Prietista and member of the Socialist party executive, took over the undersecretaryship of the interior. When urging him to accept the post, Negrín—according to Vidarte—made the following comment: "Look here, Vidarte, I made Zuga [Zugazagoitia] minister of the interior because Prieto asked me to. In reality, this is as though Prieto had two ministries. I know little about Zuga; he is not a friend of mine. He is Prieto's man. On the other hand, the Communists asked me to give the general direction of security to [Lieutenant] Colonel Ortega, who is an unconditional supporter of theirs. . . . Whom do I have in the administration? I am not offering you a post. I am asking you a favor."[21] In his book, Zugazagoitia, who speaks of Ortega's "rapid evolution from moderate Republican to enthusiastic Communist," refers to him as his "theoretical subordinate" and states that *he* did not appoint him to the position of director general of security.[22] This is confirmed by Justo Martínez Amutio, a Caballero Socialist, onetime governor of Albacete and secretary of the Socialist

Federation of Valencia, who states that, when Zugazagoitia took possession of the ministry of the interior, Negrín "at the bidding of the Communists" had already appointed Colonel Ortega to his post as director general of security and had also made appointments to the command positions in the security services in Madrid, Barcelona, and Valencia. The entire police corps, he added, underwent a "massive upheaval that resulted in its total domination by the Communists."[23] Even more convincing evidence of the predominance of the PCE in the police administration is that of Negrín's friend Vidarte, who quotes his boss, Julián Zugazagoitia, as saying that the ministry of the interior and the general direction of security were "nests of spies and confidants of the GPU [NKVD]."[24]

The Communists of course did not acknowledge publicly their penetration of the police apparatus, but their control is implicit in their official history, which states that the government "adopted a series of forceful measures designed to strengthen public order, concentrating in its hands all the levers of power."[25]

The moderate complexion of the cabinet was also deceptive in another way. Although Indalecio Prieto held the defense ministry, the philo-Communist Julio Alvarez del Vayo kept his post as head of the General Commissariat of War. As Prieto complained to Azaña on 29 June, this institution was "almost entirely Communist," and "Alvarez del Vayo acts as straw man."[26] In addition, Largo Caballero's executive order dismissing all political commissars whose appointment and rank had not been confirmed by 15 May was shelved, leaving the Communists entrenched in that vital body. It will be recalled that one of the Communist party's conditions for participating in the new government was that the General Commissariat of War should enjoy autonomy in all matters relating to the appointment and political direction of the commissars. According to Vidarte, when newsmen asked Negrín if any personal friend of Largo Caballero was going to join his administration, Negrín replied: "Of course, no one other than the chief commissar, Señor Alvarez del Vayo." Vidarte's comment: "Everyone knew . . . that no one at that time was more detested by Largo Caballero than his former minister of foreign affairs, whom he had flayed mercilessly in the cabinet. But Negrín combined the seriousness of a scientist with the sense of humor of a man of the world."[27]

Furthermore, Lieutenant Colonel Antonio Cordón, a Communist party member, whom Largo Caballero had discharged from the technical secretariat of the undersecretaryship of war, was reappointed to that post;[28] Major Manuel Estrada, also a party member, whom Largo Caballero had removed from the war ministry general staff, reemerged in the defense ministry; Captain Eleuterio Díaz Tendero, the philo-Communist, who had been dismissed from the highly sensitive information and control department, was reinstated; and Miaja's eminently capable chief of staff, the enigmatic and politically adaptable Colonel Vicente Rojo, was made chief of the central general staff.[29] All these appointments were undoubtedly made in accordance with a prior agreement between Prieto and the Communists as a condition of his heading the defense ministry.

At the same time, the process of reorganizing the inefficient and undisciplined militia into units of the Popular Army was accelerated under Prieto thanks largely to the unremitting efforts of the PCE, which perceived in the centralization, efficiency, and discipline of the new army not only the sine qua non of victory but an essential prerequisite for the control of the state. On 23 June, a decree was published suppressing the last of the militia headquarters.[30] "In this way," writes the official Communist history, "all the armed forces were subordinated to the general staffs of their respective fronts and these in turn were subordinated to the central general staff. Thanks to these and other measures adopted by the government of Dr. Negrín the militia were incorporated into the regular army on all fronts and discipline and the single command were established throughout loyalist territory."[31]

Finally, although Alvarez del Vayo was replaced in the foreign ministry by former premier José Giral, a close friend of Azaña's, he left behind him a legacy of Communist functionaries in the ministry and in its various dependencies, including the foreign propaganda press agency, the Agencia Española, and the Foreign Press Bureau. In addition, Federico Melchor, who had joined the PCE in November 1936, was made director general of propaganda.[32]

The Communists had good reason to be elated at the course of events. In fact, in a report to Moscow on 30 August 1937, Palmiro Togliatti stated that the overthrow of the Largo Caballero government had "undoubtedly gone to the heads of some of the comrades." They believed, he wrote, that their success was due entirely to the party and forgot that the centrists, together with Prieto, had played "a very important role both in the preparation and the solution of the crisis." "That erroneous assessment," he continued, "has given rise to the opinion that the party is already in a position to raise the question of its *hegemony* and to fight openly for that hegemony in the government and in the country."[33]

The idea that the PCE at this stage should throw off all restraint and make an open bid for power was at variance with Stalin's advice to Largo Caballero in December 1936 that everything possible should be done to secure the support of Azaña and his middle-class Republicans "in order to prevent the enemies of Spain from regarding her as a Communist republic." This policy had not changed, and it was Togliatti's task, as Comintern delegate, to see that the Spanish Communist leadership toed the Kremlin line. "One has only to speak with our comrades," his report to Moscow continued, "and listen to their discussions to realize that even today (August 1937) they lack sufficient clarity on the matter. One of our tasks is to explain this to them and help them to understand it." In Catalonia, the "confusion" was such that some comrades had suggested that their principal task was to "fight for the destruction of all capitalist elements" and "to prevent their resurgence and reinforcement" and had come to the conclusion that this policy could be realized "only by a proletarian and communist government." "It is clear," Togliatti observed, "that with this point of view, these confused comrades were not able to appreciate that after the fall of Caballero their task was to exert pressure on the government to carry out a Popular Front policy [i.e., a policy behind which the party could continue to disguise its hegemonic aims] and to broaden the government's base by creating, through adequate political work, a split in the ranks of the anarchists and Caballero Socialists."[34]

What all this meant in the arcane realm of Comintern politics will be seen in subsequent chapters.

47

The PSUC Supersedes the CNT and FAI
as the Dominant Force in Catalonia

*I*n Catalonia, where the May events had resulted in the taking over of public order and defense by Valencia, the political victory of the PSUC was consolidated by the formation of the Negrín government. The liberal Republican, General Sebastián Pozas, head of the Civil Guard at the outbreak of the war, who had quietly entered the Communist party in October 1936, when he was commander of the Army of the Center, and who, on 5 May, had been made military commander of Catalonia and of the eastern army in neighboring Aragon, openly joined the PSUC[1] and in the months to come gave the Communists free rein. Pozas was aided by two Communist party members: his chief political commissar, Virgilio Llanos, a former Caballero Socialist; and Antonio Cordón, recently appointed chief of staff of the eastern army by Indalecio Prieto.[2] Furthermore, Lieutenant Colonel Emilio Torres, who was sympathetic toward the CNT and FAI and whom interior minister Angel Galarza had appointed police chief of Barcelona during the fighting in order to facilitate the passage of the assault guards through Catalonia, was replaced on 8 June by former police chief of Madrid Lieutenant Colonel Ricardo Burillo, a Communist party member.[3]

The growth in the political power of the PSUC after the May fighting was evidenced by the increased stridency of its attacks on the CNT and FAI. In a speech on 1 June that exceeded in ferocity anything that he had previously delivered, secretary Juan Comorera condemned the "forced collectivizations in town and country" that had been carried out "with a sinister policy of coercion, violence, and, on occasions, assassinations" and railed against the "dictatorial will of powerful unions [that] dominated the mass of workers, who were literally hunted through the streets of Barcelona," and "denounced and executed." These powerful unions, he asserted, had attacked "the lower middle classes, undermined the economic fabric, the industrial, commercial, and banking reserves, the very reserves that form the basis for the reconstruction of our economy." And last of all, there had been "the systematic organized smuggling out of precious metals, of merchandise, and the hoarding of money."[4]

(There was of course some truth in these accusations. For instance, the CNT and FAI did indeed export precious metals in order to purchase arms and supplies, but in strict fairness it must be stated that the amounts involved were infinitesimal as compared with the massive shipment of gold to the Soviet Union, which, as we have seen, constituted the financial reserves of the nation.[5] A more genuine grievance against the CNT by its opponents was its control of the main ports and the Franco-Spanish border, a control that enabled it to ship abroad through its own export entities valuable agricultural products that yielded large quantities of foreign exchange.[6] Whereas the Anarchosyndicalists regarded this control as an inalienable conquest of the Revolution, the central government viewed it as an impingement on the indefeasible power of the state. In the long run, this political and ideological conflict could only be resolved by force, as demonstrated when Juan Negrín dispatched his carabineers to the Franco-Spanish border in April and May 1937 to wrench control from the revolutionaries. The heart of the matter was that no government, regardless of its political composition, could afford to relinquish these important elements of authority if it hoped to function as a sovereign power. Hence, it is not surprising that from the moment he entered the finance ministry in September 1936, Negrín, an implacable opponent of the left wing of the Revolution, should have found himself at odds with the CNT. Julián Zugazagoitia, the moderate Socialist, who became interior minister under Negrín in May 1937, claims that the premier and finance minister "preferred not to have Anarchists in the government" because he wished "to dismantle all the export organizations created by the CNT" and "to end once and for all" the loss of foreign exchange resulting from the shipment abroad of almonds, oranges, and saffron.[7])

While the opponents of the PSUC followed their own line "with its negative results," Comorera's diatribe continued, "we have kept to our line and in such a way that, today, the balance of forces is not the same as it was at the beginning of the war. . . . Today, as a result of experience, the great masses have been able to prove by the light of daily events, the correctness and honesty of our political line. Today the scales are turned. The balance of forces has changed and the change is profound."

And touching on one of the most sensitive issues for the libertarian movement, Comorera inveighed against the CNT's control of public utilities and services. Urging that the provisional government formed during the May events should be replaced by a new government that would give "every facility to the city councils to municipalize immediately all public services, especially transport, gas works and water works, public entertainment, housing, slaughter houses and markets," he added: "It is said that to talk of municipalizing transport, for example, is counterrevolutionary, because it would mean taking from the workers what they now have in their power. . . . Do we want to create a privileged caste? Do we want to create a new aristocracy, a new bourgeoisie? Have thousands of workers died at the battle fronts so that in the end we can substitute CNT-FAI Tramways Ltd. for Barcelona Tramways Ltd.?"[8]

On the other hand, the Anarchosyndicalists argued that they were not against municipalization. "We have already stated and will repeat as often as necessary," said *Solidaridad Obrera*, "that municipalization is in keeping with our principles. But it must be guaranteed by city councils freed from bureaucratic inertia and cleansed of the immoralities inherent in old-time politics."[9] This was just another way of saying that they would not agree to municipalization as long as they did not control the city councils. Despite its increased strength, the PSUC in this instance did not get its way, for when the question of municipalization came up for discussion in the Barcelona city council, the Esquerra, frightened that the PSUC was gaining too much power, sided with the CNT in declaring that "in its opinion [municipalization] could not be carried out unless it had the firm collaboration and understanding of the comrades of the working class."[10] Nevertheless, both the PSUC and PCE continued to press for municipalization[11] as they did for the nationalization of the basic industries[12] with a view to breaking the economic power of the CNT and FAI.

Meanwhile, the *patrullas de control*, or patrols, the police squads created in the early days of the Revolution—whose attempted dissolution and absorption into a single internal security corps had been one of the main causes of the political deadlock in Catalonia in March and April—came under renewed assault by the PSUC.[13] They were dissolved on 4 June by an executive order of the Esquerra councillor of the interior, Carlos Martí Feced,[14] in accordance with the legislation approved in March providing for the dissolution of the patrols and the Assault and National Republican guards and for their incorporation into a single internal security corps, legislation that *Solidaridad Obrera* had denounced as "completely alien to the struggles and aspirations of the working people."[15] Martí Feced, it will be recalled, was one of the four members of the provisional government formed on 4 May during the fighting in Barcelona. But his real authority as head of the Generalitat's forces of public order was ephemeral, for, after the central government had assumed control of public order on 5 May, he became a simple auxiliary of the delegate of public order appointed by Valencia. After observing that the delegate had informed him that the services of the patrols were no longer needed, his executive order stated that in accordance with the legislation approved in March, the individual members of the patrols could apply for admission into the single internal security corps. In view of the fact that the single internal security corps had never been formed and that nothing was said of the dissolution of the Assault and National Republican guards,[16] it was clear that the March legislation was invoked only to give legal support to the dissolution of the patrols. A few days later, the delegate of public order, José Echevarría Nova, announced that he had issued instructions to ensure that "within forty-eight hours" the members of the patrols handed over whatever equipment and barracks they possessed.[17] Although it took more than forty-eight hours to overcome their resistance,[18] they disappeared for good by the end of June as an organized force of the Revolution.

It is noteworthy that Colonel Eduardo Cuevas de la Peña, a member of the

PCE, who had been placed in charge of the assault guards in Barcelona and who in April 1938 became director general of security under Negrín,[19] claims personal credit for the executive order and the subsequent dissolution of the patrols. The Catalan authorities, he asserts (in an obvious reference to the timidity of the Esquerra councillor of the interior) at first argued against the measure because of the dangers it presented: "Perhaps some [militia] units would abandon the front and march on Barcelona. They did not convince me. My decision was unshakeable. . . . The next day the order was published and we seized the barracks without serious incidents. Once again, Barcelona was able to breathe freely."[20]

During the preceding weeks, the CNT—hoping to foil any attempt to suppress the patrols—had argued that they had remained neutral during the fighting.[21] This was a flawed argument, for the POUM publicly announced that the patrols had suffered fifty-seven casualties including seventeen fatalities.[22] Equally ineffectual was the gesture made by the patrols themselves, offering their services to Lieutenant Colonel Torres and to the Catalan government, a gesture that, although supported by Torres, was rejected by President Companys.[23] His rebuff was not surprising, for now that the central government had assumed control of public order, he no longer placed his hopes of political survival in an accommodation with the CNT and FAI but in the swift destruction of their armed power in the expectation that this would induce Valencia to restore the control of public order to the Generalitat, salvaging his honor as the recognized champion of Catalan autonomy. Thus, while expressing the view that the central government should not have taken over the administration of public order but, instead, should have provided the Generalitat with reinforcements,[24] he nevertheless advocated the rapid disarming of the rear and the seizure of arms depots and urged Valencia to proceed with the "cleaning up and disarming" of the frontier posts.[25] The work of reclaiming control of the Franco-Spanish border, it will be recalled, had already begun before the May fighting with the arrival of Negrín's carabineers, and on 2 June the "frontier militias" of the CNT-FAI and POUM were officially dissolved.[26] But, in the sequel, Companys was disappointed, for not only did the central government take swift advantage of its seizure of the frontier posts by the carabineers to recover the control of foreign trade from Catalonia,[27] but in November 1937 it moved to Barcelona, shattering his hopes that the administration of public order would be restored to the region.

If the dissolution of the patrols, the disarming of the rear, and the seizure of the frontier posts were a heavy blow to the CNT and FAI, no less so was the loss of their power in countless towns and villages in the region. On 15 May, the revolutionary committees—that had hitherto resisted the Generalitat's decree of 9 October 1936 providing for their replacement by municipal councils, in which the various organizations were to be seated in proportion to their representation in the cabinet[28]—were declared illegal by the Catalan government.[29] In fact, many of the committees were overturned by the newly arrived guards and carabineers even before they were outlawed in mid-May. Furthermore, the CNT was excluded from some of the town councils that had already been set up in accordance with the decree of 9 October,[30] and on 5 July the congress of the Esquerra of Tarragona province voted to eliminate from the city councils all those elements who had played an active part in the May events and had not condemned them.[31]

The decline in the revolutionary power of the Anarchosyndicalists exacerbated the animosity of the more extreme elements toward the moderate leadership. In its first issue published in the latter part of May, *El Amigo del Pueblo*, the mouthpiece of the recently formed radical group, the Friends of Durruti, accused the regional committees of the CNT and FAI of having "betrayed the workers and the revolution" by their "incompetence and cowardice."[32] The regional committees lost no time in excommunicating the radicals and issued a declaration denouncing the accusation as "very grave calumnies" and ordering the expulsion from the CNT and FAI of all those belonging to the Friends of Durruti "who do not publicly declare themselves against the stand taken by this group."[33] It was symptomatic of the growing dissensions within the Anarchist movement that the Local Federation of the Libertarian Youth of Barcelona, the regional committee of the Libertarian Youth, and the Local Federation of Anarchist Groups of Barcelona refused to sign the declaration.[34]

By mid-June a new shakeup in the Catalan government appeared inevitable. The provisional government formed during the May fighting was ineffectual. In his denunciatory speech of 1 June, Juan Comorera called for an end to "this transitional political situation" and for the formation of a "stable government" that could "fulfil the duties imposed by the war and meet the problems of economic reorganization."[35] On 19 June, *Tierra y Libertad*, the FAI organ, published the text of a "confidential political report" purportedly sent by the central committee of the PSUC to local units outlining its plans for a change. The new government, the report said, would be a "strong government of the Popular Front." Its mission would be "to pacify emotions and make those who were responsible for the counterrevolutionary movement pay for their deeds." The CNT would be offered posts in the government, "but in such a manner that it will feel compelled to reject participation." Although the authenticity of the report cannot be proved, it is curious that the CNT soon found itself maneuvered out of office in the way suggested.

During the negotiations that began at the end of June for the formation of a new cabinet, it was at first agreed that the Esquerra, the CNT, and the PSUC would each have three portfolios and the Unió de Rabassaires one, while President Companys himself would assume the premiership.[36] But at the last moment, overruling the objections of the CNT, Companys gave a seat to the distinguished anthropologist Pedro Bosch Gimpera, a member of Acció Catalana Republicana, a small middle-class party and ally of the Esquerra, thus increasing the relative strength of the left Republicans. The CNT denounced the action as a "maneuver," a "disloyalty," and informed Companys of its "absolute disagreement with the appointment."[37] Failing to perceive what may indeed have been a maneuver, the CNT declared categorically that it would not participate in the government if Companys did not withdraw the appointment.[38]

Clearly, the Anarchosyndicalist leaders did not realize to what degree the political balance had tipped against them and may have harbored the illusion that Companys would not attempt to govern without them. But the time had now passed when he was forced to take their wishes into account as in the heyday of the Revolution. Abandoning his role as shrewd conciliator, he took a firm stand and left the CNT out in the cold. "I am the President of Catalonia," he declared over the radio, "named by parliament, and ratified explicitly and repeatedly by all the trade-union and political organizations." But an attempt was being made, he said, to deny him the right to form his own government. "Catalans! Enough! The new government of the Generalitat is a Popular Front government and here is its composition." Companys then read the following list of names and portfolios:

Luis Companys	ERC	President
Antonio María Sbert	ERC	Interior
José Tarradellas	ERC	Premier and Finance
Carlos Pi Sunyer	ERC	Culture
Juan Comorera	PSUC	Economy
Rafael Vidiella	PSUC	Labor
Miguel Serra Pàmies	PSUC	Supplies
José Calvet	Unió de Rabassaires	Agriculture
Pedro Bosch Gimpera	Acció Catalana	Justice[39]

But it should be mentioned that the dispute over Bosch Gimpera was not the only reason why the CNT leaders decided against participation in the cabinet. According to Valerio Más, the CNT councillor in the previous administration, there were other factors. Two are worth recording: (1) the growing dissension between the CNT leaders who favored governmental collaboration and the anticollaborationists "who day by day saw their revolutionary conquests being wrenched from them," and (2) "the difficulty in finding comrades willing to collaborate . . . in a government that destroyed rather than reinforced the economic achievements of the CNT." "When I was a councillor," Más informed me after the war, "I succeeded in having forty industrial groupings legalized, but because of pressure by the PSUC on Companys and the Rabassaires, the remainder were not legalized, although they had already been approved by the Council of Economy, in which all the parties and organizations were represented."[40]

It is indeed most likely that the anticollaborationists exerted pressure on the CNT leaders and that Companys's unexpected appointment of Bosch Gimpera provided the CNT negotiators with a face-saving opportunity to decline participation. In any event, the anticollaborationists did not disguise their satisfaction over the outcome of the crisis.

"The maneuver has been exposed," declared *Tierra y Libertad*. "The CNT, with more than a million affiliates in Catalonia,[41] is no longer in the government. This is because Anarchosyndicalism cannot get involved with professional politicians and cannot humble itself before anyone. . . . [It] refuses to defile itself with this kind of dirty politics."[42]

Far more direct and combative was *Juventud Libre*, the national organ of the FIJL, which declared on 3 July: "Up to now the directors of the counterrevolution have achieved their aims. . . . They have removed the CNT from the central government and from the government of Catalonia. They have not hesitated to use any means, no matter how despicable or jesuitical, to betray the Revolution. They have jeopardized and continue to jeopardize the war in their desire to satisfy their shameful appetites. . . . But the Spanish people see their game and will no longer permit the further advance of the counterrevolution.

"Revolutionary Socialists, sincere Republicans, and Anarchosyndicalists must form rapidly a powerful alliance that will descend on the enemies of the revolutionary Spanish people and crush them for ever. . . .

"The Revolution is in danger. The conquests that you have won at the cost of infinite sacrifice and loss of life are being betrayed by our enemies in the rear. Do not allow them to snatch those conquests from you."

Despite these revolutionary outbursts, which expressed the feelings of a large segment of the libertarian movement, the CNT leaders made several attempts— even as late as December 1938—to reenter the Catalan government,[43] but their efforts were unavailing.[44] In any case, their participation would have had no significant impact on the course of events, for real authority in Catalonia since the May upheaval had passed to the central government and, in the last analysis, to the Communists, thanks to their assumption of police and military power in the region.

Just how much the power relations in Catalonia had changed since May has been accurately recorded by Manuel Cruells, a staff reporter at the time on the *Diari de Barcelona*, the organ of Estat Català, which represented the small separatist movement among the Catalan middle classes: "Despite the semblance of continuity created by the presence of Companys and his party in the government of the Generalitat, political ascendancy had passed [from the Anarchosyndicalists] to the PSUC. . . . And thanks to this absolute ascendancy, the PSUC was able to impose on the government of the Generalitat total obedience—humiliating at times—to the directives of the central government over which Dr. Negrín presided until the end of the Civil War."[45]

The change in power relations was clearly discernible on the streets. Writing immediately after the May events, Robert Louzon, a French revolutionary syndicalist and eyewitness, notes: "During the first months of the revolution, Barcelona was filled with workers bearing arms. Later, only those entrusted with special functions could be seen, but they were still workers. Today (except perhaps in a few exclusively proletarian districts) not a single worker carrying arms can be observed: only assault guards, assault guards with rifles, assault guards on every corner as in the heyday of bourgeois power." Even the apparel on the streets reflected the decline in the predominance of the CNT. "[The] exclusively working-class attire, which I noted in August," Louzon continued, "and which was still being worn in February, has given way in the central districts almost completely to bourgeois or at least petty bourgeois dress. A still more striking fact is that red and black have almost totally disappeared. Before May, everyone sported the colors of the CNT. . . . Today, in contrast, those who have the courage to wear the insignia of the CNT are rare. No longer can red and black flags be found outside trade-union buildings. As for caps and kerchiefs, which were once the most popular, . . . none at all can now be seen."[46]

48

Communist Repression of the Anarchists and the POUM

*I*n the weeks and months following the May events, the story of Catalonia—the former power center of the CNT-FAI and POUM—was one of arbitrary arrests, of detentions in clandestine jails, of tortures, kidnappings, and assassinations, as well as of the destruction of agricultural collectives. The spontaneous, undirected terror of the CNT and FAI during the height of the Revolution had now given way to the more sophisticated, centrally directed, and, hence, more fearful terror of the Communists. "A wave of blood and terror has swept over the communities of Catalonia . . . ," declared the national committee of the CNT in mid-June 1937. "Our libertarian movement has kept silent . . . not out of cowardice, but out of discipline and a sense of responsibility. . . . With incomparable stoicism it has endured the assault on the collectives, on the constructive work of the proletariat."[1]

"From May up to the present time," declared the regional committee of the CNT at the end of June, "the provocations against the CNT of Catalonia have not ceased. Our militants have been persecuted; they have been indicted and assassinated; our locals have been closed and collectives destroyed; outrages have been committed in order to drive the Catalan CNT to the point of desperation, yet we have remained calm in spite of this hurricane of repression and provocation. We do not want to ignite a fratricidal war. We do not want to destroy the antifascist coalition, which is already split by the vile maneuvers of certain elements."[2]

This forbearance riled the more radical spirits in the libertarian movement. On 1 July, the underground newspaper *Anarquía*, in its first issue, expressed the growing cleavage between the leadership of the movement and a large segment of the rank and file. "In face of the serious situation confronting our organization, in face of the barbarous repression unleashed against us, in face of the assault on and destruction of our collectives and our revolutionary work, . . . we must sound a cry of alarm and urge the militant comrades [that is, the leaders] of the CNT and FAI, who optimistically believe that our revolution is advancing and that we are still a force to be feared and respected . . . that they should let the scales fall from their eyes. The repression in the rural areas is incredible. The hatred of the CNT and FAI has reached unsuspected heights. In an orgy of bloodletting, the assault guards, sent to maintain order, attack the villages and destroy everything, imprisoning and assassinating our comrades."[3]

For months, the repression in Catalonia and other regions of the Republican zone continued unabated. In September, the national committee of the CNT affirmed that there were thousands of "proven revolutionaries and antifascists" in prison,[4] and, in November, *Solidaridad Obrera* gave a figure of fifteen thousand.[5] How many assassinations of CNT affiliates occurred during this period will always remain a matter of speculation, since no trustworthy figures have ever been published.[6] However, there can be little doubt that the number of assassinations was substantial, if we take into account those committed both at the front and in the rear.

Despite the repression, national secretary Mariano Vázquez, addressing the AIT congress in Paris in December 1937, painted a rosy picture. In an attempt to counter the pungent criticism of the CNT leadership by certain foreign Anarchists, among whom was the prominent Russian emigré Alexander Schapiro, Vázquez declared, according to the minutes of the congress: "The growth of the Communist party, the arbitrary acts of the reactionaries, the presence of our militants in Republican jails, etc., might suggest that our movement is declining and deceive some ill-informed observers. But the fact is that the CNT is on a good course, with a growing membership, with renewed combativeness and realism, and absolutely united in its point of view. For the moment, our concern is to win the war. Once this has been achieved, we shall resume the offensive in the social sphere and then—our friends must believe us—the revolution will be achieved without delay! Neither communism nor the bourgeoisie can frighten us. We alone can conquer. We shall win and we shall have in Spain the total dominion [*totalitarisme*] of the CNT."[7]

According to Jaap Kloosterman of the International Institute for Social History, Amsterdam, the congress of the AIT was a "secret" extraordinary congress held between 6 and 17 December 1937, and the minutes (in French), published only in part, were all that ever appeared "if one excepts the very tendentious summary printed by the CNT national committee in 1938."[8]

Despite the optimistic assessment of the situation given by Mariano Vázquez, the truth of the matter is that the repression directed against the libertarian movement, which represented half the working class, had already begun to take its toll on the revolutionary exultation of the first months of the Civil War. "[In] the rear," wrote Ricardo Sanz, the CNT militia leader, "things are not going as well as they did in the early days of the [revolutionary] movement. . . . The workers no longer think of working long hours to help the front. They only think of working as little as possible and getting the highest possible wages. This, on the whole, represents a degenerating situation."[9]

While the repression against the CNT was still in progress, the POUM was being threatened with extinction. On 16 June, Ricardo Burillo, a lieutenant colonel of the assault guards and Communist police chief of Barcelona, acting on instructions from Lieutenant Colonel Antonio Ortega, the Communist director general of security, seized the POUM headquarters in Barcelona and other buildings of the party, arresting most of its top leaders and taking them to prisons in Valencia.[10] On the same day, José Rovira, the commander of the POUM's Twenty-ninth Division and a member of the party's executive committee, was summoned to Barcelona by General Pozas and quickly arrested by the Communist police.[11]

Obeying secret orders received directly from the NKVD in Valencia[12]— Alexander Orlov's headquarters—Ortega withheld all knowledge of the impending coup from his immediate superior, interior minister Julián Zugazagoitia.[13] As an additional precaution, so that the operation would not be thwarted, he dispatched to Ciudad Real, on a false alarm, the subdirector general of security, the moderate Socialist Gabriel Morón, whom Zugazagoitia had appointed to keep him apprised of "whatever might happen" in the police department because of his distrust of the director general.[14]

At this point it is appropriate to relate a personal experience that confirms the primary involvement of the NKVD, the Soviet secret police, in the coup. I was at that time the United Press correspondent in Valencia and sympathetic to the Communist party line. On 18 June, two days after the arrest of the POUM leaders, an NKVD agent, who went by the name of "Irma," and to whom I had been introduced by Orlov,[15] handed me a document, which she claimed was an advance copy of a communiqué soon to be released by the director general of security.[16] The announcement stated (1) that "a vast conspiracy against the security of the state" had been discovered as well as numerous documents that proved "irrefutably" the suspected links between the POUM and the enemy, among them a plan of Madrid, on the back of which was written in invisible ink a message by one of General Franco's agents referring to an interview with the leaders of the POUM, including "N—" (an obvious reference to Andrés Nin, the POUM secretary);[17] and (2) that this "espionage organization" informed Franco's general staff of present and future military operations and that two hundred arrests had already been made.

Although the accusations of espionage against the POUM taxed my credulity, I felt sure I had a major scoop that I should telephone without delay to the United Press. There was only one hitch. The agent stated emphatically that I could not use the director general of security as the official source. I argued that in that case the United Press would conclude that I was personally endorsing the charges of espionage without any serious evidence and would question my credibility. "So you do not believe that the POUM is an organization of spies in the service of Franco?" she retorted suspiciously. I reiterated my objections and each time her suspicion and agitation grew. Fearing that I might not be given the scoop, I agreed to bear in mind her restrictions but secretly decided to use the source. But, when I delivered my typewritten story an hour later to Constancia de la Mora, the Communist censor at the Foreign Press Bureau, she deleted my opening sentence, "The director general of security has issued the following communiqué." She had obviously been forewarned by the NKVD. Finally, however, she agreed that I could use the vague expression, "it is stated that. . . ."[18]

In looking back at this incident with the benefit of subsequent knowledge, I have reached the following conclusions: (1) the NKVD was anxious to give the maximum publicity through a wire service to the alleged conspiracy without involving the government, which had not been informed and whose reaction it was difficult to foretell; (2) the communiqué had not been issued by the director general, as I had been told, but originated in the offices of the NKVD in the Soviet embassy in Valencia, where the incriminating documents were fabricated;[19] (3) attributing the communiqué to the director general was a ploy designed to ensure my confidence, for, after all, I was not a long-term sympathizer, least of all a party member; (4) by omitting any mention of the director general, it was hoped to avoid, or at least delay, any punitive action against him by the minister of the interior, who had not been apprised of the impending coup; and (5) the Foreign Press Bureau, officially under the control of the ministry of foreign affairs—now occupied by José Giral, a left Republican and loyal friend of President Azaña—was actually controlled by the NKVD through the Spanish Communists, who received their guidelines from the headquarters in Valencia. It is doubtful whether Giral was aware of this when he took office, for, as we have seen, he simply inherited from Alvarez del Vayo the staff of the foreign ministry and its various dependencies, but he must certainly have known Constancia de la Mora's political sympathies when he made her chief of the Foreign Press Bureau a few months later.

Although news of the arrest of the POUM leaders was published in *Mundo Obrero*, the Madrid Communist daily, on 18 June, it was not until 22 June that the Communist press in Barcelona mentioned the alleged espionage organization linking the POUM with General Franco. "A few days ago," said *Las Noticias*, the PSUC-UGT organ in Catalonia, "the police discovered in Barcelona an organization of enormous importance dedicated to espionage in various countries. . . . The most elementary caution compelled us . . . to remain silent with respect to this important police action, for otherwise we might have damaged the success of the entire operation. But now . . . we can give our readers some of the facts regarding this vast spy organization, whose best elements had infiltrated the POUM.

"The first step taken by the police was to arrest all the POUM leaders as well as a large number of foreigners of both sexes, who, it appears, had the closest contact with this espionage service. At present, the number of persons arrested is estimated at three hundred.[20] . . . During the seizure of the party's buildings, documents of such great importance were found . . . that the culprits cannot in any way deny their guilt."

During the weeks and months that followed, the PCE and PSUC, in the press and on the platform, increased their denunciations of the POUM as spies and traitors and likened them to the "Trotskyists" and "saboteurs" in the Soviet Union.

On 25 June, *Frente Rojo* declared:

From the very inception of the war . . . at meetings and in the press, and in official government bodies, our party constantly demanded the adoption of severe measures against spies, agents of fascism, and *agents provocateurs*. If we had not already known from historical experience the way fascist espionage operates, we would have gained sufficient knowledge by observing the trials in the USSR against Trotskyists and saboteurs in the service of Hitler. . . . However, with an indifference and a lack of awareness that are punishable [a reference to Largo Caballero], months were allowed to pass by without any effective action being taken. . . . Today, however, under the present government, this attitude has been rectified and now we have the proof of the correctness of our accusation. . . . As our comrade Stalin stated admirably many years ago, Trotskyism is no longer a faction within the working-class movement, but a band of assassins, saboteurs, and spies, who operate in the pay of and under the direction of the Gestapo. Is it surprising that the Trotskyists [in this country], the so-called POUMists, who are no different from the renegades and traitors in the USSR, are in the service of Franco? . . . The present government has clamped down on spies and traitors and we are sure that it will tighten its grip implacably. The fate of our cause demands that we show no weakness or consideration. Anyone who serves the enemy in one way or another must perish.[21]

After the arrest of the leaders of the POUM and the subsequent apprehension of many of its members and foreign supporters,[22] some of whom were assassinated or held without formal charges in clandestine jails,[23] the repression spread to other cities and shortly thereafter to the POUM's armed forces on the Aragon front, where its Twenty-ninth Division was dissolved.[24] Some members of the division took refuge in CNT units; others were jailed or executed, including one of the division's most respected political commissars, Marciano Mena,[25] while many were drafted into government-controlled units.

The reaction of the CNT was not slow in coming. In a long censorious article entitled "Are We Now Being Presented with the First Bill?" Juan López, CNT minister of commerce in Largo Caballero's government, declared that although he was an opponent of both the official and dissident Communists, he was filled with indignation when he saw how men who had devoted their entire lives to the fight against capitalism were now being represented as allies of Hitler. "Our revolution cannot be dragged so low as to make the elimination of antifascist parties an established practice. . . . Spain has not yet mortgaged its political independence to the point of paying such a high price for the help we accept and appreciate, provided it is given in a disinterested manner, but are forced to reject when handed the bill. By creating a new insufferable persecution, the very spirit of the Spanish revolution is being adulterated. . . . To the Communist comrades, it will come as no surprise if we tell them that even the very stones of Spain will rise against them the day the Spanish people realize the danger of the imported dictatorship they represent."[26]

On the first anniversary of the defeat of the military insurrection in Catalonia, *La Batalla*, in a clandestine issue, published the following manifesto:

Twelve months after that heroic exploit . . . hordes of opportunists . . . , deadly enemies of the working class, have descended like an avalanche on the organizations of the revolutionary proletariat. These despicable scoundrels are sheltered and directed by the ill-named Communist Party of Spain and the PSUC.

To justify their crimes, they cunningly exploit the well-worn labels of "uncontrollables" and "spies." But the truth is very different. Moaning and rotting in different jails in Barcelona—some of which are filthy dungeons without light and air—there are hundreds of workers and peasants—some of them recently arrived from the front and affiliated, for the most part, with the CNT and POUM. . . .

They have committed no crime. Nothing that is punishable in the eyes of the workers weighs on their consciences. They have been incarcerated by that very policy that is in the service of the Communist party and its offshoot, the PSUC, for the simple reason that they are militants of organizations that do not go down on their knees . . . before the reactionary bosses who carry Communist membership cards.[27]

George Orwell, who served in the POUM militia and managed to escape from Barcelona during the repression, wrote to a friend in July 1937: "[Nearly] all our friends and acquaintances are in jail and likely to be there indefinitely, not actually charged with anything but suspected of 'Trotskyism.' The most terrible things were happening even when I left, wholesale arrests, wounded men dragged out of hospitals and thrown in jail, people crammed together in filthy dens where they have hardly room to lie down, prisoners beaten and half starved etc., etc. Meanwhile, it is impossible to get a word about this mentioned in the English press, barring the publications of the ILP [the Independent Labor Party], which is affiliated to the POUM."[28]

In the roundup of POUM leaders on 16 June the prime target and the first to be arrested was Andrés Nin, the party secretary[29] and Stalin's most coveted prey.[30] Internationally known in working-class circles, author and translator of numerous works, he had held a key post as secretary in charge of the Spanish-speaking countries, Italy, and France in the early days of the Profintern, the Red International of Trade Unions (Krasnyi Internatsional Profsoiuzov).[31] Taken to one of the NKVD's secret prisons near Madrid, he was subjected to horrendous torture in a vain attempt to extract a confession of espionage on behalf of General Franco, Hitler, and Mussolini, essential to a successful Moscow-style show trial in Spain.[32] He was never seen again.

"What Stalin and his hirelings of the NKVD wanted," writes Julián Gorkin, a member at the time of the POUM executive, who was one of those arrested and taken to Valencia, "was not the assassination, pure and simple, of Nin and his principal comrades . . . , but our prosecution at a public trial, our conviction, and immediate execution, under the guise of republican legality—a trial on the model of the trials in Moscow and, later, of those in the so-called people's democracies. This appearance of legality was contained in the decree published on 23 June 1937[33] [a few days after the arrest of the POUM leaders], and its scope was both broad and precise enough to imprison, and even liquidate, all opponents of the Negrín government. . . . This decree had not received the approval of parliament and, furthermore, the Tribunals of Espionage and High Treason created by it were composed of three civilian and two military magistrates appointed by the government itself [and empowered to sit in secret session]. Its dictatorial or, if one prefers, its executive character is therefore obvious. The decree set forth the following categories of crimes: 'the commission of hostile acts against the Republic both in Spain and abroad; the defense and propagation of news and opinions unfavorable to military operations and to the reputation and authority of the Republic; meetings and demonstrations aimed at weakening public morale; the demoralization of the army or undermining of collective discipline.' The punishments ranged from a minimum sentence of six years [and one day] in prison to the death penalty. . . . But the most serious thing of all was the retroactive character of the decree."[34]

The police action against the POUM and the frightening scope of the decree, which provided for secret hearings and "the very summary procedure" established by the code of military justice, alarmed the opponents of the Negrín government. On 28 June, in a statement addressed to the president of the Republic, the president of the Cortes, the premier, the interior and justice ministers, and to the national committees of all parties and organizations, Mariano Vázquez protested on behalf of the CNT national committee that the "dangerous course initiated by the elimination of the POUM" would be followed by the annihilation of other minority parties, and that the decree of the minister of justice "establishing special tribunals with trials behind closed doors" appeared to be "one more concession" to the designs of the PCE and Russia. "We feel that Spanish liberal opinion cannot consent to this."[35] That same day, Vázquez publicly declared his opposition to the political aspect of the decree. All opponents of the government, he said, or anyone who might talk or demonstrate against it came within its scope. "This means, for example, that at this very moment I am in jeopardy, that tomorrow I could be arrested and, behind closed doors—so that you would not be aware of or blush at the crimes I had [allegedly] committed—I could be condemned to six months and one day in jail or to death."[36] And the organ of the Friends of Durruti, *El Amigo del Pueblo*, declared: "The espionage suit that has been cooked up against the comrades of the POUM on orders of the Comintern is outrageous. And, paradoxically, it is a Catholic minister [the Basque Nationalist minister of justice, Manuel de Irujo] who is entrusted with the preparation of this concoction, which is half Spanish and half Russian. . . . We shall not tolerate the maneuver against the POUM. We must bear in mind that before long it will be the militants of the CNT and FAI who will appear before the same Tribunal."[37]

The CNT and FAI had ample reason for alarm even though their immediate organic destruction was not on the agenda. Shortly after the arrest of the POUM leaders, the agit-prop section of the PCE asserted that the documents found in the buildings of the POUM provided "sufficient evidence of treason by the Trotskyists." It then proceeded to challenge the CNT. "What do the comrades of the CNT who have ventured publicly to defend the Trotskyists now say? What do the newspapers of the CNT that have protected and defended the POUM now say? After the overwhelming proof of treason by the Trotskyists discovered by the police, anyone who dares to raise his voice today in their defense must be named as an accomplice. . . . [The] Anarchist comrades who may perhaps have honorably defended the POUM are obliged to make a public and categorical declaration of their error and demand the implacable punishment of the traitors with the same loyalty and energy as all true antifascists are demanding."[38]

The decree was sharply denounced by the foreign friends of the POUM in a dogged campaign in Europe and America to save the leaders of the party. "The very decree under which the POUM leaders are now being accused was issued . . . after the alleged commission of the 'crimes' charged against them," declared the *Workers' Age*, the organ of the Communist party of the U.S.A. (Opposition), which was associated with the POUM, like the British Independent Labor Party, through the International Bureau for Revolutionary Socialist Unity. "In other words, the POUM leaders are being tried under an ex post facto law, a gross act of judicial tyranny by those very standards of liberal democracy which the Stalinists pretend to hold so sacred."[39]

An international deputation headed by James Maxton, M.P., the chairman of the Independent Labour party and representing the parties in various countries affiliated with the International Bureau, visited Spain to exert pressure on the government to find Andrés Nin and to provide legal safeguards, including a public trial, for the other POUM leaders who had been arrested. During the delegation's first visit in August, defense minister Indalecio Prieto revealed the dilemma of the government when he told the French delegates Marceau Pivert and Daniel Guérin that the deputation represented "only those countries that have done little for Spain" whereas "the Russians send the arms that enable the Spanish Republic to resist." From this insinuation, the members of the delegation gained "the clear impression that the minister was alluding to the *political compensation* demanded by Russia in exchange for her support."[40]

As no progress was made, a second delegation comprising Professor Felicien Challaye of Paris University and John McGovern, Independent Labour party M.P., visited Spain in November. "[We] had no word of the trial by the end of November," McGovern reported, "and we were greatly disturbed not only by the continued imprisonments, but by the disappearance of individuals and by the open threats of death to Señor [Benito] Pabon, the famous Spanish lawyer, who was engaged to defend the POUM prisoners [and was forced to flee abroad]. The evidence of Checa [secret police] brutality grew."[41]

Although justice minister Manuel de Irujo tried to be helpful, he was powerless to get permission for the delegation to see the POUM prisons. "The mask was off," McGovern wrote. "We had torn aside the veil and shown where the real power lay. The Ministers were willing, but powerless. The Cheka was unwilling, and it had the power. We realized that if we pressed further we ourselves would be in danger. . . . In return for Russian assistance in arms, [the] Comintern has been given this tyrannical power and she uses it to imprison, torture and murder Socialists who do not accept the Comintern line. . . . It is my firm conviction, born of study and experience of Communist tactics, that to assist them to win a place in the workers' movement is criminal folly. For my part I cannot excuse or apologize for their acts. Human decency demands an exposure of their brutal methods."[42]

Communist methods contrasted with the moderate aims professed by the party and had a pernicious effect in the democratic countries whose help it sought. In a letter to the centrist executive of the PSOE, Enrique de Francisco, a prominent leader of the Agrupación Socialista Madrileña and supporter of Largo Caballero, stated that broad sections of liberal and working-class opinion perceived "a Communist hegemony" in the government and that recent events in the field of public order had "alarmed the conscience of the world."[43] At the same time, Largo Caballero's mouthpiece, *La Correspondencia de Valencia*, argued that the "despicable exclusivist policy" of the PCE was responsible for the decline of enthusiasm in democratic circles abroad and that neither the democratic countries themselves nor the popular masses could be inspired by a country in which the Communists "push and control" and exercised what in effect was "a Communist propaganda dictatorship."[44]

In his famous (and last) speech in Spain in the Teatro Pardiñas in Madrid in October 1937, Largo Caballero took advantage of the occasion to stress the damage being done to the Republican cause abroad. "You all know," he said, "that there have been unfortunate cases, which have still not been resolved, of persons who have disappeared as a result of the action of elements who are not part of the government and who represent a State within a State. Things have reached such a point, comrades, that representatives of the Internationals [the International Bureau and the Second International] have come to Spain expressly to ascertain the truth and have told me personally: 'After what has happened we cannot arouse enthusiasm abroad among our comrades, because they suspect that those who have influence and that those who dominate here are Communist elements—they say so clearly—and everyone is asking whether they should help Spain only to have the Communists control her destiny."[45]

Meanwhile, the fate of Andrés Nin, who had been taken to a secret prison in Alcalá de Henares, near Madrid, had been decided. Having failed to extract the required confession for a show trial in Spain, his tormentors had no alternative but to dispose of him. Julián Gorkin states that Enrique Castro, onetime member of the Communist party's central committee, assured him, after he had left the party, that "the personal executioner of Nin" had been his former comrade in the Fifth Regiment, Carlos Contreras (Vittorio Vidali), and that Orlov had selected him as "his immediate collaborator in the case of Nin."[46] But since Nin was internationally known, his disappearance had to be explained. Hence, according to former politburo member Jesús Hernández, Vidali simulated a Nazi assault to "liberate" Nin from his secret place of captivity in Alcalá de Henares, the sham assault being executed by ten German members of the International Brigades, who carried him off, leaving behind incriminating documents purporting to show his connection with the Nazi secret police.[47]

The alleged liberation of Nin by the Gestapo was the version adopted by the Communists to account for his disappearance whenever the question was asked, "Where is Nin?" In fact, it was this version that Vidali himself tried to impress upon me when I met him in Mexico in 1939. It was also the one given by Mikhail Koltzov. "The accused Nin . . . ," he wrote, "was spirited away by a group of armed fascists, Spanish and German Gestapo agents, who broke into the provincial transit prison, where he was being held temporarily under a very weak guard."[48]

A not too dissimilar version of Nin's release that did not explicitly mention the alleged involvement of the Gestapo was publicized by one of the most zealous pro-Soviet propagandists of the time, the representative in Spain of the French Communist daily, *L'Humanité*, Georges Soria, who wrote a series of articles in the Comintern organ *International Press Correspondence*,[49] later published in a booklet under the title *Trotskyism in the Service of Franco*. Forty years later, however, in an attempt to exculpate the Spanish Communists from responsibility for the death of Nin, he stated that "the accusations levelled against Nin in Spain in the form of the couplet: 'Where is Nin? In Salamanca or Berlin?'" were "purely and simply . . . an extension into the international arena of the methods that constituted the most somber aspect of what has since been called Stalinism." It was clear from the mass of evidence, Soria added, that the disappearance of Nin was due to the "machinations of the ominous figure of Orlov." This "flagrant intervention in the internal affairs of Spain had serious consequences." "[The] PCE vigorously denied any connection with the matter. But this did not diminish the polemics that were unleashed and that vitiated the relations of the PCE with the other parties and organizations. From an historical standpoint this question elicits two observations: On the one hand, the charge that the leaders of the POUM, among them Andrés Nin, were 'agents of the Gestapo and Franco' was no more than a fabrication, because it was impossible to adduce the slightest evidence. On the other hand, although the leaders of the POUM were neither agents of Franco nor agents of the Gestapo, it is true that their relentless struggle against the Popular Front played the game *nolens volens* of the Caudillo [General Franco]."[50]

Soria's attempt—as well as that of other writers—to exonerate the PCE by shifting responsibility for the crusade against the POUM and for the disappearance of Nin to the phenomenon of "Stalinism"—in keeping with the Eurocommunist trend in the 1970s toward de-Stalinization[51]—cannot withstand serious investigation; for the campaign was conducted religiously by every leader of the party and by every Communist daily and periodical, both local and national, from the earliest months of the Civil War. That the roots of the campaign originated in Moscow is immaterial, for, as Ignacio Iglesias, a POUM leader, affirmed later: "[If] the repression against the POUM and the assassination of Nin perpetrated by the Stalinist police services was possible, this was due to the enthusiastic and wholehearted collaboration of the Spanish Communists, the PCE, the PSUC, and the JSU, all working in harmony."[52]

It was José Díaz, the party secretary, it will be recalled, who declared immediately after the May events—only five weeks before the coup—that the POUM was "a gang of spies and *provocateurs* in the service of international fascism" and that the Trotskyist "vermin" should be swept out of all civilized countries. Moreover, it will also be recalled that the coup was ordered by the Communist director general of security, Lieutenant Colonel Ortega, in accordance with secret instructions from the NKVD, and executed by Lieutenant Colonel Burillo, the Communist police chief in Barcelona, and that it was also Spanish Communist police who took Andrés Nin to a secret prison in Alcalá de Henares to meet his fate.

The exact form of Nin's death has never been established. Nor is it known for certain whether he was assassinated in Spain or shipped to Russia alive or dead. The moderate Socialist Juan-Simeón Vidarte, then undersecretary of the interior, relates in his memoirs that he and interior minister Zugazagoitia sent a special police agent to Madrid to investigate Nin's disappearance. The agent reported that Nin had been taken to a private home in Alcalá de Henares used as a "Communist checa," whence "screams and moans" had been heard, that one morning a large car picked up a crate and proceeded to Alicante, where it stopped alongside a Soviet ship, and that, in the agent's opinion, Nin left Spain alive.[53]

Forty years later, this version received some support, but by no means conclusive, from a certain Javier Jiménez, who, when interviewed by *Cambio 16*, the Madrid weekly, claimed that he had belonged to a special police unit in Madrid [a Brigada Especial] that was sent to Barcelona at the time of the coup against the POUM. He asserted not only that he had witnessed in Madrid the fabrication of documents with Nin's signature, designed to implicate the POUM in enemy espionage, but that, after the Civil War, he met the chauffeur who had driven him and other members of the unit to Barcelona and who had confessed that he had later taken Nin from Alcalá de Henares to Valencia, "where a Soviet ship was waiting."[54]

Whatever the fate of Nin, the Communists and their friends clung tenaciously to their version that he had been freed by a Nazi commando group. The Gestapo, they argued, could not afford to have such a valuable agent interrogated by the Republican police regarding its activities in Spain.[55]

The NKVD chief, Alexander Orlov, who defected to the United States in 1938 and exposed and condemned many of the violent crimes of Stalin and the NKVD in other countries, remained silent on those committed in Spain. Nowhere in his books, articles, or testimony before the U.S. Senate subcommittee does he mention either the POUM or the disappearance of Andrés Nin. However, in private conversation many years after his defection, when Bertram D. Wolfe asked him point-blank, "Did you have a hand in the assassination of Nin?" Orlov replied that he did not, that he did not even know him, that his role in Spain had been "limited to counterespionage and guerrilla warfare in rebel territory"—his stock description of his activities[56]—and that he had never been given a "murder job."[57] It was, of course, unlikely that he would incriminate himself. It is also unlikely that he personally assassinated Nin; there were others who could do the job.

In 1953, after the publication of his article "The Ghastly Secrets of Stalin's Power" in *Life* magazine, Orlov denied that he had anything to do with Nin's murder. The denial was made on his behalf by the editors of *Life* in reply to a letter by Jaume Miravitlles, a Catalan liberal Republican: "He could not have carried out his 'diplomatic' job (to direct counterintelligence and guerrilla activities), if also involved in assassinations. These were carried out, Orlov says, by a task force of secret liquidators sent from Moscow, one of whom, Bolodin, was probably the agent who did away with Andrés Nin."[58] But fifteen years later, in response to Stanley G. Payne's oft-cited questionnaire, Orlov placed the entire blame on the Spanish Communists, avoiding any hint that the Kremlin, through its NKVD apparatus in Spain—for whose activities, as head operative, he must of necessity be held responsible—had in any way been involved. "The leaders of the Spanish Communist party," he stated, "had an axe to grind with the POUM," and "the disappearance of Nin was an act of political vengeance."[59]

The disappearance of Andrés Nin dealt a heavy moral blow to Negrín's administration, which had hoped to establish for itself a reputation for constitutional procedure in the eyes of the Western world. The premier's desk was piled high with telegrams and letters of protest from abroad.[60] Negrín was disturbed by the international reverberations and was at first outraged by the stigma on his government only a month after its formation.[61] Nevertheless, to judge from the memoirs of Vidarte, one of his supporters, his concern seems to have had more to do with the illegal nature of the repression rather than with the repression itself. "I believed at the time, and I still believe, after more than thirty years," writes Vidarte, "that there probably existed between Negrín and the Communists some kind of tacit understanding, whereby in return for the unconditional political support they had promised him and for the shipment of arms that Spain needed more than ever because of the loss of the North and Malaga . . . , Negrín would permit them to carry out *within the law* the liquidation, ordered by Stalin, of a rival party that had taken up arms against the government."[62] That Negrín had backed the Communists' demand for the dissolution of the POUM even before he became prime minister was clear from his stance during the cabinet crisis on 13 May as attested by Manuel Azaña.

Jesús Hernández—who claims that he was unaware of the whereabouts of Nin and that he had opposed the NKVD's projected operation against the POUM on the grounds that it would provoke a "tremendous political scandal" because the minister of the interior, Zugazagoitia, had not been informed[63]—confirms Negrín's vexation when he learned of Nin's disappearance.

"What have your people done with Nin?" Negrín asked him. "With obvious anger, Negrín told me that the interior minister had informed him of a whole series of abuses committed in Barcelona by the Soviet police, who behaved as though they were in their own country and didn't even trouble to notify the

Spanish authorities, even as an act of courtesy, of the arrests of Spanish citizens, who were transferred from one place to another without judicial warrant, and were imprisoned in private prisons, totally beyond the control of the legal authorities. . . . I didn't know what to answer him. I could have told him that, like him, . . . I was also wondering where Nin was and that I detested Orlov and his gang of police. But I decided not to. I could see the storm descending on our party and resolved to defend it even though, in this case, the defense of the party meant implicitly defending a possible crime."[64]

Although there is no confirmation that Hernández was as indignant as he claims, there is no doubt about the initial reaction of Negrín. Nor is there the slightest doubt about the indignation of Zugazagoitia and the minister of justice, Manuel de Irujo, who were unable to locate Nin in any of the official prisons maintained by the government. Irujo attests that he appointed a special judge to handle the case, that he ordered the arrest of a "considerable number of policemen who were suspect," that some of them "found refuge in the Russian Embassy," and that a few days later a special police unit (*brigada especial*) attempted to arrest the judge. It was then that Irujo raised the matter "bluntly" in two cabinet meetings and threatened to resign.[65]

The two cabinet meetings at which the disappearance of Nin was discussed were described by the minister of the interior as "almost savage."[66] According to Hernández, the minister wanted to know whether his jurisdiction was to be "determined by the advice of certain Soviet 'technicians.' "[67] "The Communist ministers," Zugazagoitia testifies, "defended their colleague [director general of security Ortega] with extraordinary passion. I stated that the director general could remain at his post, but in that case I would relinquish mine. Prieto, adopting a firm stand, reproached the Communists for the manner in which they conducted the debate and declared, in support of my position, that he would add his resignation to mine in the event Ortega were not replaced."[68]

"No one [in the cabinet] believed in our sincerity," writes Hernández, "when we stated that we did not know the whereabouts of Nin. We defended the presence of Soviet 'technicians' and 'advisers' as an expression of 'disinterested' help. . . . We emphasized once again how much the supply of arms from the USSR and the assistance we were receiving in the international arena from the Soviet Union meant to our cause. As the atmosphere remained hostile . . . I compromised by agreeing to the removal of Colonel Ortega—a scapegoat—for overstepping his functions and for not duly informing the minister, but I threatened to make public all the incriminating documents against the POUM and the names of all those persons in and outside the government who, for 'simple questions of procedure,' protected the spies of that party." This tactic was "demagogic and disloyal," Hernández acknowledges. "Negrín was conciliatory and proposed that the debate be suspended until . . . we had all the evidence to which the Communist ministers referred and the ministry of the interior could give us concrete news of the whereabouts of Nin. We had weathered the first and most perilous storm!"[69]

Lieutenant Colonel Ortega was replaced in the General Direction of Security by the moderate Socialist, Gabriel Morón,[70] who, the reader will recall, had been appointed to the post of subdirector by Zugazagoitia to keep him apprised "of whatever might happen" in the police department. But his new appointment, which lasted only a few months, was ill-starred from the outset; for, according to his revealing but little-known memoir, his efforts to carry out a rigorous reorganization in the police corps were "aborted by Communist resistance." The Communist party, he asserts, decided to have recourse to every possible means, even to the point of "having me 'ejected' from the department." In this it was successful because of "the timidity, complicity, and restraint of the Socialist ministers in respect to the scandalous affair [of Andrés Nin]." Morón inveighs with particular vehemence against defense minister Indalecio Prieto, the most prestigious politician in the government, with whose centrist faction of the PSOE he had always been identified: "Better than anyone else, he could have taken advantage of the opportunity offered him to remove Communist influence from the security department once and for all. . . . But the fact is that the illustrious parliamentarian was not in the least bit interested."[71]

Morón also has harsh words for Manuel de Irujo, the justice minister: "Señor Irujo, the entire cabinet, the public prosecutor and I knew perfectly well where to find the only person responsible for the abduction of Nin." But Irujo and the judges under him, Morón alleges, thought they could discharge their duty by allowing the hand of the law to fall on minor police officials. Morón told Zugazagoitia that if he really intended to bring to justice the person directly responsible for Nin's disappearance, he had taken all the necessary measures to this end. "But the minister of the interior, deeply grieved and embittered by the distressing situation in which he had been caught, decided 'that nothing more could be done.' It was in these circumstances that I left the General Direction of Security."[72]

From the timorousness of the cabinet ministers, it was obvious that they were not inclined to investigate the disappearance of Andrés Nin too closely. Confirmation comes from Vidarte, the undersecretary of the interior. Morón, he says, "blew his top," telling the minister of the interior: " 'Since the premier is so determined to learn the truth, you can tell him that the abduction of Andrés Nin was planned by the Italian [Vittorio] Codovila, by Comandante Carlos [Vittorio Vidali], Togliatti and by the leaders of the Communist party including [party secretary] Pepe Díaz. The order to torture him was given by Orlov. Tell this to Negrín. If he wants me to arrest them, I'll put them all in jail first thing in the morning.' The minister was confounded. Because of the political implication of such arrests, he refrained from making any comment. Undoubtedly, he must have told [Dr. Negrín] immediately and the question of responsibility for the abduction or assassination of Nin was not mentioned again. And there things remained."[73]

It is clear from the reluctance of interior minister Zugazagoitia and other cabinet ministers to act forcefully that despite the initial outrage over the disappearance of Nin they were loath to pursue the investigation to its ultimate consequences—the exposure of Alexander Orlov and his close collaborators—for fear of antagonizing the Soviet Union, the sole purveyor of arms and the custodian of Spanish gold. If it is true, as Prieto later alleged, that when Zugazagoitia started an investigation into the disappearance of Nin and "the shameful truth was about to be discovered," Negrín ordered the suspension of the investigation,[74] then it is equally true that the premier was expressing the mood of submission and futility that paralyzed his cabinet. Only a few weeks later, on 14 August, the minister of the interior, in an effort to silence any press criticism of the Soviet Union, issued a stern warning from which it was evident that the government would never seriously investigate the disappearance of Nin and expose its Soviet authorship.

After stating that there appeared to be "a deliberate attempt to offend an exceptionally friendly nation, thus creating difficulties for the government," the warning said that some newspapers had equated the USSR with those countries "that are invading the national territory." "Such intemperance, which is absolutely reprehensible, cannot be permitted by the censorship and must cease forthwith." If the order were not observed "scrupulously," the offending paper would be suspended indefinitely and the censor who had read the proofs would be arraigned before "the special tribunal that handles crimes of sabotage."[75]

It was no mere coincidence that only three days earlier *Frente Rojo*, the Communist organ, warned Largo Caballero's mouthpiece, *La Correspondencia de Valencia*, to desist from any further criticism of the USSR: "Watch out, you anticommunists of the *Correspondencia de Valencia*! You are gambling with the interests of the Spanish people by allowing yourselves to be carried away by your hatreds and your malice! The Soviet Union, its Government, and its people have a special place in the hearts of all Spaniards. It is no longer permissible for anyone to make them the target of insults, slanders, and poisoned arrows. Enough! The people will call to strict account those who think that they can attack and wound its dearest friend, its most consistent defender, which is aiding it with total unselfishness and self-sacrifice. Their motive is to foster suspicion and mistrust between our two peoples. No enemy of the Soviet Union, no enemy of the Spanish people will be allowed any longer to do as he pleases. The people are vigilant and are determined to impose silence."[76]

But the most devastating and fulminatory attacks on the Soviet Union were beyond the reach of the press censorship. They were the leaflets and newspapers that circulated surreptitiously from hand to hand. On 14 August, *La Batalla*, in a clandestine issue, railed against the "interference of the Soviet police" and stated that "a special political police [unit] linked closely with the Stalinist-controlled Spanish police has subverted the State to such a point that the titular holders of government office hardly control anything and that behind their backs, and compromising them, Stalinism acts in a criminal manner." In the police station of Santa Ursula, *La Batalla* alleged, there were elements of the Russian secret police, working with "indigenous Stalinists," who had imported new methods of torture "to extract through pain and terror statements and confessions that serve the murky politics of Stalinism. . . . Everything we say is known in Valencia. It is known by the minister of the interior and the whole government. But the minister of justice and the minister of the interior can only act secretly . . . , because they are prisoners in a government held hostage by the Stalinists, who are blackmailing them with Soviet aid in the most shameful way in order to thwart our Revolution."[77]

Given the fact that the ministry of the interior and the department of security were, according to the minister himself, "nests of spies and confidants of the GPU [NKVD],"[78] it is not surprising that the removal of Lieutenant Colonel Ortega was but a minor concession, that it had little impact on Communist influence in the security services, and that Gabriel Morón, Ortega's successor, was soon forced to leave the security department.

Although the Nin scandal embarrassed the Spanish Communists, their discomfort was only a slight inconvenience. What counted was that the main objective of the Kremlin—the virtual destruction of the POUM, its most abrasive critic—had been achieved. Most of the leaders of the executive committee were in jail, many of its less well-known militants and foreign supporters had been imprisoned or shot, its press proscribed, its buildings seized, its militia dissolved, and never again would it function effectively. True, a few representatives of the POUM sat on the city councils of Castellón and Valencia until their expulsion at the end of 1937,[79] and a new executive committee was formed that not only maintained contact with members at the front and in the rear but even visited the interior minister in November 1937.[80] Furthermore, underground editions of the party newspaper *La Batalla*[81] and its youth organ *Juventud Obrera* (formerly *Juventud Comunista*) were published with the help of the CNT,[82] but the new executive was arrested in April 1938[83] and, henceforth, what remained of the party apparatus functioned only spasmodically until the end of the Civil War.[84]

Negrín's indignation over the disappearance of Nin was fleeting. Only a month later, when talking to President Azaña, he stubbornly supported the version that Nin had been abducted by the Gestapo. "He doesn't believe that it was the work of the Communists," Azaña commented in his diary on 22 July. "The Communists, of course, become indignant at the very idea. Negrín believes that Nin was abducted by . . . the Gestapo to prevent him from making revelations." " 'Isn't that too novelesque?' " the disbelieving Azaña responded. " 'No, sir,' " replied Negrín, who, to impress the president with the efficiency of the "formidable" Gestapo, proceeded to tell him of an attempt by the Nazi secret police to poison the Russian general staff in Madrid.[85]

There is no reason to assume that Negrín believed this farfetched version of Nin's disappearance any more than did his ministers of the interior and justice, who certainly possessed enough evidence of the NKVD's involvement to expose publicly the prime suspect had they not been constrained by deference to Russia. Nor is there any reason to suppose that they believed in the authenticity of the documents incriminating the POUM in acts of espionage, for, when interviewed by Nin's wife, Irujo told her: "Only the confidants of 'other ministers' can know what has happened to Nin. . . . This business of espionage is false. . . . The documents I have seen pertain to the Falange and it has been proved that the one with the letter 'N' is false, because someone removed the documents from the police archives and added everything relating to the POUM. The trial of the leaders will not be held behind closed doors and, for my part, I shall provide them with every facility so that they can defend themselves."[86]

But four months later, Irujo resigned from the ministry of justice. In his farewell speech to his staff on 11 December, he stressed the importance of maintaining "the independence of the judiciary" and his "total disagreement" with the concept that the courts could "apply the laws in accordance with the views and requirements of the government."[87] That he was alluding to attempts by the Communists to influence the judicial process is clear from the memoir written by his brother and private secretary, Andrés María de Irujo. This work, based largely on Manuel de Irujo's personal recollections, quotes approvingly from an article in *La Nación* of Buenos Aires that refers to the political tension between himself and the Communist ministers, "who were determined to modify the judicial system."[88]

Manuel de Irujo was also alluding to a fundamental disagreement with Negrín over the text of the decree published on 1 December 1937 creating the Tribunales Especiales de Guardia, which were to be set up "in those places where the government deems it necessary" and which were designed like the Special Tribunal of Espionage and High Treason to "repress flagrant crimes of espionage, treason, and defeatism," using the "very summary procedure" of the military courts[89] and, needless to say, without the regular guarantees for the defense of the accused. In a memorandum written in 1938, referring to these special tribunals, Manuel de Irujo attests that Mariano Granados, a member of the Supreme Court, was entrusted by Negrín to draft a decree creating a tribunal modeled after the repressive secret police courts of Fascist Italy.[90] At the request of Negrín, Mariano Ansó, the undersecretary of justice and a friend and admirer of the premier,[91] handed the decree to Irujo for submission to the cabinet, but the minister refrained from presenting it for approval. Negrín therefore introduced the decree himself in his capacity of premier after making a few changes that enabled him to bypass the minister of justice.[92] "The cabinet session was difficult and tumultuous like many others," Irujo's memorandum recalls. "I managed to include enough substantial amendments to convert the secret police tribunal into a court of law. Even so, I informed the cabinet after the debate was over that if the approved text were published in the *Gaceta*, I would resign the moment it appeared. I could not forget the aims pursued by the decree . . . nor the political methods employed to introduce it."[93] Although Irujo informed Azaña that he would step down if he signed the decree, the president ignored the warning and the justice minister was replaced by Mariano Ansó, Negrín's confidant.[94]

At this stage we must ask a pertinent question. What effect did the repression of the CNT-FAI and POUM and the ouster of Largo Caballero have on the conduct of the war? The answer is given by Fernando Claudín, a prominent member of the PCE for thirty years and, later, a leading analyst and critic of its policies. "[By] fulfilling the directives of Moscow to eliminate Largo Caballero from the premiership and to unleash the repression against the POUM, the PCE assumed responsibility for deepening the divisions within the working masses and greatly weakening the Republic's ability to fight."[95]

49

Highlights of the POUM Trial

Due to successive delays, the trial of the POUM leaders was not held until October of 1938.[1] Although the trial took place toward the close of the Civil War, it is necessary for the sake of thematic unity to digress briefly from the strict chronology of events.

The long delay in bringing the leaders to trial can be attributed to the following causes:

1. The principal cause, according to a report in the *Workers' Age*, the organ of the Communist party of the U.S.A. (Opposition), which was linked to the POUM through the International Bureau for Revolutionary Socialist Unity, was the question as to which kind of law, civil or military, was applicable. "This question," said the report, "has involved both the defense and the prosecution in all sorts of legal arguments." In addition, the defense attorney argued that his clients could not be tried under a law passed *after* the commission of the alleged crimes.[2] "Since it was obvious that the law was not retrospective," the report continued, "the prosecution then changed their tactics and brought the same charges under two previous laws."[3]

2. The second cause was the campaign in Europe and America for a free and open trial waged by the International Bureau with the support of the Second and Fourth Internationals and the International Federation of Trade Unions.[4] As a result of this campaign, the plans for a Moscow-style show trial in Barcelona could not proceed as rapidly as intended.

3. The third cause was the enormous difficulty in securing and retaining competent defense attorneys owing to Communist intimidation. At first, Benito Pabón, who had defended the Anarchosyndicalists in the early years of the Republic, was appointed by the national committee of the CNT to defend the POUM. But, as soon as it was learned that he was to serve as the POUM's attorney, he began to receive anonymous letters threatening him with death and eventually forcing him to flee abroad.[5] "If I were convinced that my staying in Spain would offer any guarantee to your comrades," he said in a letter to the POUM executive, "I would not hesitate in the least to remain even against my own interests. . . . Recently in antifascist Spain a theory has been adopted more

ridiculous than we ever imagined possible in the most despotic period of the Monarchy. This is the theory that a lawyer defending a case can for this reason be accused of complicity in the alleged acts of his clients. . . . Can you tell me what guarantees I would have in such an atmosphere, where calumnies are invented and documents of accusation forged overnight, that my role would not be changed from that of defending lawyer to that of one of the accused, without any possibility of defending myself against all the slander that they wish to heap upon my name?"[6]

As a result of Pabón's withdrawal, the services of Henri Torres, the most famous of French trial lawyers, were secured,[7] but the government refused him permission to assist on behalf of the accused. "We have asked for a foreign lawyer," ran an appeal by the POUM prisoners in the state prison in Barcelona. "Such a procedure is even accepted by Horthy in Hungary and by Hitler in Germany, as the cases of Rakosi and Dimitrov show. The government of the Republic has denied this to us. Our lawyer . . . has been hounded by Stalinist threats of violence and has had to resign and flee to a foreign country. Other lawyers, even though they manifested great sympathy for us, did not dare to undertake our defense. One accepted upon the condition that we guarantee the safety of his family! That is how far the fear of Stalinist terror has gone. . . . We are in jail, paying the bill, paying it in part, for the help Russia has given to the Spanish government. If we have not paid with our lives yet, we owe this to the solidarity of the international labor movement. Fortunately, the working class of the world understands. They know what is at stake."[8] Because of these problems, the young Socialist attorney, Vicente Rodríguez Revilla, who had been retained by the POUM in a junior capacity, assumed full responsibility for the defense. There is more than a little irony in the fact that the Communist *Daily Worker* (London) reported from Barcelona that the trial had been postponed several times "in order to allow the defense to prepare its case."[9]

As the opening day approached, the Spanish Communists intensified their efforts to influence the course of justice. "Signatures were obtained in plants and workshops, in cafés, and in official circles, demanding the death penalty . . . ," writes Julián Gorkin, one of the accused. "Signatures were also obtained at the fronts. Officers and men who refused to sign were threatened with the worst reprisals."[10] In their campaign the Communists were aided by a widely diffused book, *Espionaje en España*, purportedly written by a Max Rieger and published in Spain and France shortly before the trial with the object, as Jordi Arquer, another of the accused, put it, of "preparing the public for our guilt and for the necessity of exemplary punishment."[11] The book was dignified by the inclusion of a preface by José Bergamín, the well-known dissident Catholic intellectual, who described the POUM as an espionage organization that was an integral part of the international fascist organization in Spain.[12]

The author of the book, which was translated into French by the famous writer Jean Cassou, regarded at the time as a "regimented" Communist, and published by Denoël, was totally unknown and never properly identified.[13] He was referred to by the Communist *Frente Rojo* simply as a "Socialist worker," who had fought in the International Brigades.[14] There can be no doubt from internal evidence that the book was authored by the NKVD with the help of the PCE[15] and that José Bergamín knew exactly what role he was playing. "One of the most dangerous kinds of enemies of the revolution and of socialism . . . ," said *Spartacus*, a left Socialist journal published in Alicante, "are those Catholics described as 'Christians of advanced spirit and free from prejudice.' . . . And one of the most prominent elements in this category in Spain is José Bergamín."[16]

Bergamín's intimate association with the Spanish Communists by whom he was surrounded when he emigrated to Mexico in 1939[17] suggests that he was one of the precursors of the theology of liberation that came into being in Latin America many years later. His importance to the Communists can be gauged by a letter sent by Constancia de la Mora, a member of the PCE, to Eleanor Roosevelt in July 1939 praising Bergamín's cultural activities in Mexico. This was indicative, she told the president's wife, of the way "the real tradition of Spanish culture," which was "essentially democratic," could be kept alive.[18]

The trial of the POUM leaders began in Barcelona before the Tribunal of Espionage and High Treason on 11 October 1938 and lasted until 22 October, although the judgment was not announced until 2 November.[19] The trial was held in open court in the presence of the foreign press and not in secret as originally feared, a concession that was due to the international campaign on behalf of the POUM.[20] In a report to Moscow, Togliatti complained that during the trial Paulino Gómez, the moderate Socialist minister of the interior, "prohibited any campaign in the press against the Trotskyist traitors,"[21] but the fact is that he allowed *Frente Rojo* to flout the prohibition with impunity when, among other violations, it declared in front-page headlines: "THE PEOPLE DEMAND PUNISHMENT FOR THE SPIES OF FASCISM" and "THE LEADERS OF THE POUM ARE GUILTY OF HIGH TREASON."[22] "It can be proved beyond doubt," wrote Juan Peiró, former CNT minister of industry, "that while the CNT-FAI press was prohibited from commenting on the details of the trial and its whys and wherefores, the Communist and pro-Communist press enjoyed absolute freedom to continue heaping mud on the accused especially during the days following the trial, when the tribunal was deliberating the sentence."[23]

But a more serious attempt to influence the course of justice is said to have been made by Juan Negrín. Luis Araquistáin claims that Mariano Gómez, the president of the supreme tribunal, told him that *during the trial* Negrín went to see him to demand the death penalty for some of the accused, asserting that otherwise "the fronts would collapse." This was "Communist phraseology," says Araquistáin. "Mariano Gómez resisted this attempt at coercion with dignity."[24] A longer and slightly different version, which does not state whether the incident occurred before or during the trial, is given by Gorkin and is allegedly confirmed in a letter from the president of the supreme tribunal to Indalecio Prieto. According to this version, Negrín summoned Mariano Gómez to his office, together with the minister of justice, the public prosecutor, and the president of the Tribunal of

Espionage and High Treason, and placed a pile of telegrams on his desk. "The army demands the death penalty for the accused," he told them. "The situation at the fronts is very delicate and the morale of the troops has declined somewhat. I consider it essential to give satisfaction to the army. . . . If necessary I shall place myself at the head of the army against the Tribunal." When Mariano Gómez and Ramón González Peña, the minister of justice, protested, Negrín "changed his tone" and allegedly stated: "The international situation compels me to demand this sacrifice of you, señores. If you pronounce the death penalty, I undertake not to apply it."[25] This version is also given by Jacinto Toryho, onetime director of *Solidaridad Obrera*, who claims that after the war Mariano Gómez, then in Buenos Aires, recounted the episode to him personally.[26]

It is impossible to ignore this testimony from three different sources, but in all fairness it must be stated that the key evidence—Mariano Gómez's letter to Indalecio Prieto—has not yet come to light. The only significant document I have found is a telegram preserved in the Civil War section of the Archivo Histórico Nacional in Salamanca, the main repository of Republican documents captured during the war. The telegram is dated 22 October 1938, the last day of the trial, sent by Negrín to one of his aides, José García Valdecasas, asking him to deliver "by hand" and "with the utmost urgency" a message to the president of the supreme tribunal, the public prosecutor, and the minister of justice requesting them to see him that day and to let him know their reply "urgently," so that if they could not come he would try to visit them.[27]

Whatever may have been the significance of this urgent telegram and Negrín's role in the trial, there can be no question about the efforts of the PCE to pervert the course of justice. According to Jordi Arquer, Manuel Hernando Solana, one of the presiding magistrates, told him when he visited him in 1950 that he suggested in chambers that all those persons who had sent letters, telegrams, and petitions to the court demanding the death penalty should be prosecuted for exerting pressure on the judiciary and that the prisoners should be exonerated. This proposal, said Hernando, caused "a commotion" among his colleagues who replied "alarmed" that if it were implemented "the Communists would assassinate them [the prisoners]."[28] Nothing could express more tellingly the atmosphere of intimidation in which the trial was held.

Despite the pressure on the judges, the charges of espionage and of desertion from the Aragon front during the May events by the POUM's Twenty-ninth Division were dismissed. There was no evidence, the judgment stated, that the accused had furnished information of any kind to the enemy about the battle fronts or the rear. "On the other hand," it continued, "their conduct shows that they are all definite antifascists (*con una marcada significación antifascista*), that they contributed to the struggle against the military uprising and that their sole aim was to go beyond the democratic republic and to institute their own political beliefs."[29] This remarkable statement proves that there were members of the judiciary who refused to bow completely to intimidation.

Several factors helped to absolve the POUM from the charge of espionage:

1. The manifest forgery of the documents, particularly the one in invisible ink, bearing the initial "N,"[30] which made a mockery of the trial. Says Jesús Hernández, a politburo member at the time, "The trial was a crude comedy based on falsified documents and on statements extracted from wretched spies of Franco who were promised their lives—although afterward they were shot—provided that they declared that they maintained contact with the leaders of the POUM. . . . The 'evidence'—in whose documentary 'preparation' W. Roces [Wenceslao Roces, at one time Hernández's undersecretary of education][31] played a very active part—was so hollow and false that not one [of the POUM leaders] could be sent before a firing squad."[32]

2. The testimony in their favor by Araquistáin, Caballero, Irujo, Montseny, and Zugazagoitia.[33]

3. The spirited defense by the accused.[34]

4. The failure of the NKVD to extract a confession from Andrés Nin. The importance of this is stressed by Wilebaldo Solano, the secretary of the POUM's youth organization and later secretary of the party in exile. "[T]he resistance of Nin to his executioners upset the plans of the GPU [NKVD] and its Spanish collaborators. A 'confession' from Nin would have created a dramatic situation for the POUM and its imprisoned leaders, for it would have enabled the NKVD to operate as in the USSR and show the world that there were also 'Trotskyist traitors who recognized their crimes.' . . . But thanks to the heroic sacrifice of Nin, a 'Moscow trial' could not be mounted in Spain."[35]

Although the POUM leaders were absolved from the charges of espionage and desertion, they were sentenced to various terms of imprisonment for their participation in the May events. Enrique Adroher, Juan Andrade, Pedro Bonet, and Julián Gorkin were sentenced to fifteen years imprisonment for attempting to take advantage of the "rebellious movement" in order "to implement their plans to seize power . . . and to set up the social and economic system they advocate," while Jordi Arquer, the political commissar of the Twenty-ninth Division, was sentenced to eleven years in prison. Although he did not participate in the events in Barcelona, the judgment said, "he pursued the same conduct as his colleagues on the executive committee in order to prepare and benefit from any movement that served to advance the POUM's revolutionary program." Two of the accused were acquitted and the party as well as its youth organization (JCI), both of which had long been unable to function openly, were officially dissolved.[36] An attempt was made by the foreign friends of the POUM to overturn the sentences, but Barcelona fell three months later and the prisoners managed to escape to France.[37]

The judgment was a moral and political victory for the POUM leaders, for it clearly stated that they were all "definite antifascists" and that there was no evidence they had provided the enemy with information. In the opinion of Gorkin, the sentence was a compromise. This was apparent, he claims, from the words of the minister of justice: "If [the POUM leaders] had been freed, they would have been assassinated in the streets by the NKVD. We've already had enough with the Nin scandal!"[38]

The foreign supporters of the POUM were of course triumphant over the outcome of the trial. "[Where] does all this leave the Stalinist poison-pen artists?" asked *Workers' Age.* "That the POUM is a 'Trotskyist-fascist' organization, 'working hand in hand with the Gestapo,' has for a year and a half been a cardinal point in Stalinist propaganda. 'Charges' have been deliberately concocted, 'evidence' brazenly manufactured out of thin air, and given worldwide currency in thousands of columns of newspaper space and thousands of copies of pamphlets. And now, the POUM stands vindicated of these 'charges' and the 'evidence' itself is thrown out by the court, by a court of the Negrín government. What will the Stalinists do now? Will they withdraw their shameless slanders against the POUM? . . . Or will they—as we have every reason to believe—continue their poison-pen campaign despite everything that has happened?"[39]

That the result of the trial was a bitter pill for the Comintern is evidenced by Togliatti. In a report to Moscow, he described the sentence as "outrageous" since "no serious punishment"[40] was meted out. The result was also an acute disappointment for the PCE, but it made the best of a bad situation by not publishing the judgment and by continuing to attack its opponents during the last few months of the war and in the years in exile as "Trotskyist" agents and "traitors" in the pay of General Franco.[41]

50

The Destruction of the Agricultural Collectives and the Council of Aragon

*I*n order to follow the descending course of the Revolution, we must now return to the spring of 1937, when the collectivization movement, initiated with such evangelical élan in July 1936 by the peasant unions of the CNT and UGT, was coming under increased attack.[1]

Encouraged by the decree of 7 October 1936, issued by Communist minister of agriculture Vicente Uribe—giving legal status to expropriations carried out at the inception of the Revolution, but exempting from confiscation properties belonging to landowners who had not identified themselves with the military rebellion—many owners who had been forced to accept collectivization were now demanding the restitution of their land. Furthermore, to the anguish of both Anarchosyndicalists and left-wing Socialists, the Communists used the decree to encourage tenant farmers and sharecroppers, who before the war had been in conflict with the rural wage workers but had been swept up involuntarily by the collective farm movement, to recover their former parcels. Many of these farmers, it will be recalled, had belonged to right-wing parties before the war, especially in the province of Valencia, where fifty thousand joined the Peasant Federation organized by the PCE.

At the height of the offensive against the collective farms at the end of May 1937, left-wing Socialist Ricardo Zabalza, a loyal follower of Largo Caballero and general secretary of the National Federation of Land Workers affiliated with the UGT, declared: "Our most fervent aim today is to guarantee the conquests of the Revolution . . . against which a world of enemies is rising up, namely, the reactionaries of yesterday and those who held land on lease because they were lackeys of the political bosses, whereas our members were either denied land or evicted from their wretched holdings. Today these reactionaries, protected by the famous decree of 7 October, are endeavoring to take by assault the collectivized estates with the object of dividing them up . . . and putting an end to the agrarian revolution."[2]

And on 6 June, *Adelante*, the mouthpiece of the left-wing Socialists, who controlled the National Federation of Land Workers, declared: "For the bourgeois Republicans, who wish to limit the struggle to one against feudalism, the policy of the Communist party is the most beneficial. Not so for the working-class parties and organizations." The Communists, it protested, wished to destroy the constructive work of the collectives, using as an excuse the excesses committed against the legitimate interests of small farmers loyal to the regime. "[It] is one thing to defend the existing peasant owners . . . , but it is an entirely different thing to create a small rural bourgeoisie by destroying the peasant collectives."

Early in June, the Anarchist newspaper *Ideas* claimed that "terror and death" were being spread among "our best comrades, particularly in the agrarian collectives."[3] And a few weeks later, the general secretary of the CNT Peasants Federation of Castile declared: "We have fought terrible battles with the Communists, especially with brigades and divisions under their control, which has assassinated our best peasant militants and savagely destroyed our collective farms."[4]

An Andalusian peasant recalls: "If the Communists did not destroy the collectives of the CNT by force . . . they sent groups of unconditional supporters to seize their work mules on the pretext that they required the meat to feed the army. . . . [Their] aim was to control everything without opposition as in a totalitarian regime."[5]

The attacks on the collectives damaged both rural economy and morale, for as the campaign reached its peak before the summer harvest, the agricultural laborers abandoned their work in many places. Vicente Uribe, the Communist minister of agriculture, then issued a decree at the beginning of June promising help to the collectives to avoid "economic failure that might chill the faith of the land workers in the collective forms of cultivation they chose freely when they confiscated the land" and granting them legal status during the *current* agricultural year.[6] Commenting on the decree, the PCE organ *Frente Rojo* ignored the fact that the status of legality had been given only temporarily. "[The decree]," it affirmed, "grants to the agricultural collectives . . . an indestructible legal position. . . . What began as a spontaneous impulse among a large section of the agricultural workers has now been converted by virtue of the decree into a legal form of agricultural labor."[7] Nevertheless, as noted in an earlier chapter, the minister of agriculture, who remained in charge of the department until the end of the war, never granted the collectives permanent legal status.

Although the decree of June 1937 offered no protection beyond the current agricultural year, it produced a feeling of relief in the countryside, thus achieving its immediate purpose. But no sooner had the crops been gathered than foreboding again set in. On 11 August, the central government dissolved the Anarchist-dominated Regional Defense Committee of Aragon that had been established in Caspe in October 1936 to direct the Revolution in that area of Aragon occupied by the anti-Franco forces, predominantly libertarian. "The real masters of Aragon," states the official Communist history of the Civil War and Revolution, "were the Anarchists, who, with the help of the militia of the Catalan CNT, instituted an Anarchist dictatorship in that region. . . . The forced collectivization imposed by the Anarchists in Aragon, the plunder, crime and disorder that prevailed in the region caused profound discontent and unrest among the workers. To silence the disquiet and give their domination greater respectability—without using the 'abominable' label of government—the FAI leaders thought up the Regional Committee of Aragon and created a bureaucratic and police apparatus that would preserve their power."[8]

These criticisms were not entirely without substance. By October 1936, the uncontrolled requisitioning of food and animals by the militia columns, the majority libertarian, had become so serious as to threaten, according to Joaquín Ascaso, the Anarchist president of the council, the "total ruin" of the region. This, he said, impelled the council to prohibit the heads of the columns from making requisitions without its prior approval. "We hope that everyone, without exception, will abide by this order, thus avoiding the lamentable and paradoxical circumstance of a free people hating its liberty and its liberators, and the no less sad situation of a people totally ruined by the Revolution for which it has always yearned."[9]

In a report to Largo Caballero in November 1936, in which he justified the creation of the council, Joaquín Ascaso stated that the absence of all governing organs in the three provinces of Aragon and the occupation of part of this region by militia, "not all subjected to the necessary and desirable discipline," had given rise to a chaotic situation that threatened economic ruin in the rear and disaster at the front. For these reasons, he added, it had been essential to create a body that would assume all the functions exercised by the former organs of administration, "a body adequate both in its structure and functioning to the present situation."[10]

Initially, the council had been made up solely of representatives of the CNT and FAI and had operated as a completely independent entity. "The creation of an autonomous organ of power that was exclusively libertarian could not satisfy a central government formed of representatives of all the political parties," writes César M. Lorenzo, the son of Horacio M. Prieto, who, it will be recalled, was secretary of the national committee of the CNT until November 1936 and one of the principal advocates of CNT participation in the government. "Nowhere else in the loyalist zone was there a local body in the hands of one single segment of opinion. . . . The Council of Aragon thus became a choice target of the Republicans, the Socialists, and the Communists, who did not hesitate to denounce it as a camouflaged dictatorship and to accuse it of cantonalism.[11] The disapproval was so widespread that even the leaders of the CNT proclaimed their dissatisfaction." Lorenzo adds that they thought the creation of the council not only rendered their efforts to join the government more difficult, but that the council itself was "illegal" because it had been created without the approval of the CNT national committee and had not been ratified by any plenum or regular congress. The Aragonese Anarchists, he affirms, were not slow to recognize the problems created by their "high-handed conduct." They realized that in order to survive they must obtain the authorization of the government at all costs. "Benito Pabón, the well-known leader of the Syndicalist party[12] and a great friend of the CNT, devoted his efforts to persuading them to . . . request openly the legalization of the council of Aragon even at the cost of their own pride. He showed them that the complexity of the international situation required a total reorganization of the council because the great powers would not help the Republic if the predominance of the extreme left were advertised ostentatiously, and he convinced them that it was essential to maintain certain bourgeois democratic appearances."[13]

As a result, the Defense Council of Aragon agreed to give representation to other organizations in return for recognition by the central government.[14] The CNT and FAI nevertheless retained in their hands the key posts: presidency, public order, propaganda, agriculture, economy, transport, and supplies.[15] Although the Communists were given two seats, they could not live with an arch-revolutionary body that fomented libertarian communists in the countryside and pursued a policy of collectivization of the holdings of the small proprietor and tenant farmer.[16] But only after the power of the CNT and FAI had been broken in the neighboring region of Catalonia in May 1937, and after Largo Caballero had been replaced by Juan Negrín in the premiership, and Indalecio Prieto in the defense ministry was it possible for the central government—now disencumbered of the CNT—to dissolve the council.

The cabinet was united in its hostility to the council, and a decree providing for its dissolution was handed to President Azaña for signature on 12 July. As usual he was timorous. He was fearful that the operation might "turn out badly," because of the predominance of the CNT forces in Aragon,[17] but on 6 August Negrín assured him that "all possible precautions" had been taken and expressed the hope that the matter would be resolved "without serious incidents."[18] A month earlier, on 4 July, Azaña, encouraged by the precipitous decline of Anarchosyndicalist power in Catalonia, had asked Negrín when the council would be dissolved. "He is ready to do it," the president noted in his diary, "and to put them in jail, for which there is more than sufficient reason."[19]

Interior minister Julián Zugazagoitia claims that the council's "irregular" acts were "bloodcurdling."[20] But it is clear from the dissolution decree that the principal objection was that it escaped the authority of the government. "The region of Aragon," ran the preamble to the decree, which was not published until 11 August, ". . . suffers more than any other region from the effects of the diffusion of power. . . . The government holds that only by remedying the crisis of authority in Aragon will it achieve its goal of concentrating power in its hands."[21]

Since Aragon was the last remaining bulwark of the Anarchosyndicalists against the central power and they controlled three of the five divisions in the region—the Twenty-fifth, Twenty-sixth, and Twenty-eighth, formerly the Jubert, Durruti, and Ascaso columns—it was essential to proceed with secrecy and to delay the publication date until after the actual dissolution of the council. On 5 August, Prieto summoned Enrique Líster, the Communist commander of the Eleventh Division, one of the most efficient and best-armed units of the Popular Army, to the defense ministry and told him that the government had resolved to dispatch a military force to Aragon capable of carrying out its decision. "Prieto told me," Líster testifies, "that there would be no written orders regarding my mission and no reports issued on its fulfillment; that it was a secret between me and the government, and that I was to liquidate without compassion and without bureaucratic or legalistic procedures everything I deemed necessary."[22] Since Líster was a member of the central committee of the PCE,[23] we can assume that Prieto was acting in concert with the party.

Líster claims that he prepared a plan of "psychological attack"—infantry maneuvers with artillery fire on the outskirts of Caspe and the parade of a tank battalion through the streets—that produced the desired result. "Hated by the people," he writes, "the Council of Aragon collapsed without the firing of a single shot. And when the next day, 11 August, the dissolution decree appeared in the *Gaceta* the council had ceased to exist."[24] Commenting on the decree, *Adelante*, mouthpiece at that time of the moderate Socialists in the government, stated: "Perhaps the change that took place yesterday in Aragonese territory may not have extraordinary repercussions abroad. No matter. It deserves to have them because by this action the government offers the firmest testimony of its authority."[25]

"The population of Aragon, especially the peasants," recounts the official Communist history of the Civil War, "acclaimed the dissolution of the council with indescribable enthusiasm,"[26] but Ricardo Sanz, the Anarchosyndicalist commander of the Twenty-sixth Division, paints a less radiant picture. The Eleventh Division, he claims, took by assault the official centers in Caspe and arrested the majority of the office workers, dissolving the Council of Aragon by force. "It took harsh measures against all the villages, attacking the peasant collectives. It despoiled them of everything—work animals, food, agricultural implements, and buildings—and initiated a fierce repression and persecution of the members of the collectives."[27]

After the war, José Duque, one of the two Communist members of the Defense Council, stated, when he was no longer a member of the party but still a critic of the council's radical agrarian policies, that in his opinion Líster's measures were more severe than they need have been.[28] Manuel Almudí, the other Communist on the council, agreed, speaking as a Communist: "Líster's measures in Aragon were very harsh. He could have acted with greater discretion. Great ill feeling was aroused as a result of his conduct."[29]

In September, a clandestine issue of *El Amigo del Pueblo*, published in Barcelona, stated that Líster had announced in Caspe that "the collectives in Aragon would disappear from the face of the earth." "The fascist mentality of the Stalinists," it added, "has seized hold of our brotherly region. It is distressing and provoking to observe how the entire work of the CNT in Aragon has been destroyed by the agents of the USSR."[30]

Líster alleges that upon his return to Valencia, Prieto, "using all his hypocritical skill," began to shout reproaches at him so that the thirty or forty people in the waiting room could hear him. "What have you done in Aragon? You have killed the Anarchists and now they are demanding your head. I shall have to give it to them, otherwise another civil war will erupt." Líster denied that anyone had been executed (this is contradicted by Almudí, who told me that "Líster did not kill many"[31]), and he agreed to free the prisoners. "Prieto hated the Anarchists, but he hated the Communists just as much. He was also a defeatist regarding the outcome of the war. If his plan had succeeded, he would have killed two birds with one stone: He would have opened up a new civil war between the Communists and the CNT, in which the two organizations would have destroyed each other, and he would have put an end to the war [against Franco] in keeping with his ideas."[32] But the truth is that the Communists required no prodding from Prieto to break the power of the CNT and FAI.

Antonio Cordón, the Communist chief of staff of the eastern army in Aragon under General Sebastián Pozas, alleges that Prieto's behavior was in keeping with his plan to mount "an anti-Communist offensive, which from that time on was becoming clearer every day."[33] This was true as events will testify. It is also true, as José Duque, the Communist party secretary in Aragon, said a month after Líster's sweep through the region, that certain Republicans and Socialists had profited from the situation to tell the Anarchists that the Communists were responsible for the campaign against them.[34] That the Republicans and Socialists should attempt to throw the blame entirely on the Communists is not surprising, but the Anarchists had no difficulty in identifying their most dangerous opponents. "[The] XIth Division under the Communist Líster," said the peninsular committee of the FAI, "was sent to [Aragon] to undertake a repressive and punitive action. . . . Its purpose was not only to destroy the collectives, but to provoke a violent reaction on the part of CNT-FAI comrades or a revolt by the CNT divisions so as to bring about the maximum repression. The calm but forceful behavior of our responsible committees prevented a disaster."[35]

There is evidence that a part of the PSUC-controlled Twenty-seventh Division stationed on the Aragon front joined in the assault on the collective farms.[36] Under the circumstances, one may wonder why the three Anarchist divisions remained inert during the Communists' forays through Aragon. Juan Manuel Molina, who, it will be recalled, was CNT undersecretary of defense in the Generalitat government during the May events and who had fought "tooth and nail" to prevent a large motorized column of the CNT from leaving the front for Barcelona, states that the 127th Brigade of the Twenty-eighth Division "was burning with desire to go into action against the Communists." "I was able to convince the men," he attests, "that before such a step were taken I should leave for Valencia and inform the national committee of the CNT." He would also see Negrín and would launch a military offensive on his return if the "demented repression" had not stopped. On arriving in Valencia he found the national committee busy "stamping membership cards" totally unaware of the "gigantic operation under way to end once and for all the influence of the CNT." He then called on Negrín accompanied by CNT secretary Mariano Vázquez who "passed the time discussing trivialities" until the premier, looking at his watch, said it was time for lunch. "I stood up, approached Negrín, and said with some embarrassment: 'Excuse me, Señor Presidente, we have not yet explained the purpose of our visit. . . . If this intolerable situation does not cease immediately our divisions will enter into action . . . , which means that this could well be the end of the war, of your premiership, and of the Republic.' " Negrín told Molina that he was "not aware" of the gravity of the situation and would give orders for the release of the CNT prisoners immediately. "Tomorrow morning," he said, "I shall leave for that front to inform myself personally and if any irregularities have been committed they will be remedied." On being informed of the interview with Negrín, the CNT national committee said that it was satisfied and that it considered the problem solved. "As was to be expected," observed Molina, "Negrín did not go to Aragon as he had promised, but the arrests ceased, the members of the regional committee and the other prisoners were freed, the terror imposed by the Communists diminished. However, their objectives were achieved and the CNT had lost *one more* battle—the dissolution of the Council of Aragon—without a fight."[37]

On 12 August, while the repression and the destruction of the collective farms were still in progress, the CNT sent a delegation to President Azaña to complain. He could hardly be expected to lend a sympathetic ear. After listening to its grievances, he suggested "soberly," as he puts it, that the delegation should take them to the government! One of the three delegates, Azaña observes, demanded representation in the cabinet, while another stated that they did not want any ministries. "They ask not to be persecuted," runs the entry in his diary, "that 'there be understanding' and respect for what the CNT represents. They referred repeatedly to the demoralization and discontent of the 'comrades' and [stated that] if another episode like the one in May should occur their efforts to settle it peacefully might be useless. The common goal was to win the war, but if this policy of persecution were to bring about the destruction or subjection of the CNT . . . then it would be *better if everything should sink.*"[38]

Despite these ominous words, the leaders of the peninsular committee of the FAI, at a general meeting in Bujaraloz representing the CNT units, "decided not to take any retaliatory action."[39] There can be little doubt that at the back of the minds of most of the CNT-FAI leaders, bedeviled by political setbacks, by ideological constraints, and by ambivalence toward governmental collaboration, there lay the hope of salvaging what they could of the Revolution by rejoining the cabinet. César Lorenzo claims, clearly reflecting his father's thinking, that the CNT committees "wanted to collaborate with Negrín and avoid provoking any serious conflict apt to poison their relations."[40] On 29 August, David Antona, CNT secretary in the central zone, announced that the regional committees had unanimously agreed to "offer the Government of the Republic everything they possessed"—"their organizations and means of production"—because it was the "inescapable duty" of everyone to support the government and to "exercise the right to participate in the responsibilities of power."[41] But the government felt that it could manage very well without the CNT and rejected the overture on the grounds that it did not consider the moment "opportune."[42]

Meanwhile, the repression in Aragon was continuing. On the same day that the government published its dissolution decree, it appointed José Ignacio Mantecón, a former member of the council, as governor general of the region. Officially a member of Izquierda Republicana, he was an ambitious fellow traveler, who in the words of Enrique Líster, was "an intelligent, dynamic, forceful and courageous man." "From the first day," he adds, "we understood each other perfectly and we gave him all our collaboration and help in his difficult task."[43] However, according to Azaña, Mantecón was not always as accommodating as Líster would have liked. On 24 November 1938, he made the following notation in his diary: "Líster suggested [to Mantecón] that he should execute [*dar el paseo a*] the members of the Regional Council of Aragon. He refused. 'The game was clear,' he told me. 'I would have shot them and then [Líster] would have thrown the blame on me, representing himself as the champion of the working class.' "[44]

That Mantecón was not the ideal paradigm of the accommodating fellow traveler is attested by José Duque, although it is true that he was inducted into the Communist party after the Civil War.[45] In a report, on 17 August, to the central committee of the PCE, Duque criticized Mantecón for "excessive legalism" and for his "abundant weaknesses and vacillations." The governor, he complained, was not attending "forcefully and decisively" to such problems as the "disarming of the rear, the struggle against espionage, provocators [and] hidden enemies."[46] Despite this criticism, Mantecón—aided by the Eleventh Division and by two companies of assault guards—continued the ruthless destruction of the collective farms initiated by Líster. Ricardo Sanz recalls: "This petty individual, cleverly manipulated by the Communist party, was charged with the final liquidation of the collectives. . . . He savagely persecuted the genuine antifascists and revolutionaries who were said to have acted . . . with excessive violence in the early days . . . , [and] he dissolved all the remaining collectives."[47] According to a report of the Aragon CNT, the land, farm implements, horses, and cattle confiscated from right-wing supporters were returned to their former owners or to their families; new buildings erected by the collectives, such as stables and hen coops, were destroyed, and in some villages the farms were deprived even of the seed necessary for sowing, while six hundred members of the CNT were arrested.

Of this repression the tenant farmers and small owners who had entered the collective farms in the early weeks of the Revolution, when the power of the CNT and FAI in Aragon was undisputed, took full advantage. They divided up the land as well as the crops and farm implements, and, with the aid of the assault guards and Communist military forces, even raided those collectives that had been established in accordance with the wishes of their members.

The situation became so serious that the Communists, although evading personal responsibility, later acknowledged that a dangerous policy had been adopted. José Silva, general secretary of the Institute of Agrarian Reform and a Communist party member, wrote:

It was in Aragon where the most varied and strange experiments in collectivization and socialization were made, where undoubtedly the most violence was used in order to compel the peasants to enter the collective farms, and where a manifestly false policy tore open serious breaches in rural economy. When the government of the Republic dissolved the Council of Aragon, the governor general tried to allay the profound uneasiness in the hearts of the peasant masses by dissolving the collectives. This measure was a very grave mistake and produced tremendous disorganization in the countryside. Under cover of the order issued by the governor general, those persons who were discontented with the collectives—and who had good reason for being so, if the methods employed in forming them are taken into account—took them by assault, carrying away and dividing up the harvest and farm implements without respecting the collectives that had been formed without violence or pressure, that were prosperous, and that were a model of organization, like the one in Candasnos.

It is true that the governor's aim was to repair injustices and to convince the workers of the countryside that the Republic was protecting them, but the result was just the opposite from that intended. The measure only increased the confusion, and violence was exercised, but this time by the other side.[48] As a result, labor in the fields was suspended almost entirely, and a quarter of the land had not been prepared at the time for sowing.[49]

"The danse macabre of the Communists and reactionary owners resulted in the ruin of agriculture in Aragon," José Peirats, the Anarchosyndicalist historian, charges. "The collectivists who were not in jail were either persecuted or took refuge in other regions or sought protection in the CNT divisions. In these circumstances the hour arrived to prepare the soil for the next harvest. The small owners who had been triumphant could not work with their own hands the properties they had occupied. [On the other hand], the dispossessed peasants—intransigent collectivists—refused to work under a regime of private property, or, worse still, to hire themselves out for wages."[50]

On 9 October, at a meeting of the agrarian commission of the Aragonese Communist party, José Silva emphasized "the little incentive to work of the entire peasant community." "It is necessary to end this situation. We must raise the morale of the peasants and we must do this through the Agrarian Commission of the Communist party." The situation brought about by the dissolution of the collectives, he added, was "grave and critical," because "our enemies are taking advantage of these circumstances to hurt production."[51] Only a few days earlier the Communist-controlled Regional Delegation of Agrarian Reform acknowledged that "in the majority of villages agricultural work was paralyzed causing great harm to our agrarian economy."[52]

Indeed, the situation created by the Communist party's own actions was so alarming that in order to redress the situation it had once again to change its policy and restore some of the dismantled farms. "The recognition of the rights of the collectives," said Silva, "and the decision to return what had been unjustly taken away from them, together with the efforts of the governor general of Aragon in this direction, brought things back to normal. Tranquillity returned, and enthusiasm was revived among the peasants, who gave the necessary labor for sowing the abandoned land."[53]

According to Peirats, although there is no complete information on the effect of Communist repression on what he calls the "second stage of collectivization," the comparative figures of delegates who attended the two congresses of collectivists held in Aragon in 1937—five hundred in February, before the breakup of the collective farms, and two hundred in September, after their dissolution and the subsequent reversal of Communist policy, when some of the dismantled collectives had been restored—are significant. "It is very possible," he concludes, "that this second stage of collectivization reflected more faithfully the sincerity of its adherents. They had been subjected to a hard test, and those who had been capable of withstanding it were collectivists inured to all adversities. However, it would be foolish to characterize all those who abandoned collectivization during the second stage as anticollectivist. Fear, official coercion, and uncertainty of the future weighed heavily in the decisions of an important segment of the Aragonese peasantry."[54]

But, while the economic situation in Aragon improved in some degree after the Communists had modified their policy, the hatreds and resentments generated by the breakup of the collectives and by the repression that followed were never wholly dispelled. Nor was the resultant disillusionment that sapped the spirit of the Anarchosyndicalist forces on the Aragon front ever entirely removed, a disillusionment that no doubt helped to contribute to the collapse of that front a few months later. Peirats writes: "The collective farms were once again authorized. The prisoners were released. Collectivization got under way. The new sowings were prepared. But this time it was Franco who reaped the harvest. In the spring of 1938, the whole of Aragon, and parts of Catalonia and Valencia would be invaded by the fascist armies. One cannot play the game of demoralizing a front and its rear with impunity."[55]

Part VII

*The Eclipse of Largo Caballero
and Indalecio Prieto*

51

Indalecio Prieto Challenges the PCE

At this point it should be stressed that the decision of the Communists to halt the attacks on the collective farms stemmed not only from the damage to rural economy and morale but from growing friction with Indalecio Prieto and the need to find an accommodation with the CNT—as will be seen in the next chapter—in preparation for the inevitable showdown with the defense minister; for although it is true that Prieto had allied himself with the Communists against Largo Caballero, his perennial adversary, he soon made it clear that he would not be their puppet.

"Shortly after taking over the ministry of national defense . . . , the two Communist ministers, Uribe and Hernández, came to see me," Prieto told the national committee of the Socialist party a year later. "They said that they wanted to work closely with me." But when Hernández suggested that he visit Prieto "every day with suggestions, ideas, and views of the politburo on military matters," the defense minister replied bluntly that if Hernández had anything to say regarding military policy, he could present it to the entire cabinet. "You are mistaken," Prieto told him, "if you assume that you can carry on the kind of struggle with me as you did with Largo Caballero. . . . You cannot manipulate me and I will not put up with disputes such as you had with Largo Caballero in cabinet meetings that evoke such unpleasant memories."[1]

Equally disconcerting to the Communists was Prieto's attitude toward the fusion of the Socialist and Communist parties. Despite his assurance to Vittorio Codovila, the Comintern delegate, and to Pietro Nenni, the Italian Socialist leader, before the ouster of Largo Caballero, that he was ready to work for the merger of the two parties, he made it clear after he became defense minister that he would not yield to the hectoring demands of the Soviet ambassador Leon Gaykis that he support the fusion. To be sure, in July, at one of the weekly meetings of the Socialist party executive, he appeared to have second thoughts about the matter. Juan-Simeón Vidarte, a member of the executive, records Prieto's thinking: In his opinion the Communists were gaining a large number of allies. The principal cause was the "betrayal of the democracies." Since Russia was the only country that sent arms to Spain, Republican sympathy turned toward her, and the Communists derived the utmost benefit by appropriating key positions everywhere. Career officers, who had been among his best and most loyal friends, such as air force chief Ignacio Hidalgo de Cisneros and many others, were now Communists. Finally, Prieto expressed the opinion that "the time had arrived to think about the advisability of merging the Socialist and Communist parties before it was too late and we find ourselves displaced from the political leadership of the working class."[2]

Although Prieto may indeed have made this statement in a moment of exasperation over the "betrayal" of the democracies, it is questionable whether he ever seriously envisioned the possibility of fusion. Just twelve months earlier his mouthpiece *El Socialista* had condemned the campaign for the fusion of the two parties as the "fraud of unification" and had denounced the merger of the two youth movements as "the absorption of the Socialist youth by the Communist party." In any event, it is inconceivable that a man as independently minded as Prieto would ever have assented to the Communists' conditions. In a letter to the PSOE executive, published on 7 July 1937, the politburo laid down the following fundamental rules and principles for the fusion: (1) the United party would be the "monolithic vanguard of the workers with a single will"; (2) once taken, a decision, whether on a debated issue or on a course of action, would be binding upon everyone; (3) all those subject to the mandate of the party (ministers, deputies, governors, newspapers, etc.) would be obligated to carry out the decisions and directives of its supreme organ; and (4) all members guilty of sabotaging the party's work or conducting activities that threatened the unity of the party would be liable to "expulsion and public condemnation."

"The responsibility that weighs upon us is immense," the politburo warned. "It is essential to achieve the political unity of the Spanish proletariat, to create the powerful United Party through the IMMEDIATE FUSION of the two working-class parties. This is the duty that History imposes on us. This is the burning desire, the firm will, the imperative and unanimous clamor of the Socialist and Communist workers."[3]

Apart from the fact that such important local units of the party as Madrid, Valencia, Alicante, and Jaen, which represented its left wing, were not taken into account, it was unlikely that the center faction would agree to the politburo's conditions. Indeed, so strong was the opposition to the proposal for immediate fusion within the executive committee that even its secretary, the ambitious, subtle, manipulatory, and intelligent Ramón Lamoneda,[4] who at this time was warily supporting the Communists, did not venture to go beyond a qualified pledge of future unification when addressing the national committee of the Socialist party on 17 July 1937: "We are in favor of fusion into a single party of the Spanish proletariat . . . ," he declared, "[but] with adequate guarantees that if that unity is realized it will not be broken immediately by failure to foresee all the aspects of the problem."[5]

In making this statement, Lamoneda was responding not only to his own apprehensions (and to his personal ambition to secure for himself a leading post in the united party by deftly playing his hand)[6] but also to the fears of other leaders of the center faction who saw in the unification of the two parties the inescapable absorption of the Socialists by the PCE. Although the National Liaison Committee, formed in April, in which Lamoneda represented the PSOE, urged that the two parties should work "with total enthusiasm" for unification,[7] the Socialist executive, according to the official history of the PCE, "tenaciously opposed the creation of the Single Party of the Proletariat in spite of its asseverations in favor of unity."[8] It was this opposition—spearheaded by Prieto, with the backing of a majority of the executive, which included such loyal supporters as Manuel Albar, Manuel Cordero, Francisco Cruz Salido, and Anastasio de Gracia—that led the Comintern, as we have seen, to conclude in July 1937 that the Communists "should not force amalgamation" and that "those Socialists who were already prepared to join the Communist party should be persuaded that it would be more beneficial to continue to work within the Socialist party to strengthen unity of action and prepare for the amalgamation of the workers' parties."[9]

The well-known British author Ralph Bates, an outstanding authority on the Spanish working-class movement, who at one time worked for the Comintern and served as assistant commissar in the Fifteenth International Brigade, made the following remarks in a letter to me in 1940 regarding the Communist drive for the United party: It aroused "furious, envenomed opposition" in the Socialist party that went right down to the intelligent rank and file. "You must remember that Lamoneda and Co., who declared for it, were not 'ordinary' socialists. They were in large part communists; either socialists who had been won over and who had been instructed to remain in the SP—the Party was reproved for the inadvertent 'waste' of M. Nelken[10]—or a mere handful of genuine socialists who had been convinced of the necessity upon 'war-grounds' rather than final acceptance of theory." The majority of the Socialist party members, Bates added, viewed the whole unity campaign as "a mere absorptionist effort on the part of the CP." They believed that they would lose control of the UGT, be submerged in the new party, which would virtually become a CP, controlled by the Comintern, and that the Socialist tradition would be lost. "Certain it is that *never* was there any real mass clamor, on the part of the socialists, for the fusion with the CP. It antagonized the CNT-FAI, frightened the I.R. [Izquierda Republicana] and the republicans in general. It was therefore a colossal blunder. Fortunately, the CP was never very insistent. I believe the C.I. [Communist International] understood the dangers and did not push the Spanish CP very hard on this point. I know that Luis [pseudonym for Codovila], the most able of the C.I. delegates in Spain, disliked the whole thing."[11]

It was now obvious to Stalin, who had undoubtedly regarded the fusion of the Communist and Socialist parties as an essential step toward the establishment of a single party state, that more time was needed to bring about the merger. But despite this indefinite deferment, fortune continued to smile benignly on the Communist party, which by now had far outstripped the Socialists and Republicans in political influence. In the vast literature on the Spanish Civil War, no one has described the party's spectacular ascent more authoritatively than Eudocio Ravines, the Peruvian Communist leader who was appointed by Codovila to edit *Frente Rojo*, the most important Communist newspaper in Spain. Writing after he had left the party, and drawing on firsthand experience in Spanish Communist circles, he offers the following picture of its stunning growth and the concomitant perquisites of success:

The political defeat of Largo Caballero increased communist influence and gave it the halo, if not of power, at least of the administration of power. Communist adherents multiplied, coming from every field—from the republican army, from the employees of the ministries and from the black markets, from the storerooms of spongers and speculators of every kind. . . .

. . . Men who until yesterday had suffered prison and torture for the communist cause and for the defense of the workers' rights had now become important communist directors with houses outside of town where they could sleep undisturbed by sirens, men who ate well while hunger brought the civil population to the point of exhaustion. They were members of a kind of confraternity of the elect, for whom this war provided the most comfortable hour of their lives. . . .

For the party leaders . . . the war was a period of great comfort. It was an easy life of which they had no doubt dreamed in their hours of misfortune. Comfortable dwellings, cellars full of fine wines, cars at the door, chauffeurs, beautiful women, blond and brunette, with green eyes or brown eyes, short-haired or long-haired, painted or not painted. For men like [Manuel] Delicado [a member of the central committee] those were the days of the fatted calf. But not for the Spanish people—not by any means. . . .

The communist preponderance in the republican government increased its power and influence over the military to the end that the republican troops might be transformed into an authentic Red Army, which would take its orders from the party. At the same time an attempt was made to absorb, subjugate or liquidate the most important nuclei of the socialists and anarchists. As for the Marxist Workers' party of Catalonia [POUM], the Central Committee declared them trotskyites and decreed that they should be dealt with as they had been in Russia.

The anarchists offered the strongest resistance. In the Republican Left [Izquierda Republicana] something was happening very similar (always allowing for conditions and distance) to what had taken place in the radical party in Chile. There were even similar personalities. Kind, intelligent, ingenuous men had cooperated in good faith and given disinterested service, only to find themselves trapped and without the courage to shake off the communist yoke or to free themselves from their willingly contracted servitude. Besides these, there were rogues dominated by the desire for money, high position, good situation. . . . There were also thousands of poor devils who served humbly and devotedly without asking or receiving anything, on condition only of being left in peace in some little government post with a miserable little salary and haunted by the nightmare of dismissal. There were numerous traders of the type of straperlo;[12] traffickers in jewels and hunger, miniatures and narcotics, false passports and human blood. These knew well enough that help given to the communist party was at that time a good investment, which paid dividends and which at some moment might save them from ruin or even from death. With such filth the directors of the Central Committee and the Soviet leaders built up what they considered the greatness of the communist party of Spain, its undisputed and totalitarian authority.

The socialists had already abandoned all frontal attack against the communist party. . . . While their forces diminished or remained stationary, those of the communist party had grown by leaps and bounds. The socialists accused the communists, each time more weakly, of the crime of "proselytization." The communists denied it or promised to change, but they continued to use the most violent and shameless pressures to get new adherents. Everything served: the offer of a job in a ministry, the threat of dismissal, the hope of promotion, the promise of a transfer. Sometimes for six or seven hundred pesetas a month, paid out of the treasury, a whole family would join the ranks of the glorious party of Marx, Engels, Lenin, Stalin and Pepe Díaz. . . .

It was clear that the large communist group was sunk in shamelessness, crime and cynicism. Facing the situation honestly, we could not help seeing that the procedures of fascism and communism differed only by a hair's breadth. It was becoming clearer every day that this violent terrorism was accepted without repugnance by constantly widening circles, as more and more people joined the victorious party.[13]

It was in the midst of this phenomenal growth of the Communist party that Indalecio Prieto took up the campaign against it that Largo Caballero had initiated shortly before he was maneuvered out of office. Provoked by its proselytizing efforts in the armed forces and by its crescent power, he issued on 28 June a ministerial order forbidding all propaganda among the air, land, and naval forces aimed at encouraging officers and men to join a specific party or trade-union organization. "The proposal or mere suggestion by a superior to his inferior that he change his political or trade-union affiliation," the order stated, "will be regarded as a coercive act and will result in the demotion of the offender without prejudice to the criminal responsibility he might incur."[14]

On Communist party orders, Constancia de la Mora, the chief censor in the Foreign Press Bureau and wife of air force chief Ignacio Hidalgo de Cisneros, refused to allow foreign journalists to send information about Prieto's order abroad. "I had to suppress it," she told me after the war, "because it would have created a bad impression. Prieto forced me to resign."[15] The intrusive and ubiquitous Louis Fischer, who claims that he was instrumental in getting her the job through Alvarez del Vayo, the foreign minister, in January 1937, went to great lengths with both Prieto and Negrín to get her reinstated. "[It] would be difficult to find a substitute for her and Loyalist propaganda abroad would suffer," he pleaded with Prieto. "[It's] up to Negrín. Let him do as he pleases," was Prieto's atypically meek reply.[16] As a result, Constancia de la Mora returned to her post and within a few months she was made chief of the Foreign Press Bureau by the then minister of foreign affairs, the left Republican José Giral.[17] "Prieto hated me," she said shortly after the war, "because he believed that I had influenced Ignacio to join the Communist party."[18]

While the Socialist and Anarchist newspapers roundly applauded Prieto's attempt to curb proselytism in the armed forces,[19] *Mundo Obrero*, the Communist organ in Madrid, attacked "the malcontents," who, instead of examining the reasons why the Communist party had won the sympathy of most of the combatants, "engage in all kinds of speculation and consider this support to be abnormal, a product of who knows what kind of pressure and coercion, perhaps even of deception." These malcontents, *Mundo Obrero* continued, were not doing the heroic sons of the people any favor by regarding those who had entered the Communist party with enthusiasm "as weak individuals, turncoats, incapable of adhering firmly to their ideals." "We must bear in mind some of the reasons why thousands upon thousands of the most heroic combatants have entered the Communist party. We do not want to dwell on the allegations that these soldiers of liberty have allowed themselves to be coerced. That is puerile and ridiculous. The truth is that the Communist party has set an example. By this we do not wish to say that the other parties and organizations have not contributed to the struggle to the extent of their possibilities, but the fact is that from the first days of the fighting the Communist party has occupied very important posts, frontline positions, and places of the greatest danger." Finally, the paper asked, who is harmed by the growth of the Communist party? "Certainly not the Socialists, because very shortly we shall merge the two parties and shall create—for this is the desire of Communists and Socialists, and of the working class in general—the United Party of the Proletariat. No antifascist organization is harmed, because the growth of our party signifies the strengthening of the Popular Front."[20]

That the PCE was undaunted by the opposition of the "malcontents" to its drive for predominance is evident from the following passage in a report by Togliatti to Moscow on 20 August 1937: "The party has understood one thing clearly: it must carry forward a coherent struggle to expand and strengthen its position in the army, in the police, and in the state apparatus, etc. The strengthening of the positions of the party . . . is one of the principal guarantees of victory. . . . We must not lose any of the positions we have conquered in all areas and we must continue conquering new ones."[21] This recommendation was an unmistakable prescription for the ultimate conquest of power by the PCE and the eventual destruction of every element of political democracy.[22]

Under cover of the Popular Front the Communists continued their proselytizing activities without intermission, converting Prieto's order forbidding proselytism in the armed forces into the "worthless piece of paper" that the Anarchosyndicalist *CNT* had hoped it would not become.[23] Two months after the promulgation of the order, Prieto's mouthpiece, *El Socialista* censured the partiality shown in the delivery of certain newspapers at the front and the favors bestowed upon the readers of those newspapers.[24] *CNT* had a simple solution:

"Proselytism in the army. . . ," the headlines stated, *"can be eliminated only by execution squads."* In this way, it argued, no one would ever again disturb "the mutual understanding and the happiness of our soldiers with disruptive under-handed maneuvers and with absorptionist pretensions."[25]

But the Communists were not deterred either by Prieto's decree or by the facile solution proposed by *CNT*. "Every one of our comrades," declared La Pasionaria before the central committee of the PCE, "must bear in mind that neither decrees nor restrictions can prevent them from carrying out their work of political education on behalf of the Popular Front aimed at raising the level of political consciousness among the mass of soldiers. I do not believe that anyone can interpret this decree as a measure designed to curb the political rights of the soldiers to the prejudice of the Popular Army. Obviously, that is something all of us wish to avoid."[26]

Pursuing his offensive against the politicalization of the army, Prieto published the following executive order on 5 October:

1. Army chiefs and officers are forbidden to take part in public meetings of a political character.

2. They are also forbidden to make statements to the press or to make radio broadcasts. Newspapers that violate this order by publishing interviews with army chiefs or officers without the prior approval of the ministry of national defense will be severely punished.

3. No inspections or military parades shall take place without the express permission of the ministry.[27]

Largo Caballero's mouthpiece, *La Correspondencia de Valencia*, rejoicing at this turn of events, praised the efforts of the new defense minister "to nip in the bud the havoc created in the army by certain political elements" and urged him to "act with inflexible energy."[28]

Prieto needed no encouragement, for, in addition to the two ministerial orders curbing proselytism and political propaganda in the army, he attempted to redress the predominance of the Communist political commissars. Largo Caballero, it will be recalled, had vainly attempted to rectify this predominance shortly before his ouster from the government, when he issued his directive dismissing all commissars who had been provisionally appointed by Alvarez del Vayo and whose appointment and rank had not been confirmed by 15 May. Although the measure had been shelved after Caballero's removal from the war ministry, Prieto refused to ratify the appointment of hundreds of commissars until he could determine their political affiliation. His failure to confirm the appointments was vigorously condemned by the Communist party. In her report to the central committee of the PCE on 13 November, La Pasionaria declared that the conduct of the ministry of national defense, in failing to ratify "the appointments of hundreds of commissars with an exemplary history of struggle since the outbreak of the war" was "incomprehensible" and had resulted in "the sad experience of commissars who have died at the front and left their families in the utmost misery, because their appointments had not been ratified." This situation must be remedied, she added, and every commissar should understand that regardless of whether his appointment had been officially ratified or not, he should continue his work as commissar "because the maximum efficiency of the army depends on it."[29]

The barbed issue of the political commissars was raised by Prieto at a meeting of the Higher War Council, which, after the fall of Largo Caballero, had been reorganized and now comprised Juan Negrín, José Giral, Vicente Uribe, and Indalecio Prieto. In a letter to Negrín after the war, Prieto recalls that during the meeting he read detailed figures relating to the political affiliation of the commissars. These figures, he said, revealed that the percentage of commissars *officially* listed as Communists was "infinitely higher" than that to which the PCE was entitled based on its relative strength. In addition to the *official* Communists, he told Negrín, there were many commissars who belonged to the JSU and to the PSUC as well as other commissars who disguised their affiliation with the simple appellation of "UGT."[30] "As a result of the analysis I made in everyone's presence, I proposed that equilibrium be reestablished by a fair distribution of posts among all the political and trade-union organizations. . . . Vicente Uribe vigorously opposed this equitable proposal and you supported his negative stand."[31]

Undaunted by this resistance, Prieto issued a decree on 21 October restricting the rank of political commissar, in the case of men subject to the draft, to that of company, battalion, and brigade commissar. Among the most prominent Communists subject to the current draft were Santiago Alvarez, the twenty-four-year-old divisional commissar of Líster's Eleventh Division, and Francisco Antón, the twenty-seven-year-old lover of La Pasionaria, and inspector-commissar of the Madrid front, whom Prieto replaced with the Socialist Fernando Piñuela.[32] According to the official Communist history of the Civil War, Prieto's decree was aimed primarily at those commissars who belonged to the Communist party, the PSUC, and the JSU: "A substantial number of the latter, who despite their youth held the position of commissar in units larger than a brigade and who from the first moment of the military rebellion had voluntarily joined in the struggle, were compelled to leave their posts."[33]

Hernández and Uribe, both politburo members, made a special effort to spare Francisco Antón the humiliation of being demoted from the rank of inspector-commissar of the Madrid front (where there were several army corps) to that of brigade commissar on the inactive and unpublicized Teruel front, but Prieto refused to budge and Antón had no choice but to vacate his post. "The uproar created over the fact that a commissar had to accept a lower rank and join a combat unit instead of meddling with two or three armies was really childish," Prieto commented later.[34] "Antón," wrote Carlos Contreras in a laudatory article published in the Communist press, "has left the political commissariat of the largest army of the Republic to join a brigade, and has done so with that open and honest smile, which encouraged us in the most tragic times."[35] But Antón, with the backing of the politburo, did not report for duty at his brigade headquarters and was dismissed by Prieto on 1 April 1938 from the corps of commissars "for not yet occupying his post in the 49th Mixed Brigade of the 47th Division, Fifth Army Corps, 15 December 1937."[36] Before being discharged, he emerged, without Prieto's authority, as a civilian attaché to General Vicente Rojo, the chief of the central general staff.[37] It was not without cause that Rojo once told Enrique Castro, a member of the central committee of the PCE: "Prieto thinks that I am an instrument of yours."[38]

Meanwhile, the general commissar of war, the philo-communist Socialist Julio Alvarez del Vayo, disquieted by the defense minister's campaign, asked Enrique Castro—who had replaced Antonio Mije, a member of the politburo, as subcommissar general of organization[39]—if he thought the party might make some concessions to Prieto. "Don Julio," Castro reported, "I am surprised at your question. Do you by any chance believe that the party will allow its political hegemony in the army to be taken away from it when it knows that the very existence of an army capable of victory depends on its hegemony? No, Don Julio! The party will fight Prieto just as it fought Caballero." "I believe that we should make some concessions to placate Prieto and the Socialist party," del Vayo responded. "After all, I am a member of the Socialist party." "No!" was Castro's final answer.[40]

That same night the matter was taken up at a special meeting of the politburo attended by Alvarez del Vayo who, according to Castro, was given short shrift by party secretary José Díaz:

"Does it mean nothing to you, Comrade Del Vayo, that Castro has replaced a member of the politburo [as subcommissar of organization]?"

"Comrade Díaz, I believe . . ."

"Comrade Del Vayo . . . If you had asked Comrade Castro what he thought about those words 'I believe', he would have said, in keeping with his duty: 'What you believe, Comrade Del Vayo, means nothing. . . . The important thing is what the party believes, what the party demands, what the party thinks. . . . Isn't that so, Comrade Castro?"

"That's true, Comrade Díaz."

"But . . ."

"No, Comrade Del Vayo. . . . No! If Castro for a single moment were to question the party or to disagree with the party, he would not represent the party in the Political Commissariat for one moment. . . . Don't forget that, Comrade Del Vayo! When you speak to Comrade Castro, forget about Comrade Castro. You are addressing the party. And Castro is right: one concession leads to another concession. No! Castro is the party. Prieto is the anti-party. Don't forget that, Comrade Del Vayo, don't forget that!"

On leaving Communist headquarters, del Vayo observed to Castro: "Every interview with the party leadership is a marvellous lesson."[41]

Shortly afterward—on 18 November—Prieto removed Alvarez del Vayo from his post of commissar general, appointing in his stead Crescenciano Bilbao, a moderate Socialist.[42] During the following weeks, in addition to discharging from the corps of commissars a large number of commissars of lesser rank, whose names filled columns in the *Gaceta de la República* and the *Diario Oficial*,[43] Prieto ousted a number of prominent Communist or pro-Communist political commissars and army officers, including Carlos Contreras (Vittorio Vidali),[44] a founder of the famous Fifth Regiment and now chief political commissar of Líster's Eleventh Division; Alejandro García Val, the director general of transportation, whom Prieto himself had appointed;[45] the now familiar Eleuterio Díaz Tendero of the highly sensitive information and control department; the equally familiar Antonio Cordón, formerly technical secretary of the undersecretaryship of war, but now chief of staff of the eastern army under General Pozas;[46] and Luis Doporto, a subcommissar general of the General Commissariat of War.[47] Cordón acknowledges that Prieto removed him for having participated in a political meeting commemorating the twentieth anniversary of the Russian Revolution.[48] Both Díaz Tendero and Cordón, it will be recalled, had been removed by Largo Caballero but were reappointed by Prieto when he assumed control of the defense ministry.[49]

In addition to his post as head of the information and control department, Díaz Tendero was also a member of the recently created Junta de Mandos, which made recommendations to the defense minister regarding officer appointments and promotions, and in which the chief of the general staff, Vicente Rojo, had the final word. In appraising Rojo's services on behalf of the PCE during the Civil War, no memoir is more valuable than that of Colonel Jesús Pérez Salas, a Republican officer of unquestioned loyalty and honesty, yet no work of equal solidity has been so neglected or conveniently ignored.[50] In his account of the Junta de Mandos, Pérez Salas, whom Prieto appointed to replace Díaz Tendero,[51] affirms that Rojo was the "most able assistant" of the Communists and organized the army in conformity with their wishes. This, he says, was an act of disloyalty toward the minister, who placed his trust in Rojo.[52] Díaz Tendero, he adds, "slavishly obeyed the suggestions and orders of the Communist party." The only person on the junta who was "absolutely loyal to the minister" was his undersecretary Antonio Fernández Bolaños, who belonged to the corps of engineers, but "as he was always in the minority and did not know any professional officers other than those who belonged to his branch of the service, he was invariably defeated and, on most occasions, was deceived when it came to the matter of appointments."[53]

Clearly, the Communists, aided by the connivance of Rojo and by the inside knowledge of Díaz Tendero, had the advantage of possessing more complete knowledge than Fernández Bolaños of the career officers whose appointments or promotions they favored or wished to hinder.

Because Prieto was aware of Díaz Tendero's identification with the Communists, he did not automatically approve all the nominations and promotions presented to him. His failure to do so stemmed from his conviction, as he averred after the war, that the Communist party was only interested in gaining predominance in the army, because this would give it "complete power if we were victorious."[54] His attempt to block Communist ambitions was exasperating not only to the party but to Vicente Rojo, who has consistently presented himself in his books as a professional officer aloof from party politics. Evidence of his true position in this baneful feuding comes from air force chief Hidalgo de Cisneros, who remained loyal to the Communist party until his death in Prague in 1966. On several occasions Rojo told him that "he could not stand Prieto" and that he would like to resign from the central general staff "because he could do nothing useful" in view of Prieto's pessimism and animus toward Communist officers.[55]

No less vexing to the Communists and their allies was Prieto's hostility to the Communist militia leaders who had risen to officer rank, such as Enrique Líster, Juan Modesto, El Campesino, and Manuel Tagüeña. La Pasionaria affirms: "Prieto did not believe in the military capacity of the commanders who had risen from the people. Nor did he have any faith in the career officers, although he supported and protected them. On the other hand, he lost no opportunity to oppose the militia commanders, especially if they were Communists. At the root of Prieto's attitude, apart from his inveterate anti-communism, there was something that he did not acknowledge but that kept him awake at night: He knew that the Popular Army . . . was an immense revolutionary force that would play *a decisive role in determining the future political structure of Spain*."[56]

It was undoubtedly for this very reason that Prieto was ready to go to great lengths to combat Communist predominance in the armed forces. It has even been alleged by Captain Alberto Bayo, his adjutant, in a book published in Mexico in 1944, that the former defense minister offered to cede to Great Britain three strategic locations in Spain in return for military assistance in order to counteract the influence of Russia. This offer, which, to my knowledge, was never denied by Prieto, who was living and writing extensively in Mexico at the time the book was published, was allegedly made in February 1938 to two British air force officers, Colonel R. V. Goddard and Major H. M. Pearson. According to Captain Bayo, who was present at a meeting with Prieto, when the two officers visited the defense minister just before returning to London, Prieto made the following statement through his secretary Gisela, who served as translator:

> The government is convinced that if England looks unfavorably on us, we shall lose the war. When these gentlemen return to their country . . . I would like them to make on behalf of my government a confidential proposal, to which I shall anxiously await a reply.
>
> My proposal is the following: If England allows us to win by tilting the scales in our favor, which it can do at any time and which, moreover, it should do, so that we will not be beholden to Russia, which is the only country that is helping us with war material at the present time, Spain, through my intermediacy, will hand over to England the impregnable naval base of Cartagena, the superb naval base of Mahon, and the magnificent Vigo estuary, which is spacious enough to shelter the entire British fleet.

With these three positions, England will see its power reinforced in the Mediterranean and in the Atlantic, and Spain will be indebted to British protection, throwing off forever all possibility of Russian influence.[57]

Although I corresponded with Pearson in 1948 (then group captain and air attaché in the British embassy in Lima, Peru), I was unable to confirm Bayo's story. "I am afraid that my reply will be a little disappointing to you," his letter ran, "but you will understand that even now I am not at liberty to pass on the text of any conversation of a confidential nature even if I were to remember it. The main purpose of the visit which Goddard and I made to Spain was Air Intelligence; that is to study the air tactics and equipment which were being used in that theatre of war. However, it was a common habit of our hosts at all levels to let the conversation drift or be diverted towards the international and political implications of the conflict. The Foreign Office is the only authority which can confirm or deny whether the proposition of Prieto mentioned by Bayo was in fact made to the British Government through Goddard, and whether it was answered."[58]

Whatever the accuracy of Bayo's allegation, no one can seriously doubt that it was Prieto's drive to prevent the Communists from achieving dominion over the armed forces, rather than his "pessimism" and "defeatism," that was responsible for their decision to oust him from the defense ministry and to install Juan Negrín, just as it was the main reason for their offensive against Largo Caballero rather than the latter's alleged ineptitude and senility. To the apologists and eulogizers of Negrín, to those historians and writers who make much of his supposed political independence and romanticize his activity during the Civil War, it should be instructive that after he replaced Prieto in the defense ministry in April 1938, the fierce battles such as those the Communists had waged against Largo Caballero and Prieto in order to gain control of the armed forces came abruptly to an end. This fact alone should carry more weight in attesting to Negrín's amenability to the PCE than all the documentary evidence assembled in this volume.

Before his ouster from the defense ministry, which will be discussed in a later chapter, Prieto had shown his intractability on another vital issue connected with Communist control of the armed forces. This was his effort to prevent the newly created Military Investigation Service—Servicio de Investigación Militar (SIM) —from falling irremediably into the hands of the Spanish Communists and their Soviet friends. In his speech before the national committee of the PSOE he acknowledged that although he had agreed to the creation of the SIM at the suggestion of "certain Russian technicians," he at first resisted the idea on the ground that "such a sensitive service would be taken over by elements outside the control of the government as had recently occurred in the General Direction of Security."[59]

In reply to Stanley G. Payne's questionnaire, from which I have already quoted, NKVD chief Alexander Orlov stated: "[Strange] as it may seem, [Prieto] resisted my insistent requests that he let me organize a Military Intelligence Service. . . . Once I told him bluntly that his [resistance] was unfair not only to the Spanish troops, but also to our Russian soldiers—pilots, tankists, artillery men—who were fighting and dying in Spain. . . . 'Why,' I asked him, 'are you dodging the issue?' . . . The answer he gave almost knocked me down. 'I am afraid,' he said with a roguish smile, 'that having the Intelligence apparatus in your hands, you will come one day, arrest me and the other members of the government and install our Spanish Communists in power.' . . . [I] said that he might appoint his own man as chief of Military Intelligence and that I would supply only advisers who would provide the know-how. This seemed to satisfy him."

As a result, Prieto published a decree on 9 August in the *Diario Oficial del Ministerio de Defensa Nacional*, creating the SIM, whose official mission it was "to combat espionage, prevent acts of sabotage and carry out duties of investigation and vigilance within the armed forces dependent on the ministry." Prieto claims that he personally drafted the decree "as I didn't want to follow servilely the project that was handed to me."[60] Under the terms of article 2, the appointment of all chiefs, inspectors, and agents of the SIM was to be the exclusive prerogative of the defense minister. Nevertheless, Prieto did not limit his appointments to non-Communists. As he told the Socialist national committee, he named Gustavo Durán—whom the PCE itself has since identified as a member of the party, as we shall see shortly—to head the Madrid zone on the recommendation of the "sponsors of the project."[61] Durán was a gifted composer and linguist, who had been a commander of the famous Communist Fifth Regiment,[62] then interpreter and chief of staff to the Soviet general, Emilio Kléber, of the Eleventh International Brigade.[63] Later he would be promoted to commander of the Twentieth Army Corps under Negrín.[64] "It was not concealed from me that the nominee was a Communist," Prieto told the Socialist national committee. "I knew that he was, but I nevertheless appointed him."[65]

Orlov affirms that he told Durán that the defense minister was afraid of Communists and that he should not appoint too many to his staff. " 'Use the same ratio that exists in the Council of Ministers. There are only two Communist members in the cabinet,' I said. A day or so later, Prieto called me up and said that he would like to appoint a personal friend of his, a Socialist, as deputy to Durán. He hoped I would not object. Of course, I did not. 'Send as many Socialists and friends of yours as you can,' I told him, 'there is work for everybody.' "[66]

It is of course dubious whether Orlov urged Durán to appoint too many Communists, for, according to Prieto, Durán appointed several hundred Communists as his agents and only four or five Socialists. This was "intolerable," Prieto said, and he fired Durán, reassigning him to his post as commander of the Fortyseventh Division.[67] Durán went immediately to Orlov. "I have just been fired," he told him. "I could hardly believe it," Orlov affirms. Within fifteen minutes the NKVD chief was in Prieto's office. " 'Why did you do this?' I asked Prieto. His eyelashes fluttered. His smooth tongue began to stammer. 'Durán had appointed too many Communists, only Communists, in fact.' 'This is not true,' I retorted. 'Here is the list of the new officers with their party affiliations. There are four times as many Socialists as Communists here.' But Prieto was obdurate. . . . I insisted that he rescind his order and reinstate Durán." Prieto then looked at his watch and said he would resume the discussion next day. " 'There is nothing more to discuss,' I said. 'I can tell you only one thing: *If you don't reinstate Durán, I will never come to see you again.*' I got into my car and this was the last time I spoke to Prieto. This happened on Thursday, October 22, 1937."[68]

Prieto's version of this incident, as given to the national committee of the Socialist party, is substantially the same as Orlov's. He told Orlov that he had dismissed Durán because he lacked "authority to make appointments." To this, Orlov replied: "Durán can make provisional appointments."

"Neither provisional nor definite appointments!" was Prieto's response. "Here in Spain, furthermore, the provisional becomes definite." Prieto undoubtedly had in mind the hundreds of provisional appointments of Communist political commissars made by Alvarez del Vayo, when Largo Caballero was war minister.

"In any case, I have come to demand the immediate reinstatement of Major Durán as head of the SIM in Madrid."

"I am very sorry, but I cannot agree."

"If you do not agree to Durán's reinstatement I shall break my relations with you."

"I regret, but Major Durán will continue at the head of his division and will not return to the SIM. Your behavior is unjustified and I will not cave in to you."[69]

Because of the many years of unresolved controversy that raged in the United States over the alleged Communist affiliation during the Civil War of Gustavo Durán, who became an American citizen after two years' residence instead of the usual seven under current requirements and was employed in sensitive posts by the U.S. State Department in the early 1940s, it is important to record that he is now clearly identified as a wartime member of the Spanish Communist party in its official history of the Civil War, published in Moscow in 1977,[70] and that, to my personal knowledge, he was held in the highest esteem by the leading Communists I met and interviewed during the Civil War and during the postwar years in Mexico. Alexander Orlov's insistence that Durán should continue as head of the SIM in the Madrid zone is indicative of the unqualified trust that the NKVD and the Spanish Communist party placed in him. However, when he emigrated to the United States after the war and was investigated first by the Parnell Thomas Committee on Un-American Activities (U.S. House of Representatives) and then by Joseph McCarthy of the Senate Committee on Government Operations, he denied that he had ever been a Communist or an agent of the NKVD. Shortly after entering the country, he was employed by Spruille Braden of the State Department, from which he resigned under pressure in 1946. He then became an official of the United Nations in the International Refugee Organization program.

In hearings before the loyalty board of the U.S. Civil Service Commission, he explained his relations with the Communists in the following manner: "I must add in this connection, even at the risk of being misunderstood, that during the first year of the Spanish Civil War all I saw of Communist behaviour was the performance on the front line of those individual Communists who were among the military units that I commanded, and that from the point of view of courage and discipline their performance was in accordance with recognized military standards. As a result (a natural result in times of war), my attitude towards them, like the attitude of practically all the Republican military leaders at that time, was friendly. It became increasingly hostile as I gradually learned of the ruthless methods and duplicity of the Communists, of their attempts at complete control of any situation in which they happened to participate, of the fact that their primary allegiance went not to the Government they professed to serve but to their party, and finally that the instructions that that party received were not founded in any idealism but in very specific interests which were far from identical with those of the Spanish people."[71]

Although Orlov claims that after his altercation with Prieto over Durán's reinstatement he recalled his advisers and that they "had nothing more to do with the SIM,"[72] this is untrue. As Gabriel Morón, who was director general of security at the time, attests: "[The] SIM, like everything else, fell under the CAMOUFLAGED control of our good Russian friends, who ended up trampling on the minister's terrain, taking over the inalienable function and authority of making appointments and transferring personnel."[73]

It was about this time, when Prieto's opposition to the Communists had assumed threatening proportions, that Orlov, according to Jesús Hernández, decided to have the defense minister assassinated. Hernández claims that he heard of the plot through the chief of his bodyguard, Mena—who had received the information from Antonio Zubiaurren, a Spanish operative of the NKVD—and that he apprised Codovila and Gaykis just in time to save Prieto's life. "Listen here," he said to the Soviet ambassador, "if Orlov, after the tremendous scandal of Nin's abduction and 'disappearance' commits the crime he is planning against Prieto, I myself will denounce the criminal."[74] Although the historian must pick his way carefully through Hernández's evidence, there is no reason to believe that the idea of assassination—so congenial to the NKVD—never entered Orlov's mind.

At all events, it was now clear to the Communists that Prieto, like Caballero before him, would never be their pawn and that it was imperative to replace him.

52

The PCE Courts the CNT

As noted in the previous chapter, the decision of the Communists to restore some of the dismantled collectives stemmed not only from the injury inflicted on rural economy and morale and from the threat presented by Largo Caballero's provisional alliance with the CNT but from the growing friction with defense minister Indalecio Prieto. Indeed, Prieto's resolve to thwart the PCE's inexorable thrust toward dominion over the armed forces now impelled the PCE to devise his removal from the defense department and to bolster its position by seeking a temporary accommodation with the CNT. For, although the PCE had championed the interests of those segments of the rural and urban middle classes threatened with economic ruin, it could not allow them to become too strong lest with the aid of the moderate Socialists and Republicans, who were now emboldened by the recoil of the Revolution, they should attempt to take the reins of government into their own hands. In order to guide domestic and foreign policy, the PCE had to be supreme, and this was possible not only by controlling the police and army but by a skillful balancing of the various factions and class forces, exploiting to the full their mutual antagonisms and inherent self-interest.

Former politburo member Jesús Hernández writes:

> In our political struggle, we could rely upon something the other organizations lacked: discipline, the concept of blind obedience, absolute submission to hierarchical control. . . . What did the others have in face of this granite monolith? A broken, divided, fragmented Socialist party, working in three different directions, with three representative figures: Prieto, Caballero, and Besteiro, who fought among themselves and to whom another was added shortly afterward: Negrín. We managed to exploit their suicidal antagonisms for our own ends. One day we supported one side against the other. The next day we reversed our position and supported the opposite side. And today, the next day, and every day we incited one side against the other so that they would destroy one another, a game we played in full view and not without success. Thus, to destroy Francisco Largo Caballero we relied principally on Negrín and, to a certain extent, on Prieto. To get rid of Prieto we utilized Negrín and other prominent Socialists, and *had the*

war lasted we would not have hesitated to ally ourselves with the devil in order to exterminate Negrín if he had obstructed us.[1] . . . Among the Anarchosyndicalists the panorama was no better. . . . Although their ranks were tighter and more compact than those of the Socialists, we managed nevertheless to create a breach. We helped to deepen the schism—a product of evolution—that was developing in the CNT by drawing into government collaboration a large part of the Anarchist movement, which thereafter experienced a process of internal strife. . . . Nor did the republican parties . . . present a solid and homogeneous front. Cowed by the violent and disorderly character of the popular reaction to the [military] rebellion during the first days of the fighting, they allowed themselves, to a large degree, to be influenced and won over by our policy of order and discipline. Their value to us lay more in their name than in their effectiveness. For that reason we respected and defended them, but not without taking advantage of their good faith, using them like a Trojan horse when we had difficulty with other forces of the Popular Front.[2]

The experiences gained in Spain during the Civil War indubitably served the Kremlin well in helping it to achieve absolute power in Eastern Europe after World War II. In Hungary, for example, where Mátyás Rákosi, the Communist leader, was advised and supervised by Ernö Gerö, the former Comintern delegate in Catalonia, the Communists gained power thanks largely to the splitting tactics that had been honed to perfection during the Spanish Civil War. It was in Hungary that these methods first became known as "salami tactics." Paul Ignotus, a well-known liberal political writer in prewar Hungary, who spent the war years in London on the BBC staff and the years of the Rákosi-Gerö dictatorship (1949–1956) in Hungarian jails, has described the classic process. In a moment of "captivating sincerity," he writes, Rákosi "boasted that he 'sliced off' the non-Communist partners in the [Hungarian government] coalition 'like pieces of salami.' Indeed these 'salami tactics' of his were most effective, and little else was needed to insure his success except perhaps a lack of scruples and a 'knife' to cut the 'salami.' "[3] Few historians and political scientists in the West have recognized how the process of splitting parties and organizations so as to feed on their decay—a process practiced and preached by Lenin long before the Russian Revolution—was first applied most successfully outside Russia in the political laboratory of the Civil War in Spain.

Just as important as these salami tactics in the Communists' drive for power was their ability to exploit the fears of the small and middle peasants, of the small tradesmen, handicraftsmen, and manufacturers, who at the outset of the Civil War had turned to the PCE for protection against the tidal wave of collectivization, and whose political allegiance before the war had been divided among the Republican and right-wing parties. Although the Republicans served the purpose of the PCE in strengthening its power base, it could not regard them as permanent allies. Nor, for their part, could the Republicans have lasting faith in the party's defense of their property rights. Moreover, the party did not believe that the

Republican middle classes could be relied upon to support a protracted struggle, since they lacked the revolutionary incentive of the working classes and suspected that even if the war were won they would be politically and economically annihilated. This mutual distrust was confirmed by Edmundo Domínguez, a member of the UGT executive, who succumbed quite early in the war to the blandishments of the PCE. In his book, *Los vencedores de Negrín*, published shortly after the war and revised along party lines by Margarita Nelken,[4] Domínguez wrote: "The Republicans, who at the beginning of the war had been swept along by the popular tide rather than by their own impulse, lacked the steadfastness to endure a prolonged fight of indefinite duration. . . . The nature of our struggle and the political factors it involved led them to suspect that even if the war were carried to a victorious conclusion they would be superseded. This diminished their very limited spirit of resistance."[5]

To retain the upper hand, the Communists had not only to balance one rival faction against the other but to neutralize and efface them one by one. With every step up the ladder of power, they left fresh adversaries behind. "When we broke with Caballero," Hernández writes, "we broke with the preponderant force of the Socialist party. . . . When we provoked the Caballero crisis . . . we made mortal enemies of more than a million men organized in the CNT. . . . The offensive against Prieto affronted the republican parties, which saw in the Socialist leader the brain that more than any other represented their republican policy in Spain. . . . If, during this period, a total collapse of our position did not occur, it was because all the forces that hated the Communists were incapable of forming a united front."[6]

Faced by Prieto's enmity, which reached its peak after he assumed control of the defense ministry, the Communists needed a temporary truce with the CNT in order to maintain their balancing position in the scale of power and to prepare for the approaching showdown with the Socialist leader. This change of policy was now doubly necessary, for, as will be seen presently, Largo Caballero was attempting to restore his own position by concluding an alliance with the CNT.

In a report to the Comintern on 30 August 1937, Togliatti criticized the PCE for not appreciating soon enough the need for a change in tactics. After the fall of Caballero, he wrote, the party did not understand the importance of "getting the Anarchosyndicalists to draw close to us and of preventing another rapprochement [of the CNT] with the supporters of Caballero."[7] How the party could have improved its relations with the CNT in the midst of the destruction of the collective farms and the repression against the libertarian movement is not explained by Togliatti. He also criticized the party for committing other errors. "On the way from Barcelona to Valencia," he stated, "I raised the question [of the Anarchists] with the comrades who accompanied me. Their opinion was very simple: 'the Anarchists have lost all influence. . . . We hope they will organize another *putsch* and then we shall put an end to them for good.' This attitude, unfortunately, is widespread in the party, especially in Catalonia, and when such opinions are held a policy of drawing closer to the Anarchist masses and divorcing them from their leaders cannot be achieved. The members of the party . . .

know nothing about the CNT, its leaders, its internal problems, its factions, its crises, etc. I have yet to find a single comrade who can tell me the names of the members of the national committee of the CNT."[8]

It is interesting to note that Togliatti attributed the failure of the PCE to improve its relations with the CNT to Vittorio Codovila, whom he had recently replaced as head of the Comintern delegation. In a letter to Georgi Dimitrov and Dmitri Manuilsky, dated 15 September, he criticized Codovila for not pursuing a "coherent policy" with respect to a "rapprochement with the anarchists and the isolation of Caballero" and urged them not to allow him to return to Spain. "I do not want to make hasty judgments," he said, "but I believe that I have now concluded that *his presence hurts the party*."[9]

It was no doubt due to Togliatti's advice that the party softened its tone toward the CNT. In a conciliatory gesture, La Pasionaria declared in her speech in the Cortes on 1 October that "we should not ignore the importance of the CNT in our country" and "must consider the possibility of getting the sincerely revolutionary workers in its ranks to share in the responsibilities of power."[10] On another occasion, José Díaz declared that "those who think or say that we cannot talk of revolution today because we are at war are profoundly mistaken."

A few days later, El Campesino, the Communist military commander on the central front, who had risen from the ranks of the militia, embraced his counterpart, Cipriano Mera, the Anarchist commander, at a public meeting in Madrid.[11] "This embrace," observed *Frente Rojo*, the Communist organ, "should be extended to all the workers of our Fatherland."[12] In his speech on this seemingly historic occasion, El Campesino declared that "unity cannot be just another slogan or a subject for discussion. It has to be achieved by actions and by an overall change of policy. In this way, the necessary confidence among those who fight and those who work together will develop."[13] But it was palpable from Mera's speech, in which he condemned "proselytism and sectarian activities capable of destroying or weakening the unity sealed with blood in the trenches"[14] that more than a symbolic embrace was needed to convince the libertarian movement of the Communists' sincerity.

For months the CNT-FAI press had been denouncing the PCE as "counterrevolutionary." The PCE, said *Solidaridad Obrera*, was not inspired by "the Iberian ideals that distinguish our Revolution" and it puts "a Russian stamp on all its work."[15] "Anyone who glances through the Communist press," wrote *Frente Libertario*, "must get the impression that except for the militants of the hammer and sickle there is only garbage and scum in Spain. Only these militants are intelligent, loyal, heroic, capable of overcoming all difficulties and showing the people the road to victory. . . . The Communist party must convince itself once and for all that it has taken the wrong path, a path that can end in irreparable disaster in which the party itself will be the first to go under."[16] Even after the first signs of the Communists' conciliatory line began to appear, *Frente Libertario* cautioned: "We cannot accept the words about unity as sincere when the facts show criminal intentions to wage war on the working class."[17]

The PCE was not deterred by this hostile reception and attempted to allay suspicions. The desire of the party to secure the collaboration of the CNT in the leadership of the war and revolution, declared *Mundo Obrero* reassuringly, was not due to "a fleeting or opportunistic policy, but to the firm conviction that it will strengthen the Antifascist Popular Front" and accelerate victory. "We congratulate ourselves on the fact that throughout the country some successes have been achieved in improving relations among all the anti-fascist forces. . . . And perhaps the perfect expression of this reconciliation is the fraternal and enthusiastic embrace . . . of comrades Campesino and Mera. Our fervent desire and the desire of all workers is that not many days will pass before the relations between the CNT and other parties and organizations of the Popular Front are completely normalized."[18]

This was too sanguine an expectation. Not only did the Communist party lack credibility within the libertarian movement, but there was another obstacle to a tactical rapprochement with the CNT. This was Caballero's control of the UGT executive in which he had resumed his post as secretary general shortly after leaving the government,[19] determined to continue his struggle against the Communists. "[I am] in my element," he wrote, "in constant communication with members of my class. . . . They are not professionals of intrigue and political maneuvering. . . . My concern today is what will be the fate of Spain. What are those men, who lack scruples and conscience and whose only thought is power, going to do with Spain? . . . Poor Spain! Your fate is in the hands of ambition, disloyalty, and treason, and I envision your moral and material ruin. This is my soliloquy in my moments of solitude."[20]

Hoping to shore up his political fortunes against his inveterate opponents, Largo Caballero had signed a provisional alliance on 30 July 1937 with the national committee of the CNT. Among other things, both labor unions agreed to renounce violence against each other and to grant the workers absolute freedom to join whatever organization they saw fit.[21] Although there was no mention of such important issues as nationalization on which the two labor unions had divergent views, this historic agreement between the two rival unions strengthened the position of the left Socialists and the Anarchosyndicalists vis-à-vis their Communist antagonists, who characterized the agreement as "an offensive alliance directed against the political parties and the government."[22] In the opinion of Togliatti, expressed in a report to the Comintern on 30 August, the PCE's opposition to the agreement was a grave error, because Caballero "now appears as the champion of trade-union unity." The party, he added, did not understand that if it had taken the lead in the movement for a rapprochement between the two unions, "the pact directed against us could have been used against its inspirers."[23]

In any event, the pact imperiled the Communist party's immediate goal of establishing a temporary truce with the leadership of the CNT in preparation for the approaching showdown with Prieto. Equally serious was Largo Caballero's control of the UGT executive which blocked the party's ultimate goal of bringing the Socialist trade-union organization into its domain. It was therefore essential to dislodge him from his citadel.

53

The Political Demise of Largo Caballero. The UGT and CNT Sign a Pact of Unity.

To dislodge Largo Caballero from his bastion in the UGT executive, the PCE had simply to exploit the differences between the left and center factions in the Socialist labor federation and to bring into play its own accrued influence; for not only had it made inroads into the rank and file, but several influential members of the national committee, including Amaro del Rosal, Edmundo Domínguez, Antonio Pretel, and José Rodríguez Vega,[1] had been drawn into the orbit of the party. This boded ill for Caballero, for the national committee had the statutory power to appoint a new executive.

The asperities and dissensions within the UGT became especially visible in May, when the national committee disapproved of the stand taken by the executive, which had proclaimed its opposition to any government in which Caballero was not both premier and war minister. Tensions increased in June, when Amaro del Rosal, a member of the executive and president of the Federación Nacional de Banca, who was one of the first of Largo Caballero's outstanding followers to shift his allegiance to the PCE, resigned from the executive after criticizing its policies.[2] In July, the atmosphere became more acrid when Largo Caballero rejected an invitation to attend a meeting commemorating the first anniversary of the Civil War. "If the Communist party were not going to be present," he replied, "the UGT would without a shred of doubt be represented, but from the very moment that *Frente Rojo* [the Communist organ] declared on 10 July that 'the executive committee was a band of enemies of unity, of enemies of the people, of persons who are washed-up and resentful, who represent no one and who place their rancor and personal passions above the sacred interests of the people,' we cannot participate in the same meeting with the Communist party."[3]

This reply, said the politburo, was the best proof of *Frente Rojo*'s claim that the majority of the members of the UGT executive did not represent the will of the masses. "Nevertheless," it stated, "more than ever before, in view of the international situation after one year of war, the strictest unity should prevail among all parties and organizations, [which] should reinforce that unity on the basis of their common objective to win the war as soon as possible and develop the popular revolution."[4]

The expression "popular revolution"—which the PCE many years later called the "national revolutionary war"—was a sop for domestic consumption and had recently been put into circulation by the PCE to placate those critics who had given a hostile reception to the slogan calling for a "democratic and parliamentary republic of a new type."[5] The precise nature of the "popular revolution" was no more clearly defined than the "democratic and parliamentary republic of a new type" and did not allay the suspicion that if the Communists extended and consolidated their power the élan of the July revolution would continue to decline and the future configuration of society, regardless of slogans, would be determined by the PCE.

That the left Socialists distrusted the PCE's slogans on the nature of the revolution was clear from the speeches of prominent members of the PSOE and UGT who had remained loyal to Largo Caballero. At a public meeting in September, Carlos de Baraíbar, undersecretary of war in Caballero's government, railed against those who were trying to put a brake on the "revolutionary thrust" of the people. "To say that we are fighting for the democratic republic lessens the enthusiasm of the combatants and of those in the rear." At the same meeting Carlos Rubiera, former undersecretary of the interior and secretary of the UGT's National Federation of Clerical Workers (Empleados de Oficina) declared: "Today many Spaniards are asking themselves where are the illusions of July 18. Why don't the streets throb as they did then? The reason is that there has been a recoil. We must not forget the rhythm of the revolution, because without the revolution the triumph of liberty cannot be achieved. . . . There are many people who want to devitalize the impulse of the revolution, to adulterate the content of July 18. The Spanish working class must react to this situation. Much has been said of the popular revolution, but what is a popular revolution without a social revolution?"[6]

In passing, it is noteworthy that the Communist-controlled Foreign Press Bureau considered its own slogan "popular revolution" too radical for moderate opinion abroad. For instance, on 7 July, Constancia de la Mora, the Communist censor, deleted the following italicized phrase from a dispatch I sent to the United Press quoting a passage from a letter of the politburo to the PSOE urging the fusion of the two parties "as a guarantee of military victory and as the essential prerequisite for the triumph and *consolidation of the popular revolution.*"[7]

In the opinion of the politburo the time was close at hand for the final onslaught against Caballero. There can be little doubt that the provisional alliance that the UGT executive and the CNT signed on 30 July increased the urgency. Acting in concert, the Communists and their allies requested the executive to convoke a plenary session of the national committee. The undeclared but obvious purpose of the convocation was to elect a new executive. In mid-August—at the apogee of the offensive against the collective farms and several weeks before the Communists made their conciliatory gesture to the CNT—*Frente Rojo* complained that the executive committee had made common cause with the Anarcho-syndicalists by allowing the plants, the workshops, and public services to remain under the control of committees and trade unions "without governmental intervention." This, it argued, was one of the fundamental reasons for the disorganization of production. "Instead of following the line laid down by the national committee, the principal leaders of the group that controls the executive have yielded more and more to the syndicalist policy of the CNT and this reversal, which prompted the protest of comrade Amaro del Rosal within the executive, explains why the decisions of the national committee regarding confiscations, nationalization of the basic industries, and workers' control are not obeyed." The executive, *Frente Rojo* continued, had gone even further in its antagonism to the national committee. Instead of consulting the committee with regard to a rapprochement with the CNT, the executive had gone right ahead and concluded a national alliance "to reinforce the syndicalizing tendencies and to combat the government of the popular front." "Where will this policy lead if the executive continues to operate without any control by our great labor union? It could result in the UGT becoming a tool of a small group guided solely by its own personal ambitions. To prevent this from happening, it is essential that the national committee should meet urgently."[8]

Several times during the ensuing weeks, the national committee, in accordance with the statutes of the UGT, called on the executive to convoke a plenary session of the committee, but Largo Caballero, foreseeing the danger, either ignored the requests or found a reason to reject them. "In reply to one of our requests," writes Amaro del Rosal, "the executive stated that they should be countersigned by each federation. This was irregular. The members of the national committee had never had to submit to this procedure."[9]

In a desperate move to salvage his position, Largo Caballero expelled ten of the forty-two federations represented on the national committee on the purely technical grounds that they had not paid their dues.[10] "No effort, however monstrous," declared *Frente Rojo*, "can halt the executive of the UGT in its frenzied drive toward a schism. On the pretext of non-payment of dues—a pretext fabricated by the executive itself, because it has refused to accept back payments[11]—it has expelled ten national federations." But the expulsion, it affirmed, was not a matter of complying with regulations but "a maneuver to obtain an absolute majority on the national committee."[12]

On 29 September, the national committee brought matters to a head, demanding that a plenary session be held within forty-eight hours.[13] To this Caballero replied tartly: "It is our duty to remind you that the national committee cannot meet if it has not previously been convoked by the executive. If the meeting you announce were to be held, it would be regarded as rebellious."[14] Undaunted, the national committee announced that a plenary session would be held on 1 October. The national committee, said the announcement, will meet in accordance with article 33 of the statutes " 'when the majority of the delegates deem it pertinent,' which is now the case."[15] To this, the executive responded that it viewed the manner of convoking the national committee as an "act of indiscipline and provocation" and threatened to suspend the rights of those federations that had "either signed the request to hold the meeting or might attend it."[16] The next day, the press published a list of twenty-nine federations either expelled or suspended by the Caballero-controlled executive.[17]

This frantic attempt to outmaneuver the national committee was doomed to failure, for Largo's adversaries simply ignored the expulsions and suspensions. True, he may still have enjoyed, as he later claimed, the support of the majority of the rank and file,[18] but the hostile members on the national committee commanded a majority of the votes. On 1 October, at a hastily improvised gathering on the stairway of the UGT's headquarters, the national committee members elected a new executive.[19] Ramón González Peña, a Prietista and famed leader of the Asturias rebellion in 1934, was made president, and the following supporters of the Communists, all members of the PSOE, were given the remaining key posts placing the PCE in effective control of the new executive: Edmundo Domínguez, vice-president; José Rodríguez Vega,[20] secretary general; Amaro del Rosal, vice-secretary; Felipe Pretel, treasurer.

The coup was a stupendous victory for the Communists, who before the Civil War had merged their small CGTU (Confederación General del Trabajo Unitaria) with the UGT and until the outbreak of the conflict had enjoyed scant influence within the unions. As Juan-Simeón Vidarte, a Prieto Socialist and later a Negrinista, frankly acknowledged in his memoir: "They lacked roots and prestige" and during the war exercised their influence by using persons "who had nothing Socialist about them except their membership cards and who were more valuable to the Communists in our party than in their own."[21]

There is no inkling in the writings or public declarations of Indalecio Prieto as to what role he may have played in the political undoing of his longtime rival or as to how he felt about this victory of the Communists, with whom he was locked in combat for the control of the army. In major political manuevering Prieto had always preferred to remain anonymous, but there is evidence in Azaña's diary that the entire cabinet, in which Prieto was still a dominant figure, was united in its desire to pulverize the left Socialist leader. That this might enhance the power of the PCE seemed less important to the moderate Socialists (and even to the Republicans) than settling old scores and stripping Largo Caballero of the last vestige of his authority in the UGT. On 23 August, five weeks before the coup, Azaña recorded that Negrín told him the cabinet had agreed unanimously to postpone the opening of the Cortes until October: "Negrín gave me many reasons. Most were flimsy and all were secret. The strongest, on which there appeared to be unanimity, was that it suited the government to wait until Largo Caballero was no longer secretary of the UGT. Negrín assured me that the national committee at its next meeting would replace the executive." Negrín also told Azaña that since Caballero intended to oppose the government in the Cortes, he and his ministers believed that it was advisable to delay the opening of parliament until he had been replaced, "so that once relieved of his functions, Largo would not be able to say that he was speaking in the name of one million workers." Dissimulating his own animus toward Caballero, Azaña argued perfunctorily that the postponement might hurt the government as it could not publicly divulge the reasons, but he nonetheless agreed with Negrín to delay the opening until the first of October.[22]

On 28 August, according to Azaña's diary, the president received another visit from Negrín informing him that Caballero, together with Luis Araquistáin and other colleagues, had called on Diego Martínez Barrio, the speaker of the Cortes, to protest the postponement: "They wanted to criticize the performance of the government in both the political and military spheres; in the political sphere because of the preponderance of the Communists and the Russians and because of the persecution to which they considered the CNT was being subjected." "Negrín assures me," Azaña noted parenthetically, "that a tight rein is now being kept [on the Russians and the Communists] and that never have they had less control."[23] How Azaña reacted to this transparent piece of misinformation is not recorded in his diary.

The date of 1 October set for the opening of the Cortes was providential, for it fell on the very day that the national committee met to name the new executive and when Largo Caballero was too preoccupied with the internal crisis of the UGT to attend the session. Thus, not a breath of dissension over the growth of Communist power penetrated the Cortes. As usual, the Comintern apparatus harped on the government's observance of the Constitution. "On October 1," the *International Press Correspondence* reported, ". . . the Spanish Parliament resumed its work. . . . [The] Negrín government . . . shows itself to be one of the most faithful defenders of the Constitution. . . . In face of unjustified accusations of 'Bolshevism,' 'Red Spain,' etc., etc., whereby the allies of the Spanish fascists attempted to frighten the democratic peoples, . . . the parties of the People's Front, and above all the Communist Party, have repeated untiringly day by day that 'We are fighting for a democratic parliamentary republic with a new social content.' For this reason, the Parliament . . . is an irrefutable confirmation of the character of our struggle: the struggle of democracy against fascism."[24]

But behind this simplistic definition of the conflict, there lay the continuing struggle for survival of those elements in the Republican camp that were still opposing the hegemonic aims of the Communist party.

Despite his manifest defeat, Largo Caballero refused to recognize the new executive committee. As a result, both executives subsisted side by side in a state of unconcealed belligerency. "We have reason to suspect," Caballero declared at a public meeting in Madrid two weeks later, "that it is planned to do with the UGT what has been done in Catalonia. You all know that in Catalonia there is the United Socialist Party, which is not a United Socialist Party, but the Catalan Communist Party. . . . Right from the start it joined the Third International and those who direct [it] are Communists. . . . The fact of the matter is that since the UGT in Catalonia is in the service of the Communists and since our party is, in effect, also in the service of the Communists, the only organization that can stand in opposition is the UGT. Therefore they want to take possession of it. We cannot allow this to happen. We want it to remain free."[25]

To bring pressure to bear on the Socialist leader, the government decided, according to Largo Caballero's memoir, *Mis recuerdos*, "to intercept and confiscate all correspondence addressed to the UGT including that addressed to me personally." Francisco Giner de los Ríos, the Republican minister of communications, he alleges, "lent himself to this indecent stratagem." "As if that were not enough, the government ordered the banks not to hand over any union funds so that we could not pay our overhead expenses."[26]

Caballero's opponents simultaneously opened fire from other directions. Negrín, Prieto, and Zugazagoitia, he asserts, were responsible for removing him from his two parliamentary posts—as chairman of the Socialist Minority and as a member of the Permanent Commission of the Cortes. "They would not permit any opposition [and] systematically expelled me from all my posts. They didn't attempt to remove me from the Madrid Socialist organization [the Agrupación Socialista Madrileña, over which he presided], because they themselves would have been expelled."[27] Indeed, throughout the war, the Madrid Socialist organization remained loyal to the left Socialist leader, who after the government shakeup in May traveled from Valencia to Madrid every Sunday to attend the meetings, accompanied by Luis Araquistáin, José Díaz Alor, and Pascual Tomás, his close associates. The Prieto-controlled executive of the PSOE, Caballero claims, tried to "subject the Agrupación to its reckless policy," but it did not succeed because "Madrid does not yield to tyranny."[28]

In Valencia, however, where the Caballero Socialists controlled the provincial committee of the Federación Socialista Valenciana, the second largest federation, the Prieto Socialists were more fortunate. Since the removal of Largo Caballero from the government, the Valencia federation had become the main focus of opposition to the centrists and the PCE. On 9 and 10 July, the provincial committee met under the chairmanship of its general secretary Justo Martínez Amutio and approved a series of resolutions. The two most provocative were as follows:

1. "After examining closely the problems created in the countryside as a result of the formation [by the PCE] of the Valencia Peasant Federation, the provincial committee of the Federación Socialista Valenciana resolves that any organization created on the fringe of the UGT and CNT should be considered schismatic . . . and orders the expulsion from the party of all members affiliated with the Peasant Federation, which was formed for the sole purpose of dividing the workers in the countryside and is directed by elements who have resuscitated the most contemptible and despotic features of Spanish politics."[29]

2. "We regard the speeches of Hernández and Pasionaria against Largo Caballero as an assault on unity because of their slanderous nature.[30] We therefore agree to dissolve immediately the so-called liaison committees of the Socialist and Communist parties in the province until such time as the offensive statements are retracted."[31]

On 16 July, *El Socialista*, the organ of the PSOE executive committee, condemned the dissolution of the liaison committees formed in April to facilitate the fusion of the Socialist and Communist parties and asked, "Do we have to put up with the disgrace of seeing the cancer of irresponsibility grow within our party?" The answer was soon forthcoming. On 25 July, the Socialist party executive, in agreement with the centrist minister of the interior Julián Zugazagoitia, decided to take action. The newly appointed governor of the province, the centrist Manuel Molina Conejero, acting on orders from the minister, removed the committee of the Valencia Socialist federation and appointed another "to the taste," as Largo Caballero put it, of the government and the governor.[32] Martínez Amutio, the general secretary of the deposed committee, attests: "At midday, a police inspector accompanied by a squad of carabineers [under the authority of Negrín's ministry of finance] presented himself at the headquarters of the Valencia federation and at the editorial offices and printshop of *Adelante* [its daily newspaper and Largo Caballero's mouthpiece] carrying a letter from the Socialist executive and an order signed by minister of the interior, Julián Zugazagoitia . . . ordering us to hand over the offices, documents, and funds. . . . When we tried to resist this outrage, the inspector informed us . . . that he had instructions to take us to the Provincial Prison if we did not obey the order."[33]

A few days later, the PSOE executive publicly announced the reason for deposing the provincial committee. The Valencia federation, it said, had for two years adopted a "rebellious attitude," but no disciplinary steps had been taken because its "demagogic platform made it appear fervently revolutionary."[34] *Frente Rojo* commended the Socialist executive for acting "promptly and forcefully" and denounced "the enemies of proletarian and socialist unity." "This group," it declared, ". . . inflamed the distrust of the workers and constantly stirred up everything that might divide the Socialist and Communist workers and obstruct the creation of the United Party of the Proletariat."[35]

The seizure of *Adelante* left Largo Caballero and his supporters with only one daily newspaper—the very inferior *Correspondencia de Valencia*, the local organ of the UGT—to defend his position in the whole of Spain. At the very outset of the war, he had lost *Las Noticias*, the mouthpiece of the Catalan UGT, when the PSUC brought the regional trade-union organization under its control, and less than one year later he had been divested of *Claridad*, his mouthpiece in Madrid. It was now essential to strip him of his last daily medium of communication. In a letter to Moscow on 15 September, Togliatti reported that *La Correspondencia de Valencia* was waging "the dirtiest campaigns" against the PCE and that the matter had been taken up by the party secretariat. "The comrades," he stated, "guarantee every day that they will throw the Caballeristas out of the regional leadership of the unions and out of the editorial staff of the newspaper." Their plan, he said, was to come to an agreement with the centrists in the local leadership of the UGT and "to carry out a kind of semilegal coup against the paper, throwing out the Caballerista editors and forming a new editorial staff. They assure me that the matter can be settled with the help of the authorities within 24 hours. For my part, I am prodding them and pushing them along these lines." But, he complained, it turned out that the party secretariat had "never been promised any help by the authorities," and the centrists of the local UGT organization were not ready to carry out a coup. "In this way, a whole month has been lost in conversations with the Socialists, with the authorities, etc., etc., and during that period the most elementary work among the masses—the mobilization of the workers in plants and trade-union assemblies against the newspaper and its staff—has been completely forgotten."[36]

Faced with the timidity of the centrists in the local UGT, the newly formed national executive decided to intervene and, with the aid of a small force of Negrín's carabineers commanded by Enrique Puente, then a trusted collaborator of the premier,[37] occupied the offices of *La Correspondencia de Valencia* early in November.[38] Before he was divested of this last daily medium of expression, Largo Caballero made a bold attempt to reach a mass audience. On 17 October, he passionately denounced his opponents at a public meeting in Madrid, but he exhibited no statesmanship and offered no solutions or directives. Nevertheless, the response was resounding and univocal and showed that the old Socialist leader still had a large following. As he stepped onto the platform, a man shouted, "Paco, don't worry, all your old friends are here with you." This show of support convinced Caballero, according to Ginés Ganga, the left Socialist Cortes deputy, that "the people continued to have confidence in him."[39] The meeting was held in the capacious Ciné Pardiñas, which, in spite of its size, proved inadequate for the crowd, and two other theaters had to be equipped with loudspeakers. "The enthusiasm was indescribable," Caballero recorded.[40]

Although Caballero planned to hold mass meetings in several other cities, he was not allowed to speak publicly again. He was placed under strict surveillance by Zugazagoitia and was stopped at gunpoint by assault guards when on his way to Alicante for the first of a series of mass meetings accompanied by Luis Araquistáin, Rodolfo Llopis, Wenceslao Carrillo, Pascual Tomás, and Ginés Ganga, all Socialist deputies and close associates.[41] "Despotism, outrage, and injustice triumphed," Largo Caballero commented bitterly.[42]

A few days later, on 29 October, Azaña discussed the matter with Negrín, who told the president that Largo Caballero had been asked not to make the trip so as to avoid any "disagreeable incident." "As he insisted on going," Azaña records, "the minister of the interior and the prime minister decided to prevent him. . . . Negrín assures me that Largo has very little or no public support. He will not allow Caballero or his acolytes and advisers to do any harm even if he has to put them in jail and bring them before the special Tribunal [of Espionage and High Treason], because in Valencia they are disseminating 'defeatism.'[43] . . . I stressed that his organizations should observe prudence and tolerance and not carry matters to the breaking point."[44]

On 26 October, Largo Caballero had addressed a letter to Diego Martínez Barrio, in which he informed the speaker of the Cortes of the humiliating treatment to which he and the other Socialist deputies had been subjected on route to Alicante, describing it as an "affront" to all the deputies of loyalist Spain.[45] The matter was taken up by the permanent commission of the Cortes (from which Largo Caballero had recently been removed), but the action of the government was approved by all of the sixteen members present with the exception of Luis

Araquistáin. Ramón Lamoneda, the secretary of the PSOE, praised the "delicacy" with which Zugazagoitia had handled the situation, and La Pasionaria argued that the government had fulfilled its duty in preventing "certain public meetings that might cause disorders."[46]

Nevertheless, it is noteworthy that Vidarte, the moderate Socialist undersecretary of the interior, claims that when he heard that Caballero was under police surveillance, he asked the otherwise timorous minister of the interior Zugazagoitia[47] if this was true and was "painfully surprised" when the minister retorted: "That's nothing! I am going to put Largo Caballero and his friends in jail. . . . My orders are not open to discussion."[48] Despite this threat, Caballero's adversaries could not afford to go to this extreme, but he was effectively silenced for the duration of the war and was never able, either in the press or on the platform, to appeal to the court of public opinion. "The dictatorial regime of the Negrín government," he wrote in his "Notas Históricas," "did not allow any expression of disagreement in newspapers and meetings with the conduct of the Communist party. Nor could the complicity of the executive committees of the UGT and the Socialist party with all the monstrosities committed by the Communist party be denounced publicly."[49]

Even before the final muzzling of Largo Caballero, the left-wing Socialists were incensed by the combined efforts of the Communists and the centrists in their own party to deprive him of every medium of communication and remove him from every level of public life. No published polemics express more vividly the feelings of mutual revulsion that separated the two sides than three long letters exchanged between the leaders of the Agrupación Socialista Madrileña and the executive committee of the PSOE in mid-October and from which the following passages have been excerpted:[50]

The Agrupación Socialista Madrileña [ran the first missive addressed to the executive committee] which has always been the vanguard of the Spanish working class, would be truant to its traditions and historical obligations if at this grave moment for the Republic it did not tell the truth about what is happening by pointing unequivocally to the errors and responsibility of those who have brought us to our present pass.

A political organization, which first and foremost is striving for the expansion of its political power with the secret aspiration of becoming during and after the war the sole power, is dangerously undermining the morale of those who . . . are trying to liberate the country from every form of national and foreign despotism and endow it with the kind of social and political regime that the people, especially the proletariat, the largest class, should have complete liberty to decide. . . .

Until three months ago there was real antifascist unity in Spain. All the parties and trade-union organizations were collaborating in the government and in the responsibilities of the war. Today this antifascist unity is broken. . . . Who is responsible? In the first place the Communist party, which conspired to dislodge from power the men and organizations that did not submit to its imported slogans and then demolished the figures, which yesterday it deified, as soon as it saw in them an obstacle to its sectarian work in the army and in all the departments of the State. It justifies itself with the splendid antimarxist theory that the parties, and above all the Communist party, are privileged entities, almost of divine origin, whose mission it is to direct policy, whereas the mission of the trade unions is only to work and blindly obey the new élite. . . . [The PCE] has declared war to the death on those in the UGT and CNT who oppose its totalitarian policy. . . .

This divisive party, which is a brutal enemy of antifascist unity . . . sets itself up as the champion of the political unity of the Spanish working class. . . . The example of absorbing the [Socialist] youth and the Catalan Socialist party by handing them over tied hand and foot to the Communist International is no incentive for the fusion of the two working-class parties. Nor are the innumerable acts of coercion and persecution carried out by the Communist party at the front and in the rear favorable examples. . . .

We must also point out the disastrous international consequences of this policy. Some believed that the elimination of the trade-union organizations and of the left Socialists from the government as a result of the May crisis would stimulate the sympathy of the European and American democracies for the cause of the Republic. The very opposite has occurred. The international situation is more unfavorable today than ever and for these reasons:

On the one hand, the reactionary classes of these democracies perceive in the change of government and policy a weakening of the Spanish antifascist front and therefore a greater chance of victory by the rebels. . . . On the other hand, broad segments of liberal opinion in those democracies, including the great mass of the international working class, perceive in the present government the hegemony of the Communist party. This belief has grown and deepened owing to certain events relating to public order, which have alarmed the conscience of the world, and to the outrageous campaign of persecution waged by the Spanish Communist press. All this has helped to alienate a large part of the international support we enjoyed. This is due primarily to the Communists, who are mainly responsible for the crisis. . . .

However, it would not be fair to ascribe to the Communist party the entire responsibility for what is happening. It is the main culprit, but it is not the only one. There is another party that docilely supports the spectacular, divisive, and defamatory campaigns of the Communist party even against its own members. We shall not mention its name. We do not want to embarrass ourselves by the wretched behavior of those with whom we share a common lineage. But the immense majority of the members of the Socialist party know to whom we are referring, because they are aware of a certain inexplicable complicity, whose authors will have to render an account one day to Spanish Socialism and to history itself. We are acquainted with infinite forms of betrayal, but liquidating one's own party for the benefit of another is unheard of. This is equivalent to submitting to that party's orders and to tolerating in silence, if not with actual pleasure, its indignities. Only an antirevolutionary, antidemocratic minority [a reference to the executive committee of the PSOE] without scruples is capable of this deed, a minority concerned only with power for power's sake.

In response, the executive committee of the PSOE stated:

If [your letter] did not bear the heading of the veteran Agrupación Socialista de Madrid, we should have believed that it was a copy of the document recently disseminated by the CNT; so similar are the arguments. Your language perhaps is more insidious and aggressive, which explains the great publicity given by the Anarchist press. . . .

Hence, your letter is in accord with a persistent campaign against the present government . . . , against Russia and against our own party. The fact that the Negrín government has the very explicit support of the national committees of the [PSOE] and the UGT should be sufficient for a local Socialist committee to abstain from attacking it. . . .

According to the Anarchists and yourselves . . . we are faced with a new tyranny, an anti-Spanish despotism, for which you hold the Communist International primarily responsible. Salamanca and Rome say the same thing. You call it despotism in government, but that is what loyalist Spain demands: a government that governs, not one that must ask permission every day of the ungovernables. You who are Socialists—orthodox Socialists!—uphold an antiauthoritarian or libertarian opinion in a time of war when a Socialist should not only be authoritarian, in keeping with his doctrine, but also a fervent advocate of the greatest possible concentration of power without going to the extreme, as you did not much more than a year ago, of calling for the dictatorship of the proletariat. . . .

Anti-Spanish despotism! It is true that Spain must not lose faith in its own destiny, but it requires the help of Russia if it is not to lose its independence. With the help of the very country, which according to you, the Trotskyists, and Franco, wants to colonize us, we are saving ourselves from colonialization. . . . You attack the Communist party—you, the Bolsheviks of yesterday—alleging that it carries to extremes its work of expansion and its efforts to secure posts for its members. This is not the moment to discuss the legality or illegality of that policy. It is a subject for the meetings of the liaison committees [of the two parties]. . . .

The Communist party, which you call supra-national, despotic and incompetent, is a model of energy, of calm deliberation, and of responsibility. Yet, while attacking it, you tighten your bonds with the Anarchists. You are incapable of forgetting your grievances with the Communists, but, on the other hand, your capacity to bury your differences with the Anarchists is inexhaustible. . . .

The government, in your opinion, has alienated the sympathies of the democracies. . . . Why are the democracies alarmed? Because, like yourselves, although for different reasons, they believe in the specter that stalks the world: the specter of Communism. Now, when they read your very timely document, they will believe in it even more. . . .

You violate Socialist doctrine and discipline and betray them both when you accuse this executive of complicity with the Communist party. Fortunately, it is complicity in the reassuring company of the national committees of the UGT and the PSOE, which we believe count for more than a local committee. It is a complicity that raises the problem of unification in the same terms as does, for example, the French Socialist party with its Action and Unification Committees. You allude to the example of the PSUC and the [JSU]. We do not repudiate them. You contributed not a little to their becoming a reality. We had nothing to do with it, but are opposed to dissolving them.

In a third letter, which appears to have been the last in the exchange, the Agrupación Socialista Madrileña stated:

On reading your letter, . . . our first impulse was to treat it as though it had not been received, because we believed that it had been drafted not by a Socialist but by a Communist and because it seemed incomprehensible to us that such apologetics and flattery, bordering on servility, could be piled so generously on a party that is not one's own. . . . But such is the accumulation of falsehoods both in fact and doctrine that appear in the letter . . . that it would not be right or wise to allow them to remain unanswered. . . .

On occasions you describe us as national socialists and on others as Trotskyists. Even in this respect you imitate the Communists who are apparently your mentors in everything. You believe, as they do, that by hurling derogatory and incongruous words at a group of men you can liquidate them. This is the most childish tactic, because even children laugh at it. If you seek to identify us with the national socialism of Hitler, which is a rabid anti-Socialist chauvinism, the laughter will be heard as far as Canton. But if you wish to say that we believe in Spanish Socialism, in a Socialism that could be instituted in our country despite foreign intervention, . . . by the sovereign will of our people and in the form it pleases, then, that Spanish Socialism, although it is not universal, that national Socialism, without being international, is ours. If not, then why do our Socialist combatants shed their blood? Why did Russia, which also suffered foreign invasions at the beginning of its revolution, not renounce its program of establishing Socialism in its territory and not wait for the outbreak of world revolution?

Do you not believe that Socialism in one country is possible? That is the fundamental doctrine of Trotsky. Consequently, you, not we, are Trotskyists. The fact is that you do not believe in the socialist revolution in a single country nor in all of them at the same time, because you have lost faith in Socialism and because you have never had faith in the proletariat as a class destined to bring about and consolidate the Socialist revolution. . . .

Quite simply, we are Marxist Socialists, namely, revolutionary Socialists, affiliated with a party which, because of its long and fruitful history and its political maturity has the task of directing the Spanish revolutionary war despite the deviations of many people who call themselves Socialists, but who are Socialists in name only.

In the same letter, the Agrupación excoriated the executive for "vilely despoiling" the left Socialists of their daily press with the help of the police and of "unscrupulous individuals and traitors,"[51] whereas the Communist party in Madrid alone had five or six official or unofficial daily newspapers.

No less galling to the left Socialists than the seizure of their press was the free rein given to Communist newspapers, which were able to express themselves without constraint. "Largo Caballero and his lieutenants," declared *Frente Rojo*, "are the enemies of the UGT, repudiated by all the workers. They are enemies of trade-union unity, enemies of the CNT, enemies of the Popular Front."[52]

Meanwhile, the conflict over the two rival executives of the UGT boiled on until January 1938, when the dispute was arbitrated by Léon Jouhaux, the French trade-union leader—then partial to the Communists—who decided that the new executive should be enlarged to include four Caballeristas.[53] But as the key positions remained with the men appointed by the national committee in October and inasmuch as the executive comprised fifteen members, the four Caballero representatives posed no threat to the Communists' control of the union.[54] Caballero, who had been urged by Jouhaux to join the new executive in order "to strengthen unity,"[55] declined. His decision was welcomed by his opponents. "The truth is," writes Amaro del Rosal, "that given Caballero's character and the amount of political venom fed to him by his 'advisers,' it would have been quite impossible for him to collaborate with the new executive presided by González Peña, who was also president of the PSOE, with whose leadership Caballero was in a state of war."[56]

No sooner had the new executive consolidated its victory over Largo Caballero than it appointed Edmundo Domínguez and Amaro del Rosal (both philo-Communists) and César García Lombardía, the secretary of the teachers' federation, the Federación Española de los Trabajadores de la Enseñanza (who was expelled from the party in January 1939),[57] to start negotiations with the national committee of the CNT with a view to drafting "a broad program for united action."[58] Meanwhile, the Communists, who had initiated their friendly overtures to the CNT in October, continued to sing their siren song. "We shall not allow the revolution to be turned back in its course," La Pasionaria declared on 5 January.[59]

In a memorandum to Moscow, dated 25 November 1937, Togliatti had stressed the importance of a pact with the CNT and had reported that the party's overtures to the national committee had been encouraging. "It is essential," he said, "to avert the possibility that the CNT might pursue an adventurous course," and "we must seek a bond with the healthy portion of the CNT as a point of support in the struggle against capitulators and traitors [i.e., Prieto, Azaña, and Largo Caballero]. The leaders of the CNT (Vázquez) are favorable to a pact with us."[60]

It is of course true that Mariano Vázquez, the secretary of the national committee of the CNT, and other moderates—convinced that the Communists now had the upper hand, that the provisional alliance with Largo Caballero was a lost cause, and that isolation would be fatal to the libertarian movement—had decided on a policy of conciliation with their opponents. Nevertheless, Togliatti reported to Moscow on 28 January 1938 that both the PCE and the UGT were proceeding "too slowly toward a rapprochement with the Anarchist masses and organizations." They did not understand, he said, that the "turnaround of the CNT made the question of unity with the Anarchists an urgent matter" and that it was "precisely that unity that will permit the final defeat of Anarchism." If, on the other hand, he warned, "we do not carry out a policy of unity, the CNT will grow in strength . . . , because its cadres are more active than those of the UGT and it has the advantage from the viewpoint of a segment of the workers of being outside the government." The party, he added, had already been in touch with Mariano Vázquez but so far had not reached an accord. The principal task at this moment, he concluded, was to convince the Socialists of the need for the closest collaboration between the two unions and "we are now concentrating our efforts on this task."[61]

Shortly after this report was sent to Moscow, the first formal meeting between the leaders of the two labor federations (at which Mariano Vázquez, Horacio M. Prieto, and Federica Montseny represented the CNT) was held,[62] but it was not until 18 March, under pressure of a crushing enemy offensive on the Aragon front and the rapidly deteriorating military situation, that the differences in the draft proposals put forward by the two sides were finally reconciled.[63]

Although the pact affirmed that workers' control was one of the most valuable of the workers' conquests and called for the legalization of the collectives, it was a complete negation of Anarchist doctrine, for it recognized the ultimate power and authority of the state not only in these two issues but in such important matters as the nationalization of industry and the regular army.[64] Nevertheless, the pact was enthusiastically received by the CNT press,[65] even by some groups of the FAI, such as the regional committee of the center,[66] but in the long run neither workers' control nor the collectives were ever granted legal status. Hence, in retrospect, the pact appears to have served the ends only of the Communists and their allies in strengthening their position vis-à-vis the leadership of the CNT and ensuring them of its support in the approaching crisis with Indalecio Prieto, whose removal from the defense ministry was the PCE's next objective. Still, the pact was welcomed by a segment of the rank and file weary of the bitter factional strife and the endless chain of military defeats, but the enthusiasm was largely stifled by the dissident voices in the libertarian movement. "We know," declared national committee secretary Mariano Vázquez at a public meeting called to celebrate the pact, "that many [comrades] were annoyed when they learned that . . . the UGT and CNT had agreed on a broad program uniting them on the measures we must take to win the war and reconstruct our shattered economy. But we are indifferent to these malcontents. . . . I embrace comrade Rodríguez Vega, the secretary of the UGT, as a symbol of the unity of the Spanish working class."[67]

Horacio M. Prieto—a vigorous opponent of the FAI's antistatism, who, it will be recalled, had been instrumental in bringing the Anarchosyndicalists into the government of Largo Caballero—declared after the war with evident satisfaction that the CNT-UGT pact was a "triumph without precedent for Spanish Anarchism," for it represented "its definitive defeat" as an apolitical ideology. "The national state," he added, "was officially recognized" and "doctrine was sacrificed to reality, which does not recognize theoretical subtleties."[68]

In spite of its enthusiastic reception in the CNT press, the pact exacerbated the dissensions within the libertarian movement between the collaborationists and the purists, who regarded the acceptance of government control as a denial of Anarchist doctrine and a victory for the Marxists. "The Communist party," wrote Abad de Santillán, a prominent member of the peninsular committee of the FAI, who during much of the war was engaged in a bitter feud with members of the CNT national committee, "endeavored to lure the CNT leaders in order to manipulate and exploit these rubber stamps in the interest of its hegemonic policy. The more the comrades of the national committee heeded these advances, the more the peninsular committee of the FAI found itself at odds with the leadership of the CNT."[69]

But, for the moment, this opposition was muted by a sense of relief that the conflict between the rival unions may at last have ended. "The CNT-UGT pact," observed *Frente Rojo*, ". . . is one of the strongest levers for mobilizing the people and consolidating its granite-like unity in the struggle against the common enemy and in the immense and glorious tasks that lie ahead. The workers and all the popular layers know this [and] are ready to defend the unity of the proletariat and to reinforce the Popular Front against all maneuvers to which the enemies of unity may resort in shameful desperation."[70]

The Removal of Indalecio Prieto
from the Defense Ministry

*E*ncouraged by their rapprochement with the national leaders of the CNT and by the political eclipse of Largo Caballero, the Communists now felt strong enough to come to grips with Indalecio Prieto.

In their campaign against the defense minister, the military situation played a crucial role. On 23 December 1937, the Republicans captured Teruel, their first major successful offensive action since the start of the Civil War. But only two months later, on 22 February, after a grueling battle, fought in the snow and in subzero temperatures, they were forced to evacuate the city, ending abruptly the mood of exultation that had briefly suffused the Republican camp and raised the standing of the defense minister.[1] Then, on 9 March General Franco, aided by an overwhelming superiority in aviation of four to one,[2] launched in Aragon the most spectacular offensive seen so far in the Civil War. "The month of March was calamitous," records interior minister Julián Zugazagoitia. "All our lines collapsed. The enemy's motorized columns advance without difficulty. Hour by hour we lose positions, fortified heights, villages. . . . The commissar general of the Eastern Army . . . sends a report to Prieto in which the situation is described as hopeless: The morale of the men has fallen precipitously due to the difficulty of supplying food and ammunition and to the threat from the air."[3] Santiago Alvarez, the Communist chief political commissar of the 144th Mixed Brigade (Forty-fourth Division), informed the central committee of the PCE on 18 March of the "apathy," "indifference," the "panic of the majority of professional officers," and the "absolute lack of good intermediate cadres." In many cases, he added, the situation resembled the early days of the militias when there were neither officers nor organization.[4]

The plight of the International Brigades, now partially integrated into Spanish units, was no better. Sandor Voros, an American commissar in the Fifteenth Brigade, writes: "The terror in the International Brigades is on. To halt the Fascist offensive, we need air power, artillery, tanks, armored cars, transport, trained officers, noncoms, and men. The Kremlin leaders think differently; although they supply us with some material they base their main reliance on terror. Officers and men are ruthlessly executed on orders. The toll is particularly high among the Poles, Slavs, Germans, and Hungarians, especially among those who came to Spain from Moscow. These are summary executions, carried out in most cases secretly by the SIM."[5] His evidence of extensive arrests and executions of members of the International Brigades is corroborated by Carlo Penchienati, former commander of the Garibaldi Brigade, who claims that the " 'Cheka' was functioning at full capacity" at that time.[6]

The terror was simply an extension of what had been going on for a long time in Albacete, where André Marty, the organizer of the brigades, known as the "butcher of Albacete," had set up the NKVD's headquarters, according to former German Communist Gustav Regler and political commissar of the Twelfth International Brigade. "The result," Regler informed me, "was that the French brigade, whose political commissar was a young ambitious Communist of Marty's creation, sent all dissident elements down to the base, where they were jailed and some shot. The same insinuation [*sic*] came to my brigade, where it was rejected violently, even by my Communist general Paul Lukacz, who died at my side in 1937. The regime of Albacete was the regime of terror; there was even a punishment company there in which Jef Last [a Dutch Communist] served for a while; I got details from him that proved how Albacete was used as an execution place and in the end no one in the staff was of any other party than the C.P."[7]

In those military units, in which the CNT, FAI, POUM, and left Socialists were strongly represented and the factional strife and attacks on the Revolution had done more to undermine morale than in other forces, the lack of combativity cannot be ascribed solely to military reasons. The collapse of the Aragon front, ran an unpublished report by the peninsular committee of the FAI on 1 April, was also due to the "undeclared and fierce battle between parties and factions." There were parties and groups, it affirmed, whose sole aim was "the pursuit of their own hegemony." "In such circumstances, it is easy to understand that the courage and combativity of the soldiers of the people are practically annulled. . . . It is a terrible tragedy that our combatants have to face a most powerful enemy with the feeling they are led by traitors, by enemies of the people's cause."[8]

On 15 April—within six weeks of the onset of the offensive—the enemy reached the Mediterranean coast, splitting the Republican territory in two. "No one has yet explained," President Azaña wrote shortly after the war, "why in March 1938, when the [enemy] took Lérida he did not take Barcelona [the seat of the government since November 1937].[9] Between the two cities there were no forces at all."[10] An explanation for the failure of the Nationalists to exploit their military advantage lies in Hitler's decision, as we have already noted, to prolong the war and encourage Italy to make a major military investment in Spain in order to bind Mussolini closer to Germany. This would divert his attention from Austria and Czechoslovakia, whose absorption into the German Reich was essential to the consummation of Nazi aims in Eastern Europe. It was surely no coincidence that on 13 March, four days after the start of the Aragon offensive, in which German

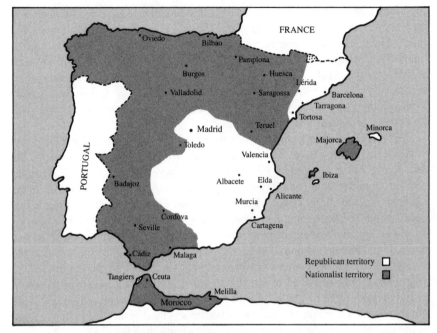

Map 4. Division of Spain, 15 April 1938

aviation, tanks, and artillery played a major role, Hitler occupied Austria without a word of protest from Mussolini, who, in 1934, had been ready to defend it against a Nazi assault. But it was not until after the Munich Pact in September 1938, in which Mussolini supported Hitler's demands on Czechoslovakia, that the führer resolved to end the war in Spain as soon as possible and concentrate his attention on Eastern Europe.

Meanwhile, in the Republican zone, even before the start of the Nationalist offensive on 9 March, the fate of Indalecio Prieto had been decided. "It was necessary," wrote Jesús Hernández, "to dig a deep grave for him, in which all his measures against Communist predominance in the army would be buried. By removing him from the defense ministry, all the levers of military control not held directly by the Communists would be concentrated in the hands of Dr. Negrín, Moscow's man of confidence."[11]

"But how could Prieto be removed?" asks El Campesino, the commander of the Forty-fourth Division, in a book written after he had escaped from Russia. "His prestige was high, especially after the successful operation of Teruel." The former Communist alleges that "Kremlin agents" decided to sacrifice the city in order to discredit Prieto. He also asserts that when his own division was surrounded in Teruel, he was deliberately abandoned by the Communist commanders Enrique Líster and Juan Modesto as part of the conspiracy to discredit Prieto but managed to escape with most of his men.[12] Líster, for his part, claims that El

Campesino fled from Teruel when it was not yet surrounded and "cowardly" abandoned his forces.[13] Because of the political animosity between the two men, their testimony must be treated with caution. Nevertheless, it is noteworthy that when El Campesino informed Prieto by letter in October 1950 that he had been used as a scapegoat to oust the defense minister, Prieto asserted that certain army chiefs had told him at the time that the Communists had devised the loss of Teruel in order to destroy him. "But," he affirmed, "despite the many indications that their assertion was well-founded, I did not believe it, because I could not believe it. Impossible! Now, El Campesino, in his letter of 10 October 1950, appears to confirm it. So many things that I once believed impossible have turned out to be true!"[14]

Although it is debatable whether the Communists went to the extreme of ordering the abandonment of Teruel in order to destroy Prieto, there is no question that the loss of the city was the starting point for their drive against him. Just as they had once launched an insidious campaign against Largo Caballero—spreading the epithets "stupidity," "ineptitude," "vanity," and "senility" from mouth to mouth—so too did they use what means they could to discredit Prieto. "The entire front and rearguard were filled with rumors," Hernández claims: " 'Prieto is a capitulator,' 'Prieto does not want Soviet aviators to take part in our war,' 'Prieto says that without French aid it is stupid to continue the war,' 'Prieto has asked the English government for a destroyer to flee to England,' 'Prieto wants to hand over the entire central-southern zone of the Republic to Franco on the pretext of fortifying ourselves in Catalonia,' etc., etc."[15]

"We must make use of the loss of Teruel to liquidate Prieto," the Comintern delegate Pedro told a meeting of the politburo, Hernández asserts. "Stefanov, who had just made a very quick trip to Moscow, brought back precise instructions and supported [Pedro] with the following words: 'The comrades of the "Casa" [Moscow] recommend that the army be supplied with new reserves that will make it possible to prolong resistance.[16] In this way, the struggle can be continued with a view to an eventual world conflict that could change the entire panorama of the war. Resist! Resist! Resist! That is the directive of the "Casa." . . . Do you believe that's possible with Prieto in charge of the defense ministry?"[17] The question was purely rhetorical, for, as Togliatti remarked, Prieto's pessimism was the chief obstacle to a policy of all-out resistance.[18] He was of course correct, for Prieto's pessimism was notorious. Ignacio Hidalgo de Cisneros, the chief of the air force and onetime intimate of Prieto's, told me after the war that he frequently had to caution the defense minister not to speak pessimistically before his subordinates. "Prieto," he said, "claimed that a responsible pessimist was worth more than an irresponsible optimist. He spoke like a pessimist, but worked like an optimist. That was one of his contradictions."[19]

Prieto's pessimism expressed itself in various ways. A few days after the formation of the Negrín government in May 1937 he refused to speak over the radio. "Anyone could do a better job than I in addressing the Spanish people," he told the cabinet, "because no matter how hard I might try to disguise my thoughts they would be transparent to my listeners."[20] At another time, his pessimism led him to contemplate declaring war on Germany. On 31 May, the German fleet had shelled the Republican port of Almería in retaliation for the bombing of the German pocket battleship *Deutschland*, one of the naval vessels involved in the international patrol scheme. At a cabinet meeting, Prieto proposed a massive aerial attack on the fleet "even though it might provoke a war and, consequently, a European conflagration." "My cabinet colleagues and the chief of state," he affirmed, "regarded my idea as foolhardy and rejected the proposal. It was the proposal of a pessimist, who saw no possibility of winning the war." Half the Spanish nation, he said, was fighting the other half aided not only by Italy, Germany, and Portugal, but by the indifference, if not the hostility, of the rest of Europe. "By declaring war on Germany," he added, "I sought a solution through an international conflict, because the Western nations, faced by the danger of an open conquest of Spanish territory by Italy and Germany, might decide to intervene."[21]

One might have thought that Prieto's proposal would have been welcomed by Moscow in view of the Kremlin's desire to involve Britain and France in the Spanish conflict.[22] It was not. According to Hernández, during a cabinet recess before the arrival of President Azaña, who had been asked to preside over the second half of the meeting, the Communist apparatus "within five minutes put everything into motion to find out the 'line.' Codovila went to the Soviet Embassy. Togliatti proceeded to El Vedat, a small village near Valencia, where, in a 'farm' lost in a beautiful orange grove, the Soviet delegation had set up a very powerful radio station with which it maintained direct contact with France and Moscow. . . . Moscow's orders were categorical: 'Prieto's provocation must be prevented at all costs.' " Hernández, who claims that he believed, like Prieto, that the war was "an agony without hope," alleges that his "disappointment was tremendous" and that his conscience battled with the conflicting feelings of subservience to Moscow and loyalty to Spain, but that obedience to Moscow prevailed.[23]

It must be said in passing that the attack on the *Deutschland* was carried out by a Soviet pilot (G. K. Livinski). This was revealed by Major General G. Prokofiev, the Soviet air force adviser to Republican Spain. "I had the opportunity of making several flights with him," he wrote twenty-eight years later. "[Livinski] was an excellent bombardier and his skill was soon proved by a direct hit on the German battleship *Deutschland*."[24] Obviously, one cannot infer unequivocally from this statement that Livinski was acting on specific orders from the Kremlin to attack the *Deutschland*, then lying at anchor off Ibiza, but, if he were, the question arises, Why did Moscow, which was intent on involving Britain and France in the Spanish conflict, veto Prieto's proposal? The answer may be that the Kremlin, seeing that the reaction of Britain and France to the bombardment of Almería was cautious and apprehensive, may have concluded that Prieto's proposal, if adopted, would have been counterproductive in that it would undoubtedly have resulted in a massive increase in German aid to Franco without any change in the policy of nonintervention on the part of Britain and France and would have been condemned as a deliberate attempt to ignite a conflict in Western Europe. Referring to a meeting of the nonintervention subcommittee on the day of the bombardment of Almería, Ivan Maisky, the Soviet ambassador, who attended the session, writes: "The committee should have been protesting . . . [but] the diplomats of the so-called 'democratic' countries were scared to death that the whole farce of 'nonintervention' would now collapse like a house of cards."[25] The fact is that distrust rather than fear governed the behavior of the British and French diplomats. The request made by the British ambassador of the German foreign minister on 31 May "not to do the Reds the favor of expanding the conflict in Spain into a world war"[26] and the remark by British foreign secretary Anthony Eden to the U.S. ambassador on 3 June that "it looked as if the Soviet government wanted the British to pull its chestnuts out of the fire and would not be disturbed if Germany was at war with England and France, leaving Russia with a comparatively free hand on the other side,"[27] reveal the true feelings of the British government. Nor was the French government less suspicious. According to the German ambassador in Paris, Socialist premier Leon Blum allegedly gave the Soviet chargé d'affaires to understand that "a repetition of such incidents would encounter the sharpest disapproval of the French government and would create a very grave situation."[28]

Although Moscow opposed Prieto's proposal to bomb the German fleet, its relations with him were not affected by the incident or by his self-avowed pessimism, which it could have tolerated had he been less refractory. Far more disquieting was his determination to curtail Communist predominance in the armed forces.[29] While recognizing that his pessimistic nature "was proverbial and bordered at times on defeatism," the official Communist history acknowledges that his administration of the defense ministry "had unquestionably positive features" but that "his tendency to depoliticize the Popular Army constituted one of the most negative aspects of his work."[30]

At this point it is appropriate to remind the reader of the following statement by Hernández, cited in a previous chapter, regarding the party's attitude toward Prieto before he became defense minister:

"When the politburo discussed the pros and cons of accepting Prieto as head of the defense ministry, we took into account his great prestige in moderate political circles at home and abroad. In this respect Prieto was useful to us. We also took into consideration the negative side of his character. He was a pessimist; he had no faith in victory. To entrust him with the maximum responsibility for prosecuting the war was an anomaly. . . . The members of the politburo hesitated to support his candidacy. Togliatti gave us the following advice: 'By supporting the candidacy of Prieto we shall bring him under our control. If he doesn't agree to serve us, we shall exploit his notorious and self-proclaimed pessimism to bring about his removal, whenever it is convenient to us. . . . [We] shall try to envelop him in such a heavy shroud of disrepute that he will be rendered useless as an outstanding Socialist leader. One enemy less.' "[31]

Hence, the loss of Teruel on 22 February provided a felicitous occasion to initiate an all-out offensive against the defense minister, who, like Manuel Azaña and Julián Besteiro, the right-wing Socialist, looked more and more to mediation to end the conflict. Many feelers were put out in 1937 and 1938,[32] but General Franco, backed to the hilt by Germany and Italy and confident of ultimate victory, would consider nothing but unconditional surrender.

The opening salvo against Prieto was fired by La Pasionaria on 27 February, five days after the loss of Teruel. Eusebio Cimorra, a staff writer on the Communist organ *Mundo Obrero* in 1936 and, later, political secretary to Hernández in the ministry of education, wrote after the war: "For the Communists, for Pasionaria, who regarded Prieto's measures prohibiting proselytism by the political commissars as a relentless policy against the Communists, the failure of the Teruel operation was an opportunity delivered on a silver platter to discredit the defense minister."[33] Without mentioning Prieto by name, or any other Socialist or Republican known to favor mediation, La Pasionaria declared:

> Who are these people who spread defeatism and talk about the inefficiency of our army? . . . They are incompetents and cowards, people who burn one candle to God and another to the devil, people who stand with one foot here and the other in the camp of the rebels. . . .
>
> We must tell them that our men did not go to the front in order to preserve the privileges of the landlords and bankers; we must tell them that our women did not give their sons in order to return to the old slavery. . . . Those who plan to destroy the revolutionary gains of our people won during nineteen months of sacrifice are not qualified to speak of democracy. . . .
>
> [When] the general commissariat of war pursues a policy . . . of removing political commissars who are cited for heroism . . . and enjoy the confidence of the soldiers . . . , then we who are inspired solely by the desire to win the war and defeat fascism must say that we will not allow this policy to continue.[34]

During the next few days, the Communist offensive against Prieto continued without letup, picking up momentum when General Franco's forces began their lightning advance toward the Mediterranean coast, and no one knew where the rout would end.

On 16 March, in an atmosphere of impending disaster, Eilrick Labonne, the French ambassador, visited Negrín to apprise him of his government's willingness to serve as mediator in the conflict. The same day, the ambassador reported to Paris that those members of Negrín's cabinet who favored mediation relied principally on the argument that Italian and German intervention was so overwhelming as to leave the Republicans with no hope of victory regardless of outside help. It was therefore better, they held, to give up while there was still time, "because mediation offered the best possible opportunity of safeguarding the ideals and even the lives of the Republicans." On the other hand, Labonne reported, Prime Minister Negrín replied that the stubborn resistance shown by the Spanish people on previous occasions would allow time for the development of a more favorable international situation. Mediation, Negrín said, was condemned to failure, because even if Franco agreed, the Germans and Italians would impose their veto and the only result would be to undermine army confidence and morale in the rear. "At this point," stated Labonne, "the prime minister, in a burst of temper and with eyes flaming, exclaimed: 'In resistance there is no room for vacillation! I can handle the situation. No matter how highly placed the opponents of resistance may be, they will be crushed.' "[35]

Negrín then convened a meeting of his cabinet. "It was rumored," recalls Carles Pi Sunyer, former mayor of Barcelona and now Esquerra councillor of culture in the Catalan government, "that the question of peace would be raised and that some ministers, particularly Prieto, would demand that negotiations should begin. As a result of these rumors, and as though obeying a single slogan, telegraphed messages from the army began to arrive at the prime minister's office, demanding the resignation of the wavering ministers."[36]

According to interior minister Zugazagoitia, Negrín informed the cabinet of Labonne's offer and of his decision to continue the struggle to the end. No one suggested peace negotiations and Negrín's view prevailed. "Only Irujo [Manuel de Irujo, the Basque Nationalist minister][37] . . . brought up the advisability of studying the military situation so that, if we were convinced of the inevitability of defeat, we could reduce the agony of prolonging a hopeless war. As for Giral [foreign minister and president Azaña's spokesman in the cabinet] . . . he suggested that it would be advisable not to reject the offer outright, since it might be welcome if the need arose."[38] Giral's recommendation, Prieto told Zugazagoitia after the meeting, was due to a visit he had received from the French ambassador, who "had offered him a warship to evacuate the President of the Republic and the cabinet, suggesting, in return, that we should send our aviation to French airfields and the units of our fleet to Bizerte [Tunisia]."[39]

"Why harbor any illusions that we can wait for the arrival of French war material, as Negrín suggested," Prieto commented bitterly. "It is obvious from the French ambassador's proposals that his government regards us as dead."[40]

After a short recess, the cabinet reconvened at 6 P.M. in the Palace of Pedralbes under the chairmanship of Azaña, who, as expected, raised the question of peace negotiations. He condemned the government's rejection of the French proposal and asked the ministers if they didn't consider it "more prudent not to close the door to negotiations that we would need if the optimism of the head of the government did not materialize."[41] Knowing that Prieto was as pessimistic as he, Azaña asked him to report on the military situation. The defense minister replied that the army was "demoralized" and was "fleeing in all directions, abandoning arms and ammunition."[42] His words simply reinforced Azaña's argument that the war was lost.[43]

Meanwhile, as rumors of capitulation began to spread, the Communist party, backed by Mariano Vázquez, the secretary of the national committee of the CNT, organized a demonstration, headed by assault guards, which marched through the principal streets of Barcelona toward the Pedralbes Palace. "The Communist party," recalls La Pasionaria, "mobilized the population of Barcelona . . . demanding that the government continue to resist."[44] "The coercive character" of the demonstration, observed Zugazagoitia, was patent.[45] The following day, *Frente Rojo* declared that the working class of Barcelona "representing all the workers of our fatherland and the thousands of heroic combatants . . . resoundingly proclaimed its will to prosecute the struggle until final victory and to expel from our midst the cowards, vacillators, and traitors." Members of the food workers' federation, the newspaper reported, closed all bars, cafés, and restaurants. "Other groups of comrades entered the movie houses and theaters, where they exhorted the audiences to join the demonstration."[46] As Prieto later put it, the "demonstration was formed by emptying the theaters and cinemas so that, whether they wanted to or not, the spectators would join it, and the same was done with passengers on the trams and buses."[47]

As the demonstrators tumultuously entered the gardens of the palace, cries of "Down with the treacherous ministers!" "Down with the minister of defense!" were heard by the assembled ministers.[48] Zugazagoitia affirms that Prieto told him that he was convinced that Negrín had advised the Communists to hold the demonstration "in order to coerce the President of the Republic" and "to impose his will in advance so as to thwart any weakness of Azaña."[49]

Togliatti informed Moscow that the Republican parties had complained that the demonstration was organized without them and, in fact, directed against them. "The fact is that to have invited the Republicans would have meant sabotaging everything." A few days earlier, he added, the Republican parties had met in order to form their own coordinating committee, "thus taking an initiative outside the Popular Front," and had raised the matter of a political change. "All this was undoubtedly inspired by the President of the Republic and in preparation for a pronunciamiento against Negrín and in favor of surrender. The demonstration of 16 March brought the Republicans back to reality, making them understand that the working class and its organizations will not tolerate any form of capitulation and that nothing can be done without them. Indeed, since 16 March, the Popular Front has begun to function again almost regularly and the official position of the Republicans has improved."[50]

As for the CNT, Togliatti complained to Moscow that its support of the demonstration had been fleeting. Its representatives, he reported, had formed part of the commission that had presented the demonstrators' demands to Negrín, but the next day *Solidaridad Obrera* ignored the demonstration. "This can be explained," he said, "partly by bad communications (the leaders of the CNT who were in contact with the party remained almost the entire night in party headquarters to escape a bombardment and could not communicate with the editors) and partly by the usual duplicity of the Anarchists and the dissensions within the leadership."[51]

Juan-Simeón Vidarte, the undersecretary of the interior and a partisan of the premier, confirms Negrín's advance knowledge of the demonstration. The Socialist executive, Vidarte states, received a telephone call from Negrín announcing that a demonstration was being organized in favor of the government and that he personally had authorized it. "Shortly afterwards, a commission of the Communist party arrived, which was more explicit than the premier: 'There was a far-reaching maneuver to overthrow Negrín and place at the head of the government an accommodating individual who would agree to unconditional surrender. . . . They could not allow Negrín to be stabbed in the back and, as they were convinced that the people were on the side of the government, they had taken the initiative in organizing the demonstration in his favor. . . . Not a minute should be lost. The demonstration should coincide with the meeting of the cabinet.' " To this, Manuel Cordero, the veteran Socialist and Prietista retorted: "Let us speak clearly. The truth is that the purpose of the demonstration is to coerce the President of the Republic." "No!" the Communists responded. "The purpose is to prevent the throats of half a million patriotic Republicans from being cut." Their argument was overpowering, and the Socialist executive appointed Vidarte to represent the party at the demonstration. "We are always complaining about the Communists," Cordero grumbled, "but all we do is dance to the piper's tune."

At the Pedralbes Palace, Vidarte and Negrín had the following exchange: "Are you happy with this 'spontaneous' demonstration that has been so well organized?" Vidarte asked banteringly. "Believe me," Negrín answered, "it was necessary to avoid the danger of unconditional surrender." "In that case, I am glad I came," Vidarte replied; he then asked, "Do you believe that Azaña is capable of [surrendering]?" and Negrín responded, "No less than he was on 18 July."[52]

As on 18 July 1936, Azaña's hopes of a compromise settlement were shattered by a mass demonstration. Even so, there was no likelihood that General Franco would have considered a negotiated peace at a time when total victory appeared so close at hand. Furthermore, according to Vidarte, the Socialist executive was in complete accord with Negrín that it was "impossible to achieve a compromise settlement that would end the war honorably, for the simple reason that Franco would not accept anything but unconditional surrender, namely, the destruction of the Republican armed forces."[53]

In a letter written shortly after the war, Azaña stated that he had done everything possible since September 1936 to bring about a compromise solution, because the idea of defeating the enemy was a "fantasy." No prime minister, no defense minister, no foreign minister, no important ambassador, he affirmed, was ignorant of his position. "The extremists were not ignorant of it when they organized demonstrations outside the Pedralbes Palace against the Republican *traitors*. Those were the days when the president was accused of being a defeatist and of wanting to concoct a deal [*un pastel*]. Today, none of them would mind if that deal had been made."[54]

Although, at the call of the national committee of the CNT, the Anarchosyndicalist workers in Barcelona participated in the demonstration, there had already developed a profound cleavage of opinion in the libertarian movement over the advisability of prosecuting the war to the bitter end. The CNT historian José Peirats, himself a witness to this torturous dilemma, states that in face of the reconquest of Teruel and the subsequent invasion of Aragon, Levante, and Catalonia "some militants began to ask themselves if there was anything left to sacrifice and to what end." Two tendencies, he says, stood out: "that of the national committee of the CNT [headed by Mariano Vázquez which, . . . in order to escape the torture of doubt, sought the necessary optimism in Negrín's drug of all-out resistance, and that of the peninsular committee of the FAI, which tried to save its honor by a ceaseless and systematic opposition to the advance of the counterrevolution and even . . . thought of bringing about an armistice in mid-1938."[55]

To what degree disenchantment and confusion had begun to pervade the libertarian movement, which represented half the working class, was apparent from a speech by Horacio M. Prieto, the former secretary of the CNT. At a national plenum of the organization held in March, he declared that the war was lost and that the CNT should use its influence to profit from the defeatism of the Socialists and Republicans and to arrive at an honorable peace by "ceasing to play unconsciously the game of the Russians who were interested in waging a war that was ruining Spain and that was bleeding the [libertarian] movement for a cause that was ours only in appearance. In this way, we would save a large number of lives, spare our men great suffering and could rebuild our movement after less damage had been done than if we continued to resist vaingloriously."[56] Finally, the delegates decided "to offer their full support to the defense minister and put an end to the ascendancy of the Communists by a test of force."[57] Nothing came of this decision. Although Indalecio Prieto acknowledges that he received the support of the CNT leadership,[58] he does not mention a "test of force." Indeed, it is barely conceivable that Prieto would have allied himself with the CNT against the Communist party even in the last extremity.

Meanwhile, the role of Mariano Vázquez, the secretary of the CNT, who had recently signed the pact of unity with the new Communist-controlled executive of the UGT and had marched with the Communists against Prieto, was disconcerting to the PCE. "Vázquez adopted an equivocal position," Togliatti told the Comintern. "He demanded that the composition of the cabinet should remain unchanged except that it should be enlarged to include representatives of the unions. In other words, he defended Prieto against Negrín and the Communists."[59] This unexpected switch astounded some of the leaders of the CNT, among them José García Pradas, the director of the Madrid newspaper *CNT* and delegate at the national plenum in Barcelona, who records that shortly after the demonstration Vázquez shifted his position and proposed that the national committee should inform Prieto that "we would be happy if he remained in the defense ministry."[60] Such waverings and inconsistencies characterized Vázquez's behavior throughout the war and contrasted with the firm line of the PCE, which knew precisely what it wanted.

Despite Vázquez's ephemeral support of the defense minister, Prieto's political career was now in its twilight hours. In an article entitled "Unrepentant Pessimist," that appeared in both *Frente Rojo*, the Communist organ, and in *La*

Vanguardia, the mouthpiece of Juan Negrín, Jesús Hernández delivered a scorching assault on the defense minister.[61] Although he used the pseudonym of "Juan Ventura," the author's true identity was clear. At a cabinet meeting on 29 March, Prieto declared: "If these were normal times . . . , I would immediately resign, because in view of my concept of cabinet solidarity, . . . I regard the attack on me by the minister of education as inadmissible. However, the present situation prevents me from resigning. Duty ties me to my post. To abandon it of my own free will, even for such a powerful reason, would be equivalent to desertion and I do not desert. Hence, I shall remain minister of national defense, but in the knowledge that from now on I shall be occupying the post without authority and without respect."[62]

Nevertheless, Prieto did not have to suffer further indignities as defense minister, for Negrín, according to Togliatti, had now arrived at the same conclusion as the PCE: "It was essential to remove Prieto from the military leadership of the country in order to avoid a catastrophe."[63] Although the premier affirmed that the decision was his own, Prieto insisted that he had yielded to the demands of the Communist party.[64] "My decision to replace you as defense minister," Negrín stated in a letter to Prieto, his old friend and former mentor, "was exclusively and strictly personal. I reached this decision on the night of 29–30 March after a painful and difficult inner struggle. It was a result of the cabinet meeting of 29 March, . . . when, with your great eloquence, your personality, your customary dramatization, and with the authority of your post, you completely demoralized our cabinet colleagues by portraying events in the darkest tones of desperation."[65] Clearly, there was no longer any place for Prieto in the cabinet, for Negrín, fostering the hope, like the Communists, that the conflict would eventually merge with a European conflagration, could no longer tolerate as his minister of defense a man who was convinced that the war was lost. In a speech some years later, Negrín declared: "It has been bandied about that my decision [to remove] Prieto was the result of outside pressures, concretely, the Communist party and the Soviet government. This is false, absolutely false. Those who say this do not know me. I swear to you on the graves of our war dead that there is not a word of truth in it."[66]

In his report to Moscow, Togliatti stated that Negrín had called a meeting of the Socialist leadership and declared that he could no longer continue with Prieto in the defense ministry as he was "a defeatist who deserved to be shot." He also stated that he wished to free himself of Giral [Azaña's confidant], who, like Prieto, was telling everyone that the war was lost "thus making it impossible to receive any help from abroad." The Socialist party leadership, Togliatti added, "gave Negrín a free hand to reorganize the cabinet."[67] This was the nadir of Prieto's influence in the Socialist executive. From now on, many of those who had been known as "Prietistas" became metamorphosed overnight into "Negrinistas," although sometimes of dubious loyalty. In informing Prieto of its decision to support Negrín, the Socialist executive was mildly apologetic. "The fact that you are leaving the defense ministry," said Ramón González Peña, the party's president, "is almost an indignity, but in view of the present political situation we have no option but to accept the sacrifice."[68]

While the composition of the new administration was still under discussion, the politburo was debating a Comintern proposal that the PCE should withdraw its two ministers from the government. In this way, affirms the official Communist history of the civil war, the Communist International believed that "the position of the Republic would be strengthened by destroying the argument used by Spanish and foreign reactionaries in their slanderous campaign against the Popular Front government branding it as Communist." On the other hand, the Spanish politburo argued that "the departure of its ministers from the government would not be understood by the people and would not strengthen the Republic especially after the loss of Teruel when capitulationist tendencies were rampant." It was precisely these circumstances, it claimed, that made the presence of the Communists all the more necessary.[69] According to José Duque, a member of the central committee, one of the principal objections of the politburo was that Negrín and del Vayo (who was to resume his post as foreign minister) were not strong enough to control the cabinet without the backing of the Communists.[70]

The tactic of withdrawing Communist participation, Togliatti told the politburo, was aimed at "convincing English and French public opinion that the Communists are not interested in the conquest of power, not even in Spain, where we could do so with comparative ease. . . . In this way, we shall strengthen Anglo-French ties with the Soviets. If Hitler should decide on war he will have to wage it against the USSR and the Western democracies."[71] Hernández claims that he opposed the tactic. "The hatred and hostility for our party and Negrín," he wrote after he had left the party, "were shared unanimously by all the forces of the Popular Front. Negrín could govern only by relying completely on the Communist party's military and political power. To withdraw our ministers would have meant death to the resistance policy."[72] Hernández's opposition is corroborated by Togliatti: "In a tone of despair, Hernández objected: 'This will mean the loss of everything.' "[73] Nevertheless, a compromise was reached: Hernández alone would withdraw, leaving Vicente Uribe as the only minister representing the PCE. This reduction in Communist representation, Hernández announced at a press conference (while still a member of the politburo), demonstrated once again "the dishonesty of those persons inside and outside the country who have played on the existence of a terrible Communist danger, seeking to provoke distrust and division among the antifascist forces in Spain and to impress world opinion with blustering threats of Communist influence in the state machinery. My removal from the government is clear proof to the contrary."[74]

Part VIII

Communist Influence Crests

55

The Second Negrín Government.
Communist Predominance in the Army.

*T*he composition of the second Negrín administration, formed on 5 April 1938, was as follows:

Juan Negrín	Socialist	Premiership and Defense
Julio Alvarez del Vayo	Socialist	Foreign Affairs
Paulino Gómez	Socialist	Interior
Ramón González Peña	UGT	Justice
Vicente Uribe	Communist	Agriculture
Segundo Blanco	CNT	Education and Health
Francisco Méndez Aspe	Left Republican	Finance and Economy
Antonio Velao	Left Republican	Public Works
Bernardo Giner de los Ríos	Republican Union	Communications and Transportation
Jaime Aiguadé	Esquerra	Labor
José Giral	Left Republican	Minister without portfolio
Manuel de Irujo	Basque Nationalist	Minister without portfolio[1]

The request of the CNT for representation in the cabinet was only partially satisfied by the appointment of a single Anarchosyndicalist, Segundo Blanco, who replaced Jesús Hernández in the ministry of education. Although the CNT newspaper, *Fragua Social*, described Blanco as an "unfailing revolutionary,"[2] his libertarian opponents later characterized him as just "another Negrinista."[3] The UGT also joined the government and was represented by Ramón González Peña, the Socialist president of the pro-Communist executive.

Togliatti welcomed the return of the CNT to the government. He informed

Moscow that it created "a new relationship with the Anarchists" and reduced "the danger of an Anarchist revolt."[4] *Solidaridad Obrera*, the once-fiery voice of the revolutionary CNT, but now the mouthpiece of the more politicized and chastened elements led by Mariano Vázquez, declared that the new government with its enlarged representation would "help to raise the morale of our soldiers" and that the participation of the CNT and UGT "opened up new courses of action that inspire everyone with confidence, serenity, and a spirit of sacrifice."[5]

For cosmetic reasons, Indalecio Prieto was urged to remain in the cabinet, since his presence would have been reassuring to both foreign and domestic opinion. The Communist party, La Pasionaria claimed after the war, made every effort to keep him in the government, but he rejected all proposals.[6] Negrín also tried to retain him in the cabinet, but, as he told his Socialist colleague Vidarte, the only portfolio Prieto would accept was that of finance so that he could mobilize all available funds and resources for purposes of emigration. "I could not agree to that request," Negrín stated. "As long as the war lasts the ministry of finance . . . cannot have its own policy independent of the prime minister's. . . . I know how much Prieto means to the [Socialist] party and I have done all I can to keep him at my side."[7]

As for Hernández, whose departure from the cabinet was designed to convince British and French opinion that the Communists were not interested in the conquest of power, he was named chief political commissar of the central-southern region, which embraced 80 percent of the land forces.[8] "In order to facilitate the reorganization of the government as a government of national union," declared La Pasionaria a few weeks later, "our party made every sacrifice. . . . This refutes those who disseminate stupid myths that our country is on the way to a dictatorship of the proletariat and who sow seeds of suspicion and disunity by representing the Communists as masters of the government and the state. Our participation in the government is simply a result of circumstances and expresses our support of the democratic republic. . . . The Communist party has never fought for positions in the government or regarded them as fundamental; nor will it ever do so."[9]

Even though the PCE held only one portfolio, it now controlled more levers of command than hitherto. This was clear not only from the return to the foreign ministry of Julio Alvarez del Vayo, the crypto-Communist par excellence—who, in addition to maintaining Communist control in the foreign propaganda and foreign press bureaus, gave Manuel Sánchez Arcas, a party member, the key post of undersecretary of propaganda[10]—but above all from the assumption of the defense ministry by Premier Juan Negrín, anathematized in the postwar years by Jesús Hernández as "Moscow's man of confidence"[11] and by El Campesino as "the Communists' ambitious and docile tool."[12] These epithets have been vigorously challenged by Negrín's Spanish and foreign admirers, whose extravagant praise contrasts sharply with the savage denunciations of some of his Socialist critics. Whereas Largo Caballero asseverated that he had surrendered himself "body and soul" to the Communist party[13] and Luis Araquistáin branded his government as "the most despotic and unscrupulous suffered by Spain even during the darkest days of the Austrian and Bourbon dynasties,"[14] Professor Juan Marichal of Harvard University has since claimed that "few men in European history during the last century and a half have displayed such a combination of intelligence and character, of moral integrity and intellectual capacity."[15] For his part, the Spanish historian Angel Viñas has described him as "one of the most clearsighted and extraordinary politicians of the entire Republican era" and the "great statesman of the Republic."[16] These encomia were later transcended by the U.S. historian Edward Malefakis, who affirmed that Negrín was "without equal in Spain since Olivares in the XVIIth century" and of the same caliber as such wartime leaders as Winston Churchill.[17]

Of the foreign admirers of Negrín, the most notable was Herbert Matthews, who, for over thirty years, was the authority on Spain of the *New York Times*, and whose books on the Civil War profoundly influenced public opinion. In 1957, he claimed that Negrín had "made a mark on Spanish history of which future generations will have a reason to be proud,"[18] and, in 1973, he wrote: "Dr. Negrín used and worked with the Communists simply for practical reasons which had nothing to do with 'leftism' or any ideology. He had no political coloration or preference for any political party as such."[19] Since the historiography of Spanish Republican politics has been so skewed by Negrín's disciples in their attempts to raise him to the status of a national hero and conciliator, it must be recorded that Matthews's portrayal of the premier bears comparison with his portrayal of Fidel Castro in 1964: "The belief fostered by Washington and Cuban exiles that Fidel Castro is a prisoner of the Cuban Communist apparatus or a puppet of Moscow is a myth. He is, by character, incapable of accepting orders or even advice. . . . Now that five years have passed, it is surely time for American officials and the American public to realize that . . . he is one of the most extraordinary men of our age."[20]

My own judgment of Negrín, based on oral and written testimony garnered and digested over fifty years, is that he did more than any other politician, whether willingly or unwillingly, to extend and consolidate the influence of the Communist party in the vital centers of power—the army and the security services[21]—during the final year of the war. This does not imply that in all matters he was totally amenable to the PCE, but on the fundamental issue of armed power—on which the future political structure of the Spanish state depended—he allowed himself, as will be seen shortly, to be guided and directed by the Communist party. It is true that the party's control of Negrín did not extend into every sphere, for the PCE, appreciating his singular value as a moderate cover for its hegemonic aims, could not afford to alienate him by attempting to impose all of its proposals.

One of the important witnesses to the control that the PCE exercised over Negrín was Enrique Castro—a subcommissar general of war in 1938—whose informative and deeply introspective memoir *Hombres made in Moscú*,[22] from which I have quoted previously, is one of the most valuable books on the Civil

War in its treatment of some of the nonparty men upon whose innocence, ignorance, connivance, or plain good will the PCE was able to build its immense
power. Castro's account of the premier and defense minister is therefore worth
recalling. While acknowledging that in the early stages of his tenure of the
premiership and defense ministry Negrín "appeared excessively considerate toward the old timers [in the Socialist and Republican parties] who embodied the
old methods," Castro nevertheless affirms that the premier was controlled by the
Communist party, "by the party directly and by two of his closest collaborators: a
certain Benigno [Rodríguez], who was director of *Milicia Popular*, the organ of
the Fifth Regiment, and [Manuel] Sánchez Arcas, a good architect, marvellous
person, blindly obedient to the party, who occupied the undersecretaryship of
propaganda."[23] According to Antonio Cordón whom, as will be seen shortly,
Negrín elevated to the undersecretaryship of the army and who was a faithful
member of the PCE until his death in 1969, Sánchez Arcas was "enthusiastically
supported in his work by Benigno Rodríguez, who directed the political department linked to the prime minister's office."[24] Furthermore, as mentioned in an
earlier chapter, Benigno Rodríguez was made political secretary of Negrín "on
party orders," and, in the words of Cordón, the prime minister "appreciated
Benigno's great merit, his talent, his enormous capacity for work, his unshakeable enthusiasm and always showed him, even after the war, great affection and
consideration."[25]

It was precisely because the premier was so closely shepherded by his Communist entourage that Comintern delegate Palmiro Togliatti, who had expressed
doubts regarding Negrín's reliability in a memo to Moscow on 25 November
1937—describing him as a "man without scruples"[26]—affirmed categorically in a
report on 21 May 1939 that the second Negrín government "*was undoubtedly the
one that collaborated most closely with the leadership of the Communist party
and accepted and implemented more fully and more rapidly than any other the
proposals of the party.*"[27]

Despite this tribute, Togliatti was not entirely satisfied with the premier's
performance, for, in the same report, he criticized his "disorganization," even his
moral conduct—"a bohemian not without a sign of depravity (women)" and
likened his style of work to that of "an undisciplined intellectual."[28] This description of Negrín by the leading representative of the Comintern in Spain is compatible with what non-Communists, who were well acquainted with him, have said
about his eating and working habits. With regard to the latter, Julián Zugazagoitia, who became general secretary of the defense ministry under Negrín, states
that official papers would pile up without receiving attention and that during the
premier's trips, his private secretaries would follow him with "seven suitcases
bursting with files. . . . They came and went, upstairs and downstairs, without
his finding the time or being in the mood to open them. The irregularity of his
hours further complicated things."[29] As to Negrín's gargantuan eating habits,
which Prieto and others have colorfully described, Justo Martínez Amutio, the
left Socialist leader, says that Soviet agents were aware quite early in the war of

Negrín's love of "feasts"—often converted into "wild parties." "They had sized him up," he alleges, "and began to 'work on' him in order to use him in their plans."[30] In any event, there can be little doubt that he dissipated his energy on personal indulgence that undermined his capacity for work.

In his report of 21 May 1939, Togliatti criticizes Negrín for tolerating, in the economic life of the country, especially in the area of foreign trade, "the presence of a series of thieves, speculators, and saboteurs" and for denying the Communists positions of decision important in the economic field.[31] This refusal may conceivably have had the direct support of Stalin, who may have preferred to deal with Negrín through his commercial representatives, such as Arthur Stashevsky, rather than subject his clandestine transactions to the scrutiny of the Spanish Communist party.[32] Togliatti also criticized Negrín for his weakness in dealing with the Socialist leadership, inspired, as he stated, "by ever increasing hostility to the Communist party." The leadership of the PCE, he pointed out, "always attempted to encourage Negrín to overcome difficulties by taking the leadership of his party into his own hands and to collaborate more closely with the unions of the UGT . . . , but Negrín, an intellectual by nature, not having participated actively in the life of his party, never agreed to follow this course."[33] As a result, he resolved problems by making "continual concessions . . . to those whom he knew were his enemies and who defended mistaken policies."[34]

How genuine or accurate were these complaints? It is hard to say with assurance, for it is evident from Togliatti's reports to Moscow that he never failed to present himself in the best possible light even at the expense of the two other Comintern delegates—Vittorio Codovila and Boris Stefanov—and of the PCE itself.[35] At all events, from his long report of 21 May 1939, there emerges a picture of Negrín that reveals a man pushed and pulled by conflicting emotions, by his desire to accommodate the Communist party—"the only party that supported [him] loyally"[36] and to which, he affirmed, "he owed a debt of honor"[37]—and by his fear of totally alienating the Socialist executive.

Antonio Cordón—who denies, as have most loyal Communists and sympathizers for half a century, that Negrín was in any way controlled by the party—stresses the fact that the premier was afraid of being called a "philo-Communist" and that this fear acted as "a brake on his behavior."[38] This is no doubt true. In a report to Moscow, dated 21–22 April 1938, Togliatti refers to attacks upon Negrín as an agent of the Communists. "The Socialists, the Republicans and the CNT," he stated, "pose grave difficulties for Negrín. He is accused of being a Communist agent and any proposal to appoint forceful men to posts of maximum responsibility is opposed. Any forceful man anxious to work in order to win the war is called a Communist. . . . The result: delay in the solution of elementary problems, a week to accomplish things that could be achieved in 24 hours. The party insists on a more rapid pace, but it has to take the situation into account and cannot force matters."[39] There can be little doubt that Negrín's fear of being labeled a philo-Communist and of breaking with the Socialist leadership explains why he appeared to Cordón and others "who had the opportunity to observe him closely, strong in most cases in his conception and explanation of the correct slogans, but weak, in not a few cases, in their application."[40]

To be sure, the Communists would have preferred a man after their own heart, whose very life and soul revolved around the party, but their policy required both a moderate and a Socialist—at least in name. They had raised Negrín from relative obscurity to national and international prominence, and despite his "weaknesses," they did not hesitate to support and extol him as long as he furthered their primary objective: the control of the army and the security services. Not that they had any choice in the matter, for there was not a Socialist of distinction who could meet their requirements and adequately replace him. As the Communist commander of the Sixth Army Corps, Ignacio Gallego, confirms: "There was no other man in the Socialist party—and he had to come from the Socialist party—who could lead the government. As an alternative to Negrín, we never rejected any other candidate who we could say today offered better qualifications. I do not want to give names, but who was there? The only man who for a long time believed in victory and fought to achieve it was Negrín. That is why we supported him. Furthermore, he was loyal and his conduct clean."[41]

Even in 1945, six years after the Civil War, the Russians, according to Alvarez del Vayo, the premier's indefatigable supporter, "still held him in great esteem." "Some months earlier," he added, "I talked with Oumansky, the very intelligent and charming Soviet ambassador to Mexico. . . . He made it clear that in Moscow no one thought anyone could replace Negrín [as head of a government in lieu of General Franco]. I got the same impression in San Francisco when I had dinner with Manuilski [former head of the Comintern]. . . . His opinion on Spanish affairs was carefully heeded in Moscow. Manuilski expressed himself in the most laudatory terms about Negrín."[42]

During the Second World War, Ivan Maisky, the Soviet ambassador in London, was on intimate terms with Negrín, who was then living in emigration in England. "He had taken a very pleasant English country house at Bovingdon, not far from London," the ambassador recalls, "with its own garden, vegetable allotment, outhouses and even an English manservant, who had been left there by the owner of the house." Negrín suggested that Maisky and his wife be his guests on weekends. "We did, in fact, try at the following weekend and were most satisfied. Thereafter Bovingdon became our regular resting-place on weekends."[43] Negrín had arrived in England from France on 25 June 1940 during the German invasion, accompanied by other Spaniards including Francisco Méndez Aspe, his former finance minister, and Benigno Rodríguez, his Communist political secretary.[44] He had been granted permission "for a visit of not more than three weeks and subject to the proviso that he should not indulge in any political activities while here."[45] Sir Samuel Hoare, the British ambassador to Spain, and the Foreign Office were seriously concerned over relations with General Franco and were fearful that Negrín might remain in England and engage in political activity hostile to the Nationalist regime.[46] Maisky did his best to extend Negrín's stay. In a conversation with R. A. Butler, parliamentary undersecretary of state at the Foreign Office on 25 July 1940, Maisky said that "he trusted that Dr. Negrín would not have to leave for America—he thought that this would be deplorable." On the memorandum recording the conversation, there is a handwritten comment signed "B," presumably Butler, stating that since the Soviet government was not doing anything to help, "M. Maisky's intervention was rather impertinent." There is also a handwritten comment by S. Williams, private secretary to Alexander Cadogan, permanent undersecretary at the Foreign Office, observing: "It is a pity Sr. Negrín cannot be persuaded to go to Russia where he should be welcome."[47] Nevertheless, Maisky's intervention must have carried considerable weight, for, thanks to the protests by some leftist leaders alerted by the Soviet ambassador, Negrín was allowed to remain in England after his application for a U.S. visa was rejected on 20 July by Franklin D. Roosevelt, who was no doubt concerned about alienating conservative Catholic voters in the approaching presidential elections.[48]

Despite Negrín's value to Moscow and the PCE during the Civil War and his friendly relations with the Soviet ambassador, it would be a mistake to argue that during the Spanish conflict he blithely offered his services to Moscow and that he did nothing to preserve a measure of political independence for himself. He was a pragmatist who believed that the war was lost without Soviet arms and that eventually Paris and London would be forced to intervene in defense of their own interests.[49] But the question must be asked, How far was he willing to yield to Communist pressure in order to secure Soviet aid? It would also be a mistake to argue that he had no apprehension or qualms of conscience about the role he was playing, for he had willfully contributed to the destruction of the two leading Socialists in Spain and to the virtual prostration of his own party as well as to that of the entire opposition upon which any form of democratic system depended. If he had any knowledge at all of the fate of so many of those who had served the Kremlin, he could not but envision the possibility that one day, as his friend Vidarte put it to him, he too might be "sacrificed to the Moloch of Stalin." "Do you imagine that this odious servitude does not weigh upon me as heavily as anyone else?" Negrín retorted. "But there is no other course. When I speak to our friends in France, I hear only promises and fine words. . . . Our only course, no matter how painful it may be, is to accept the help of the USSR or surrender unconditionally. The [Socialist] party cannot count on me for unconditional surrender. . . . I will not deliver hundreds of thousands of defenseless Spaniards who are fighting heroically for the Republic so that Franco may enjoy the pleasure of shooting them."[50]

That Negrín may have genuinely believed that he had been cast by history to play a heroic role as the "savior of Spain" is suggested by his emotional outburst after the bombing of the Catalan town of Granollers. "The whole town," writes Zugazagoitia, "was spattered with blood and strewn with human remains. The prime minister, who witnessed the spectacle, does not conceal his emotions from me. He speaks of the orphaned children who run through the streets stealing in order to live. He falls silent and looks at the garden. His eyes are shining, moist with tears." Then, according to Zugazagoitia, Negrín soliloquized:

It is terrible, terrible!

What deep suffering this discharge of duty causes me. I have to conceal it from others, because, for them, I have to be the motivating force, the animator, the spur. But, on whom can I lean? I can only reveal my weakness to you. How terrible it all is, especially as I have arrived at the conviction that everyone, absolutely everyone, Socialists, Communists, Republicans, Falangists, Francoists, all of them, are equally contemptible. If it were just a matter of a fight among themselves I would voluntarily step aside, because none of their disputes is worth the sacrifice of a single life. But it is a matter of Spain! Of Spain! I very much fear that it will end up being dismembered by the European powers in a final diplomatic deal thanks to our stupidity, because we regard ourselves as Basques, Catalans, Galicians, Valencians. This fear gives me strength. If I did not believe that I must oppose the disappearance of Spain I would have ceased asking for sacrifices some time ago and resigned with great pleasure. The spectacle of those children in Granollers, so common these days, destroys me morally.

Still, we must go on fighting![51]

It is possible that Negrín did indeed believe that in enduring his "odious servitude" he was pursuing the only honorable course open to him, since Largo Caballero and Prieto had also accepted Soviet aid and made concessions. But what distinguished him from his predecessors was the degree to which he was willing, in order to secure that aid, to contribute to the growth of the Communists' power and eventual enthronement of their party. Was Negrín so ingenuous that he was not aware of this possibility? Largo Caballero and Prieto were certainly aware of it when they fought to depoliticize the army.

In his report to Moscow of 21 May 1939, Togliatti gives Negrín credit for having changed the military policy of Prieto "in accordance with the requirements of the party."[52] Among the important changes mentioned by Togliatti were the "maximum reinforcement" of the party's positions in the army and the "revaluation" of the political commissariat of war.[53] Prieto's blunt accusation, shortly after the war, that Negrín had pursued an "insensate policy of assuring the military predominance of a single party"[54] is bolstered not only by Togliatti's recognition of Negrín's services in reversing Prieto's policy but by the markedly political nature of Negrín's appointments as soon as he took charge of the defense ministry—appointments that were made in spite of the demand by the Socialist leadership that it supervise "all appointments made by him in the army and in the ministries."[55] For example, he elevated Antonio Cordón, whom Prieto had removed as chief of staff of the eastern army because of his political activity, to the undersecretaryship of the army,[56] which was the most important subordinate position in the defense ministry; he promoted Carlos Núñez Maza, air force chief of staff, to the undersecretaryship of air[57] and appointed Pedro Prados to the post of navy chief of staff—all three members of the PCE.[58] True, in order to placate the Socialist party, he elevated Alfonso Játiva to the undersecretaryship of the navy[59] and retained Bruno Alonso as chief political commissar of the fleet—both confirmed Socialists. On 21 May 1939, Togliatti reported to Moscow: "In spite of the proposals [regarding the navy] made to Negrín by the party and approved by him . . . nothing was done until January [1939] and [even then] the reorganization of the naval command was inadequate. The [political] commissariat of the navy remained in the hands of a Socialist (Bruno Alonso), a bitter enemy of the resistance policy and one of those mainly responsible for the inactivity of the fleet during the war."[60] This tolerance by Negrín of Socialists in key positions in the navy was a prime example of what Togliatti had in mind when he informed Moscow that Negrín's concessions caused him "to make many wrong decisions and to compromise between the Communists' wise proposals and the demands of our adversaries."[61]

But, aside from the navy, the PCE had the situation in the defense ministry well in hand. Carlos Núñez Maza, the air force undersecretary, and Antonio Cordón, the army undersecretary, were two of the most trusted members of the party. Zugazagoitia, who was assigned the purely decorative post of secretary general of national defense as a sop to the Socialist leadership, says of Cordón: "His unpopularity outside the circle of his coreligionists was immense. Rarely did an officer visit me who did not display his absolute disagreement with the undersecretary, accusing him of tireless and tenacious political proselytism.[62] . . . The argument against his Communist fanaticism made no impression on Negrín, who regarded the Communists as his best allies. When he weighed their defects against their virtues, he found the latter more abundant than the former."[63] Such was the confidence that Negrín reposed in Cordón that, according to the undersecretary's own testimony, Negrín delegated to him the resolution "of the largest possible number of matters relating to the army with the exception of executive orders that required his signature or questions of *political importance on which I considered he should be consulted.*"[64]

Furthermore, Eleuterio Díaz Tendero, ousted by Prieto from the vital information and control department, reappeared as head of the personnel section of the defense ministry,[65] to which the department of information and control was made subordinate.[66] At the head of this department stood Manuel Estrada, a party member, who had been removed in the spring of 1937 by Largo Caballero from his post as chief of the central general staff.[67] Díaz Tendero, it will be recalled, had belonged to the Junta de Mandos, which made recommendations to the defense minister regarding officer promotions and appointments and over which the pro-Communist chief of the central general staff, Vicente Rojo, exercised the maximum authority. As head of the personnel section—with information at his fingertips on the political antecedents and present political persuasion of every officer in the army—Díaz Tendero resumed his crucial role in the Junta de Mandos.

Rojo, Cordón, Estrada, and Díaz Tendero were now able—with the blessing of Negrín—to make whatever appointments and promotions served the interests of the Communist party. As Jesús Pérez Salas, Cordón's predecessor in the undersecretaryship of the army and in the Junta de Mandos, affirms in his much-neglected memoir, "all the positions necessary to carry out the reorganization of the army were occupied by Communists."[68]

With the immense power of the undersecretaryship of the army in their hands, the Communists were soon able to recoup the positions they had lost under Prieto and to enhance their predominance in the army. A tactic particularly exasperating to non-Communists that was used to ensure the rapid promotion of party members and their friends was employed by Cordón as soon as he took possession of the undersecretaryship. This tactic involved the notices for tests for admission to the officers' training schools (*convocatorias*). The dates of these examinations were published in the *Diario Oficial del Ministerio de Defensa Nacional*, and priority was given to all frontline combatants. "But before the notices were published," writes the Anarchosyndicalist historian José Peirats, "the Communist brigades were alerted by the party so that aspirants could prepare themselves in advance. Normally, the *Diario Oficial* arrived late at the front. As a result, the non-Communist combatants always made their applications late. This maneuver was the work of Antonio Cordón."[69]

Peirats also cites an example of how rapidly the Communists and their supporters were able to advance their military careers: During the month of May 1938, 1,280 promotions (corporals, sergeants, lieutenants, captains, and commissars of all ranks) were made in the Twenty-seventh Division, formerly the Carlos Marx Division, commanded by José del Barrio, a PSUC member. "The men who were newly promoted were posted to vacancies in other divisions, brigades, and battalions. . . . In this way, the Communists conquered new positions in the Anarchist, Socialist, Republican, and non-party units."[70]

Because of the unfettered authority of the undersecretaryship of the army, it is not surprising that, according to an unpublished report by the military section of the peninsular committee of the FAI, dated 30 September 1938, 5,500 of the 7,000 promotions since May 1938 involved members of the PCE.[71] Nor is it surprising that the CNT, which commanded 8 of the 52 divisions of the Popular Army in November 1937,[72] controlled only 9 out of a total of 70 in September 1938.[73] Hence, Jesús Hernández's claim that, in the spring of 1938, the Communists held 70 percent of the commanding positions in the army seems reasonable enough.[74] "Proselytism by means of corruption, cajolery, promotions, favors, and coercion of all kinds, even in the trenches," testifies Diego Abad de Santillán, "created an atmosphere of resentment and decomposition that weakened the combativity and efficiency of the military apparatus."[75]

As for the larger units that comprised the Popular Army, data provided by the official Communist history of the Civil War reveals that in the winter of 1938–39 eight of the seventeen army corps (including the Agrupación Toral) in the central-southern region had Communist commanders while five of the remainder had Communist commissars in charge of their political orientation.[76] In other words, thirteen of these seventeen units were under the direct military command or political control of the PCE. In addition, the four army corps of the Army of the

Ebro in eastern Spain were commanded by Communists—José del Barrio, Enrique Líster, Manuel Tagüeña, and Etelvino Vega.

No less alarming to the Anarchosyndicalists than the PCE's overwhelming predominance in the military commands was its attempt to destroy the homogeneity of their combat forces by transferring CNT members to other units. "[CNT affiliates] were deliberately separated from the army corps and divisions to which they had always belonged," testifies Peirats. "The integrity of the large Anarchist units obstructed the hegemonic aims of the Communist party."[77] On 26 June 1938, an unpublished report issued by the military secretary of the FAI charged that it had "irrefutable proof" that the PCE was systematically persecuting CNT combatants, using every possible weapon, including the weapon of "assassination employed in the midst of [military] operations."[78] It also charged that the Communist party used calumny and denunciation with the help of "unconditional supporters" in the military tribunals and that Vicente Rojo, the chief of the central general staff, assigned positions of command in the CNT units in accordance with orders received from the Communist party.[79]

Especially infuriating to the Anarchosyndicalists (and to all those who opposed the Communists) was the treatment they received in the field hospitals, which were now mainly administered by the PCE, thanks to Dr. Juan Planelles, a party member, who was appointed director general of health, when Juan Negrín took over the defense ministry.[80] Personal physician to Largo Caballero at the beginning of the war, Planelles rose to prominence when he became the chief medical officer of the Communist Fifth Regiment in 1936, then undersecretary of health in May 1937.[81] In 1938, he was named chief medical officer of the Army of the Center,[82] comprising four army corps, to which he appointed, in the words of Alfredo Nistal, a CNT political commissar, "a plethora of subordinate civilian personnel, who belonged either in their entirety or in their immense majority, to the Communist party."[83]

We have already seen that one of the manifold complaints of the left Socialists during the first year of the war was the preferential treatment given in the hospitals to members of the PCE. Their testimony is worth repeating. "[In] some hospitals," testifies Largo Caballero, "just as the priests and nuns had once acted toward noncommunicants, non-Communists were not taken care of. They were neither treated properly nor fed properly; all the attention was given to Communist party members and future converts."[84] And Carlos Rubiera, the left Socialist Cortes deputy for Madrid, declared: "[In] the [military] hospitals the same thing goes on as in the days of the nuns, when, in order to get a stew or chicken, or whatever there was, you had to wear and venerate the scapular or the cross. Now you need the hammer and sickle."[85]

To judge from an unpublished document of the CNT and FAI, comprising five separate reports, the situation had deteriorated since the previous year. "THE WORST THING," stressed one of the reports, dated 8 July 1938, "IS THE LARGE NUMBER OF MEN WHO DIE FROM THE NEGLIGENCE, INCOMPETENCE OR BREACH OF

TRUST ON THE PART OF THE STAFF. WE HAVE SEEN SHAMEFUL CASES . . . THAT AROUSE FEARS OF DELIBERATE AND PREMEDITATED SABOTAGE." After listing a series of inexplicable deaths, the report continued: "We, who have a heart, who possess a high sense of moral responsibility, cannot permit such cases to recur. Our soldiers are too valuable to remain at the mercy of elements who can kill with absolute impunity."[86]

In a brief preamble to the five reports, the document fulminated against the PCE: "Enormous is the record of crimes committed by the Communist Party of Spain. . . . Can anyone conceive of assassinating the wounded, of trafficking politically with the sick, the wounded, and the maimed? Can even the basest human being imagine that directors, doctors, nurses, etc. in the hospitals, acting on the orders of the party, pay more attention to the membership cards of the wounded than to their injuries? Well, one of the most brutal and despicable episodes is occurring in this very area. In the health services, this policy of the Communists has reached unimaginable proportions."[87]

The rancor prevailing among the Anarchosyndicalists and left-wing Socialists, although silenced by the press censorship and by the seizure in 1937 of the entire left Socialist press, was expressed in the unpublished reports and circulars issued by the FAI for the internal consumption of the movement. In a circular dated 13 July, the secretariat of the peninsular committee excoriated the entire work of the PCE in the army: "Aided by Russian blackmail, a party composed of upstarts, cleverly manipulated by the emissaries of the Bolshevik government, has taken control of the war, of the appointment of officers, and the organization of the army. Officers have been selected on the basis of their readiness to accept a Communist party membership card. Only these pliable individuals have been able to stay afloat, to obtain promotions, to receive considerations and commanding positions far exceeding their ability. . . . Meanwhile, many individuals of merit have either been jailed or deprived of their commands, criminally accused of irresponsibility, or kept in positions where their talents are neglected."[88]

Nor were the moderate Socialists less concerned. At a gathering of centrist leaders in Negrín's residence in March 1938, shortly before the removal of Prieto, Communist behavior was denounced as intolerable. "Negrín tried to belittle the importance of the matter," Prieto told the national committee of the Socialist party a year later. "However, comrade Zugazagoitia, in a display of sincerity, exclaimed: 'Don Juan, let us take off our masks. Our comrades are being assassinated at the fronts because they refuse to accept membership cards in the Communist party.' "[89]

Hence, when Negrín became defense minister in April, he was fully aware of the rankling resentment and hostility of the Socialists and felt compelled to make concessions. But some of these concessions, which were undoubtedly made with the acquiescence of the PCE, were pure make-believe. As part of the entire panoply of fraud and dissimulation designed to placate the Socialists and Republicans, Negrín appointed Bibiano Fernández Ossorio y Tafall, officially a member of Izquierda Republicana, to the key post of general commissar of war,[90] which had been held by Julio Alvarez del Vayo until his replacement in November 1937 by Antonio Crescenciano Bilbao, a Prietista.[91] A Cortes deputy and undersecretary of the interior at the outbreak of the Civil War, later director of the left Republican organ *Política* in Madrid and elected secretary general of Izquierda Republicana in November 1936,[92] Ossorio y Tafall was now a fair-weather ally of the Communists.[93] And it was to them, rather than to Negrín, that he owed his new appointment. When the party asked Enrique Castro, at that time subcommissar general of organization in the General Commissariat of War, whether he could suggest someone who could serve the Communists "as scrupulously as 'Don Julio' " and if he knew Ossorio, he replied:

"I think he is a faker and a womanizer. No. He won't be an obstacle to us. It's simply a matter of satisfying his vices and weaknesses."

"Then go with [Francisco] Antón to see him. He should accept, *but it should be made clear to him that he owes his assignment to the party*."

And they left to see Señor Ossorio y Tafall, who at that time was secretary of Izquierda Republicana. They found him in his office. He received them warmly, affecting the airs of an important personage. As they watched him, the others laughed to themselves. . . .

"Do you think I can be of use?"

"You can rely on our help."

A few days later Bibiano Ossorio y Tafall arrived at the Commissariat of War. . . . He was never an obstacle. He knew who had made him what he was. It was only necessary to remind him from time to time, because in those days the Republicans, beginning with don Manuel Azaña, were nothing more than a Republican decoration in a situation that had very little Republican about it.[94]

In addition to the sham appointment of Ossorio y Tafall, Negrín attempted to appease the Socialist leadership by creating a few high-sounding positions in the military apparatus for members of the executive. He named Zugazagoitia to the post of secretary general of the ministry of national defense "to coordinate and administer"[95] the services of the three undersecretaryships and appointed Francisco Cruz Salido, also a leading member of the executive, to assist him. Cordón at first suspected that Zugazagoitia would become "the watchful eye of Prieto," but Negrín reassured him, "with a few pats on the back," that the post was "in practice an honorary one with very slim possibilities for any effective action."[96] This, of course, was true because the two most important undersecretaryships were held by Cordón and Núñez Maza, who obeyed only the mandate of the PCE.

Negrín also appointed Manuel Albar, another prominent member of the Socialist executive and one of Prieto's close friends, as "special delegate" to coordinate the various branches of the General Commissariat of War,[97] a purely nominal post without any substantive authority in practice. In a polemical letter to Prieto after the war, Negrín laid stress on these three appointments as examples of his impartiality in selecting non-Communists for high office and claimed with regard to the post of secretary general of the ministry of national defense that its influence on administrative and political functions was "very obvious and not exactly favorable to the Communist party."[98]

Prieto replied by listing the names of well-known Communists to whom Negrín had assigned the top positions in the army, air force, and the police.[99] "The facts are most eloquent," he rejoined. "And the strength of those facts is not destroyed by the names of Julián Zugazagoitia, Manuel Albar, and Francisco Cruz Salido, with which you try to shield yourself, because these comrades did not discharge any effective functions with which to counteract Communist predominance in the smallest degree. You kept them there as decorative figures."[100]

Zugazagoitia's purely symbolic role was obvious to him from the outset. "I went to greet Zugazagoitia," Cordón writes. "He received me affably and offered to help me in my work, although he could not see very well how he could do so." Cruz Salido was not so humble. "The factotum in the general secretaryship," Cordón notes, "was Cruz Salido, who could not avoid putting an anti-Communist stamp on everything he said or did." Cordón refused to tolerate this interference and informed Negrín. "I explained the circumstances in detail. Negrín agreed with me and told me to placate Zugazagoitia, so as to avoid political complications, seeing that the secretary general had expressed his desire to tender his resignation." Zugazagoitia told Cordón that he was thinking of resigning "because he did not understand how the undersecretaryships functioned and believed that his post was purely nominal." Cordón then requested him not to create "new difficulties" for the prime minister. "I don't know whether my visit influenced him or not . . . , but the matter was resolved and he continued to exercise his functions as theoretically as always until the loss of Catalonia [in February 1939]."[101]

Although Zugazagoitia retained his sterile post, he made no secret of his sense of impotence. "You have no idea how bored I am," he wrote to the Socialist executive in December 1938. "When I wish to learn something about the war, I have to buy a newspaper or ask a friend."[102] And after the war he wrote, "Neither my presence in the general secretaryship nor the post itself made the slightest sense."[103]

Then why did Zugazagoitia endure this self-abasement? Colonel Pérez Salas writes: "It is incomprehensible why Zugazagoitia tolerated such a humiliating situation. It was not a question of vanity . . . , because for someone who had been a minister until recently, the post was more in the nature of a demotion. His reason was undoubtedly to avoid creating problems for Negrín." Then peering more deeply into the heart of the matter, he observes: "Intoxicated by holding in his hands the reins of political and military power, Negrín thought that he had been chosen by the gods to save Spain. . . . Confronted with this danger, the Socialist and Republican parties became alarmed. . . . Everyone believed that if Negrín were removed by the President of the Republic or by a vote of no confidence in the Cortes, a coup d'état would follow in which the premier would rely on the armed forces, whose Communist officers supported him almost in their entirety. Only because of this belief can the submissiveness of the parties and [Cortes] deputies, who acknowledged, sotto voce, the false course of the Republic, be explained."[104]

56

Communist Ascendancy in the Security Services

*I*n the spring and summer of 1938, the power of Juan Negrín and his Communist promoters reached its apogee. If it is true, as Colonel Jesús Pérez Salas affirms, that the quiescence of the Republican and Socialist parties was due to the fear that the removal of Negrín would trigger a coup backed by the Communist-controlled units of the army;[1] if it is true, as Prieto informed the Socialist executive, that Azaña "no longer had any freedom to change republican policy, because all the military commands were cornered by the Communists and they would resist,"[2] it is no less true that this fear was compounded by the dread of the SIM, the Military Investigation Service.

Although the SIM's official functions were "to combat espionage, prevent acts of sabotage and carry out duties of investigation and vigilance *within the armed forces*,"[3] the investigation service, under the guiding hand of NKVD chief Alexander Orlov,[4] soon invaded the entire fabric of the left camp. "[The] fearsome police of the Military Investigation Service, organized by the 'tovarich,'" writes Jesús Hernández, "was omnipotent. Politicians and magistrates, soldiers and generals trembled before it. An accusation that a person was suspect or hostile to the regime would strike him like lightning. Without an attorney willing to assume the risk of defending him, he could be assassinated in a dungeon or riddled with bullets in a ditch."[5]

A carefully researched account of the SIM's extralegal activities is furnished by José Peirats, the Anarchosyndicalist historian and active participant in the Civil War. The SIM, he attests, was a police network that operated not only in all the units of the army, large and small, but also kept a close watch on the activities of the members. "The government departments themselves were honeycombed by the SIM. At the battle fronts, the agents who were located at various levels of the military hierarchy had as much authority as or even more authority than the political commissars and commanders. . . . In the rear, the agents of the SIM were feared by the secret police itself. Behind each visible agent, there stood an invisible one, keeping watch over him."[6] And on another occasion he stated that the SIM's espionage activity within other organizations was so "complete" that their agreements and plans were immediately transmitted to the politburo.[7]

As we have seen, Indalecio Prieto at first resisted Orlov's "insistent requests" that he be allowed to organize a military investigation service but finally yielded on the understanding that the NKVD chief "would supply only advisers who would furnish the know-how."[8] We have also seen that although Prieto had made the appointment of all chiefs, inspectors, and agents his exclusive prerogative,[9] Gustavo Durán, the chief of the Madrid zone, named hundreds of Communist agents without consulting him[10] and that after the defense minister dismissed the offending chief and refused to reinstate him, Orlov later claimed that he recalled his advisers and that they had "nothing more to do with the SIM."[11] This was false, for, as previously noted, Gabriel Morón, the director general of security at the time, testifies that "the SIM, like everything else [including his own department] fell under the CAMOUFLAGED control of our good Russian friends."[12] Moreover, Santiago Garcés Arroyo, who was made subchief of the SIM by Negrín in April 1938, after the fall of Prieto, acknowledges the presence of Russian advisers in the service, specifically, Orlov and Belayev.[13]

Prieto's inability to control the SIM was due not only to the enrollment of a large number of Communists and fellow travelers who had previously belonged to the various intelligence units and police squads improvised at the beginning of the Revolution but to his failure to find a reliable man with some expertise to head the service. First, he appointed Angel Díaz Baza, a Socialist and personal friend, who proved incompetent,[14] then Prudencio Sayagües, a Republican, who remained only two months in office,[15] and, finally, Lieutenant Colonel Manuel Uribarry, a Socialist and former member of the Civil Guard, who ended up betraying him, escaping to Cuba—allegedly with money and jewels.[16] Prieto told the national committee of the Socialist party in 1938 that Uribarry was a "Socialist of long standing," who at first served him loyally and who rejected the invitation of Orlov's "lieutenant" to consult "directly and constantly with him" without the knowledge of the defense minister. However, Prieto asserted, Uribarry, "whose mental instability had increased because of his enormous responsibilities as head of the SIM—in which he worked four to five days on end without sleep—changed his behavior and came to terms with the people who had asked him to work with them behind my back."[17]

Some authors have speculated that Uribarry may have been manipulated or trapped by the Communists, who wished to get rid of him.[18] This may not be inconsistent with claims by Uribarry's friends in the SIM, according to an unpublished report by the CNT-FAI, dated 6 June 1938, that he fled Spain for reasons of "personal safety after he discovered that the Unified Socialist Youth had carried out several fraudulent operations amounting to twenty-two million pesetas."[19] Furthermore, he appears to have attempted to remove the Communists from the SIM.[20] In any event, his departure opened the way for the promotion of the former Prieto Socialist and baker by trade, Santiago Garcés Arroyo, the subchief of the SIM who (at the age of twenty-two) became provisional head (*jefe acciden-*

tal) of the organization after the flight of Uribarry.[21] Since no permanent chief was ever appointed, Garcés's "provisional" appointment became permanent, and he remained at the headship of the SIM until the end of the war. In a letter to the Spanish historian Heleno Saña, dated 20 October 1974, Santiago Garcés stated that he was appointed to head the SIM by Negrín to keep him informed on the activities of "Prieto's creatures" in the SIM and to "improve" its operation,"[22] although he told D. Pastor Petit, the well-known Catalan writer and authority on Spanish intelligence operations, that he was reluctant to accept the position as he was "allergic" to everything relating to police work. "I did all I could," he said, "not to assume the headship of the SIM and explained my attitude to the official and private 'entourage' of Dr. Negrín, but without success." Only as a result of a private interview with the premier, he claimed, was he persuaded to take the post.[23]

His appointment was a boon for the NKVD, for, according to José Muñóz López, whose invaluable testimony I have cited on several occasions, Garcés, officially a Socialist, had already been inducted unofficially into the service of the PCE.[24] In later years, while retaining an unswerving loyalty to Negrín, he expressed hostility for the Russians and the Spanish Communists as demonstrated in an interview he gave to Heleno Saña in Mexico in 1974,[25] but it goes without saying that during the war he could not have held his pivotal position without their backing. Saña, who met Garcés several times in connection with his interview and whose judgment I respect, comments in a letter to me: "[Garcés] was above all a Negrinista and a crypto-Communist only to the extent that Negrín pursued a policy favorable to the Communists. When I knew him and dealt with him [in 1974] nothing remained of this alleged crypto-Communism. His declarations were unequivocal in this regard."[26]

A captain of the carabineers (Negrín's favored police corps) and a devotee of the premier, Garcés asserted when interviewed by Saña that during the war Negrín "paid no attention to the PCE" and usually spoke disparagingly of the Communists. "On the other hand [Negrín] got along very well with the Russian political leader in Spain, Arthur Stashevsky [officially the Soviet trade envoy, who was involved with Negrín in the massive gold shipment to Russia] and ate with him every day." Garcés also stated that he was present at many of the meals.[27] If this is true, then we must infer that his close association with Negrín long antedated his appointment as head of the SIM, since Stashevsky was recalled to Russia and disappeared in mid-1937, long before Garcés was made subchief and provisional head of the SIM (April 1938). In his letter to me, Saña expressed the opinion that the pharmacologist Dr. Rafael Méndez—an intimate of Negrín's and director general of carabineers from May to September 1937,[28] who had made Garcés a captain in the corps and also his personal adjutant—was the "connecting thread" that led to the promotion of Garcés and to his role as "one of Negrín's men of confidence."[29] In the CNT-FAI archives in the International Institute of Social History in Amsterdam, there is an interesting document, dated 27 June 1938, alleging that Méndez (who was made undersecretary of the interior by Negrín in

April 1938) was responsible for the promotion of Garcés to his high office and intended to keep him there so as to be able to control the SIM.[30]

After Garcés replaced Uribarry, the SIM distinguished itself by silencing all criticism of the Negrín government. As Colonel Pérez Salas, whom I have often cited, confirms: "The Military Investigation Service, grossly violating its mission, possessed a network of secret agents charged with spying on all persons who dared to speak ill of the prime minister and of the way the war was going. They were arrested as opponents of the regime. Serious criticism, which very often is constructive and even necessary, was absolutely forbidden and civil liberties, even though certain restrictions are required in time of war, were totally abolished."[31] In other words, the rights of free expression, public assembly, and protection from arbitrary arrest, search, and seizure were suspended. Few could believe that these rights would ever be restored.

The SIM was especially feared in Barcelona—where the Communist apparatus was strongest after the transfer of the government from Valencia in November 1937—and reached the peak of its power after the formation of the second Negrín administration in 1938. At that time, attests Pastor Petit, the SIM was "totally controlled by the PCE."[32] In Madrid, on the other hand, where Communist influence gradually declined after the transfer of the party leadership to Barcelona, Socialist strength in the various secret police departments, according to a confidential Communist report dated May 1938, was equal to that of the PCE. The report also stated that in all the departments, with the exception of the SIM, the relations between the Socialists and the Communists were generally cordial.[33] When Communist influence declined still further during the final months of the war, as we shall see later, owing to the general demoralization of the mass of the people, Angel Pedrero, the head of the SIM in the central zone and a member of the PSOE, who initially had collaborated with the PCE, distanced himself from the party and in March 1939 supported Colonel Casado's coup against Negrín and the Communists.[34]

Immediately after the war Negrín denied the existence of the SIM's secret prisons and torture chambers, or *checas*, as they were called, to Henry Buckley of the London *Daily Telegraph*, but admitted his "error" to the same journalist ten years later.[35] This is not to say that he personally sanctioned them, but there can be no doubt that through Garcés or Méndez he was aware of their existence and, for whatever motives, turned a blind eye to them. "The dungeons of the SIM," testifies José Peirats, "were sometimes concealed inside palatial mansions surrounded by formal gardens and railings. The Spanish people gave the name of 'checas' to all types of secret prisons. In the early days of the SIM, the checas were dark and gloomy, installed in old houses and convents. The system of torture was the classical brutal type: beatings with rubber piping followed by very cold showers, mock executions and other painful and bloody torments. The 'Russian advisers' modernized these old techniques. The new cells were smaller, painted in vivid colors with floors constructed with sharp tiles set on edge. . . . Recalcitrants were locked in a 'cold storage room' or 'a noise box' or tied to an 'electric chair.' . . . The prisoner was submerged in icy water hour after hour until he was ready to say what [his tormentors] wanted him to say."[36]

Not surprisingly, neither the PCE nor Santiago Garcés has ever publicly acknowledged the existence of the SIM's secret prisons and torture chambers, some of which were photographed by the Nationalists after they captured Barcelona in January 1939.[37] In two letters to Pastor Petit, dated 1 and 10 August 1977, Garcés claimed that he was unaware of their existence.[38] He also affirmed in the above-mentioned letter to Heleno Saña of 20 October 1974 that, as head of the SIM, he ordered the dissolution of the infamous interrogation committee (*comisión de interrogatorios*) headed by Alexander Orlov. He also makes the remarkable assertion that when he assumed control of the SIM, he expelled Orlov from Spain and gave Negrín an official typewritten memo on the matter, explaining that the NKVD chief was a "fanatical proselytizer" and "served no purpose" as his technical adviser. This, he claims, he was able to ascertain from the dozens of questions he asked Orlov on everything relating to the organization of the SIM.

It is just not plausible that Garcés expelled Orlov from Spain, for such a startling event could not have remained unpublicized and would have had serious repercussions. Had it occurred, it would soon have become common knowledge. In any event, Negrín would have used it to advantage in his postwar polemical exchanges with Prieto in which he employed every available argument to demonstrate his political impartiality and independence.[39] Furthermore, Garcés himself would certainly have boasted about it during his 35 years in exile in Mexico, before he wrote his letter to Saña in 1974,[40] and, once known, it would most assuredly have been used by every Negrín supporter and apologist thirsting for any scrap of evidence pointing to Negrín's political nonalignment. But there is no evidence, not even a hint of it, in the immense bibliography of the Civil War. Not until Saña revealed the purported expulsion to me in 1986, when I first corresponded with him, did I learn of Garcés's remarkable assertion. Hence, I am forced to conclude that the alleged episode is a product of Garcés's imagination.[41]

However, in all fairness, it is necessary to point out that in his political maneuverings Garcés attempted on at least one occasion to outwit the Russians. According to a memorandum in the CNT-FAI archives, dated 6 July 1938, he offered a post on an advisory committee to a member of the CNT—"possibly on the authority of the undersecretary of the interior, Méndez, to whom he owes everything"—with the proviso that the CNT representative sit on the committee as a member of one of the Republican parties so as to avoid arousing Russian "suspicions." It was clear, the memorandum added, that the "power of Moscow's intervention" was such that Garcés was forced "to have recourse to tricks of this kind in order to restrain it" and that "if his position as head of the SIM were stronger, he would impose his own rules." The fact that he could not act independently showed that he was "subject to foreign influence."[42] But it should be mentioned in passing that despite his maneuver, Garcés had no intention of giving any real power to the CNT and only intended to make use of it, for on 6 August another memorandum complained that "he insists on the idea of using CNT-FAI elements as common informers or executioners." This, said the memorandum, could not be permitted on any account. "Our comrades must enter the SIM legally and officially with all the rights and prerogatives enjoyed by other agents of the corps. We insist once again that it is absolutely essential to demand and obtain the resignation of this MULE Garcés."[43]

Although Garcés's maneuver to delude the Russians suggests that he may have chafed under Russian supervision and would have preferred a modicum of independence in dealing with the CNT, it by no means supports his assertion that he expelled Orlov from Spain. Indeed, it bears out the opposite conclusion that in his relations with the NKVD he acted cautiously, if not with extreme timidity.

According to his own testimony, Orlov defected to the United States on 13 August 1938, one month after leaving Barcelona, where he occupied a mansion with his staff up to 12 July.[44] Despite his departure, the torture chambers and tribunals continued to function at full throttle. Fortunately, the historian does not have to rely solely upon the evidence of POUMists, Anarchosyndicalists, and Nationalists to uncover the truth about the SIM's crimes; for, in the eyes of the Communists and their supporters, this evidence is too tainted to merit a place in the historiography of the Civil War. That the SIM, aided and abetted by the *tribunales especiales de guardia*—the special tribunals proposed by Negrín—was indeed guilty of heinous crimes even after Orlov's departure on 12 July is attested by moderate Republicans holding high office, whose denunciations of its transgressions cannot be easily dismissed.

The crimes committed by the SIM are amply confirmed by Manuel de Irujo, the representative of the moderate Basque Nationalist party in the government, who resigned on 11 August 1938.[45] In an acrimonious cabinet meeting the previous day, he described the kinds of torture practiced by agents of the SIM. He also condemned as "cruel and inhuman" the procedure of allowing weeks and months to elapse during which "hundreds and thousands of citizens" were separated from their families—"women from their husbands, children from their parents"—without the families being informed as to whether the arrestees were alive or dead, in which prisons they were held, and what charges had been brought against them. "With this system of fascist cruelty," he declared, "we shall lose the war." He also stated that he had brought his accusations to the attention of Garcés, who had assured him these "irregular and brutal procedures" would not be allowed to continue. At this point, Negrín left the meeting to speak to Garcés and returned a few moments later informing the ministers that he had given strict orders that "all forms of torture must cease" and that violators would be held accountable.[46] These assurances must have afforded little comfort to Irujo, for in a memorandum written after his resignation in August he states that the SIM in the hands of Negrín became "too arbitrary and dangerous an instrument for the safety of the individual" and that he had threatened to resign several times, each time receiving "promises and guarantees."[47]

If further evidence of the SIM's crimes is needed, there is the testimony of Carlos Pi Sunyer, a member of the moderate Esquerra Republicana de Catalunya and mayor of Barcelona until he became councillor of culture in the Generalitat government: "[The SIM], which was initially entrusted with the investigation of cases of espionage, extended its sphere of activity and became a political instrument that soon gained a sinister reputation because of the cruelty of its methods." Simultaneously, the special tribunals functioned "day and night employing summary procedures" and "distinguished themselves by the severity of their sentences." For this reason, he affirms, the Catalan authorities made numerous protests to the government of the Republic, expressing their deep concern over the deterioration of justice, the abuses of the SIM, and the increasing number of death penalties. These, he added, were one of the principal reasons for the August crisis of 1938.[48]

Equally important is the evidence of the Catalan councillor of justice, Pedro Bosch Gimpera, the distinguished anthropologist and rector of the University of Barcelona. The special tribunals, he affirms, became a "cover" for the lawless behavior of the SIM. "Our protests [in 1938] were of no avail and our inquiries about the arrests that we knew were unjustified went unheeded. The tribunals were formed by a professional judge, by a military man representing the defense ministry (generally a member of the SIM), and by a 'representative of the services of public order,' in other words, a policeman. . . . [The] conviction was always based on the confession of the accused—not always legally obtained by the SIM—or on dubious testimony of one of its agents. Hence, I had no course but to speak unofficially with our friends, the ministers [in the government], Irujo, Giral, Aiguadé, but there was little they could do. . . . The methods of the SIM, the irregular procedures of the special tribunals and the unjustified arrests were the object of protests by the [Catalan] councillor of justice as were the invasion of our prison in Figueras [under Catalan jurisdiction] and the disappearance of persons who were afterwards found dead in such places as Igualada and Cervera."[49] And, in a letter to Hugh Thomas, Bosch Gimpera stated: "During the last year of the Civil War, we spent a good deal of the time struggling against the military tribunals and the SIM."[50] This statement leaves little doubt that despite Negrín's reassurances at the cabinet meeting of 10 August, the SIM's abuses continued to cause serious disquiet in Catalonia.

It should now be apparent that the Military Investigation Service under the control of Negrín's aide, Santiago Garcés, became the most dreaded security force in the left camp, casting its shadow over every aspect of political and social life. According to the little-known memoir of Colonel Eduardo Cuevas de la Peña, who was appointed director general of security on 16 April 1938[51] and who at the time was a member of the PCE, the "SIM also invaded the spheres of activity of the regular police, seriously damaging its reputation."[52]

Although the moderate Socialist Paulino Gómez Sáez, a staunch Prietista, now headed the ministry of the interior, the Communists retained all the key posts in the police administration that they had assiduously acquired since the early months of the war. Moreover, Colonel Cuevas points out that the minister's functions were "subject to the control of his undersecretary [Dr. Rafael Méndez, the above-mentioned director general of carabineers in 1937], Negrín's right-hand man,"[53] and that Negrín's influence had a "disastrous effect" on the minister's conduct of affairs.[54]

Though a member of the PCE, Colonel Cuevas—who had been head of the uniformed security services in Catalonia and had helped to destroy the power of the CNT and FAI in the region[55]—was not a doctrinaire Communist. Attracted into the orbit of the PCE quite early in the war, his story is similar to that of other Republican officers who joined the party. While serving on the Madrid front, he was made an honorary commander of the Communist Fifth Regiment and later was invited to attend a meeting:

> The utmost good sense inspired the speakers: They repudiated crime as a revolutionary weapon. Pillage was to be prosecuted mercilessly. . . . Their military policy was clear: immediate organization of a regular army, creation of officers' training schools, intensive building of fortifications, creation of reserves, and a single command. *A few days later I joined the party.* . . .
>
> The Communist party was the only party that publicly launched the slogan that all officers loyal to the Republic should be respected. That initiative should have been taken by the [Giral] government, but lacking authority and fearful of making itself unpopular, it abandoned the officers to their fate. It behaved in this way with other servants of the state and this was the reason that the Communist party's small cadres at the beginning of the war grew rapidly and became at times the animating force. . . .
>
> Its policy of winning over supporters was successful. It waged a vigorous campaign of propaganda to the effect that the party was not fighting to impose its ideology but only to defend constitutional legality.[56]

"But," he asked himself, "were their words sincere? Only time would tell."[57] Cuevas alleges that he broke with the party on the very day he became director general of security in April 1938, when a representative of the Catalan Communist party summoned him to a meeting of the party to discuss his future duties. "My reply was categorical: I owed my loyalty to my post and would not permit outside pressure. That day our relations were broken off. A few days later I received a visit from some Russians, offering their collaboration. Very courteously I bade them farewell and they never returned to my office."[58]

While it might be correct and even comforting to believe that Cuevas had the courage to defy the party at the height of its power and on the very day he became director general of security, the question must be asked, Why did it not expel him and remove him from office? Or did he simply chafe under its brazen interference and never openly express his irritation, secretly deciding to pursue his own course? There is flimsy evidence in support of this conjecture in Togliatti's oft-cited letter to the Comintern of 21 May 1939, written two months after the end of the Civil War. Referring to Cuevas, he wrote: "[In] spite of the instructions, in spite of the pressure and suggestions by the party, he allowed its enemies to take over the police forces in the central zone."[59] But this criticism relates solely to the police administration in an area over which Cuevas exercised virtually no control because of its geographical and political isolation after the Nationalists reached the Mediterranean coast on 15 April 1938, splitting the Republican territory in two. Furthermore, Togliatti does not even hint at such a significant event as Cuevas's alleged break with the PCE, while former politburo member Jesús Hernández specifically includes the department of security as one of the key centers of power in the hands of "active members of the Communist party."[60] Hence, it is not unreasonable to conclude that Cuevas's version is evasive at best and that Togliatti, in criticizing the colonel, whom he identifies pejoratively as a Mason, as he does other Communist officers, was simply adding to his list of scapegoats in explaining the successful coup against Negrín and the PCE in March 1939, as we shall see in a later chapter.

At this point, it is worth mentioning that, in attributing the success of the coup partially to the betrayal of the Masons, Togliatti was also expressing the Communist movement's traditional distrust of any secret society outside its purview. In an earlier report, dated 25 November 1937, Togliatti wrote: "There are many Freemasons in the party and I realize that they are Masons first and Communists second. The Communist police officials who are Masons hold 'fractional' meetings as Masons before attending party meetings. I have been informed of such cases in the army. There is proof that a very well-known member of the party leadership has concealed and still conceals the fact that he is a Mason."[61] And in a later report, dated 28 January 1938, he stated: "In the PSUC there are many Freemasons, especially among the leaders. No less than three belong to the executive committee; two to the secretariat. The organizational secretary in Barcelona is probably a Mason. Although Freemasonry in Spain plays a different role from that in other countries, I believe that this situation should concern us."[62]

Whatever the motive behind Togliatti's insinuation that there were Masons in the party who secretly deferred to a higher authority, the fact is that the Communists were so firmly entrenched in April 1938 in the secret and uniformed police in Catalonia, the seat of government, that the Socialist minister of the interior Paulino Gómez Sáez was all but impotent. One area, however, in which he succeeded in exercising a measure of control was the domestic press censorship, which, according to Togliatti, was "for a long time in the hands of the enemies of the party [i.e., the Socialists]."[63] The Communists, he said, took their complaints to Negrín, who "acknowledged that our protests were justified and agreed to a plan of reorganization presented by the party." The plan would have placed the censorship under the direct control of the premier's office, but Negrín "did not implement it out of fear of a rupture with the Socialist party."[64]

Nevertheless, Negrín did not give Paulino Gómez free rein. On one occasion, when the censors allowed *El Socialista*, the organ of the Socialist executive, to publish an article critical of his administration and of his personal newspaper, *La Vanguardia*, he ordered Paulino Gómez to arrest them. "Thus, the voice of protest against *La Vanguardia* was silenced on the spot," Prieto observed in a letter to Negrín after the war. "The Socialist party could not say what it thought; only the opinion of Juan Negrín was allowed free expression."[65] There was a singular contrast, he said, between *El Socialista*, the organ of the party, to which the head of the government belonged, and *La Vanguardia* with "its abundance of paper, costly pictorial supplements printed on de-luxe paper imported from abroad and paid for in foreign exchange needed for the purchase of food for the civilian population."[66]

It has now been seen that the power and authority of Dr. Juan Negrín reposed directly on the military and police forces controlled by the PCE and indirectly on the submission or repression of his opponents, who now included not only the revolutionary left—the Anarchosyndicalists, Caballeristas, and POUMists—but also the Prieto Socialists and left Republicans, not to mention the pathetic figure of Manuel Azaña, the president of the Republic. It is true that Negrín, to the manifest irritation of Togliatti, had on occasion shown restraint and circumspection in dealing with the Socialist executive,[67] but it would be erroneous to argue that he was biding his time until he could slough off the Communist connection. This was the contention some thirty years later of Dr. Rafael Méndez, who—to use his own words—was Negrín's "best and most devoted friend for many years."[68] "One of the premier's set ideas," he claimed, "was to break up the Communist military units quickly once the war was over. These units he supported and even allowed to grow because the Soviet Union was our only source of supply." Méndez also asserted that shortly after the Munich crisis in the late summer of 1938 Negrín told both the British ambassador and the head of the British secret service in Republican Spain that, if Britain and France would sell the Republican government the war material it needed to win the war, *not only would he remove the two Communist ministers from the government but he would outlaw the PCE and replace the Communist officers holding command positions in the army with non-Communists.*[69]

It is impossible to accept these assertions at face value and to attribute to them anything but tactical significance, for in the most crucial matter of all—the control of the army and security services—Negrín furthered the cause of the Communist party, "the only party," according to Togliatti, "that loyally supported [him]."[70] What forces then could Negrín have mustered to destroy the armed power of the PCE? It was not without cause that the Socialists, Republicans, and Anarchosyndicalists accused Negrín, as Togliatti attests, of being "an agent of the Communists."[71] Even in the case of the carabineers, which Negrín had been instrumental in transforming into a powerful force of public order, he revealed his partiality for the Communists when, a few days before Prieto's ouster from the cabinet, he appointed Marcelino Fernández, a PSUC member, to head the corps in place of Prieto's close friend, Víctor Salazar.[72]

The appointment was a palpable act of defiance of the Socialist executive, for when Negrín became minister of finance in September 1936, it was understood that he would transform the carabineers into an elite corps under the exclusive control of the moderate Socialists. In fact, in February 1937, he reaffirmed existing regulations that prohibited members of the corps from engaging in political activity,[73] and, in May 1937, he allegedly told Rafael Méndez, whom he had just named director general of carabineers, that the corps should be "impenetrable to Communist infiltration."[74] To be sure, we have only Méndez's word for this assertion, but it may indeed be true, since Negrín had at that time not yet completely severed his umbilical attachment to Indalecio Prieto, his friend and mentor. Méndez's other assertion—that when he became undersecretary of the interior in April 1938 after Prieto's ouster, Negrín advised him "to counter Communist influence in the police, in the information service, and the assault guards"[75]—runs counter to all we know about Negrín's support of the Communist party during the last year of the war. Moreover, according to José Múñez López of the SIM, whose reliable testimony I have frequently cited, Méndez was not only a Negrinista but a friend of the Communists.[76] It may be for this reason that in September 1937, only three months after Méndez had been appointed director general of carabineers, Prieto—then in the midst of his conflict with the PCE over the control of the army—had Negrín remove him and replace him with Víctor Salazar, his close political associate.[77]

The Communists, of course, had supported the use of the carabineers by Negrín when they seized the Catalan-French border from the Anarchosyndicalists and the POUM in April and May 1937 and sequestered the offices and printing presses of the Caballero Socialists in Valencia a few months later. But, seeking dominion over all the armed forces of the state, they could not allow for long the independence of so powerful a force. Hence, when Negrín decided to oust Prieto and make common cause with the PCE, an opportunity arose to curb their power. This would not prove easy, because the carabineers had their own political commissars called *delegados de hacienda* or treasury delegates, who like the commanders were mainly Socialists, whereas Communist influence in the corps, to judge from a report by the security commission of the Madrid party organization, was "minimal."[78] Emilio Pérez, the Communist head of the politicomilitary commission of the Army of the Levante explained Negrín's dilemma to me. Negrín, he said, became a "victim of the very force he had created. . . . Later [after breaking with Prieto], when he wanted to change things, serious political problems arose because the commanders of the carabineers were linked with the Socialist party."[79] This explains why members of the PCE and PSUC were encouraged to join the carabineers and what the former member of the PSUC executive, Miguel Serra Pàmies, implied when he said to me: "Many members of the PSUC joined the carabineers. Negrín played our game and we played his."[80]

Hence, Negrín's appointment of the Communist Marcelino Fernández to head the carabineers in place of the Socialist Víctor Salazar was one more significant contribution to the Communists' ultimate objective: the control of all of the armed forces of the state.

57

Catalonia and the August Crisis

The transfer of the Negrín government from Valencia to Barcelona in November 1937 exacerbated the discord between the regional and central authorities especially in the field of public order.

Ever since the popular explosion in May 1937 had ended, discontent had been smoldering over the retention of police authority by the central government. Although President Companys had agreed under the press of hostilities to the assumption of public order by Valencia and to the dispatch of thousands of assault guards to the region, he had harbored the belief that Catalonia would soon recover her lost autonomy.[1] When José Tarradellas, finance councillor in the Catalan government formed in June 1937, complained to President Azaña on 29 July that the central government had sent "an army of occupation that lives at the cost of the region," he was expressing the vexation of Companys and the majority of Catalans, but he received no encouragement from the president.[2] A few weeks later, when Pedro Bosch Gimpera, councillor of justice, complained in similar terms to Azaña, the president, who had not forgotten his painful experience in Barcelona during the May events,[3] noted in his diary: "Bosch loses sight of the fact that if there is now an 'army of occupation' in Catalonia (as they like to call it)—an army of the legal government that finally saved Catalonia . . . from the claws of banditry—that region was for months under an army of occupation of patrols, 'controls,' clandestine tribunals, etcetera, etcetera, to the indignation, shame, and martyrdom of the majority of Catalans."[4]

The transfer of the central government to Barcelona not only sharpened the discord between the Catalan and central governments, but it also inflamed the regionalist sentiments of the Catalans, both of the separatists of Estat Català and of the moderate autonomists of the Esquerra Republicana de Catalunya. Particularly goading was the obtrusive presence of ministers and officials and families and friends, who expected and demanded preferential treatment. "I told [Negrín]," writes Enrique Líster, the Communist military commander, "that the abuses of quite a number of high officials in the government, including certain ministers, were no secret and that everybody knew that these officials had brought their mistresses and their families, for whom they had requisitioned splendid houses. Similar requisitions had been made by governmental agencies without considering the Catalan government or its departments. This naturally angered the Catalans."[5] And the former Communist director general of security, Eduardo Cuevas de la Peña, attests: "The seizure of housing was carried out with impunity in the most unconscionable way."[6]

President Companys had personal as well as political reasons for exasperation. Jordi Arquer, himself a fervent Catalanista and a member of the POUM executive, had several meetings with the distraught president. Despite political differences, they had established close personal ties in prison after the abortive coup in Barcelona against the rightist government of Lerroux-Gil Robles in October 1934. Says Arquer: "Companys complained to me about the illegal activities of the central bureaucracy that had arrived in Catalonia with the government; the unjust manner in which the censorship was exercised; the armed assault on public buildings belonging to the Generalitat and the Barcelona City Council; and the interference with the [Catalan] police and judicial bodies. . . . [He] told me that every night he had to empty the drawers of his desk in his presidential office, because the guards or other employees, who belonged to the PSUC, searched everything he had and took anything away that interested them." He also told Arquer that he had to change the guards assigned to him "because, instead of protecting him, they spied on him."[7]

The complaints of the Catalan leaders against the central authorities were unending. Pedro Bosch Gimpera records that the central government evinced "complete disregard of Catalonia in matters of justice, ignoring the powers that belonged to the region [under the Statute of Catalan Autonomy]." Typical examples, he says, were the creation of a state prison in Barcelona; the appointment of judges; the creation of special tribunals, against whose procedures and sentences the Catalan authorities had frequently to protest; and the seizure of prisons that were under the jurisdiction of the Generalitat.[8] The Catalan economist José María Bricall has pointed out that from the second half of 1937 the central government regulated foreign trade and that from January 1938 it controlled food supplies and determined taxes.[9] In other words, Catalonia was divested not only of the powers granted to it under the Statute of Catalan Autonomy but also of the prerogatives it had arrogated to itself as a result of the Revolution. The Anarchosyndicalist leader and former justice minister, Juan García Oliver, lists a number of other grievances: "the requisition of family belongings, such as a wedding ring, a sweetheart's earrings, a grandmother's broach; the shipment of stocks of textiles to the Soviet Union; the looting of machinery and equipment from our manufacturing centers on the instructions of Stashevski. . . . And a thousand other things increased hatred and resentment."[10] In an unpublished report by the FAI for the internal use of the libertarian movement, the peninsular committee stated in September 1938 that the Communist party had "facilitated the acquisition [by the Soviet Union] of our stocks of merchandise at the most ridiculous prices and the theft of our industrial secrets by Russian espionage."[11]

Diego Abad de Santillán, a former councillor of economy in the Catalan government, observes: "Nothing is known of the gold reserves of the Bank of Spain, whether anything remains of them or whether they have been totally depleted. But one thing speaks out eloquently: Russia has acquired the stocks of textiles and other manufactured products of Catalonia valued at hundreds of millions of pesetas and it is suspected that these acquisitions are used to guarantee payments. Since the outbreak of the war, the financial policy of the Government of the Republic had been conducted with a secrecy that has never been seen in history, not even in the regimes of imperial despotism."[12]

There can be little doubt that all these complaints, added to the offensive presence of the central authorities and of the massive bureaucracy of the PCE that had moved to Barcelona with the government, irritated the fierce regionalist sentiments of the Catalans. It also nettled those Catalanist leaders of the PSUC who at heart deeply resented their enforced submission to the Comintern leaders and the Spanish Communist party[13] as well as the attempt by the PCE to absorb posts that strictly belonged to Catalans.[14] At a plenary meeting of the central committee of the PCE in June 1938, Rafael Vidiella, a founder-member of the PSUC, lectured the wayward members of his party. To win the war, he declared, there can be only one political and economic leadership. For the PSUC to ensure the unity of Catalonia with the rest of the Republic "it is necessary that we correct our deficiencies and struggle against certain ideological survivals and certain residues of petty-bourgeois nationalism that still exist within our party. These ideological survivals and residues are understandable if we take into account the youth of the PSUC and the fact that it is the product of a fusion [of four Catalan organizations]." Nevertheless, petty-bourgeois nationalism, he warned, had to be fought. "The [PSUC] must mobilize itself to make all its militants and all its cadres understand the correct Marxist-Leninist line on the national question, because if the party itself doesn't understand this truth then it cannot make the masses understand it, and, instead of ensuring the close unity of Catalonia with the rest of the Republic, the party may at some moment be drawn into a collision between Catalonia and the rest of Spain."[15] Stripped of its Marxist-Leninist terminology, this admonition meant that all PSUC leaders should forget their kinship with Catalonia and submit to the rule of a national state dominated by the Spanish Communist party.[16]

If it is true that the Catalans were angered by the presence of an "army of occupation" and by the "invasion" of a host of government and party officials, it is no less true that the centralists were exasperated by the growth of regionalist sentiments. Negrín, himself a centralist, viewed the complaints of the Catalans with misgiving and was impatient of any manifestation of regionalism or separatism, as he preferred to call it. "I am not carrying on the war against Franco in order to see the revival of a stupid and parochial separatism," he fulminated in July 1938, when his friend and undersecretary of the interior, Rafael Méndez, asked him for instructions with regard to the "strong resurgence of nationalism" observed in the activities of the Catalan government. "I am waging the war because of Spain and for Spain; because of her grandeur and for her grandeur.

Those who believe otherwise are mistaken. There is only one nation: Spain! This persistent whispering campaign cannot be permitted and must be nipped in the bud, if I am to continue to direct government policy, which is a national policy."[17]

Whether Negrín was willing to acknowledge it or not, the deepest grievance of all social layers in Catalonia was the pervasive terror of the SIM and its special tribunals, and of the Communist-controlled police apparatus, a subject already discussed in the previous chapter. In a long letter addressed to the prime minister on 23 April 1938, Luis Companys enclosed reports from the Catalan councillors of the interior and justice denouncing events that "injure the morale and confidence of the rear." The following pregnant passages need to be recorded:

> With regard to the document of the councillor of justice, it should be made clear that the official who denounced the alleged abuses, and who is said to have committed suicide, was in fact found dead the next day, but from three bullet wounds. The courts have investigated the matter, but I must protest the summary procedure of some police forces of the Government of the Republic, who, armed with machine guns, entered the prison of Figueras [which was under Catalan jurisdiction] and still remain there. This outrage was carried out in contempt of the Generalitat and without prior consultation, notification, or legal complaint.[18]
>
> As to the state of affairs outlined in the councillor of the interior's report, besides the many incidents constantly recurring, of which there is abundant evidence, many others could be added. With sorrow, I am obliged to emphasize the gravity of some events, which, on becoming public knowledge, have increased the state of disquiet and alarm among our people.
>
> A few weeks ago, nineteen corpses were found in the municipal boundary of Sitges. They were tied up and bore documents showing that they were prisoners from the "Villa de Madrid." Previously the bodies of other persons who had been arrested were found in Igualada and, subsequently, there have been isolated cases of prisoners and other people who have disappeared. Only yesterday, I was informed that the police chief of Cervera armed a group of individuals of questionable antecedents who carried out searches and arrests and executions of alleged suspects. This practice of arming certain individuals was employed a few weeks ago in the town of Badalona and in other places.
>
> The courts of law and the so-called special tribunals that function in Catalonia under the direct authority of the central government . . . fulfil their mission using the summary procedures established by decree of the Government of the Republic. And this week the number of death penalties imposed has reached almost one hundred. This summary and inexorable justice . . . has increased—if that were possible—the anguish and revulsion over abuses of such magnitude.[19]

Carlos Pi Sunyer, the Catalan councillor of culture, attributes the worsening relations between the Generalitat and the central government to the "abuses of the SIM," the "growing number of death penalties," and "the crimes of uncontrolled elements."[20] But he also stresses the government's centralizing drive as the principal divisive issue. "[It] is undeniable," he affirms, "that the Republican government pursued a persistent and deliberate policy of progressive centralization reminiscent of the old policy against Catalonia."[21] In fact, it was this centralizing thrust, added to all the other grievances over the curtailment or elimination of Catalan powers, that prompted the resignation of Jaime Aiguadé, the Esquerra representative in the government. As Raymond Carr, Britain's leading authority on Spanish history, writes: "[The] Catalan minister resigned from the government in protest against the steady erosion of the powers of the Generalitat, with its competence reduced to the level of 'folklore.' The vision of a pluralistic Spain had finally vanished in a Communist-dominated centralized state, as obnoxious to Catalanists as any of its predecessors."[22]

The immediate development that prompted the resignation of Aiguadé and that of Manuel de Irujo, the Basque Nationalist minister, in an act of solidarity, was the approval by the cabinet on 11 August of three decrees: the militarization of the war industries by the central government (which were essentially a Catalan preserve run by the CNT with the intervention of the Catalan government), the militarization of the ports, and the militarization of the courts of law.[23] "These decrees," records the official Communist history of the Civil War, ". . . although temporary measures for the duration of the war and for the sake of victory, reduced the powers of the autonomous government of Catalonia and increased the distrust of many Catalans."[24] At the same meeting, sixty-four death sentences, according to José Giral, were also approved after "an extremely violent discussion."[25] Councillor of finance José Tarradellas telephoned Azaña to ask him not to sign the death penalties, but Azaña, according to the councillor's biographer, "paid no attention."[26] The fact of the matter is that Azaña was helpless; for, when Tarradellas informed him on 12 August that fifty-eight persons had been executed on the previous day, the president made the following notation in his diary: "Horrible! I am outraged. Only eight days after speaking of pity and pardon [a reference to a grandiloquent address to the nation entitled *Piedad, Perdón y Paz*] they throw 58 executions at me without telling me anything or asking my opinion. I found out about it only through the press. From the 18th of July [1938] I have not seen the prime minister, nor has he even spoken to me on the telephone."[27]

This disregard of the president by Negrín was no doubt a painful reminder to Azaña of the "glacial indifference" that former premier Largo Caballero had displayed toward him during the May events. It was also a rude letdown from the early days of Negrín's first administration, when the new prime minister charmed the president with his self-confidence and intelligence and gave him the feeling, as he chose to put it, that he was no longer "speaking to a corpse."

As no member of the Esquerra or of the Basque Nationalist party—the traditional representatives of the two autonomous regions—could be found to replace Irujo or Aiguadé in order to maintain the illusion of a "government of national union," Negrín summoned a meeting of the PSUC leaders, including party secretary Juan Comorera, Miguel Valdés, and Rafael Vidiella.[28] According to Vidiella's memoirs, preserved in the archives of the PCE, Negrín (who wished to avert a full-scale cabinet crisis) stated: "My opinion is that a Catalan and a Basque can be replaced by another Catalan and a Basque. I ask you to give me a minister to represent the PSUC, since the Esquerra is not the only party that represents Catalonia. Your party can also represent it."[29]

The dialogue that ensued is recorded by Vidiella:

Valdés: We have agreed that Comorera should be our minister.

Negrín (with a gesture of displeasure and without giving the matter a moment's thought): Ah, no! Neither Comorera nor Vidiella. They both are already too well known as Communists. I removed one of the two Communists in the previous government precisely because I wished to make concessions to those who believed that Communist representation was excessive.[30] And now, if I put another one in the government using the door of Catalonia, they will say that I am deceiving them. Give me a man who is not a known Communist.

Comorera: Moix.

Negrín: Who is Moix?

Comorera: The fact that you ask who he is shows that he is not a well-known Communist. He is a trade-unionist.[31]

Negrín: Agreed.[32]

As for the vacant seat left by Manuel de Irujo, this was filled by Tomás Bilbao, a member of the little-known Basque Nationalist Action party, who was regarded as a Negrinista[33] and whose party had never mobilized any significant following or electoral force.[34] On 17 August, the premier's press office released the following communiqué: "The Government of the Republic takes special interest in reaffirming its unwavering respect for the rights and individuality of the autonomous regions and takes pride in seeing the continued representation of the Basques and Catalans in the government, thus maintaining its character as a Government of National Union."[35]

But the patched-up crisis could not conceal the absence from the cabinet of the two parties most closely identified in the public mind with regional autonomy. Even the Spanish Communist party, generally prone to so much double-talk, confessed some years later that "the inclusion of the PSUC did not compensate for the absence of the Esquerra" and that Tomás Bilbao's group was "a long way" from representing a force equivalent to the Basque Nationalist party.[36]

One reason why Negrín was able to avert a major showdown was the failure of the four Republican ministers representing Izquierda Republicana and Unión Republicana to support Irujo and Aiguadé. The Catalan Republican leader Pi Sunyer has censured them for not resigning and for behaving with "an unconcerned passivity" that gave Negrín "a free hand to put together whatever combination he chose."[37] Another reason is given by La Pasionaria, who claims that it was "the resolute attitude" of the PCE that enabled Negrín to confront the situation by advising him not to open a full-scale ministerial crisis—which would have meant placing the solution in President Azaña's hands—"but simply to replace the two outgoing ministers."[38]

There is a theory, advanced by the PCE, that the resignation of Aiguadé and Irujo was part of a conspiracy to overthrow Negrín. Julián Besteiro, the highly esteemed right-wing Socialist, who was known to favor a negotiated settlement, was said to be involved in the plot together with Azaña, other Socialist and Republican leaders, Catalan and Basque nationalists, and certain Anarchist factions.[39] There is little evidence to support this theory, although the sudden arrival from Madrid of the famed Socialist leader—long stigmatized as a "capitulationist" by the PCE—to see Azaña in the midst of the crisis gave rise to unwarranted speculation.[40] Nothing is known of the meeting between the two men and even Azaña's private secretary, Cándido Bolívar, was not privy to the talks.[41] They must certainly have discussed ways to end the war, because this subject had dominated their minds since the early days of the conflict, but both men, according to Bolívar, were "herméticos."[42] There is no evidence to suggest an actual conspiracy to overthrow Negrín. The passivity of the four Republican ministers and the meekness of Azaña himself rule out the possibility. In fact, it is hard to imagine that Azaña, now a beaten man and no longer living in a make-believe world of delusory constitutional power, would have had the fortitude to oppose Negrín. "I stand for less than that bowl of flowers," he confessed to a visiting delegation of the CNT.[43]

Nevertheless, neither Negrín nor the Communists were prepared to risk a major cabinet shakeup. On 13 August, while the crisis was still unresolved, Antonio Cordón, Negrín's Communist undersecretary of the land forces, informed all the army chiefs that the SIM had uncovered a plot to overthrow the Republican army by inciting the men to assassinate their officers. "Through absolutely reliable channels," ran his telegram to all divisional commanders, "the following instructions addressed by the rebels [to the Republican forces] have come into the hands of the SIM: 'On the night of 14–15 August, in every position, in every command post, in every village behind the lines, in every military storage park, in every airfield—in other words, everywhere—you should, regardless of the means, immediately put out of action your commanders and their men of confidence by taking advantage of your invincible superiority of ten to one. At the break of day, raise a white flag wherever you are in control, we shall be on the lookout, so that we can free you forever from the criminal oppression of the reds. Patriots! Spanish brothers of the red zone! Until the morning of the 15th when we can embrace!' "[44]

While this telegram with its crude instructions was being read in all divisional headquarters, tank units of the Eighteenth Army Corps, commanded by the Catalan Communist and PSUC leader, José del Barrio, received orders to proceed immediately to Barcelona. On arrival, they paraded through the streets while aircraft roared overhead.[45] The same day, the Communist organ *Frente Rojo* declared in banner headlines: "IN FACE OF ALL MANEUVERS, THE WORKERS, THE COMBATANTS, THE ENTIRE PEOPLE ARE FIRMLY AT THE SIDE OF THE GOVERNMENT OF NATIONAL UNION AND ITS PRIME MINISTER NEGRIN."[46]

It was against this background of military coercion and a flood of telegrams from army commanders to Azaña supporting Negrín that the premier, on the night of 16 August, handed the president for his signature the two decrees appointing the new ministers. Although Azaña eschews any details in his memoirs about this humiliating encounter, his friend Pi Sunyer records: "During the interview, Negrín told [the president] that since the crisis was only a partial one and simply required the replacement of the two ministers, it was within the competence of the prime minister to resolve it without consulting the President. Azaña, of course, could reject the solution, but he should bear in mind the consequences given the attitude of the army. Yielding once again to coercion, Azaña signed the decrees appointing the two ministers.[47] In referring to this painful scene in his memoirs Azaña devoted only a single phrase of four words: 'Entrevista para no olvidada' [an unforgettable interview]!' "[48]

In a postwar letter to Negrín, Indalecio Prieto refers to the "ignominious parade of military forces through the streets of Barcelona" and to the "shameless deluge of telegrams to strangle the will of the Head of State." The uniformity of the messages and their simultaneous transmission, he added, pointed clearly to a "directing hand."[49] As for the alleged plot, it was "a fraud." The document, he said, referred to an alleged invitation by the rebels to the Republican soldiers to assassinate their officers and to raise the white flag. "Was this the reason why it was necessary to take precautions in Barcelona, a hundred kilometers from the battle fronts? I didn't hesitate to express my opinion to the person who showed me the document: it had sordid political aims. In the final analysis, why did the precautions have to include a spectacular and alarming parade of military forces through the streets of Barcelona with armored cars and equipment while squadrons of planes threatened from the sky?"[50]

The next day the press published the composition of the new government:

Juan Negrín	Socialist [pro-Communist]	Premiership and Defense
Julio Alvarez del Vayo	Socialist [crypto-Communist]	Foreign Affairs
Paulino Gómez	Socialist [Prietista]	Interior
Ramón González Peña	Socialist [Negrinista]	Justice
Vicente Uribe	Communist	Agriculture
Segundo Blanco	CNT [Negrinista]	Education and Health
Francisco Méndez Aspe	Left Republican [Negrinista]	Finance and Economy
Antonio Velao	Left Republican [Negrinista][51]	Public Works
Bernardo Giner de los Ríos	Republican Union	Communications and Transportation
José Moix	PSUC [Communist]	Labor

| José Giral | Left Republican [Azañista] | Minister without portfolio |
| Tomás Bilbao | Basque Nationalist Action [Negrinista] | Minister without portfolio |

This cabinet, more heavily weighted in favor of Negrín and his Communist backers than any previous cabinet, would be the last wartime government.

Part IX

Doubts, Divisions, and Disasters Proliferate.
Communist Influence Wanes.

58

Internecine Conflicts Grow

While the political drama in Barcelona was still unfolding, the role of the libertarian movement was negligible. Riven by discord over inconsistencies between theory and practice, it had neither the unity nor the power to influence the course of events.

Earlier in the year, when the CNT reentered the government, with Segundo Blanco replacing Jesús Hernández as minister of education, the national committee, headed by secretary Mariano Vázquez, had expressed high hopes. In a circular addressed to the local unions on 8 April, it affirmed that by collaborating with the Negrín government, the CNT would be able to reconquer the political positions lost in May 1937 and to stop the repression against the movement. It urged all militants to be disciplined and to accept the government's decisions, which might appear "restrictive or arbitrary" but were necessary in view of the gravity of the military situation. If the CNT had only a single minister, it declared, this was in order "to reassure the bourgeois democracies" and to deter France from closing her borders to the passage of war material.[1]

The increasingly accommodative trend of the national committee clashed with the mood of the more radical spirits in the libertarian movement. As a result, the national committee decided to take drastic and exemplary action against Jacinto Toryho, the director of *Solidaridad Obrera*, the leading mouthpiece of the CNT, expelling him without ceremony on 7 May from the post he had held since 8 November 1936. In a bitter reply, Toryho inveighed against "the most incredible indifference of the so-called higher committees" in face of the arrest of Anarchosyndicalist militants and the destruction of the best collectives of the CNT. *Solidaridad Obrera*, he said, had been subject to "intolerable" censorship and to suspensions and seizures without anything being done by these committees "to put a stop to the unjust governmental measures." Hence, to keep the movement apprised of the true situation, he decided on 30 April to send copies of the censored articles to the unions so that they could see for themselves that the "defects of the newspaper were the result of forces beyond its control." This action, he claimed, was the reason for his "immediate expulsion" from the directorship of the paper.[2]

Following Toryho's ouster, *Solidaridad Obrera* pursued a policy of unqualified governmental collaboration,[3] but it never expressed itself as iconoclastically as Horacio M. Prieto, Mariano Vázquez's mentor and former secretary of the CNT, who proclaimed that *apoliticismo* was dead and libertarian communism only a distant goal. Described by José García Pradas, a FAIista and director of the Madrid newspaper *CNT*, as a "man of extraordinary moral and intellectual gifts" and as "one of the best minds in the CNT," but "dangerous to our movement,"[4] Prieto had been instrumental in bringing the CNT into the government of Largo Caballero in November 1936. At a plenary assembly, he had opposed the CNT's campaign to replace the central government with a national council of defense and had urged the delegates to "put an end to so many scruples, moral and political prejudices, and so much semantic fuss."[5] He now characterized the FAI—once the sacrosanct ideological guide of the libertarian movement—as a mere "phantom, a war cry, a special form of revolutionary infantilism" and accused it of inconsistencies: It defended "proletarian militarism" and "a controlled economy," he said, and had army officers, prison wardens, and its own representatives in minor organs of the state, but while admitting all this it believed that it could "free itself of impurities by not participating in the government." He also criticized the resolution approved at the FAI plenum held in July 1937, creating "a new organic structure," as nothing but "a vague utterance" and accused the peninsular committee of "mental incompetence and moral weakness" for denying the "political character" of the FAI. The Anarchosyndicalist movement, he argued, should create a libertarian Socialist party that would participate in every organ of the state.[6]

During the August crisis, the FAI endeavored to assert its much-eroded authority by urging the leaders of the CNT to withdraw Segundo Blanco from the government, but to no avail. Writes Diego Abad de Santillán, the FAI purist: "They insisted on keeping a useless minister in the government, who was not consulted nor told anything of vital interest. . . . [The] supposed representatives of the CNT stuck to their guns in spite of all the humiliations to which they were subjected."[7]

Although Segundo Blanco appears to have made a face-saving attempt to oppose the decrees militarizing the war industries, the ports, and the courts of law—to judge from his somewhat defensive response to libertarian critics[8]—he was unsuccessful, for, as Azaña noted tersely in his diary, "Negrín subdued him."[9] This was to be expected, for Blanco was not a man of strong doctrinal convictions and was dubbed by fellow Anarchosyndicalists just "another Negrinista." Furthermore, when the CNT national committee concluded its alliance with the Communist-dominated executive of the UGT in March, it had gone a long way toward recognizing the ultimate power and authority of the government. Hence, it could not easily reverse its stand, and its voice remained publicly silent on the decrees. As Juan Gómez Casas, the Anarchist historian, puts it, this silence was not surprising, for the CNT's pact with the UGT "gave the green light to every whim of the State to devour and centralize."[10] For its part, the peninsular committee of the FAI denounced the decrees as "an assault on the people's democratic achievements," which were "the minimum guarantee against the blatant trend toward the dictatorship of a single party."[11]

The underlying differences between the two factions erupted savagely at the national plenum of the libertarian movement held in Barcelona between 16 and 30 October 1938, two months before the fall of Catalonia. Emma Goldman, the famous American Anarchist, who had lived through the Bolshevik Revolution and had witnessed the destruction of the Anarchist movement, was invited to attend. She read the material prepared in advance by the peninsular committee of the FAI "setting forth its opposition to the growing encroachment of the Negrín government on the libertarian achievements and the critical attitude to the timid stand of the [CNT] national committee," but not wishing to remain one-sided in her judgment, she listened to a long explanation by secretary Mariano Vázquez. "I realized," she wrote at the time, "that the relations between him and the comrades of the peninsular committee had become very strained. Not for a moment could I doubt the personal integrity of the contending comrades. I had found them all of sterling quality, deeply sincere and passionately devoted to the struggle. True, their temperamental differences had no doubt contributed to the quarrel. Comrade Vázquez's rough-hewn manners and thunderous voice easily roused antagonism.[12] I myself had at first been shocked by them until I learned to know his earnestness and his fine qualities back of his savage exterior. . . . [The comrades of the FAI] had prepared a formidable dossier powerfully documented of some of the outrageous acts against the libertarian ranks. . . . I conceded the justification of the criticism and demands of our comrades of the FAI. Still, I felt like a hen for her chicks. I trembled for them."[13]

The belligerent tone of the plenum was set by Horacio Prieto and Mariano Vázquez of the CNT and by Pedro Herrera of the FAI. According to the unpublished record of the debates used by José Peirats in his two important works on the libertarian movement, Prieto adopted a position of "undisguised reformism bordering on Marxism," "underrated contemptuously the doctrines of Kropotkin," and "affirmed that truly effective action" was possible only from "organs of power." Finally, he asserted that the errors incurred by the libertarian movement were due to its "naivity" and "its lack of concrete plans."[14]

Vázquez was equally censorious: "We must jettison our literary and philosophical baggage in order to achieve hegemony tomorrow. The refusal of our comrades to accept the militarization [of the militia] is responsible for the few positions we now hold [in the army]. . . . The collectives would have fared better if they had submitted to official tutelage. They have already received eight million pesetas in credits, which would have been considerably greater had our comrades decided to take advantage of them." Vázquez then defended the government of Negrín "for facing up to the Communist party" and for its military successes and declared that no man could replace him.[15] In the caustic words of Peirats, "the CNT, with Vázquez at the head, clung like a leech to Negrín's gang."[16] "[At] that time," writes Gómez Casas, "[Vázquez] had come a very long way from the posture he once held as secretary of the building trades union. Political collaboration had had a devastating effect upon him."[17]

Incensed by the assault at the plenum on Anarchism's venerated precepts, the FAI delegate, Pedro Herrera, riposted: "We must thwart those who deprecate our principles. Those who are devoid of ideas should not be in the vanguard of our movement. . . . The 'philosophical baggage' and the 'outdated literature' to which they allude must not be disparaged by those who boast that they are still Anarchists. If anyone belittles our doctrines, . . . he should leave us. . . . The policy of Negrín does not merit our confidence. On more than one occasion, we have expressed our concern about it, but we have not been heeded. . . . Not for a moment should we forget our genuine revolutionary objectives."[18] And in response to a proposal that the CNT should "enter the state apparatus in order to destroy it," another FAI delegate stated: "This is the same as saying that in order to abolish prostitution we should support the idea of placing our wives and sweethearts in the brothels."[19]

Despite their vehement insistence that collaboration with the government was a bankrupt policy, the dissidents had little impact on the outcome of the plenum. In the end, a resolution was approved reaffirming the Anarchosyndicalists' commitment to "circumstantial political collaboration."[20]

It would be erroneous to leave the reader with the impression that Vázquez and his supporters on the national committee consciously served the ends of Negrín and the Communists. Even Togliatti, in his letter to Moscow of 21 May 1939, stated: "Unfortunately, our party had no possibility of directly influencing the Anarchist unions from the inside. . . . Vázquez's group never wanted to link itself with us lest it be accused of working for the Communists."[21] Federica Montseny, a member of the peninsular committee of the FAI, who claims that the CNT's support of the Negrín government was leading to a "disaster," says in extenuation of Vázquez's position: "Mariano believed that we should prolong our resistance, because he thought that world war would break out and that it would create a favorable situation for us. If he agreed with Negrín and the Communists on this question, it does not mean that he had surrendered himself to them. . . . Even today I ask myself who was right: we or he. If war had broken out at the beginning of 1939 instead of in September, the entire position of Mariano would have been redeemed. But the fact is that the Spanish people at that time could not stand any more and that any solution aimed at saving lives and the interests of the people—at least a minimum of those interests—looked like a collective salvation. How strange! Those days, the FAI, Azaña, and Indalecio Prieto coincided in their views."[22]

No debate among the upper echelons of the CNT and FAI, such as occurred at the plenum of the libertarian movement in October 1938, could have illustrated more dramatically the contradictions and unbridgeable divisions that had developed within the libertarian movement since the beginning of the Civil War and Anarchism's insoluble dilemma that in order to survive it must compete for power, yet by so doing it must negate hallowed principles. But now, after twenty-

eight months of war and uninterrupted decline of the Anarchosyndicalist movement, which represented half the working class, doctrinal disputes had become
patently academic to the rank and file. "The people, debilitated by hunger," writes
Peirats, "had grown morally weary of the war. In order to reanimate them a
fundamental political change would have been necessary by removing Negrín."[23]
Illustrative of the hostility to the premier are the following lines written to me by
Abad de Santillán: "[If] the war had ended with Negrín and his crew in the
government, we would have had to suffer annihilation in the name of the Republic
instead of annihilation in the name of fascism."[24]

It was of course impossible to remove Negrín from the premiership and
defense ministry, not only because of the dissensions within the libertarian movement, but because of the emasculation of the Socialists, whose party and trade-
union movement were irrevocably split into warring factions, and because of the
supineness and weakness of the Republican middle-class parties. After more than
two years of war, *Política*, the organ of Izquierda Republicana, the largest of these
parties, made the following confession: "The middle classes . . . have been
pushed aside, passed over, and shattered during the war. They have only themselves to blame, because they have not managed to create an organization adequate to the defense of their own existence."[25] It is true that President Azaña, the
titular head of the Republican middle classes, had the constitutional power to
remove Negrín, but when a delegation of FAI leaders visited him and urged him,
according to Peirats, "to get rid of the dictator . . . he was already utterly
intimidated."[26]

In any event, who could have replaced Negrín? What leading Republican or
Socialist enjoyed the confidence of Moscow and the Spanish Communists and
would have been willing to accept the unenviable task of prosecuting the war, as
Stalin wished, to the bitter end? The left Republican leader, José Giral, Azaña's
intimate, thought only of a negotiated settlement as did the president himself and
the Socialist leaders Julián Besteiro and Indalecio Prieto. As for Largo Caballero,
when a group of Anarchosyndicalists invited him to "reinforce" the authority of
the government with persons of "political integrity . . . so as not to lose the war,"
he replied that they were inviting him to a "funeral" and he could not attend. The
war was lost, he told them, they knew it as well as he, and he could not lend
himself, "after all that had happened, to share with Negrín and Company the
responsibility for the catastrophe that was drawing near."[27]

Largo Caballero's case deserves further examination, not only because it
throws light on the personal drama of the most prominent political figure in the
Republican camp during the first ten months of the war, but because it helps to
explain the depth of the schism within the Socialist movement. After being
removed from office in May 1937 and divested of his press and all his posts, he
refused to consort with his opponents and declined to attend any official function
of the PSOE or the UGT. "The brand-new executive of the UGT," he wrote,
"offered a banquet to various foreign delegates and sent me an invitation to which
I did not reply. Did they believe that with dinners and banquets I would forget

what they had done to me? What kind of mood would I be in at these fine spreads (*cuchipandas*)? What I call dignity, they call pride and arrogance."[28] On another occasion, several members of the executive asked him to speak at the anniversary of the founding of the PSOE in order to "*demonstrate the unity of the party.*" "I expressed my surprise at the invitation [and] told them that I could not speak, because in discussing the history of the party I would have to condemn the monstrosities that the government was committing and would be obliged to denounce its prime minister as responsible for the feud [within the Socialist movement] and as the upholder of the Communist party. Besides, before I could speak they would have to retract all the stupidities and lies uttered against me so that we would not appear like men without shame or dignity."[29] The next day, Caballero sent the following letter to the organizing committee confirming and amplifying his reasons for refusing to participate:

> As some may have forgotten . . . I joined the party on March 9, 1893, that is to say, forty-five years and five months ago. My affiliation with the UGT was earlier, in 1890, forty-eight years ago. I do not mention this as any special virtue, but to indicate that I have never been a passive member; from the first day of my affiliation I devoted my whole life to the service of the party and the UGT. In both organizations I have been placed in posts of the highest responsibility, both at home and abroad; my actions have never called forth censure. Nevertheless, and especially since the political crisis of May 1937, a crisis which was provoked by the Executive Committee, the latter and most of the Socialist press controlled by that committee have, with the able assistance of the Communist Party, waged a campaign of defamation against me such as has never been known in the annals of the Spanish labor movement. If special newspaper articles and official statements or speeches at meetings and conferences were to be believed, I was a breaker of discipline, a troublemaker, a bad Socialist, an Anarchosyndicalist and a nefarious splitter of the Socialist Party and of the working class—practically a traitor.
>
> I had been suffering all these insults and slanders in silence for many months and when I finally decided to speak out publicly, I was permitted to hold the first meeting, because it was expected to be a failure; but since it turned out to be just the opposite, a Socialist minister, backed up by the Executive Committee, prohibited me from continuing my speeches.[30] I was even confined to my residence so as to prevent me from getting in touch with Socialists. Furthermore, with the aid of the police and assault guards, Socialist newspapers and organizations which protested against these abuses were forcibly taken over.[31] I was summarily ousted, without any explanation, from the secretaryship of the UGT, to which I was unanimously elected at the 1932 Congress. I was also ousted from the presidency of the parliamentary minority and of the permanent committee of the Socialist parliamentary delegation. . . .[32]
>
> What has been done to me can only be done to a bad Socialist. Am I one? In that case I cannot take part in such an important and historic event as is being

planned. And if, on the other, I am a good Socialist, deserving the confidence of the party administration, let it be declared publicly and let the campaign against me be rectified beforehand. . . .

As you can see, the matter is more serious than it appears at first sight. . . . For these reasons, then, and for many others I could cite, it is with sincere feeling that I must say to you that I cannot take part in the meeting you are planning. Moreover, I am convinced that my absence will in no way influence the course of the war.[33]

The political impotence of the Republicans, Socialists, and Anarchosyndicalists increased their frustration and heightened their animosity toward Negrín and the PCE. Their antagonism was not always apparent in the heavily censored daily press, but it was the inevitable topic of discussion in party and trade-union locals. In his report to Georgi Dimitrov of 21 May 1939, Togliatti mentioned "the growing hostility [in mid-1938] of a large part of the Republican Socialist, and Anarchist leaders" and stressed the fact that "the Communist party was the only party that supported Negrín loyally."[34] Even such a circumspect chronicler of the Civil War as Julián Zugazagoitia did not attempt to conceal the extent of the prevailing hostility. The critics of Negrín, he wrote, claimed that he had a secret pact with the Communists and that he was serving them "in total disregard of the general interest. . . . According to [his] opponents, he acts exactly like a dictator and in every crisis, by one means or another, manages to frighten Azaña, sequestrate his will, and get him to reaffirm his confidence. There remains the parliament, which is convened simply to observe constitutional formalities, but it cannot muster the courage to veto Negrín's powers. . . . The strength of Negrín, say his political opponents, is not exactly based on trust. His continuance in power is due to his dictatorial resources. He leans heavily on the Communist portion of the army."[35] And, in a later passage, he states: "The Republicans are angered; so are the Basques and Catalans, and among the Socialists there is a faction, by no means insignificant, that would support any action aimed at bringing about the defeat of Negrín. They abominate his policy, branding it as Communist."[36]

If this was the atmosphere in Barcelona in mid-1938, what was the mood of Madrid? According to José Giral, "the spirit of Madrid had changed to such a point that it was necessary to restrain the people to stop them from breaking all relations with the Communists and declaring them enemies of the Republic. This impression was general and was confirmed to me by the military who arrived from the central zone."[37]

The internecine dissensions were now so apparent that they could not be disguised even by Negrín's principal propagandist abroad. Wrote Louis Fischer in August 1938: "There are Socialists who accuse the Communists of wishing to monopolize jobs and propaganda. The Communists charge that the Socialists work too little and complain too much. The truth is that the Communists' saving dynamism and discipline can have unpalatable by-products. The Socialists, as a midway group, are ground between bourgeois republicans and Communists. Those who dislike both, sulk or dream of a bridge to the Anarchists, whom they formerly reviled."[38]

Given the state of disunity in the Republican camp, what indications are there of Negrín's much-vaunted talent as a statesman? Because of his identification with the Communist party, he was not in a position to mitigate the pessimism and distrust even within his own party. "For a long time I have been saying," Luis Araquistáin wrote to his daughter, "that whether we are defeated or whether we win the war the independent Socialists will have to emigrate, because in the first case we should be assassinated by Franco or in the second by the Communists,"[39] while Julián Besteiro, the prestigious leader of the right wing of the PSOE, who had remained in Madrid aloof from the intraparty struggle, declared on 15 November 1938: "If we should win, Spain will become Communist. The whole democratic world would be hostile to us and we should only be able to count on Russia. . . . And if we were defeated, then the future would be terrible."[40]

Even in May, only a few weeks after the formation of Negrín's "Government of National Union," La Pasionaria acknowledged "the bitter and violent polemics" between the Socialist and Communist parties and declared that it was essential that "we all put forth a genuine effort to end them."[41] Despite this exhortation, the relations between the two parties steadily deteriorated. They became more difficult every day, she records in her autobiography. "The Socialist leaders, including those who were more inclined to an understanding with us [for example, Ramón Lamoneda, the party secretary] systematically refused to attend meetings of the coordinating committee of both parties. Relations with the Socialist leaders were reduced to a few conversations with Lamoneda, . . . who, on various pretexts, opposed any joint action."[42]

This aloofness of Ramón Lamoneda—the inimitable opportunist, whose political allegiance had oscillated since 1921 between the PSOE and the PCE—was a clear indication of the declining influence of the Communists in the fall of 1938, occasioned not only by what Louis Fischer euphemistically called their "saving dynamism and discipline" but by the disastrous course of the war.

Another indication of their waning fortunes was the growing discord within the JSU, the United Socialist Youth Federation, formed through the fusion of the Socialist and Communist youth movements before the Civil War and which for two years had been one of the main props of Communist policy. It had been agreed in March 1936, as noted in an earlier chapter, that until a national congress of unification had determined democratically the principles, program, and definitive structure of the united organization and had elected a directive body, the fusion would be effected on the basis of the entry of the Young Communists into the Socialist Youth Federation. But no congress was ever held. Instead, Santiago Carrillo, the secretary of the united organization, and other young Socialists who had joined the PCE in November 1936, convened a national conference in January 1937, to which he appointed as delegates not only the representatives of the local sections of the JSU but a large number of young Communists from the fronts and factories, a stratagem that enabled him to secure the election of both a national and executive committee packed with Communist party nominees. "Instead of holding a congress," wrote Antonio Escribano, the delegate from Alicante province, "the Communists convened that 'hoax,' the Conference of Valencia. They gave it the full weight of a 'democratic' congress of unification, but the truth is quite the opposite."[43] And in a letter to me after the war, Escribano stated: "Those of us who were loyal to Caballero did not raise any objections at the conference for two reasons, both fairly ingenuous when I look back on them today, although justifiable at the time. These reasons were: 1. 90 percent of the young Socialists who attended the conference did not know that Carrillo, Lain, Melchor, Cabello, Aurora Arnaiz, etc., had gone over outright to the Communist party. We believed that they were still young Socialists. . . . Had we known that this group of recreants had betrayed us, I can assure you that an entirely different situation would have arisen. 2. The atmosphere and the manner in which the conference was conducted took us by surprise, and when we wished to react the assembly had already come to an end."[44]

Nevertheless, two of Largo Caballero's steadfast supporters, José Gregori Martínez, secretary of the provincial committee of the Valencia JSU, and Rafael Fernández, secretary of the JSU of Asturias, declined the seats on the national committee to which they had been appointed, and shortly afterwards Escribano, the delegate for Alicante, resigned from the executive committee after denouncing the other members for surrendering themselves to the Communists.[45] During the great surge of influence and power of the PCE in 1937 and early 1938, the voices of dissent were to a large degree quieted. "The war provided a thick smoke screen that concealed the greatest abuses and the greatest political calamities," wrote Escribano. "If anyone tried to say anything against the mass of abuses, he was denied the right on the ground that it was harmful to the war effort. What a convenience the war was for many people! . . . It is very important to stress this fact in order to understand why many genuine young Socialists did not destroy the united organization from the very moment of its birth."[46] However, in Murcia, according to Togliatti, the dissension had already gone so far in September 1937 that there were two rival leaderships in the JSU: "one Caballerista, with headquarters in the House of Youth, and the other Communist, in the offices of the party."[47]

As the hostility toward the PCE increased in late 1938, a growing number of dissidents in the JSU attempted to recover the former political identity of the Socialist youth, especially in the provinces of Alicante, Jaen, Murcia, and Valencia. Virtually nothing was reported in *Ahora*, the national organ of the JSU, about the danger of a schism, but the mounting number of attacks on the "enemies of unity" and the warning that "no one can tear the JSU apart [because] six hundred thousand young members would prevent it"[48] revealed the threat presented by the dissidents. Alarmed by their activity Carrillo tried "to bribe the visible heads of the opposition with promises of posts in the army and the JSU,"[49] but he was unsuccessful. In October 1938, despite a show of military strength by the Communists, who brought some of their members from the front, the Socialists elected in Jaen a new provincial committee.[50] In a thirty-seven-page typewritten letter to Norman Thomas, the leader of the American Socialist party, dated 1 January 1939, describing the hegemonic ambitions of the PCE, Luis Araquistáin wrote: "In the JSU, the Juventudes Socialistas Unificadas or 'Ursificadas,' as some humorists call them [a play on URSS, the Spanish equivalent of USSR], there has been a strong reaction against absorption by the Communists, and in several provinces the young Socialists have already deleted the deceitful 'U' from the name of their organization and recovered their former independence."[51]

But it was in Madrid, the bulwark of the left Socialists, where the greatest threat to the leadership of the JSU emerged. Toward the end of 1938, a "Commission of Young Socialists" was set up with Socrates Gómez, the son of José Gómez Ossorio, the civil governor of Madrid, as president, and Antonio Escribano as secretary.[52] Santiago Carrillo, who had moved the national committee of the JSU to Madrid to head off the danger, made one more attempt to check the movement but failed. This may explain why, after the fall of Catalonia, he did not return to the central zone. In November, the Commission of Young Socialists convened a national conference in Madrid attended by delegates from almost every province. Several delegates, Escribano testifies, demanded an immediate break with the Communists and the re-creation of the Socialist Youth Federation, but no action was taken because of the enemy offensive then under way against Catalonia.[53] Meanwhile, in the fall of 1938, Ramón Lamoneda, seeing the schism within the JSU approaching, had set up a Youth Secretariat (Secretariado Juvenil) attached to the executive of the PSOE, as well as youth secretariats in several provinces, in the hope that if the dissidents were successful he could gain control of the revived Socialist youth movement, but the collapse of Catalonia and his flight to France abruptly ended whatever ambitions he may have harbored in that direction.[54]

In view of the compelling evidence of increasing hostility to the PCE, it is by no means essential to have recourse to the testimony of prominent ex-Communists, whose works are on the index of the Communist faithful and their apologists. But to ignore their testimony entirely would be tantamount to yielding to those who would exclude all books from the historiography of the Civil War that do not conform to the party line. One such book is *Comunista en España y antistalinista en la URSS* by Valentín González (El Campesino), the well-known Communist militia commander, who escaped from the Soviet Union after World War II. Despite numerous inaccuracies and distortions, like countless books on the Civil War, it nonetheless contains material of undoubted historical value, which deserves recording.

(My use of this book on a previous occasion was criticized by Herbert R. Southworth, the well-known writer and polemicist on the Spanish Civil War.[55] In replying to Southworth, Robert Conquest, the famous sovietologist, stated: "Mr. Southworth is very choosy about evidence. Everything written by ex-Communists, but also by anyone else 'connected' with Western organizations, thought to have been involved in the 'Cold War,' is to be ruled out. Cold War here signifies as usual the voicing of opinions or retailing of facts unpalatable to the Soviet leadership. Anyone who has been concerned with a broader view of the period knows that *some* defector material is false . . . , when it comes to the disputed issues; any real historian must pick his way very carefully. On the other hand, neither the opinion, nor even the imperfect character, of one or another witness in themselves refute his testimony. Nor are we to exclude those who may tend to put themselves in a better light than we might accept—to do so would be to disqualify virtually the entire human race. Mr. Southworth's criteria, even if they were not so patently partisan, would enable him to exclude anyone he wished, under cover of an insistence on immaculate certainties."[56])

Referring to the formation of the second Negrín government in April 1938, El Campesino states: "From then on morale at the front and in the rear continued to decline and we went from defeat to defeat. . . . The hatred of the Communists by the mass of the people reached such a point that during a meeting of the politburo one of the leaders had to declare: 'We cannot retreat. We must carry on and stay in power at all costs, otherwise we shall be hunted like predatory animals through the streets.' "[57]

To reinforce their position, the Communists were compelled to rely more and more on their military and police power. At the front, cajolery, coercion, and violence grew from day to day. "Thousands upon thousands of our comrades," said a report issued by the peninsular committee of the FAI in October 1938, "confess that they are more afraid of being assassinated [at the fronts] by the adversaries at their side than of being killed by the enemies they face."[58] And another report issued in Stockholm, the headquarters of the world Anarchosyndicalist movement, declared: "One cannot assassinate antifascist officers and men just because they belong to the libertarian working-class movement . . . without the masses beginning to ask what distinguishes the regime of Negrín from that of the fascists under Franco. One cannot behave in this manner without causing demoralization and decay, without undermining the will to fight."[59]

Not only the Anarchosyndicalists lived in dread of assassination at the battlefronts, but all who resisted the will of the PCE. For refusing to accept the line of the JSU, ran a report by a dissident group of young Socialists, dated 1 June 1939, "an infinite number" of young Socialists were shot on the front lines and "a large number" were imprisoned, downgraded, or denied the possibility of becoming political commissars.[60] "At the front our comrades are being assassinated, because they do not want to accept a Communist party membership card," Zugazagoitia had told Negrín.[61] Nor were the young Republicans at the front spared the terror. According to Colonel Jesús Pérez Salas, the leaders of the Republican Youth, seeking protection for their "persecuted members," went to his headquarters with the request that they be allowed to enlist in the Twenty-fourth Army Corps, which he was then organizing. "During one of these visits, they gave me a copy of a 'secret and confidential' document addressed to the commander or commissar . . . of a Communist brigade which stated *that it was necessary to wipe out all those who oppose Communist authority and even eliminate them physically if necessary.*"[62]

While intimidation and terror reigned at the battlefronts, the dread of the SIM and secret police silenced all but the faintest criticism. From now on Negrín, backed by Communist propaganda and Russian supplies, became the symbol of resistance. Soviet aid, limited by logistics and by Stalin's resolve not to become too enmeshed in the conflict, was predicated on the belief that Britain and France would eventually be forced to intervene in defense of their own interests and that the Spanish conflict would eventually merge with a general war in Western and Central Europe. "[Moscow] will try by every means to avoid being isolated, to force the Western democracies to fight Hitler, if war is the only course," Boris Stefanov, the Comintern adviser, told the Spanish politburo.[63]

In May 1938, in keeping with Kremlin policy, the central committee of the Spanish Communist party declared in a resolution published in the Comintern organ, *International Press Correspondence*:

> Republican Spain is gaining sympathy and prestige every day. Our struggle is mobilising the proletarian, democratic, and liberal forces of the whole world. Our resistance is spurring on the determination of the liberal public in Great Britain, the United States, France, etc., to oppose a firm and united barrier to the fascist barbarity which is driving [the world] to war.
>
> The Communist party confirms once more its standpoint with regard to the *democratic character* of the Spanish revolution, and condemns all dangerous, extremist, and adventurous experiments which can only serve . . . to prevent the strengthening and consolidation of the democratic achievements. We are fighting for the *democratic parliamentary Republic*, which is based upon the will of the people and on the people's army, which secures the free political activities of all antifascist parties and organizations.[64]

59

Why Are the People Fighting?

*I*n keeping with its policy of courting the Western democracies, the Negrín government attempted to conciliate foreign capital.

On 27 April, it decreed the dissolution of the Serveis Electrics Unificats de Catalunya,[1] which had been formed on the initiative of the CNT to control all the foreign hydroelectric enterprises operating in Catalonia. Under the terms of the decree each enterprise was to recover its status as a stock company (*personalidad propia*) with the aim of returning it to its former owners. At the same time, the workers' committees formed at the inception of the Revolution were dissolved, and a government controller (*interventor*) was appointed to each enterprise. "The CNT unions," writes José Peirats, the Anarchosyndicalist historian, "vigorously protested this bold attack on the Collectivization Decree [approved by the Catalan government in October 1936].[2] Certain Catalanist political groups also protested what they regarded as interference by the central government in the autonomy of Catalonia."[3]

The decree, wrote the Barcelona correspondent of the *New York Post*, "suggests that the government is taking drastic steps to conciliate big foreign capital and thereby the important financial interests which exert so much influence on the foreign policies of Britain and France."[4] But, confident of General Franco's ultimate victory, the companies involved ignored the gesture. Quite early in the war, the international combine based in Toronto, the Barcelona Traction, Light, and Power Company, known as *La Canadiense*—which in Catalonia owned the Riegos y Fuerzas del Ebro, Compañía Barcelonesa de Electricidad, Electra Reusense, Hidro-Eléctrica del Segre, Manresana de Energía Eléctrica and Alumbrado de Poblaciones—had moved its headquarters to Saragossa in Nationalist territory. In a letter to H. Malcolm Hubbard, a company executive in London, dated 10 August 1936, Fraser Lawton, the manager in Barcelona, stated: "Things look worse and worse here every day; not a bright spot in sight at present. . . . We are up against every conceivable difficulty in business and private life."[5] It was not likely that the decree of 27 April would lure him back to Barcelona now that General Franco's victory appeared so close at hand.

Without specifically mentioning the decree, *Tierra y Libertad*, the FAI organ, warned that "a morale of victory" was possible only by recognizing the working class as "a factor of prime importance"; that it would be "downright madness to attempt under any pretext to wrest from [the working class] what it most desires, . . . to nullify what it is principally defending. The 19th July 1936 marked a new era in the history of Spain. For the proletariat, it opened . . . the road to its emancipation. . . . With the means of production, it initiated a new historical epoch by creating and testing new forms of socialization.[6] When we speak of a morale of victory we think of the workers. Isn't it absurd how much is being done to demoralize them by seizing their revolutionary gains, the gains that strengthen their will to fight, multiply their efforts, and make them invincible in the defense of liberty?"[7]

While the attempt to appease foreign capital was under way, government controllers were appointed to decollectivize and nationalize a few Spanish enterprises, a policy that was promoted to a limited extent in the industrialized region of Catalonia by the department of economy under the PSUC leader Estanislao Ruiz Ponsetti.[8] In addition, other firms were returned to their original owners. "The instigators of this trend," decried *Solidaridad Obrera*, did not possess the "degree of prudence and responsibility" of the organized proletariat and were seeking the "restoration of certain privileges and even the creation of new ones" without worrying about the morale of thousands of workers and combatants.[9] Although only a few enterprises were restored to their former proprietors, because many owners had been executed or had fled to nationalist territory at the outbreak of the Civil War, the Communist-controlled foreign press censorship, which in the past had attempted to minimize the scope of the Revolution, allowed foreign press correspondents to make great play with the handful of restitutions.

"If the loyalist republic were ever really 'Red,' as its enemies call it," observed the correspondent of the *New York Post*, "the great work of handing back factories and mines to their original owners certainly shows that the label cannot now be properly applied. As a matter of fact, a great number of industrial properties were never collectivized and have continued to run under private management and ownership. Hundreds of others, which were taken over by soviets of workers, in the early days of the civil war, have been restored to the owners. The rest, a government official told me, also will be 'decollectivized' in the course of time. This official asserted that the Negrín government has become more conservative and capitalistic than the government existing before the Aragon offensive, and predicted that any future cabinet shifts would turn it even further to the right. What this official did not add was that the government in decollectivizing had a political motive. It demonstrated thereby, for the benefit of Britain, France, and the United States, that the loyalist government is not a 'Red' Government."[10]

The article had obviously been inspired by official sources for propaganda purposes, for the actual number of restitutions was "minimal, insignificant," to use the words of Cardona Rosell, a member of the CNT national committee,[11] but the mere threat of rolling back the workers' gains and the failure of the central government to approve any laws institutionalizing the revolution created doubts and anxieties among the rank and file of the libertarian movement. This threat had loomed large since the decree of 2 September 1937, signed by Juan Negrín, in his capacity as finance minister, making the industrial collectives subject to state taxes but without conferring on them legal status.[12]

Particularly threatening was the decree of 11 August 1938, militarizing the war industries, which the Anarchosyndicalists regarded as being no less odious than nationalization.[13] Although the plants involved had been collectivized by workers' committees and their seizure subsequently legalized by the collectivization decree of the Generalitat in October 1936, this measure was never recognized by the central government. "The immediate result of the [militarization decree]," writes Peirats, "was the appointment of technicians, on the basis of political criteria, and the creation of a vast bureaucracy of inspectors and advisers, many of them Russian, subservient to a political party, whose directives could not be questioned. The consequences were necessarily deplorable: the progressive demoralization of the workers because of their loss of control and the replacement of real technicians by specialists in political proselytism. All this had a detrimental effect on production."[14] The decree, he stated in a later passage, was issued by a government in which the CNT was represented. "If the upper echelons of the CNT appeared to give their blessing, this was not so in the case of the rank and file, for there is abundant proof of tenacious resistance among the workers to the handing over of the war industries."[15]

Evidence of this resistance can be found in a brief record of the session of 15 October 1938 of the national plenum of the CNT, during which fears were expressed by the Catalan delegate that the control of the war industries by the Communist-controlled undersecretaryship of armaments would result in the absorption of the CNT by the UGT, since the Anarchosyndicalists would be "displaced" from the management of the factories and shops they controlled. "All this," said the delegate, "with the acquiescence of the national committee! We must give warning that this is the road that leads to the abyss and to disaster."[16]

No less disturbing to the workers of the CNT and FAI was the knowledge that some enterprises were being returned to their original owners. In an article headlined "Why Are the People Fighting?" *Tierra y Libertad* declared: "The whole world knows that the Spanish people will not revert to the regime that ended in July 1936. Everything that is said to the contrary notwithstanding, everything that is done to put a brake on the wheels of progress, in order to placate international reaction and the social classes that have been divested of their privileges, undermines our fighting morale and the spirit of sacrifice indispensable for victory."[17]

It was evident that the uncertainties regarding the future course of the revolution weighed heavily on the minds of the workers. "We have rejected as a pernicious error, or worse still, as a dangerous maneuver, the tendency to sacrifice the most vital and precious conquests of our people for foreign aid, which is necessarily hypothetical," wrote *Solidaridad Obrera*.[18] Such a sacrifice, it declared on another occasion, would mean "a vertical collapse of morale in the rear and, consequently, at the battle fronts. It would be equivalent to telling the combatants that they should renounce the most essential reasons for the struggle."[19]

It is fitting at this point to raise the question as to whether those historians (and present-day political activists, such as the Veterans of the Abraham Lincoln Brigade) who portray the Civil War as essentially a conflict between democracy and fascism fully comprehend or intentionally distort the true nature of the conflict in the Republican camp and the real purpose of Soviet intervention, as well as the seismic proportions of the revolution that shattered the democratic Republic of 1931.[20] For some historians, the revolution was not an event of the first magnitude unparalleled in depth and scope in European history but rather a lamentable phenomenon, which, in the words of Angel Viñas—who typifies this school of thought—"brutally tarnished the image of the Republic abroad" and "was fatal to the Republic and its foreign policy." It was for this reason, he said, when interviewed in 1979, that he attributed such importance to the policy of Stalin and the Spanish Communist party in "curbing the revolution," in prosecuting the war "exclusively," in "improving the image of the Republic in the eyes of the British and French governments in order to bring about a much more favorable attitude toward the Republic, if not their direct intervention." In the end, he added, this objective was not achieved. "But of course Stalin saw the problem from the first moment. . . . His famous letter to Largo Caballero bears witness to this. . . . I do not believe, contrary to what is currently affirmed in the literature, that it signified Soviet interference in the internal affairs of the Republic or that Largo Caballero was offended by it. At least, this is not documented. But to revert to the theme of the revolution, it is true that its outbreak could not be avoided and that this sealed the fate of the Republic. However, war is waged with enthusiasm. As long as there was revolution, there was enthusiasm. When the revolution was checked, the enthusiasm in many sectors declined. Taking everything into consideration, it is clear that, in the last analysis, the war could not be won by recourse to a revolution."[21]

In view of the ambiguity of this statement, it is important to clarify some of the fundamental issues by quoting a few passages from the analytical work *La crisis del movimiento comunista*, of Fernando Claudín, who was a prominent member of the PCE for nearly thirty years until he parted company with its secretary, Santiago Carrillo, in 1964:

> If the war had been only a technical and military undertaking, it would be difficult to fault the contribution of the trinomial PCE-CI-USSR to the struggle of the Spanish people against fascism. . . . The PCE's thesis that "if we do not win the war, no revolution is possible" was clarity itself, but the other thesis that always accompanied the first, "when we win the war, we shall have won the revolution,"[22] was ambiguity itself, because . . . each of the political and trade-union organizations in the republican camp had its own idea of the "revolution." . . .

The entire future of the Republic would be strongly conditioned by the type of social and political regime that prevailed during the Civil War. The military forces established by the PCE, the Comintern, and Soviet aid basically served two political objectives: military resistance to the rebels, and ensuring that the "bourgeois democratic" type of republic acceptable to the bourgeois republicans, and supposedly acceptable to the "western democracies" would prevail. But, in implementing the second objective, the military forces of the PCE, Comintern and USSR came into conflict with the reality of the revolution and with the majority of the proletariat, who saw this reality as their greatest gain. Such a conflict was bound to weaken the military power of the republic. The two political objectives . . . were not complementary but contradictory. The second undermined the positive effects of the first. . . .

In the early months of 1937, the Caballeristas, Anarchosyndicalists, and POUMists became convinced that their adaptation to the Moscow line had no positive effect on the attitude of the "western democracies." On the other hand, it resulted in the continual recoil of the initial "proletarian content" of the revolution and strengthened the PCE, reformist socialists and bourgeois republicans in the political and military structure. . . .

Great social revolutions, like the Spanish revolution, either advance decisively to their ultimate conclusion, or they retreat equally decisively and end in counterrevolution. Long before the fascist troops broke into Barcelona and Madrid, counterrevolution was silently being established in the republican zone. The longer the Civil War dragged on, with its wake of deprivation and sacrifice, the more the military relationship of forces changed in the enemy's favor (for they were receiving much more aid from Germany and Italy than the Republic was receiving from the USSR), and the more defeatism and despair spread among the petty-bourgeois layers of town and country, infecting groups of the proletariat. Azaña's and Prieto's capitulationist policy gained a broader and broader social base, while the last ditch resistance advocated by the Communists encountered growing skepticism. The PCE desperately tried to check this deterioration of the situation, but neither propaganda, nor its measures designed to strengthen the army or intensify arms production, could fill the vacuum left by the loss of what had in the early months been the decisive reservoir of the people's combativity: its revolutionary enthusiasm.[23]

Claudín then touches upon a little-known development, which partly explains the symptoms of demoralization within the PCE that manifested themselves shortly before the end of the war. After stating that the most radical section of the proletariat felt rejected and betrayed and that within the Communist party itself, "doubt and vacillation appeared behind an optimistic façade," he continues: "Critical voices were raised [in the PCE] against the policy of alliance with the bourgeois republican leaders and the reformists of the PSOE, and the idea was expressed that the only way out of the situation was for the party to take the conduct of the war completely into its own hands. These tendencies were associated with a conviction that gained ground among many Communists that the hopes placed in aid from the 'western democracies' had proved totally illusory."[24]

Whatever the extent of this deviation, which reflected the growing sense of dubiety within the party, it was never strong enough to cause a change of policy and was quickly corrected by Togliatti. In his report to the Comintern, dated 21–22 April 1938, he stated: "The tendency against which I have had to take a stand on several occasions is the belief that all problems can be solved if the party takes into its hands all the levers of power and that it should do so as soon as possible. There was indecision also on the part of Pepe [party secretary José Díaz] regarding the idea of a purely working-class government. But this was rapidly overcome."[25]

In spite of this evidence, La Pasionaria emphatically denied, when interviewed years later, that there had ever been any deviationist tendency within the party. "We never raised the question of socialism during the war," she stated, "only the question of the defense of the Republic and democracy. . . . There was never any vacillation within the party on this matter."[26] Nevertheless, the deviationist trend made an ephemeral public appearance in Madrid, when *Mundo Obrero*, which was not closely supervised by the politburo in Barcelona, ventured to assert: "We cannot say, as another paper affirms, that 'the only possible outcome of the war is for Spain to be neither fascist nor Communist, because this is the way France wants it.' The Spanish people will win though the capitalists oppose us."[27] The reply of the politburo was categorical. Signed by José Díaz, but undoubtedly inspired, if not actually written, by Togliatti himself, it said:

> The statement that "*the only possible outcome of the war is for Spain to be neither fascist nor Communist*" is absolutely correct. To remove the slightest doubt, we must repeat one more time that the Spanish people are fighting this war *for their national independence . . . and for the defense of the democratic Republic*. . . . Our party has never thought of establishing a Communist regime after the war. If the working masses, the peasants, and the small urban bourgeoisie follow us and trust us it is because they know that we are the stoutest defenders of national independence, of liberty, and the republican Constitution. . . . To raise the question of establishing a Communist regime would be to divide the people, because a Communist regime could never be accepted by all Spaniards, not by any means, and our party will never do anything to divide the people. . . . You affirm that "the Spanish people will win though the capitalists oppose us," . . . but, politically, this also is not in accord with the situation or with the policy of our party and the Communist International. In my report to the November plenum of the central committee, I stated: "There are grounds on which all the democratic States can unite and act together . . . : the grounds of defense against war, which threatens all of us." When I spoke of "all the democratic States" I was thinking not only of the Soviet Union, where there is a Socialist democracy, but of France, England, Czechoslovakia, the United States, etc., which are democratic countries, but capitalist ones. We want these States to help us; we think

they would be defending their own interests by defending us. . . . The position you take in your article is very different and is incorrect. The error you make is that you forget the international character of our struggle.[28]

It was clear from this unequivocal response that the Spanish politburo, directed by the Comintern, intended to present the same moderate façade as it had presented since the inception of the conflict.

60

Negrín's Thirteen War Aims

*I*n a move designed to influence the Western democracies and the moderate segment in General Franco's territory, the government issued on 30 April 1938 the following statement to Spanish and foreign journalists:

The Government of National Union, which enjoys the confidence of all parties and trade-union organizations in Loyalist Spain . . . solemnly proclaims for the knowledge of its compatriots and for the information of the world the following war aims:

1. To assure the absolute independence and complete integrity of Spain, a Spain completely free from all foreign interference whatever its nature and origin . . .

2. Liberation of our territory from the foreign military forces that have invaded it, as well as from those elements who have come to Spain since July 1936 and who, under the pretext of technical collaboration, intervene and attempt to dominate the legal and economic life of Spain for their own benefit. [To avoid misunderstanding, the Communist organ *Mundo Obrero* made it clear that this paragraph was directed at German and Italian military forces and technicians and at those "who have been placed at the head of all kinds of foreign industrial enterprises established by the invaders in the rebel zone."[1]]

3. A People's Republic represented by a strong State based on *principles of pure democracy* and acting through a government endowed with full authority by the votes of its citizens enjoying *universal suffrage* . . .

4. The legal and social structure of the Republic shall be determined by the will of the nation freely expressed in a plebiscite to take place immediately after the conclusion of the war. The plebiscite shall be held with full guarantees and with no restrictions or limitations, ensuring those who participate in it against any possible reprisal.

5. Respect for regional liberties without prejudicing the unity of Spain . . .

6. The Spanish State will guarantee full civil and political rights, freedom of conscience, and the free exercise of religious beliefs and practices. [According to A. Lizarra (pseudonym for Andrés María de Irujo) this point was inspired by his

brother, Manuel de Irujo, a practicing Catholic and, at the time, Basque National minister without portfolio.²]

7. Within the limits imposed by the supreme interests of the nation, the State shall guarantee legally acquired property and the protection of the producers. Without reducing individual initiative, it shall prevent any accumulation of wealth that might lead to the exploitation of the citizen and the infringement of collective rights, endangering the State's control over social and economic life. To this end, the State shall encourage the development of small business, guarantee family property and stimulate all measures conducive to moral, economic and racial improvement among the producing classes.

The property and legitimate interests of those foreigners who have not aided the rebellion shall be respected, and the question of compensation for damages involuntarily caused during the war will be studied. . . .

8. Agrarian reform shall liquidate the old semifeudal aristocratic estates, which lack all human, national, and patriotic feeling and have always formed the major obstacle to the development of the country's great possibilities. A new Spain based on a broad, solid democracy of the peasants, who shall be the owners of the land they till.

9. The State shall guarantee the rights of the worker by means of advanced social legislation in accordance with the specific needs of the life and economy of Spain.

10. Cultural, physical and moral improvement of the race will be the prime and basic concern of the State.

11. *The Spanish army . . . shall be free from all hegemony by any party or tendency. . . .*

12. The Spanish State reaffirms its constitutional doctrine renouncing war as an instrument of national policy. . . .

13. A broad amnesty for all Spaniards who wish to cooperate in the immense task of the reconstruction and aggrandizement of Spain. . . .³

Negrín's mouthpiece, *La Vanguardia*, affirmed that the program would be put into effect "the very day the war ended."⁴ The premier's enthusiasm for the thirteen war aims, wrote Julián Zugazagoitia, "is almost delirious. He attaches the utmost importance to them and regards them as a valuable tool in Franco's territory and abroad."⁵ But if the promise of "pure democracy" and of an army "free from all hegemony by any party or tendency"—the two fundamental conditions on which a multiparty system depended—had any substance at all, there was little evidence in the conduct of the premier and defense minister and even less in the policies pursued by the PCE, as indicated in previous chapters. Even after the formal enunciation of the program, the PCE continued its drive for dominion over the armed forces and resumed its campaign in favor of a "Single Party of the Proletariat." The single party, it asseverated on 13 May, would benefit "all tendencies, all the antifascist forces," and no one could view it "with anything but extreme sympathy." Communists and Socialists, it exhorted, should work "with the utmost haste and intensity for a single membership card."[6] In the light of similar mergers—the JSU and PSUC—it cannot be overemphasized that if this amalgamation had been achieved, it would have been a giant stride toward the establishment of a single party state and rendered null and void the two basic points of the program pledging "pure democracy" and an army "free from all hegemony."

The maximum publicity was given to the program at home and abroad. Foreign minister Alvarez del Vayo, at the next session of the League of Nations, laid special emphasis on the promise of the "free exercise of religious beliefs and practises,"[7] which had been suppressed since the outbreak of the Revolution.[8] In the succeeding months a number of reforms were introduced. On 25 June, Negrín restored religious practices in the land, sea, and air forces and ordered the chiefs of the three services to provide spiritual aid to those requesting it.[9] On 17 October, for the first time since the outbreak of the Civil War, Barcelona witnessed the astonishing spectacle of a religious funeral procession in honor of a Basque captain making its way along the Gran Vía Diagonal with "raised cross," "priests meticulously vested," and with participants "chanting ritual responses."[10] The leading article in *El Día Gráfico*, written by Negrín's press secretary Francisco Aguirre, stated: "The Catholic funeral held yesterday afternoon provided the military members controlling the withdrawal of foreign combatants with a moving spectacle.[11] The respect that was shown will enable them, when their stay here is over, to take away with them a totally different impression of Spain than the one that has been given until recently, namely, a lamentable example of fanaticism and intolerance. . . . The funeral of the Basque hero, Vicente de Eguía Sagarduy, was a political event of enormous importance. . . . The Catholics, who are fighting on the side of the Republic, know that their right to express their religious beliefs enjoys today, as never before, . . . not only the protection of the government, but the respect of all citizens. If evidence of this has been lacking, it was proved yesterday and the news films will make it known to the world."[12] Finally, on 8 December, Negrín issued a decree setting up a "General Commissariat of Religion" in his own offices entrusted with all matters relating to religious activities.[13] His mouthpiece, *La Vanguardia*, whose editorial comment was flanked on both sides by laudatory statements of such moderate politicians as the Basque Nationalist Julio Jáuregui and the Socialist Manuel Cordero, stressed the "guarantee of religious freedom" furnished by the decree and the effect on foreign countries, which would "discern the liberal spirit of the Republic."[14] To head the commissariat, Negrín appointed his friend and fellow physiologist, Dr. Bellido Golferich of the University of Barcelona.[15] Whether or not Negrín would have reopened the churches in Barcelona cannot be said with certainty, for the city was occupied by General Franco only a few weeks later.

Meanwhile, the thirteen war aims became the programmatic frontispiece of the Negrín government. "The Thirteen Points," wrote Louis Fischer, Negrín's chief propaganda agent abroad, ". . . became the cardinal principles of the Republic. Negrín frequently referred to them in speeches. They were communicated officially to foreign governments and pro-Loyalist propaganda abroad often took them as its text."[16]

In a radio address aimed at foreign opinion and reported in the weekly propaganda bulletin *The News of Spain*, edited by Herbert R. Southworth, an unfaltering supporter of Negrín for fifty years,[17] the prime minister declared: "We wish to assure the independence of Spain and the liberty of the Spanish people. . . . We want the legal aspects of the Spanish State within the bounds of tolerance, liberty and individual guarantees to be outlined by the Spanish people themselves through a plebiscite. We assure everyone that once the war is over there will be a full amnesty. We want a strong firm government of democratic origin. . . . Our proposals are guaranteed by a government which has known how to restore order, create an army, . . . unify the people, defend its territory and which has been the first government in authority for many generations that has succeeded in linking its authority with the aspirations of the people."[18]

Foreign fellow travelers, such as the celebrated German playwright and poet Ernst Toller, helped to disseminate the thirteen points abroad. In a broadcast to the United States from Radio Madrid, controlled by the PCE, he stressed that private property was protected. "You may own a shop, a department store. You may own a textile factory or a jeweler's. Nobody will interfere with your work."[19] In the *Volunteer for Liberty*, the organ of the English-speaking battalions of the Communist-controlled International Brigades, a contest of articles was held on the merits of the declaration. "It is a dignified statement which must profoundly move all decent humane people throughout the world," ran the winning article. "It will succeed in convincing many wavering elements both in Spain and abroad that the cause of the Republic is in capable hands and is bound to succeed. . . . All liberal-minded people—all who believe in human justice and freedom—must support these points and must recognise their own obligations, their duty to the Republic assailed by foreign invaders."[20] The thirteen-point program was also favorably and optimistically discussed by non-Communists, including some prominent leaders of Izquierda Republicana and Unión Republicana,[21] and by distinguished foreign scholars.[22]

In view of the immense publicity received by the program, its genesis is worth noting. According to Louis Fischer, whose evidence is crucial in the matter, the program was inspired by Ivor Montagu, the British film producer, whom Fischer prudently avoids identifying as a member of the Communist party of Great Britain and as an editor of the London *Daily Worker*.[23] "Throughout my stay in Barcelona," he writes in the U.S. edition of *Men and Politics*, "I visited the Foreign Office every day, and every day I saw Ivor Montagu sitting in del Vayo's antechamber still waiting for permission from the War Department to take moving pictures at the front. . . . Once he said to me, 'You know, it seems to me that the Loyalist government ought to enunciate its war aims, a sort of Fourteen Points program like Woodrow Wilson's.' 'Wonderful idea,' I said, 'why has it never occurred to anybody?' I passed the idea on to del Vayo. . . . He talked to Negrín. Negrín said, 'Fine, write them.' Vayo drafted ten points and showed them to

Negrín. Negrín said, 'We must have thirteen to show that we are not superstitious,' and he added three himself."[24] Negrín's frivolity says little for the genuineness of the entire program.

It is noteworthy that in the English edition of Louis Fischer's book, all reference to Ivor Montagu—who since 1929 had been a prominent member of the British Communist party[25]—was omitted, and the thirteen-point episode was "touched up," as Salvador de Madariaga puts it, to adapt to "English tastes."[26] "For some time," ran the expurgated English version, "the Loyalist leaders had considered the advisability of announcing their social peace aims. They hoped they would undermine morale in Franco territory and reinforce sympathy for Loyalist Spain in foreign countries. Del Vayo and Negrín drafted most of the war aims and they were finally approved at a solemn session of the Cabinet."[27] Writes Alvarez del Vayo: "It was a Cabinet meeting which did credit to the Government and to the country, and which in itself gave the lie direct to all those who tried to represent loyalist Spain as a country dominated by foreign influence, demagogues, and revolutionaries."[28] And some years later the official Communist history of the Civil War affirmed: "The thirteen points demonstrated the falsity of the campaigns abroad that we were fighting for Communism, Socialism, or for an Anarchist regime in Spain and without democratic principles."[29]

As though it had not been directly involved in the elaboration of the thirteen war aims, the PCE issued two weeks after their publication the following formal announcement: "The Politburo of the Central Committee of the Communist Party has examined the thirteen points and proclaims its agreement with them. The document corresponds with the character of the struggle of the Spanish people who are defending republican democracy and national independence and constitutes the foundation upon which all the antifascist forces of our country should unite. . . . We encourage all our comrades, all the combatants, and the entire antifascist people to continue working and fighting for a democratic Spain, in which the people enjoy to the full the rights that have always been denied them and in which they will achieve their aspirations of liberty, peace, justice, and social progress."[30]

At the cabinet meeting of 30 April at which Negrín announced his program, there was only one hesitant voice. According to a circular issued the next day by the national committee of the CNT to the regional committees of the organization, Segundo Blanco, the lone CNT minister, suggested that the program be submitted to the various parties and organizations for prior approval, but Negrín objected for the following reasons: (1) It had to be published the same day and delivered to the British embassy. (2) Its object was to demonstrate abroad, "especially in France and England," that there were "no extreme policies or any red danger" in Republican Spain. (3) If it were submitted to all the organizations "none would be in agreement with it, since it could not satisfy their respective doctrinal points of view." Finally, Negrín pointed out that the declaration "should not be taken literally, because it was not something that would be applied in its entirety but rather a declaration that was timely and necessary for abroad."[31]

On 3 May, in a circular addressed to the regional committees of the FAI, the peninsular committee expressed its foreboding. There was no doubt, it said, that the program was designed to effect a change in international policy toward antifascist Spain, but it was also "the first openly acknowledged step" toward the liquidation of the Revolution. The fact that it had been announced by a government in which the CNT was represented raised "a very grave problem" of responsibility, since it would appear that the CNT had given "its consent to the renunciation of all the revolutionary conquests we have defended until now." Then, in a more conciliatory tone, the peninsular committee added: "We accept the declaration as an inescapable fact, as something imposed by more powerful forces, which we cannot openly oppose lest we put ourselves in the position of causing a veritable catastrophe for antifascist Spain. . . . But in no way . . . do we lend ourselves to the game of the bourgeois and reformist groups who are using the international situation in order to blackmail the working class into renouncing its revolutionary gains. It would have been preferable had our revolutionary trade-union organization not shared responsibility for the declaration. Nevertheless, what it has done has avoided greater evils and is in accord with its representation in the government. The FAI, which is free from these commitments, should continue and can continue to be the vehicle for attaining Anarchism's yearnings and aspirations."[32]

This artful attempt to distance itself from the ideological transgressions of the CNT and to salvage its own historic responsibility, while condoning the CNT's action in order not to exacerbate the dissensions within the libertarian movement, was not supported by the more radical elements; for, three days later, the peninsular committee issued another circular divorcing itself completely from the program: "From point 3, which establishes a parliamentary regime, to point 13, which promises amnesty to the supporters of Franco, the whole document clashes violently not only with our ideas . . . but with the reality of the situation created on 19 July [1936]. . . . We do not find in the text a formula that guarantees the conquests of the workers and peasants: the right to working-class control of production and to the collective cultivation of the soil. On the other hand, the State guarantees private property, private enterprise, the free exercise of religion, the development of small business, the compensation of foreign capital, etc., etc. It is difficult to conceive of a more counterrevolutionary program at this time."[33]

On 19 May, the national committee of the CNT, controlled by the two outstanding moderates, Mariano Vázquez and Horacio M. Prieto, secretary and former secretary, respectively, tried to assuage the anxieties rampant in the libertarian movement. In a circular summarizing the reaction of the regional committees to the thirteen-point program, it stated: "[The] militants . . . intuitively see dangers, but at times some of the comrades exaggerate, . . . because the declaration contains much that is profitable." It then explained each point in a positive manner as indicated by the following examples:

1. *To assure the absolute independence and complete integrity of Spain.* This has been repeatedly affirmed by us since the 19th of July. If anybody should feel concern it should be the Communists since the document refers to a Spain "free from all foreign interference WHATEVER ITS NATURE AND ORIGIN." . . .

6. *The Spanish State will guarantee the free exercise of religious beliefs and practices.* Is it possible to say anything else? It is essential to record our respect for religion, when we know the important role it plays especially in North America and England.

7. *The State shall guarantee legally acquired property and shall encourage the development of small property.* We would prefer to see a declaration in favor of socialization, collectivization, etc., but how can we forget that these issues are the "crux" of our problem abroad? Can we suddenly ignore the fact that neither England, nor France, nor America, nor any democracy can look kindly on or assist in the victory of a regime based on collectivization, socialization, or even nationalization by the workers? . . .

11. *The Spanish army shall be free from all hegemony by any party or tendency.* This is just a repetition of what we have been saying all along in face of the tactics and absorbing tendencies (*absorcionismos*) of the marxists.

"We have taken the document apart point by point," the circular continued. ". . . It is not as counterrevolutionary as may appear at first sight. This we have demonstrated, but it is not the fundamental matter. The important thing is that it has been proclaimed at an opportune time for the benefit of foreign opinion. . . . In France, in North America, in England, it is a formidable tool in the hands of those who wish to help us. That is all. It has fulfilled its mission."[34]

In spite of the massive publicity given to the program, it made no impression on the democratic powers. Horacio M. Prieto, the most influential and forceful member on the national committee of the CNT, who together with Mariano Vázquez was largely responsible for determining CNT policy and for the committee's endorsement of the program, nonetheless brashly declared after the war: "Neither in the foreign offices nor in bourgeois circles abroad did anyone pay the slightest attention to the mendacious propaganda of our governments, which were the victims of a stupid naivety in trying to hide what was as clear as the light of day: On the one hand, the workers of the CNT carrying out sporadic attempts at socialization and, on the other hand, the marxists, lying in wait for the hour of victory in order to bolshevize Spain."[35]

Nevertheless, until General Franco's all-out offensive against Catalonia in December 1938, the hope still lingered among a significant segment of the Spanish left that Britain and France might reverse their policy and that the latent antagonisms between Germany and the Western democracies would erupt into a general European conflict that would save Republican Spain. For obvious diplomatic reasons, this hope could not be publicly acknowledged. Even after the collapse of the eastern front in the spring of 1938, when everything appeared to be fusing into disaster, La Pasionaria declared: "There are still people in our country who cherish too many illusions regarding the international situation, and every day expect some extraordinary event that will suddenly change the European outlook and put an end to the invasion of our country. We do not share these naive illusions and warn everyone against them. [If] a European war should break out the fascists who are invading our soil would not hesitate to make use of the most barbarous weapons of destruction to crush our people in their eagerness to conquer Spain and gain control of the Mediterranean. We must not have any illusions that a European war would operate in our favor and bring the end of the war nearer."[36]

Despite this asseveration, foreign minister Alvarez del Vayo, whose thoughts reflected the politburo's expectations, made no secret in private conversation that he based his hopes on a European conflict. According to Azaña's brother-in-law, Cipriano Rivas-Cherif, del Vayo "assured" José Giral that war was imminent and that it would have "a favorable and decisive influence on our fate,"[37] while Elya Ehrenburg, the Soviet journalist and writer, recalls that the foreign minister assured him in the summer of 1938 that "war between Germany on the one hand and France with her allies on the other was inevitable."[38]

This of course was the hope of Joseph Stalin and the personal conviction of Juan Negrín, the symbol of the resistance policy, who, according to Herbert Matthews, a friend and enduring admirer of the premier, "realized that if he could only hold out long enough the greater conflict would come along and save Republican Spain."[39]

61

Hopes of Anglo-French Intervention Fade

*I*f Britain and France refrained from challenging Italy and Germany in Spain, this was not because they were blind to the threat to their strategic interests;[1] it was because they feared that a general war in Western Europe, whether they won or lost, could only redound to the benefit of Russia. This point has already been stressed in earlier chapters,[2] but is important enough to warrant further evidence.

In a policy summary drafted by Gladwyn Jebb, private secretary to Alexander Cadogan, permanent undersecretary of the Foreign Office since January 1938, and based partly on the papers of William Strang, head of the Central Department—all three men supporters of Prime Minister Neville Chamberlain—Jebb observed that the objection to collective security was that it would "provoke war in which defeat would be disastrous and victory hardly less so."[3]

At a session, on 15 March 1938, of the Comité Permanent de la Défense Nationale, Edouard Daladier, the French minister of defense, stated that "one would have to be blind not to see that intervention in Spain would start a general war."[4] As to what he envisioned by a general war was expressed by him apocalyptically three months later, when, as the reader will recall, he told Count von Welczech, the German ambassador: "[The] catastrophic frightfulness of a modern war would surpass all that humanity had ever seen, and would mean the utter destruction of European civilization. Into the battle zones, devastated and denuded of men, Cossack and Mongol hordes would then pour, bringing to Europe a new 'Culture.' "

Hence, the nonintervention policy of Britain and France during the Civil War was determined not only by their hostility to the social revolution and by later Communist domination, of which they were fully informed through their diplomatic and secret agents, but by the fear that a general war would bring in its wake the enthronement of Communism in the whole of Europe. Consequently, no effort at dissimulation or persuasion, no attempt by successive Spanish governments to curb or roll back the revolution could have affected Anglo-French policy. To prove this point beyond cavil it is imperative to resume our study of the diplomatic game discussed in earlier chapters[5] so that the reader will understand why Stalin's "democratic" masquerade in Spain was bound to fail.

We have already seen that the policy of appeasement of Germany was pursued with greater vigor from the time Neville Chamberlain succeeded Stanley Baldwin in the premiership in May 1937 and that the new prime minister perceived the Soviet Union as the major long-term threat to British interests and the Western world. For this reason, a political settlement with Germany was the cornerstone of Chamberlain's policy, and it was visionary to believe that Britain would come to the aid of Republican Spain at the risk of a war in Western Europe.

That some members of the PCE in the spring of 1938 had begun to question the assumption that Britain and France would eventually be drawn into the conflict has already been seen in a previous chapter,[6] but such doubts, inadmissible in Communist circles, had to be squelched if morale were to be sustained, particularly at the battlefronts. "I never for a moment believed that the Spanish government would get real help from Britain and France," Ralph Bates, the British author and assistant commissar of the Fifteenth International Brigade, wrote in 1940 after he had severed his connections with the Communists. He was "tremendously censured," he said, by the English representative of the Communist party in Madrid for dealing with the problem, even implicitly, in the brigade organ *Volunteer for Liberty*—of which he was editor—and was "charged with exposing the boys to the possibility of this thought coming up in their minds." "In so far as we damped down the revolution in Spain," he added, "in the interests of collective security, then we miscalculated. I feel compelled to face that fact. Not all our soft-pedalling won [Britain and France] to our side. Might we have got more out of the CNT and FAI if we had not soft-pedalled so much?"[7]

The extent to which Chamberlain and his supporters were prepared to pursue the appeasement of Germany is evident from a conversation that Lord Halifax held with Adolf Hitler on 19 November 1937. At that time, Halifax was Lord Privy Seal and later, as foreign secretary,[8] formed part of Chamberlain's "Inner Cabinet" with Sir Samuel Hoare and Sir John Simon. According to a German foreign ministry memorandum, Halifax recognized that Hitler "had not only performed great services in Germany" but also had been able "by preventing the entry of Communism into his own country, to bar its passage further West." Halifax stated that on the English side "it was not necessarily thought that the status quo must be maintained under all circumstances." He then spoke of "possible alterations in the European order which might be destined to come about with the passage of time. Amongst these questions were Danzig, Austria, and Czechoslovakia. England was interested to see that any alterations should come through the course of *peaceful evolution* and that methods should be avoided which might cause far-reaching disturbances [i.e., war in Western Europe]."[9] Since Austria was the gateway to Czechoslovakia, and Danzig the key to Poland, these remarks must have encouraged Hitler to believe that his territorial ambitions in Eastern Europe would encounter scant opposition.

"Halifax's remarks," writes the British historian A. J. P. Taylor, "if they had any practical sense, were an invitation to Hitler to promote German nationalist agitation in Danzig, Czechoslovakia, and Austria; an assurance also that this agitation would not be opposed from without."[10] Hitler also received similar assurances from the French government. "[I] was amazed to note," Franz von Papen, the German ambassador in Austria, told Hitler on 10 November 1937 after a visit to Paris, "that, like [foreign minister] Bonnet, Premier [Camille Chautemps] considered a reorientation of French policy in Central Europe as entirely open to discussion. . . . [He], too, had no objection to a marked extension of German influence in Austria obtained through evolutionary means."[11] And, on 4 December, in a letter to state secretary von Weizsäcker, the head of the political department in the German foreign ministry, von Papen stated: "I found it very interesting to note that neither Bonnet nor Chautemps raised any objections to an evolutionary extension of German influence . . . in Czechoslovakia, on the basis of a reorganization into a nation of nationalities."[12]

In pursuit of his appeasement policy, Chamberlain removed Sir Robert Vansittart, the permanent undersecretary of state for foreign affairs, the most forceful exponent of anti-German opinion in the Foreign Office, and assigned him to the newly created post of "Chief Diplomatic Adviser," where, according to the earl of Birkenhead, "he found himself trapped in a gilded cage" and where he "ceased to exert any effective influence on foreign affairs."[13] Commenting in a letter to his sister on all the months Stanley Baldwin had "wasted in futile attempts" to push Vansittart out of the Foreign Office, Chamberlain remarked: "[It] is amusing to record that I have done it in three days. . . . I am afraid his instincts were all against my policy. . . . I suspect that in Rome and Berlin the rejoicings will be loud and deep."[14]

The way was now open for a more vigorous pursuit of appeasement by circumventing the Foreign Office, which, according to Sir Horace Wilson, Chamberlain's intimate colleague and chief diplomatic adviser, represented an obstruction to the prime minister's policy of coming to terms with the dictators.[15] "The old-established machine of the Foreign Office," wrote Lord Templewood (Sir Samuel Hoare), in his published memoir of the period, "did not seem to [Chamberlain] to move quickly enough for the crisis that threatened Europe."[16] More expressive of Hoare's true attitude toward the Foreign Office was the candid letter he sent to Neville Chamberlain on 17 March 1937, shortly before Stanley Baldwin's resignation from the premiership. After suggesting that Chamberlain should not copy "Baldwin's slipshod, happy-go-lucky quietism" he continued: "Do not let anything irrevocable or badly compromising happen in foreign politics until you are in control. I say this because I am convinced that the FO [Foreign Office] is so much biased against Germany (and Italy and Japan) that unconsciously and almost continuously they are making impossible any sort of reconciliation. I believe myself that when once you are Prime Minister it will be possible greatly to change the European atmosphere."[17]

On 3 March 1938, the British ambassador to Berlin, Sir Nevile Henderson, who bypassed the regular Foreign Office channels and plied the prime minister directly with letters and visits,[18] told Hitler that the aim of British policy was "to establish the basis for a genuine and cordial friendship with Germany." Lord Halifax, Henderson added, had already admitted that changes in Europe could be considered "quite possible," provided they were the product of "higher reason" rather than "the free play of forces."[19] This policy was certainly not one that Henderson "had worked out for himself," as William N. Medlicott affirms in his preface to volume 18 of *Documents on British Foreign Policy, 1919–1939*, second series, in a "revisionist" interpretation of appeasement.[20] As British historians Keith Middlemas and Ian Colvin have pointed out, Henderson was a disciple of Chamberlain's and one of the principal exponents of his policy.[21] Medlicott's assertion is all the more remarkable in that he quotes Henderson's own testimony from the latter's memoir *Failure of a Mission*, in which the former ambassador states: "Both Mr. Chamberlain and Mr. Baldwin, whom I had seen earlier, agreed that I should do my utmost to work with Hitler and the Nazi Party as the existing government of Germany. . . . Mr. Chamberlain outlined to me his views on general policy towards Germany, and I think I may honestly say that to the last and bitter end I followed the general line which he set me, all the more easily and faithfully since it corresponded so closely with my private conception of the service I could best render in Germany to my own country."[22]

In this connection, it is worth quoting from a memorandum by Henderson to the Foreign Office, dated 10 May 1937, in which he stated: "[Eastern Europe] is neither definitely settled for all time nor is it a vital British interest, and the German is certainly more civilized than the Slav, and in the end, if properly handled, also less potentially dangerous to British interests—one might even go so far as to assert that it is not even just to endeavour to prevent Germany from completing her unity or from being prepared for war against the Slav, provided her preparations are such as to reassure the British Empire that they are not simultaneously designed against it."[23]

On 10 March 1938, two days before Hitler's annexation of Austria, German foreign minister von Ribbentrop reported to Hitler during a visit to London that Lord Halifax had told him that "Chamberlain and he, Lord Halifax, were determined to reach an understanding with Germany" and that in advocating this policy "Chamberlain had assumed a great responsibility in the eyes of the British people and a great risk as well." Ribbentrop then stated: "Germany wished to be and had to be strong. . . . Germany must be armed for defense against Soviet Russian attacks.-. . . The Führer did not wish to request aid at the outset from the great Western Powers, if some day the steamroller of world revolution should be set in motion against Germany." At this point Lord Halifax interjected that "England was well aware of Germany's strength and that she had no objection to it whatever." Then Ribbentrop continued: "Germany wished to obtain the right of self-determination for the 10 million Germans living on her eastern border, i.e., in Austria and Czechoslovakia. . . . In this connection . . . the Führer had been pleased when Lord Halifax had shown understanding for that, too, at Berchtesgaden and when he had declared that the status quo in Eastern Europe could not be maintained unconditionally forever."[24] The next day, Ribbentrop reported that Chamberlain had "very emphatically requested" that he inform the Führer of "his most sincere wish for an understanding with Germany."[25]

Hitler's annexation of Austria had no effect in London—it had, in fact, been regarded as inevitable[26]—and Chamberlain pursued his appeasement of Germany with unruffled self-assurance. Nevertheless, it was essential that Hitler achieve his next territorial objective by peaceful means lest Great Britain be drawn into a European conflict through France's treaty obligations. On 22 May, during the mounting crisis over Czechoslovakia, Lord Halifax instructed Nevile Henderson to inform Ribbentrop of this dangerous contingency: "If a resort is had to forcible measures, it is quite impossible for me or for him to foretell the results that may follow, and I would beg him not to count on this country's being able to stand aside if from any precipitate action there should start a European conflagration. Only those will benefit from such a catastrophe who wish to see the destruction of European civilization."[27] At the beginning of September, there was mutual understanding. Theodor Kordt, the German chargé d'affaires in London, reported to ambassador Dirksen on a conversation with Chamberlain and Sir Horace Wilson: "The conversation took place in an exceedingly friendly atmosphere. [Wilson] was visibly moved (as far as an Englishman can betray such feelings at all) when at the end he shook my hand and said: 'If we two, Great Britain and Germany, come to agreement regarding the settlement of the Czech problem, we shall simply brush aside the resistance that France or Czechoslovakia herself may offer to the decision."[28] At the end of the month there followed the Munich settlement, the result of British pressure on Czechoslovakia to cede the Sudeten territory.[29]

By now, it must have been obvious to Stalin that the policy of collective security that he had indefatigably pursued since the USSR joined the League of Nations in 1934 in the hope of warding off the German threat might fail and that the slender hope that Britain and France would risk a conflict over Spain was fading. He therefore renewed his interest in the possibility of negotiating a nonaggression pact with Hitler in order to divert German military might against the West. We have already seen that quite early in the Civil War, his trade representative David Kandelaki had initiated negotiations for an agreement with Germany but that these tentative efforts had been rebuffed by Hitler. In fact, it was not until after the overthrow of Juan Negrín on 6 March 1939,[30] that Stalin finally gave up all hope of involving Britain and France in a war with Germany over the Spanish conflict and revived his plans for a compact with Hitler.

At this stage it is important to anticipate the course of events in Spain and even to probe the diplomatic intrigues among the European powers beyond the close of the Spanish Civil War, in order fully to appreciate the perilous game being played and the real concerns of British policymakers during the war itself.

In his report to the eighteenth congress of the Soviet Communist party on 10 March 1939, Stalin inveighed against Britain and France for encouraging Germany to embroil herself in a war with the Soviet Union, in which "they would appear on the scene with fresh strength . . . to dictate conditions to the enfeebled belligerents"[31]—precisely the role of arbiter that Stalin had reserved for the Soviet Union should the Spanish Civil War develop into a Western European conflict—and for the first time he threw out the first open hint of his desire for a rapprochement with Germany. "Marshal Stalin in March 1939," testified the former Reich foreign minister, Joachim von Ribbentrop, during his trial at Nuremberg, "delivered a speech in which he made certain hints of his desire to have better relations with Germany. I had submitted this speech to Adolf Hitler and asked him whether we should not try to find out whether this suggestion had something real behind it. Hitler was at first reluctant, but later on he became more receptive to this idea. Negotiations for a commercial treaty were under way, and during these negotiations, with the Führer's permission, I took soundings in Moscow as to the possibility of a definite bridge between National Socialism and Bolshevism and whether the interests of the two countries could not at least be made to harmonize."[32]

The extremely cautious manner in which both sides broached the question of a political settlement from the time of Stalin's speech, as revealed by documents found in the archives of the German foreign office,[33] stemmed no doubt from the fact that each side feared that the other might use any concrete proposal for a political agreement to strengthen its own bargaining position vis-à-vis Britain and France. In fact, up to 30 May 1939, less than three months before the signing of the German-Soviet nonaggression pact (in August) and the Secret Protocol that touched off the German attack on Poland and World War II, these documents indicate that matters had not gone beyond vague soundings. On that date state secretary Weizsäcker wired the German embassy in Moscow: "Contrary to the policy previously planned we have now decided to undertake definite negotiations with the Soviet Union."[34]

Although Stalin did not open formal negotiations with Hitler until the middle of 1939, he was not backward during the Spanish Civil War—apart from the overtures made by Kandelaki—in letting Hitler know that it would be to Germany's advantage to have him as a partner rather than an enemy. This is borne out by the testimony of Alexander Orlov: "The fourth line of Soviet intelligence," he wrote, "is so-called *Misinformation*. . . . Misinformation is not just lying for the sake of lying; it is expected to serve as a subtle means of inducing another government to do what the Kremlin wants it to do. . . . During the Spanish Civil War . . . the Misinformation desk was ordered to introduce into the channels of the German military intelligence service information that the Soviet planes fighting in Spain were not of the latest design and that Russia had in her arsenal thousands of newer planes, of the second and third generation, possessing much greater speed and a higher ceiling. This was not true. Russia had given Spain the best and the newest she had (though in insufficient quantities). This misleading information greatly impressed the German High Command. . . . Evidently, Stalin wanted to impress on Hitler that the Soviet Union was much stronger and better armed than he thought and that it would be wiser for Germany to have Russia as a partner rather than an opponent."[35]

Four months before the signing of the German-Soviet nonaggression pact in August, Walter Krivitsky claimed that Stalin's foreign policy in the Western world was predicated upon a profound contempt for the "weakling" democratic nations and that his international policy had been a series of maneuvers whose sole purpose was to place him in a favorable position for a deal with Hitler.[36] This is by no means certain, for Stalin could not rely entirely on a problematical agreement with Hitler on which to base his foreign policy. For this reason, he was careful to keep open his other option of collective security in the hope that the Western powers would eventually confront Hitler, whether in Spain or Czechoslovakia, and deflect German aggression away from Russia's borders. It was because Stalin held open both these options that even after the loss of Catalonia in February 1939 he still hoped, as we shall see later, that Britain and France might reverse their policy of neutrality and instructed the Spanish politburo to continue the struggle in the fading expectation that the latent antagonisms in the West would finally burst into flame.

It would be false to convey the impression that only Stalin, Negrín, and the Spanish Communists placed their hopes of victory in the Civil War in the eventual outbreak of a European conflict, for these hopes were also entertained, as we have seen, by some leaders of the CNT.[37] They were also entertained for some time by certain prominent Socialists. Referring to the occupation of the Basque provinces and Asturias by General Franco in the summer and autumn of 1937, Wenceslao Carrillo, a supporter of Largo Caballero and director general of security in his government, wrote: "Nevertheless, the hope of victory that the Communist party and the Negrín government held out to us, based on the possibility of world war, had not disappeared. Neither France nor England, they argued, can consent to an out-and-out triumph of fascism in Spain because that would put them in a critical position in the Mediterranean. As I am ready to tell the whole truth, I refuse to conceal the fact that, in the beginning, I too shared this belief. . . . But I did not think of profiting from war; nor was I in the service of interests other than those of my country."[38]

On the other hand, President Azaña, like Julián Besteiro, the right-wing Socialist, who hoped for a negotiated settlement, frowned on the prospect of a European conflict. In reply to Juan-Simeón Vidarte, a member of the Socialist executive and a Negrín supporter, Azaña once stated: "I already know that there is someone among you who believes that the just cause of the Republic would be saved by a world war. That war would be a catastrophe of inconceivable dimensions and it is not right for us to seek salvation in the martyrdom of millions of human beings. . . . I see that you are infected by the Negrín thesis. . . . Suppose that at the end of the war Communism were implanted in Western Europe just as it was implanted in Eastern Europe at the end of the last war. To the majority of Republicans and, I suppose, Socialists that solution would be repugnant."[39]

If the hope that a general conflict would eventually erupt was disappointed, this was not because those who determined policy in Britain and France contemplated lightly the extension of Italo-German power in the Mediterranean; it was because the purview of their foreign policy went beyond the Spanish problem and embraced the whole of Europe. If Britain and France refused to challenge Germany in Spain; if, moreover, they sacrificed the independence of Austria and Czechoslovakia; if, finally, Neville Chamberlain, as will be seen shortly, secretly proposed—before being outmaneuvered by the Hitler-Stalin pact—a political settlement with Germany that would free Britain from her guarantee to Poland, it was because they knew that the frustration of German aims at this stage, even if it did not lead to war, would weaken the Nazi regime and enhance Russia's influence on the continent. Above all, those who molded policy in Britain and France wished to avoid war in the West until Germany had weakened herself in the East. To have resisted Germany before she had blunted her teeth on Russian soil would have left the Soviet Union arbiter of the continent, infinitely more powerful than if she had to bear the main burden of the fighting.

Of course, in the long run, Britain and France could no more have desired Germany to obtain a complete mastery over the greater part of Europe than they could Russia. They wished for the domination of neither. Of this, German leaders were supremely conscious. Hence, if, after the occupation of Poland, Germany invaded Belgium, France, and the Netherlands before attacking the Soviet Union, this was because the subjection of Western Europe and the control of its coastline were, in the German mind, indispensable prerequisites for war on the Soviet Union; for although Britain and France might encourage German ambitions in Eastern Europe, Germany could not feel certain that once she was involved in an exhausting struggle on Soviet soil, these powers would not attempt to restore the balance in their favor. Undoubtedly the conviction that Germany would attack the West before assailing Russia lay at the root of some of the opposition in Britain and France to the policy of giving Germany a free hand in Eastern Europe.[40]

Although the direction of the German thrust seemed unmistakable, there is evidence that both the British and French leaders were not unmindful of the danger that appeasement might backfire and that Germany might march west instead of east. On 1 November 1938, one month after the Munich agreement, Lord Halifax, in a letter to Sir Eric Phipps, the British ambassador in Paris, outlined his thoughts: "Henceforward, we must count with German predominance in Central Europe. . . . In these conditions, it seems to me that Great Britain and France have to uphold *their* predominant position in Western Europe by the maintenance of such armed strength as would render any attack upon them hazardous. . . . It is one thing to allow German expansion in Central Europe, which to my mind is a normal and natural thing, but we must be able to resist German expansion in Western Europe or else our whole position is undermined."[41]

The possibility that Germany might attack Western Europe before marching East was conveyed to Halifax by Sir G. Ogilvie-Forbes, the British chargé d'affaires in Berlin, in a dispatch dated 6 December 1938. There was a school of thought, he stated, that believed that "Herr Hitler will not risk a Russian adventure until he has made quite certain that his western flank will not be attacked while he is operating in the east, and that consequently his first task will be to liquidate France and England, before British rearmament is ready."[42] Equally disturbing was a report by William Strang, Halifax's assistant undersecretary of state, dated 18 January 1939, in which he referred to "reports we have had of

Hitler's intention to attack in the West this Spring. . . . Germany cannot conduct a war on two fronts in present circumstances, and material conditions will make it easier for her to operate in the West than in the East."[43]

That French leaders were aware of the dangers is also evident. In a letter to French foreign minister Georges Bonnet on 19 March 1939, a few days after the Nazi invasion of Czechoslovakia, the French ambassador in Moscow, Robert Coulondre, stated that the Nazi leaders saw two ways open to them: "Either to proceed without intermission in the subjugation of east and south-east Europe" or to "attack France and Britain before these two Powers have, with American help, caught up with German armaments. . . . This second possibility is not at present the more probable. But we must reckon with the risk of seeing Germany engaged in such an undertaking."[44]

The general assumption, however, after the occupation of Czechoslovakia on 15 March 1939 was that Hitler's next move would be against Poland. But despite Chamberlain's treaty guarantees to defend Polish independence—guarantees hastily given under pressure from the parliamentary Opposition and the aroused state of British public opinion—he did what he could to evade his commitments. This is clear from the meticulously documented study by the British historians Martin Gilbert and Richard Gott of British treaty obligations to Poland, of the subsequent efforts to wriggle out of them, and the eight-month "phoney" war,[45] during which Chamberlain still hoped for an Anglo-German agreement that would avert war in Western Europe.[46] It is also clear from the secret proposals that Sir Horace Wilson, his chief collaborator and adviser, made to Helmut Wohlthat, Hermann Goering's emissary in London, in mid-July 1939, and the conversations a few days later between Wilson and Herbert von Dirksen, the German ambassador to London.

These "back-stair negotiations," as the British historian Sir Lewis Namier called them, in which the prime minister "unwisely engaged" without the knowledge of the Foreign Office,[47] were the zenith of the appeasement policy. Wilson's proposals were recorded by von Dirksen in a long memorandum written after the outbreak of war, which was found on his estate at Gröditzberg by the Soviet army, and also in a shorter "strictly secret" report dated 21 July 1939 drawn up at the time of his ambassadorship.[48] The authenticity of the proposals is beyond doubt, not only because Dirksen later confirmed them in every important detail in a work published in London in 1951,[49] but because Wohlthat himself refers to them in his report to Goering.[50] Moreover, Wilson's proposals (which quite naturally he concealed from the Foreign Office)[51] have never been challenged by a single British historian. Although conveniently ignored by many historians (for example, William N. Medlicott,[52] Robert Skidelsky,[53] and Simon Newman[54]) in their revisionist assessments of Chamberlain's foreign policy, they have been accepted without question by others, notably, Ian Colvin,[55] Sir Lewis Namier,[56] and A. J. P. Taylor.[57] Nevertheless, they have not been accorded the significance they deserve.

While not directly related to the Spanish Civil War, the Dirksen memoranda shed more light than any other documents on the mainspring of appeasement—to divert German aggression eastward—and illustrate how far Chamberlain was prepared to go in order to reach a political settlement with Germany in order to preserve peace in Western Europe. Therefore they are particularly relevant to the Civil War since they demonstrate the futility of Stalin's efforts to provoke a conflagration in Western Europe by involving Britain and France in the Spanish conflict and are the clearest proof of the inevitable failure of his attempts to influence Western governments by distorting the true nature of the revolution. For this reason, they merit inclusion in this volume.

In the longer of the two documents, Dirksen testifies:

When Herr [Helmut] Wohlthat [emissary of Goering] was in London for the whaling negotiations in July [1939], Wilson [Sir Horace Wilson] invited him for a talk, and, consulting prepared notes, outlined a program for a comprehensive adjustment of Anglo-German relations. . . .

In the political sphere, a non-aggression pact was contemplated, in which aggression would be renounced in principle. The underlying purpose of this treaty was to make it possible for the British gradually to disembarrass themselves of their commitments towards Poland, on the ground that they had by this treaty secured Germany's renunciation of methods of aggression. . . .

The importance of Wilson's proposals was demonstrated by the fact that Wilson invited Wohlthat to have them confirmed by Chamberlain personally, whose room was not far from Wilson's. Wohlthat, however, declined this in order not to prejudice the unofficial character of his mission. . . .

In order to avoid all publicity, I visited Wilson at his home on August 3 [one month before Hitler's invasion of Poland] and we had a conversation which lasted nearly two hours. . . . Again Wilson affirmed, and in a clearer form than he had done to Wohlthat, that the conclusion of an Anglo-German entente would practically render Britain's guarantee policy nugatory. Agreement with Germany would enable Britain to extricate herself from her predicament in regard to Poland on the ground that the non-aggression pact protected Poland from German attack; England would thus be relieved of her commitments. Then Poland, so to speak, would be left to face Germany alone.

Sir Horace Wilson, on my insistence, also touched on the question of how the negotiations were to be conducted in face of the inflamed state of British public opinion [resulting from Hitler's seizure of Czechoslovakia in March 1939]. . . . He admitted quite frankly that by taking this step Chamberlain was incurring a great risk and laying himself open to the danger of a fall. But with skill and strict secrecy, the reefs could be avoided. . . .

The tragic and paramount thing about the rise of the new Anglo-German war was that Germany demanded an equal place with Britain as a world power and that Britain was in principle prepared to concede. But whereas Germany demanded immediate, complete and unequivocal satisfaction of her demand, Britain—although she was ready to renounce her eastern commitments, and therewith her encirclement policy, as well as to allow Germany a predominant position in east and south-east Europe and to discuss genuine world political partnership with Germany—wanted this to be done only by way of negotiation and a *gradual* revision of British policy. This change could be effected in a period of months, but not of days or weeks.[58]

A. J. P. Taylor, one of the few British historians who have ventured to mention Sir Horace Wilson's proposals, writes: "Wilson produced a memorandum on 10 Downing Street notepaper, which, not surprisingly, has disappeared from the British records. This proposed an Anglo-German treaty of non-aggression and non-interference. . . . A pact of this kind 'would enable Britain to rid herself of her commitments vis-à-vis Poland.' . . . [It] is inconceivable that these proposals were made without Chamberlain's knowledge or approval."[59]

Although Wilson's proposals met with no response in Berlin and were "simply thrown into the wastepaper basket," as von Dirksen put it,[60]—undoubtedly because Hitler, impatient to dispose of the Polish problem before the onset of winter, favored a pact with Stalin that offered immediate territorial gains rather than a pact with Britain that would have required a long period of uncertain negotiations in view of the inflamed state of British opinion—they were the culminating effort, the final desperate gamble of the British government to direct Germany's course away from Western Europe.

Oddly enough, A. J. P. Taylor questions whether the British and French governments intended that Nazi Germany should destroy the "Bolshevik menace." "This was the Soviet suspicion, both at the time and later. There is little evidence of it in the official record, or even outside it. British and French statesmen were far too distracted by the German problem to consider what would happen when Germany had become the dominant Power in Eastern Europe. Of course they preferred that Germany should march east not west, if she marched at all. But their object was to prevent war, not to prepare one; and they sincerely believed—at any rate Chamberlain believed—that Hitler would be content and pacific if his claims were met."[61] If this be so, then the policy of the British government of encouraging German rearmament from the beginning of 1935, of conniving at the German reoccupation of the Rhineland in 1936, of forcing Czechoslovakia to submit to German demands in 1938, and of secretly attempting to negotiate a settlement with Germany at the expense of Poland in July 1939, makes positively no sense and becomes a succession of moronic moves in the perilous diplomatic game being played by Britain and Russia in the prewar years. It is impossible to believe that there was no strategic thinking behind Chamberlain's policy of appeasement and that he did not take into account what might happen once Germany became predominant in Eastern Europe and established a common border with Russia.

The British military expert Liddell Hart acknowledges in his *History of the Second World War* with reference to the strategic situation after the German invasion of Poland that "the best hope [of Britain and France] now that Germany and Russia faced each other on a common border, was that friction would develop between these two mutually distrustful confederates and draw Hitler's explosive force eastward, instead of westward."[62] Although Liddell Hart does not relate this hope to any prewar strategy, it is unimaginable, given the massive evidence presented in this and previous chapters, that British and French leaders long before the outbreak of World War II "were far too distracted by the German problem [as A. J. P. Taylor puts it] to consider what would happen when Germany had become the dominant Power in Eastern Europe" and a common border between Germany and the Soviet Union had been established.

Of course it would be idle to suggest that in the prewar years British leaders in pursuit of their policy of appeasement were not influenced to some degree by other considerations than the fear that a Western European conflagration would redound to Russia's benefit. Among these considerations, according to the earl of Birkenhead, were the conclusions of the chiefs of staff in their report to the Committee of Imperial Defense in the late summer of 1938 that Great Britain was not ready for war and that she could not fight a war on three fronts—German, Italian, and Japanese—without powerful allies.[63] "[Chamberlain and Halifax]," Lord Birkenhead affirms, "were apprehensive of the situation in the Far East, of what action Japan might take there if Great Britain became involved in a war with Germany in the West; and they were at all times uneasily conscious of America's neutrality and of the unpalatable fact that no help could be looked for from that quarter in case of trouble. The British Government was also alarmed about the attitude of the Dominions to involvement in war. South Africa had decided to remain neutral, should it come; the Australian Labour Party were against intervention and there was grave doubt whether [Prime Minister] Mackenzie King could bring the Canadian people into war."[64] Furthermore, the British historian Charles L. Mowat states that since World War I the policy of the dominions had been one of no commitments "and certainly they were not going to be bound by Britain's commitments. . . . [They] naturally opposed involvement in war and rejoiced that appeasement was keeping the threat of war at a distance."[65] But all these considerations, although used by various historians to explain the policy of appeasement, pale before the single most important consideration: the deep-rooted fear of Russia.

That the wells of appeasement lay in this fear of Russia, in the conviction that Nazi Germany was a barrier against the spread of Communism, and that a war in Western Europe could only benefit the Soviet Union by extending her power and influence has been amply demonstrated in this and other chapters. But these cardinal elements in the policy of appeasement have been underrated or almost totally ignored by the British historical establishment.

There are two reasons for this failure by British historians to come to terms with their country's diplomatic past. Firstly, there is the accepted tradition not to attribute to their government Machiavellian designs against a foreign power. Hence, no matter how patriotic or realistic Chamberlain and his supporters may have felt themselves to be in attempting to spare Western Europe the ravages of war and revolution, they should not be accused of conspiring to pit one totalitarian power against the other. "Of course," writes Robert Skidelsky, the British neorevisionist historian, "there were a number of groups in Britain who . . . advocated the bargain that Hitler must always have hoped for—'a German deal with the British Empire at the expense of the Soviet Union.' But such cynicism (or realism) was foreign to the British Establishment."[66] Secondly, because of the ideological divide between East and West, no establishment historian (despite Stalin's own Machiavellian aims) wishes to play into the hands of the Soviet Union by acknowledging Britain's share of responsibility for the rebirth of German militarism and the calamity of the Second World War.

This failure to expose the main roots of appeasement is unfortunate not only for the historiography of this crucial period in world history, but for those seeking a true understanding of the Spanish Civil War and Revolution and of the reason why Stalin's democratic camouflage in Spain was doomed to failure.

62

The Fall of Catalonia

*I*t should now be apparent that no stratagem devised by Negrín or the Comintern could have induced Britain and France to enter the conflict on the side of the Republicans. The much-publicized thirteen-point program—the high-water mark of Negrín's diplomatic effort—made no impression on the democratic powers. Nor did the much-flaunted restitution of certain foreign and domestic properties make the slightest impact.

Despite these frustrations, despite the immolation of Czechoslovakia, despite the disastrous Battle of the Ebro (which began on 25 July 1938 with the intrepid crossing of the river and ended on 16 November with the loss of all the captured territory and some sixty thousand to seventy thousand dead and wounded),[1] and despite the total collapse of Catalonia in February 1939,[2] Moscow instructed the Spanish politburo to continue the resistance policy.

On 23 February 1939 the politburo declared:

> It is a profound error to believe that we can hope for nothing or for very little from abroad and that the democratic countries, which have allowed Catalonia to be invaded by the Germans and Italians, will not help us now that we have lost such an important position. The international situation has never been more unstable than it is today. Furthermore, the successes of the fascist invaders in Catalonia have increased their boldness, encouraging them to reveal still more clearly their plans of conquest, plunder, and war, and this in turn opens the eyes of those who until now have not wanted to face reality and increases the possibilities of direct and indirect aid for the Spanish people. On the side of the Spanish Republic is the Soviet Union, that powerful country, the firm defender of liberty, justice, and peace throughout the world. The working class, as well as the sincerely democratic countries, have until now given Spain very substantial material aid and will continue to do so. What they have not been able to do, partly because of lack of unity and determination in the struggle and partly because they have not yet completely understood the importance to them of a just solution of the Spanish problem, is to change radically in our favor the policy of their governments. But what has not been achieved up to now can still be accomplished if we increase our resistance.

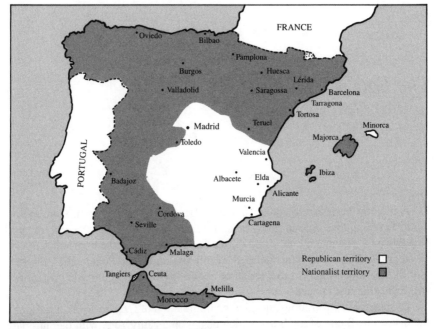

Map 5. Division of Spain, March 1939

For all these reasons, we say that resistance is not only necessary but possible, and we affirm that, as on previous occasions when many persons believed that everything was lost . . . , our resistance can change the situation. It will permit new factors to develop, both in Spain and abroad, that will redound to our advantage and will open the prospect of victory.[3]

Beneath this seeming optimism, the politburo was undoubtedly aware of the misgivings that assailed the summits of the party. In *Hombres made in Moscú*, Enrique Castro recaptures his thoughts even before the disastrous Battle of the Ebro and the fall of Catalonia:

He knew that the war could no longer be won.

He knew that the USSR and the international Communist movement wished to prolong republican resistance in order to check Hitler's plans in Europe.

He knew that by prolonging resistance many would die and that villages and towns would be destroyed.

What did that matter?

A revolution always exacts a high price. To be afraid of that seemed to him absurd. What was Spain worth? He didn't know exactly, but if the price of a breathing spell for the USSR, if the price of a postponement of aggression against the USSR was Spain, what did it matter? . . .

For Castro there was only one fatherland: the socialist fatherland. There was no other choice. Only Russia existed.[4]

And referring to the state of mind prevailing in the rear after the Ebro battle, he wrote: "The rear was the barometer of the tragedy. It was useless for Negrín and the Communist party to try to make the people believe that the Ebro had been the scene of a great military victory that had saved Valencia. People did not believe it. They did not say so openly, because it was still too dangerous. . . . The people were no longer thinking of the war. They were thinking of the victors. Fear began to penetrate the body and soul of millions of people whose faces reflected a great sadness and a great effort not to weep; because this was not only the death of an illusion; it was also the beginning of a terrible calvary."[5]

No less important in the inexorable process of disenchantment than the military defeats and the grueling privations of the civilian population was the conviction that, whatever the outcome, the cause of freedom was lost. We have already seen that the SIM, the dreaded Military Investigation Service, arrested those who "dared speak ill of the prime minister and of the way the war was going." We have already seen that the majority of the people, working class and middle class, now perceived no future for the Republic even in the event of victory: "[Whether] we are defeated or whether we win the war," Luis Araquistáin had confided to his daughter, "the independent Socialists will have to emigrate, because in the first case we should be assassinated by Franco or in the second by the Communists,"[6] while Diego Abad de Santillán expressed the forebodings of the Anarchosyndicalists when he wrote that if the war had ended with the victory of Negrín, "we would have had to suffer annihilation in the name of the Republic instead of annihilation in the name of fascism."[7] As for the moderate Socialists and liberal Republicans, who represented a large segment of the middle classes, Julián Besteiro, as we have seen, gave voice to the thoughts they shared but feared to utter, when he declared at a meeting of the executive of the Socialist party on 15 November 1938: "If we should win the war, Spain will become Communist . . . , and if we should be defeated then the future will be terrible."[8]

That the fear of victory stemmed mainly from the conviction that Communist preponderance in the army would determine the future polity of Spain can be open to no doubt. "I do not know what the odds were that the Communists would have been able to impose their system if we had won the war," wrote Colonel Pérez Salas, "but I do know that they would have tried to strengthen and consolidate their power, because they were aware that never again would such an opportunity present itself. If this is not the case, why were they so interested in dominating the armed forces? If they were more willing to risk losing the war than losing their predominance in the army, what was their reason? Their conduct cannot be excused on the ground that they fought better and thus had a greater chance of winning the war for all of us. This is untrue, except in the sense that they had more power since they were better armed and had accumulated more positions of command, but this predominance sapped the fighting spirit of other Spaniards who were far more numerous."[9]

Because the fear of Communist military predominance plagued the opposition, Negrín was forced to broach the subject in the Cortes on 1 October 1938, five months after his pledge to free the army "from all hegemony by any party or tendency." Responding to criticism before a generally cowed assembly, he offered no apologies or hope of redress. To insinuate that the army was dominated by a single party, he said, to speak of favoritism or partiality, was an "insult" to the head of the government, to the minister of defense, and to the army. "We must put an end to these damnable insinuations," he added menacingly. "To ventilate them in parliament is a crime against the State [*lesa patria*]. Besides, señores diputados, they are false. I do not doubt there have been mistakes. That is human. But to speak of a biased leadership, of favoritism, is false, completely false. These assertions do terrible harm, such terrible harm that even if they were true they should not be made. How happy our enemies will be tomorrow when they can reproduce in large print some of the things that have been said here by persons who should have had a greater sense of responsibility!"[10]

But there was another matter of even greater import that could not freely be discussed either inside or outside the parliament: the demoralization of the working people upon whose sacrifice any hope of victory depended. That the policies pursued by Negrín and the PCE were among the decisive factors in the decline of proletarian morale was acknowledged by British novelist Ralph Bates, a Comintern organizer in Spain for many years and assistant commissar of the Fifteenth International Brigade. In a letter written to me in 1940 shortly before his rupture with the Communists, he wrote: "Imagine [the] bitterness [of the Anarchosyndicalists], now when all their revolutionary sacrifices, all their concessions to the C.P., all their detestation of the petty bourgeois who smothered their army, as they called their militia, took away their factory committees, when all of this still did not win British and French approval, when after all the Comintern's analysis turned out to be incorrect. . . . I fear that the party, and with it the future, have been terribly damaged by many things that occurred. For instance, I have talked with many Spanish Socialists. They all have an undying hate for the C.P. That is a catastrophe. . . . I am sure you have no conception of the violent hatred of whole political strata of the Spanish workers for the party."[11]

An expression of this hostility has been conserved for posterity in a letter by Araquistáin to his daughter. Written during the final days of the Nationalist offensive against Catalonia, it stated: "This end is dreadful, but it was easily foreseen and we said so clearly to everyone who wished to listen to us. . . . [The Communists] alone are responsible for this terrible disaster. If they and the Socialists, like Vayo and Negrín, who served them slavishly, had a hundred lives, they could not expiate so many crimes and stupidities."[12]

In contrast, Negrín presented at the end of the war to the Permanent Deputation of the Cortes (Diputación Permanente de las Cortes), in a session held in Paris on 31 March 1939, a visionary's picture of what might have happened "if the war material we received late had arrived sooner." "If we had received that matériel four months earlier," he said, "perhaps the Ebro offensive would have meant the end of the war. If we had received it just two months earlier, Catalonia would not have collapsed the way it did. Even after the fall of Borjas Blancas—when the Army of Catalonia had 37,000 rifles—it is almost certain that Barcelona would not have been lost if we had received what we needed. . . . Even after the fall of Barcelona, Catalonia could have been saved and then we would have won the war, because I do not have the slightest doubt that things would have changed completely if we had been able to resist six, eight or ten months longer."[13]

The start of General Franco's offensive against Catalonia on 23 December 1938 and the capture on 26 January of Barcelona, the largest industrial center in Spain, once the impregnable fortress of the CNT and FAI and the pulsating center of regional autonomy, climaxed the demoralization and defeatism of the Catalan workers. As for the Catalan middle classes, upon whose good will and confidence the Communists had risen to power in 1936 and 1937 by their drive against the revolutionary inroads of the labor unions, the policy of resistance and the thirteen-point program with its hollow promise of "respect for regional liberties" were meaningless. Pi Sunyer, the mayor of Barcelona and a leader of the Esquerra Republicana, told President Azaña that "the Catalans no longer knew why they were fighting, because of Negrín's anti-Catalan policy."[14] The reigning mood of defeatism is recalled by Manuel Cruells, the editor in chief of the *Diari de Catalunya*, himself a Catalan autonomist: "The men loyal to the policy of Negrín spoke in terms we could clearly understand, but what they said meant nothing to us. We were told to resist, but 'where and with what do we resist?' we asked ourselves. 'And why resist?' The reasons and the objectives of a resistance to the bitter end [*resistència numantina*] that they proposed were not clear enough to us. Negrín had emptied his entire politico-military policy of any Catalan content; he had dislodged Catalonia from the decisive posts of the war in accordance with the continuous and never-ending tendency to absorb and centralize."[15]

Catalonia's supreme crisis was now at hand. Chief of the general staff Vicente Rojo, a steadfast supporter of Negrín and the PCE, describes the "tremendous contrast" between Barcelona in January 1939 and Madrid in November 1936: "What a difference in the atmosphere! What enthusiasm then . . . and what disheartenment now! Forty-eight hours before the enemy entered Barcelona, it was a dead city. . . . [It] was lost, purely and simply, because there was no will to resist, either in the civilian population, or in the troops contaminated by the atmosphere."[16]

While Rojo ignores the large share of responsibility that must be assigned to Negrín and the PCE for the demoralization of the working class, which formed the backbone of the opposition to General Franco, and for the disenchantment of the Catalan middle classes, the PCE has furnished its own version of the Catalan debacle. "The government of the Generalitat," it stated on the second anniversary of the fall of Catalonia, "instead of organizing the defense of [the region], instead of mobilizing its resources to prevent the enemy from invading the soil of Catalonia, devoted itself to maneuvering inside and outside of Spain against the government of the Republic, subverting its authority. Lacking faith in the strength of its people, the Catalan separatists preferred to seek salvation in conversations, behind the back of the Republican government, with the imperialist, so-called democratic governments, . . . who were helping the victory of Franco."[17]

There is no evidence that the government of the Generalitat engaged in secret conversations with foreign governments, although there can be little doubt that there were separatist elements in Catalonia who would have gladly negotiated a separate peace had there been the slightest chance. But Franco had all but won the war, and the world knew it. Nevertheless, the Comintern continued its efforts to enlist the military aid of the democratic powers. In January 1939, while the Nationalist forces were sweeping all before them in their relentless march on Barcelona, the Comintern organ *World News and Views*, published in several languages like its predecessor *International Press Correspondence*, published an urgent appeal signed by sixteen Communist parties:

> War threatens France, Europe and the world. We sound the alarm. *Help Spain in order to help ourselves!*
>
> To all the peoples of the world, to men who love liberty and peace, to sincere democrats, we issue this urgent appeal for *vigorous help for Republican Spain.*
>
> For more than two years and a half, on their national soil, invaded by the bloody hordes of Italian and German troops, the sons of the Spanish people have heroically resisted the steel avalanche of Hitler and Mussolini. . . .
>
> *The Italian war against France has started. The march on Barcelona is the culminating point of the first stage of this war.* . . .
>
> To make war recede, to save peace, to preserve the conquest of civilisation and human culture, *Republican Spain must be helped.*
>
> Republican Spain will win. But for this, the peoples must immediately . . . obtain restoration of international law, the delivery of arms, munitions, guns and planes to the defenders of Madrid and Valencia, to the Republican troops of Catalonia.
>
> This is the right of the Republican Government of Spain, a legal Government brought to power by the will of the people, expressed by universal vote. . . .
>
> The hour has come for the peoples to take into their own hands the foreign policy of their countries. Words of sympathy and platonic demonstrations of solidarity are not enough.
>
> *This is the hour for effective action by the people.*[18]

But nothing could be done either inside or outside Spain to reverse or even to check the steamroller advance of Franco's forces. Long passed were the heroic days when the CNT-FAI and POUM workers of Barcelona with the help of loyal Assault and Civil guards had suppressed the rebel garrisons. Long passed were the heroic days of the defense of Madrid, when the Communist, Socialist, and Anarchosyndicalist workers with the aid of the International Brigades and Soviet weaponry had saved the threatened capital. As Colonel Pérez Salas pointedly remarks: "There had not yet occurred the bloody fighting in the rear, nor the assassinations at the front, nor the unfair predominance of the Communists in the army. . . . [This] lowered substantially the combative spirit of the other parties, which found themselves dominated by an insignificant minority, only because it had the arms."[19]

Isolated and anathematized, the Communists envisioned a lone heroic gesture. Manuel Tagüeña, the Communist commander of the Fifteenth Army Corps, relates that at 4 A.M. on 26 January, several hours before the first units of Franco's army penetrated the outskirts of Barcelona, he was visited by political commissar Francisco Antón and youth leader Santiago Carrillo. "They told me that the Communists and the JSU were going to make the maximum effort to defend the capital of Catalonia, mobilize the population and thus gain time to stabilize the front. They wanted to repeat the miracle of Madrid. Conditions, however, were entirely different. The Communist leadership was well aware of this and was most certainly convinced of the futility of such directives, but it had to issue them in order to continue to be the organization that maintained resistance to the end. . . . To believe that the population of the Catalan capital would rise up in its defense was completely illusory. In the final days, despite all appeals, scarcely one thousand of the million inhabitants could be assembled to build fortifications. Barcelona accepted the defeat with sorrow and saw no purpose at all in prolonging the fight. We were no longer in 1936."[20]

Nevertheless, Soviet premier Leonid Brezhnev, speaking in 1967, painted a highly imaginative picture of "thousands of Soviet volunteers who to the last day, together with the Spaniards, fought at the Barcelona barricades and in the skies of Madrid."[21] But, in truth, all but a handful of Soviet citizens had been withdrawn from Spain. José Fernández Sánchez, in a short, well-documented study based on Soviet sources, states that in October–November 1938 "all the Soviet citizens who had participated directly in the military actions as aviators and tank operators" had left Spain and that in 1939 only thirty Soviet specialists comprising professional officers, interpreters, and auxiliary personnel remained. "When the capture of Barcelona by Franco's troops appeared imminent," he claims, "all the Soviet advisers gathered in the city and left it in the early morning of 26 January 1939."[22]

There can be no doubt that Stalin now entertained few illusions about the possibility of continuing the war much longer, especially in view of the overwhelming military superiority of the Nationalist forces, supplied freely and lavishly with arms by Italy and Germany. His recall of all but a few Soviet advisers and their assistants, not to mention the withdrawal of most of the volunteers of the International Brigades,[23] was indicative of his diminishing interest in the Civil War and of his intention to reduce his involvement. Nevertheless, it was important for his twofold strategy to continue the resistance policy, while leaving the door ajar for a possible deal with Hitler.

Meanwhile, six weeks before the start of the Nationalist offensive against Catalonia, Negrín had written a long letter to Stalin on 11 November 1938 urging a speedy implementation of his requests for arms. Addressed to "My renowned comrade and great friend," Negrín stressed that "without the interest you have taken in our struggle, we should have succumbed long ago" and "the future and fate of Liberty and Democracy in our country would already have been irrevocably lost." Although the first half of the eighteen-page missive contains tedious

comments on European statesmen, on whom Stalin—the wiliest and best informed of all on big-power diplomacy—had infinitely more knowledge than
Negrín, the remainder of the communication contains passages of sufficient
historical interest to merit reproduction here (the italics are mine):

In our domestic policy a unity has been achieved, which, although not perfect, is nonetheless satisfactory, if we take into account the period of anarchy
through which we have passed. This unity has been accomplished despite *the difficulties inherent in a situation in which we have had to govern with a heterogeneous coalition of parties* subject to the influence of the rebels and of countries
that are our enemies whether open or not. It is possible that what may have been
interpreted at times as weakness was in reality nothing more than an acknowledg-
ment that *we did not yet possess the necessary strength to carry out a project.
The function of a statesman, especially when he does not have a strong homogeneous party behind him* [presumably an allusion to the "heterogeneous coalition
of parties" previously mentioned] *is not to sacrifice power by attempting prematurely to realize an aim. I believe that in applying this rule I have been
successful.*

*Because of foreign influence and enemy propaganda, because of the resent-
ment of parties that have lost vitality or have not established roots among the
people, a hard and fierce campaign is still being waged against the Communists.*
I should not conceal this fact from you, nor should I hesitate to tell you that *the
Communists are my best and most loyal collaborators*, the most inclined to self-
sacrifice and self-denial in the cause of victory. But the fact is that the slightest
excuse is used to poison the atmosphere in order to give the impression that the
government is manipulated by foreign influences. . . . *As yet we are unable
to respond adequately, because it would create a new conflict.* Nevertheless,
the domestic situation does not worry me and I am sure it will continue to
improve. . . .

[As for the army,] . . . there has been considerable improvement during the
last few months: Increase in reserves, formation of cadres, technical advances.
Everything has been improving, above all the army's fighting qualities. However,
from the verbal reports that [air force chief] General Hidalgo de Cisneros will be
giving you, your government will appreciate the decisive effect that the rapid execution of our orders (copies of which I enclose) may have on the outcome of the
war.[24] To be totally effective, massive rather than piecemeal shipments will be
necessary. . . . Once our needs have been met, it will be possible to defeat the
rebels before the end of the spring. . . .

I shall not close without assuring you that the reconstruction and recovery of
Spain will be possible within a few years by our own efforts. This is not the time
to tell you about my plans for our recovery, but, believe me, such an undertaking
will be easy with a united country and *a government in strong hands* given the
resources of Spain.

In the end we shall be stronger than before. Many traditional obstacles will have been erased. *With men of energy and authority forged by the war, with a powerful army and with the industrial potential of our shipyards, we shall be able to create a considerable merchant marine and navy and to provide [ships] to other countries. It will always be for many Spaniards an honor to know that if, at some given time, there exists at this extreme end of western Europe a powerful military and naval force capable of collaborating in the common cause of human progress with the USSR,* it was due in large measure to the encouragement, collaboration, and help given to us in a disinterested way by our Soviet friends. And then we shall be able to speak frankly of the noble and generous contribution of the Soviet people, of the sacrifice of their sons, and of the genial vision of the statesmen that lead their country.

From one end of Europe to the other, my dear Comrade Stalin, I shake your hand as a symbol of unity and as a sign of appreciation and gratitude.[25]

From the italicized passages, I draw the following four conclusions.

First, Negrín was anxious to impress Stalin with his political acumen, with his support for the PCE and the Soviet Union, and with his leadership capabilities.

Second, he was irked by the multiparty system and, given the right circumstances, would have been willing to replace it with a "strong homogeneous party." In other words, he was willing to go beyond the mere fusion of the Socialist and Communist parties, long advocated by Stalin and by the Spanish Communists, and by himself in June 1937, when he declared that he had always been in favor of merging the two parties and that there was "nothing incompatible" in their programs.[26] It may be argued that Negrín made this statement simply to ingratiate himself with the PCE, but there is evidence in Togliatti's report to the Comintern of 21 May 1939 that Negrín attributed the "weaknesses" of his government to the multiparty system (*regimen de partidos*) and that he proposed to the PCE on 2 December 1938 the creation of a "national front in which *all parties would disappear*."[27] In this way, Togliatti observed, Negrín thought that it would be possible to "govern without having to take into account at every moment the demands and threats of certain political groups." The party, Togliatti continued, advised Negrín against the idea, "which would not have yielded the desired results."[28] In his unpublished memoir, politburo member Vicente Uribe confirms Negrín's thought of merging all parties into a national front. "He argued that with such a merger or movement [the Communists], because of our strength and practical experience, would succeed in imposing our orientation. To form this single party of Negrín, administrative measures would not be excluded, because once formed, all other parties in the republican zone would be proscribed."[29]

Among the myths propagated during the last half-century that must be laid to rest is one begotten by Dr. José María García-Valdecasas, a collaborator and disciple of Negrín. According to the Catalan author Juan Llarch, García-Valdecasas told him that toward the end of the Battle of the Ebro (November 1938), Russia offered Negrín "unlimited military aid" if he agreed to impose a totalitarian Communist regime in Spain. "Negrín categorically refused. . . . The

Russian offer to Negrín, unknown until now [1985] . . . was revealed to his most intimate collaborators and friends in Figueras when the army was already seeking to cross the French border [February 1939]."[30] This tale, which no other champion of Negrín has ever mentioned in the course of fifty years of legend-making, runs counter to the "moderate" policy pursued by Stalin in the hope of involving the democratic powers in the conflict. Far more plausible is the assertion by Santiago Garcés, the head of the SIM, that Negrín sent a letter to Stalin through Hidalgo de Cisneros "consulting him on the possibility of dissolving the Communist party so as to attract the sympathies of the European democracies."[31] But the only support for this assertion comes from an article written three years earlier by Rafael Méndez—another devotee of Negrín's and Santiago Garcés's benefactor—who claimed, as we have seen in an earlier chapter, that Negrín told the British ambassador and the head of the British secret service in Republican Spain that if Britain and France would sell the Republican government the arms it needed to win the war, he would not only remove the two Communist ministers from his government, but he would outlaw the Communist party and replace the Communist officers holding command posts in the army with non-Communists. However, as stated earlier, it is impossible to accept these assertions at face value and to attribute to them at best anything but tactical significance.

My third conclusion is that in the event of victory, Negrín would have relied on the "men of energy and authority forged by the war," who, given his reliance on the PCE, would have been mainly Communists and who were in his own words his "best and most loyal collaborators."

Fourth, Negrín hoped to induce Stalin to speed up the delivery of weapons by holding out two enticing possibilities in the event of victory: (a) the provision of merchant and naval vessels and (b) the existence in Western Europe of a "powerful military and naval force capable of collaborating in the common cause of human progress with the USSR."

In sum, the letter is particularly significant in that it reveals to what degree Negrín was willing to collaborate in the postwar period with the Soviet Union, a degree of collaboration that because of his dependence on the PCE may have turned Spain into the first Soviet satellite in Western Europe, the forerunner of the People's Democracies established in Eastern Europe after World War II.

La Pasionaria herself has retrospectively provided some insight into what kind of regime the PCE had in mind in the postwar era if the Republicans had won. "During the war," she wrote in her memoirs, "and with the backing of the people in arms, the bourgeois democratic republic was transformed into a Popular Republic, the first in the history of contemporary democratic revolutions." Whereas in the Russian revolution of 1905, she said, the working class created soviets, "the most democratic form of proletarian power," in the "national revolutionary war" in Spain, the Spanish people created "the popular democracy, which after the second world war was in some countries one of the forms of peaceful transition to socialism."[32]

Although Negrín's letter was dated 11 November, Hidalgo de Cisneros—

who, as we have seen, was to give Stalin a verbal report on the military situation—did not leave for Moscow until a few days before the start of the offensive against Catalonia on 23 December. In his memoirs, he gives no explanation for this delay nor does he discuss the arms previously ordered. Negrín, he writes, telephoned him early one morning to go to his home as soon as possible. On his arrival, the prime minister informed him that the "only way to avoid or delay the loss of Catalonia was to ask the Soviet Union to send to Spain a large shipment of war material" and ordered him to leave for Moscow the same day with a list of weapons that were needed, which included 250 airplanes, 250 tanks, 4,000 machine guns, and 650 pieces of artillery. "Negrín told me," he says, "that it was a matter of life and death for us and that the negotiations should be conducted by a person of his absolute confidence."[33] Since Hidalgo de Cisneros does not allude to any of the previous orders, one is left with the impression that he was carrying to Moscow an entirely new list of requirements.

His description of his interview with Stalin and other Soviet leaders merits recounting: He was seated between Stalin and the interpreter with (chairman of the council of people's commissars Vyacheslav) Molotov and (defense commissar Kliment) Voroshilov facing them. "I felt somewhat embarrassed," he says, "when we began to read the list of requests, because they appeared astronomical and unrealistic to me. With surprise and joy I saw Stalin give his approval." Before rising from the table, Voroshilov asked Hidalgo de Cisneros how the sum of approximately $103 million was to be paid inasmuch as the Spanish government had a balance of less than $100,000 in the Soviet Union. " 'We shall have to find a solution to cover the difference,' Voroshilov stated. 'Tomorrow you will speak with the minister of commerce, Comrade Mikoyan, to finalize the matter.' " It was agreed, Hidalgo claims, to cover the cost of the weapons by a loan to the Spanish government secured "solely by my signature." "When we consider the shameful conditions," he observes, "imposed by certain countries on some governments before giving them a few million dollars and compare those conditions with the rapidity and naturalness with which the Soviets gave us $100 million without any security or commitment . . . it is understandable why I speak with enthusiasm of the generosity and unselfishness of the Soviet Union toward our country."[34]

In evaluating this statement, one should bear in mind the difficulty Negrín and his ambassador in Moscow, Marcelino Pascua, had experienced in March 1938 in obtaining a credit of $70 million. At that time, the Russians had insisted that half the amount be secured by gold and repaid in two years and the unsecured balance be repaid in four years. It is unlikely that Stalin would have agreed to less stringent terms purely on the basis of Hidalgo de Cisneros's signature, especially at a time when defeat appeared inevitable.

Hidalgo de Cisneros also claims that the Soviets began to prepare the shipment of arms immediately and that they were loaded onto seven Soviet vessels that sailed for French ports. He says, however, that the French government raised "all kinds of objections" and delayed the shipment across France up to the last moment. "When [the weapons] began to arrive in Catalonia, it was already too late. We no longer had any airfields where we could assemble the planes or territory to defend ourselves."[35]

From the available evidence it would be rash to assume that any weapons that arrived in Catalonia at the height of the Nationalist offensive were those allegedly shipped from Murmansk in late December or January. Ignacio Iglesias, former political editor of the POUM organ *La Batalla*, raises doubts as to whether this war material, if in fact it ever existed, could have reached Spain before the fall of Catalonia. To have done so, he argues, it would have had to be assembled, shipped to Murmansk, then loaded onto the seven ships, which would have had to navigate the Arctic Ocean down the long coast of Norway before entering the Atlantic Ocean and the North Sea, sail through the English Channel, and unload their cargo at Bordeaux for transport by rail across France—"all this in the record time of less than a month and a half."[36] Angel Viñas, on the other hand, a staunch Negrinista, objects that Iglesias "in his anticommunism" found it necessary to question whether the material really existed.[37]

In the dispute over the weaponry that was allegedly shipped as a result of Hidalgo de Cisneros's trip to Moscow in December 1938, one fact deserves special notice. The official Soviet history of the Second World War, *Istoriia vtoroi mirovoi voiny, 1939–1945*, published in Moscow in 1974, which gives precise figures (II, 54) regarding the arms shipments to Spain during the Civil War, does not even mention the purported shipment; yet, when the book was published, the USSR had no reason to understate its help to the Spanish Republic. In the text and in an accompanying table, the authors claim that the Soviet Union "managed to send" (*udalos' napravit'*) to the Spanish Republic fifty-two ships between 1 October 1936 and 1 August 1937 as compared with thirteen ships between 14 December 1937 and 11 August 1938 and *only three ships between 25 December and 28 January 1939* (see table).

These official figures, which were furnished by the Institute of Military History of the Soviet Union, make it impossible to give credence either to Hidalgo de Cisneros's claim that seven ships sailed from Murmansk (sometime in December or January) carrying 250 airplanes, 250 tanks, 4,000 machine guns, and 650 pieces of artillery or to Angel Viñas's unsubstantiated assertion that at the end of 1938 new material was shipped to Spain from the USSR "in large quantities."[38] Nor can any credence be given to Viñas's other assertion that the USSR resumed supplies "on a large scale" after the Munich Pact (signed on 30 September 1938). "This materiel," he asserts, "began to arrive toward the end of 1938, and one can only believe that if Stalin had truly abandoned the Republic [as has been argued] these shipments would not have been made."[39] Moreover, in view of Negrín's letter to Stalin of 11 November and a later communication addressed to Molotov on the 26th, urging him to do what was necessary "to send us immediately the merchandise we have contracted to purchase,"[40] it is clear that Hidalgo's mission to Moscow was not to acquire new war material, as he would have us believe, but rather, as Viñas himself acknowledges, "to support the requests previously made."[41]

Soviet Arms Shipments to Spain, 1936–1939

Weapons	1 October 1936– 1 August 1937	14 December 1937– 11 August 1938	25 December 1938– 28 January 1939	Total
Airplanes	496	152	—	648
Tanks	322	25	—	347
Armored vehicles	60	—	—	60
Artillery	714	469	3	1,186
Machine guns	12,804	4,910	2,772	20,486
Rifles	377,793	125,020	35,000	497,813

As for the alleged credit of $103 million, there is not a shred of evidence from Soviet sources that such a large loan was ever granted. The only evidence that the official Spanish Communist history of the Civil War is able to produce is deceptive, since it rests on an article written in April 1970 by Marcelino Pascua, Negrín's wartime ambassador to Moscow, in which he refers to a request for a loan of $60 million *in the summer of 1938*,[42] in other words, *six months before Hidalgo de Cisneros left for Russia*. Moreover, on 5 April 1957, *Pravda* claimed that the Spanish government owed $50 million of $85 million in Soviet credits extended in 1937 and 1938 but made no mention of any other loan. It is equally significant that on 18 February 1939, Negrín, according to the official Spanish Communist history of the Civil War, requested politburo member and minister of agriculture Vicente Uribe to send a letter to the Soviet government to inquire "whether the USSR was willing to continue sending armaments to the Spanish Republic and to grant it the loan it had requested, which was absolutely necessary in order to continue the resistance."[43] This loan, whatever its size or purpose, was never granted, for although, according to the same official Communist source, the Soviets offered assurances that "if the Republic kept up its resistance, the USSR would continue as always to provide the necessary help,"[44] the Negrín government was overthrown a few days later.

Despite contradictory statements regarding the quantity and type of arms that reached Catalonia or France during the Catalan offensive, there is no dispute that they arrived too late to hinder General Franco's crushing offensive and his capture of Barcelona on 26 January. This catastrophe was of such magnitude that it triggered the disintegration of the entire administrative machinery of state. Palmiro Togliatti, who remained the most authoritative Communist figure in the left zone until the total breakdown of Communist power, gave the following version of the Catalan disaster in his report to the Comintern on 21 May 1939, in which he made an obvious attempt to make a scapegoat of the premier:

After [the loss of] Barcelona the state apparatus completely collapsed amidst unheard-of disorder and panic. Eight days before its fall, Negrín had given the order to evacuate all the ministries to the Gerona-Figueras region and advised all political leaders to leave. But neither he nor any of the ministers took practical measures to organize the evacuation and to maintain a functioning governmental apparatus. For this reason the flight was disorganized. The officials carried away in trucks their women, children, and friends, their beds and mattresses, even their desks and inkwells. A tragic and grotesque spectacle, which contributed to the demoralization of the entire city. The roads that lead to the frontier were clogged for ten days. In the Gerona-Figueras region nothing had been prepared and this mass of humanity ended up camping in the fields and along the roads around the castle of Figueras and inside the castle itself, which became the temporary seat of government and the center of the most appalling chaos.

Nothing functioned any longer, neither the telephone nor telegraph service, neither rail nor road transportation, nor the [political] commissariat of war. The apparatus of the carabineers and assault guards, who had been trained as the last reserve of the government to handle a situation such as this, collapsed. The carabineers contributed to the creation of the panic. The assault guards put up somewhat more resistance, but disappeared in their turn in the confusion. The recruiting centers and the few reserves that still existed also disappeared. Only the general staff retained a liaison apparatus with the front and some ability to function, but with great difficulty and without facilities. With a rear guard in total disarray, pounded in turn by waves of panic, the army was no longer able to fight. But despite everything, it still resisted in front of Granollers (the XIth Division) and around Gerona, withdrawing in comparative order and executing systematically the plan for the destruction of highways, bridges, ammunition depots, etc., etc., thus permitting the civilian population and all the weaponry to be evacuated toward France.

Negrín was completely overwhelmed. He did not adopt a single concrete measure of organization on his own initiative. *He did, however, give the party a free hand.* Every day he had to contend with the offensive of the capitulators in the cabinet, which was in almost permanent session. They then comprised, quite openly, all the ministers with the exception of Uribe.[45] Comrade Moix, the minister of labor and a member of the PSUC, could find nothing better to do than to weep at a cabinet meeting on 30 January, during which Negrín, after reading a perfidious letter from Rojo about our friends,[46] asked for a vote of confidence leaving him free to decide when the government should move to the central zone. The other ministers, the President of the Republic, nearly all the leaders of the other parties, the non-Communist military chiefs, etc., all demanded that Negrín should put an end to the war, acknowledging the impossibility of any future resistance and requesting Britain and France to obtain "honorable" terms from

Franco. What these terms might be no one knew or attempted to specify: in general it was thought that we might be allowed to evacuate from the central zone several thousand leaders who were in jeopardy, but nothing more. . . . It was clear that Negrín had lost confidence in the continuation of the struggle, but still adhered to his former political line of resistance. . . .

What was contradictory in Negrín's position was that, although he reaffirmed the [policy of] resistance in a platonic manner, he did nothing later to organize it. His major responsibility was his failure to give the necessary orders during the last days in Figueras [eighteen kilometers from the French border] to transfer to Valencia and Madrid at least some of the arms that were reaching us.[47]

This last accusation does not rest on solid ground, for not only was Figueras cut off from the central zone by land and sea, except for a few fishing communities that could have been quickly destroyed by enemy action, but the defense ministry was to all intents and purposes under the control of the PCE. It is therefore difficult not to conclude that this accusation, like other criticisms of Negrín in Togliatti's report[48]—parts of which later became the raw material from which the official line was hewn—were to some degree an attempt to clear himself of any responsibility for the final disaster. It is equally difficult not to conclude that La Pasionaria, who years later repeated some of Togliatti's criticisms of Negrín—notably that he had "lost confidence in the struggle, although he appeared to maintain his former political line of resistance,"[49] and that he did nothing "to send to the central-southern zone the largest possible quantity of war material"[50]—intended, like Togliatti, to make a scapegoat of the premier.

Although Togliatti and La Pasionaria both accuse Negrín of having lost confidence in the possibility of resistance, an unidentified "comrade Sa."—who, to judge from Togliatti's references to him in his report to the Comintern, was a Soviet military adviser—told him two days after the fall of Barcelona that "Catalonia was irremediably lost and that, once lost, he considered resistance in the central zone impossible and collapse inevitable." That was the opinion, Togliatti noted, "of all the career officers both Communist and non-Communist."[51] Hence, it is not surprising that no steps were taken by anyone to ship arms to the central zone.

On 1 February, in the castle of Figueras, the Cortes that had been elected in 1936 met for the last time. Of its original 473 members, only 62 were present at this final session.[52] Some had sided with the military uprising; some had fled the country; others had been given diplomatic posts; a few were unable to attend or refused to attend, such as Largo Caballero and Araquistáin; while others, finding themselves on the wrong side at the outset of the Civil War, had long since been imprisoned or executed.

This final gathering of the Cortes was more than the usual constitutional façade. It was symbolic of the tragic fate of the Second Republic proclaimed in the spring of 1931 with joy and hope. Few of the attending deputies would ever set foot again on Spanish soil. Most would die in exile during the thirty-six years of General Franco's rule, but one in particular, the moderate Socialist Julián Zugazagoitia, would be handed over to Franco in 1940 by the Gestapo during the German occupation of France—as were other prominent figures such as Luis Companys and Juan Peiró—and executed, joining thousands of anonymous victims of the repression during the Franco dictatorship.

The ministers and deputies gathered in the intense cold in an underground chamber of the castle. Most of the ministers wore their overcoats and huddled together on a short plain bench. The Republican flag was displayed and cheap carpets were strewn across the stone floor for the occasion. Diego Martínez Barrio, the speaker of the Cortes, standing behind a makeshift tribune covered with red brocade, opened the session at 10:30 P.M.[53] "Señores diputados," he said, "this constitutional gathering of the Republican parliament is being held in difficult circumstances. We are holding it on a piece of Catalan soil that is stained and trampled down under the foot of foreign invaders and their national collaborators and underlings. . . . All I expect of you is that you restrain whatever passions dwell in your hearts. . . . This session will probably be historic . . . in the life of Spain."[54]

"Negrín was the first speaker," writes an eyewitness and friend of the premier, "and the only one who mattered. Those of us who knew his state of physical exhaustion and discouragement wondered whether he would be able to keep on talking. Several times he had to stop to pull himself together, and sometimes he seemed almost too dazed to express his thoughts coherently, especially after his notes gave out when he was half way through, and had to speak extemporaneously."[55]

According to the official record, Negrín declared that the Chamber was meeting in "a harsh atmosphere of war," although "spirits were now quieted and fears calmed." But the truth, he said, was that for some days "a wave of panic was on the point of asphyxiating our rear guard, contaminating our army and destroying the entire machinery of government. However, let us be fair. Neither order, nor authority was in danger. . . . Despite the provocations of the enemy, there was nothing resembling a revolt, a mutiny, or an uprising against the authority of the government." After referring to the difficulties—"insuperable at times"—that his government had experienced in acquiring arms abroad, while the enemy backed by the industrial might of Italy and Germany had "received everything it needed even to excess," he continued:

> Peace is never won solely on the battlefield. It is achieved cultivating a psychological factor among the combatants on the enemy side and also by disseminating abroad the issue of what we are defending. From the very first moment the desire of the Spanish government has been to make the world see what is being disputed here and to make our fellow citizens on the other side, friends and enemies alike, understand our aims. Don't have any illusions, señores diputados. We Spaniards are not engaged in a civil war over a question of ideas, over some ideological problem. No, we are fighting for the independence of our country, because we

know that if we do not triumph we shall be enslaved. . . . [We] are defending the interests of Spain and those of other countries. . . . It has been the mission of the Spanish government to try to show these neutral and friendly countries not only where their interests lie, but how mistaken they have been to allow themselves to be carried away by the maneuvers of our enemies. . . . To save the peace of Europe they allowed Austria to be devoured. To save the peace of Europe they allowed Czechoslovakia to be carved up. . . . I do not believe that their blindness could reach such a point as to imagine that with the strangulation of Spain they could satiate an appetite that becomes more ravenous the more they try to appease it.

The premier then named only three conditions for peace culled from his thirteen war aims: (1) a guarantee of national independence free from all foreign influence, (2) a guarantee that the Spanish people would have the right to determine their own regime and their own destiny, and (3) a guarantee that once the war was over all persecutions and reprisals would stop. These were the indispensable prerequisites, he said, for ending the war. "It horrifies me to think what the victory of Italy and Germany would mean to our country." There was the danger that their domination would result in the loss of Spain's national identity and that it would take generations to recover it. "[For] this reason we must fight to the last breath. We shall fight in Catalonia . . . and if we lose here, we shall still have the central-southern zone, where we have hundreds of thousands of combatants ready to continue the fight for those fundamental causes that are worth dying for."[56]

Representatives of each of the major parties then addressed the assembly. Martínez Barrio presented a brief resolution supporting Negrín's peace terms, which was passed unanimously by acclamation. The Cortes broke up at 12:45 A.M.[57]

Although nobody opposed the peace proposals, everyone knew that the gesture was hopeless, for even after the victorious crossing of the river Ebro by the Republicans on 25 July 1938, when the final outcome of the battle was still uncertain, Franco had rejected outright any settlement other than total victory. It was chimerical, he said, to believe that "criminals and their victims" could live in peace. "Nationalist Spain," he asserted, "had conquered and will not allow its victory to be torn from it or adulterated by anyone or anything."[58]

Clearly, Negrín was now in no position to lay down terms of peace to an enemy in full glow of victory. Even the confidence of chief of the general staff Vicente Rojo—who had told the premier on more than one occasion that "he would remain at his side and share his fate as long as he retained his trust"[59]—had evaporated. "Was it not an illusion to believe anymore in foreign help? Was it not an illusion to believe that a military success was still possible?" he asked after the war. "Perhaps to more than one observer of our struggle such questions may appear defeatist, but I know that all those who went through that unhappy experience also asked them. . . . At that time they were careful to remain silent and perhaps it was their political duty to do so; but I had the military duty to ask these questions and to reply to them. . . . It was already very clear that every country except the USSR . . . had turned its back on us and that the majority of them were anxiously awaiting the end of the war."[60]

Togliatti, forever on the lookout for scapegoats, reported Rojo's defeatism to Moscow: "We now know that Rojo, immediately after the fall of Barcelona, proposed to Negrín that he put an end to the war by giving all battalion leaders written orders to raise the white flag and pass over to the enemy. Negrín, however, said nothing about this either to the party or to comrade Sa. General Rojo, at the cabinet meeting of 29 January, and also afterwards, claimed that resistance was impossible. Although he remained at his post and continued to give orders, he did nothing to salvage the situation, which he regarded as desperate."[61]

On 2 February, the politburo issued in Figueras its notorious manifesto, drafted by Antonio Mije, a leading member of the politburo,[62] denouncing all its enemies—Catalan autonomists, deserters, defeatists, fifth columnists, and Trotskyists—who, in the lexicon of the PCE, now virtually encompassed the entire population of Spain. After declaring that the fall of Barcelona had created the most serious situation since the beginning of the war and represented a "veritable catastrophe for the democratic peoples of France and England," the manifesto continued:

> We must openly condemn the fact that this situation was facilitated by the criminal and treasonable behavior of elements who, because of the enemy's success, have lost faith and confidence in our people, in our country, and in the possibility of continuing the struggle. In their great majority, these elements are the same as those who have contributed to the decline of resistance by their intrigues and vacillations, by their opposition to unity, by disseminating discord, and by sabotaging the labor of others and the work of government. . . .
>
> In face of this situation, the Communist party has used all its strength in the Catalan region to avoid errors, overcome weaknesses and defects in order to re-establish discipline at the fronts and in the rear and denounces with indignation these acts of disunity and open treason. It asks the government and all the organizations of the people to take forceful and exemplary measures as soon as possible. Any official, any commander, who has abandoned his post or abandons his post at this time should be treated in the same way that traitors and deserters are treated at the battle fronts. . . .
>
> The Politburo specifically denounces the shameful flight from national territory of Largo Caballero who—surrounded by a small group of enemies of unity, of enemies of the Spanish people and of its organizations—has done everything in his power to sabotage the work of the government and destroy the unity and resistance of our people and now crowns his criminal career by fleeing.[63] The Politburo also hopes that the antifascist organizations and the people will denounce with indignation the behavior of those men who, after rendering difficult the vital work of mobilizing all the resources of Catalonia by their mistaken separatist or

autonomous policies . . . can only think of escaping abroad. The people will see that these cowards and traitors are brought to justice. . . .

Confronted with this very grave situation, the Communist party reaffirms its confidence in the victory of the Spanish people and declares that as long as there remains a piece of Catalan territory it will be successfully defended by the rapid reorganization of our army and the restoration of morale and discipline at the front and in the rear.

The Communist party emphatically rejects the criminal conduct of the deserters, defeatists, trotskyists, and fifth columnists in abandoning Catalan territory without fighting. . . .

Our party, whose sacred objective is the defense of the democratic Republic and the independence of Spain, is in the vanguard of the struggle. It places at the disposal of the government all its men and all its resources and urges its militants . . . to provide rapidly the utmost assistance in order to solve the military and political problems of the moment, placing themselves without discussion at the orders of the civilian and military authorities. . . .

The Communist party declares that it will fight without pity against all those who at this time obstruct this task and who intrigue against unity. . . .

Finally, on behalf of all the Communists of Spain, the Politburo sends its heartfelt greetings to the working class and the people of Barcelona who are being brutally treated by the ferocity and savagery of the invaders. We shall continue to fight until victory for the liberation of Barcelona and of all the invaded territory.

Everyone must work and fight at the front or in the rear: all Communists, all workers, all antifascists!

No mercy to deserters, cowards, and enemies of unity![64]

By 10 February, the war in Catalonia was over. General Vicente Rojo, the president of the Republic, the premier and his ministers, the Cortes deputies, the members of the Generalitat government, the politburo, and high-ranking members of all organizations, as well as some 400,000 refugees, including the defeated Army of Catalonia, had crossed the border into France. "I, like many another," wrote Lawrence Fernsworth, the correspondent of the *Times*, "hoped never again to behold such a spectacle. . . . The fleeing hordes of Spaniards, each one the embodiment of an individual tragedy, spilled over the mountainous borders, immense avalanches of human debris."[65]

"The situation in Catalonia is good," Count Galeazzo Ciano, Mussolini's foreign minister, wrote jubilantly in his diary on 22 February. "Franco improved it with a very painstaking and drastic housecleaning. Many Italians were taken prisoner: Anarchist and Communist. I informed the Duce about it, and he ordered that they all be shot, adding, 'Dead men tell no tales.' "[66]

Part X

The End of the Resistance Policy

63

Negrín Returns to the Central-Southern Zone

On 10 February, as the curtain was falling on the final scene of the Catalan drama, Negrín flew from Toulouse to Alicante accompanied by Julio Alvarez del Vayo, his foreign minister, and by Santiago Garcés Arroyo, the head of the SIM.[1] He was followed by the other members of his cabinet with the exception of José Giral, who remained in France with Manuel Azaña, and Francisco Méndez Aspe, who stayed behind to attend to financial matters.

On arriving in Alicante, Negrín announced that Madrid would be the official seat of government and that his administration, "inspired by popular sentiment," would fight to the very end for "the principles of national independence, self-determination and unity of all Spaniards." It was essential, he declared, to ensure that the struggle "would not end in foreign domination or in an atmosphere of savage hatred and reprisals."[2]

His decision to leave for the central-southern zone was not acclaimed by all the members of his cabinet, the majority of whom at first refused to leave Toulouse. Only after he admonished the recalcitrants did they follow his example.[3] However, according to Togliatti, they "continued to do in Madrid what they had done in Figueras: to call for cabinet meetings in order to demonstrate the impossibility of further resistance and the need to capitulate."[4]

The mood of the army generals in the central-southern zone was no less defeatist. "When I landed at the airfield in Alicante," Negrín told the permanent committee of the Cortes a few weeks later, "I immediately got in touch with the military authorities: General Miaja, General Matallana, the chiefs of the various Armies and the commander of the fleet. I was able to perceive from the tenor of our telephone conversations that the arrival of the head of the government caused great confusion and even great displeasure as though it disrupted something they had agreed upon. I noticed especially the cold, dry tone of my interlocutors."[5] Alvarez del Vayo records that the morale of the military leaders depressed him and that during a conversation at General Miaja's headquarters in Valencia he and Negrín observed their "skepticism" with regard to the possibility of future resistance. "Our words of encouragement found no echo in their hearts, which were dead to all vigorous reaction, and longing only for an early end to the hostilities."[6]

All this could have come as no surprise. On 30 January, General Miaja, in reply to a request by Negrín for information on the military situation, had reported that the forces were "poorly armed," that the percentage of unusable material was "truly distressing," and that the population after two and a half years was "tired of the war."[7]

Togliatti reported to Moscow: "The conviction was general that the army in the central zone could not contain an enemy attack. This was because of his overwhelming numerical superiority and *our army's lack of weapons, aviation and transport, and its organic weakness.*" All the professional officers, including those who were Communist, were of the opinion that "*resistance was impossible.*" As for Colonel Antonio Cordón, the undersecretary of the army, General Ignacio Hidalgo de Cisneros, the chief of the air force, and Colonel Carlos Núñez Maza, the undersecretary of air—all career officers and members of the PCE— they stated "openly" that they did not believe in further resistance. "I believe," Togliatti added, "that the conviction that we could not resist any longer was also fairly widespread among the commanders who had risen from the ranks of the militia. The same conviction was also general among the cadres of the Anarchist, Republican, and Socialist parties, and in the police and state apparatus. *Hence, the problem was no longer how to organize resistance, but how to put an end to the war 'with honor and dignity.'*" There was one point, he said, upon which everyone agreed: the Communists were the "sole obstacle" to peace. "Among the masses, war weariness and suffering expressed themselves in a profound and general desire for peace. *The whole country was waiting for a new development that would put an end to the war. No longer was there any thought of victory.*"[8] (The words I have italicized in this once "strictly confidential" report to the Comintern should be borne in mind by the reader when evaluating all claims by Negrín and his supporters that significant resistance was feasible.)

Togliatti blamed General Miaja—who had recently been appointed commander in chief of the land, sea and air forces and government delegate in the central-southern zone[9]—for making the situation "even worse" by appointing Colonel Ricardo Burillo to command the police forces in the region.[10] Burillo, a former member of the PCE and police chief of Barcelona at the time of the coup against the POUM in June 1937, had been appointed commander of the Army of Estremadura in November 1937.[11] In September of 1938, he was removed from his command[12] and expelled from the party. He is described by Togliatti in his report to Moscow of 21 May 1939 as "an ex-Communist and Mason animated by a fierce hatred toward the party."[13] Under his direction, Togliatti asserts, the assault guards, which were previously "one of the police corps trusted by the party," reverted to "their old traditions and reactionary make-up." As for the carabineers, who were "controlled by Socialist cadres and capitulators," they could be "easily mobilized" for a struggle against the party. "Hence a situation was created in which the real apparatus of power was directed against us in a struggle that was no longer undeclared and secret, but open and continuous."[14]

Even before the fall of Catalonia, the influence of the PCE in the central-southern zone had begun to wane. "The transfer of the leadership of the party to Catalonia in order to be near the government," La Pasionaria later acknowledged, "prejudiced us more than it favored us, because all the propaganda and organizational work in the central-southern zone, especially in Madrid, was severely weakened. Our adversaries took advantage of this deficiency in order to strengthen their own positions."[15] In fact, as we have already seen, the mood in Madrid—once the bastion of the PCE—had changed to such a point in August 1938 that, according to José Giral, "it was necessary to restrain the people to stop them from breaking all relations with the Communists and declaring them enemies of the Republic."

It was against this background of political decline and dissolution that the principal Communist leaders arrived in the central-southern zone to participate in the final act of the Spanish drama. They were accompanied by Togliatti, the guiding spirit and de facto leader of the party, who, in the words of the official Communist history, returned to Spain to "continue to help his Spanish comrades with his experience."[16] Boris Stefanov, the other Comintern delegate, and three of the politburo members, Jesús Hernández, La Pasionaria, and Pedro Martínez Cartón, were already there, but José Díaz, the party secretary, was seriously ill in Russia.[17] Although the declared aim of the PCE was to pursue the policy of resistance, Ettore Vanni, the Italian Communist and director of *Verdad*, the party organ in Valencia, who was in close touch with the Communist leaders and the Soviet delegation in the city, affirms: "Deep down, everyone felt within himself the inanity of a struggle that had cost the Spanish people innumerable casualties on both sides. Only later did I realize that the 'will to resist,' which characterized the Communists' official stand, was no more than a purely formal acceptance of the Russian catchphrase: 'resistance to the end.' "[18]

It is doubtful whether Negrín actually shared the largely showcase optimism of Alvarez del Vayo, his pro-Soviet foreign minister, that a general war was near at hand and that resistance should be prolonged until war erupted;[19] for not only does Togliatti allege that the premier had "no faith in the possibility of further resistance,"[20] but Cordón, Negrín's undersecretary of the army, asserts that he returned to Spain "not as a government leader resolved to take the reins firmly in his hands in order to direct the resistance, but as an honorable man who wishes to ease his conscience and accept the necessary sacrifice, although convinced of its futility."[21]

Whatever may have been Negrín's intimate thoughts, few can doubt that he was torn by conflicting sentiments. Some hint of his inner torment can be gleaned from his self-justificatory letter to Indalecio Prieto of 23 June 1939: "I tried to raise spirits, reestablish services, gather all the necessary elements for effective resistance [and] to continue fighting, *because, if we could not win, this was the only way to save what could be saved, or, at least, to save our honor.*"[22] It is reasonable to assume that Negrín's speedy return to Spain was prompted by some of the following considerations: (1) his loyalty to the Communists, to whom, in his own phrase, he owed "a debt of honor";[23] (2) the desire to save his self-respect by not shirking his responsibilities; (3) the hope that his immediate return to Spain would raise morale and set an example to those military leaders who had crossed the border into France and were now convinced that further resistance was chimerical; (4) the hope that resistance would win a promise of clemency from General Franco or, failing such a promise, that resistance would allow time for those of his followers, whose lives were most in jeopardy, to escape abroad; (5) the fading expectation that, if resistance were maintained, the Civil War might eventually merge with a general European conflict; and (6) the belief that if resistance proved impossible, he could shift the burden of surrender and stigma of defeat onto his opponents.

Negrín's anguish was heightened by the knowledge that apart from those officers dedicated to the PCE few military leaders supported the resistance policy.[24] Negrín was correct, writes Juan Modesto, when he said that the commanders and commissars who arrived from France at his request were all Communists. "But it is important to emphasize that this occurred not because of our party's desire to dominate, but because many of the others had deserted."[25] In fact, according to Cordón, the majority of the top-ranking military commanders and high-level government officials—undersecretaries, directors, inspectors general, the members of the general staff, and military chiefs—"did not want to return to Spain, using one pretext or another."[26] Conspicuous among those who did not return were Colonel Patricio de Azcárate, the inspector general of engineers; Colonel Eduardo Cuevas de la Peña, the director general of security, who along with other members of the PCE had been expelled at the end of January from the party "for desertion in the face of the enemy";[27] Colonel Eleuterio Díaz Tendero, head of the personnel section of the defense ministry; Colonel José Luis Fuentes, the inspector general of artillery; General Juan Hernández Sarabia; General Enrique Jurado (who replaced Hernández Sarabia as the overall commander of the armies of the East and of the Ebro); and General Sebastián Pozas, onetime commander of the Army of the East and, more recently, military governor of Figueras.[28] But more important than all these defections was that of General Vicente Rojo, the chief of the central general staff, whose easy relations with Negrín and the Communists had never been marred by political disagreement during their two years of close cooperation.

Although these officers—except Hernández Sarabia, an Azañista—had supported the PCE when the political winds were in its favor or, like General Pozas and Colonel Cuevas, had joined the party, they had now lost all faith in future resistance. After the fall of Barcelona, Rojo had informed Azaña that there was "a shortage of all resources and that morale was totally lacking." And, he added, "nothing can be done."[29] Explaining his decision not to proceed to the central-southern zone, Rojo wrote in his first book written shortly after the war: "Apparently, the view that we should persist in the policy of resistance was imposed because it might cause a change in the international situation. The same hope that had sustained us during a year of sacrifice! But now without the slightest foundation! Let us ignore the sacrifices! Resistance! A sublime formula for heroism when it is nurtured by hope and bolstered by an ideal! But when the will that holds aloft the flag of that ideal collapses . . . [resistance] is no longer a military gesture. It is an absurdity. *How could we resist? What reason did we have to resist?*"[30]

Rojo then makes a grave accusation that has been carefully ignored by Negrín and his supporters: "If it is true that the war was to be seriously continued in the central zone, why were the stocks of food, raw materials, and armaments accumulated in France liquidated? This was too obvious and significant not to be disconcerting.[31] On the one hand, the war was being wound up economically by the sale of stocks; on the other hand, the order to resist was being given without providing the necessary means even in food supplies."[32]

After the war, Negrín claimed that there were enough "material means" in the central-southern zone for an organized defense for "six months or more," but he disregarded Rojo's total disbelief in further resistance. Instead, he praised his "inflexible sense of duty," his "absolute integrity," and his "irreproachable chivalry" and "enlightened patriotism."[33] Nor have the Communists publicly censured Rojo for not returning to Spain. In fact, their official history is mute on this crucial matter.[34] Clearly, neither Negrín nor the PCE wished to lock horns with the man whom they had elevated to the top military post[35] and awarded with the *laureado*, the highest decoration, and who knew more about the military situation than any single person. To have condemned his defeatism and defection openly would have provided ammunition to their opponents and undermined the legend that has been fostered for half a century that the loss of the war was due entirely to "traitors and capitulators."

Apart from Rojo's cognizance of the military odds against the Republic, of the liquidation of stocks in France, and of the defection of the high-ranking officers who opted to remain in France, there was yet another factor that influenced his decision not to return to Spain. "The conduct of many leaders of lower rank filled me with distrust. Everything they did was . . . contrary to what they should have done if the slogan of resistance were to be realistic and effective. But the most serious thing of all was that they themselves were convinced that the famous slogan had neither feasibility nor substance."[36]

Given the state of mind of the officers and officials in the upper and middle echelons of the army and the government, who elected to remain in France, it is no wonder, as Hidalgo de Cisneros averred, that the last six airplanes that flew to Spain were "nearly empty." As for those Communists who returned to Spain, they did not go there, he affirmed, "to win laurels, for *we knew the situation was almost hopeless. We went there because of party discipline.*"[37] Some prominent Communists, however, did not go back to Spain. Manuel Tagüeña, the Communist commander of the Fifteenth Army Corps, attests: "They included leaders of the PCE and the JSU, like [Francisco] Antón, [Antonio] Mije, [Luis Cabo] Giorla and Santiago Carrillo."[38] Enrique Líster corroborates this charge: "In the airplane in which I left Toulouse for the central-southern zone on the night of 13–14 February," he states, ". . . there were thirteen passengers despite the fact that there was room for thirty-three. . . . The point is that the aforementioned members of the Politburo and the JSU executive . . . regarded the war as lost."[39] Although when Líster made this accusation he was trying to wrest control of the party from Santiago Carrillo, then its general secretary, Carrillo's own explanations of his failure to return are too riddled with contradictions to be trustworthy.[40]

Of all the leaders who stayed in France, none was more openly defeatist than Manuel Azaña, the president of the Republic, now in temporary residence in the Spanish embassy in Paris.[41] Even before crossing the border into France he had told Negrín that he would not return to Spain. "Absolutely not," he said. "If I were to go to the central zone, I would be giving support and approval to the resistance policy, which I disapprove. I shall remain [in Catalonia] until the government agrees that I should leave, but if I cross the frontier you cannot rely on me for anything except to make peace. On no account will I return to Spain."[42]

Fearing that Azaña might resign the presidency and that Britain and France would immediately recognize General Franco's administration as the sovereign government of Spain, Negrín had del Vayo fly to Paris on 12 February to inform the president that the government viewed his presence in Spain as "indispensable."[43] But in vain. "My only duty is to make peace," Azaña told him. "I refuse . . . to prolong a senseless struggle. We must try to get the best possible guarantees for humane treatment and then finish everything as soon as we can."[44] Negrín then sent Azaña two telegrams, the second, according to Diego Martínez Barrio, the speaker of the Cortes, "more discourteous and mortifying than the first." He accused the president of "abandoning his constitutional duties and demanded 'in the name of the Spanish people' his immediate return to the Republican zone."[45] But the president had resolved not to return, least of all, "to enter Madrid accompanied by Negrín and Uribe with la Pasionaria and Pepe [José] Díaz on the running board."[46]

Although Azaña had told del Vayo that the only course was to make peace and obtain the best possible guarantees for humane treatment, there is evidence from his own pen that he regarded a settlement without reprisals as a delusion.[47] Ever since 18 July 1936, when he had appointed Diego Martínez Barrio to head a "government of conciliation," in an effort to avert civil war, he had hoped to secure a mediated peace.[48] But now all possibility of a settlement without reprisals finally evaporated when General Franco published on 13 February his terrifying Law of Political Responsibilities. The scope and severity of the measure, which filled twenty-four pages of the Nationalist official bulletin, were evident from its preamble, which stated that the law was directed against all those who by "action or grave omission had fomented the Red subversion" and had "hindered the historic and providential victory of the National Movement." Under the provisions of the law all political parties, trade-union organizations, and all affiliated groups that had opposed the National movement were proscribed and anyone over the age of fourteen who, between 1 October 1934 and 18 July 1936, had contributed to "the subversion of public order" or had resisted the movement "by passive or definite acts" was subject to the penalties of the law.[49] As one prominent historian observed, at least half of all Spaniards came within its scope.[50]

No wonder the law caused tremors of consternation. Only the previous day Negrín had issued a proclamation in Madrid calling for further resistance, for the "rebirth of the spirit that immortalized Madrid during the memorable days of November 1936," and for the "passionate collaboration of everyone above party interests." In no other way, he declared, could the government ensure the independence of Spain and prevent the country from being "submerged in a sea of blood, hatred, and persecution."[51]

But it was fanciful to imagine that the popular forces would rally around Negrín and the PCE for another spell of sacrifice. When the Communist leaders arrived in Madrid from France, they found that the factions of the left had coalesced against them. Embittered by political injury and oppression, demoralized by the attacks on the Revolution, as were the left Socialists and the Anarchosyndicalists, and exhausted by a protracted war that offered no hope of victory, they execrated the Negrín government—which the Socialist Luis Araquistáin described as the "most cynical and despotic" in Spanish history[52]—as much as they detested its resistance policy.

"Resist? What for? That is the universal question," wrote Zugazagoitia, the moderate Socialist. "The fall of Barcelona and the loss of Catalonia . . . have destroyed the hopes even of those who delude themselves the most: the Communists. The front-line troops see the relaxation of discipline and desertions increase alarmingly. Those who do not desert to the enemy leave the trenches and find their way home. . . . Does Negrín perceive the new reality? Does anyone try to apprise him of the virulence of the germs of decomposition? The persons who surround the premier are, like the premier himself, tied to his resistance policy: they are all Communists."[53]

"Only men blinded by pride and arrogance," wrote the Besteiro Socialist Trifón Gómez, president of the UGT National Federation of Railroad Workers and head of the quartermaster corps, "could ignore the fact that everyone was hostile to them when they returned to the central-southern zone—everyone, that is, but the group of Communists who continued to manipulate Negrín. . . . It cannot be denied . . . that the conquest of Catalonia was a military walkover. In view of this, the policy of resistance advocated by the Negrín government lacked support among the people. . . . The truth is . . . that the government was a phantom. Not a single ministry functioned; the titular heads of the various departments had not the slightest desire to establish themselves; they were obsessed with the thought of assuring for themselves the means by which they could leave Spain."[54]

As Jesús Hernández aptly put it: the government was "a mute, paralytic phantom that neither governed nor spoke and that lacked the machinery of government and a fixed place of residence."[55]

What was the feeling of the cabinet members whom Negrín had forced to return to Spain? The minister of justice, Ramón González Peña, a Prietista, told Wenceslao Carrillo, the left Socialist leader and director general of security under Largo Caballero: "Procure passports for all the comrades who run any risk when Franco seizes what still remains of the Republican zone and let them all out! . . . Here there remains nothing to be done in spite of all that Negrín says. Bear in mind that he is dominated by the Communist party to such an extent that he only informs Uribe and del Vayo as to what he is doing. We the other ministers are nobodies."[56]

Most conspicuous among the opponents of Negrín and the PCE in Madrid were the Caballero Socialists who, according to the official Communist history, "waged a fierce campaign of slander" against the Communist party, Negrín and his government, and the executive committee of the PSOE. "They tried to take control of the leadership of the PSOE and the UGT [both dominated by Negrinistas and Communists]. . . . Apart from Madrid, the Socialist elements hostile to the government enjoyed the greatest ascendancy in the provinces of Alicante, Murcia, and Jaén."[57]

A factor contributing to the poisoning of the political environment was the manifesto issued by the politburo in Figueras a few days before the fall of Catalonia condemning "the shameful flight" of Largo Caballero, to which reference was made in the previous chapter. In reporting to Moscow, Togliatti refers to the declaration as a violent denunciation of the "intrigues and treason of the cowards and capitulators." The principal blow, he said, was directed against Caballero for having fled to France two days after the fall of Barcelona. "This was all right . . . [but] the BP [politburo] decided on an illegal mass diffusion [of *Mundo Obrero*, the Communist organ in Madrid, which reproduced the manifesto in most of its issues and posted it on walls in defiance of the military censorship].[58] The consequences were a rupture of relations [with the PCE] by the Socialist party in a whole series of provinces, beginning with Madrid, and a public resolution by the FP [Popular Front] of Madrid condemning and denouncing the PCE as an opponent of unity. In other provinces the party was expelled from the Popular Front. . . . The fact is that the document was presented to the masses by our enemies as proof that the Communists did not want peace."[59]

Boris Stefanov, Togliatti's Comintern colleague, who was in Madrid at the time of the Figueras manifesto episode, confirms the hostile reaction of the opposing factions in a "top secret" (*sovershenno secretno*) report to the Comintern, a copy of which is now available in the Archivo Histórico del Comité Central del PCE in Madrid.[60] "The comrades, who drafted the manifesto," he said, "were not familiar with the prevailing political conditions in the central-southern zone. It became a pretext for the creation of the broadest anti-Communist coalition. . . . I personally feared that this would happen and recommended a delay in the distribution if only for twenty-four hours. This was done, but, on further consideration, it was decided to distribute a huge number of copies." Owing to the reaction among the various segments of the Popular Front, Stefanov continues, it became obvious to the politburo that "our party was isolated [and] was the only one demanding a far-reaching policy of firm resistance." This isolation, he says, was aggravated by the fact that the military apparatus, the police, the labor unions, and the press had already begun to assume a sharp anti-Communist stance. "In this situation, it was necessary to react and maneuver quickly in a way that would break the anti-Communist coalition."[61]

Negrín was at first irritated by the manifesto, but his annoyance was fleeting; for after the publication of a second declaration on 26 February,[62] the final draft of which, according to Togliatti, was "personally corrected by Negrín, he got to work and gave the party much more than it had requested."[63] Togliatti also reported to Moscow that the party made other errors: The "whole tone," he said of the party conference in Madrid at the beginning of February (before his arrival on the sixteenth),[64] was "mistaken" because it did not take into account "the new conditions of the struggle and the mood of the masses [i.e., their desire for peace]." The speech of La Pasionaria, he added, which was "clear and violent in its denunciation of the conspiracy of the capitulators" was not understood by the people and "increased our isolation from all the other political forces in Madrid."[65] Years later, Santiago Carrillo, when head of the PCE in exile, expressed the opinion that Togliatti's criticism of the party (an opinion that might easily apply, as we shall see directly, to Togliatti's criticisms of Boris Stefanov) "could have been influenced by the fear that the Italian leader might become the scapegoat of the Soviet leaders for the Spanish defeat."[66]

In contrast to Togliatti, Stefanov, who undoubtedly had a hand in setting the tone of the party conference, defended the party line in his secret report to the Comintern. "It is true," he acknowledged, "that little was said at the Madrid conference about peace. . . . Perhaps more should have been said and differently. Nevertheless, I consider the line of the Madrid conference and Dolores's speech absolutely correct. . . . Because of the confusion, intrigue, demoralization, defeatism, conspiratorial activity, . . . hunger and general exhaustion . . . the Madrid conference was the greatest political act of the Communist party at that time. . . . The party members in Madrid were clearly aware of the gravity of the situation. They understood that their days of trial had begun. . . . They ignited the spirit of enthusiasm and determination to carry on the fight no matter what. . . . The Madrid conference was the most important step taken toward overcoming the isolation of the party. It would therefore be absolutely wrong to attribute this isolation to the conference. . . . The meeting at which Dolores spoke drew more people than ever before. If we had organized conferences in Albacete, Alicante, and other cities with speeches by Dolores and other party leaders, if we had organized in Madrid other meetings, then the masses would have been on the side of the Communist party and the coalition of Casado with the Caballeristas, Anarchists, and Republicans would never have taken place."[67]

In his report to Moscow, in which he criticized the party, Togliatti reprehended Stefanov, his Comintern colleague, for the tone of the Madrid conference and accused him of "total passivity and political blindness." In fact, according to Stefanov's report to Moscow, Togliatti, in the presence of Comintern leader

Dmitri Manuilsky, said that "the most colossal political mistake committed by the party and by me was the fact that the central question of peace was not decided upon at the Madrid conference."[68] On the other hand, Togliatti took personal credit for the change in the party line after the conference, initiated after his arrival in Madrid on 16 February. "Comrade Checa [leading member of the politburo] was the first to understand the need to rectify matters . . . and immediately accepted the advice and suggestions in that sense. The rectification [which was reflected in the declaration by the politburo of 23 February[69]] openly raised the question of peace, stating that we, like all the people, wanted peace . . . , that it was possible on the basis of the points enunciated by Negrín in Figueras, but that in order to ensure their recognition [by General Franco] it was essential to continue the resistance."[70] The new declaration held out the possibility of direct and indirect help from the democratic powers—as can be seen from the passage quoted in the previous chapter—and made an urgent appeal for "unity and antifascist brotherhood," proclaiming that the PCE would never abandon its policy of unity and close collaboration "with all the parties, all the leaders, all the trade-union, political, and military bodies."[71]

But the declaration did nothing to lessen the animosities between the opposing sides, and both Negrín and the Communist leaders who had arrived from France on the tenth and sixteenth of February, fearing that they might be cornered in Madrid, decided on the twenty-seventh to leave the capital.[72] "Madrid was like a trap that we all tried to leave while the door was still half open," attests Manuel Tagüeña. ". . . The hostility of our enemies and former allies was such that we could not help but notice it."[73] Negrín, who was also afraid of being trapped in the capital, moved to Elda, a small community in the coastal province of Alicante, 382 kilometers from Madrid, with an airstrip nearby at Monóvar. He was accompanied by his constant companions, Benigno Rodríguez, his political secretary, and Manuel Sánchez Arcas, the undersecretary of propaganda, both extraordinarily competent and devoted members of the PCE, as well as by Major Julián Soley Conde, his adjutant, who was also a member of the party.[74] They set up their headquarters in an old palace known as El Poblet, which was given the code name of "*posición Yuste*."[75] The palace, together with other buildings, had been commandeered by Santiago Garcés earlier in the month,[76] and an elite guard of one hundred Communist commandos of the Fourteenth Army Corps, a partisan unit under Major Domingo Ungría, a PCE member, was entrusted with the protection of the buildings used by the government and the Communist leadership.[77] "Negrín," writes Colonel Stanislav A. Vaupshasov, Ungría's Soviet adviser, "settled in the town of Elda and withdrew from everything. He didn't want to meet anyone [and] did nothing. His depressed state suited the defeatists and traitors."[78] Enrique Líster, in line with the party's tactic of making Negrín a scapegoat, also criticized the premier for moving to Elda—"a place remote from any large urban center"—although it was obviously the party that had given him the protection of the elite guerrilla guard. "This was the best way," Líster said, "to give the conspirators a free hand and to isolate himself voluntarily from the people and the military forces."[79] In his unpublished memoir, politburo member Vicente Uribe, the Communist minister of agriculture, was equally censorious of Negrín. In the short period between the arrival of the ministers and their departure from Spain, he wrote, Negrín convened the government only two or three times and "hardly discussed anything." Shortly after arriving in Madrid, he "disappeared" for some days without letting the party know his whereabouts. "Previously, all his important measures, especially those of a political nature, were known to us and he would seek our opinion. On this occasion he maintained complete secrecy and did not say one word of what he was going to do and what he planned." Subsequently, Negrín informed the party that he had met with military leaders—"among whom Masons abounded"—and that they had given proof of a "violently anticommunist state of mind." Nevertheless, Uribe testifies, "Negrín remained passive and did not adopt a single measure."

In another passage, he states: "Between the Negrín of March 1938 and the Negrín of the final phase there lay an abyss. Previously, he had shown determination and confidence. He sought our help and our views. Now, without breaking with us, he did not seek our support. He listened to our proposals like someone listening to the rain and during the time he remained in the republican zone he did not adopt a single measure that displayed any desire to prosecute the war. To continue the struggle . . . and to unite all the forces and all energies, he had only one party that firmly supported him: ours. In my opinion, he did not rely on the party, because he considered that the war was lost. He did not direct his attention to continuing the struggle, but rather to placing himself in a position whereby he could end his premiership in the best possible way."[80]

While Negrín and his Communist entourage withdrew to Elda on 27 February, members of the politburo led by Togliatti left for El Palmar, just south of Murcia on the main road to the capital and located about eighty kilometers from Elda.[81] "We remained near Murcia," Togliatti reported to Moscow, "so that we could rely on a party organization of some significance."[82] On the other hand, La Pasionaria offers a dubious explanation. The comrades had agreed, she writes, to move to this intermediate point between Elda and Madrid "in order to be quickly informed of the government's decisions and to act in the capital, because telephone and telegraph communications were becoming difficult."[83] It is difficult to see how the politburo could operate effectively in El Palmar, 382 kilometers from the capital. One plausible reason for the move, in addition to the one given by Togliatti, was the proximity of El Palmar (43 kilometers) to the naval base of Cartagena, where it was feared that the fleet would desert and deprive the central-southern zone of the principal means of evacuation.

Although, when he moved to Elda, Negrín was a beaten man, he attempted to make a show of strength. Cordón attests that the premier told him that he wanted to give "the country and the army the feeling that the government was still functioning,"[84] but the general impression was that it was only an appellation lacking material substance. In any case, Negrín was at loggerheads with the members of his cabinet. According to Líster, who saw him on 16 February, "he heaped abuse on some of his ministers, whom he described as cowards who did nothing but quarrel among themselves about paltry questions." Only Uribe, Moix, and Vayo, he said, "continued to conduct themselves with dignity."[85] The picture that emerges from the testimony of eyewitnesses of a spectral or at best a palsied government is confirmed by the philo-Communist Edmundo Domínguez, recently appointed inspector-commissar of the Army of the Center by Negrín.[86] Despite his assertion that the arrival of the government in the central-southern zone was welcomed with jubilation,[87] he acknowledges that no one was certain of its whereabouts.[88] "During its twenty-three days in the central-southern zone," Stefanov reported to Moscow, "the government did nothing to make the army and the people feel that there was a government in control of the country."[89] This picture of political impotence is completed by PCE loyalist Vicente Uribe, who states that the ministers "did absolutely nothing" and "didn't even bother to set up their respective ministries." On the other hand, he adds, "they were quite active in cabarets and similar places." But even when the ministers first arrived in the central-southern zone they were viewed with disdain. "When we all went to visit Miaja, the commander in chief, he received us in pajamas. . . . This showed us that in his opinion the government counted for less than nothing. To receive anyone in pajamas indicates a lack of consideration and respect, but when a military man receives his superiors in pajamas, it is the height of contempt."[90]

It is now necessary to describe in more detail the most disquieting problem that faced Negrín from the moment he arrived in Spain on 10 February. Two days later, he met with Colonel Segismundo Casado, the chief of the Army of the Center, who even before Negrín's arrival had been conspiring to bring the war to a rapid end.[91] Although Casado's chronicle of the last two months of the war is in some cases confused or inaccurate, his version of his conversation with Negrín has not been contradicted. Asked by the premier to give him an account of the general situation, Casado stressed the following points:

1. The loss of Catalonia had reduced the production of war material by 50 percent, and the shortage of raw materials had created an alarming situation. "Under the circumstances we cannot produce the indispensable minimum for continuing the struggle."

2. Tanks, antitank guns, artillery, and automatic weapons were in very short supply and the air force had been reduced to three squadrons of Natachas, two of Katiuskas, and twenty-five fighters. It would be suicide, he said, for the Republican pilots to confront the Nationalist air force, which was far superior in quantity and quality. The troops in the Sierras as well as in Páramos de Cuenca and Guadalajara were suffering the rigors of winter without warm clothing and in sandals because it was impossible to supply them with boots.

3. During the entire war, the problem of food supplies had been serious but now it was "extremely grave and without hope of relief."[92] There was no transportation to bring food from the Levante, and spare parts, accessories and particularly tires were lacking.

4. The civilian population of Madrid, which had shown great courage and self-sacrifice, was now saying openly that "it is fed up with the war and wants peace."

5. In contrast to this somber picture, the enemy "with a high morale of victory" was concentrating his forces south of Madrid in order to unleash the final offensive with a minimum of twenty-five divisions and with great masses of tanks, artillery, and aviation. "In such conditions, the fall of Madrid is inevitable causing enormous loss of lives, which will be sacrificed in vain."

In reply, Negrín stated: "I agree with you that the situation is extremely grave, but . . . circumstances demand that we continue fighting. It is the only solution, because since May of 1937 I have tried repeatedly to enter into negotiations with the enemy, using my friendship with prominent Nationalists, but I failed in all these efforts.[93] I therefore suggested to the British government that it should act as mediator . . . , but unfortunately this attempt was also fruitless."[94]

Negrín was undoubtedly referring to peace proposals he had made to Ralph Stevenson, the British chargé d'affaires, and to Jules Henry, the French ambassador, on 6 February, offering to end the war on the three conditions approved by the Cortes in Figueras.[95] Although it was rather too soon to expect a response, Negrín must have anticipated that the conditions would be rejected out of hand by his triumphant adversary. The fate of these peace proposals is worth recording. On 16 February, Oliver Harvey, private secretary to British foreign secretary Lord Halifax, stated in his diary that Negrín's offer was telegraphed to Burgos on 14 February and that Halifax's view was that "while he did not want to bargain over the diplomatic recognition of Franco," he would like to get Franco to do something that would "ease" the British position. Another telegram was sent to Burgos stating that his majesty's government would be "greatly assisted if Franco could make 'some restatement of policy already in mind,' i.e. that when the fighting was over he would not allow unauthorised or general reprisals." "Today," Harvey noted, "we had a further message through Azcárate [Pablo de Azcárate, the Spanish ambassador in London] offering surrender if only assurance against reprisals and permission to escape to leaders were given." This message was undoubtedly a feeler put out by Azcárate on his own initiative inasmuch as Harvey recorded in his diary that [the Foreign Office] decided to "draft a further telegram to Burgos in this sense, but before sending it we asked Azcárate to get authority of his people [i.e., Negrín]."[96]

Alvarez del Vayo states that he and Azcárate repeatedly telegraphed Negrín to obtain his consent but received no reply. "The key to the mystery," he claims, "must have lain in Madrid, where—as Negrín afterwards supposed—subversive elements . . . who, under Colonel Casado, were preparing a military rising, had intercepted the cables."[97] However, Azcárate claims that a favorable reply was received on 25 February, but too late. "The Foreign Office," he affirms, "informed me on the 21st that if it did not receive a reply the following day, the 22nd, it would recover its freedom of action."[98] On the twenty-second, Oliver Harvey entered the following note in his diary. "Still no reply from Azcárate and he has now been told that we cannot wait indefinitely and if we do not receive a reply shortly we must go ahead and recognise [General Franco]. We have telegraphed Paris proposing that we should, in fact, recognise at the earliest moment, not later than February 24th, basing ourselves on a statement by Franco that he will not accept foreign domination and that reprisals are alien to his Government, although he must insist on unconditional surrender."[99]

The vague statement by General Franco on the question of reprisals, upon which the British based their recognition of his government, is given by Azcárate. The main points were: (1) "Nationalist Spain has won the war and the vanquished have no course but to surrender unconditionally." (2) "The patriotism, chivalry, and generosity of the Caudillo [Franco] . . . are a firm guaranty for all Spaniards who are not criminals." (3) "By prolonging this criminal resistance, the red leaders continue sacrificing more lives and shedding more blood exclusively in their own interests. *Since the spirit of reprisal is alien to the Nationalist government and the Caudillo*, all that [the red leaders] will achieve by prolonging this insane resistance will be to increase their own responsibility."[100] It was difficult to believe, writes Azcárate, that Chamberlain, Halifax, or any of the officials of the Foreign Office could attribute the slightest value to Franco's statement.[101]

The famous Spanish writer Luis Romero, who went to great lengths in an attempt, through correspondence and interviews, to get to the root of Negrín's delay in replying to Azcárate, points out that it has never been satisfactorily explained. "Don Pablo de Azcárate," he writes, "who afterwards maintained good relations with Negrín, received from him an evasive and not very convincing reply: that the telegram did not reach him until the last moment, when it no longer served its purpose (cuando había perdido su virtualidad)." (In a footnote, Romero states that Azcárate told him that "Negrín did not wish to explain to him the reasons for his silence and that he responded evasively and with a smile to a direct and concrete question, indicating that the matter was now water under the bridge.") "What really happened?" Romero asks. "Did Negrín decline to become the man who would publicly and officially preside over the liquidation of the war? . . . Did he expect to prolong the war for some time? Was he motivated by the hope that others would shoulder the burden of defeat?"[102]

During his conversation with Colonel Casado on 12 February, Negrín of course had not yet received Azcárate's telegram, but he was no doubt convinced that Franco would insist on unconditional surrender. "We have no alternative but to resist," he told Casado. In order to do this, he said, there were arms in France salvaged from the Catalan retreat as well as a considerable quantity of artillery, automatic weapons, and airplanes recently acquired in other countries. It was possible, he added, that all this weaponry would be allowed to enter Spain, "although actually we do not yet know France's decision on the matter." (In the English edition of his book, published in 1939, Casado stated that Negrín claimed that there were ten thousand machine guns, six hundred airplanes and five hundred pieces of artillery "waiting in France."[103] These figures do not appear in the Spanish edition published almost thirty years later.) As for the troops interned in France, Negrín stated that he was negotiating for their repatriation but that his negotiations had not yet borne fruit. Finally, he assured Casado that in order to resolve the problems of food and transportation "he would quickly take the necessary measures."

Casado replied that there was no solution to the last two problems. "As for the considerable quantity of weaponry you say is in France, I do not believe that [the French] will allow it to leave the country and even in the unlikely event that they do, the unloading would be very difficult. [The official Communist history confirms that "neither the weaponry nor the men of the Army of Catalonia in France could be transferred to the central-southern zone."[104]] I believe we should speak clearly. . . . We know that both Great Britain and France, which have had unofficial representatives in the Nationalist camp for some time,[105] are on the side of Franco and are anxious to recognize him. Hence, we should not delude ourselves and must consider these two countries as our enemies. Under the circumstances, if resistance is materially impossible, if all peace overtures have failed, I would suggest that you call a meeting of all the army and air force chiefs and the Admiral of the Fleet, so that each one of them can express his opinion as to what should be done. In this way, you will be able to spare yourself or limit the historical responsibility that weighs upon you at this tragic time."[106]

Negrín acquiesced in the proposal, and a meeting was held on 16 February at the small airport of Los Llanos, two kilometers south of Albacete.[107] Present at the meeting were the following army, navy, and air force leaders: Lieutenant General José Miaja, commander in chief of the land, sea, and air forces;[108] General Manuel Matallana, commander of the army group of the central-southern region, comprising the armies of the Center, Levante, Estremadura, and Andalusia; Colonel Segismundo Casado, commander of the Army of the Center; General Leopoldo Menéndez, commander of the Army of the Levante; General Antonio Escobar, commander of the Army of Estremadura; Colonel Domingo Moriones, commander of the Army of Andalusia; Colonel Antonio Camacho, commander of the air force of the central-southern region; General Carlos Bernal, commander of the naval base of Cartagena; Admiral Fernández Buiza, commander of the Republican fleet.

According to Casado's account of the meeting,[109] Negrín repeated what he had told him a few days earlier regarding the war material in France, the problems of food and transportation, and his abortive efforts to negotiate an end to the war. Since every possibility of negotiating peace had been exhausted, he concluded, the only solution was to fight on. Of those assembled only General Miaja, who was "visibly disturbed," said that he was in favor of "resistance at all costs." This must have come as a shock to Casado, Matallana, and Menéndez, with whom Miaja had met in Valencia on 2 February, when he had agreed, according to Casado, to join them in overthrowing Negrín.[110] It is not unlikely that Miaja felt beholden to Negrín for having promoted him in the meantime to the rank of lieutenant general or simply hesitated to speak openly in the presence of the premier. In any case, he again changed his position a few days later and sided with Casado.[111] The other leaders agreed with General Matallana, who stated that since the fall of Catalonia the people and the army were defeatist and wanted to end the war rapidly.[112] Colonel Camacho, the air force chief in the central-southern zone and a member of the PCE,[113] said that he had only five squadrons of worn-out planes and some fighters and that "it would be folly to confront the well-equipped Nationalist aviation with such material." Peace, he said, was the only solution.[114] The most alarming statement was made by Admiral Buiza, the chief of the fleet. "This chief," records Casado, "reported that the fleet had decided to abandon Spanish jurisdictional waters if peace were not made quickly," because a commission representing the crews had informed him that they were "convinced that the war was lost and were not disposed to tolerate any longer the intensive daily bombardments, since they lacked any anti-aircraft defense." In Buiza's judgment "the war was irremediably lost and it was advisable to negotiate peace with the utmost urgency."[115]

In his report to the permanent committee of the Cortes in Paris a few weeks later, Negrín summed up the defeatist and hostile attitude of the military leaders. "These gentlemen," he said, "took the liberty of urgently demanding that, as head of the government, I should end the war soon." Above all, Negrín distrusted Casado, who followed his every movement. "I suspected that a trap was being prepared for me and of course I managed to escape along with the entire government from Casado's hands."[116]

Shortly before Negrín's departure from Madrid two developments occurred that made the policy of resistance untenable.[117] On 27 February, Britain and France recognized General Franco's administration as the sovereign government of Spain, and, within hours, Manuel Azaña, who had been anxiously awaiting this event, resigned the presidency, liberating himself at long last from his puppet role as constitutional cover, first, for the popular revolution of July 1936 to May 1937, and, then, for the incipient dictatorship of Negrín and the Communists that had loomed every day more threateningly in the spring and summer of 1938. Azaña's letter of resignation, which avoided any allusion to his humiliating role during the Civil War, stated that the recognition of General Franco had deprived him of the "international juridical representation necessary to convey to foreign governments . . . not only what my conscience as a Spaniard tells me but what is the profound desire of the immense majority of our people," that the political apparatus of the state had disappeared, and that under the circumstances, it was impossible "to retain, even nominally, an office that I did not relinquish the very day I left Spain, because I hoped to see the time employed for the benefit of peace."[118]

Diego Martínez Barrio, the speaker of the Cortes and leader of the moderate Unión Republicana party, who, according to Negrín, should "automatically" have succeeded Azaña in keeping with the Constitution—a point of view not shared by

Barrio—played a dilatory game. He convened the permanent committee of the Cortes on 3 March in a restaurant in Paris to discuss the juridical and political aspects of the crisis. The committee decided that it would cooperate with Negrín only if he intended to liquidate the war with "the least possible damage and sacrifice."[119] Martínez Barrio then notified the premier that unless this condition were met he would be faced with the painful necessity of declining the presidency. Although Negrín affirmed that the message was read and approved at a cabinet meeting, Martínez Barrio claimed that he never received a reply.[120] He also asserted that just as he was preparing to leave for Spain—despite "serious doubts as to how useful and effective the trip might be"—the coup against Negrín occurred.[121] He was thus providentially relieved of any further responsibility.

The recognition of General Franco and the resignation of President Azaña, Togliatti informed Moscow, "contributed to the demoralization of the leaders and of the people."[122] In addition, the events gave added impetus to those who believed that further resistance was futile and who were conspiring to overthrow the government of Juan Negrín.

64

Segismundo Casado, Cipriano Mera, and the Libertarians

At the center of the movement to end the war was Colonel Segismundo Casado, toward whom the adversaries of Negrín and the PCE now gravitated. Although disliked by the Communists and the Soviet military advisers,[1] his professional competence and loyalty to the Republic were never impugned during the war. A steadfast Republican and commander of Manuel Azaña's presidential guard at the outbreak of the Civil War, Casado had been on hostile terms with the PCE since the early months of the conflict. In fact, at the pressing instance of the party, he had been dismissed by war minister Largo Caballero from the post of operations chief of the central general staff because of his criticism of the inequitable distribution of Soviet arms. However, in a gesture of defiance, Caballero soon reinstated him, and at the end of 1936 he appointed him to organize the mixed brigades of the Popular Army with the aid of a Soviet general and two Soviet colonels.[2] When Indalecio Prieto assumed control of the defense ministry in May 1937, Casado was given the command of the Eighteenth and Twenty-first Army Corps and of the Army of Andalusia in that order.

Although Casado never succumbed to Communist blandishments, he maintained tolerable relations with the party during the spring and summer of 1938 after Negrín became premier and defense minister and the Communist Antonio Cordón was made undersecretary of the army in virtual control of the land forces. Indeed, in May, Casado was appointed commander of the prestigious Army of the Center,[3] comprising the First, Second, Third, and Fourth Army Corps, the first three under the professional army officers, Luis Barceló, Emilio Bueno, and Antonio Ortega, respectively, all members of the PCE,[4] and the fourth under the well-known Anarchist militia leader Cipriano Mera. The military historian Ramón Salas Larrazábal is undoubtedly correct when he says that in the spring and summer of 1938 Casado "dreamt not of surrender but of victory."[5] *Mundo Obrero*, the Communist organ in Madrid, applauded Casado's appointment, praised his "loyalty to the Republic and the people," and described him as "an antifascist, a liberal," and as "an opponent, long before the military uprising, of the reactionary castes that governed our country."[6]

In the succeeding months, as the internecine struggle continued to heat up, Casado's relations with the PCE steadily deteriorated, and his hostility to the party became the glue that bound him to its opponents. "The support for Casado," writes Manuel Tagüeña, the former Communist and commander of the Fifteenth Army Corps, "was based on the animosity that many Socialists, Anarchists, and Republicans nurtured against the Communists during the bitter political struggles of the war."[7] Thus, two essential factors combined to make Casado the man of destiny during the climactic weeks of the Civil War: his pivotal position as commander of the Army of the Center and his animosity to the PCE. It is dubious, as Gabriel Morón, the moderate Socialist and former director general of security, suggests, that the task of initiating the revolt could have been undertaken by anybody else,[8] for there was no one in sight either willing or able to shoulder the responsibility. Certainly, General José Miaja—the manufactured hero of Madrid, now lieutenant general and supreme commander of the armed forces in the central-southern zone—was not the man, for he lacked the moral fiber to confront the political and military machine of the PCE which was still intact in the Madrid zone. Nor is it likely that any of the disaffected commanders who attended the meeting at Los Llanos on 15 February would have assumed the burden.

Even before Negrín's return to Spain, Casado had resolved to take matters into his own hands. "We could not continue to sit with folded arms," he writes, "without making a decision."[9] He spoke to the commanders of the army and to the heads of the parties—"with the exception of course of the Communist party." "They all agreed that the war should be brought to an end as soon as possible, but they buried their faces, hoping that someone else would do the job."[10] On 2 February, he had met with generals Miaja, Matallana, and Menéndez, and informed them of his decision to overthrow Negrín and that he would attempt to establish contact with the Nationalist government as soon as possible. "Without discussion," he adds, "the three generals regarded themselves as committed to the decision with all its consequences."[11]

Casado also records that the next day, he met with Julián Besteiro, the right-wing Socialist and academic Marxist, now the most respected and prestigious Socialist leader in Spain. As head of the Junta de Reconstrucción de Madrid, a purely symbolic post, he had remained in the capital through the war almost totally removed from the vortex of intraparty strife. Quintessentially a man of peace, he had served as Azaña's emissary at the coronation of Edward VIII in June 1937 and conveyed to the British the president's desire for a negotiated settlement. Although at odds with the Caballeristas and Prietistas before the war and during the first two years of the conflict, he had gained enormously in prestige and popularity as the war ground on and the urge for peace became overwhelming. When Casado requested his collaboration, he replied that he would support him "*unconditionally*," but "*only in order to make peace*."[12]

The most important of Casado's allies upon whom the success of the coup would depend were the Madrid organizations of the CNT and FAI and Cipriano Mera's Fourth Army Corps. "Although Communist power had been increasing and threatened to engulf the libertarians," writes Luis Romero, the famous Spanish historian and literary figure, "[the CNT and FAI] had retained a certain vigor and their ranks had not suffered from the desertions that had undermined the Socialist and bourgeois republican parties, which had been attracted by the personalist policy of Negrín or had either swollen the ranks of the PCE or had been drawn into its orbit. . . . Between Casado and the libertarians . . . a sympathy of mutual attraction had developed, whose deepest roots lay in the colonel's antagonism to the Communists."[13]

Especially important in Casado's relationship with the CNT was his rapport with Cipriano Mera, who had long shed his philosophical opposition to discipline and militarization, as seen in a previous chapter.

Luis Romero says: "Cipriano Mera [was] one of the most prominent leaders that rose from the ranks of the militias, one of those singular personalities who from time to time erupt in the history of the Spanish people, the authentic and unfortunate Spanish people. Because of his libertarian affiliation, Mera has had no renowned or adequate biographer and it is unlikely that he will have.[14] Nor was he exalted by propaganda as were others. He was born in 1896 and, although young, the few published photographs show an aging face, deeply furrowed from hard work, deprivation, and suffering, but illumined by the ideals that inspired him."[15]

And in an earlier passage, Romero writes:

> Before the war, Cipriano Mera . . . had been the secretary of the construction workers' union. A man of unquestionable integrity, he began in the militias and rose in rank until he became lieutenant colonel in command of the IVth Army Corps, defending the Guadalajara and Cuenca fronts. A bricklayer by trade, a person of very limited culture, he managed to surround himself with professional military men of proven fidelity. . . . He applied himself to the study of military science to the best of his ability, for he understood that to fight an army it was essential to have an army. He was an idealist of a combative and ascetic type gifted with a military instinct like our great popular leaders in days gone by. The IVth Army Corps was predominantly libertarian, but the discipline Mera imposed on himself and on his men was strict. . . . Although their family origins were far apart, . . . Casado and Mera coincided in their military outlook, in their view of the course of the war and in the austerity of their behavior. . . . They respected each other and between the two military men, one from the professional army and the other from the militias, there developed a friendship based on mutual trust.[16]

Above all, they questioned the validity of the resistance policy. When Casado met with Negrín, as we have seen, on 12 February, he did not disguise his pessimism. Nor was he influenced by Negrín's vague hopes that the war material and men interned in France would be allowed to reenter Spain. Equally pessimistic was Cipriano Mera during a similarly fruitless meeting with Negrín toward the end of February. Their conversation, as related by Mera, deserves recording:

Mera: You know perfectly well, Señor Negrín, that the combatants in France . . . will not return and that the weapons in possession of the French authorities will not reenter Spain. Besides, you also know that no government will help us and that we shall not receive arms from anywhere. . . . Our position of inferiority has become worse since the loss of Catalonia, because we can no longer count on its industry or on the assistance of the Armies of the Ebro and the East, which have both disappeared forever in the defeat. Our Army of the Center is still intact and well prepared, but without the necessary armament and for months without sufficient food. . . . The morale of the men has continued to decline because of the defeatist mood of the civilian population and the disorganization of the republican government, if indeed it still exists. You must know that my pessimism is more than justified.

Negrín: . . . I have done everything possible to begin negotiations with the enemy, including a request to the British government to serve as mediator, but without achieving anything. For this reason, there is no other policy but that of all-out resistance. To achieve this policy we have thousands of pieces of artillery, machine guns, and mortars, more than five hundred planes, as well as large quantities of ammunition of all kinds.

Mera: And where is all this enormous quantity of material, Señor Negrín?

Negrín: I have it in France. . . .

Mera: Yes, of course, in France. But we are in Spain. Do you sincerely believe that you can have it shipped to Madrid?

Negrín: I think so.

Mera: You say that you "think so," which means that you are not very sure.[17]

Mera's gloom was shared by the overwhelming majority of libertarians in the central region. This was manifest from the proceedings of a special plenum of the CNT held in Madrid toward the end of February. José García Pradas, the director of the Anarchosyndicalist daily CNT, who was present and has given us the best published though imprecise account of the meeting and of the subsequent activities of the CNT leaders in the Madrid region, describes the mood: "We regarded the situation as so disastrous that it seemed impossible either to resist or to make peace." Everyone agreed on the necessity of avoiding "the horror of a military catastrophe followed by the dislocation of our rear driven insane by desperation and panic as occurred in Málaga, Santander, Asturias, and Catalonia."[18]

In the hope of averting a total breakdown, the plenum decided to form a regional committee of defense comprising military, police, and propaganda sections with "extraordinary powers." Its members included Eduardo Val, the secretary, Manuel González Marín, Manuel Salgado, Manuel Amil, and José García Pradas, all prominent militants of the regional organization. "Two or three days later," attests García Pradas, "I spoke to Val and Amil. I told them that we were losing time . . . and that we were running the risk that Negrín and the Communists . . . might rise up and crush us . . . ; that a coup d'état was in the air and that unless we acted first we would be on the receiving end."[19]

The fear of a preemptive coup by the PCE was undoubtedly uppermost in the minds of the leaders of the CNT, for the Communists, as the reader will recall, controlled three of the four army corps that comprised Casado's Army of the Center. According to García Pradas, the CNT defense committee took up the matter with Casado to decide on "the method of a rebellion, which everyday was becoming more and more urgent and inevitable."[20] The committee also approached leaders of other organizations. "We spoke with José del Río and other leaders of the Unión Republicana who were ashamed of the behavior of their chief, Don Diego Martínez Barrio [who had remained in France], and we agreed on all issues. The same thing happened with representatives of Izquierda Republicana in Madrid, who did not forgive Azaña for resigning and for his hypocritical and whining declaration. The members of both parties said terrible things about Negrín, but we knew that to oust him we could count only on our own forces." The committee also met with Hilario de la Cruz and Gómez Egido, leaders of the Agrupación Socialista Madrileña, the largest of the local organizations of the Socialist party. "They believed that we were heading for a disaster from which nothing and no one would be saved. . . . They stated that they accepted our plans without reservation, and discreetly incited us to launch a rebellion for which they lacked the means. . . . They saw in our movement the only force capable of initiating a successful revolt. . . . Two or three times a day, Val and Salgado communicated our decisions to Casado, and during these meetings the smallest details for the rising were worked out. Segismundo [Casado]—Segis, as we called him—took charge of contacting the military leaders whom we felt were necessary. He enjoyed the maximum prestige among them, because of his professional gifts, his republican past, his keen and perceptive intelligence, and his opposition to any maneuvers against the people and antifascist unity."[21]

Meanwhile, Colonel Casado had for some time been secretly negotiating an end to the war with General Franco's intelligence service in Madrid, which had made the initial approach. The negotiations have been chronicled by the highly esteemed military historian, Colonel José Manuel Martínez Bande, who consulted the pertinent nationalist documents in the Servicio Histórico Militar de Madrid.[22] The following brief account of these negotiations up to the first week of March 1939 are based exclusively on his findings.[23]

At the end of January, according to a report by Julio Palacios, a professor at the University of Madrid, who was an agent of the Nationalist intelligence organization, the Servicio de Información y Policía Militar (SIPM), Antonio de Luna, also a university professor and SIPM agent, was given a special mission "to sound out the state of mind of Colonel Casado." Shortly afterward, in an attempt to win over Casado, the agents made known to him "the guarantees that General Franco was offering to the military who laid down their arms and who had not committed common crimes."[24]

On 1 February, Palacios received Casado's terse response to this overture: "Informed, agree, and the sooner the better."

On 11 February, Colonel José Ungría, national chief of the SIPM in Burgos, received a report from his agents stating that "Casado in agreement with Besteiro asks that the lives of honorable career officers (militares decentes) be respected."

On 16 February, a report was sent to Burgos, which quoted Casado as saying, "I hope to form a Besteiro cabinet, in which I shall hold the portfolio of war. . . . If this should not take place, it does not matter. I shall sweep everyone aside. I propose fifteen days as the maximum delay for the entry of the Nationalist forces in Madrid." After noting that Casado asked for "compassion" for his staff, the report added: "It will not be possible to prevent the flight of some prominent red leaders, although [Casado] assures us that many will remain in Madrid and that he will proceed with their arrest."

Nevertheless, there were suspicions regarding Casado's good faith, for Palacios informed Burgos of his "artfulness" and claimed that "he was continuing his devious and procrastinating policies" at a time when "Madrid was fully aware of an imminent Communist coup."

It was at this point that Burgos decided that "what was really needed was the participation in the negotiations of a responsible military chief of absolute confidence." This man was Lieutenant Colonel José Centaño de la Paz, the head of Artillery Park No. 4 in Madrid and head of the spy ring known as "Lucero Verde."[25]

On 20 February, Centaño, accompanied by Manuel Guitián, another important agent of the SIPM in Madrid, visited Casado.[26] During this meeting, as reported to Burgos by the SIPM (and I continue to quote from Martínez Bande), "Casado receives the visitors 'with extraordinary warmth' and does not give them time to speak 'in his desire to prove that he is an implacable enemy of the vile procedures of the Soviet leaders and the cruel and unjust masses who have followed them.' He presents himself as a liberal, a fervent Republican, a bitter adversary of Azaña [whom he had recently condemned as a "coward" for remaining in France[27]], of Alvarez del Vayo, and above all, of the Communists whom he covers with insults." Because of the "Communist danger," Centaño and Guitián urged Casado not to delay his coup. "The Army [of Franco] cannot allow any delays," they told him, to which Casado replied that undue haste would result in "horrible bloodshed." As for the political leaders, Casado said that the best thing would be to allow them to leave Spain: "The more, the better. In this way, there will be less bloodshed and less resentment." According to the same report, Casado stated that "he prefers not to be in charge of their pursuit and arrest; besides, he intends to leave the country." At this point Centaño and Guitián presented Casado with the document outlining the concessions that General Franco was prepared to make to those officers who surrender.[28] "Casado reads it carefully, showing signs of extraordinary satisfaction: 'Magnificent, magnificent!'" he exclaimed, according to the report. "He appears moved, 'expressing his explicit approval and exhibiting enthusiasm.'" This enthusiasm, Martínez Bande observes, "was less than sincere." The two SIPM agents then pressed Casado to set a definite date for the surrender of the Republican army. Casado replied that it could be carried out "in about fifteen days." Commenting on

Casado's attitude, Centaño stated in his report: "He does not feel the Nationalist cause. For that reason he is thinking of going into exile after the war has been liquidated, but he is willing to serve the cause, because he understands it is the only course to follow as it is honorable, logical, humane, and Spanish."

On 22 February, Manuel Guitián visited Casado for the second time. "He urges him once again," Martínez Bande chronicles, "to fix a definite date for the coup he is preparing. Casado replies that at the end of the month he will 'begin to liquidate the matter.' He asks the Nationalists to delay their offensive, which is now almost completely prepared, because he cannot be responsible for the bloody outrages that would occur in Madrid and because, if the offensive were to begin, 'he will have to act as a Republican officer who fulfils his duty as such to the end.' Finally, he requests time and confidence so that 'not one more drop of blood will be shed.' The report on the interview is as optimistic as the previous one. 'We have the impression,' it said, 'that Casado CAN REALIZE HIS PLAN WITH COMPLETE SUCCESS AND WITH ALL SECURITY.' "[29]

But General Franco was not satisfied with the slow progress of the negotiations. On 25 February, he informed his staff that "the surrender must be without conditions" and that the Nationalist army had more than sufficient means to occupy Madrid "by force, when and how it pleases." Casado was clearly under increasing pressure to set a firm date for his coup and eventual surrender to the mercy of General Franco.

On 27 February, Franco's headquarters received the following message from the SIPM in Madrid: "Tomorrow, Tuesday, a Junta of Liquidation will be formed. We request permission for Besteiro and Colonel Ruiz Fornells [one of Casado's staff officers] to fly to the Nationalist zone with agents of the [SIPM] to formalize quickly the capitulation." The reply from Burgos was categorical. "We must emphasize that Nationalist Spain will not accept anything but unconditional surrender. . . . One or two professional officers may come here, but only for the purpose of being informed of the way in which the surrender is to be carried out. . . . The presence of Besteiro or other civilians is unacceptable."

On 2 March, the SIPM in Madrid sent Franco the following message: "Casado has received the reply from H.E. the Generalissimo and the instructions. It appears that there is some apprehension among the politicians and that Casado's Military-Civilian Junta is not materializing at least for the moment. . . . With this Junta, the politicians hoped to obtain what they call *an honorable capitulation*, which would allow the free exit of those who wish to leave." On 4 March, Burgos received another message: "Everything depends on the flight of the leaders so that Casado does not appear to be a traitor."

Casado was now under tremendous moral pressure from his own side to negotiate an honorable settlement that would protect the lives of those who were in danger and wished to flee the country. But the prospect of such a settlement was bleak indeed, for Franco had already made it clear by his notorious Law of Political Responsibilities of 9 February that he would not consider anything but unconditional surrender and had reiterated his intransigent position during the negotiations.

Nevertheless, Casado may have believed that the removal of Negrín and the Communists would mollify Franco's attitude to the point that he would allow those who wished to flee the country the right to do so and would also grant other concessions. Antonio Cordón alleges that when he went to see Casado in February, the colonel, affecting "a mysterious air," told him—but without giving any hint of his secret negotiations to end the war—that "Franco would not only yield on the matter of reprisals, but would allow only Spanish forces to enter Madrid and would recognize the ranks of the Republican chiefs and officers." Cordón also alleges that Casado informed him that on several occasions "persons of absolute reliability, Englishmen," had visited him and told him that sufficient ships to evacuate twenty thousand persons had been readied and the terms of peace, as outlined by Casado, "would be imposed on Franco."[30]

There is no documentary evidence that the British gave any assurances either officially or unofficially. At least, there is no hint of any in the large number of documents consulted by the British historian Michael Alpert in the public records office in England.[31] This of course does not exclude the possibility that some documents may have been removed from public scrutiny. Still, the idea that the British would attempt to "impose" certain terms on Franco runs counter to the whole trend of British policy of maintaining good relations with General Franco.[32] It is true that a certain Denys Cowan visited Casado on a number of occasions and has been accused by the pro-Communist Edmundo Domínguez of attempting to negotiate the surrender of Madrid with the chief of the central army.[33] All we know for sure is that Cowan was the liaison officer of the Chetwode commission appointed by the British government to negotiate an exchange of prisoners. "Casado," says Alpert, "was very concerned about the Nationalist sympathizers in prison and warned the Nationalists, during his peace talks the following month, that the prisoners might be killed if he were obliged to put up a desperate resistance. In the feverish atmosphere of Madrid, Cowan's visits were noticed, but there is apparently no proof that he played any part in convincing Casado that he should surrender."[34] Alpert has since informed me (1987) that he is "not as definite in his views" as he was when he first studied the matter some years ago and now regards it as an "open question."[35]

It is indeed probable that he is right when he conjectures that "Cowan might have been told, in general conversations before he went to Spain, that if he got a chance, he should try to encourage Casado to come to terms with Franco."[36] If this should be true, then Cordón's allegation that Casado told him that the British had given him certain assurances may be accurate. It is also likely that when Casado told Cordón about them, he hoped to win his support against Negrín just as he apparently attempted to influence the Communist air force chief Hidalgo de Cisneros by using the same alleged assurances. When interviewed by me in 1940, Cisneros claimed that Casado told him at the end of February that the "English representative" in Madrid had "guaranteed" that Franco would agree to "good terms of peace." On 2 March, Casado also told Cisneros, according to the shorthand record of my interview: "I can assure you that Franco will never negotiate with Negrín, but I am absolutely certain that if several honorable military leaders deal directly with him, we shall get the following terms: 1. Neither Moors nor volunteers [Italian and German soldiers] nor the Foreign Legion will enter Madrid. 2. Anyone who wishes to leave Spain will be able to do so and Franco will provide facilities for this purpose. 3. Franco will not take reprisals against those who remain in Spain. 4. The ranks of the professional officers will be recognized by Franco's army."[37]

In his memoirs published in 1964, Hidalgo de Cisneros claims that when he asked Casado who had given these assurances, "he replied very solemnly that England had arranged the guarantee to the last detail, and that he had personally held various interviews with the English representative, to whom Franco had expressly promised to fulfil these commitments with only one condition: that we get rid of the Republican government and that we—the professional officers—would take charge of the situation and deal directly with him."[38]

Whatever the truth of these alleged commitments, the question now arises: Were Negrín and the Communist leaders aware of the threat presented by Casado? Most certainly. Not simply because Cordón and Cisneros claim that they informed Negrín of Casado's attempt to lure them into his conspiracy,[39] nor because it was their bounden duty as Communists to inform the party leadership immediately, but especially because the official PCE history states that the Madrid Communist leaders on the eve of Casado's rebellion (5–6 March) "had information for some weeks that a conspiracy was being hatched."[40] As Manuel Tagüeña testifies, information on Casado's disaffection reached the top Communist leaders as soon as they arrived from France: "From the first moment, the party [in Madrid] apprised us of the possibility of a coup headed by Colonel Casado. . . . As I was the military chief of highest rank [among the Communists] who had arrived from Catalonia and who remained in Madrid [after the others had left for El Palmar], Domingo Girón, the secretary of the [Madrid] Communist organization . . . , kept me up to date on everything that was being plotted by Colonel Casado."[41]

And what about Negrín? Was he likewise aware of the conspiracy? Of this there can also be no doubt, not only because he was obviously informed by his Communist entourage but because of his own declaration (part of which I have quoted previously) to the permanent committee of the Cortes in Paris shortly after he escaped from Spain. "I soon grasped from a series of indications [after arriving in Madrid] what was being plotted," he also stated. "In the first place, Casado was anxious that I should live in a house that he had prepared for me in the Paseo de Ronda, because [he said] it was very safe. In the second place, he tried to furnish me with a special guard that he had personally selected. In the third place, Señor Casado followed my movements not only in the [Army of the] Center, which he commanded, but in every other Army I visited. I suspected that a trap was being prepared for me and of course I managed to escape along with the entire government from Casado's hands."[42]

65

In Search of Scapegoats

It has now been firmly established on the strength of the PCE's and Negrín's own testimony that they were fully aware of the threat presented by Colonel Casado. What measures then did they take to foil his conspiracy? Or did they decide after the diplomatic recognition of General Franco and the resignation of President Azaña on 27 February to allow Casado's plans to mature in the hope of personally avoiding the stigma of surrender?

In analyzing the conduct of Negrín and the top Communist leaders during their transitory presence in the central-southern zone from mid-February until 6 March, it is important to remember that whatever their private apprehensions there was no hint of defeatism in the politburo's resolution of 23 February cited in a previous chapter.[1] The declaration, whose "final draft," according to Togliatti, "was personally corrected by Negrín,"[2] gave an optimistic assessment of the international situation: it had never been more unstable and this instability increased the possibilities of direct and indirect aid to the Spanish people. Hence, resistance was not only necessary but possible and would permit new factors to develop both in Spain and abroad, opening the prospect of victory.

One other important factor must also be borne in mind. On *25 February*—two days before the recognition of General Franco and the resignation of President Azaña—the *Gaceta de la República* published a decree, signed by Negrín, promoting Colonel Casado, the very nerve of the conspiracy, to the rank of general. Behind this astonishing promotion there lay, according to Antonio Cordón, Negrín's undersecretary, an ulterior objective. Negrín, he says, told him that "it was necessary to act with caution" and that he "was thinking of appointing Casado to the post of chief of staff of the army" and then replacing him with Lieutenant Colonel Emilio Bueno, the Communist commander of the Second Army Corps.[3] The purpose of this maneuver, according to Benigno Rodríguez, Negrín's Communist political secretary, was to remove Casado from "direct control" of the Army of the Center.[4]

The official Communist history claims that the idea of substituting Casado for Bueno originated with the politburo, which had proposed to Negrín on 24 February that he remove and prosecute Casado because of his "dubious conduct" and replace him "provisionally" either with Lieutenant Colonel Bueno or Lieutenant Colonel Luis Barceló, commander of the First Army Corps, who like Bueno was also a member of the PCE.[5] Togliatti, on the other hand, states that the original proposal was to place Colonel Juan Modesto, the well-known Communist, in command of the Army of the Center but that Negrín objected to the idea.[6] More cautious than the party, Negrín may have feared that the appointment of Modesto would have been a provocation to Casado, for he was the most prominent of the Communist military leaders who had risen from the ranks of the militia and a bone-deep party member trained in Moscow, whereas Lieutenant Colonel Bueno was a career officer who, like many others, had embraced the PCE unobtrusively. In any case, as we shall see, no serious attempt was made to replace Casado, who remained in charge of the Army of the Center until the end of the Civil War.

In his long report to the Comintern on 21 May 1939—which, as noted in an earlier chapter, furnished some of the raw material from which the party's postwar attitude toward Negrín was hewn—Togliatti criticized the premier for promoting Casado to the rank of general "instead of removing him and substituting him on the basis of the abundant incriminating evidence that exposed him."[7] He also made the following accusation: "My opinion is that during these months [Negrín] behaved like a man trying to save himself from a situation he considered desperate, but who did not want to betray our party or his past openly. If he let the traitors have their way, this was due not only to weakness and to a mistaken political orientation, but also because the coup d'état of the traitors appeared to offer him the possibility of freeing himself from personal responsibility. Also his disorderly life and physical fear took their toll."[8]

No matter how harshly one may judge Negrín's private life or his political conduct, he cannot fairly be accused of cowardice or fear. Even Casado has attested to his personal courage, which, in his words, "was put to the test in my presence at the battle fronts on various occasions."[9] Moreover, there is good reason to believe that some of the criticisms leveled against Negrín after the war by Togliatti and the party were intended, as already suggested, to make a scapegoat of the premier. For example, the official *Historia del partido comunista de España*, written in Moscow by a commission headed by La Pasionaria, which included Manuel Azcárate, Antonio Cordón, and Irene Falcón (La Pasionaria's secretary), and published in France in 1960, charges that during the final stage of the war Negrín "refused to listen to Communist proposals, that he was no longer interested in continuing the struggle and gave a free hand to the capitulators."[10]

Despite these criticisms, which were omitted from the final volume of the official Communist party history of the Civil War, published in 1977—at a time when an attempt was being made both inside and outside the PCE to enhance the statesmanlike qualities of Negrín—there is ample evidence from Communist sources that, except for Negrín's promotion of Casado to the rank of general and for his alleged opposition to the appointment of Modesto to the command of the Army of the Center, he yielded to most of the party's demands and even went beyond its wishes. Togliatti himself acknowledges in his report to Moscow that toward the end of February Negrín "gave the party much more than it demanded."[11] Furthermore, Cordón attests that the premier and defense minister told him, also toward the end of February, that he should centralize in his hands as far as possible the military apparatus, "so as to make the government's presence felt in the army commands."[12] But more significant is the fact that when Cordón informed Negrín on 3 March of "strange and suspicious" measures being adopted in the headquarters of the Army Group of the Central-Southern Region (Grupo de Ejércitos de la Zona Centro-Sur), the premier replied: "Cordón, I am fed up with all these things. Do, in my name, what appears best to you."[13]

Perhaps the most important evidence of Negrín's withdrawal and self-efface-ment at this time and of his willingness to surrender to the PCE whatever was left of his authority were the measures that appeared in the now historic issue of the *Diario Oficial del Ministerio de Defensa Nacional* of 3 March. These measures, according to Togliatti, were presented to Negrín three or four days after he himself had arrived in the central-southern zone on 16 February.[14] However, most were not signed by Negrín until 2 March. Togliatti does not explain the delay, but it may be attributed to Negrín's fear of precipitating a coup by Casado. In any event, Togliatti and the politburo pressed for the implementation of the measures. "The party," attests the official *Historia del partido comunista de España*, "was aware of the intrigues of the capitulators and *insisted* that the premier should take forceful action against them. Finally, on 2 March 1939, Negrín dictated measures designed to strengthen the army in the central-southern zone, putting it in a fit condition to implement the policy of resistance."[15]

The measures "dictated" by Negrín were of course those proposed ten days earlier by the party. Although published in the *Diario Oficial* of 3 March, it was not until more than thirty years later that they could actually be verified, when a copy of the *Diario Oficial* of that date was discovered in the Hemeroteca Munici-pal de Madrid in the early 1970s.[16] Meanwhile, the absence of any precise knowledge of the measures gave rise to appalling confusion and speculation and to the legend that Negrín and the PCE had launched a full-scale coup d'état from the pages of the *Diario Oficial* aimed at giving them complete control of the army and the state.[17] Apart from the fact that coups are not generally heralded in official government journals, a critical examination of the measures that actually appeared lends little substance to the legend, which became firmly rooted in the historiography of the Civil War for more than three decades. After seeing a copy of the *Diario Oficial* in the early 1970s, Ramón Salas Larrazábal, the military historian, affirmed that "there was no coup d'état,"[18] and this conclusion is well sustained by the measures that actually appeared.

Included among them were the following reassignments:

General José Miaja, commander in chief of the army, navy, and air force, was made inspector general of the three armed services. Although this new assign-ment effectively reduced his powers of command, it is doubtful whether it could have alarmed Casado, who distrusted Miaja because of his equivocal behavior at the Los Llanos meeting on 16 February.

General Manuel Matallana, the commander of the army group of the central-southern region, with headquarters in Valencia, comprising the armies of the

Center (Segismundo Casado), Levante (Leopolde Menéndez), Estremadura (Antonio Escobar), and Andalusia (Domingo Moriones), was appointed "provisionally" chief of the now defunct central general staff in place of Vicente Rojo, who had refused to return to Spain. Neither this assignment nor the dissolution of the army group itself—also announced in the *Diario Oficial* of 3 March—effected any change in Communist command positions in the Madrid region, where Casado's conspiracy was centered, for three of the four commanders of the army corps constituting Casado's Army of the Center were led, as we have seen, by Communist commanders. More important still was the fact that no order for Casado's substitution appeared.

Colonel *Félix Muedra* and *Lieutenant Colonel Antonio Garijo*,[19] two staff officers attached to the above-mentioned army group, who were suspected of disaffection and of spying on behalf of General Franco,[20] were assigned to posts where they were rendered ineffectual. Garijo was assigned to Miaja, while Muedra was named provisionally chief of the organizational section of the undersecretaryship of the army under the vigilant eye of Cordón. Neither of these transfers could have been viewed by Casado as an impediment to his plans.

The *Diario Oficial* of 3 March also published the following promotions of Communist officers:

Colonel Juan Modesto was given the rank of general.

Lieutenant colonels Luis Barceló, Emilio Bueno, Francisco Galán and *Enrique Líster* were promoted to the rank of colonel. Líster's promotion was dated 28 January. It had not appeared earlier, because the *Diario Oficial* had suspended publication on 24 January just before the fall of Barcelona. But neither Modesto nor Líster, the two most prominent Communist commanders who had returned to Spain, was given any assignment, while Barceló and Bueno—despite the proposal to substitute Casado for one of them as chief of the Army of the Center—remained in command of their respective units. Only Francisco Galán was given an assignment, as will be seen shortly.

So far then it is hard to picture anything resembling a coup d'état. As for the appointments, only those of six Communist officers are worth mentioning:

Antonio Cordón (whom Negrín had promoted to general at the end of February)[21] was named—in addition to his existing post as undersecretary of the land forces—secretary general of the ministry of national defense, an empty title formerly held by Julián Zugazagoitia who had refused to return to Spain,[22] while *Ernesto Navarro Marquez* was made his technical secretary. These two appointments did no more than reaffirm the Communists' long-standing control of the defense ministry, now virtually a spectral body confined to Negrín's temporary headquarters in the estate known as El Poblet (*posición Yuste*) in Elda, and protected by Communist guerrillas of the Fourteenth Army Corps.

In contrast, the four other appointments of Communist officers had real significance, but not as part of a coup in Madrid, the center of the conspiracy:

Colonel Francisco Galán was given the command of the naval base of Cartagena.

Lieutenant Colonel Etelvino Vega was placed in charge of the military command of Alicante, an important port thirty-seven kilometers from Elda.

Lieutenant Colonel Leocado Mendiola was appointed military commander of Murcia, a strategic location on the main road from Madrid to Cartagena.

Major Inocencio Curto was named military commander of Albacete on the main highway from Madrid to both Alicante and Murcia. It was in Albacete that chief of the air force Hidalgo de Cisneros had set up his headquarters on returning to Spain.[23]

When Cordón handed the last three appointments to Negrín for his signature, the premier stated: "All three are Communists, right?" "Yes, sir," was Cordón's response. "I am not proposing them because they are Communists but rather because I do not know of any others who have equal or even similar leadership qualities."[24]

Clearly, the last four appointments were not aimed at removing Casado. Their essential purpose was to secure the most important escape routes to the coast in case a mass evacuation became necessary. This eventuality loomed more threateningly every day as General Franco prepared for his final offensive. No wonder the adversaries of the Communists were alarmed by these appointments. In the naval base of Cartagena, where General Carlos Bernal received word that he was to be relieved by Francisco Galán, apprehension was widespread, for it was feared that the Communists, as Bruno Alonso, the Socialist commissar general of the fleet, asserts, "would assassinate their enemies" and prevent those whose lives were most in jeopardy from fleeing the country.[25]

Whatever the legitimacy of these fears, there can be no doubt that the Communists had similar apprehensions, for they too were afraid, in the prevailing climate of hatred and revenge, that unless they secured the principal avenues of escape they themselves might be assassinated or prevented from evacuating their political, trade-union, and military cadres. Luis Romero expresses the magnitude of the drama: "In the final stages of a war . . . bloody events can occur and old disputes, political rivalries, and even personal differences may be settled by expeditious methods. One such method would be to deprive both individuals and groups of the means of evacuation, leaving them at the mercy of the vengeful justice of an implacable enemy that loomed ever closer."[26]

A factor that had muddled the historiography of this crucial period was the inclusion by Casado in the Spanish version of his chronicle, published in 1967 and in a serialized account that same year,[27] of the following five appointments of Communist officers which he claimed appeared in the *Diario Oficial* of 3 March but were strangely absent from the English version published in 1939: General Cordón, supreme chief of the land, sea, and air forces; General Modesto, chief of the Army of the Center; Colonel Líster, commander of the Army of the Levante; Lieutenant Colonel Valentín González (El Campesino), commander of the Army of Estremadura; Lieutenant Colonel Tagüeña, commander of the Army of Andalusia.

But the truth is that none of these appointments appeared in the *Diario Oficial*

of 3 March. To be sure, this was not known until the early 1970s, when, as we have seen, a copy of the missing issue was located in the Hemeroteca Municipal of Madrid. This valuable discovery, however, did not put an end to all speculation, for in subsequent years it was conjectured that the five appointments must have appeared in the issue of 4 March; but as no copy could be found, Casado's listing could not be verified. Hence, when José Manuel Martínez Bande published his definitive account of the final days of the war early in 1985, he concluded that all available copies of this "mysterious" issue of 4 March had been hidden or burned.[28] It was not until September of that same year—forty-six years after its publication—that a copy was located thanks to the diligent efforts of my research assistant, Carmen de la Cal Mata—working for me at that time in the Archivo Histórico Nacional, Salamanca—and to the invaluable help of José Manuel Mata and Margarita Vázquez de Parga of the Centro de Información Documental de Archivos of the ministry of culture, Madrid, to all of whom I am greatly indebted.

Contrary to expectations, this long sought-for issue contains none of the five crucial appointments. Nor does it contain any significant appointment or promotion of Communist officers. Furthermore, *none* of the books written by the officers in question—Cordón, Modesto, Líster, González, and Tagüeña—offers the slightest hint of the purported appointments. It cannot reasonably be conjectured, as one former member of the PCE suggested to me in 1985, that perhaps the five officers may have been told to remain silent on the matter, for both González and Tagüeña wrote their books after leaving the PCE. Nor can we assume that Casado had the appointments removed from the *Diario Oficial* before it was published in Madrid, for he would most certainly have revealed this important fact instead of claiming that they appeared in the issue of 3 March. Hence, one must conclude that the five appointments were apocryphal and that Casado was either relying on a faulty memory or on unconfirmed reports[29] or that he falsified the facts in order to bolster his claim against Negrín and the Communists that they intended to seize power in the central-southern zone.

Togliatti makes no mention in his report of the *Diario Oficial* of 4 March and asserts in reference to the issue of 3 March that "if all the measures belatedly agreed to by Negrín had been put into effect the coup d'état by Casado would have been impossible."[30] He also censured Negrín for publishing all the measures at one time in what he describes as an "extraordinary" issue of the *Diario Oficial*. "Almost exclusively," he said, "it contained decrees promoting and appointing Communists, beginning with the promotions of Modesto and Cordón to the rank of general and of Líster to the rank of colonel, etc. Provocators could not have done a better job. The issue was used by [our] enemies as proof that the Communists, in agreement with Negrín, were preparing to take complete power."[31]

In her memoirs published in 1962, La Pasionaria also criticizes Negrín for allegedly delaying the implementation of the measures proposed by the Communists. "[These measures]," she writes, "which at another moment would have been effective in improving the situation, were counterproductive at a time when the conspiracy was already in progress [and] caused profound indignation among the plotters, who felt that their plans were going to fail. But they were able to rely upon an ally they did not suspect, namely Negrín himself, who inexplicably kept at his side the comrades he had appointed. Nearly all the political and military cadres that had arrived from France began to concentrate in Elda on instructions from Negrín awaiting assignments that were never given."[32]

At least one of these accusations is demonstrably false, for the Communist officers, whose appointments to command positions appeared in the *Diario Oficial* of 3 March (Galán, Vega, Mendiola, Curto), all received their assignments. On the other hand, it is true that both Líster and Modesto claim in their memoirs that when they visited Negrín in Elda to request command posts for themselves he delayed taking any action.[33] But how reliable are their allegations that Negrín alone was responsible for this dillydallying? The reader will remember that the premier had to all intents and purposes relinquished his military powers to Antonio Cordón, the party's most trusted career officer. Additionally, it should be noted that when Líster and Modesto wrote their memoirs in the 1960s they were both in good standing with the party and that its policy at that time was to blame Negrín for certain errors and omissions which, in its opinion, contributed to the loss of the war.

La Pasionaria's claim that Negrín kept the military cadres of the PCE immobilized in Elda "awaiting assignments that were never given"—an accusation that does not appear in the final volume of the official Communist history of the Civil War, published in 1977—is even more bizarre if we take into account the fact that he was surrounded in Elda solely by dedicated members of the party, such as Benigno Rodríguez, his political secretary; Sánchez Arcas, his undersecretary of propaganda; Major Julián Soley Conde, his adjutant, who had previously been Modesto's aide;[34] and of course Antonio Cordón. Under the circumstances, it is not unreasonable to suggest that if Togliatti and the politburo had really wanted to appoint Modesto and Líster to positions of command no one in Elda would have stopped them. As for the political cadres of the party that arrived from France it is implausible to ascribe their immobility to Negrín. As we have already seen, La Pasionaria herself has testified that when Negrín moved to Elda, she and other members of the politburo left for El Palmar, south of Murcia, where it is obvious that they were subject not to the orders of Negrín but to those of Togliatti. For this reason alone, it is not only implausible but senseless to place the blame solely on Negrín for their inactivity.

Despite the attempts by La Pasionaria and Togliatti to saddle Negrín with the main burden of responsibility for failing to thwart the conspiracy, it is evident from Togliatti's report to the Comintern that the PCE was faced with grave disciplinary problems that, whatever its plans, seriously affected its ability to function effectively. After affirming that "if all the measures belatedly agreed to by Negrín had been put into effect, the coup by Casado would have been impossible," Togliatti continues: "But at that time there occurred the first disquieting and fatal phenomenon: the failure of the cadres on which the party relied. Lieutenant

Colonel Bueno refused to assume command of the Army of the Center. We thus lost what should have been the key to our preventive action. Mendiola, named military commander of Murcia, declined, and Curto, named military commander of Albacete, declined. Paco [Francisco] Galán, named commander of Cartagena, arrived there two days late and, disobeying the orders of the party not to enter the city except at the head of an infantry brigade placed at his disposal . . . , entered by car and without a bodyguard. This allowed the others to arrest him." Unable to resist the urge to hold the Masons partly responsible for the breakdown in party discipline, Togliatti added that as far as Bueno, Mendiola, and Curto were concerned, their failure could only be explained "by a direct or indirect link, probably Masonic, to the military preparing the coup d'état."[35]

But even more expressive of the gravity of the crisis that faced the party is the following passage from Togliatti's report to Moscow on 29 May 1939:

> In face of the impotence and shortcomings of the government, could our party on its own initiative have taken the necessary measures to prevent the coup by force? When we saw that the situation was getting worse day by day we discussed the question. I even asked for instructions, but received no reply due to technical reasons.

> [Togliatti was no doubt referring to an attempt to seek advice from Moscow through the Soviet delegation's radio station in Valencia. In this connection, it should be noted that, according to Stefanov's secret report to the Comintern, it had been decided at a meeting of the politburo held in Madrid two days after Togliatti's arrival on 16 February[36] that Stefanov should proceed to Moscow "as quickly as possible" to request directives on a number of "acute, burning tactical matters." These questions, which, according to Stefanov, were "formulated orally by Togliatti and written down by me," included the crucial issue as to what should be the position of the party if the government, ignoring the PCE, should decide to capitulate in agreement with the military and the trade unions. "Should it attempt to continue fighting alone?"[37] Since Stefanov's trip to Moscow apparently did not materialize, given the fact that Togliatti does not even refer to it in his long report to Moscow of 29 May 1939, we may have to conclude that the momentous decision whether or not to continue the struggle was left entirely in Togliatti's hands. However, it should be mentioned that the Italian Communist Ettore Vanni, who was close to Togliatti and director of *Verdad*, the Communist party organ in Valencia, states in his memoir that early in March "Luisa"—Rita Montagnana, Togliatti's wife—arrived in Valencia with directives from Moscow.[38] As the date of her departure from Moscow is not given by Vanni, it is impossible to judge whether at the time she left for Spain the coup against Negrín had already occurred. Furthermore, as Togliatti says nothing of these instructions in his lengthy report to Moscow, they cannot be confirmed and the exact attitude of Moscow *at the time of the coup* cannot be determined with certainty.]

Our view [Togliatti's report continues], and mine in particular, was that we could not use force for the following reasons: we were no longer in the same position as we were in Figueras [in Catalonia], when everyone with his eyes fixed on the frontier allowed us to do as we wished. . . . Here, on the other hand, we were faced by a state apparatus, civil and military, mobilized against us, whose hostility and resistance could only be smashed by brute force. For such an act of force, *we could not rely on a single ally; everyone would have been against us*. We should have had to take power in the name of the party. This would have implied politically that the party would have had to assume responsibility for destroying the Popular Front by force. The entire leadership of the party was against the idea. Moreover, there was another reason even more profound that impelled me to advise the party against [the use of force]. I was convinced, because of my knowledge of the party and the state of its forces at the time, that we would have been rapidly and hopelessly defeated, because the masses, who were disoriented and *whose only wish was for peace, would not have followed us. Not even the military forces commanded by Communists would have supported us with the necessary energy and determination. Very probably, some of them would have aligned themselves against us. And it is even very likely that a section of the party would have wavered*.[39]

The full import of the statement that "not even the military forces commanded by Communists would have supported us with the necessary energy and determination" can only be appreciated if we consider that according to the official Communist history, eight of the seventeen army corps that comprised the army group of the central-southern region—the First, Second, Third, Seventh, Fourteenth, Nineteenth, Twentieth, and Twenty-first—had Communist commanders and that five of the others—the Eighth, Ninth, Seventeenth, Twenty-second, and Twenty-third—had Communist commissars in charge of their political orientation. In addition, a reserve unit, the Agrupación Toral, comprising five divisions, was commanded by Hilamón Toral, a party member.[40]

But in spite of the frank admission by Togliatti that the party could not rely even on the military units commanded by Communists for a "preventive action" against Casado and that the masses "whose only wish was for peace would not have followed us," he nevertheless asserted in another lunge at Negrín: "We were all convinced, on the other hand, that if [he] . . . had given us the opportunity of occupying a whole series of decisive posts it would have been possible to prevent the coup or crush it with one swift stroke. This would have had the support of the masses and the army as it would have assumed the form of a struggle in defense of the government and the Popular Front."[41] It is impossible to reconcile this assertion with Togliatti's other frank acknowledgments that the party could not abort the conspiracy by force as "everyone would have been against us" and that it would have been "rapidly and hopelessly defeated," because the "masses, who were disoriented and whose only wish was for peace, would not have followed us."

In view of this telling admission and of all the other evidence of the collapse of Communist power and influence, what validity is there in the postwar claims of the PCE and its supporters that but for the vacillations and apathy of Negrín and the treachery of Casado the Republicans could have resisted until the outbreak of war in Europe in September 1939 and that the victory of General Franco could have been averted? In her memoirs, La Pasionaria fastens responsibility squarely on Negrín for the Casado coup and avoids any mention of the party's immobility and impotence. "In his secret thoughts," she writes, "he wanted to relieve himself of the burden of government and find a scapegoat. . . . The passivity and indifference with which he received the news of the activities of the capitulators led us to the conviction that he wanted events to run their course."[42] This may well be true, but the crucial question is not whether La Pasionaria's accusation has any validity in fact but whether her charge that Negrín was looking for a scapegoat does not apply with equal force to the party. In fact, it is significant that Stefanov, in his secret report to Moscow, blames the party leaders for not showing greater independence with regard to Negrín. "Although they did not believe that Negrín showed any sign of resoluteness," he wrote, "they expected everything from him and placed their hopes in him."[43]

"[I] have reached the conclusion," writes Ettore Vanni, "that despite all appearances at least some of the leaders of the party firmly intended not to do anything to change the course of events."[44] Even in Madrid, the focal point of the conspiracy, the politburo, which had retired to El Palmar, south of Murcia, made no attempt to thwart Casado before its departure. Tagüeña, who remained in Madrid until he was ordered to proceed to Elda on 5 March, affirms that the inaction of the party was so apparent that "it completely confirmed my suspicions that it was not thinking of taking the initiative [and] was going to await the development of events as it did not wish to be responsible for any action that would lead to the collapse of the teetering Popular Front."[45]

If it is true, as La Pasionaria asserts, that Negrín was looking for a scapegoat and was relieved that his long ordeal was ending, it is no less true that Togliatti and the PCE were also seeking scapegoats in both Casado and Negrín. This is not to argue that when Togliatti and the politburo returned to Spain in mid-February, they did not intend to continue the policy of resistance in the hope that Britain and France, in spite of the loss of Catalonia, would eventually confront Italy and Germany and that the Civil War would merge with a general war in Western Europe. We have already seen that on 23 February the politburo, despite the demoralization and desire for peace that were universal, had issued its optimistic manifesto presaging help from the democratic powers if the anti-Franco forces continued to resist. Furthermore, the proposal to remove Casado from the command of the Central Army was made to Negrín on 24 February and was presumably aimed at reviving the spirit of resistance in the critical war zone of Madrid.

What then occurred to cause the politburo to withdraw permanently from Madrid to El Palmar and to impel Negrín to move to Elda only days before the Casado rising? The answer is simple. On 27 February, Britain and France had recognized General Franco's administration as the sovereign government of Spain, ending any hope of assistance from these two powers. And, on the same day, Azaña had resigned the presidency. "These two events, added to all the others," Togliatti reported to Moscow, "contributed to the demoralization of the leaders and the people. While some regarded the loss of a 'legal' government as ending the possibility of aid [*la posibilidad de "contar"*], the others gave up what little hope they had that the international situation would change in our favor."[46] And why, one may further ask, did the Communist leaders who had moved to El Palmar receive orders on the very eve of the rebellion, as we shall see shortly, to concentrate in Elda with its airfield at Monóvar conveniently close by? Again, the answer is simple. Firstly, the military and political apparatus of the party showed signs of crumbling as evidenced by Togliatti's report to Moscow. Secondly, on 4 March, Franco's Fifth Column staged an uprising at the naval base of Cartagena, and the next morning Admiral Buiza (who had warned Negrín at the Los Llanos meeting that the navy would abandon Spanish jurisdictional waters if peace were not made quickly) ordered the fleet to put out to sea and then to sail for North Africa, leaving the entire coastline undefended and thousands of people without means of escape.[47]

In spite of these and other adverse developments, the myth has been disseminated for half a century that resistance could have continued until the outbreak of war in Europe in September 1939. "[The Civil War] could have finally been won," wrote Alvarez del Vayo, "if we had held on six months longer, waiting for the Spanish War to become a part of World War II."[48] This was no idle dream, he later wrote. All that was needed was "the strengthening of public morale, the reorganization of the services, and the removal from posts of authority of certain unreliable and defeatist elements."[49] Among the leading historians who have helped to perpetuate this myth is Hugh Thomas, who asseverated in his popular work on the Civil War: "Had the republic lasted intact, with Negrín and Casado still in one camp, for even so short a time as two weeks longer, their international position might have altered. On 15 March, Hitler marched into Prague. Even Chamberlain spoke in protest, on 18 March. By the end of the month, the Anglo-French guarantee to Poland had transformed the international situation. A united republic could have taken advantage of the opportunity thus opening out."[50] This remarkable assertion totally ignores, among other things, the impact of the diplomatic recognition of General Franco by Britain and France, the resignation of President Azaña, and, above all, the fact that the British guarantee to Poland was, as shown in a previous chapter, a bogus document from which Neville Chamberlain and Sir Horace Wilson did all they could to extricate themselves.

By the end of February, there was no faith in further resistance even among the Communists themselves. Togliatti knew it and so of course did Stalin, whose focus of diplomatic interest since the Munich agreement in September 1938 was no longer the Spanish Civil War but rather the possibility of a nonaggression pact with Hitler that would deflect German aggression away from Eastern Europe. And since the war was lost and resistance offered no salvation, why not allow the conspiracy free rein? Why not leave to Colonel Casado the unpalatable task of negotiating what terms he could with a ruthless and vengeful victor? In this way, the Communists would be spared the dishonor and historic responsibility of surrender.

Thus, on 5 March, even before Casado had announced his coup, the Communist leaders who had left Madrid for El Palmar were ordered to proceed to Elda, where they congregated in a large building code-named *posición Dakar*,[51] already occupied by Antonio Cordón and other Communists. To Enrique Líster, it was obvious that the members of the politburo regarded the war as lost. "Only in this way can it be explained," he affirmed in the early 1970s, when he was at loggerheads with the party leadership, but still a Communist, "that they locked themselves up in Elda and that they gave some of our military leaders, who had returned from France, the order to go into seclusion there, far from the battle fronts, from the large industrial centers, where the working masses were located, and, above all from Madrid, which had been our fortress and was then the center of the conspiracy against the Republic."[52]

In 1966, in keeping with the then party line, Líster also claimed that the measures published in the *Diario Oficial* were a provocation for which Negrín was responsible. "On seeing the *Diario Oficial*," he wrote, "I could not conceal my indignation at this stupidity, because to the conspirators it was like a banderilla, which was immediately exploited by them as proof that we Communists had returned from France to seize the command posts and to conduct the war in our own way. Did Negrín fail to see the consequences? I do not think so."[53]

On the other hand, politburo member Jesús Hernández, who was chief political commissar of the armies of the central-southern region, asserted after he had left the PCE that "the measures adopted by Negrín at the insistence of the politburo," were inspired by Moscow and were "a cunning political provocation, an incitement to defiance and rebellion, the spark that was to ignite the powder keg of the rebellion."[54] But the truth is that although the measures may have added body and color to the prevailing suspicion that the Communists might attempt to seize power and have given greater urgency and impetus to the conspiracy, Casado's coup would have occurred without any provocation by the Communists. In fact, neither in the official communiqué broadcast by the Casado rebel junta on the night of the rebellion on 5–6 March nor in any of the speeches by the conspirators was there any allusion to the measures or to a planned coup by Negrín and the Communists.[55] Furthermore, the conspiracy had been brewing, as we have seen, ever since Casado had entered into negotiations with Nationalist agents at the beginning of February, before the return of Negrín and the politburo to Spain, and had gained momentum after the serious events of 27 February and the leaders of the CNT in Madrid, with the backing of Cipriano Mera's Fourth Army Corps, had aligned themselves with Casado.

At all events, we now know that by the end of February the PCE had given up all hope of continued resistance. This is also true of Negrín. One piece of testimony relating to the dramatic events of the last days of Negrín and the Communist leaders in Elda is that of Jesús Hernández. Although the reader should be reminded that his evidence has on occasions proved untrustworthy, it is essential to point out that this particular testimony concurs in some important respects with Togliatti's report to Moscow and with what I heard from several leading Communists in Mexico shortly after the Civil War, who were at Negrín's side to the very end. Although Hernández's evidence may not in all instances be reliable, the following testimony should not be rejected out of hand simply because it is fashionable among some historians to ignore the evidence of ex-Communists while uncritically accepting that of others.

Referring to the early morning of 5 March, Hernández recounts that he went to Elda to see Negrín:

> At 3 A.M. Negrín appears. . . . He looks like a tramp, unshaven, with his hat pulled down over his ears. . . . He seems extremely tired. . . .
>
> "My friend, Hernández," he said with a soft voice. "When I left France for the central-southern zone I believed there was a ninety-five per cent chance that I would leave my skin here, but now that percentage has risen to ninety-nine per cent. . . . There is nothing for us to do here. I do not want to preside over a new civil war among Franco's opponents."
>
> "But your decision will reduce everything to the most infernal chaos," I said.
>
> "No more so than now! The uprisings have already started. Now it is Cartagena and the fleet. Tomorrow it will be Madrid or Valencia. What can we do? Crush them? I don't believe it's worth the trouble. The war is definitely lost. If others want to negotiate peace, I shall not oppose them."
>
> "Then what was the purpose of the series of appointments in the *Diario Oficial?*" I asked him, confused and curious.
>
> "They were due to the demands of your comrades. I tried to please them, knowing that everything would be useless and even prejudicial."
>
> I could see that Negrín, the man of resistance, the premier and defense minister, who most loyally and effectively had embodied the magnificent fighting spirit of our people in the periods of greatest difficulty, was already dead.

Later in the day, Togliatti and La Pasionaria arrived in Elda and met immediately with Hernández, who posed several questions. "Togliatti removed his glasses," recounts Hernández, "and, as always, when getting ready to listen, busied himself cleaning them."

> "The first question I would like to ask you is whether, as a member of the politburo, I have the right to know what decisions are adopted? In Madrid, I learned third hand that you had decided to take a whole series of measures while *awaiting* events. I was not told what these measures were, nor do I understand why it is necessary to *wait* for uprisings to occur and not to anticipate them and abort them."
>
> "The second question," I continued, "is what are the *advantages* of Elda over Madrid or Valencia as a fixed place of residence for the leadership of the party?
>
> "And the third is what are the political reasons for the dismissals and appointments that appeared in the *Diario Oficial* yesterday?"[56]

Togliatti continued cleaning his glasses. From time to time he looked fixedly at me with his myopic eyes like a fish in an aquarium. . . . Although I had finished speaking neither Togliatti nor Pasionaria decided to answer me. Finally, La Pasionaria opened fire.

"Comrade Hernández knows perfectly well why he was not asked to attend the meetings of the politburo. We had all agreed that in order to avoid the suspicion of the military and the criticism of the other parties he should not attend the politburo meetings while at the head of the commissariat of the Group of Armies [of the central-southern zone]."

"That is true, but the complementary agreement is no less true that you would keep me apprised of everything decided by the politburo and would consult with me previously on all matters of definite importance," I explained.

La Pasionaria pretended not to be listening to me and continued:

"The politburo decided to move to Elda in order to be near the government at all times and to be able to react with the requisite speed in face of any contingency. And, finally, the appointments that we recommended to Negrín, which were published in the *Diario Oficial*, were in keeping with our clear policy of cleansing the army of traitors and vacillators, of putting a barrier around the capitulators and intriguers, the defeatists and conspirators, and substituting them for men of trust, who have proved themselves in a hundred battles, faithful to the death to the people's cause. Now, is that clear?" she ended provocatively.

"What is clear to me," I replied, "is that if reasons of insecurity made it advisable for the party leadership to leave Madrid, the move should never have been made to Elda but rather to Valencia, a city that is a strategic center of the republican territory, that has an excellent network of communications and would guarantee rapid action against the conspirators. And it is also clear that, if we expect the principal coup to take place in Madrid, it is there that one or two of our most prestigious military men should be posted together with one of the members of the politburo. And what to me is even clearer is the irreparable blunder of the appointments recommended to Negrín unless you foresaw the terrible consequences. If we had done all that with the deliberate intention of provoking a rebellion, we could not have done a better job. Can you tell me why Modesto, Líster, Vega, Mendiola, and the others are not already at their new posts?[57] May I know what they are doing in Elda? Or is their mission here to *await* events?"

Pasionaria lashed out with her claws like a lioness in heat.

"I will not allow comrade Hernández to call us provocators. . . ."

Togliatti felt obliged to intervene.

"I am convinced that Hernández did not wish to call us provocators." . . . His voice was cold, calm, as if he were discussing the disintegration of the atom. And he continued in his jesuitical manner: "This combination of military appointments and precautionary measures is unfortunately a little late. . . . We tried to rectify with a single stroke all the harm caused by the vacillating policy of Negrín with respect to the cleansing of the focal points of conspiracy and treason. Things had gone too far. But what other measures could we have taken?

. . . To allow things to take their course would have been catastrophic. . . . I agree that our comrades should leave immediately to take charge of their new posts and that we should consider the advisability of moving to Valencia and setting up the government there. Although Negrín is downcast, we shall encourage him. In Madrid everything has been taken care of so that not even a rat can move. If they attempt to rebel, they will be crushed in half an hour."[58]

From this dialogue we may surmise that Hernández was unaware that the Communist leaders who had been called to Elda would soon be instructed by Togliatti to leave the country. Indeed, it is conceivable that none of the Spanish Communist leaders knew the exact script and that only Togliatti, who was burdened with the full responsibility of winding up the PCE's involvement in the war, had any definite plans regarding the next act of the drama.

66

The Flight of Negrín and the End of the Third Republic

While the Communist leaders were gathering in Elda, Colonel Casado and his co-conspirators were finalizing their plans to oust the government. "At 7 P.M. [Sunday, 5 March]," records Casado, "I established myself in the building of the former ministry of finance. . . . This very old building lent itself to a good plan of defense in the event of a Communist uprising."[1] At 8 P.M., most of the other plotters arrived and the various posts on a rebel junta, named the National Council of Defense, were assigned. The venerable Socialist Julián Besteiro, the most distinguished figure among the conspirators, stated that as the army was the sole legitimate authority, Colonel Casado should occupy both the presidency and the defense department. However, Casado agreed to head the council only provisionally until the arrival from Valencia of General Miaja, recently appointed inspector general of the three armed services who, after his initial vacillation, had now firmly committed himself to the rebellion.[2]

The final distribution of seats was as follows:

General José Miaja	Former PCE member	Presidency
Julián Besteiro	Socialist	Foreign Affairs
Colonel Segismundo Casado	Republican	Defense
Wenceslao Carrillo	Socialist	Interior
Miguel San Andrés	Izquierda Republicana	Justice and Propaganda
Eduardo Val	CNT	Communications and Public Works
José González Marín	CNT	Finance and Economy
José del Río	Unión Republicana	Education and Health[3]
J. Sánchez Requena	Syndicalist	Secretary[4]
Antonio Pérez	UGT	Labor[5]

At 11:30 P.M., the Seventieth Brigade, commanded by the Anarchosyndicalist Bernabé López of the Fourth Army Corps under Cipriano Mera, who had helped to plan the coup with Casado, took over the protection of the ministries of war, interior, and communications, as well as the central telephone exchange, the Bank of Spain, and the general direction of security.[6] Shortly after midnight (6 March), Miguel San Andrés, the left Republican, broadcast a manifesto on behalf of the council: "Spanish Workers! People of Antifascist Spain! . . . As revolutionaries, as proletarians, as Spaniards, and as antifascists, we cannot continue to accept passively any longer the improvidence, the lack of direction, and the senseless inactivity of the government of Dr. Negrín. . . . We cannot tolerate that while the people struggle, fight, and die, a few privileged persons prepare to live abroad.

"To prevent this, . . . to prevent desertion at the most critical moment, the National Council of Defence has been formed. . . . The authority of Dr. Negrín's government has no juridical basis. Under these circumstances, we . . . affirm our own authority as honest and genuine defenders of the Spanish people, as men who are ready to offer their lives as a guarantee and to make their destiny that of everyone, so that nobody shall escape the sacred duties that are incumbent on all alike."[7]

Julián Besteiro then spoke. Because of the resignation of President Azaña, he said, the Republic had been decapitated. "Constitutionally, the Speaker of the Cortes [Diego Martínez Barrio] cannot replace the President except with the strict obligation of arranging presidential elections within a maximum period of eight days. As this constitutional requirement is impossible under present circumstances, the Negrín government, without presidential authority and the support of the Cortes—to which it would be futile to attempt to give a semblance of life—lacks legitimacy." On the other hand, he added, "the Army of the Republic has unquestionable authority. . . . The Negrín government, with its concealment of the truth, its half-truths, and its insidious aims could only hope to gain time. . . . Its policy of procrastination could serve no other purpose than that of encouraging the morbid belief that complications in international affairs would provoke a catastrophe of universal proportions, a catastrophe in which the proletarian masses of many nations would perish with us."[8]

The next speaker was Colonel Casado, who addressed himself to Spaniards on both sides of the trenches: "Compatriots, . . . the people have had the courage and gallantry to seek . . . the way of peace through conciliation with independence and liberty. . . . We want a country free of foreign domination. . . . Spaniards in the invaded zone, you must choose between foreigners and compatriots. . . . The Spanish people will not lay down their arms until there is a guarantee of peace without crimes. . . . You must choose. If you offer us peace you will find our generous Spanish hearts open. If you continue to wage war on us, you will find our heroic fighting spirit implacable, unshakable, hard like the tempered steel of our bayonets. Either peace for Spain or a struggle to the death! . . . Spaniards, long live the Republic! Long live Spain!"[9]

Finally, Cipriano Mera, the CNT commander of the Fourth Army Corps, spoke. In an impassioned onslaught on the "criminal and perfidious conduct" of Juan Negrín, he described the deposed premier as "unworthy of the combatants and the workers" and declared that his policy had "no other aim than that of fleeing with the national treasure, while the people remain tied hand and foot to face the enemy. . . . This officer, who is now speaking to you with emotion stirred by the memories of his hard and austere life as a manual laborer, believes that one can only serve with discipline a person who serves his country and that it is essential to oppose anyone who despoils or betrays it. . . . For this reason I join these men of good will with an immaculate past . . . who comprise the National Council of Defense. . . . From now on, fellow citizens, Spain has a government and a mission: An honorable peace based on principles of justice and brother-hood. . . . But, if unfortunately for everyone, peace is lost in the void of misun-derstanding, then I must also tell you calmly that as soldiers we are at our posts ready to fight to the finish defending the independence of Spain. Workers and combatants! . . . Long live invincible Spain, independent and free! We are all ready to defend the lives and honor of the people who entrusted us with this mission. Long live the National Council of Defense!"[10]

Despite the tenor of the addresses, none of the speakers could have felt certain that an honorable peace was achievable. They may of course have been heartened by the hope that once Negrín and the Communist leadership had been deposed, the council would be able to negotiate reasonable terms with General Franco despite his insistence until now on unconditional surrender.

As soon as the broadcast was over, Casado was called to the telephone by Negrín. Casado has given three almost identical versions of the conversation. The following version appeared in *Pueblo*, 2 November 1967.[11]

> Negrín: General, what is happening in Madrid? [In the first of the three ver-sions published in London in 1939, Casado says that he told Negrín, "I am no more than a Colonel. I do not admit the promotion to General which you have given me, because it is no more legal than your government."[12]]
>
> Casado: I have rebelled.
>
> Negrín: Against whom? Against me?
>
> Casado: Yes, against you!
>
> Negrín: I have heard the manifesto and it seems to me that what you have done is madness.
>
> Casado: I feel at peace with myself because I have done my duty as a soldier and as a citizen. All the political and trade-union representatives on the Council are also at peace, because they are convinced that they have rendered Spain a service.
>
> Negrín: I hope you will reflect, because we can still reach a settlement.
>
> Casado: I don't understand what you mean, for I believe that everything has been settled.
>
> Negrín: At least you should send a representative so that I may hand over the powers of government or I shall send one to Madrid for this purpose.

Casado: Don't worry about that. You cannot hand over what you don't have. Actually, we have already assumed the powers that you and your government have relinquished.

Negrín: Then you do not accede to this request?

Casado: No!

At about 1 P.M., Casado received four telephone calls from Elda in quick succession: from the minister of communications (Bernardo Giner de los Ríos), the minister of the interior (Paulino Gómez), the undersecretary of the armed forces (Antonio Cordón), and the chief of the air force (Ignacio Hidalgo de Cisneros), each of whom tried in the name of the prime minister to convince him that he should accept the transfer of power.[13] "I told all of them that the refusal I had given Dr. Negrín was irrevocable and asked them not to insist, as it would be useless. (They wanted to hand over to me a putrefying corpse—the powers of that Government.)"[14]

Julián Zugazagoitia emphatically denies that Negrín offered to transfer his powers and claims that Casado was "fantasizing," but he was not in Elda at the time and does not reveal his sources.[15] The official Communist history is silent on the matter, nor does La Pasionaria say anything about it in her memoir, *El único camino*; but two partisans of Negrín (one a PCE member) give substance to Casado's claim. One is Santiago Garcés, who states that he was with Negrín at the time of the premier's telephone call to Madrid and that the premier suggested to Casado that Trifón Gómez, the well-known Besteiro Socialist, should carry out the *legal transfer* of powers;[16] the other is Colonel Francisco Ciutat, operations chief to General Leopoldo Menéndez, the commander of the Army of the Levante. In a report to the central committee of the PCE, dated 3 May 1939, Ciutat says that Cordón, on instructions from the government, asked Menéndez to telephone Casado "to take steps *to legalize what he had done*" and "to accept the powers of the government in order to ensure republican legality." But Casado "refused to accept any transfer of authority from someone who had none to give, because the government was not legally constituted."[17] Negrín's attempt to contrive a "legal" transfer of power after the coup was an astute maneuver, for, if successful, it would have removed the stigma of being ousted from office and having to flee Spain with undignified haste to save his life. But Casado was not inclined to render Negrín this service.

The news of Casado's coup reached Negrín and his ministers in Elda during a short recess of the cabinet. When the ministers reassembled, affirms the official Communist history, volume 4, published in Moscow in 1977, Uribe asked what measures should be taken against the rebels. "Negrín called Hidalgo de Cisneros and ordered him to have bombers ready at dawn."[18] It is improbable that such an order was given, for Togliatti states in his letter to Moscow of May 1939, thirty-eight years earlier, that during the cabinet meeting Negrín did not raise the question of "repression" but, on the contrary, "declared himself against the idea of an open conflict."[19] In fact, when I interviewed Hidalgo de Cisneros in 1940, he said nothing of the alleged order, but recalled that when the coup occurred, Negrín said to him: "Our job now is to try to gain time. On no account quarrel with Casado."[20]

There is no reason to believe that at this juncture Togliatti and the politburo were opposed to Negrín's attempt to gain time—time to prepare for their flight from Spain—for this is clearly implied in one of two proposals, as we shall see later, that the politburo made to Negrín on the advice of the Comintern delegate. If it is true that Negrín was convinced that further struggle was futile and relieved that his ordeal was ending, it is no less true that the Communist leaders in Elda had similar feelings. At meetings held in Moscow in the spring and summer of 1939, Enrique Líster claims that he accused members of the politburo of defeatism. "That alone explains why they locked themselves up in Elda. . . . In one of those meetings . . . I said that I could never forget the painful impression I received on the morning of 6 March when, arriving at Elda from Cartagena . . . a few hours after Casado had rebelled, I found Dolores and other party leaders preparing to leave by plane instead of studying what response they should give to the traitors of the Casado Junta."[21]

The artful role played by Togliatti during the final stage of the war lends credence to the following conversation that Jesús Hernández claims he held in Moscow with Comintern leader Dmitri Manuilsky shortly after the Civil War. The dialogue cannot be authenticated, but it is quoted here because it is in keeping with the whole course of events before the coup, which have been fully documented in the previous chapter.

> Manuilsky: The war was irremediably lost for you. With good judgment the
> party continued its slogan of resistance, although it is evident that not even a
> miracle could have averted the defeat confronting the Republic. The hope of a
> European conflagration was an illusion, because it could not break out until the
> Spanish situation was totally resolved.
>
> Hernández: That's not what you told us then.
>
> Manuilsky: If it wasn't explained to you, that was the fault of our delegation.
>
> Hernández: You told us the exact opposite.
>
> Manuilsky: In any case, that doesn't change the basic situation. Once the in-
> evitability of defeat had been acknowledged, it was essential to save the prestige
> of the party from the discredit into which all the organizations of the Popular
> Front had fallen during the war because of their intrigues. It would have been un-
> fair if our Spanish party had shared the same responsibility as the others, for it
> was our party that had made the greatest contribution in enthusiasm and blood
> during the war. [Togliatti] employed a tactic that I consider was very clever. On
> the one hand, he kept alive the slogan of resistance, thus demonstrating that the
> Communists would not lay down their arms in the struggle against Franco; and,
> on the other hand, he left the field wide open to those who showed when they re-
> belled that they were ready to end the resistance—which they believed useless—
> and seek a negotiated peace with Franco, which was downright madness at that

time. Ercoli allowed events to unfold as expected. The Casadistas fell into the trap . . . [and] the party was spared the responsibility for the final catastrophe. . . . Now that the Spanish masses are feeling the brutality of Franco's bloody repression, it is logical for them to think that it would have been better to have followed the advice of the Communists to resist to the death if necessary. . . . And they will turn in anger against the Anarchists and Socialists, against the members of the Junta of Casado. [Togliatti's] maneuver has saved the political future and prestige of the Spanish Communists.[22]

Because of their seclusion in Elda, Negrín and the Communist leadership could not have taken any effective action to thwart the coup even if they had wished to do so. In any case, wasn't the purpose of their presence in Elda to prepare for their flight from Spain? "All the military commands in the provinces were taken over by the rebels," Negrín informed the permanent committee of the Cortes a few weeks later when in exile. "The government had no possibility of communicating with anyone. Our emissaries were arrested and we knew that the controls on the highways were being taken over so that the government would be caught in a trap."[23]

It was in these circumstances, says the official Communist history, that the government decided to leave Spain as soon as possible. The Communist ministers (Uribe and Moix) said that they "were at the disposal of the party and would follow its directives." Accompanied by Cordón and Hidalgo de Cisneros, they went to "posición Dakar," the party's headquarters in Elda, where the Communist leaders were now concentrating in preparation for their own flight abroad. They had no course but to leave Spain immediately, Stefanov affirmed. "If the comrades had not left on 6 March, Dolores, Modesto, Líster, and Uribe would most certainly have been executed during the next two or three days. . . . Their execution would have been an irreparable loss and caused confusion within the ranks of the party. . . . Their departure was necessary because nothing useful or practical could have been done under those conditions in that completely isolated trap. The mistake was to allow the party leaders and a considerable group of prominent Communist officers to get bogged down in Elda, where they did not have a single loyal supporter among the population and where they had hardly any means of maintaining contact with the party organizations and the army. It would have been stupid and criminal in the extreme to have allowed the leaders of the party to stay under those conditions."[24]

While most of the cabinet ministers proceeded to Monóvar airfield early on 6 March to await the arrival of the planes that were to take them from Spain, Negrín and Vayo, according to the official Communist history, went to *posición Dakar* to bid farewell to the party leadership. They were accompanied by Manuel Sánchez Arcas (the Communist undersecretary of propaganda), Bibiano Fernández Ossorio y Tafall (the pro-Communist chief political commissar), Santiago Garcés Arroyo (Negrín's devotee and head of the once powerful SIM) and by other "high-ranking officials." In the building, they found La Pasionaria, José Antonio Uribes

(Communist deputy for Valencia), Angelín Alvarez, a Communist officer, and several other PCE military commanders as well as Benigno Rodríguez (Negrín's inseparable Communist political secretary), Irene Falcón (La Pasionaria's secretary), and other "collaborators." Pedro Checa and Manuel Delicado (both politburo members) as well as Togliatti, all of whom had been in Murcia, arrived around 8 A.M.[25] In the beguiling words of Vayo, *posición Dakar* was filled to overflowing with people who had turned its terrace into "the most public and democratic of meeting places."[26]

Vayo asserts that Casado speeded up his plans to rebel in order to prevent Negrín from broadcasting a speech, from which the whole population would have learned of the "pending negotiations" and his efforts to make "an honorable peace." Vayo also claims that Casado had heard about the planned speech from the lips of the prime minister himself and that the broadcasting of the speech would have deprived Casado's rebellion of its whole raison d'être. "Hence the determination to stifle the voice of the government."[27] Although the official history states that Negrín had planned to speak over the radio in order to explain to the people the situation arising from the recognition of Franco by Britain and France and from the resignation of Azaña and why it was advisable to continue the resistance "in order to obtain an honorable peace," it says nothing about the "pending negotiations."[28] Nor is there the slightest evidence in Togliatti's and Stefanov's long reports to the Comintern that Negrín was negotiating for peace.

Significantly, Vicente Uribe, who was both a politburo member and a cabinet minister, also says nothing of the purported negotiations in his unpublished memoir and criticizes Negrín and the government for "lack of will" for failing to come to grips with the situation and deciding to leave Spain. He asserts that he spent a good part of the night of 5–6 March trying to discourage Negrín and Vayo from leaving, but "it was not worth the trouble, because they had already made up their minds."[29] This may be true, but, in any event, the official Communist line for many years to come was to ascribe most of the responsibility for the success of Casado's coup to the passivity of Negrín and his cabinet ministers, to their isolation in Elda, and to their decision to leave Spain, as though the PCE leadership, which had provided the detachment of one hundred guerrilla fighters for the protection of the government and the Communist leaders, as well as three airplanes "to serve the party leadership,"[30] had not been directly involved in the preparations for the flight from Spain.

Commenting on Negrín's visit to Communist party headquarters at *posición Dakar* just before leaving Spain, Togliatti wrote: "It appeared that Negrín did not wish to abandon the Communists to whom he said he owed a debt of honor."[31] Togliatti, on the other hand, felt no such debt toward Negrín. Although Negrín, as premier and defense minister, had done more than any man outside the party to enhance its strength and stature, although he had sacrificed his friends and reputation in the Socialist movement by linking his political fortunes with those of the Communist party, Togliatti did not spare him. In a letter to the Spanish politburo, written on 10 March, a few days after Negrín and the Communist leaders had fled Spain, he lay down the policy to be pursued toward the man who had done so much to promote the interests of the party. "[The flight of Negrín]," he said, "was in my opinion, a tragic error, an error so inexplicable that I have come to suspect Negrín of direct complicity with Casado. Your relations with him abroad, your declarations regarding him, etc., must be *very guarded*."[32]

Even Enrique Líster, a party zealot, did not swallow Togliatti's treacherous accusation. "Togliatti's opinion was curious," he wrote. "He was the delegate in Spain of the Communist International, whom the entire politburo obeyed without a murmur." It was Togliatti, he said, who arranged for the departure by plane for Africa (Oran) in midmorning of 6 March of Dolores Ibárruri, Jesús Monzón (a Communist deputy), Stefanov, and Jean Cattelas, a French Communist deputy. "In other words, these persons left Spain about five hours before Negrín, who departed at 2:30 P.M." In her memoir, *El único camino*, La Pasionaria confirms that she left several hours before the entire government,[33] although the official history, volume four, written under her supervision and published ten years later, obscures this important detail. "Togliatti," Líster continues, "later organized the departure of the members of the politburo who remained [in Elda] . . . as well as the group of Communist officers who had arrived from France. What instructions was Togliatti fulfilling? Did the Casado uprising favor only Negrín's plans to abandon the fight, or did it also favor other plans to put an end to the war?"[34]

Togliatti's accusation that Negrín was in league with Casado was not sustained by the party. In 1971, Santiago Carrillo, then secretary of the PCE, while affirming that Negrín received the news of the Casado coup "with a certain relief," described the accusation as "too severe."[35] Even La Pasionaria, who echoed so many of Togliatti's criticisms of Negrín, rehabilitated the prime minister in 1977. "When the history of Spain, the true history, is written," she predicted, "the personality of Negrín will appear with all the vitality that it deserves from the point of view of what he did, what he attempted to do, and what he was able to accomplish."[36] It is not surprising that this rehabilitation came after the death of General Franco in 1975, when the PCE and Negrín's supporters seem to have believed that the time had come to find a national hero for the Civil War.

In spite of Togliatti's criticisms of Negrín, it is clear from his report of May 1939 that when he arrived at *posición Dakar* in the morning of 6 March, no one was in any mood to challenge the national council, least of all to continue the resistance policy: "The confusion was complete. Everyone was in a state of despair. Our liaisons with the rest of the country no longer existed."[37] After brief consultations with the party leaders, he advised them to make two proposals to Negrín, both of which the premier approved. The first was to send a message to Casado suggesting that the junta should appoint one or more persons to settle all differences in a "friendly and patriotic" way and that "any transfer of authority should take place in a normal and constitutional manner."[38] This proposal, Togliatti explains, was made "so that Negrín would remain and in order to gain a few hours."[39] "Without saying a word," recounts the official Communist history, "Negrín wrote out a few pages roughly expressing these ideas. Benigno Rodríguez, the prime minister's secretary, then took charge of the text and went to broadcast it. However, the radio station had already been dismantled as well as the teletypewriter. There was no alternative but to communicate the text by telephone from the military command in Elda to General Menéndez [commander of the Levante army] for retransmittal to Casado."[40] It is not known for sure what happened to the message, for Casado makes no reference to it in his chronicle of the events. On the other hand, Uribe states that Madrid refused "absolutely to have any dealings with [Negrín]."[41] The second proposal, which was designed to secure the vital escape routes, also came to nothing because the "fateful news" was soon received that Alicante, just thirty-seven kilometers southeast of Elda, had been taken by Casado's supporters.[42] The loss of Alicante, Togliatti commented, paralyzed "the entire action we had planned."[43]

But even as these two proposals were being made to Negrín, Togliatti had his next move in mind. "We decided to get Dolores out of Spain, because under existing circumstances we could not guarantee her life. Moreno [Stefanov] left with her. I didn't consider his presence useful, because he did not possess any of the qualities necessary for this type of situation. During the entire night he was unable to offer a single piece of advice to the leadership."[44]

The adversities of the PCE continued throughout the day. According to the official history, the government received word that Casado had ordered the arrest of Negrín, La Pasionaria, del Vayo, Uribe, Modesto, Líster, and all the members of the politburo. Even more threatening was the news that assault guards supporting Casado had begun to occupy the outskirts of Elda.[45]

Alvarez del Vayo recounts that he and Negrín waited until 2:30 P.M. for Casado's reply to Negrín's proposal for "a normal and constitutional" transfer of authority and that they were warned several times from the airfield that if the planes were delayed any longer they would fall into Casado's hands. When they arrived at Monóvar airfield it was already past 3 P.M. "This worried me, for I wanted at all costs to avoid the humiliating fate of being taken just at the point when we were about to make good our departure. . . . We were greeted by the justified, if restrained, indignation of our [cabinet] colleagues, who like ourselves had had nothing to eat, and who had, besides, been waiting for six hours in the blazing sun."[46]

According to the official history, Negrín told the Communists in Elda just before his departure with Vayo: " 'We cannot remain here a moment longer, because we shall be arrested. I believe we should all leave.' " Both shook hands emotionally with those present and left. "From then on, the circle around Elda began to tighten. . . . The military commander of Elda, a Communist, was arrested and replaced by an Anarchist."[47] Around 5 P.M., says Togliatti, news was received that air force chief of staff Lieutenant Colonel Luis Alonso Vega, a Communist, had allied himself with Casado. "Thus, Albacete, our principal point of support on the highway from Madrid, was lost."[48]

Before his flight from Spain, Negrín met with Colonel Stanislav A. Vaupshasov, the Soviet adviser to Domingo Ungría, the commander of the Fourteenth

Army Corps, whose elite guerrilla forces, it will be recalled, had been assigned to protect the government and the Communist leadership in Elda. Vaupshasov was accompanied by Brigadier Mikhail Stepanofich Shumilov, known as "Shilov," who had replaced Gregoriy M. Shtern, the chief Soviet military adviser. "While waiting for our turn to be evacuated," writes Vaupshasov, "[we] met with Negrín, the former premier of the Republic, in one of the farmhouses near the small town of Elda, and asked him to appropriate for our use two Douglas airplanes. Negrín replied with embarrassment that he no longer had any power and that all he could do was to thank us for our services. A lot of good that could do us! Nevertheless, the ex-premier wrote a letter of introduction to the commander of the air base near Albacete, Colonel [Manuel] Cascón, but we could not use his amiable letter, because there was not a single airplane on the base. While we were speaking, Negrín's adjutant reported that the rebels had taken Albacete and that it was necessary to hurry to the airfield at Monóvar, where a plane was waiting for the former premier. Negrín quickly shook hands with us and, almost running, proceeded to his car."[49] Despite Negrín's helplessness, Vaupshasov, Shumilov and other advisers and interpreters managed to leave Alicante for Oran, North Africa, in a French plane provided by Soviet representatives in Paris.[50]

Meanwhile, in Elda at about 10 P.M. (6 March), in one of the buildings of the Monóvar airfield, the politburo—with the other leaders of the party present—met under the chairmanship of Togliatti for the last time in Spain. It was decided that a small group would remain to organize clandestine work "in view of Franco's imminent victory," to evacuate those persons who were most in jeopardy and to set up a new leadership "of little-known comrades."[51]

"Everyone's morale was quite low," Togliatti reported to Moscow. "I asked Modesto and Líster if they thought it possible to regain control of the military situation. [Here, Togliatti appeared to be covering himself in case the two Communist military leaders should at some future date criticize him for not attempting to continue the fight.] Both replied that . . . without the support of the government the party could do nothing.[52] I nevertheless insisted that some of the comrades who were present should not leave. . . . The politburo then reconvened on its own and decided that Checa, Claudín, the secretary of the JSU, and I should remain."[53]

Air force chief Hidalgo de Cisneros, who had arranged for the flight of the government and the party leaders, recalls the drama of those final hours. "At midnight the first trucks sent by Casado began to arrive to capture us dead or alive. . . . The comrades decided to reconvene to make the final decisions. . . . It was already 3 A.M. [7 March] and it would be daylight at 4:30. If the planes did not leave by then, nothing could be done, for they could be put out of action with a few shots. My state of mind was contradictory. On the one hand, I was aware of the urgency and was angered by the sangfroid that I considered excessive and dangerous. On the other, I felt great admiration for those comrades who, realizing the danger, were doing their duty as Communists with the utmost responsibility. . . . There was now only one half hour left before dawn. . . . All accepted the decisions without the slightest protest: One group of comrades would leave for Toulouse. The other would try to break through the circle and scatter in different directions."[54]

Protected by the commandos, the planes took off and Togliatti, Checa, and Claudín managed to slip through the tightening circle of assault guards into Casado territory.[55] Not for thirty-eight years would the PCE again function legally in Spain.

Because of the breakdown of telephone and telegraph communications, writes the official history, the Madrid Communists "were unaware of the decisions and measures taken by the politburo in Elda and of the reaction of Negrín and his government. Nevertheless, they did not vacillate; they decided to defend themselves and to defend the government and the Republic with the means at their disposal."[56] In contrast, Togliatti's version is categoric about the directives given by the politburo: "[The Madrid Communists] did not hesitate for one moment to set to work to overthrow the Junta. *These were the instructions they had received from the politburo*."[57] There is no corroborative evidence that the Madrid Communists were given any precise instructions by the politburo on how to react if the anticipated rebellion by Casado should materialize. Nevertheless, they decided to fight the council, employing some of their military forces in Madrid to this end. On the third day of hostilities *Mundo Obrero* denied that the government had fled: "The Government of the Republic, headed by Dr. Negrín, is today at its post as it was during the critical days in Catalonia. Those who deny this are not telling the truth."[58] Fighting continued for several days,[59] ending only when two Anarchist divisions called in by Casado inflicted a humiliating defeat on the party. "The plan to crush the Junta by a very rapid action had failed," says Togliatti's oft-cited report to the Comintern of 29 May 1939. "This meant that we had been defeated."[60]

In a letter written on 10 March 1939 to the Spanish politburo based on information he received while in hiding in Albacete,[61] Togliatti stated: "[The comrades in Madrid] believed that the government was resisting in another part of the country. I don't yet know all the details, but it seems that after deciding to defend themselves by every possible means our comrades lacked decision. Their sense of responsibility, of course, prevented them from calling in reinforcements from the front. [They were also uncertain of their dependability, as will be seen shortly.] This gave the Junta time to bring into Madrid some Anarchist divisions from other fronts and to overpower us. The majority of our commanders conducted themselves well, but the men did not fight, because they did not understand the reason for the struggle against other republican soldiers. In contrast, Mera's men, accustomed to turning tail, fought with determination and spirit against us."[62]

In the same letter, Togliatti expressed the dilemma of the Madrid Communists and his own lack of faith in the reliability of the troops: "We believed that the most serious error that the party could commit would be to capitulate to its enemies by allowing itself to be decapitated, isolated, and declared illegal. On the other hand we dismissed the idea of a coup to overthrow the Junta and seize power for the following reasons. We could be successful only if we transferred several army corps from the front, in other words, if we opened the front to the enemy. This we would never do for obvious reasons. Moreover, *we were not sure that these forces would support us.*[63] A part of them would not respond as they would not understand the reason for the conflict. In short, we would lack the support of the masses who would also not understand the motive for the struggle. This means that we could hold the rear only by methods of terror: mass executions of the leaders of other parties, etc., etc., methods that are inadvisable in the present situation. To execute such a coup we would virtually be without *a single ally* and the responsibility for ending the war in the most bloody chaos imaginable would fall upon us."[64]

Togliatti reveals in his report to the Comintern of May 1939 the degree to which the military power of the Communists in Madrid had eroded and how little they could rely even on those officers who were members of the party: "The Communist professional officers, on whom the military action against Casado inevitably depended, did not respond. . . . [Emilio] Bueno (IInd Army Corps) refused to take command of the Madrid front. [Luis] Barceló (Ist Army Corps) did likewise. Both refused to give the party the necessary forces to crush Casado within a few hours. . . . [Antonio] Ortega (IIIrd Army Corps) not only failed to supply the necessary forces, but permitted the transit through his sector . . . of two Anarchist divisions from Estremadura. It was these divisions that crushed our comrades in Madrid. Ortega furthermore misled the party with erroneous information and remained all the time in contact with Casado. All three (Bueno, Barceló and Ortega) were masons."[65]

Because of this attempt to denigrate the three leading professional officers in Madrid, all of whom were members of the PCE, it is worth recording that Barceló never wavered in his loyalty to the party and paid for this loyalty with his life when arrested and executed on 13 March by the junta.[66] Colonel Bueno was arrested and imprisoned for many years in Francoist jails, while Colonel Ortega, who managed to escape to Alicante, was later arrested by Franco's forces and executed by the *garrote vil*.[67]

Overthrow of Negrín was only the initial goal of the Defense Council, its principal objective being to place the government in the hands of moderates and of professional military officers who would be in a position to negotiate peace with Franco on terms more lenient to the Republicans. Like all Republican governments since 1931, this represented a coalition of differing forces and points of view. Some of its members were willing to try to continue the war a little longer in order to obtain better terms, while others came to insist that peace must be made almost immediately, even if on Franco's conditions.

On 12 March, as the final resistance of Communist units in the Madrid district was being put down by the council's forces, its members met to draft a statement of the principles on which they would be willing to make peace. These included:

1. Direct negotiations with Franco's government

2. "National independence and integrity"

3. A guarantee of no reprisals and no prosecutions other than by regularly constituted civil courts

4. Freedom to leave Spain of all those in the Republican zone who so desired over a period of twenty-five days

5. Guarantee of the lives, liberty, and commission of regular army officers and of the lives and liberties of other military personnel and Republican functionaries, unless guilty of common civil crimes

6. Guarantee that no foreign troops (i.e., Italians and Moroccans) enter Republican territory after the surrender.[68]

This document rested on the fundamental error of the Defense Council from the beginning—the supposition that military officers and nonradicals would be acceptable to Franco in mutual negotiation of the terms of surrender.

Franco had always refused the slightest compromise or negotiation with the Republican authorities—even when proposed by the Vatican itself—during the months when the outcome of the Civil War lay completely in doubt. He had not the slightest intention of changing his position now that the remaining Republican forces were on the verge of collapse. He was well aware that morale had disappeared and that the People's Army was totally unprepared either militarily or psychologically to resist a major assault, which he was rapidly preparing.

As mentioned in the preceding chapter, since January, Casado had personally been in contact with Franco's military intelligence network (SIPM) in the Madrid area. This was operated by Colonel José Ungría, attached to Franco's own headquarters staff, and its Madrid command post and transmitter were set up in the small town of Torre de Esteban Hambrán, in Toledo not far from the capital. To encourage the anti-Communist revolt, a set of "Concessions of the Generalissimo," providing some minimal terms for surrender, had been signed by Franco on 6 February and quickly transmitted to Casado. These stated:

I. Nationalist Spain . . . will be generous to those who have not committed crimes but have been deceived into participating in the conflict.

II. Commanders and officers who voluntarily lay down their arms and are not guilty of the deaths of their comrades or of other crimes will be guaranteed their lives, and will enjoy greater benevolence the more important the service which they lend the cause of Spain in these final moments or the less their role or malice in the war.

III. Those who lay down their arms to prevent sterile sacrifice and are not guilty of murder or other major crimes will obtain a safeconduct to enable them to leave our territory, while enjoying full personal security.

IV. Protection and assistance will be given to Spaniards who rehabilitate their lives abroad.

V. Mere service in the Red forces or having been a member of political groups alien to the National Movement will not be a matter of criminal responsibility.

VI. Only courts of justice will have jurisdiction over crimes committed during the Red domination. Civil penalties will be lightened in favor of the families of those condemned.[69]

These vague, unreassuring terms were followed on 9 February by Franco's promulgation of a new Law of Political Responsibilities for all Spanish citizens, stipulating diverse categories of fines, imprisonment, and confiscation of goods for those judged guilty of political as distinct from civil crimes retroactive to 1 October 1934. Taken together, these measures could only further arouse the anxiety of members of the Defense Council, leaving them desperate to clarify Franco's "concessions" in the interest of more specific guarantees concerning freedom from prosecution and the right to emigrate, particularly with regard to professional officers. On 12 March the SIPM informed Franco's headquarters in Burgos that Casado and General Matallana, the Republican army central zone commander, wished to fly north immediately to negotiate terms, subsequently transmitting a document drawn up by the Defense Council that day. Franco replied tersely that he "required unconditional surrender and in the shortest possible time."[70]

On 14 March, Casado addressed the Republican zone by radio, assuring them that the council's goal was an honorable peace and then told a press conference of foreign and domestic reporters that in the event of a new Nationalist offensive the Republican army would resist until it had gained appropriate terms.[71] This public announcement infuriated Franco. When Casado repeated to SIPM agents on the following morning that he and Matallana were eager to fly to Burgos for negotiations, Franco responded categorically that "there is no other solution but unconditional surrender" and that they could not expect to "play politics at the expense of Nationalist Spain." He added that "with the attitude reflected in their statements, *they should send no one*" and "should be responsible for the consequences they have created in making them."[72]

During the next three days Franco's headquarters received reports of growing restlessness in Madrid, with the return of sporadic executions and appearances of corpses in public places.[73] At the same time, Casado indicated that firm measures were being taken to maintain order, and on the seventeenth dissolved the Republican military intelligence service (SIM) and eliminated the red star as Republican army emblem.[74] All the while Besteiro and other council members sought to place inquiries with friendly governments for assistance in evacuation procedures.[75]

After the virtual breakdown in communication on 15 March, Casado reiterated to SIPM agents two days later his concern to fly to Burgos,[76] and in a radio address of the eighteenth, Besteiro read a public declaration of the Defense Council to the Nationalist government urging "negotiations to assure an honorable peace" as soon as possible.[77] The response late that night from Burgos was that there was no point in Casado and Matallana coming to negotiate and that "to regulate the details of surrender it is sufficient for one professional commander with full powers to come."[78]

Still hoping to gain both time and some sort of guarantees, Casado prepared a message for Franco's headquarters on 20 March which began by recognizing categorically that "the war has been won by the Nationalist government" but warning that if the Defense Council was not able to negotiate an orderly surrender with rights of evacuation, new disorders might erupt in the Republican zone bringing reprisals against Nationalist sympathizers.[79] On the following day he proposed to the council that two medium-rank Republican staff officers, Lieutenant Colonel Antonio Garijo and Major Leopoldo Ortega, be dispatched to Burgos to meet Franco's representatives. He prepared a new statement of "themes to treat," which asked for little more than extension of the "concessions" to include "means of evacuation" from the Nationalist government. It also requested that foreign troops not be permitted to parade in Madrid and that the surrender be a carefully phased operation proceeding day by day through a series of geographical zones to assure order and security.[80] When asked to accept this mission on the basis of the "concessions" of 6 February, Franco quickly agreed to receive it on the morning of the twenty-third.[81] In the interim, however, Nationalist agents insisted on clarification of what the council meant by further discussion of the "concessions." To prevent any further breakdown, the new Republican government responded on 22 March that the "Council accepts the surrender without conditions generosity Caudillo [Franco] and urges Service [SIPM] to shorten time,"[82] thus largely abandoning the illusion that any real negotiation with Franco was possible. Even then the categorical nature of his requirements was, however, fully grasped.

While agents of the Defense Council desperately sought foreign shipping to assist in the immediate evacuation of political refugees, the two staff officers, Garijo and Ortega, arrived at Gamonal airport outside Burgos at 11 A.M. on the morning of 23 March to meet with Colonel Ungría of the SIPM and Colonel Luis Gonzalo, representing Franco's headquarters. The reports subsequently prepared by Garijo and Gonzalo for their superiors give somewhat differing accounts of the tenor and details of this meeting.[83] Both versions agree that Garijo pressed energetically for clarification of Franco's "concessions," most specifically as to whether point 5 referred to crimes as defined by the criminal code in effect on 18 July 1936. He also asked if such responsibility was to be defined in individual or collective terms and repeatedly stressed that the Defense Council had no interest in protecting those guilty of common crimes. The point defended most tenaciously by the Republican representatives was the need to obtain valid passports for those who wished to emigrate, a figure that Garijo placed optimistically at no more than four thousand to five thousand, but which other participants were inclined to double. Gonzalo reported that the Republicans were given some encouragement on these issues, after which he presented Franco's "Norms for the surrender of the enemy's army and occupation of its territory," which required that all planes in the Republican air force fly unarmed to be surrendered at Nationalist airports on 25 March, and then gave detailed instructions for surrender of the entire Republican army two days after that. Though Casado's proposal was accepted for transmission to Franco, the Republican plan for a phased surrender by zones that would take twenty-five days was rejected, even though the Defense Council's representatives stressed that an immediate surrender might lead to violent outbursts by leftist diehards in which more Nationalist sympathizers could be slain.

The council met in Madrid at 11 P.M. that same day and again at 6 P.M. on the twenty-fourth. Garijo reported in detail the verbal clarifications provided by Gonzalo and Ungría, but these remained uncertain and not formally binding, all the more since the council's request for a written agreement had been rejected. There was considerable resistance to immediate surrender of the air force, which Casado declared to be technically impossible of accomplishment in less than forty-eight hours, and much objection to Franco's refusal of any written guarantees.[84] Pressure was even more intense because of the failure of the council to gain much foreign assistance in evacuation, the French consul in Madrid having avoided any commitment by his government concerning evacuation facilities or the admission of refugees, and the British being only slightly more helpful.[85] In a desperate gesture, Casado dispatched a personal letter to Franco which Nationalist agents transmitted immediately. This missive asked for consideration of the council's position, for more time, and guaranteed evacuation but only prompted a refusal by radio from Franco's headquarters shortly before 10 P.M. on the twenty-fourth.[86]

Another frenzied meeting of members of the council took place early on the morning of 25 March. After heated disagreement, Casado prepared yet another proposal to Franco. This accepted surrender on the terms of the "concessions," but asked at least for a written document which would guarantee them, together with a pledge concerning evacuation. Though still hoping for some delay in the surrender, the council proposed to begin by handing over the air force three days later.[87] Its final proposal was carried by Garijo and Ortega to a second meeting at Gamonal airfield on the afternoon of the twenty-fifth.

According to Garijo, the reaction by the Nationalist liaison officers was more cordial than it had been two days earlier. The Republicans presented the council's newest document but had to respond evasively when pressed as to whether the Republican air force was about to begin its surrender immediately. Garijo urged that some sort of capitulation document be signed providing guarantees concerning legal responsibilities, if for no other reason than to placate the council's enemies in the Republican zone. The Nationalist representatives took note of the main points in the conversation and after further discussion agreed to allow the Republican officers to draw up a detailed memorandum concerning certain clarifications in the "concessions" that had earlier been defined. While they were in the process of doing so, the Nationalist officers conferred once more with their superiors and then menacingly informed Garijo and Ortega that the conversation was fruitless and that they must fly back to Madrid while there was still time.[88]

As soon as the Republican officers returned to Madrid, it became clear that the last hope of negotiation had ended and that Franco's final offensive would begin at any moment. In one last effort to stave it off, a radio dispatch was sent to Burgos at 2:40 A.M. on the morning of the twenty-sixth, declaring that the surrender of the Republican air force would take place later that day. It came too late.

Franco had been planning his final "Ofensiva de la Victoria" since mid-February and, given the disparity of forces, the issue was never in doubt. In planes alone the Nationalists outnumbered the Republicans at this point approximately five hundred to one hundred. The plan was for assaults at major points all along the remaining battleline, but the main thrust was aimed south of Madrid, to achieve a complete breakthrough, seal off the former capital, and then proceed to seal off Valencia to the east as well.

The offensive began at dawn on 26 March. For two months the final Republican plan had been based on the concept of a *repliegue escalonado* (phased retreat), in which the vastly outgunned and dispirited remnants of the People's Army would attempt to fall back in orderly fashion step by step through a series of four defensive zones, the last focusing on the Cartagena naval base in the southeast, final redoubt for mass evacuation. In fact, there was no more than sporadic opposition, as entire units often surrendered en masse. Republican officers, responsible for maintaining resistance, were in many cases apparently brought to surrender by a widely distributed Nationalist propaganda announcement, called "Concessions of the Generalissimo," which promised enemy officers that the more they did to bring resistance to an end the less likely they were to be prosecuted. By 27 March, thousands of troops on the Madrid front laid down their arms and walked away to the southeast, melting into the civilian population, in some cases riding the Madrid subway all the way across the city to disappear on the opposite side. Late on the twenty-seventh the Defense Council moved to Valencia, with the exception of the austere Besteiro, who refused to abandon Madrid, which was officially surrendered at 1 P.M. on the twenty-eighth.[89] At approximately the same time orders to cease fire and prepare to surrender were issued by the commanders of the principal Republican army corps. In the larger cities Falangists and other members of the Nationalist Fifth Column moved confidently into the open and began to take control of municipal services.

The roads east and southeast of Madrid were full of refugees seeking a way to leave the country, and on 28 March the Defense Council set up an official "Junta de Evacuación" in Valencia. Thus far it had enjoyed little success in gaining foreign assistance, save for the commitment of a few British ships. Only a handful of vessels were available to carry refugees from Republican ports on the twenty-eighth and twenty-ninth, though a small number of officers and other notables escaped in airplanes, sometimes commandeered by force, to seek asylum in French Algeria. By the evening of the twenty-ninth, Casado and the other council members had fled, the former aboard a British cruiser. A rumor meanwhile spread that only Alicante was remaining open as a port of evacuation, and by the morning of 30 March some twelve thousand refugees were massed near its docks, waiting for evacuation vessels that never arrived.

By 29 March resistance had effectively ceased and Nationalist units were moving rapidly through the former Republican zone. Tens of thousands of Republican soldiers were allowed to throw away their uniforms and return to their homes. The first units to reach Alicante, which instead of Cartagena had become the only thing approaching a Republican redoubt, were the Hispano-Italian forces commanded by the Italian General Gambara. Ironically, though the Defense Council had sought to avoid any foreign participation in the surrender process, Gambara was more lenient than Franco and recognized a temporary "neutral zone" around the Alicante docks, from which refugees would be allowed to leave freely provided that shipping arrived for them soon. As soon as word of this reached Burgos, Franco immediately canceled the order, directed Gambara to occupy the entire area as soon as possible, and hurried other Nationalist units to Alicante to guarantee that his command was fully carried out. By 31 March virtually the entire Republican zone was under Nationalist control.

On 1 April, General Franco issued his final communiqué: "Today the Nationalist troops, having captured and disarmed the Red army, have achieved their final military objective. The war has ended."[90] For Republicans, the years of external exile and internal repression were at hand. The Defense Council had had good reason to fear the effects of the retroactive Law of Political Responsibilities. Eight months after the fighting ended, and long after most ordinary rank-and-file Republican soldiers had been released, Spanish jails were bursting with 270,000 prisoners, most of them political detainees. During the next few years military courts would dictate approximately 50,000 death sentences, of which about half were actually carried out.[91] Both the Republic and the Revolution had been defeated, and the era of Franco had begun.

Notes

Chapter 1

1. See *Le contrat de travail dans la république espagnole*, 18.

2. *España*, 513. See also Edward E. Malefakis, *Agrarian Reform and Peasant Revolution in Spain*, 366–67; Antonio Ramos Oliveira, *Politics, Economics and Men of Modern Spain, 1808–1946*, 493; Richard A. H. Robinson, *The Origins of Franco's Spain*, 204–5.

3. *Discursos frente al parlamento*, 224.

4. "The socialist-controlled mixed juries [labor courts] caused trouble. The jury of Salamanca province permitted employment of UGT [socialist union] members only and forbade dismissals. Reapers were to be paid 12 pesetas for an eight-hour day, and since overtime was inevitable at harvest-time the daily wage rose to 19.65 pesetas, more than was earned by a skilled urban worker. With prices depressed, small holders simply could not pay these sums and joined the ranks of the unemployed laborers" (Robinson, 121). "The law of mixed juries," wrote the left Socialist politician and intellectual, Luis Araquistáin, "was aimed fundamentally at ending the system of starvation wages which had obtained for centuries in the country districts of Spain. When the Republic was inaugurated, wages of one-and-a-half and two pesetas were current for a day's work from sunrise to sunset, and that only for five or six months of the year. During the rest of the year unemployment was almost absolute. Even during the first year of the republican régime the average agricultural daily wage rose to five or six pesetas, and at harvest time to eight or ten pesetas, and even more in certain districts, thanks to the work contracts arranged by mixed juries" (*Foreign Affairs*, Apr. 1934).

5. For the three most complete works on the Popular Front, see Víctor Alba, *El frente popular*; Santos Juliá, *Orígenes del frente popular en España, 1934–1936*; and Javier Tusell, *Las elecciones del frente popular en España*; also Chapter 8 of this volume.

6. For the most complete study of the CEDA, its structure, its various components, its strength in the different regions, its ideology and its attitude toward labor and agrarian reform, see the monumental fifteen-hundred-page work of José R. Montero, *La CEDA*, I, II.

7. Statement made to *El Defensor*, Cuenca, as quoted in ibid., II, 206.

8. *El Debate*, 6 Mar. 1936.

9. "In the two and one-half months between 1 May and the outbreak of the civil war on 18 July, the Ministry of Labor recorded 192 agricultural strikes, as many as during the whole of 1932 and almost half as many as during that entire year of trouble, 1933. The scale of the strikes was considerably greater than it had been previously" (Malefakis, 371).

10. Editorials in *El Obrero de la Tierra* protesting against the procrastination of the government can be found in the issues of 28 Mar., 11, 25 Apr. 1936. For the best study of the crisis in the countryside during the months before the Civil War, see Malefakis, 364–87, 375–78. This magisterial work, which won the American Historical Association's Adams prize as the best book on any aspect of European history to be published in 1970, provides the most thorough study in any language of land tenure, agrarian reform, and peasant revolution in Spain in the years before the Civil War.

11. Speech, reprinted in José Díaz, *Tres años de lucha*, 162.

12. Malefakis, who, as stated in note 10, has made the most thorough study of the agrarian crisis before the war, considers the figure of ninety villages excessive (369, n. 17).

13. César Falcón in *La Correspondance Internationale*, 9 May 1936. See also Pedro Checa, ibid.; E. Varga, ibid., 4 June 1936; the Spanish refugee periodical, *El Socialista* (Algiers), 16 Oct. 1944; *Times*, 15 Apr. 1936 (Madrid correspondent); Gerald Brenan, *The Spanish Labyrinth*, 312; José María Capo, *España desnuda*, 87–89; Horsfall Carter in *Listener*, 29 Apr. 1936; José Plá, *Historia de la segunda republica española*, IV, 356–57; Ramos Oliveira, 539. The work by Capo acquires greater authority from the commendatory preface by Marcelino Domingo, minister of education in the government formed after the February 1936 elections.

14. Paul Nizon in the *International Press Correspondence*, 1 Aug. 1936. Although published in August, this article was written before the outbreak of the Civil War.

15. Malefakis, 373–74, 383, and n. 69. See also Salvador de Madariaga, *Spain*, 452–53; speech in the Cortes by José Maria Cid, the right-wing Agrarian party deputy, giving his version of the situation in the countryside, *Diario de las Sesiones de Cortes*, 1 July 1936, 1743–53; Ricardo de la Cierva, *Historia de la guerra civil española*, 697.

16. Within the limits of this brief account, it is impossible to do more than give a rough idea of the magnitude of the strike wave; even to enumerate all the strikes would require many pages. The general picture given here is based on reports in the following Spanish newspapers: *El Adelanto* (Salamanca), *La Batalla* (Barcelona), *Claridad* (Madrid), *El Día Gráfico* (Barcelona), *Diario de Burgos* (Burgos), *La Libertad* (Madrid), *Mundo Obrero* (Madrid), *El Noticiero* (Saragossa), *Política* (Madrid), *El Socialista* (Madrid), *El Sol* (Madrid), *Solidaridad Obrera* (Barcelona), *Unión* (Seville). According to Malefakis, 371, n. 31, from 1 May to 17 July 1936 there were 719 industrial strikes, more than in the whole of any previous year.

17. *Gaceta de Madrid*, 1 Mar. 1936.

18. See, for example, the manifesto signed by their various associations, *El Sol*, 1 Mar. 1936; also Joaquín Arrarás, *Historia de la segunda república española*, IV, 79–80; *Dictamen de la comisión sobre ilegitimidad de poderes actuantes en 18 de julio de 1936*, 54–55; Robinson, 269. The liberal historian Gabriel Jackson says: "Anarchist pistoleros occasionally forced employers to take on men who had never been their employees" (*The Spanish Republic and the Civil War, 1931–1939*, 213).

19. *Rio Tinto Company Limited: Report of the Transactions at the Sixty-Third Ordinary General Meeting*, 7.

20. *ABC* (Seville), 20 Jan. 1937.

21. For accounts of the stoppage, apart from the local press, and of the conflict between the Socialist and Anarchosyndicalist unions, see Arrarás, *Historia*, IV, 327–29; Pierre Broué and Emile Témime, *La révolution et la guerre d'Espagne*, 79–80; Juan Gómez Casas, *Historia del anarcosindicalismo español*, 200–202; Santos Juliá, *La izquierda del PSOE, 1935–1936*, 256–64; also Eduardo de Guzmán in *Triunfo*, 19 July 1976.

22. For information covering this period I am indebted to the following sources: Arrarás, *Historia*, IV, 441–67; Raymond Carr, *Spain, 1808–1939*, 626–36; José María Gil Robles, *No fué posible la paz*, 134–41; Jackson, 121–68; Alejandro Lerroux, *La pequeña historia*, 260–65; Madariaga, *Spain*, 421–43; Ramos Oliveira, 487–547; Robinson, 134–92; Hugh Thomas, *The Spanish Civil War* (1965 ed.), 112–24.

23. Robinson, 135.

24. Quoted in ibid., 140.

25. Ibid., 141–42.

26. For accounts of the October rebellion, see materials cited in n. 22; also Adrian Shubert, *Hacia la revolución*.

27. Clara Campoamor, *La révolution espagnole vue par une républicaine*, 71–72.

28. Jackson, *The Spanish Republic and the Civil War*, 167.

29. See, for example, speech on 11 Apr. 1936 by the secretary of the Communist party, demanding the imprisonment and execution of Lerroux and Gil Robles, as reprinted in Díaz, 162.

30. Cierva, *Historia de la guerra civil española*, 693–94; Stanley G. Payne, *Falange*, 99–100.

31. Payne, *Falange*, 100; Robinson, 387, n. 97.

32. Vicente Palacio Atard, essay in Vicente Palacio Atard et al., *Aproximación histórica a la guerra española, 1936–39*, 151; see also Stanley G. Payne, *Politics and the Military in Modern Spain*, 316.

33. In preparing this summary of events the newspapers mentioned in note 16, as well as the following materials, were consulted: Arrarás, *Historia*, IV, 66–67, 82–89, 114–15, 122–37, 186–89, 205–8, 228–30, 323–68, 371–73; Broué and Témime, 65–82; *Causa general: La dominación roja en España*, 13–24; Cierva, *Historia de la guerra civil española*, 692–740, 792–95; Díaz, 172–73; José Díaz de Villegas, *Guerra de liberación, 1936–39*, I, 420–57; Gil Robles, *No fué posible la paz*, 630–707, 748–58, 761–65; *Guerra y revolución en España, 1936–1939*, I, 92–93, 102–3; Jackson, *The Spanish Republic and the Civil War*, 196–232; Lerroux, *La pequeña historia*, 464–77; K. L. Maidanik, *Ispanskii proletariat v natsionalno-revoliutsionnoi voine, 1936–1937*, 64–66; Stanley G. Payne, *The Spanish Revolution*, 185–214; Plá, IV, 290–300, 311–23, 341–56, 375–83, 411–22; Indalecio Prieto, *Convulsiones de España*, I, 157–62, III, 133–34, 144; Ramos Oliveira, 539–41, 546–47; Robinson, 274–75, 392–93, n. 149; Carlos Seco Serrano, *Historia de España*, VI, 128–45; Thomas (1965 ed.), 136–54, 170–77.

34. *The Politics of Modern Spain*, 168.

35. José Martín Blázquez, *I Helped to Build an Army*, 67.

36. "Peasants, Politics, and Civil War in Spain, 1931–1939," in Robert J. Bezucha, ed., *Modern European Social History*, 192–227.

37. Felipe Bertrán Güell, *Preparación y desarrollo del alzamiento nacional*, 116; see also Cierva, *Historia de la guerra civil española*, 763–64. The official history of the rising, Joaquín Arrarás, ed., *Historia de la cruzada española*, II, 467, reveals that a meeting of generals was held early in March "to prepare a defensive action should a situation of very grave danger for the country arise as was feared by the course of events." See also Arrarás, *Historia*, IV, 94–95; Manuel Goded (son of General Goded, leader of the revolt in Barcelona), *Un "faccioso" cien por cien*, 26.

38. Bertrán Güell, *Preparación*, 99–100.

39. Reported in the *Manchester Guardian*, 4 Dec. 1937. See also reproduction of documents in the handwriting of Goicoechea, recording his interview with Mussolini on 31 March 1934, in *How Mussolini Provoked the Spanish Civil War*, 6–9.

40. *Memorias de la conspiración, 1931–1936*, 34–41. A documented account of this meeting with the Italian government can be found in John F. Coverdale's excellent work, *Italian Intervention in the Spanish Civil War*, 50–54.

41. Lizarza, 40.

42. Essay in Palacio Atard, *Aproximación*, 73.

43. Lizarza, 40–41.

44. Julio Romano, *Sanjurjo*, 188. For other conspiracies before and after the elections, see Cierva, *Historia de la guerra civil española*, 763–64. Because of his prestige and seniority, Sanjurjo was leader-designate of the military rebellion in July 1936, but was killed in a plane crash at the outbreak of the war when flying to Spain from Portugal, where he had been in exile. Leadership of the revolt was subsequently taken over by General Francisco Franco who, by decree of 29 September 1936, was named generalissimo of all the armed forces and head of state by the rebel Junta de Defensa Nacional set up in Burgos at the outbreak of the Civil War.

45. Quoted in Cierva, *Historia de la guerra civil española*, 740.

46. José Gutiérrez-Ravé, chief press officer of Renovación Española, wrote some years later: "On Monday, the 17th, a few hours after the elections, outrages begin in the streets of Madrid and in the provinces provoked by 'popular jubilation.' . . . Terrified, many governors hand over their posts to the revolutionary committees while the mobs of the Popular Front take possession of local councils" (*Las cortes errantes del Frente Popular*, 29).

47. Gil Robles, *No fué posible la paz*, 492–93.

48. Arrarás, *Historia de la cruzada*, II (Tomo 9), 441.

49. For information on the crisis, see Arrarás, *Historia*, IV, 50–51, 56–61; Manuel Azaña, *Obras completas*, IV, 563–64, 718–19; Cierva, *Historia de la guerra civil española*, 639–41; Estado Mayor Central del Ejército, *Historia de la guerra de liberación, 1936–39*, 420–22; Maximiano García Venero, *El general Fanjul*, 219–23; *Guerra y revolución*, I, 81–82; Payne, *Politics*, 310–13; Indalecio Prieto, *De mi vida*, 300; Robinson, 250–51, 384–85; Fernando de Valdesoto, *Francisco Franco*, 98–99. For a stinging criticism of Portela by Alejandro Lerroux, former premier and leader of the Radical party for leaving the power "in the middle of the street," see *La Pequeña historia*, 447–49. In a guarded account of his own somewhat equivocal role during the crisis, the president of the Republic acknowledges that he advised Portela "for the time being not to institute martial law," urging

"prudence and calm," and attacks him for fleeing his responsibilities, portraying him as a man stricken with fear and panic (*Memorias*, 346–48). In an interview given at a much later date to Lawrence Fernsworth of the London *Times*, Portela offers a more heroic version: "I was first of all a Spaniard, and my duty was to see that the interests of Spain were safeguarded. I felt they could best be served now by my immediate resignation and my delivering the power into the hands of the newly elected leaders of the Left, who could then carry on in accordance with the popular will" (Lawrence A. Fernsworth, *Spain's Struggle for Freedom*, 182–84).

50. Speech, 23 Feb. 1936, as reprinted in Díaz, 151.

51. Lizarza, 95–106; General Carlos Martínez de Campos, *Ayer: 1931–1953*, 41. See also Martin Blinkorn, *Carlism and Crisis in Spain*, 243–50; Cierva, *Historia de la guerra civil española*, 767. For the directives issued by Mola to the conspirators, see ibid., 769–85. Martínez, who was chief of the Central General Staff (1939–41) under General Franco, writes: "The posting of Brigadier General Emilio Mola to Pamplona was a critical error of the Cabinet or was inspired by those persons who foresaw the possibility of his working with the Carlists. The matter is not clear. The only thing that is evident is that Mola assumed command of the military forces in Navarre with adequate time to establish himself comfortably and to negotiate secretly with the principal traditionalist leaders" (Martínez de Campos, 41).

52. Ramos Oliveira, 544–45; Payne, *Politics*, 314.

53. *Politics*, 314–15. See also Cierva, *Historia de la guerra civil española*, 757–58.

54. Essay in *Aproximación*, 152–54.

55. *El Sol*, 19 Mar. 1936.

56. 19 Mar. 1936, "Para la Seguridad del Régimen."

57. Because of the peculiarities of the electoral system, which favored large coalitions, the Popular Front won 258 seats in the Cortes, the center 62, and the right 152, although the number of votes cast was as follows: Popular Front, 4,206,156; center, 681,047; right, 3,783,601 (figures given by Madariaga, *Spain*, 445). While the figures given by various other sources differ, they nonetheless reveal that the popular vote was fairly equally divided between the Popular Front and the center-right. See, for example, Arrarás, *Historia*, IV, 75–76; Jackson, 193–94; Payne, *Politics*, 311; Robinson, 248; Manuel Tuñón de Lara, *La crisis del estado: Dictadura, república, guerra, 1923–1939*, 214–15, and Gil Robles who comments on the figures given by a number of foreign historians, *No fué posible la paz*, 525–26. For the most careful analysis of the election results province by province, see Javier Tussell, *Las elecciones del frente popular en España*, II, 308–41. His total figures differ from those given by several prominent historians (13–15), but reinforce the conclusion that the parties of the right and center received at least half the votes as do the figures given by Ramón Salas Larrazábal, *Los datos exactos de la guerra civil*, 40–51, 256–57. See also Tussell in *Historia 16*, Feb. 1977; Víctor Alba (a supporter of the left), who gives a slight edge to the center-right, *El frente popular*, 391–97; and *El Sol*, 3 March 1936.

58. *La Libertad*, 16 Jan. 1936.

59. *Gaceta de Madrid*, 25 Apr. 1934.

60. Ibid., 24 Mar. 1935.

61. *Política del frente popular en agricultura*, 14. See also *Claridad*, 5, 26 Oct. 1935; *Democracia*, 22 Nov. 1935; *La reforma agraria en España*, 40–41; Robinson, 202–3.

62. *España*, 512. See also E. Allison Peers, *The Spanish Tragedy*, 145–46; Robinson, 161.

63. Robinson, 266–67. For Communist attacks on the church, demanding the end of subsidies and the expropriation of its wealth, see Díaz, 155, 163, 177, 191–92, 216.

64. Robinson, 266–67. See also Arrarás, *Historia*, IV, 224–26. After the outbreak of the Civil War, Barnés published a decree directing local authorities to take possession, in the name of the state, of all religious schools (*Gaceta de Madrid*, 28 July 1936).

65. For examples of this hostility, see Cierva, *Historia de la guerra civil española*, 758–59.

66. For a balanced account of these grievances by a liberal Republican officer, see Colonel Jesús Pérez Salas, *Guerra en España, 1936–1939*, 22, 47–53, 85. For a varied assortment of views on Azaña's military reforms, see Michael Alpert, *La reforma militar de Azaña, 1931–1933*; Eduardo Espín in *Revista del Occidente*, Nov. 1981, 39–57; Jackson, *The Spanish Republic*, 66–88, 171; Emilio Mola, *Obras completas*, 1048–1101; Stanley G. Payne, *Politics*, 266–76, 281, 284–85, 294, 300–304; Ernesto Portuondo, *La segunda república*, 27–36; Jorge Vigón Suerodíaz, *Milicia y política*, 287–96.

67. Speech in the Cortes, *Diario de las Sesiones de Cortes*, 3 Apr. 1936, 222.

68. José Manuel Liébana and G. Orizana, *El movimiento nacional*, 5.

69. Interview reported in *La Libertad*, 21 Feb. 1936.

70. *Diario de las Sesiones de Cortes*, 3 Apr. 1936, 223–24.

71. Ibid., 15 Apr. 1936, 288–89.

72. *Anecdotario*, 190.

73. *Politics*, 318.

74. *Diario de las Sesiones de Cortes*, 15 Apr. 1936, 293, 297. An excellent account of Calvo Sotelo's policies is given in Robinson, to whose book I am indebted for bringing to my attention Calvo Sotelo's speech from which the above excerpts have been taken.

75. Robinson, 270–71, 394, n. 168.

76. Gil Robles, *No fué posible la paz*, 573–74, 623, n. 63. "Little by little," writes Cierva, "Gil Robles began to lose control of his most aggressive militants, who abandoned the ranks of the CEDA *en masse* to join Falange Española or the National Front [comprising the Alphonsine and Carlist monarchists]" (*Historia de la guerra civil española*, 741).

77. See Robinson, 169, 173, 206, 208–12, 214, 244–45. I am greatly indebted to this superb chronological and analytical study of Gil Robles's policies during the 1933–36 period.

78. *Historia de la guerra civil española*, 740.

79. Robinson, 194, 226. In his memoirs, Gil Robles states that he turned down all suggestions by friends and collaborators that the CEDA should abandon its legal tactic (*No fué posible la paz*, 574).

80. José María de Fontana, *Los catalanes en la guerra de España*, 43. See also Gil Robles, *No fué posible la paz*, 623, n. 63, in which he mentions that the youth movement of the Derecha Regional Valenciana, one of the parties belonging to the CEDA, "agreed enthusiastically . . . to give their resolute support to those who were preparing the rising."

81. Cierva, *Historia de la guerra civil española*, 743–44.

82. *Diario de las Sesiones de Cortes*, 15 Apr. 1936, 300.

83. *No fué posible la paz*, 688, n. 25.

84. *Diario de las Sesiones de Cortes*, 19 May 1936, 696–97.

85. Quoted in Gil Robles, *No fué posible la paz*, 684.

86. *Historia de la guerra civil española*, 787.

87. Essay in Raymond Carr, *The Republic and the Civil War in Spain*, 190. On the other hand, it should be pointed out that Javier Jiménez Campo, in his published doctoral thesis, *El fascismo en la crisis de la II República*, 318, while recognizing that from February 1936 the Falange "had initiated a new penetration of the army," claims that "the presence of military men among the membership . . . remained minimal."

88. *No fué posible la paz*, 684–85.

89. Gil Robles, *No fué posible la paz*, 686, n. 23.

90. Ibid., 607, 787–89, 794, 797–99.

91. Ibid., 730.

92. Ibid., 798, n. 50. For further information on the transfer of 500,000 pesetas to General Mola, see Arrarás, *Historia de la cruzada*, III, 456–57; Arrarás, *Historia*, III, 317; Félix Maíz, *Mola aquel hombre*, 230–35.

93. Quoted by Marqués de Luca de Tena, *ABC* (Madrid), 1 May 1968; see also Cierva, *Historia de la guerra civil española*, 742–43.

94. Cierva, *Historia de la guerra civil española*, 741; see also Gil Robles, *No fué posible la paz*, 789.

95. Gil Robles, *No fué posible la paz*, 788.

96. Ibid., 789.

97. Agustín Calvet's political sympathies for Azaña are mentioned by Arrarás, *Historia*, IV, 325, who quotes from this article, and were confirmed to me by Pedro Voltes Bou, the director of the Instituto Municipal de Historia de Barcelona, to whom I am indebted for a reproduction of the entire article.

Chapter 2

1. The belief of the leaders of the rebellion that after declaring martial law everything would be plain sailing is confirmed by Juan Antonio Ansaldo, who helped in the preparation of the insurrection (¿Para que . . . ?, 120). "Some of the leading officers responsible for the July rising," affirms Ricardo de la Cierva, "were fearful, even before the event, of the possibility of a long and bloody war, but the great majority hoped that victory would follow their coup almost immediately" ("The Nationalist Army in the Spanish Civil War," essay in Raymond Carr, The Republic and the Civil War in Spain, 190).

2. Speech reported in Solidaridad Obrera (Barcelona), 22 Dec. 1936.

3. Ibid., 17 Jan. 1936.

4. Ibid., 2 Apr. 1936.

5. In his diary, on 4 Jan. 1933, Azaña, premier at the time, describes Casares Quiroga, who was interior minister as "this good friend who is the best I have in the government" (Joaquín Arrarás, Memorias íntimas de Azaña, 109). Julián Zugazagoitia, the moderate Socialist leader, director of El Socialista at the time, says that Azaña felt it necessary to entrust the formation of his first cabinet to Casares Quiroga who was linked "to his policy and to his person by a devotion, which it is not exaggerated to say bordered on idolatry" (Historia de la guerra en España, 3–4).

6. La Libertad, 16 Jan. 1936. In the matter of agriculture, the program promised reduction of rents and taxes, suppression of usury, increase of agricultural credits, revaluation of agricultural produce, stimulation of exports, irrigation and afforestation, settlement of families on the land, and the repeal of the law of leases and the law providing for the return of their estates to landowners implicated in the Sanjurjo rising.

7. See his speeches, reported in El Socialista (Madrid), 2 May 1936; La Libertad, 26 May 1936; also quotations from Prieto in Joaquín Arrarás, Historia de la segunda república española, 205–7.

8. Historia de la guerra en España, 4–5; see also Gabriel Morón, Política de ayer y política de mañana, 25.

9. Largo Caballero signed the document on behalf of the UGT, while Juan-Simeón Vidarte and Manuel Cordero signed on behalf of the Socialist party (La Libertad, 16 Jan. 1936).

10. El Socialista, 14 Jan. 1936.

11. Edward E. Malefakis, Agrarian Reform and Peasant Revolution in Spain, 254–55.

12. Ibid., 393. "[The] Popular Front government was essentially bourgeois and its reforms tended to respect private property. This delayed the Agrarian Reform and the distribution of land, forcing the peasants to occupy the estates in order to satisfy their need for land and work" (Manuel Requeña Gallego, Los sucesos de Yeste, 126).

13. Pp. 273–74.

14. For a critical account of the attempt to "Bolshevize" the Socialist movement and for the intraparty struggle among the three factions, headed by Julián Besteiro (right-wing), Indalecio Prieto (center), and Francisco Largo Caballero (left-wing), see Gabriel Mario de Coco, Anti-Caballero: Crítica marxista de bolchevizacíon del partido socialista, 1930–1936. See also Arrarás, Historia, IV, 139–41, 249–66; Richard A. H. Robinson, The Origins of Franco's Spain, 260–61, 271–72.

15. See Marta Bizcarrondo, Octubre del 34: Reflexiones sobre una revolución, who reproduces the pamphlet on pp. 83–156. On p. 50, she states that the first edition was signed by Carlos Hernández Zancajo, as president of the Socialist youth federation, and that the second, enlarged edition included the signature of its secretary, Santiago Carrillo. "But," she adds, "it does not appear that those who signed officially were the real authors. Apparently, the writing was entrusted to Santiago Carrillo and Amaro del Rosal, who were in the Model Prison in Madrid." In a footnote, she adds that, according to Rosal, thirty-six of the pamphlet's ninety-eight pages were written by him.

16. Ibid., 156.

17. See, for example, Amaro del Rosal (a supporter of Largo Caballero at the time), Historia de la UGT de España, 1901–1939, II, 609; also Fernando Claudín, La crisis del movimiento comunista, 173. Before the Civil War, Claudín was a member of the Communist youth, which merged with the Socialist youth organization in April 1936 to form the JSU, the United Socialist Youth Federation. He was a member of the latter's executive committee. In 1937, he became a member of the central committee of the Communist party and a member of the politburo in 1947. He was expelled from the party in 1964.

18. See, for example, Julián Gorkin, *Caníbales políticos*, 62; Salvador de Madariaga, *España*, 547; Federica Montseny and Indalecio Prieto in *Francisco Largo Caballero, 1869–1946*, 71, 138; Rosal, *Historia*, II, 524–609; Andrés Saborit in *Adelante*, Marseilles, 3 May 1946; Zugazagoitia, *Historia*, 208.

19. H. Edward Knoblaugh, *Correspondent in Spain*, 17. Knoblaugh was Associated Press representative in Madrid and took the precaution of submitting his cable to Largo Caballero, who "heartily approved it." That Caballero's statement was fully in keeping with his attitude at the time was confirmed to me by one of his former supporters, the Socialist deputy for Orense, Galicia, Alfonso Quintana de la Pena, who claimed, when interviewed by me in 1963, that he "distanced himself" from Largo "for allowing himself, without protest, to be called the Spanish Lenin." Nevertheless, in his unpublished memoirs, Largo Caballero affirms that he "emphatically rejected" the label and describes it as an effort by the Communists to "capture" him ("Notas Históricas sobre la Guerra de España," 264–65). The evidence, however, suggests that Luis Araquistáin, Largo Caballero's influential political adviser, had more to do with creating the myth of the "Spanish Lenin" than the Communists (see, for example, his prologue to Francisco Largo Caballero, *Discursos a los trabajadores*, dated 2 March 1934, where in the final paragraph [xv] he draws a parallel between the historic role of Lenin before the October Revolution of 1917 and that of Largo Caballero in 1934). According to Andrés Saborit, the right-wing Socialist, the myth originated in this prologue (letter to me, Hoover Institution).

20. *Claridad*, 19 Mar. 1936.

21. See, for example, speech in Oviedo, *La Libertad*, 16 June 1936.

22. Speech on 3 Aug. 1933, as given in Andrés Saborit, *Julián Besteiro*, 336. His position had not changed in 1936. See, for example, José María Gil Robles, *No fué posible la paz*, 657; Salvador de Madariaga, *Spain*, 697, who stated in a letter to the *Times*, London, in July 1939, that Besteiro—who had just been given a thirty-year prison sentence by the victorious Franco regime—"was a consistent opponent of violent methods of opposition throughout the Republican days, and in the councils of the Socialist party he stood courageously against the hotheads who have brought the country to the present plight."

23. For well-documented biographies of Besteiro, see Saborit, *Julián Besteiro* and *El pensamiento político de Julián Besteiro* (Prólogo de Emiliano M. Aguilera); also Ignacio Arenillas de Claves, *El proceso de Besteiro*; Carlos Díaz, *Besteiro: El socialismo en libertad* and E. Lamo de Espinosa, *Filosofía y política en Julián Besteiro*. His early parliamentary speeches have been assembled by Fermín Solana in *Historia parlamentaria del socialismo: Julián Besteiro*, I, II.

24. Interview given to Mikhail Koltzov (*Pravda*'s special correspondent) on 26 Aug. 1936, as published in *Novyi Mir*, Apr. 1938, 40. The interview was part of Koltzov's diary, which *Novyi Mir* serialized between April and September 1938 under the title "Ispanskii Dnevnik" (Spanish Diary). It was published in book form in 1957, fifteen years after his liquidation by Stalin, as Volume 3 of *Izbrannye proizvedeniia* (Selected Works) and translated into Spanish by Ruedo Ibérico, Paris, in 1963, under the title *Diario de la guerra de España*. The diary is hereafter referred to as Koltzov, "Ispanskii Dnevnik," *Novyi Mir*. In the diary, Koltzov frequently refers to a Mexican Communist, Miguel Martínez. This is undoubtedly a pseudonym for the author.

25. Pp. 145, 153.

26. See, for example, Zugazagoitia, 4; Indalecio Prieto, *Convulsiones de España*, III, 158–59, 164; *Claridad*'s version of the incident (31 May 1936), as given in Fernando Díaz-Plaja, *La historia de España en sus documentos. El siglo XX. Dictadura . . . República 1923–36*, 870–72.

27. *Spain*, 455–457. This was also the view expressed to me after the war by some Socialists. In the opinion of Alfonso Quintana y Pena (interview, 1963), "There would have been no possibility of a military uprising had the Socialist party maintained its unity."

28. See speech by Wenceslao Carrillo (a Largo Caballero Socialist), *La Correspondencia de Valencia*, 4 Sept. 1937.

29. *Claridad*, 19 Mar. 1936; *La Libertad*, 4 Apr. 1936.

30. José Díaz, *Tres años de lucha*, 165, 190, 194, 206.

31. *The Spanish Revolution*, 166–67. See also Largo Caballero's letter to José Bullejos, 20 Nov. 1939, as given in Largo Caballero, *¿Qué se puede hacer?*, 20–24.

32. See, for example, interview reported in *Claridad*, 7 Dec. 1935; speech, ibid., 11 Apr. 1936.

33. See article by José Díaz, general secretary of the Communist party, in *Correspondencia Internacional*, 17 Apr. 1936, as reprinted in Díaz, *Tres años*, 133–39.

34. Ibid.

35. Speech on 11 Apr. 1926, as reprinted in Díaz, 165.

36. Speech in Cortes, *Diario de las Sesiones de Cortes*, 15 Apr. 1936, 311.

37. Article in *Correspondencia Internacional*, 17 Apr. 1936, as reprinted in Díaz, *Tres años*, 133–39.

38. Manuel, 164.

39. Koltzov, "Ispanskii Dnevnik," *Novyi Mir*, Apr. 1938, 42.

40. José Duque, who became a member of the central committee of the PCE in 1937, confirmed to me in 1945 that in the months before the Civil War leading Communists were secretly hostile to Largo Caballero's policy.

41. See José Bullejos (a former secretary of the PCE), *Europa entre dos guerras, 1918–1938*, 191–92.

42. *International Press Correspondence*, 9 May 1936.

43. *Claridad*, 9 Apr. 1936.

44. *El Socialista*, 3 July 1936.

45. Ibid., 2 July 1936.

46. Article in *Correspondencia Internacional*, 17 Apr. 1936, reprinted in Díaz, *Tres años*, 133–39.

47. *El Mercantil Valenciano*, 16 May 1936.

48. Eduardo Ortega Gasset, quoted in Gil Robles, *No fué posible la paz*, 450.

49. Zugazagoitia, 275.

50. Niceto Alcalá-Zamora, *Memorias*, 360–73, and article in *Journal de Genève* reproduced in *Spanish Liberals Speak out on the Counter-Revolution in Spain*, 11–13; Arrarás, *Historia*, IV, 103–8, 175–78; Joaquín Arrarás, *Historia de la cruzada española*, II, 477, 488; Gil Robles, *No fué posible la paz*, 585, 592–96; Largo Caballero, *Mis recuerdos*, 155; Alejandro Lerroux, *La pequeña historia*, 462; Joaquín Maurín, *Revolución y contrarrevolución en España* (epilogue, 1965), 237–38; Prieto's speech in the Cortes, *Diario de las Sesiones de Cortes*, 7 Apr. 1936, 242–50.

51. See Morón, 60–63.

52. See, for example, Gil Robles, *No fué posible la paz*, 450; Miguel Maura, *Así cayó Alfonso XIII*, 58, 153, 216–22.

53. *El Socialista*, 2 May 1936. For further information on Prieto, see biography by Alfonso Carlos Saíz Valdivielso, *Indalecio Prieto: Crónica de un corazón*.

54. As given in Arrarás, *Historia*, IV, 157.

55. José Plá, *Historia de la segunda república española*, IV, 384.

56. Maura, 222.

57. See statement issued by the executive, *El Socialista*, 8 May 1936.

58. According to Diego Martínez Barrio, the speaker of the Cortes, sixty deputies supported Largo Caballero and forty Indalecio Prieto (*Memorias*, 303).

59. *Palabras al viento*, 279.

60. Speech in Mexico City, 21 Apr. 1940, as published in Indalecio Prieto, *Inauguración del círculo "Pablo Iglesias" de México*, 19–20. See also his statement in *El Mercantil Valenciano*, 16 May 1936.

61. *La izquierda del PSOE, 1935–1936*, 108–9.

62. *Obras completas*, Introduction, III, xxi–xxii.

63. *Yo fui ministro de Negrín*, 112.

64. *Mis recuerdos*, 155.

65. Article by Araquistáin in *Leviatán*, Mar. 1936, as given in *Leviatán: Antología*, 317. Araquistáin's optimism regarding the success of a Socialist revolution in Spain is summarized by Santos Juliá: "He believed that the European powers were so preoccupied with their own internal problems that they would not have time to devote the slightest attention to Spain. The Spaniards would be able to devote themselves with complete liberty to their own problems and carry out the socialist revolution 'without my being unduly concerned about the counterrevolutionary dangers from abroad.' This inevitable revolution would be safe, because in the worst case the USSR would not stand idly by if the European states were to intervene against a socialist Spain" (*La izquierda del PSOE, 1935–1936*, 167).

66. Speech on 24 Jan. 1947, as given in Saborit, *Julián Besteiro*, 364.

67. *No fué posible la paz*, 617–19. See also Arrarás, *Historia*, IV, 274–76; Robinson, 263–64, 391, n. 137.

68. *Diario de las Sesiones de Cortes*, 19 May 1936, 1690–94.

69. See, for example, General Núñez de Prado, as quoted by Diego Martínez Barrio in *Hoy*, 13 Apr. 1940; Major Aberri, ibid., 29 July 1939; Dolores Ibárruri (La Pasionaria), *El único camino*, 238, 252, 268; Largo Caballero, *Mis recuerdos*, 162–63, and *Escritos de la república*, 304–5; Prieto, *Convulsiones*, III, 143–44, and *Palabras al viento*, 279–81; Zugazagoitia, 41.

70. Zugazagoitia, 23.

71. *El Sol* published six articles by Maura between 18 and 27 June.

Chapter 3

1. Vicente Palacio Atard, essay in Palacio Atard, *Aproximación histórica a la guerra española, 1936–1939*, 152; Ricardo de la Cierva, *Historia de la guerra civil española*, 807; José María Gil Robles, *No fué posible la paz*, 743–44.

2. *Palabras al viento*, 279. The radical Marxist politician, Joaquín Maurín, reviewing the political panorama many years later, comments: "The prime minister, Casares Quiroga, whom Azaña appointed, was a nonentity; and the minister of the interior, Juan Moles, whom he selected, was a supernonentity. The military were able to continue calmly their preparations for the rebellion which led to the Civil War and the fall of the Republic" (*España Libre* [New York], Sept.–Oct. 1971). For the futile efforts by Ignacio Hidalgo de Cisneros, Casares Quiroga's aide de camp, to impress upon the prime minister and President Azaña the imminent danger of a military uprising and the need to take effective measures, see Constancia de la Mora (wife of Hidalgo de Cisneros), *In Place of Splendor*, 222, 229–32. On one occasion Casares responded: "Don't be an alarmist, Cisneros. I have everything under control. We have taken all the necessary measures to meet any attempt at an uprising. You'll see. Let them rebel, let them rebel! And the sooner the better!" (ibid., 233). Casares's attitude is recorded by Indalecio Prieto, who also warned him of the danger. "I noted the anger my warnings provoked, but I felt obliged to put up with it. But one afternoon I put an end to it, when . . . the prime minister, unable to contain his annoyance, replied sharply: 'Stop bothering me. What you imagine is only the product of your menopause.' I didn't visit him again until 17 July, when the rebellion had already started in Morocco" (*Convulsiones de España*, I, 163).

3. Essay in Palacio Atard, *Aproximación*, 163–64. See also Cierva, *Historia de la guerra civil española*, 765, 807. As Verle B. Johnston observes, "In several cases assuming command necessitated the removal of superior officers of strong republican sympathies. This is one facet of the rebellion which has not always been appreciated by students of the Civil War" (*Legions of Babel*, 20). Richard A. H. Robinson, *The Origins of Franco's Spain*, 376, n. 3, makes the following important point: "Conspirators were, in the main, *africanistas* removed from active commands in late February 1936; they had in most cases to get rid of Azañista garrison-commanders before 'pronouncing' against the government."

4. Azaña, *Obras completas*, Introduction, III, xxxii.

5. Julián Zugazagoitia, *Historia de la guerra en España*, 5–6.

6. José María Gil Robles, *No fué posible la paz*, 608.

7. Robinson, 288.

8. José Díaz, *Tres años de lucha* (speech, 1 June 1936); 199–200 (article in *Mundo Obrero*, June 1936).

9. Stanley G. Payne, *Politics and the Military in Modern Spain*, 330–31.

10. Reproduced in Manuel Aznar, *Historia militar de la guerra de España*, 31–32.

11. Ibid., 30. On the other hand, Guillermo Cabanellas, the son of General Miguel Cabanellas, one of the conspirators, says: "That letter of loyalty to the government gives the impression that its author was sitting on the fence before deciding on which side it suited him to descend" (*Cuatro generales: Preludio a la guerra civil*, I, 439–40). And elsewhere he defines Franco's ambiguous position in the years before the war as opportunistic (ibid., 446, n. 49).

12. Cierva, *Historia de la guerra civil española*, 785, 803; Payne, *Politics*, 334–35; Robinson, 288.

13. Payne, *Politics*, 332; Robinson, 288, 405, n. 274.

14. Robinson, 287–88. See also Guillermo Cabanellas, n. 11 above.

15. As given in Cierva, *Historia de la guerra civil española*, 785. For the negative attitude of some officers toward the idea of a coup against the government, see ibid., 787; Palacio Atard, essay in Palacio Atard, *Aproximación*, 160–61, quoting General Queipo de Llano; Gil Robles, *No fué posible la paz*, 716–17; Antonio Olmedo Delgado and Lieutenant General José Cuesta Monereo, *General Queipo de Llano*, 85.

16. Pp. 735–816.

17. Ibid., 736–37.

18. Ibid., 437, n. 1. For other accounts of the conspiratorial activities of military leaders and their disagreements, see essay by Cierva in Palacio Atard, *Aproximación*, 72–79; Joaquín Arrarás, *Historia de la segunda república española*, IV, 295–322, 391–402; Jaime del Burgo, *Conspiración y guerra civil*, 521–52; Maximiano García Venero, *El General Fanjul*, 215–83; Gil Robles, *No fué posible la paz*, 709–87; *Guerra y revolución en España, 1936–1939*, I, 96–102; Antonio de Lizarza Iribarren, *Memorias de la conspiración, 1931–1936*, 61–142; Payne, *Politics*, 314–40; Stanley G. Payne, *Falange*, 89–115; Robinson, 277–88; Carlos Seco Serrano, *Historia de España: Gran historia de los pueblos hispanos*, VI, 145–52; Hugh Thomas, *The Spanish Civil War* (1965 ed.), 153–80; General Jorge Vigón, *General Mola*, 87–110. Especially important for the secret activities of General Mola is the work by B. Félix Maíz, Mola's confidant and close collaborator in the preparation of the military uprising, *Mola, aquel hombre*, 63–311.

19. Antonio Ramos Oliveira, *Politics, Economics and Men of Modern Spain, 1808–1946*, 547. For accounts of the assassinations of Castillo and Calvo Sotelo, see General Felipe Acedo Colunga, *José Calvo Sotelo*, 329–51; Arrarás, *Historia*, IV, 345–68; *Causa general: La dominación roja en España*, 13–24; Cierva, *Historia de la guerra civil española*, 792–95; Estado Mayor Central del Ejército, *Historia de la guerra de liberación, 1936–39*, I, 451–57; Gil Robles, *No fué posible la paz*, 746–56; Eduardo de Guzmán, *Triunfo*, 17 July 1976; Prieto, *Convulsiones*, I, 157–62, III, 133–34, 144; Fernando Rivas, *El frente popular*, 359–81; Zugazagoitia, 28–34. But see also the most recent works: Ian Gibson, *La noche en que mataron a Calvo Sotelo*, and Luis Romero, *Por qué y cómo mataron a Calvo Sotelo*.

20. *Historia*, 740.

21. Ibid., 792.

22. Article in *El Liberal*, 14 July 1936, quoted in Arrarás, *Historia*, IV, 362–63.

23. *El Sol*, 14 July 1936.

24. Zugazagoitia, 16–17.

25. As quoted in José Gutiérrez-Ravé, *Las cortes errantes del frente popular*, 99–100. "The accusation that the crime had been committed by the government's own agents," he writes, "was deleted from the official record at the request of the president of the Cortes, Diego Martínez Barrio, and did not appear in the official *Diario de las Sesiones de Cortes*" (ibid., 100).

26. Quoted in Arrarás, *Historia*, IV, 366; Aurelio Joaniquet, *Calvo Sotelo*, 278; Fernando de Valdesoto, *Francisco Franco*, 108; Zugazagoitia, 16.

27. See Díaz, *Tres años*, 156, 165.

28. Indalecio Prieto in *Correo de Asturias*, 1 May 1943.

29. His announcement was not published at the time, but is quoted by Martínez Barrio in *Hoy*, 20 Apr. 1940.

30. Zugazagoitia, 40.

31. Interview in Mexico in 1940. For corroborative testimony, see General José Asensio in *Nuestra España*, Nov. 1939; the official Communist history of the Civil War, *Guerra y revolución en España, 1936–1939*, I, 150; José Martín Blázquez, *I Helped to Build an Army*, 112; Juan Modesto, *Soy del quinto regimiento*, 51, 61; Ramón Salas Larrazábal, *Historia del ejército popular de la república*, I, 127.

32. *El General Miaja*, 124–25.

33. When interviewed by me in Mexico in 1940. My shorthand notes taken during this interview are in the Hoover Institution. It is noteworthy that Antonio López Fernández, General Miaja's secretary and admirer, states that the general did not approve of the manner in which the weapons were handed over (*Defensa de Madrid*, 64). The opposition of General Miaja to the distribution of arms was confirmed many years later by Núñez Maza himself to M. Teresa Suero Roca (*Militares republicanos*

de la guerra de España, 297–98) and in the unpublished memoirs of artillery captain Urban Orad de la Torre (ibid., 298, n. 5).

34. *Hoy*, 20 Apr. 1940.

35. César Falcón, *Madrid*, 60.

36. See, for example, Cierva, *Historia de la guerra civil española*, 608.

37. A transcript of my interview is in the Hoover Institution. Campoamor, 42, 133, n. 1, confirms and supports Martínez Barrio's opposition to the distribution of arms. Clara Campoamor was a Radical party deputy until 1934 and mixed in Madrid political circles at the time of the rising (ibid., ii).

38. *Hoy*, 20 Apr. 1940.

39. *Correo de Asturias*, 1 May 1943.

40. *Hoy*, 27 Apr. 1940. See also Diego Martínez Barrio, *Memorias*, 358–59.

41. Quoted in Bertrán Güell, *Preparación y desarrollo del alzamiento nacional*, 76; Rafael Fernández de Castro y Pedrera, *Vidas de soldados ilustres de la nueva España*, 190; Maíz, 306–7; and Joaquín Pérez Madrigal, *Augurios, estallido y episodios de la guerra civil*, 168; all were supporters of the military rising. Another general telephoned by Martínez Barrio was Miguel Cabanellas, commander of the V Organic Division, with headquarters in Saragossa, who, according to the testimony of his son, replied unequivocally, "It is too late" (Guillermo Cabanellas, *La guerra de los mil días*, 424–25, and *Cuatro generales*, II, 79).

42. Quoted in Gil Robles, *No fué posible la paz*, 791. Details of this conversation were given by Sánchez Román to someone who enjoyed Gil Robles's absolute confidence (ibid.).

43. This offer is confirmed by Ino Bernard, *Mola, mártir de España*, 77; Jaime del Burgo, *Conspiración*, 25; José María Iribarren, *Mola*, 107; Carlos de la Válgoma, *Mola*, 406; Vigón, 115. It is not mentioned by Martínez Barrio in his article in *Hoy*, 20 Apr. 1940. However, in a letter to Salvador de Madariaga, some years later, Martínez Barrio asserted that "at no time was the rebels' assistance sought" (Salvador de Madariaga, *España*, prologue to the 4th edition [1944]). All the evidence runs counter to this assertion.

44. According to Sánchez Román, quoted in Gil Robles, *No fué posible la paz*, 791.

45. Ibid.

46. *Hoy*, 27 Apr. 1940.

47. Ibid. García Venero reproduces a point-by-point program of conciliation, given to him years later by Ramón Feced, who became a member of Martínez Barrio's government, and drawn up by Sánchez Román for submission to the insurgent generals (*El General Fanjul*, 287–89). See also García Venero, *Historia de las internacionales en España*, III, 102–8.

48. The complete list of names, as given in the *Gaceta de Madrid*, 19 July 1936, was as follows: Diego Martínez Barrio, Manuel Blasco Garzón, Antonio Lara, Plácido Alvarez Buylla, Bernardo Giner de los Ríos, Felipe Sánchez Román, Justino Azcárate, Ramón Feced, Enrique Ramos, Augusto Barcia, Marcelino Domingo, José Giral, Juan Lluhi y Vallesca, and General José Miaja, commander of the Madrid military district.

49. *Hoy*, 20 Apr. 1940. See also Marcelino Domingo, *España ante el mundo*, 231.

50. Zugazagoitia, 45.

51. Olmedo Delgado and Cuesta Monereo, 98–103.

52. Cierva, *Historia de la guerra civil española*, 767.

53. Cierva, essay in Palacio Atard, *Aproximación*, 78.

54. Cierva, *Historia de la guerra civil española*, 767.

55. See *Guerra y revolución*, I, 123–26; Olmedo Delgado and Cuesta Monereo, 138; Vigón, 185.

56. Olmedo Delgado and Cuesta Monereo, 137. The proclamation was published in *ABC* (Seville), 23 July 1936.

57. See also José Manuel Liébana and G. Orizana, *El movimiento nacional*, 175.

58. See also Francisco J. de Raymundo, *Cómo se inició el glorioso movimiento nacional en Valladolid y la gesta heroica del Alto del León*.

59. See, for example, Manuel Sánchez del Arco, *El sur de España en la reconquista de Madrid*, 24; J. Guzmán de Alfarache, *¡18 de julio!*, 68, 92; Angel Gollonet and José Morales, *Sangre y fuego, Málaga*, 24–25; Olmedo Delgado and Cuesta Monereo, 110–17.

60. See, for example, Liébana and Orizana, 144–45.

61. *Politics*, 278–79. Interestingly, Payne's view that Maura was one of the few responsible, farsighted leaders produced by the Republic is very similar to that of Joaquín Maurín, a political opponent of Maura on the far left during the Republic (see *España Libre* [New York], Sept.–Oct. 1971). For Miguel Maura's own account of the creation of the Assault Guard (which he achieved with Galarza's help) and of the problems of public order during his incumbency, as well as for his unqualified praise of Galarza as "an exemplary collaborator, discreet, capable, active, and loyal," see Maura, *Así cayó Alfonso XIII*, 265–76.

62. Zugazagoitia, 134.

63. IV, 381.

64. Time given by Barrio in *Hoy*, 27 Apr. 1940.

65. *El Noticiero*, 23 July 1936.

66. *Politics*, 334–35.

67. See decree, dated 29 Sept. 1936, as given in Fernando Díaz-Plaja, *La historia de España en sus documentos: La guerra, 1936–1939*, 249–50. For information on the initial disagreements among the rebel hierarchy over the terms of the decree, see Payne, *Falange*, 129–31; Payne, *Politics*, 369–73; Thomas, 365–66.

68. See Luis Bolín, *Spain*, 10–52, for a fascinating account of this important event. It is noteworthy that according to Cierva the flight was financed by the notorious smuggler and tycoon, Juan March (*Historia de la guerra civil española*, 80). See also Gil Robles, *No fué posible la paz*, 780. In a statement issued by Gil Robles on 27 February 1942, he also claims to have had a hand in arranging the flight (published in *ABC* [Madrid], 1 May 1968). For accounts of the military insurrection in Spanish Morocco and in various parts of Spain, see Enrique Arques, *17 de julio: La epopeya de Africa*, 13–58, 89–95; Joaquín Arrarás, *Historia de la cruzada española*, II, 474–562, IV, 14–606, V, 15–560, VI, 15–436; Pierre Broué and Emile Témime, *La révolution et la guerre d'Espagne*, 82–102; Ronald Fraser, *Blood of Spain*, passim; Victor de Frutos, *Los que NO perdieron la guerra*, 13–22; García Venero, *El General Fanjul*, 294–350; *Guerra y revolución*, I, 123–32, 138–75, 180–87; Gabriel Jackson, *The Spanish Republic and the Civil War, 1931–1939*, 232–46; César M. Lorenzo, *Les anarchistes espagnols et le pouvoir, 1868–1969*, 139–44; José Manuel Martínez Bande, *La invasión de Aragón y el desembarco en Mallorca*, 15–52; Olmedo Delgado and Cuesta Monereo, 98–138; Payne, *Politics*, 341–52; Luis Romero, *Tres días de julio*, 3–616; Seco Serrano, VI, 152–64; Thomas, 131–64, 186–89; Vicente Ramos, *La guerra civil, 1936–1939, en la provincia de Alicante*, 85–111; Vigón, *General Mola*, 111–211.

69. Quoted in Valdesoto, 115–17, n. 1.

70. *Guerra y revolución*, I, 121–22.

71. Martínez Barrio, *Hoy*, 27 Apr. 1940; Dolores Ibárruri, *El único camino*, 260.

72. 18 Jan. 1936.

73. 12 Oct. 1935.

74. 2 Apr. 1936.

75. Domingo, 233. See also A. C. Márquez Tornero, *Testimonio de mi tiempo*, 1, 9. According to Zugazagoitia, 45, Isaac Abeytua, the director of *Politica*, organ of the Left Republican party, was strongly opposed to the government.

76. *Obras completas*, III, 494.

77. Eduardo de Guzmán, *Madrid, rojo y negro*, 37. See also Martínez Barrio, *Hoy*, 27 Apr. 1940; Manuél Blasco Garzón (a member of Martínez Barrio's government), in *España Republicana*, 6 Nov. 1947; Arturo Barea, *The Forging of a Rebel*, 510; *Guerra y revolución*, I, 122.

78. *Hoy*, 27 Apr. 1940. Sánchez Román, a member of the government, confirmed, when interviewed by me, that Prieto urged Martínez Barrio to remain in office, contending that the street demonstrations did not warrant his resignation. This is corroborated by Largo Caballero in *Mis recuerdos*, 167. In a letter to Salvador de Madariaga, some years later, Martínez Barrio stated: "The Martínez Barrio government died at the hands of the Caballero Socialists, the Communists, and some irresponsible Republicans" (Madariaga, *España*, prologue to the 4th edition [1944]).

79. Palacio Atard, essay in Palacio Atard, *Aproximación*, 50.

Chapter 4

1. José Giral in *La Vanguardia*, 19 July 1938. See also his speech reported in *La Voz Valenciana*, 10 Mar. 1937.

2. Speech reported in *Política*, 2 Nov. 1938. See also Manuel Azaña, *Obras Completas*, III, 487–88; *Guerra y revolución en España, 1936–1939*, I, 177; Indalecio Prieto, *Convulsiones de España*, III, 149.

3. José Giral, when interviewed by me in Mexico in 1940.

4. *Gaceta de Madrid*, 7 Aug. 1936.

5. Azaña, *Obras*, IV, 862.

6. According to a meticulous study, based on primary sources, by Ricardo de la Cierva, *Historia de la guerra civil española*, 756–57, 760. See also Vicente Palacio Atard, essay in Palacio Atard, *Aproximación histórica a la guerra española, 1936–1939*, 41–42. Although Cierva cited these figures as representing the ideological division within the army (essay in Raymond Carr, *The Republic and the Civil War in Spain*, 188), they were of necessity determined to a large degree by the territorial split, which Cierva himself does not entirely discount in his major work, *Historia de la guerra civil española*, 760–61.

7. *Nuestra guerra*, 275. Palacio Atard, a right-wing historian, puts the figure as high as thirty-five hundred. Palacio Atard, *Cuadernos bibliográficos de la guerra de España, 1936–1939: Memorias y reportajes de testigos*, 142.

8. *Freedom's Battle*, 122.

9. *Guerra en España, 1936–1939*, 259. See also Colonel Segismundo Casado, *National Review*, July 1939.

10. Essay in Carr, *The Republic and the Civil War in Spain*, 190.

11. Essay in Palacio Atard, *Aproximación*, 41–42.

12. Salvador de Madariaga, *Spain*, 487.

13. An account of the attitude of the Civil Guard in the various provinces can be found in Arrarás, *Historia de la cruzada española*. See also José Manuel Liébana and G. Orizana, *El movimiento nacional*.

14. According to a careful study by Cierva, *Historia de la guerra civil español*, 760. On the other hand, the Spanish historian, Ramón Salas Larrazábal, states that 51.36 percent of the corps remained in the Republican camp after the outbreak of the Civil War. On the basis of Cierva's total figure of 34,320 officers and men, this would mean that approximately 17,500 remained in the Republican zone (*Los datos exactos de la guerra civil*, 60, 270–71). However, numbers alone do not tell the entire story, for they do not take into account the breakdown of authority within the corps and the demoralization that set in as a result of the revolution and the assumption of police powers by the left-wing organizations.

15. See, for example, the account of Captain Reparaz of his escape together with a large body of civil guards from Jaén in Capitán Reparaz y Tresgallo de Souza, *Desde el cuartel general de Miaja, al santuario de la Virgen de la Cabeza*; report in *Solidaridad Obrera*, 18 Feb. 1937, of the attempt by forty civil guards to join General Franco's forces; and Julián Zugazagoitia, *Historia de la guerra en España*, 103.

16. According to *Mundo Obrero*, 3 Nov. 1936.

17. *Gaceta de Madrid*, 21 Aug. 1936.

18. This corps, according to information given to me in Mexico in 1950 by José Muñoz López, top-ranking official in the SIM (Military Investigation Service) in the later part of the war, ceased to function entirely at the outbreak of the rebellion and had to be re-created, only three hundred of its three thousand members remaining loyal to the government.

19. This is an approximate figure given by Cierva, *Historia de la guerra civil española*, 757. Ramón Salas Larrazábal, on the other hand, gives a figure of nearly eighteen thousand men (*Historia del ejército popular de la república*, I, 74).

20. Some of the provincial capitals where the assault guards supported the rising were Burgos, Huesca, Saragossa, Valladolid, Cáceres, Granada, León, Logroño, Pamplona, Salamanca (Liébana and Orizana, 209–10, 154, 201–2, 192, 216, 193 respectively), Oviedo (Oscar Pérez Solís, *Sitio y defensa de Oviedo*, 24; Germiniano Carrascal, *Asturias*, 52), and Teruel (Arrarás, *Historia de la cruzada española*, IV, 238). According to Ramón Salas Larrazábal, 70 percent of the guards remained

at the disposal of the government (*Los datos exactos*, 61). However, it should be borne in mind that a large number of the assault guards joined the revolutionary militia as did many of the members of the Civil Guard.

21. For frank accounts of the absolute impotence of the remnants of the government police corps in the first days of the war, see speech by the Socialist politician Angel Galarza (*La Correspondencia de Valencia*, 5 Aug. 1937), who became minister of the interior in September 1936; speech by Juan García Oliver, the Anarchist leader, who was made minister of justice in November 1936 (*Fragua Social*, 1 June 1937). See also Jesús de Galíndez (a friend of the Republic), *Los vascos en el Madrid sitiado*, 15–19, and the preamble to the minister of the interior's decree of 26 Dec. 1936 in *Gaceta de la República*, 27 Dec. 1936.

22. *Freedom's Battle*, 261.

23. Ibid., 224.

24. Dolores Ibárruri, *Speeches and Articles, 1936–38*, 214. "The republican state," writes Fernando Claudín, a Communist at the time, "collapsed like a house of cards. . . . The means of production and political power in effect passed into the hands of the working-class organizations" (*La crisis del movimiento comunista*, 179–80). No less explicit is Vicente Uribe, a member of the Spanish politburo, who affirms in his unpublished memoir that "the old republican State ceased to exist and only the external symbols remained" ("Memorias"), 12.

25. Zugazagoitia, 47.

26. Angel Ossorio y Gallardo, *Vida y sacrificio de Companys*, 179, also 169. Should further corroborative testimony from the Republican camp on the collapse of the state still be needed, see Manuel Azaña, *Madrid* (speech of 13 Nov. 1937), 7–8; *Política*, 16 July 1938 (editorial); *La Correspondencia de Valencia*, 5 Aug. 1937 (speech by Angel Galarza); *El Poble Català*, 2 Feb. 1940 (article by Major Josep Guarner).

27. Speech reported by *El Día Gráfico*, 2 Dec. 1937.

28. *Treball*, 22 July 1936. See *La Humanitat*, 6 Aug. 1936, for the control of the entire Catalan French border from Bausén to Port-Bou by the working-class militia.

29. M. Sterling (Mark Sharron) in *Modern Monthly*, Dec. 1936. See also Walter Duranty in the *New York Times*, 17 Sept. 1936; R. Louzon in *La Révolution Prolétarienne*, 10 Aug. 1936; Alvarez del Vayo, *Freedom's Battle*, 164; H. E. Kaminski, *Ceux de Barcelone*, 11; John Langdon-Davies, *Behind the Spanish Barricades*, 90–91; Pérez Salas, 122.

30. Bruno Alonso, *La flota republicana y la guerra civil de España*, 25.

31. Zugazagoitia, 157. For the lack of discipline in the Republican fleet, see article by N. Kuznetsov, Soviet naval attaché and adviser to Antonio Ruiz, chief of the Cartagena Naval Base, in *Pod znamenem ispanskoi respubliki, 1936–1939*, 198. See also Admiral Francisco Moreno, chief of General Franco's fleet during the Civil War, for reference to the assassination of officers, the failure of the sailors at the naval base of El Ferrol to defeat the military uprising, the ineffectualness of the Republican fleet and the principal naval operations during the war, *La guerra en el mar*, 69–70, 78–279. For additional information on the events in the principal naval bases and units of the fleet, see Manuel D. Benavides, *La escuadra la mandan los cabos*; Luis Carrero Blanco, *España y el mar*, I, 562–66; José Cervera Pery, *Alzamiento y revolución en la marina*, 41–127, 129–237, 260–64, 269–77; and Daniel Sueiro, *La flota es roja*, 121–247. An invaluable contribution, the best in English, is the dissertation of Willard C. Frank, Jr., "Sea Power, Politics, and the Onset of the Spanish Civil War, 1936," University of Pittsburgh (546 pp.), which is the first part of a larger work in progress that examines the role of sea power and politics in the entire Civil War.

32. An exception must be made of the Basque provinces, where the population reacted with greater moderation than elsewhere due, in large measure, to the influence of the Catholic Basque Nationalist party. See Manuel de Irujo, "La guerra civil en Euzkadi antes del estatuto," 23–25, 45–46, 50–52, 64–65, and report to the central government by José Antonio Aguirre, premier of the autonomous Basque government, 2–4, 7–8, 10–11, 13–15, 17–18, 22. See also Aguirre, *Veinte años de gestión del gobierno vasco, 1936–56*, 28–29, 49; José María Arenillas, *Euzkadi, la cuestión nacional y la revolución socialista*; A. de Lizarra, *Los vascos y la república española*, 58–59 and passim; Payne, *Basque Nationalism*, 178–81.

33. Juan López, speech published in *CNT* (Madrid), 21 Sept. 1936. See also his article in *Cultura Proletaria*, 8 Jan. 1938, and speech reported in *Fragua Social*, 29 May 1937. In Valencia, for example, the real organ of government during the first months of the revolution was the Popular

Executive Committee, in which the trade-union organizations were the principal ruling force (Alfons Cucó, *El valencianismo político, 1874–1939*, 205–6). "The immediate result of the military uprising," writes a Communist author, "was the collapse of the institutions of the state in the areas where it failed. This was the case in Valencia. A total power vacuum occurred in the former governmental bodies: neither the army, nor the police, nor the Civil Guard, nor the municipal council, nor the Deputation, nor the law court retained a minimum of power that would permit them to exercise the simplest function of public order. . . . [The] Popular Executive Committee . . . assumed the functions of a state body" (Carlos Llorens, *La guerra en Valencia y el frente de Teruel*, 40).

34. *Spartacus*, Sept.–Oct. 1938.

35. *La revolución en los ayuntamientos*, 16–17.

36. *Boletín de Información, CNT-FAI*, as given in *El Día Gráfico*, 16 Aug. 1936.

37. *Politics, Economics and Men of Modern Spain, 1808–1946*, 595. See also speeches by the Socialist politician, Angel Galarza, *La Correspondencia de Valencia*, 2 Feb. 1937, 5 Aug. 1937, and R. Louzon in *La Révolution Prolétarienne*, 10 Aug. 1936; César M. Lorenzo, *Les anarchistes espagnols et le pouvoir, 1868–1969*, 182–204; Carlos M. Rama, *La crisis española del siglo XX*, 294.

38. Speech reported in *Fragua Social*, 1 June 1937.

39. *The Forging of a Rebel*, 536, see also, 545–47. For an account of the collapse of the administration of justice in the region of Catalonia by a Cortes deputy, a member of the Esquerra Republicana de Cataluña, see Mariano Rubió i Tudurí, *La justicia en Cataluña*, 13.

40. For the names of those assassinated, see *Causa general: La dominación roja en España*, 352–54; also Francisco Lacruz, *El alzamiento, la revolución y el terror en Barcelona*, 159.

41. For the destruction in November 1936 of the principal judicial records in Madrid by the Anarchist leader, Juan García Oliver, see deposition by Luis Palud Clausó, as given in *Causa general*, 363–65. For the burning of judicial records in Barcelona and Castellón respectively, see Rubió i Tudurí, 13, and *Datos complementarios para la historia de España*, 237.

42. See decrees of 23 and 25 Aug. 1936, *Gaceta de Madrid*, 24, 25 Aug. 1936; see also decree of 6 Oct. 1936, ibid., 7 Oct. 1936.

43. Ibid., 7 Oct. 1936.

44. *Convulsiones*, II, 314–16.

45. For information on the opening of deposit boxes in Madrid and of various decrees providing for the surrender to the Bank of Spain of certain valuables, see Angel Viñas, *El oro español en la guerra civil*, 160–67; also Amaro del Rosal, *Historia de la UGT de España, 1901–1939*, 510.

46. Galíndez, 10. See also Julián Gorkin, *Caníbales políticos*, 120, for the release of prisoners from the Model Prison, Madrid.

47. *Spain*, 496.

48. See, for example, the memorandum presented to the Largo Caballero government by Manuel de Irujo, Basque Nationalist minister, as reproduced in Lizarra, 200–204.

49. 15 Aug. 1936.

50. *Ruta*, 14 Nov. 1936.

51. *Tierra y Libertad*, 13 Aug. 1936.

52. 29 July 1936. For confirmatory testimony by non-Anarchist, but pro-Republican sources, on the destruction of ecclesiastical property, see Ramos Oliveira, 571; essay by Lawrence Fernsworth in Frank Hanighen, *Nothing but Danger*, 13–47.

53. *The Fellow-Travellers*, 1. In a necrology from London, the *New York Times* reported on 23 Oct. 1966: "He was variously described as a Communist, a crank and a saint—sometimes all three. . . . He once declared in a sermon that if Jesus were alive today, he would have been a Communist. Such remarks were especially embarrassing because outside England he was often confused with the Archbishop of Canterbury, the Primate of all England."

54. Cardenal Isidro Gomá y Tomás, *Pastorales de la guerra de España*, 169.

55. *Freedom and Catholic Power in Spain and Portugal*, 11–12.

56. For confirmation by a pro-Republican source of the imprisonment and killing of thousands of members of the priesthood and religious orders, see memorandum presented to the Largo Caballero government by Manuel de Irujo, Basque Nationalist minister, as reproduced in Lizarra, 200–204. Irujo also stated that in the Basque provinces nobody attacked the church or interfered with religious worship because, in contrast with the rest of the left camp, the clergy in those provinces sympathized with democratic and Republican institutions. The most reliable study of the assassination of members

of the priesthood and religious orders, the result of many years of diligent research, can be found in Antonio Montero's *Historia de la persecución religiosa en España, 1936–1939*, 762–883, which lists the names, places, and dates of assassination of 6,832 religious personnel. See also Angel García, *La iglesia española y el 18 de julio*, 309–12; Albert Manent i Segimon and Josep Raventós i Giralt, *L'Església clandestina a Catalunya durant la guerra civil, 1936–1939*; and José M. Sánchez, *The Spanish Civil War as a Religious Tragedy*.

57. For criticism of these Republicans by Fernando Valera, a Cortes deputy and prominent member of Unión Republicana, see speech, reported in *El Pueblo*, 27 Jan. 1937. See also article by Juan J. Domenichina, a leading intellectual of the Republican Left party, in *Hoy*, 28 Dec. 1940.

58. *Obras*, IV, 624. Among the outstanding Republicans who had left Spain and to whom Azaña was undoubtedly alluding were: Plácido Alvarez Buylla, Augusto Barcia, Manuel Blasco Garzón, Marcelino Domingo, Salvador de Madariaga, Gregorio Marañón, José Ortega y Gasset, Ramón Pérez de Ayala, Mariano Ruiz Funes, and Claudio Sánchez-Albornoz. Sánchez-Albornoz, the famous Republican intellectual and a member of the conservative wing of Izquierda Republicana, Azaña's own party, writes: "Azaña envied us from the depths of his soul. But this envy turned into resentment. The closer our political relationship, the greater was his resentment" (*Anecdotario político*, 227).

59. *International Law and Diplomacy in the Spanish Civil Strife*, 157.

60. *Los sucesos de España vistos por un diplomático*, 338.

61. *Freedom's Battle*, 240.

62. *Asilos y canjes durante la guerra civil española*, 19–20.

63. *Diplomat in Roten Madrid*, 59.

64. T. G. Powell, *Mexico and the Spanish Civil War*, 77.

65. As quoted by Javier Tusell in his Preliminary Study of Araquistáin in Luis Araquistáin, *Sobre la guerra civil y en la emigración*, 22. The original letter is in the Archivo Histórico Nacional, Madrid.

66. Federica Montseny in *La Revista Blanca*, 30 July 1936.

67. Diego Abad de Santillán, *La revolución y la guerra en España*, 176.

68. Galíndez, 9–10. In 1977, Ramón Salas Larrazábal published his painstaking monograph *Pérdidas de la guerra*, in which he gives estimates of the deaths from all causes province by province. He computes the executions and homicides at 58,000 in the Nationalist zone and at 73,000 in the Republican zone. Until the publication of this work, there appeared to be little likelihood that figures even remotely approaching accuracy would ever be available in view of the palpable exaggerations and contradictions by both sides. As Hugh Thomas points out (*The Spanish Civil War* [1965 ed.], 789), Nationalist estimates of the number of assassinations in the Popular Front zone ran initially as high as 3–400,000. A figure of more than 300,000 laymen assassinated is given by the Spanish bishops in their collective letter, dated 1 July 1937 (Gomá y Tomás, 169). But these estimates were subsequently revised downward to about 60,000. On the other hand, *Causa general*, 390, which was first published by General Franco's ministry of justice in 1943 and contains a mass of evidence concerning executions in the left camp, gave the number of those "duly investigated" as 85,940. In contrast, Gabriel Jackson, *The Spanish Republic and the Civil War, 1931–1939*, 533, arrives at a "most tentative estimate" of 20,000 deaths by assassination in the Popular Front zone, an extremely low figure if one takes into account the 6,832 religious personnel assassinated.

Reasonably accurate estimates were likewise unavailable for the number of wartime killings in Nationalist Spain. The figure of 750,000 executions named by the Spanish Republican writer, Ramón Sender, for the whole of Nationalist Spain to mid-1938 (Thomas [1965 ed.], 223) and that of 150,000 for the military territory of the Second Organic Division given by Antonio Bahamonde, former propaganda chief to General Queipo de Llano, commander of the division, comprising the provinces of Badajoz, Cadiz, Cordova, Granada, Huelva, Malaga, and Seville (*Memoirs of a Spanish Nationalist*, 90) appear definitely exaggerated to Thomas (1965 ed.), 223, who considers that Nationalist assassinations "are unlikely to have numbered more than 50,000" (789). On the other hand, Jackson, 535, citing estimates given to him by a notary and former member of the Catholic CEDA, names figures of 47,000 for the province of Seville alone and 32,000 and 26,000 respectively for the provinces of Cordova and Granada. More sober estimates for the number of killings in some of the provinces controlled by the Nationalist and Popular Front forces are given by a Basque priest, Juan José Usabiaga, using the pseudonym of Juan de Iturralde, in *El catolicismo y la cruzada de Franco*, 96–155. For the repression in Burgos, the seat of the Nationalist government, and in the province of Granada, see Antonio Ruiz Vilaplana (dean and president of the College of Judicial Commissioners until he fled abroad in 1938), *Burgos Justice*, 72–77, 84–85, 92–95, and Ian Gibson, *La represión nacionalista de Granada en 1936 y la muerte de Federico García Lorca*, 58–59, 137–39.

In the light of Salas Larrazábal's study mentioned at the beginning of this note, most of the earlier figures appear grossly exaggerated, although it should be pointed out that his methodology and the accuracy of his estimates have been questioned. For example, Antonio Hernández García, author of *La represión en la Rioja durante la guerra civil*, claims in this three-volume work devoted to the Nationalist repression in the communities located in La Rioja in Logroño province (Aragon), based on oral and documentary evidence, that Salas's reliance on the data in the civil registers led him to underestimate the total number of assassinations on both sides by as much as 110 percent. Many entries in the registers, he asserts, falsified the cause of death: a shot in the head was described as "cerebral hemorrhage" and shots in the chest as "cardiac arrest." "Furthermore," he adds, "it is public knowledge that not all the assassinations were faithfully recorded in the public register" (I, 16–17).

A chapter on the gruesome nature and extent of the repression in the Nationalist camp can be found in Stanley G. Payne, *Politics and the Military in Modern Spain*, 409–20, which originally supported Jackson's contention that during the wartime period Nationalist executions exceeded those carried out by the left. However, in a later work (*The Spanish Revolution*, 225) Payne states: "Though the Red Terror may have taken more lives than the Nationalist repression while the war lasted, the victors were subsequently able to complete the task at their leisure." These postwar executions were confirmed by Bernard Malley of the British Embassy in Madrid, who was in Spain during the Second World War, and who affirmed that there were daily trials and executions throughout 1939, 1940, and 1941 (Brian Crozier, *Franco*, 296), and by Count Galeazzo Ciano, Mussolini's foreign minister, who recorded in a memorandum on 19 July 1939 after a week's stay in Spain: "The number of executions is still very large: In Madrid alone, 200 to 250 a day, in Barcelona, 150; in Seville, which was never in the hands of the Reds, 80. . . . [More] than 10,000 men already condemned to death wait in their cells for the inevitable moment of execution" (*Les archives secrètes du Comte Ciano, 1936–1942*, 294). For additional information on the "White Terror," see Guillermo Cabanellas, *La guerra de los mil días*, II, 838–67. The most serious research into the executions carried out by the Nationalists in Catalonia from the time of their first entry into the region in 1938 is that of Josep M. Solé i Sabaté, *La represió franquista a Catalunya, 1938–1953*. In this 600-page work, Solé lists the name, birthdate, political affiliation, occupation, and the date and place of execution of each individual, the total number, according to my count, exceeding ten thousand.

In the paroxysm of barbarity that convulsed the country, one man, in particular, distinguished himself by his humanity. This was the Anarchist Melchor Rodríguez, who became director of prisons in December 1936, and who saved the lives of hundreds of supporters of the right in the Cárcel Modelo, Madrid, where some of the worst atrocities in the left camp had occurred. Arsenio de Izaga, one of the inmates, testifies: "He was appointed on 4 December. . . . He amazed those of us who were not aware of the integrity of his conscience and the nobility of his heart. That date, which all inmates should engrave on their minds, marks the fortunate and definite end of the horrendous mass executions" (*Los presos de Madrid*, 280). See also Rafael Abella, who states: "As the war advanced . . . the safety of the prisoners in the central zone increased thanks to the arduous work of the admirable Melchor Rodríguez from Seville. A former bullfighter and pure anarchist, he showed exceptional courage in his post of director of prisons . . . , protecting the penal population at a time when the increase in Nationalist bombings incited such horrifying events as the 'train of death,' a grievous episode in which hundreds of persons lost their lives when being transferred from Jaén to Alcalá" (*La vida cotidiana durante la guerra civil*, 105). And the Basque priest, Juan de Iturralde, writes: "[When] Alcalá de Henares was bombed and the people wanted to take the prison by assault to lynch the inmates, Melchor appeared at the gates of the jail, harangued the mob and managed to save the lives of the prisoners, among whom was the secretary of the Falange, Raimundo Fernández Cuesta" (*El catolicismo*, 129). The humanitarian conduct and courage of Melchor Rodríguez are also attested to by the Republican sympathizer and Basque Nationalist, Jesús de Galíndez, *Los vascos en el Madrid sitiado*, 66, n. 10. Galíndez summarizes the gruesome state of affairs prevailing in the Madrid prisons before the appointment of Rodríguez: "During the night of 6 November, the records of some six hundred prisoners in the Cárcel Modelo were summarily reviewed. Having established that they were fascists, they were executed in the small village of Paracuellos del Jarama, near Alcalá de Henares; two nights later four hundred prisoners were executed, making a total of 1,020. On succeeding days, until 4 December, the clean-up continued in the temporary jails, although in smaller numbers. The clean-up in the prison on General Porlier street lasted several days, the most bloody of which was on 24 November; in the prison of San Antón the clean-up was carried out on 27 and 30 November; and in Ventas, 30 November and the first days of December. The only jails spared were the Duque de Sesto and the Mujeres del Asilo San Rafael" (ibid., 66). For further information on Melchor Rodríguez, see Ian Gibson, *Paracuellos: Como fue*, 150, 164, 174, 175–84, 191, 236–37; *Indice* (Madrid), 1 Mar. 1972; and his interview given to *Ya*, 21 Apr. 1939, three weeks after Franco entered Madrid. For information on the Paracuellos del Jarama massacre, see Carlos Fernández, *Paracuellos del Jarama: ¿Carrillo culpable?*; Gibson, *Paracuellos: Como fue*; *Datos complementarios para la historia de España*, 240–41 and Anexo VII; also article in *Cambio 16*, 21 Feb. 1983 ("¿Qué pasó en Paracuellos?").

69. *La velada en Benicarló*, 96. This book is in the form of a dialogue. Garcés, a former minister, who makes the above statement, expresses ideas commonly attributed to Manuel Azaña.

70. The same, of course, is true of the Government of the Generalitat in the semiautonomous region of Catalonia, which, in the words of Angel Ossorio y Gallardo, *Vida y sacrificio de Companys*, 172, had become a "purely nominal organ," the real power in the region having been assumed by the Central Antifascist Militia Committee.

71. Confirmation of this was given to the author by several trade-union leaders.

72. Barea, 660.

73. See, for example, *Boletín de Información, CNT-FAI*, 25 Aug. 1936; *Solidaridad Obrera*, 31 July 1938.

74. See, for example, Indalecio Prieto, *Palabras al viento*, 281, and his article in *Correo de Asturias*, 15 Aug. 1942; Alvarez del Vayo, *Freedom's Battle*, 262; César Falcón, *Madrid*, 122; Major Josep Guarner in *El Poble Català*, 2 Feb. 1940; Pérez Salas, 113; Zugazagoitia, 47.

75. Unión General de Trabajadores and Confederación Nacional del Trabajo respectively.

76. An exception must be made of the province of Vizcaya in the Basque Country. "Vizcaya," writes Stanley G. Payne, "was practically the only sector of the Republican zone where there were virtually no revolutionary changes in the basic structure of the economic system. State control (*intervención*) was established over industrial and commercial assets of those known to support Franco's Spanish Nationalists, and all aspects of military production were placed under state supervision. . . . Wartime regulations were imposed on the general economy by the end of October, including strict rationing and price controls, but in general there was no change in the legal basis of property. The relative social conservatism of Basque nationalism combined with the diplomatic cautiousness of the Communists and Socialists (who were eager not to offend British interests and foreign opinion) to prevent genuine revolutionary changes in Vizcaya" (*Basque Nationalism*, 181). And summarizing the contrast between the Basque Country and the rest of Republican Spain, Rafael Abella writes: "As compared with the tumultuous outburst that took place in republican Spain in response to the military coup, the Basque Country represented a rare oasis in the midst of the antireligious obsession and the frenzy of seizures of property. The administrative councils held their meetings, the banks were respected, the industrial plants continued to function without collectivist experiments; religion was practised freely and the excesses that occurred were the work of outside elements such as the dreadful attack on the jails after a bombardment" (*La vida cotidiana durante la guerra civil*, 114). See also Maximiano García Venero, *Historia del nacionalismo vasco*, 611–12. This is not to say that there was no revolutionary activity on the part of the workers' organizations (see, for example, Arenillas, 7–13; Manuel Chiapuso, *El gobierno vasco y los anarquistas: Bilbao en guerra*, and Chiapuso, *Los anarquistas y la guerra en Euzkadi: La comuna de San Sebastián*), but, on the whole, the basic structure of the economic system, as Payne affirms, remained unchanged.

77. *Half of Spain Died*, 121.

78. Speech, 9 May 1937, José Díaz, *Tres años de lucha*, 428.

79. *Treball*, 9 Apr. 1937. See also Antonio Mije (member of the politburo), *Por una potente industria de guerra*, 3; Federico Melchor (member of the executive committee of the JSU, the Communist-run Unified Socialist Youth Federation), *Organicemos la producción*, 4.

80. *Pravda*, 26 Sept. 1936.

81. See the preamble of a decree published in the official *Gaceta de la República* (formerly *Gaceta de Madrid*), 22 Oct. 1937. For earlier references to the destruction of property records, see speech by the undersecretary of finance, Jerónimo Bugeda, as reported in *El Día Gráfico*, 9 Feb. 1937; article by

Federica Montseny in *Tierra y Libertad*, 29 Oct. 1936; report of the Committee of War of the Iron Column, *Nosotros*, 16 Feb. 1937; *Solidaridad Obrera*, 13 Aug. 1936 (article on Pina).

82. Report to the central committee of the Communist party, 5–8 Mar. 1937, in Díaz, *Tres años*, 351.

83. *Tribuna*, Oct. 1948.

84. Franz Borkenau, *The Spanish Cockpit*, 148.

85. For some of the institute's reports listing confiscated properties, see *Claridad*, 12, 14 Oct. 1936; *CNT*, 15, 18, 19 Aug. 1936; *Mundo Obrero*, 8 Aug. 1936; *Política*, 11, 14, 23, 27, 28, 30 Aug.; 1, 16, 17, 23–25, 27 Sept.; 10, 15, 28 Oct. 1936; *El Socialista*, 29 Aug., 29 Sept. 1936.

86. *Boletín de Información, CNT-FAI*, 25 Aug. 1936.

87. Statement issued by the Barcelona Traction, Light, and Power Company, Limited, on 3 Sept. 1936; see also statement issued on 16 Nov. 1936.

88. On the question of the confiscation and control of property by the unions and also by the left-wing parties a great deal could be written based on left sources alone. But considerations of space do not permit more than a brief reference to some of these sources under each of the following heads:

Railroads. "The boards of directors disappeared," said one trade-union report, "and works councils were formed in which the working-class organizations were directly represented" (*CNT* [Madrid], 2 Oct. 1936). This control of the railroads by the working-class organizations is confirmed in the preamble of a government decree published in the *Gaceta de Madrid*, 16 Aug. 1936. See also *Avant*, 26 July 1936; *La Batalla*, 18 Aug. 1936; *Boletín de Información, CNT-FAI*, 26 Aug. 1936; *CNT* (Madrid), 5 Oct. 1936; *Cultura Proletaria*, 15 June 1940 (article by Gaston Leval); *El Día Gráfico*, 24 Sept. 1936; *Fragua Social*, 7 Apr. 1937; *Solidaridad Obrera* (Barcelona), 11, 19 Aug. 1936; *La Vanguardia*, 14 Oct. 1936; *De julio a julio* (article by Juan de Arroyo), 165–68; Gaston Leval, *Espagne libertaire, 1936–1939*, 277–78; Leval, *Né Franco né Stalin*, 97–111; Agustín Souchy and Paul Folgare, *Colectivizaciones: La obra constructiva de la revolución española*, 55–61; Matilde Vázquez and Javier Valero, *La guerra civil en Madrid*, 78.

Other sections of the transport industry. According to Víctor Zaragoza, secretary of the national committee of the CNT National Transport Federation, when interviewed by me, every important transport enterprise was appropriated by the labor unions. This excludes the Basque provinces, where there were fewer changes in the economic field (see, for example, G. L. Steer, *The Tree of Gernika*, 73). For the confiscation of some of the most important transport enterprises in Barcelona, Madrid, and Valencia, see *Boletín de Información, CNT-FAI*, 7, 26 Aug. 1936, also article reproduced from this paper in *El Día Gráfico*, 18 Aug. 1936; *CNT*, 7, 10 Aug. 1936; *La Noche*, 6 Aug. 1936; *Nosotros*, 8, 19 July 1937; *Política*, 8 Aug. 1936; *Solidaridad Obrera*, 1, 4 Aug., 13 Oct., 19 Nov., 17 Dec. 1936; *Tierra y Libertad*, 1 May 1937; *La Vanguardia*, 8 Oct. 1936; Leval, *Né Franco né Stalin*, 111–22; Vicente Ramos, *La guerra civil, 1936–1939, en la provincia de Alicante*, I, 153; Souchy and Folgare, 61–71. For the control of the shipping companies by the unions, see Hugh Thomas, *The Spanish Civil War* (1977 ed.), 530.

Public utilities. According to Mariano Cardona Rosell, a member of the national committee of the CNT, every public utility enterprise in the left camp was taken over by the CNT and UGT (letter to me). Some of the most important were: Compañía Catalana de Gas y Electricidad, Compañía Hidroeléctrica Española, Compañía Madrileña de Gas, Cooperativa Electra, Electra Valenciana, Eléctrica Santillana, Empresa Concesionaria de las Aguas Subterráneas del Río Llobregat, Gas Lebon, Riegos y Fuerzas del Ebro, Saltos del Duero, Sociedad Anónima de Fuerzas Eléctricas, Sociedad General de Aguas de Barcelona, Unión Eléctrica Madrileña. For details on some of these enterprises, see *La Batalla*, 2, 23 Aug. 1936; *Boletín de Información, CNT-FAI*, 27 July 1937; *CNT*, 31 Aug. 1936; *Luz y Fuerza*, Jan. 1938; *Nosotros*, 3 July 1937; *Solidaridad Obrera*, 13, 15 Aug. 1936, 10 Jan. 1937; Leval, *Espagne libertaire, 1936–1939*, 261–66; Leval, *Né Franco né Stalin*, 127–31; Vicente Ramos, I, 153–54; Souchy and Folgare, 125–36; Vázquez and Valero, 77–78.

Manufacturing, mining, and banking enterprises. See *Acracia*, 24 Oct. 1936; *La Batalla*, 22 Sept. 1936; *Boletín de Información, CNT-FAI*, 7 Aug., 30 Sept. 1936, also articles reproduced from this paper in *El Día Gráfico*, 5, 6, 14, 25 Aug. 1936; *Claridad*, 1 Mar. 1937 (speech by Vicente Uribe); *CNT*, 23 Sept., 5–7 Oct. 1936; *CNT* (Paris), 26 Dec. 1947, 3 Dec. 1948, 20 Nov. 1949; *CNT-FAI-AIT Informationsdienst*, 15 Aug. 1936; *La Correspondencia de Valencia*, 2 Mar., 14 Aug. 1937; *Cultura Proletaria*, 25 Nov. 1939; *El Día Gráfico*, 6 Dec. 1936; *Diario Oficial de la Generalitat de Catalunya*,

28 Oct. 1936 (see preamble of the collectivization decree); *Documentos Históricos de España*, July 1938; *L'Espagne Antifasciste*, no. 8 (no date) and 21 Nov. 1936 (article by Christian Couderc); *España Libre* (Toulouse), 18 Sept. 1949; *Fragua Social*, as given in *Tierra y Libertad*, 13 Feb. 1937; *El Mercantil Valenciano*, 30 Aug. 1936, 11 May 1937 (statement by Belarmino Tomás); *Mundo Obrero*, 20 Aug. 1936; *Nosotros*, 6, 14 July 1937, also article reproduced from this paper in *Boletín de Información, CNT-FAI*, 16 June 1937; *La Révolution Prolétarienne*, 25 Sept. 1936 (article by Jean Leunois); *El Socialista*, 27 Aug. 1937; *Solidaridad Obrera*, 7, 18, 22 Aug., 4, 16, 19, 25, 29, 30 Sept., 21, 23 Oct., 18–21 Nov., 2, 5, 11, 15, 17, 19 Dec. 1936, 21, 28 Jan., 1, 24 Apr., 30 June, 15 Aug. (article by Cardona Rosell), 23 Oct. 1937; *Solidaridad Obrera* (Paris), 16 July 1949; *Spanish Revolution*, 5 Sept. 1936, 6 Aug. 1937; *Tierra y Libertad*, 30 Jan., 27 Mar., 24 July, 9, 16, 30 Oct., 13 Nov. 1937; *Treball*, 6 (speech by Angel Estivill), 13 Dec. 1936; *La Vanguardia*, 21 Apr. 1938 (interview with Vidal Rosell). See also John Brademas, *Anarchosindicalismo y revolución en España, 1930–1937*, 189–96; José Díaz, *Tres años de lucha*, 350–66; Kaminski, *Ceux de Barcelone*, 223–27; Leval, *Espagne libertaire, 1936–1939*, 241–61; Leval, *Social Reconstruction in Spain*, 6–7, 10, 22–23, 32; Peter Merin, *Spain between Death and Birth*, 233–35; Vicente Ramos, I, 122, 154; Souchy and Folgare, 73–124; Vázquez and Valero, 77. According to reliable information given to me by Antonio Villanueva, secretary at one time of the CNT metal workers' union of Valencia, the following firms were taken over by his union: Brunet, Davis, Mateu, Sanz, Torras, and Unión Naval de Levante.

Urban real estate and buildings of right-wing organizations. See, for example, *La Batalla*, 23 Sept. 1936; *Boletín de Información, CNT-FAI*, 26 Aug., 26 Sept., 7 Nov. 1936; *Claridad*, 22 July 1936; *CNT*, 10 Aug. 1936; *El Día Gráfico*, 24 July, 29 Aug. 1936; *Mundo Obrero*, 19–20 Nov., 2, 5, 17, 19 Dec. 1936, 20 Jan. 1937, 5 June 1938; *Tierra y Libertad*, 23 Jan. 1937 (article by Gaston Leval); decree of the minister of finance, published in the *Gaceta de Madrid*, 29 Sept. 1936, which confirms the appropriation of urban real estate by trade-union and political organizations; also statement to the press by the minister of finance, *El Pueblo*, 24 Dec. 1936; J. Oltra Picó, *Socialización de las fincas urbanas y municipalización de los servicios*; Vicente Ramos, I, 155; Vicente Sáenz, *España en sus gloriosas jornadas de julio y agosto de 1936*, 18; Lazarillo de Tormes (Benigno Bejarano), *España, cuña de la libertad*, 67; Vázquez and Valero, 78–79.

Motion-picture theaters and legitimate theaters. See *La Batalla*, 9, 29 Aug. 1936; *Claridad*, 17 Aug. 1936; *CNT-AIT-FAI Informationsdienst*, 15 Aug. 1936; *La Humanitat*, 12 Sept. 1936; *Solidaridad Obrera*, 15 Aug., 19 Nov. 1936, 10 Feb. 1937; *Tiempos Nuevos*, 1 Dec. 1936 (article by A. Souchy); *Ultima Hora*, 6 Aug. 1936; *La Veu de Catalunya*, 29 Oct. 1936; R. Louzon, *La contra revolución en España*, 34; Vicente Ramos, I, 152; Vázquez and Valero, 112.

Hotels, restaurants, bars, and department stores. See *Acracia*, 24 Oct. 1936; *La Batalla*, 27 Feb. 1937; *Boletín de Información, CNT-FAI*, as given in *El Día Gráfico*, 21 Aug., 25 Nov. 1936; *CNT*, 7 Oct. 1936; *El Día Gráfico*, 24 July 1936; *Pravda*, 26 Sept. 1936 (article by Mikhail Koltzov); *Mundo Obrero*, 2 Oct. 1936; *Política*, 15 Aug. 1936; *Solidaridad Obrera*, 1 Nov. 1936; *Spanish Revolution*, 6 Aug. 1937; *Tierra y Libertad*, 30 Oct. 1937; *Umbral*, no. 14, as given in *Documentos Históricas de España*, Mar. 1938; *La Vanguardia*, 24 Nov. 1937; Diego Abad de Santillán, *Por qué perdimos la guerra*, 80; Leval, *Social Reconstruction*, 32; Louzon, 34; *Collectivisations*, 27.

Newspapers and printing shops. See *Claridad*, 24, 26 July 1936; *CNT*, 24 July, 1 Sept., 7 Oct. 1936; *El Día Gráfico*, 28 July 1936; *Mundo Obrero*, 21, 23 July, 27 Aug. 1936; *Tiempo de Historia*, June 1979 (Eduardo de Gúzman, "Periódicos y periodistas de Madrid en guerra"); *Treball*, 25 July 1936; Vázquez and Valero, 80–81.

For additional information on the control by the labor unions of various branches of industry and trade, see Walther L. Bernecker, *Anarchismus und Bürgerkrieg*, 137–211; Josep María Bricall, *Política económica de la Generalitat, 1936–1939*; Sam Dolgoff, *The Anarchist Collectives*; Ronald Fraser, *Blood of Spain*, 209–36; Leval, *Espagne libertaire*, 241–352; Frank Mintz, *L'autogestion dans l'Espagne révolutionnaire*, 210–36; Albert Pérez-Baró, *30 mesos de col·lectivisme a Catalunya, 1936–1939*; Vicente Ramos, I, 336–47 (for the names of 333 small manufacturing and commercial establishments sequestered in the province of Alicante by the UGT and CNT); Vázquez and Valero, 126–30; *Economies et Sociétés* (Paris: ISEA), Tome VI, Sept.–Oct. 1972 (article by Bricall, "L'Expérience Catalane d'Autogestion Ouvrière durant la Guerre Civile, 1936–1939"). Also, an unpublished manuscript by Michael Seidman, "Workers' Control in Barcelona in the Spanish Civil War, 1936–1938," which uncovers new sources (a copy of the manuscript is in the Hoover Institution, Bolloten Collection).

For the intervention by the ministry of industry and commerce in certain concerns in Madrid, see the *Gaceta de Madrid*, 27 July 1936; also *CNT*, 3 Aug. 1936; *Mundo Obrero*, 1 Aug. 1936; Política, 18 Aug. 1936; and *Guerra y revolución en España, 1936–1939*, I, 269–71. It should be observed that the immense majority of these firms had previously been taken over by the labor unions. See, for example, Mikhail Koltzov in *Pravda*, 26 Sept. 1936.

89. *Obras*, III, 497.

Chapter 5

1. These confiscations, to be sure, were often carried out without the approval of the national leaders of the UGT. For criticisms by Pascual Tomás, its vice-secretary, of the confiscation of small property by local UGT unions, see *La Correspondencia de Valencia*, 21 Dec. 1936; *Adelante*, 13 Feb. 1937; *Spartacus*, July–Aug. 1938.

2. See *Claridad*, 27 Aug. 1936; *CNT*, 7 Oct. 1936.

3. See speech by the local Communist party trade-union secretary, reported in *Frente Rojo*, 30 Mar. 1937. In a letter to the author, Antonio Villanueva, a member of the Valencia CNT, stated that the premises and equipment of nearly all the printers, cabinetmakers, tailors, dressmakers, barbers, beauticians, bootmakers, and other leather goods producers were taken over by the unions of that city. For the collectivizations of the bakeries, confectioneries, hotels, cafés, and bars in Valencia, see *Nosotros*, 27 Nov., 3 Dec. 1937. For seizures and collectivizations of industries and public utilities in the region, see Aurora Bosch Sánchez, *Ugetistas y libertarios: Guerra civil y revolución en el país valenciano, 1936–1939*, 23–31, and Albert Girona i Albuixec, *Guerra i revolució al país Valencià*, 135–222.

4. See Vicente Ramos, *La guerra civil, 1936–1939, en la provincia de Alicante*, I, 336–47, who lists the names of 333 small manufacturing and commercial establishments confiscated by the UGT and CNT.

5. The revolutionary developments in this region are dealt with in chapters 38 and 43.

6. See the Anarchosyndicalist organ, *Solidaridad Obrera*, 19 Dec. 1936; also speech by Federico Melchor, a Communist, as reprinted in Melchor, *Organicemos la producción*, 4–5.

7. *Solidaridad Obrera*, 23, 24 Dec. 1936.

8. Ibid., 29 Dec. 1936.

9. Ibid., 7 Oct. 1936.

10. See account in *Tierra y Libertad*, 21 Aug. 1937.

11. Ibid.

12. *Solidaridad Obrera*, 15 Dec. 1936.

13. See, for example, *CNT*, 10 Aug. 1936 (Madrid province); *Tierra y Libertad*, 23 Jan. 1937 (Carcagente); *Orientaciones Nuevas*, 6 Feb. 1937 (Montmeló).

14. See articles on the CLUEA (Consejo Levantino Unificado de la Exportación Agrícola) in *Fragua Social*, 31 Jan., 7 Feb. 1937; *Nosotros*, 19 Apr. 1937; also Franz Borkenau, *The Spanish Cockpit*, 197–200; María Josepa Cucó Giner et al., *La qüestió agrària al país Valencià*, 49–53; Girona i Albuixec, *Guerra i revolució*, 181–94; Manuel Villar, *España en la ruta de la libertad*, 51. Although the UGT was represented in the CLUEA, the CNT was the dominant influence.

15. For examples not already given in this chapter, the reader is referred to the following publications: *Acracia*, 24 Oct. 1936, 17 Nov., 3 Dec. 1937; *La Batalla*, 3 Oct. 1936; *Boletín de Información, CNT-FAI*, 14, 17, 23 Sept., 8 Oct., 7 Nov. 1936; *CNT*, 10 Aug., 19, 23 Sept., 7, 8, 16 Oct. 1936; *Cahier de l'Humanisme Libertaire* (Les Pêcheurs de Roses), March 1974; *Cultura Proletaria*, 8 Jan. 1938; *El Día Gráfico*, 4 Sept., 25 Nov. 1936; *España Libre* (Toulouse), 18 Sept. 1949 (article by A. Costales); *Espoir*, 18 Aug. 1963 (article by Manuel Jiménez); *Ideas*, 7 Jan. 1937; *Nosotros*, 15 Feb., 15 Nov. 1937; *El Noticiero Universal*, 11 Sept. 1936; *La Nouvelle Espagne Antifasciste*, 2 Dec. 1937; *Orientaciones Nuevas*, 30 Jan., 6 Feb. 1937; *La Révolution Prolétarienne*, 25 June 1937 (article by R. Louzon); *Solidaridad Obrera*, 13 Aug., 24 Sept., 18–20, 22 Nov., 2, 5, 11, 15, 17, 19, 25, 27 Dec. 1936; 20 Jan., 23 Apr., 30 June, 3 Aug. (article by Mariano Cardona Rosell) 1937; *Solidaridad Obrera* (Paris), 10 Feb. 1951 (article by Gaston Leval); *Tierra y Libertad*, 23 Jan. (article by Gaston Leval), 27 Feb., 17 Apr., 25 Dec. 1937; 15 Jan. 1938; *Umbral*, 24 July 1937; Gaston Leval, *L'indispensable révolution*, 192; Gaston Leval, *Né Franco né Stalin*, 131–42 and passim; Gaston Leval, *Social Reconstruction in Spain*, 10–11; Ramos, I, 336–47. See also Chapter 6.

16. 4 Feb. 1937.

17. *Solidaridad Obrera*, 1 Sept. 1937; see also *Las Noticias*, 1 July 1937.

18. *Solidaridad Obrera*, 1 Sept. 1937.

19. Ibid., 2 Oct. 1937.

20. Ibid., 24 Dec. 1936; see also *La Batalla*, 22 Jan. 1937; *Boletín de Información, CNT-FAI*, 25 Dec. 1936; Aristide Lapeyre, *Le problème espagnol*, 22–23.

21. *Boletín de Información, CNT-FAI*, 10 Apr. 1937; see also *CNT* (Paris), 17 July 1949.

22. *Tierra y Libertad*, 23 Jan. 1937; see also *Solidaridad Obrera*, 20 Jan. 1937.

23. *Solidaridad Obrera*, 23 Nov. 1938; *Ultima Hora*, 28 Sept. 1936; Aristide Lapeyre, 22; Agustín Souchy and Paul Folgare, *Colectivizaciones: La obra constructiva de la revolución española*, 137–43. Not all the CNT militants were in agreement with this rationalization of the barber shops and beauty parlors. "The working class showed a splendid sense of initiative," said Sebastián Clara, as recorded by Ronald Fraser in his oral history. "But that isn't to say there weren't stupid collectivizations. Take the barber shops. What in reality was being collectivized? A pair of scissors, a razor, a couple of barber's chairs. And what was the result? All those small owners who on their own would have supported the fight against fascism, now turned against us. Worse than having the enemy in front of you is the enemy in your midst" (*Blood of Spain*, 233).

24. For this information I am indebted to Antonio Villaneuva, a member of the Valencia CNT. For details of the collectivized clothing industry in that city, see *Nosotros*, 21 Oct. 1937. See also interview with the representative of the carpenters' union in the provincial secretariat of the Valencia UGT, stating that he considered the socialization of the woodworking industry "an error," especially in view of the large number of small owners who had not supported the military rebellion (*Frente Rojo*, 27 Feb. 1937).

25. Gaston Leval, *Espagne libertaire, 1936–39*, 351–52.

26. *Solidaridad Obrera*, 20 Oct. 1936.

27. *CNT*, 23 Sept. 1936; Leval, *L'indispensable révolution*, 192–93; Leval, *Social Reconstruction*, 32.

28. Leval, *Social Reconstruction*, 32.

29. *Boletín de Información, CNT-FAI*, 18 Aug. 1937.

30. Ibid., 15 Jan. 1937.

31. Ibid., 17 Sept. 1936; *Dialéctica*, Feb. 1938; José Peirats, *La CNT en la revolución española*, I, 174–75.

32. According to Mariano Cardona Rosell, member of the national committee of the CNT, in a letter to me, Hoover Institution.

33. See *Tierra y Libertad*, 23 Jan. 1937 (article by Gaston Leval).

34. Leval, *L'indispensable révolution*, 192; Leval, *Social Reconstruction*, 11.

35. Speech by Tomás Cano Ruiz at the closing session of the November 1936 congress of the Valencia CNT, quoted in *Fragua Social*, 17 Nov. 1936.

36. *Solidaridad Obrera*, 7 Apr. 1937. See also ibid., 4 Oct. 1936, 4 Feb. 1937.

37. The opposition of countless small businessmen to the collectivization movement in Catalonia was frankly admitted in an official report of the CNT; see report of the Junta del Control del Comité Económico, as given in Confederación Regional del Trabajo de Cataluña, *Memoria del congreso extraordinario de la confederación regional del trabajo de Cataluña celebrado en Barcelona los días 25 de febrero al 3 de marzo de 1937*, 363–65.

38. Albert Pérez-Baró, *30 mesos de col·lectivisme a Catalunya, 1936–1939*, 49. The author of this valuable book states that he was active in the syndicalist movement until 1926, but "politically independent" thereafter. Although commendably objective in his approach, bringing out both the positive and negative aspects of the collectivization movement, he clearly sympathizes with it. During the war, he was an official in the Secretaría de la Comisión de Aplicación del Decreto de Colectivizaciones del Consejo de Economía de Cataluña (see introduction to the Spanish-language edition, *Treinta meses de colectivismo en Cataluña, 1936–1939*, 29).

39. As recorded by Fraser, 221.

40. In a letter to Juan López, 8 March, 1940, Pérez-Baró, *30 mesos*, 25. See n. 38 above, for information on Pérez-Baró.

41. *Solidaridad Obrera*, 9 Sept. 1936.

42. 29 Aug. 1936. See also ibid., 8 Aug., 3 Sept., 8 Oct. 1936; statement issued by the regional committee of the Catalan CNT and by the peninsular committee of the FAI, as given in *El Día Gráfico*, 26 Aug. 1936.

Chapter 6

1. For data on some of the agricultural collectives in different parts of the left camp, the following newspapers and periodicals published during and after the Civil War may be consulted: *Acracia*, 19 July 1937 (Vallfogona, Castelló de Farfaña, Bellmunt de Urgell, La Portella, Os de Balaguer), 16, 17, 29, 30 Nov. 1937 (Belvis de Jarama, Alguaire, Serós, Mayals, Roses de Llobregat), 16 Dec. 1937 (Palau de Anglesola); *La Batalla*, 26 Aug. 1936 (Raimut); *Boletín de Información, CNT-FAI*, 16, 23, 29 Sept. 1936 (Cabanes, Pont de Molins, Llardecans, Granadella), 8 Oct. 1936 (Palafrugell, Caldes de Malavella), 24 Mar. 1937 (Cabra del Campo), 4, 17 Aug. 1937 (Candasnos, Peñarroya de Tastavins), 11 Feb. 1938 (Bujaraloz); *Cahiers de l'Humanisme Libertaire*, Nov.–Dec. 1936 (Ballobar); *Castilla Libre*, 16 Apr. 1937 (Membrilla), as given in *Documentos Históricos de España*, Nov. 1937; *Claridad*, 14 Dec. 1936 (Guadasur), 16 Feb. 1937 (Badajoz); *CNT*, 10, 17 Aug. 1936 (Puente de Arganda, Belvis de Jarama, Paracuellos de Jarama, Cobena, Villas Viejas), 1, 19 Sept. 1936 (Navilucillos, Utiel), 7–9 Oct. 1936 (collectives in the central region and Mestanza and Hellin), 19 June 1937 (Alcalá de Henares); *CNT* (Paris), 5, 12 Nov. 1938 (Madrid, García), 7, 28 Jan. 1949 (Hijar, Caspe, Angües, Fraga, Torrente de Cinca, Utillas, Peñalba, Farlete, Lécera, Aznara, La Fresnada, Mas de las Matas, Alarcón, Maella), 25 Dec. 1949 (Bot), 29 Jan. 1950 (Cerviá); *CNT* (Toulouse), 23 Nov. 1946 (Tivisa), 6 Sept. 1947 (Hospitalet de Llobregat), 17 Dec. 1950 (Villas Viejas); *Colectivismo*, 15 Aug. 1937 (Infantes), 15 Sept. 1937 (Iniesta), 15 Oct. 1937 (Castuera, Valdepeñas), 15 Dec. 1937 (Ibi), Jan.–Feb. 1938 (Marchamalo), 15 Mar. 1936 (Manises), 1 May 1936 (Los Estados de Santo Tomé), 1 June 1938 (Venta del Charco), 1 Aug. 1938 (Rafelguaraf), 1 Sept. 1938 (Villarubia de Santiago), 1 Dec. 1938 (Marchal); *La Correspondencia de Valencia*, 19 Oct. 1937 (Castuera); *Cultura Proletaria*, 2 Oct. 1937 (Peñarroya), 8, 29 Jan. 1938 (Perales de Tajuña, Hospitalet de Llobregat), 23 Apr. 1938 (Valencia province), 21, 28 Oct., 4, 11 Nov. 1939 (Calanda), 7, 21 Feb. 1948 (Farlete, Binéfar, Altamira, Fraga, Alcorisa, Monzón, Hijar, Alcañiz, Caspe), 28 Jan. 1950 (Ballobar); *Cultura y Acción*, 6 Aug. 1937 (Binéfar), 1 May 1937 (Alcañiz); *Documentos Históricos de España*, Dec. 1938 (Liria); *Espoir*, 4 Aug. 1963 (Amposta), 30 July 1972 ("La Révolución Libertaria en el Campo Andaluz"); *El Día Gráfico*, 26 Aug. 1936 (Rubi); *Fragua Social*, 17 June 1937 (Utiel), 28 Aug. 1937 (Cullera), 2 Dec. 1937 (Gramanet del Besós), 26 Feb. 1938 (Sueca); *Juventud Libre*, 31 Oct. 1936 (Utiel); *Le Libertaire*, 23 July 1948 (the Levante zone); *Mujeres Libres*, July 1937 (Calanda, Cabeza del Buey, Herrera del Castillo, Siruela); *Nosotros*, 19 Feb. 1937 (Simat de Valldigna), 24 June 1937 (Benaguacil), 1 Dec. 1937 (Madrid); *La Nouvelle Espagne Antifasciste*, 25 Nov. 1937 (Balsareny); *Orientaciones Nuevas*, 6 Feb. 1937 (Montmeló); *La Révolution Prolétarienne*, 10 Sept. 1937 (Segorbe); *Solidaridad Obrera*, 14 Aug. 1936 (Bujaraloz), 6 Oct. 1936 (La Figuera), 17, 19, 22, 28 Nov. 1936 (Valjunquera, Tarrassa, Premiá de Dalt, Martorell), 5, 11, 19, 27 Dec. 1936 (Serdanyola Ripollet, Villanueva y Geltrú, Sadurni de Noya, Rubi), 20 Jan. 1937 (Amposta), 26, 30 June 1937 (Oliete, Plá de Cabra), 10 Nov. 1937 (Lérida), 25 Dec. 1937 (Caravaca), 10 Dec. 1937 (Vilaboi); *Solidaridad Obrera* (Paris), 10 Feb. 1951 (Tamarite de Litera); *Tierra y Libertad*, 27 Aug. 1936 (Maella), 16 Jan. 1937 (Carcagente, Vallforguna de Balaguer, Pina de Ebro, Palafrugall), 13 Feb. 1937 (Llivia); *Umanità Nova*, 8 Jan. 1950 (Triana); *Umbral*, 24 July 1937 (Amposta); *Vida*, as given in *Solidaridad Obrera*, 22 Oct. 1937 (Beniopa, Oliva, Teresa, Tabernes de Valldigna, Benifairó, Simat). For additional data on rural collectives, see *Timón*, July 1938 (article by Agustín Souchy); Bernecker, *Anarchismus und Bürgerkrieg*, 45–72; Franz Borkenau, *The Spanish Cockpit*, 148–51; Julián Casanova, *Anarquismo y revolución en la sociedad rural aragonesa, 1936–1938*, 177–219, 323–37; *Las colectividades campesinas, 1936–1939*; Confederación Nacional del Trabajo, *Realizaciones revolucionarias y estructuras colectivistas de la comarcal de Monzón* (Huesca); María Josepa Cucó Giner et al., *La qüestió agrària al país Valencià*, 58–62; Sam Dolgoff, *The Anarchist Collectives*; Ronald Fraser, *Blood of Spain*, 347–73; Luis Garrido González, *Colectividades agrarias en Andalucía: Jaén (1931–1939)*, 27–174; José Luis Gutiérrez Molina, *Colectividades libertarias en Castilla*, 9–113; Gaston Leval, *Le communisme*, 60–66; Gaston Leval, *Espagne libertaire, 1936–39*, 83–256; Gaston Leval, *Né Franco né Stalin*, 143–300;

Frank Mintz, *L'autogestion dans l'Espagne révolutionnaire*, 51–78, 98–111, and the latter's bibliography on collectivization published by Archives Internationales de Sociologie de la Coopération et Développement (supplément à *Communauté*, July–Dec. 1967); José Peirats, *Los anarquistas en la crisis política española*, 147–72; José Peirats, *La CNT en la revolución española*, I, 302–26, 331–53; Antonio Rosado, *Tierra y libertad: Memorias de un campesino anarcosindicalista andaluz*, 149–205; Rafael Sardá, *Las colectividades agrícolas*; Agustín Souchy, *Entre los campesinos de Aragón*; Souchy and Folgare, *Colectivizaciones: La obra constructiva de la revolución española*, 145–55, 193–94; 201–2, 205–6, 223–36; also materials given in n. 42 below. By far the most serious study of rural collectivization to appear in recent years, but restricted to the region of Valencia, is that of Aurora Bosch Sánchez, *Ugetistas y libertarios: Guerra civil y revolución en el país valenciano, 1936–1939*. Her work is especially valuable in that it deals with various facets of the collectives, with voluntary and forced collectivization, and with the confrontations between the proponents of individual and collective farming.

2. *Agrarian Reform and Peasant Revolution in Spain*, 386, n. 75. Malefakis also points out that where the military rebellion was successful, the settlers placed by the Republic were for the most part ousted from their holdings: "The official Nationalist position distinguished between settlements made under the Popular Front, which were immediately undone on the grounds that they were illegitimate, and the lesser settlements made earlier, the legitimacy of which was accepted until 1941, when the entire legacy of the IRA was liquidated. In some areas, however, particularly those under the control of General Queipo de Llano, the yunteros, who had received temporary grants of land in the spring of 1936 were also allowed to remain on their holdings until the end of the war" (ibid., 386, n. 76).

3. Garrido González, *Colectivadades agrarias*, 28–30. This carefully researched book is a valuable corrective to the impression widely held that the collective farm movement was limited largely to CNT-dominated areas. Out of the 104 collectives that Garrido was able to identify in Jaén, 38 (36.53 percent) were run by the UGT; 19 (18.26 percent) by the CNT; 18 (17.3 percent) jointly by the UGT-CNT; 14 (13.46 percent) by the Communists (ibid., 33; see also ibid., 5). The full history of the collective farm movement has not yet been written, but it is becoming increasingly apparent from such recent studies as those of Garrido González, Cucó Giner, *La qüestió agrària*, and Gutiérrez Molina, *Colectividades libertarias*, that the movement was far more extensive than its antagonists were willing to admit during the war and immediately thereafter. The evidence that emerges strongly suggests that in spite of wartime difficulties, political opposition, and many cases of coercion and violence, it was to a large degree successful and spontaneous.

4. See, for example, J. Valery, in *Fragua Social*, 23 July 1937.

5. 16 Jan. 1937.

6. *Tiempos Nuevos*, Sept. 1938.

7. *La revolución y la guerra en España*, 107–8. See also *Solidaridad Obrera*, 4 Sept. 1936; *Frente Libertario*, 7 June 1937.

8. See, for example, "Cómo trabajan nuestros técnicos," *Colectivismo*, 15 Nov. 1937; also statement by a local secretary of the National Federation of Land Workers, in *Adelante*, 16 June 1937.

9. *Adelante*, 1 Apr. 1937.

10. *El Obrero de la Tierra*, 30 Aug. 1936, as reprinted in *Adelante*, 21 July 1937. In December 1936, however, the national committee of the federation resolved that each of its members who were opposed to the collectivization of the large estates would receive a proportionate piece of land (quoted in *Por la revolución agraria*, 8).

11. *Juventud Libre*, 3 July 1937. See also speech by Juan J. Domenech, *Solidaridad Obrera*, 7 Jan. 1937; report from Barbastro signed by Cosme Sampériz, ibid., 1 Sept. 1936; article by Gaston Leval on Carcagente, *Tierra y Libertad*, 16 Jan. 1937.

12. See *CNT*, 5 Apr. 1937 (CNT Peasant Congress of Castile); *Fragua Social*, 15 Nov. 1936 (8th Session of the Congress of the Valencia CNT); *Solidaridad Obrera*, 8 Sept. 1936 (Congress of the CNT Peasants' Union of Catalonia); *Adelante*, 10 Mar. 1937 (resolution approved by the provincial congress of the UGT Land Workers of Valencia); *Claridad*, 16 Dec. 1936 (editorial); *La Correspondencia de Valencia*, 21 Dec. 1936 (speech by Pascual Tomás, vice-secretary of the UGT); resolution and manifesto of the National Federation of Land Workers, December 1936, as reprinted in *Por la revolución agraria*, 5–13, 29–33, see also 38–39.

13. *Verdad*, 8 Jan. 1937.

14. See *CNT*, 5 Apr. 1937 (CNT Peasant Congress of Castile); *Cultura y Acción*, 18 Feb. 1937

(Congress of Agricultural Collectives of Aragon); *Fragua Social*, 15 Nov. 1936 (8th Session of the Congress of the Valencia CNT); *Solidaridad Obrera*, 8 Sept. 1936 (Congress of CNT Peasants' Union of Catalonia); *Adelante*, 10 Mar. 1937 (provincial congress of the UGT Land Workers of Valencia); *Claridad*, 25 Oct. 1936 (provincial congress of the UGT Land Workers of Granada); resolution and manifesto of the National Federation of Land Workers, December 1936, as reprinted in *Por la revolución agraria*, 5–13, 29–33.

15. See, for example, what happened in the village of Guadasur, which was controlled by the UGT and CNT, *Claridad*, 14 Dec. 1936; also resolution approved by the delegates of twenty-one villages controlled by the CNT in Aragon, as given in *Solidaridad Obrera*, 16 Aug. 1936. Of the village of Calanda, Gaston Leval, the well-known foreign Anarchist, wrote: "The individualists were allowed a minimum of freedom. They could possess land because that is what they desired, but they could not trade with the fruit of their labor. They could not speculate and compete disloyally with the young collective" (*Cultura Proletaria*, 4 Nov. 1939). It is not undeserving of notice that after the formation early in 1937 of the National Peasants' Federation affiliated with the CNT, this organization became, at least theoretically, the sole distributor of the agricultural produce of the individual cultivators and collective farms that came under its jurisdiction (see *Estatutos de la federación nacional de campesinos*, 13).

16. See *Adelante*, 21 Apr. 1937; also article by Ricardo Zabalza, general secretary of the National Federation of Land Workers, published in *CNT*, 26 May 1937.

17. Isaac Puente, *Finalidad de la CNT*, 3. See also resolution on libertarian communism approved at the Extraordinary Congress of the CNT held in Saragossa in May 1936, as given in *Solidaridad Obrera*, 12 May 1936. Commenting on this resolution in an interview given to *Tiempo de Historia* in its issue of January 1980, the Anarchosyndicalist militant and historian, José Peirats, made the following observation: "Nowadays, this document may appear ingenuous or romantic and make a lot of people laugh. The fact is that we regarded ourselves as the last romantics . . . and without underestimating the obstacles that society would place in the path of our aspirations, we understood that it was necessary to indicate our goal. . . . I have already said that the resolution on libertarian communism may appear childish . . . because society has changed since 1936, but that change does not represent absolute progress, for there are many negative aspects. Although the resolution related to a semifeudal or underdeveloped society, such as Spain, there still exists a desire for perfection and a faith in the eternal values of humanity that the sarcastic critics of today do not take into account."

18. Puente, *Finalidad de la CNT*, 4. See also ibid., 24–26, and *La Revista Blanca*, 25 Jan. 1937.

19. Puente, *Finalidad de la CNT*, 4.

20. Federico Urales, *La anarquía al alcance de todos*, 29.

21. Isaac Puente in *Tierra y Libertad*, supplement, Aug. 1932, as reprinted in Puente, *Propaganda*, 101.

22. *Die Soziale Revolution*, no. 3, Jan. 1937. "The men and women who stormed the convents [in Barcelona] burned everything they found inside, including money. How well I remember that rugged worker who proudly showed me the corner of a burned thousand peseta bill" (Federica Montseny, "19 de Julio Catalán," *Fragua Social*, 19 July 1937, as reprinted in *De julio a julio*, 22).

23. Agustín Souchy in *Tierra y Libertad*, 6 Aug. 1938.

24. An Anarchist report on Fraga elaborates on the revolutionary experiment carried out in that small community:

"The product of one's own labor—wheat, fruit, olives—is freely available. To cover the rest of its needs, each family receives a weekly sum which increases in accordance with the number of members in the family and the number of adult workers.

"This sum is not paid in bills of the Bank of Spain, for the simple reason that they would be useless, because they have no value in the village. Small slips printed by the union with a nominal value that varies between ten céntimos and twenty-five pesetas are used as purchase vouchers. These are only accepted by the barber, the shoemaker and the office for the distribution of food products. . . .

"A traveller who wishes to spend the night or remain in Fraga must go to the Committee to convert his Spanish Republican money into local vouchers. If an inhabitant wants to leave the town he must also go to the Committee, indicating the reason for his journey and the amount he needs; the Committee then changes his local vouchers into Spanish bills" (Souchy and Folgare, *Colectivizaciones*, 230–31). For the difficulties created by the collectivist experiment in Mas de las Matas, an Aragonese village of twenty-three hundred inhabitants, see Fraser, *Blood of Spain*, 351–58. The oral testimony that Fraser cites, furnished by CNT survivors many years later, presents a well-balanced picture of life in the village.

25. Kaminski, *Ceux de Barcelone*, 118–21.

26. Ibid., 121–22.

27. Borkenau, *The Spanish Cockpit*, 166–67.

28. Quoted from dissertation (University of London) entitled, "Anarchist Ideology and the Working Class Movement in Spain (1880–1900); with Special Reference to the Ideas of Ricardo Mella," 237, n. 12. Esenwein also states: "For examples of this [puritanical] tendency, see *El Productor* (Barcelona, 1887–93); *El Socialismo* (Cádiz, 1886–91); and *La Solidaridad* (Seville, 1888–89). Later, puritanism was promoted in such prestigious and influential Anarchist journals as *La Revista Blanca* (Madrid, 1898–1905 and 1923–36). A vivid portrait of the self-abnegating revolutionary type is found in Vicente Blasco Ibáñez, *La Bodega*, in which the character Fermín Salvatierra is modeled after the legendary Anarchist, Fermín Salvochea." My own personal recollection is that middle-class Spaniards scoffed at those Anarchists who closed down the brothels in the cities and put the prostitutes to useful work. But for Anarchist purists the cleaning up of society was an article of faith. In his oral history, Ronald Fraser tells of the young Eduardo Pons Prades, who, in the CNT woodworkers' union headquarters in Barcelona, just off the Parelelo, with its music-halls, nightclubs and bars, heard the men discussing what had to be done: " 'Listen, what about all the people who work in these dens of iniquity?' 'We've got to redeem them, educate them so they can have the chance of doing something more worthy.' 'Have you asked them if they want to be redeemed?' 'How can you be so stupid? Would you like to be exploited in that sort of den?' 'No, of course not. But after years at the same thing, it's hard to change.' 'Well, they'll have to. The revolution's first duty is to clean up the place, clean up the people's consciousness' " (137). Of the village of Mas de las Matas, in Aragon, Fraser writes: "All the taverns were closed. 'We libertarians were always hostile to bars because they were the cause of vice, arguments and fights,' recalled Sevilla Pastor. . . . Only the large room in the CNT center was left open and there people could drink coffee or non-alcoholic beverages. Wine was distributed as part of the ration for private consumption at home. Gambling was suppressed" (ibid., 354–55).

29. *Tierra y Libertad*, 30 Jan. 1937.

30. Agustín Souchy, *Entre los campesinos de Aragón*, 73.

31. 13 July 1934, 8 June 1934, respectively.

32. *Cahiers de l'Humanisme Libertaire*, Mar. 1968.

33. Alardo Prats, *Vanguardia y retaguardia de Aragón*, 85–93.

34. Souchy and Folgare, 233–34.

35. *Entre los campesinos*, 92.

36. Fraser, 368, n. 1.

37. Ibid., 371.

38. *Entre los campesinos*, 84–85.

39. Confederación Nacional del Trabajo, *Comarcal de Valderrobres (Teruel)*, 73.

40. Souchy and Folgare, 45–47.

41. 24 Sept. 1936.

42. *Entre los campesinos*, 66. "The wage differential between men and women mentioned by Souchy," writes George Esenwein, "points to one of the important cleavages between Anarchist theory and practice that emerged during their collectivist experience. The Anarchists had for many years claimed that men and women were equal in every way. Their commitment to this proposition was reiterated on the eve of the Civil War at the Saragossa Congress of 1936, at which it was declared confidently that the economic differences existing between men and women under capitalism would disappear with the advent of revolution, making both sexes equal as regards their rights and obligations (see *El Congreso Confederal de Zaragoza [CNT]*, Madrid: Zero, 1978, 237–38). Recent scholarship has shown that even though the Anarchists made great strides towards achieving these goals in some collectives, their overall record on women's rights was inconsistent with their libertarian principles. See, for example, Martha A. Ackelsberg, 'The Practice of Anarchist Revolution: The Position of Women in Spanish Anarchist Collectives,' unpublished paper, 1980; Bernecker, *Anarchismus und Bürgerkrieg . . .* , Hamburg: Hoffmann und Campe, 1978, 106–10; Temma Kaplan, 'Spanish Anarchism and Women's Liberation,' in *Journal of Contemporary History*, vol. 6, no. 2, 1971, 101–10; Mary Nash, ed., *'Mujeres Libres.' La doble lucha de la mujer*, Barcelona: Tusquets,

1975, and her 'Una gran conciencia feminista (entrevista con Mary Nash),' in *Tiempo de Historia*, año II, no. 19, May 1976, 43–47; María Pino, '"Mujeres Libres," un movimiento feminista en plena Guerra civil' (ibid., 36–42); Geraldine Scanlon, *La polémica feminista en la España contemporánea*; Concepción Sonadellas, *Clase obrera y revolución social en España, 1936–1939*, 149–74." This note, based on Esenwein's own research, was written at my request.

Obviously no attempt has been made to cover in detail all aspects of the libertarian collectives. The interested reader should consult the following materials: *Boletín de Información, CNT-FAI*, 20 Feb. 1937 (Tabernes de Valldigna), 17 Aug. 1937 (Peñarroya de Tastavins); *Cahiers de l'Humanisme Libertaire*, Nov.–Dec. 1963 (Ballobar), 1 Mar. 1968 (Magdalena de Pulpis); *CNT*, 7 Oct. 1936 (Membrilla), 27 May 1937 (Torrevelilla); *CNT* (Paris), 24 Dec. 1948 (Binéfar), 27 Nov. 1949 (Santa Magdalena de Pulpis); *CNT*, 23 Aug. 1947 (Graus), 22 July 1951 (Ballobar); *Cultura y Acción*, 13 Mar. 1937 (Mosqueruela); *L'Espagne Antifasciste*, 21 Nov. 1936 (Alcoy, Enguerra, Játiva); *Fragua Social*, 6 Apr. 1937 (Bujaraloz), also article from this paper on Utiel, reproduced in *Boletín de Información, CNT-FAI*, 19 June 1937; *Juventud Libre*, 14 Nov. 1936 (Pedrilla); *Le Libertaire*, 15 July 1937, as given in *Spanish Revolution*, 6 Aug. 1937; *Mar y Tierra*, 15 Aug. 1937 (La Nucia); *Mujeres Libres*, July 1937 (Calanda); *Nosotros*, 24 Feb. 1937 (Beniopa); *Solidaridad Obrera*, 13, 17, 19 Nov. 1936 (Bujaraloz, Velilla de Ebro, Lécera, Farlete); *Solidaridad Obrera* (Mexico City), 17 May 1947 (Graus); *Solidaridad Obrera* (Paris), 24 Feb., 10 Mar. 1951 (Mas de las Matas), 7, 14, 21 Apr. 1951 (Graus), 23, 29 June 1951 (Alcolea de Cinca), 7, 14 July 1951 (Alcorisa); *Tierra y Libertad*, 17, 24 Sept. 1936 (Maella), 30 Jan. 1937 (Magdalena de Pulpis); *Tierra y Libertad* (Mexico City), 25 Jan. 1947 (Asco), 10 July 1947 (Ballobar); *Umanità Nova*, 25 Dec. 1950 (Santa Magdalena de Pulpis); Borkenau, *The Spanish Cockpit*, 166–67; Julián Casanova Ruiz, *Anarquismo y revolución en la sociedad rural aragonesa, 1936–1938*, 177–219, 323–37, and *Caspe, 1936–1938*, 55–56; *Las colectividades campesinas, 1936–1939*, 122–42; Confederación Nacional del Trabajo, *Realizaciones revolucionarias y estructuras colectivistas de la comarcal de Monzón (Huesca)*; Confederación Regional de Aragón, Rioja y Navarra (CNT), *Comarcal de Valderrobres (Teruel)*; José Duque, "La situación de Aragón al comienzo de la guerra," 2–4; Fraser, *Blood of Spain*, 347–73; José Gabriel, *La vida y la muerte en Aragón*, 146; Félix García, *Colectivizaciones compesinas y obreras en la revolución española*, 23–32; Kaminski, *Ceux de Barcelone*, 118–25; Aristide Lapeyre, *Le problème espagnol*, 18–20; Leval, *Espagne libertaire, 1936–39*, 85–126; Leval, *Né Franco né Stalin*, 143–300; Leval, *Social Reconstruction in Spain*, 12–13, 15, 17–18; Xavier Paniagua, *La sociedad libertaria*, 99–114; Peirats, *La CNT en la revolución*, I, 319–26; Alardo Prats, *Vanguardia y retaguardia de Aragón*, 84–93; Souchy, *Entre los campesinos*; Souchy and Folgare, *Colectivizaciones*, 223–42.

43. Quoted in Diego Abad de Santillán, *Timón*, Aug. 1938.

44. Quoted in Abad de Santillán, *La bancarrota del sistema económico y político del capitalismo*, 53.

45. *Bog i gosudarstvo*, 16.

46. 5 June 1936.

47. 5 Aug. 1936. See also *Solidaridad Obrera*, 15 Aug. 1936.

48. Souchy, *Entre los campesinos*, 87–88.

49. Report from Albalate de Cinca in *Solidaridad Obrera*, 26 Aug. 1936.

50. *Cultura y Acción*, 18 Feb. 1937.

51. Paraphrase by *Solidaridad Obrera*, 9 Sept. 1936, of a passage in a speech by Ramón Porté, delegate for Tarragona province and member of the regional committee of the Catalan CNT. He drew attention in this passage to similar warnings by previous speakers.

52. See, for example, *Castilla Libre*, 30 Mar. 1937; *CNT*, 10 Aug. 1936; *Cultura y Acción*, as given in *Boletín de Información, CNT-FAI*, 4 Aug. 1937; *Nosotros*, 24 June 1937; *Solidaridad Obrera*, 19 Dec. 1936, 13 May 1937; *Tierra y Libertad*, 16 Jan. 1937; *Timón*, July 1938 (article by Souchy).

53. *Juventud Libre*, 10 July 1937. See also ibid., 14 Nov. 1936 (article on Pedralba).

54. *Solidaridad Obrera*, 19 Nov. 1936. See also Souchy and Folgare, 224, and article on Calanda in *Mujeres Libres*, July 1937.

55. This is the figure given by the Anarchosyndicalist leader, Abad de Santillán, *Por qué perdimos la guerra*, 94. It was confirmed to the author by José Duque and José Almudí, the two Communist members of the Defense Council of Aragon, the principal administrative organ in the region during

the early months of the Revolution (interviews in Mexico in 1939; shorthand notes taken during Almudí interview are in Hoover Institution). See also Prats (a Socialist), 81, who says that 70 percent of the land was collectivized.

56. Figure given by César Martínez Lorenzo, *Les anarchistes espagnols et le pouvoir, 1868–1969*, 152, n. 17; Peirats, *Los anarquistas en la crisis*, 300; Prats, 81.

57. It is noteworthy that the Anarchists did not refer to the foremost men of their movement as leaders because this term implied authority and control. Instead, they used the words "representatives," "delegates," and "militants." Still, as these men possessed the qualities of leadership in their ability to guide and influence the members of the CNT and FAI, and, indeed, were leaders by almost every test that distinguishes the leadership of a movement from the rank and file, I prefer to use this term.

58. Quoted in *CNT*, 6 Oct. 1936.

59. *Solidaridad Obrera*, 17 Nov. 1936.

60. *Fragua Social*, 6 Apr. 1937.

61. In the village of Gelsa, for instance, a proclamation was issued as soon as the revolutionary regime was instituted, stating that "those persons who do not deposit food and clothing of all kinds [in the communal warehouse], but keep them to enrich themselves, will suffer the maximum penalty" (*Solidaridad Obrera*, 16 Aug. 1936).

62. See resolution approved at the Congress of Agricultural Collectives of Aragon, as given in *Cultura y Acción*, 18 Feb. 1937; also preface by Agustín Souchy to *Collectivisations: L'oeuvre constructive de la révolution espagnole, 1936–1939*, 20, and *Frente Libertario*, 25 Dec. 1937.

63. See statement by the councillor of agriculture of the Catalan government, *El Día Gráfico*, 3 Jan. 1937; also notice issued by the Peasant Federation of Valencia province, *Verdad*, 21 Jan. 1937.

64. An interesting example was the collective of Prat de Llobregat. According to an account in *Tierra y Libertad*, the FAI organ, 1 July 1938, it was set up in October 1936 by one thousand farm laborers, tenant farmers, and peasant owners who had agreed "almost unanimously" to the collective cultivation of the soil. But no sooner had the political situation changed to the disadvantage of the CNT and FAI than the tenant farmers and peasant owners demanded the restoration of their properties, the original collective, according to this account, being reduced to a quarter of its former size.

65. *Timón*, July 1938.

66. Interview published in *Tiempo de Historia*, Sept. 1978.

67. See, for example, *Cultura y Acción*, 6 Aug. 1937; *Juventud Libre*, 10 July 1937 (statement by Criado, general secretary of the CNT Peasants' Federation of Castile); *Solidaridad Obrera*, 11 July 1937; also Abad de Santillán, *La revolución*, 103, and Leval, *Social Reconstruction in Spain*, 13.

68. Article in *Estudios*, quoted in Henri Rabasseire, *Espagne: creuset politique*, 130. See also *Frente Libertario*, the CNT newspaper, 25 Dec. 1937. For further evidence of coercion and violence in the creation of some collective farms, see oral testimony given to Fraser by CNT militants, 362, 366–71.

69. 10 Sept. 1936.

70. Article in *Llibertat*, 29 Sept. 1936, as reprinted in Juan Peiró, *Perill a la reraguarda*, 102–3; see also ibid., 107–10, 158–59, and Joaquín Ascaso (the Anarchist president of the Defense Council of Aragon) in *Cultura y Acción*, 28 July 1937. In the preface to Juan Peiró, *Trayectoria de la CNT: Sindicalismo y anarquismo*, Peiró's son, José, writes: "In those days, when the life of a human being had such little value and when the extrarevolutionary executions perpetrated because of personal jealousies, hatreds, and disputes were common currency, countless people owed their lives to the sensibility of Juan Peiró, a sensibility that was not sentimentality—as some claim—but the product of a profound feeling of justice. Peiró, a CNT militant, had suffered so much from the injustice of reactionary capitalist regimes that he could not allow the most immoral 'popular justice' to be committed in the name of 'revolutionary justice,' in which he sincerely believed. . . . [Defying] danger, he fought all opposition in order to impose respect for the human personality and his emancipatory Ideal. His sensational press campaign [in *Llibertat*] in those days of convulsive passions was a veritable monument to his revolutionary steadfastness" (28–29).

71. *Il Risveglio Anarchico*, 30 Nov. 1929.

72. *Unmanità Nova*, 14 Oct. 1922, as given in Luis Fabbri, *Vida y pensamiento de Malatesta*, 220.

73. See, for example, Abad de Santillán, *Por qué*, 71. Of particular interest are the following

replies some forty years after the event by Federica Montseny, the CNT-FAI leader, to questions posed by Agustí Pons regarding the Patrullas de Control, the revolutionary police squads formed in Barcelona by the Anarchosyndicalists and other left-wing organizations.

"Pons: 'In retrospect, what is your opinion of the Patrullas de Control?'

"Montseny: 'The problem affected all organizations not only ours. . . . The fact of the matter is that the most capable men remained in the collectives. It was they who kept the plants operating. The most audacious and the most idealistic went to the front. . . . The type of man that was left was neither intrepid nor capable. . . . The majority of our comrades were idealists. They were repelled by police work and did not want to do it. . . . This is not to say that there were not some worthy individuals who did police work because they believed that a "nettoyage" was necessary. . . . But they were a minority.'

"Pons: 'Wasn't the activity of the Patrullas de Control a decisive factor in the sense that a sizable portion of the handicraftsmen and small bourgeoisie who, in the beginning, were in favor of the Republic ended up being more or less sympathetic to the entry of Franco's troops?'

"Montseny: 'What happened was that the Patrullas de Control became corrupt. The persons who joined them turned into professional policemen and developed an obsession about conspiracies, espionage, and the enemy. . . . I have come to one conclusion: whether you call them Patrullas de Control, GPU or any other name, you are lost once you give them police powers, even though they are a product of the revolution, because you have created a police mentality. This happened not only in our case, but in that of Russia and the French Revolution. And it will happen in all revolutions . . . and there will always be excesses that later we all regret' " (Pons, *Converses amb Frederica Montseny*, 141–45).

74. *Gosudarstvennost i anarkhiia* (State and Anarchy), 234–35.

75. "A Contribution to the History of the Question of Dictatorship," *Communist International*, no. 14, 6 Nov. 1920, in *Collected Works*, XXXI, 326 (4th Russian edition), as quoted by Bertram Wolfe, *Khrushchev and Stalin's Ghost*, 9.

76. "Marxism and the Russian Revolution," in Milorad M. Drachkovitch, *Fifty Years of Communism in Russia*, 32.

77. This was not the first occasion that the Spanish Anarchists contradicted their stated principles. The libertarian historian, César M. Lorenzo, writes: "On 18 January 1932, groups of the FAI staged an insurrection in the mining region of the upper Llobregat and Cardoner, where the working conditions were deplorable and the workers were harshly exploited. In Berga, Cardona, Figols, Sallent, Suria, libertarian communism was 'proclaimed.' But the movement did not spread beyond that part of Catalonia. This permitted the government to crush it easily within five days. . . . In all those places where the libertarians had the situation briefly in hand and attempted to make the social revolution, they ran counter to their principles. Wishing to abolish laws, to institute a society without authority and without restraints, and to give free rein to the spontaneous creativity of the masses, they were compelled to set up executive committees charged with maintaining order and watching over malcontents or opponents. They imposed their rule by force through decrees they modestly called 'proclamations.' Far from realising 'Anarchism,' the leaders of the Revolution, armed and supplied with dynamite, established what one would characterize as the 'dictatorship of the proletariat' without taking into consideration the views of the peasants and the small bourgeoisie" (Lorenzo, 73–74). The author of this work is the son of Horacio M. Prieto, secretary in 1936 of the CNT national committee, who both before and during the Civil War had serious differences with the FAI. Although Lorenzo— who does not reveal his relationship to Prieto—makes a special effort to defend his father's attitudes, the book is nonetheless an extraordinarily valuable contribution to the history of the Spanish libertarian movement.

78. Adrian Shubert and George Esenwein, *The Spanish Civil War: War of Many Wars*.

79. See interview given by José Peirats to *Tiempo de Historia*, Jan. 1980, in n. 17 above.

80. *Anarchism: History of Libertarian Ideas and Movements*, 398.

81. The failure of liberal historians to stress the magnitude of the social revolution and the total collapse of the Republican state in July 1936 prompted Noam Chomsky to attack the school of "liberal scholarship" in *American Power and the New Mandarins* (1967), 23–158. His criticisms were aimed mainly at Gabriel Jackson's *The Spanish Republic and the Civil War, 1931–1939* (1965), and Hugh

Thomas's *The Spanish Civil War* (1961), which, as Chomsky indicates, "barely refers to the popular revolution" (138, n. 59). Jackson later attempted to rectify the omission, though only partially, in his paper "The Living Experience of the Spanish Civil War Collectives," presented at the meeting of the American Historical Association, Washington, D.C. (30 Dec. 1969), later published in the *Newsletter of the Society for Spanish and Portuguese Historical Studies* (1 Apr. 1970), and in the chapter "Revolución Social in la Zona Republicana" in his book *Entre la reforma y la revolución* (1980), 218–68, which consists of long excerpts from various works dealing with the Revolution. Thomas, on the other hand, added an eleven-page chapter on the collectives to the revised Penguin edition of his book (1965) and a year later published an essay on the same subject in Gilbert, *A Century of Conflict, 1850–1950*, 247–63, which was reprinted in a slightly modified form in Raymond Carr, *The Republic and the Civil War in Spain*, 239–55. Although in his essay Thomas disparages all independent and Anarchist accounts of the life of the collectives as either prejudiced, incomplete, or premature in their judgments, he nevertheless bases his work entirely on these sources. Furthermore, he makes no use of the dozens of additional references in my book, *The Grand Camouflage* (55–56, 61), but in a footnote to the original essay he seeks to impair the objectivity of my research by describing me "as a good anticommunist . . . apparently attracted" to the collectives (249, n. 1).

Chapter 7

1. From a radio address reported in *Solidaridad Obrera*, 20 Sept. 1936.

2. Clara Campoamor, *La révolution espagnole vue par une républicaine*, 103. See also Manuel Azaña, *Obras completas*, III, 499.

3. John Langdon-Davies, *Behind the Spanish Barricades*, 123–24. See also Louis Fischer, *Men and Politics*, 353; Jésus de Galíndez, *Los vascos en el Madrid sitiado*, 22; Frank Jellinek, *The Civil War in Spain*, 380; H. E. Kaminski, *Ceux de Barcelone*, 30–31; Megan Laird in *Atlantic Monthly*, Nov. 1936; E. Puig Mora, *La tragedia roja en Barcelona*, 52; *CNT*, 28 May 1937 (article by J. García Pradas); *Solidaridad Obrera*, 11 Aug. 1936 (article by Sixto), 13, 17 Aug. 1936 (manifestoes by the hat section of the Clothing Union urging the public to wear hats in order to save the industry); *Ultima Hora*, 16 Oct., 14 Dec. 1936.

4. 11 Aug. 1936.

5. *Personal Record: 1920–1972*, 311.

6. Federica Montseny in *La Revista Blanca*, 30 July 1936.

7. *Mis Memorias*, 226.

8. Speech reported in *Política*, 6 Dec. 1938. See also ibid., 13 Jan. 1937. For criticism of the laissez-faire attitude of the Republican parties by a Republican officer, see Jesús Pérez Salas, *Guerra en España, 1936–1939*, 135.

9. Some historians have given the number as sixteen. The correct figure is seventeen (see Eduardo Comín Colomer, *Historia del partido comunista de España*, 169, 732, who gives the names and constituencies of the seventeen deputies represented in the Cortes).

10. This figure is given by Manuel Delicado, a member of the central committee, as the 18 July 1936 membership (*La Correspondencia Internacional*, 23 July 1939). However, some twenty-five years later, Dolores Ibárruri (La Pasionaria), then secretary, in Moscow, of the PCE in exile, claimed that the membership had risen from 30,000 in January to more than 100,000 in July 1936 (*El único camino*, 375). This figure is likewise given in the official Communist history, *Guerra y revolución en España, 1936–1939*, I, 87 (published in Moscow in 1956 and in whose preparation La Pasionaria had a leading hand), which also claims that because of the number of its members "the Communist party was already at that time [July 1936] the strongest party of Spanish democracy." On the basis of my own research I am inclined to accept the lower figure of 40,000 as being closer to the true membership in July.

11. See report to the central committee in March 1937, by José Díaz, general secretary of the party, in Díaz, *Tres años de lucha*, 390.

12. Antonio Ramos Oliveira, *Politics, Economics and Men of Modern Spain, 1808–1946*, 599.

13. 27 July 1936.

14. This hostility of a large part of the small bourgeoisie to the Revolution was acknowledged in an official report of the CNT: see report of the Junta del Control del Comité Económico, as given in

Confederación Regional del Trabajo de Cataluña, *Memoria del congreso extraordinario de la confederación regional del trabajo de Cataluña celebrado en Barcelona los días 25 de febrero al 3 de marzo de 1937*, 363–65.

15. 8 Aug. 1936. For other Communist statements and articles in the first months of the war in defense of the urban middle classes, see *Mundo Obrero*, 5, 13–15, 20, 31 Aug., 16 Sept. 1936; *Treball*, 17 Aug., 22 Sept., 22 Dec. (speech by Sesé) 1936; Díaz, *Tres años*, 273, 311, 331. The following lines, taken from an article by a former foreign Communist, who served in the International Brigades in Spain, are worth quoting: "In Murcia and elsewhere I saw that our placards and leaflets appealed for shopkeepers' membership with the promise of absolute support of private property" (Henry Scott Beattie in *Canadian Forum*, Apr. 1938).

16. This figure is given by Antonio Mije, a member of the politburo of the Communist party, *Frente Rojo*, 21 Oct. 1937; see also Miguel Ferrer, secretary-general of the Communist-controlled UGT of Catalonia, in *La Vanguardia*, 9 Apr. 1938.

17. 25 Apr. 1937.

18. Lenin, *Sochineniia* (Moscow, 1950), XXIX, 133, as quoted by Ivo J. Lederer, "Soviet Foreign Policy," in Milorad M. Drachkovitch, *Fifty Years of Communism in Russia*, 177.

19. Speech reported in *Política*, 19 Apr. 1937.

20. Article in *Amanecer Rojo*, reprinted in *Verdad*, 2 Dec. 1936.

21. *Verdad*, 8 Dec. 1936.

22. Ibid., 1 Dec. 1936. For other speeches by Communist leaders in support of the small and middle peasant, see *El Mercantil Valenciano*, 24 Jan. 1937 (Uribe); *Treball*, 20 Oct. 1936 (Comorera), 7 Feb. 1937 (Colomer); Segis Alvarez, *La juventud y los campesinos*; Díaz, *Tres años*, 272, 309–11, 326–27; *El partido comunista por la libertad y la independencia de España*, 181–91.

23. Julio Mateu, general secretary of the federation, *La obra de la federación campesina*, 7.

24. *Claridad*, 14 Dec. 1936. See also article by Santiago Bosca in the left-wing Socialist *Adelante*, as given in *CNT*, 15 May 1937, and letter from the Valencia secretariat of the UGT National Federation of Land Workers to the Peasant Federation, published in *Fragua Social*, 12 Aug. 1937. For a strong attack by an Anarchosyndicalist on the well-to-do farmers who entered the Peasant Federation, see *Nosotros*, 5 June 1937.

25. *Adelante*, 18 Apr. 1937.

26. Although the UGT was represented in the CLUEA, the CNT was the dominant force. The CNT's control of this important segment of the economy, providing large sums of foreign exchange, gave rise to sharp criticism not only from the PCE but from the left-wing Socialists, who, like the Communists, held that the export trade was a function of government not of the unions (see *Adelante*, 6, 8 Feb. 1937, and *La Correspondencia de Valencia*, 24 Dec. 1936, 9 Apr. 1937). The CLUEA was also censured for allegedly underpaying the peasants for their crops and was characterized by Jesús Hernández, when he was still a member of the PCE, "as the administrative center through which the plundering of the peasants' crops was channelled" (*Negro y rojo*, 363). For articles in the CNT press defending the CLUEA, see *Fragua Social*, 7 Feb., 1, 4 Sept., 9 Oct. 1937. No serious study has yet been published on this organization and information is scattered, fragmentary, and highly partisan. A short, evenhanded account of the controversies that swirled around the CLUEA is given in Franz Borkenau, *The Spanish Cockpit*, 198–200.

27. Mateu, 9–10.

28. *Mundo Obrero*, 30 July 1936.

Chapter 8

1. Executive Committee of the Communist International, *XIII Plenum IKKI. Stenograficheskii Otchet* (Thirteenth Plenum of the Executive Committee of the Communist International; Stenographic Report), 531. See also "The Struggle against Fascism, the Struggle for Power, for the Workers and Peasants' Republic in Spain," *Communist International*, 5 Dec. 1934, and the electoral program of the Spanish Communist party, 30 October 1933, which included among the "most important revolutionary measures that the workers' and peasants' government would immediately carry out," the following: "Confiscation and nationalization of industry and large trusts; control of production and distribution by soviets; nationalization of the banks, railways, and all means of transportation and

communication in the hands of the big capitalists (shipping, street cars, busses, airplanes, telegraph, telephone and radio companies); suppression of the Civil and Assault Guards and of all the armed forces of the capitalists and big landowners; general arming of the workers and peasants; liquidation of the bureaucracy hostile to the people and election of public officials by the soviets; suppression of the regular army as an instrument in the hands of the capitalists and landowners; liquidation of the generals and of the officer corps; democratic election of commanders by the soldiers; election by the soldiers of delegates to the workers', peasants' and soldiers' committees; and creation of a workers' and peasants' Red Army, which would defend the interests of the popular masses and the revolution" (as given in Miguel Artola, *Partidos y programas políticos, 1808–1936*, II, 479–80). This ultrarevolutionary program is totally ignored by the official *Historia del partido comunista de España*, which was written by a commission of the party's central committee presided over by La Pasionaria (Dolores Ibárruri). For a meticulous study of the Spanish Communist party before the Civil War, from 1931 to 1937, see dissertation by Bernard Bayerlein, "Die Kommunistische Partei Spaniens als Sektion der Kommunistischen Internationale vor dem Spanischen Bürgerkrieg, 1931–1936" (Ruhr-Universität Bochum 1978).

2. *Stalin*, 415.

3. 4 Mar. 1933.

4. Speech at the Fourth Session of the Central Executive Committee of the Soviet Union, as reported by *Izvestiia*, 29 Dec. 1933.

5. 12 Oct. 1934. For a more detailed Soviet explanation of the shift in policy toward the league, see Xenia Joukoff Eudin and Robert M. Slusser, *Soviet Foreign Policy, 1928–1934: Documents and Materials*, 664–72.

6. Speech at the Seventh Congress of the Soviets of the USSR, reported by *Izvestiia*, 29 Jan. 1935.

7. André Géraud (Pertinax), *The Gravediggers of France*, 244–45, 342–43; Geneviève Tabouis, *Blackmail or War*, 90.

8. Tabouis, *Blackmail*, 91–93; Winston Churchill, *The Gathering Storm*, 134–35; Louis Fischer, *Russia's Road from Peace to War*, 264–65; Henri de Kerillis, *Français! Voici la guerre!*, 111–12. For a well-documented account of the French Communist party's opposition to the defense program before the signing of the Franco-Soviet pact, see Maurice Ceyrat, *La trahison permanente*, 26–41. After the conclusion of the treaty, Stalin gave public approval to the program (see official communiqué as published in *Le Temps*, 17 May 1935), and sometime afterward the French Communist party executed a turnabout.

9. Max Beloff, *The Foreign Policy of Soviet Russia, 1929–1941*, I, 157; Churchill, *Gathering Storm*, 135; Fischer, *Russia's Road*, 265; I. K. Koblyakov, *USSR: For Peace against Aggression, 1933–1941*, 57–58; Paul Reynaud, *La France a sauvé l'Europe*, I, 115ff. In his book *De la place de la Concorde au cours de l'Intendance*, Fabry, minister of war at the time of the signing of the Franco-Soviet pact, reveals that both he and Pierre Laval, the prime minister, were opposed to the idea of a military convention (quoted by Paul Reynaud in his testimony before the Parliamentary Commission of Inquiry set up in 1947 to investigate the events that took place in France between 1933 and 1945, *Les événements survenus en France de 1933 à 1945*, 89–90).

10. See Beloff, I, 160; Kerillis, 117; Charles A. Micaud, *The French Right and Nazi Germany, 1933–1939*, 67–84; Geneviève Tabouis, *Ils l'ont appelée Cassandre*, 244–45.

11. U.S. Department of State, *Documents on German Foreign Policy, 1918–1945*, III, 67. See also report to German foreign minister von Neurath by Johannes Welczek, the German ambassador to Paris, on 26 Dec. 1936, stating that "notwithstanding all the slaps in the face the French have received in the past year, they are even now ready to negotiate with a view to an understanding" and that "in the event of a German-French rapprochement, the Franco-Russian treaty would be gradually reduced in value to the level of the Rapallo treaty. That was the expression Delbos used in our last conversation."

12. *L'Humanité*, 17 May 1935. See also ibid., 16 May 1935, article by M. Magnien.

13. *Candide*, 28 Nov. 1925.

14. Cited by Micaud, 73. "The refusal by the majority of the Right to accept the pact," Micaud writes, ". . . revealed a break in the traditional policy of the French nationalists [of keeping Germany within her existing frontiers], which may be interpreted as the prelude to the appeasement of Germany at the expense of Eastern Europe" (ibid., 70).

15. *The Time for Decision*, 321. For a documented account showing the support of Nazism by banking and industrial interests in the United States, see Antony C. Sutton (onetime Research Fellow of the Hoover Institution, Stanford), *Wall Street and the Rise of Hitler*.

16. *Ambassador Dodd's Diary*, 241. According to the British historian Martin Gilbert, "[Lord Lothian] believed that by helping Hitler to reverse the Versailles Treaty, gather all German-speaking people within his frontiers, expand eastwards, and regain colonial territory, Britain would soon change Nazism from a vicious to an acceptable creed. As he wrote to [Lord] Asquith's widow in 1936: 'My view is quite simple. I loathe all the dictatorships. I think Mussolini and the Pope are the worst. I think after that Litvinov with his intrigue all over Europe to keep the European powers on the edge of war or to drive them into war is the next, and that Hitler, who is a visionary rather than a gangster, is by far the least evil of the lot' " (*The Roots of Appeasement*, 164–65). The letter is dated 7 May 1936 and is in the Lothian Papers. On 2 May 1935, Lothian wrote to a friend: "Unless we are prepared to stand in the way of [Germany's] course in the East, which this country certainly is not, the only real answer is that the oceanic democracies should be strong and prepare themselves to stand together to prevent the dictatorship from interfering with their own liberty and coming out into their own zone" (cited by J. R. M. Butler, *Lord Lothian (Philip Kerr), 1882–1940*, 209). See also ibid., 214.

17. 28 Nov. 1933.

18. *The British Press and Germany, 1936–1939*, 32, 25–26.

19. *Parliamentary Debates*, Vol. 295, Fifth Series, 919–20.

20. Schweppenburg, *The Critical Years*, 86.

21. *Fellow Travellers of the Right: British Enthusiasts for Nazi Germany, 1933–39*, 139.

22. *Nine Troubled Years*, 350.

23. Quoted in Londonderry, *Wings of Destiny*, 171.

24. Pp. 8, 129. See also ibid., 21.

25. That these were the thoughts at the time of leading members of the French government is confirmed by German documents published after World War II.

26. *Combat*, Nov. 1938. See also article by Léon Bailby, *Le Jour*, 24 Sept. 1936.

27. Quoted in Londonderry, *Wings of Destiny*, 187. It is of historical interest that in February 1920, Churchill, who had been the most prominent leader of intervention against the Soviet Union, declared: "No one knows what is coming out of the Russian cauldron, but it will almost certainly be something full of evil, full of menace for Britain, France and the United States. It seems to me therefore that our dangers . . . have not finally been removed by the war, and that, after a few years, they may come back again in a new, but still in a grave form. In order to prevent this we ought to try to make a real and lasting peace with the German people" (reported in the *Times*, 16 Feb. 1920, as given in Martin Gilbert, *Britain and Germany between the Wars*, 130).

28. Maisky, *Who Helped Hitler?*, 61. See also ibid., 55–56, and Ian Colvin, *Vansittart in Office*, 34, who says: "There were those in the Conservative Party in England, and in the amorphous strata beneath it, who saw Germany as the future policeman of Europe, while others thought that Hitler could be turned conveniently eastwards to exhaust his energies in conflict with Soviet Russia."

29. Quoted in Sir Harold Nicolson, *King George the Fifth: His Life and Reign*, 529. On 28 April 1936, Nicolson wrote: "I lunched alone with Robert Vansittart at his house. . . . His view is that a German hegemony in Europe means the end of the British Empire and that we have no right to buy Germany off for a generation by offering her a free hand against the Slav countries. Once she has established herself in an unassailable position she will turn round upon us and we shall be too weak to resist her. I think he is right in theory, but in practice it would be quite impossible for us to get the British people to fight Germany for the sake of the Czechs" (*Diaries and Letters, 1930–1939*, 259). And on 16 July 1936, Nicolson made the following significant entry in his diary: "Foreign Affairs Committee. Winston argues from the premise, which everyone accepts, that our main duty is to defend the British Empire and the Rhine frontier. This in itself, in modern conditions, is 'a gigantic task.' What we have got to ask ourselves is whether that task would in the end be facilitated by our telling Germany that she could take what she likes in the East. Were we to say this, Germany, within the course of a single year, would become dominant from Hamburg to the Black Sea, and we should be faced by a confederacy such as had never been seen since Napoleon. The general impression left was that the majority of the National Party are at heart anti-League and anti-Russian, and that what they

would really like would be a firm agreement with Germany and possibly Italy by which we could purchase peace at the expense of the smaller states. This purely selfish policy would to my mind make an Anglo-German war quite certain within twenty years" (ibid., 269).

30. P. 55. According to Neville Chamberlain's biographer, Keith Feiling, Lord Lloyd was one of the "powerful elements" in Prime Minister Baldwin's following (*Life of Neville Chamberlain*, 285).

31. *Kommunisticheskii internatsional: Kratkii istoricheskii ocherk*, 359.

32. For the evolution of some of the sections of the Comintern toward a Popular Front line, see ibid., 349–400.

33. Ibid., 351–53, 356, 360–63. See also Philippe Robrieux, *Histoire intérieure du parti communiste, 1920–1945*, 452–58.

34. See Alba, *El frente popular*, 277–81; David T. Cattell, *Communism and the Spanish Civil War*, 29–31; Ricardo de la Cierva, article in Vicente Palacio Atard, *Aproximación histórica a la guerra española, 1936–1939*, 61–64; Francisco Largo Caballero, *Escritos de la república*, 254–61; Santos Juliá, *Orígenes del frente popular en España, 1934–1936*, 27–55.

35. *International Press Correspondence*, 19 Sept. 1935.

36. *The Times*, 7 Feb. 1935.

37. Quoted in Churchill, *Arms and the Covenant*, 249. See also Churchill, *The Gathering Storm*, 137–41. "[The] British not only accepted the 35 percent ratio but also agreed that Germany should be allowed a 45 percent ratio in submarine strength" (Gordon A. Craig, *Germany: 1866–1945*, 686). For the British government's argument in favor of the agreement, see Viscount Templewood (Sir Samuel Hoare), *Nine Troubled Years*, 139–48. Hoare was foreign secretary at the time.

38. *Who Helped Hitler?*, 64.

39. Beloff, I, 133–34.

40. See Churchill, *The Gathering Storm*, 189.

41. *International Press Correspondence*, 19 Sept. 1935.

42. Ibid.

43. As given in Richard Crossman, *The God That Failed*, 54–55.

44. *Kommunisticheskii internatsional: Kratkii istoricheskii ocherk*, 408.

45. Dimitrov, *The United Front: The Struggle against Fascism and War*, 75.

46. Cattell, *Communism and the Spanish Civil War*, 30.

Chapter 9

1. U.S. Department of State, *Documents on German Foreign Policy, 1918–1945*, Series D, III, 1–2 (hereafter cited by title). For a meticulously researched study, based largely on German documents and oral testimony, of General Franco's efforts to obtain Hitler's help during the first days of the Civil War, see Angel Viñas, *La Alemania nazi y el 18 de julio*, 312–401. According to Viñas, Hitler decided to give his support on the night of 25–26 July.

2. See Werner Beumelburg, *Kampf um Spanien*, 22–29; Wulf Bley, *Das Buch der Spanienflieger*, 23–27, 31–32; Max Graf Hoyos, *Pedros y Pablos*, 15–22; Otto Schempp, *Das autoritäre Spanien*, 69–71; Rud Stache, *Armee mit geheimen Auftrag*, 10–26; Hannes Trautloft, *Als Jagdflieger in Spanien*, 29; official account of German intervention published in the German press (as reported in the *Daily Telegraph*, 31 May 1939); special number of *Die Wehrmacht* entitled *Wir kämpften in Spanien*, issued in May 1939 by the German High Command; *Voelkischer Beobachter*, 31 May 1939. According to the aforementioned official account published in the German press, the first armored car detachment was sent out in October 1936. It consisted of staff, two companies, and a transport company and, in addition to taking part in the fighting, formed a school of instruction for Spaniards in the use of armored cars, guns, and flamethrowers. In November, according to the same account, a complete air force corps arrived in Spain, composed of combat, pursuit, and reconnaissance planes, as well as intelligence and antiaircraft detachments. In an article published in the special number of *Die Wehrmacht*, mentioned above, General Sperrle stated that 6,500 German "volunteers" reached Spain at the beginning of November 1936.

3. International Military Tribunal, *The Trial of German Major War Criminals*, Part IX, 93.

4. According to Viñas, the first of these planes arrived in Tetuan on 28 July and its pilot, Alfred Henke, "devoted himself to making the round trip Tetuan-Seville several times a day . . . with his machine overloaded with troops" (Viñas, *La Alemania nazi*, 385–86).

5. Ibid., 353.

6. See memorandum by the acting state secretary of the German foreign office, Hans Heinrich Dieckhoff, as reprinted in *Documents on German Foreign Policy, 1918–1945*, Series D, III, 155–56; also ibid., 168, 222, 230, 265, 391–92, and Ernst von Weizsäcker, *Memoirs of Ernst von Weizsäcker*, 113–14.

7. *"Es spricht der Führer." 7 exemplarische Hitler-Reden*, 173.

8. According to a memorandum by the German diplomat Hans Stille, dated 2 June 1942, cited in Viñas, *La Alemania nazi*, 363.

9. *Documents on German Foreign Policy, 1918–1945*, Series D, III, 279. See also excerpt of a report by the German ambassador in Rome to the Wilhelmstrasse, dated 18 December 1936, on the interests of Germany and Italy in the Spanish conflict (quoted later in this chapter).

10. Léon Bailby in *Le Jour*, 24 Sept. 1936. See also Pierre Bernus in *Journal des Débats*, 15 Aug. 1936; Pierre Gaxotte in *Candide*, 27 Aug. 1936; Pierre Dominique in *La République*, 8, 9 Oct. 1936.

11. The nonintervention system is extensively studied by Norman J. Padelford, *International Law and Diplomacy in the Spanish Civil Strife*. For violations of the Non-Intervention Agreement, see David T. Cattell, *Soviet Diplomacy and the Spanish Civil War*; also Dante A. Puzzo, *Spain and the Great Powers, 1936–1941*.

12. *Daily Worker*, 9 Sept. 1936. For further evidence of Soviet fears, see Cattell, *Soviet Diplomacy*, 15–16.

13. See, for example, Joaquín Arrarás, *Historia de la segunda república española*, IV, 266–70; Manual Aznar, *Historia Militar de la guerra de España*, 25–30; *Exposure of the Secret Plan to Establish a Soviet in Spain*.

14. *No fué posible la paz*, 705–6.

15. *El mito de la cruzada de Franco*, 247–58.

16. *Historia de la guerra civil española*, I, 709. See also Cierva, *Los documentos de la primavera trágica*, 428.

17. *Historia de la guerra civil española*, 713–20.

18. José Díaz, speech 11 Apr. 1936, as reprinted in José Díaz, *Tres años de lucha*, 165.

19. José Díaz, speech in Cortes, *Diario de las Sesiones de Cortes*, 15 Apr. 1936, 311.

20. Díaz, speech, 5 Apr. 1936, as reprinted in Díaz, *Tres años*, 155.

21. Article in *La Correspondencia Internacional*, 17 Apr. 1936, as reprinted in Díaz, *Tres años*, 133–39; see also article in *Mundo Obrero*, 1 May 1936, in Díaz, *Tres años*, 184–85.

22. Díaz, speech, 1 June 1936, as reprinted in Díaz, *Tres años*, 188; article in *Mundo Obrero*, June 1936, as reprinted in Díaz, *Tres años*, 199.

23. Díaz, speech, 5 July 1936, as reprinted in Díaz, *Tres años*, 215.

24. See *Mundo Obrero*, 6, 8–11, 13, 15–17 July 1936; also José Bullejos (a former secretary of the Communist party), *Europa entre dos guerras, 1918–1938*, 189–90.

25. *La crisis del movimiento comunista*, 168.

26. See, for example, General Francesco Belforte, *La guerra civile in Spagna*, III, 28; Guido Mattioli, *L'aviazione legionária in Spagna*, 22–28; *Le Forze Armate* (official organ of the Italian War Office), 8 June 1939. According to the latter publication, Italian warships assisted General Franco's forces in the defense of Majorca and the occupation of the neighboring island of Ibiza in September 1936. With regard to Italian ground forces, the first contingent of black shirts, numbering three thousand, did not leave Italy until 18 December 1936 (see telegrams from the German ambassador in Rome to the Wilhelmstrasse, as given in *Documents on Germany Foreign Policy, 1918–1945*, Series D, III, 169, 173. The first shipment of Italian artillery, antiaircraft guns, and armored cars, however, reached Spain toward the end of September (Aznar, 316). The entire question of Italian aid to General Franco is covered most thoroughly in John F. Coverdale, *Italian Intervention in the Spanish Civil War*.

27. *Fu la Spagna*, 63.

28. Bolín, *Spain*, 53, 159–72. For a copy of the document signed by General Franco, see photograph, ibid., between pp. 38 and 39.

29. *No fué posible la paz*, 713.

30. III, 126. Bolín does not mention in his book the presence of Goicoechea in Rome during the negotiations. For the best account of Mussolini's initial hesitancy to enter the Spanish conflict, see Coverdale, 68–88; also Viñas, 308–10, for the full text of a little-known anonymous report on Goicoechea's visit to Rome now in the archives of the Servicio Histórico Militar, Madrid. According

to this report, the Italians demanded payment in advance of more than one million pounds sterling for twelve Savoia aircraft, which sum was made available by the famous Spanish financier and "smuggler" Juan March.

31. Pierre Cot, *Triumph of Treason*, 340–41.

32. U.S. Department of State, *Foreign Relations of the United States*, II, 467.

33. *Documents on German Foreign Policy, 1918–1945*, Series D, III, 170–73. The motives for Italian intervention are discussed in Coverdale, 74–84.

34. *Documents on German Foreign Policy, 1918–1945*, Series D, III, 155. How many other such proposals were made by Faupel cannot be said with certainty, but there is substantial evidence that at a conference in Berlin on 21 December Faupel asked without success for three German divisions (Gerhard L. Weinberg, *The Foreign Policy of Hitler's Germany, 1933–36*, 297–98).

35. *Documents on German Foreign Policy, 1918–1945*, I, 37.

36. *The Foreign Policy of Hitler's Germany, 1937–1939*, 143–44.

37. Weinberg, ibid., 144, nn. 5 and 8, cites two examples: 1. "Cloverdale [164] argues that the evidence on Hitler's policy should be read differently but merely concludes that 'Hitler did not do everything he might have to shorten the war, but that is a far cry from deliberately prolonging it.'" 2. "The comment by Manfred Merkes, *Die deutsche Politik gegenüber dem spanischen Buergerkrieg, 1936–1939*, 2d ed. (Bonn: Rohrscheid, 1969), 102, that the proposals of the German commanders in Spain with the object of bringing speedy victory to Franco 'dissolve' the argument that Germany wanted a long war is . . . based on a confusion between the tactical proposals of men on the spot—who had no interest in seeing their soldiers killed in a drawn-out combat—and the broader objectives of Hitler." In his earlier work, Weinberg (*The Foreign Policy of Hitler's Germany [1933–36]*, 299, n. 149), stated: "Since Merkes does not understand the general line of German policy in this matter, he asserts (127–28) that those who accept the statement in the Hossbach memorandum have been misled; in fact it is Merkes who has misled himself as has already been pointed out by Detwiler (141–42, n. 31)." Those historians who have been misled by Merkes would do well to read the long footnote to which Weinberg refers. The full reference is: Donald S. Detwiler, *Hitler, Franco und Gibraltar* (Wiesbaden: Franz Stiner Verlag, 1962).

38. *Canaris*, 172–73.

39. Krivitsky's claim that Stalin's goal was to reach an understanding with Germany was made long before the signing of the Soviet-German nonaggression pact of 23 August 1939. See his articles in *Sotsialisticheskii Vestnik*, 31 Mar. 1938, and *Saturday Evening Post*, 22 and 29 Apr. 1939.

40. *In Stalin's Secret Service*, 80–81.

41. See, for example, the *New Masses*, 9 May 1939, and the reply to these accusations by the *Saturday Evening Post*, 24 June 1939. Isaac Don Levine, Krivitsky's literary agent, writes: "The campaign of vituperation attained such an hysterical pitch that some published stories maintained Krivitsky did not even exist and was a literary fabrication. The truth, presented in rebuttal in the socialist *New Leader* and similar publications, was like a voice crying in the wilderness. Suzanne La Follette pointed out that when Krivitsky announced his break with Stalin in December 1937, the Communist press had given him the silent treatment. She emphasized that his initial public statement began: 'The undersigned, Samuel Ginsberg, bearing in the U.S.S.R. as a Soviet citizen the name of Walter Krivitsky and the political pseudonym Walter . . .' And it was signed: 'Samuel Ginsberg (Krivitsky).' Others, like Max Schachtman, the editor of the Trotskyite *Socialist Appeal*, called attention to the use of 'Shmelka' for Samuel as a Hitlerite way of describing him as 'a dirty Jew' and challenged the leading editors of the [Communist] *New Masses*, Abe Magil, Joseph North, Theodore Draper, Robert Forsythe, Joseph Freeman, Michael Gold, and William Gropper, to reveal their real names, 'middle initials included'" (*Eyewitness to History*, 186).

42. *Sotsialisticheskii Vestnik*, 18, 31 Mar., 15, 29 Apr. 1938; *Saturday Evening Post*, 15, 22, 29 Apr., 17 June, 4 Nov. 1939; Krivitsky.

43. For the best but not always concordant accounts of the Krivitsky affair, see Paul Wohl in the *Commonweal*, 28 Feb. 1941; Flora Lewis in the *Washington Post*, 13 Feb. 1966; Gordon Brook-Shepherd, *The Storm Petrels*, 141–81; Isaac Don Levine, 182–200; Victor Serge, *Mémoires d'un révolutionnaire*, 374; and Elisabeth K. Poretsky, *Our Own People*, whose husband Ignace Reiss, alias Ludwik, a leading NKVD operative in Europe with close ties with Krivitsky, was assassinated in Switzerland in 1937 after defecting. Poretsky knew Krivitsky personally and has numerous references

to him in her book. In contrast to some of Krivitsky's other acquaintances and friends, she holds that his suicide was genuine (270). Angelica Balabanoff, a secretary to Lenin and the first secretary of the Comintern, who soon broke with the Soviet leader (see "Angelica Balabanoff and V. I. Lenin" by Bertram D. Wolfe, *The Antioch Review*, Summer 1964), informed Ella Wolfe, the wife of the famed sovietologist, that Krivitsky told her in New York, just before leaving for Washington, that if she heard that he had committed suicide, she would know that he was "suicided" (information given to me by Ella Wolfe in 1979).

44. *Sotsialisticheskii Vestnik*, 25 Feb. 1941. Nicolaevsky's testimony is bolstered by the fact that he knew Krivitsky intimately. See also Paul Wohl in the *Commonweal*, 29 Feb. 1941, who also knew him well. Krivitsky described his official position as that of chief of Soviet military intelligence (GRU or so-called Fourth Administration) in Western Europe (Krivitsky, 75), but it is now clear that at the time of his defection he was NKVD "resident" in The Hague and that the exalted title of Chief of Soviet Military Intelligence in Western Europe was part of the publicity buildup in the United States, for which Isaac Don Levine, his imaginative literary agent, must be held partly responsible, since, according to Elisabeth Poretsky, Krivitsky who was "unable to write English . . . had to rely on ghost-writers" (270). As Nicolaevsky points out, Krivitsky did at one time work in Soviet military intelligence. This is confirmed by Poretsky, but she also states that "neither the Fourth Department [GRU] nor the NKVD ever had a centralized control post in Europe. The resident in each country had an area for which he assumed full responsibility. He in turn was responsible only to 'the centre,' or headquarters, in Moscow, not to any West European section chief" (Poretsky, 139 and 148, n. 2). In the publicity campaign for his writings, Krivitsky was described as a general in the GRU. On this matter, Gordon Brook-Shepherd, the distinguished British author and journalist, writes: "Walter Krivitsky was never a general in the GRU. . . . He had for many years held lower ranks in that service, but had been transferred from it in 1933 or 1934 to the NKVD. [Poretsky states that he received the pay of a captain in the NKVD as he had in the Fourth Administration, (185, n. 1).] It was as NKVD 'resident' in Holland, with liaison responsibilities for other western European countries, that he had defected in 1937. He himself is known to have been embarrassed by being labeled with the false title of general, which seems to have been part of the publicity build-up in America for his writings" (Brook-Shepherd, 154, n. 3). For information on the GRU, see John Barron, *KGB*, 15, 343–45; David Dallin, *Soviet Espionage*, 4–5; Richard Deacon, *A History of the Russian Secret Service*, 223–25; Peter Deriabin, *Watchdogs of Terror*, 215; *McGraw-Hill Encyclopedia of Russia and the Soviet Union*, 245–46.

45. *The Spanish Civil War* (1961 ed.), 263, n. 1. I am indebted to John Amsden for giving me a copy of his unpublished manuscript, "Krivitsky," in which he critically discusses the attitudes of various Spanish Civil War historians (including Thomas) toward Krivitsky. The copy of the manuscript has been deposited with the Hoover Institution.

46. *The Spanish Civil War* (1965 ed.), 337, n. 1.

47. Joan Llarch, *Negrín: ¡Resistir es vencer!*, 104.

48. Poretsky, 75, n. 2; 124, n. 1; 146, n. 1; 171, n. 1; 204, n. 1; 211, n. 1. None of these alleged errors and exaggerations, however, relates to the Spanish Civil War.

49. Article, *Saturday Evening Post*, 29 Apr. 1939; see also Krivitsky, 21.

50. *The Communist Party of the Soviet Union*, 485, n. 2. Schapiro expresses his indebtedness to John Erickson of St. Andrews University for a copy of the document, dated 11 February 1937. I, too, am most grateful to Professor Erickson for giving me the reference to this document and to other important papers relating to Kandelaki's overtures, dated, 6, 17, 19, and 20 February 1937, namely, "Kandelaki Mission," Auswärtiges Amt. Film Serial 1907 H/429294-324 (National Archives, Washington, D.C.), and for bringing to my attention his imposing work, *The Soviet High Command*, published in 1962, in which he discusses the secret negotiations and Kandelaki's role therein (396–97, 432, 453, 458, 464, 731, n. 79). Why these important papers were not included in the official *Documents on German Foreign Policy, 1918–1945*, Series D, III (1950), since of all the volumes published it would have been the most appropriate, has not been satisfactorily explained. Were they inadvertently omitted or were they considered too embarrassing to the Soviet government at the time the selection was made? The reason given to me by one authority regarding the document of 11 February, to which Schapiro refers (that "it was deleted—or missed—from the collections," because "no one had paid much attention to it since it came generally under 'trade discussions.' And, in any

event, who would know the name Kandelaki?") was far from satisfactory. In 1962 and 1966, two volumes were published (IV and V, Series C, of *Documents on German Foreign Policy, 1918–1945*), which contain numerous documents referring to Kandelaki and his trade negotiations with the Germans between 9 April 1935 and 6 May 1936. Some of these reveal the Soviet desire for improved political relations between the two countries (IV, 28–29, 453–54, 783–84, 870–71, 967–72; V, 488–91, 512, 571–73), but none as important as the document of 11 February 1937, which finally saw the light of day in 1983 (*Documents on German Foreign Policy, 1918–1945*, Series C, VI, 403–4), thirty-three years after the publication of the volume on the Spanish Civil War. Other documents found in the German archives, which fell into Allied hands in 1945 but were not published until 1963 (*Survey*, Oct. 1963), reveal meetings in 1935 and 1936 between Yevgeni Gnedin, a member of the Soviet embassy in Berlin, and Duercksen (not to be confused with von Dirksen), an official of the foreign political office of the Nazi party (APA), during which Gnedin is reported to have "expressed his regret that the two countries . . . were not able to arrive at a better relationship" and stated that he had come to Germany "with specific instructions to study the possibility of an improvement" in their relations. Gnedin also made the significant comment that although "the ideologies of the Comintern and of the Soviet Union were the same, the *Realpolitik* of the USSR had nothing to do with the Comintern." *Survey* gives the source of these documents as EAP 250-d-18-15, Aussenpolitisches Amt, Amt Osten, available in microfilm T 81/14 (Washington). For additional information on Kandelaki and Soviet attempts to improve political relations with Germany, based on official documents, see Karlheinz Niclauss, *Die Sowjetunion und Hitlers Machtergreifung*, Chapter XIV, "Die Brücke zum Stalin-Hitler-Pact," 182–99; also, for further information on the origins of the Nazi-Soviet pact of 1939, see Louis Fischer, *Russia's Road from Peace to War*, 240–49, and Fischer's reply to Alexander Dallin in the *Saturday Review*, 16 Aug. 1969.

51. *Documents on German Foreign Policy, 1918–1945*, Series C, VI, 404 (1983).

52. *German-Soviet Relations between the Two World Wars, 1919–1939*, 141.

53. *Sotsialisticheskii Vestnik*, 31 Mar. 1938. In one of his articles in the *Saturday Evening Post* (29 Apr. 1939), Krivitsky claimed that he was in Moscow in April 1937 when Kandelaki brought with him the "draft of an agreement" with the Nazi government. This is most unlikely in view of the above-quoted passage from Neurath's message to Schacht of 11 February 1937 revealing Hitler's suspicions of Soviet overtures.

54. *Soy del quinto regimiento*, 235–36. See also Ignacio Hidalgo de Cisneros, *Memorias 2*, 332; Koblyakov, *USSR for Peace against Aggression, 1933–1941*, 69; Maisky, *Spanish Notebooks*, 116, 119.

55. Academy of Sciences of the USSR, *International Solidarity with the Spanish Republic, 1936–1939*, 329–30. For attacks and sinking of Soviet vessels, see East European Fund, Program on the USSR, *Soviet Shipping in the Spanish Civil War*, Mimeographed Series, No. 59.

56. "Nakanune voiny," *Istoriia vtoroi mirovoi voiny, 1939–1945*, II, 54.

57. *The Last Days of Madrid*, 51.

58. *Así fue la defensa de Madrid*, 213.

59. See Manuilsky's report to the Eighteenth Congress of the Communist Party of the Soviet Union on 10 March 1939, as given in *The Land of Socialism Today and Tomorrow*, 57–100.

60. *Brigate internazionali in Spagna*, 30. An indispensable contribution to the study of the International Brigades, their origins, recruitment, transportation to Spain and the number of participants is R. Dan Richardson's *Comintern Army: The International Brigades and the Spanish Civil War*.

61. *Las brigadas internacionales*, 49.

62. See Academy of Sciences of the USSR, *International Solidarity with the Spanish Republic, 1936–1939*, 370, which states: "Historical records give various estimates of the total number of international volunteers in the Spanish Republican Army. The most frequently named figure is 35,000, although a thoughtful and competent military leader like General Walter (Karol Swierczewski), commander of the 35th Division of the Republican Army, considers 42,000 as a quite probable figure. He attributes the difficulties in the question to the poor recording of personnel at the Albacete base and in the International Brigades themselves."

63. *Agoniia beloi emigratsii*, 173.

64. Krivitsky, 80, also 85.

65. Academy of Sciences of the USSR, *International Solidarity with the Spanish Republic, 1936–*

1939, 312–13. For additional information on attacks on Soviet vessels, see East European Fund, Program on the USSR, *Soviet Shipping in the Spanish Civil War*, Mimeographed Series, No. 59.

66. *The Secret History of Stalin's Crimes*, 238.

Chapter 10

1. See, for example, speeches at the Radical party congress, reported in *L'Ere Nouvelle*, 25 Oct. 1936.

2. See, for example, the *Daily Herald*, 10 Oct. 1936.

3. R. Palme Dutt in *Labour Monthly*, Aug. 1936.

4. Joan Estruch, *Historia del P.C.E., 1920–1939*, I, 95.

5. Claudín, *La crisis del movimiento comunista*, 180–81.

6. David T. Cattell, *Communism and the Spanish Civil War*, 58.

7. *L'Humanité*, 4 Aug. 1936; *Communist International*, Oct. 1936; *International Press Correspondence*, 8 Aug. 1936; *Daily Worker*, 5 Aug. 1936. It is interesting to contrast Marty's phrase—"The few confiscations that have been made"—with a statement by Ivan Maisky, Soviet ambassador in London during the Civil War, that appeared in his book *Spanish Notebooks* thirty years later. On p. 118, he affirms that requisitions "by the state, municipalities, or, most often, the trade unions . . . assumed sweeping proportions from the very first months of the war, taking in tens of thousands of enterprises."

8. *L'Humanité*, 3 Aug. 1936.

9. Ibid.

10. *International Press Correspondence*, 8 Aug. 1936.

11. Mar. 1937, 174.

12. Franz Borkenau, *The Spanish Cockpit*, 110.

13. *Mundo Obrero*, 8 Aug. 1936.

14. *Mundo Obrero*, 18 Aug. 1936; *International Press Correspondence*, 29 Aug. 1936. Despite these quotations, most of which appeared in the text or footnotes of my work, *The Grand Camouflage*, 101–3, demonstrating that the Communists attempted to minimize or conceal from the outside world the depth of the social revolution that had swept the country, Herbert R. Southworth ridicules my thesis that there was an attempt at concealment (*El mito de la cruzada de Franco*, 155).

Chapter 11

1. Frank E. Manuel, *The Politics of Modern Spain*, 164.

2. José Díaz, *Tres años de lucha*, 352.

3. André Marty, *En Espagne . . . où se joue le destin de l'Europe*, 34. In a letter to me, dated 4 November 1948, former politburo member Jesús Hernández said that Marty's statement was not correct. "It is true," he added, "that there were extreme tendencies within the left wing of the Socialist party . . . , but they never formally raised the question of proclaiming a 'socialist republic' " (Hoover Institution).

4. Reported in *Mundo Obrero*, 9 Sept. 1936.

5. Letter to me, 4 Aug. 1948 (Hoover Institution). Other prominent left-wing Socialists simply ignored my written requests for information on this matter.

6. Report from London, *La Humanitat*, 13 Aug. 1936.

7. "While it is not mandatory under international law for other governments to allow an established, friendly government seeking to suppress a rebellion to purchase arms and supplies in their markets, it is generally acceded to in practice" (Dante A. Puzzo, *Spain and the Great Powers, 1936–1941*, 149–50). On the other hand, Julio Alvarez del Vayo, the pro-Communist foreign minister in the government that succeeded Giral's cabinet in September 1936, wrote: "Juridically there was no possible defense for Non-Intervention. To refuse a legitimate government, with whom the United Kingdom and France were maintaining normal diplomatic relations, their indisputable right to acquire the material necessary to subdue the revolt of a few rebel generals was the very extreme of arbitrary conduct" (*Freedom's Battle*, 44).

8. Public Record Office, Foreign Office 371/20573.

9. *Guerra y revolución en España, 1936–1939*, I, 265. See also Antonio Cordón, *Trayectoria*, 248.

10. "Memorias," 11.

11. Araquistáin Papers, Leg. 32/L 30[a].

12. *The Invisible Writing*, 372.

13. "Ispanskii Dnevnik," *Novyi Mir*, Apr. 1938, 41–42. For information on "Ispanskii Dnevnik" (Koltzov's diary), see chapter 2, n. 24.

14. Clara Campoamor, *La révolution espagnole vue par une républicaine*, 143–46; cf. Henri Rabasseire, *Espagne: creuset politique*, 98. See also Pierre Broué and Emile Témime, *La révolution et la guerre d'Espagne*, 180–81, and Fernando Claudín, *La crisis del movimiento comunista*, 610, who give credence to this version.

15. *Guerra y revolución*, II, 45–46. Nevertheless, there is no corroborative evidence that Araquistáin or Baráibar agitated more or less publicly at this time in favor of a working-class dictatorship, as claimed by the official Communist history. The only evidence that even remotely approaches this claim is Araquistáin's letter to Caballero.

16. "Ispanskii Dnevnik," *Novyi Mir*, Apr. 1938, 39–40.

17. *La guerre d'Espagne*, 146. See also Amaro del Rosal, *Historia de la UGT de España, 1901–1939*, 500. Ramón Sender, the famous Spanish writer, who knew Prieto personally, told me that he was "the only man with energy among the Republicans and Socialists during the first few weeks of the war" and that in the Navy Ministry "he animated the others." (Interviewed in Mexico in 1939.)

18. "Ispanskii Dnevnik," *Novyi Mir*, Apr. 1938, 40.

19. This spectacular advance is described in great detail by Colonel José Manuel Martínez Bande, *La marcha sobre Madrid* (rev. ed., 1982). This work is based on documents in the archives of the Servicio Histórico Militar in Madrid.

20. 4 Sept. 1936. When interviewed by me in 1940, Giral stated that, as he lacked the support of the working class, he proposed that Largo Caballero should head a new administration.

21. The condition that he would not form a government unless the Communists shared the responsibilities of office is corroborated by a variety of sources: Alvarez del Vayo, *Freedom's Battle*, 212; Jesús Hernández, *Yo fui un ministro de Stalin*, 47; *Guerra y revolución*, II, 47; *Historia del partido comunista de España*, 139. The last two volumes are official histories of the Civil War and Spanish Communist party written by commissions presided over by La Pasionaria.

22. "Ispanskii Dnevnik," *Novyi Mir*, Apr. 1938, 46–47.

23. *Madrid*, 159.

24. Julián Zugazagoitia, *Historia de la guerra en España*, 137.

25. "Memorias," 14.

26. *Yo fui un ministro de Stalin*, 47. Why this unexpected decision on the part of Moscow? Hernández does not explain it. Fernando Claudín, the former Communist leader, writes: "For the working class, Largo Caballero at the head of the government served as a guarantee for the revolution. For Azaña and Prieto, just as for Stalin and his representatives in Spain, the premiership of Largo Caballero might serve as a guarantee that the revolution would collaborate in its own transformation in the restoration of the bourgeois-democratic republican state" (*La crisis del movimiento comunista*, 184). This raises the following questions: Did Stalin really want to restore bourgeois democracy in Spain or simply use its outward forms to disguise his real intentions? And was Largo Caballero a suitable instrument for Stalin's policy? Francisco Giral, the son of Prime Minister Giral, writes that because of the "indifference" of the League of Nations "the leaders of the Republican government are aware that a critical situation has arrived. The only card they have left to play is the USSR and my father knew that [the Soviet Union] would not support a politician of the Left Republican party such as my father. It then occurred to both sides that they should support a Socialist of the 'extreme left.' The only possible man was don Francisco Largo Caballero" (*Tiempo de Historia*, Jan. 1980). This version flies in the face of the Kremlin's concern for foreign opinion and its support of the moderate Giral government. A more plausible explanation is that the Kremlin, faced by the Giral government's lack of popularity, was forced to yield to the intransigence of Largo Caballero until such time as he could conveniently be replaced by a moderate politician. This is actually what happened when Juan Negrín succeeded Largo Caballero in the premiership eight months later, as will be seen in a subsequent chapter.

27. Stefanov, "Las causas de la derrota de la República española," 19.

28. *Historia de la guerra en España*, 135.

29. As given in the official *Gaceta de Madrid*, 5 Sept. 1936.

30. Memorandum written by José María Aguirre found among Araquistáin's papers (Araquistáin Papers, Leg. 75/7).

31. *Gaceta de Madrid*, 16 Sept. 1936.

32. Ibid., 26 Sept. 1936.

33. *Why Spain Fights On*, 37. See also excerpt from article by Marcel Rosenberg (Soviet ambassador to Spain until April 1937) in the *Journal de Moscou*, as quoted by *Le Temps*, 1 May 1937.

34. Jesús de Galíndez, *Los vascos en el Madrid sitiado*, 19.

35. This passage is on p. 68 of Aguirre report.

36. Actually, the only Catholic was Manuel de Irujo, a member of the Basque Nationalist party, as indicated above in the list of cabinet members.

37. *Guerra y revolución*, II, 49.

38. *The Spanish Revolution*, 235.

Chapter 12

1. José Díaz, *Tres años de lucha*, 390. It is worth mentioning that in a report to the Comintern, dated 28 January 1938, Palmiro Togliatti, the Comintern delegate in Spain, stated that the membership of 339,000, claimed at that time by the organizational section of the party, should be viewed with some skepticism and should not be published. "339,000 is the figure given in the communications sent by the central committee to the local organizations," he added, "and not that of members who are actually paying their dues. The real numerical strength of the party, I consider, is slightly mor than 200,000, but this is not a precise estimate" (Togliatti, *Escritos sobre la guerra de España*, 174).

2. *Politics, Economics and Men of Modern Spain, 1808–1946*, 599.

3. *Nation*, 7 Aug. 1937.

4. *The Forging of a Rebel*, 706.

5. *La bestia contra España*, 95.

6. See, for example, *Política*, 24 Nov., 1 Dec. 1936.

7. *La crisis del movimiento comunista*, 186.

8. Henry Buckley, *Life and Death of the Spanish Republic*, 402.

9. 6 Nov. 1936.

10. Speech, *La Voz Valenciana*, 10 Mar. 1937.

11. Speech, 21 Apr. 1940, as given in Prieto, *Inauguración del círculo "Pablo Iglesias" de México*, 13. See also article by Juan López, *CNT* (Madrid), 19 June 1937.

12. *Yo, comunista en Rusia*, 29.

13. *The Spanish Labyrinth*, 326.

14. *Les anarchistes espagnoles et le pouvoir, 1868–1969*, 96–97, n. 78.

15. Ibid., 210–11.

16. Ibid., 211–12.

17. Ibid., 236–37.

18. Carlos de Baráibar, *Via Libre*, 5 Aug. 1939. See also his article in *Timón* (Buenos Aires), June 1940.

19. Barea, 579.

20. For an account by a left-wing Socialist of how the Socialist party in the provincial capital of Alicante, where it was the strongest political organization, had failed to compete successfully with the Communists and Anarchists for the control of leading positions, see Ferrándiz Alborz, 64–65.

21. Report to the Labor and Socialist International dated 23 May 1939, published in special issue of *Independent News* (June 1939?).

22. *Política de ayer y política de mañana*, 79, 88. It is interesting to note that five years after the publication of his book, Gabriel Morón himself entered the Communist party (see announcement in the Spanish Communist refugee newspaper *Frente Popular*, Mexico City, 11 Apr. 1947).

23. *Yo fui un ministro de Stalin*, 135. Hernández was expelled from the party in 1944. See his book *En el país de la gran mentira*, 215–27. In later years, he was roundly condemned by the party and its

supporters. The most curious attack was made by the crypto-Communist Amaro del Rosal in 1977: "Because of the negligence of his own comrades, who were aware of his moral character and his past history, [he] was elevated to the post of minister [of public education and fine arts]. . . . During a journey by train from Prague to Warsaw, Vicente Uribe [Communist minister of agriculture in Largo Caballero's cabinet] informed me in detail of certain antecedents of Jesús Hernández: an exploiter of women, a professional loafer and a filcher of alms boxes from churches" (*Historia de la UGT de España, 1901–1939*, II, 525). If the party was indeed aware of his moral character, as depicted by Rosal, one wonders how he became a member of the politburo and director of the party organ *Mundo Obrero* in 1931, and a Cortes deputy and minister of public education in 1936.

24. See his letter to José Bullejos, 20 Nov. 1939, as given in Francisco Largo Caballero, *¿Qué se puede hacer?*, 20–24.

25. For reference to this by Largo Caballero, see his speech as given in Francisco Largo Caballero, *La UGT y la guerra*, 32.

26. See Largo Caballero, *La UGT y la guerra*, 32, also *Adelante*, Largo Caballero's organ in Valencia, 8 Apr. 1937.

27. For complaints in the left-wing Socialist press regarding some of these methods, such as flattery, offers of material gain, and coercion, see article in the *Boletín de la Unión de Trabajadores*, as given in *Claridad*, 11 Mar. 1937; also article by S. Esteve Gregori in *Adelante*, 27 Mar. 1937.

28. See report by Wenceslao Carrillo to the Labor and Socialist International, 23 May 1939, in which the Communist sympathies of Domínguez, Rosal, and Pretel are mentioned, as published in special issue of *Independent News* [June 1939?], also Largo Caballero, *Mis recuerdos*, 212. For Rosal's criticism of Largo Caballero's "anti-Communist" and "anti-Soviet" position in 1937, which he ascribes largely to the influence of "Caballero's eminence grise, Luis Araquistáin," see his book, *Historia de la UGT de España, 1901–1939*, II, 611–31. Although Rosal followed the Communist line throughout the war and in the postwar years, it was not until 1948 that he entered the PCE (see his letter requesting admission in *Nuestra Bandera*, Paris, June–July 1948).

29. See article by the left Socialist leader Rodolfo Llopis, *Tribuna*, Mar. 1949, Carlos Llorens, *La guerra en Valencia y en el frente de Teruel*, 158–59, and Zugazagoitia, 170. Years later, Federica Montseny, the Anarchist leader, who, together with La Pasionaria and Margarita Nelken, was one of the three most prominent women during the Civil War, made the following observation: "Perhaps [Nelken] hoped to occupy in [the Communist party] the position that belonged to her because of her qualities, infinitely superior from an intellectual standpoint to those of Dolores Ibárruri. But the position was already taken and La Pasionaria defended it with tooth and nail. Margarita remained in the background, losing the prestige she had in the Socialist party and failing to become an influential figure in the Communist party. It was an error for which she paid dearly" (*Espoir*, 14 Apr. 1968). In letters to me (9 Mar. 1981, 20 Oct. 1982), Julián Gorkin, a leader of the POUM states that Nelken was already veering toward the PCE after the October rebellion in 1934.

30. Francisco Montiel, *Por qué he ingresado en el partido comunista*, 4. In 1937 Montiel became a member of the central committee of the PCE (see Pedro Checa, *A un gran partido, una gran organización*, 23).

31. Juventudes Socialistas Unificadas.

32. See José Díaz in *International Press Correspondence*, 9 May 1936; Segis Alvarez, *Nuestra organización y nuestros cuadros*, 7; also *Mundo Obrero*, 2, 6 Apr. 1936.

33. *En marcha hacia la victoria*, 13.

34. See his speech, *Frente Rojo*, 2 Apr. 1937.

35. He did, however, acknowledge in a letter, dated 1 January 1939, to Norman Thomas, leader of the U.S. Socialist party, that he had been one of the proponents of unity with the Communists, but that this unity had ended in the absorption and destruction of the Socialists as in the case of the JSU and PSUC, "which are now nothing but Communist organizations" (Araquistáin Papers, Leg. 58/V7[b]).

36. Codovila is the correct spelling, although several Spanish and foreign writers have referred to him as Codovilla.

37. *El comunismo y la guerra de España*, 9. For an account of Santiago Carrillo's trip to Moscow at the beginning of March 1936, together with Federico Melchor and José Lain, both members of the Socialist Youth Federation, and with Trifón Medrano, the secretary general of the Union of Young

Communists, see Fernando Claudín (a leader at the time of the Communist youth), *Santiago Carrillo: Crónica de un secretario general*, 35–39.

38. *Historia de la UGT*, II, 622.

39. See Santiago Carrillo's tribute to Largo Caballero for his help in effecting the fusion (speech, reported in *Mundo Obrero*, 6 Apr. 1936); also an open letter from the central committee of the PCE to "Comrade Francisco Largo Caballero" hailing him as "the most vigorous champion" of the unity of the Socialist and Communist youth and conveying to him "cordial Bolshevik greetings," ibid., 2 Apr. 1936.

40. Passages from this statement are quoted by Carlos Hernández Zancajo (president of the Socialist Youth Federation), *Tercera etapa de octubre*, 9–11. For the entire text, see Ricard Viñas, *La formación de las juventudes socialistas unificadas, 1934–1936*, 145–46.

41. See Luis Romero Solano, *Vísperas de la guerra de España*, 77. Romero Solano represented Estremadura on the national committee of the Socialist Youth Federation.

42. That of Antonio Escribano, organizational secretary of the JSU in Alicante province, in a letter to me, 23 May 1950 (Hoover Institution). It will be recalled, however, that Santiago Carrillo, the general secretary of the JSU, gives forty thousand as the figure for the *combined* membership at the time of the fusion, but the ratio of three to fifty may be fairly accurate. The Communist writer, Evgenii S. Varga, in his book *Ispaniia v revoluitsii*, 117, gives the number of young Communists alone as fifty-one thousand, obviously an exaggerated figure.

43. See, for example, his article in *Claridad*, 13 May 1936; speech in Saragossa, reported in ibid., 1 June 1936.

44. According to information given to me by Alfonso Quintana y Pena, a former Socialist deputy.

45. For example, Alfredo Cabello, José Cazorla, José Lain, Federico Melchor, and Serrano Poncela. According to Enrique Castro, onetime commander in chief of the Communist Fifth Regiment and former member of the party's central committee, both Santiago Carrillo and José Cazorla joined the party on 6 November 1936 (*Hombres made in Moscú*, 439). See also Fernando Claudín, *Santiago Carrillo*, 48 and the Spanish Communist refugee periodical *España Popular*, 15 June 1940. For Carrillo's defense of their action, see Carrillo, *La Juventud, factor de la victoria*, 14.

46. According to Pedro Checa, a member of the politburo, in a speech in March 1937 (*A un gran partido*, 23). See also *Juventud de España*, 7 June 1940. Fernando Claudín states that Carillo was made deputy member (miembro suplente) of the politburo in March 1937 (*Santiago Carrillo*, 48).

47. *Demain l'Espagne*, 51.

48. As quoted by Andrés Carabantes y Eusebio Cimorra, *Un mito llamado Pasionaria*, 163–64.

49. "Notas Históricas sobre la Guerra de España," 264–65.

50. *Timón* (Buenos Aires), June 1940.

51. *Demain l'Espagne*, 43. Isaac Don Levine says of Codovila: ". . . a short, chunky and almost neckless Italian-born founder of the Argentine Communist party. Affiliated for a quarter-century with the Soviet underground, he had risen to the top as Comintern boss in South America" (*The Mind of an Assassin*, 70).

52. Claudín, *Santiago Carrillo*, 48.

53. Ibid., 44, 56.

54. According to José Duque, a member of the central committee of the Spanish Communist party, the word "instructors" was later dropped in favor of "collaborators," which was considered more diplomatic (when interviewed by me after the war).

55. *Hombres made in Moscú*, 374.

56. *La gran estafa*, 307.

57. Ibid., 309–10. For further information on Stefanov, see Branko Lazitch and Milorad M. Drachkovitch, *Biographical Dictionary of the Comintern*, 383–84, and Justo Martínez Amutio (the left-wing Socialist, who knew him personally), *Chantaje a un pueblo*, 269–80. The latter states (271–72): "He had offices reserved exclusively for himself, furnished luxuriously and ostentatiously in flats in Barcelona, Valencia and Madrid. At his side was his secretary and interpreter, the mysterious Angelita, a militant Communist, a real demon, beautiful, but cold and cruel. . . . Another of his adjutants was the sinister 'Carmen la Gorda' (Carmen, the Fat), a Russian, whose mere appearance and gestures produced repugnance. She was named 'Chief of Cadres' of the JSU and later of the

Spanish Communist party. . . . Her *nom de guerre* was of her own choosing." I met "Carmen la Gorda" in Spain and later in Mexico, where she married the diminutive Pedro Martínez Cartón, a member of the politburo, who, as I personally observed, lived in fear of her.

58. For this information I am grateful to a number of Spanish Communist refugees, whom I met in Mexico in the 1940s.

59. *Memorias de un luchador*, 432. Valentín González (El Campesino), the well-known Communist militia leader, wrote after he left the party: "During the Spanish Civil War, the man who in effect directed the Communist party was 'Alfredo,' the famous Palmiro Togliatti, one of the top-ranking figures in the Comintern. . . . José Díaz and the entire Politburo did nothing more than carry out his directives" (*Comunista en España y antistalinista en la U.R.S.S.*, 92).

60. U.S. Congress, Senate, Committee on the Judiciary, *Scope of Soviet Activity in the United States*, 3446.

61. From an unpublished commentary on Verle B. Johnston's "The International Brigades in the Spanish Civil War, 1936–1939" (Hoover Institution, Bolloten Collection).

62. *Togliatti-Díaz-Carrillo. Los comunistas y la revolución española*, 144.

63. *Demain l'Espagne*, 64. See also Cordón, 467.

64. *Chantaje a un pueblo*, 345–46.

65. *Comunista en España*, 99.

66. *J'ai perdu la foi à Moscou*, 130.

67. *La crisis del movimiento comunista*, 178.

68. Víctor Alba, *El frente popular*, 511. On the other hand, La Pasionaria, referring many years later to Togliatti, denied that the party submitted to his will: "Togliatti was not a man to interfere with our policy. He would say: 'You are the ones who must lead; no one from outside can resolve the problem.' In other words, he would talk with us and give us advice along certain lines, but on no account would he meddle with the policy of the party or with its work. He was a very intelligent, capable and cultured man" (Jaime Camino, *Intimas conversaciones con La Pasionaria*, 45).

69. From an unpublished article (No. 1) given to me by Antonio Escribano (Hoover Institution).

70. As given in *Nuestra lucha por la unidad*, 34. See also Santiago Carrillo, *Somos la organización de la juventud*, 6–9.

71. Letter to me, 28 May 1950 (Hoover Institution).

72. Carrillo, *En marcha*, 9.

73. Letter to me, 28 May 1950 (Hoover Institution).

74. See, for example, articles by Sócrates Gómez in *Adelante*, 25 June 1937, and *CNT*, 11 June 1937.

75. The letters were published in *La Correspondencia de Valencia*, 31 Mar., 1 Apr. 1937, respectively. See also statement by José Gregori Martínez in *Adelante*, as given in *La Correspondencia de Valencia*, 9 Apr. 1937.

76. *Blood of Spain*, 333.

Chapter 13

1. *Mis recuerdos*, 212. See also ibid., 230. Luis Araquistáin, *El comunismo y la guerra de España*, 8, and his letter to Diego Martínez Barrio, as given in *Vía Libre*, 15 May 1939; also Carlos de Baráibar in *Timón* (Buenos Aires), June 1940; Wenceslao Carrillo in ibid., Nov. 1939; Indalecio Prieto in *Correo de Asturias*, 10 July 1943. The handwritten draft of Araquistáin's letter to Martínez Barrio is in the Archivo Histórico Nacional, Araquistáin Papers, Leg. 33/M66[b].

2. See *Claridad*, 15 Mar. 1939; also report of Wenceslao Carrillo to the Labor and Socialist International, 23 May 1939, as given in the special issue of *Independent News* [June 1939?].

3. See his articles in *Claridad*, 5 Oct., 9 Nov. 1935; also *Times*, 2 Mar. 1936 (dispatch from Madrid); speech reported in *Verdad*, 13 Aug. 1937, showing his position prior to the war.

4. See his articles in *Frente Rojo*, 19 June 1937, and speech, *Verdad*, 13 Aug. 1937; also Dolores Ibárruri's reference to him in her speech at the plenary session of the central committee of the Communist party, 17 June 1937 (*Frente Rojo*, 21 June 1937).

5. Julio Alvarez del Vayo, *The Last Optimist*, 323. "The devil in the piece of the *Nation*'s degeneration," wrote Lewis Corey, for thirteen years a *Nation* contributor, "is Alvarez del Vayo and

his fatal influence on Freda Kirchwey [editor and publisher]. This man promotes every twist and turn of Soviet Communism and imperialism" (quoted, Peter Viereck, *Shame and Glory of the Intellectuals*, 179).

6. Ibid., 228.

7. Quoted in Enrique Castro, *Hombres made in Moscú*, 659. In spite of the overwhelming documentary proof of Alvarez del Vayo's services to the Communists and their Soviet allies presented in my previous works, the leftist Spanish historian Julio Aróstegui claims, without adducing any evidence, that I have "falsified" the pro-Communist stance of Alvarez del Vayo, Miaja, Rojo, and Negrín (see Manuel Tuñón de Lara, *La guerra civil española: 50 años después*, 72).

8. Castro, *Hombres*, 553.

9. *Men and Politics*, 457.

10. *Dva goda v. Ispanii, 1937–39*, 115. See also Lillian Hellman, *Three*, 97.

11. Later in the war, he appointed Constancia de la Mora, a Communist party member and granddaughter of the famous conservative Prime Minister Antonio Maura, to head the foreign press bureau (see Constancia de la Mora, *In Place of Splendor*, 340).

12. Article in *Socialist Review*, Sept. 1937. Oak was a member of the American Communist party until 1936 and denounced the Comintern in 1937 (see his letter dated 16 January 1950 to Bertram D. Wolfe [Hoover Institution]). I can personally corroborate with documentary evidence Liston Oak's statement that foreign correspondents were not permitted to write freely of the revolution. In a dispatch to London, dated 31 December 1936, I quoted from a speech by Juan García Oliver, then Anarchosyndicalist minister of justice, in which he stated that "the revolution must be carried on simultaneously with the war" and that it was "necessary to renovate every branch of Spanish life." These lines were deleted by Rubio Hidalgo, who had been made chief of the foreign press bureau by Alvarez del Vayo. See Bolloten, "Dispatch to the London Bureau of the United Press, 31 Dec. 1936" (Hoover Institution). See also my dispatch from Valencia, 7 July 1937, from which the words "consolidation of the popular revolution" were deleted by Constancia de la Mora, the Communist censor (Hoover Institution).

13. See letter by Simone in *Tiempo*, 27 Aug. 1943; also Claud Cockburn (alias Frank Pitcairn, reporter for the Communist London *Daily Worker* during the Civil War), *A Discord of Trumpets*, 305–9, and *Crossing the Line*, 26–28; Hellman, *Three*, 91–92; Arthur Koestler, *The Invisible Writing*, 400–401, 409. After World War II Simone became editor of the Czech Communist newspaper *Rude Pravo* during the Stalinist-controlled regime of Klement Gottwald and was placed on trial and hanged in 1952 with ten other prominent Communists, mostly Jews, including Rudolf Slansky, former secretary general of the Czech Communist party and premier, after "confessing" to crimes of "sabotage, treason, and espionage" (see Arthur G. London, a Communist and former vice-minister of foreign affairs, who, with two other leading Communists, was sentenced during the same trial to life imprisonment, *L'aveu*, 277–324). Sixteen years later, in 1968, Simone and all the other convicted men were "rehabilitated" (ibid., 324).

14. Koestler, 333. For a fascinating profile of Otto Katz, see ibid., 255–56. Both "Otto" and "Willy" are mentioned in three letters by Alvarez del Vayo, dated 24, 25 Dec. 1936, 10 Mar. 1937, addressed to Luis Araquistáin, the Spanish ambassador in Paris (Araquistáin Papers, Leg. 23/A108[a] A109[a] and A117[a]).

15. Koestler, 333, 335.

16. Because of his services to the Communist cause, some Spaniards have concluded that at the beginning of the war he was a member of the left wing of the Socialist party. This is untrue. See, for example, Julián Zugazagoitia (a moderate Socialist), *Historia de la guerra en España*, 138, who shows that he was a follower of Prieto's, and Justo Martínez Amutio (a supporter of Largo Caballero), *Chantaje a un pueblo*, 41.

17. *Mis recuerdos*, 230.

18. Raymond Carr, *Modern Spain*, 144.

19. See, for example, Aróstegui, n. 7 above; also Dante A. Puzzo, *Spain and the Great Powers, 1936–1941*, 186, 267, n. 48 (whose authority for Negrín's alleged independence of the Communists is no other than Alvarez del Vayo), and Herbert R. Southworth in *Tiempo de Historia*, Oct. 1978 (interview by María Ruipérez), and the *Times Literary Supplement*, 9 June 1978. "In order to understand Southworth's steadfastly loyal and therefore uncritical support of Negrín," writes George

Esenwein, "one must bear in mind that he served as an important propagandist for the Negrín government. Between February 1938 and February 1939, he edited in New York *The News of Spain* (see *Contemporary Authors*, vols. 85–88, 557), a bulletin which, if not financed by or otherwise officially associated with the Spanish Republican government, was unmistakeably a mouthpiece for its policies." Excerpt from a careful study of a complete collection of the bulletin.

20. See, for example, Angel Viñas (interview published in *Tiempo de Historia*, May 1979, 9, 13).

21. *Autobiografía de Federico Sánchez*, 17, 24. My italics.

22. *Hombres made in Moscú*, 660. Sánchez Arcos was appointed to the post of undersecretary of propaganda on 22 January 1938 by José Giral, then minister of foreign affairs and member of Izquierda Republicana (*Gaceta de la República*, 25 Jan. 1938). He succeeded Federico Melchor, a member of the Communist-controlled JSU executive and a PCE member since 1936.

23. See Palmiro Togliatti, *Escritos sobre la guerra de España*, 280. For further information on Rodríguez, see the official Communist history of the Civil War, *Guerra y revolución en España, 1936–1939*, I, 301, IV, 296–97. I met Rodríguez in Mexico City in 1939 through the Italian Communist Vittorio Vidali, known in Spain as Carlos Contreras, and one of the principal organizers of the Fifth Regiment. Vidali was undoubtedly an important agent of the NKVD (the Soviet secret police), who, to judge from the authority he exercised over the Spanish Communist refugees, must have been instructed by Moscow to keep them in line. It was through my contact with Vidali that I met most of the leading Spanish Communists in Mexico and was able to appreciate Rodríguez's intimate association with Negrín. Rodríguez had accompanied Negrín to Mexico on urgent matters connected with the prodigious Spanish treasure shipped from Spain at the close of the Civil War. He was Negrín's right-hand man during the negotiations with President Lázaro Cardenas.

The Spanish treasure shipped from Spain to Mexico consisted of gold, precious stones, foreign currency, stocks, bonds, and art objects seized during the war from safe deposit boxes and the homes of opponents of the regime. (For information on the opening of deposit boxes in Madrid and on various decrees providing for the surrender to the Bank of Spain of certain valuables, see Angel Viñas, *El oro español en la guerra civil*, 160–67). The treasure was shipped to Veracruz in the luxury yacht, the *Vita*, formerly the property of Alfonso XIII, and was used for the financial support of Spanish refugees. Through his finance minister, Francisco Méndez Aspe, Negrín had placed the treasure during the voyage to Mexico in the custody of Enrique Puente, a trusted aide, whom he had promoted during the war to the rank of colonel of the carabineers. Puente was to have delivered the precious cargo to Negrín's friend, Doctor José Puche, in Mexico, but he switched allegiance and turned it over to Indalecio Prieto (see Gabriel Morón, *Política de ayer y política de mañana*, 171), at that time Negrín's archenemy, who administered the proceeds through the Junta de Auxilio a los republicanos Españoles (JARE). Later, owing to the infighting among the refugees, the Mexican government, by decree signed by President Manuel Avila Camacho on 21 January 1941 (text given in Amaro del Rosal, *El oro del Banco de España y la historia del Vita*, 155–62), transformed the JARE into an "economic entity subject to Mexican laws" composed of Spanish and Mexican representatives. However, because of the friction between the Spanish and Mexican delegates, Avila Camacho issued a new decree on 27 November 1942, forming a commission that gave the Mexican authorities greater control over the administration of the funds (ibid., 192–97). Rosal, the president of the UGT bank employees' union, the Federación Nacional de Banca, initially a left-wing Socialist who abandoned Largo Caballero for the Communists and who, in his own words, became "a direct collaborator of Dr. Negrín and of his finance minister, Francisco Méndez Aspe" (Rosal, *Historia de la UGT de España, 1901–1939*, 538), was also director general of the Caja de Reparaciones, which had custody in Spain of the confiscated valuables. (See Viñas, *El oro de Moscú*, 198–202, for information on the Caja de Reparaciones. For Rosal's account of the *Vita* episode, see *El oro del Banco de España*, 81–235, and his article "El Tesoro del Vita" in *Historia 16*, Mar. 1984.) According to Prieto, the treasure shipped on the *Vita* represented a "very small portion of the confiscated valuables that were stored in disorder in the Spanish embassy in Paris. Franco was able to recover the rest without any difficulty" (*Convulsiones de España*, III, 144). Louis Fischer, who was very close to Negrín, claims that the entire treasure was kept in a fortress in Figueras near the French border and that, as the front crept nearer to Figueras, Negrín gave orders to have it transported to a chic villa in Deauville. "One night in the second week of February 1939, the well-dressed inhabitants of the Deauville villa put on working clothes and carried huge cases filled with diamonds, sapphires, emeralds, pearls, and gold and platinum jewelry down to the sea and loaded them on the yacht *Vita*. The estimated value of the jewels was $50,000,000. The cargo also contained strong boxes packed tight with stocks and bonds" (*Men and Politics*, 596–97). For further information on the *Vita* episode and the JARE, see Alvarez del Vayo, *The Last Optimist*, 292–97; José Borrás, *Políticas de los exiliados españoles, 1944–1950*, 86–88; José Fuentes Mares, *Historia de un conflicto: El tesoro del "Vita"*, 173–91; Enrique Líster, *Memorias de un luchador*, 413–22; Salvador de Madariaga, *Spain: A Modern History*, 589–91; Prieto, *Convulsiones*, III, 97–110, 123–28; Lois Elwyn Smith, *Mexico and the Spanish Republicans*, 229–30, 233–36, 270, 274–75.

24. *Trayectoria*, 391. Cordón remained a member of the Communist party until his death in 1969. See also the pro-Communist Amaro del Rosal, *Historia de la UGT en España, 1901–1939*, II, 626.

25. Cordón, *Trayectoria*, 411.

26. *Del triunfo a la derrota*, 369.

27. See *Claridad*, 15 Mar. 1939; also report of Wenceslao Carrillo to the Labor and Socialist International, 23 May 1939, as given in the special issue of *Independent News* [June 1939?].

28. See Angel Galarza in *El Socialista Español*, 2 Dec. 1946, and Martínez Amutio, 40–42.

29. The interested reader can find in the writings of the following top-ranking Socialists and in the other sources cited such a profusion of corroborative evidence of Negrín's cooperation with the Communists as to leave not a scintilla of doubt: Luis Araquistáin (letter to Martínez Barrio, as given in *Via Libre*, 15 May 1939; *El comunismo*, 14, 17); Carlos de Baráibar (*Timón* [Buenos Aires], June 1940); Wenceslao Carrillo (speech in May 1946, as given in *Segundo congreso del partido socialista obrero español en el exilio*, 95–107; Carrillo, *El último episodio de la guerra civil española*, 10); Martínez Amutio, 60; Gabriel Morón, *Política de ayer y política de mañana*, 108–9; Indalecio Prieto, *Cómo y por qué salí del ministerio de defensa nacional*, prologues to the Mexican and French editions, 12, 25; Prieto, *Convulsiones*, II, 141, III, 219; *Epistolario, Prieto y Negrín*, 17, 99–100; article in *Correo de Asturias*, 10 July 1943; article in *El Socialista* [Paris], 9 Nov. 1950; interview given by Prieto to the United Press, reported in *El Universal*, 30 July 1939; Andrés Saborit, *Besteiro*, 398–99; Zugazagoitia, 408, 464, 535. But see also the testimony of Segismundo Casado, *The Last Days of Madrid*, 101, 281, and Jesús Pérez Salas, *Guerra en España, 1936–1939*, 141, 162, both moderate Republican officers, as well as editorials in *Política*, organ of the Left Republican party, 16, 20 Mar. 1939. For an Anarchist profile of Negrín, see Diego Abad de Santillán, *Por qué perdimos la guerra*, 210–13. Two former leading Communists describe Negrín as the Communists' "ambitious and docile tool" and as "Moscow's man of confidence" (Valentín González [El Campesino], article in *Solidaridad Obrera* [Paris], 11 Mar. 1951, and Jesús Hernández, *Yo fui un ministro de Stalin*, 157, respectively).

30. *My Mission to Spain*, 358.

31. *The New Leader*, 5 July 1954.

32. Letter to Sender. "Before the war and in its early stages," Bowers wrote, "I am sure Negrín was not a fellow traveler. I thought he had made terms under necessity at a critical stage and when I saw him in Paris after the war ended he talked frankly and I thought honestly about the Communists. I have changed my mind about him now. The letter I wrote him asking certain information relative to the Communists he has not so much as acknowledged." A copy of this letter to Sender is in the Joaquín Maurín Collection, Hoover Institution (Container 3).

33. *The Tragedy of Manuel Azaña and the Fate of the Spanish Republic*, 182.

34. *The Yoke and the Arrows*, 58.

35. *Half of Spain Died*, 225–26. Alvarez del Vayo, with whom Matthews maintained a friendly relationship for many years, wrote: "Rarely has there been a politician less disposed to be anybody's puppet than Negrín. The Spanish Communists were the first to know this. . . . To assume that Negrín can be 'managed' or 'manipulated' by Moscow or anybody else is not to know the kind of man he is" (*The Last Optimist*, 290). In the false picture of Negrín that Matthews presented to the American public, his writings bear comparison with his tendentious handling of Fidel Castro in 1964: "The belief fostered by Washington and Cuban exiles that Fidel Castro is a prisoner of the Cuban Communist apparatus or a puppet of Moscow is a myth. He is, by character, incapable of accepting orders or even advice. . . . The path he has chosen forces him into conformity to most needs and desires of the Soviet bloc, but that is a different matter. Now that five years have passed, it is surely time for American officials and the American public to realize that whatever they want to think of Fidel Castro,

he is one of the most extraordinary men of our age" (*Return to Cuba* [special issue of the *Hispanic American Report*, 1964]).

36. This view of Negrín as a "strong" man is not shared by the Communist Antonio Cordón, whom Negrín appointed to head the vital undersecretaryship of the army in April 1938. Although an admirer of his "extraordinary fortitude and vitality," Cordón states: "[Negrín] appeared to be a man of strong character. To judge from my observations during the period I was close to him, I do not believe he was. He frequently had those spectacular outbursts of bad temper that are typical of weak characters" (*Trayectoria*, 390–91).

37. *The Spanish Civil War* (1965 ed.), 556 and n. 1.

38. P. 669.

39. In the preface to Pablo de Azcárate's book, *Mi embajada en Londres durante la guerra civil española*, 17, Manuel Azcárate, his son, says of his father: "Perhaps Negrín was the political figure who exercised the greatest influence on him. In spite of the serious discussions and differences between us, he always respected the choice I had made to join the Communist party in 1934." In a letter to me, dated 23 January 1949 (Hoover Institution), Luis Araquistáin, who was Spanish ambassador to Paris from September 1936 to June 1937, stated that the son had "great political influence" on his father and that the latter "always collaborated closely with the Russians."

40. *Españoles de mi tiempo*, 414.

41. 1965 ed., 557; 1977 ed., 669.

42. *Yo fui ministro de Stalin*, 135. My italics.

43. *In Stalin's Secret Service*, 96–97. See Chapter 9 for information on Krivitsky.

44. *Triunfo*, 22 June 1974.

45. Krivitsky, 99–100.

46. *Epistolario, Prieto y Negrín*, 104. In this postwar exchange of correspondence, Negrín does not deny Prieto's assertion regarding Louis Fischer's receipt of funds. See also Cipriano Rivas-Cherif (Azaña's intimate friend and brother-in-law), *Retrato de un desconocido: Vida de Manuel Azaña*, 291. "How much did Fischer receive?" asked Araquistáin in the preface to an unpublished work ("NO nos callamos durante la guerra"). "This is not easy to ascertain. During the early months of the war, at the request of and with the signature of Alvarez del Vayo, he was given $600,000 ($300,000 were authorized by Negrín, then minister of finance in Valencia; the other $300,000 he was to pick up in New York) to recruit volunteers in the United States. I heard Fischer say that it cost $100 to transport each volunteer from New York. Thus, if this entire amount were invested, 6,000 North American volunteers should have gone to Spain. Later, he was given further sums." (Fischer himself acknowledges that he "obtained considerable sums of money for the transportation of volunteers to Spain" [*Men and Politics*, 547].) Araquistáin also states that he was told by a former foreign Communist that Fischer had been entrusted with the distribution to certain newspapers in Paris, London, and New York certain funds that Negrín had given him to "feed the flame of his improvised glory as a statesman" (Araquistáin Papers, Leg. 75/5[a]). It is of course impossible to verify all of Fischer's alleged activities, but in view of the important but little-known role he played during the Civil War, the following biographical information must be recorded. He was born in Philadelphia on 29 February 1896 (*Who Was Who, 1961–1970*). He lived with his wife, Markoosha, and their two children in Moscow from 1927 to 1939 in housing conditions reserved only for the privileged (see Markoosha Fischer, *My Lives in Russia*, 45–46, 87–88, 112, 114). During that period he wrote several pro-Soviet books and contributed to the *New York Post* and the *Nation*. After breaking with Moscow in 1940, he affirmed that he had never been a member of any party (*Men and Politics*, 160). "This disavowal of party membership," said an obituary in the *New York Times* (17 Jan. 1970), "meant little to those who chided Mr. Fischer for neglecting to reveal the extent of Stalinist purges and tyranny in his writing from Russia in the 1920s and '30s." For his support of Russia, see David Caute, *The Fellow Travellers*, 66, 85, 123, 178–79, 189, and his letter to Largo Caballero in which he mentions his "devotion to the Soviet Union" (*Men and Politics*, 372). In Spain, during the Civil War, a certain aura of mystery surrounded him. Justo Martínez Amutio, a longstanding associate of Caballero, who became governor of Albacete, headquarters of the International Brigades, to which Fischer was appointed quartermaster by André Marty (*Men and Politics*, 386) and who knew Fischer personally, writes: "The only thing that could be confirmed with certainty was that he served as a Soviet agent, although he said he was not a Communist and that no one had sent him to Spain from Moscow. . . .

[But] Luis Araquistáin, who knew him well, when he was Republican ambassador in Berlin, warned that he was actually a crypto-Communist and a direct agent of Stalin. His activity in the form of visits and interviews . . . was very intense. . . . Although Fischer wished to appear simple and courteous, he was overbearing especially with the Spanish Communists. . . . He was seen with great frequency with Dr. Negrín, with whom, he said, he had made friends years before when they met in Paris and Berlin. It was he who introduced Stashevsky to Negrín, before Negrín became minister of finance . . . and long before the arrival [in September 1936] of the [Soviet] Ambassador [Marcel] Rosenberg, who was also a great friend of Fischer's (*Chantaje a un pueblo*, 367–68; see also ibid., 39–40, 42). In the previously mentioned preface to his unpublished work, Araquistáin wrote: "It would not surprise me if it were Fischer who 'discovered' Negrín and recommended him as the future prime minister to those who directed Spanish politics in Moscow" (Araquistáin Papers, Leg. 75/5[a]). It is noteworthy that Fischer claims that he often saw the speeches prepared by Alvarez del Vayo and Pablo de Azcárate, the Spanish ambassador in London, for delivery at the League of Nations and "occasionally offered suggestions which were included in the final draft" (*Men and Politics*, 450).

47. *Nation*, 13 Jan. 1940. According to Martínez Amutio (see n. 46 above), it was Fischer who introduced Stashevsky to Negrín.

48. *The Last Optimist*, 291. He adds on p. 292: "[A point that] Negrín considered essential to the maintenance of good relations with the Russians was a clear understanding that he would not tolerate, from anyone, even the suggestion of intervention in the affairs of the Republican government or in the internal policy of Spain. . . . [The Russians] must have been the first to laugh over the charge of some Spanish leaders that overnight Negrín had become a 'tool of Moscow.' "

49. Ansó, *Yo fui ministro de Negrín*, 188.

50. Interview, Heleno Saña in *Indice*, 15 June 1974.

51. Interview in *Tiempo de Historia*, May 1979.

52. *El oro español*, 212–13, n. 69, 226, 235, 261, 278, 281. This six-hundred-page volume, published in November 1976 and based largely on classified documents found in the Bank of Spain and the ministry of finance in 1973, is the most important work published to date on the mobilization of the Spanish gold reserves and on other aspects of Republican finances during the Civil War. Viñas has since completed a more popular work (*El oro de Moscú*, 1979), based on the documentation of the first.

53. *El oro español*, 212–13, n. 69. See also Viñas, *El oro de Moscú*, 184, n. 14. In a letter to me Viñas contends that Stashevsky's role has been overestimated.

54. Krivitsky, 99–100.

55. Orlov gives 13 August 1938 as the date he received political asylum in the United States, one month after leaving Spain (Orlov, *The Secret History of Stalin's Crimes*, xv). In *The Legacy of Alexander Orlov*, prepared by the U.S. Senate Subcommittee on Internal Security after Orlov's death in the United States on 10 April 1973, which contains a photograph of Orlov, his name at birth is given as Leon Lazarevich Feldbin and his party name as Lev Lazarevich Nikol'skiy (3–4). Orlov informed the subcommittee on 28 September 1955 that he was sent by the politburo to Spain in September 1936 (16). "I had arrived in Madrid on September 16, 1936, about two months after the outbreak of the Spanish Civil War," he wrote in 1966, "to head a large Soviet mission on intelligence and of military experts. As a general in the Intelligence Service (NKVD), I was chief Soviet adviser to the Republican government on intelligence, counterintelligence and guerrilla warfare, a post I was to hold for nearly two years" (*Reader's Digest*, Nov. 1966).

56. *Reader's Digest*, Nov. 1966. Viñas, *El oro español*, 190, states that Negrín was the "driving force" in the decision to send the gold to Russia, but in a subsequent reference to the subject, he leaves open the question as to whether the idea originated with Spanish or Soviet authorities (*European Studies Review*, Jan. 1979, 112).

57. See article by Gonzalo Moya, "Don Marcelino Pascua: Un gran médico socialista olvidado," *Triunfo*, 9 July 1977. Luis Araquistáin describes Pascua as "an obscure doctor of medicine," appointed to Moscow "at the behest of Negrín," "a man of [Negrín's] absolute confidence . . . tied to him by an almost slavish loyalty" (*El comunismo y la guerra de España*, 28). The Republican jurist Angel Ossorio y Gallardo, not generally given to namecalling, characterizes the ambassador as "Communist or pro-Communist" (*Mis memorias*, 242). Little has been written about Marcelino Pascua. His papers were acquired by the Archivo Histórico Nacional, Madrid, and were to be opened in 1989.

58. See Pascua, article in *Cuadernos para el Diálogo*, June–July 1970; Viñas, *El oro de Moscú*, 288.

59. Viñas, *El oro español*, 76, gives the weight of the gold actually sent to Russia as 510 metric tons.

60. Pascua, article in *Cuadernos para el Diálogo*, June–July 1970.

61. Ibid.

Chapter 14

1. For General Franco's spectacular advance toward Madrid, see Colonel José Manuel Martínez Bande, *La marcha sobre Madrid* (rev. ed., 1982), which is based on documents in the Servicio Histórico Militar in Madrid.

2. Angel Viñas, *El oro español en la guerra civil*, 140, and *El oro de Moscú*, 108–9.

3. The text of the decree is reproduced in *Causa general*, Anexo XIII. See also Viñas, *El oro español*, 133–34. In his memoirs published in Mexico in 1954, Largo Caballero states that Negrín requested authority from the cabinet to remove the gold stocks from the Bank of Spain and to take them to "a safe place without stating where" (*Mis recuerdos*, 203). This is likely since the utmost secrecy had to be observed, but it does not imply that he did not inform the prime minister of their destination. In fact, Largo Caballero unequivocally approved the transfer of the gold reserves to Cartagena and later to the Soviet Union. Hence Angel Viñas, who, as we have seen, is a vigorous supporter of Negrín, is hardly justified in pointing to Largo Caballero's statement as one of the reasons why the memoirs "must be read with caution" (*El oro de Moscú*, 143, n. 50). On the other hand, he is justified in criticizing the following assertion by Caballero relating to the orders that were sent to Moscow to sell portions of the gold: "Negrín and I had to sign them. I signed two or three. Afterwards, without giving me any explanation, Negrín alone signed them" (*Mis recuerdos*, 204). As Viñas correctly points out, Caballero countersigned "each and every one of the orders for the sale of gold issued during his encumbency comprising the first six orders that covered the period between 16 February and 23 April 1937" (*El oro de Moscú*, 314). However, Caballero's erroneous assertion, which, according to Viñas, is "one of the myths that have blackened the character of Negrín," hardly gives Viñas license to state, without adducing the slightest evidence, that *Mis recuerdos* was "conveniently retouched" (*El oro de Moscú*, 314) or to make other unfounded allegations calling into question the authenticity of the memoirs (ibid., 138, n. 12).

4. Viñas, *El oro español*, 146–47, states that the ten thousand cases of gold were transported by rail between 15 and 21 September and gives the exact times of departure of the trains. See also Viñas, "Gold, the Soviet Union, and the Spanish Civil War" in *European Studies Review*, Jan. 1979.

5. Viñas, *El oro español*, 139, 137.

6. Ibid., 129.

7. Ibid., 76.

8. For a detailed account of the shipments to France and for other related information, see ibid., 47–89; also Viñas, *El oro de Moscú*, 83–101, and "El mito del oro de la guerra civil," *Historia 16*, Mar. 1977.

9. For a list of the principal recipients of funds, together with the sums they received, see Viñas, *El oro español*, 87; see also 121–23 for additional information.

10. Quoted in ibid., 84–85.

11. Quoted in ibid., 99.

12. Ibid., 101–5.

13. Ibid., 105–21, 114–15, 119. See also the official communiqué issued by General Franco, *Heraldo de Aragón*, 15 Oct. 1936.

14. *El oro español*, 35. For some of the provisions of this law, see ibid., 33–34. In order to circumvent the law, both the Giral and Largo Caballero cabinets approved certain confidential decrees relating to the export of gold and allocation of foreign exchange, although after the gold shipments to France had already begun (ibid., 38–39, 132). See also 553–57, for the confidential decree of 29 April 1938, by which the gold sales were made legal. It was approved long after the gold reserves in their entirety had been shipped abroad, leaving the paper currency in circulation without any gold backing. According to Viñas, no Republican leader ever acknowledged the existence of this decree

(article in *Historia 16*, Mar. 1977). This is not surprising, for had the decree been divulged it would have rendered the peseta to all intents and purposes worthless on the international exchange markets.

15. *The Last Optimist*, 284.

16. Viñas, *El oro español*, 227. In the opinion of Viñas, who recognizes—but subsequently denies—the political disadvantages of shipping the bulk of the gold reserves to Russia (ibid., 187), the gold could not have been sent to any other country and mobilized as effectively for the war effort (ibid., 182–86). See also Mariano Ansó, *Yo fui ministro de Negrín*, 309–11. In his article, "Oro español en Moscú," Marcelino Pascua, the former Spanish ambassador to Moscow, discusses the reason why it was considered impractical or unwise to ship the gold to England, France, Switzerland, the United States, or Mexico (*Cuadernos para el Diálogo*, June–July 1970).

17. See, for example, Prieto, *Convulsiones*, II, 156.

18. For the secrecy that surrounded the bank's operations and its failure to publish any records of the accounts held by the Republican government, see Viñas, *El oro español*, 362. For additional information relating to this bank, see ibid., 81, 227–29, 460–61. See also his statement at the Spanish Institute, New York. Readers interested in the financial involvement of this bank with the French Communist party, its leaders, and its press in recent years should consult the remarkable work by Jean Montaldo, *Les secrets de la banque soviétique en France*. According to the author, the bank "has the reputation of being the most impenetrable in France." Nevertheless, he was able to collect "thousands of original documents." "My investigation was not simple; I came up against the extraordinary system of precautions typical of the Soviets who are masters in the art of secrecy" (11).

19. Cipriano Rivas-Cherif, Azaña's brother-in-law, says that Negrín was Pascua's "medical colleague and steadfast protector in exchange for a contemptible subservience" (*Retrato de un desconocido: Vida de Manuel Azaña*, 316).

20. Article in *Cuadernos para el Diálogo*, June–July 1970.

21. *El oro de Moscú*, 311.

22. Ibid., 382, n. 10.

23. U.S. Congress, Senate, Committee on the Judiciary, *Scope of Soviet Activity in the United States*, 3430.

24. *El oro del Banco de España y la historia del Vita*, 36–37.

25. According to Viñas, *El oro español*, 147–50, 1,998 cases went to France and 202 were sent to the ministry of finance in Valencia. See also his article in *Historia 16*, Mar. 1977.

26. Luis Bolín, *Spain: The Vital Years*, 375–82, reproduces the official eight-page receipt in its French version.

27. The figures of $518 million and 460.52 metric tons are given by Viñas, *El oro español*, 207–10.

28. Ansó, 313–30. The Spanish edition of Luis Bolín's book, *España! Los años vitales*, contains copies of several documents turned over to the Franco government that are not in the English edition.

29. Ansó, 325–29. Viñas claims that Ansó's version regarding the units of the Spanish fleet is incorrect. "They had been embargoed," he writes, "in Odessa in order to secure payment of certain sums owing to Soviet commercial agencies. The Soviet authorities had tried to acquire them or lease them. Finally, in February 1939 [one month before the end of the war] the Republican government decided to accept a Russian offer to buy them" (notes in letter to me, 15 Jan. 1978, Hoover Institution). See also Viñas, *El oro de Moscú*, 356, 412, 425, nn. 32–33. In note 33, Viñas states that on 21 February 1939 Méndez Aspe notified Negrín from Paris that the Russians wished to purchase four ships for 607,000 pounds sterling. "Méndez Aspe considered the transaction advisable and was only waiting urgently for Negrín's authorization in order to finalize it." A month later, on 24 March 1939, Méndez Aspe informed Eliodoro de la Torre, a member of the Basque government, with whom he met to discuss the question of providing more financial aid to the Basque refugees in France, that "the amount in question had not yet been credited by the Soviets" (according to a memorandum of the meeting quoted by the Spanish historian Javier Rubio in *Historia 16*, Jan. 1980). Neither Viñas nor Rubio indicates whether the Russians ever paid for the ships. See also Cipriano Rivas-Cherif, *Retrato de un desconocido*, 324–25.

30. Alvarez del Vayo claims that the coldness between Negrín and the Russians began in 1945 and "became sharper at the time of the death of Jan Masaryk in Prague [where, a few days after the Communist coup d'état in February 1948, it was officially announced that he had committed suicide

by throwing himself from a window]. Negrín and Masaryk were united by a warm friendship that went back to the time of their exile in London during the Second World War" (*Give Me Combat*, 193). During that time, Negrín was on very friendly terms with Soviet ambassador Ivan Maisky and his wife, both of whom stayed with him frequently at his country house at Bovingdon, not far from London. Says Maisky: "Bovingdon became our regular resting place at weekends" (*Memoirs of a Soviet Ambassador: The War, 1939–43*, 117–18).

31. *Reader's Digest*, Nov. 1966. It is hard to believe that Orlov, so alert to everything that was going on, was not aware of the whereabouts of the gold reserves.

32. Letter to me, 15 Dec. 1979, Hoover Institution. Martínez Amutio was secretary of the Valencia Federation of the Socialist party, the second largest federation.

33. U.S. Congress, Senate, *Scope of Soviet Activity*, 3431–32.

34. *The Last Optimist*, 285–86.

35. *Por qué perdimos la guerra*, 105–6.

36. Ibid., 113.

37. *Todos fuimos culpables*, 503.

38. *Obras Completas*, IV, 704.

39. *Reader's Digest*, Nov. 1966.

40. U.S. Congress, Senate, *Scope of Soviet Activity*, 3431–32. Amaro del Rosal confirms Méndez Aspe's "state of 'agitation' . . . which was in keeping with his personality" (*El oro del Banco de España*, 35).

41. See article by N. Kuznetsov, Soviet naval attaché and adviser to Antonio Ruiz, chief of the Cartagena naval base, in *Pod znamenem ispanskoi respubliki, 1936–1939*, 241–244. The number of Soviet vessels is confirmed by Pascua, article in *Cuadernos para el Diálogo*, June–July 1970, and by Rosal, *El oro del Banco de España*, 38.

42. Viñas, *El oro de Moscú*, 262.

43. The weight of each case, according to Rosal, was 65 kilos (*El oro del Banco de España*, 30).

44. Walter Krivitsky, *In Stalin's Secret Service*, 112–13.

45. Pascua, article in *Cuadernos para el Diálogo*, June–July 1970, and Viñas, *El oro de Moscú*, 285, 298, n. 25, 304, n. 65.

46. The estimated fine gold value is given by Viñas, *El oro español*, 206, table 14.

47. My italics. Bland's letter is in the Hoover Institution.

48. I am deeply grateful to Roger Bland for his assistance and regret that I failed to acquaint him at the time with this important piece of information.

49. For the charge of melting and refining, see Viñas, *El oro español*, table 18 (between pp. 242 and 243). For other costs charged to the Spanish government, such as "maintaining the military guard" for protecting the gold, namely $14,500 a month), see Viñas, *El oro de Moscú*, 293.

50. *The Yoke and the Arrows*, 98.

51. See Viñas, *El oro español*, table 19 (between pp. 244 and 245), for a detailed account of the melting and refining, based on official Soviet figures that he found in the Bank of Spain, of varying amounts of gold that were sold in accordance with fifteen orders received from the Spanish treasury.

52. Ibid., 235. The first six orders, it will be recalled, were also signed by Largo Caballero.

53. *El oro de Moscú*, 381, n. 6. Until Viñas attributed their enforced stay in Moscow to a decision by Negrín and Méndez Aspe, it had always been assumed that only the Russians were responsible for their prolonged sojourn. Viñas also states: "The subject of the officials gave rise to many accusations, but it appears that their retention in Moscow was due to the fact that the Republican authorities themselves did not desire their return. . . . When the Republican government decided to repatriate them, the Russians, after a certain hesitation, acceded" (notes in letter to me, 15 Jan. 1978, Hoover Institution).

54. Ibid., 285 and n. 66; 381, n. 6.

55. *El oro español*, 197, n. 57.

56. According to Martínez Amutio, when the four Spaniards, who had been told that their absence from Spain would not last longer than a month, asked Pascua to intercede on their behalf, he "promised to intervene immediately and advised them to remain at their posts without protesting to the Soviets or creating problems. . . . The Spanish officials lodged further complaints with the ambassador. When, after nearly two months, no one received any explanation, they were made to change their

lodgings, so that they could not communicate with one another. Even the trips from their lodgings were made separately and each one was accompanied by a Russian who quite obviously belonged to the secret police. . . . The way Ambassador Pascua conducted himself was worse than negligent: Obvious subservience to and complicity with the Soviets, because, although the complaints of the officials reached Spain, he replied that they were exaggerating their situation" (Justo Martínez Amutio, *Chantaje a un pueblo*, 56–57). See also ibid., 63. According to Prieto, the four bank employees were able to leave Russia thanks to Manuel Martínez Pedroso, the chargé d'affaires: "[His complaints] to our ambassador, Don Marcelino Pascua, were in vain. They were not given permission to leave; they had to remain in Russia with their families. At the end of two years, when the war was drawing to an end, the chargé d'affaires Don Manuel Martínez Pedroso put an end to their confinement. But the four bank officials were not repatriated; they might say too much. To prevent this from happening they were scattered throughout the world" (*Cómo y por qué salí del ministerio de defensa nacional* [preface to the Mexican edition], 16). With respect to the role of Martínez Pedroso, Viñas disagrees with Prieto. "Martínez Pedroso," he claims, "arrived in Moscow in the summer of 1938, when the repatriation was practically decided" (notes in letter to me, 15 Jan. 1978, Hoover Institution).

57. *El oro de Moscú*, 381, n. 6.

58. Pp. 217, 313. The date of 15 March 1938 is confirmed by the *Bolshaia sovetskaia ent-siklopediia*, the Great Soviet Encyclopedia (vol. 7, 1972, and vol. 13, 1973), but the cause of death is not mentioned. Prieto says: "The high-ranking Soviet officials who participated in the matter [of the Spanish gold] disappeared from the scene: finance minister Grinko; the director of the Grosbank [State Bank] Marguliz [sic]; the subdirector Cagan [sic]; the representative [in the State Bank] of the finance ministry, Ivanovski; the new director of the State Bank, Martinson. All lost their jobs, several went to prison, and Grinko was shot" (*Cómo y por qué*, 16). In two instances Prieto is in error regarding the posts held by the aforementioned officials. According to an official Soviet document (in French) reproduced by Viñas (*El oro de Moscú*, in the section entitled "Documentación Gráfica," 17), J. V. Margoulis was director of the Section of Precious Metals of the People's Commissariat of Finance and O. I. Kagan was director of the Section of Foreign Exchange of the People's Commissariat of Finance.

59. *El oro español*, 229–59. See also Viñas, *El oro de Moscú*, 328, 375, 377, 380, 388.

60. From my notes taken at the meeting (Hoover Institution).

61. *El oro de Moscú*, 366.

62. Ibid., 420.

63. Jan. 1979.

64. Martínez Amutio, 62.

65. Article in *Cuadernos para el Diálogo*, June–July 1970.

66. In *Half of Spain Died*, published in 1973, 171, Herbert Matthews wrote: "Dr. Negrín told me in 1954 that the purchases from the Soviet Union did not use up the full amount of the gold sent and that Moscow therefore owed Spain a sum that had to be calculated, partly because the Russians, without asking permission, had melted down the more valuable English gold sovereign coins into bars, and *partly because Spanish raw materials were shipped to Russia in partial payment of the purchases*" (my italics). See also Abad de Santillán, *Por qué*, 253, for reference to textile and other manufactured goods shipped to Russia.

67. Matthews writes: "A final shipment of arms, worth about $60,000,000, was, with many delays and with reluctance, allowed through France at the very end of the Civil War, but so late that none of it could be used and it was then shipped back to Russia. A credit was due for this" (*The Yoke and the Arrows*, 117). Viñas, however, gives a different version: "New supplies began to arrive in Spain [from Russia] during the early days of 1939. It was already too late: the Nationalist offensive on Catalonia advanced so rapidly that distribution of part of the materiel was hindered; another part was disabled or destroyed; still another was captured by the Franco troops; and the rest remained in France" (*European Studies Review*, Jan. 1979). It is not known whether the shipment of arms, worth about $60 million, was connected with the Soviet credit of the same amount.

68. On the question of the alleged transfer of plant machinery, see Abad de Santillán, *Por qué*, 253, 265, n. 1. and García Oliver, *El eco de los pasos*, 526. I have not been able to locate any additional evidence.

69. The interested reader will find in the illuminating work of Dominique Grisoni and Gilles Hertzog, *Les brigades de la mer*, an abundance of information on the organization, covert ownership, and activities of this shipping company. According to the authors, the company was formed on 15 April 1937 and, within eight months, owned sixteen vessels with a gross weight of 310,000 tons (417). "The USSR," they affirm, "had everything to gain by placing the burden of shipping arms to the Spanish Republicans on a reliable foreign company. The first argument in favor was a practical one: from the fall of 1936, the Soviet Union had been sending arms to Spain and, in most cases, had been using Soviet ships. . . . Inevitably, they were spotted by 'observers' placed in the Bosphorus. Any ship that was assumed to be carrying arms to the Republicans became a target for Italian submarines, which kept a close watch over the narrow passage between Sicily and Tunisia. It is estimated that over a period of one year nearly thirty Soviet vessels were sunk. This was a serious hemorrhage for the Republican combatants, to be sure, but it was also a considerable loss for the Soviet Union. . . . The second argument in favor was linked to the fiction of nonintervention. . . . The ships of France-Navigation, which were less conspicuous than those flying the red flag, would be able to elude the perils of the sea more easily and would draw less attention . . . to the violations by the Soviets" (121). For additional information on attacks on Soviet vessels, see East European Fund, Program on the USSR, *Soviet Shipping in the Spanish Civil War*, Mimeographed Series, No. 59.

70. *Convulsiones*, II, 146–47. See also *Cómo y por qué*, 12–14.

71. Ansó, 328; Alvarez del Vayo, *The Last Optimist*, 284.

72. Prieto later claimed that not until 1954, several years after Largo Caballero's death, when the latter's memoirs, *Mis recuerdos*, were published, did he learn that Largo Caballero was aware of and approved the shipment to Russia (*Convulsiones*, III, 221).

73. *Cómo y por qué*, 15. Nevertheless, Marcelino Pascua claims that Negrín told him that Prieto's presence in Cartagena was the result of a prior agreement between the two men (article in *Cuadernos para el Diálogo*, June–July 1970).

74. *Convulsiones*, II, 125. Prieto does not explain why he signed the permit.

75. U.S. Congress, Senate, *Scope of Soviet Activity*, 3433. My italics. See also article by Orlov in *Reader's Digest*, Nov. 1966.

76. *The Last Optimist*, 284.

77. Ibid., 283. My italics.

78. *Convulsiones*, II, 124–25.

79. Ibid., 131–33.

80. Ansó, 312.

81. Article by N. Kuznetsov in *Pod znamenem*, 241–44. This evidence disposes of Marcelino Pascua's claim that it was decided that the four Soviet vessels should leave Cartagena at night and sail to Odessa unescorted so as not to arouse the suspicion of the enemy (article in *Cuadernos para el Diálogo*, June–July 1970).

82. *The Last Optimist*, 285. Marcelino Pascua claims that Negrín told him repeatedly that Azaña had never objected to the gold shipment to the USSR (article in *Cuadernos para el Diálogo*, June–July 1970).

83. *Convulsiones*, II, 133.

84. Article in *Cuadernos para el Diálogo*, June–July 1970.

85. *Mis recuerdos*, 203–4. This quotation should dispose of Viñas's charge that Largo Caballero accused Negrín of sending the gold to Russia without consulting him (*El Socialista* [Madrid], 12 Aug. 1979).

86. *El oro español*, 187.

87. *El Socialista* (Madrid), 12 Aug. 1979.

88. Grisoni and Hertzog, 59, 120.

89. U.S. Congress, Senate, *Scope of Soviet Activity*, 3431, 3433–34.

90. Article in *Life*, 27 Apr. 1953.

Chapter 15

1. Casado, *The Last Days of Madrid*, 52.

2. Ibid., 54.

3. *El comunismo y la guerra de España*, 24–25.

4. Ibid., 26.

5. Louis Fischer claimed in 1941 that "at no time were there more than 700 Soviet Russians in Spain" (*Men and Politics*, 498). This figure was more or less confirmed in 1973 by a Soviet source, which stated: "In Western literature one finds fantastically exaggerated figures about Soviet participation in the military operations in Spain. In fact, only a little more than 2,000 Soviet volunteers fought and worked in Spain on the side of the Republic *throughout the whole war*, including 772 airmen, 351 tank men, 222 army advisers and instructors, 77 naval specialists, 100 artillery specialists, 52 other specialists, 130 aircraft factory workers and engineers, 156 radio operators and other signals men, and 204 interpreters. What is more, there were never more than *600 to 800 present in Spain at one time*" (Academy of Sciences of the USSR, *International Solidarity with the Spanish Republic, 1936–1939*, 328–29, my italics). However, in 1978, the Soviet Military Encyclopedia gave a figure of "approximately 3,000 Soviet volunteers" (*Sovetskaia voennaia entsiklopediia*, V, 550). For a list of more than 300 Soviet participants, both civilian and military, gleaned from published sources, see José Luis Alcofar Nassaes, *Los asesores soviéticos en la guerra civil española*, 153–62.

6. Ignacio Hidalgo de Cisneros, the Spanish chief of the air force, when interviewed by me in 1940, stated that Soviet pilots were relieved every few months and that altogether one thousand flew in Spain during the war. (Shorthand notes of this interview are in the Hoover Institution.) The German pilots were also relieved frequently to gain experience, according to Hermann Goering, Hitler's air force chief.

7. *Cómo y por qué salí del ministerio de defensa nacional* (prologue to the French edition), 24–25.

8. 4 Oct. 1936.

9. Quoted by Julián Gorkin (POUM leader) in *Workers' Age*, 31 May 1939. See also Gorkin's letter to me, dated 7 July 1946 (Hoover Institution).

10. Excerpts from his statement, which was made on 4 December 1936, were given to me by the delegation itself when I was representing the United Press in Valencia and were approved for transmission to the United Press office in London by the foreign press censorship. They were not published in any of the newspapers I consulted (see Bibliography: "Burnett Bolloten. Dispatch from Valencia to the United Press").

11. See, for example, the *Manchester Guardian*, 25 Nov. 1936. It is not surprising that *Pravda* of the same date displayed this news item prominently. See also Largo Caballero's statement to the Duchess of Atholl and other women members of Parliament as given in *Claridad*, 22 Apr. 1937.

12. *Discurso del presidente del consejo de ministros, Francisco Largo Caballero, el 1º de febrero de 1937*, 9, as given in Carlos M. Rama, *La crisis española del siglo XX*, 260.

13. *Política*, 5 Sept. 1936. My italics.

14. 1 Oct. 1936.

15. The Left Republican party was not the only liberal party that attempted to conceal the changes in the economic, social, and political life of the left camp. See, for example, radio address to world opinion by Diego Martínez Barrio, vice-president of the Republic and leader of the Republican Union party, as reported in *Política*, 2 Aug. 1936.

16. *Política*, 2 Dec. 1936. My italics.

17. Article in *Left News*, Jan. 1943.

18. Salvador de Madariaga, *Españoles de mi tiempo*, 407–14.

19. *Obras completas*, III, 558. In a letter to Robert A. Friedlander, Prieto, who was very close to Azaña, affirmed that from the very first month of the Civil War the president "foresaw Republican defeat" (*Historian*, Nov. 1965). See also Josefina Carabias (a confidant of Azaña's), *Azaña: Los que le llamábamos Don Manuel*, 245–46.

20. *Anecdotario político*, 228–29.

21. *Mis recuerdos*, 187. In his unpublished memoirs, "Las Notas Históricas sobre la Guerra de España," 482, Largo Caballero claims that he and Azaña agreed that the president would establish his residence in Valencia. "On the way there," he adds, "the President of the Republic decided to go to Barcelona without consulting anyone. Why he made that decision is still unknown." On the other hand, Azaña claims that he and the cabinet agreed to move to Barcelona and that he left Madrid expecting to find the ministers in Barcelona the next day. "They delayed their departure," he affirms, "and, without telling me of the change in the agreement, they later established themselves in Valencia.

I remained in Barcelona seven months in the belief that my presence there would be useful" (*Obras*, IV, 817–18). According to minister without portfolio José Giral, an Azañista (when interviewed by me in November 1939), Barcelona was only one of several possible locations. In mid-October, five ministers left Madrid to investigate alternative cities: Alicante, Cartagena, Barcelona, and Valencia. "Caballero wanted to leave for Barcelona," Giral told me. "Originally, it had been decided that the Government should leave for Barcelona on 15 October. That is why Prieto went there to see how the land lay, [but] it is possible that there was opposition on the part of the Catalan Generalitat. For this reason the Government did not go" (transcribed copy of shorthand interview, Hoover Institution). The final decision (to leave for Valencia) was not made until the beginning of November. Meanwhile, Azaña had left Madrid on 19 October and may have believed, as his brother-in-law claims, that Largo Caballero had decided to move to Barcelona (Cipriano Rivas-Cherif, *Retrato de un desconocido: Vida de Manuel Azaña*, 271).

22. Carabias, 243.

23. *Palabras al viento*, 140.

24. The reader should be reminded of Azaña's criticism of the large number of "outstanding and even eminent Republicans" who had left Spain and whom, he claimed, he had raised from nothing by making them "deputies, ministers, ambassadors, undersecretaries, etcetera, etcetera." One prominent member of Azaña's party who had been foreign minister in Giral's government, and who decided to leave Spain was Augusto Barcia (see Ansó, *Yo fui ministro de Negrín*, 158). Referring to the Republican party deputies, Teresa Pàmies wrote in 1975: "[Reading] today the *Diario de las Sesiones [de Cortes]*, we can verify the absences, the defections of deputies elected on 16 February 1936. To the normal absence of the right must be added that of the lukewarm, timid, demoralized and mortified Republicans. When the Republican parliament was obliged to leave Madrid for Valencia, it had ceased to reflect the political forces that had [originally] comprised it" (*Una española llamada Dolores Ibárruri*, 81–82). And Cipriano Rivas-Cherif, Azaña's intimate friend and brother-in-law, testifies: "[Azaña] was extremely grieved by the way the Republicans had abandoned him and the Republic along with him, thus greatly strengthening the argument with which the rebels justified their treachery, namely, that the Government lacked the power to oppose the demagogic and anarchic revolution, which, according to them, had been engendered by the regime against whose legitimacy they had risen in revolt" (Rivas-Cherif, 226–27).

25. *The Tragedy of Manuel Azaña and the Fate of the Spanish Republic*, 174–75. For more information on some of the most prominent intellectuals who left Spain, see Ricardo de la Cierva, *Historia básica de la España actual, 1800–1974*, 428.

26. III, xxxiii.

27. *Freedom's Battle*, 214.

28. *Mis recuerdos*, 187.

29. *Memorias 2: La republica y la guerra de España*, 457.

30. *Así cayó Alfonso XIII*, 167, also 230. For more information on Azaña's fear, see Ernest Udina, *Josep Tarradellas*, 210–11.

31. Rivas-Cherif, 161–62.

32. Ansó, 154–55.

33. Sánchez-Albornez, *Anecdotario político*, 226–27.

34. Ossorio's exact words (according to Rivas-Cherif, 261): "He spoke to me even about resigning. I told him what I had to tell him."

35. Sedwick, 169.

36. The full text of the letter in French—the language of diplomacy—is in Madariaga, *Spain*, 672–74. It was first published in English, however, together with a facsimile of the first and last pages, in an article by Luis Araquistáin that appeared shortly after the war in the *New York Times* of 4 June 1939. The letter is reproduced in Russian, together with a Spanish translation, in the official Spanish Communist history of the Civil War, *Guerra y revolución en España, 1936–1939*, II, 100–102. My italics.

37. *Historia de la UGT de España, 1901–1939*, 629.

38. For a photostatic copy of the reply (in French), see *Guerra y revolución en España, 1936–1939*, II, between pp. 102 and 103.

39. As given in Azaña, *Los españoles en guerra*, 33. Speech on 21 January 1937.

Chapter 16

1. *Documents on British Foreign Policy, 1936–37*, Second Series, XVII, 496.
2. J. V. Stalin, *Sochineniia*, VII, 14.
3. Gustav Hilger and Alfred G. Meyer, *The Incompatible Allies*, 306–7.
4. *Munich: Prologue to Tragedy*, 392.
5. Cited by Iain Macleod (his biographer) in *Neville Chamberlain*, 273. See also Keith Feiling, *Life of Neville Chamberlain*, quoted in Chapter 17.
6. *Documents on German Foreign Policy, 1918–1945*, Series D, II, 608 (memorandum on the conversation sent by Kordt to Ernst von Weizsäcker, state secretary in the German foreign ministry). In his covering letter, Kordt describes Wilson (who had a room in 10 Downing Street while Chamberlain was prime minister) as "Chamberlain's most intimate colleague," and adds, "[He] is generally considered to be one of the most influential men in the British Government. He does not like to appear in the limelight. It is an established fact that Neville Chamberlain asks for his advice on all matters. This man, who is opposed to all outward show, commands respect from all who come into contact with him. He is an embodiment of Moltke's idea: 'To be more than you appear to be' " (ibid., 605). A full-scale biography of this extremely competent and controversial civil servant, who was regarded by his opponents as Chamberlain's eminence grise, has yet to be written. In a brief biographical account of Wilson, the British historian Keith Middlemas provides the following information: "The evidence of official archives suggests that his activities were more subordinate than were alleged in the polemical wartime book, *Guilty Men*. He had been brought into Downing Street in 1935 by [Prime Minister] Baldwin as a 'wise counsellor,' somewhat against his own will. . . . [As] Permanent Under-Secretary to the Ministry of Labour he had taken a heavy part in the General Strike. . . . His reputation as a skilled and subtle negotiator was unrivalled in Whitehall. From 1931 to 1939 the bulk of his work concerned domestic policy or his duties as unofficial counsellor to the Prime Minister. Involvement in foreign policy developed only slowly. . . . In Wilson, Chamberlain inherited a 'fluid person' . . . of great seniority and experience with an exceptionally lucid mind, who . . . owed the Prime Minister primary loyalty. Wilson was the perfect man for unofficial duties. . . . Chamberlain could use him as an emissary to the German Embassy, who would deliver an impressionistic view of British aims, informing the other side without the commitment inherent in diplomatic interchanges; at the same time he would sense the atmosphere of German thinking. . . . Naturally, his activities were resented in the Foreign Office. . . . [Until] the summer of 1938 and the Munich Conference he seems to have been no more than an efficient civil servant carrying out the Prime Minister's instructions to the limit. . . . Perhaps the fairest comment is Lord Woolton's: 'He had more detailed knowledge of what was happening in Government circles than anyone else. He was deeply conscious of the strain under which Prime Ministers work. . . . His insight and his high competence as a civil servant were invaluable, but I believe the greatest help he gave to the Prime Minister was that of his sympathy. . . . With his knowledge and his understanding he enabled the Prime Ministers to have somebody to whom they could talk and upon whom they could rely' " (*Diplomacy of Illusion*, 83–84). Additional information on Wilson can be found in the following works: Anthony Eden (Earl of Avon), *Facing the Dictators*; Andrew Boyle, *Montagu Norman*; Ian Colvin, *The Chamberlain Cabinet* and *Vansittart in Office*; Martin Gilbert and Richard Gott, *The Appeasers*; Charles L. Mowat, *Britain between the Wars, 1918–1940*; Viscount Templewood (Sir Samuel Hoare), *Nine Troubled Years*; Lord Vansittart, *The Mist Procession*.
7. C. A. MacDonald, *The United States, Britain and Appeasement, 1936–1939* (Bullitt to Roosevelt, 20 December 1936). 8.
8. U.S. Department of State, *Foreign Relations of the United States*, II, 575. On 2 September 1938, during the crisis over Czechoslovakia, British ambassador Eric Phipps in Paris informed Foreign Minister Lord Halifax that Bullitt felt that "Russia's great wish is to provoke a general conflagration in which she herself will play but little part, beyond perhaps a little bombing from a distance, but after which she will arise like a phoenix, but out of all our ashes, and bring about a world revolution" (*Documents on British Foreign Policy, 1919–1939*, Third Series, II, 219).
9. *Documents on British Foreign Policy, 1919–1939*, Second Series, XVIII, 975.
10. Cabinet Minutes, 23/29, p. 27.
11. Ibid., 29.

12. Public Record Office, Richmond, C1935/95/62 FO371//21626. I am indebted to Middlemas's *Diplomacy of Illusion* for this reference, which I have personally consulted.

13. *Documents on British Foreign Policy, 1919–1939*, Third Series, I, 341.

14. *The Critical Years*, 56, 86.

15. *Documents on German Foreign Policy, 1918–1945*, Series D, II, 25. In a report to Foreign Secretary Lord Halifax, dated 2 September, Sir Eric Phipps, British ambassador in Paris, stated that, according to Bonnet, "Russia's one wish is to stir up general war in the troubled waters of which she will fish. He here confirms the opinion expressed to me by Mr. Bullitt" (*Documents on British Foreign Policy, 1919–1945*, Third Series, II, 220).

16. *Documents on German Foreign Policy, 1918–1945*, Series D, II, 267.

17. Ibid., 327.

18. Ibid., 713. "I hope with all my heart," the French ambassador to Moscow told his German counterpart, "that it will not come to a German-French conflict. You know, as well as I do, for whom we are working if we come to blows" (ibid., 631).

19. General Maurice Gamelin, *Servir*, II, 343.

20. Wheeler-Bennett, 389–90. "If there is any fighting to be done, I should like to see the Bolsheviks and the Nazis doing it," Prime Minister Baldwin told Churchill in July 1936 (quoted by Middlemas, 54).

21. *Diaries and Letters, 1930–1939*, 250. About the same time Prime Minister Baldwin stated privately, according to his biographer, that "a Germany crushed by France and Russia would be a Communist Germany" (G. M. Young, *Stanley Baldwin*, 223). Should there be any doubt in the reader's mind as to the ability of Britain and France to drive Hitler back across the Rhine, the following quotations from authoritative sources should be helpful. General Gamelin, who at the time was chief of the French general staff, wrote in his memoirs: "In 1936, if we had shown ourselves determined to fight, [the Germans] would have retreated. And their entire program might have been jeopardized, even the prestige of the 'Führer' " (*Servir*, II, 193). Winston Churchill writes: "MM. Sarraut [French premier] and Flandin [foreign minister] had the impulse to act at once by general mobilisation. . . . But they appeared unable to move without concurrence of Britain. This is an explanation, but no excuse. The issue was vital to France and any French Government worthy of the name should have made up its own mind and trusted to the Treaty obligations. . . . Be this as it may, they did not meet with any encouragement to resist the German aggression from the British. [This is confirmed by the Earl of Avon (Anthony Eden, foreign secretary at the time), who writes: "Though personally friendly to France, (Prime Minister Baldwin) was clear in mind that there would be no support in Britain for any military action by the French. I could only agree" (*Facing the Dictators*, 385).] On the contrary, if they hesitated to act, their British allies did not hesitate to dissuade them. . . . If the French Government had mobilised the French Army . . . there is no doubt that Hitler would have been compelled by his own General Staff to withdraw, and a check would have been given to his pretensions which might well have proved fatal to his rule. . . . In fact she remained completely inert and paralysed, and thus lost irretrievably the last chance of arresting Hitler's ambitions without a serious war. Instead, the French Government were urged by Britain to cast their burden upon the League of Nations" (*The Gathering Storm*, 193–95). "[One] cannot help thinking," writes the former military attaché to the German embassy in London, General Baron Geyr von Schweppenburg, "that it was indeed a misfortune for the German people that the Western Powers put up no energetic military counter-action at a moment when everything favoured it" (*The Critical Years*, 68). And, finally, we have the testimony of Sir Samuel Hoare (Viscount Templewood), a member of Neville Chamberlain's "Inner Cabinet," and one of the principal advocates of appeasement: "I am now certain that if we and our ally had intervened, we could certainly have driven Hitler back, and inflicted a crushing blow on his growing prestige" (*Nine Troubled Years*, 201). It was, however, the social consequences in Germany and the rest of Europe that might follow the "crushing blow" to Hitler's position that held Britain and France back from opposing the remilitarization of the Rhineland. At all events, France's failure to act proved devastating to her position in Europe. Charles A. Micaud is undoubtedly correct when he concludes that March 1936 was the turning point in her foreign policy and that she changed from "the foremost power in Europe to a mere satellite of England" (*The French Right and Nazi Germany, 1933–1939*, 97).

22. *Diaries*, 273.

23. Ibid., 313.

24. Ibid., 346.

25. Ibid., 359.

26. John Harvey, *The Diplomatic Diaries of Oliver Harvey, 1937–1940*, 222.

27. *Geoffrey Dawson and Our Times*, 362.

28. J. R. M. Butler, *Lord Lothian*, 331.

29. *Appeasement*, 32.

30. *Retrospect*, 202–3.

31. *The Roots of Appeasement*, p. 162.

32. *Documents and Materials Relating to the Eve of the Second World War*, I, 14–45. This record of the conversation is a Soviet translation into English of the German document. The words in italics do not appear in the British translation of the document in *Documents on German Foreign Policy, 1918–1945*, Series D, I, 55–67. Otherwise, the two texts are substantially the same. Halifax's own account of that part of the conversation dealing with Communism is given as follows: "I was not blind [he told Hitler] to what he had done for Germany and to the achievements from his point of view of keeping Communism out of his country, and, as he would feel, of blocking its passage West" (*Documents on British Foreign Policy, 1919–1939*, Second Series, XIX, 543).

33. *A Diary with Letters, 1931–1950*, 202, 209. This is an extremely valuable work for those interested in the political influence Jones attempted to exert upon Baldwin. A. L. Rowse, an acquaintance of Jones, writes: "[He] was a great busybody and contacts-man. . . . If I had known the dirty work he was doing for Ribbentrop [German ambassador to London, later foreign minister], I should have been less affable to T. J. . . . I knew he was on that side, but I never knew to what a degree he lent himself to Ribbentrop's purposes until his *Diary with Letters* came out" (Rowse, *All Souls*, 35).

34. Young, Baldwin's biographer, writes: "In Cabinet, he would ostentatiously close his eyes when foreign affairs were under discussion. 'Wake me up,' he would say, 'when you are finished with that' " (*Stanley Baldwin*, 63).

35. According to Thomas Jones, 231.

36. Hoare to Foreign Office, covering minute by Lord Chatfield, the first sea lord, Public Records Office, W7781/62/41 FO371/20527. I am grateful to Lawrence R. Pratt's *East of Malta, West of Suez* for this and other references, which I have personally consulted.

37. Hankey ("secret" memorandum), Public Records Office, W11340/79/98 FO371/20475. See n. 41 for Lawrence R. Pratt.

38. Pratt's footnote to this statement reads in part as follows: "Vansittart [permanent undersecretary of state for foreign affairs] to Chatfield, 16 February 1937. Chatfield Papers. The British Consul in Barcelona, Norman King, had denounced 'Red Spain' and impressed Backhouse with the need to crush the revolution" (*East of Malta*, 43).

39. 29 Nov. 1936.

40. Pertinax (André Géraud) in prologue to E. N. Dzelepy, *The Spanish Plot*, vii. See also Maurice Pujo in *L'Action Française*, 25 July 1936; Vicent Auriol, quoted by Indalecio Prieto in *España Republicana*, 17 July 1948; Claude Bowers, *My Mission to Spain*, 281; Fenner Brockway, *Workers' Front*, 159–60; Pierre Lazareff, *Deadline*, 134; Hugh Thomas, *The Spanish Civil War* (1965 ed.), 331; Alexander Werth, *Which Way France?*, 397.

41. See Joel Colton, *Léon Blum*, 235 and n. 6, 241–42. Blum told Hugh Dalton, chairman of the National executive of the British Labor party, that the policy of nonintervention in Spain was *his* policy. "It was he and not Eden [British foreign secretary], as some alleged, who had first proposed it" (Hugh Dalton, *The Fateful Years*, 95).

42. Colton, 236 and n. 9, 239. See also Pierre Cot (air minister), *Le Nouvel Observateur*, 3 Aug. 1966; Jules Moch, *Rencontres avec . . . Léon Blum*, 191, and secret communication of Robert Coulondre, adjutant director of political affairs, to Yvon Delbos, dated 23 July 1936, *Documents diplomatiques français, 1932–1939*, III, 37.

43. Colton's source for this quotation is Blum's speech to the Socialist conference, 1946, *Le Populaire*, 19 July 1950.

44. Colton's footnote regarding this conversation reads as follows: "Blum, private remarks at a dinner, March 27, 1939, at which Blumel [André Blumel, chef de cabinet] was present: typed memorandum, Blumel files." For a slightly different version, see Blumel memorandum, Georges

Lefranc, *Histoire du Front Populaire*, 462. Jules Moch, secretary general in the government of Léon Blum, attributes the following statement to Neville Chamberlain, at that time chancellor of the Exchequer in the British government: "We British hate fascism. But we also hate Bolshevism. Therefore, if there is a country where the two kill off each other, it is a great good for humanity" (as given in John E. Dreifort, *Yvon Delbos at the Quai d'Orsay*, 46).

45. In his memoirs *Facing the Dictators* (450–51), the Earl of Avon (former foreign secretary Anthony Eden) wrote: "Although Blum was under pressure to support the Government in Madrid, he announced on July 26th that France was in no way able to intervene. He and Delbos knew only too well that any other course of action would sharply divide France, while open intervention by the great powers could lead to a European war. We agreed with this French decision of policy." There was also another reason why Britain was opposed to intervening on behalf of the Republican forces. On 20 August 1936, Sir Alexander Cadogan, deputy undersecretary of state in the Foreign Office (1936–37) under Anthony Eden, and later permanent undersecretary (1938–46), wrote the following minute, quoted earlier in this volume: "In more normal circumstances—i.e., if the 'existing Government' exercised real control and had any chance of surviving—I should say that, failing international agreement, we should most scrupulously observe our regular and normal policy of allowing or licensing shipments to the established Government and not to the rebels. In the present state of Spain, or in the situation that is likely rapidly to develop, the ordinary rule cannot be blindly followed. What is the existing Government? How far do those in power in Barcelona recognise the Madrid Authorities? How far, in effect, have the latter control of Madrid itself? . . . Apart from the international aspect of the matter and our desire to avoid 'alignments,' it may well be that in the near future it will become clearer, even to our Labour people, that the 'existing Government' is becoming less and less deserving of their sympathy" (Public Record Office, Foreign Office 371/20573).

46. *Léon Blum*, 241–42. See also Dreifort, 31–54, and M. D. Gallagher, "Léon Blum and the Spanish Civil War," *The Journal of Contemporary History* 6, no. 3 (1971). It is noteworthy that David Carlton, the British historian, denies that there was any British pressure, basing his arguments on the absence of evidence in the official archives of the British government and in the French foreign ministry documents he consulted ("Eden, Blum, and the Origins of Non-Intervention," ibid.). On the other hand, Glyn A. Stone, lecturer in international history at Bristol Polytechnic, England, argues that although "at first sight, Carlton's refutation would appear to be soundly based . . . further investigation of the published and unpublished sources . . . demonstrates that it is by no means conclusive" ("Britain, Non-Intervention and the Spanish Civil War," *European Studies Review* 9, no. 1 [January 1979]). The British military tactician and historian, Liddell Hart, who was the military correspondent of the conservative London *Times* during the Civil War, but a friend of the Spanish Republic, asserts that on 8 August 1936 the British government delivered "a virtual ultimatum that if France did not promptly ban the export of war material to Spain, and a war with Germany ensued, Britain would consider herself absolved from her obligations, under the Locarno Treaty, to aid France" (*Memoirs*, II, 128). However, he does not cite any source in support of this assertion, which appears quite plainly to have been copied almost verbatim from the first edition of Hugh Thomas's history of the Civil War (1961), 258. For his part Thomas cites only the testimony of the crypto-Communist Alvarez del Vayo and the pro-Communist Pablo de Azcárate, which leaves the reliability of the charge in doubt, since no sound evidence has yet been produced that such crude pressure was used. For a rebuttal to Thomas's assertion, see David Carlton, *The Journal of Contemporary History* 6, no. 3 (1971).

47. According to Louis Lévy, an intimate of Léon Blum, *Vérités sur la France*, 114.

48. See his testimony before the Parliamentary Commission of Inquiry set up in 1947 to investigate the events that took place in France between 1933 and 1945, as given in *Les événements survenus en France de 1933 à 1945*, I, 216–27. At the Radical party congress held in October 1936 a resolution was approved commending the government for having "averted a grave international peril" by proposing the Non-Intervention Agreement (see *L'Ere Nouvelle*, 24 Oct. 1936).

Researchers seeking a comprehensive picture of the attitudes of the different political parties and factions in France during the Spanish Civil War, as seen through the French press, will find David Wingeate Pike's meticulous *Les français et la guerre d'Espagne, 1936–1939* invaluable. Pike's vast array of quoted material, based on the study of thousands of newspaper and magazine issues, will spare students and historians an endless amount of drudgery. See also his earlier studies *Conjecture*,

Propaganda, and Deceit and the Spanish Civil War and *La crise espagnole de 1936 vue par la presse française*. Another valuable work of more recent publication that focuses mainly on the attitude of French business and financial publications toward the Spanish Civil War is that of José María Borrás Llop, *Francia ante la guerra civil española: Burguesía, interés nacional e interés de clase*.

49. *Léon Blum*, 317.

50. "The foreign policy of the Popular Front was weakened by the fact that the Franco-Soviet Pact, which should have been its solid basis, was really accepted only by the Communist deputies, by a small part of the Socialist party, and by barely half the Radicals. Were not the arguments of Léon Blum himself, in his articles in the *Populaire*, perhaps the most difficult to dismiss by those who wished to see the pact ratified? His policy was one of weakness. His personal views on collective security— 'Fundamentally, can we logically be expected to run the risk of a war now in order to avoid another later on?'—were floating around more than ever" (Geneviève Tabouis, *Ils l'ont appelée Cassandre*, 297).

51. 6 July 1936. According to Franklin Reid Gannon (*The British Press and Germany, 1936–1939*), "*The Times* was incomparably the most important British newspaper of the 1930's." Although it gained the reputation of being an "official spokesman for the British Government," it was "an independent conservative newspaper which had independently and characteristically arrived at a policy towards Nazi Germany which happened to coincide with that pursued by the Baldwin and particularly the Chamberlain Governments" (56, 70, 73–74). Its reputation of being the mouthpiece, official or unofficial, of the British government derived to a large degree from the close rapport between its editor, Geoffrey Dawson, for a long time a champion of appeasement, and leading Tory politicians. According to Gannon, one of the main criticisms leveled against Dawson was that he was a "sinister figure, the villain of the appeasement piece. His position at the head of the crustiest and most infuriating organs of the Establishment was enough to make him such for radical newspapers, leftist dons and Communist propagandists" (ibid., 64). According to the British historian A. J. P. Taylor, "Dawson was superbly confident in his own righteousness. . . . He was . . . ruthless for reconciliation with Germany. He turned *The Times* into a propaganda sheet and did not hesitate to suppress, or to pervert, the reports of his own correspondents" (*English History, 1914–1945*, 418). See also Rowse, *Appeasement*, 5–13. Dawson's biographer writes: "Geoffrey was certainly influenced . . . by the thought that Nazi Germany served as a barrier to the spread of Communism in the West" (John Evelyn Wrench, *Geoffrey Dawson and Our Times*, 376). In a letter written in May 1937, Dawson stated: "I do my utmost, night after night, to keep out of the paper anything that might hurt [German] susceptibilities. I can really think of nothing that has been printed now for many months past to which they could possibly take exception as unfair comment" (ibid., 361).

52. 20 Dec. 1936. According to Gannon (*British Press*, 55), the *Sunday Times* was one of the two quality Sunday newspapers—the other being the *Observer*—whose major spokesman on foreign affairs from 1929 to 1940 was "Scrutator" (Herbert Sidebotham). In the words of R. C. K. Ensor, who was Sidebotham's successor, no articles then written were "more widely and attentively read by influential people" (ibid.).

53. 1 Nov. 1936. Of Garvin and the *Observer*, Gannon writes: "As one of the two quality Sunday papers, the Observer's influence was undoubtedly great. . . . [Garvin's] contempt for the Treaty of Versailles was boundless: the whole kind of system of international affairs it represented—based upon British involvement with France in Europe—seemed to him repugnant and dangerous to British interests. Although Garvin by no means condoned the racial policies of the Nazis, he clearly felt that agreement between Germany and Britain was possible and desirable" (*British Press*, 51). For a brief abstract of some of Garvin's principal articles revealing his fear of Communism and sympathy for Nazi Germany, see Margaret George, *The Warped Vision*, 146–50.

54. Ian Colvin, *The Chamberlain Cabinet*, 109. Colvin's source for this information is given as Cab. 27.623 [British cabinet documents], 164.

55. As given in Middlemas, *Diplomacy of Illusion*, 18. The source is CID (Committee of Imperial Defense) 1385-B Chiefs of Staff Sub-committee, Strategic Review 1937.

56. Middlemas, 18–19. The source for the quotation is Cab. 50-37 (British cabinet papers), "Note on the situation of Germany vis-à-vis the other European Powers" 13 March 1938.

57. Colvin, *The Chamberlin Cabinet*, 110.

58. *A Diary with Letters*, 181.

59. *Survey of International Affairs*, 1936, 280–81.

60. Basil Henry Liddell Hart, *The Memoirs of Captain Liddell Hart*, I, 221.

61. *Munich: Prologue to Tragedy*, 295–96. In contrast, it is worth quoting from the British historian Professor Robert Skidelsky, an adherent of one of the revisionist schools that have grown up in the postwar era and have done more to obfuscate than illumine this crucial period of world history. Writing in *Encounter*, in July 1972, he stated: "Had the British really been determined to give Germany a 'free hand' in the East, as many politicians and Foreign Office officials discussed in private, then Britain could have brought strong pressure on the French to break their guarantees—and also the Franco-Soviet Pact—in exchange for a much firmer British military guarantee of the defense of France itself. The reason this alternative was never seriously pursued was that Britain had no intention of washing its hands of Central and Eastern Europe. . . . Of course, there were a number of groups in Britain . . . who advocated the bargain that Hitler must always have hoped for—'a German deal with the British Empire at the expense of the Soviet Union.' But such cynicism (or realism) was foreign to the British Establishment." Skidelsky would have done well to remember that the British government under Neville Chamberlain did indeed wash its hands of Central and Eastern Europe, when it decided that the independence of Czechoslovakia was not worth defending and when, a few months later, it secretly proposed to Germany a political settlement that would have freed Britain from its guarantee to go to Poland's assistance, a proposal, as we shall see that came to grief only because Hitler, fortified by his pact with Stalin, was bent on an immediate military settlement of the Polish question. Skidelsky also failed to remember that the British did exert pressure on the French to disentangle themselves from their alliance with Czechoslovakia. Oliver Harvey, private secretary to Lord Halifax, Chamberlain's foreign minister, made the following entry in his diary on 19 September 1938, a few days before the Anglo-French surrender to Hitler's demands at Munich: "I must record my view that Phipps [British ambassador] in Paris had done his utmost to discourage the French from anything resembling positive action in fulfillment of their treaty with Czechoslovakia. . . . He has given the definite impression that [His Majesty's Government] wish to hold France back (which of course is true). Again over Spain he has consistently supported the Franco side and done his utmost to stop the French Government from helping Barcelona [the seat of the Republican government in 1938]. Whilst it is true that the French Government now are just as anxious as H.M.G. to avoid war at any price, it is also true that the French . . . caught their defeatist note from us" (John Harvey, *The Diplomatic Diaries of Oliver Harvey, 1937–1940*, 188). Four months earlier, Sir Alexander Cadogan, permanent undersecretary of state in the Foreign Office, made the following entry in his private diary: "H. [Halifax, foreign secretary under Neville Chamberlain] wants to sever French-Czech and Czech-Soviet connections. He's quite right" (*The Diaries of Sir Alexander Cadogan*, 80).

Chapter 17

1. Letter dated 6 Feb. 1937, quoted in *Mission to Moscow*, 57–60. See also letter dated 19 Feb. 1937, ibid., 77–79.

2. In a frank account published after the Civil War of Italian assistance to General Franco, *Le Forze Armate*, the official organ of the Italian war office, revealed (8 June 1939) that between mid-December 1936 and mid-April 1937 the navy had transported 100,000 men to Spain in addition to 4,370 motor vehicles, 40,000 tons of war material, and 750 heavy guns. The journal also revealed that units of the Italian fleet had been employed in the early stages of the war not only in escorting Italian transports from Italian to Spanish ports but in naval operations against the Republican fleet and coast as well as against ships bringing cargoes to Republican ports, many of which had been sunk. For an equally frank account of German intervention in the early part of the war, see the special number of *Die Wehrmacht* entitled *Wir kämpften in Spanien*, issued in May 1939 by the German High Command. For further information on attacks on merchant ships, see East European Fund, Program on the USSR, *Soviet Shipping in the Spanish Civil War*, Mimeographed Series, No. 59.

3. See reference in the *Daily Herald*, 13 Jan. 1937, to the labor party's appeal to the labor movement to "establish unity within its own ranks and not by association with organizations in conflict with the aims of the party." See also article by Harry Pollitt, secretary of the British Communist party, *Left Review*, Dec. 1936.

4. According to Miguel Serra Pàmies, a member of the central committee, whom I interviewed in Mexico in 1944.

5. *El Día Gráfico*, 31 Jan. 1937.

6. *Treball*, 2 Feb. 1937.

7. Among the documents of Luis Araquistáin, the Spanish ambassador in Paris, acquired by the Archivo Histórico Nacional in Madrid, there are two letters from Alvarez del Vayo, dated 31 January and 7 February 1937 (Araquistáin Papers, Leg. 76/146, Leg. 23/A112[a]) that touch on the Moroccan proposal. In the first letter Vayo also states that if England were interested in naval bases in the Balearic Islands, "we shall construct them in common accord." However, as will be seen later, the official memorandum sent to London and Paris makes no mention of naval bases and refers only to the transfer of Spanish Morocco. In the same letter, Vayo stresses the advantages of offering Spanish Morocco to Britain and France over a plan favored by Araquistáin to "neutralize" Germany by means of a loan financed "in large part by Spanish money," a plan that, in Vayo's opinion, "would be the same as throwing money into the sea." Araquistáin's plan is outlined by him in a report dated 12 January 1937 (Araquistáin Papers, Leg. 76/119) and further discussed by him in a letter to Largo Caballero, dated 9 March 1937 (ibid., Leg. 76/118).

8. For this information I am grateful to Miguel Serra Pàmies.

9. *Yo fui un ministro de Stalin*, 75.

10. *Mi embajada en Londres durante la guerra civil española*, 73. For the full text of the memorandum, see ibid., 266–68. That both Vayo and Azcárate were involved in the drafting of the memorandum is clear from a letter written by Vayo to Luis Araquistáin on 31 January 1937 (Araquistáin Papers, Leg. 76/146).

11. See, for example, *Daily Telegraph* and *Le Temps*, 11 Jan. 1937.

12. *Yo fui un ministro de Stalin*, 75–76.

13. *Convulsiones de España*, II, 92.

14. *Mi embajada en Londres*, 75, n. 4.

15. Araquistáin Papers, Leg. 23/A112[a].

16. See the *Times*, 12 Apr. 1937.

17. *El Adelanto*, 17 Mar. 1937.

18. Araquistáin Papers, Leg. 76/152.

19. Ibid., Leg. 23/A122[a].

20. *El Adelanto*, 17 Mar. 1937.

21. *Freedom's Battle*, 235.

22. For the British and French replies, see the *Times*, 22 Apr. 1937, and Azcárate, *Mi embajada en Londres*, 74–75. "Contrary to the calculations of the Kremlin's 'strategists,' " writes Jesús Hernández, former politburo member, "neither France nor England nibbled at the bait" (*Yo fui un ministro de Stalin*, 76).

23. "When after Munich, it became clear that the British government had decided to follow very closely the policy of friendship with Rome which had already been initiated with the Anglo-Italian Agreement of the previous April," Alvarez del Vayo writes (*Freedom's Battle*, 255), "the Spanish government—in spite of its tremendous opposition to Italian intervention in Spain—did not hesitate to inform the British government categorically that if the latter would put an end to this intervention the victory and consolidation of the Republic in Spain would afford no obstacle whatever to a policy of collaboration with Italy in the Mediterranean. They even went as far as to declare that they would themselves be willing to collaborate with Italy on the basis of natural respect for the integrity and political independence of either state. This declaration, which I communicated personally to M. Fouques Duparc, the French chargé d'affaires in Barcelona, was also ignored by the British government."

24. Ibid., 238–39.

25. Quoted in Hernández, *Yo fui un ministro de Stalin*, 159.

26. *Frente Rojo*, 30 Mar. 1938, as reprinted in José Díaz, *Tres años de lucha*, 559.

27. Address in May 1939 before the Council of Foreign Relations in New York, quoted in Alvarez del Vayo, *Freedom's Battle*, 76.

28. *Halifax*, 362. In 1935, when he was chancellor of the Exchequer in Baldwin's cabinet, Chamberlain made the following notation in his diary: "I am more and more carrying this government on my back. The P.M. is ill and tired . . . and won't apply his mind to problems. It is certainly time there was a change" (Keith Feiling, *Life of Neville Chamberlain*, 242).

29. *Halifax*, 362, 375. In a family letter written in Nov. 1937, Chamberlain stated: "I don't see why

we shouldn't say to Germany—'Give us satisfactory assurances that you won't use force to deal with the Austrians and Czechoslovakians and we will give you similar assurances that we won't use force to prevent the changes you want, if you can get them by peaceful means" (quoted by Ian Colvin, *Vansittart in Office*, 156).

30. See memorandum written by Herbert von Dirksen, German ambassador to London, quoted in Chapter 61.

31. Colvin, *Vansittart in Office*, 12.

32. The British historian Charles Loch Mowat writes: "Chamberlain relied on him heavily, gave him an office adjoining his own, and for three years went for a walk with him daily in the park" (*Britain between the Wars, 1918–1940*, 598 and n. 4).

33. Ian Colvin, *The Chamberlain Cabinet*, 9. In a chapter on British cabinet records, Charles Loch Mowat points out in *Great Britain since 1914*, 76, that one of the difficulties for historians "arises from the loss of documents" including the "declaration of friendship signed by Hitler and Neville Chamberlain on the night of the Munich treaty." "It does not follow," he adds, "that papers transferred to the Public Record Office and falling within the thirty-year rule, are necessarily open for research; *any 'sensitive' subject is likely to be closed for fifty, seventy-five or even 100 years*." My italics.

34. *The Origins of the Second World War*, 244.

35. *English History, 1914–1945*, 627.

36. *The War Path: Hitler's Germany, 1933–1939*, 156, 191. See also ibid., 56, for the disappearance of the captured transcripts of Ribbentrop's interviews with prominent Englishmen. This controversial work, the product of extraordinary research, is based on fifteen hundred pages of source-notes (xiii) and uses sources untapped by previous historians (see foreword, ix–xviii). The fact that all documents relating to the Duke of Windsor (ex-king Edward VIII), whose pro-German sentiments are well documented (see, for example, *Edward VIII* by Frances Donaldson) have been excluded from public scrutiny, further tends to hinder research into the appeasement era as does the decision by the supreme allied commander, General Dwight D. Eisenhower, to cooperate with the British in 1945 in ordering his chief of intelligence, Major General Edwin L. Sibert, to hand over to him all documents found in archives captured by the United States army that related to the Duke of Windsor. According to his own testimony, Sibert subsequently passed along a small collection found in German foreign minister von Ribbentrop's home and the documents were "either destroyed or their whereabouts concealed" (Anthony Cave Brown and Charles B. MacDonald, *On a Field of Red: The Communist International and the Coming of World War II*, 554). According to Irving, "Ribbentrop found in the Duke 'something akin to a British National Socialist.' Unfortunately, the record of their meeting has vanished from the captured files" (*War Path*, 59). It is significant that during the discussions between the British and U.S. representatives toward the end of World War II as to what was to be done with the Nazi leaders when captured, Sir John Simon, lord chancellor in Churchill's wartime cabinet and formerly a member of Chamberlain's Inner Cabinet, argued strenuously in favor of summary execution and against a full-scale trial, which he felt would produce endless debate and open up a Pandora's box of legal and political problems "with a reaction we can hardly calculate" (Bradley F. Smith, *The Road to Nuremberg*, 179). For other references to the British position, see 45–46, 64, 171–75, 178–79, 185–88, 192–93, 219. At one point during the Anglo-American discussions, Smith records, Sir John Simon presented a paper that concluded with a paragraph that it would be "valuable" if, at the moment of capture, Hitler was presented with a paper chronicling his evil deeds, as long as it was understood that there would be no hearing or trial on the basis of this paper" (ibid., 197). The conclusion one must draw from Smith's remarkable book is that had it not been for the persistence of Secretary of War Henry L. Stimson and Assistant Secretary John J. McCloy, there may never have been any Nuremberg trials at all. The British position against a trial and in favor of summary execution is confirmed by Henry L. Stimson and McGeorge Bundy in *On Active Service in Peace and War*, 587: "To Stimson's great surprise the principal opposition to legal proceedings came from the British, who for a long time urged direct military executions instead. But with firm French and Russian support, the American view prevailed and in August 1945, there was signed at London a four-power agreement chartering the International Tribunal which met at Nuremberg the following November." Even so, the trials did nothing to clarify British prewar foreign policy any more than they did to illuminate Soviet foreign policy maneuvers against the West. "History since 1945," writes David Irving, "has been plagued by the effects of the Nuremberg Trials—by the prosecution teams' methods

of selection of exhibits, by the subsequent publication of the selected documents in neatly printed and indexed volumes, and by the incineration in a Bavarian forest pit of documents that, it was felt, would hinder the Allied prosecution effort. Exhibits were chosen less for their representative nature than because they displayed Axis criminality" (*War Path*, xi). A similar view is held by British historian A. J. P. Taylor: "The documents were chosen not only to demonstrate the war-guilt of the men on trial, but to conceal that of the prosecuting Powers. If any of the four Powers who set up the Nuremberg tribunal had been running the affair alone, it would have thrown the mud more widely. The Western Powers would have brought in the Nazi-Soviet Pact; the Soviet Union would have retaliated with the Munich conference and more obscure transactions" (*The Origins of the Second World War*, 13). For an idea of just how incomplete are the available documentary records of the period and of the burden this deficiency places on the historian, see essay by T. Desmond Williams in Esmonde M. Robertson, *The Origins of the Second World War*, 37–64.

37. *Diplomacy of Illusion*, 54.

38. *Observer*, 16 Sept. 1962 ("The Foreign Secretary Speaks Up").

39. *Life of Neville Chamberlain*, 325.

40. Ibid., 347.

41. Ibid., 403. See also Sir Samuel Hoare (Viscount Templewood), a member of Chamberlain's inner group, *Nine Troubled Years*, 342–43.

42. *Appeasement*, 83, 63. The U.S. historian William R. Rock, while failing to reveal the principal motive force of appeasement, presents a more objective picture of Neville Chamberlain: "Born to a prominent political family [his father was Joseph Chamberlain], he had entered business in Birmingham, attaining considerable stature among Midland industrialists and serving in various public capacities, including that of lord mayor, before his election to parliament in 1918. First entering the cabinet as postmaster general (1922), he later achieved an outstanding record as minister of health (1924–29) and served capably as chancellor of the exchequer (1931–37) during a time of severe economic stress. What he lacked in imagination and personal appeal he made up in efficiency, administrative skill, dedication and a willingness to assume assignments shunned by other men. His interests and strength lay largely in domestic politics (social, economic, health, and welfare problems); it is the irony of history that, as prime minister, he was preoccupied almost exclusively with foreign policy. He was certainly not ignorant of foreign affairs, as some have held, but he had no real 'touch' for a diplomatic situation, did not always grasp the full implications of foreign policy problems, and relied too heavily on his own judgment" (*British Appeasement in the 1930s*, 55–56).

43. *Halifax*, 363. Even Duff Cooper (later Viscount Norwich), who resigned from the Chamberlain cabinet on account of his opposition to the Munich agreement that resulted in the dismemberment of Czechoslovakia, throws no light on Chamberlain's strategy and reduces the whole question of appeasement to absurdity: "Chamberlain had many good qualities but he lacked experience of the world, and he lacked also the imagination which can fill the gaps of inexperience. He had never moved in the great world of politics or of finance [yet he had been chancellor of the Exchequer for six years before becoming prime minister!], and the continent of Europe was for him a closed book. He had been a successful Lord Mayor of Birmingham, and for him the Dictators of Germany and of Italy were like the Lord Mayors of Liverpool and Manchester, who might belong to different political parties and have different interests, but who must desire the welfare of humanity, and be fundamentally reasonable, decent men like himself. This profound misconception *lay at the root of his policy and explains his mistakes* [my italics]" (*Old Men Forget*, 200). The British historian Keith Middlemas, who has written what is perhaps the best study of the workings of the Chamberlain government, but fails to come to grips with the real essence of appeasement, does not subscribe to this deceptive portrayal of the prime minister as an artless politician: "His approach to foreign affairs was by no means the myopic view from the Birmingham town hall with which Lloyd George, among many detractors, liked to amuse himself." And in a later passage, he stated: "It would be wrong to depict Chamberlain as a helpless innocent, shuffling sheeplike among the crooked leaders of the Third Reich. He was used to rough bargaining and in the past, in British domestic politics, he had shown himself as tough and ruthless as any leader of the twentieth-century Conservative Party. It was unfortunate that his only previous experience of foreign negotiation should have been in the relatively mild climate of Lausanne in 1932, where concession appeared to be wisdom" (*Diplomacy of Illusion*, 47, 339).

44. Preface to *Documents on British Foreign Policy, 1919–1939*, Second Series, XVIII, ix. My italics.

45. Valediction, *Hansard*, 12 Nov. 1940, reproduced in Robert Rhodes James, *Winston S. Churchill: His Complete Speeches, 1897–1963*, VI, 6307. Perhaps the most objective description of Chamberlain comes from the pen of the French historian François Bédarida: "Although seventy-one years old [in 1940], he carries the weight of his manifold tasks and responsibilities breezily, coping with documents, meetings and parliamentary debates, and backed by an unflagging faith in his mission. Not without vanity, he usually displays confidence in himself, even arrogance, and this self-assurance is apparent not only in his relations with the French, but also in the way he judges his compatriots. . . . He is secretive, high-handed and efficient. All this explains his ascendancy over his cabinet. . . . In additon, he is able to rely on his long experience in politics as well as on his remarkable capabilities: clarity of exposition, lucidity of reasoning and strength of logic. These qualities leap to the eye from the Minutes of the Supreme Council [the Conseil Suprème Interalliée which met between 12 September 1939 and 27 April 1940]. There we see a debater without equal, a perceptive, shrewd, and sometimes crafty interrogator" (*La stratégie secrète de la drôle de guerre*, 66–67).

46. Middlemas, 60–61, 65.

47. As given in *Acción Socialista*, 15 Jan. 1952. For Hernández's expulsion from the party in 1944, see his book, *En el país de la gran mentira*, 215–27.

48. *Solidaridad Obrera* (Paris), 11 Mar. 1951. The Communists and their supporters claim that El Campesino's articles and books were ghost-written by Julián Gorkin, one of the leaders during the Civil War of the anti-Stalinist Partido Obrero de Unificación Marxista (POUM). This is true. El Campesino was to all intents and purposes an illiterate and incapable of giving literary expression to his thoughts and experiences. After the close of the Civil War, El Campesino took refuge in Russia, whence he escaped ten years later completely disillusioned. See his book *La vie et la mort en U.R.S.S., 1939–1949*, which was written by Gorkin on the basis of El Campesino's oral testimony after the latter's escape from Russia (see Gorkin's letter to me of 18 Oct. 1984, Hoover Institution). It is important to record that during the Civil War El Campesino's brutality in carrying out Communist policy was proverbial (see, for example, J. García Pradas in *Cultura Proletaria*, 5 May 1946).

Chapter 18

1. See Chapter 4.

2. See, for example, *Tierra y Libertad*, the FAI organ, 29 Oct. 1938; Horacio M. Prieto, secretary in 1936 of the national committee of the CNT, *Marxismo y socialismo libertario*, 62–64. Juan García Oliver, a prominent member of the FAI, writes: "[The FAI's] aim was to prevent reformist and political adventurism from seizing control of the CNT" (*El eco de los pasos*, 115).

3. George Esenwein, an authority on Spanish Anarchism, writes: "According to Adolfo Bueso (*Cómo fundamos la CNT*), the CNT was formally constituted at the Second Congress of the syndicalist organization Solidaridad Obrera—called the 'Congreso de Bellas Artes'—held in Barcelona between 30 October and 1 November 1910. It was not formed in September 1911 as erroneously recorded in the works of Manuel Buenacasa, *El movimiento obrero español, 1886–1926*, 39, and José Peirats, *La CNT en la revolución española*, I, 3. Peirats later rectified his error in *Los anarquistas en la crisis política española* (1964 edition), 13–14, 20 (n. 4). See also the revised n. 4 in the 1976 edition. For further information on the founding of the CNT, see, especially, Confederación Nacional del Trabajo, *Congreso de constitución de la confederación nacional del trabaja (CNT)*, prólogo de José Peirats, which is a reprinting of the full text of the proceedings of the 'Congreso de Bellas Artes' first published in *Solidaridad Obrera*, 4 November 1910, and Xavier Cuadrat, *Socialismo y anarquismo en Cataluña, 1899–1911: Los orígines de la CNT*, 441, et seq." I am grateful to George Esenwein for having prepared this note especially for this volume.

4. *Les anarchistes espagnols et le pouvoir, 1868–1969*, 66–68.

5. *Espoir*, 3 Apr. 1977. The best account of the history of the FAI from its foundation in 1927 to its eclipse at the end of the Civil War in 1939 is in Juan Gómez Casas, *Historia de la FAI*.

6. See Confederación Nacional del Trabajo, *Memoria del congreso extraordinario celebrado en Madrid los días 11 al 16 de junio de 1931*, 38.

7. See, for example, *Solidaridad Obrera*, 18 Apr., 8 May 1937, also interview with Federica Montseny in *Tiempo de Historia*, June 1977. It is noteworthy that in his review of the Mexican edition of my book *The Grand Camouflage (La revolución española)*, Diego Abad de Santillán, the CNT-FAI leader, objected to my use of the word "domination" (*Reconstruir*, Jan.–Feb. 1965).

8. For example, Victor Zaragoza, secretary of the national committee of the CNT National Transport Federation, when interviewed by me in Mexico in 1940. See also "La última entrevista con Gaston Leval" by Antonio Albiñana and Mercedes Arancibia, *Tiempo de Historia*, Sept. 1978.

9. *Los anarquistas en la crisis política española*, 276–77.

10. See, for example, Lorenzo, 68–70, 79, 93.

11. See, for example, letter of Luis Araquistáin, published in *Left News*, Dec. 1942, on the opposition of Juan Negrín to Anarchosyndicalist participation in the government.

12. Diego Abad de Santillán, *La bancarrota del sistema económico y político del capitalismo*, 55.

13. 3 July 1936.

14. Fernando Claudín, *La crisis del movimiento comunista*, 176.

15. *Gosudarstvennost i anarkhiia* (State and Anarchy), 234.

16. Article in *L'Adunata dei Refrattari*, 12 Mar. 1932.

17. *Mañana*, May 1930, as given in Abad de Santillán, *El anarquismo y la revolución en España: Escritos 1930–38*, 58.

18. *Tierra y Libertad*, 15 Sept. 1933.

19. Ibid., 27 Oct. 1933.

20. Germinal Esgleas in *La Revista Blanca*, 18 Jan. 1935.

21. José Bonet in *Tierra y Libertad*, 22 Sept. 1933.

22. Isaac Puente in *CNT*, 19 June 1933, as reproduced in Puente, *Propaganda*, 129–30.

23. See, for example, Germinal Esgleas in *La Revista Blanca*, 18 Jan. 1935.

24. 27 Oct. 1933.

25. *CNT*, 24 Oct. 1933, as reproduced in Puente, *Propaganda*, 126.

26. 10 Nov. 1933.

27. See *Solidaridad Obrera*, 17 Jan. 2 Apr. 1936.

28. See speech by Juan López in *Fragua Social*, 16 Feb. 1937; also Federica Montseny, *María Silva*, 28; Ricardo Sanz, *El sindicalismo y la politica*, 262–63.

29. Diego Abad de Santillán, the CNT-FAI leader, makes this point clear in both *Por qué perdimos la guerra*, 36–37, and *La revolución y la guerra en España*, 30. In the former he also states that the right "endeavored by every means to encourage us to abstain from voting, as in the case of Cádiz . . . , where [it] offered us half a million pesetas to carry on our usual antielectoral propaganda."

30. The following news item datelined Barcelona appeared in the Monarchist daily *ABC* on 17 February: "At 4 P.M. yesterday, the general impression in the working-class districts was that the left front would undoubtedly win by an enormous majority . . . [because] of the decisive role played by the [Anarchosyndicalists] in the election."

Chapter 19

1. *The Spanish Labyrinth*, 224.

2. Francisco Largo Caballero, *Presente y futuro de la Unión General de Trabajadores de España*, 43.

3. As given in José Andrés-Gallego, *El socialismo durante la dictadura, 1923–1930*, 322.

4. Ibid., 323.

5. As given in Dámaso Berenguer, *De la dictadura a la República*, 52.

6. Quoted in Helmut Ruediger, *Ensayo crítico sobre la revolución española*, 25. During the Civil War Ruediger was representative in Spain of the International Workingmen's Association, with which the CNT was affiliated.

7. *The Spanish Labyrinth*, 258–59. See also César M. Lorenzo, *Les anarchistes espagnols et le pouvoir, 1868–1969*, 76–77; S. Cánovas Cervantes, *Durruti y Ascaso*, 15; José Peirats, *La CNT en la revolución española*, I, 35–36; Richard A.H. Robinson, *The Origins of Franco's Spain*, 120–21.

8. Jacinto Toryho, a prominent CNT-FAI member, in *Vía Libre*, 19 May 1940.

9. See, for example, Rudolf Rocker, *Anarcho-Syndicalism*, 116.

10. "Declaración de principios de la Asociación Internacional de Trabajadores," as reproduced in *Internacional*, May 1938.

11. In *Solidaridad Obrera*, 15 Apr. 1932, as given in Puente, *Propaganda*, 132.

12. Speech published in *Claridad*, 11 Apr. 1936.

13. *Solidaridad Obrera*, 24 Apr. 1936.

14. Ibid., 7 June 1936.

15. See, for example, *Claridad*, 7, 9 July 1936.

16. Frank E. Manuel, *The Politics of Modern Spain*, 167.

17. 3 June 1936.

18. For some idea of these, see the following materials: speeches by Pascual Tomás, vice-secretary of the UGT, as reported in *La Correspondencia de Valencia*, 21 Dec. 1936, 17 Feb. 1937; *CNT*, 26 Feb., 3 Mar. 1937; *Claridad*, 13 Apr. 1937; document signed by the national committee of the CNT and the executive committee of the UGT, dated 26 Nov. 1936, as given in Peirats, *La CNT*, I, 252–53; excerpts from speeches of delegates at a meeting of the CNT unions of the central region, as given in *CNT*, 8 Oct. 1936.

19. 25 Oct. 1936.

20. Lorenzo, 222; also *Claridad*, 27 Oct. 1936.

21. 28 Oct. 1936.

22. I realize that some persons may not accept the whole of this statement, but it has not been made without careful research. In *The Grand Camouflage*, published in 1961, I said the following: "The total number of persons in the anti-Franco camp belonging to each federation may have been between 1.5 million and 1.75 million, but no figures on the wartime membership can be given with any degree of exactitude. Estimates above and below these figures by sources siding with one organization or the other have been made, but as there is no way of checking their accuracy nothing would be gained by burdening the text with them." Since then, José Luis Guinea, in his work *Los movimientos obreros y sindicales en España de 1833 a 1978*, 94–95, gives the figure of the UGT membership in 1938, based on the dues paid to the International Federation of Trade Unions, as 1,904,569.

23. Lorenzo, 222.

24. Ibid.

25. 5 Sept. 1936.

26. Lorenzo, 222–23.

27. Ibid.

28. Ibid., 224.

29. "Notas Históricas sobre la Guerra de España," 261–62.

30. Lorenzo, 224.

31. *El anarquismo español en la pucha política*, 7.

32. See resolution published in *CNT*, 17 Sept. 1936.

33. From an unpublished work by Lazarillo de Tormes (Benigno Bejarano), "Les morts ne vous pardonnent pas," 69.

34. Lorenzo, 249.

35. The most prominent foreign Anarchist who condemned the CNT for entering the government and for other reasons was the Russian emigré Alexander Schapiro. For his caustic criticisms of CNT policies during the first year of the war, see his articles in *Le Combat Syndicaliste*, 28 May, 27 August, and 19 November 1937. See also Alexander Schapiro and Albert de Jong, *Waarom verloren wij de revolutie?* Emma Goldman, the famous American Anarchist, also criticized the CNT, but was less rigid. In an address to the congress of the International Workingmen's Association, she stated: "The participation of the CNT-FAI in the government, and concessions to the insatiable monster in Moscow, have certainly *not* benefited the Spanish Revolution, or even the anti-Fascist struggle. Yet closer contact with reality in Spain, with the almost insurmountable odds against the aspirations of the CNT-FAI, made me understand their tactics better, and helped me to guard against any dogmatic judgment of our comrades" (*Red Emma Speaks: Selected Writings and Speeches*, 375–77). See also *Nowhere at Home: Letters from Exile of Emma Goldman and Alexander Berkman*, 271–72, and "Where I Stand," *Spain and the World*, 2 July 1937.

36. *Internacional*, July–Aug. 1938.

37. See resolution published in *CNT*, 17 Sept. 1936.

38. 25 Sept. 1936. This ingenuous attempt to delude foreign opinion probably originated in a directive issued on 4 September 1936 by Jacinto Toryho, the secretary of the propaganda department of the regional committees of the CNT and FAI in Catalonia. According to the well-known Anarchist Floreal Ocaña, the order instructed all speakers of the libertarian movement not to refer to libertarian communism in their propaganda. "Obviously quite a number of libertarian propagandists paid no attention to this folly, for which we felt we would have to pay dearly if we had observed it, and we continued . . . speaking and writing as Anarchists" (*Cultura Proletaria*, 17 Aug. 1940). See also Severino Campos, ibid., 25 Jan. 1941. Gaston Leval, the French Anarchist, who was active in Spain, wrote at the time: "Because of the need for arms and ammunition, the necessity for their being obtained abroad, and the necessity for relying on democratic public opinion (in the bourgeois sense of the word), all creative work of the Spanish people has been passed over in silence. This has been an error which has made the international proletariat feel less drawn to the Spanish people than they would have otherwise been" (*Social Reconstruction in Spain*, 3).

39. Lorenzo, 227–28.

40. For some of the most interesting editorials in the Anarchosyndicalist press, see *CNT*, 19 Sept., 6 Oct. 1936; *Solidaridad Obrera*, 30 Sept., 2, 4 Oct. 1936.

41. For the attitude of the Republicans and Communists, see, for example, *El Mercantil Valenciano*, 8 Oct. 1936 (speech by Angel Moliner, Cortes deputy representing the Left Republican party); *Treball*, 1 Oct. 1936; *Verdad*, 22 Sept. 1936.

42. 30 Sept. 1936.

43. 31 Oct. 1936.

44. Letter to me.

45. Interview with Federica Montseny, the CNT-FAI leader, *Tiempo de Historia*, June 1977.

46. *El anarquismo español en la lucha política*, 6; also 7.

47. 23 Oct. 1936.

48. See *CNT*, 30 Oct. 1936, and Largo Caballero's statement to the correspondent of the *Daily Express*, published in *Claridad*, 29 Oct. 1936.

49. The new appointments and the shifts they entailed are given in the *Gaceta de Madrid*, 5 Nov. 1936.

50. Lazarillo de Tormes (Benigno Bejarano), *España, cuña de la libertad*, 83.

51. See *Claridad*, 25 Oct. 1936. "The grave problems created by the encirclement of Madrid and the urgent necessity of avoiding internal disorders had decided Caballero to bring the CNT into the government, thereby forming a bloc of all the antifascist forces of the country" (Julio Alvarez del Vayo, *Freedom's Battle*, 215).

52. Francisco Largo Caballero, *Mis recuerdos*, 187.

53. *Freedom's Battle*, 216.

54. *Mis recuerdos*, 188.

55. *Freedom's Battle*, 215–16. In his "Notas Históricas," 261, Largo Caballero refers to a telephone conversation between José Giral and Azaña, but does not say that he himself spoke to the president. However, the mayor of Barcelona, Carlos Pi Sunyer, confirms that Largo Caballero telephoned Azaña to say that he was going to form a government with four CNT ministers. See subsequent text.

56. *Obras completas*, IV, 592.

57. *La república y la guerra*, 418–19.

58. Julián Zugazagoitia, *Historia de la guerra en España*, 181.

59. *De mi vida*, 324–25.

60. "Notas Historicos," 481–82.

61. Alvarez del Vayo's version of this incident is in *Freedom's Battle*, 217–18.

62. *De mi vida*, 324–25.

63. Ibid., 325–26.

64. *Guerra, exilio y cárcel de un anarcosindicalista*, 74–77.

65. As César M. Lorenzo points out, "All the directive organs of the political and trade-union organizations left Madrid about the same time, 7 November, the day of the government's departure" (255, n. 2).

66. Ibid., 254–55. See also article by Horacio M. Prieto in *España Libre* (Paris), 3 July 1949. For a

biographical article on Mariano Vázquez, known familiarly as Marianet, see article by Federica Montseny in *CNT* (Paris), 24 June 1949.

67. See resolution approved by the regional congress of the Catalan CNT in April 1937, as given in article by P. Bernard (Bernardo Pou), *Universo*, 1 May 1948, in which this fact is mentioned; also report of Mariano Vázquez (secretary of the national committee of the CNT from 19 Nov. 1936), to the extraordinary congress of the AIT, as reproduced in *L'Espagne Nouvelle*, 15 Mar. 1939, and J. Capdevila in *Solidaridad Obrera* (Paris), 7 Apr. 1951.

68. 4 Nov. 1936. The CNT militant, Adolfo Bueso, attributes this explanation and justification of the CNT's entry into the government to the FAI leader Abad de Santillán ("the most intransigent of the libertarians")—but does not say that the article appeared in *Solidaridad Obrera* (*Recuerdos de un cenetista*, II, 213).

69. See manifesto issued by the Regional Federation of Anarchist Groups of Catalonia, as given in *Tierra y Libertad*, 19 Dec. 1936. A manifesto issued by the Federation of Anarchist Groups of the Central Region affirmed that in spite of the CNT's entry into the government, "there is not the slightest contradiction with our doctrines" (as given in *Cultura Proletaria*, 20 Mar. 1937). See also speech by Juan López (CNT minister of commerce), *Solidaridad Obrera*, 11 Feb. 1937; *Tierra y Libertad*, 22 May, 30 Oct. 1937, and the manifesto of the peninsular committee of the FAI, addressed to the international libertarian movement, as reproduced in *Cultura Proletaria*, 23 Oct. 1937.

70. *Internacional*, Oct. 1938.

71. José Peirats, *Los anarquistas en la crisis política española*, 216.

72. Speech in Alicante, as given in *El Día Gráfico*, 22 Dec. 1936.

73. Her parents were the famous Anarchists Federico Urales (Juan Batista Montseny) and Soledad Gustavo.

74. As given in *Fragua Social*, 8 June 1937.

75. The letter is dated 27 Oct. 1950 (Hoover Institution).

76. Her letter, dated 31 May 1950, is in the Hoover Institution. For a detailed account of the leading role played by Horacio Prieto in the selection of the CNT-FAI representatives, see Lorenzo (his son), 232–34.

77. *Inquiétudes*, special number, July 1947. See also article by Montseny in *Espoir*, 9 Jan. 1966.

78. Speech in Barcelona, *Solidaridad Obrera*, 5 Jan. 1937. See also her speech reported in *Fragua Social*, 8 June 1937.

79. Letter to me, dated 7 Dec. 1950 (Hoover Institution).

80. Reported in *Boletín de Información, CNT-FAI*, 23 Dec. 1936.

81. *Internacional*, June 1938. See also resolution approved by the regional congress of the Catalan CNT in April 1937, as given in article by P. Bernard (Bernardo Pou) in *Universo*, 1 May 1948.

82. Speech reported in *Le Libertaire*, 24 June 1937.

83. Speech reported in *Fragua Social*, 29 May 1937.

84. Lorenzo, 235.

Chapter 20

1. See, for example, *Los soviets en España*.

2. 9 Sept. 1936. See also *Verdad*, 30 Dec. 1936.

3. 20 Dec. 1936. The text given here is a retranslation from the Anarchosyndicalist German-language periodical *Die Soziale Revolution* (Barcelona), no. 5–6, Feb. 1937. The Spanish text was unavailable.

4. Letter to me, dated 21 April 1951 (Hoover Institution).

5. Article in *Política*, 23 Feb. 1937.

6. Solano Palacio in *Tiempos Nuevos*, 28 Sept. 1938.

7. See speech by Juan López, CNT minister of commerce, reported in *Fragua Social*, 29 May 1937.

8. See *Gaceta de la República*, 25 Dec. 1936, 7 Jan. 1937.

9. Ibid., 26 Dec. 1936. None of these decrees, it should be noted, applied to the semiautonomous region of Catalonia, where events took a different course.

10. See, for example, Matilde Vázquez and Javier Valero, *La guerra civil en Madrid*, 289–90.

11. Joan Estruch, *Historia del P.C.E., 1920–1939*, I, 103.

12. For attacks by the Communists on the committees for levying taxes and requisitioning harvests, see *Verdad*, 1, 8, 30 Dec. 1936, 12 Jan. 1937 (speech by Juan José Escrich); *Frente Rojo*, 31 Mar. 1937.

13. 19 Feb. 1937. See also speech by Largo Caballero at the session of the Cortes held on 1 February 1937, as reported in *El Día Gráfico*, 2 Feb. 1937. For other criticisms of the committees by moderate as well as by left-wing Socialists, see *Claridad*, 16 Feb. 1937 (article by Leoncio Pérez); *La Correspondencia de Valencia*, 30 Nov. 1936 (speech by Molina Conejero), 1 Feb. 1937 (speech by Jerónimo Bugeda), 2 Feb. 1937 (speech by Angel Galarza), 16 Feb. 1937 (speech by Rodolfo Llopis); *El Socialista*, 2, 10, 11 Mar. 1937 (editorial articles); *Verdad*, 9 Jan. 1937 (speech by Juan Tundidor).

14. 25 Dec. 1936.

15. Speech reported by *Solidaridad Obrera*, 29 Nov. 1936.

16. 30 Mar. 1937.

17. *Verdad*, 26 Jan. 1937.

Chapter 21

1. See Chapter 4.

2. Speech reported in *La Correspondencia de Valencia*, 5 Aug. 1937.

3. 18 Sept. 1936.

4. *The Forging of a Rebel*, 536. For testimony by opponents of the military rebellion on the excesses committed by the left during this early period of revolutionary terror, see speech by Wenceslao Carrillo in *La Correspondencia de Valencia*, 4 Aug. 1937; Juan José Domenichina in *Hoy*, 30 Nov. 1940; Jesús de Galíndez, *Los vascos en el Madrid sitiado*, 15–19, 42–43, 67–69; Miguel Peydro in *Correo de Asturias*, 25 Jan. 1941; Indalecio Prieto in ibid., 15 Aug. 1942; Sánchez Roca, interview published in *Solidaridad Obrera*, 17 Sept. 1937; Julián Zugazagoitia, *Historia de la guerra en España*, 111–12. For information on the revolutionary *milicias de retaguardia*, which were set up in Madrid in the first days of the Civil War to carry out arrests of enemies of the regime, see Matilde Vázquez and Javier Valero, *La guerra civil en Madrid*, 113–15.

5. *Gaceta de Madrid*, 31 Aug. 1936.

6. Speech reported in *La Correspondencia de Valencia*, 5 Aug. 1937.

7. Ramón Salas Larrazábal gives a figure of 15,251 (article in Vicente Palacio Atard et al., *Aproximación histórica a la guerra española, 1936–1939*, 100). Ricardo de Cierva (*Historia de la guerra civil española*, I, 760) provides the following breakdown: 700 officers, 1,090 noncommissioned officers, and 13,000 men, a total of 14,790, of which 8,750 were in the left camp on 20 July 1936. Diego Abad de Santillán (*Por qué perdimos la guerra*, 236) gives a total figure of 15,570.

8. James Minifie in the *New York Herald Tribune* (dispatch from Valencia), 28 Apr. 1937. See also Henry Buckley, *Life and Death of the Spanish Republic*, 311. On 23 September, a decree was approved empowering the minister of finance to recruit 8,000 additional men for the corps (*Gaceta de Madrid*, 24 Sept. 1936) and a month later that number was raised to 20,000 (ibid., 24 Oct. 1936). In mid-November, Negrín estimated that the corps would soon number 30,000 (*Gaceta de la República*, 18 Nov. 1936).

9. Buckley, 311.

10. *The Spanish Civil War* (1977 ed.), 666–67.

11. Reported in *Verdad*, 27 Dec. 1936. In February 1937, Negrín issued a circular order reminding all carabineers that, in conformity with existing decrees, they should abstain from political activity and confine themselves to the "enthusiastic fulfillment of their duty toward the legal government of the democratic Republic" (*Gaceta de la República*, 20 Feb. 1937). It will be seen in a later chapter that Negrín, as he drew closer to the Communists, ignored this prohibition and recruited new members for the carabineers from the PCE and PSUC. Miguel Serra Pàmies, a member of the PSUC executive, told me in 1944, after he had left the party: "Many members of the PSUC joined the carabineers. Negrín played our game and we played his." A shorthand record of the interview is in the Hoover Institution.

12. See, for example, speech by Fidel Miró, reported in *Ruta*, 18 Feb. 1937.

13. 28 Apr. 1937.

14. William Rust in the *Daily Worker*, 1 Mar. 1938.

15. Abad de Santillán, *Por qué perdimos la guerra*, 236.

16. *Política*, 15 Nov. 1938.

17. Louis Fischer, *Men and Politics*, 415.

18. The comment by Vidali was made to me after the war in Mexico shortly after Puente's betrayal.

19. *¡Alerta los pueblos!*, 186. This displeasure was confirmed to me after the war by Gabriel García Maroto, a former subcommissar general of war. For information on García Maroto, see Chapter 28.

20. Rojo, *¡Alerta los pueblos!*, 109.

21. Chapter 55.

22. *Gaceta de Madrid*, 17 Sept. 1936.

23. Ibid.

24. See speech by Angel Galarza, reported in *La Correspondencia de Valencia*, 5 Aug. 1937. The decree did not apply to Catalonia.

25. Resolution approved at the congress of the Valencia CNT in November 1936, *Fragua Social*, 18 Nov. 1936. See also *Frente Libertario*, 10 Apr. 1937.

26. For protests against the disarming and arrest of Anarchosyndicalists and the occupation of villages by the police, see speech by Tomás Cano Ruiz at the closing session of the congress of the Valencia CNT, reported in *Fragua Social*, 7 Nov. 1936; manifesto issued by the CNT of the central region, published in *El Día Gráfico*, 23 Dec. 1936; *Fragua Social*, 23 Apr. 1937; *Nosotros*, 13 Mar., 5, 7, 8, 10 Apr. 1937. See also Federación Anarquista Ibérica, *Memoria del pleno regional de grupos anarquistas de Levante celebrado en Alicante, durante los días 11, 12, 13, 14 y 15 del mes de abril de 1937*, 128–31, 133; Confederación Regional del Trabajo de Levante, *Actas del congreso regional de sindicatos de Levante celebrado en Alicante, en el Teatro Verano, los días 15, 16, 17, 18 y 19 de julio de 1937*, 199–205.

27. See, for example, instructions published in *La Correspondencia de Valencia*, 15 Feb. 1937; also *Gaceta de la República*, 13 Mar. 1937.

28. *Gaceta de Madrid*, 24, 26 Aug. 1936; see also ibid., 7 Oct. 1936.

29. See speech by García Oliver, CNT-FAI minister of justice in the Largo Caballero government, reported in *Fragua Social*, 1 June 1937.

30. See, for example, *Frente Libertario*, 10 Mar. 1937; also General José Asensio on Margarita Nelken as quoted by Julián Gorkin, *Caníbales políticos*, 218; interview given to *CNT* by Wenceslao Carrillo, director general of security from December 1936 to May 1937, as reported in *La Correspondencia de Valencia*, 11 Aug. 1937; Justo Martínez Amutio, *Chantaje a un pueblo*, 213; Jesús Pérez Salas, *Guerra en España, 1936–1939*, 160.

31. Martínez Amutio, 205–13.

32. Julio Aróstegui and Jesús A. Martínez, *La junta de defensa de Madrid*, 228, 236.

33. For the information on Luis Omaña Díaz, I am grateful to José Muñoz López, a member of the secret police and later a high-ranking official of the SIM, Military Investigation Service (interviewed by me in Mexico in 1950). As for Appellániz, a profile can be found in Martínez Amutio, 211, 228–30, and additional information in *Datos complementarios para la historia de España*, 266–67.

34. For all of this information I am likewise indebted to José Muñoz López (see previous note). In letters to me, dated 7 August and 18 December 1951, Wenceslao Carrillo, the director general of security under Largo Caballero, confirmed the political affiliation of Adám and Torrijos (Hoover Institution). At the end of April 1937, Juan Galán was made inspector of the armed forces under the control of the ministry of the interior (see *Gaceta de la República*, 30 Apr. 1937).

35. There are many references to Sloutsky (also spelled Sloutsky) in Alexander Orlov, *The Secret History of Stalin's Crimes*; Elisabeth K. Poretsky (the wife of the assassinated NKVD agent, Ignace Poretsky, alias Ignace Reiss, alias Ludwik), *Our Own People*, and in U.S. Congress, Senate Committee on the Judiciary, *The Legacy of Alexander Orlov*. In the graphic section of Viñas, *El oro de Moscú*, 14–17, there is a copy of a confidential protocol, drawn up in Moscow on 7 November 1936, relating to the arrival in the Soviet capital of the Spanish gold reserves. One of the signatories was A. A. Sloutsky, whose title at that time was Commissar of State Security.

36. Because the Soviet secret police was variously referred to in the 1930s as the GPU, OGPU, or NKVD, the following information taken from the *McGraw-Hill Encyclopedia of Russia and the Soviet Union*, 502, should clarify the matter. By a decree of February 1922, a State Political Administration (GPU) was established in the People's Commissariat of Internal Affairs (NKVD). In 1923 the GPU was taken out of the NKVD and transformed into a Unified State Political Administration (OGPU) attached to the Sovnarkom (Council of People's Commissars). In 1934 a new reorgani-

zation took place. By a decree of 10 July, the functions of the OGPU were transferred to the NKVD. Nevertheless, long after 10 July 1934, the Soviet secret police was still commonly referred to as the GPU, or OGPU, probably, in many instances, through force of habit. The involved sequence of naming and renaming is covered in more detail by the famous sovietologist David Dallin in *Soviet Espionage*, 1–2 (footnote). See also Hugo Dewar, *Assassins at Large*, 200–203.

37. *In Stalin's Secret Service*, 82.

38. P. 4. His full party name is given as Lev Lazarevich Nikolsky.

39. Article in the *Reader's Digest*, Nov. 1966.

40. *Men and Politics*, 361.

41. I am grateful to Payne for having furnished me with a copy of the reply signed by Orlov. The copy is in the Hoover Institution.

42. Orlov also asserted in reply to Payne's questionnaire that Krivitsky "had never been chief of intelligence in all of Europe." This is true, but then Krivitsky claimed only that he was "chief of Soviet military intelligence in western Europe." It is noteworthy that when Benjamin Mandel, director of research for the U.S. Senate subcommittee, during his interrogation of Orlov, referred (on 28 Sept. 1955) to Krivitsky as a "ranking NKVD official" Orlov did not contradict him (U.S. Congress, Senate Committee on the Judiciary, *The Legacy of Alexander Orlov*, 29).

43. David T. Cattell observes: "It may be true that the Communists instigated the terror and took an active lead in it, but in their activities they received the cooperation and assistance of the Socialist and Republican groups" (*Communism and the Spanish Civil War*, 134–35). It would have been more accurate had he said "of *some* Socialist and Republican groups."

44. *La crisis del movimiento comunista*, 196. See also Jesús Hernández, *Yo fui un ministro de Stalin*, 111.

45. My italics.

46. See, for example, Orlov, "Answers to the Questionnaire of Professor Stanley G. Payne"; article in *Reader's Digest*, Nov. 1966; *The Secret History of Stalin's Crimes*, x.

47. *Men and Politics*, 361.

48. Santiago Carrillo, *Demain l'Espagne: Entretiens avec Régis Debray et Max Gallo*, 56.

49. Krivitsky, 102. See also ibid., 106–7, and Chapter 48 of this work. The tale of arrests without judicial warrant, of detentions in clandestine jails, of tortures, kidnappings, and assassinations by the NKVD and the Communist-controlled Spanish secret police is amply confirmed by left-wing sources; see, for example, AIT, *Boletín de Información*, Service d'Information Français de l'AIT, Special Edition, 11 May 1937, p. 4 (mimeographed), cited in Cattell, *Communism*, 133, 237, n. 3; *Castilla Libre*, 15–18 Apr. 1937; *CNT*, 17 Apr. 1937 (statement by Melchor Rodríguez); *La Correspondencia de Valencia*, 24 Feb. 1937 (open letter of the provincial secretariat of the Valencia UGT); *Cultura Proletaria*, 25 Sept., 18 Dec. 1937; *L'Espagne Nouvelle*, 17 Sept. 1937 (article by Ethel MacDonald); *Fragua Social*, 16, 17, 28 Apr. 1937; *Frente Libertario*, 9 Apr. 1937; *Independent News*, 7 Nov., 4 Dec. 1937; *Modern Monthly*, Aug. 1937 (article by Hugo Oehler), Sept. 1937 (article by Anita Brenner); *El Pueblo*, 11, 17 Apr. 1937; *La Révolution Prolétarienne*, July 1947 (article by Jordi Arquer); *El Socialista* (Madrid), 20 Apr. 1937; *Solidaridad Obrera* (Barcelona), 20, 23, 25 Apr. 1937; *Worker's Age*, 22 Feb. 1937 (article by George Kopp), 15 Jan. 1938 (excerpt from report by John McGovern); Abad de Santillán, *Por qué perdimos la guerra*, 183, 185–90; *L'assassinat de Andrés Nin*, 18–19; Franz Borkenau, *The Spanish Cockpit*, 239–40; Fenner Brockway, *Workers' Front*, 123–24; Pierre Broué and Emile Témime, *La révolution et la guerre d'Espagne*, 275–86; Claudín, *La crisis del movimiento comunista*, 188; "El Campesino" (Valentín González), *La vie et la mort en U.R.S.S., 1939–1949*, 206; Louis Fischer, *Russia's Road from Peace to War*, 284; Gorkin, *Caníbales políticos*, 133, 176–79, 184, 227–40, and *El proceso de Moscú en Barcelona*, 53–56, 61, 106–266; Krivitsky, 72–73; Katia Landau, *Le stalinisme en Espagne*, 14–17, 24, 27, 33–34, 45–48; John McGovern, *Terror in Spain*, 5, 9; Gabriel Morón, *Política de ayer y política de mañana*, 99; Patrik v. zur Mühlen, *Spanien war ihre Hoffnung*, 143–77; G. Munis, *Jalones de derrota*, 388–90; José Peirats, *Los anarquistas en la crisis política española*, 265–73. See also letter, dated 26 January 1939, from George Kopp, a former commander of the militia of the POUM, to Harry Milton, also a former combatant in the POUM militia, stating that he personally had been in "17 secret GPU [NKVD] prisons." I am indebted to Harry Milton for a copy of this letter, which has been deposited with the Hoover Institution.

Chapter 22

1. The full text of the decree appeared in the official *Gaceta de Madrid* on 3 Aug. 1936.

2. For the intervention by the ministry of industry and commerce in industrial concerns in Madrid both before and after the publication of the decree of 2 August, see *Gaceta de Madrid*, 27 July 1936; *CNT*, 3 Aug. 1936; *Mundo Obrero*, 1 Aug. 1936; *Política*, 18 Aug. 1936.

3. *Guerra y revolución en España, 1936–1939*, I, 271.

4. See statement issued by the executive committee of the UGT metallurgical federation, *La Correspondencia de Valencia*, 2 Mar. 1937.

5. See, for example, *Verdad*, 8 Dec. 1936 (speech by José Díaz), 17 Dec. 1936 (Communist party manifesto), 23 Dec. 1936 (editorial); speech by José Díaz on 8 Feb. 1937, as given in *Tres años de lucha*, 325; *Frente Rojo*, 27 Feb. 1937 (editorial), 19 Mar. 1937 (manifesto of the central committee of the Communist party).

6. Diego Abad de Santillán, *After the Revolution*, 122. See also *Boletín de Información, CNT-FAI*, 21 June 1937; speech by Juan López in *Fragua Social*, 6 Oct. 1936; *Solidaridad Obrera*, 25 Sept. 1936 (interview with España Industrial); manifesto of the Communist party, as given in *Verdad*, 17 Dec. 1936; report of Helmut Ruediger, representative in Spain of the International Workingmen's Association, with which the CNT was affiliated, *Informe para el congreso extraordinario de la AIT, el día 6 de diciembre de 1937*; Albert Pérez-Baró, *30 meses de col·lectivisme a Catalunya, 1936–1939*, 43.

7. See joint statement issued by the national committees of the CNT and UGT textile federations, as given in *Claridad*, 3 Mar. 1937; *Tierra y Libertad*, 2 Jan. 1937; speech by Jesús Hernández in May 1937, as given in Hernández, *El partido comunista antes, durante y después de la crisis del gobierno Largo Caballero*, 41; speech by Antonio Mije, as given in Mije, *Por una potente industria de guerra*, 4.

8. "Work and Revolution: Workers' Control in Barcelona in the Spanish Civil War, 1936–38," 45–46. See also ibid., 28–29, 39–44. A copy of this unpublished manuscript has been deposited with the Hoover Institution, Bolloten Collection.

9. Pérez-Baró, *30 mesos*, 43–44.

10. "Inside the Revolution," part 5 of the TV series "The Spanish Civil War," edited by historians Ronald Fraser, Hugh Thomas, and Javier Tusell.

11. As will be seen in a later chapter, the CNT entered the Catalan regional government before it joined the central government.

12. Quoted by Ronald Fraser, *Blood of Spain*, 11.

13. The full text of the decree is reproduced in Pérez-Baró, *30 mesos*, 228–36. For an illuminating account of collectivization in Barcelona, see Fraser, 109–36, 575–76.

14. Letter to Pérez-Baró, quoted by Fraser, 212, n. 1.

15. Abad de Santillán, *Alfonso XIII, la II república, Francisco Franco*, 360. See also letter to me, dated 25 Sept. 1971 (Hoover Institution).

16. Taped interview shown in the TV series "The Spanish Civil War," part 5 ("Inside the Revolution"). See also Fraser, 211, n. 1. On the occasion of the fiftieth anniversary of the Civil War, Tarradellas affirmed that without the council of economy and the collectivization decree the conflict "would have lasted a very short time, since they were an incentive to the whole of Spain in the struggle to achieve our fervent hopes. No one should ignore the fact that the victory we obtained during the early days of the [military] rebellion would not have had positive and lasting results without the profound changes that occurred in our economy" (*El País*, 21 July 1986).

17. *Men and Politics*, 421. According to Juan Ferrer, secretary of the CNT commercial employees' union, Negrín refused to recognize the collectivization decree of Catalonia. "He, and the majority of the central government along with him, were determined not to accept it, nor allow the CNT in particular to control any part of the economy" (as quoted by Fraser, 576). See also José Peirats, *Los anarquistas en la crisis política española*, 263–64, and the decree of 2 Sept. 1937 (*Gaceta de la República*, 3 Sept. 1937) signed by Juan Negrín in his capacity as finance minister, making the industrial collectives subject to state taxes but without conferring on them legal status. For valuable comments on the decree, see Pérez-Baró, *30 mesos*, 141–42.

18. See statement by the secretary of the national committee of the CNT at the extraordinary

congress of the Catalan CNT in *Memoria del congreso extraordinario de la confederación regional del trabajo de Cataluña celebrado en Barcelona los días 25 de febrero al 3 de marzo de 1937*, 197; see also Juan Negre, *¿Qué es colectivismo anarquista?*, 5.

19. See, for example, *Tierra y Libertad*, 26 Dec. 1936 ("Posición de la FAI" and article by Gaston Leval), 30 Jan. 1937 ("Se impone la socialización" and "Hacia nuevas realizaciones"), 6 Feb. 1937; also *Boletín de Información, CNT-FAI*, 23 Dec. 1936; Mariano Cardona Rosell, *Aspectos económicos de nuestra revolución*, 3, 6; *Collectivisations*, 13–16.

20. *Nosotros*, 9 Mar. 1937. See also *Tierra y Libertad*, 14 Aug. 1937.

21. For data from Anarchosyndicalist sources on the development of these tendencies, see *Boletín de Información, CNT-FAI*, 21 June 1937 (speech by C. Bassols); *Cultura y Acción*, 24 July 1937 (article by Maximo Llorca); *Regeneración*, 15 Mar. 1938 (article by H. N. Ruiz); *Solidaridad Obrera*, 24 Apr. 1937 (speech by Playan); *Tierra y Libertad*, 1 May 1937 (article by Juan P. Fàbregas); Pierre Broué and Emile Témime, *La révolution et la guerre d'Espagne*, 145–46; Fraser, 231–34; César M. Lorenzo, *Les anarchistes espagnols et le pouvoir, 1868–1969*, 246–47.

22. *Espoir*, 13 Sept. 1964.

23. For other examples, see *Documentos Históricos de España*, Mar. 1938; *Tierra y Libertad*, 9, 16 Oct., 13 Nov. 1937. Socialization did not necessarily solve the economic problems. In the shoemaking industry in the province of Alicante, the situation was "so catastrophic," according to the Communist *Nuestra Bandera*, that the only solution was nationalization, "otherwise we shall die of hunger" (as given in Vicente Ramos, *La guerra civil 1936–1939 en la provincia de Alicante*, I, 272.

24. See, for example, *Las Noticias*, 14 Apr. 1937 (speech by Riera); *Solidaridad Obrera*, 24 Apr. 1937 (speech by Playan); also *Tiempos Nuevos*, Sept., Oct. 1937.

25. The moderate Socialist Manuel Cordero, a member of the PSOE executive, declared: "There are some who put a wrong interpretation on the revolution by believing that the expropriation of the capitalists was carried out in order to favor certain collectivized enterprises. They are mistaken. [The plants] that were abandoned by the enemies of the Republic and expropriated, but have not yet been taken over by the State, will have to be taken over" (*La Vanguardia*, 21 Oct. 1938). See speeches by Pascual Tomás, the left-wing Socialist and vice-secretary of the UGT, in *La Correspondencia de Valencia*, 21 Dec. 1936, 11 Jan., 17 Feb., 9 Apr. 1937, and other references by him to nationalization in *Adelante*, 13 Feb. 1937, and *Claridad*, 6 Apr. 1937.

26. Letter to me (Hoover Institution).

27. For information on the enlarged national economic plenum, see *Fragua Social* for the month of January 1938 and the letters to me from Mariano Cardona Rosell, the chief delegate of the CNT national committee, in the Hoover Institution.

28. See, for example, J. Jiménez, *Solidaridad Obrera*, 3 Dec. 1936; *Tierra y Libertad*, 30 Oct. 1937 (statement by the treasurer of the Sindicato de la Alimentación e Industrias Gastronómicas); *Treball*, 27 Mar. 1937.

29. *La Batalla*, 31 Jan. 1937.

30. 31 Jan. 1937.

31. *El Día Gráfico*, 28 Feb. 1937.

32. Even in July 1938, the question of a Banco Sindical or Trade-Union Bank was still being discussed.

33. See his statements published in *La Correspondencia de Valencia*, 6 Jan. 1937, and in *El Día Gráfico*, 9 Feb. 1937; also his decree on state intervention in industrial enterprises, as given in *Gaceta de la República*, 24 Feb. 1937, and his order of 2 Mar. 1937, ibid., 7 Mar. 1937.

34. Peiró, *Mi gestión en el ministerio de industria*, as given in *Guerra y revolución*, II, 276. See also Josep M. Bricall, *Política económica de la Generalitat, 1936–1939*, 200, n. 75.

35. *Guerra y revolución*, II, 276.

36. *Los anarquistas*, 263–64. The decree to which Peirats refers was signed by Largo Caballero on 5 March 1937 (*Gaceta de la República*, 7 Mar. 1937). It provided for a credit of 30 million pesetas. For the difficulty the CNT encountered in obtaining funds from the government for its collectivized enterprises, see Juan López, "Evolución del sindicalismo español," in *Comunidad Ibérica*, Nov.–Dec. 1964, 32, quoted in Lorenzo, 244, n. 11; prologue to speech by Peiró (*De la fábrica de vidrio de Mataró al ministerio de industria*), quoted in Lorenzo, 257, n. 6.

37. *Treball*, 13 Apr. 1937.

38. Report to the central committee of the Communist party in March 1937, reprinted in Díaz, *Tres años*, 353.

Chapter 23

1. Speech reported in *Frente Rojo*, 30 Mar. 1937.
2. Speech in January 1937, as given in Melchor, *Organicemos la producción*, 6–8.
3. Article in *Stato Operaio*, 11 Nov. 1936, as given in Togliatti, *Escritos políticos*, 336.
4. Speech reported in *Mundo Obrero*, 18 May 1938. It is noteworthy that in Catalonia, where the CNT and FAI were dominant, there was opposition during the first few months of the war within the Communist-controlled PSUC to the slogan of the "democratic republic," for it was feared, according to Miguel Serra Pàmies, onetime member of the executive, that "it would hurt the growth of the party among the working class." In Madrid, he added, "it was easier to launch the slogan, because the Communists were strong and the Caballero Socialists supported it, but, in Catalonia, there was revolutionary ferment and the slogan could not be launched during the early months" (quoted from shorthand notes taken during my interview with Serra Pàmies in 1944, deposited in the Hoover Institution).
5. Carrillo, *Demain l'Espagne: Entretiens avec Régis Debray et Max Gallo*, 53.
6. Carrillo, *En marcha hacia la victoria*, 10.
7. *El frente de la producción, una industria grande para ganar la guerra*, 13, quoted in David T. Cattell, *Communism and the Spanish Civil War*, 62.
8. Open letter to Carrillo published in *La Correspondencia de Valencia*, 1 Apr. 1937.
9. Letter published in *Juventud Libre*, 1 May 1937. See also article by Federico Fernández López in *Adelante*, 28 May 1937.
10. Letter to me, dated 31 May 1950 (Hoover Institution).
11. See, for example, speech by Juan López, 7 Feb. 1937, reprinted in López, *Concepto del federalismo en la guerra y en la revolución*, 3–4.
12. *CNT*, 19 June 1937.
13. 19 Jan. 1937.
14. 2 Feb. 1937. See also *Juventud Libre*, 6 Feb. 1937; *Solidaridad Obrera*, 9 Feb. 1937; *Tierra y Libertad*, 23 Jan. 1937.
15. 3 Feb. 1937. See also *Mundo Obrero*, 5 Feb. 1937.
16. Díaz, *Tres años de lucha*, 349–52. See also his speech at the plenary session of the central committee of the PSUC, reported in *Treball*, 9 Feb. 1936.
17. 10 Apr. 1937. A few days earlier, the Communist-dominated Frente de la Juventud de España, which comprised the JSU and the Republican Youth, denounced its rival, the Frente de la Juventud Revolucionaria, as "Trotskyist." The greatest damage committed by Trotskyism, it declared, was its distortion of the "character of our war of independence." "We raise the alarm among all young men who defend our cause, especially our brothers of the libertarian youth, and urge them to remove these false friends [the Trotskyists], these saboteurs of our victory" (*Política*, 7 Apr. 1937).
18. Speech at a meeting of the Libertarian Youth, reported in *CNT*, 4 May 1937.
19. 22 May 1937. For other attacks in the libertarian press accusing the Communists of trying to return to the Republic of 1931, see *Juventud Libre*, 9 May 1937; *Ruta*, 1, 17 Apr. 1937.
20. José Sandoval and Manuel Azcárate, *Spain, 1936–1939*, 85; see also Dolores Ibárruri, *El único camino*, 436.
21. *Hombres made in Moscú*, 448.

Chapter 24

1. *Gaceta de Madrid*, 8 Oct. 1936.
2. 10 Oct. 1936.
3. One hectare is equivalent to approximately two and a half acres.
4. 20 Mar. 1937.
5. Article in *CNT*, 26 May 1937.
6. That Morayta was a Communist party member is confirmed by Enrique Castro, the Communist

director general of the Institute of Agrarian Reform, under whom he served (Castro, *Hombres made in Moscú*, 386). For an edifying account of Morayta's disillusionment with the party and its leaders ("You are all men of a Stalinist mold, men driven insane by a dogma, by a terrible machine, by an animal discipline, and by a hatred that has rotted your souls," he told Castro), see ibid., 499–504. He was replaced by José Silva, also a party member, in the spring of 1937.

7. *Tribuna*, Oct. 1948.

8. José Sandoval and Manuel Azcárate, *Spain, 1936–1939*, 89.

9. 12 Oct. 1936.

10. *Por la revolución agraria*, 44.

11. Speech, *Juventud Libre*, 24 July 1937. See also article in *Castilla Libre*, 30 Mar. 1937, quoting a member of the provincial committee of the CNT of Ciudad Libre (formerly Ciudad Real) as saying that a delegate of the minister of agriculture in that province had demanded the return of their land to persons who were not fascists; and letter sent to the minister of agriculture by Ricardo Zabalza, general secretary of the National Federation of Land Workers (published in *Adelante*, 29 May 1937), complaining that a delegate of the Institute of Agrarian Reform had ordered the restoration of a large estate to its original owner in the village of Garvayuela, Badajoz.

12. *Claridad*, 14 Dec. 1936. See also article "En Desprestigio de los Hombres de la Federación Española de Trabajadores de la Tierra" in Largo Caballero's organ, *La Correspondencia de Valencia*, 18 Aug. 1937.

13. For indications of the hostility created among left-wing Socialists, see replies of various provincial secretaries of the National Federation of Land Workers to questions posed by the Socialist newspaper, *Adelante*, regarding Communist policy in the countryside, as given in *Adelante*, 17, 20 June 1937, and *CNT*, 14, 21 June 1937. See also *Colectivismo*, 1 May 1938 (article by A. Fernández Ballesteros).

14. See, for example, speech by minister of agriculture Vicente Uribe, reported in *Verdad*, 8 Dec. 1936.

15. 16 Dec. 1936.

16. Pp. 395, 397. In setting the tone for his book, Castro says on the pretitle page: "To know [the Communists] well you must first of all not heed them, so as to avoid being poisoned. Secondly, you must look at them day and night until you penetrate their innermost being where other men have a soul. Thirdly, you must see their socialism through the man and not through propaganda and statistics. I got to know them by looking at myself. I therefore believe that this book will be of use."

17. Ibid., 407.

18. Speech at the national conference of the Unified Socialist Youth Federation in January 1937 (Carrillo, *En marcha hacia la victoria*, 41).

19. *Adelante*, 3 July 1937.

20. Ibid. See also *Por la revolución agraria*, 42–43, and statement by Ramón Arcos Arnau, provincial secretary of the Madrid section of the Federation of Land Workers, as given in *CNT*, 14 June 1937.

21. *Por la revolución agraria*, 42–43. See also *Adelante*, 17 June 1937 (reply by Jesús Pérez Salas to questions posed by the newspaper regarding Communist policy in the countryside); *Colectivismo*, 15 Sept. 1937; Jan.–Feb. 1938; 1 May 1938 (article by A. Fernández Ballesteros).

22. Interview given to *Adelante*, reprinted in *Solidaridad Obrera*, 28 May 1937. See also his letter to minister of agriculture, *Adelante*, 29 May 1937, and articles by José España in *Cultura y Acción*, 5 June 1937, and in *Nosotros*, 3 June 1937.

23. *Castilla Libre*, 10 Apr. 1937. See also Zabalza's letter to the minister of agriculture, *Adelante*, 29 May 1937.

24. *Castilla Libre*, 10 Apr. 1937. See also ibid., 31 Mar. 1937 (article by Isabelo Romero); *CNT*, 26 Mar., 29 May 1937; *Frente Libertario*, 20 Mar., 6 Apr. 1937; *Spanish Revolution*, 2 July 1937.

25. Interview given to *Juventud Libre*, 10 July 1937. See also *Acracia*, 19 Mar. 1937 (article by M. Salas); *CNT*, 29 May 1937; José Peirats, *La CNT en la revolución española*, I, 320–23.

26. *Los anarquistas en el gobierno, 1936–1939*, 160–61.

27. *¡Teníamos que perder!*, 157.

28. *Triunfo*, 19 Nov. 1977.

29. Letter, 1940 (Hoover Institution). This evidence of Ralph Bates is all the more convincing in

that, since 1923, when he was sent to Spain as a Communist organizer, he had been a member of the British Communist party. It can be safely argued that in those years, few foreign writers understood Spain and its revolutionary mood better than he. His break with the Communist party came in 1939, at which time I met him in Mexico. His enlightening views on fundamental aspects of the Spanish Revolution had a profound influence on my own and it is regrettable that the full-scale novel on the Spanish Civil War that he planned came to nothing, largely, I suspect, because he did not have the heart to tell all he knew. His feeling about my own work, *The Grand Camouflage* (1961), was that it should not have been written, since it tended to "destroy the illusions" of Spanish Republican supporters. For information on Bates, as a writer and political activist, see Katharine Bail Hoskins, *Today the Struggle*, 125–29. On p. 124 she states: "Unlike many of the leftist writers of the period, Bates was a relatively long-time Communist, and his background was working-class. He started working in a factory at the age of sixteen and served throughout World War I as a private. He joined the British Community Party shortly after it was founded, and when he went to Spain in 1923 it was as a Communist organizer."

30. Anibal Ponce, *Examen de la España actual*, 75, says there were nearly fifty; José María Capo, *España desnuda*, 88, puts the number at thirty-five. See also *Claridad*, 7, 9 Apr. 1936.

31. Cayetano Cordova Iturburu, *España bajo el comando del pueblo*, 154.

32. *Gaceta de la República*, 9 June 1937.

33. 11 June 1937.

34. See, for example, interview given to *Juventud Libre*, 10 July 1937, by the general secretary of the CNT Peasants' Federation of Castile; report on the Madrid Congress of the Libertarian Youth, ibid., 31 July 1937; *Castilla Libre*, 30 Mar. 1937 (article on Ciudad Libre); *Fragua Social*, 21 Oct. 1937; Juan López, "Evolución del sindicalismo español," in *Comunidad Ibérica*, Nov.–Dec. 1964, quoted in César M. Lorenzo, *Les anarchistes espagnols et le pouvoir, 1868–1969*, 244, n. 11.

35. Letters to me (Hoover Institution).

36. See the composition of the department, as given in the decree of 30 January 1937 (*Gaceta de la República*, 2 Feb. 1937). For a long, informative article by Cardona Rosell on the National Service of Agricultural Credit, in which he urged the CNT collectives to use the service, see *Solidaridad Obrera*, 25 Mar. 1937.

37. For figures on the number of collectives recognized by the Institute of Agrarian Reform, the number of hectares confiscated and the credits granted to the collectives in each province (with the exception of Catalonia), see Pascual Carrión, *La reforma agraria de la segunda república y la situación actual de la agricultura*, 135–37.

38. My italics.

39. 11 June 1937.

40. Reprinted in *Alianza CNT-UGT*, 131–41.

41. 3, 21 Oct., 3 Dec. 1938.

42. See letter to me, dated 9 Apr. 1950, from Mariano Cardona Rosell, representative of the CNT national committee on the National Service of Agricultural Credit (Hoover Institution).

43. See, for example, *Frente Rojo*, 4 Aug. 1937; *Verdad*, 5 Aug. 1937; *Fragua Social*'s comments, 5 Aug. 1937; Duque, "La situación de Aragón," 30–43; José Peirats, *Los anarquistas en la crisis política española*, 291–94. The matter of the dissolution of the Defense Council and of the agricultural collectives in Aragon is discussed in more detail in Chapter 49, although some of the material has been used here.

44. Líster, *Nuestra guerra*, 151–55.

45. Ibid., 152; see also Ricardo Sanz, *Los que fuimos a Madrid*, 154.

46. *Nuestra guerra*, 155.

47. 12 Aug. 1937.

48. See the Spanish Communist refugee periodical, *España Popular*, 23 Jan. 1948; also Peirats, *Los anarquistas*, 294.

49. *Nuestra guerra*, 160.

50. Sanz, *Los que fuimos a Madrid*, 157.

51. *Fragua Social*, 23 Oct. 1937. Accounts by other libertarian sources of the dissolution of the Defense Council and the repression that followed can be found in *Acción Libertaria*, 22 Sept. 1937; *Cultura Proletaria*, 17 Jan. 1948 (article by Miguel Jiménez); *Documentos Históricos de España*,

May 1939 (summary of a report by the Aragon CNT to the central government); *L'Espagne Nouvelle*, 1, 29 Oct. 1937; *Frente Libertario*, 27 Aug. 1937; *Juventud Libre*, 4 Sept. 1937; *Spanish Labor Bulletin*, 3 Feb. 1938; *Spanish Revolution* (New York), 22 Oct. 1937, 28 Feb. 1938; Peirats, *Los anarquistas*, 283–302; Alardo Prats, *Vanguardia y retaguardia de Aragón*, 157–58.

52. He replaced Rafael Morayta in the spring of 1937 (see n. 6 above).

53. *La revolución popular en el campo*, 17–18. See Chapter 50 for more information on this subject.

54. See, for example, *Frente Rojo*, 27 Jan. 1938.

Chapter 25

1. *Obras completas*, III, 487–88.

2. See José Martín Blázquez (an officer in the war ministry), *I Helped to Build an Army*, 189; Jesús Pérez Salas, *Guerra en España, 1936–1939*, 115.

3. Pérez Salas, 259. See also L. Romero Solano, *Vísperas de la guerra de España*, 380.

4. *Gaceta de Madrid*, 28 July 1936.

5. Ibid., 3 Aug. 1936.

6. Ibid., 18 Aug. 1936.

7. Azaña, *Obras*, III, 488.

8. Antonio Cordón, *Trayectoria*, 249.

9. Information given to me by Giral, who also stated that Largo Caballero had a "violent temper" and "put up a terrible opposition to the formation of the volunteer army." For Azaña's testimony, see *Obras*, IV, 862.

10. 20 Aug. 1936.

11. According to Giral, when interviewed by me during the war.

12. 21 Aug. 1936.

13. *Gaceta de Madrid*, 27 Aug. 1936.

14. See *Política*, 19 Aug. 1936.

15. "Ispanskii Dnevnik," *Novyi Mir*, Apr. 1938, 41–42.

16. *Obras*, III, 488–89.

17. Archives of the Servicio Histórico Militar, cited by José Manuel Martínez Bande, *La campaña de Andalucía*, 84.

18. H. E. Kaminski, *Ceux de Barcelone*, 244.

19. *Historia militar de la guerra de España*, 601–2. See also ibid., 106. For materials on the matter of discipline, see, for example, Pérez Salas, 145; verbatim report of a meeting of political and military leaders on the Aragon front in September 1936 (listed in Bibliography); speech by Enrique Líster, quoted in *Mundo Obrero*, 12 Oct. 1936; for a frank account of the behavior of the Socialist militia on the Toledo front, see Romero Solano (former Socialist deputy for Cáceres), 308–10.

20. Pérez Salas, 131–32. See also César M. Lorenzo, *Les anarchistes espagnols et le pouvoir, 1868–1969*, 247.

21. Miguel González Inestal in *Internaciónal*, July–Aug. 1938.

22. *The Forging of a Rebel*, 536–37.

23. This typically Spanish insult is what Major Aberri implies.

24. *Hoy*, 12 Aug. 1939. Italics in text.

25. Martín Blázquez, 143.

26. *Freedom's Battle*, 28. See also Romero Solano, 308, and speech by Rodolfo Llopis reported in *La Correspondencia de Valencia*, 13 Aug. 1937.

27. Antonio Vilanova, *La defensa del Alcázar de Toledo*, 122–23.

28. See decree published in the *Gaceta de Madrid*, 3 Aug. 1936, and subsequent amendments, ibid., 20 Sept., 4 Oct. 1936.

29. See, for example, Martín Blázquez, 131–34, whose testimony was amply confirmed to me by Alejandro García Val, who became director of road transport later in the war.

30. See José Carreño on the Madrid transport problem, as recorded in the minutes of the Madrid Defense Council, session of 23 Nov. 1936 (*Actas de las sessiones de la junta de defensa de Madrid*, 456, Library of Congress). The library does not have copies of the minutes of all the sessions. A

complete record, assembled from the Library of Congress, the Archivo Histórico Nacional, Madrid, and the Servicio Histórico Militar, Madrid, can be found in Julio Aróstegui and Jesús A. Martínez, *La junta de defensa de Madrid*, 291–454; the minutes concerning the transport problem are on 325–26 of Aróstegui and Martínez.

31. See, for example, Víctor de Frutos (a Communist militia commander), *Los que NO perdieron la guerra*, 51–52.

32. See, for example, Manuel Azaña, *La velada en Benicarló*, 107.

33. When interviewed by me in Mexico in 1939.

34. This is confirmed by German diplomats in General Franco's territory. See Hans Hermann Voelckers's and Lieutenant General Wilhelm Faupel's communications to the German foreign ministry, as given in U.S. Department of State, *Documents on German Foreign Policy, 1918–1945*, III, 137–39, 159–62. "Franco owes the successes of the first few weeks to the fact that his Moroccan troops were not opposed by anything of equal quality, and also to the fact that there was no systematic military command on the Red side" (Faupel to the German foreign ministry, 10 Dec. 1936, ibid., 160). It is worth noting that the Carlist (monarchist) and Falangist (fascist) militia units, which in the early months of the war were not subordinate to the regular army, suffered from some of the defects that afflicted the left-wing militia (see Faupel's report, ibid., 161). See also Ramón Serrano Súñer, foreign minister and member of the Falange, *Entre Hendaya y Gibraltar*, 43.

35. Although Russian bombers reached Spain in October, the first combat planes did not arrive until 2 November.

36. For accounts by eyewitnesses in the anti-Franco camp of the siege of the Alcázar of Toledo, see Louis Fischer, *Men and Politics*, 359–62, 365–69; Luis Quintanilla, *Los rehenes del Alcázar de Toledo*; article by Clara Candiani in *La Dépêche*, 3 Oct. 1936.

37. At a meeting of political and military leaders on the Aragon front in September 1936 (see verbatim report, Hoover Institution, Bolloten Collection).

Chapter 26

1. 22 June 1934.

2. 22 Aug. 1936.

3. *Fragua Social*, 18 Nov. 1936.

4. For further details see the Anarchist *Nosotros*, 16 Feb., 12, 13, 15–17 Mar. 1937; the CNT papers, *Fragua Social*, 8 Sept., 14, 18 Nov. 1936, and *Solidaridad Obrera*, 24 Sept. 1936; also Lazarillo de Tormes (Benigno Bejarano), *España, tumba del fascismo*, 82.

5. On the Madrid front the group consisted of twenty men (Eduardo de Guzmán, *Madrid, rojo y negro*, 78).

6. On the Madrid front there were also battalions composed of a certain number of centuries (ibid.).

7. See, for example, resolution passed at the regional congress of the Valencia CNT establishing a uniform structure for the CNT-FAI columns formed in that region (*Fragua Social*, 18 Nov. 1936).

8. Ibid.

9. Ibid. See also statement by Buenaventura Durruti in *CNT*, 6 Oct. 1936.

10. *Boletín de Información, CNT-FAI*, as given in *Spanish Revolution* (New York), 8 Jan. 1936.

11. *Fragua Social*, 8 Sept. 1936. See also Cipriano Mera, *Guerra, exilio y cárcel de un anarcosindicalista*, 108.

12. Alberto Bayo, *Mi desembarco en Mallorca*, 103–4.

13. 7 Aug. 1936.

14. *Fragua Social*, 21 Nov. 1936. For other appeals for discipline, see ibid., 17 Nov. 1936 (speech by Juan Peiró), 24 Nov. 1936 (article by Claro J. Sendón); *Solidaridad Obrera*, 1 Oct. 1936 (article by Jaime Balius), 3 Oct. 1936 (editorial note), 27 Oct. 1936 (article by Luka-Zaga), 5 Dec. 1936 (speech by García Oliver); *CNT*, 3 Oct. 1936 (editorial), 5 Oct. 1936 (report by the CNT of the central region), 8 Oct. 1936 (speech by Federica Montseny).

15. *España Libre* (Toulouse), 11 Sept. 1949. Durruti's death on the Madrid front, where he transferred his column when the fall of Madrid appeared imminent, remains a mystery to this day. Even the Anarchosyndicalists themselves cannot agree as to whether he was killed by an enemy bullet or by one of his own men. See, for example, Federica Montseny, ibid., 21 Nov. 1976. Both Mera, 90–

92, and Ricardo Sanz (one of the principal organizers of the Durruti column), *Los que fuimos a Madrid*, 118, are positive he was killed by an enemy bullet. For biographies of this legendary hero of the libertarian movement, see Hans Magnus Enzensberger, *El corto verano de la anarquía: Vida y muerte de Durruti*; Raimundo Ferrer, *Durruti*; Joan Llarch, *La muerte de Durruti*; Abel Paz, *Durruti: Le peuple en armes*. See also articles in *Ercilla*, 30 Mar. 1960; *Espoir*, 17 Nov. 1963, 1 Dec. 1963, 13, 20, 27 Sept., 4 Oct. 1964, 23 July 1967; *Tiempo de Historia*, Nov. 1976. For an allegation that Durruti's Soviet adviser on the Madrid front, Mamsurov Judji-Umar, may have been involved in his death, see *Carta del Este*, 16 Sept. 1978. Although Durruti sent warm greetings to the Russian working class on the occasion of the nineteenth anniversary of the Russian Revolution (*Tierra y Libertad*, 5 Nov. 1936), there is absolutely no reliable evidence that before his death he was veering toward the Communists as asserted by an *Izvestiia* correspondent, who stated in an article datelined Barcelona: "Durruti passed through a period of political transformation and his views came to approach closely those of the Communist party. Before his recent departure for the [Madrid] front he said with pride, 'Yes, I feel I am a Bolshevik and I am ready to have Stalin's portrait on the wall of my working room'" (*Izvestiia*, 22 Nov. 1936). This crude fabrication was undoubtedly designed to capitalize on Durruti's death. I interviewed him in his makeshift headquarters on the Aragon front only a few weeks before he died. He said not one word about the Soviet Union or Stalin and spoke only of the ultimate victory of the Anarchist revolution, on which he gave me a long ecstatic lecture. I was struck by his spontaneity, extraordinary simplicity, and friendliness and saw no evidence of what Hugh Thomas, who was too young to know him, calls his "dreams of grandeur" (*The Spanish Civil War*, 1977 ed., 316).

16. A. G. Gilabert in *Tierra y Libertad*, 12 Dec. 1936.

17. Published in *CNT*, 3 Oct. 1936.

18. *El sindicalismo y la política*, 281.

19. *Frente Libertario*, 20 Oct. 1936.

20. *Ruta*, 28 Nov. 1936.

Chapter 27

1. That it did exist is proved by the following extract from an article in a Communist military paper: "There are still cases, though not as frequent as before, of comrades who have no sense of responsibility, who abandon their posts in order to roam around the town, and we know that the result of such excursions is the purchase of liquor" (*Pasaremos*, 31 Dec. 1936).

2. 22 July 1936.

3. Juan Modesto, *Soy del quinto regimiento*, 47, 50, 61–62.

4. In an interview in 1977, Líster (still a staunch supporter of Moscow), a stonemason by occupation before the Civil War, stated: "[I] had much more military knowledge than colonels, majors, captains, especially in unequal combat, in street fighting and things of that nature, for which I had been preparing myself for fourteen months in a special school in Moscow. But I couldn't say [publicly] that I had this professional knowledge, nor could Modesto who was in the same position. And during our war everyone believed that it was a marvel of intuition that this stonemason or that carpenter could demonstrate a military wisdom that appeared to have dropped from heaven" (*Triunfo*, 19 Nov. 1977).

5. *Nuestra guerra*, 61–62.

6. *A Discord of Trumpets*, 296.

7. *Hombres made in Moscú*, 434. Enrique Castro was first introduced to the reader as the director of the Institute of Agrarian Reform. Because of the different posts he held during the war, they are listed here chronologically to avoid confusion. July 1936: director of *Mundo Obrero* (the Communist party organ in Madrid) and commander in chief of the Fifth Regiment (*Mundo Obrero*, 28 July 1936). September 1936: director of the Institute of Agrarian Reform (ibid., 9 Sept. 1936). November 1936: chief of the operations section of the Junta de Defensa de Madrid (*Claridad*, 11 Nov. 1936). August 1937: subcommissar of war in the General Commissariat of War (*Pasaremos*, 9 Aug. 1937). July 1936–March 1939: Agricultural secretary of the provincial committee of the Madrid Communist party organization and a member of the party's central committee.

8. *Trayectoria*, 277.

9. *Chantaje a un pueblo*, 337–43. For additional information on Vidali-Contreras (known in the U.S.A. as Ernea Sormenti), see Isaac Don Levine, *The Mind of an Assassin*, 70–71, 79–80; Vittorio Vidali, *El Quinto Regimiento* and *Spagna lunga battaglia*, 29–94, also *Milicia Popular: Diario del 5⁰ Regimiento de Milicias Populares*. The entire collection of this newspaper containing articles and speeches by Vidali was published in Milan in 1973. See also Vittorio Vidali, *Diary of the Twentieth Congress of the Communist Party of the Soviet Union* and the introduction by Robert G. Colodny (professor of history, University of Pittsburgh), which concludes with the following paragraph: "In your years, Carlos, the trajectory of world history has been shifted. That Red Star which in your youth just appeared on the horizon now moves toward its meridian. And in years to come, Carlos, when your grandchildren are as weighted with the years as you are, they will be able to say, there was a man who spoke; there was a man who pioneered the way." After World War II, Vidali became the leader of the alleged involvement in the assassination of Andrés Nin, the leader of the dissident POUM, and in the violent deaths of Carlo Tresca, Julio A. Mella, and Tina Modotti (María Ruiz), see Julián Gorkin, *El asesinato de Trotsky*, 235–40, and Gorkin's letter to me, dated 25 February 1977 (Hoover Institution).

10. See, for example, *Política*, organ of the Left Republican party, 30 July 1936.

11. Anna Louisa Strong, *Spain in Arms*, 41–43. For further information on the regiment from Communist sources, see *Guerra y revolución en España, 1936–1939*, I, 298–306; Líster, *Nuestra guerra*, 61–73, and interview with him in *Triunfo*, 19 Nov. 1977; Modesto, 54–56; my interview with Vidali, Hoover Institution. An excellent, nonpartisan account of the regiment is in Michael Alpert, *El ejército republicano en la guerra civil*, 51–57.

12. As given in *Guerra y revolución*, I, 304.

13. Carlos Contreras, speech reported in *Mundo Obrero*, 21 Dec. 1936; see also José Díaz, *Tres años de lucha*, 297 (speech, 27 Jan. 1937).

14. Simone Téry, *Front de la liberté*, 182.

15. *Nuestra guerra*, 62. This is also the figure given in *Guerra y revolución*, I, 304.

16. *Historia del ejército popular de la república*, I, 1147–48.

17. Quoted in Jesús Hernández, *Negro y rojo*, 332.

18. *New Republic*, 20 Oct. 1937.

19. At the outbreak of the conflict, Barceló was aide-de-camp to Casares Quiroga, the left Republican premier and war minister (see José Martín Blázquez, *I Helped to Build an Army*, 121). Although he figured publicly as a member of the Left Republican party (see his speech in *La Libertad*, 11 Aug. 1936), his real allegiance was to the Communist party, of which he had actually been a member, according to a Spanish Communist refugee newspaper (*España Popular*, 11 Mar. 1940) since 1935. This paper erroneously refers to him as Eduardo instead of Luis Barceló, but there is no mistaking his identity. For further information on Barceló, see letter to me from Colonel Jesús Pérez Salas, dated 1 Nov. 1949 (Hoover Institution).

20. See notices issued by the Inspección General de Milicias published in *Claridad*, 19, 25 Aug. 1936.

21. See, for example, Jesús Pérez Salas, *Guerra en España, 1936–1939*, 146.

22. For the success of the Communist party in recruiting professional officers, see *Guerra y revolución*, I, 299–300.

23. Martín Blázquez, 205. See also Pierre Broué and Emile Témime, *La révolution et la guerre d'Espagne*, 212–13, both opponents of the party.

24. According to information given to me by Vidali. See interview, Hoover Institution.

25. *The Last Days of Madrid*, 51.

26. Speech reported in *Pasaremos*, 31 Jan. 1937.

27. *Nuestra guerra*, 75.

28. Letter to me, 1940 (Hoover Institution). This preferential treatment of Communist units was confirmed to me by the former German Communist Gustav Regler, political commissar of the Twelfth International Brigade in a letter, dated 10 May 1948, in which he stated: "I know that we got most of the weapons" (Hoover Institution). See also Martínez Amutio, 54–55, 125–66. For complaints by the CNT that its units on the Madrid front were being discriminated against in the distribution of arms, see, for example, *Frente Libertario*, 24, 27 Oct. 1936.

29. According to information given to me by Vidali (interview, Hoover Institution).

30. As quoted in *Guerra y revolución*, I, 305. See also Díaz, *Tres años*, 297 (speech, 27 Jan. 1937); Líster, *Nuestra guerra*, 62; Pasionaria, speech reported in *Frente Rojo*, 20 Feb. 1937.

31. 6 Feb. 1937. See also El Campesino (former Communist), *La vie et la mort en U.R.S.S., 1939–1949*, 12.

32. *El único camino*, 389.

33. See his book, *J'ai perdu la foi à Moscou*.

34. *Hombres made in Moscú*, 277. For information on this book, see Chapter 24, n. 16.

Chapter 28

1. See, for example, *Mundo Obrero*, 17 Sept. 1936.

2. See *Gaceta de Madrid*, 29, 30 Sept., 16, 30 Oct. 1936.

3. *Men and Politics*, 354.

4. *Hombres made in Moscú*, 449.

5. See editorials and speeches published in *Mundo Obrero*, *Verdad*, and *Milicia Popular* of the period.

6. *Hombres*, 465.

7. *Guerra y revolución en España, 1936–1939*, I, 305.

8. See *Milicia Popular*, 17, 19, 28 Dec. 1936; also *Volunteer for Liberty*, 1 June 1937, which gives an account of the disbanding of the Fifth Regiment.

9. So called because they were composed of infantry, cavalry, artillery, and basic services (see Enrique Líster, *Nuestra guerra*, 75; José Martín Blázquez, *I Helped to Build an Army*, 293; Colonel Segismundo Casado in *National Review*, July 1939, who, according to his book, *The Last Days of Madrid*, 52, helped to organize the brigades). The word "mixed" was also appropriate in another sense because, in addition to the old militia volunteers, the brigades consisted of recruits, professional army officers, members of the police corps, and *carabineros* (excise and customs officials). The military historian, Colonel Ramón Salas Larrazábal, writes: "The general staff embarked on the task of forging a new army. Its first structural measure was dated 9 October [1936] and specified that the basic unit of the new army was to be the mixed brigade. All units, whether of the militia, the regular or volunteer army, were to be integrated into these units. Initially, 25 were to be formed, of which five were to be international. Eight brigades were organized immediately, six of them national and two international. . . . All had an identical structure: a headquarters staff with 13 men; four infantry battalions with 633; a cavalry squadron with 141, artillery and medical sections with 519 and 145 [respectively]; a mixed company of engineers with 346, a quartermaster corps with 42, and munitions supply section with 138—a total of 3,876 combatants" (*Los datos exactos de la guerra civil*, 123–24). See also Alpert, *El ejército republicano en la guerra civil*, 82–85; José Martín Blázquez, 293; and Colonel José Manuel Martínez Bande, *La intervención comunista en la guerra de España, 1936–1939*, 42–43, and n. 28, which states that the mixed brigade was "a unit of Russian inspiration, of which there was no precedent in Spain. Strictly speaking, it was a true division, but reduced in size, capable of carrying out independent tactical actions."

10. Louis Fischer, *Men and Politics*, 383, gives the name of this officer as "Fritz"—a pseudonym. His real name was Pavel Batov, and he joined Líster's First Brigade in October 1936 before helping to organize the International Brigades (*Pod znamenem ispanskoi respubliki, 1936–1939*, 281–84, 307). Batov was succeeded briefly by Kirill A. Meretskov, in later years a marshall and Red Army chief of staff.

11. See *Milicia Popular*, 17 Oct. 1936; Líster, *Nuestra guerra*, 74.

12. Information given to me after the war by Contreras.

13. This may not be quite accurate, as the jacket on a book by Galán stated that he joined the party in 1937 (*Cuestiones varias del Carrillismo*).

14. Letter to me (Hoover Institution).

15. *Nuestra guerra*, 74–75.

16. A few weeks later Cordón was made head of the technical secretariat of the undersecretaryship of war, which controlled the personnel, matériel, army pay, audit, coordination, court-martial, engineering, and supply departments as well as the war experiments committee. See Martín Blázquez

(one of two technical secretaries who assisted Cordón), 279; also *Diario Oficial del Ministerio de la Guerra*, 2 Nov. 1936. Cordón's membership in the Communist party is confirmed by the official Communist history of the Civil War, *Guerra y revolución en España, 1936–1939*, I, 300. See also Cordón, *Trayectoria*, 289–97, for García Val's and his own Communist party membership as well as for information on Martín Blázquez, 236, 389–90.

17. This department examined the antecedents of every man before he could enter the army (see Martín Blázquez, 121; Casado, 49–50). Before the war, according to Cordón, 235, Díaz Tendero kept a "running file on the military with precise information on the personal, professional, and political characteristics of every man." With regard to the information and control department, M. Teresa Suero Roca (*Militares republicanos de la guerra de España*, 150), writes: "[From] the very beginning [of the war], in the barracks and various military centers in Madrid, classification commissions were set up that devoted themselves to investigating and purging the personnel. The work of these commissions was centralized in the information and control department headed by Díaz Tendero, who was its creator and organizer, and who had a profound distrust for his comrades. . . . The file he had kept of all the officers in the army was of great help to him as well as the records of the UME [the right-wing Unión Militar Española], which he managed to get hold of."

18. *Guerra y revolución*, I 66; Juan Modesto, *Soy del quinto regimiento*, 43–47. See also Vicente Palacio Atard et al., *Aproximación histórica de la guerra española, 1936–1939*, article by Ramón Salas Larrazábal, 104–5; Ricardo de Cierva, *Historia de la guerra civil española*, 758.

19. He was appointed to this post when Largo Caballero became war minister (*Diario Oficial del Ministerio de la Guerra*, 5 Sept. 1936). His adjutant was Alejandro García Val, the Communist party member mentioned above, who, in accordance with the procedure governing such appointments, was nominated by Largo Caballero on the proposal of the chief of the general staff.

20. For this information I am indebted to Communists as well as non-Communists. For further details regarding these officers, see Enrique Castro, *Hombres*, 553–54; Cordón, 273, 288, 296; and Martín Blázquez, 320.

21. See circular order signed by Largo Caballero, *Gaceta de Madrid*, 16 Oct. 1936. The Communists later claimed that, on repeated occasions, they had urged the war minister to establish the commissariat (see, for example, Francisco Antón in *Nuestra Bandera*, Jan.–Feb. 1938).

22. *Mundo Obrero*, 26 Apr. 1937. See also *Informaciones*, 8 Aug. 1936; *Claridad*, 15 Oct. 1936.

23. See, for example, José Díaz's speech, 22 Oct. 1936, as reprinted in Díaz, *Tres años de lucha*, 255.

24. See circular orders signed by Largo Caballero, *Diario Oficial del Ministerio de la Guerra*, 16 Oct. 1937; also regulations issued by the general commissariat of war, published in *Claridad*, 5 Nov. 1936.

25. "The political commissar must make his men understand the necessity of a conscious and iron discipline," ran one of the regulations issued by the general commissariat of war. "By constant work he must ensure this discipline as well as obedience to the officers" (published in *Claridad*, 5 Nov. 1936).

26. "The political commissar," said the organ of the CNT Defense Committee of Madrid, "must at every moment analyze the psychological condition of his troops, so as to harangue them in moments of moral depression" (*Frente Libertario*, 20 Feb. 1937).

27. *Verdad*, 27 Jan. 1937.

28. Ibid.

29. *Frente Rojo*, 17 Apr. 1937.

30. The other three subcommissariats were held by Crescenciano Bilbao, a moderate or Prieto Socialist, Angel Pestaña, the leader of the Syndicalist party, and Angel G. Gil Roldán, a CNT member (see *Diario Oficial del Ministerio de la Guerra*, 16 Oct. 1936).

31. See Carlos de Baráibar (left Socialist leader) in *Timón* (Buenos Aires), June 1940; Castro, *Hombres*, 553–58; Julio Martínez Amutio (left Socialist), *Chantage a un pueblo*, 170. For other references to Alvarez del Vayo's and Pretel's pro-Communist activities in the commissariat of war, see Wenceslao Carrillo (left Socialist leader), *Timón* (Buenos Aires), Nov. 1939; Luis Araquistáin (left Socialist leader), *El comunismo y la guerra de España*, 8; Francisco Largo Caballero, *Mis recuerdos*, 212, "Notas Históricas sobre la Guerra de España," 816, and *La UGT y la guerra*, 10–11; Indalecio Prieto (moderate Socialist leader) in *Correo de Asturias*, 10 July 1943; Casado, 57; also for Communist praise of Alvarez del Vayo's work in the commissariat, see *Frente Rojo*, 16 Apr., 19 May 1937, and *Pasaremos*, 8 May 1937.

32. See *Nuestra lucha por la unidad*, 35; also Pedro Checa, *A un gran partido, una gran organización*, 23, and Martínez Amutio, 170–71.

33. This was only a small party, formed by dissident members of the CNT, and had no influence on the course of events.

34. After the war (1939), he showed me his party membership card, although he did not say for how long he had been a member.

35. Conversation with me after the war.

36. See Carlos de Baráibar in *Timón* (Buenos Aires), June 1940.

37. Pablo Clavego, *Algunas normas para el trabajo de los comisarios políticos* (Communist party handbook on the commissar's functions), 24.

38. From speech by Antonio Mije, member of the politburo, reported in *Mundo Obrero* (Madrid), 9 Sept. 1936.

39. *Acción Socialista*, 15 Mar. 1952.

40. *Correo de Asturias*, 10 July 1943. See also Indalecio Prieto, *Inauguración del círculo "Pablo Iglesias" de México*, 22.

41. *Guerra en España, 1936–1939*, 144.

42. Casado, *The Last Days of Madrid*, 57–58.

43. *Gaceta de Madrid*, 7 Oct. 1936.

44. *El comunismo*, 24.

45. *National Review*, July 1939. See also Casado, 53–54.

46. Quoted by Luis Araquistáin, *El comunismo*, 25, from Largo Caballero's unpublished memoirs.

47. Article in *Argentina Libre* (Buenos Aires), 13 Mar. 1941, as given in Pablo de Azcárate, *Mi embajada en Londres durante la guerra civil española*, 313–15.

48. *Pod znamenem ispanskoi respubliki, 1936–1939*, 89. This important book, which contains articles written by some of the principal Soviet officers who served in Spain during the war and who survived Stalin's purges, was published in Moscow in 1965 and translated into Spanish under the title *Bajo la bandera de la España republicana*. I am greatly indebted to Hilja Kukk of the Hoover Institution, Stanford, for translating portions of the Russian text, for her invaluable biographical research on Soviet officers and civilian personnel who served in Spain, and for her work in translating excerpts from many other Soviet sources.

49. See n. 47.

50. Kirill A. Meretskov, *Na sluzhbe narodu: stranitsy vospominaniia*, 136.

51. *Unos . . . y . . . otros . . .*, 193. See also Regina García, *Yo he sido marxista*, 282.

52. *The Forging of a Rebel*, 585. See also ibid., 604 and the portrait of him by Martínez Amutio (who knew him personally), 291–300.

53. P. 233.

54. P. 162.

55. Bolloten, *The Grand Camouflage*, 272–73.

Chapter 29

1. *Milicia Popular*, 6 Sept. 1936.

2. Enrique Castro in *Mundo Obrero*, 10 Sept. 1936; see also ibid., 8 Sept. 1936.

3. Ibid.; see also letter to Asensio from Alejandro García Val on behalf of the Fifth Regiment, notifying him of its decision to make him an honorary commander, published in Asensio, *El General Asensio*, 105.

4. So said Alejandro García Val when interviewed by me after the war. García Val, a Communist officer in the Fifth Regiment, later became a member of the operations section of the general staff. For his communist affiliation, see Antonio Cordón, *Trayectoria*, 289.

5. See César Falcón, *Madrid*, 177. Falcón was director during the first few months of the war of the Communist daily, *Mundo Obrero*.

6. Segismundo Casado, *The Last Days of Madrid*, 75–76.

7. *El Socialista* (Madrid), 12 Mar. 1939. See also Bruno Alonso, *La flota republicana y la guerra civil de España*, 89–90.

8. See, for example, José Martín Blázquez, *I Helped to Build an Army*, 264, 280, 291; also the Communist Antonio Cordón, 282–84, who, although a vehement opponent of Asensio's, credits him

with considerable ability as well as with many practical accomplishments in building the Popular Army; the pro-Communist Amaro del Rosal, *Historia de la U.G.T. de España*, 616, who describes Asensio as a great military man; and Alvarez del Vayo, (n. 12 below), who says that Asensio was "unquestionably one of the most capable and intelligent officers in the republican army."

9. See, for example, Julián Zugazagoitia, *Historia de la guerra en España*, 141–43, 152–53; Martín Blázquez, 263.

10. Fischer, *Men and Politics*, 372–74. In his long letter, which he reproduces verbatim, Fischer says: "You probably know my devotion to the Soviet Union and to the interests of anti-Fascist Spain. Because I am your friend I assume the liberty of writing to you frankly and freely."

11. *Freedom's Battle*, 126.

12. Ibid.

13. As given in Asensio, 107.

14. *Mis recuerdos*, 192. Asensio's appointment was published in the *Gaceta de Madrid* and in the *Diario Oficial del Ministerio de la Guerra*, 23 Oct. 1936. For a biographical essay on Asensio, see M. Teresa Suero Roca, *Militares republicanos de la guerra de España*, 27–52.

15. *Diario Oficial del Ministerio de la Guerra*, 23 Oct. 1936.

16. Casado, 51. For Casado's reinstatement by Largo Caballero, see *Mis recuerdos*, 63.

17. According to Enrique Castro, a former member of the central committee, in a letter to me, dated 2 May 1949 (Hoover Institution). See also his book, *Hombres made in Moscú*, 553–54, and Ramón Salas Larrazábal, *Historia del ejército popular de la república*, I, 684–85. Estrada was made head of the information section of the central general staff (ibid.). After the fall of Largo Caballero, he became (on 28 June 1937) chief of staff of the Fifth Army Corps under Juan Modesto (ibid., II, 1208, n. 7).

18. *Diario Oficial del Ministerio de la Guerra*, 23 Oct. 1936.

19. "Ispanskii Dnevnik," *Novyi Mir*, Apr. 1938, 123–24.

20. Prieto, *De mi vida*, 324–25; Zugazagoitia, 162; *Guerra y revolución en España, 1936–1939*, II, 141–42.

21. As quoted in *Guerra y revolución*, II, 161.

22. Ibid.

23. 8 Nov. 1936.

24. *La révolution et la guerre d'Espagne*, 213.

25. Antonio López Fernández, *Defensa de Madrid*, 88.

26. *Así fué la defensa de Madrid*, 48. Rojo discusses what might have happened if the mistake had not been discovered early enough. See also Cordón, 178–79, for an interesting account of this incident.

27. *Así fué la defensa de Madrid*, 48.

28. For the full text of the instructions, see ibid., 247; also *Guerra y revolución*, II, 148–49; Rojo (*Así fué la defensa de Madrid*, 47–48) analyzes certain contradictions in the instructions.

29. For some idea of the disorganization on the central front, see Rojo, ibid., 23–24, 36–37; also Rojo, *España heroica*, 47–51.

30. Zugazagoitia, 181.

31. *España heroica*, 47.

32. Zugazagoitia, 181. See also López Fernández (General Miaja's aide), 83–84.

33. For General Pozas's account of this episode, see my transcribed shorthand notes of an interview with him in Mexico in 1939 (Hoover Institution).

Chapter 30

1. Julio Aróstegui and Jesús A. Martínez, *La junta de defensa de Madrid*, 75.

2. "Ispanskii Dnevnik," *Novyi Mir*, May 1938, 56.

3. *Los que NO perdieron la guerra*, 53–55.

4. Interviewed by me in Mexico in 1939. The shorthand notes are in the Hoover Institution. Menéndez was president of the ill-starred Popular Olympiad, which was to be held in Barcelona in July 1936 in protest against the Olympic Games in Germany but was canceled because of the military uprising. He was adjutant to Gustavo Durán, commander of the hastily improvised "Machine-Gun Motor Cycle Battalion" formed during the first few weeks of the war.

5. Vincent Brome, *The International Brigades*, 77–78. See also Andreu Castells, *Las brigadas internacionales de la guerra de España*, 102.

6. Article in *Triunfo*, 6 Nov. 1977.

7. Bernard Knox, the British author, himself a member of the Eleventh International Brigade, writes: "The three battalions of the XIth are credited with numbers ranging from 1,700 to 3,500; the likeliest figure is 1,900 but no one will ever know for certain, since the brigade went into action without records, without proper identification papers. The only statistic history agrees on is the butcher's bill: more than 50 percent losses by November 23, when Franco called off the first offensive. The English section was typical; we were sixteen strong on November 8 and by December 31 eight were dead and three badly wounded" (*New York Review of Books*, 6 Nov. 1980).

8. This is also the approximate figure given to me by Ludwig Renn, the German writer and commander of the Thaelmann Battalion, one of the three battalions comprising the Twelfth International Brigade, the two others being the Franco-Belge and the Garibaldi Battalions. The latter was led by Randolfo Pacciardi (see his book *Il battaglioni Garibaldi*). The Twelfth Brigade was commanded by the Hungarian novelist Mate Zalka, known in Spain as General Lukácz, who was killed on the Aragon front in June 1937 (see Mijaíl Tijomírov, *El general Lukács: Novela*, 361–65, and Gustav Regler [political commissar of the Twelfth], *The Owl of Minerva*, 312, who was wounded on the same occasion). Zalka's Soviet adviser, General Batov, was also wounded (*Pod znamenem ispanskoi respubliki, 1936–1939*, 308). Renn gave the size of the Brigade as "between 1,500 and 1,600." These figures are taken from his diary, parts of which (6 Oct. 1936 to 22 May 1937) he dictated to me when I met him in Mexico in 1939. My shorthand record is in the Hoover Institution.

9. *The Spanish Civil War* (1965), 412–13. For an eyewitness account of this event by a former member of the Libertarian (Anarchist) Youth, who participated in the defense of Madrid, and pays tribute to the International Brigades, see Ernesto Méndez Luengo, *Tempestad al amanecer: Le epopeya de Madrid*, 167–75.

10. In his oral history, *Blood of Spain* (262), Ronald Fraser quotes one Madrileño as saying: "This was the moment we liked the Russians. It was marvellous to see those Russian fighters knocking the German planes out of the sky. The streets were full of people cheering and clapping. The Russians had come to our defense, we felt great sympathy for the U.S.S.R. Later, things changed."

11. *The Struggle for Madrid*, 144. The saga of the International Brigades lies of necessity beyond the scope of this work. Hundreds of books and articles have been written on the subject, among which Vincent Brome's *The International Brigades*, Verle B. Johnston's *Legions of Babel*, and R. Dan Richardson's *Comintern Army: The International Brigades and the Spanish Civil War* (the most recent and best-documented work) are recommended. *Legions of Babel* was badly mutilated by the editors through the elimination of a significant amount of amplifying and qualifying material, but fortunately a copy of the original typescript has been deposited with the Hoover Institution, Bolloten Collection. These three works, which contain much valuable information on the brigades, have extensive bibliographies, as do Colodny's *The Struggle for Madrid* and Thomas's *The Spanish Civil War* (1965). The exact date of the Eleventh International Brigade's entry into action is still uncertain. Brome (80), Colodny (66–67), Richardson (81), Thomas (412–13), and Vittorio Vidali, *Spagna lunga battaglia* (203) state that it first came under fire on the evening of 8 November—a date also given by the official Spanish Communist history of the Civil War (*Guerra y revolución en España, 1936–1939*, II, 168), but Johnston (168, n. 23) adduces evidence (including that of Luigi Longo, political commissar of the Twelfth International Brigade), that puts the date at 9 November. To add to the discrepancy, Vicente Rojo, Miaja's chief of staff, states categorically that the Eleventh Brigade did not go into battle until 10 November (*Así fué la defensa de Madrid*, 222). However, Andreu Castells (*Las brigadas internacionales de la guerra de España*, 161–62, n. 7) criticizes Rojo for "warping" the truth. For differing opinions regarding the highly controversial subject as to whether or not the brigades saved Madrid, see, for example, *Guerra y revolución*, II, 170–71; Rojo, *Así fué la defensa de Madrid*, 84, which agree that they did not; also Verle Johnston, *Legions of Babel*, 56, 171, n. 40, who cites Louis Fischer, Gustav Regler, and Julián Zugazagoitia, on the one hand, as saying that the brigades "did save Madrid," and Pietro Nenni, Dolores Ibárruri, and Tom Wintringham, on the other, who "agree that the brigades were only one of several important factors."

12. Federico Bravo Morata, *Historia de Madrid*, III, 276.

13. Sandor Voros, *American Commissar*, 283. Even such an uncompromising Stalinist as Alvah Bessie, a veteran of the Abraham Lincoln Battalion—who risked his life a hundred times on the

battlefields of Spain and never exposed the totalitarian aims that lay behind the catchwords of "Popular Front" and "democracy"—could not help touching on the early revolutionary illusions for which so many foreign Communists fought and died in Spain: "Never before in the history of the world," he wrote in 1939, "had there been such a body of men—a spontaneously gathered international volunteer army, drawn from every stratum of human life and every human occupation, handworkers and professionals, intellectuals and farmers. The very existence of this army, that had played so crucial a role in this Spanish war, was the guarantee of international working-class brotherhood; the final proof that those who perform the work of the world possess a common interest and an identical obligation" (*Men in Battle*, 343).

14. Letters dated 2 Jan., 7 Feb. 1986 (Hoover Institution). In a paper delivered at Siena College, Loudenville, New York, on 6 June 1986, Herrick stated: "The irony is that though nearly all of my comrades in the International Brigades were Leninists and Stalinists, believers in the great proletarian revolution, only a few (I, I am proud to say, among them) recognized that what had taken place in Catalonia and Aragon led by the ridiculed Anarchists and abetted by the hated POUMists was that very proletarian revolution, the thought of which permeated every moment of our lives. It would seem that our greatest loyalty was to the Communist Party and Joseph Stalin and not to our ideals." A copy of this paper is in the Hoover Institution.

15. See text of official letter Rojo received from General Miaja, dated 6 November, notifying him of his appointment by Largo Caballero (as given in Rojo, *Así fué la defensa de Madrid*, 248).

16. Antonio López Fernández, *Defensa de Madrid*, 105.

17. Cecil D. Eby, *The Siege of Alcázar*, 144.

18. *Historia del ejército popular de la república*, I, 574–75.

19. "Ispanskii Dnevnik," *Novyi Mir*, May 1938, 86. For other praise of Rojo, see Antonio Cordón, *Trayectoria*, 429, and Gustav Regler, the former German Communist and political commissar of the Twelfth International Brigade, who confirms that "the real organizational work" in the defense of Madrid was carried out by Rojo (letter to me, dated 30 October 1948, Hoover Institution). For Rojo's extraordinary ability and capacity for work and for his vital role in the defense of Madrid, see also the Nationalist historian Ramón Salas Larrazábal, *Historia del ejército*, I, 574–75, 642. Strangely enough, despite his glowing praise of Rojo in vol. I, Salas refers to him in vol. II (1808) with such pejorative expressions as "the overrated Vicente Rojo" and "his mediocrity" without satisfactory explanation.

20. "Ispanskii Dnevnik," *Novyi Mir*, June 1938, 33–34. Some of the major problems that confronted Rojo are given in his work, *Así fué la defensa de Madrid*, 59–60.

21. "Ispanskii Dnevnik," *Novyi Mir*, June 1938, 54–55.

22. *Give Me Combat*, 269.

23. *Causa general*, 289–90.

24. In a letter to me, dated 20 April 1949.

25. *Mis recuerdos*, 213–14. This is confirmed in Largo Caballero's unpublished memoirs, "Las Notas Históricas sobre la Guerra de España," 510–12. See also José María Gil Robles (a former minister of war), *No fué posible la paz*, 708. It is worth recording that after Diego Martínez Barrio had failed to persuade General Mola to join his government of conciliation on 18 July, Miaja telephoned him at his headquarters in Pamplona. According to B. Félix Máiz, an industrialist and close collaborator of Mola, the latter replied: "I cannot accept any of your offers because within three hours I am going to rebel . . . in defense of Spain, against a government whose system is leading it to ruin and dishonor. You thought the same way, at least when you urged me on repeated occasions to join the Unión Militar Española at the time you did" (*Mola, aquel hombre*, 307).

26. See, for example, the Nationalist historian, Manuel Aznar, *Historia militar de la guerra de España*, 200, and Ramón Salas Larrazábal, *Historia del ejército*, I, 574–75.

27. Testimony given to me by Carlos Contreras (Vittorio Vidali) in Mexico in 1939. Koltzov, on the other hand, says that Rojo "placed himself immediately at the disposal of the government" ("Ispanskii Dnevnik," *Novyi Mir*, June 1938, 34).

28. Evidence of Luis Fernández Castañeda, a subordinate at the time of Miaja, as quoted by Maximiano García Venero, *El General Fanjul*, 289–90.

29. I am obliged to Giral for this information, which was given to me during an interview in Mexico in 1939. A transcribed copy of my shorthand notes is in the Hoover Institution.

30. A copy of my transcribed shorthand notes is in the Hoover Institution.

31. P. 369.

32. Cordón, 317.

33. For the best documented account of the siege of the Santuario de la Virgen de la Cabeza, see Colonel José Manuel Martínez Bande, *Los asedios*, 107–200. Other important works on the subject are Capitán Reparaz y Tresgallo de Souza, *Desde el cuartel general de Miaja al Santuario de la Virgen de la Cabeza* and José Rodríguez de Cueto, *Epopeya del Santuario de Santa María de la Cabeza*. For the Republican offensive in April, which ended the siege, see the long oral account (in shorthand) given to me by Pedro Martínez Cartón, the commander of the Fifteenth Brigade, which headed the assault (Hoover Institution). For some information on Miaja's difficulties on the Cordova front in August, see the comments of Arturo Perucho (a combatant at the time and later editor of *Treball*, the PSUC organ) in an interview given to me (Hoover Institution). Valuable information on the siege can also be found in Cordón, 315–40.

34. *Gaceta de Madrid*, 18 Aug. 1936.

35. This information was given to me by General Sebastián Pozas, who was well acquainted with the incident. A transcribed copy of my shorthand notes is in the Hoover Institution. This incident was also confirmed to me by General Ignacio Hidalgo de Cisneros (interview, Hoover Institution). See also M. Teresa Suero Roca, *Militares republicanos de la guerra de España*, 242–44.

36. *Diario Oficial del Ministerio de la Guerra*, 23 Oct. 1936.

37. See, for example, Julio Aróstegui and Jesús A. Martínez, *La junta de defensa de Madrid*, 71.

38. *The Owl of Minerva*, 283.

39. *International Press Correspondence*, 17 May 1938.

40. Zugazagoitia, 197.

41. *The Last Days of Madrid*, 63–64. See also Castro, *Hombres made in Moscú*, 452–53, and Largo Caballero, *Mis recuerdos*, 192.

42. *España Popular*, 9 Nov. 1940. See also Cordón, 288 and 278–79, for this Communist officer's account of Miaja's undistinguished career. In a letter to the Comintern, dated 21 May 1939, Togliatti describes Miaja as "completely stupefied by drugs and alcohol" (*Escritos sobre la guerra de España*, 273).

43. *Nuestra guerra*, 288. Many years later, Santiago Carrillo (a member of the junta) said that, in the defense of Madrid, "General Miaja played a certain role, but he was essentially a decorative figure" (*Demain L'Espagne*, 59).

44. Cordón, 287–88.

45. *Eve of War, 1933–41*, 146, 235.

46. *Pod znamenem*, 152.

47. *Hombres*, 452. See also ibid., 440–41.

48. *The Education of a Correspondent*, 143–44. It is noteworthy that Ramón Salas Larrazábal (*Historia del ejército*, I, 576), whose meticulously documented four-volume history of the People's Army deserves the highest praise, credits Miaja with greater intelligence, political independence, and military ability than reflected in these pages. My own knowledge of Miaja gleaned through considerable research prevents me from subscribing to this assessment, least of all to the view that Miaja was a "great chief."

49. *Mis recuerdos*, 213.

50. See Martínez Cartón, member of the central committee of the Communist party, in *International Press Correspondence*, 17 May 1938; also Edmundo Domínguez (*Los vencedores de Negrín*, 203), who likewise confirms the guiding role of Antón. Domínguez, a left-wing Socialist and secretary of the UGT National Federation of Building Workers in July 1936, followed Communist policy during the war, finally becoming inspector-commissar of the central front.

51. *Men and Politics*, 593.

52. *Todos fuimos culpables*, 755.

53. P. 245.

54. "Notas Históricas sobre la Guerra de España," 512.

55. Jesús Hernández, *El partido comunista antes, durante y después de la crisis del gobierno Largo Caballero*, 24. The mass of evidence cited above should satisfy Hugh Thomas, who claims that Miaja was not a party member (*The Spanish Civil War* [1965], 460). It may also persuade José

Aróstegui, who has consistently denied that Miaja was a Communist (see his essay in Manuel Tuñón de Lara, *La guerra civil española: 50 años después*, 72, and his book *La junta de defensa de Madrid*, 75).

56. *Obras completas*, IV, 589.

57. *Así fué la defensa de Madrid*, 33.

58. 10 Nov. 1936.

59. Although he was not a member of the party when the junta was formed, Miaja, as we have already seen, joined the party shortly thereafter.

60. Although Frade figures in the list as a Socialist, he was actually a Communist, according to information given to me by José Bullejos, a former secretary general of the PCE (letter, dated 24 February 1950, Hoover Institution). See also Arturo Barea (a Socialist), *The Forging of a Rebel*, 579, and the pro-Communist historian Colodny, 51, 173 n. However, Aróstegui and Martínez deride Barea's evidence and deny that Frade was a Communist (141, 251–52, n. 135).

61. Carrillo joined the Communist party on 7 November 1936, the day he became a member of the junta, according to Fernando Claudín, *Santiago Carrillo*, 48.

62. Although officially representing the UGT, the Socialist labor federation, Yagüe's membership in the Communist party is not disputed. See, for example, Aróstegui, 68, 251, n. 133.

63. For more information on this question, see Aróstegui, 90 and 55 ff. Largo Caballero's dissatisfaction with the independence of the junta, and with Miaja and the Communists can be seen in *Mis recuerdos*, 191–92.

64. Aróstegui, 91–92.

65. The composition of the junta is given in ibid., 93, but I am responsible for the affiliations as listed. See also ibid., 116–17.

66. Although I have no evidence that Máximo de Dios was a Communist or a Communist sympathizer, it is worth mentioning that in a conversation in 1984 with Lorenzo Iñigo, who represented the CNT on the reorganized junta, Aróstegui was informed by Iñigo that Dios was a Communist (ibid., 140, 255, n. 106).

67. The Spanish Communist refugee periodical *España Popular* of 15 June 1940 gives the date of Cazorla's entry into the Communist party as 7 November 1936. He was elected to the central committee in March 1937 (*Juventud de España*, 7 June 1940).

68. Luis Nieto had been deputy supplies councillor to Pablo Yagüe in the previous junta and replaced him after an Anarchist attempt on his life on 23 December 1936. Nieto, like Yagüe, was undoubtedly a Communist, for it is inconceivable that Yagüe, a member of the party (see n. 62 above) would have appointed as his deputy anyone but a Communist or at least a trusted sympathizer. It is noteworthy that Aróstegui, who implies on p. 140 that he was a Communist, later states on p. 251, n. 133: "[We] know that he was a member of the JSU, but we cannot say for sure that he was also a member of the PCE."

69. See Félix Albin, *The Socialist Unity Party of Germany* (title page); *Who's Who in the Socialist Countries*, 206. The Communists also gained control of the foreign press censorship in Madrid, when Koltzov arbitrarily placed it under the direct authority of the General Commissariat of War, which, as we have seen, was firmly in their hands. See Barea, 585–86.

70. See Aróstegui, 245, n. 4.

71. Ibid., 140.

72. Ibid., 68.

73. Ibid., 140.

74. *Hombres*, 447.

75. With regard to the question of "key posts," it is worth recording that the Anarchosyndicalist historian César M. Lorenzo (who, it will be recalled, was the son of Horacio M. Prieto, onetime secretary of the CNT) states that the department of war industries occupied by the Anarchist youth leader, Lorenzo Iñigo, "was purely symbolic, because at that time Madrid had no industrial infrastructure" (*Les anarchistes espagnols et le pouvoir*, 216).

76. P. 281.

77. Victor Alba, *El marxismo en España, 1919–1939*, II, 491.

78. Pp. 13–14.

79. Pp. 125, 130.

80. P. 130. See also minutes for the session of the junta on 8 and 11 Nov. 1936 (293–96). According to Julián Gorkin, when he and Juan Andrade, both members of the POUM executive, tried to join the junta, "the antifascist parties and organizations [at first] approved our entry," but "the Stalinists imposed their veto" (*Caníbales políticos*, 90–91).

81. P. 141. See also Gorkin, *Caníbales políticos*, 90–91.

82. P. 141. The statement by Manuel Alba can be found in Pierre Broué and Emile Témime, *La révolution et la guerre d'Espagne*, 215, n. 30.

83. See minutes for 29 January, as given in Aróstegui, 376. No doubt more provoking to the Communists was *El combatiente Rojo*'s vociferous championship of "proletarian revolution" (4 Dec. 1936) and its defense of "our comrade Trotsky" against Soviet persecution (11 Dec. 1936). In a letter to premier Largo Caballero, dated 22 February 1937, General Miaja, president of the junta, stated that the measures against the POUM were taken because of "the reiterated and unjustified attacks on the Junta and on the government . . . and the need to maintain discipline in the rear at all costs and to avoid anything that might undermine authority." In his reply the next day, Largo Caballero stated that he approved of the measures, but pointed out that the junta's decisions were Miaja's exclusive responsibility. Copies of both letters (the originals of which are in the Library of Congress, Manuscript Division) are in the Hoover Institution, Bolloten Collection.

84. Aróstegui, 376.

85. Ibid., 141. Aróstegui and Martínez describe González Marín as an "extraordinary polemicist," which is borne out during his confrontation with Cazorla at the session of the junta on 15 April 1937 (see minutes, ibid., 440–54).

86. Ibid., 285. My italics.

87. Aróstegui, 121. For the discussion of the letter in the session of the junta of 8 February, see minutes, as given in ibid., 396–400.

88. 16 Feb. 1937.

89. *Hombres*, 489.

90. See minutes, as given in Aróstegui, 400.

91. P. 139. My italics.

92. *Boletín de la Junta de Defensa de Madrid*, 13 Nov. 1936, as given in Aróstegui, 87.

93. All were prominent members of the JSU. Luis Rodríguez Cuesta, for example, was a member of its national committee.

94. Pp. 94, 228, 236.

95. For details of the confrontation, see minutes of the 15 April session, as given in Aróstegui, 440–54. The hostility to Cazorla was reflected in the CNT-FAI press in Madrid, which denounced him as "an *agent provocateur* in the service of fascism" (*Castilla Libre*, 15 Apr. 1937) and demanded his immediate removal from the junta (*CNT*, 17 Apr. 1937).

96. There is some evidence of this apprehension in the minutes of the 15 April session of the junta, as given in Aróstegui, 440–54.

97. P. 139.

98. For Largo's communication to General Miaja, in which he notified him of his decision to dissolve the junta, see *Mundo Obrero*, 24 Apr. 1937. The communication stated that the general's functions would henceforth be strictly military, that he would therefore be relieved of civil authority, and that the new city council would take care of the needs of the municipality. For the executive order, dated 18 April 1937, providing for the formation of the new city council, which was to comprise thirty-two members representing the major organizations, see *Gaceta de la República*, 21 Apr. 1937. André Marty, the C.I. delegate, wrote some months later that Largo Caballero, by separating the civilian from the military authority, "very considerably weakened" the defense of the city and that for certain factions and members of the government the enemy was "no longer fascism but communism" (Marty, *Heroic Spain*, 15).

99. See excerpts from his diary, "Ispanskii Dnevnik," text to nn. 19–22, this chapter, and his article in *Pravda*, 13 Dec. 1936.

100. See *Pod znamenem*, published in Moscow in 1966 (articles by Marshals Voronov and Malinovsky, 95, 166–67, 183); Marshal Kirill A. Meretskov, *Na sluzhbe narodu*, 144. Meretskov also states that Rojo's outlook "was considerably more to the left than Miaja's."

101. *Guerra y revolución*, II, 152.

102. *The Siege of the Alcázar* (see "Sources," 235–59). Since the publication of this book in 1961, two works have appeared that throw additional light on the subject: Luis Quintanilla, *Los rehenes del Alcázar de Toledo* (1967) and Angel Lamas Arroyo, *Unos . . . y . . . otros* (1972).

103. *The Siege of the Alcázar*, 148. This account is based in part on a document signed by Moscardó and published in *Causa general*, Annexe X. There is no reason to question the accuracy of the document. Rojo, who had ample opportunity to reply to it, never discussed it in any of his books or articles on the civil war. According to this evidence, Rojo stated that "his wife and children were in Madrid and if he did not return they would be killed," and that, on bidding farewell to the insurgent officers, he was "visibly moved" and said, "I wish you all very good luck. Viva España!" (327). In a biographical essay on Rojo, M. Teresa Suero Roca records that on a Spanish television program in September 1978, "General Valencia affirmed that he had heard his father [who was among those in the Alcázar] say that Rojo urged [the defenders] to continue to resist, told them that the Republic had very few arms available and gave them great encouragement" (*Militares republicanos*, 62, n. 5).

104. *Información Española* (Resumen de la Prensa Española), 18 June 1966.

105. When questioned by me after the war.

106. "Ispanskii Dnevnik," *Novyi Mir*, June 1938, 35.

107. *Diario Oficial del Ministerio de la Guerra*, 20 Mar. 1937; *Diario Oficial del Ministerio de Defensa Nacional*, 21 Oct. 1937.

108. *Diario Oficial del Ministerio de Defensa Nacional*, 21 Oct. 1937. For a laudatory article on Rojo, see the Communist daily, *Frente Rojo*, May 20, 1937.

109. Pérez Salas, 147, 152, 169–70, 185. It is worth mentioning that Largo Caballero refers to Rojo's support of the Communists and even claims, though without supporting evidence, that he was a Communist (*Mis recuerdos*, 195–214).

110. For information on Garcés, see Chapter 55.

111. *Indice*, 15 June 1974.

112. For example, Thomas (1965), 460.

113. See Castro, *Hombres*, 317–18, 554.

114. José Martín Blázquez, *I Helped to Build an Army*, 283. See also Aznar, 428; Francisco Casares, *Azaña y ellos*, 256.

115. *Hombres*, 554.

116. Ibid., 318.

117. *Militares republicanos*, 92–93.

118. Quoted in Tsvetan Kristanov, *Za svobodu Ispanii*, 335.

119. *In Stalin's Secret Service*, 97. David Dallin, the famous sovietologist, states that Kléber, under the name of Mark Zilbert, was chief of Soviet military intelligence in the United States in the early 1930s (*Soviet Espionage*, 396–98), but I am unable to offer any corroborative evidence.

120. For example, Pierre Broué and Emile Témime, *La révolution et la guerre d'Espagne*, 354, n. 21; Colodny, 62, 179–80, n. 101; Ypsilon, *Pattern for World Revolution*, 422.

121. When questioned by me in Mexico in 1939.

122. Letter to me, dated 30 Oct. 1948 (Hoover Institution).

123. Zugazagoitia, 198.

124. *Der spanische Krieg*, 69.

125. *Two Wars and More to Come*, 210.

126. Krivitsky, 97–98.

127. Conversation in Mexico City in 1939. Shorthand notes in Hoover Institution.

128. Johnston, 57. A French officer by the name of "Vincent," in charge of the "1st sector" of the front in the Casa de Campo under General Kléber, made the following comments to me in late November or early December 1936: "The [Spanish] Communist party is afraid of the International Column. . . . The International Column doesn't want to be under the command of the Spaniards, and the Spaniards do not want to be under the command of the International Brigades. The situation is hopeless. The Spaniards are afraid of the publicity given to the International Column." He added that he was "discouraged" and was returning to Paris (shorthand notes, Hoover Institution).

129. When questioned by me in Mexico City in 1939. Shorthand notes in Hoover Institution.

130. See, for example, Carlo Penchienati, a commander of the Garibaldi Battalion, *Brigate internazionali in Spagna*, 112–13; also Gustav Regler, political commissar of the Twelfth International Brigade, letter to me, dated 10 May 1948 (Hoover Institution).

131. *Men and Politics*, 401.

132. *Así fué la defensa de Madrid*, 215.

133. P. 55.

134. Rojo gives the full text of his letter on pp. 253–55, with comments on p. 223.

135. *Nuestra guerra* and *El único camino*, respectively.

136. *Guerra y revolución*, II, 169. On the other hand, Carlos Contreras (Vittorio Vidali), the Italian Communist and chief political commissar of the Fifth Regiment, refers favorably to Kléber twice in *Spagna lunga battaglia* (203, 304), as does José María Galan, the Communist commander of the Third Brigade, in the Soviet historical journal *Voenno-Istoricheskii Zhurnal*, no. 7 (1961): 85–86, although he does not mention Kléber's outstanding contribution to the defense of Madrid. It is of interest that he states that Kléber's two brothers, Leo Stern and Wolfe Stern, "fought along with him [Kléber]" on the Madrid front, but does not say what became of them. This is the first mention I have seen of these two brothers.

137. *The Spanish Cockpit*, 274–75.

138. For example, Brome, 143; David T. Cattell, *Communism and the Spanish Civil War*, 130–31; Thomas (1965), 455.

139. *The Spanish Cockpit*, 275. For a critical analysis of Borkenau's version see Colodny, 215–16.

140. Verbal evidence from Carlos Contreras, from the British Communist, journalist, and writer Claud Cockburn (alias Frank Pitcairn), and from Gabriel García Maroto of the General Commissariat of War.

141. When questioned by me after the war. Rojo himself refers to Kléber's dismissal, but does not state why or by whom he was dismissed (*Así fué la defensa de Madrid*, 223).

142. Fischer, *Men and Politics*, 405. See also *Pod znamenem*, 463, n. 4.

Chapter 31

1. See Stanley Weintraub, *The Last Great Cause*, 235; also Fischer, *Men and Politics*, 412, 427.

2. *Men and Politics*, 395, 398. Fischer reaffirmed this view in 1969, twenty-eight years later (*Russia's Road from Peace to War*, 278).

3. Personal conversation.

4. It is noteworthy that Gorev's tank commander, General Pavlov, who apparently was not liquidated until 1941, is referred to several times in the diary under the Spanish pseudonym of "Del Pablo" ("Ispanskii Dnevnik," *Novyi Mir*, June 1938, 53, 78–79, 87), but there is no reference to Gorev even under an assumed name. When published in book form in 1957, after Stalin's death, as volume 3 of *Izbrannye proizvedeniia* (Selected Works), the diary still contained no reference to Gorev, but then it was not until the 1960s that Soviet works revealed the true names of many Soviet officers who had served in Spain.

5. See "Ispanskii Dnevnik," *Novyi Mir*, June 1938, 33–34, 37.

6. *Eve of War, 1933–41*, 146. For other accounts of Gorev, see Arturo Barea, *The Forging of a Rebel*, 628–30; Enrique Castro, *Hombres made in Moscú*, 453–54; Fischer, *Men and Politics*, 363, 395, 398; O. Savich (Tass correspondent in Spain from 1937 to 1939), *Dva goda v Ispanii, 1937–1939*, 138.

7. *Así fué la defensa de Madrid*, 31, 214–15. According to Rojo, Gorev was a colonel, but was promoted to the rank of general before leaving Spain (ibid., 214). However, two Soviet officers (N. Voronov, who reached Madrid in October 1936, and Rodion Malinovsky, who arrived in December 1936 or January 1937) refer to Gorev as a brigadier general at the time of their arrival (*Pod znamenem ispanskoi respubliki*, 72, 146).

8. For example, Pierre Broué and Emile Témime, *La révolution et la guerre d'Espagne*, 346, n. 8; Robert Colodny, *The Struggle for Madrid*, 165; Gabriel Jackson, *The Spanish Republic and the Civil War, 1931–1939*, 319.

9. *Bortsy Latvii v Ispanii, 1936–1939*, 516; Ilya Ehrenburg, *Eve of War, 1933–41*, 152, 176; Alexander Orlov, *The Secret History of Stalin's Crimes*, 235. It is strange indeed that the unusually well-informed Koltzov, in a conversation with Louis Fischer in Madrid at the end of October 1936, did not identify Ian K. Berzin, the top Soviet military adviser correctly. "One evening," writes Fischer, "Mikhail Koltzov took me to dinner in the special Soviet restaurant in Madrid's elegant Palace Hotel. It was unusually full. Soviet military personnel had arrived—all dressed in ill-fitting, Moscow-made

blue serge suits. 'Who,' Koltzov asked, 'is the top officer here? Guess.' I indicated a tall, gaunt man with a thick mat of gray hair. 'No,' Koltzov corrected, 'that's General Jan [Ian] Berzin. The commanding general is this one,' and he nodded in the direction of a shorter person with a ruddy, kindly face and silver hair. I subsequently met him, General 'Grishin,' in the headquarters of the Spanish General Staff" (*Russia's Road from Peace to War*, 277–78).

10. *Pod znamenem*, 145–46 (article by Marshal Malinovsky, in which he mentions Gorev's dual capacity); ibid., 74–75 (photographs of Gorev and Berzin, captioned "Soviet military attaché in Spain" and "Principal military adviser," respectively); Nikolai G. Kuznetsov (Soviet naval attaché and adviser to the Spanish Republican fleet in 1936–37), *Na dalekom meridiane*, 232, and *Bortsy Latvii v Ispanii, 1936–1939*, 407. Actually Walter Krivitsky, (*In Stalin's Secret Service*, 96), the Soviet defector, had revealed as far back as 1939 that Ian Berzin was the top military adviser in Spain, but the Communist offensive denouncing him as an imposter undermined his evidence at the time. For additional information on Berzin, see *Bortsy Latvii*, 7, 407–10, 422, 426, 516–17; David Dallin, *Soviet Espionage*, 4, 5, 16, 46–47.

11. *Soviet Espionage*, 4–5. The *Sovetskaia voennaia entsiklopediia* (Soviet Military Encyclopedia), vol. 1 (1976) and the *Bolshaia sovetskaia entsiklopediia* (Great Soviet Encyclopedia), vol. 3, 3rd edition (1979) state that Berzin's service with Soviet military intelligence began in April 1921, that he was its chief from 1924 to 1935 and from July 1937 to November 1937. Only the first of these two volumes states that in 1936–37 he was head military adviser to the Spanish government. For further information on Berzin, see *Radio Liberty Research*, 2 Feb. 1979, 3, 15. For information on the GRU, see John Barron, *KGB*, 343–45; Richard Deacon, *A History of the Russian Secret Service*, 223–25; Peter Deriabin, *Watchdogs of Terror*, 215; and *McGraw-Hill Encyclopedia of Russia and the Soviet Union*, 245–46.

12. See review by General P. Batov of the Soviet book *Ia ne boius'ne byt'* (Moscow: Politizdat, 1982) in *Pravda*, 27 March 1983.

13. *Witness*, 398–99.

14. See Castro, *Hombres*, 456–58; Castro, *J'ai perdu la foi à Moscou*, 124; Carlo Penchienati (commander of the Garibaldi Brigade), *Brigate internazionali in Spagna*, 34; *Pod znamenem*, 146.

15. *Pod znamenem*, article by Marshal Malinovsky, 161.

16. Ibid., article by Voronov, 74.

17. Ibid., article by Major General of Aviation G. Prokofiev, 537. For additional information on Smushkevich and his successor, E. S. Ptukhin, see Dmitrii Ia. Zilmanovich, *Na orbite bolshoi zhizni*, 174, 178, 262, 282–83.

18. These were the reasons they both gave me after the war. The same reasons are also given by Hidalgo de Cisneros in his *Memorias*, II, 315, 317, who informed me that he joined the party January 1937. For Constancia de la Mora's entering the party, see ibid., 330, and obituary in *Mundo Obrero* (Paris), 9 Feb. 1950. Hidalgo de Cisneros was promoted from colonel to general by Juan Negrín in September 1938 (see *Gaceta de la República*, 14 Sept. 1938, and *Frente Rojo*'s laudatory article, 15 Sept. 1938).

19. *Nuestra guerra*, 100.

20. *Pod znamenem*, 537.

21. Zilmanovich, 178.

22. Ehrenburg, *Eve of War, 1933–41*, 152; *Who Was Who in the USSR*, 512; Louis Fischer in the *Nation*, 13 Jan. 1940.

23. Nikita Khrushchev, *Speech at a Session of the 20th Congress of the Communist Party of the Soviet Union on February 25, 1956*, 31.

24. *Eve of War, 1933–41*, 152.

25. *Russia's Road*, 300. See also Robert Conquest, *The Great Terror*, 230.

26. Ehrenburg, *Eve of War, 1933–41*, 166, 290, 202.

27. See Patricia Cockburn, *The Years of the Week*, 208. Patricia's husband, Claud, was one of Koltzov's closest friends (ibid.).

28. P. 290.

29. P. 597. Efimov gives the date of his brother's death as 4 March 1942 (ibid.) as opposed to 4 April 1942 given by *Who Was Who in the USSR*.

30. II, 484.

31. *Men and Politics*, 494–95. It is probable that Koltzov, who had for a time enjoyed Stalin's confidence, may have incurred his disfavor partly because of his arrogant self-assurance. Koltzov himself told his brother Boris Efimov after an audience he had with Stalin in 1937 before his final recall to Moscow: " 'Do you know what I read in the eyes of the boss, when I prepared to leave. . . ?' 'What?' 'I read: He has too much nerve.' " During the audience the following "strange conversation" took place. " 'Do you have a revolver, Comrade Koltzov?' . . . 'Yes, I have, Comrade Stalin,' I answered, astonished. 'But you are not preparing to shoot yourself?' 'Of course not,' I answered even more astonished, 'and I have no intention of doing so.' 'Well, that's excellent!' he said, 'excellent!' " (Beliaev, *Mikhail Koltsov: Kakim on byl: vospominaniia* [article by Efimov], 66). I am grateful to Robert Conquest for having brought this rare book to my attention.

32. Ibid., 302.

33. Patricia Cockburn (Cockburn's wife) recalls: "[Claud] knew that Koltzov was a man who had a reckless kind of arrogance in expressing his opinions. Above all, he had a reckless and savagely biting sense of humour. He never even tried to restrain his love of satire. And these qualities, as Claud had seen in Spain, made him a fresh crop of enemies almost every week. In Claud's opinion these qualities were in themselves quite enough to get a man shot in the climate of Moscow in 1939" (Patricia Cockburn, 262).

34. *A Discord of Trumpets*, p. 304–5. For further data on Koltzov, see General Heinz Hoffman, *Mannheim. Madrid. Moscau* (published in East Germany), 378–79; A. Rubashkin, *Mikhail Koltsov*, and *Molodoi Leningrad*, 386–92, for Rubashkin's review of Koltzov's diary, in which he points out that the Mexican Communist, Miguel Martínez, mentioned frequently in the diary, is in reality Koltzov.

35. P. 67. According to the same source, he was posthumously rehabilitated.

36. Vol. 1, 1976.

37. Vol. 3, 3d ed., 1970.

38. *Eve of War, 1933–41*, 176, 190.

39. I am indebted to Robert Conquest's *The Great Terror*, 231, for bringing this issue of *Komsomolskaya Pravda* to my attention. In an article by S. Goliakov and V. Ponizovskii, the writers say simply, "Today we observe the seventy-fourth birthday of Ian K. Berzin, whose life was ended twenty-seven years ago [1937] by Beria's hirelings."

40. P. 410.

41. Krivitsky, 114.

42. Although the functions of the OGPU were transferred to the NKVD in 1934, the NKVD was for some still commonly referred to as the OGPU or GPU.

43. Krivitsky, 96–97, 106–7.

44. Ibid., 113–14. See also Elisabeth K. Poretsky, *Our Own People*, 211–13.

45. The following allegation by Elisabeth Poretsky, the wife of Ignace Reiss, the slain NKVD operative, is worth recording: "It was the job of Orlov-Nikolsky, NKVD commandant in Spain, to see that anyone Moscow wanted returned alive got there. Soviet ships were standing by in the harbour of Barcelona to take those who were needed to Moscow or to dispose at sea of those who were not" (Poretsky, 193).

46. *Eve of War, 1933–41*, 190.

47. Fischer, *Men and Politics*, 392.

48. Kuznetsov, 32.

49. *The Secret History of Stalin's Crimes*, 235–36. The only reference I have been able to find in Soviet sources to either of these two officers is a brief mention in Savich, 136, who states that Valua and Petrovich were "the chief advisers" on the Madrid front in 1937. In 1940, Manuel Schwarzmann, a Rumanian volunteer, who served under the Russians in the DECCA, the antiaircraft defense unit on the Madrid front, informed me that Valua, a colonel, was responsible for the organization of the Guadalajara counteroffensive launched in March 1937 that resulted in the rout of the Italian forces supporting General Franco.

50. *Bol'shaia sovetskaia entsiklopediia*, 3d ed., vol. 5, 1971; *Sovetskaia voennaia entsiklopediia*, vol. 2, 1976; Seweryn Bialer, *Stalin and His Generals*, 639.

51. The *Sovetskaia voennaia entsiklopediia*, vol. 4, 1977, states that he was born in 1890 and died on 24 August 1950; that in 1940 he was promoted to the rank of marshal; that in March 1942 he held

the position of major general [presumably a demotion], and that in 1957 [four years after the death of Stalin] was restored posthumously to the rank of marshal. For further information on Kulik, see also Bialer, 633.

52. *Prominent Personalities in the USSR*, 341; *Bol'shaia sovetskaia entsiklopediia*, vol. 13, 1973; Bialer, 633–34.

53. Pp. 512, 520, 466. The *Bol'shaia sovetskaia entsiklopediia* gives the date of Shtern's and Smushkevich's deaths as 28 Oct. 1941 (3d ed., vol. 29, 1978, and vol. 23, 1976, respectively). According to Louis Fischer, General Maximov, Shtern's successor, who helped direct the victorious Ebro offensive in the summer of 1938, was arrested after his return to Russia (*Nation*, 13 Jan. 1940).

54. *The Aim of a Lifetime*, 79.

55. Both the *Bol'shaia sovetskaia entsiklopediia* (vol. 23, 1976) and the *Sovetskaia voennaia entsiklopediia* (vol. 7, 1979) give the promotions and the date of Smushkevich's death, but do not state how he died.

56. *Eve of War, 1933–41*, 176. Ehrenburg does not mention the date of Pavlov's death, but the *Bol'shaia sovetskaia entsiklopediia*, 3d ed., vol. 19, 1975, and the *Sovetskaia voennaia entsiklopediia*, vol. 6, 1978, both give the date as July 1941, but do not explain the cause of his death. Bialer, 635, says he was "accused of treason and shot."

57. *Pod znamenem*, 275, 313, 446–47, 483, 485, 503. See also the *Bol'shaia sovetskaia entsiklopediia*, 3d ed., vol. 3, 1970, for Batov, and vol. 22, 1975, for Rodimtsev.

58. For information on Malinovsky and Meretskov, see *Who Was Who in the USSR*, 365; *Prominent Personalities in the USSR*, 403; Bialer, 634–35; *Bol'shaia sovetskaia entsiklopediia*, vols. 15, 16, 1974; *Sovetskaia voennaia entsiklopediia*, vol. 5, 1978.

59. See his memoirs, *Na sluzhbe narodu*, 130, 136, 141, 143, 166. See also P. Ia Egorov, *Marshal Meretskov*, 40–52.

60. According to the Soviet journalist Egor Iakovlev, who interviewed Mamsurov many years later, Mamsurov told him that at the urging of Koltzov he spent three days giving Hemingway information on his activities in Spain for the novel *For Whom the Bell Tolls* (*Piat istori iz piati stran*, Moscow, 1968, as given in *Carta del Este*, 16 Sept. 1978). In the same issue, *Carta del Este* quotes at length the portions of the interview that specifically deal with Hemingway, 10–13).

61. *Eve of War, 1933–41*, 154. See also *Guerra y revolución en España, 1936–1939*, II, 174, and n. 2, which states: "On arriving in Madrid, Buenaventura Durruti [the famous Anarchist leader who had transferred his men from the Aragon front to assist in the defense of Madrid] asked for a Soviet adviser. The war ministry granted his request and appointed Mamsurov Jadjji-Umar, an officer from the Caucasus." Pavel Batov (the Soviet officer who fought in Spain) wrote many years later: "In Spain, our dear Ksanti (the name by which he was known there) helped the defenders of the Republic to set up espionage and counterespionage services. Unfortunately, the moment has not yet arrived to speak openly about his activities. But when it does arrive, people will be amazed and delighted that personalities like Ksanti live among us" (*V pokhodakh i boiakh*, 15). I am indebted to *Carta del Este*, 16 Sept. 1978, for bringing this valuable book to my attention. The same issue of *Carta del Este*, which refers to Egor Iakovlev's interview with Mamsurov (see previous note), says in connection with the death of Durruti that during the interview Mamsurov insisted "time and again" on his innocence and affirmed that Durruti was assassinated by "them," alluding "undoubtedly to the Anarchists." *Carta del Este*, which was published in Madrid for several years, was edited by Gabriel Amiama who, as a child, was sent to Russia during the Civil War, but managed to leave the country after World War II.

62. Regler gives the name of Maximovich as the leader of the Russian delegation. This may have been a pseudonym as I have not found any reference to a Maximovich in Spain in February 1937. There was a General Maximov, who succeeded Shtern (Grigorovich) as the highest Soviet adviser (see Fischer, *Men and Politics*, 543), but that was not until 1938.

63. *The Owl of Minerva*, 294–95.

64. Ibid., 292–93. As the journalist Philip Knightly points out, Hemingway, as a war correspondent, never wrote a word in his dispatches of what he knew about Marty's spy mania and executions. "In the end, Hemingway did write it all, in *For Whom the Bell Tolls*, but from a war correspondent the reader has the right to expect all the news the correspondent knows at the time, not as interpolations in a work of romantic fiction published when the war is over. The truth was that Hemingway, for all his

compassion for the Spaniards, for all his commitment to the Republican cause, used the war to gain a new lease on his life as a writer. As Baker [Carlos Baker, Hemingway's biographer] says, 'Refusing to waste the best of his materials in his newspaper dispatches . . . he had gathered and salted away a body of experience and information which he described . . . as 'absolutely invaluable.' For a novelist, this was understandable. For a war correspondent, it was unforgiveable" (*The First Casualty*, 213–14).

65. Generalnyi Shtab RKKA, *Upravlenie voiskami i rabota shtabov v ispanskoi respublikanskoi armii*, 125.

66. Essay by Julián Gorkin in Jeane J. Kirkpatrick, *The Strategy of Deception*, 196. John Dos Passos, who visited Spain during the Civil War, wrote some years later: "It was in the Spanish operation that the pattern laid down for infiltration, subversion and seizure of power . . . was used to such victorious effect in Czechoslovakia and in China a few years later" (*The Theme Is Freedom*, 151).

67. P. 444.

68. A photostatic copy of the original letter in French is reproduced in *Guerra y revolución*, II, between 102 and 103.

69. Letter of 21 December 1936.

70. *Actas de las sesiones de la junta de defensa de Madrid*, 422–23, Library of Congress, and Julio Aróstegui and Jesús A. Martínez, 310.

71. When interviewed by me in Mexico in 1940. Shorthand notes in Hoover Institution.

72. *The Last Days of Madrid*, 54. See also ibid., 55–57; Casado's article in the *National Review*, July 1939; and Largo Caballero, *Mis recuerdos*, 206.

73. Justo Martínez Amutio, the Socialist governor of Albacete, headquarters of the International Brigades and training center of the new mixed brigades, writes: "There was blatant discrimination among the recently organized units of the army in the distribution of war material. . . . It was natural that the effects of this discrimination went beyond the units involved and provoked suspicion and rivalry as well as political confrontations when it was confirmed that only units commanded by Communists received preferential treatment. . . . [We] had to intercede in conflicts, sometimes violent ones, caused by this blatant discrimination and favoritism. The great blackmail that would be used by the Communist Party of Spain to achieve its exaggerated growth and hegemony had begun" (*Chantage a un pueblo*, 54–55). Alejandro García Val, Communist party member who was made chief of the transport section of the general staff in November 1936, told me after the war that when Russian trucks reached Spain he organized with the aid of party members and sympathizers in the UGT the first three militarized motor transport battalions composed of six hundred vehicles and three thousand men.

74. For non-Communist praise of Spanish Communist units, see, for example, *Política* (organ of the Left Republican party), 11 Nov. 1936, and Colonel Segismundo Casado (whom no one can accuse of being partial to the Communists), *The Last Days of Madrid* 96, who says that there were "plenty of communist units which distinguished themselves by their impetuous fighting."

75. See, for example, Diego Abad de Santillán, *La revolución y la guerra en España*, 131–32.

76. See also Jesús Pérez Salas, *Guerra en España, 1936–1939*, 128, Julián Zugazagoitia, *Historia de la guerra en España*, 195, and Eduardo de Guzmán, *Madrid, rojo y negro* (director of the CNT organ in Madrid, *Castilla Libre*), 164, 200, who praises the courage, intelligence, discipline, and military skill of the International Brigades and gives full credit to the example they set to the Anarchosyndicalist militia on the Madrid front: "[Our men]," he commented, "observe them, and, with that wonderful power of adaptation the Spanish people possesses, they imitate them without losing any time."

77. 25 Nov. 1936.

78. *Politics, Economics and Men of Modern Spain, 1808–1946*, 599.

79. *Yo fui un ministro de Stalin*, 80.

80. *Hombres*, 457.

81. For Malinovsky, see *Who Was Who in the USSR*, 365.

82. *Pod znamenem*, 151.

83. See, for example, the official (Franco) history of the Civil War, Joaquín Arrarás, *Historia de la*

cruzada española, IV, 381, 391; *Política*, 23 Oct. 1936. When interviewed by me after the war, Captain Aniceto Carbajal, son-in-law of Pozas, stated that a few days after the February elections, when General Franco was still chief of the general staff, he tried through his intermediary to purchase Pozas's support for a "National Government" by offering him a sum of money deposited in a Swiss bank.

84. See speech by Jerónimo Bujeda, *El Socialista*, 19 July 1937.

85. Louis Fischer, who was in a position to know, stated in 1937, when still a Communist supporter, that Pozas was a member of the party (*Why Spain Fights On*, 39). In his dogged attempt to manipulate the facts, Julio Aróstegui ignores this troublesome evidence (see his essay in Manuel Tuñon de Lara, *La guerra civil española: 50 años después*, 72) just as he ignores similarly bothersome evidence in the case of General Miaja.

86. See Pérez Salas, 141–42; Zugazagoitia, 406.

87. According to Alejandro García Val, Communist member of the general staff, when interviewed by me in Mexico in 1939.

88. Pérez Salas, 146–47.

89. *La flota republicana y la guerra civil de España*, 38.

90. Martín Blázquez, 241.

91. *Common Sense*.

92. *The Theme Is Freedom*, 127–29.

93. Ibid., 130. For the effect of the Civil War on the friendship between Hemingway and Dos Passos, see John P. Diggins, *Up from Communism*, 88–90.

94. Quoted in Julián Gorkin, *Caníbales políticos*, 217. In an article in *Francisco Largo Caballero, 1869–1946*, 74, Federica Montseny, a cabinet colleague, refers to his "unipersonal" conception of power.

95. An employee in the war ministry who was in intimate contact with José María Aguirre, Largo Caballero's politicomilitary secretary, informed me that the relations between the Russian officers and Largo Caballero became very bad after December 1936 and that the Russians were particularly concerned about the political orientation of the army.

96. *El comunismo y la guerra de España*, 10.

97. *Hoy*, 5 Dec. 1942.

98. P. 190. Even the latest edition of the *Bolshaia sovetskaia entsiklopediia* contains no reference to any of them.

99. *Obras*, IV, 701.

100. Ibid., 711.

101. Vittorio Vidali, *Diary of the Twentieth Congress of the Communist Party of the Soviet Union*, 137.

102. My own personal judgment during a luncheon interview in March 1937, arranged for me by Mirova, the Tass news agency representative, herself a later victim, as has been noted, of Stalin's purges.

103. Speech in the *Centro Republicano Español* (Mexico City), 29 Mar. 1946, as given in *Adelante* (Mexico City), 1 Apr. 1936.

104. See *Fragua Social*, 6, 9, 18 Mar. 1937.

105. José Díaz, *Tres años de lucha*, 377–79. See also declaration by La Pasionaria as reported in *El Socialista*, 11 Mar. 1937.

Chapter 32

1. 27 Oct. 1936.

2. Speech, reported by *Fragua Social*, 18 Oct. 1936.

3. 11 Feb. 1937.

4. As given in *Solidaridad Obrera*, 12 May 1936.

5. 5 Aug. 1936.

6. Speech reported in *CNT*, 12 Sept. 1936.

7. Speech in January 1937 reprinted in *En marcha hacia la victoria*, 51.

8. Resolution approved at a plenary meeting of representatives of the regional committees of the CNT, as given in *CNT*, 17 Sept. 1936.

9. "We failed to transform as rapidly as we should have done the spontaneous columns of the first days into regularly organized units. Positions were lost by us and taken by the Communists" (Mariano Vázquez, secretary of the national committee of the CNT, speaking at an AIT congress, reported in supplement of *Espagne Nouvelle*, 15 Mar. 1939).

10. *Internacional*, June 1938.

11. Speech at Valencia CNT congress, November 1936, reported by *Fragua Social*, 17 Nov. 1936.

12. Ibid.

13. Indeed, this was the opinion given to me by Gabriel García Maroto, a friend of Alvarez del Vayo, who became a member of the new body (interview in Mexico in 1939).

14. *Gaceta de la República*, 10 Nov. 1936.

15. Ibid.

16. In a demonstration held on 14 February 1937, the Communists in a ten-point petition presented to Largo Caballero demanded inter alia that the Higher War Council should be allowed to fulfill "the mission for which it was created," and two weeks later their organ, *Frente Rojo*, urged that it "should meet methodically and as often as necessary for discussing and reaching agreement upon all questions of war," among which it included "the appointment and control of officers and the cleansing of the army of all hostile and incapable elements" (quoted in *Mundo Obrero*, 2 Mar. 1937).

17. *Fragua Social*, 19 Nov. 1936.

18. Eduardo de Guzmán, *Madrid, rojo y negro*, 200.

19. *Fragua Social*, 14 Nov. 1936.

20. "Unpublished Article by a Regular Army Corporal" (Hoover Institution, Bolloten Collection).

21. *Mi desembarco en Mallorca*, 113–14. After the Civil War, Bayo, a Cuban, emigrated to Mexico, where he became an instructor at the School of Military Aviation. In 1956, at the request of Fidel Castro, who was then in Mexico organizing his forces, Bayo began to train the men who would invade Cuba in guerrilla warfare (see Fidel Castro, *Revolutionary Struggle, 1947–1958*, I, 78–79, and Mario Llerena, *The Unsuspected Revolution*, 206).

22. *Solidaridad Obrera*, 1 Dec. 1936.

23. *CNT* (Madrid), 20 Sept. 1937. See also his proclamation to the Anarchosyndicalist militia on the Madrid front, published in *Castilla Libre*, 17 Feb. 1937.

24. Pp. 107–9. See also 109–11, 113, 116.

25. *Así fué la defensa de Madrid*, 115–17.

26. 14 Jan. 1937.

27. Guzmán, *Madrid, rojo y negro*, 200. See also the Anarchist Ricardo Sanz, *Los que fuimos a Madrid*, 108–9, for the example set by the International Brigades. Despite this tribute to the brigades, there was considerable resentment and hostility in the libertarian movement as well as fear that they would strengthen the hand of the Communists. Diego Abad de Santillán claims that the CNT and FAI turned back more than a thousand volunteers at the Catalan-French border, who had to be shipped to Spanish ports controlled by the central government (*Por qué perdimos la guerra*, 175). See also Abad de Santillán, *La revolución y la guerra en España*, 133. In a letter to me in 1940, Ralph Bates, assistant commissar of the Fifteenth International Brigade, stated that frequently the volunteers who crossed the border into Catalonia had to travel in trains with drawn blinds (Hoover Institution). "We considered it an injustice and a crime," wrote Abad de Santillán, "to leave our militiamen—whose bravery and fighting spirit are unparalleled—without arms and, simultaneously, to form large foreign combat units equipped with everything and treated with special consideration" (*Por qué*, 175).

28. *CNT*, 23 Feb. 1937.

29. *Mundo Obrero*, as given in *Fragua Social*, 26 Sept. 1937.

30. *Bulletin de la Généralité de la Catalogne* (issued by the Propaganda Department of the Catalan government), 30 Mar. 1937, as quoted in *Le Libertaire*, 8 Apr. 1937. See also Máximo Llorca in *Ideas*, 29 Apr. 1937.

31. See speech by Mariano Vázquez, secretary of the national committee of the CNT, published in Confederación Regional del Trabajo de Cataluña, *Memoria del congreso extraordinario de la confederación regional del trabajo de Cataluña celebrado en Barcelona los días 25 de febrero al 3 de marzo de 1937*, 178–85.

32. *Fragua Social*, 1 June 1937.

33. That the Anarchosyndicalists were in a minority was emphasized by Mariano Vázquez in a speech published in Confederación Regional del Trabajo de Cataluña, *Memoria del congreso extraordinario*, 178–85.

34. Reply to a questionnaire sent to García Oliver at my request by the German Anarchist Agustín Souchy. The reply, dated 23 August 1949, is in my file of correspondence with Souchy (Hoover Institution).

35. *I Helped to Build an Army*, 299. In his book, Cordón, a Communist, also speaks highly of García Oliver's work in the officers' training schools (*Trayectoria*, 282).

36. See, for example, *CNT*, 28 Apr. 1937.

37. Ibid., 10 Apr. 1937.

38. As given in J. García Pradas, *Antifascismo proletario*, 46.

39. Máximo Llorca, in *Ideas*, 29 Apr. 1937.

40. *La tragedia del norte*, 135.

41. *CNT*, 1 Mar. 1937.

42. *Cipriano Mera, revolucionario*, 60.

43. Two Republican officers confirm this: Martín Blázquez, 295, and Segismundo Casado (article in *National Review*, July 1939), who, while criticizing the mixed brigades on technical grounds, says: "[The government] committed the very serious initial mistake of accepting the opinion of the 'friendly Russian advisers.'" In his book, Casado, who was appointed to organize the first brigades, writes: "One Russian general and two Russian colonels were chosen to help me in this mission by order of the minister [Largo Caballero]" (*The Last Days of Madrid*, 52).

44. Martín Blázquez, 297.

45. A short account of the military reasons for the creation of mixed brigades is given by Martín Blázquez, 293–95. For a criticism on technical grounds, see Colonel Segismundo Casado in *National Review*, July 1939.

46. A typewritten copy of this report, the original of which was loaned to me by Ruediger, is in the Hoover Institution.

47. *Elementos distinados al pleno de la AIT del 11 de junio de 1937 en vista de la discusión sobre la situación española*, as given in *Guerra y revolución en España, 1936–1939*, III, 63, n. 1.

48. In letters to me (see file, Hoover Institution).

49. Hoover Institution, Bolloten Collection.

50. Although officially the organ of the Valencia FAI and unofficially the organ of the Valencia Libertarian Youth, *Nosotros* was also the mouthpiece of the Iron Column by virtue of the help these two organizations received in money and men from the column (see César M. Lorenzo, *Les anarchistes espagnols et le pouvoir, 1868–1969*, 187). Abraham Guillén, the director of *Nosotros*, became the theoretician of the Tupamaros, the urban guerrilla organization in Uruguay, in the 1960s.

51. 11 Feb. 1937.

Chapter 33

1. *Fragua Social*, 14 Nov. 1936.

2. In his book *Anarquismo y revolución en la sociedad rural aragonesa, 1936–1938*, 106–7, Julián Casanova Ruiz argues that the Iron Column was less hostile to the state than described by me in *El gran engaño* (1975), in which I use exactly the same phraseology that I employ here. Unfortunately, he bases his argument on a gross misinterpretation of an editorial in the Madrid newspaper *CNT*, which was reproduced on 5 October 1936 in *Linea de Fuego*, the mouthpiece of the column. Contrary to what Casanova affirms, the editorial does not advocate the participation of the CNT in the central government, but in a national council of defense, which was proposed as a *substitute* for the government. The reader may recall that in September and October 1936 the CNT was waging a vigorous campaign for the creation of a national council, but because of Largo Caballero's opposition reversed its stand and joined the government at the beginning of November. I have reconsulted all available issues of *Linea de Fuego* and have found nothing to justify modifying my description of the Iron Column. Curiously enough, Casanova, who delivers a gratuitous lecture to historians on the "extraordinary value" of such primary sources as *Linea de Fuego*, not only flagrantly misinterprets the

CNT editorial reproduced in its issue of 5 October but also fails to note that on 5 November 1936 the paper virulently attacked the CNT leaders for entering the government.

3. *Fragua Social*, 14 Nov. 1936.

4. This was the figure given by an Iron Column delegate at a CNT congress, reported in ibid.; see also José Martín Blázquez, *I Helped to Build an Army*, 296.

5. *Nosotros*, 16 Feb. 1937.

6. This was admitted to me by a Valencia Anarchosyndicalist who had been in close contact with members of the column.

7. In a letter to me, dated 21 April 1951, Federica Montseny, who was a member of the national committee of the CNT, emphasizes this friction and states that the Valencia CNT demanded that the column should purge itself of the malefactors in its ranks (Hoover Institution).

8. 4 Nov. 1936. See n. 2 above.

9. This information was given to me by a well-informed member of the Valencia CNT.

10. As given in *Cultura Proletaria*, 7 Nov. 1936.

11. Rafael Abella, *La vida cotidiana durante la guerra civil: La España republicana*, 111. See also Adolfo Bueso, *Recuerdos de un cenetista*, II, 220.

12. Cited by Abella, 111.

13. Carlos Llorens, *La guerra en Valencia y en el frente de Teruel*, 50–51.

14. 5 Nov. 1936.

15. Martín Blázquez, 296.

16. Report to the General Commissariat of War, dated 18 February 1937 (Hoover Institution, Bolloten Collection).

17. This was confirmed to me by Rodolfo Llopis, Largo Caballero's undersecretary in the premiership in his reply to a questionnaire (Hoover Institution). See also Francisco Largo Caballero, *La UGT y la guerra*, 10–11.

18. See statement published in *Nosotros*, 2 Jan. 1937.

19. Ibid., 16 Feb. 1937.

20. *Diario Oficial del Ministerio de la Guerra*, as given in *La Correspondencia de Valencia*, 3 Mar. 1937.

21. Martín Blázquez, 323.

22. Ibid.

23. *El Pueblo*, 13 Mar. 1937. For an account of the events by the national committee of the CNT, see *Boletín de Información y Orientación Orgánica del Comité Peninsular de la Federación Anarquista Ibérica*, 1 May 1937. Although neither of these reports mentioned the role of the Iron Column in the events, its members were, as everyone knew at the time, among the principal participants.

24. 23 Mar. 1937.

25. Issued 6 Mar. 1937; published in *Nosotros*, 9 Mar. 1937.

26. *Frente Rojo*, 19 Mar. 1937.

27. 12–13, 15–17 Mar. 1937.

28. In Spanish the second person singular is used for familiar address.

29. See *Nosotros*, 24 Mar. 1937.

30. Ibid., 27 Mar. 1937.

31. When interviewed by me early in 1937, a few weeks after his arrival in Spain, Siqueiros stated: "I shall not paint another picture until the war is over, because I consider that . . . my military experience is more valuable to Spain at this time than my talent. . . . If Franco were to win, his victory would give tremendous moral support to those reactionary forces in Mexico who wish to destroy the social gains the masses have won in twenty-six years of fighting. I therefore believe that by fighting for Spain, I am fighting for Mexico. Mexico is the vanguard of Latin American countries. . . . A victory here would give a tremendous boost . . . to all the progressive revolutionary forces in the whole of Latin America." Taken from my shorthand notes, Hoover Institution.

32. *Me llamaban el coronelazo (memorias)*, 322–23.

Chapter 34

1. Hoover Institution, Bolloten Collection. Other important documentation on the Malaga disaster can be found in the International Institute of Social History, CNT-FAI Archives, Paquete 63, Documentación General. 1. Asuntos Especiales. 1. Malaga. Photocopies are in the Bolloten Collection.

2. I, 803–57.

3. Pp. 139–242.

4. Antonio Cordón, *Trayectoria*, 293. See also 264, 292–95.

5. The text of the indictment against Villalba is reproduced in Martínez Bande, *La campaña de Andalucía*, 218–24. Justo Martínez Amutio, an intimate of Largo Caballero's, alleges that Cayetano Bolívar, the Communist deputy for Malaga and chief political commissar on the Malaga front, was largely responsible for the disaster in that "he interfered in military plans" by "instigating capriciously the removal of officers and chiefs who did not belong to the Communist party" (*Chantaje a un pueblo*, 155).

6. *La Vanguardia*, 3 Nov. 1938. At the outbreak of the Civil War, Colonel Villalba was commander of the Barbastro garrison in Aragon. His failure to join the military revolt was a heavy blow to Emilio Mola, the organizer of the conspiracy on the Peninsula, for it gave the CNT-FAI militia in the adjoining region of Catalonia sufficient time to occupy a large part of Aragon. Mola later accused Villalba of having demanded 100,000 pesetas as his price for bringing his troops into the conspiracy (speech, Jan. 1937, in Mola, *Obras completas*, 1188), but although Iribarren, Mola's secretary, mentions this (Stanley G. Payne, *Politics and the Military in Modern Spain*, 508, n. 59), it is not, to my knowledge, corroborated by any other source. For further information on Villalba, see Cordón, 292–95, and Lieutenant Colonel Vicente Guarner, *Cataluña en la guerra de España, 1936–39*, 169–72.

7. Pp. 258–59. In a letter to Luis Araquistáin, dated 11 February 1937, Alvarez del Vayo claims that at 7 A.M. on the eighth, Negrín sent several trucks to Malaga to collect the silver believed to be there and that the trucks entered Malaga and did as they pleased without seeing the enemy anywhere (Araquistáin Papers, Leg. 23/A113[a]).

8. See editorials and speeches published in *Mundo Obrero*, *Verdad*, and *Milicia Popular* of the period.

9. "Ispanskii Dnevnik," *Novyi Mir*, June 1938, 71.

10. *Na sluzhbe narodu*, 134.

11. Cordón, 258.

12. Ibid. Cordón's testimony is supported by that of Margarita Nelken, a onetime staunch supporter of Largo Caballero: "[He] used to leave his office at 8:30 P.M. and return at 8:30 A.M. Meanwhile, it was impossible to communicate with him. . . . The undersecretaries never allowed it" (interview, 1940, Hoover Institution).

13. "Ispanskii Dnevnik," *Novyi Mir*, June 1938, 71.

14. *Gaceta de Madrid*, 30 Sept. 1937.

15. See article in *Claridad*, Largo Caballero's newspaper, 20 Aug. 1936.

16. Quoted in A. and D. Prudhommeaux, *Catalogne libertaire, 1936–1937*, 19–20. See also statements by the delegates of Puertollano and the Madrid Printers' Union at the CNT Plenum of the Central Region reported in *CNT*, 5 Oct. 1936.

17. Quoted by Máximo de Dios at a meeting of the Madrid Defense Council on 19 Feb. 1937 (*Actas de las sesiones de la junta de defensa de Madrid*). See also Julio Aróstegui and Jesús A. Martínez, *La junta de defensa de Madrid*, 403–4.

18. *Gaceta de Madrid*, 30 Oct. 1936.

19. *La Correspondencia de Valencia*, 11 Feb. 1937.

20. *Gaceta de la República*, 21 Feb. 1937. See also Jesús Hernández's statement to the press, published in *CNT*, 17 Feb. 1937.

21. Notice published in *Cultura y Acción*, 3 Mar. 1937.

22. *Diario Oficial del Ministerio de la Guerra*, 9 Mar. 1937.

23. *Fragua Social*, 16 Mar. 1937.

24. 21 Apr. 1937.

25. See, for example, Communist party statement issued after the fall of Malaga, *Frente Rojo*, 10 Feb. 1937; also ibid., 12 Feb. 1937.

26. *Hombres made in Moscú*, 489.

27. *Mis recuerdos*, 192–93.

28. Ibid., 193 and "Notas Históricas sobre la Guerra de España," 599–600; Baráibar, articles in *Timón* (Buenos Aires), June 1940, and *España Libre* (New York), 1 Jan. 1942; Wenceslao Carrillo, open letter to Indalecio Prieto, published in *Mundo*, Aug. 1943; Martínez Amutio, 214–16.

29. *Hoy*, 5 Dec. 1942.

30. "Notas Históricas," 599–600. Shortly after this incident, Moscow announced that Rosenberg had been appointed to a new post and would be succeeded by Leon Gaykis (see dispatch from Moscow reported in *CNT*, 20 Feb. 1937; also the *Times* [London], 22 Feb. 1937). He left for Moscow and disappeared without a trace.

31. *Mis recuerdos*, 193.

32. *Historia de la UGT de España, 1901–1939*, II, 636.

33. Ibid., 616.

34. Cordón, 296. See also ibid., 284, 292–93, 295.

35. A photostatic copy of his reply, in French, is reproduced in *Guerra y revolución en España, 1936–1939*, II, between 102 and 103.

36. Amaro del Rosal, the former Caballerista, writes: "The slogan of unification—of unity—was promoted before the war and in its early stage by Caballero and by the whole Caballero group, of which Araquistáin was the spiritual director" (*Historia de la UGT*, II, 629–30).

37. *El comunismo y la guerra de España*, 27–28. See also Largo Caballero, *Mis recuerdos*, 225–26.

38. See *Claridad*, 19 Mar. 1936; *La Libertad*, 4 Apr. 1936.

39. As published in *Claridad*, 12 Mar. 1936.

40. Speech in Madrid, 17 Oct. 1937, as reprinted in Francisco Largo Caballero, *La UGT y la guerra*, 41.

41. *Tribuna*, Mar. 1949. See also Rodolfo Llopis's speech, reported in *La Correspondencia de Valencia*, 13 Aug. 1937.

42. See article by Ginés Ganga in *Hoy*, 12 Dec. 1942; also Largo Caballero's speech in Madrid, Oct. 1937, as given in Largo Caballero, *La UGT*, 5, and Largo Caballero, *Mis recuerdos*, 225.

43. *Mis recuerdos*, 223–26. See also Largo Caballero, "Notas Históricas," 264–65, and Chapter 13, n. 57, above.

44. Personal recollection. How effective this campaign was among foreign journalists, who were for the most part totally unaware of the political struggle between Largo Caballero and the Communists, can be judged from the following comment by Philip Jordan, a contributor to the London *News Chronicle* and other publications, who passed through Valencia hurriedly on his way to Madrid in March 1937: "Two days later, my business was finished and I went to Madrid. I had shaken hands with that shabby myth, Largo Caballero, whose vanity did so much to dissipate the early strength of Republican Spain" (*There Is No Return*, 18).

45. *Hombres*, 489–90.

46. Ibid., 490.

47. In a letter to Largo Caballero, dated 7 October 1945, Luis Araquistáin refers to Llopis as "our very lazy friend" ("nuestro gran perezoso"). Araquistáin Papers, Leg. 75/12.

48. This unattractive portrayal of Aguirre is based on my personal knowledge of him, on information given to me by Ricardo del Río, the head of the Febus news agency in Valencia, who was in daily contact with him, and from the Communists and Socialists who knew him personally.

49. Araquistáin Papers, Leg. 23/A28[a]. An account of the acquisition of this private collection is given in Luis Araquistáin, *Sobre la guerra civil y en la emigración*, 14, n. 3. Tusell's work is a valuable digest of that part of the collection relating to the Civil War and the period of emigration. A catalog of the documents (organized under the direction of María Teresa de la Peña Marazuela) has been published under the title *Papeles de D. Luis Araquistáin Quevedo en el Archivo Histórico Nacional*, prólogo de Javier Tusell.

50. Speech in Madrid, Oct. 1937, as given in Largo Caballero, *La UGT y la guerra*, 5–6.

Chapter 35

1. *Freedom's Battle*, 126.

2. Ibid.

3. Letter dated 22 Aug. 1950 (Hoover Institution). After the war Juan García Oliver (one of the four CNT-FAI members of the cabinet), in reply to a question I posed through Agustín Souchy, claimed that the four Anarchosyndicalist ministers had voted in Asensio's favor. This of course runs counter to Montseny's honest admission to the contrary and to the hostile attitude of the entire CNT-FAI press.

4. 21 Feb. 1937.

5. *Gaceta de la República*, 21 Feb. 1937.

6. For attacks in CNT-FAI newspapers, see *Castilla Libre*, 19 Feb. 1937; *CNT*, 17 Feb. 1937; *Fragua Social*, 23 Feb. 1937; *Frente Libertario*, 16 Feb. 1937; *Solidaridad Obrera*, 20, 25, 27 Feb. 1937.

7. José Martín Blázquez, *I Helped to Build an Army*, 217. See also J. García Pradas, *¡Teníamos que perder!*, 196.

8. *Gaceta de la República*, 21 Feb. 1937.

9. Ibid., 23 Feb. 1937.

10. That he was a sympathizer was confirmed to me by Alejandro García Val, himself a Communist party member and adjutant of Major Manuel Estrada, the former chief of the general staff (interview, Mexico City in 1939).

11. *Gaceta de la República*, 21 Feb. 1937.

12. Martín Blázquez, 320. Cordón, *Trayectoria*, 296, affirms that the dismissals were a "form of reprisal" against the Communist party by Largo Caballero, "undoubtedly on the advice of the general [General Asensio]."

13. Martín Blázquez, 121; Segismundo Casado, *The Last Days of Madrid*, 49–50.

14. Interviewed by me in Mexico in 1939. See Jesús Pérez Salas, *Guerra en España, 1936–1939*, 147, who confirms Díaz-Tendero's pro-Communist activities later in the war. However, Cordón, 288, stresses the fact that he was not a Communist, by which he no doubt means a member of the party.

15. *The Spanish Revolution*, 321.

16. *Militares republicanos de la guerra de España*, 150.

17. Letter to me, dated 7 Dec. 1949 (Hoover Institution).

18. These were, according to the *Gaceta de la República*, 23 Feb. 1937, José Díaz Alor, Luis Barrero Hernando, Mariano Muñoz Sánchez, Carlos Hernández Zancajo, Manuel Arias Fernández, and Julio de Mora Martínez.

19. Specific reference was made to the general commissar (Alvarez del Vayo), the secretary general (Felipe Pretel), who were both secret Communist supporters, and to the subcommissars of war, the chief of whom was Antonio Mije, a member of the politburo of the Communist party.

20. See circular order published in the *Gaceta de la República*, 23 Feb. 1937.

21. See *Frente Rojo*, 24 Feb. 1937.

22. This information was given to me in Mexico in 1939 by Carlos Contreras (Vittorio Vidali), chief political commissar of the Fifth Regiment, who was well acquainted with Díaz-Tendero. The accuracy of this information was confirmed forty-four years later in a letter dated 28 Feb. 1937, from José María Aguirre, Largo Caballero's politicomilitary secretary, to Luis Araquistáin (Araquistáin Papers, Leg. 23/A28 [a]). These archives were not open to scholars until 1981. For a biographical essay on Díaz-Tendero, see Suero Roca, *Militares republicanos*, 143–60, who states that he joined the PCE in exile.

23. Letter to me, dated 16 Nov. 1949 (Hoover Institution).

24. Ibid.

25. *Adelante*, 24 Feb. 1937.

26. Ibid.

27. 25 Feb. 1937.

28. *La Correspondencia de Valencia*, 2 Mar. 1937.

29. 25 Feb. 1937.

30. *Claridad*, 28 Feb. 1937. See letter from Aguirre to Araquistáin, n. 22 above.

31. This information can be found both in *Claridad* and in Aguirre's letter to Araquistáin cited in n. 22 above.

32. See Confederación Regional del Trabajo de Cataluña, *Memoria del congreso de la confederación regional del trabajo de Cataluña celebrado en Barcelona los días 25 de febrero al 3 de marzo de 1937.*

33. Report to the AIT, dated 8 May 1937.

34. The text of the indictment is given in his book, *El General Asensio*, 29–62. This book in defense of his position was written in jail.

35. See his letters to Asensio, ibid., 110–11. In January 1939, Asensio was appointed military attaché in Washington (*Diario Oficial del Ministerio de Defensa Nacional*, 16 Jan. 1939). After his release from jail in May 1938, he was not given any military command by Juan Negrín, who was defense minister at the time.

36. As an example of Largo Caballero's concern for foreign opinion because of Communist influence in the army, see his speech, Oct. 1937, *La UGT y la guerra*, 16.

37. Ibid., 5.

38. *Adelante*, 13 Feb. 1937.

39. *Claridad*, 27 Feb. 1937.

40. Hernández, *El partido comunista antes, durante y después de la crisis del gobierno Largo Caballero*, 11.

41. See, for example, *Mundo Obrero*, 1 Mar. 1937.

42. *El Día Gráfico*, 28 Feb. 1937.

43. *Guerra y revolución en España, 1936–1939*, I, II, III.

44. Orlov, "Answers to the Questionnaire of Professor Stanley G. Payne," 15–16.

45. Claudín, *Santiago Carrillo*, 57.

46. *Yo fui un ministro de Stalin*, 66–71.

47. Orlov, "Answers to the Questionnaire of Professor Stanley G. Payne," 15–16. "Those familiar with Stalin's policy of manipulating the foreign communist parties (always through the machinery of the Comintern)," Orlov writes, "will recognize at once the absurdity of Hernández' assertion that two Soviet diplomats—Gaikis and I—were present at a Politburo meeting of the Spanish Communist Party." Hernández, it will be recalled, makes a special point of mentioning that they were attending such a meeting "for the first time."

48. *Yo fui un ministro de Stalin*, 90.

49. *Slavic Review*, June 1969 (letter to the editor). Elizabeth K. Poretsky, the wife of the NKVD operative Ignace Reiss, who was assassinated by Soviet agents in 1937, claims that there were two Alexander Orlovs in Spain in different capacities and that the one who defected to the United States, whom she says she met near Moscow in 1932, had worked with the Soviet commercial services in Valencia. As for the other Orlov, the NKVD chief, both she and Krivitsky, she asserts, were sure that he had been "ordered home to Moscow from Spain and shot there with the others" (*Our Own People*, 258–59 and n. 1). Her assertion, which is vague and entirely unsubstantiated, has nonetheless been given credence by some writers (see, for example, article by Ignacio Iglesias, "¿Existe un Misterio Orlov?," in *Historia y Vida*, Sept. 1976, who accepts Poretsky's version and elaborates upon it), but there is no doubt in my mind, after carefully studying Orlov's testimony before the U.S. Senate subcommittee and his published writings, that he was too well informed on the activities of the NKVD to have held only a minor post in the Soviet embassy in Valencia. Nor was there any doubt in the mind of Bertram D. Wolfe, who had numerous long, penetrating interviews with Orlov, that he was the high-level functionary he claimed to be (according to his widow, Ella Wolfe, who knew Orlov equally well; conversation with me in 1980).

50. *J'ai perdu la foi à Moscou*, 40. Unfortunately, I realized the importance of the description, which appeared as long ago as 1950, only thirty years later. This leaves the identity of the "tall, elegant, and polished" individual unestablished. Orlov and Belayev, to judge from the evidence available, worked in close cooperation, their names being linked together on three separate occasions, although the spelling of Belayev's name varies. Louis Fischer stated that, in September 1936, the Soviet ambassador in Madrid introduced him to "two Embassy secretaries, Orlov and Belayev," whom he guessed were "GPU [NKVD] men" (*Men and Politics*, 361); Julián Gorkin (a leader of the POUM, the anti-Stalinist Partido Obrero de Unificación Marxista), who was arrested in June 1937 on the orders of the NKVD, gives the name of the Russian next in rank to Orlov, as "Bielov" (*El proceso de Moscú en Barcelona*, 173), the source of his information being the former Communists Enrique Castro and Valentín González (letter from Gorkin to me, 9 Apr. 1977, Hoover Institution); and,

finally, Hernández refers to a certain "Vielayev," who, it would appear from the context, was intimately associated with Orlov (*Yo fui un ministro de Stalin*, 59, 90). Since Bielov and Vielayev are so close to Belayev in pronunciation, especially if we take into account the similarity in the sound of the Spanish *B* and *V*, there can be little doubt that they relate to the same person. The former Peruvian Communist Eudocio Ravines, who worked on the editorial staff of *Frente Rojo*, the Communist morning newspaper in Valencia, refers frequently in his book to a "Colonel Bielov" (known as General Popov) of the NKVD, whom he knew personally, but does not mention Orlov (*La gran estafa*, 338, 340, 346, 349, 358, 374–78). For his part, the Italian Communist Ettore Vanni, who was editor in chief of *Verdad*, the Communist evening newspaper in Valencia, refers to "comrade Veláiev, who kept an eye not only on all the functionaries in the [Soviet] Embassy, but, through his men of confidence, on the apparatus of the party leadership" (*Yo, comunista en Rusia*, 14), and Valentín González says that "Bielov" was one of the "principal components of the apparatus of the Comintern and the NKVD" (*Yo escogí la esclavitud*, 230).

51. *Yo fui un ministro de Stalin*, 90–94. There are references to Orlov by name also on 66, 89, 95–98, 109–13.

52. *Conversando con Togliatti*, 261.

53. Orlov, "Answers to the Questionnaire of Professor Stanley G. Payne," 16.

54. Palmiro Togliatti, *Escritos políticos*, prologue by Adolfo Sánchez Vázquez, 11.

55. *Yo fui un ministro de Stalin*, 33–36, 49, 79–84.

56. *Chantaje a un pueblo*, 245.

57. *El proceso*, 79–80, n. 7.

58. P. 191.

59. Palmiro Togliatti, *Escritos sobre la guerra de España*, 146.

60. *Yo fui un ministro de Stalin*, 66.

61. Date given in José Díaz, *Tres años de lucha*, 341.

62. *Yo fui un ministro de Stalin*, 73.

63. It should be noted that Hernández's speech of 7 March 1937 was mild as compared with the fierce onslaught on Caballero that he delivered on 28 May after the fall of the government. Hence, it is not unlikely that he had in mind the more vehement speech when writing his book many years later. The full text of the speeches can be found in Hernández, *Todo dentro del frente popular* and *El partido comunista*.

64. *Yo fui un ministro de Stalin*, 73.

65. Ibid., 85.

66. For this information I am indebted to the staff of the Febus news agency, which was in daily contact with persons having close relations with members of the government and the Higher War Council.

67. 2 Mar. 1937.

68. Largo Caballero, "Notas Históricas sobre la Guerra de España," 600–601. Cf. Largo Caballero, *Mis recuerdos*, 195. In a letter to Araquistáin, Alvarez del Vayo, whose opinions, not surprisingly, coincided with those of the PCE, described Martínez Cabrera as a "real nitwit" ("verdadero atún") in contrast to Prieto's opinion that he was "No. 1" of the "Escuela Superior de Guerra" (Araquistáin Papers, Leg. 23/A113).

69. In his unpublished memoirs, Largo Caballero reproduces the replies of both Rojo and Miaja ("Notas Históricas," 600–601). For the cancellation of Rojo's appointment, see *Gaceta de la República*, 16 Mar. 1937.

70. For a war ministry announcement paying tribute to Martínez Cabrera, see *El Mercantil Valenciano*, 16 Mar. 1937. Although Largo Caballero says that he did not fill the vacancy (*Mis recuerdos*, 195), there is evidence that Martínez Cabrera was replaced, at least provisionally, by Colonel Alvarez Coque, a Republican (see article by Vicente Guarner, *España Nueva*, 18 Mar. 1950; also Ramón Salas Larrazábal, *Historia del ejército popular de la república*, I, 1075–76). Rojo was made chief of the central general staff after the fall of Largo Caballero in May 1937 (see *Guerra y revolución*, III, 88).

71. *Mis recuerdos*, 195.

72. *Así fué la defensa de Madrid*, 216.

73. See his speech of 28 May 1937 in Hernández, *El partido comunista*, 24.

74. *Mis recuerdos*, 195.

Chapter 36

1. Article in *Timón* (Buenos Aires), June 1940.
2. Ibid.
3. *Vía Libre*, 5 Aug. 1939.
4. Article in *Timón* (Buenos Aires), June 1940.
5. Ibid.
6. *Vía Libre*, 5 Aug. 1939.
7. *Mis recuerdos*, 209.
8. Speech reported in *Fragua Social*, 7 July 1937.
9. *El Socialista*, 25 Feb. 1937.
10. Article in *Timón* (Buenos Aires), June 1940.
11. 28 June 1937.
12. For this information I am indebted to a member of the staff of José María Aguirre, Largo Caballero's politicomilitary secretary.
13. Article in *Timón* (Buenos Aires), June 1940.
14. Ibid.
15. *Frente Rojo*, 29 Mar. 1937.
16. See letter sent by *Claridad*, at that time still a Largo Caballero Socialist organ, to Francisco Antón, the secretary of the Madrid Communist party organization and inspector-commissar of the central front, charging that the Madrid section of the commissariat of war, which he controlled, was obstructing the distribution of that paper at the front (published in *Claridad*, 1 Mar. 1937). See also *Frente Libertario*, 20 Feb. 1937, complaining that the CNT-FAI newspapers were not reaching the front regularly owing to sabotage.
17. See Largo Caballero, "Notas Históricas sobre la Guerra de España," 797. At the beginning of March, Pascual Tomás, supporter of Largo Caballero and vice-secretary of the UGT, declared that political commissars who tried to make converts, "often using methods in opposition to all sense of decency," should not be allowed to remain in their positions a moment longer (*La Correspondencia de Valencia*, 3 Mar. 1937). See also interviews with Tomás published in *El Pueblo*, 16 Feb. 1937; *Claridad*, 16 Feb. 1937; and his article, ibid., 6 Apr. 1937. Even Antonio Mije, Communist head of the subcommissariat of organization, admitted in April 1937 that there had been some "overstepping of powers" by commissars (see *Frente Rojo*, 15 Apr. 1937).
18. *Gaceta de la República*, 26 Nov. 1936.
19. For this information I am grateful to Gabriel García Maroto, head of the subcommissariat of propaganda.
20. *Mis recuerdos*, 212; see also Largo Caballero, *La UGT y la guerra*, 10–11. In his "Notas Históricas" (819), written before *Mis recuerdos* and with the help of documentation, Largo Caballero gives the number of commissars appointed without his signature as "more than one thousand." "How can it be explained," he asks, "that two men (del Vayo and Pretel), endowed with [my] confidence could have acted in this manner? The only explanation is that they had delivered themselves totally to the Communist party, thus betraying not only the person who appointed them, but our party and Spain as well."
21. *Freedom's Battle*, 127.
22. *Give Me Combat*, 179–82.
23. For Alvarez del Vayo's own account of this incident, see *Freedom's Battle*, 219–20; for Prieto's, see Prieto, *Convulsiones de España*, II, 141.
24. *Correo de Asturias*, 10 July 1943.
25. *Gaceta de la República*, 17 Apr. 1937.
26. 16 Apr. 1937.
27. 17 Apr. 1937.
28. *Frente Rojo*, 17 Apr. 1937. For criticism of the order in *Mundo Obrero*, the Madrid Communist organ, see, for example, issues for 24, 29 Apr. 1937.
29. 20 Apr. 1937.
30. 20 Apr. 1937 (*Frente Rojo* was an evening paper).
31. 22 Apr. 1937. For charges by *Adelante* that Francisco Antón, inspector-commissar of the

central front and secretary of the Madrid Communist party organization, had replaced Socialist commissars with Communist ones, see issues 23–25 Apr. 1937. For *Frente Rojo*'s replies, see issues of 23, 24 Apr. 1937.

32. Araquistáin Papers, Leg. 23/A124[a].

33. 25 Dec. 1936. See also *CNT*, 25 Feb. 1937.

34. 22 Apr. 1937. For other articles approving the war minister's order, see issues of 23, 26, 27 Apr. 1937; also *Fragua Social*, 27 Apr. 1937.

35. See, for example, report by José Díaz to the central committee of the Communist party, 8 Mar. 1937, as reprinted in Díaz, *Tres años de lucha*, 363–64; speech by Francisco Antón, *Mundo Obrero*, 18 Mar. 1937; manifesto of the central committee of the Communist party, *Frente Rojo*, 19 Mar. 1937; editorials, ibid., 23, 31 Mar., 8, 13 Apr., 18 May 1937.

36. *Gaceta de la República*, 17 Feb. 1937. Cordón (259) asserts that Largo Caballero "hindered in every way he could the rapid promotion of the militia to command positions."

37. On 27 January 1937, at a public meeting held to celebrate the formal dissolution of the Fifth Regiment, José Díaz had declared that the posts of generals and other officers whose hearts were not in the war "should be occupied by the new talents discovered in the Fifth Regiment" (speech reprinted in Díaz, *Tres años*, 297). Although, after the publication of the decree of 16 February, the Communists frequently referred to the question of promotions and implicitly criticized Largo Caballero's policy (see, for example, José Díaz's report to the central committee of the Communist party, 8 Mar. 1937, ibid., 367, the resolution of the central committee, *Mundo Obrero*, 7 Apr. 1937, also *Frente Rojo*, 21 Apr. 1937), there was no open criticism of the decree itself until January 1938 (ibid., 5 Jan. 1938), when the provision restricting the promotion of militia leaders was annulled (*Gaceta de la República*, 5 Jan. 1938). For sharp criticism of the decree in the official Communist history of the Civil War, see *Guerra y revolución en España, 1936–1939*, III, 62–63.

38. *Guerra y revolución*, III, 63.

39. Quoted in *Castilla Libre*, 31 Mar. 1937. For *Frente Rojo*'s reply to an attack on Uribe by *Adelante*, see issue for 21 Apr. 1937. For all details regarding Hernández and Uribe not contained in the above newspapers I am indebted to members of the staff of the Febus news agency.

40. 22 Apr. 1937.

41. 22 Apr. 1937.

42. 23 Apr. 1937.

Chapter 37

1. *El Socialista*, 3 July 1936.

2. Ibid., 2 July 1936.

3. Article in *Correspondencia Internacional*, 17 Apr. 1936, reprinted in José Díaz, *Tres años de lucha*, 133–39.

4. 15 Apr. 1936, pp. 3, 6.

5. In 1921, as a prominent though youthful member of the PSOE, Lamoneda, who had acclaimed the Bolshevik Revolution, urged the executive commission unsuccessfully to vote for affiliation with the Comintern. Shortly afterward, he left the PSOE, and the following year he occupied the post of secretary of the interior in the recently formed PCE (see Gerald H. Meaker, *The Revolutionary Left in Spain, 1914–1923*, 114, 365–66, 448). In the course of his ideological and political odyssey, he rejoined the PSOE before the advent of the Republic in 1931, was elected a deputy to the Cortes, and, before the outbreak of the Civil War, he became—thanks to the maneuvering of Indalecio Prieto—secretary of the staunchly anti-Communist executive commission of the party. Although nominally a Prietista during the first year of the war, he walked cautiously arm in arm with the Communists, ultimately supporting Premier Juan Negrín against Prieto. His power base was the printers' union, the Federación Gráfica Española, of which he was president. I am indebted to Andrés Saborit, a former secretary of the executive commission of the PSOE and a member of the Cortes, for confirmation of Ramón Lamoneda's pro-Communist stance (correspondence, Hoover Institution). Saborit had a reputation in his party of keeping meticulous records of the political trajectory of party and trade-union leaders. For Lamoneda's political fluctuations, see Luis Romero Solano (a Socialist representative in the Cortes during the Republic), *Vísperas de la guerra de España*, 176–77; Justo Martínez Amutio,

Chantaje a un pueblo, 66–69; Gabriel Morón, *Política de ayer y política de mañana*, 110–11; Amaro del Rosal, *Historia de la UGT de España, 1901–1939*, II, 623–24. The authors of the last three works, as we have seen, were all prominent Socialists, although Rosal transferred his allegiance to the PCE quite early in the war.

6. As quoted in *Guerra y revolución en España, 1936–1939*, III, 51–53. In a speech reported in *Claridad*, 3 May 1937, Lamoneda expressed himself more openly: "We know that a single party that defines the tasks of socialism is necessary. For that reason, the Socialists have no objection to merging with the Communists" (quoted by Rosal, *Historia*, II, 634).

7. *Guerra y revolución*, III, 51–53.

8. Ibid.

9. See Morón, 106–7.

10. See Constancia de la Mora (Hidalgo de Cisneros's wife), *In Place of Splendor*, 179–80, 195.

11. Statement to me when interviewed in Mexico in 1940 (shorthand notes are in the Hoover Institution).

12. This was well known in Communist circles and was confirmed to me by José Duque, a member during the war of the central committee of the PCE, when interviewed by me in Mexico in 1944.

13. Nenni, *La guerre d'Espagne*, 67, n. 2. There is further evidence of this extraordinary political deviation on the part of Prieto: At a meeting of the executive committee of the Socialist party in the summer of 1937, Prieto is said to have come out flatly in favor of fusion on the ground that the only help the government could hope to receive was from Russia (see the pro-Communist Julio Alvarez del Vayo, *Freedom's Battle*, 67, and *The Last Optimist*, 288, n. 2, and the centrists Gabriel Morón, 107, and Juan-Simeón Vidarte, *Todos fuimos culpables*, 620–21, who states that Prieto "believed that the time had arrived to think about the desirability of merging the Socialist and Communist parties before it was too late and we should find ourselves displaced from the political leadership of the proletariat").

14. *El Socialista* (Paris), 9 Nov. 1950. According to Claudio Sánchez-Albornoz, José Giral (who became foreign minister when Prieto took over the war ministry) told him that when Soviet war material arrived in Spanish Republican ports "it was not unloaded unless the government agreed beforehand to give the Communists important police and military posts" (*Anecdotario político*, 233). I have found no other evidence in support of this charge.

15. *Mis recuerdos*, 153. See also José María Gil Robles, *No fué posible la paz*, 657.

16. Statement to me when interviewed in Mexico in 1940 (Hoover Institution).

17. His attitude is reflected in the editorials of *Informaciones*, his mouthpiece, and of *El Socialista* (Madrid), the organ of the PSOE executive. See, for example, *Informaciones*, 5 Aug. 1936, and *El Socialista*, 2, 10, 11 Mar. 1937. The director of the latter, Julián Zugazagoitia, was Prieto's man of confidence.

18. See also Indalecio Prieto, *Convulsiones de España*, III, 163–64.

19. Speech in Mexico City, 21 Apr. 1940, as published in Prieto, *Inauguración del círculo "Pablo Iglesias" de México*, 13.

20. These methods were the subject of sharp and even violent criticism in *El Socialista*, the organ of the PSOE executive. See, for example, articles published on 14 Jan., 20, 25 Feb., 6 Mar., 22, 23, 25 Apr., 15 May 1937; also circular letter of the executive committee, 28 Mar. 1937.

21. Ravines, *La gran estafa*, 311. Ravines worked on the editorial staff of *Frente Rojo*, the Communist organ in Valencia (ibid., 309).

22. *Frente Rojo*, 29 Mar. 1937.

23. See announcement published in ibid., 26 Apr. 1937.

24. See speeches by Ramón Lamoneda, reported in *El Socialista*, 16 July 1937; *Adelante*, 3 Aug. 1937.

25. P. 443. In the English-language edition (*Outline History of the Communist International*, 420), the four words "greater benefit to them" are used instead of the two words "more beneficial," which is an accurate rendering of the Russian. The difference in the meanings of the two phrases is worth pondering. Cf. *Guerra y revolución en España, 1936–1939* (the official Communist history), III, 218.

Chapter 38

1. Reply to my questionnaire, Hoover Institution. See also García Oliver, *El eco de los pasos*, 170–71.

2. *Al servei de Catalunya i de la república: La victòria, 19 de juliol 1936*, 286–87; also ibid., 425–26. For a biographical essay on Escofet, see M. Teresa Suero Roca, *Militares republicanos de la guerra de España*, 95–120. Vicente Guarner, police chief of Barcelona at the time of the military rebellion, informed Jordi Arquer after the war that the number of civil guards garrisoned in the city on 19 July was 2,000 and that the assault and security guards totaled 1,920 (see Arquer's letter to me of 24 May 1946, Hoover Institution).

3. Both generals were executed by General Franco after the war for not joining the military rebellion. For a biographical essay on Escobar, see Suero Roca, 267–86.

4. Even opponents of the CNT and FAI have acknowledged their important role: "I shall never forget the decisive part they played" (Luis Companys, president of Catalonia, to Jean Richard Bloch, *España en armas*, 34); "In the first days of the revolt Anarchists bravely stormed the Franco garrisons in Barcelona and quickly suppressed the mutiny" (Louis Fischer, *Why Spain Fights On*, 41); "The CNT [took] the lead in the fighting" (Frank Jellinek [*Manchester Guardian* correspondent in Barcelona], *The Civil War in Spain*, 325).

5. See Escofet, *Al servei de Catalunya*, also Xavier Febrés (Escofet's biographer), *Frederic Escofet: L'últim exiliat*, 178.

6. The reader may recall that before the war, as a precautionary measure, Azaña's government had transferred General Goded, then inspector general in the war ministry, to the minor post of garrison commander in the Balearic Islands, where it was felt he could do no harm. However, on 19 July he flew to Barcelona to take command of the garrison. Shortly after his surrender, he was tried and shot.

7. *Contribución a la historia del movimiento obrero español*, 323–24. See also Abad de Santillán, *Alfonso XIII, la II república, Francisco Franco*, 319.

8. The aim of the decree, which was issued by the Giral government, was to free the men from any obligation to obey the orders of the rebel officers, but, according to José Tarradellas, a leading Catalan politician, it was a "monumental error" (letter to me of 24 March 1971, Hoover Institution). The Madrid government, Tarradellas added, believed that the decree would influence the men under the command of the insurgent officers, but the opposite occurred. "In other words, this incomprehensible measure was heeded only by the soldiers on the Republican side who abandoned their weapons and returned to their homes, creating disorder on our side." See also Escofet, *Al servei de Catalunya*, 402–3.

9. *Cataluña en la guerra de España, 1936–39*, 139–41. For a biographical essay on Guarner, see Suero Roca, 121–42.

10. *La república y la guerra*, 386–87.

11. See Chapters 4 and 5 for material on the economic revolution in Catalonia.

12. Jonathan Galassi, *Understand the Weapon, Understand the Wound: Selected Writings of John Cornford*, 174. The International Brigade newspaper, *Volunteer for Liberty*, 3 Jan. 1938, stated: "John Cornford, a young poet and brilliant university student, met his death on his twenty-first birthday. He was the most prominent leader of the student movement in England and his efforts, more than those of any other single individual, helped forge unity of the left wing student organizations. . . . Comrade Cornford was one of the very first international volunteers to arrive in Spain in the late summer of 1936. He took part in the defense of Madrid [and later] in the action on the Cordova front where he met his death."

13. Article in *Vu*, 29 Aug. 1936.

14. According to Pérez Farràs, the commander of the corps, it comprised four hundred men in October 1934 (*Full Català*, Oct. 1942). Since that date it had not increased in size.

15. As quoted by García Oliver in article, "El Comité Central de las Milicias Antifascistas de Cataluña," published in *De julio a julio*, 194–95.

16. Escofet, *Al servei de Catalunya*, 406–7.

17. Ossorio y Gallardo, *Vida y sacrificio de Companys*, 170–71; Benavides, *Guerra y revolución en Cataluña*, 185–86; Pi Sunyer, 391–92.

18. Article in *De julio a julio*, 193–94.

19. *Por qué perdimos la guerra*, 53.
20. 17 June 1933.
21. *La Continental Obrera*, Feb. 1935.
22. Pi Sunyer, 391–92.
23. *Catalunya*, 143.
24. Article in *De julio a julio*, 195.
25. Reported in *La Publicitat*, 17 Oct. 1936. See also his statement in *El Liberal*, as given in *Ultima Hora*, 1 Sept. 1936.
26. *La revolución y la guerra en España*, 148. See also statement by Sebastián Clara, former director of *Solidaridad Obrera*, as given in *Las Noticias*, 22 Aug. 1936.
27. See, for example, *La Publicitat*, 26 July 1936; *La Humanitat*, 1 Aug. 1936; *Treball*, 26 Aug. 1936.
28. *Vida*, 189. See also Lluhi Vallescà, *Lluis Companys Jover*, 58; *España Republicana*, 25 Oct. 1941. This humanitarian conduct did not help Companys when in 1940, after the German occupation of France, he was turned over to General Franco and executed (see, for example, Domènec de Bellmunt, *Lluis Companys*, 136–49; Indalecio Prieto, "Homenaje a Luis Companys," *España Libre*, 12 Dec. 1943). Many lives were saved in Barcelona by other Republicans; see, for example, Pi Sunyer, 402–3, and Ramon Salas Larrazábal, *Historia del ejército popular de la república*, I, 1023–24, on Escofet, the general commissioner of public order.
29. See, for example, speeches by Juan Casanovas, first councillor (prime minister) in the Catalan government, as given in *La Humanitat*, 29 July 1936; *El Día Gráfico*, 19 Aug., 15 Sept. 1936; Ventura Gassol, councillor of culture, as given in *La Humanitat*, 30 July 1936; Carlos Pi Sunyer, mayor of Barcelona, as given in *Ultima Hora*, 22 Aug. 1936.
30. See, for example, 30 July, 11, 13 Aug. 1936; also 26 Aug. 1936, as quoted by *La Batalla*, 27 Aug. 1936; and 24 Sept. 1936, as quoted by *El Noticiero Universal*, 24 Sept. 1936.
31. *La Revista Blanca*, 30 July 1936.
32. *La revolución*, 43.
33. Article in *Timón*, Aug. 1938. See also *Solidaridad Obrera*, 19 July 1938 (Federica Montseny interview); *Tiempo de Historia*, June 1977 (José Peirats interview); Isidro Guardia Abella, *Conversaciones sobre el movimiento obrero*, 39–40; Jacinto Toryho, article in *Rumbos Nuevos*, 1 Aug. 1939.
34. Article in *De julio a julio*, 195–96.
35. *Noir et Rouge*, June–July 1967, as cited in César M. Lorenzo, *Les anarchistes espagnols et le pouvoir, 1868–1969*, 104, n. 3.
36. *El eco de los pasos*, 190–91. Agustín Souchy, who was the AIT representative in Casa CNT-FAI (Anarchosyndicalist headquarters in Barcelona) and in close touch with the principal CNT-FAI leaders, informed me after the war that during the meeting García Oliver proposed taking "complete power" in Catalonia, but that Abad de Santillán opposed the idea on the grounds that the British warships in Barcelona would bombard the city and that "we would be finished off immediately." "The moderates," said Souchy, "prevailed." Interview in San Diego, California, in 1950. My shorthand notes are in the Hoover Institution.
37. *Noir et Rouge*, June–July 1967, as cited in Lorenzo, 104–5, n. 3.
38. See Abad de Santillán, *El anarquismo y la revolución en España: Escritos, 1930–38*, 350; Lorenzo, 105, n. 4 (FAI report); *Solidaridad Obrera*, 16 Aug. 1936, 19 July 1938; *Tierra y Libertad*, 2 Apr. 1937; Federica Montseny in *Boletín de Información*, *CNT-FAI*, 22 July 1937, and in *Tiempo de Historia*, June 1977 (interview).
39. *La Revista Blanca*, 26 July 1935.
40. Escofet, *Al servei de Catalunya*, 405.
41. *Internacional*, July–Aug. 1938. Ruediger was also director of the German-language papers *CNT-FAI-AIT Informationsdienst* and *Die Soziale Revolution*, both published in Barcelona.
42. For the names of the committee members and the organizations they represented, see *Solidaridad Obrera*, 21 July 1936.
43. Article in *De julio a julio*, 195–96.
44. *Vida*, 171.
45. *Por qué perdimos la guerra*, 69.
46. *Tiempos Nuevos*, May–June 1937.

47. Ernest Udina, *Josep Tarradellas*, 128–29. For a tribute to Tarradellas's political acumen, see Miquel Caminal, *Joan Comorera*, II, 28–32.

48. Letter to me of 24 March 1971, Hoover Institution.

49. Baltasar Porcel, *Conversaciones con el honorable Tarradellas*, 52.

50. On 23 July it issued a decree empowering it to intervene in the operations of the private banks (*Butlletí Oficial de la Generalitat de Catalunya*, 25 July 1936), and a month later, by the terms of a decree dated 27 August 1936 (*Ultima Hora*, 28 Aug. 1936), it assumed control of the branches of the Bank of Spain.

51. *Butlletí Oficial de la Generalitat de Catalunya*. Its name was changed to *Diari Oficial* on 26 August 1936.

52. Taken from my shorthand notes of interview with Serra Pàmies in Mexico in 1944 (Hoover Institution).

53. Ibid.

54. Letter to me, Hoover Institution.

55. *Butlletí Oficial de la Generalitat de Catalunya*, 24 July 1936.

56. Ibid., 26 July 1936.

57. Ibid., 31 July 1936.

58. Ibid., 7 Aug. 1936.

59. Ibid., 11 Aug. 1936.

60. Ibid., 31 July, 6, 7, 12, 16, 18 Aug. 1936, and in *Diari Oficial*, 26, 29 Aug. 1936.

61. For appointments of comptrollers or *interventores* by the Generalitat government, see *Butlletí Oficial*, 12, 13, 16, 17, 25 Aug. 1936, and *Diari Oficial*, 26, 28, 30, 31 Aug. 1936.

62. *Boletín de Información, CNT-FAI*, as given in *Las Noticias*, 11 Aug. 1936.

63. For the collectivization of small business enterprises in Catalonia, see Chapter 5.

64. 10 Sept. 1936. See also Juan Peiró, *Perill a la reraguarda*, 102–3.

65. 29 Aug. 1936.

66. *La Batalla*, 3 Oct. 1936.

Chapter 39

1. 8 Aug. 1936.

2. *Treball*, 10 Sept. 1936.

3. See Largo Caballero, *La UGT y la guerra*, 32; also *Adelante*, Largo Caballero's organ in Valencia, 8 Apr. 1937. According to the Comintern organ, *International Press Correspondence*, 27 Nov. 1937, the GEPCI possessed no right of representation at the UGT congresses.

4. *Solidaridad Obrera*, 8 Apr. 1937. For other criticisms, see ibid., 3, 6 Apr. 1937; *Acracia*, 5 Apr. 1937; and *La Batalla*, 29 Apr. 1937.

5. *Treinta meses de colectivismo en Cataluña*, 150.

6. Interview in Mexico, 1944.

7. See Ralph Bates, *Daily Worker*, 12 Dec. 1936.

8. *Treball*, 27 July 1937.

9. *La formación del partit socialista unificat de Catalunya*, 100.

10. Interview, 1944. My italics. This firsthand testimony by a man who played a leading role in the negotiations is especially important in view of the fact that Comorera's opposition to affiliation with the Comintern is not mentioned in two authoritative works that deal with the process of unification, namely, Miquel Caminal, *Joan Comorera*, I, 229–38, and Josep Lluis Martín i Ramos, *Els origens del partit socialista unificat de Catalunya, 1930–1935*, 226–35. Caminal, II, 170–71, states that Serra Pàmies was "one of the most influential figures in the PSUC leadership during the war."

11. See Joan Gilabert (who was in touch with former PSUC leaders, Víctor Colomer and Miguel Serra Pàmies, in Mexico) in *Butlletí del Partit Socialista Català*, 31 Mar. 1943.

12. I am grateful to Reiner Tosstorff (letter, 31 May 1982, Hoover Institution) for having brought to my attention the fact that Vidiella ceased to be a loyal supporter of Largo Caballero in December 1935, when, according to Santos Juliá (*La izquierda del PSOE, 1935–1936*, 84, 165), he was the only left-wing Socialist to remain on the national committee of the party after Largo Caballero and his followers resigned in protest against Prieto's tactics.

13. Interview with Serra Pàmies in Mexico in 1944. Shorthand notes of this interview are in the Hoover Institution. Although Pàmies stressed the point that Vidiella at first opposed adherence to the Communist International, there is evidence in Santos Juliá (*La izquierda del PSOE*, 166) that in the spring of 1936 he was in favor of affiliation. It is important to record that the Prieto faction within the Federació Catalana del PSOE refused to enter the PSUC (see Caminal, I, 238) and that the fusion took place without the prior consent of Largo Caballero. When Rafael Vidiella and Joaquín Almendros (both members of the Catalan Federation) visited the left Socialist leader in August 1936 to inform him of the merger, a "very disagreeable" conversation ensued, during which Caballero referred to the fusion as "a coup d'état" (Almendros, *Situaciones españolas, 1936–1939: El PSUC en la guerra civil*, 160).

14. *Justicia Social*, 27 June 1936, as given in Caminal, I, 264, n. 373. *The Communist International* reported in its issue of February 1937 (199): "As far back as June, 1936, Comrade Comorera . . . declared at the Madrid conference of the Spanish Communist Party: 'The four parties . . . are in very close contact, and I can assure you that in a month's time these four parties will merge into one on the basis of the Statutes of the Third International. . . . We hope that our example will be followed not only in Spain but throughout the rest of the world.' "

15. *El marxismo en España, 1919–1939*, I, 294, n. 4.

16. *International Press Correspondence*, 22 June 1934. My italics.

17. *Situaciones españolas*, 110–11.

18. *La formación*, 99. For the composition of the central committee of the PSUC, see *Treball*, 27 and 28 July 1936. Short biographies of some of the leading figures can be found in Roger Arnau, *Marxisme català i qüestió nacional catalana, 1930–1936*, II, 315–24.

19. Comorera, *Cataluña, en pie de guerra*, 15.

20. *La formación*, 101.

21. *Ideas*, 24 June 1937.

22. Comorera, *Informe presentado en la primera conferencia nacional del partido socialista unificado de Cataluña*, 30.

23. Colomer, *Informe presentat a la primera conferencia nacional del partit socialista unificat de Catalunya I. C.*, 30.

24. Evidence of Serra Pàmies (a member of the PSUC's executive committee) during an interview in Mexico in 1944 (shorthand notes, Hoover Institution).

25. Branko Lazitch and Milorad M. Drachkovitch, *Biographical Dictionary of the Comintern*, 117–18; *Uj Magyar Lexikon*, III, 55.

26. See Pedro Checa (a member of the politburo of the PCE), *A un gran partido, una gran organización*, 23.

27. Lazitch and Drachkovitch, 117; Rudolf L. Tökés, *Béla Kun and the Hungarian Soviet Republic*, 257.

28. Tökés, 257.

29. *Situaciones españolas*, 111–12. This hostile testimony is not mentioned by Caminal in his biography of Comorera.

30. Information given to me by Serra Pàmies (interview in Mexico, 1944). See also Caminal, II, 172–75.

31. Article by Felipe Matas in *Nuestra Bandera*, 31 Dec. 1943. A few years later, Comorera himself fell into disfavor. According to Víctor Alba, he returned to Spain "when his comrades of the PSUC in exile removed him from the leadership. He hoped to link up with the clandestine cadres of the party, although what he found there was a denunciation to the Spanish police by his own 'friends,' and an open letter from his daughter accusing him of being a traitor" (*El marxismo en España*, II, 496–97). For an article by Virgilio Llanos, the PSUC leader, denouncing Comorera as a traitor and enemy agent, see *Lluita* (the PSUC organ in exile), 16 Feb. 1950. Among other things, he accused Comorera of "taking advantage of every occasion to speak badly to me of Negrín, whom he identified with the PCE." The Soviet historian Ponamariova writes (*La formación*, 99–100, n. 186): "During the time he occupied the general secretaryship, Comorera committed various grave errors of a nationalist character and in 1949 was expelled from the PSUC (*Mundo Obrero*, 10 Nov. 1949). Later, he returned secretly to Spain, but in June 1954 he was arrested by the Franco authorities and sentenced to thirty years imprisonment by a military tribunal in Barcelona. He died in prison. The politburo of the PCE

and the executive committee of the PSUC published in 1957, during the trial, a statement protesting the arbitrary action taken by the Franco authorities against Comorera and other antifascists (*Pravda*, Aug. 11, 1957)." For Comorera's services to Moscow in Latin America after the Civil War and for his relationship with the publishing house Editorial 'Atlante' in Mexico, which distributed Soviet propaganda in that country and in Central America, see Karl Rienffer, *Comunistas españoles en America*, 104–12.

32. Testimony of Serra Pàmies (interview in Mexico, 1944).

33. See Julián Gorkin, *Caníbales políticos*, 81–83, and *El proceso de Moscú en Barcelona*, 51, in both of which Gorkin gives what appears to be a reliable account of Pedro's authority over the Soviet consul general. Colonel Vicente Guarner states that NKVD chief Alexander Orlov, according to secret service reports, delegated to Gerö the creation of a Soviet-style secret police organization in Barcelona and that Gerö "put an end to Antonov-Ovseenko by sending him to his death in Moscow" (*L'aixecament militar i la guerra civil a Catalunya, 1936–1939*, 213). In November 1917, Antonov-Ovseenko had directed the storming of the czar's winter palace and arrested the provisional government. Recalled to Russia in 1937, he vanished in the purges. *Who Was Who in the USSR*, 24, states that he died in prison in 1938 and was posthumously rehabilitated. The *Bol'shaia sovetskaia entsiklopediia*, 3d ed., vol. II, published in 1970, gives the date of his death as 1939, but does not say that he had been imprisoned. On the other hand, Ilya Ehrenburg claimed that when he arrived in Moscow in December 1937 he found out about "the fate" of Antonov-Ovseenko (*Eve of War, 1933–41*, 190).

34. For the composition of the government, see *Treball*, 1 Aug. 1936. The date of 2 August given by the official Communist history (*Guerra y Revolución*, II, 19) is erroneous.

35. *Guerra y revolución*, II, 19. For information in the local press on the solution of the crisis and the creation of a new government without PSUC participation, see *La Humanitat*, *La Publicitat*, *Solidaridad Obrera*, and *Treball*, 7 Aug. 1937.

36. *Les anarchistes espagnols et le pouvoir, 1868–1969*, 117, n. 25.

37. Article by Marcos Alcón, who was present at the meeting, *Cultura Proletaria*, 20 Feb. 1943.

38. *Por qué perdimos la guerra*, 116.

39. *Tierra y Libertad*, 29 Oct. 1936. See also ibid., 22 May 1937; Agustín Souchy, *Tiempos Nuevos*, Sept. 1938, and Helmut Ruediger, *Ensayo crítico sobre la revolución española*, 24, 27.

40. Vernon Richards, *Lessons of the Spanish Revolution*, 63.

41. Mariano Ansó, *Yo fui ministro de Negrín*, 182. See also Caminal, II, 28–32.

42. Although Artemio Aiguadé presided over the Junta de Seguridad, the real chief was the secretary general, Aurelio Fernández, of the CNT. For more information on the duality of police functions, see Josep Coll and Josep Pané, *Josep Rovira*, 155–56.

43. *Butlletí Oficial de la Generalitat de Catalunya*, 11 Oct. 1936.

44. Ernest Udina, Tarradellas's biographer, writes: "The policy [of Tarradellas] was to urge moderation upon the Anarchists and possibly to prevent the involvement of the PSUC in the strategy of the PCE, so as to safeguard the predominance and political authority of the Generalitat" (*Josep Tarradellas*, 187). See also Tarradellas's letter to me of 24 March 1971 (pp. 1, 6) regarding the policy he pursued with respect to the CNT and FAI (Hoover Institution).

Chapter 40

1. For information on Maurín and Nin, see Víctor Alba and Stephen Schwartz, *Spanish Marxism vs. Soviet Communism: A History of the POUM*. This work includes considerable material on the party's origins in the Catalan working-class movement. In addition, the German historian Reiner Tosstorff will shortly be publishing in West Germany his dissertation, "Die POUM während des Spanischen Bürgerkriegs, 1936–1939." A copy is in the Hoover Institution, Bolloten Collection. Tosstorff's work, a university dissertation, is a thoroughly researched and extremely detailed account of the POUM during the Civil War. These two books must be considered the basic authorities on the history of the POUM and should be consulted by future researchers interested in matters relating to the POUM and the Trotskyist movement in Spain that are not dealt with in this book. See also Alba, *Dos revolucionarios: Joaquín Maurín, Andreu Nin*; Francesc Bonamusa, *Andreu Nin y el movimiento comunista en España, 1930–1937*; George Esenwein in Robert A. Gorman, *Biographical Dictionary*

of Marxism, articles on Maurín and Nin; Antoni Monreal, *El pensamiento político de Joaquín Maurín*; Andrés Nin, *Els moviments d'emancipació nacional, Los problemas de la revolución española*, and *La revolución española, 1930–1937*; Pelai Pagès, *Andreu Nin: Su evolución política, 1911–1937* and *El movimiento trotskista en España, 1930–1935*.

2. Report to the central committee of the POUM in Nin, *La revolución española*, 232.

3. "At the time, Norway was under Soviet pressure to expel Trotsky," writes George Esenwein, "and it may well be that his past relations with Nin and Andrade had something to do with the POUM's decision to seek asylum for him. As the dissident Marxist Victor Serge wrote in his memoirs, Nin, Andrade and other prominent POUMists 'had serious disagreements with Trotsky, but viewed him with comradely admiration' (*Memoirs of a Revolutionary*, 335). On the other hand, Julián Gorkin, a member of the POUM's executive committee at the time, has written that the POUM's invitation to Trotsky was nothing more than a gesture of solidarity that was extended to him because, thanks to the diplomatic pressures being exerted by the Soviet Union, Trotsky was finding it increasingly difficult to secure refuge in Europe (Gorkin letter to Burnett Bolloten, 24 May 1981, Hoover Institution). In any event, the POUM's plans to bring Trotsky to Catalonia never materialized. Early in August 1936, Trotsky himself wrote to Jean Rous, the representative of the International Secretariat of the Fourth International, who was negotiating with the POUM on Trotsky's behalf, that he would be 'very happy' to receive a visa to go to Barcelona (letter published in *La Batalla* [Paris], Jan.–Feb. 1971). Yet Rous never received this message as it was intercepted by OVRA (Italian secret police) agents then operating in Barcelona. (This letter was not discovered until some years later by the Italian historian Paolo Spriano, who found it while conducting research in the archives of the Italian secret police, ibid.) But even if Trotsky's ill-fated message had reached its destination, it is highly improbable that he would have been permitted to stay in Catalonia. For although the POUM executive announced their invitation to Trotsky in *La Batalla* (Paris) on 3 September 1936—and in their Madrid daily, *El Combatiente Rojo* on the 20th of that month—their proposal was rejected by the President of the Generalitat, Luis Companys (Gorkin, letters to Bolloten, 9 Mar., 24 May 1981). There can be little doubt that Companys was in no position to grant Trotsky a visa at this time, largely because the Anarchosyndicalists, whose power in the region was predominant, would not have tolerated his presence. Not only were the Anarchosyndicalists implacably opposed to Marxists generally, but they hated Trotsky in particular for having ruthlessly persecuted the Anarchists during the Bolshevik Revolution. Julián Gorkin has pointed out in his letter to Bolloten (of 24 May 1981) that Companys' negative reply may well have been based on other considerations. For example, the PSUC was no less hostile to Trotsky than were the Anarchosyndicalists and it would have pressured Companys to keep him out of Spain. Moreover, Companys himself, according to Gorkin, was doubtless aware that Trotsky's presence in Spain would have seriously undermined the republican efforts to obtain aid from the Western democracies." I am grateful to Esenwein for researching this matter at my request.

4. See, for example, *La Batalla*, 24 Dec. 1936; ibid., 24, 27 Apr. 1937 (articles by Gorkin). For Nin's break with Trotsky in 1934, see Gorkin, *El proceso de Moscú en Barcelona*, 38.

5. See, for example, "El Trotsquime, el millor agent de Hitler-Mussolini-Franco," *Treball*, 17 Jan. 1937, and "El trotskismo en acción. Los que trabajan para el enemigo," *Las Noticias*, 29 Jan. 1937. In this campaign the Communists were joined by Mikhail Koltzov, *Pravda*'s special correspondent in Spain. See, for example, his article in *L'Humanité*, as given in *La Batalla*, 27 Jan. 1937.

6. For Maurín's odyssey and the efforts of his wife, Jeanne, to secure his release, see Jeanne Maurín, *Cómo se salvó Joaquín Maurín*.

7. James W. Cortada, *Historical Dictionary of the Spanish Civil War, 1936–1939*, 328. For the letter from Iglesias to Alba, see Víctor Alba, *El marxismo en España, 1919–1939*, I, 291–92. After Maurín's death in the United States in 1973, his documents were acquired by the Hoover Institution.

8. According to Alba, there were only 250 to 300 members in Nin's Communist Left at the time of the fusion as compared with 7,000 in Maurín's party, in other words, a ratio of one to twenty-eight or, at best, one to twenty-three (*Dos revolucionarios*, 389).

9. Ibid., 390–91.

10. See, for example, Trotsky, *La révolution espagnole, 1930–40*, 273–307; Trotsky, *Escritos sobre España*, 123–32; article in *Unser Wort*, mid-February 1936; and English translation in *New Militant*, 15 Feb. 1936; also *Unser Wort*, early May 1936. A valuable book, written by one of the founders of the POUM, is *Léon Trotski y España, 1930–1939* by Ignacio Iglesias. Pelai Pagès, in his

study of the Trotskyist movement in Spain, states that "Trotsky's campaign against the new party, and especially against Nin and Andrade, did very little to help the Spanish Revolution and created among those elements of the POUM who came from the Trotskyist movement a fresh dissension that rendered their consolidation as leaders of the new party even more difficult" (*El movimiento trotskista*, 289).

11. The Bolshevik Leninists never publicly revealed the number of their adherents during the war, but in the minutes of the founding conference of the Fourth International, held at Lausanne on 3 September 1938, the membership of the Spanish section was said to be between ten and thirty (*Documents of the Fourth International: The Formative Years, 1933–40*, 289). I am grateful to Stephen Schwartz, a former English-language representative between 1977 and 1982 of Manuel Fernández Grandizo (G. Munis), for bringing these figures to my attention and for reading this chapter and making valuable suggestions. In a letter to me, dated 4 January 1986, Pierre Broué, the foremost living authority on the world Trotskyist movement, provides useful information on the number of members at the front and in the rear during the first year of the war (Hoover Institution). Trotsky himself acknowledged on 14 April 1937: "[The] Trotskyites in Spain are not numerous—the genuine Trotskyites. I regret it, but I must confess, they are not numerous. There is a powerful party, the POUM, the Workers' Party of Marxist Unification. . . . The youth of that party has sympathy with our ideas. But the policy of that party is very opportunistic, and I openly criticize it" (*The Case of Leon Trotsky*, 294).

12. Mid-August 1937. In a letter to me in 1948, Manuel Fernández Grandizo (known as G. Munis) informed me that he founded the Spanish section of the Fourth International in November 1936 and that the POUM expelled from the party those members who were sympathetic to the ideas of the Bolshevik Leninists. In a letter to Trotsky, dated 11 October 1937, Harry Milton, himself a Trotskyist at the time, who fought with the POUM militia on the Aragon front, stated that Moulin (Hans Freund), "the leading comrade of our group," had been expelled from the POUM at the beginning of the year (Harry Milton, "Copies of correspondence with Leon Trotsky and George Kopp" [Hoover Institution]). I am grateful to Harry Milton for these copies. However, according to Stephen Schwartz there is "no evidence that Moulin was ever a member of the POUM" (conversation with Schwartz, who bases his claim on Broué and Tosstorff). Paul Thalmann, another Trotskyist and onetime secretary of the Communist youth in Switzerland, who fought with the POUM militia, alleges in an interview published in 1976: "There was a strong right wing in the POUM that made short work of the Trotskyists; they also shot some—this, one should also know" (Clara Thalmann and Paul Thalmann, *Revolution für die Freiheit*, 380). However, when questioned by me in 1984, Clara Thalmann stated emphatically that she had no knowledge of the executions alleged by her husband, Paul.

According to information given to Stephen Schwartz by Pierre Broué (see n. 11 above), the POUM organ, *La Batalla*, published the expulsion of one Karl Herbert Lenz ("Kampenski"). I have found no information on other Trotskyists expelled. On 13 November 1936, Andrés Nin—in reply to a formal request by the Bolshevik Leninists for entry into the POUM as a group with the rights of a fraction— informed them on behalf of the executive committee that they could join the POUM as individuals but not as a group and that since membership in the POUM was "incompatible with affiliation to any other political organization" they must leave the Bolshevik Leninist organization. He also stated that those who joined the POUM must "publicly disassociate themselves and disagree with the campaign of calumny and defamation carried on against our party by the publications of the would-be 4th International" (*Information Bulletin*, International Bureau for the Fourth International, July 1937). These terms were unacceptable to the Bolshevik Leninists. Then, in April 1937, in an open letter to the POUM executive, they again applied for entry as a group with the rights of a fraction, at the same time sharply criticizing the leadership: "The lack of a party, not merely revolutionary, but bolshevik, capable of taking a resolute class position with regard to the capitalist State supported by the Popular Front seriously threatens to leave the road open to reaction. When we wrote our first letter, this danger loomed in the distance. . . . Today we have only a short time, but we still can regain what has been lost. You cannot argue that the POUM is a truly revolutionary party, because not even the members of the E.C. believe that. Your slogans for a Workers and Peasants Government and a Revolutionary Workers Front, which are irreconcilable, belie this; but you have been able to launch both of them because you see in the Revolutionary Workers Front a sort of bureaucratic agreement with the CNT, which will achieve the Workers and Peasants Government by means of dividing the portfolios of the Generalidad between the CNT and the POUM. In the face of this opportunist confusionism, we support the slogan of the dictatorship of the proletariat based on the committees of workers, peasants and combatants. . . .

"We beg you to reflect, comrades of the E.C. It must be recognized that the POUM has committed, and is committing, fundamental errors that bar the way to revolution. A full discussion of principles is indispensable to give the proletariat the theoretical direction it needs. . . . Only an opportunist leadership can fear fractions. Under the present conditions of the class struggle, and especially the internal conditions of the POUM the first duty of a revolutionary leadership is to pose the ideological, that is, factional struggle" (ibid.). There is no record that the POUM executive even considered this second request for admission of the Bolshevik Leninists to agitate freely within the party as a fraction.

13. *Civil War in Spain*, 68–70. See also *Workers' Age*, 11 Dec. 1937, "What Is Trotskyist View of Spain," by Jim Cork (Harry Goldberg). For Andrade's and the POUM's differences with the Trotskyists during and after the Civil War, see his paper presented in Paris on 10 Jan. 1970 (Juan Andrade, "Conferencia leída el 10 Enero de 1970, en el Centro de Estudios sobre el Movimiento Obrero Español, de Paris"; copy in Hoover Institution, Bolloten Collection).

14. *Unser Wort*, early Dec. 1936.

15. Essay in *Quatrième Internationale*, "L'Espagne Livrée," May 1939, published in book form under the title of *La guerra de España*. I wish to express my appreciation to George Esenwein for writing the following note: "When Casanova wrote this booklet, he ignored the differences that existed within the POUM over the advisability of entering the government. (For these differences, see Alba, *El marxismo*, I, 320–24.) He also ignored the fact that Juan Andrade, a member of the executive committee, was opposed to the liquidation of the Central Antifascist Militia Committee and, consequently, to the POUM's decision to collaborate with the Generalitat government. Alba does not mention Andrade by name, but states that within the executive *two* votes were cast against joining the government and that within the larger central committee several members were opposed. He also affirms that both the executive committee and the central committee accepted the proposal to enter the government 'in principle,' although there is some question as to whether Nin, the political secretary, took it upon himself to make the final decision without submitting the government's program to the executive 'for further ratification.' According to Ronald Fraser, who interviewed Andrade some years after the war, Andrade was pressured into accepting the decision, for despite his personal opposition to the POUM's collaboration with 'a bourgeois government,' he 'knew that he would be expelled from the party if he voted against it' (*Blood of Spain*, 341). Andrade has explained why the POUM decided to join the government: 'On the one hand, the immense majority of the sections of the party would not have accepted a break with the other working-class organizations, which would have meant our isolation. In practical terms, we would no longer have received material and economic support for our militia and would have lost all the positions that our sections held locally. In short, the party would have been reduced to nothing and would also have been in an illegal position. On the other hand, almost half the battle would have been won by the Stalinists, who would have profited from the occasion to proclaim our illegality. There were many factors that required careful consideration. For this reason, the executive committee of the party resolved to submit the final decision to the central committee, which met two days later' (unpublished paper presented on 10 Jan. 1970 at the Centro de Estudios sobre el Movimiento Obrero Español in Paris); I am grateful to Andrade's widow, María Teresa García Banús, for providing me with a copy of this paper." A copy of the Andrade paper is in the Hoover Institution, Bolloten Collection (Juan Andrade, "Conferencia leída el 10 de Enero de 1970 en el Centro de Estudios sobre el Movimiento Obrero Español, de Paris").

16. *La Batalla*, 24 Oct. 1936. For differences of opinion within the POUM itself as to the advisability of entering the government, see Alba, *El marxismo*, I, 320–24. The POUM, in fact, was buffeted by eight "ideological currents," according to Russell Blackwell (Rosalio Negrete), a Trotskyist sympathetic to the POUM. See his letters to Hugo Oehler in Brandeis University, Hugo Oehler Papers.

17. *Jalones de derrota: Promesa de victoria*, 288. For information on Munis's activity in the I.C., see Bonamusa, *Andreu Nin*, 185.

18. The FOUS was formed on 1 May 1936. It was made up of the local trade-union federations of Lérida, Tarragona, and Gerona (which had been expelled from the CNT) and a number of autonomous unions (see Pedro Bonet, its first assistant secretary, in *La Batalla* [Paris], Feb.–Mar. 1972, Mar. 1976).

19. Walter Held, *Die spanische Revolution*, 15; see also Trotsky, *Leçon d'Espagne*, 67–68, and his letter of 10 Mar. 1939 to Daniel Guérin, in the *New International*, May 1939, charging that the POUM "refrained from penetrating into the midst of the [CNT] in order not to disturb relations with the summits of this organization." For one of the most polemical attacks by a Trotskyist on the entire policy of the POUM leadership during the Civil War, see Felix Morrow, *Revolution and Counter-Revolution in Spain*, 40–102. An invaluable document in response to Trotsky's attacks on the POUM and its leaders is the unpublished paper presented on 10 January 1970 by Juan Andrade, a former Trotskyist and later member of the executive committee of the POUM (see n. 15 above).

20. *La Batalla*, 15 Oct. 1936.

21. Before the Civil War, the Catalan Federation of the UGT was one of the smallest sections of the Socialist labor union. According to Rafael Vidiella, the leader of the Catalan Federation of the PSOE, one of the four groups that had merged to form the PSUC (see Chapter 39), the membership of the Catalan UGT before 19 July was only 25,000 (*Las Noticias*, 17 Aug. 1937), but even this figure appears to be exaggerated. See, for example, Frank Jellinek (a pro-UGT observer), *The Civil War in Spain*, 335, who gives a figure of 12,000. On the other hand, according to Helmut Ruediger, secretary of the AIT, the prewar membership of the Catalan CNT was between 150,000 and 175,000 (Report to the AIT, dated 6 May 1937). Both labor unions grew rapidly during the war because most people felt safer carrying a union card. This led to extravagant and totally unverifiable claims by both the CNT and UGT regarding the number of their affiliates in Catalonia. On 10 October 1936, the Catalan CNT stated that its membership had risen to 360,977 (*Solidaridad Obrera*). Ten days later, the UGT claimed 436,299 members, pointing out that its demand for parity of representation in the government and in the municipal councils was therefore perfectly justified (Ramón Fuster in *Treball*, 20 Oct. 1936). A few months later, the UGT claimed 475,000 affiliates, to which *Solidaridad Obrera* (2 Mar. 1937) replied that the CNT had 1 million.

22. H. E. Kaminski, *Ceux de Barcelone*, 167, interview with Nin. See also article by Nin in *La Batalla*, 23 Sept. 1936, "¿Por qué los sindicatos de la FOUS ingresan en la UGT?"

23. See *La Batalla*, 15, 18 Oct., 25 Nov., 2, 13, 19, 22 Dec. 1936; 3, 16, 22, 30 Jan., 5 Feb., 17 Apr., 12 May 1937.

24. 27 Jan. 1937. See also "¿Por qué ha sido desautorizada la Junta del Ramo de la Madera de la UGT?", *La Batalla*, 4 Mar. 1937.

25. *La Batalla*, 14 Nov. 1936.

26. *Treball*, 2 Feb. 1937.

27. See *La Batalla*, quoted by Alba, *El marxismo*, I, 316.

28. Alba, *El marxismo*, I, 317.

29. Munis, 286.

30. See Alba, *Historia de la segunda república española*, 255; *El marxismo*, I, 317.

31. 25 Jan. 1937.

32. 27 Jan. 1937.

33. In 1921, Gorkin founded the Communist Party of Valencia, of which he became secretary general. In 1929 he broke with the Communist party machine and thereafter was denounced as a Trotskyist. Some years later, he wrote: "This accusation remained the excuse for a savage persecution. . . . It is true, though, that during the struggle for power between Trotsky and Stalin my sympathies were entirely with the first. It is also true that between 1928 and 1932 I translated into Spanish several works by the organizer of the Red Army. . . . But I never belonged to any Trotskyist organization. I must add that my relations with Trotsky, to the day of his death, had been entirely polemical" ("My Experiences of Stalinism," *The Review*, Oct. 1959, published by the Imre Nagy Institute, Brussels). In his book, *El movimiento trotskista en España, 1930–1935*, 40–41 and nn. 23–24, Pelai Pagès produces evidence that contradicts Gorkin's claims.

34. 15 Sept. 1936.

35. *En marcha hacia la victoria*, 11.

36. According to Juan Comorera, PSUC secretary, in a speech reported in *Treball*, 22 Dec. 1936.

37. Reported in *Solidaridad Obrera*, 9 Dec. 1936.

38. Ibid., 10 Dec. 1936.

39. Until December 1936 one looks in vain in the Esquerra newspapers, *La Humanitat* and *Ultima Hora*, for anything even remotely approaching the aggressiveness of the PSUC.

40. 11 Dec. 1936.

41. Andrade's radical attitudes occasionally caused dissension within the POUM leadership. Julián Gorkin, who wrote most of the editorials for *La Batalla*, informed me that Andrade sometimes filled in for him. "On one occasion," he stated, "this gave rise to a conflict, for on returning from Paris I found that he had written an editorial denouncing the Largo Caballero government as counterrevolutionary at a time when the Stalinists had already increased their maneuvers against it. Both the executive committee and the central committee condemned the Trotskyist tenor of the article, but I did not want the matter to become a public issue" (letter to me dated 2 June 1977, Hoover Institution). See also George Esenwein in Robert A. Gorman, *Biographical Dictionary of Marxism*, article on Andrade. For Andrade's as well as the POUM's differences with the Trotskyists during and after the Civil War, see his paper presented in Paris on 10 Jan. 1970 (Juan Andrade, "Conferencia leída el 10 de Enero de 1970 en el Centro de Estudios sobre el Movimiento Obrero Español, de Paris." A copy is in the Hoover Institution, Bolloten Collection).

42. As given in Juan Andrade, *Algunas "notas políticas" de la revolución española*, 7.

43. *Treball*, 13 Dec. 1936.

44. Ibid., 22 Dec. 1936.

45. Article by N. Molins y Fábrega, *La Batalla*, 16 Dec. 1936.

46. Ibid., 13 Dec. 1936. A full meeting of the Generalitat council was held on 14 December under the presidency of Luis Companys, who stated that he would begin consultations the next day with a view to forming a new government and that he would try "to harmonize existing differences" (Generalidad de Cataluña, *Actas de Reuniones del Consejo de la Generalidad, 3 Nov.–23 Dec. 1936*. A photocopy is in the Bolloten Collection, Hoover Institution). The minutes throw little light on the nature of the ideological and political dissensions. This fact demonstrates the vital importance of the Republican press as a primary source of information. Without a careful study of the thousands of editorials, speeches, articles, and manifestoes that appeared in the daily press of the various parties and organizations, the historian would be hard-pressed to understand the factional struggles that raged during the war.

47. See n. 18 above for reference to the FOUS, the POUM's trade-union organization, which was made up almost entirely of unions that had been expelled from the CNT.

48. See, for example, *La Batalla*, 19 Sept., 3, 15, 27 Oct., 28 Nov., 8, 12 Dec. 1936. See also *Spanish Revolution* (Barcelona), English-language paper of the POUM, 21 Oct., 25 Nov., 20 Dec. 1936, and Santiago Palacín, *La revolución y el campo*, 21. This criticism flies in the face of the accusations of foreign Communists and their supporters to the effect that the POUM (or the "Trotskyists") favored the immediate collectivization of small business enterprises and farm properties. See Winifred Bates, *Daily Worker* (London), 24 Feb. 1937; J. R. Campbell, *Soviet Policy and Its Critics*, 357; Louis Fischer, *Men and Politics*, 378, *Why Spain Fights On*, 44–45; Mikhail Koltzov, *Pravda*, 16 Aug. 1936; and Georges Soria, *International Press Correspondence*, 11 Dec. 1937. For the agrarian policy of the POUM, see Víctor Alba, *La revolución española en la práctica*, 256–68. In its defense of the small urban bourgeoisie, the POUM made a distinction between its own policy and that of the PSUC: "[It] is one thing to attract the middle classes to the revolution and another to form a coalition giving them a decisive role as a governing force . . . , but we uphold their economic claims . . . within the framework of the revolution" (*La Batalla*, 23 Feb. 1937).

49. Interview in Mexico in 1944. The shorthand notes taken during the interview are in the Hoover Institution. It was not until 1986, when re-reading these notes, that I discovered this important statement.

50. Rudolf Rocker, *Extranjeros en España*, 91. This allegation was also made by another foreign Anarchist (see *Vanguard*, June 1937), but I have found no confirmation by Spanish Anarchist leaders of any direct threat. David T. Cattell says: "Soviet aid was used to discriminate against the revolutionaries in Catalonia in several ways. There is good circumstantial evidence that the Soviet Union set these conditions for aiding Catalonia: that the dissident Communist POUM should not be allowed to participate any longer in the Catalonia Generalitat, and that the Catalonian government should submit to the over-all program set down by the central government" (*Communism and the Spanish Civil War*, 109). As will be seen, the POUM firmly believed at the time that its ouster was due to Soviet pressure.

51. *La Batalla*, 15 Dec. 1936.

52. Ibid., 18 Dec. 1936.

53. See list of central committee members elected at the beginning of March 1937, as given in Pedro Checa, *A un gran partido, una gran organización*, 23.

54. See Chapter 39 for Abad de Santillán's reason for entering the government.

55. 17 Dec. 1936.

56. *La Batalla*, 18 Dec. 1936.

57. Ibid., 20 Dec. 1936.

58. Ibid., 23 Dec. 1936.

59. 27 Dec. 1936, as given in Nin, *La revolución española*, 24.

Chapter 41

1. *La Batalla*, 5 Jan. 1937.

2. George Esenwein, in a note prepared at my request, writes: "The statement provoked the Soviet Consulate General to declare publicly that 'the communication published in *La Batalla* of 5 January, under the title, *Warning Note!*, was based on false material.' Furthermore, the Consulate claimed that the Transocean Agency did not exist in the USSR and that 'in the Soviet press there is not and cannot be any space for an attack on the fraternal workers' movement organized in the National Confederation of Labor [CNT]' (quoted in *La Batalla*, 9 Jan. 1937). The POUM attempted to prove the validity of the news release by reproducing the page of *Universal Gráfico*, where it had originally appeared (ibid.), although it never produced any extract from either *Pravda* or *Izvestiia* of 17 December 1936 containing the disputed quote. In fact, the Consulate General was right in saying that no such attack had appeared, for the only article on the subject of Spanish Trotskyism was one published in *Pravda* called 'Slanderous Maneuvers of the Trotskyists in Catalonia,' which was simply a reproduction of an article in *Mundo Obrero*. But while this article is censorious of the POUM, it does not contain the quote that *La Batalla* took from *Universal Gráfico*. In any case it is hard to imagine that the Kremlin at that time would publicly proclaim its intention to destroy the Anarchosyndicalists, for Vladimir A. Antonov-Ovseenko, the Consul General, was attempting to curry favor with the CNT-FAI leaders (see, for example, Diego Abad de Santillán, *Alfonso XIII, la II república, Francisco Franco*, 360–61, also 426–27). It is noteworthy that the apocryphal POUM quote was later attributed to *Pravda* of 17 December 1936 and was used in a pivotal way by countless writers and historians, including Diego Abad de Santillán, Gerald Brenan, Julián Gorkin, and Hugh Thomas (although it was eliminated from the 1977 edition of the latter's work on the Spanish Civil War). I am grateful to Hilja Kukk of the Hoover Institution for having carefully examined *Pravda* and *Izvestiia* for the 15th, 16th, and 17th December 1936. A similar account of the apocryphal nature of the *Pravda* article appears in Frank Mintz, *L'autogestión en la España revolucionaria*, 227–28, which was consulted after this note was written."

3. See *Ultima Hora*, 28 Dec. 1936; *La Humanitat*, 29 Dec. 1936.

4. *La Humanitat*, 29 Dec. 1936.

5. 30 Dec. 1936. See also *Solidaridad Obrera*, 29 Dec. 1936.

6. For this information I am indebted to Felipe Ubach, an aide in the premier's office, when interviewed by me in Mexico in 1945. Cf. Tarradellas's letter to me, dated 24 Mar. 1971, pp. 3, 6, Hoover Institution.

7. *Boletín de Información, CNT-FAI*, 26 Mar. 1937.

8. *Solidaridad Obrera*, 6 Feb. 1937. For Tarradellas's support of the CNT, see Miquel Caminal, *Joan Comorera*, II, 96–97.

9. *Treball*, 18 Mar. 1937.

10. *Tiempos Nuevos*, Feb. 1937.

11. Baltasar Porcel, *Conversaciones con el honorable Tarradellas*, 55.

12. *España Popular*, 30 May 1940.

13. For a PSUC reference to its influence over the CADCI, see Víctor Colomer, *Informe presentat a la primera conferencia nacional del partit socialista unificat de Catalunya I.C.*, 15. On 19 September 1936, the PSUC organ, *Treball*, stated that the Unió de Rabassaires had fifty thousand members.

14. Caminal, *Comorera*, II, 150.

15. *Treball*, 22 Dec. 1936.

16. *Solidaridad Obrera*, 21 Apr. 1937.

17. *La Batalla*, 23 Apr. 1937.

18. Ibid., 29 Dec. 1936. See also ibid., 1 Jan. 1937.

19. For a glowing tribute to Aiguadé by the Spanish Communists after the war, see *España Popular*, 7 Dec. 1946.

20. For more information on Rodríguez Salas, Aiguadé, and Martín Rouret, see Josep Coll and Josep Pané, *Josep Rovira*, 151–60. Rodríguez Salas was appointed on 17 December (*El Día Gráfico*, 18 Dec. 1936). Coll was secretary general of the Comisaría General de Orden Público and a POUM member. See also CNT dossier on Rodríguez Salas in International Institute of Social History, CNT-FAI Archives, Paquete 005, Caja 305. B. Informes. Dossier 90. Copies of these documents are in the Hoover Institution, Bolloten Collection.

21. See Chapter 40.

22. *Treball*, 1 Jan. 1937.

23. 28 Jan. 1937.

24. *La Batalla*, 24 Feb. 1937.

25. See *Diari Oficial*, 4 Mar. 1937.

26. In announcing the approval of the decrees, which had been heatedly debated during five cabinet sessions, Premier Tarradellas stated, according to *Treball*, the PSUC organ, that they had been "carefully studied and approved by all the councillors and their respective organizations" (2 Mar. 1937). On the other hand, *La Batalla*, the POUM organ (3 Mar. 1937) reported Tarradellas as saying that there had been agreement among all the cabinet members "on the majority of the provisions in the decrees," which was another way of saying that there had been disagreement on some.

27. *La Batalla*, 3 Mar. 1937.

28. 4 Mar. 1937.

29. Statement to the press by Tarradellas, *Treball*, 17 Mar. 1937.

30. Ibid.

31. Ibid., 10 Feb. 1937.

32. *El Día Gráfico*, 1 Nov. 1936; also communiqué issued by the Defense Council published in ibid., 3 Nov. 1936.

33. Quoted in A. and D. Prudhommeaux, *Catalogne libertaire, 1936–1937*, 19–20.

34. José del Barrio in *Treball*, 3 Feb. 1937.

35. *Solidaridad Obrera*, 13 Feb. 1937.

36. Ibid., 19 Feb. 1937.

37. *La Batalla*, 21 Feb. 1937. For Trotskyist criticism of the POUM's "vacillating" policy in the military arena, see G. Munis, *Jalones de derrota*, 369.

38. *Treball*, 27 Feb. 1937.

39. *El Día Gráfico*, 2 Mar. 1937.

40. *Treball*, 5 Mar. 1937.

41. 6 Mar. 1937.

42. Little information relating to the accords was ever published and then only in general terms. See, for example, *El Día Gráfico*, 4 Mar. 1937; *La Batalla*, 5 Mar. 1937; *Ultima Hora*, 5 Mar. 1937. Ramón Salas Larrazábal, *Historia del ejército popular de la república*, I, 1042–45, however, sheds some light on this matter, but, despite his diligent research, he was unable to find any official order merging the Catalan militia with the Popular Army.

43. See *Treball*, 20 Mar. 1937. The dates were set as follows: 1934–36 classes, 22, 23, 25, 27, 30 March; 1932–33 classes, 5 April.

44. Ricardo Sanz, the CNT militia leader, who assumed command of the Durruti Column after the death of its leader in Madrid, wrote after the war that Largo Caballero gave neither arms nor ammunition to the libertarian units, "because of his fear of I don't know what" (*Los que fuimos a Madrid*, 151). *Solidaridad Obrera*, the CNT organ in Barcelona (30 Jan. 1937), charged that the Aragon front was deliberately deprived of arms so that Anarchosyndicalism would fail in Catalonia (see also ibid., 6 June 1937; *Ideas*, 10 Mar. 1937; *Juventud Libre*, 17 Apr. 1937, *Ruta*, 28 Jan. 1937, and *La Batalla*, 31 Jan., 29 Apr. 1937). There can be no doubt that the hostility to the CNT and FAI was partly responsible for the paucity of arms and inactivity of the front during the first year of the war. The following comment by Walter Krivitsky is worth recording: "Stalin was determined to support with arms and man power only those groups in Spain which were ready to accept without reservation his leadership. He was resolved not to let the Catalonians lay hands on our planes, with which they

might win a military victory that would increase their prestige and thus their political weight in the republican ranks" (*In Stalin's Secret Service*, 91–92). But there were other important reasons for the inactivity of the Aragon front: the political rivalry among the various units, the lack of discipline, the absence of a single command (see Chapter 25), and the tensions in Barcelona and other cities in Catalonia, where more arms were held than at the front. "We cannot silence the fact," wrote the CNT-FAI militant, Diego Abad de Santillán, "that whereas we had only 30,000 rifles on the Aragon front, in the rear there were about 60,000 in the possession of the various parties and organizations with more ammunition than at the front. Not once, but dozens of times, we suggested that the libertarians hand over their arms. . . . They argued that we could not disarm our own people while the other parties and organizations were preparing to attack us in the back" (*Por qué perdimos la guerra*, 68). While it is true that political strife was partly responsible for the paucity of light arms on the Aragon front, this cannot be said of heavy weaponry, which Valencia either deliberately withheld or preferred to send to the threatened Madrid front. George Orwell, who fought with the POUM militia, gives the following vivid picture of the plight of the Aragon front: "Sometimes I used to gaze around the landscape and long—oh, how passionately!—for a couple of batteries of guns. One could have destroyed the enemy positions one after another as easily as smashing nuts with a hammer. But on our side the guns simply did not exist. . . . There were machine-guns at the rate of approximately one to fifty men; they were oldish guns, but fairly accurate up to three or four hundred yards. Beyond this we had only rifles, and the majority of the rifles were scrap-iron. . . . Ammunition was so scarce that each man entering the line was issued with fifty rounds, and most of it exceedingly bad. . . . We had no tin hats, no bayonets, hardly any revolvers or pistols, and not more than one bomb between five or ten men" (*Homage to Catalonia*, 41–42).

45. The article appeared under Enrique Adroher's pen name of "Gironella."

46. *El Día Gráfico*, 19 Mar. 1937; see also ibid., 4 Mar. 1937.

47. See letters from Balius to me, dated 10, 24 June and 15 July 1946, for detailed information on the group (file "Los Amigos de Durruti," Hoover Institution).

48. *The Civil War in Spain*, 541.

49. *La Lutte Ouvrière*, 3 Mar. 1939. For material dealing with the creation and activity of the Friends of Durruti, see file "Los Amigos de Durruti," containing letters from Balius to me, written after the war, and photostatic copy of Jordi Arquer's typewritten data on the organization based primarily on interviews with Balius and other members (Hoover Institution). See also Frank Mintz and Miguel Peciña, *Los amigos de Durruti, los trotsquistas y los sucesos de mayo*; Paul Sharkey, *The Friends of Durruti: A Chronology*; and Jaime Balius, *Hacia una nueva revolución*. George Esenwein writes: "The Friends of Durruti represented an extremist group within the CNT-FAI movement with significant support on the Aragon front and in Barcelona. By vigorously opposing militarization of the militias as well as the dissolution of the defense committees and the Anarchist-dominated patrols, the group hoped to stem the rising counterrevolutionary tide. From a theoretical standpoint, the Friends of Durruti challenged the reformist posture that had been increasingly assumed by the CNT-FAI leadership. According to a principal spokesman of the group, Pablo Ruíz, 'the primary objective of the new organization was to preserve intact the tenets of the CNT-FAI as of 19 July so as to ensure that the trade-union organization would assume the leadership of socio-economic affairs without the participation of the political parties' (*La Noche*, 24 Mar. 1937, as cited in Mintz and Pecina, 11–12). It is difficult to assess the extent to which the Friends of Durruti influenced the Anarchosyndicalist movement at this crucial juncture of the war. The group did not bring out its own journal, *El Amigo del Pueblo*, until May, and even though circulation figures are not available, Balius claimed that the second issue had a distribution of around 15,000. According to Balius, the group managed to publish the paper until the end of 1938 and, that same year, his pamphlet *Hacia una nueva revolución* [without the author's name, but later published in English with his name under the title *Towards a Fresh Revolution*] was distributed clandestinely, with an estimated circulation of between thirty and fifty thousand (file 'Los Amigos de Durruti,' Hoover Institution, Bolloten Collection). Besides Balius, the vice-president, and Félix Martínez, the secretary, other prominent members included Pablo Ruíz, Francisco Carreño, and Eleuterio Roig. Inflicted with paralysis at an early age, Balius abandoned his medical training to become a political activist. At first, he belonged to the separatist Estat Català party until 1931 and was briefly a member of Joaquín Maurín's BOC, the Bloque Obrero y Campesino (Jordi Arquer's letter to Bolloten, 16 July 1971, Hoover Institution; however, his membership in the

BOC is strongly contested by Alba and Schwartz in their forthcoming work). In 1932, he joined the CNT, eventually becoming an editor of *Solidaridad Obrera* and, during the war, editor-in-chief of the Anarchosyndicalist evening paper, *La Noche* (see Pablo Ruíz, 'Elogio posthumo de Jaime Balius,' in *Le Combat Syndicaliste*, 7 Jan. 1981, which also appeared in English in *The Alarm*, San Francisco, Feb.–Mar. 1982). No doubt the creation of the Friends of Durruti owed a great deal to Balius's leadership abilities, which have been described by the Swiss Trotskyists, Clara and Paul Thalmann, in the following way: 'Even at our first meeting with Balius and his friends the dominant impression was that he had an extraordinary gift in handling men. His appraisal of the situation was simple: the Anarchist leadership, because of its participation in the Popular Front government, had abandoned the firm ground of revolutionary Anarchist policy and had become an appendage of Communist strategy' (*Revolution für die Freiheit*, 189)." I am indebted to Esenwein for this note written at my request.

50. Although Isgleas resigned on 23 March, the crisis was not officially disclosed until 26 March.

51. FAI manifesto published in *Tierra y Libertad*, 3 Apr. 1937.

52. *Treball*, 30 Mar. 1937.

53. Comorera, speech at public meeting, *Treball*, 9 Apr. 1937; see also Tarradellas, statement to the press, ibid., 3 Apr. 1937; Sesé, secretary of the Catalan UGT, statement to *El Noticiero Universal*, as given in *La Publicitat*, 3 Apr. 1937.

54. *Solidaridad Obrera*, 4 Apr. 1937.

55. *Treball*, 28 Mar. 1937.

56. Caminal, *Comorera*, II, 93, 107–8.

57. *Treball*, 8 Apr. 1937.

58. 8 Apr. 1937.

59. Speech, 9 Apr. 1937, published in *La Batalla*, 11 Apr. 1937.

60. Caminal, *Comorera*, II, 117.

61. Luis Companys, "Notes and Documents on the Fighting in Barcelona, 3–7 May 1937." A copy of this invaluable material was given to me during the war by Ricardo del Río, the head of the Febus news agency in Valencia (Hoover Institution). Its authenticity was confirmed to me by Felipe Ubach, an aide to Premier Tarradellas, who claims that he saw and read a copy in the possession of the premier. Furthermore, Angel Ossorio y Gallardo, the Republican jurist, obviously had a copy to judge from the short excerpts quoted in his biography of Companys, *Vida y sacrificio de Companys*, 177–78. Ricardo del Río received the document from the famous liberal journalist and Catalanist Francisco Aguirre. For an obituary on Aguirre, see *España Republicana*, 24 Oct. 1942.

62. *La Batalla*, 17 Apr. 1937.

63. Ibid., 18 Apr. 1937.

64. For the restructuring of the militia units, see Salas Larrazábal, *Historia*, I, 1043, and Sanz, *Los que fuimos a Madrid*, 126–27. What was the true strength of the forces on the Aragon front? Propaganda estimates were as high as 150,000, but this figure was grossly exaggerated. Michael Alpert, in his scholarly monograph, *El ejército republicano en la guerra civil*, 45–47, states, on the basis of the limited data available, that "it appears improbable that the total number of men on the front exceeded 25,000 at any one time." This is supported by Helmut Ruediger in his report to the Anarchosyndicalist AIT of 8 May 1937, who states that in mid-April the number of CNT militiamen was 16,000 as compared with 9,000 belonging to other organizations, and by Moulin (Hans Freund), one of the leading Trotskyists in Barcelona, who gives the figure of 23,000, made up as follows: CNT-FAI, 13,000; UGT-PSUC, 5,000; and POUM, 5,000 (*Fight*, 10 Oct. 1936). He does not include the Esquerra militia.

65. *El Día Gráfico*, 25 Apr. 1937; *Treball*, 25 Apr. 1937.

66. *Treball*, 27 Apr. 1937. On the other hand, Ramón Liarte, secretary general in 1937–38 of the Libertarian Youth of Catalonia, asserts, although without corroborative evidence: "The Communists themselves had Roldán Cortada assassinated, throwing the blame on the 'uncontrollables of the FAI.'" It was necessary, he alleges, to find a "'moral' justification" for igniting "the antifascist powder keg"—an allusion to the May fighting in Barcelona (*Entre la revolución y la guerra*, 239).

67. 27 Apr. 1937.

68. 27 Apr. 1937.

69. *Treball*, 27 Apr. 1937.

70. Ibid., 28 Apr. 1937.

71. *Solidaridad Obrera*, 28 Apr. 1937; see also ibid., 29 Apr. 1937.

72. Article by Juan Andrade, *La Batalla*, 28 Apr. 1937.

73. For the best account of the incident, see Mariano Puente (a member of the CNT) in Nancy Macdonald, *Homage to the Spanish Exiles*, 171–88. See also *Solidaridad Obrera*, 29 Apr. 1937 (editorial and statement issued by the secretary of the councillor of internal security); *El Día Gráfico*, 1 May 1937; *Ruta*, 14 May 1937; Adolfo Bueso, *Recuerdos de un cenetista*, II, 227; the Communist writer Manuel D. Benavides, *Guerra y revolución en Cataluña*, 401–13; and Ramón Liarte (secretary general of the Catalan Libertarian Youth), *Entre la revolución y la guerra*, 236–38.

74. *El Día Gráfico*, 1 May 1937. According to the official Communist history of the Civil War, the carabineers actually began to arrive at the border region on 17 April and "during the ensuing days proceeded to disarm the gangs of 'uncontrollables' and to take possession of the frontier in the name of the central government" (*Guerra y revolución en España, 1936–1939*, III, 72). On 4 May, Indalecio Prieto informed Manuel Azaña by teletype that Negrín had left Valencia for the border on 30 April ("Azaña-Prieto Tapes," 11. Information on these teletyped messages is given in Chapter 42). However, according to a teletyped conversation between Comorera and Negrín on the evening of 2 May, quoted by Benavides, *Guerra y revolución*, 423, the finance minister was still in Valencia on that date. Negrín asked Comorera if he should take any special precautions to reach the frontier through Barcelona, to which Comorera replied: "I have already told you that in Catalonia and [in Barcelona] serious things may happen. You must postpone the trip." "I'll take a 'penknife' to defend myself," answered Negrín. "Don't tell anyone about my intention." To this Comorera replied: "It will all end well and would have ended well sooner if we had been given the means to purchase a lot of 'penknives.'"

75. *Gaceta de la República*, 16 Apr. 1937.

76. For the conflict between the CNT-FAI and the central government over the control of foreign trade and the flow of arms from the French border to the rest of Spain during the early part of the war, see letter of Largo Caballero to Spanish ambassador in Paris, Luis Araquistáin, dated 7 April 1937, stating that he had received reports denouncing the seizure of war material at the border by "uncontrolled elements" (Araquistáin Papers, Leg. 32/L40). See also Abad de Santillán, *Por qué*, 103, 112, 130; Louis Fischer, *Men and Politics*, 427; and statement by finance minister Juan Negrín, published in *El Día Gráfico*, 2 Dec. 1937. The above-cited letter of Largo Caballero also refers to problems with the International Brigades representative at the port of Barcelona, who refused to turn over to the war ministry cargoes that he claimed were the property of the brigades.

77. *La Vanguardia*, 28 Apr. 1937; *La Humanitat*, 28 Apr. 1937; *Diari de Barcelona*, 29 Apr. 1937.

78. *La Publicitat*, 30 Apr. 1937.

79. Agustín Souchy, *La verdad sobre los sucesos en la retaguardia leal*, 11; Orwell, 160.

80. Orwell, 157.

81. Some years later, Andrade flayed the Friends of Durruti as "a monument of ideological confusion," whose "ultrarevolutionary words" had no political effect (see his paper, "Conferencia leída el 10 de Enero de 1970, en el Centro de Estudios sobre el Movimiento Obrero Español, de Paris," Hoover Institution, Bolloten Collection).

82. *La Batalla*, 1 May 1937. On the same day, the tiny group of Bolshevik Leninists issued a lengthy manifesto directed against the CNT-FAI and POUM leadership and the "reformists" of the PSUC. It stated in part: "On 19 July the working class lacked the essential revolutionary leadership for the conquest of political power. . . . Anarchosyndicalism completely denied the necessity of political power. . . . Nor did there exist, nor does there exist, a genuine Marxist vanguard. On the other hand, the reformist movement unmasked itself as the mainstay of the liberal, capitalist bourgeoisie. . . .

"'Without the world revolution we are lost,' Lenin said. This applies even more to Spain. To lead the working class of the world toward insurrection we must show it the way by setting an example. . . .

"To get the masses oppressed by fascism to rise up, it is essential to show them the socialist way and not make pacts with our own bourgeoisie.

"The war and revolution are inseparable. More precisely, the war cannot be won without the revolution and, even more accurately, only the dictatorship of the proletariat can win the war.

"What is the dictatorship of the proletariat? The domination of the immense majority over the exploiting minority. . . .

"Who will form the dictatorship of the proletariat? The democratic organs of the masses, the committees of workers, peasants, and combatants, their assemblies, local, regional and national congresses and the revolutionary executive committees. The labor unions must organize the economy, but the entire working class must take into its hands the destiny of society.

"The emancipation of the working class can be the task only of the working class itself.

"DOWN WITH THE BOURGEOIS REPUBLIC!

"LONG LIVE THE DICTATORSHIP OF THE PROLETARIAT!"

I am indebted to Stephen Schwartz for a copy of this manifesto, which has been deposited in the Hoover Institution.

83. *La Batalla*, 1 May 1937.

Chapter 42

1. *ABC*, 7 May 1937; *El Adelanto*, 5 May 1937; *Diario de Burgos*, 5 May 1937; *Heraldo de Aragón*, 5 May 1937; *Ideal*, 6 May 1937; *El Norte de Castilla*, 5 May 1937; *El Noticiero*, 6 May 1937; *El Pensamiento Navarro*, 5 May 1937.

2. 10 May 1937.

3. 6 May 1937.

4. 8 May 1937.

5. May 1937.

6. See, for example, *Manchester Guardian*, 5 May 1937; *New York Times*, 8 May 1937; *L'Osservatore Romano*, 6 May 1937; *Le Temps*, 6 May 1937; *The Times* (London), 5 May 1937.

7. 11 May 1937.

8. 6 May 1937.

9. 7 May 1937.

10. *IV Internacional* (Mexico City), June 1937.

11. *Le Temps*, 8 May 1937. For the complete text of the statement in Spanish, as drafted by ambassador Luis Araquistáin, see Araquistáin Papers, Leg. 73-19; also Leg. 73/20A for a reply by Araquistáin to a protest in the Anarchosyndicalist daily *Solidaridad Obrera* entitled "La Embajada española en Paris contra Nosotros."

12. 11 May 1937.

13. *El Comunista*, 15 May 1937.

14. National committee report as given in Jacinto Toryho, *La independencia de España*, 308–17; see also "Manejos Separatistas en Cataluña," *Boletín de Información* (CNT National Committee, Valencia), 19 June 1937, and "El Separatismo en Cataluña," ibid., 24 June 1937.

15. When interviewed after the war by Jordi Arquer, a member of the executive committee of the POUM, Artemio Aiguadé accepted full responsibility for the assault on the *telefónica*. He stated that he had given the order personally to Rodríguez Salas and that he had not informed the government because he was acting within the confines of his authority. (Typewritten notes on this interview are in my file "Arquer Documents on the May Events" in the Hoover Institution.) According to Ronald Fraser, Pere Riba, Comorera's close associate, "recalled that he had known of the decision [to raid the telephone exchange] since a party executive committee meeting several days before" (*Blood of Spain*, 377). The two statements are not incompatible in view of the widely known cooperation between Aiguadé and the PSUC.

16. *Solidaridad Obrera*, 29 Jan. 1937.

17. Ibid., 4 May 1937.

18. *Catalunya*, 4 May 1937.

19. Barcelona correspondent of *Cultura Proletaria*, 12 June 1937.

20. The full text of the decree is reproduced in Albert Pérez-Baró, *30 mesos de col·lectivisme a Catalunya*, 228–36.

21. Speech, *Treball*, 2 June 1937.

22. Luis Companys, "Notes and Documents on the Fighting in Barcelona, 3–7 May 1937" (see Chapter 41, n. 61).

23. *Por qué perdimos la guerra*, 133.

24. See n. 15 above; also *Solidaridad Obrera*, 4 May 1937; Manuel Cruells, *Mayo sangriento*, 48. Cruells was a staff reporter in May 1937 on the *Diari de Barcelona*.

25. The official Communist history of the Civil War claims that Aiguadé was given authority to

occupy the telephone exchange during a meeting of the Generalitat government "despite Anarchist opposition" (*Guerra y revolución en España, 1936–1939*, III, 72). Miquel Caminal states that Rafael Vidiella, the PSUC leader, told him in 1979 that it was President Companys, in the presence of several councillors, including Juan Domènech of the CNT, who ordered Artemio Aiguadé to seize the *telefónica* but that Domènech warned them of the consequences (*Joan Comorera*, II, 120 and n. 193). On the other hand, the CNT claimed that everyone in the government later agreed that "Aiguadé had overstepped his authority" (report on the May events by the national committee of the CNT, *Cultura Proletaria*, 19 June 1937). See also *Boletín de Información* (CNT National Committee, Valencia), 24 June 1937; *Solidaridad Obrera*, 12 May 1937 (report by regional committees of the CNT, FAI, and FIJL). Furthermore, President Azaña states, apparently on the evidence of Tarradellas, that Aiguadé did not inform the other councillors of his decision (*Obras completas*, IV, 576). This is confirmed by José Coll, the general secretary of the General Commissariat of Public Order, who also states that Companys had no advance knowledge of the coup (Josep Coll and Josep Pané, *Josep Rovira*, 158).

26. Azaña, *Obras*, IV, 576.

27. Ibid., IV, 577.

28. CNT national committee report, *Cultura Proletaria*, 19 June 1937.

29. *La CNT en la revolución española*, II, 192. Felipe Ubach, an aide to Premier Tarradellas, told me in Mexico in 1939 that the premier was opposed to the raid on the *telefónica* but nevertheless sided with Companys during the cabinet debate out of loyalty to the president.

30. Cruells, *Mayo sangriento*, 55–56. See also his article in *Historia 16*, April 1977, on the May events.

31. *Cultura Proletaria*, 12 June 1937.

32. *Homage to Catalonia*, 169.

33. *La Batalla*, 4 May 1937.

34. After the cessation of hostilities the CNT defense committee in Sans released four hundred national republican guards, whom it had arrested at the inception of the fighting (see *Solidaridad Obrera*, 9 May 1937).

35. *La revolución y la guerra en España*, 144. President Azaña records: "All the working-class suburbs were in the hands of the rebels. The Generalitat, the departments of the interior and finance, etcetera, etcetera, were besieged" (*Obras*, IV, 579).

36. Interview, *Fragua Social*, 15 May 1937. The Anarchosyndicalist historian José Peirats, who witnessed the events, informed me that "the barracks controlled by the CNT did not intervene during the fighting" (letter dated 12 Sept. 1951, Hoover Institution).

37. Evidence from Cándido Bolívar, when interviewed by me in Mexico in 1940.

38. CNT national committee report, *Cultura proletaria*, 19 June 1937.

39. This accusation is not borne out by Carlos Pi Sunyer, the mayor of Barcelona and an Esquerra member: "As soon as the fighting began, Companys suggested to Azaña that he and his wife should move to the Generalitat. Perhaps fearful of taking the risk of making his way through the streets of a city in turmoil, Azaña preferred to remain in the Parliament building" (*La república y la guerra*, 444).

40. *Obras*, IV, 577–78. Jaime Miravitlles, a member of the Esquerra, who accompanied Tarradellas on his hazardous trip through Barcelona to the parliament building to see Azaña, writes: "The interview with Azaña was distressing. We found a man physically and morally destroyed" (*Episodis de la guerra civil espanyola*, 148).

41. *Obras*, IV, 578.

42. *Caníbales políticos*, 69–70. For a more detailed account by Gorkin of what transpired at this historic meeting, see his typewritten "Nota sobre las 'Jornadas de Mayo de 1937,'" in the Hoover Institution, Bolloten Collection. See also Juan Andrade's unpublished paper, "Conferencia leída el 10 Enero de 1970, en el Centro de Estudios sobre el Movimiento Obrero Español, de Paris," and typewritten notes, "Les Jornades de Maig de Barcelona," by Narcís Molins i Fàbrega, a member of the POUM executive, who was present at the meeting (Bolloten Collection). The Trotskyist leader in Barcelona, G. Munis (Manuel Fernández Grandizo), writes: "[The POUM leaders] claim that they made very militant and revolutionary proposals during their interview with the [CNT] regional committee. We believe them without further proof. But a revolutionary leadership does not distinguish itself solely by its revolutionary *proposals* but rather by its *efforts* to execute them when the other leaders oppose them. The POUM leaders constantly trailed the Anarchist leadership out of fear

of separating themselves from it when it refused to go along with the masses" (*Jalones de derrota*, 304).

43. Companys, "Notes and Documents." The date of the telephone conversation is given erroneously as Tuesday, 7 May, instead of Tuesday, 4 May.

44. Orwell, 174–75.

45. No attempt is made in this chapter to provide a detailed account of the street fighting. Firsthand reports can be found in the following: *La Batalla, Boletín de Información, CNT-FAI, Catalunya, El Día Gráfico, Las Noticias, El Noticiero Universal, La Publicitat, Solidaridad Obrera, Treball, Ultima Hora*, and *La Vanguardia* (all of which were published almost every day during the events); Abad de Santillán, *Por qué*; Cruells, *Mayo sangriento*; Marcel Ollivier, *Les journées sanglantes de Barcelone*; Orwell; Agustín Souchy, *Le verdad sobre los sucesos en la retaguardia leal.*

46. Interview, *Fragua Social*, 15 May 1937. In a document on the May events compiled from various sources after the war, Jordi Arquer, a former member of the POUM executive, states that Abad de Santillán was arrested on 4 May when on his way by car to the Generalitat Palace and was taken to the office of police commissioner Rodríguez Salas, where the two men embraced. Abad de Santillán, the document alleges, was somewhat timorous and afraid for his life. He told Rodríguez Salas that it was necessary to stop the fighting and that he was going to the Generalitat Palace precisely for that purpose. He was then allowed to proceed and the police were given orders not to fire on his car ("Notes sobre els Fets de Maig," Hoover Institution, Bolloten Collection). It is worth noting that Abad de Santillán states that after the fighting had ended he decided it was an error to have called for a cease-fire "without resolving pending matters." He met with Mariano Vázquez and García Oliver in the belief that "there was still time to recover lost positions." It was impossible to reach agreement, he says. "They replied that we had done the right thing . . . and that nothing could be done except await developments and adapt ourselves to them as best as possible" (*Por qué*, 138).

47. *La revolución*, 147.

48. As given in Rudolf Rocker, *Extranjeros en España*, 130; see also Souchy, *La verdad*, 19.

49. Statement made to Charles Orr, editor of the *Spanish Revolution*, English-language bulletin of the POUM (quoted in Felix Morrow, *Revolution and Counter-Revolution in Spain*, 100).

50. Orwell, 208.

51. The full text of the declaration can be seen in Víctor Alba, *La revolución española en la práctica: Documentos del POUM*, 155–62, and Andrés Nin, *La revolución española, 1930–1937*, 281–90.

52. 4 May 1937.

53. 9 May 1937, article by E. Tamarin.

54. This request for reinforcements is confirmed by Indalecio Prieto, who told Azaña in a teletyped conversation at 3 P.M. that Angel Galarza, the minister of the interior, had received a message from the councillor of internal security "stating that the situation was becoming more serious and urging him again to send substantial reinforcements." The original tapes of these conversations have been preserved by the Servicio Histórico Militar in Madrid. I am indebted to José Clavería Prenafeta for providing me with a microfilm copy of the eighty-nine pages. The above-quoted excerpt can be found on p. 12. Hereafter the tapes will be referred to as "Azaña-Prieto Tapes." They are published, in part, by Colonel José Manuel Martinez Bande, *La invasión de Aragón y el desembarco en Mallorca*, 282–92. My copy is in the Hoover Institution.

55. CNT national committee report, *Cultura Proletaria*, 19 June 1937. Article 9 of the Statute of Catalan Autonomy set forth the powers of the central government in the matter of public order as follows: "The Government of the Republic, by virtue of its powers and its constitutional functions, may . . . intervene in the maintenance of internal order in Catalonia under the following circumstances: 1. At the request of the Generalitat. 2. On its own initiative, when it considers that the general interests of the State or its security is in jeopardy" (C. Massó i Escofet and R. Gay de Montellà, *L'estatut de Catalunya*, 66).

56. CNT national committee report, *Cultura Proletaria*, 19 June 1937.

57. Ibid.

58. Both Carlos Hernández Zancajo and Mariano Muñoz Sánchez, it may be recalled, were appointed by Largo Caballero in February 1937 to scrutinize the work of officers and commissars of every rank.

59. Companys, "Notes and Documents."

60. Ibid. Under the provisions of the statute, Madrid was empowered to take control of internal order in Catalonia if the interests of the state were threatened. See n. 55 above.

61. Companys, "Notes and Documents."

62. See n. 55 above.

63. Azaña-Prieto Tapes, 12.

64. Ibid.

65. A copy of this document was loaned to me by Jordi Arquer, to whom I am indebted for much scrupulous research. A typewritten copy is deposited in the Hoover Institution. The Spanish Communists were obviously unaware of the existence of this document when they published a glowing tribute to Aiguadé in their refugee newspaper, *España Popular*, on 7 Dec. 1946. That Comorera remained at Companys's side during the four days of fighting and may have influenced his decisions was corroborated by Artemio Aiguadé when interviewed by Jordi Arquer (see n. 15 above). Agustín Souchy, the AIT representative in Casa CNT-FAI, Anarchosyndicalist headquarters in Barcelona, who was in touch with the CNT-FAI leaders during the events, confirmed Comorera's influence over Companys during the fighting when I interviewed him in San Diego in 1950. The shorthand notes of this interview are in the Hoover Institution.

66. Prieto, *Palabras al viento*, 203.

67. Azaña-Prieto Tapes, 3.

68. Ibid., 11.

69. Ibid., 20–29. In 1940, Hidalgo de Cisneros informed me that Prieto instructed him to proceed to the Catalan air base at Reus with a detachment of ground forces for its defense and with two bomber and two fighter squadrons "for operations against the region in the event the insurrectionists should win" (interview, shorthand record, Hoover Institution).

70. Information given to me in May 1940 in Mexico. The messages were read by her in the navy and air ministry. I have no way of knowing whether she was referring to the Azaña-Prieto Tapes, which came to my attention forty years later, or to other teletyped messages from Azaña. The first appeal for help recorded in the Azaña-Prieto Tapes was on Tuesday, 4 May, at 9 A.M. In a message to Largo Caballero's undersecretary of war, Azaña stated: "I want the government to be aware of the situation directly from me, a situation that I consider delicate both with regard to public order and my position with no means of defense other than a few dozen soldiers whose only weaponry are rifles. I expect to be informed of the government's opinion regarding these circumstances" (1–2).

71. *Obras*, IV, 580.

72. *La Vanguardia*, 5 May 1937.

73. *La verdad*, 19.

74. 4 May 1937.

75. National committee report, *Cultura Proletaria*, 19 June 1937.

76. Ibid.

77. Azaña-Prieto Tapes, 20.

78. *Solidaridad Obrera*, 5 May 1937.

79. Ibid.

80. *Cultura Proletaria*, 12 June 1937.

81. *Ensayo crítico sobre la revolución española*, 23–24.

82. National committee report, *Cultura Proletaria*, 19 June 1937.

83. *La Voz Valenciana*, 5 May 1937.

84. Companys, "Notes and Documents."

85. Statement issued by national committee of the CNT, published in *Fragua Social*, 7 May 1937.

86. *Fragua Social*, 15 May 1937.

87. For an account by the Trotskyists, Clara and Paul Thalmann, of the efforts by Moulin, one of the most active militants of the Bolshevik Leninists, to influence Jaime Balius, the vice-secretary of the Friends of Durruti, "in all-night discussions," to abandon his "innate Anarchist mistrust of the Marxists" and to collaborate with the Trotskyists, see *Revolution für die Freiheit*, 189–90.

88. As given in *Information Bulletin* of the International Bureau of the Fourth International, July 1937. See also Frank Mintz and Miguel Peciña, *Los amigos de Durruti, los trotsquistas y los sucesos de mayo*, 41–42.

89. As reproduced in *La Batalla*, 6 May 1937. See also Fenner Brockway, *Truth about Barcelona*, 10; Morrow, *Revolution*, 82; Mintz and Peciña, 49; Munis, *Jalones de derrota*, 305; Orwell, 207; Paul Sharkey, *The Friends of Durruti: A Chronology*, 13.

90. 6 May 1937. See also *Treball*, 6 May 1937, for the PSUC's criticism of *La Batalla*.

91. See Hugo Oehler, *Barricades in Barcelona*, 10. Oehler was national secretary of the Revolutionary Workers League of the United States.

92. I am grateful to Esenwein for his permission to use this excerpt from his personal research. In an interview published in *La Lutte Ouvrière* on 3 March 1939, Munis (the leader of the Bolshevik Leninists) said of the Friends of Durruti: "This group of young revolutionary workers represented the beginning of the evolutionary process of anarchism toward marxism. They had come to replace the theory of libertarian communism with that of the 'revolutionary junta' (soviets) as the embodiment of proletarian power democratically elected by the workers." However, in another part of the interview, Munis criticizes the Friends of Durruti for their "lack of political clarity."

93. There is no record in any of the newspapers of the period of any appeal over the radio by POUM leaders for a cease-fire.

94. 19 May 1937.

95. This appears to be a reference to the conference held on the night of 3 May.

96. *Revolution*, 94, and footnote. For a long criticism of the CNT-FAI and POUM leaders for not attempting to take power during the May events, see the Trotskyist *La Lutte Ouvrière* of 10 June 1937. A copy of this issue together with a point-by-point rebuttal by Jordi Arquer, a former member of the POUM executive, can be found in the Hoover Institution, Bolloten Collection (file "*La Lutte Ouvrière* and Jordi Arquer"). Arquer's rebuttal is part of a letter written to me in 1950. See also article by Lois Orr in the *Information Bulletin* of the International Bureau for the Fourth International, July 1937.

97. *Vanguard*, Feb. 1939.

98. Léon Trotsky, *La révolution espagnole, 1930–1940*, 425. See also Munis (leader of the Bolshevik Leninists), 301. For a POUMist's criticism of the Trotskyists, see Juan Andrade, "Conferencia leída el 10 de Enero de 1970, en el Centro de Estudios sobre el Movimiento Obrero Español, de Paris" (Hoover Institution, Bolloten Collection).

99. *IV International*, 1 June 1937.

100. *Service d'Information et de Presse por la Quatrième Internationale*, June 1937. See also Munis, 303–4, for a sharp criticism of the POUM's conduct during the May events.

101. *Unser Wort*, mid-March 1939.

102. Speech on 9 May 1937, as given in Díaz, *Tres años de lucha*, 432. This speech is quoted more fully at the beginning of Chapter 44.

103. 9 May 1937.

104. 10 May 1937. See also his article in *Labour Monthly*, Aug. 1937. Arthur Koestler, a member of the Communist party at the time, confirms that Langdon-Davies was also a member and secretary of the Communist front organization the Spanish Relief Committee "composed, as usual, of a panel of distinguished and unsuspecting personalities—Philip Noel-Baker, Lord Faringdon, Eleanor Rathbone, Professor Trent, and others" (*Invisible Writing*, 394). It is interesting to note that the *News Chronicle* had on its staff three party members covering events in Spain: Arthur Koestler, Langdon-Davies, and William Forrest, the later having previously represented Lord Beaverbrook's *Daily Express* in Spain (*Sunday Times*, 2–8 Jan. 1982). For Forrest's affiliation, see Koestler, 409.

105. 5 Oct. 1937.

106. *International Press Correspondence*, 11 Nov. 1937. Forty years later, Soria—without mentioning his own important role in disseminating the accusation that the POUM leaders were agents of Franco (see his pamphlet *Trotskyism in the Service of Franco: A Documented Record of Treachery by the POUM in Spain*, published in 1938)—states that the charge was a "fabrication" and an "extension into the international arena of the methods that constituted the most somber aspect of what has since been called Stalinism. . . . On the other hand, although the leaders of the POUM were neither agents of Franco nor agents of the Gestapo, it is true that their relentless struggle against the Popular Front played the game *nolens volens* of the Caudillo [Franco]" (*Guerra y revolución en España*, III, 79). This five-volume, profusely illustrated work, which closely follows the Spanish Communist party line during the Civil War, except when it ascribes certain unpleasant episodes to "Stalinism," is replete with distortions. Nonetheless, Soria claims wide recognition. "One of the greatest French historians

of the twentieth century, Pierre Vilar, who is a very good friend of mine," he said when interviewed by *Tiempo de Historia* (Nov. 1978), "has paid me the very great honor of reading my book from beginning to end and of agreeing to his name appearing in the book. . . . Just as I feel very happy to be in the company of Pierre Vilar, so too do I feel very happy in the company of very courageous people like [Herbert R.] Southworth and other historians." In a dual review of Soria's work and the French edition of the expanded version of my book *The Grand Camouflage*, Southworth observed: "[The] first Communist general history of the Spanish Civil War [by Soria] published in France for some years certainly deserves to be read, not merely looked at. It is superior to the work begun some years ago in the Soviet Union by the group headed by Señora de Ibárruri [*Guerra y revolución en España, 1936–1939*]. Soria treats the social revolution and the events of May 1937 with more nuances than did the Moscow team but his conclusions are, as expected, contrary to those of Bolloten" (*Times Literary Supplement*, 9 June 1978). On 19 May 1984, the Soviet news agency Tass reported that Soria, director at that time of the Paris agency for literary and artistic exchanges, had been awarded the Order of Friendship of Nations by the Soviet government (*Pravda*, 29 May 1984).

107. *My Mission in Spain*, 356.

108. *Documents on German Foreign Policy, 1918–1945*, Series D, II, 284–86.

109. See, for example, Dolores Ibárruri, *El único camino*, 366–67; also *Historia del partido comunista de España*, 162–63.

110. *La révolution espagnole* (Ruedo Ibérico, Paris).

111. 13 Oct. 1978.

112. *Times Literary Supplement*, 17 Nov. 1978.

Chapter 43

1. Editorial, reviewing events, 14 May 1937.

2. 6 May 1937.

3. According to Companys, the news that the government had taken over public order was received at 12:30 P.M. ("Notes and Documents on the Fighting in Barcelona, 3–7 May 1937").

4. As given in *Cultura Proletaria*, 19 June 1937. The *Boletín de Información, CNT-FAI* alleged: "Companys and Tarradellas, as well as the UGT [PSUC] representatives, did everything possible to delay all the negotiations, so that the fighting would continue. Their pleasure could be seen whenever the fratricidal struggle increased in intensity and, on the other hand, they looked dismayed whenever they noted any pacification" (21 May 1937, as given in Agustín Souchy, *La verdad sobre los sucesos en la retaguardia leal*, 59).

5. Interview in Mexico, 1944. The shorthand notes are in the Hoover Institution.

6. In his diary, Azaña states that during his teletyped exchange with Prieto he threatened to make a decision of "incalculable consequences" unless the government remedied the situation. He also says that he instructed Prieto to give this message to Martínez Barrio (*Obras completas*, IV, 581).

7. Azaña-Prieto Tapes, 29–37. For information on these tapes, see Chapter 42, n. 54.

8. According to information given to me by Cisneros in Mexico in 1940 (shorthand notes, Hoover Institution).

9. *Obras*, IV, 581.

10. Azaña-Prieto Tapes, 59.

11. *La Correspondencia de Valencia* (evening newspaper), 5 May 1937.

12. *El Día Gráfico*, 15 June 1937.

13. *La Vanguardia*, 6 May 1937.

14. Companys, "Notes and Documents."

15. According to Miguel Serra Pàmies, a member of the PSUC's central committee and councillor in the Generalitat government after the May events (personal interview, 1945).

16. Within a few days after the fighting had ended and the region had been occupied by twelve thousand assault guards, Companys expressed the hope in an interview given to *Ce Soir* (Paris) that the administration of public order would be returned to the region (as given in *Hoja Oficial del Lunes*, 17 May 1937).

17. *La revolutión y la guerra en España*, 148–50.

18. *Solidaridad Obrera* (Barcelona), 6 May 1937.

19. Reports on the fighting in these places can be found in *Anarquía*, 12 July 1937; *Solidaridad Obrera*, 12, 15, 16 May 1937; and *Treball*, 14 May 1937. See also Companys, "Notes and Documents"; Manuel Cruells, *Mayo sangriento*, 89; and Souchy, *La verdad*, 49–50.

20. Josep Coll and Josep Pané, *Josep Rovira*, 171–73.

21. *El proceso de Moscú en Barcelona*, 60. See also POUM document, "El Comité Executiu del POUM dona ordres que no venguin a Barcelona forces del front" (Hoover Institution, Bolloten Collection).

22. The CNT activist Isidro Guardia Abella writes: "On the orders of President Companys and with the written approval of the CNT-FAI committees, [Molina] handed to General Pozas, flanked by his Communist staff, the military command of Catalonia (*Conversaciones sobre el movimiento obrero: Entrevistas a militantes de la CNT*, 109).

23. *Alfonso XIII, la II república, Francisco Franco*, 424–25. See also Abad de Santillán, *Por qué perdimos la guerra*, 136–37; *La revolución*, 147; and Souchy, *La verdad*, 32.

24. Dolores Ibárruri, *El único camino*, 371–72. A report, dated 15 May 1937, drawn up by the juridical department for the Aragon front at the request of General Pozas, now a member of the PCE, states that on 5 May between fifteen hundred and two thousand men belonging to the CNT and POUM forces "abandoned the front and proceeded in the direction of Barcelona with all kinds of armament" but were halted outside Lérida by air force ground forces under the command of Lieutenant Colonel Alfonso Reyes ("Informe que emite la Asesoría Jurídica del Frente de Aragón en virtud de la Orden Telegráfica del General Jefe del Ejéricto del Este," Servicio Histórico Militar, Armario 62, Leg. 768, Carpeta 1). A photocopy is in the Hoover Institution, Bolloten Collection.

25. 5 May 1937.

26. He was replaced by Rafael Vidiella, the PSUC-UGT leader.

27. *Cultura proletaria*, 19 June 1937.

28. *Frente Rojo*, 6 May 1938. See also speech by Rafael Vidiella, ibid., 4 June 1938.

29. *La verdad*, 30–31. According to Miguel Serra Pàmies (interviewed by me in Mexico in 1944), Sesé may indeed have been killed by members of the PSUC. At one time, he said, Sesé had been a "Bullejista" (a follow of José Bullejos, former PCE secretary, who was expelled from the party and joined the left wing of the PSOE). "The Communists," he added, "made things difficult for Sesé in the UGT. They only tolerated him there. He had been a member of the BOC long before the Civil War" (taken from my shorthand notes, Hoover Institution).

30. *El Noticiero Universal*, 6 May 1937.

31. *El Día Gráfico*, 6 May 1937.

32. George Esenwein writes: "Official word of the assassination of Berneri and Barbieri did not appear until 8 May (*Boletín de Información, CNT-FAI*). No doubt because of the truce called on 6 May, the details of the murder were not reported by *Solidaridad Obrera* until 11 May, some days after the fighting had ended. Who exactly was responsible for the deaths of Berneri and Barbieri has never been conclusively established. There are three plausible versions of how they occurred. At the time, most sources sympathetic to the Anarchosyndicalists attributed the assassinations to the Communists. It was well known at the time that Berneri had repeatedly antagonized the Communists as a result of his criticisms of their policies in Spain. In an article published in *Guerra di Classe*—an Italian Anarchosyndicalist periodical that Berneri and other Italian libertarians residing at the 'Casa Malatesta' in Barcelona had been publishing since October 1936—Berneri maintained that Russia had sent arms and cadres to Spain in order to 'control the antifascist struggle and to arrest the development of the social revolution in the armed struggle against fascism' (16 Dec. 1936, as reprinted in *Anarchist Review*, no. 4, 1978, 54). According to Rudolf Rocker, this article 'gave rise to a protest from the Russian Ambassador in Barcelona [presumably the Soviet consul-general, Antonov-Ovseenko] and from that moment the agents of Moscow declared a war to death upon him' (*Extranjeros en España*, 132). In view of Berneri's and the Anarchosyndicalists' longstanding conflict with the Communists before the May events, and given the Communists' method of liquidating their political opponents, it is not surprising that they were blamed for his murder. According to Agustín Souchy, Berneri and Barbieri were killed in the following manner: 'On Wednesday, 5 May, at about 5 in the afternoon . . . twelve men went [to their flat], half of them Mozos de Escuadra [Generalitat Guards] and the other half members of the PSUC, apparently members of the UGT, wearing red arm bands. The leader of the group, when asked for his name, showed his identification card with the number 1109. Two of the

group remained in the flat and carried out another search. . . . The following night [Berneri and Barbieri] were killed by machine gun bullets, as the autopsy revealed. It was a cold-blooded calculated murder. . . . The evidence is irrefutable. Berneri and Barbieri were assassinated, because they were Anarchists, by Mozos de Escuadra and members of the PSUC, i.e., by the Communist party affiliated to Moscow' (*Los sucesos de Barcelona*, 24–25). A similar account was given by 'Brand' (Enrico Arrigoni), the free-lance correspondent of the American Anarchist paper *Cultura Proletaria*, who, like Souchy, was also in Barcelona at the time. Moreover, he claims to have been with the wives of Berneri and Barbieri when they identified their husbands' badly mutilated bodies (*Cultura Proletaria*, 12 June 1937, and Arrigoni, *Freedom: My Dream*, 323–24). Several weeks after the May events, the belief that Berneri was murdered by the Communists was given credence by an article that appeared on 29 May 1937 in *Il Grido del Popolo*, the organ of the Italian Communist party in France. Above all, the article attempts to assign responsibility for the May disturbances. Berneri himself is falsely accused of having been a member of the so-called uncontrollable elements who, it is asserted, provoked 'the bloody uprising against the Popular Front government in Catalonia.' The article goes on to affirm that, as a member of the *provocateurs*, Berneri got 'his just deserts in that revolt.' Although the article in no way suggests that the Communists had a hand in Berneri's death, it does demonstrate their strongly-felt contempt for him. It also clearly reflects the Communist view current at the time that the suppression and even killing of anti–Popular Front elements was justifiable. Since the war, a number of writers have accepted the version that the Communists were responsible for Berneri's murder, the most notable being his son-in-law, Vernon Richards (*Lessons of the Spanish Revolution, 1936–1939* [1983 ed.], 250); Abad de Santillán (*Alfonso XIII*, 425); and Pier Carlo Masini and Alberto Sorti (in Berneri, *Pietrogrado 1917/Barcellona, 1937*, 239–54).

"The official Anarchist account of Berneri's murder was presented by the National Committee of the CNT. In a manifesto issued in June 1937 the National Committee blamed the May Day tragedy and by extension the deaths of Berneri and Barbieri on the separatist Catalan party *Estat Català* (see *Boletín de Información, CNT-FAI*, 14 June 1937). According to this manifesto, Berneri was killed because of his intimate knowledge of Italian fascist activities in Spain and elsewhere in the Mediterranean. Significantly, the manifesto strongly suggests that the men who arrested Berneri and Barbieri were not PSUC members but rather pro-fascist elements of the *Estat Català* disguised as the police and who were allegedly working in collusion with the OVRA (Mussolini's secret police).

"A variation of the fascist conspiracy theory of Berneri's murder has more recently been put forward by the historian Carlos Rama, who painstakingly researched the subject and produced his findings in several publications. (See, for example, *Fascismo y anarquismo en España contemporánea*). Put very briefly, Rama believes that Berneri was most likely assassinated by Francoist fifth columnists on orders from the OVRA. In support of his view, Rama points out that the Italian historian Pier Carlo Masini has unearthed documents in the Casellario Político Centrale at the Ministry of Interior in Italy that prove that, while he was in Barcelona, Berneri was constantly under the surveillance of Italian police agents. These agents, Rama goes on to say, could have infiltrated the ranks of the foreign Anarchosyndicalist groups operating in Barcelona. Rama explains that the OVRA's intense interest in Berneri's movements was understandable: not only was he well-known for his anti-fascist writings (for example, his *Mussolini a la conquista de la Baleares*), but he was also reputedly involved in a plot to assassinate Mussolini. It is essential to note in this connection that there is concrete evidence that OVRA agents were, in fact, active in Barcelona during the Civil War. For example, we now know that a letter to Jean Rous from Leon Trotsky was intercepted by OVRA agents, for it was discovered years later in the Italian police files (see Chapter 40, n. 3 above).

"Rama's theory obviously challenges the belief still popular among many Anarchists that Berneri was killed by the Communists. Yet there are some libertarians, like Juan García Oliver, who subscribe to a view similar to that of Rama's. In his autobiography, *El Eco de los Pasos* (1978), García Oliver remarks that the Anarchists instinctively accused the PSUC of killing Berneri due to their intense hatred of the Communists. On the other hand, he speculates that, given the confusion reigning in Barcelona during the May events, it would have been possible for OVRA agents to have carried out such an operation. He also finds it noteworthy that Berneri's execution was strikingly similar to those of his compatriots Carlo and Nello Rosselli, who were killed shortly after the May events in France by French Cagoulards on orders from the OVRA (see *New York Times*, 24 Sept. 1944, which reports that the Rosselli murders were ordered by Count Galeazzo Ciano).

"In a letter to Burnett Bolloten (July 1979), Federica Montseny stated that the assassination of Berneri 'remains and will always remain a mystery.' She reached this conclusion after discussing the subject with Rama: 'According to Rama, the authors of the assassination could have as easily been Fascists as Communists. Mussolini never forgave Berneri . . . for the campaigns against fascism that our unfortunate comrade conducted during his years of exile in France. And the deed committed one month later—in June 1937—by the paid killers of fascism who assassinated Carlo and Nello Roselli in Paris in the horrible circumstances that are well-known raises certain doubts. In fact, Berneri had distinguished himself more by his attacks on fascism than by his opposition to the Communists. The seed of doubt that Rama implanted in me as a result of our conversation compels me, as a matter of conscience, not to dismiss a question that has its pros and cons.'

"For further information on Berneri, see Víctor Alba, *El marxismo en España, 1919–1939*, II, 429, 448–49; Camillo Berneri, *Mussolini a la conquista de las Baleares*, 3–6; Giovanna Berneri, *Lezione sull'antifascismo*, 109 ff., cited by Hugh Thomas, *The Spanish Civil War* (1977 ed.), 658, n. 5; Julián Gorkin, *Caníbales políticos*, 96; Francisco Madrid Santos, *Camillo Berneri, un anarchico italiano, 1897–1937*; Marcel Ollivier, *Les journées sanglantes de Barcelone*, 27; Randolfo Pacciardi, *Il battaglione Garibaldi*, 223; Max Sartin, *Berneri en Ispagna*; Paul Sharkey, *The Friends of Durruti: A Chronology*; Carlos Semprún-Maura, *Revolution et contre-revolution en Catalogne*, 240–42; Paolo Spriano, *Storia del partito comunista italiano*, III, 154, 209; *L'Adunata dei Refrattari*, 13 Aug. 1938; *La Batalla*, 11, 13 May 1937; BEIPI (Paris), 16–31 July 1955; *Boletín de Información, CNT-FAI*, 14 June 1937 (Report to the national committee of the CNT); *CNT* (Paris), 22 Oct. 1950; *Cultura Proletaria*, 3, 10, 17 May 1941; *L'Espagne Nouvelle*, 10 June 1938; *Man!*, June 1937; *Le Reveil* (Geneva), 29 May 1937; *Solidaridad Obrera*, 13 June 1937; *Spanish Revolution* (New York), 4–18 June 1937; *Tierra y Libertad*, 11 May 1937; and *Vanguard*, June, Aug. 1937. (Burnett Bolloten and I are indebted to David W. Pike for providing us with some of the bibliographical sources listed above.)" I am indebted to George Esenwein for this valuable piece of research.

33. Azaña, *Obras*, IV, 580–81.

34. Ibid., 585, 587.

35. P. 7.

36. *Diario de las Sesiones de Cortes*, 15 Mar. 1933, as given in Jerome R. Mintz, *The Anarchists of Casas Viejas*, 247. Of all the books written on this subject, this work, based on three years of field research, is by far the best.

37. Manuel Azaña, *Una política, 1932–1933*, 230–31.

38. *Obras*, IV, 584.

39. Ibid., 585.

40. *Historia de la guerra en España*, 255–56.

41. *Obras*, IV, 585–88. Azaña's fears and hesitations are apparent in his teletyped messages to Prieto, who did what he could to persuade the president to leave the parliament building for the port (Azaña-Prieto Tapes, 70–89).

42. *La verdad*, 24.

43. 31 Sept. 1937 (*sic*). The erroneous version of the leaflet given in Cruells, 70, and quoted by me in *La revolución española*, 587, apparently originated in *Los sucesos de Barcelona*. The author of this pamphlet, although not given in the Spanish edition, was Agustín Souchy, as can be seen from the English-language translation, *The Tragic Week in May*, which bears his name. It was published by the Foreign Information Office of the CNT-FAI, which Souchy directed.

44. *Solidaridad Obrera*, 6 May 1937. George Esenwein writes: "The acrimony between the CNT-FAI leadership and the Friends of Durruti continued after the May events. At the beginning of June, the Friends of Durruti joined the POUM and some sections of the Libertarian Youth in distributing a manifesto—*Manifiesto de Unión Comunista*—that was highly critical of the CNT-FAI leadership, attacking it, above all, for ordering the Anarchosyndicalists to withdraw from the streets and return to work (see Juan Gómez Casas, *Historia de la FAI*, 246–48). This provoked the CNT organ *Fragua Social* into branding Jaime Balius [the group's most prominent leader] a Marxist. Although he adamantly rejected this label in *El Amigo del Pueblo* (22 June 1937), he never succeeded in wholly dispelling the Marxist stigma from the Friends of Durruti. It is noteworthy that the controversy surrounding the group continued long after the war. José Peirats, who is regarded by many as the official historian of the CNT-FAI (*La CNT en la revolución española*), does not conceal his hostility in

his popularized account of the Anarchosyndicalists during the war (*Los anarquistas en la crisis política española*, 229). More critical of the Friends of Durruti was Helmut Ruediger, AIT representative in Barcelona, who characterized some of its policies as being 'bolshevik-fascist' (*Ensayo crítico sobre la revolución española*, 28). On the other hand, one of the books that has attempted to rescue the Friends of Durruti from such criticisms is the short but interesting study by Frank Mintz and Miguel Peciña, *Los amigos de Durruti, los trotsquistas y los sucesos de mayo*." I am grateful to George Esenwein for this note.

45. A copy of this manifesto is on file at the Hoover Institution (Bolloten Collection).

46. *Revolution and Counter-Revolution in Spain*, 95.

47. *Homage to Catalonia*, 183–84.

48. *El Noticiero Universal*, 6 May 1937.

49. *El Día Gráfico*, 6 May 1937.

50. *El Noticiero Universal*, 6 May 1937.

51. *Solidaridad Obrera*, 6 May 1937.

52. *El Noticiero Universal*, 6 May 1937.

53. *Cultura Proletaria*, 19 June 1937.

54. The full text of the resolution can be seen in Víctor Alba, *La revolución española en la práctica: Documentos del POUM*, 155–62, and Andrés Nin, *La revolución española, 1930–1937*, 281–90.

55. See Chapter 41, n. 61. The date of the discussions is given erroneously as Tuesday, 7 May, but it is obvious from internal evidence that the date should have been Thursday, 6 May.

56. See *Diario Oficial del Ministerio de la Guerra*, 12 May 1937. Torres was regarded as being friendly to the CNT and FAI (Abad de Santillán, *Por qué*, 136; Alba, *El marxismo*, II, 448; R. Louzon, *La contrarrevolución en España*, 123, n. 6; Ramón Salas Larrazábal, *Historia del ejército popular de la república*, I, 1039–40). At all events, he was replaced a few weeks later, after the fall of the Largo Caballero government, by Lieutenant Colonel Ricardo Burillo, a Communist party member and former police chief of Madrid (*Gaceta de la República*, 8 June 1937).

57. The appointments made by Galarza, published in the *Gaceta de la República*, 11 May 1937, were as follows: José Echevarría Nova, delegate of public order; Emilio Torres Iglesias, police chief of Barcelona; José María Díaz de Ceballos, general commissioner of security.

58. *Cultura Proletaria*, 19 June 1937.

59. *Solidaridad Obrera*, 16 May 1937; *Treball*, 14 May 1937; also Companys, "Notes and Documents," and Cruells, *Mayo sangriento*, 89.

60. 16 May 1937.

61. *Solidaridad Obrera*, 7 May 1937.

62. 9 May 1937. Julián Zugazagoitia, the moderate Socialist leader, writes: "Barcelona gave a very warm welcome to the assault guards. I noticed it in the streets and in the cafés. And numerous persons of different political beliefs with whom I spoke confirmed this to me. The autonomists [i.e., the liberal Republicans of the Esquerra] will forgive me if I affirm on the basis of my own information that Barcelona felt relieved on learning that the State had assumed the task of ensuring order" (*Historia de la guerra en España*, 261).

63. Barcelona correspondent, *Times*, 12 May 1937. *Solidaridad Obrera*, 9 May 1937, reported that five thousand assault guards arrived on the evening of 7 May.

64. The number of casualties during the May events has been variously estimated. The highest figures were given by PCE secretary José Díaz and by CNT-FAI leader Abad de Santillán. The former stated that 900 persons had been killed and 2,500 wounded (*Daily Worker* [London], 11 May 1937) and the latter, 1,000 killed and several thousand wounded (*Por qué*, 138). On the other hand, *Solidaridad Obrera*, 9 May 1937, reported a death toll of 400. The only serious research into this matter has been done by J. M. Solé and J. Villarroya ("Les Víctimes dels Fets de Maig" in *Recerques*, No. 12, 1982). Using the Civil Register of Deaths (Registre Civil de Defuncions de Barcelona) and the Register of the City Morgue (Registre del Dipòsit Judicial) as their main sources of information, they arrive at a figure of 218 deaths for Barcelona. They do not give any estimate of the number of wounded.

Chapter 44

1. Santiago Carrillo, *Demain l'Espagne*, 52–53.
2. Reprinted in Díaz, *Tres años de lucha*, 431–33. See also *Frente Rojo*, 10, 11, 13 May 1937; *Treball*, 15 May 1937.
3. 11 May 1937.
4. *Guerra y revolución en España, 1936–1939*, III, 79.
5. Azaña, *Obras completas*, IV, 587–88.
6. Ibid., 591–92.
7. Ibid., 585.
8. Ibid., 588–89.
9. *The Spanish Tragedy*, 175.
10. *Obras*, IV, 592–93.
11. Ibid., 595–96.
12. See his speech in October 1937, giving his account of this episode, reprinted in Largo Caballero, *La UGT y la guerra*, 8; also Juan Peiró (CNT minister of industry at the time), *Problemas y cintarazos*, 201–2.
13. P. 1184. See Chapter 45, n. 19, below, for information on these memoirs.
14. Largo Caballero, *La UGT y la guerra*, 8.
15. *Yo fui un ministro de Stalin*, 85.
16. *Adelante* (Mexico City), 1 Apr. 1946.
17. *Historia de la guerra en España*, 274.
18. *Adelante* (Mexico City), 1 Apr. 1946. See also Indalecio Prieto, *Convulsiones de España*, II, 94.
19. *Mundo Obrero* (Paris), 25 Sept. 1947.
20. *Política de ayer y política de mañana*, 85.
21. Togliatti, *Escritos sobre la guerra de España*, 136.
22. Largo Caballero, "Notas Históricas," 1184.
23. *Obras*, IV, 595.
24. Ibid.
25. Ibid., 596. See also ibid., 613–14, 616–17. For the Communist view of the project, see *Guerra y revolución*, III, 80 and n. 3; ibid., I, 225. On 26 March 1937, Carlos de Baráibar, then visiting Paris, noted in a letter to Spanish ambassador Luis Araquistáin that Largo Caballero "has entrusted me with the mission of carrying back to [Valencia] the sum of 3,300,000 French francs in bills of 1,000 regarded as necessary for the immediate development of a plan of agitation and propaganda in North Africa" (Araquistáin Papers, Leg. B. 30).
26. That the offensive was planned by Asensio and Martínez Cabrera is confirmed by the Nationalist military historian Ramón Salas Larrazábal (*Historia del ejército popular de la república*, I, 1076), who states that Alvarez Coque, who succeeded Martínez Cabrera as provisional head of the general staff, "inherited" the plans of these two generals relating to the operation.
27. *Obras*, IV, 589.
28. *El comunismo y la guerra de España*, 13.
29. Salas Larrazábal, *Historia*, I, 1077–78. According to Azaña, Largo Caballero told him that seventy-five thousand men would take part (*Obras*, IV, 590). The Estremadura plan of operations is published in Colonel José Manuel Martínez Bande's *La ofensiva sobre Segovia y la batalla de Brunete*, 237–40.
30. *Historia*, I, 1083.
31. For a scrupulously documented account of the precise units to be used in the operation and for the delays in its execution, see ibid., I, 1075–83. The American historian Gabriel Jackson states that, in connection with the Estremadura plan, Julio Just, the left Republican minister of public works in the Caballero government, told him that "he had prepared dozens of portable bridges and dispatched numerous supply trains to Ciudad Real," but that, on the other hand, Prieto told him that "upon taking office as minister of defense on May 27, he found absolutely no practical dispositions looking toward an offensive in Estremadura" (*The Spanish Republic and the Civil War, 1931–1939*, 372, n. 13).
32. See Miaja's communication, dated 1 May 1937, to Largo Caballero (Library of Congress);

Azaña, *Obras*, IV, 590–91; Segismundo Casado, *The Last Days of Madrid*, 71–72; Francisco Largo Caballero, *Mis recuerdos*, 215; Salas Larrazábal, *Historia*, I, 1078–80. Miaja's disobedience is also confirmed in Largo Caballero's unpublished memoirs, "Notas Históricas," 1158, in which he states that the general "began to boycott the dispatch of the troops requested."

33. *El comunismo*, 13. See also Largo Caballero, *Mis recuerdos*, 215.

34. Casado, *The Last Days*, 72–73.

35. Martínez Bande gives the source of his information as A.G.L. (Archivo de la Guerra de Liberación)—D.R. (Documentación Rojo)—Ejército del Centro—L.673-C.3 and L.691-C.1 (*La ofensiva sobre Segovia*, 56, n. 60).

36. *Mis recuerdos*, 214–15.

37. *Yo fui un ministro de Stalin*, 79–85.

38. *Obras*, IV, 595.

39. Ibid., 596–97.

40. *Mis recuerdos*, 219.

41. *Obras*, IV, 597.

42. *El comunismo*, 14.

43. *Mis recuerdos*, 219.

44. *El Mercantil Valenciano*, 22 July 1937.

45. *El comunismo*, 14.

46. *Todos fuimos culpables*, 656.

47. Morón, 60–63.

48. *Mis recuerdos*, 220.

49. *Obras*, IV, 598.

50. Ibid.

51. See, for example, ibid., 598, quoting Martínez Barrio; Largo Caballero, *Mis recuerdos*, 219–22.

52. *Obras*, IV, 598.

53. Ibid., 600–601.

54. See document issued by the party's central committee, published in *El Mercantil Valenciano*, 16 May 1937.

55. See point 6 of its declaration, published in *El Socialista*, 18 May 1937. The Socialist executive's support of Prieto for the ministry of national defense is confirmed by Largo Caballero in his unpublished memoirs, "Notas Históricas," 1187.

56. Article in *España Popular*, 11 Mar. 1940.

57. *Claridad*, 15 May 1937.

58. *Obras*, IV, 602.

59. Letter to José Bullejos, 20 Nov. 1939, published in *¿Qué se puede hacer?*, 20–24.

60. *Mis recuerdos*, 222–23.

61. *Frente Libertario*, 17 May 1937.

62. *Fragua Social*, 16 May 1937.

63. *Solidaridad Obrera*, 16 May 1937.

64. *Fragua Social*, 16 May 1937.

65. See his plan, as given in *La Correspondencia de Valencia*, 17 May 1937.

66. *Fragua Social*, 18 May 1937.

67. See his plan, as given in the evening newspaper *La Correspondencia de Valencia*, 17 May 1937.

68. See letter published in the evening newspaper *Frente Rojo*, 17 May 1937.

69. See letter to Largo Caballero published in *El Socialista*, 18 May 1937.

70. Reply to Largo Caballero, as given in the evening newspaper *Frente Rojo*, 17 May 1937.

71. Azaña, *Obras*, IV, 602.

72. See report from Valencia by the Febus news agency, "Una referencia de la reunión celebrada en la Presidencia de la República," published in *Mundo Obrero*, 17 May 1937.

Chapter 45

1. *Obras completas*, IV, 602.
2. Indalecio Prieto, *Convulsiones de España*, II, 94.
3. *Adelante* (Mexico City), 1 Apr. 1946.
4. *Todos fuimos culpables*, 663.
5. *Obras*, IV, 603. See also Julián Zugazagoitia, *Historia de la guerra en España*, 274. "For the majority of people," writes Mariano Ansó, a close friend of Negrín's, "Negrín was little more than a straw man for Prieto, the figurehead of the government that was to be piloted by Prieto. This belief was so widespread that during the first months [of the new administration] it was called the Prieto-Negrín government, the name of the minister preceding that of the premier. Negrín was aware of this and smiled. He did not feel humiliated. It seemed quite natural to him that because of Prieto's strong personality his name was placed ahead of his—a name that was still unknown. Undoubtedly, the Communists saw in him the malleable person they needed" (*Yo fui ministro de Negrín*, 190).
6. "Un hombre singular" in *Convulsiones*, III, 219–21. The eating habits attributed to Negrín by Prieto were common knowledge among those who knew him and were confirmed to me by several reliable sources. For additional published testimony, see Segismundo Casado, *Así cayó Madrid*, 134–35; Antonio Cordón, *Trayectoria*, 390; José García Pradas, *¡Teníamos que perder!*, 209; Justo Martínez Amutio, *Chantaje a un pueblo*, 368; Carles Pi Sunyer, *La república y la guerra*, 474; Frank Sedwick, *The Tragedy of Manuel Azaña and the Fate of the Spanish Republic*, 183 (who describes Negrín as a "tactless, indecorous, disorganized and unscrupulous man, whom even his friends admit to have been a kind of Rasputin-of-the-stomach-and-sex in his personal life"); Togliatti, *Escritos sobre la guerra de España*, 231; Zugazagoitia, 336.
7. *In Stalin's Secret Service*, 100–101.
8. *Nation* (New York), 13 Jan. 1940.
9. *The Last Optimist*, 291.
10. Ansó, 188.
11. *Indice*, 15 June 1974.
12. Interview in Mexico, 1944. It will be recalled that in March 1937 Togliatti, according to Jesús Hernández, had also favored Largo Caballero's successor.
13. *Triunfo*, 22 June 1974. This hyperbolic characterization of Negrín by Juan Marichal and his continuing effort, along with other well-known historians, such as Manuel Tuñón de Lara, Angel Viñas, José Aróstegui, and Herbert R. Southworth, to revamp the figure of Negrín may be regarded almost as a "crusade" to "*reubicar*" or "resituate" Negrín historically by clearing him of any stigma of pro-Communism. In a letter to me, dated 4 November 1982, Viñas asserted that in his opinion no one was interested in "resituating [*reubicar*] Negrín historically," yet in *Tiempo de Historia* of May 1979, he described Negrín as "the great statesman of the Republic," adding that "he left no memoirs (or, at least, if he left any, they have not been published), as a result of which the task of resituating him historically out of an underbrush of contradictory data and opinions makes it doubly exciting." In a review of the French revision of my book *El gran engaño*, Herbert R. Southworth, an unwavering admirer of Negrín, stated (*Times Literary Supplement*, 9 June 1978): "I think I can discern on the horizon unmistakable signs that History is beginning to take a second look at Juan Negrín. . . . Angel Viñas's book on the Spanish gold shipped to Moscow vindicates Negrín's actions, long viewed by writers of Bolloten's school with a jaundiced (non-auriferous) eye. . . . It is ardently to be hoped that Juan Marichal will soon find the time and documents necessary to continue his projected life of Negrín." Southworth has never explained his own dogged support of Negrín. George Esenwein writes: "In order to understand Southworth's steadfastly loyal and therefore uncritical support of Negrín one must bear in mind that he served as an important propagandist for the Negrín government. Between February 1938 and February 1939, he edited *The News of Spain* (see *Contemporary Authors*, vols. 85–88, p. 557), a bulletin published in New York, which, if not financed by or otherwise officially associated with the Spanish Republican government, was unmistakeably a mouthpiece for its policies. Several themes recur which identify it as such. 1. News of events in Spain is focused on the achievements of the Negrín administration. Thus, the opening of a church was cited as an example of the government's commitment to religious tolerance. 2. Other events, no matter how controversial, were always presented as somehow reflecting the positive aspects of the Negrín government. An

example of this is found in the bulletin's report of the POUM trial in October 1938. Using information derived from reporters like Herbert Matthews or other sources either sympathetic or close to Negrín, the bulletin attempted to portray the trial as a model of 'Republican justice.' The 'facts' of the case are all given from this point of view and are therefore heavily weighted against the POUM defendants. For instance, although the bulletin does not openly assert that the POUMists on trial were traitors, it clearly implied that the accused were guilty of treason and espionage. Accordingly, rumors circulated by the Communists, who were responsible for staging the trial, are repeated without qualification, e.g., that Andrés Nin and José Rovira, the political secretary of the party and the former commander of the XXIXth division respectively, had taken refuge in 'Rebel territory' (2 November 1938). 3. Finally, the Republican figures who received most attention (in the form of biographical sketches and the like) were pro-Communists associated with Negrín, such as Vicente Rojo, Alvarez del Vayo and José Bergamín, the Catholic writer, who was personally involved in goodwill campaigns abroad on behalf of the Negrín government and who, in the preface to a book, *Espionaje en España*, widely diffused by the Communists and written by an unknown author 'Max Rieger,' had described the POUM as an espionage organization and an integral part of the international fascist organization in Spain. Foreign personalities who were also Negrinistas and frequently appeared in the bulletin's columns were Herbert Matthews, Louis Fischer, Gustav Regler and Frank Jellinek. It is interesting to note that Southworth has not discussed the role he played as editor of *The News of Spain*. When interviewed about the Civil War in *Tiempo de Historia* (October 1978), he did not allude to the fact that he was a propagandist for the Negrín government, but he did describe the premier as 'the most outstanding personality during the war in the Republican camp,' and argued that the time had come to reassess his achievements as a political figure." I am indebted to George Esenwein for this important piece of research undertaken at my request in 1984.

After the death of General Franco in 1975, Southworth appeared prominently on Spanish TV as a leading authority on the Spanish Civil War, of which he gave his own particular version to viewers, most of whom, because of their age and the many years of press censorship during the Franco régime, had little knowledge of the complexities of the Civil War. The most recent attempt to "resituate" Negrín was on the occasion of a colloquium held in the Canary Islands in honor of the former prime minister (see *Canarias*, 17 Nov. 1985) and attended by Tuñón de Lara, Juan Marichal, José Prats, and Juan Rodríguez Doreste (the last two, onetime aides of Negrín) at which the well-known historian Javier Tusell found himself outnumbered by Negrín apologists. According to Tusell, the most "tendentious" speaker was not Tuñón de Lara but Juan Marichal (letter to me). It was because of the long-standing effort to revamp Negrín, whose principal apologists studiously avoid any testimony that conflicts with their immutable position, that I delivered a paper in Madrid at the 16th Annual Conference of the Society for Spanish and Portuguese Historical Studies on the "Strange Case of Dr. Juan Negrín." The paper was published in *Historia 16* in January 1986, together with eighty-nine source references.

In view of the controversy that still surrounds Negrín, the following passage from a fourteen-page unpublished portrait written by one of Negrín's harshest critics, Luis Araquistáin, after a five-hour visit with him in London in 1944, should be recorded lest the document escape attention. After asserting that "there is much that is pathological" about Negrín's inordinate appetite for physical enjoyment and for power, Araquistáin continues: "He always regarded himself as a potential dictator. His model during the first World War was Clemenceau. Later, it was Mussolini, and now I suspect he secretly admires Hitler and Stalin. . . . I have always been fond of this wild, unpredictable man (hombre desorbitado) as though he were a brother or, rather, a son, and I am still fond of him despite his infinitely mendacious and false character, because I feel that all his defects are a reflection of a weak, infantile nature that can only express and impose itself through lies and deceit. At the root of the severity with which I judge him lies a feeling of pity and forgiveness, because I believe he is irresponsible. However, after this visit, I also believe that there is no remedy for his misfortune and that he is a tragic figure, tragic to himself and, above all, to everyone else and that he should be treated like a sick man" (Araquistáin Papers, Leg. 52 N 10[a]). A photocopy of the original document is in the Hoover Institution, Bolloten Collection, file "Luis Araquistáin, 'Negrín.'" For a portrait of Negrín in an unpublished report by the Peninsular Committee of the FAI, see "Informe, Comité Peninsular de la FAI, Sept. 1938," International Institute of Social History, CNT-FAI Archives, Paquete 92, Caja 305, B, pp. 7–8. Photocopy is in the Hoover Institution, Bolloten Collection, file "FAI, Informe, Comité Peninsular, Sept. 1938."

14. *La vocación de Manuel Azaña*, 265.

15. Krivitsky, 100–101. See also Salvador de Madariaga, *Spain*, 515.

16. *Spain*, 521.

17. *Yo fui un ministro de Stalin*, 86–88.

18. Founded as a weekly, *Claridad* was converted into a daily in April 1936 under the control of Luis Araquistáin, Carlos de Baráibar, and Amaro del Rosal, all three prominent supporters of Largo Caballero. The sum of 250,000 pesetas for the conversion was loaned by the UGT bank employees' union, the Federación Nacional de Banca, whose president was the young and influential Rosal. After Araquistáin, who was director of the daily, became ambassador to Paris in September 1936 and Baráibar, the manager, was made undersecretary of war in February 1937, the newspaper was left in the hands of Rosal, who had been appointed delegate-adviser by his union at the time of the conversion. With both Araquistáin and Baráibar out of the way, Rosal, who had already furtively switched his support to the Communists, *Claridad* became what his two former colleagues later called "the cowardly and clumsily disguised mouthpiece of the Communist party" (*La Correspondencia de Valencia*, 1 Sept. 1937). For further information on *Claridad*, see files "Ricardo del Río, Director of Febus news agency, Valencia and Barcelona" and "*Claridad*" (Hoover Institution, Bolloten Collection); also Marta Bizcarrondo, *Araquistáin y la crisis socialista en la II república, Leviatán, 1934–1936*, 419–20; Amaro del Rosal, *Historia de la UGT de España, 1901–1939*, II, 648; Matilde Vázquez and Javier Valero, *La guerra civil en Madrid*, 374, 456–57.

19. P. 226. In view of the political significance of Largo Caballero's memoirs, *Mis recuerdos*, published in Mexico in 1954 and cited frequently in this work, it is of immense historical and historiographical importance to clear up any doubts regarding their authenticity, which Angel Viñas, a stout supporter of Juan Negrín, has called into question. When the memoirs first appeared, with a twenty-one-page introduction by Enrique de Francisco, Caballero's close friend and former secretary of the Agrupación Socialista Madrileña, no one ventured to question their authenticity or even to suggest that they had been "conveniently retouched," to use the phrase of Viñas (*El oro de Moscú*, 314).

In this connection, it is interesting to note that Indalecio Prieto, an archenemy of Largo Caballero (in an article dated 5 Dec. 1956, reproduced in Prieto, *Convulsiones*, III, 221), and Bruno Alonso, a Prietista (in a letter to Enrique de Francisco dated 3 February 1955, deposited in the Fundación Pablo Iglesias in Madrid), both sharply criticize the publication of *Mis recuerdos* but do not dispute its authenticity. Nor did Rodolfo Llopis (secretary of the PSOE in exile) question the reliability of the memoirs when, in a letter to Largo Caballero's son, Francisco Largo Calvo, on 12 May 1954, he urged him to reconsider the advisability of publishing them in view of the danger that the enemies of the party would exploit them "to sow discord in our ranks" (Araquistáin Papers, L42/140). It is no less interesting that the official *Historia del partido comunista de España* (1960), 160, in quoting a few lines from *Mis recuerdos* also does not question its authenticity. But, in recent years, in an attempt to revamp the figure of Negrín and free him from the stigma of pro-Communism, *Mis recuerdos*, which accuses him of having surrendered himself "body and soul" to the Communist party (230), has come under attack. It is unfortunate that Viñas, whose contributions to the historiography of the Civil War are substantial, allowed himself, because of his defense of Negrín, to assume the most visible role in this assault. "It is necessary to mention the possibility," he wrote in 1979 (*El oro de Moscú*, 138, n. 12), "that these memoirs were not actually written by the Socialist leader. There are strong rumors that they were doctored for political motives. However, we have not been able to find documentary proof. . . . This year the authentic ones—'las auténticas'—will be published."

The inference from this statement that *Mis recuerdos* is not authentic was vigorously condemned in letters to me by Leonor Menéndez de Beltrán and Justo Martínez Amutio, who were intimate political associates of Largo Caballero and were familiar with both *Mis recuerdos* (which was written from memory after Largo's release from a German concentration camp in 1945) and the "*auténticas*" entitled "Notas Históricas sobre la Guerra de España," comprising 1,541 typewritten pages, each signed by Largo Caballero (which were written between 1937 and 1940, when he had the benefit of documentation). A copy of the manuscript is with the Fundación Pablo Iglesias. It is regrettable that its publication has been delayed year after year by the foundation for reasons beyond its control. Because of the importance of determining the authenticity of *Mis recuerdos*, in 1982 I requested the assistance of Aurelio Martín Nájera of the Fundación Pablo Iglesias, who kindly commissioned his collaborator, Antonio González Quintana, an authority on the history of the Socialist party and the UGT, to compare

Mis recuerdos with the "Notas Históricas." After a painstaking study, González Quintana, in a twenty-seven-page report to me, made the following categorical statement: "After comparing the texts of *Mis recuerdos* and 'Notas Históricas sobre la Guerra de España,' I believe I can testify with certainty to the accuracy and similarity of both texts on fundamental and basic questions." González Quintana's report and my correspondence with Martín Nájera, Justo Martínez Amutio, Leonor Menéndez de Beltrán, and Angel Viñas are in the Bolloten Collection, Hoover Institution (file "Largo Caballero: *Mis recuerdos* and 'Notas Históricas sobre la Guerra España' "). Since the writing of this note, the first volume of the "Notas Históricas," covering the period 1917–36, has been published (Francisco Largo Caballero, *Escritos de la República: Edicion, estudio preliminar y notas de Santos Juliá*, 1985). No definite dates have been set for the publication of the two subsequent volumes covering the Civil War and postwar periods.

20. P. 1179. For important information on both the published and unpublished memoirs of Largo Caballero, see note 19.

21. *Solidaridad Obrera* (Paris), 11 Mar. 1951. See Chapter 17 for the claim that El Campesino's articles and books were ghostwritten by Julián Gorkin.

Chapter 46

1. *Gaceta de la República*, 18 May 1937.

2. *Spanish Notebooks*, 136.

3. *El Socialista* (Madrid), 18 May 1937.

4. *Solidaridad Obrera*, 18 May 1937; *Tierra y Libertad*, 29 May 1937. See also *Boletín de Información, CNT-FAI*, 22 May 1937; *CNT*, 27 May 1937; *Cultura y Acción*, 22 May 1937; *Ideas*, 27 May 1937; and *Solidaridad Obrera*, 23 May 1937, for other sharp criticisms of the government.

5. *Boletín de Información, CNT-FAI*, 25 May 1937.

6. Ibid., 1 June 1937.

7. See statement by Vázquez, ibid.; also *Fragua Social*, 2 June 1937; *Solidaridad Obrera*, 2, 3 June 1937.

8. *El Mercantil Valenciano*, 29 May 1937.

9. *Boletín de Información, CNT-FAI*, 8 June 1937.

10. *Guerra y revolución en España, 1936–1939*, III, 100.

11. *CNT*, 10 July 1937.

12. *Tierra y Libertad*, 21 Aug. 1937.

13. See Vernon Richards, *Lessons of the Spanish Revolution* (1983 ed.), 149.

14. *Esfuerzo*, No. (no. 1) 1937. For an account of the dissensions within the FAI on this issue, see Richards, *Lessons of the Spanish Revolution* (1983 ed.), 144–49.

15. Article by Gilabert in *Solidaridad Obrera*, 12 Oct. 1937.

16. The committee's decision is quoted by Gilabert, ibid.

17. I have found no record of a peninsular congress either in the CNT-FAI press or in the CNT-FAI archives now on microfilm at the International Institute of Social History, Amsterdam.

18. *Obras completas*, IV, 877; see also ibid., 880–83.

19. Ibid., IV, 603.

20. For Ortega's Communist affiliation, see, for example, Azaña, quoting Prieto, *Obras*, IV, 638; Jesús Hernández, *Yo fui un ministro de Stalin*, 89, 98; the moderate Socialist Gabriel Morón (who succeeded Ortega as director general of security), *Política de ayer y política de mañana*, quoting Zugazagoitia, 95.

21. *Todos fuimos culpables*, 670.

22. *Historia de la guerra en España*, 279–80. My italics.

23. *Chantaje a un pueblo*, 218. See also Morón, 100–102, who describes his futile efforts as director general of security to free the Dirección General de Seguridad and the police corps from Communist influence.

24. *Todos fuimos culpables*, 751.

25. *Guerra y revolución*, III, 89.

26. Azaña, *Obras*, IV, 638.

27. *Todos fuimos culpables*, 672.

28. *Diario Oficial del Ministerio de Defensa*, no. 127, as given in Ramón Salas Larrazábal, *Historia del ejército popular de la república*, II, 1206, n. 1. Cordón was later made chief of staff of the Eastern Army in Aragon.

29. *Diario Oficial del Ministerio de Defensa Nacional*, 21 May 1937. For a glowing tribute to Rojo, see *Frente Rojo*, 20 May 1937. On 21 October 1937, he was promoted by Prieto to the rank of general (*Diario Oficial del Ministerio de Defensa Nacional*, 22 Oct. 1937).

30. *Gaceta de la República*, 23 June 1937.

31. *Guerra y revolución en España, 1936–1939*, III, 88.

32. *Gaceta de la República*, 28 May 1937. See also obituary in *El País*, 16 Sept. 1985.

33. Palmiro Togliatti, *Escritos sobre la guerra de España*, 136.

34. *Escritos*, 136–37.

Chapter 47

1. Jesús Pérez Salas, *Guerra en España, 1936–1939*, 141–42; Julián Zugazagoitia, *Historia de la guerra en España*, 406.

2. For Llanos's membership in the PCE and Cordón's appointment, see Antonio Cordón, *Trayectoria*, 342, 346–47, 350. Cordón's membership is well documented in his book.

3. *Gaceta de la República*, 8 June 1937. His membership of the PCE has never been disputed and was common knowledge. See, for example, Colonel Jesús Pérez Salas (a Republican and former police chief of Barcelona), *Guerra en España*, 159. His Communist affiliation was also confirmed to me after the war by Vittorio Vidali.

4. *Treball*, 2 June 1937.

5. See Chapter 14.

6. One of these export entities was the CLUEA (Consejo Levantino Unificado de la Exportación Agrícola). See articles on the subject in *Fragua Social*, 31 Jan. 1937; *Nosotros*, 19 Apr. 1937; also Manuel Villar, *España en la ruta de la libertad*, 51. Although the UGT was represented in the CLUEA, the CNT was the dominant influence. For information on the CLUEA and the hostility of the Communist-controlled ministry of agriculture, see María Josepa Cucó Giner et al., *Qüestió agrària al país Valencià*, 49–53.

7. Zugazagoitia, 285.

8. *Treball*, 2 June 1937.

9. *Solidaridad Obrera*, 29 May 1937.

10. "La Nota de la Esquerra," *El Día Gráfico*, 6 June 1937.

11. See, for example, *Las Noticias* (organ of the PSUC-controlled Catalan UGT), 11, 12 June 1937.

12. See Chapter 22.

13. *Treball*, 12, 13, 16, 19–22 May. For retort by the CNT, see *Solidaridad Obrera*, 20 May 1937.

14. *Diari Oficial de la Generalitat de Catalunya*, 5 June 1937.

15. 4 March 1937.

16. For the CNT's reaction to this omission, see *Solidaridad Obrera*, 11 June 1937.

17. *El Día Gráfico*, 6 June 1937, and *Solidaridad Obrera*, 6 June 1937 (statement by Echevarría Nova). Two days later (see *El Día Gráfico*, 8 June 1937) Echevarría Nova was replaced by Paulino Gómez Saiz.

18. For the disarming of the patrols, see *El Día Gráfico*, 10, 18, 29 June 1937; *Las Noticias*, 9 June 1937; *Tierra y Libertad*, 12 June 1937.

19. See Chapter 55. According to his memoir, *Recuerdos de la guerra de España*, 27, he joined the Communist party in the early months of the war.

20. Ibid., 47.

21. See *Boletín de Información, CNT-FAI*, 6 May 1937; *Solidaridad Obrera*, 13, 14, 18, 19, 21, 22 May 1937; also statement by the secretary general of the patrols published in *La Batalla*, 13 May 1937.

22. *La Batalla*, 9 May 1937.

23. Luis Companys, "Notes and Documents on the Fighting in Barcelona, 3–7 May 1937." See also *Solidaridad Obrera*, 7, 11 May 1937.

24. Companys, "Notes and Documents."

25. Ibid.

26. *Diari Oficial de la Generalitat de Catalunya*, 2 June 1937.

27. See José Arias Velasco, *La Hacienda de la Generalidad, 1931–1938*, 241.

28. *Diari Oficial de la Generalitat de Catalunya*, 10 Oct. 1936.

29. See *Solidaridad Obrera*, 16 May 1937; *Claridad*, 17 May 1937.

30. See, for example, *Solidaridad Obrera*, 28 May 1937; *Treball*, 26 May 1937 (Sabadell). For unpublished reports by the CNT on its forcible exclusion from town councils and on the dissolution of its collectives, see file "Atropellos Contra Nuestra Organización," International Institute of Social History (Amsterdam), CNT-FAI Archives, Paquete 44 B/5, Caja 318. Photocopies of these reports are in the Bolloten Collection, Hoover Institution.

31. *Las Noticias*, 6 July 1937.

32. No. 1 (no date). The next issue (no. 2) was published on 26 May 1937.

33. *Solidaridad Obrera*, 28 May 1937.

34. *Nosotros*, 28 May 1937.

35. *Treball*, 2 June 1937.

36. *La Humanitat, Solidaridad Obrera, Treball, La Vanguardia*, 30 June 1937.

37. Statement by the Regional Committee of the CNT published in *Solidaridad Obrera*, 30 June 1937. Parts of this statement were censored. The full text is in the *Boletín de Información, CNT-FAI*, 30 June 1937.

38. Letter to Companys from the Regional Committee of the CNT, *El Día Gráfico*, 1 July 1937. The letter is mentioned by Companys in his radio address published in *La Vanguardia*, 30 June 1937.

39. *Las Noticias*, 30 June 1937. For further information on the government crisis, see ibid., 26, 27, 29 June 1937, *La Humanitat, Solidaridad Obrera* and *Treball*, 26, 27, 29, 30 June 1937; also *Guerra y revolución en España, 1936–1939*, III, 101–3; José Peirats, *La CNT en la revolución española*, II, 306–11; Carlos Pi Sunyer (a member of the new cabinet), *La república y la guerra*, 445–47.

40. Letter to me, dated 5 Jan. 1950, Hoover Institution.

41. This figure is undoubtedly a gross exaggeration. On the other hand, the membership figures given by the UGT for the two rival unions are equally unreliable (see *Las Noticias*, 30 June 1937).

42. 3 July 1937.

43. See *Solidaridad Obrera*, 2, 3, 13, 15, 21 Dec. 1938.

44. Peirats, *La CNT en la revolución española*, III, 325–26.

45. Manuel Cruells, *El separatisme català durant la guerra civil*, 162–63. See also Miquel Caminal (*Joan Comorera: Guerra i revolució, 1936–1939*, II, 140–41), who states that the PSUC became the "hegemonic force in Catalonia."

46. *Le Libertaire*, 17 June 1937.

Chapter 48

1. *Fragua Social*, 12 June 1937. See also *El Amigo del Pueblo*, 20 July 1937.

2. The quoted passage was deleted by the censor from *Solidaridad Obrera*, 30 June 1937. The full text is in the *Boletín de Información, CNT-FAI*, 30 June 1937. For unpublished reports by the CNT on the repression, see file "Atropellos Contra Nuestra Organización," International Institute of Social History (Amsterdam), CNT-FAI Archives, Paquete 44 B/5, Caja 318. Photocopies of these reports are in the Bolloten Collection, Hoover Institution.

3. See also *Anarquía*, 8 July 1937, for further information on the repression. Copies of both clandestine issues are in the Hoover Institution.

4. *Fragua Social*, 9 Sept. 1937. For other Anarchosyndicalist accounts of the repression, see *Le combat Sindicaliste*, 6 Aug. 1937; *Frente Libertario*, 7 Aug. 1937; *Le Libertaire*, 22 July 1937.

5. 5 Nov. 1937. The famous Russian-born Anarchist, Emma Goldman, went to Spain in September 1937 to see for herself "how far the new found freedom of the Spanish masses had been annihilated by Stalin's henchmen. I went straight to Valencia and there discovered that 1,500 CNT members, comrades of the FAI and the Libertarian Youth, hundreds of the POUM and even members of the International Brigade were filling the prisons of Valencia. . . . I soon discovered that the same situation was repeated in every town and village I visited. Thousands of comrades and other genuine

revolutionaries were filling the prisons under the Negrín-Prieto and Stalinist regime" (article in *Man!*, Jan. 1938). For excerpts from articles, speeches, interviews, and letters by Emma Goldman relating to the Civil War, see *Vision on Fire*.

6. After the Civil War, Diego Abad de Santillán, reporting to the AIT, with which the CNT was affiliated, alleged that "thousands" of assassinations of workers and soldiers, who belonged "in nearly all instances to our organizations," had been committed during the war, but there is absolutely no evidence to support this allegation.

7. The minutes of the congress were not published until March 1939 (see supplement to *Espagne Nouvelle*, 15 Mar. 1939; Alexander Schapiro and Albert de Jong, *Waarom verloren wij de revolutie*, 20–21, and n. 3, which discusses the surprising use of the word *totalitarisme*).

8. Letter to me, 11 Apr. 1980 (Hoover Institution).

9. *Los que fuimos a Madrid*, 137–38.

10. *Las Noticias*, 22 June 1937. See also *La Batalla* (clandestine issue), 14 Aug. 1937; Julián Gorkin, *Caníbales políticos*, 99–131, and *El proceso de Moscú en Barcelona*, 106–40; Jesús Hernández, *Yo fui un ministro de Stalin*, 98; Katia Landau, *Le stalinisme en Espagne*, 13; Andrés Suárez (Ignacio Iglesias), *El proceso contra el POUM*, 83–84. For profiles of the principal POUM leaders arrested, see *Autour de procès du POUM*, 2–7.

11. Josep Coll and Josep Pané, *Josep Rovira*, 203–4. See also "Informe sobre la represión llevada a cabo contra el Partido Obrero de Unificación Marxista (POUM)," July 1937, and copy of a report on Rovira's arrest sent to the ministry of national defense by the Twenty-fifth, Twenty-sixth, Twenty-eighth, and Twenty-ninth Divisions. Both documents are in the Servicio Histórico Militar, Armario 47, Leg. 71, Carpeta 10. Copies are in the Hoover Institution, Bolloten Collection, file "POUM, Informe sobre la represión llevada contra el POUM." Fenner Brockway, secretary of the British Independent Labour party, states that he saw a telegram from Prieto, the defense minister, to the Twenty-ninth Division, stating that the arrest of Rovira was made "without his authority or knowledge" (*New Leader*, 16 July 1937). This means that General Pozas acted at the request of the Communist police, when he summoned Rovira to Barcelona. According to the aforementioned POUM document, Prieto, when informed of Rovira's arrest, ordered his release (pp. 4, 11–14). Rovira was rearrested in October 1938 but managed to escape from prison with other POUM leaders just before the capture of Barcelona on 26 January 1939 (see next chapter).

12. Gabriel Morón (subdirector general of security under Ortega), *Política de ayer y política de mañana*, 98. See also Gorkin, *El proceso*, 98; Indalecio Prieto, *Convulsiones de España*, II, 117.

13. Morón (see previous note), 96–98. See also Víctor Alba, *Dos revolucionarios* (memorandum of Olga Nin), 490; Gorkin, *El proceso*, 98, 162; Hernández, *Yo fui un ministro de Stalin*, 90–91; Suárez, 102–4; Julián Zugazagoitia, *Historia de la guerra en España*, 278. However, Orlov, in reply to Stanley G. Payne's questionnaire ("Answers to the Questionnaire of Professor Stanley G. Payne"), says that Zugazagoitia "signed a warrant for the arrest of Andrés Nin and the other members of the central committee of the POUM." This, of course, was totally untrue, for no warrant for the arrest of the POUM leaders or for the seizure of the party's building was issued by anyone (see POUM document [p. 2] cited in n. 11 above).

14. Morón, 95–98, in which he describes the maneuver to remove him from Valencia while the Communist coup was in progress.

15. I have already pointed out that when I met Orlov in 1937 I was not aware of his real identity. It was not until after his death in the United States in 1973, when the U.S. Government Printing Office published a photograph of him, that I was able to identify him beyond a shadow of doubt.

16. I regarded "Irma" as a valuable news source, as important as the Tass representative, Mirova, and the British and U.S. diplomatic representatives, with whom I maintained friendly relations. Colonel Stephen Fuqua, the U.S. military attaché, for example, invited me to "exchange" information with him. The document handed to me by "Irma" was undoubtedly given to the Valencia correspondent of *The Times*, London (Lawrence Fernsworth), to judge from a dispatch from Valencia dated 18 June (see the *The Times*, 19 June 1937), and to the *New York Times* correspondent in Madrid, Herbert L. Matthews (see the *New York Times*, 19 June 1937).

17. In the trial of the POUM leaders in October 1938, this document, which was demonstrably a forgery, was used as prime evidence by the prosecution (for the indictment, see Suárez, 197), but the charge of espionage could not be sustained.

18. The censored typewritten copy of my telephoned dispatch in English, stamped by the censor, and the modified opening paragraph on a separate slip of paper have been deposited in the Hoover Institution (see "Bolloten, Dispatch from Valencia to the United Press, 18 June 1937"). It is noteworthy that *The Times* correspondent (see n. 16 above) also used the phrase "it is stated" and that no source was given by the *New York Times* correspondent in his dispatch from Madrid.

19. In this connection, it is worth recording that Ettore Vanni, the Italian Communist, who was editor in chief of *Verdad*, the Communist evening newspaper published in Valencia, states that "Valáiev" (variously referred to in this book as Belyaev or Vielayev), who was closely associated with Orlov in Valencia, informed him, when he met him again in Moscow in 1940, that he "organized that colossal fraud, the trial of the Spanish Trotskyists, even concocting copious photographic material" (Vanni, *Yo, comunista en Rusia*, 14).

20. In subsequent weeks the number of arrests of POUM members, according to a report by the regional committee of the Levante, rose to one thousand, "Informe del Comité Regional de Levante del Partido Obrero de Unificación Marxista sobre la Represión llevada a cabo contra Dirigentes y Secciones del Partido" (Servicio Histórico Militar, Madrid, Armario 47, Leg. 71, Carpeta 10, Documento 1). A copy of this document is in the Hoover Institution, Bolloten Collection. The figure of one thousand is also given by Katia Landau, *Le stalinisme en Espagne*, 8. For the names of some of the POUM members in prisons and labor camps and of others assassinated, see *Independent News*, 22 Nov. 1938; *Workers' Age*, 22 Oct. 1938. In Barcelona, the police acted with such extraordinary speed and efficiency on 16 and 17 June that the POUM leaders and many of their foreign supporters were taken by surprise. "We have been asked time and again 'How was it possible for a revolutionary party such as the POUM to be so thoroughly and quickly suppressed?' " wrote Charles Orr, the editor of *Spanish Revolution*, the English-language bulletin of the POUM. "In the first place the POUM was woefully unprepared for underground activity. . . . For months, but especially since the May Days, suggestions had come from the rank and file urging preparation for illegal activity . . . , but Nin and the executive committee remained as ever optimistic. . . . The other reason . . . lies on the side of the police. No one foresaw, though a revolutionary marxist might have been expected to foresee it, the wonderfully organized police action. It can be said that never in Spain . . . was a round-up so well organized. And in fact this one was not organized by Spaniards, but was planned and carried through under the direction of Russian experts. These we saw and spoke with in prison" (Charles Orr, "Some Facts on the Persecution of Foreign Revolutionaries in 'Republican' Spain." A copy of this document is in the Hoover Institution, Bolloten Collection.).

21. Similar attacks on the POUM appeared in the entire Communist press throughout the war. The interested reader should consult *Frente Rojo*, *Mundo Obrero*, *Las Noticias*, *Treball*, and *Verdad* covering that period.

22. See Víctor Alba, *El marxismo*, II, 521–29, and Víctor Alba and Stephen Schwartz, *Spanish Marxism vs. Soviet Communism* (forthcoming), which contains an extended account of the persecution of foreigners in the POUM. See also *Independent News*, 20 Nov. 1937; Lois Cusick (Orr), "The Anarchist Millennium: Memories of the Spanish Revolution, 1936–1937" (typescript, Hoover Institution), 304–12; A. de Lizarra, *Los vascos y la república española*, 144–45 (see n. 65, below, for information on this book); Helmut Ruediger, *Informe para el congreso extraordinario de la AIT, el día 6 de diciembre de 1937. Paris, 1937*; Charles Orr, "Some Facts on the Persecution of Foreign Revolutionaries in 'Republican' Spain" (Hoover Institution, Bolloten Collection); and Suárez, 87–99. See also Landau, 32–48, for the arrest of foreign supporters of the POUM including herself and her husband, Kurt Landau (a former Trotskyist known by the pseudonym of Wolf Bertram), who was later assassinated. For information on Kurt Landau, see ibid.; Gorkin, *Caníbales políticos*, 226–27, and Hans Schafranek in *Cahiers Leon Trotsky*, 1er trimestre 1980, 75–95. In a letter to me, Katia Landau pointed out certain errors in the Hans Schafranek article. A copy of her letter has been attached to the aforementioned issue of *Cahiers Leon Trotsky* in the Hoover Institution. For information on the Belgian Georges Kopp, see *POUM: Hasta vencer o morir*, 8. As for the small group of Bolshevik Leninists, the leaders, Manuel Fernández Grandizo (G. Munis) and Adolfo Carlini, were arrested and tortured and due to be placed on trial but managed to escape to France before the Nationalists entered Barcelona in January 1939. See *Vanguardia* (Mexico City), Jan. 1939; *Socialist Appeal*, 21 Jan., 3 Mar., 28 May, 1939. Two other Trotskyists, Erwin Wolf and Hans Freund (Moulin) were also arrested but disappeared without a trace (Alba and Schwartz [forthcoming]; Landau, 45–47; Georges Vereeken, *The GPU in the Trotskyist Movement*, 168–74).

23. For the location of some of these secret prisons, see *La Batalla* (clandestine issue), 27 Nov. 1937 (Hoover Institution); *Independent News*, 4 Dec. 1937; Julián Gorkin, *Caníbales políticos*, 183; Landau, 14–27. Many years after the war, Santiago Carrillo, when secretary of the PCE, acknowledged that there were NKVD (GPU) prisons in Spain (Santiago Carrillo, *Demain l'Espagne*, 56).

24. "Nuestra gloriosa Division Lenin ha sido disuelta," *La Batalla* (clandestine issue), 14 Aug. 1937 (Hoover Institution).

25. See Gorkin, *Caníbales*, 195; Víctor Alba, *El marxismo en España, 1919–1939*, II, 526; Josep Coll and Josep Pané, *Josep Rovira*, 202; *Independent News*, 30 Aug. 1937, 30 Apr. 1938; *The New Leader*, 3 Sept. 1937. POUM members were singled out for punishment in other military units. A particularly revolting and cold-blooded murder committed by two Mexican Communists, Colonel Juan B. Gómez, commander of the Ninety-second Mixed Brigade, and the famous Mexican artist David Alfaro Siqueiros, commander of a motorized brigade in the southern zone, is described by Siqueiros himself in *Me llamaban el coronelazo: Memorias*, 333–36.

26. *Nosotros*, 19 June 1937.

27. 19 July 1937 (Hoover Institution).

28. Letter to Rayner Heppenstall, as given in Sonia Orwell and Ian Angus, *An Age like This: 1920–1940*, 279.

29. Gorkin, *El proceso*, 108.

30. Hernández, *Yo fui un ministro de Stalin*, 111.

31. For information on Nin, see Chapter 40, n. 1.

32. *El proceso*, 157, 171–73; Hernández, *Yo fui un ministro de Stalin*, 124–26. See also *L'assassinat de Andrés Nin*, 17–23, and Gorkin's letter to me dated 25 Feb. 1977 (Hoover Institution).

33. *Gaceta de la República*, 23 June 1937.

34. *El proceso*, 157–58. Gorkin's summary of the decree, which can be seen at length in the *Gaceta de la República*, 23 June 1937, has been verified by me. It was approved by the cabinet and signed by Manuel de Irujo, the Basque Nationalist minister of justice, on 22 June. There is no way of knowing whether Irujo realized at the time the decree was published that it would be used retroactively against the POUM leaders. For a criticism of the decree by the Anarchosyndicalists, see *CNT*, 23 July 1937.

35. *Boletín de Información, CNT-FAI*, 7 July 1937. The statement is dated 28 June 1937.

36. Speech delivered on 28 June 1937 (*Fragua Social*, 2 July 1937).

37. 12 Aug. 1937.

38. *Nuestra programa y el de la CNT*, 54, n. 1.

39. 29 Sept. 1937. See also *The New Leader*, organ of the Independent Labour party, 13 Dec. 1937.

40. *Le Populaire*, 7 Sept. 1937. See also report by the delegation published in *Independent News*, 15 Dec. 1937.

41. John McGovern, M.P., *Terror in Spain*, 5. Pabón was a Cortes deputy for Saragossa representing the small Partido Republicano Federal and before the Civil War had acted as defense attorney for the CNT. In December 1936, he became general secretary of the Regional Defense Council of Aragon and Syndicalist party leader.

42. Ibid., 13.

43. Araquistáin Papers, 73/117. The letter was approved by the Agrupación Socialista on 21 August 1937.

44. 24 Aug. 1937.

45. Francisco Largo Caballero, *La UGT y la guerra*, 16–17.

46. *El proceso*, 15, 168, and n. 1. For a profile of Vidali, see Gorkin, *L'assassinat de Trotsky*, 167–73; also Benjamin Gitlow, *The Whole of Their Lives*, 270.

47. *Yo fui un ministro de Stalin*, 126. In response to this allegation, Vidali told Giorgio Bocca, author of a biography of Palmiro Togliatti: "So many things have been said about me, but this is a stupidity. Why put on that stage show? In those days, if an anarchist or a Poumist had to be executed, it was done without so much fuss. Can you imagine, then, why I was necessary?" (as given in Francesc Bonamusa, *Andreu Nin y el movimiento comunista en España, 1930–1937*, 377). See also Vidali, *La caduta della repubblica*, 62–71, which gives his version of the Nin affair.

48. Article in *International Press Correspondence*, 4 Sept. 1937. See also Koltsov in *Pravda*, 25 Aug. 1937.

49. 16 Oct. 1937–4 Dec. 1937.

50. Georges Soria, *Guerra y revolución en España, 1936–1939*, III, 78–79.

51. One of these writers is the well-known pro-Communist historian Manuel Tuñón de Lara (see *Historia de España*, IX, 368).

52. Article by Ignacio Iglesias in *NADA, Cuadernos Internacionales*, no. 1 (Spring 1979).

53. *Todos fuimos culpables*, 728–29.

54. 10–16 Oct. 1977.

55. See, for example, Manuel Azaña (quoting Negrín), *Obras completas*, IV, 692; Zugazagoitia (quoting Antonio Ortega), 278–79, also 280–81.

56. See, for example, his article in *Reader's Digest*, Nov. 1966, and his book, *The Secret History of Stalin's Crimes*, x.

57. Information given to me by Wolfe.

58. The article was published on 15 April, and the letter by Miravitlles along with *Life*'s reply appeared on 11 May. For further information, see Juame Miravitlles, *Episodis de la guerra civil espanyola*, 192–94.

59. Orlov, "Answers to the Questionnaire of Professor Stanley G. Payne," 1 Apr. 1968, 8–9.

60. Hernández, *Yo fui un ministro de Stalin*, 119.

61. Information I gathered in Valencia toward the end of June 1937.

62. *Todos fuimos culpables*, 731.

63. *Yo fui un ministro de Stalin*, 91, 97, 101. On pp. 90–94 of this book, Hernández reproduces a long, acrimonious discussion that he claims he had with Orlov with regard to the operation against the POUM. However, since his description of Orlov is inaccurate, his testimony must be taken with extreme caution.

64. Ibid., 109.

65. A. de Lizarra, 150. This book is based largely on the memoirs of the minister of justice. Andrés María was his brother and private secretary.

66. Zugazagoitia, 281.

67. *Yo fui un ministro de Stalin*, 112.

68. Zugazagoitia, 281.

69. *Yo fui un ministro de Stalin*, 113.

70. In a communiqué issued on 19 July, the ministry of the interior stated: "The minister of national defense has expressed his urgent desire to the government that Lieutenant Colonel Ortega should resume the military activities he temporarily suspended when the government assigned him to head the General Direction of Security" (*Adelante*, 21 July 1937).

71. *Política de ayer*, 100–102, 104–5.

72. Ibid., 102–4.

73. *Todos fuimos culpables*, 732–33.

74. *Convulsiones*, II, 117. Prieto claims that he learned of this from Zugazagoitia after he (Prieto) had left the government. See also Indalecio Prieto, "Reply to Jordi Arquer's questionnaire" (Hoover Institution, Bolloten Collection).

75. *El Socialista*, 15 Aug. 1937.

76. 11 Aug. 1937.

77. A microfilm copy of this clandestine issue of *La Batalla* is in the Hoover Institution, Bolloten Collection.

78. Recorded by Vidarte, *Todos fuimos culpables*, 751, who says that Zugazagoitia made this statement to the police officer who had been sent to Barcelona to investigate the disappearance of Marc Rein, the son of the Russian Menshevik leader Abramovich.

79. *Fragua Social*, 25 Dec. 1937, and *Independent News*, 1 Jan. 1938. See also Alba and Schwartz on the POUM's municipal activities after the May events.

80. See *El Día Gráfico*, 23 Nov. 1937, and *Frente Rojo*, 24 Nov. 1937.

81. The first number of the underground edition of *La Batalla* was published on 10 July 1937. A microfilm copy is in the Hoover Institution, Bolloten Collection. Five subsequent issues on microfilm are also available: 19 July, 5, 14 Aug., 20, 27 Nov. 1937. For information on the POUM's clandestine newspapers, see Alba, *El marxismo en España, 1919–1939*, II, 563–64.

82. Ibid., 565.

83. Ibid., 562–63.

84. Wilebaldo Solano, the secretary general of the POUM's youth organization, the JCI, and a member of the second executive committee of the party, points out in a document prepared by him relating to the organization's clandestine activity: "The majority of historians speak of the 'liquidation of the POUM,' when referring to the police coup of 16 June 1937. In general, they refer to the disappearance of the POUM as a result of the repression as though it were an established fact. This is absolutely false and must be refuted. The POUM continued its activity in clandestinity, although under very difficult conditions" ("Notas sobre el POUM en la Revolución de 1937"). A copy of this document, dated March 1973, is in the Hoover Institution, Bolloten Collection. Until the arrest of a new executive in April, the POUM definitely appears to have been quite active. According to Togliatti, in a report to the Comintern dated 28 January 1938, "the POUM continues to be strong and carries out dangerous subversive work in the factories" (*Escritos sobre la guerra de España*, 182). On the other hand, in a report to Leon Trotsky on 6 July 1937, Erwin Wolf (later arrested and presumed assassinated by the NKVD) stated: "It is impossible to say how many active members of the POUM remain. 100, 200, 300 at the very most. It is impossible to find them. Their illegal activity—to judge from their illegal tracts—is minimal" (Letter of Erwin Wolf to L. D. Trotsky, Harvard College Library, Houghton Library, #17371). I am grateful to Stephen Schwartz for referring me to this document.

85. *Obras*, IV, 692. See also Zugazagoitia, 281, who says that Negrín tried to convince him that "everything was possible." However, many years later, Negrín, when asked by Vidarte what he thought about the Nin case, replied, "I believe the Communists killed him" (Vidarte, *Todos fuimos culpables*, 724).

86. Gorkin, *El proceso*, 163.

87. Lizarra, 188–90. See n. 65 above.

88. Ibid., 158–59. The article is dated 9 Dec. 1938. See also Vicente Palacio Atard, *Cinco historias de la república*, 90–91.

89. *Gaceta de la República*, 1 Dec. 1937.

90. In his memoirs published some thirty years later, Irujo slightly modified his testimony to read that Negrín entrusted the undersecretary of justice, Mariano Ansó, with the task of drafting a decree. Ansó, he says, consulted "a magistrate of the Supreme Tribunal," whom he asked to study the subject and who informed him that such secret police courts functioned in totalitarian countries in violation of the "fundamental democratic principle that affirms and maintains the independence of the judiciary" (*Un vasco en el ministerio de justicia: Memorias*, I, 83). See also ibid., 87.

91. See Ansó, *Yo fui ministro de Negrín*, 108–9.

92. It is noteworthy that the decree was signed by Negrín and not by the minister of justice. See also Irujo, *Un vasco*, I, 84. Not surprisingly, Negrín's domestic and foreign supporters do not mention his primary involvement in the creation of the *tribunales de guardia*. See, for example, Hugh Thomas, *The Spanish Civil War* (1977 ed.), 778.

93. "Datos Remitidos por el Señor Manuel de Irujo, Ministro Vasco en el Gobierno de la República Española," Hoover Institution, Bolloten Collection. See also letter to me from Andrés María de Irujo, dated 20 Sept. 1949 (Hoover Institution).

94. In his memoirs, Irujo states that he returned to the cabinet as minister without portfolio, following the intervention of José Antonio Aguirre, the premier of the Basque government, who believed that it would be more beneficial to the Basques if Irujo remained in the government (Irujo, *Un vasco*, I, 85).

95. *Santiago Carrillo: Crónica de un secretario general*, 57–58.

Chapter 49

1. The trial is covered fully in Víctor Alba and Stephen Schwartz, *Spanish Marxism vs. Soviet Communism* (forthcoming).

2. It will be recalled that the decree creating the Tribunal of Espionage and High Treason was published in the *Gaceta de la República* on 23 June 1937.

3. 20 Nov. 1937.

4. Some idea of the scope of this campaign can be gleaned from the following: *Independent News*,

The New Leader, *Socialist Appeal*, and *POUM: Hasta vencer o morir*, 14–18. Photocopies of some of the pages of this rare pamphlet are in the Hoover Institution.

5. John McGovern, M.P., *Terror in Spain*, 5. See also *Cultura Proletaria*, 14 Jan. 1939.

6. As given in McGovern, 14–15. The original Spanish text is given in Rudolf Rocker, *Extranjeros en España*, 174–75.

7. *The New Leader*, 19 Aug. 1938.

8. *Workers' Age*, 5 Nov. 1938 (the appeal is dated 30 Aug. 1938). See also *Vanguard*, Nov. 1938.

9. 12 Oct. 1938 (report by Peter Kerrigan).

10. *El proceso de Moscú*, 248. See also *Independent News*, 16 Dec. 1938.

11. Letter to Joaquín Maurín, dated 12 Apr. 1972 (Maurín Collection, Hoover Institution).

12. Pp. 12–13 in the Spanish edition.

13. Efforts by Jordi Arquer and by me to discover his identity were fruitless. See file "Jordi Arquer, Correspondence with Bolloten regarding the identity of Max Rieger," Hoover Institution.

14. 25 Oct. 1938.

15. It is noteworthy that Arturo Perucho, the director of the PSUC organ, *Treball*, informed me in Mexico after the war that he furnished many of the newspaper clippings reproduced in the book. For a letter from the POUM prisoners, dated 14 July 1938, to Azaña, Martínez Barrio, Negrín, and Companys, protesting the arrest and assassination of party members and sympathizers and the publication of the Max Rieger book, see CNT-FAI Archives, International Institute of Social History (Amsterdam), Paquetes 61 and 61a. A copy is in the Bolloten Collection, Hoover Institution, file "POUM Leaders. Letters from the State Prison, Barcelona."

16. Sept.–Oct. 1938.

17. Personal knowledge. He was introduced to me by Spanish Communists and was accompanied by them when he visited me and my wife Gladys in our apartment in Mexico City in 1939.

18. A facsimile of this letter, dated 14 July 1939, can be found in the rare booklet *Spanish Communists in the Kremlin and the White House*. A copy is in the Bolloten Collection, Hoover Institution. In the letter, in which Constancia de la Mora thanks Eleanor Roosevelt for "the great kindness and hospitality you showed me last Saturday [when she visited the White House with Juan Negrín]," there is a passage that is worth quoting at length: "Do you think there is some possibility of the President's Advisory Committee on Refugees taking up the question of the Spanish exiles, or of another similar committee being formed to deal only with the Spanish question? Please forgive me for putting this question so bluntly, but I am sure that some constructive plan could be worked out with the help of such a committee; a plan both to raise money and to use the Spaniards arriving in the new world to foster the democratic policies of the United States in Latin and South America. We should not forget that many of our exiles are men of the greatest prestige in all Spanish speaking countries. Their words and writings carry great weight; but they must be given the opportunity to establish themselves in their new surroundings." In view of Constancia de la Mora's Communist affiliation and her devotion to the cause, as evidenced by her husband's memoir, the quoted passage has unusual significance. I visited Constancia de la Mora and her husband, former air force chief Hidalgo de Cisneros and also a member of the PCE, in Cuernavaca, Mexico, at the beginning of 1940, and I can attest to the fact that she was still corresponding with Eleanor Roosevelt, for she asked me to mail a letter to her.

19. The full text of the indictment and the judgment is in Andrés Suárez, *El proceso contra el POUM*, 195–209.

20. For data on the trial, see Alba and Schwartz (forthcoming); Víctor Alba, *El marxismo en España, 1919–1939*, II, 576–98; *Autour du Procès du POUM*; Gorkín, *Caníbales políticos*, 267–89, *El proceso*, 251–66; also articles by Jordi Arquer in *Enllà*, June 1945, and *La Révolution Prolétarienne*, July 1947, and by Emma Goldman (who attended the trial) in *Vanguard*, Feb. 1939.

21. Palmiro Togliatti, *Escritos sobre la guerra de España*, 232.

22. 19 and 25 Oct. 1938. For other attacks on the POUM, see *Frente Rojo*, 26–28, 29 Oct., 1, 2 Nov. 1938; also supplement to *Acero* (a Communist military newspaper), 25 Oct. 1938 (a copy of this supplement is in the Bolloten Collection, Hoover Institution).

23. *Problemas y cintarazos*, 191–92.

24. Note 5 in Araquistáin's own handwriting on a typewritten copy of his open letter, dated 1 Jan.

1939, to Norman Thomas, president of the American Socialist party (Araquistáin Papers, Leg. 75/21). My emphasis.

25. *El proceso* (1971), 249 and n. 6.

26. *Del triunfo a la derrota*, 314–15.

27. Leg. 2770/1. A copy of this telegram is in the Bolloten Collection, Hoover Institution. See file "Negrín's telegram to García Valdecasas, 22 Oct. 1938."

28. See Arquer's letter to me (1950) describing his meeting with Hernando in Carcassonne, France (Hoover Institution). Emphasis in letter.

29. See Suárez, 206.

30. See Chapter 48, n. 19, also text to n. 86. Louis Fischer writes: "A prominent Soviet citizen, whose name I do not mention because he may still be alive in Russia, told me in Spain at the time that the documents were forged by the Spanish Communists" (*Men and Politics*, 428).

31. For further information on Roces, see Eduardo Comín Colomer, *Historia secreta de la segunda república*, 589–90.

32. *Yo fui un ministro de Stalin*, 127.

33. For excerpts from their testimony, see *Solidaridad Obrera*, 26 Oct. 1938, and *Tierra y Libertad*, 5 Nov. 1938; also Gorkín, *Caníbales*, 284–86, and A. de Lizarra, *Los vascos y la república española*, 151–53.

34. For an example of this, see verbatim report (ninety-five typewritten pages) of the public prosecutor's cross-examination of Jordi Arquer (Bolloten Collection, Hoover Institution).

35. Biographical essay in Andrés Nin, *Els moviments d'emancipació nacional*, 63.

36. See Suárez, 202–9, for the complete text of the judgment.

37. For a handwritten letter signed by three of the prisoners and addressed to Negrín, Companys, and González Peña on 17 January 1939, nine days before the fall of Barcelona, demanding their immediate release and the legalization of the POUM and the JCI, see CNT-FAI Archives, International Institute of Social History (Amsterdam), Paquete 59, Carpeta 5. A copy of the letter is in the Bolloten Collection, Hoover Institution, file "POUM Leaders. Letters from State Prison, Barcelona." For the story of their dramatic escape from Barcelona to France, see Gorkin, *Caníbales*, 302–35, and *El proceso*, 279–99; also *The New Leader* (Independent Labor party), 7 Apr. 1939, and *Socialist Appeal* (the official organ of the Trotskyist Socialist Workers party), 3 Mar. 1939. This issue carries a long article by Terence Phelan on the escape of the Spanish Bolshevik-Leninist and POUM leaders from Barcelona. Phelan claims that when the prison director telephoned Santiago Garcés, the head of the SIM, requesting a truck to transport the prisoners farther north, Garcés snarled: "No trucks for the POUM leadership; let the fascists finish the bastards off." See also Gorkin, *Caníbales*, 305–6.

38. *El proceso*, 265.

39. 2 Dec. 1938.

40. *Escritos*, 232.

41. *España Popular*, 28 Mar., 16 May 1940.

Chapter 50

1. The account that follows is based in part on material in Chapter 24.

2. Interview given to *Adelante*, reprinted in *Solidaridad Obrera*, 28 May 1937. The quotation is given at greater length in Chapter 24.

3. 10 June 1937.

4. Interview given to *Juventud Libre*, 10 July 1937. For a sampling of other references in the libertarian press to attacks on the collectives, see *Acracia*, 5 Aug. 1937; *Boletín de Información, CNT-FAI*, 23 June 1937; *Cultura Proletaria*, 4 Sept. 1937; *Ruta*, 17 June 1937. César M. Lorenzo alleges that in Castile "hundreds of collectivists were massacred," that "fields were devastated and homes burned down," and that "El Campesino" exceeded Líster "in savagery" (*Les anarchistes espagnols et le pouvoir, 1868–1969*, 310). Líster never denied the executions he carried out in Castile.

5. *Memorias de un campesino andaluz en la revolución española*, 105. For attacks on the collective farms in the region of Valencia in the second half of 1937, see the well-documented work of Aurora Bosch Sánchez, *Ugetistas y libertarios: Guerra civil y revolución en el país valenciano, 1936–1939*, 306–28.

6. *Gaceta de la República*, 9 June 1937. For more information on the decree, see Chapter 24.

7. 11 June 1937.

8. *Guerra y revolución en España, 1936–1939*, III, 262. See also *Historia del partido comunista de España*, 158–59.

9. *Solidaridad Obrera*, 31 Oct. 1936. It should be recorded that the ultrarevolutionary conduct of the CNT and FAI in Aragon was opposed not only by the Communists but also by the Esquerra and the POUM. The CNT activist Félix Carrasquer accuses members of the POUM of attacking some Anarchosyndicalist collectives in the proximity of Huesca and of using the party's mouthpiece, *La Batalla*, to wage a "campaign of discredit" against them (*Las colectividades de Aragón*, 72–73).

10. *Solidaridad Obrera*, 2 Nov. 1936. See also "De Julio a Julio," *Fragua Social*, 19 July 1937, as reprinted in *De julio a julio*, 9–18.

11. In this context cantonalism implies a libertarian system of administration based on the division of the national territory into small, independent administrative units or cantons without a central governing body.

12. The Syndicalist party was a small splinter party formed by Angel Pestaña, a leading member of the CNT, who in opposition to the FAI had sought unsuccessfully before the war to bring the CNT into the field of political and parliamentary activity. Angel Pestaña was the party's only representative in the Cortes in 1936. Its role during the Civil War was insignificant, particularly after Pestaña's death in 1937. A full-length biography by Pestaña's friend and comrade, Angel María de Lera (*Angel Pestaña, Retrato de un anarquista*) was published in Barcelona in 1978.

13. Lorenzo, *Les anarchistes*, 149–50.

14. Ibid., 150–51.

15. The composition of the reorganized council can be found in the *Boletín del Consejo Regional de Defensa de Aragón*, as given in the *Boletín de Información, CNT-FAI*, 24 Dec. 1936. For an excellent study, richly documented, of the formation and activity of the council, see Julián Casanova Ruiz, *Anarquismo y revolución en la sociedad rural aragonesa, 1936–1938*, 133–76.

16. For collectivization in Aragon at the beginning of the war, see José Duque, "La situación en Aragón al comienzo de la guerra."

17. *Obras completas*, IV, 677.

18. Ibid., 710.

19. Ibid., 614.

20. Zugazagoitia, *Historia de la guerra en España*, 285.

21. *Gaceta de la República*, 11 Aug. 1937.

22. Enrique Líster, *Nuestra guerra*, 152. For the secrecy in which the operation against the council was carried out, see ibid., 152–54; also Antonio Cordón, *Trayectoria*, 350–52, and Jesús Hernández, *Negro y Rojo*, 254–58.

23. His name is listed as a member of the politburo in Pedro Checa, *A un gran partido, un gran organización*, 23.

24. *Nuestra guerra*, 155.

25. 12 Aug. 1937. For other favorable reactions to the dissolution, see *Política* (organ of Izquierda Republicana) and *El Socialista* (Prieto's mouthpiece), 12 Aug. 1937.

26. *Guerra y revolución en España, 1936–1939*, III, 269.

27. *Los que fuimos a Madrid*, 154. See also Enrique Martin, *Recuerdos de un militante*, 122–23.

28. Conversation with me in Mexico in 1945.

29. Interviewed by me in Mexico in 1939. A copy of my shorthand notes is in the Hoover Institution. For a well-documented account of the dissolution of the council and the repression that followed, see Casanova Ruiz, *Anarquismo*, 264–97. See also José Borrás, *Aragón en la revolución española*, 191–216.

30. The date of the issue is given as 31 Sept. 1937 (*sic*). A copy can be found in the Hoover Institution, Bolloten Collection.

31. See n. 29 above.

32. *Nuestra Guerra*, 155–56.

33. *Trayectoria*, 352.

34. "Comité Regional de Aragón del Partido Comunista de España. Acta de la Reunión Celebrada

el día 12 de Septiembre de 1937" (Archivo Histórico Nacional, Salamanca, Leg. 616/816–21). A copy of this document is in the Hoover Institution, Bolloten Collection.

35. Report dated 1 Apr. 1938. A copy of this report, which is part of the Rudolf Rocker collection in the International Institute for Social History, Amsterdam, is in the Hoover Institution, Bolloten Collection.

36. Confederación Nacional del Trabajo, *Realizaciones revolucionarias y estructuras colectivistas de la Comarcal de Monzón*, 143–56.

37. Letter from Molina to Joan Llarch as reproduced in Llarch, *Negrín: ¡Resistir es vencer!*, 204–7.

38. *Obras*, IV, 733. Later, the CNT Regional Committee of Aragon sent a detailed report to the government on Líster's repressive measures. The final lines stated: "Up to now the Aragonese people have given proof of seriousness and good citizenship by not responding to the provocation, because they have one goal: to fight fascism and not to demoralize the combatants. . . . [We] demand that such outrages and every kind of persecution cease, that all stolen property be returned, and the appropriate punishment be meted out" (as given in *Cenit*, Apr. 1983).

39. *Cenit*, Apr. 1983.

40. *Les anarchistes espagnols*, 307.

41. As given in Peirats, *La CNT en la revolución española*, II, 367.

42. Ibid., 368.

43. *Nuestra guerra*, 160. See also Cordón, 352.

44. *Obras*, IV, 897.

45. See the Spanish Communist refugee periodical, *España Popular*, 23 Jan. 1948; also Peirats, *Los anarquistas*, 294.

46. José Duque, "Informe de José Duque, Secretario General de la Comisión Agraria al Comité Central del P.C. 17-VIII-37" (Archivo Histórico Nacional, Salamanca, Leg. 616/816-6). A copy of this document is in the Hoover Institution, Bolloten Collection.

47. *Los que fuimos a Madrid*, 157.

48. Antonio Rosel, an Aragonese Communist and a member of the party's regional committee, told Ronald Fraser many years later: "We went from an anarchist dictatorship to a communist one. People who had been, and always would be, enemies of the working class because their interests were fundamentally opposed, were now given encouragement and support simply because of their hostility to the CNT. Later, these same people turned their hostility on the communist party and the republican government" (*Blood of Spain*, 391).

49. *La revolución popular en el campo*, 17.

50. *Los anarquistas*, 301.

51. "Reunión de la Comisión Agraria del Partido Comunista celebrada en Caspe el día 9 de Octubre de 1937" (Archivo Histórico Nacional, Salamanca, Leg. 616/816-3. A photocopy of this document is in the Hoover Institution, Bolloten Collection.

52. "Proyecto que la Delegación Regional de Reforma Agraria Presenta para su Aprobación al Comité Regional del Frente Popular de Aragón" (Archivo Histórico Nacional, Salamanca, Leg. 616/816-3. A photocopy of this document is in the Hoover Institution, Bolloten Collection.). During the national plenum of the regional peasant federations of the CNT (Pleno Nacional de Federaciones Regionales de Campesinos) held in Valencia on 20–23 October 1937, the Aragonese delegates referred to "the little enthusiasm and lethargy in the villages" in the region of Caspe (Servicio Histórico Militar. Armario 47, Leg. 71, Carpeta 4, as quoted by Julián Casanova Ruiz, *Caspe, 1936–1938*, 65). Four months later, the situation had not changed. According to the minutes of the municipal council of Caspe of 25 February 1938, the CNT representative, Braulio Serrano, affirmed that "the abandonment of the activities in the countryside by a large number of peasants is alarming" (quoted, ibid., 66).

53. *La revolutión popular en el campo*, 17–18.

54. *Los anarquistas*, 300–301.

55. Ibid., 301–2.

Chapter 51

1. Indalecio Prieto, *Cómo y por qué salí del ministerio de defensa nacional*, 37–38. This incident is confirmed by Manuel Azaña in an entry in his diary on 17 September 1937, *Obras completas*, IV, 785.

2. *Todos fuimos culpables*, 620. For Hidalgo de Cisneros's joining the Communist party, see Chapter 31.

3. *Frente Rojo*, 7 July 1937.

4. This description was given to me by Alfonso Quintana y Pena, a former Socialist Cortes deputy, who knew Lamoneda well and portrayed him as a "man without ideals, never a real Socialist or Communist, whose supreme ambition was to manipulate people" (interview in San Francisco in 1979). See also Alvarez del Vayo, who describes Lamoneda as "extremely intelligent and honorable" (*Give Me Combat*, 183).

5. As given in *Guerra y revolución en España, 1936–1939*, III, 212. On a previous occasion, Lamoneda stated: "It is indubitable that we shall have to achieve not only unity of action, but also organic unity. We must, however, first pass through a trial period of common action" (*Claridad*, 1 May 1937).

6. It must be remembered that Lamoneda was a skilled politician with considerable practical experience both in the Communist and Socialist movements and that in the early days of the Comintern he had held the post of secretary of the interior in the PCE (see Chapter 37).

7. *Guerra y revolución*, III, 217.

8. *Historia del partido comunista de España*, 167.

9. *Kommunisticheskii internatsional: Kratkii istoricheskii ocherk*, 443. On 30 August 1937, Togliatti informed the Comintern that "the resistance of the Socialist leadership [to the fusion]—I refer to the centrists, since the Caballeristas, as we know, obstinately oppose it—is still very strong" (*Escritos sobre la guerra de España*, 137).

10. Margarita Nelken, who had joined the PCE openly quite early in the war.

11. Letter (pp. 1–4) in Hoover Institution, Bolloten Collection.

12. The word *straperlo* was added to the Spanish language during the Lerroux administration in 1935, when a Dutch adventurer persuaded certain ministers to agree to a new type of roulette wheel known as *straperlo* that would guarantee profits. After the scandal broke, the word passed into the language to signify blackmarketing or any kind of dishonest dealing.

13. *The Yenan Way*, 202–3, 210–12.

14. *El Diario Oficial del Ministerio de Defensa Nacional*, 28 June 1937.

15. Interview in Cuernavaca, Mexico, March 1940.

16. *Men and Politics*, 456–60. As Fischer points out, there is no mention of her dismissal from the Foreign Press Bureau in her autobiography, *In Place of Splendor*.

17. Mora, 340.

18. Interview in Cuernavaca, Mexico, March 1940.

19. See, for example, *Adelante* (Caballerista), 3 July 1937; *CNT*, 24 July, 6 Sept. 1937; *La Correspondencia de Valencia* (Caballerista), 7, 31 July 1937; *Fragua Social* (CNT), 3 Aug. 1937; *Juventud Libre* (Libertarian Youth), 10 July 1937; *El Socialista* (Prietista), 2 July, 5 Sept. 1937.

20. 2 July 1937.

21. *Escritos*, 135–36.

22. Togliatti's statement should give an accurate measure of the sincerity of his desire for a "genuine participatory democracy" in Spain, attributed to him by Joan Barth Urban in her work *Moscow and the Italian Communist Party: From Togliatti to Berlinguer*, 122–23. She bases her misleading interpretation of Togliatti's thinking on the following passage from his report of 20 August 1937 (*Escritos*, 133–34) but does not quote the key passage on the question of armed power cited by me in the text to n. 21 above: " 'The thing that above all strikes the eyes is the absence of those democratic forms which permit the vast masses to participate in the life of the country and in politics. In present-day Spain Parliament represents almost no one. . . . The municipal councils and provincial councils have been formed from above. . . . The committees of the popular front have ceased in fact to exist. . . . There are factory committees, but it is very difficult to establish whether they have been elected or nominated from above by the leadership of the trade unions: it seems to me that for the most part they have been nominated from above. In the trade unions, which have become a powerful

economic organization, there is very little democracy. . . . The [political] life of the country develops beyond the control of the masses.' "

"The irony of sending such a dispatch to Stalin's Russia of 1937," she observes, "was evidently lost on Togliatti. Yet this only heightens the light it shed on his own vision of the ideal society as well as his illusions regarding Soviet reality" (122–23). The fact is that Togliatti perceived democracy in Spain during the Civil War as a means of PCE penetration of the unions and other organs of local power. The interested reader should study carefully all of Togliatti's reports to Moscow during his sojourn in Spain *in relation to the prevailing situation* before making any judgment about his interest in a "genuine participatory democracy."

23. 24 July 1937.

24. 5 Sept. 1937.

25. 6 Sept. 1937.

26. Report to the plenum of the central committee of the PCE on 13 November 1937, as given in Ibárruri, *En la lucha*, 213.

27. *Diario Oficial del Ministerio de Defensa Nacional*, 5 Oct. 1937.

28. 6 Oct. 1937.

29. Ibárruri, *En la lucha*, 214.

30. According to Azaña, Prieto told him on 15 September 1937 that 33 percent of the commissars were Communists and that 16 percent were members of the JSU "which is also a Communist organization" (*Obras*, IV, 786).

31. *Epistolario Prieto y Negrín*, 94, letter dated 3 July 1939. Italics in text. The CNT of course was also interested in redressing the balance. On 23 October 1937, Miguel González Inestal, the new subcommissar general representing the CNT in the General Commissariat of War, who had replaced Angel González Gil Roldán, the former CNT representative (*Diario Oficial del Ministerio de la Defensa Nacional*, 6 Oct. 1937), submitted to the defense minister a long "plan of organization," which included the following bold but unrealistic proposal: "To reestablish equilibrium the appointment of commissars shall be as follows: Socialists, 33%; Libertarians, 33%; Communists, 14%; Republicans, 10%; Syndicalist party, 5%; Regional parties, 5%." This document, which is in the Servicio Histórico Militar of Madrid, is printed at length in Ramón Salas Larrazábal, *Historia del ejército popular de la república*, III, 3011–16.

32. For a profile of Piñuela, see Regina García, *Yo he sido marxista*, 218–19. In the commissariat of war in Madrid, Regina García held the posts of chief of propaganda and press and director of *La Voz del Combatiente*, ibid., 214.

33. *Guerra y Revolución*, IV, 69.

34. *Cómo y por qué*, 42.

35. *Frente Rojo, Verdad*, 21 Dec. 1937.

36. *Diario Oficial del Ministerio de Defensa Nacional*, 2 Apr. 1938. See also Salas Larrazábal, *Historia*, II, 1630, n. 14; Prieto, *Cómo y por qué*, 43.

37. According to Tomás Mora, a Socialist inspector-commissar, when interviewed by Robert Fraser, *Blood of Spain*, 462.

38. *Hombres made en Moscú*, 554.

39. *Diario Oficial del Ministerio de Defensa Nacional*, 22 June 1937.

40. *Hombres*, 555.

41. Ibid., 557–58.

42. *Diario Oficial del Ministerio de Defensa Nacional*, 18 Nov. 1937. Alvarez del Vayo states that Prieto "made" him submit his resignation (*Give Me Combat*, 182). There is some evidence but unconfirmed that Crescenciano Bilbao, although officially a Prieto or moderate Socialist, may have been under Communist influence. This testimony comes from Palmiro Togliatti, who, in a memorandum dated 25 November 1937, expressed the view that "the new comissar general is better, for us, than the previous one" (Togliatti, *Escritos*, 156). This reflection on Alvarez del Vayo (the previous commissar general) is illuminating inasmuch as it demonstrates that despite his myriad services to the PCE, del Vayo had not gained the confidence of Togliatti, although he had won the trust of other Communist leaders. "The opinion," said Togliatti, "that our comrades and especially Louis [pseudonym for Vittorio Codovila] have of del Vayo as a man almost completely won over to our policy, but weak, I personally consider mistaken: [del Vayo] has not broken off his relations with Caballero, he

intrigues and plays a role that is not very clear" (ibid.). Togliatti's view regarding Crescenciano Bilbao clashes with the evidence of Enrique Castro, the subcommissar of organization, who told the PCE on a later occasion that Bilbao was "too much of a Socialist to serve us [as commissar general]" (*Hombres made in Moscú*, 659).

43. See, for example, *Gaceta de la República*, 4, 30 March 1938.

44. Ibid., 5 Jan. 1938. See also report by Vidali to the central committee of the PCE in Miscellaneous Documents, Vol. IV (Hoover Institution, Bolloten Collection), in which he states that Prieto also discharged the entire personnel of the propaganda section of the General Commissariat of War, including all its Communist commissars. The report is a typewritten copy of the original loaned to me by Vidali in Mexico in 1939.

45. García Val informed me after the war that Prieto also dismissed all the Communists under his authority. He was replaced by the Socialist Coello de Portugal.

46. See Jesús Pérez Salas, *Guerra en España, 1936–1939*, 165.

47. *Gaceta de la República*, 8 Feb. 1838.

48. *Trayectoria*, 371–72. Cordón says: "At the same time [Prieto] dismissed other officers of the Eastern Army, but only those who were Communists. Some of those dismissed had not even attended the meeting, for example, all the members of the information section of the general staff" (ibid.).

49. In an interview I had with Hidalgo de Cisneros in Cuernavaca, Mexico, in March 1940, he told me that Díaz Tendero had been a personal friend of Prieto's until the defense minister's campaign against the Communists. The entire interview, consisting of 111 pages, mainly in shorthand, is in the Hoover Institution.

50. *Guerra en España*. Later, Prieto named Pérez Salas (at the time a lieutenant-colonel) undersecretary of the army in place of Colonel Antonio Fernández Bolaños (see his laudatory comments in *El Día Gráfico*, 29 Mar. 1938).

51. *Guerra en España*, 165.

52. For further evidence of Rojo's role in promoting Communist predominance in the army, see ibid., 147, 152, 158, 162, 165–66, 169–72, 185–86, also Chapter 30 of this book. Although Hugh Thomas refers to Pérez Salas's book, he asserts, without adducing any solid evidence, that Rojo was not pro-Communist and was a "technician pure and simple" (*The Spanish Civil War* [1977 ed.], 836).

53. Pérez Salas, 147.

54. Letter to Negrín, dated 3 July 1939, as given in *Epistolario, Prieto y Negrín*, 93.

55. Interview, Cuernavaca, Mexico, in March 1940.

56. *El único camino*, 389. My italics. See also her report to the central committee on 13 Nov. 1937, *En la lucha*, 197.

57. *Mi desembarco en Mallorca*, 340–41.

58. Pearson letter, dated 25 Nov. 1948, Hoover Institution, Bolloten Collection.

59. *Cómo y por qué*, 76.

60. Ibid., 77.

61. Ibid.

62. *Milicia Popular*, 3 Sept. 1936.

63. See Ramón Salas Larrazábal, *Historia*, I, 605, 635.

64. Ibid., II, 1926, 1937, 2086, 2184, 2261. See also the official Communist history of the Civil War, *Guerra y revolución*, IV, 230.

65. *Cómo y por qué*, 77.

66. Orlov, "Answers to the Questionnaire of Professor Stanley G. Payne, 1 April 1968," Hoover Institution, Bolloten Collection.

67. *Cómo y por qué*, 78.

68. Stanley G. Payne's questionnaire. The emphasis is Orlov's.

69. *Cómo y por qué*, 78.

70. *Guerra y revolución*, IV, 230.

71. Gustavo Durán, "Testimony for the International Organizations Employees Loyalty Board of United States Civil Service Commission" (duplicate manuscript), 1954, as given in Günther Schmigalle, *André Malraux und der spanische Bürgerkrieg*, 152. For further information on Durán, his activities, and his problems with the U.S. investigatory committees during the 1940s and early 1950s, see Schmigalle, 139–59; also William F. Buckley, Jr., and L. Brent Bozell, *McCarthy and His Enemies*, 140–46, 274, 367–68, 386; Durán, *Una enseñanza de la guerra española*; Karl Rienffer,

Comunistas españoles en América, 52–53, 91–92; Michael Straight, *After Long Silence*, 90, 186, 265–72 (Durán was married to the sister of Straight's wife); Simone Téry, *Front de la liberté*, 146–52; U.S. Congress, Senate Committee on the Judiciary, *Hearing before the Subcommittee to Investigate the Administration of the Internal Security Act*, 83d Cong., 1st sess., 1953.

72. Stanley G. Payne's questionnaire.

73. Morón, *Política y ayer y política de mañana*, 92. Orlov's statement is also controverted by the fact that Santiago Garcés, who was made chief of the SIM by Negrín when the latter became defense minister in April 1938, acknowledges the presence of "Russian advisers" in the organization after he took office (see his letter to D. Pastor Petit, *La cinquena columna a Catalunya*, 235). He also informed the Spanish historian Heleno Saña that Orlov "ran the Interrogation Commission [of the SIM] behind the scenes" (see Saña's letter to me, dated 21 Oct. 1986, Hoover Institution). For further information on the SIM, see Chapter 56.

74. *Yo fui un ministro de Stalin*, 130–31. In the same book, Hernández reveals that in 1923, when he was sixteen, he and five other members of the Communist party were just on the point of assassinating Prieto, when they were frustrated by the Civil Guard (ibid., 128–29). For Prieto's comments on Hernández's revelations, see *Convulsiones*, II, 117–18.

Chapter 52

1. My italics. Hugh Thomas, an apologist of Negrín, distorts the italicized lines in order to bolster his argument that it would be "ludicrous to suppose that so tough and independent-minded an intellectual, with so bad a temper, could ever be subservient to anyone." His paraphrased rendering reads, "Hernández later admitted that a time would have come when it would have been necessary to 'liquidate' Negrín" (*The Spanish Civil War* [1965 ed.], 556–57). This, of course, is the opposite of what Hernández stated, but the reader could not know, since Thomas omits the key words "if he had obstructed us." As will be seen later in this volume, there was no need to eliminate Negrín. In a report to Georgi Dimitrov, the secretary general of the Communist International, dated 21 May 1939, Palmiro Togliatti, who was the Comintern delegate in Spain and the de facto leader of the party, testifies that the second Negrín government formed in April 1938 "collaborated more closely with the leadership of the Communist party and accepted and implemented more fully and more rapidly than any other the proposals of the party" (Palmiro Togliatti, *Escritos sobre la guerra de España*, 229).

2. *Yo fui un ministro de Stalin*, 135–36.

3. As given in Thomas T. Hammond, *The Anatomy of Communist Takeovers*, 393–94.

4. I was assured of this by the Communists themselves, while living in Mexico, where the book was published.

5. Pp. 59–60.

6. *Yo fui un ministro de Stalin*, 140.

7. Togliatti, *Escritos*, 138.

8. Ibid., 137–38.

9. Ibid., 149. Togliatti refers to Codovila as "Louis."

10. As given in Dolores Ibárruri, *En la lucha*, 179.

11. See *CNT*, 4 Oct. 1937.

12. 5 Oct. 1937.

13. Ibid. (report datelined Madrid).

14. Ibid.

15. 19 May 1937.

16. 29 Aug. 1937.

17. 19 Sept. 1937.

18. 14 Oct. 1937.

19. *Claridad*, 2 July 1937.

20. *Mis recuerdos*, 229.

21. For the full text of the pact, see *Solidaridad Obrera*, 30 July 1937.

22. Resolution of the fourth provincial conference of the Valencia Communist party, as quoted by Diego Abad de Santillán, *Por qué perdimos la guerra*, 180. See also *Mundo Obrero*, 31 July 1937, and statement by the politburo, published in *Frente Rojo*, 1 Aug. 1937, for criticism of the alliance.

23. *Escritos*, 138.

Chapter 53

1. Rosal and Domínguez were members of both the national and executive committees.

2. It is not certain whether Amaro del Rosal resigned of his own volition or was forced to resign (see *La Correspondencia de Valencia*, 26 June, 16 July 1937, and *Frente Rojo*, 3 July 1937).

3. As quoted in a report of the politburo meeting held on 19 July 1937 (*Frente Rojo*, 20 July 1937).

4. Ibid.

5. See Chapter 23.

6. *La Correspondencia de Valencia*, 22 Sept. 1937.

7. See "Burnett Bolloten. Typewritten dispatch from Valencia to the United Press, dated 7 July 1937."

8. 16 Aug. 1937.

9. *Historia de la UGT de España, 1901–1939*, II, 655. Although this history is slanted against Largo Caballero and biased in favor of its author, its wealth of documentary material is invaluable to the student of the period. Amaro del Rosal was the last assistant secretary of the UGT during the Civil War and, according to the jacket of the book, "was for forty years the custodian, one might say the rescuer, of the greater part, and without doubt the most valuable part, of the archives of that labor organization."

10. *Frente Rojo*, 7 Sept. 1937. See also ibid., 1 Sept. 1937.

11. A few days earlier *Frente Rojo* stated that when some federations offered to pay their back dues to the treasurer, they were told that they could not do so "for lack of forms" (2 Sept. 1937). See also ibid., 23 Sept. 1937, and *Claridad*, 9 Sept. 1937.

12. *Frente Rojo*, 7 Sept. 1937.

13. Rosal, *Historia de la UGT*, II, 655; *Fragua Social*, 1 Oct., 1937.

14. Rosal, *Historia de la UGT*, II, 656.

15. *Verdad*, 30 Sept. 1937.

16. Ibid.

17. Ibid., 1 Oct. 1937. See also Rosal, *Historia de la UGT*, II, 656.

18. See manifesto of the UGT executive in *La Correspondencia de Valencia*, 9 Oct. 1937. I have not found any precise figures by left-wing sources to prove this point, but it is worth noting that the pro-Nationalist historian Ramón Salas Larrazábal, citing figures relating to the UGT plenum held in May 1937, states that the 14 federations that voted in favor of Largo Caballero represented 930,000 members, whereas the 24 that voted against him represented only 650,000 (*Historia del ejército popular de la república*, I, 1052, 1061, n. 57).

19. The composition of the new executive is given in *Verdad*, 2 Oct. 1937, and in Rosal, *Historia de la UGT*, II, 664. For an account by Largo Caballero of the stairway election, see his speech of 17 October 1937, as published in Francisco Largo Caballero, *La UGT y la guerra*, 28–29.

20. Several years before the war, Rodríguez Vega had been a member of the Communist party. He later transferred his allegiance to Indalecio Prieto. He was secretary of the printers' federation (Federación Gráfica Española), of which Ramón Lamoneda (also a former Communist) was president. According to reliable information I personally received (from Alfonso Quintana y Pena, a former Socialist Cortes deputy, and from Ricardo del Río, the head of the Febus news agency in Valencia, whose knowledge of the Socialist party was encyclopedic), Rodríguez Vega was very much under the influence of Lamoneda, who pursued a subtle pro-Communist, pro-Negrín course during the Civil War. In any event, Rodríguez Vega's pro-Communist stance was clearly evident during the last year of the conflict.

21. *Todos fuimos culpables*, 624.

22. *Obras completas*, IV, 746.

23. Ibid., 754.

24. 9 Oct. 1937.

25. Largo Caballero, *La UGT y la guerra*, 32.

26. P. 233. For a published protest by the Caballero executive, see *La Correspondencia de Valencia*, 6 Oct. 1937.

27. *Mis recuerdos*, 234–35. Cf. Vidarte, *Todos fuimos culpables*, 745.

28. *Mis recuerdos*, 230. In his "Notas Históricas," Largo Caballero states (1245): "The aim of the leaders [of the Socialist party] and the UGT has been to oust Largo Caballero from all the posts that he

held, having recourse to any procedure no matter how dishonorable. If they did not remove him from the chairmanship of the Agrupación Socialista Madrileña, it was because they were unable to; they tried."

29. For information on the Valencia Peasant Federation, which represented the interests of the small and medium farmers, many of whom had previously belonged to right-wing parties and clashed with the National Federation of Land Workers (Federación Española de Trabajadores de la Tierra) controlled by the left-wing Socialists, see Chapter 24, text to n. 12. For similar conflicts in other provinces, see *La Correspondencia de Valencia*, 18 Aug. 1937.

30. This refers to the speeches delivered after the fall of the Largo Caballero government by Jesús Hernández (see Hernández, *El partido comunista antes, durante y después de la crisis del gobierno Largo Caballero*, and Dolores Ibárruri, *En la lucha* [report to the plenum of the central committee of the PCE, 17 June 1937], 108–54).

31. *La Correspondencia de Valencia*, 14 July 1937.

32. *Mis recuerdos*, 231–32.

33. *Chantaje a un pueblo*, 70–71. For Largo Caballero's account, see Largo Caballero, *La UGT y la guerra*, 24–26, and his "Notas Históricas sobre la Guerra de España," 1013–15. Carlos de Baráibar, the director of *Adelante*, was replaced by Francisco Cruz Salido, a Prietista (*Adelante*, 27 July 1937).

34. *Claridad*, 4 Aug. 1937. See also *Adelante*, 27 July 1937.

35. 27 July 1937.

36. Palmiro Togliatti, *Escritos sobre la guerra de España*, 147–48 (letter to Georgi Dimitrov and Dimitri Manuilsky).

37. After the war Puente was placed in charge of the prodigious Spanish treasure shipped to Mexico by Negrín (see Chapter 13).

38. See Largo Caballero, *Mis recuerdos*, 232, and his "Notas Históricas," 1313–15; also Rosal, *Historia de la UGT*, II, 648.

39. *Hoy*, 19 Dec. 1942.

40. *Mis recuerdos*, 235. Several excerpts from this speech, which was published in its entirety in Largo Caballero, *La UGT y la guerra*, have already been quoted by me. The few newspapers that attempted to publish it were heavily censored. See, for example, *Nosotros*, 18 Oct. 1937.

41. See Largo Caballero, *Mis recuerdos*, 236–38; also Ginés Ganga in *Hoy*, 19 Dec. 1942.

42. *Mis recuerdos*, 238.

43. The Tribunals of Espionage and High Treason, it will be recalled, were set up after the arrest of the POUM leaders. They were empowered to sit in secret session and to try such crimes as holding meetings and demonstrations aimed at weakening public morale, in other words, disseminating "defeatism."

44. *Obras*, IV, 837.

45. International Institute of Social History, CNT-FAI Archives, Paquete 005, Caja 305, Dossier 66, Francisco Largo Caballero. A copy of the letter is in the Hoover Institution, Bolloten Collection.

46. *Diario de las Sesiones de la Diputación Permanente de la Cortes*, 3 Nov. 1937.

47. See Zugazagoitia, chap. 48, 1204–5.

48. Vidarte, *Todos fuimos culpables*, 746.

49. P. 1367.

50. Araquistáin Papers, Leg. 73/117 (Archivo Histórico Nacional, Madrid). Copies of the letters are in the Hoover Institution, Bolloten Collection. In the preface to an unpublished work ("No nos callamos durante la Guerra") Araquistáin notes that when the draft of the first letter by the Agrupación was to be read at a closed meeting in Valencia of left Socialist leaders, Largo Caballero and Carlos Hernández Zancajo proposed that the session should not be held as long as Alvarez del Vayo was present, because he did not merit their confidence. As a result, Vayo was forced to withdraw from the session. "Regarded as an agent of the Communists in the Socialist party, to which he continued to be nominally affiliated," Araquistáin comments, "it was assumed that his presence at the meetings of his official party had no purpose other than that of favoring Communist policy and informing the Stalinist party and the Soviet embassy of its intimate affairs and agreements" (Araquistáin Papers, Leg. 75/5[a]).

51. In Luis Araquistáin's handwriting, there is a note referring to the epithet "unscrupulous individuals and traitors," which says: "This alludes to the main one among them," the Communist agent Amaro del Rosal.

52. 4 Dec. 1937.

53. Largo Caballero, *Mis recuerdos*, 233–34. For the composition of the new executive, see *Frente Rojo*, 5 Jan. 1938; Rosal, *Historia de la UGT*, II, 732. The four Caballeristas who joined the fifteen-seat executive were Pascual Tomás, Carlos Hernández Zancajo, Ricardo Zabalza, and José Díaz Alor (not to be confused with José Díaz, the secretary of the PCE).

54. For composition of the executive, see previous note.

55. *La Vanguardia*, 4 Jan. 1938.

56. *Historia de la UGT*, II, 731–32.

57. See *Frente Rojo*, 1 Feb. 1939, for notice of the expulsion of García Lombardía.

58. Rosal, *Historia de la UGT*, II, 739.

59. Speech at the Madrid Regional Conference of the PCE on 5 January 1938 (*Mundo Obrero*, 7 Jan. 1938), as given in Ibárruri, *Speeches and Articles, 1936–1938*, 184.

60. Togliatti, *Escritos*, 162.

61. Ibid., 171.

62. Rosal, *Historia de la UGT*, II, 739.

63. See Juan Gómez Casas (*Historia del anarcosindicalismo español*, 254), and José Peirats (*La CNT en la revolución española*, II, 43), who both stress the enemy offensive as a factor in hastening agreement between the two sides.

64. For the terms of the pact, see *Frente Rojo* and *Solidaridad Obrera*, 18 March 1938; *Alianza CNT-UGT*, 131–41. For libertarian criticism of the pact, see Gómez Casas, *Historia del anarcosindicalismo español*, 256–57; Peirats, *Le CNT en la revolución española*, III, 61–69; Vernon Richards, *Lessons of the Spanish Revolution*, 170–76.

65. See, for example, *Fragua Social*, 23, 25, 26, 29 Mar., 3 Apr. 1938; *Frente Libertario*, 21 Apr. 1938; *Solidaridad Obrera*, 19, 25 Mar. 1938.

66. *Solidaridad Obrera*, 31 Mar., 1938.

67. Ibid., 25 Mar. 1938. It is worth recording that, according to Severino Campos, who was secretary of the Catalan regional committee of the FAI during the war, Mariano Vásquez's "libertarian education was as deficient as it was inconsistent" (letter to me, dated 27 Oct. 1950, Hoover Institution).

68. *Posibilismo libertario*, 77–78.

69. *Por qué perdimos la guerra*, 180.

70. 30 Mar. 1938.

Chapter 54

1. The best account of this battle can be found in José Manuel Martínez Bande, *La batalla de Teruel*. See also Rafael García-Valiño y Marcen, *Guerra de liberación española: Campañas de Aragón y la batalla de Teruel, 1938–1939*.

2. According to a report by the French military attaché in Barcelona of 20 March 1938, the Nationalist victory was due to "a crushing superiority in air power." He estimated the number of Nationalist aircraft at 450 to 500 and that of the Republicans at 100 to 120 (*Documents diplomatiques français, 1932–1939*, 2ᵉ Série [1936–1939], Tome VIII, 954).

3. *Historia de la guerra en España*, 365.

4. "Informe Operaciones del 8 al 14 de Marzo de 1938" (Bolloten Miscellaneous Documents, vol. IV, Hoover Institution). See also Santiago Alvarez's report to the central committee of the PCE, dated 4 April 1938, in Hoover Institution (Santiago Alvarez, "Informe Operaciones del 22 al 27 de Marzo de 1938"). Two other important documents that throw light on the rout on the Aragon front are a report by General Sebastián Pozas, the commander of the Eastern Army, dated 17 March 1938, and a deposition by Pozas on 21 March before General Carlos Masquelet, the judge appointed to examine the debacle (Bolloten, Miscellaneous Documents, vol. II, Hoover Institution). These four reports, from which I made typewritten copies, were loaned to me by Carlos Contreras (Vittorio Vidali) in Mexico in 1939. According to Contreras (private conversation), Pozas conducted himself in a cowardly manner (see my notes, Hoover Institution). Prieto removed Pozas from his command and replaced him with Lieutenant Colonel Juan Perea (*El Día Gráfico*, 2 Apr. 1938), who was commonly regarded as a friend of the Anarchosyndicalists. Given the large number of the CNT-FAI troops on the Aragon front, the removal of Pozas—a fair-weather member of the PCE and PSUC—was undoubtedly designed to instill confidence in the Anarchosyndicalist forces.

5. *American Commissar*, 410–11.

6. *Brigate internazionali in Spagna: Delitti della "Ceka" comunista*, 125.

7. Letter dated 10 May 1948, Hoover Institution.

8. Rudolf Rocker Collection, International Institute of Social History, Amsterdam. A copy of this report as well as other unpublished CNT-FAI documents in the Rocker Collection is available in the Bolloten Collection, Hoover Institution. I am indebted to Rudolf de Jong of the Institute for photocopying this large number of rare documents for me.

9. The decision to move to Barcelona was made at the end of October (*Gaceta de la República*, 31 Oct. 1937). The aim of the transfer was to consolidate and expand the authority of the government in Catalonia (see, for example, Azaña, *Obras completas*, IV, 823). In a conversation with Azaña on 23 August 1937, Negrín stated that in order to counteract the effects of the torpedoing of Spanish ships by Italy, Catalan industry should be put into full production, but that first it was necessary to resolve a "difficult political problem in Catalonia"—a reference to the insistence of the Catalans that they control their own industry. "I had to wait several weeks to resolve the urgent matter of the Council of Aragon," Negrín added impatiently. "Now it is essential that the state put its hands on Catalan industry" (ibid., IV, 745).

10. *Obras*, IV, 537 (letter to Angel Ossorio).

11. *Yo fui un ministro de Stalin*, 157.

12. *Comunista en España y antistalinista en la URSS*, 41, 49, 65–71.

13. *Nuestra guerra*, 182.

14. Indalecio Prieto, article in *El Socialista* (Paris), 2 Nov. 1950. The article was reprinted in Prieto, *Convulsiones de España*, II, 107–12.

15. *Yo fui un ministro de Stalin*, 157.

16. On 29 March, *Frente Rojo* made an urgent call for 100,000 volunteers.

17. *Yo fui un ministro de Stalin*, 158.

18. Ibid., 159.

19. Interview, Mexico 1940 (Hoover Institution).

20. Indalecio Prieto, *Cómo y por qué salí del ministerio de defensa nacional*, 33–34.

21. Ibid., 34–35. See also Prieto, *Convulsiones*, II, 98–100; Vicente Uribe, "Memorias," 47.

22. For Soviet diplomacy and the Spanish Civil War, see Chapters 8, 10, 16, and 17.

23. *Yo fui un ministro de Stalin*, 114–16.

24. Essay by Prokofiev in *Pod znamenem ispanskoi respubliki, 1936–1939*, 539–40.

25. *Spanish Notebooks*, 140.

26. *Documents on German Foreign Policy*, Series D, III, 299.

27. Robert Bingham to Cordell Hull, 1 June 1937, U.S. Department of State, *Foreign Relations of the United States: Diplomatic Papers, 1936 and 1937*, I, 318.

28. As given in Hans-Henning Abendroth, *Hitler in der spanischen Arena*, 362, n. 203. Abendroth's reference to this document, dated 2 June 1937, is AM [Akten des Arhivs der Marine]/M 1375/80689.

29. See Chapter 50.

30. *Guerra y revolución en España, 1936–1939*, IV, 68.

31. *Yo fui un ministro de Stalin*, 88.

32. Several authors have touched on the question of mediation, including attempts by Negrín, but none have dealt with the matter in depth or produced so far any convincing documentary evidence regarding Negrín's alleged efforts. It must be borne in mind in assessing these alleged efforts that, according to Togliatti, Negrín, even after the fall of Barcelona in January 1939, "ignored the offers of mediation which, in any case, had no concrete basis and were invitations to capitulation pure and simple" (*Escritos sobre la guerra de España*, 264). For Azaña's peace feelers, see n. 54 below and Chapter 63, n. 48.

33. Andrés Carabantes and Eusebio Cimorra, *Un mito llamado Pasionaria*, 183–84.

34. Dolores Ibárruri, *En la lucha*, 248–61.

35. Ministère des Affaires Etrangères, *Documents diplomatiques français, 1932–1939*, 2ᵉ Série (1936–1939), Tome VIII, 858.

36. *La república y la guerra*, 483.

37. After resigning from the ministry of justice in December 1937, Irujo rejoined the government as minister without portfolio.

38. *Historia*, 372. For Giral's guarded pessimism regarding the military situation, see his conversation with the French ambassador, as reported by the letter to Paul-Boncour, the French foreign minister, on 25 March 1938 (Ministère des Affaires Etrangères, *Documents diplomatiques français, 1932–1939*, 2ᵉ Série [1936–1939], Tome IX, 93–96).

39. *Historia*, 372. See also Prieto's letter to Negrín, *Epistolario, Prieto y Negrín*, 107. There is no mention in Labonne's report to Paul-Boncour (see previous note) of any offer of a French warship to evacuate the president and the cabinet.

40. *Historia*, 372.

41. Ibid., 374.

42. Ibid.

43. Ibid., 375–76.

44. *El único camino*, 390.

45. *Historia*, 374.

46. 17 Mar. 1938. See also Zugazagoitia, 377.

47. *Epistolario*, 105.

48. Ibid.; Hernández, *Yo fui un ministro de Stalin*, 161; Pi Sunyer, 483.

49. *Historia*, 378–79.

50. Report dated 21–22 April 1938 as given in Togliatti, *Escritos*, 193.

51. Ibid.

52. Juan-Simeón Vidarte, *Todos fuimos culpables*, 823–35.

53. Ibid., 820–21.

54. Azaña, *Obras*, III, 558. Azaña's peace feelers are confirmed by Georges Bonnet, former French foreign minister, who says that on several occasions "he confided in various French personalities" that the defeat of the Republicans seemed "inevitable" to him and that he desired an arrangement to end the Civil War "in a manner honorable to his party" (*Défense de la paix: Fin d'une Europe*, 81). See also Chapter 63, n. 48.

55. *La CNT en la revolución española*, III, 130.

56. As given in César M. Lorenzo (Horacio M. Prieto's son), *Les anarchistes espagnoles et le pouvoir, 1868–1969*, 315–16, n. 27.

57. Ibid., 315.

58. *Epistolario, Prieto y Negrín*, 15. See also Vidarte, *Todos fuimos culpables*, 850.

59. Report dated 21–22 April 1938 as given in Togliatti, *Escritos*, 195.

60. *¡Teníamos que perder!*, 275.

61. 23 March 1938.

62. Prieto, *Cómo y por qué*, 56–57.

63. Togliatti, *Escritos*, 192.

64. *Epistolario, Prieto y Negrín*, 16.

65. Ibid., 23.

66. *Documentos políticos para la historia de la república española*, 21.

67. *Escritos*, 194.

68. Vidarte, *Todos fuimos culpables*, 849.

69. *Guerra y revolución*, IV, 75–76.

70. Interviewed by me in Mexico in 1945.

71. As given in Hernández, *Yo fui un ministro de Stalin*, 166–67.

72. Ibid., 165–66.

73. *Escritos*, 197.

74. *La Vanguardia*, 9 Apr. 1938.

Chapter 55

1. *Gaceta de la República*, 6 Apr. 1938. After his resignation from the ministry of justice in December 1937, Irujo rejoined the government as minister without portfolio.

2. 7 Apr. 1938.

3. See, for example, José Peirats, *La CNT en la revolución española*, III, 90; José García Pradas, *¡Teníamos que perder!*, 308; Juan Gómez Casas, *Historia del anarcosindicalismo español*, 255, n.

217; and Juan López, *Una misión sin importancia*, 159–61. See also Federica Montseny's letter to me, dated 7 December 1950, regarding her attitude toward Segundo Blanco and Mariano Vázquez (Hoover Institution).

4. *Escritos sobre la guerra de España*, 196 (report dated 21–22 Apr. 1938), 196.

5. 7 Apr. 1938.

6. Dolores Ibárruri, *El único camino*, 391. See also *Guerra y revolución en España, 1936–1939*, IV, 79.

7. Juan-Simeón Vidarte, *Todos fuimos culpables*, 854.

8. *Epistolario, Prieto y Negrín*, 99.

9. *¡Unión de todos los españoles!* (Report to the plenum of the central committee of the PCE, 23–25 May 1938), 19.

10. *Gaceta de la República*, 10 Apr. 1938. In January, the left Republican foreign minister, José Giral, had appointed him director general of propaganda (ibid., 25 Jan. 1938).

11. *Yo fui un ministro de Stalin*, 157.

12. *Solidaridad Obrera* (Paris), 11 Mar. 1951.

13. *Mis recuerdos*, 219.

14. Letter to Diego Martínez Barrio, published in *Vía Libre*, 15 May 1939.

15. *Triunfo*, 22 June 1974.

16. *Tiempo de Historia*, May 1979.

17. *El País* (Semanal), 20 July 1986.

18. *The Yoke and the Arrows*, 58.

19. *Half of Spain Died*, 226.

20. *Return to Cuba* (special issue of the *Hispanic American Report*, 1964).

21. Communist influence in the security services is dealt with in the next chapter.

22. For information on this book, see Chapter 24, n. 16.

23. *Hombres*, 653 and 660. For additional information on Sánchez Arcas, see Castro, *J'ai perdu la foi à Moscú*, 147–48. Sánchez Arcas was appointed undersecretary of propaganda on 6 April 1938 (*Gaceta de la República*, 10 Apr. 1938).

24. *Trayectoria*, 411.

25. Ibid. At the time of the German invasion of France in June 1940, Rodríguez accompanied Negrín to England.

26. Togliatti, *Escritos*, 154.

27. Ibid., 229. My italics.

28. Ibid., 231.

29. *Historia de la guerra en España*, 417.

30. *Chantaje a un pueblo*, 368.

31. *Escritos*, 234.

32. No serious study has yet been made on Soviet imports from Spain of finished goods and raw materials and on the alleged transfer of plant machinery. Nor will this be possible until Negrín's files have been located and analyzed and until the records of the Soviet-controlled banks in London and Paris, which handled the Spanish government's transactions, become available.

33. According to Martínez Amutio, the left Socialist leader, Negrín was "not a militant Socialist of firm ideals. He despised the unions and never had any contact with them" (letter to me, Hoover Institution). This is confirmed by Togliatti, who wrote on 25 November 1937 that Negrín "is not linked to the masses. In the PS [Socialist party] he is a rightwinger" (*Escritos*, 154).

34. *Escritos*, 231.

35. Ibid., 136–38, 141–42, 144, 146–49, 156, 160, 164, 169, 196–97, 275, 289, 300.

36. Ibid., 230–31.

37. Ibid., 288.

38. *Trayectoria*, 391.

39. *Escritos*, 200–201.

40. Cordón, 391.

41. Interview in *Tiempo de Historia*, Jan. 1980.

42. *Give Me Combat*, 192. See also Enrique Líster, *¡Basta!*, 180–81.

43. *Memoirs of a Soviet Ambassador: The War, 1939–43*, 117–18.

44. Letter from Immigration Branch, Home Office, to Foreign Office, dated 24 July 1940, Folio 108, FO 371/24527, C7501/7501/41, Public Record Office. A photocopy is in the Hoover Institution, Bolloten Collection.

45. Memorandum, dated 1 July 1940, signed by S. Williams, private secretary to the permanent undersecretary at the Foreign Office, Sir Alexander Cadogan, Folio 80, FO 371/24527, C7501/7501/41, Public Record Office. A photocopy is in the Hoover Institution, Bolloten Collection.

46. For the unsuccessful efforts to remove Negrín from England, see Folios 80–126, FO 371/24527, C7501/7501/41, Public Record Office. Photocopies of all these documents are in the Hoover Institution, Bolloten Collection. See also essay by Denis Smyth, "The Politics of Asylum, Juan Negrín and the British Government in 1940," in Richard Langhorne, *Diplomacy and Intelligence during the Second World War*, 126–45. I am indebted to Smyth's essay for the reference and register number of the aforementioned documents which greatly facilitated my research.

47. Memorandum, dated 25 July 1940, by Butler on conversation, Folio 116, FO 371/24527, C7501/7501/41, Public Record Office. A photocopy is in the Hoover Institution, Bolloten Collection.

48. Smyth, "The Politics of Asylum," in Langhorne, 129. See n. 46 above.

49. Address in May 1939 before the Council of Foreign Relations in New York, quoted in Alvarez del Vayo, *Freedom's Battle*, 76.

50. *Todos fuimos culpables*, 855.

51. *Historia*, 428–29.

52. *Escritos*, 230.

53. Ibid.

54. *Epistolario, Prieto y Negrín*, 17 (letter to Negrín, dated 17 June 1939).

55. Togliatti, *Escritos*, 201 (report dated 21–22 Apr. 1938).

56. *Gaceta de la República*, 7 Apr. 1938.

57. Ibid.

58. See Azaña, *Obras completas*, IV, 896; Cordón, 236; *Epistolario*, 29, 30, 33, 99–100; *Guerra y revolución*, I, 300; Pérez Salas, 187–88; M. Teresa Suero Roca, *Militares republicanos de la guerra de España*, 306; Togliatti, *Escritos*, 235; Zugazagoitia, 406–8.

59. *Gaceta de la República*, 7 Apr. 1938.

60. *Escritos*, 235–36.

61. Ibid., 231.

62. It is worth recalling Cordón's warning to one of his fellow officers, quoted earlier in the work: "Let me remind you that we are living in strange times, when people are killed for nothing at all. I seriously advise you to join the Communist party. It needs you, and you need it (José Martín Blázquez, *I Helped to Build an Army*, 241).

63. *Historia*, 406, 408.

64. *Trayectoria*, 389. My italics.

65. *Gaceta de la República*, 14 Apr. 1938.

66. See Pérez Salas, 188; Suero Roca, *Militares republicanos*, 159. For biographical information on Díaz Tendero not included in this book, see ibid., 143–60.

67. His position as head of this department is confirmed in a report by the military section of the peninsular committee of the FAI, dated 30 Sept. 1938 (Rudolf Rocker Collection, International Institute of Social History, Amsterdam). A copy of this report as well as other unpublished FAI and CNT documents in the Rocker Collection is available in the Bolloten Collection. I am indebted to Rudolf de Jong of the Institute for photocopying this large quantity of rare documents for me.

68. *Guerra en España*, 188. Pérez Salas was named undersecretary of the army in mid-March, replacing Fernández Bolaños who had been appointed military attaché in Paris (ibid., 185).

69. *Los anarquistas en la crisis política española*, 357. That this tactic was used by the Communist party is confirmed in a report of the military section of the peninsular committee of the FAI, dated 26 June 1938 (Rocker Collection; see n. 67 above).

70. *Los anarquistas*, 357. See also circular letter issued by the peninsular committee of the FAI, 13 July 1938 (Rocker Collection; see n. 67 above).

71. This detailed report is in the Rocker Collection; see n. 67 above.

72. Togliatti, *Escritos*, 156.

73. FAI report, dated 30 Sept. 1938 (Rocker Collection; see n. 67 above).

74. *Yo fui un ministro de Stalin*, 144. Hernández adds: "The tank and air units were the exclusive preserve of the Communists."

75. *Por qué perdimos la guerra*, 219. For other Anarchosyndicalist complaints regarding Communist activities and influence in the army, see CNT-FAI Archives, International Institute of Social History, Paquete 17, Caja 318(501), Paquete 3, Caja 320(503), Paquete 17, Caja 540, no. 7. It is important to draw the reader's attention to a circular letter of the CNT national committee, dated 14 October 1938, in which Miguel González Inestal, a CNT-FAI affiliate and subcommissar of the General Commissariat of War, to which he had been appointed by Negrín in May, is quoted as asserting that the influence of the PCE in the commissariat (and in the army as a whole) had declined considerably since September 1937 (CNT-FAI Archives, International Institute of Social History, Paquete 59, Carpeta 5. A photocopy of this document is in the Hoover Institution, Bolloten Collection, file "González Inestal, Miguel. CNT National Committee Circular, 14 Oct. 1938"). González Inestal's assertion is not supported by any substantive evidence and, in fact, is belied by the overwhelming testimony to the contrary adduced in the course of this work. His attempt to play down the preponderant position of the PCE was symptomatic of what was happening to a number of Anarchosyndicalists who had managed to attain positions of influence in the state apparatus and had become known as "Negrinistas."

76. *Guerra y revolución*, IV, 229–30. Cf. Togliatti's report to Moscow, dated 25 Nov. 1937 (*Escritos*, 156).

77. *Los anarquistas en la crisis política española*, 355. See also FAI report mentioned in n. 69.

78. See also Abad de Santillán, *Por qué*, 242–47.

79. Rocker Collection (see n. 67 above).

80. That Planelles was a Communist is confirmed by the official Communist history of the Civil War, *Guerra y revolución*, I, 301.

81. *Gaceta de la República*, 28 May 1937.

82. He was appointed to the post by Dr. José Puche, who in April 1938 was made chief medical officer (*jefe de sanidad del ejército*) by his friend Negrín (*Gaceta de la República*, 1 May 1938) and in December 1938 director general *de sanidad de guerra* (*La Vanguardia*, 11 Dec. 1938). After the war, José Puche, then in Mexico, was to have received from Negrín's trusted colonel of carabineers, Enrique Puente, the famous Spanish treasure shipped aboard the luxury yacht, the *Vita*. However, Puente unexpectedly switched his allegiance to Prieto and turned it over to his custody.

83. Report by Nistal, dated 29 June 1938, to the delegate commissar in the Inspección General de Sanidad, Rocker Collection.

84. *Mis recuerdos*, 209.

85. Speech reported in *Fragua Social*, 7 July 1937.

86. Rocker Collection.

87. Ibid.

88. Ibid.

89. Prieto, *Cómo y por qué salí del ministerio de defensa nacional*, 48.

90. *Diario Oficial del Ministerio de Defensa Nacional*, 1 May 1938.

91. See Chapter 50. Crescenciano Bilbao was relieved of his post by Negrín as soon as he became defense minister (*Diario Oficial del Ministerio de Defensa Nacional*, 9 Apr. 1938).

92. *Claridad*, 12 Nov. 1936.

93. For Ossorio y Tafall's support of the Communists, see Manuel Tagüeña (former Communist and commander of the Fifteenth Army Corps), *Testimonio de dos guerras*, 309; and José Peirats, *La CNT en la revolución española*, III, 227. See also Ossorio's speech giving a glowing account of the accomplishments of the Soviet Union (*Política*, 1 June 1938), and the excerpt from his speech in July 1937, as quoted in the official Communist history of the Civil War, in which he advocated the creation of a "great working class party that inherits the Socialist tradition and is infused with the revolutionary vitality of the Communist party" (*Guerra y revolución*, III, 209, n. 1). However, at the time of the Casado coup in March 1939, he offered his "unconditional adherence" to the National Defense Council, which overthrew Negrín and the Communists (see *Adelante* [Alicante], 7 Mar. 1939). In a letter to Prieto after the war, Negrín cites his appointment of Ossorio y Tafall "of Izquierda Republicana" as an example of his impartiality (*Epistolario, Prieto y Negrín*, 31).

94. *Hombres*, 659–60. My italics.

95. *Diario Oficial del Ministerio de Defensa Nacional*, 7, 8 Apr. 1938. See also Cordón, 394.
96. Cordón, *Trayectoria*, 394–95.
97. *Gaceta de la República*, 13 May 1938. See also *Epistolario*, 32.
98. *Epistolario*, 32–33.
99. Ibid., 99–100.
100. Ibid., 100.
101. *Trayectoria*, 395–96.
102. Quoted by Prieto, *Epistolario*, 101.
103. *Historia*, 423–24.
104. *Guerra en España*, 195, 197.

Chapter 56

1. See Chapter 54.
2. Manuel Azaña, *Obras completas*, IV, 883.
3. *Diario Oficial del Ministerio de Defensa Nacional*, 9 Aug. 1937. My emphasis.
4. See Chapter 50.
5. *Yo fui un ministro de Stalin*, 122. According to Julián Gorkin, the ministers of the interior and justice could do nothing in the face of the "Stalinist 'caretakers.'" "They have in their hands the most fearful apparatus. . . . The SIM arrests capriciously whomever it wishes. . . . The minister of justice himself feels impotent in face of the SIM. This organization terrorizes judges, lawyers, prosecutors" (*Caníbales políticos*, 170–71).
6. *Los anarquistas en la crisis política española*, 270–71. The pro-Communist Edmundo Domínguez, secretary of the UGT National Federation of Building Workers (Federación Nacional de la Edificación) and political commissar of the Army of the Center, writes: "In every unit of the Republican Army there was an agent of the SIM charged with the surveillance of the officers and men. Sometimes he was covert, sometimes he was not" (*Los vencedores de Negrín*, 101, n. 1).
7. *La CNT en la revolución española*, III, 281.
8. See Chapter 51.
9. See Chapter 51.
10. See Chapter 51.
11. See Chapter 51.
12. See Chapter 51.
13. Letter from Garcés to D. Pastor Petit, dated 18 Sept. 1977. I am deeply indebted to Pastor Petit for furnishing me with photocopies of Garcés Arroyo's letters to him. These copies are in the Hoover Institution.
14. D. Pastor Petit, *La cincuena columna a Catalunya*, 19 (evidence of Colonel Vicente Guarner) and 183.
15. Ibid. See also Ramón Salas Larrazábal, *Historia del ejército popular de la república*, II, 1585.
16. For information on Uribarry, see Justo Martínez Amutio, *Chantaje a un pueblo*, 122, 325; Pastor Petit, *La cincuena columna*, 19–20 (evidence of Colonel Vicente Guarner) and 231; Indalecio Prieto, *Cómo y por qué salí del ministerio de defensa nacional*, 79; Salas Larrazábal, *Historia del ejército popular*, II, 1585–86; Manuel Uribarri, *La quinta columna española: Revelaciones sensacionales*. This book, published in Havana in 1943, extols the SIM during the "Uribarri period."
17. Prieto, *Cómo y por qué*, 79.
18. See, for example, Martínez Amutio, 222; Pastor Petit, *La cincuena columna*, 231; and Hugh Thomas, *The Spanish Civil War* (1977 ed.), 777.
19. CNT-FAI Archives, International Institute of Social History, Paquete 52, Caja 308, Carpeta 4. A photocopy of the document is in the Hoover Institution, Bolloten Collection, file "Uribarry."
20. Report on CNT interview with Garcés on 27 May 1938 (CNT-FAI Archives, International Institute of Social History, Paquete 51, Carpeta 3, Series I 14, "Informe de Nuestra Entrevista con el Jefe del SIM Camarada Garcés, en el Día de Hoy." A photocopy of this document is in the Hoover Institution, Bolloten Collection, file "Uribarry").
21. In a letter to Pastor Petit, dated 20 June 1977, Garcés mentions his age and former trade. In a previous letter (6 June 1977), he gives the date of his appointment as head of the SIM as 7 April 1938.

He undoubtedly means his appointment as *subchief* as Uribarry did not flee Spain until the end of April or the beginning of May. There is evidence of this in the report mentioned in the previous footnote. Before the Civil War, Garcés served as a bodyguard to PSOE leaders and had gained notoriety after it was learned that he and other Socialists had accompanied the avenging assault guards on the night of 13 July 1936, when José Calvo Sotelo, the monarchist leader, was assassinated (see Ian Gibson, *La noche en que mataron a Calvo Sotelo*, 108, 117–26, 202, 210–11, and Luis Romero, *Por qué y cómo mataron a Calvo Sotelo*, 191–95).

22. I am grateful to Heleno Saña for providing me with excerpts from Garcés's letter, several of which I have used in this chapter. See Saña's letters to me, dated 21 Oct. and 6 Nov. 1986 (Hoover Institution).

23. Pastor Petit, *La cincuena columna*, 233–34. Garcés confirms his alleged reluctance to accept the post in his letter to Saña of 20 October 1974 (see previous note).

24. Conversation in Mexico in 1950.

25. *Indice* (Madrid), 15 June 1974.

26. Letter dated 21 Oct. 1986 (Hoover Institution).

27. See n. 25 above. During the interview Garcés told Saña that he did not know what the two men discussed, "because they always spoke in Russian or in other foreign languages." With respect to the relationship between the two men, he stated: "I believe that Negrín dominated the Russian and not the reverse."

28. *Gaceta de la República*, 28 May, 3 Sept. 1937.

29. Letter dated 21 Oct. 1986 (Hoover Institution).

30. Paquete 005, Caja 305, Carpeta 8, Dossier 9, p. 150. Photocopies of this and other documents relating to the SIM in the CNT-FAI archives are in the Hoover Institution, Bolloten Collection, file "SIM."

31. *Guerra en España, 1936–1939*, 199.

32. *La cincuena columna*, 222.

33. Servicio Histórico Militar, Documentación Roja, A56 Leg. 558, Carpeta 1, p. 2. A copy of this document is in the Hoover Institution, Bolloten Collection. A book by an unknown Spanish author, published in Moscow in 1957, states: "The SIM was basically in the hands of the Socialists. According to 1938 statistics, there were 113 agents from the Socialist party, 135 from the labor unions, and only two from the Communist party in the Army of the Center. Basically, a similar picture could be presented with respect to Catalonia, the Army of the Southern front, and the rest of the units" (Khose Garsia, *Ispaniia narodnogo fronta*, 166). Even if we allow for the strong likelihood that of the 135 agents who came from the labor unions many belonged to the PCE, it is impossible to take these "statistics" seriously.

34. He was never a member of the PCE, as alleged by Colonel Vicente Guarner (Pastor Petit, *La cincuena columna*, 222), although for a long time he worked closely with the party. For information on Pedrero by one who knew him well, see Regina García, *Yo he sido marxista: El cómo y el porqué de una conversión*, 220–27, 287. García was editor in chief of the Popular Army newspaper, *La Voz del Combatiente*, and was later chief of press and propaganda of the Madrid commissariat of war (ibid., 211–12). For additional information on Pedrero, see J. García Pradas, *La Traición de Stalin*, 63, 85, 86, 124.

35. Buckley's evidence to Hugh Thomas (*The Spanish Civil War* [1977 ed.], 669, n. 5).

36. *Los anarquistas en la crisis política española*, 271–72. For further information on the SIM and the special tribunals, see Gabriel Avilés, *Tribunales rojos*; Pere Bosch Gimpera, *Memòries*, 261–64; R. L. Chacón, *Por qué hice las chekas de Barcelona: Laúrencic ante el consejo de guerra*; *Datos complementarios para la historia de España*, 253–75; Julián Gorkin, *Caníbales políticos*, 168–70; Martínez Amutio, 211, 325–27; Carlos Pi Sunyer, *La república y la guerra*, 479–80, 506, 519; and Miguel Sabater, *Estampas del cautiverio rojo*. See also Rudolf Rocker Documents (International Institute of Social History), No. 53, "Las Prisiones Clandestinas: Santa Ursula en Valencia. La Cheka de la Calle de Córcega, en Barcelona," and Documentos Nos. 8, 9, 29, 56, 64, 72, 83. Copies of all these documents are in the Hoover Institution, Bolloten Collection. In the CNT-FAI archives there is a memorandum dated 14 June 1938 that says: "In view of the continuing crimes committed by the agents of the SIM, the President of the Supreme Court and the Attorney General of the Republic (Don Mariano Gómez and Don Leopoldo Garrido) have appeared repeatedly before the Minister of Justice,

Sr. González Peña . . . , vigorously protesting the conduct of the SIM" (International Institute of Social History, Paquete 005, Caja 305, Carpeta 8, Dossier 9, p. 149. Copies of all documents in this file relating to the SIM are in the Bolloten Collection).

37. For photographs of the torture chambers, see, for example, *Datos complementarios para la historia de España*, Anexo VIII, between 276 and 277.

38. Photocopies of these letters are in the Hoover Institution, Bolloten Collection. See n. 13 above.

39. See *Epistolario, Prieto y Negrín*.

40. It is noteworthy that Garcés wrote his letter after the publication in Madrid, in June 1974, of the interview given to Saña in Mexico. It appears from Saña's correspondence with me that Garcés's main purpose in writing his letter was to reply to certain accusations and rumors in circulation in Madrid regarding his conduct in the SIM. He asked Saña if the same publication (*Indice*) that had published the interview would also publish the letter, but for reasons Saña cannot recall *Indice* did not do so. See Saña's letters to me of 21 October and 6 November 1986 (Hoover Institution). It is not unreasonable to suppose that Garcés wrote his letter in order to whitewash and even embellish his role in the SIM in anticipation of his eventual return to Spain.

41. Three years later, in a letter to Pastor Petit, dated 18 September 1977, Garcés stated that Orlov was "substituted" as a result of a typewritten memo he sent to Negrín, in which he demonstrated that Orlov was "useless and counterproductive." However, he does not even mention Orlov's alleged expulsion. A photocopy of the letter is in the Hoover Institution, Bolloten Collection. See n. 13 above.

42. International Institute of Social History, Paquete 005, Caja 305, Carpeta 8, Dossier 9, p. 167. A photocopy of this document is in the Hoover Institution, Bolloten Collection, file "SIM."

43. CNT-FAI Archives, International Institute of Social History, Paquete 51, Carpeta 3, Series I 14. A photocopy of this document is in the Hoover Institution, Bolloten Collection, file "SIM." In a document, dated 18 May 1938, relating to the SIM, the CNT, which had been requesting directive positions in the investigative service, stated that it had the men and the capacity for the job. "Our capabilities in the field of vigilance and investigation exceed those that are attributed to us when we are only offered posts as concentration camp guards" (International Institute of Social History, Paquete 005, Caja 305, Carpeta 8, Dossier 9, p. 152. A photocopy of this document is in the Hoover Institution, Bolloten Collection, file "SIM").

44. *The Secret History of Stalin's Crimes*, xv.

45. It will be recalled that Irujo had resigned as minister of justice in December 1937, because of the creation of the *tribunales de guardia*, but had rejoined the government as minister without portfolio shortly afterward due to the intervention of José Antonio Aguirre, the premier of the Basque government.

46. Manuel de Irujo, *Un vasco en el ministerio de justicia: Memorias*, I, 254–57.

47. "Datos Remitidos por el Señor Manuel de Irujo, Ministro Vasco en el Gobierno de la República Española," Hoover Institution, Bolloten Collection, file "Irujo."

48. *La república y la guerra*, 479–80. See also ibid., 506, 519. The August crisis is discussed in the next chapter.

49. *Memòries*, 261–64. See also ibid., 289–90.

50. *The Spanish Civil War* (1977 ed.), 808.

51. *Gaceta de la República*, 17 Apr. 1938.

52. *Recuerdos de la Guerra de España*, 61–62.

53. See nn. 68 and 77 below for further information on Méndez.

54. *Recuerdos*, 59.

55. Ibid., 45–50.

56. Ibid., 26–27. My italics.

57. Ibid., 27.

58. Ibid., 59–60. It is noteworthy that Cuevas was expelled from the PCE at the end of January 1939 "for desertion in the face of the enemy."

59. *Escritos sobre la guerra de España*, 228.

60. *Yo fui un ministro de Stalin*, 144.

61. *Escritos*, 158.

62. Ibid., 183–84.

63. The unusually well-informed head of the Febus news agency in Barcelona, Ricardo del Río, told me that on one occasion, when the CNT sharply criticized a Communist political commissar for his conduct on the northern front, Paulino Gómez refused to allow the PCE newspapers to reply. He also told me that Vázquez Ocaña, a member of the Socialist party and director of Negrín's mouthpiece in Barcelona, *La Vanguardia*, "never carried out the instructions of the Socialist executive" and had "problems" with Paulino Gómez (from notes taken during my talks with del Río [Hoover Institution]).

64. *Escritos*, 236.

65. *Epistolario, Prieto y Negrín*, 104.

66. Ibid., 103.

67. See Togliatti's criticisms, Chapter 54; also text to n. 51 above.

68. *Indice*, Nov.–Dec. 1971. Méndez also states in the same article that in September 1936 he became private secretary to Negrín, who at that time was minister of finance. "From the end of that month until January 1937 I travelled abroad, principally to Paris and New York, as delegate of the minister. In the banks in Paris and New York there were enormous sums of money in my name for the purpose of attending to various expenses related to the war."

69. *Indice*, Nov.–Dec. 1971.

70. *Escritos*, 230–31.

71. Ibid., 200–201.

72. *Gaceta de la República*, 1 Apr. 1938.

73. Ibid., 20 Feb. 1937.

74. Article by Méndez in *Indice*, Nov.–Dec. 1971.

75. Ibid.

76. When questioned by me after the war.

77. Méndez was appointed at the end of May (*Gaceta de la República*, 28 May 1937) and resigned at the beginning of September (ibid., 3 Sept. 1937). Víctor Salazar was appointed in mid-October (ibid., 15 Oct. 1937). Ricardo del Río of the Febus news agency assured me that it was at Prieto's behest that Salazar was made director general. Méndez stated years later that he was replaced by Salazar, who was "another Socialist who enjoyed the absolute confidence of the party [PSOE]" (*Indice*, Nov.–Dec. 1971).

78. Servicio Histórico Militar, Documentación Roja, A 56 Leg. 558, Carpeta 1, p. 6. A photocopy of this document is in the Hoover Institution, Bolloten Collection.

79. Interviewed by me in Mexico in 1939. The transcribed shorthand notes are in the Hoover Institution.

80. Interview, Mexico, 1944. A shorthand record is in the Hoover Institution.

Chapter 57

1. See Chapter 43.

2. Manuel Azaña, *Obras completas*, IV, 707.

3. See Chapter 43.

4. *Obras*, IV, 771.

5. *Nuestra guerra*, 244. See also Carlos Pi Sunyer, *La república y la guerra*, 470; also Ernest Udina, *Josep Tarradellas*, 206, 212.

6. *Recuerdos de la guerra de España*, 53.

7. Letter to me. See file, "Jordi Arquer. Correspondence with B. Bolloten. Letters and Excerpts" (Hoover Institution). In his letter, Arquer explains that he visited Companys several times at his home and in the Generalitat Palace between the time he was released from prison in 1937—after being arrested by the Communist police—and rearrested in 1938 a few months before the POUM trial.

8. *Memòries*, 290–91.

9. Article in *Economies et Sociétés*, Tome VI, Sept.–Oct. 1972. See also José Antonio González Casanova, *Federalismo y autonomía*, 348–50, for an account of the encroachments by the central government on Catalan autonomy.

10. *El eco de los pasos*, 526. See also Diego Abad de Santillán, *Por qué perdimos la guerra*, 265.

11. "Informe, Comité Peninsular de la FAI, Sept. 1938." CNT-FAI Archives, International Institute of Social History, Paquete 92, Caja 305, B, p. 11. Photocopy in Hoover Institution, Bolloten Collection, file "FAI. Informe, Comité Peninsular, Sept. 1938."

12. *Por qué perdimos la guerra*, 253. Abad de Santillán also states that the Russians shipped to the Soviet Union the machinery for the manufacture of cigarette paper (ibid., 265, n. 1).

13. Almost immediately after the war many PSUC leaders left the party for this reason. See, for example, Gregorio Morán, *Miseria y grandeza del Partido Comunista de España, 1939–1985*, 30.

14. Miguel Serra Pàmies, a leading member of the PSUC executive, who left the party after the war, and was a councillor in the Generalitat government and agricultural secretary of the party, told me in Mexico in 1945 that the PCE tried to monopolize the posts in his department and that "all the political commissars on the Aragon front [presumably in PSUC units] were members of the PCE" (shorthand notes in Hoover Institution).

15. *Frente Rojo*, 4 June 1938.

16. For further information on the friction between the Catalanistas in the PSUC and the PCE, see Chapter 39.

17. Article by Rafael Méndez in *Indice*, Nov.–Dec. 1971.

18. See also Bosch Gimpera, 262, on this subject.

19. The entire text can be found in Salvador de Madariaga, *España* (4th ed. corrected and expanded), 798–801. The authenticity of the letter has never been questioned and is summarized by Carlos Pi Sunyer, who was councillor of culture in the Catalan government when the letter was written to Negrín (Pi Sunyer, 480). See also Bosch Gimpera, 262, 289–90.

20. *La república y la guerra*, 479–80.

21. Ibid., 461.

22. *The Spanish Tragedy*, 200–201.

23. For the ministers' letters of resignation, see *La Vanguardia*, 21 Aug. 1938.

24. *Guerra y revolución en España, 1936–1939*, IV, 142–43.

25. Azaña, *Obras*, IV, 887. See also Manuel de Irujo, *Un vasco en el ministerio de justicia: Memorias*, I, 89.

26. Udina, 208.

27. *Obras*, IV, 888.

28. *Guerra y revolución*, IV, 147.

29. As quoted in the official Communist history, ibid., IV, 147. The source given is "Recuerdos de Rafael Vidiella sobre el PSUC," 10. Archives of the PCE. As the official history was published in Moscow, the archives of the Spanish Communist party are presumably located there.

30. The reader will recall that it was the Comintern that had originally proposed that the Communists should withdraw from the government in order to influence foreign opinion.

31. According to the official Communist history, Moix was vice-president of the Catalan UGT in March 1937 and in exile was elected secretary general of the PSUC and later president (*Guerra y revolución*, IV, 148, n. 1).

32. Ibid., 147–48, n. 2. See also Miquel Caminal, *Joan Comorera*, II, 250, who confirms the interview.

33. José Peirats, *La CNT en la revolución española*, III, 143.

34. Stanley G. Payne, *Basque Nationalism*, 109. See also Luis María and Juan Carlos de Aberásturi, *La guerra en Euzkadi*, 248. The only reference I have been able to find to Tomás Bilbao in works dealing specifically with the Basque country are in José Luis de la Granja Sainz, *Nacionalismo y II república en el país vasco*, 65, 104, 121, 479, 485–86, 506–21, 567, and Maximiano García Venero, *Historia del nacionalismo vasco*, 624.

35. *La Vanguardia*, 17 Aug. 1938.

36. *Guerra y revolución*, IV, 148–49. For the repercussions among the Basques of Tomás Bilbao's replacement of Irujo, see Iñaki Anasagasti and Koldo San Sebastián, *Los años oscuros*, 74–76.

37. Pi Sunyer, 522.

38. *El único camino*, 408.

39. *Historia del partido comunista de España* (official party history), 191.

40. Benigno Rodríguez, Negrín's political secretary, informed me in Mexico after the war that it was believed that the Republican ministers, possibly led by Bernardo Giner de los Ríos, would

precipitate a cabinet crisis by resigning (interview in Mexico in 1939). A transcribed copy of the interview is in the Hoover Institution. As we have seen, the Republican ministers remained inert even after the resignation of Irujo and Aiguadé. In a letter to me, dated 20 Sept. 1949 (Hoover Institution), Andrés María de Irujo, the brother of the minister of justice and his personal secretary during the war, denied that the resignation of his brother had anything to do with a movement in favor of a negotiated peace.

41. Interview in Mexico City in 1940. A transcribed copy of the interview is in the Hoover Institution, Bolloten Collection.

42. Ibid.

43. Jacinto Toryho, *Del triunfo a la derrota*, 374.

44. As quoted by Julián Zugazagoitia, secretary general of the defense ministry at the time, *Historia de la guerra en España*, 456; also by Ricardo Sanz, *Los que fuimos a Madrid*, 254, both of whom received a copy of the telegram. The official histories of the Spanish Communist party and of the Civil War steer clear of any mention of the telegram as does La Pasionaria in her memoirs.

45. *Epistolario, Prieto y Negrín*, 109; Sanz, *Los que fuimos*, 254–55.

46. 16 Aug. 1938.

47. The decrees were published in the *Gaceta de la República*, 17 Aug. 1938.

48. Pi Sunyer, 523. Azaña's laconic comment is in *Obras*, IV, 890.

49. *Epistolario, Prieto y Negrín*, 105.

50. Ibid., 109. For the opinion of the peninsular committee of the FAI on the alleged plot and the precautionary measures taken, see report, dated September 1938, CNT-FAI Archives, International Institute of Social History, Paquete 92, Caja 305, B. Informes, pp. 14–15. A photocopy is in the Hoover Institution, Bolloten Collection, file "FAI. Informe, Comité Peninsular, Sept. 1938." After the war, Ignacio Hidalgo de Cisneros, the air force chief, informed me that Negrín told him at the time that the "most important thing was to raise the morale of the people of Barcelona at all costs." He also said that approximately fifty aircraft participated but that the number appeared much larger because in circling and recircling Barcelona they passed behind the Tibidabo mountain "and no one could see whether new ones were coming or not." The quoted sentences are on p. 68 of the shorthand notes taken during the two-day interview (Hoover Institution, Bolloten Collection).

51. My information is that he was totally subservient to Negrín. Alvarez del Vayo's testimonial is worth recording. "Don Antonio Velao [was] one of the most intelligent and exemplary leaders of the Republican Left" (*Give me Combat*, 191).

Chapter 58

1. As given in César M. Lorenzo, *Les anarchistes espagnols et le pouvoir, 1868–1969*, 318–19.

2. Toryho's four-page response is in the CNT-FAI Archives, International Institute of Social History, Paquete 48, Caja 308. A photocopy is in the Hoover Institution, Bolloten Collection, file "Jacinto Toryho. Destitución Fulminante del Compañero Jacinto Toryho de su Cargo de Director de *Solidaridad Obrera*."

3. See, for example, the editorial in the issue of 21 July 1938.

4. Article in *Cultura Proletaria*, 16 Mar. 1940.

5. See Chapter 20.

6. Article in *Timón*, Sept. 1938.

7. *Por qué perdimos la guerra*, 205. Although a purist, Abad de Santillán, it will be recalled, had himself in December 1936 temporarily laid aside his Anarchist principles when he entered the Catalan government as councillor of economy. For a brief account of some of the controversies surrounding him during his long career in the libertarian movement in Spain and Argentina, see article by Rafael Cid in *Historia 16*, Jan. 1984.

8. See report on the national plenum of the CNT, pp. 5–11. "Pleno Nacional de Regionales CNT. Celebrado en Barcelona el Día 15 de Octubre de 1938." CNT-FAI Archives, International Institute of Social History, Paquete 54, C. A photocopy of this document is in the Hoover Institution, Bolloten Collection, file "CNT. Pleno Nacionales de Regionales, 15 Oct. 1938."

9. *Obras completas*, IV, 888. On the other hand, the official Communist history of the Civil War says: "Segundo Blanco, who voted in the cabinet in favor of the August decrees, believed like the

national committee of the CNT that no problem had arisen in the government" (*Guerra y revolución en España, 1936–1939*, IV, 152).

10. *Historia del anarcosindicalismo español*, 262.

11. Abad de Santillán, *Por qué*, 204–5.

12. An interesting description of this controversial figure in the libertarian movement is given by Juan López, *Una misión sin importancia*, 170–71. López was CNT minister of commerce in the Largo Caballero cabinet.

13. As given in David Porter ed., *Vision of Fire: Emma Goldman on the Spanish Revolution*, 44–45.

14. *La CNT en la revolución española*, III, 304.

15. Ibid., 304–6.

16. Letter to Joan Llarch in *Negrín: ¡Resistir es vencer!*, 135.

17. *Historia de la FAI*, 282. According to Severino Campos, who was secretary of the Catalan regional committee of the FAI during the war, Vázquez's "libertarian education was as deficient as it was inconsistent," but this inadequacy was counterbalanced by two attributes: "daring and the will to work" (letter to me, dated 27 Oct. 1950, Hoover Institution).

18. Peirats, *La CNT*, III, 307–8.

19. Ibid., 309.

20. Ibid., 311.

21. Togliatti, *Escritos sobre la guerra de España*, 244.

22. Letter to me, dated 7 Dec. 1950 (Hoover Institution).

23. Peirats, *La CNT*, III, 318.

24. Letter, dated 18 March 1947 (Hoover Institution).

25. 15 Nov. 1938. See also speech by Salvador Quemades, president of Izquierda Republicana, in *Política*, 21 Nov. 1938.

26. *Los anarquistas en la crisis política española*, 351–52.

27. Francisco Largo Caballero, *Mis recuerdos*, 248–49.

28. Ibid., 247.

29. Ibid., 248.

30. See Chapter 53.

31. See Chapter 53.

32. See Chapter 53.

33. As given in *Socialist Review*, Jan.–Feb. 1939. The reply was included in a letter, dated 14 August 1938, to José Díaz Alor, a fellow Socialist. It was not published in any newspaper in Spain. The Spanish text can be found in print in the CNT-FAI Archives, International Institute of Social History, Paquetes 61 and 61A, P221.

34. *Escritos*, 230–31.

35. *Historia de la guerra en España*, 463–64.

36. Ibid., 473–74.

37. Ibid., 465.

38. *Nation*, 3 Sept. 1938.

39. Araquistáin Papers, Leg. 24/A233. I am grateful to Javier Tusell's study of Luis Araquistáin, *Sobre la guerra civil y en la emigración*, which brought this letter to my attention.

40. Spanish Communist party archives, Moscow, cited in *Guerra y revolución*, IV, 166.

41. Dolores Ibárruri, *Unión de todos los españoles*. Report to the central committee of the PCE, 23–25 May 1938.

42. *El único camino*, 410–11.

43. From an unpublished article (No. 1) given to me by Antonio Escribano (Hoover Institution). This excerpt has already been quoted in Chapter 12.

44. Letter to me (Hoover Institution). It is quoted at greater length in Chapter 12.

45. From an unpublished article (No. 1) given to me by Antonio Escribano (Hoover Institution).

46. Ibid.

47. *Escritos*, 149. In Murcia, the anti-Communist provincial committee of the JSU had its own newspaper, *Acción*, throughout the war; see Escribano's letter to me of 28 May 1950 (Hoover

Institution), quoting from his article in *Renovación* (Mexico). The article also gives the names of opposition papers in several other towns.

48. 6, 29 Nov. 1938.

49. From an unpublished article (No. 1) given to me by Antonio Escribano (Hoover Institution).

50. I am indebted to my friend and trustworthy informant Ricardo del Río of the Agencia Febus for this important information. Because of the censorship, little was said in the press about the event (see, for example, *Ahora*, the national organ of the JSU, 13 Nov. 1938). It is covered in more detail in the transcript of my shorthand notes taken during a conversation with del Río (Hoover Institution). See also unpublished article (No. 2) given to me by Antonio Escribano (Hoover Institution).

51. Araquistáin Papers, Leg. 58/v7[b].

52. Unpublished article (No. 2) by Escribano (Hoover Institution).

53. Ibid.

54. I am indebted to Ricardo del Río of the Agencia Febus for this information. See transcript of notes taken during a conversation with him (Hoover Institution); also Ramón Casteras Archidona, *Las juventudes socialistas unificadas de Cataluña*, 328–29. For further information on Lamoneda and the Secretariado Juvenil, see Escribano's letter to me of 12 June 1950 (Hoover Institution) and *Ahora*, 21 Oct. 1938.

55. See the *Times Literary Supplement*, 9 June 1978, and my reply, ibid., 17 Nov. 1978.

56. Ibid., 17 Nov. 1978.

57. P. 72.

58. As given in Peirats, *La CNT*, III, 251.

59. *AIT Servicio de Prensa*, April 1939.

60. Araquistáin papers, Leg. 72/13.

61. Quoted in Indalecio Prieto, *Cómo y por qué salí del ministerio de defensa nacional*, 48. See also letter from Prieto to Negrín, 3 July 1939 (ibid., 101–2).

62. *Guerra en España, 1936–1939*, 190.

63. Quoted by Jesús Hernández, *Yo fui un ministro de Stalin*, 159.

64. 11 June 1938.

Chapter 59

1. *Gaceta de la República*, 28 Apr. 1938.

2. See Chapter 22 for information on the decree. For CNT protests against attacks on the decree, see *Solidaridad Obrera*, 11, 31 May 1938.

3. *La CNT en la revolución española*, III, 124.

4. 16 June 1938.

5. I am indebted to Adrian Shubert for providing me with photocopies of Fraser Lawton's cables and letters from Barcelona in July and August 1936. The originals, according to Shubert, are in the possession of Jack Goering, a member of the family. The photocopies are in the Bolloten Collection, Hoover Institution.

6. See Chapter 22.

7. 14 May 1938.

8. See Josep María Bricall, *Política econòmica de la Generalitat, 1936–1939*, 346. Ruiz Ponsetti was a member of the central committee of the PSUC.

9. 9 June 1938.

10. 15 June 1938.

11. See Cardona Rosell's letter to me, dated 29 Apr. 1950 (Hoover Institution).

12. *Gaceta de la República*, 3 Sept. 1937. For valuable comments on the decree, see Albert Pérez-Baró, *30 mesos de col·lectivisme a Catalunya*, 143–44.

13. What the Anarchosyndicalists thought of nationalization is exemplified by the following quotation from one of their newspapers: "If nationalization were carried out in Spain as the Socialists and Communists desire, we should be on the way to a dictatorship, because by nationalizing everything the government would become the master, the chief, the absolute boss of everyone and everything" (*Nosotros*, 9 Mar. 1937. See also *Tierra y Libertad*, 14 Aug. 1937).

14. *La CNT*, III, 185. See also Peirats, *Los anarquistas en la crisis política*, 343–44.

15. *La CNT*, III, 187–88.

16. "CNT. Pleno Nacional de Regionales, Celebrado en Barcelona el Día 15 de Octubre de 1938," CNT-FAI Archives, International Institute of Social History, Paquete 54, C. Photocopy in Hoover Institution, Bolloten Collection, file "CNT. Pleno de Regionales, 15 Oct. 1938."

17. 20 Aug. 1938.

18. 1 Oct. 1938.

19. 28 Nov. 1938. See also *Solidaridad Obrera*, 10, 11, 20 Nov., 4 Dec. 1938, and *Tierra y Libertad*, 10 Dec. 1938.

20. See Chapter 4 for abundant testimony demonstrating the scope of the Revolution and the collapse of the Republic.

21. "Entrevista con Angel Viñas," by Ricardo Dessau in *Tiempo de Historia*, May 1979.

22. Claudín gives the source of this quotation as José Díaz, *Tres años de lucha*, 350, but does not identify the edition.

23. Pp. 187–89.

24. Ibid., 189–90.

25. *Escritos sobre la guerra de España*, 196–97.

26. Jaime Camino, *Intimas conversaciones con La Pasionaria*, 117.

27. 23 Mar. 1938.

28. *Frente Rojo*, 30 Mar. 1938. For Claudín's comments on the *Mundo Obrero* letter and on José Díaz's reply, see *La crisis*, 190–91, 618, n. 159.

Chapter 60

1. 14 May 1938.

2. *Los vascos y la república española*, 209. The author was secretary to his brother, Manuel.

3. *La Vanguardia*, 1 May 1938. My italics.

4. Ibid.

5. *Historia de la guerra en España*, 420.

6. *Mundo Obrero*, 14 May 1938.

7. Julio Alvarez del Vayo, *Deux Discours prononcés à la 101me session de la Société des Nations*, 15.

8. For an account of the clandestine religious activities in Catalonia during the war, see Albert Manent i Segimon and Josep Raventós i Giralt, *L'església clandestina a Catalunya durant la guerra civil, 1936–1939*.

9. *Gaceta de la República*, 26 June 1938.

10. Ricardo del Río, director of the Febus news agency. File "Ricardo del Río: Information on various important events written by Del Río and shorthand notes taken by Burnett Bolloten during conversations with him" (Hoover Institution).

11. For information on the withdrawal of foreign volunteers, which was conducted under the supervision of the League of Nations, see Chapter 62.

12. 18 Oct. 1938. See also Iñaki Anasagosti and Koldo San Sebastián, *Los años oscuros*, 75, n. 14.

13. *Gaceta de la República*, 9 Dec. 1938.

14. 15 Dec. 1938. See also ibid., 9, 17 Dec. 1938. For Communist press comments on the decree creating the commissariat, see *Frente Rojo*, 16 Dec. 1938.

15. File "Ricardo del Río: Information on various important events" (Hoover Institution).

16. *Men and Politics*, 492.

17. "In order to understand Southworth's steadfastly loyal and therefore uncritical support of Negrín," writes George Esenwein, "one must bear in mind that he served as an important propagandist for the Negrín government. Between February 1938 and February 1939, he edited *The News of Spain*, published by the Spanish Information Bureau, New York (see *Contemporary Authors*, vols. 85–88, p. 557), a bulletin which, if not financed by or otherwise officially associated with the Spanish Republican government, was unmistakeably a mouthpiece for its policies. Several themes recur which identify it as such. 1. News of events in Spain is focused on the achievements of the Negrín administration. Thus, the opening of a church was cited as an example of the government's commit-

ment to religious tolerance. 2. Other events, no matter how controversial, were always presented as somehow reflecting the positive aspects of the Negrín government. An example of this is found in the bulletin's report of the POUM trial in October 1938. Using information derived from reporters like Herbert Matthews or other sources either sympathetic or close to Negrín, the bulletin attempted to portray the trial as a model of 'Republican justice.' The 'facts' of the case are all given from this point of view and are therefore heavily weighted against the POUM defendants. For instance, although the bulletin does not openly assert that the POUMists on trial were traitors, this is clearly implied. Accordingly, rumor, circulated by the Communists, who were responsible for staging the trial, are repeated without qualification, e.g., that Andrés Nin and Juan Rovira, the political secretary of the party and the former commander of the Twenty-ninth division respectively, had taken refuge in 'Rebel territory' (2 November 1938). 3. Finally, the Republican figures who received most attention (in the form of biographical sketches and the like) were pro-Communists associated with Negrín, such as Vicente Rojo, Alvarez del Vayo and José Bergamín, the Catholic writer, who was personally involved in goodwill campaigns abroad on behalf of the Negrín government. [This is a good example of what Luis Araquistáin was referring to when he wrote in the *New York Times* on 25 May 1939 that "the propaganda carried out abroad only sang the praises of Dr. Negrín, Señor Alvarez del Vayo, and the Communists."] Foreign personalities who were also Negrinistas and frequently appeared in the bulletin's columns were Herbert Matthews, Louis Fischer, Gustav Regler and Frank Jellinek. It is interesting to note that Southworth has not discussed the role he played as editor of *The News of Spain*. When interviewed about the Civil War in *Tiempo de Historia* (October 1978), he did not allude to the fact that he was a propagandist for the Negrín government, but he did describe the Premier as 'the most outstanding personality in the Republican camp during the war' and argued that the time had come to reassess his achievements as a political figure." This account, which is reproduced in a previous chapter, is based on a careful analysis of *The News of Spain* collection, and was prepared specifically for me by George Esenwein in 1984. It is worth recording that after the death of General Franco in 1975, Southworth appeared prominently on Spanish TV as a leading authority on the Spanish Civil War, of which he gave his own particular version to viewers, most of whom, because of their age, had little knowledge of the complexities of the Civil War.

18. 26 October 1938.

19. *New Statesman and Nation*, 8 Oct. 1938.

20. 30 June 1938. See also issue of 7 July 1938.

21. See, for example, Diego Martínez Barrio in *La Vanguardia*, 29 May 1938, and Miguel San Andrés in *Política*, 11 May and 8 June 1938.

22. For example, William C. Atkinson in *Fortnightly Review*, Jan. 1939.

23. *Who's Who, 1973–1974*, 2268, includes the following biographical data: Born 23 April 1904, third son of 2d Baron Swaythling; film critic, editor, director, writer, producer from 1925; editorial staff *Daily Worker*, 1932–33 and 1937–47; member of the Secretariat and Bureau of the World Council of Peace, 1948–67; Lenin Peace Prize, 1959.

24. *Men and Politics*, 491–92.

25. See interview with Montagu in *Screen*, Autumn 1972.

26. *Spain: A Modern History*, 541.

27. *Men and Politics* (English edition), 465.

28. *Freedom's Battle*, 231.

29. *Guerra y revolución en España, 1936–1939*, IV, 90.

30. *Mundo Obrero*, 16 May 1938.

31. Document 59 of the Rocker Collection ("Posición de la FAI ante la Declaración del Gobierno de 'Los Trece Puntos'"), Circular No. 9, dated 1 May 1938.

32. Ibid., Circular No. 17, dated 3 May 1938.

33. Ibid., Circular No. 18, dated 6 May 1938.

34. Ibid., Circular No. 12, dated 10 May 1938.

35. From an unpublished work, quoted by his son César M. Lorenzo, *Les anarchistes espagnols et le pouvoir, 1868–1969*, 324, n. 41.

36. Dolores Ibárruri, *En la lucha*, 277 (from her report at the plenum of the central committee of the PCE, held in Madrid from 23 to 25 May 1938).

37. *Retrato de un desconocido: Vida de Manuel Azaña*, 293.

38. *Eve of War, 1933–1941*, 207.

39. *The Yoke and the Arrows*, 40. In June 1938, Azaña, when interviewed by Ehrenburg, said: "Negrín seems to believe that a world war would save Spain. There will certainly be a war. But they won't start it before they have throttled Spain" (Ehrenburg, *Eve of War, 1933–1941*, 209). See also Heleno Saña's interview with Santiago Garcés Arroyo in *Indice*, 15 June 1974.

Chapter 61

1. See, for example, "Extrait de la Note su sujet des conséquences stratégiques d'un succès du général Franco," drafted by General Gamelin, chief of the central general staff (*Documents diplomatiques français, 1932–1939*, 2e série, Tome VIII, 830–31).

2. Chapters 8, 9, 16, and 17.

3. Public Record Office, C14471 42/18 (FO 371/21659), Folio 72. The summary also stated that the "Defense of the West" (one of four alternative British policies) would mean that "the French would be pressed to denounce the Franco Soviet Pact" and that "the real—if unavowed—intention of this would be to indicate that, if Germany required further 'expansion,' she could always seek it in the Ukraine" (ibid., Folio 74). Photocopies of Folios 9 through 119 of this Foreign Office file are in the Hoover Institution, Bolloten Collection, file "Public Record Office. C14471 42/18 (FO 371/21659)."

4. *Documents diplomatiques français, 1932–1939*, 2e série, Tome VIII, 828.

5. Chapters 8, 9, 16, and 17.

6. Chapter 59.

7. Letter to me in 1940 (Hoover Institution).

8. Halifax became foreign secretary in February 1938 after the resignation of Anthony Eden. It should be noted, as a corrective to the mistaken belief by some that Eden was an antiappeaser, that in a report to the German foreign office in December 1937 von Ribbentrop stated that, according to Eden, people in England "recognized that a closer connection between Germany and Austria would have to come about sometime. They wished, however, that a solution by force be avoided" (*Documents on German Foreign Policy, 1918–1945*, Series D, I, 90). David Carlton, Eden's biographer, states: "It must be recognized that Eden had long preferred to appease Hitler in east-central Europe rather than with colonial restitution and that at no point contemplated armed British resistance to a German Anschluss with Austria, however brought about" (*Anthony Eden*, 114).

9. *Documents on German Foreign Policy, 1918–1945*, Series D, I, 56, 58, 62–63. My italics. Halifax's own version is couched in the following terms: "I said that there were no doubt other questions arising out of the Versailles settlement which seemed to us capable of causing trouble if they were unwisely handled. . . . On all these matters we were not necessarily concerned to stand for the status quo as today, but we were concerned to avoid such treatment of them as would be likely to cause trouble. If reasonable settlements could be reached with the free assent and goodwill of those primarily concerned we certainly had no desire to block" (*Documents on British Foreign Policy, 1919–1939*, Second Series, XIX, 545).

10. *The Origins of the Second World War*, 137.

11. *Documents on German Foreign Policy, 1918–1945*, Series D, I, 44.

12. Ibid., 103.

13. *Halifax*, 422, 375–76. Vansittart's biographer, Ian Colvin, describes the new assignment as a "sham position of precarious dignity" (*Vansittart in Office*, 174).

14. Letter dated 12 Dec. 1937, as given by Keith Middlemas, *Diplomacy of Illusion*, 174.

15. John Harvey, *The Diplomatic Diaries of Oliver Harvey, 1937–1940*, 75. Oliver Harvey was private secretary to foreign secretaries Anthony Eden and Lord Halifax.

16. *Nine Troubled Years*, 259.

17. Quoted by William N. Medlicott in his preface to *Documents on British Foreign Policy, 1919–1939*, Second Series, XVIII, ix, n. 1. The letter is preserved in Chamberlain's private papers at the University of Birmingham.

18. Colvin, *Vansittart in Office*, 246.

19. Memorandum of conversation between Hitler and Henderson, *Documents on German Foreign Policy, 1918–1945*, Series D, I, 241.

20. Second Series, XVIII, vi.

21. *Diplomacy of Illusion*, 71; *The Chamberlain Cabinet*, 262.

22. Medlicott quotes this passage in *Documents on British Foreign Policy, 1919–1939*, Second Series, XVIII, 695, n. 1. Oddly enough he produces other evidence in the same note that further contradicts his assertion: "Professor T. P. Conwell-Evans," he writes, "states that Sir Neville told him, when he visited him in Berlin, that he 'based his policy on instructions constantly received from 10 Downing Street and not on the views of the Permanent Head of the Foreign Office' (Ian Colvin, *None So Blind*, 72)." However, Medlicott attempts to nullify this statement by claiming that no evidence in support of it could be found in the Foreign Office archives or in Chamberlain's private papers consulted by the editors at Birmingham University. Since Chamberlain was conducting his policy behind the back of the Foreign Office and in the utmost secrecy, it is not likely that he committed these highly sensitive instructions to paper or that, if he did, they have yet been released for public scrutiny.

23. Quoted by Middlemas, 73–74. His source is Foreign Office documents 67932 (FO 371/20736), 10 May 1937.

24. *Documents on German Foreign Policy, 1918–1945*, Series D, I, 266–67.

25. Ibid., 273.

26. Sir Alexander Cadogan, who had recently replaced Vansittart as permanent undersecretary in the Foreign Office, made the following notation in his diary on 15 February 1938: "Personally, I almost wish Germany would swallow Austria and get it over. She is probably going to do so anyhow—anyhow we can't stop her" (David Dilks, *The Diaries of Sir Alexander Cadogan, 1938–1945*, 47). And, on April 22, after the Anschluss, Cadogan wrote: "Thank Goodness, Austria's out of the way. I can't help thinking that we were very badly informed about feeling in that country. I've no doubt there's a section of the population hiding in the cellars, and a number of those waving Swastika flags now may come to rue the day later, but we should evidently have been very wrong to try to prevent the Anschluss against the wishes of . . . a very considerable proportion of the population. After all, it wasn't our business: we had no particular feeling for the Austrians" (ibid., 70).

27. *Documents on German Foreign Policy, 1918–1945*, Series D, II, 320. It is worth noting that William C. Bullitt, the U.S. ambassador to Paris, stated in a letter to President Roosevelt on 20 May, according to the British historian C. A. MacDonald, that "Roosevelt should seek some means of helping France to evade its obligations. If Germany invaded Czechoslovakia, the President should summon a great power conference at the Hague. If Prague refused to accept its decisions France would be justified in refusing to fight. The United States would be accused of 'selling out a small nation . . . to produce another Hitler triumph' but this was preferable to seeing 'an Asiatic despotism established on the fields of the dead' " (*The United States, Britain and Appeasement, 1936–1939*, 87. MacDonald gives the following source: "President's Secretary's File, Franklin D. Roosevelt Library, Hyde Park, New York").

28. *Documents and Materials Relating to the Eve of the Second World War*, II, 46.

29. See, for example, John W. Wheeler-Bennett, *Munich: Prologue to Tragedy*. Since its publication in 1948, numerous historians have dealt with the Czech episode, but Wheeler-Bennett's book remains the standard work on the subject.

30. Chapters 64 and 65.

31. As given in Jane Degras, *Soviet Documents on Foreign Policy*, III: 1933–1941, 318–19.

32. International Military Tribunal, *The Trial of German Major War Criminals before the International Military Tribunal, Nuremberg*, part X, 267.

33. U.S. Department of State, *Nazi-Soviet Relations, 1939–1941*.

34. Ibid., 15.

35. *Handbook of Intelligence and Guerrilla Warfare*, 20–23. Enrique Líster, commander of the Communist-controlled Fifth Regiment and later an officer in the regular People's Army, also affirms that the Russians sent their best weapons to Spain (*Nuestra guerra*, 75–76).

36. *Saturday Evening Post*, 29 Apr. 1939. My italics.

37. According to the Anarchosyndicalist historian José Peirats, Mariano Vázquez sincerely believed in what was "very popular those days: the need to prolong resistance in the hope of merging the Civil War with a general conflict" (*Los anarquistas en la crisis política española*, 351. See also Peirats, *La CNT en la revolución española*, III, 318–19).

38. *El último episodio de la guerra civil española*, 5–6.

39. Vidarte, *Todos fuimos culpables*, 894–95.

40. See, for example, Henri de Kerillis, *Français! Voici la guerre!*, 147–48.

41. *Documents on British Foreign Policy, 1919–1939*, Third Series, III, 252.

42. Ibid., 387.

43. Ibid., 590.

44. Ministère des Affaires Étrangères, *The French Yellow Book*, 95.

45. According to these historians, the Anglo-Polish treaty had barely been signed when Britain was preparing to abandon her pledge. "The Treaty had been made as a result of great public pressure. It was a sham Treaty" (*The Appeasers*, 275–76). The hostile reaction of public opinion to the occupation of Prague was reflected not only in such large-circulation newspapers of the left as the *Daily Herald*, the *Manchester Guardian*, and the *News Chronicle*, but also in the *Times*, the *Sunday Times*, the *Daily Telegraph*, and the *Observer*, hitherto unwavering supporters of appeasement. See Franklin Reid Gannon, *The British Press and Germany, 1936–1939*, 236–61. Undoubtedly, the fear was growing in Britain that, by his use of force, Hitler was making a bid for world dominion.

46. Only when Hitler's surprise attack on Western Europe in the spring of 1940 put an end to the hope that he would march eastward and when Britain was suddenly confronted by a direct and clear challenge to her national survival was the "appeaser" Chamberlain replaced by the "antiappeaser" Churchill.

47. *Europe in Decay*, 227.

48. *Documents and Materials Relating to the Eve of the Second World War*, II, 67–72, 148–92.

49. *Moscow, Tokyo, London*, 237–41.

50. *Documents on German Foreign Policy, 1918–1945*, VI, 977–83.

51. His record of his conversation with Wohlthat communicated to the Foreign Office on 19 July omits any mention of the proposals (see *Documents on British Foreign Policy, 1919–1939*, Third Series, VI, 389–90). Unfortunately, as A. J. P. Taylor points out, Wilson's personal notes outlining the proposals, written on 10 Downing Street notepaper, have "not surprisingly" disappeared from the British records.

52. *British Foreign Policy since Versailles, 1919–1963*.

53. *Encounter*, July 1972, June 1980.

54. *March 1939: The British Guarantee to Poland*.

55. *Vansittart in Office*, 330; *None So Blind*, 330–31.

56. *Europe in Decay*, 225.

57. *The Origins of the Second World War*, 244–45.

58. *Documents and Materials Relating to the Eve of the Second World War*, II, 183–89. This important document totally invalidates the "neo-revisionist" interpretation of appeasement, of which Simon Newman and Robert Skidelsky are among the principal exponents. According to this school, "Britain never intended Germany to have a free hand in eastern Europe at all. Thus the guarantee to Poland should not be interpreted as a revolution in British foreign policy as has so often been argued, but should be seen as the culmination, or rather the explicit manifestation, of a strand of British policy going back to before September 1938 which has until recently been overlooked or ignored—the attempt to stem German expansion in eastern Europe by any means short of war but in the last resort by war itself" (Newman, 5–6; see also Skidelsky, *Encounter*, July 1972, June 1980). Both Newman and Skidelsky conveniently ignore the Chamberlain-Wilson attempt to disembarrass the government of its commitment to Poland. The aim of the "neo-revisionists" is apparently to give Chamberlain a completely new image by disposing of the orthodox and revisionist interpretations, which Newman summarizes as follows: "Most explanations of British policy towards Germany in this period postulate a dichotomy between the 'appeasement' pursued until March 1939 and the policy of 'resistance' that followed. The first of these interpretations, commonly referred to as 'orthodox,' has completely dominated the historiography of the period until recently. Its proponents believe that British inaction resulted from guilt derived from the Versailles settlement, or personal gullibility, or predisposition towards the Nazi dictatorship. . . . Neville Chamberlain and the 'appeasers' were led by the nose and lulled into complacency with continual promises of good behavior by Hitler. According to this view the 'appeasers' suddenly 'awoke' to the reality of Hitler's aggressive design for world domination following the German invasion of Bohemia and Moravia [Czechoslovakia] on 15 March 1939. Where before Chamberlain had been prepared to allow Germany a free hand in Eastern Europe (provided of

course that Hitler would abide by the rules of common decency and morality in his expansion), popular outrage now forced him to resist any further extension of German power. Thus the British guarantee to Poland was a diplomatic revolution not only in the sense that it was the first peacetime guarantee of an eastern-European state but above all because it demonstrated that Chamberlain had abandoned his old policy of 'appeasement.' The [revisionist] interpretation . . . is that British inaction before March 1939 was the inevitable result of various decisive constraints. These included military and economic weakness, the isolationist attitude of the Dominions and of public opinion, and the global 'responsibilities' which dictated the avoidance of war with Germany for fear that Japan, Italy, and even the United States would also benefit at the expense of the Empire. Chamberlain was thus far from gullible or idealistic in his view of Anglo-German relations, he was merely realistic. In this interpretation the guarantee to Poland is easy to explain, Britain was now strong enough to challenge Germany openly. Where before the 'realists' had had no choice but to abandon Eastern Europe, they were now able to reverse the process. The guarantee is still seen as a revolution of sorts, for where before Britain had done nothing, she was now able to venture forth with military guarantees" (*March 1939*, 1–2).

59. *The Origins*, 244–45.

60. *Moscow, Tokyo, London*, 242.

61. *The Origins*, 163.

62. P. 706. For the Russian view that Anglo-French diplomacy, even after the Nazi invasion of Poland and the formal declaration of war by Great Britain and France against Germany in September 1939, still aimed at pushing Germany and the Soviet Union into conflict, see Ivan Maisky (Soviet ambassador to the United Kingdom from 1932 to 1943), *Memoirs of a Soviet Ambassador*, 10–15.

63. *Halifax*, 412. See also ibid., 415, and Dilks, *The Diaries of Sir Alexander Cadogan*, 64, 93, 108.

64. *Halifax*, 416. For the attitude of the dominion prime ministers toward the Czech and Polish crises, see Ritchie Ovendale, *"Appeasement" and the English Speaking World*, 118–298. From this magnificently researched work, I quote just two of many pertinent passages: "Mackenzie King [prime minister of Canada] wrote to [Malcolm] Macdonald [secretary of state for the dominions] on 2 April [1938] of his admiration for the way in which Chamberlain had performed his task. . . . 'I am more convinced than ever that to keep the British Empire out of a European war is the one means of saving the Empire'" (123). "Hertzog [South African prime minister] was anxious that peace be preserved, almost at any cost. He seemed to feel that Germany had justifiable grievances and should be allowed to expand eastwards to satisfy these" (268).

65. *Britain between the Wars, 1918–1940*, 592.

66. *Encounter*, July 1972.

Chapter 62

1. For a variety of accounts on the Ebro battle, see, for example, Enrique Castro, *Hombres made in Moscú*, 655–99; Antonio Cordón, *Trayectoria*, 412, 422–30; Louis Fischer, *Men and Politics*, 540–50; José García Pradas, *¡Teníamos que perder!*, 298–316; Lieutenant General García-Valiño y Marcen, *Guerra de liberación*, 222–80; *Guerra y revolución en España, 1936–1939*, IV, 117–32, 186–91; Julián Henríquez Caubin, *La batalla del Ebro*; Jesús Hernández, *Yo fui un ministro de Stalin*, 171–77; Enrique Líster, *Nuestra guerra*, 201–29; Juan Llarch, *La batalla del Ebro*; José Manuel Martínez Bande, *La batalla del Ebro*; Juan Modesto, *Soy del quinto regimiento*, 245–342; Jesús Pérez Salas, *Guerra en España, 1936–1939*, 209–12; Vicente Rojo, *España heroica*, 165–95; Ramón Salas Larrazábal, *Historia del ejército popular de la república*, IV, 3287–3314; Manuel Tagüeña, *Testimonio de dos guerras*, 187–260. See also Ricardo del Río, "Account of the Political and Military Situation in Catalonia during the last few months of the Civil War" (Hoover Institution, Bolloten Collection) and transcript of shorthand notes of my interview with Daniel Tapia, adjutant to General Hernández Sarabia, commander of the Agrupación de Ejércitos (Hoover Institution). According to Louis Fischer, the Soviet general Maximov helped to direct the Ebro offensive (*Nation*, 13 Jan. 1940).

2. For information on the Nationalist offensive against Catalonia, see Cordón, 443–66; *Guerra y revolución en España, 1936–1939*, IV, 192–226; Líster, *Nuestra guerra*, 23–47; Martínez Bande, *La*

campaña de Cataluña; Modesto, 353–73; Pérez Salas, 221–38; Pi Sunyer, *La república y la guerra*, 571–631; Rojo, *¡Alerta los pueblos!*, 136–218; A. Roviri i Virgili, *Els darrers dies de la Catalunya republicana*; Jaume Sobrequés i Callicó, *Història de Catalunya*, XII, 443–82, Tagüeña, 266–99.

3. *Mundo Obrero*, 26 Feb. 1939.

4. *Hombres made in Moscú*, 655.

5. Ibid., 699.

6. Chapter 58.

7. Chapter 58.

8. Chapter 58.

9. Pérez Salas, 232.

10. *La Vanguardia*, 2 Oct. 1938.

11. Bolloten Collection, Hoover Institution.

12. Araquistáin Papers, Leg. 24/A/232.

13. *Diario de las Sesiones de Cortes.* A copy of this rare document printed in Paris is in the Araquistáin Papers, Leg. 71/6.

14. *Obras Completas*, III, 537.

15. *El separatisme català durant la guerra civil*, 203.

16. *¡Alerta los pueblos!*, 172–73.

17. *España Popular*, 13 Feb. 1941. It should be pointed out that this description of the "so-called democratic powers" (courted indefatigably by Stalin as "democracies" during the Spanish Civil War) as "imperialist" was in accordance with the Kremlin's policy after the signing of the Hitler-Stalin pact in August 1939. The line quickly changed after Germany attacked Russia in June 1941, when the "imperialist" countries allied themselves with the USSR.

18. 28 Jan. 1939.

19. *Guerra en España*, 231.

20. Tagüeña, 283–84.

21. Leonid I. Brezhnev, *Following Lenin's Course: Speeches and Articles*, 52.

22. "Los Ultimos Consejeros Rusos en España," *Historia 16*, Apr. 1984.

23. In a speech before the League of Nations on 21 September 1938, Negrín announced the decision of the Republican government to withdraw all foreign volunteers (*Volunteer for Liberty*, 23 Sept. 1938). It is dubious whether this gesture was made independently of Moscow, although evidence is lacking. Various explanations for the unilateral decision have been advanced: (1) that world opinion would force the withdrawal of German and Italian military units (Bill Alexander, *British Volunteers for Liberty: Spain, 1936–1939*, 238); (2) that the Republican government wanted "to squelch the canards regarding an alleged Comintern intervention in Spain that were aimed at justifying German and Italian intervention" (official Communist history, *Guerra y revolución*, IV, 177); (3) that Moscow "wished to deprive the Republic of any possibility of further resistance," because Stalin—realizing that "all his diplomatic maneuvers [to influence Britain and France] had been a resounding failure"— had decided "to negotiate with Berlin, offering as proof of his sincerity the corpse of the Spanish Republic" (Hernández, *Yo fui un ministro de Stalin*, 176–79). The accusation that Moscow wished to deprive the Republic "of any possibility of future resistance" clashes with the Comintern's efforts to prolong the war as long as possible. On the other hand, it is not unlikely that Stalin, realizing that the Republicans would eventually lose unless Britain and France could be induced to enter the conflict—a possibility that was becoming more and more remote—wished to save his stalwarts for future ventures.

24. Facsimiles of these documents can be found in *Guerra y revolución*, IV, between 328 and 329.

25. For a facsimile of the eighteen-page handwritten letter, see ibid. The full text in print can be found in Manuel Tuñón de Lara, *Historia de España*, XII, 529–38.

26. Interview given to Roger Klein; see *Política*, 18 June 1937. It is true that Louis Fischer, a paid propagandist for Negrín during the war and forever a supporter and apologist, asserted after the conflict was over that Negrín had asked him to tell Moscow "to call off . . . this fusion propaganda. Our Socialists are against it. We want collaboration with the Communists but we wish to retain our identity as a separate party" (*Men and Politics*, 440). There is no corroborative evidence in support of this assertion.

27. My italics.

28. *Escritos sobre la guerra de España*, 237 (report dated 21 May 1939).

29. "Memorias," 59–60.

30. Juan Llarch, *Negrín: ¡Resistir es vencer!*, 68, 108.

31. Interview by Heleno Saña in *Indice*, 15 June 1974.

32. Dolores Ibárruri, *El único camino*, 436.

33. *Memorias 2*, 445–46.

34. Ibid., 448–49, 451–52.

35. Ibid., 453. The official Communist history of the Civil War states that the Soviet war material "did not arrive in time to enable the heroic soldiers [of the Republic] to defend Catalonia" (*Guerra y revolución*, IV, 202).

36. *La fase final de la guerra*, 102–3.

37. *El oro de Moscú*, 428, n. 49.

38. Ibid., 419.

39. "Entrevista con Angel Viñas," by Ricardo Dessau, *Tiempo de Historia*, May 1979.

40. The letter is reproduced in facsimile in *El oro de Moscú* (section denominated "Documentación Gráfica"), 30.

41. Ibid., 419.

42. *Guerra y revolución*, IV, 201.

43. Ibid., 245.

44. Ibid.

45. It is extraordinary that Togliatti did not exclude Alvarez del Vayo as well as Uribe from the "capitulators," for one has only to read the foreign minister's optimistic remarks on the imminence of a general European conflict to question the accuracy of Togliatti's assertion. One example of Alvarez del Vayo's optimism is cited by Cipriano Rivas-Cherif, Azaña's brother-in-law. When the government, after the fall of Barcelona, moved to Figueras, eighteen kilometers from the French border, the foreign minister said to him: "If only we could resist just one more week! Because between now and Tuesday war between Italy and France will break out and a general European conflict will be our salvation" (*Retrato de un desconocido*, 303). And, in a letter to Angel y Ossorio y Gallardo, President Azaña recounts that Quero Morales, Vayo's undersecretary of state, told him (in February 1939) that the foreign minister "was a madman who did not understand the situation" and that he was "very optimistic, believing that a general war was imminent" (*Obras*, III, 548). In the same letter, Azaña quotes Vayo as saying "with his self-satisfied smile": "We must hold out two or three days longer. On Tuesday Mussolini will make a speech. The outcome will be a general war. Then our situation will change" (ibid., 552).

46. This letter has not yet come to light (1987). However, it may be conjectured that he made some reference to the delay in the arrival of Soviet weapons.

47. *Escritos*, 262–64. My italics.

48. Ibid., 278–84.

49. *El único camino*, 422.

50. Ibid., 431. For other criticisms of Negrín, see ibid., 433–34, 436, 438; also, the official *Historia del partido comunista de España*, 193, 195, 198, which was written by a commission presided over by La Pasionaria.

51. *Escritos*, 265. Later in the report, Togliatti records that when he saw "Sa." for the last time in Perpignan (France), after the fall of Catalonia, Sa. expressed the opinion that resistance in the central-southern zone was possible, "but on condition that a part of the army and the weapons evacuated to France and at least a part of the weapons that were on their way were transferred to the central zone" (ibid., 270).

52. The names of those present can be found in the *Diario de las Sesiones de Cortes*, no. 69 (no date of publication). I am indebted to Margarita Vázquez de Parga of the ministry of culture, Madrid, for providing me with a photocopy of this rare document, which was printed in France after the fall of Catalonia.

53. For eyewitness descriptions of the scene, see Herbert L. Matthews, *The Education of a Correspondent*, 174–75, and Julián Zugazagoitia, *Historia de la guerra en España*, 508.

54. *Diario de las Sesiones de Cortes*, no. 69. See n. 52 above.

55. Matthews, *The Education*, 175.

56. *Diario de las Sesiones de Cortes*, no. 69.
57. Ibid.
58. Francisco Franco Bahamonde, *Palabras del Caudillo*, 273.
59. Rojo, *¡Alerta los pueblos!*, 226.
60. Ibid., 229–30.
61. *Escritos*, 268.
62. Constancia de la Mora informed me in Mexico in 1940 that Mije told her that he had written the manifesto after the session of the Cortes on 1 February.
63. There is some evidence that Largo Caballero may have felt that his life was in danger and for that reason crossed the border into France with Luis Araquistáin on 28 January, two days after the fall of Barcelona (see article by Rodolfo Llopis, undersecretary of Largo Caballero during the latter's premiership, "Los últimos días que viví en España," *Cuardernos Socialistas*, Fascículo No. 3, 1948). In the letter to his daughter of 9 March 1939, from which I have already quoted, Araquistáin wrote: "[The Communists] have assassinated hundreds of Socialists and Anarchists. If they did not assassinate others, such as Largo Caballero and me, it is because we left at the right time" (Araquistáin Papers, Leg. 24/A233.
64. A photocopy of the four-page manifesto, which was delivered to the Communist press for publication on 2 February, is in the Archivo Histórico Nacional, Salamanca (Sección Guerra Civil), Sección Político-Social, Serie Madrid, Carpeta 2102. A copy, which was kindly furnished to me by Antonio González Quintana, director of the Archivo Histórico Nacional, Salamanca, is in the Hoover Institution, file "Figueras Manifesto."
65. *Spain's Struggle for Freedom*, 234. For another eyewitness account of the flight from Barcelona to the frontier, see article by Rodolfo Llopis, "Los últimos días que viví en España," *Cuadernos Socialistas*, Fascísculo No. 3, 1948.
66. *The Ciano Diaries, 1939–1943*, 32.

Chapter 63

1. For information on Garcés, see Chapter 56. His return to the central-southern zone is confirmed by Antonio Cordón, *Trayectoria*, 470.
2. *CNT*, 11 Feb. 1939 (report from Valencia, Agencia Española). See also decree of 11 Feb. 1939 (*Gaceta de la República*, 12 Feb. 1939), making Madrid the official seat of government.
3. For their initial refusal to leave France, see Palmiro Togliatti, *Escritos sobre la guerra de España*, 277; Juan López, *Una misión sin importancia* (account by Segundo Blanco, minister of education), 162–66; Santiago Garcés, interview in *Indice*, 15 June 1974; Vicente Uribe, "Memorias," 64.
4. *Escritos*, 277–78. Three years after the war, Negrín asserted that the army "wished to continue fighting to the end" (Juan Negrín, *Un discurso*, 44).
5. *Congreso de los Diputados. Diputación Permanente, Sesión celebrada [in Paris] el viernes 31 de marzo de 1939*. A copy of this rare document is in Leg. 71/6ª of the Araquistáin papers. For a photocopy, see Bolloten Collection, Hoover Institution.
6. *Freedom's Battle*, 292.
7. See Miaja's reply, dated 30 January 1939 (José Miaja Papers, "Spain. Ejército. Estado Mayor, 1936–1939," Manuscript Division, Library of Congress; photocopy in Hoover Institution, Bolloten Collection).
8. *Escritos*, 269–70.
9. *Gaceta de la República*, 9 Feb. 1939. Negrín later explained that this dual appointment was necessary because of the difficulty of communicating with the central zone after he left Barcelona. See *Congreso de los Diputados. Diputación Permanente* (n. 5 above).
10. According to the official Communist history, he was made delegate of public order (*Guerra y revolución en España, 1936–1939*, IV, 281, n. 2). Politburo member, Pedro Checa, informed me in Mexico in 1939 that the party asked Negrín to remove Burillo, but that, although he was in agreement, his decision came "too late" (shorthand notes, Hoover Institution).
11. *Diario Oficial del Ministerio de Defensa Nacional*, 29 Nov. 1937.
12. Ibid., 4 Sept. 1938.
13. *Escritos*, 272. The reasons for Burillo's removal from the party are not entirely clear. In

November 1937, when he was appointed commander of the Army of Estremadura (*Diario Oficial del Ministerio de Defensa Nacional*, 29 Nov. 1937), he was still in good standing, and on 17 and 30 March 1938 he wrote letters to Carlos Contreras, which contained no hint of any differences with the party (see Bolloten Collection, Hoover Institution). The rupture came later following a serious military defeat on the Estremadura front. See his letter of 4 September 1938 to Jesús Hernández, then chief political commissar of the central-southern region (CNT-FAI Archives, International Institute of Social History, Paquete 17, Caja 540, No. 3. A photocopy is in the Hoover Institution, Bolloten Collection, file "Burillo"); see also Julián Zugazagoitia, *Historia de la guerra en España*, 452–53. In Mexico, in 1939, Pedro Checa, a member of the politburo, gave me the following brief explanation of Burillo's removal (taken from my shorthand notes, Hoover Institution). "Burillo was removed from the Communist party, because he wrote a letter to General Queipo de Llano [Francoist general in Seville], addressing him as 'Dear Brother.' Queipo de Llano was a Mason. Burillo was a fanatical Mason and he was trying to come to an agreement with Queipo against Franco. The Communist party expelled Burillo and asked for his removal from his command of the Army of Estremadura."

14. *Escritos*, 272.

15. *El único camino*, 409.

16. *Guerra y revolución*, IV, 252, n. 4.

17. He committed suicide by throwing himself from a hospital window in Tbilisi in 1942. The reason is unknown. See Fernando Claudín, *Santiago Carrillo*, 70–71.

18. *Yo, comunista en Rusia*, 9–10.

19. Julio Alvarez del Vayo, *The March of Socialism*, 268.

20. *Escritos*, 278.

21. Cordón, 470. During an interview given to me in Mexico, in 1939, Pedro Checa, a member of the politburo, expressed the opinion that Negrín did not believe that resistance was possible after the loss of Catalonia (shorthand notes, Hoover Institution).

22. *Epistolario, Prieto y Negrín*, 37. My italics.

23. Togliatti, *Escritos*, 288.

24. The official Communist history points to Jesús Pérez Salas, a longtime opponent of the PCE, as an example of a professional officer who believed that resistance was still possible after the loss of Catalonia (*Guerra y revolución*, IV, 232) but conveniently fails to mention that in his opinion this was contingent upon a "total" change of the military commands and emancipation from "Russian tutelage" (*Guerra en España, 1936–1939*, 255–56).

25. *Soy del quinto regimiento*, 382.

26. *Trayectoria*, 468. Air force chief Hidalgo de Cisneros informed me that the only undersecretaries who returned were the Communists Cordón, Núñez Maza, and Sánchez Arcas (interview notes, 79, Hoover Institution).

27. *Frente Rojo* (Figueras), 1 Feb. 1939. An original of this rare issue is in the Archivo Histórico del Comité Central del PCE, Madrid. A photocopy is in the Hoover Institution, Bolloten Collection. Other expulsions announced included that of César G. Lombardía.

28. I am indebted to Hidalgo de Cisneros for most of these names (interview notes, 78–80, Hoover Institution). For Díaz Tendero, see M. Teresa Suero Roca, *Militares republicanos de la guerra de España*, 160.

29. Manuel Azaña, *Obras completas*, III, 539.

30. *¡Alerta a los pueblos!*, 238.

31. Wenceslao Carrillo, the left Socialist leader, stated in *Frente Libertario* (London): "After the collapse of Catalonia, Señor [Méndez] Aspe, the finance minister in Negrín's cabinet, resold 3,600 tons of frozen meat to Argentina and cancelled a contract with an English firm that had arranged to deliver 3,000 tons of codfish" (as given in *A.I.T. Servicio de Prensa*, Sept. 1939).

32. *¡Alerta a los pueblos!*, 240.

33. *Un discurso*, 45, 43.

34. *Guerra y revolución en España*, IV, capítulo XXI.

35. After the fall of Catalonia, he and José Miaja were promoted to the rank of lieutenant general, in an apparent attempt to retain their fealty (*Gaceta de la República*, 12 Feb. 1939). This was the view (with respect to Miaja's promotion) of politburo member Pedro Martínez Carton, whom I interviewed in Mexico in 1940 (see shorthand record, part 2, p. 21, Hoover Institution, Bolloten Collection).

36. *¡Alerta a los pueblos!*, 239–40.

37. Bolloten, interview notes, 79, Hoover Institution.

38. *Testimonio de dos guerras*, 303–4.

39. *¡Basta!*, 117. See also Líster, *Así destruyó Carrillo el PCE*, 16–17.

40. See Carrillo, *Demain l'Espagne*, 70–71; Claudín, *Santiago Carrillo*, 57; *¿Adónde va el partido socialista?*, 19, as given in Líster, *Así destruyó Carrillo el PCE*, 16–17. See also the official Communist history *Guerra y revolución*, IV, 260, which was published when Carrillo was the party secretary. Its explanation of his failure to return to Spain—namely, that the plan "could not be carried out because of the rapid development of events"—undoubtedly had his approval. For another explanation, see Gregorio Morán, *Miseria y grandeza del partido comunista de España, 1939–1985*, 68.

41. For his account of his last days in Catalonia, his crossing of the frontier into France, and his refusal to go to the central-southern zone, see his letter to Angel Ossorio y Gallardo in Azaña, *Obras*, III, 535–54. See also Cipriano Rivas-Cherif (his brother-in-law, who accompanied him), *Retrato de un desconocido*, 306–12, and Diego Martínez Barrio (the speaker of the Cortes), *Memorias*, 401–8.

42. Azaña, *Obras*, III, 551.

43. *Guerra y revolución*, IV, 241.

44. Alvarez del Vayo, *Freedom's Battle*, 299; *Give Me Combat*, 175; also Martínez Barrio, *Memorias*, 403.

45. *Memorias*, 406.

46. Ibid.

47. See his letter to Angel Ossorio y Gallardo in Azaña, *Obras*, III, 545.

48. During the war Azaña made several unofficial soundings with a view to a mediated settlement. See, for example, Azaña, *Obras*, III, 545–46, 558; ibid., IV, 588, 655–56, 833; *Guerra y revolución*, III, 179–84; André Saborit, *Julián Besteiro*, 404–5. See also Chapter 54 of this volume and article by Michael Albert in *Revista Política Internacional*, April 1975, in which he refers to Azaña's talk with Stevenson, the British representative in Catalonia, just before the president crossed the frontier into France. Some overtures, which were often made by Cipriano Rivas-Cherif, Azaña's brother-in-law and consul general in Geneva until May 1938, proved troublesome to Negrín and Alvarez del Vayo; for they were made without the knowledge of the government and conflicted with its policy. Despite passionate resistance from Azaña, Negrín managed to remove Rivas-Cherif (*Gaceta de la República*, 11 May 1938), but the president insisted that he be appointed *introductor de embajadores* (ibid.) in his official residence in Barcelona, where he was able to meet visiting foreign dignitaries. I am grateful to Gabriel García Maroto, a close friend of del Vayo's, for this information (interview, Mexico City, 1939; taken from shorthand notes, Hoover Institution).

49. *Boletín Oficial del Estado*, 13 Feb. 1939, 824–47.

50. Guillermo Cabanellas, *La guerra civil y la victoria*, 193. For other comments on the decree, see Rafael Abella, *La vida cotidiana durante la guerra civil: La España republicana*, 443; George Hills, *Franco*, 330.

51. *Claridad*, 13 Feb. 1939.

52. Letter to Martínez Barrio, 4 Apr. 1939, as given in Saborit, *Julián Besteiro*, 398.

53. *Historia de la guerra en España*, 534–35.

54. Quoted in *Epistolario, Prieto y Negrín*, 117–18.

55. *Yo fui un ministro de Stalin*, 183–84.

56. *Oran Socialiste*, 1 July 1939, as given in *Spain*, 2 Nov. 1939.

57. *Guerra y revolución*, IV, 262.

58. It should be noted that until Negrín declared a "state of war" on 19 January 1939, a few days before the fall of Barcelona, the press censorship had been under civilian authority. As a result, the censorship in Madrid passed under the control of Colonel Segismundo Casado, the commander of the Army of the Center, an opponent of the PCE, who suspended *Mundo Obrero* for publishing the manifesto in spite of his prohibition.

59. *Escritos*, 274–75. After the war, José Duque, formerly a member of the central committee of the PCE, told me that the people of Madrid "wanted to end the war" and that the manifesto "only increased the conviction that the Communists wanted to continue it" (shorthand notes, Hoover Institution). For various accounts of the *Mundo Obrero* incident, see Casado, *Así cayó Madrid*, 117–18; Edmundo Domínguez (pro-Communist), *Los vencedores de Negrín*, 39–45; José García Pradas (Anarchist), *La traición de Stalin*, 29–30; and Vicente Uribe (Communist), "Memorias," 65.

60. This extraordinarily valuable archive was organized by Luis and Severiano Hernández over a period of two years with funds provided by the ministry of culture, Madrid. I am greatly indebted to Antonio González Quintana, director of the Archivo Histórico Nacional, Salamanca, Sección "Guerra Civil," for providing me with a listing of the holdings, which has been deposited in the Hoover Institution, Bolloten Collection.

61. "Las causas de la derrota de la República española (en ruso)," 151, Archivo Histórico del Comité Central del PCE, Madrid, Carpeta 58. A photocopy is in the Hoover Institution, Bolloten Collection. The text of this 258-page report is in Russian. I am greatly indebted to Hilja Kukk of the Hoover Institution for carefully studying this valuable document and kindly translating certain key passages at my request.

62. *Mundo Obrero*, 26 Feb. 1939. The declaration is dated 23 February. Togliatti erroneously gives the date as the twenty-second.

63. *Escritos*, 280.

64. Ibid., 274.

65. Ibid., 275.

66. As given in Fernando Claudín, *Santiago Carrillo*, 66.

67. "Las causas de la derrota," 152–53. See n. 61 above.

68. Ibid., 151.

69. See n. 62 above.

70. *Escritos*, 275–77.

71. *Mundo Obrero*, 26 Feb. 1939.

72. On 28 February, the Madrid newspapers announced: "The Government has deemed it advisable to locate the services of the ministerial departments in the Levante zone, while retaining its residence in Madrid" (as given in José Manuel Martínez Bande, *El final de la guerra civil*, 168).

73. *Testimonio*, 306.

74. Cipriano Mera, *Guerra, exilio, y cárcel de un anarcosindicalista*, 197.

75. Vicente Ramos, *La guerra civil, 1936–1939, en la provincia de Alicante*, III, 136. See also *Guerra y revolución*, IV, 294, and Enrique Castro, *Hombres made in Moscú*, 729.

76. Cordón, 471.

77. The official Communist history confirms that the Fourteenth Army Corps was commanded by Ungría, a party member (*Guerra y revolución*, IV, 231). See also José Manuel Martínez Bande, article in *Revista Histórica y Vida*, July 1973, and Vanni, 11. Manuel Tagüeña, the Communist commander of the Fifteenth Army Corps, who was in Yuste on 6 March, states that the place "was surrounded by almost one hundred faithful commandos, well-armed soldiers selected from the units controlled by the Communists that operated behind the enemy lines" (*Testimonio*, 311). The figure of one hundred is corroborated by politburo member Manuel Delicado (see *Guerra y revolución*, IV, 300).

78. *Na trevozhnykh perekrestkakh: Zapiski chekista*, 173.

79. *Nuestra guerra*, 254.

80. "Memorias," 66–67, 71–72.

81. Marcella and Maurizio Ferrara, *Conversando con Togliatti*, 278.

82. *Escritos*, 282.

83. *El único camino*, 444.

84. *Trayectoria*, 476.

85. *Nuestra guerra*, 250. Uribe, of course, was a Communist, Moix, a leader of the PSUC, and Vayo, a philo-Communist.

86. *Diario Oficial del Ministerio de Defensa Nacional*, 5 Dec. 1938.

87. *Los vencedores de Negrín*, 100. This book was written in Oran during the spring of 1939. It was published in Mexico in 1940 and was edited and revised on the orders of the Communist party by Margarita Nelken, who, like Domínguez, was a former Caballerista (information given to me by Spanish Communists in exile in Mexico City in 1940). Domínguez was made inspector-commissar of the Army of the Center by Negrín in December 1938, replacing the Socialist Fernando Piñuela (*Diario Oficial del Ministerio de Defensa Nacional*, 5 Dec. 1938). For friction between Jesús Hernández, the chief commissar of the central-southern zone, and Piñuela, see José Miaja Papers, Manuscript Division, Library of Congress. Copies are in the Hoover Institution, Bolloten Collection.

88. Ibid.

89. Stefanov, 150.

90. "Memorias," 65, 64–65. Archivo Histórico del Comité Central del PCE, Madrid, Carp. 60.

91. This subject is dealt with in the following chapter.

92. For the shrinkage of the average ration of the Republican troops between 1936 and 1938, see Stanley G. Payne, *The Spanish Revolution*, 358, who quotes from a Soviet source. On 20 December 1938, Miaja wrote Negrín that the civilian population was in a "state of physical exhaustion due to two years of food shortages" (José Miaja Papers, Manuscript Division, Library of Congress; a copy of the letter is in the Bolloten Collection, Hoover Institution). On the same date he wrote to General Rojo, telling him that there had been two demonstrations by women in a period of three days (ibid.).

93. See Chapter 54.

94. *Así cayó Madrid*, 113–15.

95. See, for example, Alvarez del Vayo, *Freedom's Battle*, 295–97, and Michael Alpert, article in *Revista de Política Internacional*, April 1975, 55–59.

96. John Harvey, *The Diplomatic Diaries of Oliver Harvey, 1937–1940*, 254–55.

97. *Freedom's Battle*, 302.

98. *Mi embajada en Londres durante la guerra*, 126–27.

99. John Harvey, *The Diplomatic Diaries*, 256. My italics.

100. Azcárate, 137. My italics.

101. Ibid. See also Michael Alpert, article in *Revista de Política Internacional*, April 1975, 57–59.

102. *El final de la guerra*, 132.

103. *The Last Days of Madrid*, 111.

104. *Guerra y revolución*, IV, 229.

105. These were Sir Robert Hodgson and Léon Berard. See José Manuel Martínez Bande, *Los cien últimos días de la república*, 98–101.

106. *Así cayó Madrid*, 115–16.

107. The date of this meeting has been variously given as 11, 13, 16, 26, and 27 February, but it is clear from documentary evidence in José Manuel Martínez Bande's *El final de la guerra*, 138, that the correct date is the 16th.

108. Miaja was appointed to the rank of lieutenant general on 11 February 1939.

109. *Así cayó Madrid*, 122–27.

110. Ibid., 199–200. Luis Romero states that he has read a signed letter from Casado severely condemning the attitude of Miaja at the Los Llanos meeting in contradiction to his position in Valencia (*El final de la guerra*, 119).

111. An interesting sidelight is that one of Miaja's main concerns at this time, according to Hidalgo de Cisneros, was to hold on to an airplane that had always been at his disposal. When Cisneros said jokingly that he needed the plane, Miaja "nearly went out of his mind." It was in this plane that he later fled to North Africa (Bolloten, interview notes, 81, Hoover Institution). See also Cordón, 416. It is also worth recording that when Líster visited Miaja on his return to Spain, the general asked him why he had come back. "I explained my reasons," says Líster, "while he continued to look at me with surprise. The interview was sad, painful. I found myself in the presence of a man who seemed like an idiot. His words were unintelligible with no connection between them" (*Nuestra guerra*, 252).

112. For a biography of Matallana, see Suero Roca, *Militares republicanos*, 161–90.

113. That he was a Communist is confirmed by Negrín (*Epistolario, Prieto y Negrín*, 30).

114. In a long report on the state of the air force, dated 13 February 1937, and presumably read at the meeting on the sixteenth, Camacho expressed the view that "we virtually have no aviation" (see Ramón Salas Larrazábal, who reproduces the entire report, *Historia del ejército popular de la república*, IV, 3392–98).

115. *Así cayó Madrid*, 122–27.

116. *Congreso de los Diputados. Deputación Permanente, Sesión celebrada [in Paris] el viernes 31 de marzo de 1939*.

117. See n. 72 above.

118. A photographic reproduction of the letter is in Eduardo Comín Colomer, *La república en el exilio*, between 152 and 153. See also Zugazagoitia, 527. Azaña died on 3 November 1940 in Montauban, France, from a heart attack at the age of sixty. (For biographical information, see Vicente R. Pilapil in James W. Cortada, *Historical Dictionary of the Spanish Civil War, 1936–1939*, 61–67.)

119. *Congreso de los Diputados. Diputación Permanente, Sesión celebrada [in Paris] el viernes 3 de marzo de 1939.*

120. Ibid., *Sesión celebrada el 6 de marzo de 1939.*

121. For Martínez Barrio's documented account of the presidential crisis, see his *Memorias*, 408–20.

122. *Escritos*, 279.

Chapter 64

1. For a Soviet opinion of Casado, see N. Voronov, the chief of Soviet artillery in Spain, in *Pod znamenem ispanskoi, 1936–1939*, 86.

2. Segismundo Casado, *The Last Days of Madrid*, 52.

3. *Frente Rojo*, 19 May 1938.

4. Their political affiliation is given in the Communist official history, *Guerra y revolución en España, 1936–1939*, IV, 229–30, n. 1; also in Tagüeña, *Testimonio de dos guerras*, 307.

5. *Historia del ejército popular de la republica*, II, 2286.

6. 11 May 1938. For biographical material on Casado, see Michael Alpert, *El ejército republicano en la guerra civil*, 301–3; Casado, *Así cayó Madrid, The Last Days of Madrid*, and his "Las Memorias Inéditas del Coronel Casado," in *Pueblo*, 28, 30, 31 Oct., 1–4, 6–11, 13, 14 Nov. 1967; Ricardo de la Cierva, *Historia ilustrada de la guerra civil*, II, 492–511; Antonio Cordón, *Trayectoria*, 368, 471–74; Salas Larrazábal, *Historia del ejército popular*, II, 2286–89; Teresa Suero Roca, *Militares republicanos de la guerra de España*, 191–231; Cristóbal Zaragoza, *Ejército popular y militares de la república, 1936–1939*, 237–45.

7. *Testimonio*, 323.

8. *Política de ayer y política de mañana*, 139.

9. *Así cayó Madrid*, 199.

10. Ibid.

11. Ibid., 199–200.

12. Casado, *Así cayó Madrid*, 200–201. My italics.

13. *El final de la guerra*, 121–22.

14. Two biographies have, in fact, been written on Mera: Miguel González Inestal, *Cipriano Mera, revolucionario* (1943) and Joan Llarch, *Cipriano Mera: Un anarquista en la guerra civil española* (1977).

15. *El final de la guerra*, 181.

16. Ibid., 122.

17. Mera, *Guerra, exilio y cárcel de un anarcosindicalista*, 198–200.

18. *La traición de Stalin*, 47.

19. Ibid., 47–49.

20. Ibid., 54.

21. Ibid., 55–57.

22. These documents can be found in Documentación Nacional, Armario 5, Legajo 277, Carpetas 11 and 12.

23. *Los cien últimos días de la república*, 119–29, and *El final de la guerra civil*, 134–54.

24. See n. 28 below for General Franco's terms.

25. For additional information on Centaño and "Lucero Verde," see Cierva, *Historia ilustrada*, II, 493–95.

26. In the English edition of his book, published in 1939, Casado gave the date of this visit as 12 March (*The Last Days*, 207). He later changed the date to 5 February in the Spanish version published in 1968 (*Así cayó Madrid*, 203) but never explained the discrepancy. However, even the date of 5 February appears to be inaccurate to judge from Martínez Bande's study of the pertinent documents. Curiously enough, Ricardo de la Cierva, who also studied the Nationalist documents in the Servicio Histórico Militar, gives the date of the first meeting with Centaño as "one of the first days of February, probably the 5th" (*Historia ilustrada*, II, 494).

27. After Azaña decided to remain in France, Casado asked Alvarez del Vayo to tell the president that he was a coward (Cordón, 473).

28. Martínez Bande cites the terms offered by Franco to those officers who laid down their arms. Nationalist Spain, Franco stated, would be "generous" toward those who had been deceived into fighting but had not committed crimes. However, there is absolutely no hint of the broad concessions that Antonio Cordón and Hidalgo de Cisneros allege Casado told them the British would "impose" on Franco, as mentioned later in this chapter. For the text of Franco's conditions, as presented to Casado, see Martínez Bande, *El final de la guerra*, 150, n. 188.

29. Capitals in text.

30. *Trayectoria*, 474.

31. See article by Alpert in *Revista de Política Internacional*, Mar.–Apr. 1975. I am grateful to Michael Alpert for furnishing me with a copy of his invaluable piece of research, based largely on official documents in the public record office, England.

32. See previous note.

33. *Los vencedores de Negrín*, 94–95.

34. See n. 31 above.

35. Letter dated 31 Aug. 1987 (Hoover Institution, Bolloten Collection).

36. Ibid.

37. Interview notes, 83–85 (Hoover Institution). See also Julio Alvarez del Vayo, *Freedom's Battle*, 306–7 and n. 1; Cordón, 473–74. For Franco's terms to Casado, see n. 28 above.

38. *Memorias 2: La república y la guerra de España*, 464.

39. See Cordón, 474, and my interview with Hidalgo de Cisneros, 83–85 (Hoover Institution).

40. *Guerra y revolutión*, IV, 304. "However, it was difficult for them to believe it," the official history adds. "They were trained for implacable combat against fascist aggression, for combat based on unity, on the cohesion of the Popular Front" (ibid.).

41. *Testimonio*, 305–6.

42. *Congreso de los Diputados. Diputación Permanente, Sesión celebrada el viernes 3 de marzo de 1939.*

Chapter 65

1. The resolution, dated 23 February, was not published until the twenty-sixth (*Mundo Obrero*, 26 Feb. 1939).

2. *Escritos sobre la guerra de España*, 280. Togliatti erroneously gives the date of publication as 22 Feb. 1939. See n. 1.

3. *Trayectoria*, 477. See also Togliatti, *Escritos*, 282–83.

4. Conversation with me in Mexico City in 1939. (Shorthand notes, Hoover Institution).

5. *Guerra y revolución en España, 1936–1939*, IV, 258. Their respective posts and their party affiliation are given in ibid., 229–30, n. 1, although on p. 258 their posts are erroneously reversed.

6. *Escritos*, 282–83.

7. Ibid., 279.

8. Ibid., 280.

9. *Así cayó Madrid*, 133–34.

10. P. 198.

11. *Escritos*, 280.

12. *Trayectoria*, 471.

13. Ibid., 482.

14. Date given by the official Communist history, *Guerra y revolución*, IV, 252, n. 6.

15. P. 200. My italics.

16. See Ramón Salas Larrazábal, *Historia del ejército popular de la república*, II, 2333, n. 47.

17. See, for example, Bruno Alonso (moderate Socialist and commissar general of the fleet), *La flota republicana y la guerra civil de España*, 136; Wenceslao Carrillo (left-wing Socialist, former director general of security under Largo Caballero, and later a member of Casado's rebel National Council of Defense), *El último episodio de la guerra civil española*, 10; Casado, *Así cayó Madrid*, 141; González Marin (CNT member of Casado's National Council of Defense) in *España Libre* (Paris), 13 Mar. 1949.

18. *Historia del ejército popular*, II, 2333, n. 47.

19. For information on these two officers, see José Manuel Martínez Bande, *Los cien últimos días de la república*, 80; Salas Larrazábal, *Historia del ejército popular*, II, 2333, n. 47.

20. Referring to the early summer of 1938, when these officers were on General Miaja's staff, Cordón writes: "Through various channels Negrín received accusations against these two officers. They were denounced as agents of Franco, but the informers did not produce concrete evidence and both Miaja and Rojo doubted the veracity of the accusations. For this reason, Negrín decided not to take any action against [them]" (*Trayectoria*, 415). See also Hidalgo de Cisneros interview, Bolloten Collection, Hoover Institution, 63–65.

21. *Gaceta de la República*, 1 Mar. 1939.

22. The post of secretary general of the ministry of national defense had originally been held by Julián Zugazagoitia, who had refused to return to Spain. Cordón writes: "I reminded [Negrín] that when this post was first created he regarded it as more honorary than practical. Hence, in the existing situation, the post appeared to me to be completely useless. He insisted on making the appointment: 'You don't expect Zugazagoitia to return, do you? Well, I just want to put it on record that as he has not returned I have had to replace him' " (*Trayectoria*, 477).

23. See Hidalgo de Cisneros interview, 85–86 (Bolloten Collection, Hoover Institution).

24. Cordón, 478.

25. *La flota republicana*, 136–37.

26. *El final de la guerra*, 173.

27. *Así cayó Madrid*, 142, and *Pueblo*, 1 Nov. 1967.

28. *El final de la guerra civil*, 176.

29. One such report originated with General Matallana, who, according to Casado, informed him confidentially on 28 February that Negrín "had dictated the requisite orders" appointing Modesto commander of the Army of the Center in place of Casado, who was named chief of the army general staff (*Así cayó Madrid*, 131), but these orders did not appear in the *Diario Oficial*. However, they were, as we have seen, the subject of discussion and never went beyond that stage. In the English version of his book, Casado says: "In a telephone conversation which I had with the Prime Minister he denied that he had given orders for my relief, but I telephoned to the Civil Governor of Madrid, who told me that he had these orders in his hands for publication in the Gazette [*Diario Oficial*], but that the Prime Minister had told him to delay them until further orders. From this it will be seen that the Prime Minister was working with caution to avoid a false step in carrying out his plan" (*The Last Days of Madrid*, 127).

30. *Escritos*, 283.

31. Ibid., 284.

32. *El único camino*, 445.

33. Líster, *Nuestra guerra*, 252–53; Modesto, *Soy del quinto regimiento*, 385–88.

34. Cipriano Mera, *Guerra, exilio y cárcel de un anarcosindicalista*, 197.

35. *Escritos*, 283.

36. Stefanov erroneously gives the date as 14 February, but states in a "Cautionary Note" at the beginning of the report that it was written without the help of his personal notes or other documentation and consequently might contain some chronological or factual errors.

37. Stefanov, 153–54.

38. See Vanni, *Yo, comunista en Rusia*, 17–18, also 15–16.

39. *Escritos*, 280–81. My italics.

40. *Guerra y revolución*, IV, 229–30, n. 1, and 231.

41. *Escritos*, 281.

42. *El único camino*, 434, 436. In accordance with the party line, Enrique Líster wrote in 1966 that after he saw Negrín in Elda on 2 March he left him "with the conviction that he would not make any fundamental change in the command of the military forces and that he wanted to gain time and see how events developed" (*Nuestra guerra*, 253).

43. Stefanov, 153.

44. *Yo, comunista en Rusia*, 11.

45. *Testimonio de dos guerras*, 309–10.

46. *Escritos*, 279–80.

47. The complex developments at the naval base of Cartagena and the departure of the fleet for

North Africa have been touched on by numerous authors, but are best described by Luis Romero in *Desastre en Cartagena*. For accounts of these events by two Socialist participants, see Bruno Alonso (the Socialist commissar general of the fleet), *La flota republicana*, 133–56, and Miguel Peydro in *Tribuna*, Jan. 1951. The official Communist version is given in *Guerra y revolución*, IV, 281–89. The ships that sailed for North Africa comprised the cruisers *Miguel de Cervantes*, *Libertad*, and *Méndez Núñez*, eight destroyers and several smaller craft (see, for example, Admiral Francisco Moreno, *La guerra en el mar*, 280). Since the publication of Luis Romero's extraordinary work in 1971, three important reports on the Cartagena events by prominent Communist participants—Víctor de Frutos, Francisco Galán, and Joaquín Rodríguez—have come to light in the Archivo Historico del Comité Central del PCE, Madrid, Carp. 35 and 54. Photocopies are in the Hoover Institution, Bolloten Collection, file "Cartagena Events, March 1939."

48. *Give Me Combat*, 174.

49. *Freedom's Battle*, 305.

50. *The Spanish Civil War* (1977 ed.), 911.

51. *Guerra y revolución*, IV, 296.

52. *¡Basta!*, 117.

53. *Nuestra guerra*, 254.

54. *Yo fui un ministro de Stalin*, 187.

55. See next chapter.

56. Here, Hernández is mistaken. The *Diario Oficial* to which he refers appeared the day before.

57. Hernández is in error. Neither Modesto nor Líster, as we have seen, was appointed to any post.

58. *Yo fui un ministro de Stalin*, 192–95.

Chapter 66

1. *Así cayó Madrid*, 151.

2. Miaja took over the presidency the next day (Casado, *Así cayó Madrid*, 152. See also J. García Pradas, *La traición de Stalin*, 66.

3. Only the preceding names and posts appeared in the Madrid press on 7 March 1939 (see, for example, *Política*).

4. Sánchez Requena's name does not appear in the list published in the Madrid newspapers on 7 March but is given in *Guerra y revolución en España, 1936–1939*, IV, 293, and Mathilde Vázquez and Javier Valero, *La guerra civil en Madrid*, 836.

5. Antonio Pérez joined the council on 8 March (Vázquez and Valero, 836). The official Communist party history quotes from a letter by José Rodríguez Vega, the secretary general of the UGT, dated 17 March 1939, stating that the members of the UGT executive in Madrid agreed to help the council "in order to avert clashes between antifascists, especially in view of the fact that the government no longer existed" (*Guerra y revolución*, IV, 293). Edmundo Domínguez, the crypto-Communist vice president of the UGT, writes: "Antonio Pérez was appointed [at a meeting of the UGT] to represent us on the Council. Neither Vega nor I wished to accept such a post. Pérez, regretfully and angrily, had to accept an office that ran counter to his point of view. At the meeting the most violent hatred against the Communists was displayed [but] we prevented their expulsion from the unions" (*Los vencedores de Negrín*, 212).

6. Casado, *The Last Days of Madrid*, 139–40; see also José Manuel Martínez Bande, *El final de la guerra civil*, 240.

7. *El Socialista*, 7 Mar. 1939.

8. Ibid.

9. Ibid.

10. Ibid.

11. The other versions appeared in *The Last Days of Madrid* (London, 1939), 149–50, and in *Así cayó Madrid* (Madrid, 1968), 157–58.

12. *The Last Days of Madrid*, 149. It will be recalled that Negrín promoted Casado to the rank of general on 25 February 1939. See Uribe, "Memorias," 69.

13. *The Last Days of Madrid*, 153. See also Casado, *Así cayó Madrid*, 158, and *Pueblo*, 2 Nov. 1967.

14. *The Last Days of Madrid*, 153.

15. *Historia de la guerra en España*, 563, n. 1.

16. Interview, Heleno Saña, *Indice*, 15 June 1974. Italics in text.

17. "Informe al Comite Central sobre el Desarrollo de los Acontecimientos Desarrollados en España durante el Perído del Golpe de Casado," dated 3 May 1939, 15–16 (italics in text), Archivo Histórico del Comite Central del Partido Comunista de España, Madrid, Carpeta 34 (photocopy in Hoover Institution, Bolloten Collection). See also Casado, *The Last Days of Madrid*, 154.

18. *Guerra y revolución*, IV, 295.

19. *Escritos sobre la guerra de España*, 287.

20. Interview, Mexico, 1940, shorthand notes, p. 90, Hoover Institution.

21. *¡Basta!*, 117–18. The reader should be alerted to the fact that this book was written in 1971, when Líster was trying to wrest control of the party from Santiago Carrillo, then general secretary, and from La Pasionaria, its president.

22. *Yo fui un ministro de Stalin*, 255–56.

23. *Diario de Sesiones de la Diputatión Permanente de las Cortes*, Paris, 31 Mar. 1939.

24. Stefanov, 256–57.

25. *Guerra y revolución*, IV, 296. Other persons present were the famous poet Rafael Alberti and his wife María Teresa Léon, both members of the PCE (Enrique Castro, *Hombres made in Moscú*, 732).

26. *Freedom's Battle*, 315.

27. Ibid., 299.

28. *Guerra y revolución*, IV, 294–95.

29. P. 70.

30. Togliatti, *Escritos*, 290.

31. Ibid., 288. See also Stefanov, 149, who states that Negrín considered that it was "his duty and a question of honor to visit the party leaders before his departure."

32. Togliatti, *Escritos*, 205. For Togliatti's comments on the exact date of this letter, see ibid., 294.

33. P. 449.

34. *Memorias de un luchador*, 432.

35. *Togliatti-Díaz-Carrillo: Los comunistas y la revolución*, 137.

36. Jaime Camino, *Intimas conversaciones con la Pasionaria*, 143.

37. *Escritos*, 288.

38. The full text is given in *Guerra y revolución*, IV, 297, n. 1. See also Luis Romero, *El final de la guerra*, 274 and 275, n. 2.

39. *Escritos*, 288.

40. *Guerra y revolución*, IV, 297.

41. "Memorias," 70.

42. *Guerra y revolución*, IV, 298.

43. *Escritos*, 290.

44. Ibid., 289.

45. *Guerra y revolución*, IV, 299.

46. *Freedom's Battle*, 301.

47. *Guerra y revolución*, IV, 299–300.

48. *Escritos*, 290.

49. S. A. Vaupshasov, *Na trevozhnykh perekrestkakh: Zapiski chekista*, 180.

50. Ibid., 180–86.

51. *Guerra y revolución*, IV, 301.

52. See also Stefanov, 166.

53. *Escritos*, 290. See also Stefanov, 166–67.

54. *Memorias 2*, 468–70. For other eyewitness accounts of these final hours, see Castro, *Hombres*, 731–35; Manuel Tagüeña, *Testimonio de dos guerras*, 315–17.

55. They were later arrested by Casado's military police and assault guards. "This unfortunate

incident," Togliatti informed Moscow, "prevented us from influencing the course of events in any way for three to four days. The arrest was made about 1 A.M. on the night of 6–7 March. We were not in a position to contact the party and begin work until 9 March, in Albacete, after a series of complicated adventures" (*Escritos*, 291). See also Stefanov, 167 ff., and *Guerra y revolución*, IV, 303–4.

56. *Guerra y revolución*, IV, 304.

57. *Escritos*, 292. My italics.

58. 9 Mar. 1939.

59. For accounts of the fighting in Madrid, see Antonio Bouthelier and José López Mora, *8 días: La revuelta comunista, Madrid, 5–13 marzo 1939*; Casado, *Así cayó Madrid*, 170–83, and *The Last Days of Madrid*, 166–92; Dominguéz, *Los vencedores de Negrín*, 207–50; *Guerra y revolución*, IV, 304–17; Martínez Bande, *El final de la guerra civil*, 261–87; Cipriano Mera, *Guerra, exilio y cárcel de un anarcosindicalista*, 201–12; Romero, *El final de la guerra*, 323–53; Ramón Salas Larrazábal, *Historia del ejército popular de la república*, II, 2312–18 and notes.

60. *Escritos*, 294.

61. Ibid., 291, 294.

62. Ibid., 206–7.

63. My italics.

64. Ibid., 109–10. The words "a single ally" are italicized in the text.

65. Ibid., 292. See also Tagüeña, 320–21.

66. *Guerra y revolución*, IV, 317.

67. Ibid.

68. The most direct documentation on the final negotiations is the material from Spanish army archives cited in Servicio Historico Militar, *El final de la guerra*, 293–314. See also the memoir by Casado and J. M. Martínez Bande, *Los cien últimos días de la República*.

69. Quoted in Segismundo Casado, *Así cayó Madrid*, 208–9, and Ignacio Arenillas de Chaves, *El proceso de Besteiro*, 471. These "concessions" were later broadcast in radio messages and leaflets to Republican troops in the final offensive of 26 March.

70. Ramón Salas Larrazábal and Jesús María Salas Larrazábal, *Historia general de la guerra de España*, 411.

71. Servicio Histórico Militar, "Archivo de la Guerra de Liberación," Leg. 277/14/5, Intelligence report, Cuartel General del Generalísimo, 14 March 1939.

72. Ibid., Estado Mayor to SIPM, 15 March 1939.

73. Ibid., SIPM report, 18 March 1939.

74. Ibid., 17 March 1939.

75. Ibid., Italian intelligence report, Ufficio D, 18 March 1939. Trifón Gómez, the council's special representative sent to Paris, prepared a detailed "Informe" (29 May 1939) concerning his mostly fruitless efforts (Hoover Institution, Bolloten Collection).

76. Servicio Histórico Militar, "Archivo de la Guerra de Liberación," Leg. 277/14/5, SIPM report, 17 March 1939.

77. Ibid., radio information report, Ministry of the Interior, 18 March 1939.

78. Ibid., SIPM telegram, 18 March 1939.

79. Ibid., Casado to the Nationalist government, 20 March 1939.

80. Ibid., 21 March 1939.

81. Ibid., SIPM telegram, 21 March 1939.

82. Ibid., SIPM report, 22 March 1939.

83. The report by Colonel Gonzalo and Colonel Ungría, 23 March 1939, is in Martínez Bande, *El final de la guerra*, 382–86.

84. Casado, *Así cayó Madrid*, 222–35, presents the text of Garijo's report and a summary of the discussion.

85. See Michael Alpert, "La diplomacia inglesa y el fin de la guerra civil española," *Revista de Politica Internacional*, no. 138 (March–April), 53–72.

86. The text is in Martínez Bande, *El final de la guerra*, 387.

87. The two documents bearing the council's final proposals may be found in the Servicio Histórico Militar, "Archivo de la Guerra de Liberación," Leg. 277/15/5.

88. The report of Gonzalo and Ungría on the second and final interview may be found in Martínez Bande, *El final de la guerra*, 388–91.

89. The surrender of Madrid is described in Casado's memoir and in Francisco Camba's propagandistic *Madridgrado*.

90. *ABC*, April 2, 1939.

91. For a discussion of the repression imposed by the new regime, see chapter 11 of Stanley G. Payne, *The Franco Regime, 1936–1975*.

Bibliography

I. Books, Correspondence, Documents, Interviews, and Pamphlets

In the preparation of this work several thousand books and pamphlets have been consulted, but since considerations of space do not permit a complete bibliographical listing, only those sources are given here that have been cited in the text or notes or, in the opinion of the author, may be helpful to others in their research projects. Books and pamphlets published before the Civil War as well as many works dealing exclusively with Nationalist Spain, with military operations, and with the postwar period are not included unless cited in the text or notes. Two or more editions of the same book (whether in one or two languages) have been listed only in cases where revisions, additions, or deletions have made those editions significant to this author. All materials listed hereunder are available in one or more of the libraries and institutions mentioned at the beginning of this book. Materials marked with an asterisk are available only in the archives of the Hoover Institution (Bolloten Collection).

Abad de Santillán, Diego. *After the Revolution*. New York: Greenberg, 1937.
_____. *Alfonso XIII, la II república, Francisco Franco*. Gijón: Júcar, 1979.
_____. *El anarquismo y la revolución en España: Escritos 1930–1938*. Madrid: Ayuso, 1976.
_____. *Los anarquistas y la reacción contemporánea*. Mexico City: Ediciones del Grupo Cultural Ricardo Flores Magon, 1925.
_____. *La bancarrota del sistema económico y político del capitalismo*. Buenos Aires: Nervio, 1932.
_____. *Contribución a la historia del movimiento obrero español*. Puebla, Mexico: Cajica, 1965.
*_____. Correspondence with Burnett Bolloten.
_____. *Estrategia y táctica*. Puebla, Mexico: Cajica, 1971.
_____. *Memorias, 1897–1936*. Barcelona: Planeta, 1977.
_____. *El organismo económico de la revolución: Cómo vivimos y cómo podríamos vivir en España*. Barcelona: Tierra y Libertad, 1938.
_____. *Por qué perdimos la guerra*. Buenos Aires: Imán, 1940.
_____. *La revolución y la guerra en España*. Mexico City: El Libro, 1938.

Abella, Rafael. *Julio 1936: Dos Españas frente a frente.* Barcelona: Plaza y Janés, 1981.

_____. *La vida cotidiana durante la guerra civil: La España republicana.* Barcelona: Planeta, 1976.

Abendroth, Hans-Henning. *Hitler in der spanischen Arena.* Paderborn: Schöningh, 1973.

Academy of Sciences of the USSR. *International Solidarity with the Spanish Republic, 1936–1939.* Moscow: Progress, 1974.

Acedo Colunga, General Felipe. *José Calvo Sotelo.* Barcelona: AHR, 1957.

Acier, Marcel, ed. *From Spanish Trenches.* New York: Modern Age Books, 1937.

Acords del ple extraordinari del comité nacional de la unió General de treballadors. Valencia: UGT, 1937.

Acords de III congrés de la unió general de treballadors a Catalunya 13–18 de novembre de 1937. Introducció per Rafael Vidiella. Pròleg per Miguel Ferrer. Barcelona: UGT, 1937.

Actas de las sesiones de la junta de defensa de Madrid. (Archivo Histórico Nacional, Salamanca; The Library of Congress; Servicio Histórico Militar, Madrid).

Agencia Febus. Typewritten copies of dispatches received by the Febus news agency in Madrid during the first few days of the Civil War. Hoover Institution, Bolloten Collection.

Agrarian Reform in Spain. London: United Editorial, 1937.

La agresión italiana: Documentos ocupados a las unidades italianas en la acción de Guadalajara. Valencia: Ministerio de Estado, 1937.

Aguado, Emiliano. *Don Manuel Azaña Díaz.* Barcelona: Nauta, 1972.

_____. *Manuel Azaña.* Madrid: Epesa, 1978.

Aguilar Olivencia, Mariano. *El ejército español durante la segunda república.* Madrid: Econorte, 1986.

Aguirre y Lecube, José Antonio de. *De Guernica a Nueva York pasando por Berlin.* Buenos Aires: Vasca Ekin, 1943.

_____. *Freedom Was Flesh and Blood.* London: Gollancz, 1945.

*_____. Report to the central government by José Antonio de Aguirre, premier of the autonomous Basque government. A photocopy of the first ninety-five pages of this report loaned to Burnett Bolloten by Manuel de Irujo is in the Hoover Institution.

_____. *Veinte años de gestión del gobierno vasco, 1936–1956.* Durango (Vizcaya): Zugaza, 1978.

*Aiguadé, Jaime Antón. "Actuació del Govern de la Generalitat i del seu President Lluis Companys durant les Jornades de Maig de 1937." Copy of original document loaned to Burnett Bolloten by Jordi Arquer.

Aiguader, Jaime. *Cataluña y la revolución.* Madrid: Zevs, 1932.

Aims of the Spanish Republic. London: United Editorial, 1938.

Akademiia Nauk SSSR. Institut istorri. *Ispanskii narod protiv fashizma, 1936–1939 gg: Sbornik statei.* Moscow: Academiia Nauk SSSR, 1963.

Aláiz, Felipe. *Indalecio Prieto: Padrino de Negrín y campeón anticomunista.* Toulouse: "Páginas Libres," n.d.

Alba, Luz de. *19 de julio.* Montevideo: Esfuerzo, 1937.

Alba, Víctor. *Catalonia: A Profile.* London: Hurst, 1975.

————. *Cataluña de tamaño natural*. Barcelona: Planeta, 1975.

————. *Dos revolucionarios: Joaquín Maurín, Andreu Nin*. Madrid: Seminarios y Ediciones, 1975.

————. *El frente popular*. Barcelona: Planeta, 1976.

————. *Histoire de POUM*. Paris: Champ Libre, 1975.

————. *Historia de la segunda república española*. Mexico City: Libro Mex, 1960.

————. *Historia general del campesinado*. Barcelona: Plaza y Janés, 1973.

————. *Insomnie Espagnole*. Paris: Franc-Tireur, 1946.

————. *El marxismo en España, 1919–1939: Historia del BOC y del POUM*. Vols. I, II. Mexico City: Costa-Amic, 1973.

————. *El partido comunista en España*. Barcelona: Planeta, 1979.

————. *Sentencia díctada contra el POUM, 1938*. Mexico City: Costa-Amic, 1974.

————, ed. *La revolución española en la práctica: Documentos del POUM*. Madrid: Júcar, 1977.

Alba, Víctor, and Schwartz, Stephen. *Spanish Marxism vs. Soviet Communism*. New Brunswick, N.J.: Transaction Books, 1988.

Albert Despujol, Carlos de. *La gran tragedia de España, 1931–1939*. Madrid: Sánchez de Ocaña, 1940.

Albin, Felix [Kurt Hager]. *The Socialist Unity Party of Germany*. Introduction by Konni Zilliacus. London: New Germany Publications, 1946.

Alcade, Carmen. *La mujer en la guerra civil*. Madrid: Cambio 16, 1976.

Alcalá-Zamora, Niceto. *Discursos*. Madrid: Tecnos, 1979.

————. *Memorias*. Barcelona: Planeta, 1977.

————. *Pensamientos y reflexiones*. Mexico City: Porrua, 1950.

Alcofar Nassaes, José Luis. *Los asesores soviéticos en la guerra civil española*. Madrid: Dopesa, 1971.

*Alcon, Marcos. Correspondence with Burnett Bolloten.

Aldana, B. F. *Como fué la guerra en Aragón*. Barcelona: Ediciones "Como Fué," 1937.

Alexander, Bill. *British Volunteers for Liberty: Spain, 1936–1939*. London: Lawrence and Wishart, 1982.

Algarra Rafegas, Commandant Antonio. *El asedio de Huesca*. Saragossa: El Noticiero, 1941.

Alianza CNT-UGT. Barcelona: Tierra y Libertad, 1938.

Allen, David Edward, Jr. "The Soviet Union and the Spanish Civil War, 1936–1939." Dissertation, Stanford University, 1952.

Almendros, Joaquín. *Situaciones españolas, 1936–1939: El PSUC en la guerra civil*. Barcelona: Dopesa, 1976.

*Almudí, Manuel. Interview, notes taken by Burnett Bolloten.

Alonso, Bruno. *La flota republicana y la guerra civil de España*. Mexico City: Imprenta Grafos, 1944.

Alonso, Pedro Luis. *La Batalla de Teruel*. Barcelona: Bruguera, 1975.

Alpert, Michael. *El ejército republicano en la guerra civil*. Barcelona: Ibérica, 1977.

————. *La reforma militar de Azaña, 1931–1933*. Madrid: Siglo XXI, 1982.

Alvarez. Basilio. *España en el crisol*. Buenos Aires: Colección Claridad, 1937.

Alvarez, Santiago. *Castelao y nosotros los comunistas*. Coruña: Ediciós do Castro, 1984.

*_____. "Informe Operaciones del 22 al 27 de Marzo de 1938," dated 4 April 1938. Typewritten copy of original loaned to Burnett Bolloten by Carlos Contreras.

_____. *El partido comunista y el campo*. Madrid: Torre, 1977.

_____. *El pueblo de Galicia contra el fascismo*. Valencia: Partido Comunista de España, 1937.

Alvarez, Segis. *La juventud y los campesinos: Conferencia nacional de juventudes, enero de 1937*. Valencia: JSU de España, 1937.

_____. *Nuestra organización y nuestros cuadros*. Valencia: JSU de España, 1937.

Alvarez del Vayo, Julio. *Deux discours prononcés à la 101me session de la Société des Nations*. Paris: Services d'Information du Rassemblement Universel pour la Paix, 1938.

_____. *L'Espagne accuse*. Paris: Comité Franco-Espagnol, 1936.

_____. *Freedom's Battle*. New York: Knopf, 1940.

_____. *Give Me Combat*. Boston: Little, Brown, 1973.

_____. *The Last Optimist*. New York: Viking Press, 1950.

_____. *Speech at the Council of the League of Nations, May, 1938*. London: Union of Democratic Control, 1938.

Ametlla, Claudi. *Catalunya: Paradís perdut*. Barcelona: Selecta, 1984.

*"Los Amigos de Durruti." File containing three letters to Burnett Bolloten from Jaime Balius, vice-secretary of the Friends of Durruti, and a photostatic copy of typewritten data compiled by Jordi Arquer. See also Balius, correspondence with Burnett Bolloten, and *Hacia una nueva revolución*.

Among Friends. New York: Friends of the Abraham Lincoln Brigade, 1938.

Amsden, Jon. *Convenios colectivos y lucha de clases en España*. Paris: Ruedo Ibèrico, 1974.

*_____. "Krivitsky." Manuscript.

Anarcosindicalismo: Antecedentes, Declaración de principios. Finalidades y tácticas. Toulouse: Espoir, 1947.

Los anarquistas y la autogestión. Barcelona: Anagrama, 1977.

Anasagosti, Iñaki, and San Sebastián, Koldo. *Los años oscuros: El gobierno vasco—el exilio, 1937–1941*. San Sebastián: Txertoa, 1985.

Andrade, Juan. *Algunas "notas políticas" de la revolución española, 1936–1937*. Paris: La Batalla, 1969.

_____. *Apuntes para la historia del PCE*. Barcelona: Fontamara, 1979.

_____. "Conferencia leída el 10 Enero de 1970, en el Centro de Estudios sobre el Movimiento Obrero Español, de Paris." Copy in Hoover Institution, Bolloten Collection.

_____. *Notas sobre la guerra civil: Actuación del POUM*. Madrid: Libertarias, 1986.

_____. *La revolución española día a día*. Barcelona: Nueva Era, 1979.

Andrés-Gallego, José. *El socialismo durante la dictadura: 1923–1930*. Madrid: Tebas, 1977.

Un año de las brigadas internacionales. Madrid: Ediciones del Comisariado de las Brigadas Internacionales, [1937?].

Ansaldo, Juan Antonio. *¿Para qué . . . ? De Alfonso XIII a Juan III*. Buenos Aires: Vasca Ekin, 1951.

Ansó, Mariano. *Yo fui ministro de Negrín.* Barcelona: Planeta, 1976.

Antón, Francisco. *Madrid: Orgullo de la España antifascista.* Barcelona: Partido Comunista de España, 1937.

Araceli, Gabriel. *Valencia 1936.* Saragossa: El Noticiero, 1939.

Araquistáin, Luis. See also Archivo Histórico Nacional, *Papeles de Don Luís Araquistáin.*

————. *El comunismo y la guerra de España.* Carmaux (Tarn): 1939.

*————. Correspondence with Burnett Bolloten.

————. *Marxismo y socialismo en España.* Barcelona: Fontamara, 1980.

————. *Mis tratos con los comunistas.* Ediciones de la Secretaría de Propaganda del P.S.O.E. en Francia, n.d.

————. "Negrín." Unpublished article. Araquistáin Papers, Archivo Histórico Nacional.

————. *Sobre la guerra civil y en la emigración: Edición y estudio preliminar de Javier Tusell.* Madrid: Espasa-Calpe, 1983.

————. "La Verdad sobre el Comunismo en España: Carta Abierta a Norman Thomas." Barcelona, 1 Jan. 1939. Archivo Histórico Nacional, Madrid. Araquistáin Papers, Leg. 58/v7^b. Photocopy in Hoover Institution, Bolloten Collection.

————. *La verdad sobre la intervención y la no-intervención en España.* Madrid: n.p., 1938.

Les archives secrètes de la Wilhelmstrasse: De Neurath a Ribbentrop. Septembre 1937–Septembre 1938. Paris: Plon, 1950.

Archivo Histórico Nacional. *Papeles de Don Luis Araquistáin Quevado.* Organized under the direction of María Teresa de la Peña Marazuela. Prólogo de Javier Tusell. Madrid: Archivo Histórico Nacional, 1938. Photocopies of several hundred of these documents are in the Hoover Institution, Bolloten Collection.

Archivo Histórico Nacional, Salamanca. Sección Guerra Civil.

Ardiaca, Pere. *Intervenció de Pere Ardiaca del c.c. en la primera conferéncia nacional del Partit Socialista Unificat de Catalunya (I.C.).* Barcelona: Edicions del Secretariat d'Agitació i Propaganda del PSUC, n.d.

Arenillas, José. *Euzkadi, la cuestión nacional y la revolución socialista.* Paris: La Batalla, 1969.

Arenillas de Claves, Ignacio. *El proceso de Besteiro.* Madrid: Revista de Occidente, 1976.

Arias Velasco, José. *La hacienda de la Generalidad, 1931–1938.* Barcelona: Ariel, 1977.

L'armée de la république espagnole qui défend la démocratie et la paix. Paris, [1937?].

Armero, José-Mario. *España fue noticias: Corresponsales extranjeros en la guerra civil española.* Madrid: Sedmay, 1976.

Armiñán, Luis de. *Bajo el cielo de Levante.* Madrid: Ediciones Españolas, 1939.

————. *Por los caminos de guerra: De Navalcarnero a Gijon.* Madrid: Ediciones Españolas, 1939.

Arnau, Roger. *Marxisme català i qüestió nacíonal catalana, 1930–36.* Vol. II. Paris: Edicions Catalanes, 1974.

Aron, Raymond. *Entre Deux Guerres.* Vol. III. New York: Brentano, 1946.

Aróstegui Sánchez, Julio, and Martínez, Jesús A. *La junta de defensa de Madrid.* Madrid: Comunidad de Madrid, 1984.

*Arquer, Jordi. Letter to Bolloten on his meeting in 1950 with Manuel Hernando Solana (magistrate on the Tribunal of Espionage and High Treason during trial of the POUM leaders).

*_____. Miscellaneous correspondence with Burnett Bolloten.

_____. Verbatim account of public prosecutor's cross-examination of Arquer during the POUM trial in October 1938.

Arques, Enrique. *17 de julio: La epopeya de Africa*. Madrid: Reus, 1948.

Arrabal, Juan. *José María Gil Robles*. Avila: Senén Martín Díaz, 1935.

Arrarás, Joaquín. *Historia de la segunda república española*. Vols. I, II, III, IV. Madrid: Editora Nacional, 1964 and 1968.

_____. *Memorias íntimas de Azaña*. Madrid: Ediciones Españolas, 1939.

_____. *El sitio del Alcázar de Toledo*. Saragossa: Heraldo de Aragón, 1937.

_____, ed. *Historia de la cruzada española*. 12 vols. Madrid: Ediciones Españolas, 1940.

Arrigoni, Enrico [Carl Brand, pseud.]. *Freedom: My Dream*. Sun City: Western World Press, 1985.

Arsenio de Izaga, G. *Los presos de Madrid*. Madrid: Martosa, 1940.

Artal, Francesc, et al. *El pensament economic català durant la republica i la guerra, 1931–1939*. Barcelona: Ediciones 62, 1976.

Artola, Miguel. *Partidos y programas políticos, 1808–1936*. Vol. I: *Los partidos políticos*. Vol. II: *Manifiestos y programas políticos*. Madrid: Aguilar, 1974, 1975.

Asedio de Huesca. Huesca: Ayuntamiento de Huesca, [1938?].

*Asensio, General José. Correspondence with Burnett Bolloten.

_____. *El General Asensio: Su lealtad a la república*. Barcelona: Artes Gráficas CNT, 1938.

L'assassinat de Andrés Nin. Paris: Spartacus, 1939.

Assassination of Catholic Priests in the Diocese of Barcelona, Spain, under the So-called Spanish Republic, Now the Spanish Republic in Exile. Washington, D.C.: Spanish Embassy, [1946?].

Atholl, Katherine, Duchess of. *My Impressions of Spain*. Essex: Lucas, 1937.

_____. *Report of Our Visit to Spain*. London: Caledonian Press, [1937?].

_____. *Searchlight on Spain*. Harmondsworth, England: Penguin, 1938.

Aub, Max. *Ultimos cuentos de la guerra de España*. Caracas: Arte, 1969.

Aunós Pérez, Eduardo. *Calvo Sotelo: Le drame de l'Espagne contemporaine*. Paris: Éditions de France, 1943.

Autour du procès du POUM. Paris: Independent News, 1938.

Avilés, Gabriel. *Tribunales rojos: Vistos por un abogado defensor*. Barcelona: Destino, 1939.

Avilés Farré, Juan. *La izquierda burguesa en la II República*. Madrid: Espasa-Calpe, 1985.

Ayala, José Antonio. *Murcia en la II república*. Murcia: Comunidad Autónoma de Murcia, 1984.

Azaña, Manuel. *Los españoles en guerra*. Barcelona: Grijalbo, 1977.

_____. *Madrid*. London: Friends of Spain, 1937.

_____. *Obras completas*. Edited by Juan Marichal. Vols. III, IV. Mexico City: Oasis, 1967, 1968.

_____. *Una política, 1932–1933*. Madrid: Espasa Calpe, 1932.

————. *Speech by His Excellency the President of the Spanish Republic, January 21, 1937.* London: Spanish Embassy, 1937.

————. *La velada en Benicarló.* Buenos Aires: Losada, 1939.

————. *A Year of War in Spain.* London: Friends of Spain, 1937.

Azaña-Prieto tapes. Teletyped messages exchanged between Prieto and Azaña during the May events in Barcelona, 3–7 May 1937. Servicio Histórico Militar, Madrid. A microfilm copy is in the Hoover Institution.

Azaretto, Manuel. *Las pendientes resbaladizas: Los anarquistas en España.* Preface by José A. Barrionuevo. Montevideo: Germinal, 1939.

Azcárate, Pablo de. *Mi embajada en Londres durante la guerra civil española.* Barcelona: Ariel, 1976.

Aznar, Manuel. *Historia militar de la guerra de España.* Madrid: Idea, 1940.

Bahamonde y Sánchez de Castro, Antonio. *Un año con Queipo de Llano.* Mexico City: Nuestro Tiempo, 1938.

————. *Memoirs of a Spanish Nationalist.* London: United Editorial, 1939.

Bajatierra, Maura. *Crónicas de la Guerra.* Valencia: Subsecretaria de Propaganda, 1937.

Bajo la bandera de la España republicana. Moscow: Progreso, 1967.

Baker, Carlos. *Ernest Hemingway: A Life Story.* New York: Scribner's Sons, 1969.

Bakunin, M. A. *Bog i gosudarstvo.* New York: Union of Russian Workers of the City of New York, 1918.

————. *Gosudarstvennost i anarkhiia.* Petersburg-Moscow: Gosudarstvennoe Izdanie, 1922.

Balbontín, José Antonio. *La España de mi experiencia.* Mexico City: Colección Aquelarre, 1952.

Balcells, Albert. *Cataluña contemporánea II, 1900–1936.* Madrid: Siglo XXI, 1974.

————. *Crisis económica y agitación social en Cataluña, 1930–1936.* Barcelona: Ariel, 1971.

————. *Marxismo y catalanismo, 1930–1936.* Barcelona: Anagrama, 1977.

————. *El problema agrario en Cataluña: La cuestión Rabassaire, 1890–1936.* Madrid: Ministerio de Agricultura, 1980.

*Balius, Jaime. Correspondence with Burnett Bolloten.

————. *Towards a Fresh Revolution* (translation of *Hacia una nueva revolución*). The Friends of Durruti Group. Orkney: Cienfuegos Press, 1978.

Baráibar, Carlos de. *Las falsas "posiciones socialistas" de Indalecio Prieto.* Madrid: Yunque, 1935.

————. *La guerra de España en el plano internacional.* Barcelona: Tierre y Libertad, 1938.

La Barbarie Roja. Valladolid: Santarén, 1938.

Barça, J. O. *La obra financiera de la generalidad durante los seis primeros meses de la revolución.* Paris: Association Hispanophile de France, 1937.

Barcellona, Antonio María de. *Martiri della rivoluzione del 1936 nella Catalogna.* Milan-Rome: Società Editrice Internazionale, 1937.

Barcelona Traction, Light, and Power Company, Limited. Statements issued on 3 September and 16 November 1936. Public Library of Toronto.

Bardoux, Jacques. *Chaos in Spain.* London: Burns Oates and Washbourne, 1937.

————. *Staline contre l'Europe.* Paris: Flammarion, 1937.

944 · Bibliography

*Barea, Arturo. Correspondence with Burnett Bolloten.
———. *The Forging of a Rebel*. New York: Reynal Hitchcock, 1946.
*Barea, Ilsa. Correspondence with Burnett Bolloten.
Barrio, José del. *Intervención en la primera conferencia nacional del Partido Socialista Unificado de Cataluña (I.C.) celebrada durante los dias 24 a 26 de julio de 1937*. Barcelona: Agitación y Propaganda del PSU, 1937.
———. *3er congrés de la UGT a Catalunya*. Informe de Josep del Barrio. Barcelona: UGT, 1937.
Barron, John. *KGB*. New York: Dutton, 1974.
Bateman, Don. *Joaquín Maurín, 1893–1973*. Leeds, England: I.L.P. Square One Publications, 1974.
*Bates, Ralph. Correspondence with Burnett Bolloten.
———. *En la España leal ha nacido un ejército*. Mexico, [1937?].
Batov, Pavel I. *V pokhodakh i boiakh*. Moscow: Voennoe Izdatel'stvo, 1966.
Battaglione Garibaldi. Paris: Edizioni di Cultura Sociale, 1937.
Bauer, Eddy. *Impressions et expériences de la Guerre d'Espagne*. Lausanne: Imprimeries Reunies, 1938.
Bayerlein, Bernard. "Die Kommunistische Partei Spaniens als Sektion der Kommunistischen Internationale vor dem Spanischen Bürgerkrieg, 1931–1936." Dissertation. Bochum: Ruhr-Universität, 1978.
Bayo, Capitán Alberto. *Mi desembarco en Mallorca*. Guadalajara, Mexico: Imprenta Gráfica, 1944.
Bécarud, Jean. *La segunda república española*. Madrid: Taurus, 1967.
Bécarud, Jean, and Lapouge, Gilles. *Anarchistes de'Espagne*. Paris: Balland, 1970.
Bécarud, Jean, and López Campillo, E. *Los intelectuales españoles durante la II República*. Madrid: Siglo XXI, 1978.
Bédarida, François. *La stratégie secrète de la drôle de guerre*. Paris: Presses de la Fondation Nationale des Sciences Politiques et Editions du CNRS, 1979.
Bedford Jones, Nancy. *Students under Arms*. New York: North American Committee to Aid Spanish Democracy, 1938.
Bejarano, Benigno. See Lazarillo de Tormes.
Belausteguigoitia, Ramón de. *Euzkadi en llamas*. Mexico City: Botas, 1938.
Belforte, General Francesco. *La guerra civile in Spagna*. Vol. I: *La disintegrazione dello stato*. Vol. II: *Gli interventi stranieri nella Spagna rossa*. Vol. III: *La campagna dei volontari italiani*. Vol. IV: *La campagna dei volontari italiani e la vittoria di Franco*. Milan: Istituto per gli studi di política internazionale, 1938, 1939.
Beliaev, N., comp. *Mikhail Koltsov: Kakim on byl: vospominaniia*. Moscow: Sovetskii Pisatel', 1965.
Bellmunt, Domènec de. *Lluis Companys*. Toulouse: Foc Nou, 1945.
Beloff, Max. *The Foreign Policy of Soviet Russia, 1929–1941*. 2 vols. London-New York-Toronto: Oxford University Press, 1947.
Ben-Ami, Shlomó. *La revolución desde arriba: España, 1936–1979*. Barcelona: Ríopiedras, 1980.
Benavides, Manuel D. *La escuadra la mandan los cabos*. Mexico City: n.p., 1944.
———. *Guerra y revolución en Cataluña*. Mexico City: Tenochtitlan, 1946.
———. *Luz sobre España*. Mexico City: Tenochtitlan, 1944.
Bennett, Milly. Archives. Hoover Institution.

Berdión, Auxilio. *Madrid en tinieblas: Siluetas de la revolución.* Madrid-Valencia: Salmantina, 1937.

Berenguer, Dámaso. *De la dictadura a la república.* Madrid: Plus-ultra, 1946.

Bergamín, José. *Marañón's Betrayal.* n.p., [193–?].

Berlin Institut für Marxismus-Leninismus. *Der Freiheitskampf der spanischen Volkes und die internationale Solidarität.* Berlin: Dietz, 1956.

Bernanos, Georges. *Les grandes cimitières sous la lune.* Paris: Plon, 1938.

Bernard, Ino. *Mola, mártir de España.* Granada: Prieto, 1938.

Bernecker, Walther L. *Anarchismus und Bürgerkrieg.* Hamburg: Hoffmann and Campe, 1978.

―――. *Kollektivismus und Freiheit.* Munich: Deutscher Taschenbuch, 1980.

―――. *Die soziale Revolution im Spanischen Bürgerkrieg.* Munich: Ernst Vögel, 1977.

Bernecker, Walther L., and Hallerbach, Jörg. *Anarchismus als Alternative?* Berlin: Kramer, 1986.

Berneri, Camillo. *Entre la revolución y las trincheras (1936–1937, Barcelona),* No. 21. France: Tierra y Libertad, 1946.

―――. *Guerra de clases en España, 1936–1937.* Barcelona: Tusquets, 1977.

―――. *Mussolini a la conquista de las Baleares.* Buenos Aires: Servicio de Propaganda de España, 1938.

―――. *Pietrogrado 1917/Barcellona, 1937.* Milan: Sugar, 1964.

Berryer. *Revolutionary Justice in Spain.* London: Burns Oates and Washbourne, [1937?].

Bertrán Güell, Felipe. *Caudillo, profetas y soldados.* Madrid-Barcelona: Editorial Juventud, 1939.

―――. *Preparación y desarrollo del alzamiento nacional.* Valladolid: Santarén, 1938.

Bertrán y Musitu, José. *Experiencias de los servicios de información del nordeste de España (SIFNE) durante la guerra.* Madrid: Espasa-Calpe, 1940.

Bessie, Alvah. *Men in Battle.* New York: Scribner's Sons, 1939.

―――. *Spain Again.* San Francisco: Chandler and Sharp, 1975.

―――, ed. *The Heart of Spain.* New York: Veterans of the Abraham Lincoln Brigade, 1952.

Bessie, Alvah, and Prago, Albert, eds. *Our Fight: Writings by Veterans of the Abraham Lincoln Brigade, Spain 1936–1939.* New York: Monthly Review Press, 1987.

Besteiro, Julián. *Marxismo y antimarxismo.* Mexico City: Pablo Iglesias, 1966.

Bethune, Norman. *El crimen del camino Malaga-Almeria.* Valencia: Iberia, 1937.

Beumelburg, Werner. *Kampf um Spanien: Die Geschichte de Legion Condor.* Oldenburg-Berlin: Gerhard Stalling, 1939.

Bezucha, Robert J., ed. *Modern European Social History.* Boston: Heath, 1972.

Bialer, Seweryn, ed. *Stalin and His Generals: Soviet Military Memoirs of World War II.* New York: Pegasus, 1969.

Bibliothèques du front et de l'arrière en Espagne républicaine. Barcelona: Editions Espagnoles, 1938.

Bilainkin, George. *Ivan Mikhailovitch Maisky: Ten Years Ambassador.* London: Allen and Unwin, 1944.

"Bilan": Textos sobre la revolución española, 1936–1938. Barcelona: Etcétera, 1978.

Biographical Dictionary of Marxism. See Gorman, Robert A.

Birkenhead, Earl of. *Halifax: The Life of Lord Halifax.* Boston: Houghton Mifflin, 1966.

Bizcarrondo, Marta. *Araquistáin y la crisis socialista en la II república, Leviatán, 1934–1936.* Madrid: Siglo XXI, 1975.

_____. *Octubre del 34: Reflexiones sobre una revolución.* Madrid: Ayuso, 1977.

Blackstock, Paul W. *The Secret Road to World War II: Soviet Versus Western Intelligence, 1921–1939.* Chicago: Quadrangle Books, 1969.

Blackwell, Russell [Rosalio Negrete, pseud.]. Correspondence with Hugo Oehler, 1936–37. Brandeis University, Hugo Oehler Papers.

*Bland, Roger. Correspondence with Burnett Bolloten.

Blanshard, Paul. *Freedom and Catholic Power in Spain and Portugal.* Boston: Beacon Press, 1962.

Bley, Wulf. *Das Buch der Spanienflieger.* Leipzig: Hase and Koehler, 1939.

Blinkhorn, Martin. *Carlism and Crisis in Spain, 1931–1939.* Cambridge: Cambridge University Press, 1975.

_____, ed. *Spain in Conflict, 1931–1939: Democracy and Its Enemies.* London: Sage, 1986.

Bloch, Jean Richard. *Espagne, Espagne!* Paris: Editions Sociales Internationales, 1936.

_____. *España en armas.* Mexico City: Pax, 1937.

The Blodgett Collection of Spanish Civil War Pamphlets. Cambridge, Mass.: Harvard College Library, 1980. This booklet contains a listing of several hundred pamphlets. The microfiche of the entire collection is in the Hoover Institution.

Blythe, Henry. *Spain over Britain.* London: Routledge, 1937.

Bocca, Giorgio. *Palmiro Togliatti.* Rome: Laterza, 1977.

Bochot, Pierre. *Les volontaires du peuple.* Perigueux: Soleil Levant, 1947.

Bohlen, Charles. *Witness to History, 1929–1969.* New York: Norton, 1973.

Bolín, Luis. *España: Los años vitales.* Madrid: Espasa Calpe, 1967.

_____. *Spain: The Vital Years.* London: Cassell, 1967.

*Bolívar, Candido. Interview, notes taken by Burnett Bolloten.

Bollati, Ambrogio, and Bono, Giulio del. *La guerra di Spagna.* Torino: Giulio Einaudi, 1937.

*Bolloten, Burnett. Clippings from over 500 different newspapers, periodicals, and government publications arranged chronologically in 986 large envelopes and 10 bound volumes covering each day of the Civil War. Additional envelopes contain clippings covering the first years of the postwar period.

*_____. "Dispatch from Valencia to the London Bureau of the United Press, 31 December 1936."

*_____. "Dispatch from Valencia to the United Press. Excerpts from Largo Caballero's unpublished statement to British Members of Parliament on 4 December 1936."

*_____. "Dispatch from Valencia to the United Press, 18 June 1937."

_____. "Dispatch from Valencia to the United Press, 7 July 1937."

_____. *The Grand Camouflage: The Spanish Civil War and Revolution, 1936–39.* New York: Praeger, 1961, 1968. Introduction to the second printing by H. R. Trevor-Roper.

_____. *El gran engaño.* Barcelona: Caralt, 1961, 1967, 1975, 1984.

*————. Interviews: Shorthand notes taken during Burnett Bolloten's interviews with some of the leading Civil War participants. Some transcripts are available.

*————. Microfilm collection of newspapers, periodicals, government publications, books, pamphlets, and documents comprising 7,250 items.

*————. Miscellaneous Documents. Vols. I, II, III, IV. These consist of typewritten copies of directives and reports by political commissars and military leaders, manifestos and articles, as well as original passes by revolutionary organizations. The original directives and reports were loaned to Burnett Bolloten by Vittorio Vidali (Carlos Contreras).

————. *La revolución española: Sus orígines, la izquierda y la lucha por el poder durante la guerra civil.* Foreword by Gabriel Jackson. Barcelona: Grijalbo, 1980.

————. *The Spanish Revolution: The Left and the Struggle for Power during the Civil War.* Foreword by Raymond Carr. Chapel Hill: University of North Carolina Press, 1979.

Bol'shaia sovetskaia entsiklopediia. Moscow: [1st ed. 1926–47; 2d ed. 1950–60; 3d ed. 1970–].

Bombardments et agressions en Espagne: Juillet 1936–juillet 1938. Paris: Comité Mondial contre la Guerre el le Fascisme, 1938.

Bombs over Barcelona. New York: North American Committee to Aid Spanish Democracy, 1938.

Bonamusa, Francesc. *Andreu Nin y el movimiento comunista en España, 1930–1937.* Barcelona: Anagrama, 1977.

————. *El bloc obrer i camperol, 1930–1932.* Barcelona: Curial, 1974.

Bonastre. *Características fundamentales del ejército popular.* Barcelona: Publicacions Antifeixistes de Catalunya, 1938.

Bonnet, Georges. *Défense de la paix: De Washington au Quai d'Orsay.* Genève: Bourquin, 1946.

————. *Défense de la paix: Fin d'une Europe.* Genève: Bourquin, 1948.

Bookchin, Murray. *The Spanish Anarchists: The Heroic Years, 1868–1936.* New York: Free Life Editors, 1977.

Borkenau, Franz. *The Spanish Cockpit.* London: Faber and Faber, 1937.

Borrás, José. *Políticas de los exilados españoles 1944-1950.* Paris: Ruedo Iberico, 1976.

Borrás T. *Checas de Madrid.* Madrid: Escelicer, 1940.

Borrás Cascarosa, José. *Aragón en la revolución española.* Barcelona: Viguera, 1983.

Borrás Llop, José María. *Francia ante la guerra civil española: Burguesía, interés nacional e interés de clase.* Madrid: Centro de Investigaciones Sociológias, 1981.

Bortsy Latvii v Ispanii, 1936–1939: Vospominaniia i dokumenty. Riga: Institu Istori Partii pri Tsk KP Latvii. Filial Institua Marksizma-Leninizma pri Tsk. KPSS., 1970.

Bosch Gimpera, Pere. *Memòries.* Barcelona: Edicions 62, 1980.

Bosch Sánchez, Aurora. *Ugetistas y libertarios: Guerra civil y revolución en el país valenciano, 1936–1939.* Valencia: Soler, 1983.

A Boss for Spain. Madrid: SIE, 1964.

Botin, Mikhail. *Za svobodu Ispanii.* Moscow: Sovetskaia Rossiia, 1986.

Bougöuin, E., and Lenoir, P. *La finance internationale et la guerre d'Espagne.* Paris: Centre d'études de Paix et Démocratie, 1938.

Bouthelier, Antonio, and López Mora, José. *Ocho días: La revuelta comunista, Madrid, 5–13 marzo 1939.* Madrid: Editora Nacional, 1940.

Bowers, Claude. *My Mission to Spain.* New York: Simon and Schuster, 1954.

Boyle, Andrew. *Montagu Norman.* London: Cassell, 1967.

Brademas, John. *Anarcosindicalismo y revolución en España, 1930–1937.* Barcelona: Ariel, 1974.

Brandt, Willy. *Bericht über Krieg und Revolution in Spanien.* n.p.: Socialistischen Arbeiter Partei Deutschlands, 1937.

_____. *Ein Jahr Krieg und Revolution in Spanien.* Referat des Gen. Brandt auf der Sitzung der erweiterten Partei-Leitung der SAP, Anfang Juli, 1937. Paris: Sozialistischen Arbeiter-Partei Deutschlands, 1937.

Brasa, Juan. *España y la Legion.* Valladolid: Santarén, 1938.

Brasillach, Robert. *Histoire de la Guerre d'Espagne.* Paris: Plon, 1939.

_____. *Le Siège de l'Alcazar.* Paris: Plon, 1939.

Braubach, Max. *Hitlers Weg zur Verständigung mit Russland im Jahre 1939.* Bonn: Hanstein, 1960.

Bravo Martínez, Francisco. *Historia de la Falange Española de las JONS.* Madrid: Editora Nacional, 1940.

Bravo Morata, Federico. *Historia de la república.* Vol. II: *1934–1939.* Madrid: Daimon, 1977.

_____. *Historia de Madrid.* Vol. III. Madrid: Fenicia, 1968.

_____. *La reforma agraria de la república.* Madrid: Fenicia, 1978.

_____. *La república y el ejército.* Madrid: Fenicia, 1978.

Brea, Juan, and Low, Mary. *Red Spanish Notebook.* London: Martin Secker, 1937.

Brenan, Gerald. *The Face of Spain.* New York: Pellegrini and Cudahy, 1951.

_____. *Memoria personal, 1920–1975.* Madrid: Alianza, 1979.

_____. *Personal Record, 1920–1972.* New York: Knopf, 1975.

_____. *The Spanish Labyrinth.* London: Cambridge University Press, 1943.

Brenner, Anita. *Class War in Spain: An Exposure of Fascism, Stalinism, etc.* Sydney: Socialist Labour Party of Australia, 1937.

Brereton, Geoffrey. *Inside Spain.* London: London Quality Press, 1938.

Brezhnev, Leonid I. *Following Lenin's Course: Speeches and Articles.* Moscow: Progress, 1972.

Bricall, Josep M. *Política económica de la Generalitat, 1936–1939.* Barcelona: Edicions 62, 1970.

La brigada del amanecer. Valladolid: Santarén, n.d.

Brigada Internacional ist unser Ehrenname: Erlebnisse ehemaliger deutscher Spanienkämpfer. 2 vols. East Berlin: Militärverlag der Deutschen Demokratischen Republik, 1986.

Briones, Mariano. *La juventud anarquista: Factor determinativo de la guerra y de la revolución.* Barcelona: Agrupación Anarquista "Los de Ayer y los de Hoy," 1937.

Brissaud, André. *Canaris.* Paris: Tallandier, 1971.

_____. *Canaris: The Biography of Admiral Canaris, Chief of German Military Intelligence.* Translated and edited by Ian Colvin. New York: Grosset and Dunlop, 1973.

British Medical Aid in Spain. London: News Chronicle, n.d.

Brockway, Fenner. *Truth about Barcelona*. London: Independent Labour Party, 1937.

———. *Workers' Front*. London: Secker and Warburg, 1938.

Brome, Vincent. *The International Brigades*. London: Heinemann, 1965.

Brook-Shepherd, Gordon. *Anschluss: The Rape of Austria*. London: Macmillan, 1963.

———. *The Storm Petrels: The Flight of the First Soviet Defectors*. New York: Harcourt Brace Jovanovich, 1978.

Broué, Pierre. See also Trotsky, *La révolution espagnole*.

*———. Correspondence with Burnett Bolloten.

Broué, Pierre; Fraser, R.; and Vílar, P. *Metodología histórica de la guerra y revolución españolas*. Barcelona: Fontamara, 1980.

Broué, Pierre, and Témime, Emile. *La révolution et la guerre d'Espagne*. Paris: Les Editions de Minuit, 1961.

Browder, Earl. *Lenin and Spain*. New York: Workers Library, 1937.

———. *Next Steps to Win the War in Spain*. New York: Workers Library, 1938.

———. *Win the War in Spain!* New York: Workers Library, 1937.

Buckley, Henry. *Life and Death of the Spanish Republic*. London: Hamish Hamilton, 1940.

Buckley, William F., Jr., and Bozell, L. Brent. *McCarthy and His Enemies: The Record and Its Meaning*. Chicago: Regnery, 1954.

Buenacasa, Manuel. *El movimiento obrero español, 1886–1926*. Madrid: Júcar, 1977.

———. *Por la unidad CNT-UGT: Perspectivas del movimiento obrero español*. Mexico City: Salvador Segui, 1964.

Bueso, Adolfo. *Como fundamos la CNT*. Barcelona: Avance, 1976.

———. *Recuerdos de un cenetista*. Vol. II. Barcelona: Ariel, 1978.

Bullejos, José. *La comintern en España: Recuerdos de mi vida*. Mexico, D.F.: Impresiones Modernas, 1972.

*———. Correspondence with Burnett Bolloten.

———. *España en la segunda república*. Mexico City: Impresiones Modernas, 1967.

———. *Europa entre dos guerras, 1918–1938*. Mexico City: Castilla, 1945.

Bullock, Alan. *Hitler: A Study in Tyranny*. New York: Harper and Row, 1964.

Burgo, Jaime del. *Conspiración y guerra civil*. Madrid: Alfaguara, 1970.

Burns, Emilio. *La conspiración nazi en España*. Mexico City: Editorial Revolucionaria, 1938.

———. *Spain*. London: Communist Party of Great Britain, 1936.

Butler, James Ramsay Montagu. *Lord Lothian (Philip Kerr), 1882–1940*. London: Macmillan, 1960.

Les buts militaires de l'Allemagne et de l'Italie dans la guerre d'Espagne. Paris: Comité Mondial contre la Guerre et le Fascisme, 1938.

Caballé y Clos, Tomás. *Barcelona Roja*. Barcelona: Librería Argentina, 1939.

Cabanellas, Guillermo. *Cuatro generales: Preludio a la guerra civil*. Barcelona: Planeta, 1977.

———. *La guerra civil y la victoria*. Madrid: Tebas, 1978.

———. *La guerra de los mil días: Nacimiento, vida y muerte de la II república española*. Vols. I, II. Barcelona, Buenos Aires, Mexico City: Grijalbo, 1973.

Cabezas, Juan Antonio. *Asturias: Catorce meses de guerra civil*. Madrid: Toro, 1975.

Cabo Giorla, Luis. *Primera conferencia nacional del P.S.U.C*. Barcelona: Ediciones del Departamento de Agitación y Propaganda del PSUC, 1937.

Cadden, J. *Spain 1936*. New York: International Youth Commission, 1936.

Cadogan, Sir Alexander. *The Diaries of Sir Alexander Cadogan, 1938–1945*. Edited by David Dilks. London: Cassell, 1971.

Camba, Francisco. *Madridgrado*. Documental film, 2d ed. Madrid: Ediciones Espanoles, 1940.

Camillo Atrayente. Barcelona: Tierra y Libertad, 1937.

Caminal, Miquel. *Joan Comorera*. Vol. I: *Catalanisme i socialisme, 1913–1936*. Vol. II: *Guerra i revolució, 1936–1939*. Barcelona: Empúries, 1984.

Camino, Jaime. *Intimas conversaciones con la Pasionaria*. Barcelona: Dopesa, 1977.

El camino de la victoria. Valencia: Gráficas Genovés, [1936?].

Campbell, J. R. *Soviet Policy and Its Critics*. London: Gollancz, 1939.

_____. *Spain's "Left" Critics*. London: Communist Party of Great Britain, 1937.

Campbell Doherty, Julian. *Das Ende des Appeasement*. Berlin: Hess, 1973.

El Campesino [Valentín González]. *Comunista en España y antistalinista en la U.R.S.S*. Mexico City: Guarania, 1952.

_____. *La vie et la mort en U.R.S.S., 1939–1949*. Paris: Plon, 1950.

_____. *Yo escogí la esclavitud*. Barcelona: Plaza y Janés, 1977.

Campoamor, Clara. *La révolution espagnole vue par une républicaine*. Paris: Plon, 1937.

*Campos, Severino. Correspondence with Burnett Bolloten.

Cánovas Cervantes, S. *Apuntes históricos de "Solidaridad Obrera."* Barcelona: Ediciones C.R.T., n.d.

_____. *De Franco a Negrín pasando por el partido comunista: Historia de la revolución española*. Toulouse: Páginas Libres, n.d.

_____. *Durruti y Ascaso: La CNT y la revolución de julio*. Toulouse: Páginas Libres, n.d.

Cantalupo, Roberto. *Fu la Spagna*. Ambasciata presso Franco. Febbraio–Aprile 1937. Milan: Arnolde Mondadori, 1948.

Cantarero del Castillo, Manuel. *Tragedia del socialismo español*. Barcelona: Dopesa, 1971.

Capo, José María. *España desnuda*. Havana: Publicationes España, 1938.

Carabantes, Andrés, and Cimorra, Eusebio. *Un mito llamado Pasionaria*. Barcelona: Planeta, 1982.

Carabias, Josefina. *Azaña: Los que le llamábamos Don Manuel*. Esplugues de Llobregat: Plaza y Janés, 1980.

*Carbajal, Captain Aniceto. Interview, notes taken by Burnett Bolloten.

Cardona, Gabriel. *El poder militar en la España contemporánea hasta la guerra civil*. Madrid: Siglo XXI, 1983.

Cardona Rosell, Mariano. *Aspectos económicos de nuestra revolución*. Barcelona: CNT-FAI, 1937.

*_____. Correspondence with Burnett Bolloten.

Carney, William P. *No Democratic Government in Spain.* New York: America Press, 1937.

Carr, Edward Hallet. *The Comintern and the Spanish Civil War.* London: Macmillan, 1984.

————. *The Foreign Policy of Britain, 1918–1939.* London: Longmans, Green, 1939.

————. *German-Soviet Relations between the Two World Wars, 1919–1939.* Baltimore: Johns Hopkins Press, 1951.

Carr, Raymond. *Modern Spain: 1875–1980.* Oxford: Oxford University Press, 1980.

————. *Spain, 1808–1939.* Oxford: Oxford University Press, 1966.

————. *The Spanish Civil War: A History in Pictures.* New York: Norton, 1986.

————. *The Spanish Tragedy: The Civil War in Perspective.* London: Weidenfeld and Nicolson, 1977.

————, ed. *Estudios sobre la república y la guerra civil española.* Barcelona: Ariel, 1973.

————, ed. *The Republic and the Civil War in Spain.* London: Macmillan, 1971.

Carrascal, Geminiano. *Asturias: 18 julio 1936–21 octubre 1937.* Valladolid: Casa Martín, 1938.

Carrasco, C. *Como se destrozan los tanques enemigos.* Valencia: J.S.U., 1937.

Carrasquer, Félix. *Las colectividades de Aragón: Un vivir autogestionado, promesa de futuro.* Barcelona: Laia, 1986.

Carrero Blanco, Luis. *España y el mar: El mar en la guerra y en la paz hasta la II guerra mundial.* Madrid: Instituto de Estudios Políticos, 1962.

Carrillo, Santiago. *Demain l'Espagne: Entretiens avec Régis Debray et Max Gallo.* Paris: Editions du Seuil, 1974.

————. *En marcha hacia la victoria.* Valencia: Partido Comunista de España, 1937.

————. *La juventud, factor de la victoria.* Valencia: Partido Comunista de España, 1937.

————. *Somos la organización de la juventud.* Madrid: n.p., n.d.

*Carrillo, Wenceslao. Correspondence with Burnett Bolloten.

————. *El último episodio de la guerra civil española.* Toulouse: La Secretaría de Publicaciones de la J.S.E. en Francia, 1945.

Carrión, Pascual. *Los latifundios en España.* Madrid: Gráficas Reunidas, 1932.

————. *La reforma agraria de la segunda república y la situación actual de la agricultura.* Barcelona: Ariel, 1973.

Casado, Colonel Segismundo. *Así cayó Madrid.* Madrid: Guardiana, 1968.

————. *The Last Days of Madrid.* London: Peter Davies, 1939.

Casanova, M. *L'Espagne livrée.* Paris: Ligue Comuniste, 1971.

————. *La guerra de España: El frente popular abrió las puertas a Franco.* Barcelona: Fontamara, 1978.

Casanova Ruiz, Julián. *Anarquismo y revolución en la sociedad rural aragonesa, 1936–1938.* Madrid: Siglo XXI, 1985.

————. *Caspe, 1936–1938.* Zaragoza: Grupo Cultural Caspolino, 1984.

Casanovas, Joan. *Une pensée et une attitude: Discours, notes et déclarations, 1936–1939.* Paris: Grifé, [1939].

Casares, Francisco. *Azaña y ellos*. Granada: Prieto, 1938.

Castelao, Alfonso R. *Galicia mártir*. Valencia: Ministerio de Propaganda, 1937.

Castells, Andreu. *Las brigadas internacionales de la guerra de España*. Barcelona: Ariel, 1974.

Casterás Archidona, Ramón. *Las juventudes socialistas unificadas de Cataluña: Ante la guerra y la revolución, 1936–1939*. Barcelona: Hogar, 1982.

Castilla, Floreal. *El anarquismo ibérico: La FAI y la CNT*. Supplement to *Espoir*, #780. Toulouse, n.d.

Castrillo Santos, Juan. *Revolución en España*. Buenos Aires: Librería la Facultad, 1938.

Castro, Fidel. *Revolutionary Struggle, 1947–1958. Selected Works*, Vol. I. Cambridge, Mass.: MIT Press, 1972.

Castro Albarrán, A. de. *El derecho al alzamiento*. Salamanca: Henricus, 1940.

————. *La gran víctima: La iglesia española martir de la revolución roja*. Salamanca: Henricus, 1940.

Castro Delgado, Enrique. *Balance y perspectivas de nuestra guerra*. Barcelona: Partido Comunista de España, Comisión Nacional de Agit-Prop, 1937.

*————. Correspondence with Burnett Bolloten.

————. *Hombres made in Moscú*. Mexico City: Publications Mañana, 1960.

————. *J'ai perdu la foi à Moscou*. Paris: Gallimard, 1950.

Castro Marcos, Miguel de. *El ministerio de instrucción pública bajo la dominación roja*. Madrid: Enrique Prieto, 1939.

Castrovido, Roberto. *Las dos républicas: El 11 de febrero y el 14 de abril*. Barcelona: Ediciones españolas, [1938?].

Catalla, Bernard, ed. *Problèmes de la construction et du logement dans la revolution espagnole, 1936–39: Barcelone, Aragón*. Toulouse: n.p., 1976.

A Catholic Looks at Spain. London: Labour Publications Department, 1937.

Catholics and the Civil War in Spain: A Collection of Statements by World-famous Catholic Leaders on the Events in Spain. New York: Workers Library, 1936.

Catholics Reply to Open Letter of 150 Protestant Signatories on Spain. New York: America Press, [1937?].

Cattell, David T. *Communism and the Spanish Civil War*. Berkeley: University of California Press, 1955.

————. *Soviet Diplomacy and the Spanish Civil War*. Berkeley: University of California Press, 1957.

Caudet, F. *História política de Catalunya*. Barcelona: Producciones Editoriales, 1978.

Causa general: La dominación roja en España. Madrid: Dirección General de Información, 1961.

Caute, David. *The Fellow Travellers*. New York: Macmillan, 1973.

Cave Brown, Anthony C., and MacDonald, Charles B. *On a Field of Red: The Communist International and the Coming of World War II*. New York: Putnam, 1981.

Cavero y Cavero, Francisco. *Con la segunda bandera en el frente de Aragón*. Zaragoza: Heraldo de Aragón, 1938.

Cayette, André. *Sauvons la France en Espagne*. Paris: Baudinière, 1937.

Cerezo Martínez, Ricardo. *Armada española, siglo XX*. 4 vols. Madrid: Poniente, 1983.

Cervera Pery, José. *Alzamiento y revolución en la marina*. Madrid: San Martín, 1978.

Cervera Valderrama, Almirante Juan. *Memorias de guerra*. Madrid: Editora Nacional, 1968.

Ceyrat, Maurice. *La trahison permanente. Parti communiste et politique russe*. Paris: Spartacus, 1948.

Chacón, R. L. *Por qué hice las chekas de Barcelona: Laúrencic ante el consejo de guerra*. Barcelona: Solidaridad Nacional, 1939.

Chalmers Mitchell, Sir Peter. *My House in Malaga*. London: Faber, 1938.

Chamberlain, Neville. *The Struggle for Peace*. London: Hutchinson, 1939.

Chambers, Whittaker. *Witness*. New York: Random House, 1952.

Chaminade, Marcel. *Feux Croisés sur l'Espagne*. Paris: Denoël, 1939.

Chapaprieta Torregrosa, Joaquín. *La paz fue posible: Memorias de un político*. Barcelona: Ariel, 1972.

Charlton, L. E. O., Air Commodore. *The Military Situation in Spain*. London: United Editorial, 1938.

Checa, Pedro. *A un gran partido, una gran organización*. Valencia: Partido Comunista de España, Comisión Nacional de Agit-Prop, 1937.

*_____. Interview, notes taken by Burnett Bolloten.

_____. *Qué es y cómo funciona el partido comunista*. Valencia: Partido Comunista de España, n.d.

_____. *Tareas de organización y trabajo práctico del partido*. Madrid-Barcelona: Partido Comunista de España, 1938.

Chiapuso, Manuel. *Los anarquistas y la guerra en Euzkadi: La comuna de San Sebastián*. San Sebastián: Txertoa, 1977.

_____. *El gobierno vasco y los anarquistas: Bilbao en guerra*. Txertoa: San Sebastián, 1978.

Chipont Martínez, Emilio. *Alicante, 1936–1939*. Madrid: Editora Nacional, 1974.

Chomsky, Noam. *American Power and the New Mandarins*. New York: Random House (Vintage Books), 1969.

Churchill, Winston S. See also James, Robert Rhodes.

_____. *Arms and the Covenant*. London: George G. Harrap and Co., 1938.

_____. *The Gathering Storm*. Boston: Houghton Mifflin, 1948.

Ciano, Count Galeazzo. *Les archives secrètes du Comte Ciano, 1936–1942*. Paris: Plon, 1949.

_____. *The Ciano Diaries, 1939–1943*. Edited by Hugh Gibson. Garden City: Doubleday, 1946.

Cien años por el socialismo: Historia del PSOE, 1879–1979. Madrid: Pablo Iglesias, 1979.

Cierva y de las Hoces, Ricardo de la. *Cien libros básicos sobre la guerra de España*. Madrid: Publicaciones Española, 1966.

_____. *Los documentos de la primavera trágica: Análisis documental de los antecedentes immediatos del 18 de julio de 1936*. Madrid: Ministerio de Información y Turismo, 1967.

_____. *Historia básica de la España actual, 1800–1971*. Barcelona: Planeta, 1974.

_____. *Historia de la guerra civil española*. Madrid: San Martín, 1969.

_____. *Historia del socialismo en España, 1879–1983*. Barcelona: Planeta, 1983.

⸻. *Historia ilustrada de la guerra civil española.* 2 vols. Barcelona: Danae, 1971.

⸻. *La historia perdida del socialismo español.* Madrid: Editorial Nacional, 1972.

⸻. *Leyenda y tragedia de las brigadas internacionales.* Madrid: Prensa Española, 1973.

Cirre Jíménez, José. *De espejo a Madrid con las tropas del General Miaja.* Granada: Prieto, 1938.

⸻. *Memorias de un combatiente de la brigada internacional.* Granada: Prieto, 1938.

Civera, Marín. *El sindicalismo y la economia actual.* Valencia: Partido Sindicalista, 1937.

Claudín, Fernando. *La crisis del movimiento comunista.* Vol. I: *De la kominform al komintern.* Paris: Ruedo Ibérico, 1970.

⸻. *Santiago Carrillo: Crónica de un secretario general.* Barcelona: Planeta, 1983.

Clavego, Pablo. *Algunas normas para el trabajo de los comisarios políticos.* Madrid: Europa América, [1937?].

El clero y los católicos vasco-separatistas y el movimiento nacional. Madrid: Centro de Información Católica Internacional, 1940.

Cleugh, James. *Spanish Fury.* London: Harper, 1962.

Climent, Luís. *Rojos en Tarragona y su provincia.* Tarragona: Torres y Virgili, 1942.

Coates, W. P., and Coates, Z. K. *A History of Anglo-Soviet Relations.* London: Lawrence and Wishart, 1945.

⸻. *World Affairs and the USSR.* London: Lawrence and Wishart, 1939.

Cockburn, Claud. See also Pettifer, James, and Pitcairn, Frank [pseud.].

⸻. *Cockburn in Spain: Despatches from the Spanish Civil War.* Edited by James Pettifer. London: Lawrence and Wishart, 1986.

⸻. *Crossing the Line.* London: Macgibbon and Kee, 1958.

⸻. *A Discord of Trumpets.* New York: Simon and Schuster, 1956.

Cockburn, Patricia. *The Years of the Week.* London: Macdonald, 1968.

Code, Joseph B. *The Spanish War and Lying Propaganda.* New York: Paulist Press, 1938.

Las colectividades campesinas, 1936–1939. Barcelona: Tusquets, 1977.

Coll, Josep, and Pané, Josep. *Josep Rovira: Una vida al servei de Catalunya i del socialisme.* Barcelona: Ariel, 1978.

Collectivisations: L'oeuvre constructive de la révolution espagnole, 1936–1939. Recueil de documents. Preface by A. Souchy. Toulouse: CNT, 1965.

Colodny, Robert Garland. *Spain: The Glory and the Tragedy.* New York: Humanities Press, 1970.

⸻. *The Struggle for Madrid: The Central Epic of the Spanish Conflict, 1936–37.* New York: Paine-Whitman, 1958.

Colomer, Víctor. *Informe presentat a la primera conferencia nacional del partit socialista unificat de Catalunya I.C.* Barcelona: Secretariat d'Agitacio i Propaganda del P.S.U.C., 1937.

Colton, Joel. *Léon Blum: Humanist in Politics.* New York: Knopf, 1966.

Colvin, Ian. *The Chamberlain Cabinet.* London: Gollancz, 1971.

⸻. *None So Blind.* New York: Harcourt, Brace and World, 1965.

————. *Vansittart in Office: The Origins of World War II.* London: Gollancz, 1965.

Comín Colomer, Eduardo. *El comisariado político en la guerra española.* Madrid: San Martín, 1973.

————. *El comunismo en España, 1919–1936.* Madrid: Publicaciones Españolas, 1959.

————. *Historia del anarquismo español.* Vols. I, II. Barcelona: AHR, 1956.

————. *Historia de la primera república.* Barcelona: AHR, 1956.

————. *Historia del partido comunista de España.* Vols. I, II, III. Madrid: Editora Nacional, 1965.

————. *Historia secreta de la segunda república.* Barcelona: AHR, 1959.

————. *Luchas internas en la zona roja.* Madrid: Publicaciones Españolas, 1959.

————. *El 5º Regimiento de Milicias Populares.* Madrid: San Martín, 1973.

————. *La república en el exilio.* Barcelona: AHR, 1957.

"Comité Regional de Aragón del Partido Comunista de España. Acta de la Reunión Celebrada el día 12 de Septiembre de 1937." Archivo Histórico Nacional, Salamanca. Leg. 616/816–21.

Communist International. *Unity for Spain: Correspondence between the Communist International and the Labor and Socialist International, June–July, 1937.* New York: Workers Library, 1937.

Communist International Executive Committee. *XIII Plenum IKKI. Stenograficheskii Otchet.* Moscow: Communist International, 1934.

¿Cómo fortalecer nuestra democracia? Madrid-Barcelona: Partido Comunista de España, 1938.

Cómo piensa el partido sindicalista en este momento histórico de la vida española. Valencia: Cultura Popular, 1937.

Comorera, Juan. *Cataluña en pie de guerra: Discurso pronunciado en el pleno ampliado del C.C. del partido comunista de España.* Valencia: Partido Comunista de España, 1937.

————. *Informe presentado a la primera conferencia nacional del partido socialista unificado de Cataluña I.C. por su secretario general.* Barcelona: Agitación y Propaganda del P.S.U., 1937.

Companys, Luis. *Discurso pronunciado el dia 27 de diciembre de 1936.* Barcelona: Esquerra Republicana de Catalunya, 1936.

*————. "Notes and Documents on the Fighting in Barcelona, 3–7 May 1937." Carbon copy of original material given to the author by Ricardo del Río, director of the Febus news agency, who received it from Francisco Aguirre, a friend of Companys.

Los comunistas y la revolución española: Palmiro Togliatti, José Díaz, Santiago Carrillo. Barcelona: Bruguera, 1979.

Confederación Nacional del Trabajo. *Acuerdos del pleno económico nacional ampliado.* Barcelona: Artes Gráficas CNT, 1938.

————. "Atropellos Contra Nuestra Organización." International Institute of Social History, CNT-FAI Archives. Paquete 44 B/5, Caja 318. Photocopies in Hoover Institution, Bolloten Collection.

————. *Comarcal de Utrillas (Teruel): En lucha por la libertad, contra el fascismo, 1936–1939.* Toulouse: Cultura y Acción, 1971.

————. *Comarcal de Valderrobres (Teruel): Sus luchas sociales y revolucionarias.* Toulouse: Cultura y Acción, 1971.

————. Confederación Regional de Aragón, Rioja y Navarra (CNT). *Comarcal de*

Valderrobres (Teruel). Toulouse: Cultura y Acción, [1971?].

―――. *El congreso confederal de Zaragoza, 1936*. Madrid: Zero, 1978.

―――. *Congreso de constitución de la confederación nacional del trabajo (CNT)*. Prólogo de José Peirats. Barcelona: Anagrama, 1976.

*―――. *Memoria del congreso extraordinario celebrado en Madrid los días 11 al 16 de junio de 1931*. Barcelona: Cosmos, [1931?]. Photographic reproduction.

―――. "Pleno Nacional de Regionales, 15 Octubre 1938." International Institute of Social History, CNT-FAI Archives, Paquete 54, C. Photocopy in Hoover Institution, Bolloten Collection.

―――. *Realizaciones revolucionarias y estructuras colectivistas de la comarcal de Monzón (Huesca)*. Monzón: CNT, Cultura y Acción, 1977.

CNT-FAI Archives. International Institute of Social History, Amsterdam.

Confederación Regional del Trabajo de Cataluña. *Memoria del congreso extraordinario de la confederación regional del trabajo de Cataluña celebrado en Barcelona los días 25 de febrero al 3 de marzo de 1937*. Barcelona: CNT, 1937.

―――. *Memorias de la conferencia regional extraordinaria celebrada los días 25, 26 y 27 de enero 1936*. Barcelona: Confederación Regional del Trabajo de Cataluña, 1936.

*Confederación Regional del Trabajo de Levante. *Actas del congreso regional de sindicatos de Levante celebrado en Alicante, en el Teatro Verano, los días 15, 16, 17, 18 y 19 de julio de 1937*. Valencia: CNT, 1937.

Conforti, Olao. *Guadalajara: La prima sconfitta del fascismo*. Milano: Mursia, 1967.

*Congress of the Valencia CNT, November 1936. Bound collection of clippings from *Fragua Social*, organ of the CNT, Valencia.

Conquest, Robert. *The Great Terror*. New York: Macmillan, 1969.

Contemporary Authors. Detroit: Gale Research, 1980.

Contes de guerra i revolució, 1936–1939. Vols. I, II. Barcelona: Laia, 1982.

Le contrat de travail dans la république espagnole. Madrid: Ministère du Travail et de Prévoyance, Gráficas Reunidas, 1937.

Contreras, Carlos J. See also Vidali, Vittorio.

―――. *Nuestro gran ejército popular*. Barcelona: Partido Comunista de España, Comisión Nacional de Agit-Prop, 1937.

―――. *La quinta columna*. Valencia: Partido Comunista de España, [1937].

Contreras, Juan de. *La iniciación en Segovia del movimiento nacional*. Segovia: El Adelantado, 1938.

Contreras, Manuel. *El PSOE en la II república: Organización e ideología*. Madrid: Centro de investigaciones sociológicas, 1981.

Controversy on Spain. London: United Editorial, 1937.

Conze, Edward. *Spain Today*. London: Martin Secker and Warburg, 1936.

Cooper, Duff (Viscount Norwich). *Old Men Forget: The Autobiography of Duff Cooper*. London: Rupert Hart-Davis, 1953.

Las cooperativas agrícolas. Barcelona: Partido Comunista de España, [1937?].

Córdoba, Juan de. *Estampas y reportajes de retaguardia*. Sevilla: Ediciones Españolas, 1939.

Córdoba. Ayuntamiento. *Seis estudios sobre el proletariado andaluz, 1868–1939*. Córdoba: Delegación de Cultura, 1984.

Cordón, Antonio. *Trayectoria*. Paris: Ebro, 1971.

Cordonié, Rafael. *Madrid bajo el Marxismo*. Madrid: Victoriano Suárez, 1939.

Cordova Iturburu, Cayetano. *España bajo el comando del pueblo*. Buenos Aires: Acento, 1938.

Cortada, James W., ed. *The Historical Dictionary of the Spanish Civil War, 1936–1939*. Westport: Greenwood Press, 1982.

———. *Spain in the Twentieth-Century World: Essays on Spanish Diplomacy, 1898–1978*. Westport, Conn.: Greenwood, 1980.

Corthis, André. *L'Espagne de la victoire*. Paris: Fayard, 1941.

Cossio, Francisco de. *Guerra de Salvación*. Valladolid: Santarén, 1937.

Cot, Pierre. *Triumph of Treason*. New York: Ziff-Davis, 1944.

Coulondre, Robert. *De Staline à Hitler: Souvenirs de deux ambassades, 1936–1938*. Paris: Hachette, 1950.

Coverdale, John F. *Italian Intervention in the Spanish Civil War*. Princeton: Princeton University Press, 1975.

Cox, Geoffrey. *Defence of Madrid*. London: Gollancz, 1937.

Craig, Gordon A. *Germany, 1866–1945*. New York: Oxford University Press, 1980.

Craig, Gordon A., and Gilbert, Felix, eds. *The Diplomats, 1919–1939*. Vol. II: *The Thirties*. New York: Atheneum, 1977.

Cremascoli, Franco. *Inferno a Barcellona*. Milan: Mondadori, 1939.

Crossman, Richard, ed. *The God That Failed*. New York: Bantam Books, 1959.

Crowley, Edward L., ed. *The Soviet Diplomatic Corps, 1917–1967*. Metuchen, N.J.: Scarecrow Press, 1970.

Crozier, Brian. *Franco*. Boston: Little, Brown, 1967.

Cruells, Manuel. *L'expedició a Mallorca*. Barcelona: Juventud, 1972.

———. *Mayo sangriento: Barcelona, 1937*. Barcelona: Editorial Juventud, 1970.

———. *El separatisme català durant la guerra civil*. Barcelona: Dopesa, 1975.

———. *La societat catalana durant la guerra civil*. Barcelona: Edhasa, 1978.

Cuadernos bibliográficos de la guerra de España, 1936–1939. Series 1, 2, and 3. Madrid: Universidad de Madrid, 1966, 1967.

Cuadrado, Alonso Arturo. *18 julio: Diez meses de Madrid rojo*. Melilla: Artes Gráficas, 1938.

Cuadrat, Xavier. *Socialismo y anarquismo en Cataluña, 1899–1911: Los orígenes de la CNT*. Madrid: Revista de Trabajo, 1976.

Cucó, Alfons. *Republicans i camperols revoltats*. Valencia: Eliseu Climent, 1975.

———. *El valencianismo político, 1874–1939*. Barcelona: Ariel, 1977.

Cucó Giner, María Josepa, et al. *La qüestió agrària el país Valencià*. Barcelona: Aedos, 1978.

Cucurull, Félix. *Panoràmica del nacionalisme català*. 6 vols. Paris: Edicions Catalanes, 1975.

Cuevas de la Peña, Colonel Eduardo. *Recuerdos de la guerra de España*. Montauban: Forestié, 1940.

Culla i Clarà, Joan B. *El catalanisme d'Esquerra, 1928–1936*. Barcelona: Curial, 1977.

Cunningham, Valentine. *Spanish Front: Writers on the Civil War*. Oxford: Oxford University Press, 1986.

Cusick (Orr), Lois. "The Anarchist Millennium: Memories of the Spanish Revolution, 1936–1937." Typescript. Hoover Institution.

Dahms, H. Günther. *Der spanische Bürgerkrieg, 1936–1939*. Tubingen: Rainer Wunderlich, 1962.

Dallet, J. *Letters from an American Volunteer to His Wife*. New York: Workers Library, 1938.

Dallin, David J. *Russia and Postwar Europe*. New Haven: Yale University Press, 1943.

———. *Soviet Espionage*. New Haven: Yale University Press, 1955.

———. *Soviet Russia's Foreign Policy, 1939–1942*. New Haven: Yale University Press, 1942.

Dalton, Hugh. *The Fateful Years: Memoirs, 1931–1945*. London: Frederick Muller, 1957.

d'Arcangues, Pierre. *Le Destin de l'Espagne*. Paris: Denoël, 1938.

Dashar, M. [Helmut Ruediger]. *The Revolutionary Movement in Spain*. New York: Libertarian Publishing Society, n.d.

Datos complementarios para la historia de España: Guerra de liberación, 1936–1939. Madrid: 1945.

Dautun, Yves. *Valence sous la Botte Rouge*. Paris: Baudinière, 1937.

Davies, Joseph E. *Mission to Moscow*. New York: Simon and Schuster, 1941.

Deacon, Richard. *A History of the Russian Secret Service*. New York: Taplinger, 1972.

De Companys a Indalecio Prieto: Documentación sobre las industrias de guerra en Cataluña. Buenos Aires: Servicio de Propaganda España, 1939.

Decret de collectivizacions. Barcelona: Consellería d'Economía, Generalitat de Catalunya, 1936.

Decret sobre la collectivització i control de la industria i el comerç a Catalunya. Barcelona: Consellería d'Economía, Catalunya, Industries Grafiques Seix i Barral Germans, 1936.

Degras, Jane. *Soviet Documents on Foreign Policy*. Vol. III: 1933–1941. London: Oxford University Press, 1953.

De julio a julio: Un año de lucha. Barcelona: Tierra y Libertad, 1937.

Delaprée, Louis. *Le martyre de Madrid, témoignages inédits*. Madrid, 1937.

———. *Mort en Espagne*. Paris: Tisné, 1937.

Delicado, Manuel. *Comó se luchó en Sevilla*. Barcelona: Partido Comunista de España, 1937.

Dellacasa, Gianfranco. *Revolución y frente popular en España, 1936–1939*. Madrid: Zero, 1977.

Delperrie de Bayac, Jacques. *Les brigades internationales*. Paris: Fayard, 1968.

*Deltell, Louis. Correspondence with Burnett Bolloten.

Denkschrift über die Einmischung des Bolchewismus und der *Demokratien in Spanien*. Berlin-Leipzig: Nibelungen, 1939.

Deportista, Juan. *Los Rojos*. Valladolid: Santarén, 1938.

Deriabin, Peter. *Watchdogs of Terror*. New Rochelle, N.Y.: Arlington House, 1972.

Detwiler, Donald S. *Hitler, Franco und Gibralter*. Wiesbaden: Franz Stiner, 1962.

Deutsche kämpfen in Spanien. Darmstadt: Winklers, 1939.

Deutscher, Isaac. *The Prophet Outcast: Trotsky, 1929–1940*. New York: Random House, 1965.

———. *Stalin: A Political Biography*. New York and London: Oxford University Press, 1949.

Deutschland und der spanishe Bürgerkrieg, 1936–1939. Akten zur Deutschen Auswärtigen Politik, 1918–1945. Serie D., 1937–1945. Vol. III. Baden-Baden: Imprimerie Nationale, 1951.

Dewar, Hugo. *Assassins at Large.* London: Wingate, 1951.

Dez anos de política externa, 1936–1947: A naçao portuguesa e a segunda guerra mundial. Vols. I, II, III. Lisbon: Ministérios dos Negócios Estrangeiros, 1962.

Díaz, Carlos. *Besteiro: El socialismo en libertad.* Prologue by Enrique Tierno Galván. Madrid: Silos, 1976.

Díaz, José. *Tres años de lucha.* Paris: Globe, 1969.

Díaz de Entresotos, Baldomero. *Seis meses de anarquía en Extremadura.* Caceres: Editorial Extremadura, 1937.

Díaz del Moral, Juan. *Historia de las agitaciones campesinas andaluzas.* Madrid: Alianza, 1967.

Díaz del Moral, Juan, and Ortega y Gasset, José. *La reforma agraria y el estatuto catalán.* Madrid: Revista de Occidente, 1932.

Díaz de Villegas, General José. *Guerra de liberación, 1936–39.* Barcelona: Editorial AHR, 1958.

———. *La guerra revolucionaria.* Madrid: Europa, 1963.

Díaz Doin, Guillermo. *Como llegó Falange al poder.* Buenos Aires: Aniceto López, 1940.

———. *El pensamiento político de Azaña.* Buenos Aires: PHAC, 1943.

———. *236 biografías sintéticas políticas y militares.* Buenos Aires: Editorial Mundo Atlántico, 1943.

Díaz-Plaja, Fernando. *La historia de España en sus documentos: El siglo XX. Dictadura . . . república, 1923–1936.* Madrid: Instituto de Estudios Políticos, 1964.

———. *La historia de España en sus documentos: El Siglo XX. La guerra, 1936–1939.* Madrid: Faro, 1963.

Dictamen de la comisión sobre ilegitimidad de poderes actuantes en 18 de julio de 1936. Madrid: Editora Nacional, 1939.

19 julio de 1936. FAI-CNT. Barcelona: Oficinas de Propaganda CNT-FAI, [1937?].

Diego, Capitán de. *Belchite.* Barcelona: Editora Nacional, 1939.

Diego Sevilla, Andrés. *Historia política de la zona roja.* Madrid: Rialp, 1963.

Diez, Genadius. *Spain's Struggle against Anarchism and Communism.* New York: Paulist Press, [1936?].

Diéz de los Ríos San Juan, María Teresa. *Documentación sobre la guerra civil en Alicante.* Alicante: Instituto Juan Gil-Albert, 1984.

Diggins, John P. *Up from Communism.* New York: Harper and Row, 1975.

Dimitrov, Georgi. *Against Fascism and War: Report before the Seventh World Congress of the Communist International, delivered on August 2, 1935.* Sofia: Sofia Press, 1975.

———. *Las lecciones de Almería.* Barcelona: Europa-America, 1937.

———. *Spain and the People's Front.* New York: Workers Library, 1937.

———. *Spain's Year of War.* New York: Workers Library, 1937.

———. *Two Years of Heroic Struggle of the Spanish People.* New York: Workers Library, 1938.

———. *The United Front: The Struggle against Fascism and War.* New York: International Publishers, 1938.

Dingle, Reginald J. *Russia's Work in Spain*. London: Spanish Press Services, 1939.
———. *Second Thoughts on "Democracy" in Spain*. London: Spanish Press Services, 1937.
Dirksen, Herbert von. *Moscow, Tokyo, London: Twenty Years of German Foreign Policy*. London: Hutchinson, 1951. (See *Documents and Materials Relating to the Eve of the Second World War.*)
Documentos. Lo que han visto en Madrid los parlamentarios ingleses. Valencia: Ministerio del Estado, [1937?].
Documentos políticos para la historia de la república española. Vol. I. Mexico City: Colección Málaga, 1945.
Documentos secretos del ministerio de acuntos exteriores de Alemania sobre la guerra civil española. Gijón: Júcar, 1978.
Documents and Materials Relating to the Eve of the Second World War. Vol. I: November 1937–1938. Vol. II: Dirksen Papers, 1938–1939. Moscow: Ministry of Foreign Affairs of the USSR Foreign Languages Publishing House, 1948.
Documents: De la proclamació de la república al front popular. Barcelona: Disseny, 1977.
Documents diplomatiques français, 1932–1939. See France, Ministère des Affaires Etrangères.
Documents of the Fourth International: The Formative Years, 1933–40. New York: Pathfinder Press, 1973.
Documents on British Foreign Policy. See Great Britain, Foreign Office.
Documents on German Foreign Policy, 1918–1945. See U.S. Department of State, and Great Britain, Foreign Office.
Dodd, William E. *Ambassador Dodd's Diary, 1933–1938*. New York: Harcourt Brace, 1941.
Dolgoff, Sam. *La anarquía según Bakunin*. Barcelona, Tusquets, 1977.
———, ed. *The Anarchist Collectives*. New York: Free Life Editions, 1974.
Domènec de Bellmunt. *Lluis Companys*. Toulouse: Foc Nou, 1945.
Domingo, Marcelino. *España ante el mundo*. Mexico City: Mexico Nuevo, 1937.
Domínguez, Edmundo. *Los vencedores de Negrín*. Mexico City: Nuestro Pueblo, 1940.
Dommanget, Maurice. *Histoire du premier mai*. Paris: Tête de feuilles, 1972.
Donaldson, Frances. *Edward VIII*. Philadelphia: Lippincott, 1975.
Dos Passos, John. *The Theme is Freedom*. New York: Dodd, Mead, 1956.
Douglas, Roy. *In the Year of Munich*. London: Macmillan, 1977.
Drachkovitch, Milorad M. See also Lazitch, Branko.
———, ed. *Fifty Years of Communism in Russia*. Hoover Institution Publications. University Park: Pennsylvania State University Press, 1967.
Le drame du pays basque. Paris: SGIE, 1937.
Dreifort, John E. *Yvon Delbos at the Quai d'Orsay: French Foreign Policy during the Popular Front, 1936–1938*. Wichita: University Press of Kansas, 1973.
Duff, Charles. *A Key to Victory: Spain*. London: Gollancz, 1940.
Dulles, John W. F. *Brazilian Communism, 1935–1945*. Austin: University of Texas Press, 1983.
Dupré, Henri. *La "Légion Tricolore" en Espagne, 1936–1939*. Paris: Ligue Française (Mouvement social européen), 1942.
Duque, José. "Informe de José Duque, Secretario General de la Comisión Agraria al

Comité Central del P.C. 17-VIII-37." Archivo Histórico Nacional, Salamanca. Leg. 616/816-6.

*_____. "La situación de Aragón al comienzo de la guerra." Unpublished manuscript given to Burnett Bolloten by José Duque.

Durán, Gustavo. *Una enseñanza de la guerra española*. Madrid: Júcar, 1980.

Duval, Général. *Les espagnols et la guerre d'Espagne*. Paris: Plon, 1939.

_____. *Les leçons de la guerre d'Espagne*. Paris: Plon, 1938.

Dzelepy, E. N. *The Spanish Plot*. London: King, 1937.

East European Fund. Program on the USSR. *Soviet Shipping in the Spanish Civil War*. New York, 1954. Mimeographed Series of the East European Fund, No. 59.

Eby, Cecil. *Between the Bullet and the Lie: American Volunteers in the Spanish Civil War*. New York: Holt, Rinehart, 1969.

_____. *The Siege of the Alcázar*. New York: Random House, 1965.

Echeandia, José. *La persecución roja en el país vasco*. Barcelona: Fidel Rodriguez, 1945.

Echeverría, Federico de. *Spain in Flames*. London: Burns Oates and Washbourne, [1936?].

Echeverría, Tomás. *Cómo se preparó el alzamiento: El General Mola y los carlistas*. Madrid: Gráf. Letra, 1985.

Les écrivains et la guerre d'Espagne. Paris: Pantheon, 1973.

Eden, Anthony (Lord Avon). *Facing the Dictators*. London: Cassell, 1962.

_____. *The Reckoning*. Boston: Houghton Mifflin, 1965.

Edwards, Jill. *The British Government and the Spanish Civil War*. London: Macmillan, 1979.

L'Effort cultural du peuple espagnol en armes. Paris: Ministère de l'Instruction Publique de la République Espagnole, 1937.

Egorov, P. Ia. *Marshal Meretskov*. Moscow: Voennoe Izd., 1974.

Eguía Ruiz, Constancio. *Los causantes de la tragedia hispana*. Buenos Aires: Difusión, 1938.

Ehrenburg, Ilya. *Corresponsal en España*. Buenos Aires: Tiempo Contemporáneo, 1968.

_____. *España república de trabajadores*. Madrid: Júcar, 1976.

_____. *Estampas de España*. Buenos Aires: Problemas de España, 1938.

_____. *Eve of War, 1933–41*. London: Macgibbon, 1963.

_____. *No Pasarán*. London: Malik-Verlag, 1937.

Un ejército popular y democrático al servicio del pueblo. Barcelona: Ministerio de Defensa Nacional, [1938?].

Elstob, Peter. *Spanish Prisoner*. London: Macmillan, 1939.

Elwyn Jones, F. *The Battle for Peace*. London: Gollancz, 1938.

Emiliani, Angelo. *La aviación legionaria: España, 1936–39*. Madrid: San Martín, 1974.

Encinas, Joaquín de. *La tradición española y la revolución*. Madrid: Rialp, 1958.

Enríquez de Salamanca, Jesús. *La vida en el Alcázar de Toledo*. Valladolid: Santarén, 1937.

Enzensberger, Hans Magnus. *El corto verano de la anarquía: Vida y muerte de Durruti*. Barcelona: Grijalbo, 1977.

Un episode de la lutte fratricide. Paris: Archives Espagnoles, 1938.

Epistolario, Prieto y Negrín. Paris: Imprimerie Nouvelle, 1939.

Epopée d'Espagne: Brigades internationales, 1936–1939. Paris: L'Amicale des Anciens Volontaires français en Espagne Républicaine: Paris, 1957.

La epopeya de Africa 17 de julio. Ceuta-Tetuán: Imprenta Africa, 1938.

Erickson, John. *The Soviet High Command: A Military-Political History, 1918–1941.* New York: St. Martin's, 1962.

Escofet, Frederic. *Al servei de Catalunya i de la república: La victòria, 19 de juliol 1936.* Paris: Edicions Catalanes, 1973.

―――. *De una derrota a una victoria: 6 de octubre de 1934–19 de julio de 1936.* Barcelona: Argos Vergara, 1984.

*Escribano, Antonio. Correspondence with Burnett Bolloten.

Esenwein, George. "Anarchist Ideology and the Working-Class Movement in Spain (1880–1900); with Special Reference to the Ideas of Ricardo Mella." Dissertation, University of London, 1987. (Copy in Hoover Institution.)

España, Daniel. *Carceles Rojos.* Madrid: Victoriano Suárez, 1939.

España, su lucha y sus ideales: Documentos de Ossorio y Gallardo, Federica Montseny, Juan P. Fábrega, F. Martí Ibañez, García Oliver, H. Noja Ruiz. Buenos Aires: Acento, 1937.

Esperabé de Arteaga, Enrique. *La guerra de reconquista española y el criminal comunismo.* Madrid: San Martín, 1940.

Espin, Eduardo. *Azaña en el poder: El partido de Acción Republicana.* Madrid: Centro de investigaciones sociológicas, 1980.

Espinar, Jaime. *Noviembre de Madrid.* Barcelona: Unió Gráfico, 1938.

Espinosa y del Río, José María. *La Agonía de la dictadura rojo-separatista en Vizcaya.* San Sebastián: Editorial Española, 1938.

"Es spricht der Führer." 7 exemplarische Hitler-Reden. Gütersloh: Sigbert Mohn, 1966.

Estado Mayor Central del Ejército. *Historia de la guerra de liberación, 1936–1939.* Vol. I. Madrid: Servicio Histórico Militar, 1945.

Estampas de la revolución española, 19 de julio de 1936. Barcelona: Oficinas de Propaganda CNT-FAI, [1936?].

L'Estatut de Catalunya. Text oficial comentat, amb referenciès legals i notes de la discussió parlamentaría. Per C. Massó i Escofet i R. Gay de Montellà. Barcelona: Llibrería Bosch, 1933.

Estatutos de la federación nacional de campesinos. Valencia: n.p., 1937.

Esteban-Infantes, General Emilio. *General Sanjurjo.* Barcelona: AHR, 1957.

Estornés Lasa, José. *Un gudari en los frentes de Euzkadi, Asturias y Cataluña.* San Sebastián: Auñamendi, 1979.

Estruch, Joan. *Historia del PCE, 1920–1939.* Vol. I. Barcelona: Iniciativas, 1978.

Etchebéhère, Mika. *Ma guerre d'Espagne à moi: Une femme à la tête d'une colonne de combat.* Paris: Denoël, 1976.

Eudin, Xenia J., and Slusser, Robert M. *Soviet Foreign Policy, 1928–1934: Documents and Materials.* Vol. II. University Park: Pennsylvania State University Press, 1967.

Les événements survenus en France de 1933 à 1945: Temoignages et documents recueillis par la commission d'enquête parlementaire. Paris: Presses Universitaires de France, n.d.

Evidence of Recent Breaches by Germany and Italy of the Non-Intervention Agreement. London: King, 1937.

El exilio español en Mexico, 1939–1982. Mexico City: Fondo de Cultura Ecónomica, 1982.

Exposición del plan secreto para establecer un "Soviet" en España. Bilbao: Editora Nacional, 1939.

Exposure of the Secret Plan to Establish a Soviet in Spain. London: Friends of National Spain, n.d.

Fabbri, Luis. *¿Qué es la anarquía?* Toulouse: Tiempos Nuevos, n.d.

———. *Vida y pensamiento de Malatesta.* Barcelona: Tierra y Libertad, 1938.

Fàbregas, Joan P. *Los factores económicos de la revolución española.* Barcelona: Oficinas de Propaganda CNT-FAI, 1937.

———. *Els factors económics de la revolució.* Barcelona: Bosch, 1937.

———. *Les finances de la revolució.* Barcelona: Bosch, 1937.

———. *Vuitanta dies al govern de la Generalitat.* Barcelona: Bosch, 1937.

Fagen, Patricia W. *Exiles and Citizens: Spanish Republicans in Mexico.* Austin: Institute of Latin American Studies, University of Texas Press, 1973.

Falcón, César. *Madrid.* Madrid: Nuestro Pueblo, 1938.

Falsifiers of History. Moscow: Foreign Languages Publishing House, 1948.

Febrés, Xavier. *Frederic Escofet: L'últim exiliat.* Barcelona: Pòrtic, 1979.

Federación Anarquista Ibérica. "Informe, Comité Peninsular de la FAI, Sept. 1938." International Institute of Social History, CNT-FAI Archives, Paquete 92, Caja 305, B, pp. 7–8.

———. *Memoria del peninsular de regionales celebrado en Valencia los días 4, 5, 6 y 7 de julio, 1937.* Valencia: FAI, 1937.

———. *Memoria del pleno regional de grupos anarquistas de Levante celebrado en Alicante, durante los días 11, 12, 13, 14 y 15 del mes de abril de 1937.* Valencia: Nosotros, 1937.

Federación Española de Trabajadores de la Enseñanza. *Les professionnels de l'enseignement luttent pour la libération du peuple espagnol.* [Paris?]: FETE, [1937?].

Federación Regional de Grupos Anarquistas de Cataluña. *Actas del pleno regional de grupos celebrado los días 1, 2 y 3 del mes de julio de 1937.* Barcelona: Federación Anarquista Ibérica, 1937.

Feiling, Keith. *The Life of Neville Chamberlain.* London: Macmillan, 1946.

Felipe, Leon. *Poesía Revolucionaria.* Barcelona: CNT-FAI, 1937.

Fernández, Carlos. *Paracuellos del Jarama: ¿Carillo culpable?* Barcelona: Vergara, 1983.

Fernández Almagro, Melchor. *Catalanismo y república española.* Madrid: Espasa-Calpe, 1932.

———. *Historia de la república española, 1931–36.* Madrid: Editorial Biblioteca Nueva, 1940.

Fernández Arias, Adelardo. *La agonía de Madrid.* Zaragoza: Librería General, 1938.

———. *Gil Robles. ¡La esperanza de España!* Madrid: Comentarios del Momento, 1936.

———. *Madrid bajo el terror.* Zaragoza: Librería General, 1937.

*Fernández Ballesteros, Alberto. Reports to the General Commissariat of War, dated 18 Feb. and 12 Mar. 1937. Typewritten copies of original documents loaned to Burnett Bolloten by Gabriel García Maroto, subcommissar general of propaganda.

Fernández de Castro y Pedrera, Rafael. *Hacia las rutas de una nueva España.* Melilla: Artes Gráficas Postal Exprés, 1940.

––––––. *Vidas de soldados ilustres de la nueva España: Franco, Mola, Varela.* Melilla: Artes Gráficas Postal Exprés, 1937.

Fernández García, Eusebio. *Marxismo y positivismo en el socialismo español.* Madrid: Centro de Estudios Constitucionales, 1981.

Fernández Grandizo, Manuel. See Munis, G.

Fernández Santander, Carlos. *El alzamiento de 1936 en Galicia.* Coruña: Castro, 1983.

Fernsworth, Lawrence A. *Back of the Spanish Rebellion.* Washington, D.C., [1936?].

––––––. *Spain's Struggle for Freedom.* Boston: Beacon Press, 1957.

Ferrándiz Alborz, F. *La bestia contra España.* Montevideo: n.p., 1951.

*––––––. Correspondence with Burnett Bolloten.

––––––. *Francisco Largo Caballero.* Paris: Federación Nacional de Juventudes Socialistas de España en exilio, 1949.

Ferrara, Marcella, and Ferrara, Maurizio. *Conversando con Togliatti.* Rome: Edizioni de Coltúra Sociale, 1954.

Ferrer, Rai (Raimundo). *Durruti, 1896–1936.* Barcelona: Planeta, 1985.

Figuero, Javier. *Memoria de una locura: Crónica testimonial de una gran tragedia española.* Barcelona: Planeta, 1986.

Finalidad de la CNT. El comunismo libertario. Barcelona: Tierra y Libertad, 1936.

La finance internationale et la guerre d'Espagne. Paris: Centre d'Etudes de Paix et Democratie, 1938.

Financial Relations between the Spanish Government and Great Britain. London: Friends of Spain, 1937.

Fischer, Louis. *Men and Politics.* London: Cape, 1941. Some material omitted from U.S. edition.

––––––. *Men and Politics.* New York: Duell, Sloan and Pierce, 1941.

––––––. *Russia's Road from Peace to War: Soviet Foreign Relations, 1917–1941.* New York: Harper, 1969.

––––––. *The War in Spain.* New York: *The Nation,* 1937.

––––––. *Why Spain Fights On.* London: Union of Democratic Control, 1938.

Fischer, Markoosha. *My Lives in Russia.* New York: Harper and Bros., 1944.

Fontana, José María. *Los catalanes en la guerra de España.* Madrid: Samarán, 1951.

Fonteriz, Luis de. *Red Terror in Madrid.* London: Longmans, Green, 1937.

Foreign Journalists under Franco's Terror. London: United Editorial, [1937?].

Foxá, Agustín de. *Madrid de corte a cheka.* San Sebastián: Librería Internacional, 1938.

France. Ministère des Affaires Etrangères. *Documents diplomatiques français, 1932–1939.* 2e Série (1936–1939). Tomes VIII and IX. Paris: Imprimerie Nationale, 1973.

————. *The French Yellow Book, 1938–1939*. London: Hutchinson, 1940.

Francisco Largo Caballero, 1869–1946. Toulouse: Ediciones El Socialista, 1947.

Franco Bahamonde, Francisco. *Palabras del Caudillo*. Madrid: Editora Nacional, 1943.

Franco in Barcelona. London: United Editorial, 1939.

Frank, Willard C., Jr. "Sea Power, Politics, and the Onset of the Spanish War, 1936." Dissertation, University of Pittsburgh, 1969.

Fraser, Hamish. *De las brigadas internacionales a los sindicatos católicos*. Madrid: Editora Nacional, 1957.

Fraser, Ronald. *Blood of Spain*. New York: Pantheon Books, 1979.

Freemasons and Spain. New York: North American Committee to Aid Spanish Democracy, [1937?].

Der Freiheitskampf des spanischen Volkes und die internationale Solidarität. Berlin: Dietz, 1956.

Friends of Democracy and Independence in Spain. *Italians in Spain*. London: Friends of Democracy and Independence in Spain, 1937.

Friends of Spanish Democracy. *Spain*. New York: American Spanish News Service, 1936.

Frutos, Víctor de. *Los que NO perdieron la guerra*. Buenos Aires: Oberon, 1967.

Fuchser, Larry William. *Neville Chamberlain and Appeasement*. New York: Norton, 1982.

Fuentes Mares, José. *Historia de un conflicto: El tesoro del "Vita"*. Madrid: CVS, 1975.

Führing, Hellmut H. *Wir funken für Franco*. Gütersloh: Bertelsmann, 1939.

Fuller, J. F. C. *The Conquest of Red Spain*. London: Burns Oates and Washbourne, 1937.

Fundación Pablo Iglesias. *Catálogo de publicaciones periodicas, 1984*. Madrid: Editorial Pablo Iglesias, 1984.

Fusi Aizpurua, Juan Pablo. *El problema vasco en la II república*. Madrid: Turner, 1979.

Fyrth, Jim. *The Signal Was Spain: The Spain Aid Movement in Britain, 1936–1939*. London: Lawrence and Wishart, 1986.

Gabriel, Jose. *La vida y la muerte en Aragón*. Buenos Aires: Imán, 1938.

Galán, José María. *Cuestiones varias del Carrillismo*. Madrid: Futuro, 1976.

Galassi, Jonathan, ed. *Understand the Weapon, Understand the Wound: Selected Writings of John Cornford*. Manchester, England: Carcanet New Press, 1976.

*Galíndez, Jesús de. Correspondence with Burnett Bolloten.

————. *Los vascos en el Madrid sitiado*. Buenos Aires: Vasca Ekin, 1945.

Galindo Herrero, Santiago. *Los partidos monárquicos bajo la segunda república*. Madrid: Rialp, 1956.

Gallego, Ignacio. *El problema campesino en Andalucia*. Valencia: JSU, 1937.

Gamelin, Général Maurice Gustave. *Servir*. 3 vols. Paris: Plon, 1946–47.

Gamir Ulibarri, General Manuel. *La pérdida de Barcelona*. Paris: Imprimerie Moderne, 1939.

Gannes, Harry. *How the Soviet Union Helps Spain*. New York: Workers Library, 1936.

————. *Soviets in Spain*. New York: Workers Library, 1935.

Gannes, Harry, and Reppard, T. *Spain in Revolt*. London: Gollancz, 1936.

Gannon, Franklin Reid. *The British Press and Germany, 1936–1939*. Oxford: Clarendon, 1971.

Gantenbein, James W. *Documentary Background of World War II, 1931–1941*. New York: Farrar, Straus, 1975.

Garcerán, Rafael. *Falange desde febrero de 1936 al gobierno nacional*. n.p.: Secretaría General de la F.E., 1938.

Garcés Arroyo, Santiago. Photocopies of letters to D. Pastor Petit.

García, Angel. *La iglesia española y el 18 de julio*. Barcelona: Acervo, 1977.

García, Félix. *Colectivizaciónes campesinas y obreras en la revolución española*. Madrid: Zero, 1977.

García, Regina. *Yo he sido marxista: El cómo y el porqué de una coversión*. 2d. ed. Madrid: Editora Nacional, 1952.

García, Víctor. *El pensamiento anarquista*. Toulouse: CENIT, 1963.

García de Bartolomé, Santiago, and Rull, Alberto. *Republicanos: 50 años después*. Caracas: Ateneo de Caracas, 1986.

García Durán, J. *Fuentes de la guerra civil española y bibliografía*. Barcelona: Crítica, 1985.

García Escudero, José María. *Historia política de las dos Españas*. Vols. I, II, III, IV. Madrid: Nacional, 1976.

García Lacalle. *Mitos y verdades: La aviación de caza en la guerra española*. Mexico City: Oasis, 1973.

*García Maroto, Gabriel. Interview, notes taken by Burnett Bolloten.

————. *Un jefe ejército popular: Teniente Coronel Joaquín Pérez Salas*. Pozoblanco: Colectiva Linares, 1937.

García Mercadal, J. *Aire, tierra y mar*. Vols. I, II. Zaragoza: Colección Hispania, 1938, 1939.

García Morato, Joaquín. *Guerra en el aire*. Madrid: Editora Nacional, 1940.

García-Nieto, María Carmen, and Donezar, Javier M. *La guerra de España, 1936–1939*. Madrid: Guadiana de Publicaciones, 1975.

————. *La segunda república: Política burguesa y movimiento obrero, 1931–1936*. Madrid: Guadiana de Publicaciones, 1974.

García Oliver, Juan. *El eco de los pasos*. Paris: Ruedo Ibérico, 1978.

————. *El fascismo internacional y la guerra antifascista española*. Barcelona: CNT-FAI, 1937.

García Pradas, José. *Antifascismo proletario*. Madrid: Frente Libertario, n.d.

————. *Como terminó la guerra de España*. Buenos Aires: Inmán, 1940.

*————. Correspondence with Burnett Bolloten.

————. *Origen, esencia y fin de la sociedad de clases*. Rennes: Libertad, 1948.

————. *Rusia y España*. Paris: Tierra y Libertad, 1948.

————. *¡Teníamos que perder!* Madrid: Toro, 1974.

————. *La traición de Stalin*. New York: Cultura Proletaria, 1939.

————. *Tres epístolas a Horacio*. Algiers: Ediciones Libertarias Africa del Norte, 1946.

García Sánchez, Antonio. *La segunda república en Málaga: La cuestión religiosa, 1931–1933*. Córdoba: Ayuntamiento de Córdoba, 1984.

*García Val, Alejandro. Interview, notes taken by Burnett Bolloten.

García-Valiño y Marcen, Lieutenant General. *Guerra de liberación española*. Madrid: Bosca, 1949.

García Venero, Maximiano. *El General Fanjul: Madrid en el alzamiento nacional*. Madrid: Ediciones Cid, 1967.

———. *Historia de las internacionales en España*. Vol. II: *1914–1936*; Vol. III: *1936–1939*. Madrid: Ediciones del Movimiento, 1957.

———. *Historia del nacionalismo catalán*. Vols. I, II. Madrid: Editora Nacional, 1967.

———. *Historia del nacionalismo vasco*. Madrid: Editora Nacional, 1969.

———. *Madrid: Julio 1936*. Madrid: Tebas, 1973.

Garibaldini in Ispagna. Madrid: n.p., 1937.

Garrachón Cuesta, Antonio. *De Africa a Cádiz y de Cádiz a la España Imperial*. Cádiz: Establecimientos Cerón, 1938.

Garratt, G. T. *Gibraltar and the Mediterranean*. London: Cape, 1939.

———. *Mussolini's Roman Empire*. Harmondsworth, England: Penguin, 1938.

Garrido González, Luis. *Colectividades agrarias en Andalucía Jaén, 1931–1939*. Madrid: Siglo XXI, 1979.

Garriga, Ramón. *El general Juan Yagüe: Figura clave para conocer nuestra historia*. Barcelona: Planeta, 1985.

———. *La Legión Condor*. Madrid: Toro, 1975.

Garsia, Khose. *Ispaniia narodnogo fronta*. Moscow: Akademiia Nauk SSSR, 1957.

Gates, John. *The Story of an American Communist*. New York: Thomas Nelson, 1958.

*———. Twelve-page unpublished commentary on Verle B. Johnston's manuscript, "The International Brigades in the Spanish Civil War, 1936–1939."

Gaule, Jacques de. *La batalla del Ebro*. Madrid: Círculo de Amigos de la Historia, 1973.

———. *La batalla de Madrid, 1936–1937*. Vols. I, II. Madrid: Círculo de Amigos de la Historia, 1972.

———. *El frente de Aragón*. Madrid: Círculo de Amigos de la Historia, 1973.

———. *Hacia el final*. Madrid: Círculo de Amigos de la Historia, 1973.

———. *La política española y la guerra civil*. Vols. I, II. Madrid: Círculo de Amigos de la Historia, 1973, 1974.

Geiser, Carl. *Prisoners of the Good Fight: Americans against Franco and Fascism. The Spanish Civil War, 1936–1939*. New York: Veterans of the Abraham Lincoln Brigade, 1986.

Gellhorn, Martha. *The Face of War*. London: Hart-Davis, 1959.

Gemelli, Augustín Fr. *España e Italia en la defensa de la civilización cristiana contra el bolshevismo*. Avila: Imprenta Católica, 1938.

Generalidad de Cataluña. *Actas de Reuniones del Consejo de la Generalidad, 3 Nov.–23 Dec. 1936*. Servicio Histórico Militar. Archivo de la Guerra de Liberación. Sección II. Leg. 556, Apartado II, Carpeta 3. Photocopies in Hoover Institution, Bolloten Collection.

Generalnyi Shtab RKKA. *Upravlenie voiskami i rabota shtabov v ispanskoi respublikanskoi armii*. Moscow: Gosudarstvennoe Voennoe Izdatelstvo Narkomata Oborony Soiuza SSR, 1939.

George, Margaret. *The Warped Vision: British Foreign Policy, 1933–1939*. Pittsburgh: University of Pittsburgh Press, 1965.

Gerahty, Cecil. *The Road to Madrid*. London: Hutchinson, 1937.

Gerahty, Cecil, and Foss, William. *The Spanish Arena*. London: Gifford, 1938.

Gerassi, John. *The Premature Antifascists: North American Volunteers in the Spanish Civil War, 1936–39*. New York: Praeger, 1986.

Geraud, André (Pertinax). *The Gravediggers of France*. Garden City: Doubleday Doran, 1944.

Gerhard i Hortet, Carles. *Comissari de la Generalitat a Montserrat, 1936–1939*. Montserrat: Abadia de Montserrat, 1982.

Germany. Auswaertiges Amt. *Documents on German Foreign Policy, 1918–1945*. London: HMSO, 1951.

Germán Zubero, Luis. *Aragón en la II República: Estructura económica y comportamiento político*. Zaragoza: Institución Fernando el Católico, 1984.

Gibson, Ian. *La noche en que mataron a Calvo Sotelo*. Barcelona: Argos Vergara, 1982.

———. *Paracuellos: Como fue*. Barcelona: Vergara, 1983.

———. *Queipo de Llano: Sevilla, verano de 1936*. Barcelona: Grijalbo, 1986.

———. *La represión nacionalista de Granada en 1936 y la muerte de Federico García Lorca*. Paris: Ruedo Ibérico, 1971.

Gilabert, A. G. *Durruti, un anarquista íntegro*. Barcelona: Confederación Nacional del Trabajo, n.d.

Gilbert, Martin. *Britain and Germany between the Wars*. Bungay, England: Longmans, 1964.

———. *The Roots of Appeasement*. London: Weidenfeld and Nicolson, 1966.

———, ed. *A Century of Conflict, 1850–1950: Essays for A. J. P. Taylor*. London: Hamilton, 1966.

Gilbert, Martin, and Gott, Richard. *The Appeasers*. Boston: Houghton Mifflin, 1963.

Gillain, Nick. *Le Mercenaire*. Paris: Fayard, 1938.

Gil Robles, José María. *Discursos Parlamentarios*. Madrid: Taurus, 1971.

———. *No fué posible la paz*. Barcelona: Ariel, 1968.

———. *Spain in Chains*. New York: America Press, 1937.

Gil Robles, José María, and Pérez-Serrano, Nicolás. *Diccionario de términos electorales y parlamentarios*. Madrid: Taurus, 1977.

Giménez Arnau, J. A., and Giménez Arnau, R. *La guerra en el mar*. Zaragoza: Heraldo de Aragón, 1938.

Giménez Caballero, Ernesto. *Camisa azul y boina colorada*. Madrid: Los Combatientes, 1939.

———. *España y Franco*. Cegama: Los Combatientes, 1938.

———. *Genio de España*. Barcelona: FE, 1939.

———. *¡Hay Pirineos!* Barcelona: Editora Nacional, 1939.

———. *Madrid Nuestro*. Madrid: Educación Popular, 1944.

———. *Manuel Azaña*. Madrid: Turner, 1975.

———. *Los secretos de la Falange*. Barcelona: Yunque, 1939.

Giner, Vicente, ed. *Historia de la segunda república, 1931–1939*. Vols. I, II, III, IV, V. Madrid: Giner, 1985.

*Giral, José. Interview, notes taken by Burnett Bolloten.

Giral, o una historia de sangre. Spain: Ediciones Combate, n.d.

Girona. Ayuntamiento. *La guerra civil a les comarques gironines, 1936–1939*.

Girona: Cercle d'Estudis Històrics i Socials de Girona, 1986.

Girona i Albuixec, Albert. *Guerra i revolució al país Valencià*. Valencia: Biblioteca d'Estudis i Investigacions, 1986.

Gisclon, Jean. *La désillusion: Espagne 1936*. Paris: France-Empire, 1986.

Gitlow, Benjamin. *The Whole of Their Lives*. New York: Scribner's Sons, 1948.

El gobierno del frente popular abre a los trabajadores las puertas de la cultura superior. Sabadell: Ministerio de Instrucción Pública, 1937.

Godden, G. M. *Communism in Spain*. New York: America Press, 1937.

――――. *Conflict in Spain*. London: Burns Oates and Washbourne, 1937.

Godé, Antonio. *Asedio de Huesca, 18 julio 1936, 25 marzo 1938*. Huesca: Ayuntamiento de Huesca, [1938?].

Goded, Manuel. *Un "faccioso" cien por cien*. Saragossa: Heraldo, 1939.

Goldman, Emma. *Nowhere at Home: Letters from Exile of Emma Goldman and Alexander Berkman*. Edited by Richard and Anna Maria Drinnon. New York: Schocken Books, 1975.

――――. *Red Emma Speaks: Selected Writings and Speeches*. Edited and compiled by Alix Kates Shulman. New York: Vintage Books, 1972.

――――. *Vision on Fire: Emma Goldman on the Spanish Revolution*. Edited by David Porter. New Paltz, N.Y.: Commonground Press, 1983.

Gollonet, Angel, and Morales, José. *Málaga: Sangre y fuego*. Granada: Imperio, 1937.

Gomá y Tomás, Isidro. *La España heroica*. Pamplona: Bescansa, 1937.

――――. *Pastorales de la guerra de España*. Madrid: Rialp, 1955.

Gómez, Sócrates. *Los jóvenes socialistas y la JSU*. Madrid: Rivadeneyra, n.d.

Gómez Acebo, Juan. *La vida en las cárceles de Euzkadi*. Zarauz: Icharopena, 1938.

Gómez Aparicio, Pedro. *A Bilbao!* Granada: Imperio, 1937.

Gómez Bajuelo, Gil. *Málaga bajo el dominio rojo*. Cadiz: Cerón, 1937.

Gómez Casas, Juan. *Los anarquistas en el gobierno*. Barcelona: Bruguera, 1977.

――――. *Historia de la FAI*. Madrid: Zero, 1977.

――――. *Historia del anarcosindicalismo español*. Madrid: ZYX, 1969.

Gómez Málaga, Juan. *Estampas trágicas de Madrid*. Avila: Senén Martín, n.d.

Gómez Oliveros, Major Benito, in collaboration with Lieutenant General José Moscardó. *General Moscardó: Sin novedad en el Alcázar*. Barcelona: AHR, 1956.

Gómez Ortiz, Juan María. *Los gobiernos republicanos: España, 1936–1939*. Barcelona: Bruguera, 1977.

González, Ceferino. *La rébellion militaire en Espagne et l'incompréhension des démocraties européennes devant un aussi grave problème*. Bruxelles: Imp. Coop. Lucifer, [1936?].

González, Valentín. See El Campesino.

González Casanova, José Antonio. *Federalismo y autonomía: Cataluña y el estado español, 1868–1938*. Barcelona: Grijalbo, 1979.

González Echegaray, R. *La marina mercante y el tráfico marítimo en la guerra civil*. Madrid: San Martín, 1977.

González Gómez, Joaquín. *Publicaciones periódicas de la guerra civil, 1936–1939, en la zona republicana, existentes en la Hemeroteca Nacional*. Madrid: Hemeroteca Nacional, 1986.

González Inestal, Miguel. *Cipriano Mera, revolucionario*. Havana: Atalaya, 1943.

970 · Bibliography

*González Quintana, Antonio. Report to Burnett Bolloten on Largo Caballero's *Mis Recuerdos* and "Notas Históricas sobre la guerra civil." File includes Bolloten's correspondence with Aurelio Martín, Justo Martínez Amutio, Leonor Menéndez de Beltrán, and Angel Viñas regarding these two works.

Gorkin, Julián [Julián Gómez]. *El asesinato de Trotsky*. Barcelona: Aymá, 1971.

_____. *L'assassinat de Trotsky*. Paris: Julliard, 1970.

_____. *Caníbales políticos*. Mexico City: Quetzal, 1941.

_____. *Les communistes contre la révolution espagnole*. Paris: Belfond, 1978.

*_____. Correspondence with Burnett Bolloten. Two files.

_____. *España: Primer ensayo de democracia popular*. Buenos Aires: Libertad de la Cultura, 1961.

_____. *El proceso de Moscú en Barcelona*. Barcelona: Aymá, 1974.

_____. *El revolucionario profesional*. Barcelona: Aymá, 1975.

_____. *"We Conquer or Die": Two Speeches Which Sir John Simon Tried to Stop*. London: Independent Labour Party, [1936?].

Gorman, Robert A., ed. *Biographical Dictionary of Marxism*. Westport: Greenwood Press, 1986.

Gorozhankina, N. *Rabochii klass Ispanii v gody revolutsii*. Moscow: Gos. Sotsial'no-Ekonomicheskoe Izdat, 1936.

Gracia, Padre Vicente, S.J. *Aragón, baluarte de España*. Saragossa: El Noticiero, 1938.

Graham, Helen, and Preston, Paul, eds. *The Popular Front in Europe*. Houndmills, Basingstoke: Macmillan, 1987.

Grandi, Blasco. *Togliatti y los suyos en España*. Madrid: Publicaciones Españolas, 1954.

Granja Sainz, José Luis de la. *Nacionalismo y II república en el país vasco*. Madrid: Siglo Veintiuno, 1986.

Grant, Ted. *The Spanish Revolution, 1931–37*. London: Militant, 1977.

Great Britain. Cabinet Office. *Minutes, 1916–1939*. Cab. 23. Microfilm n.s. 173. Green Library, Stanford University.

_____. Foreign Office. *Documents on British Foreign Policy, 1919–1939*. Second Series XVII, XVIII, XIX. Third Series I, II, III, VI. London: HMSO, 1946 (Third Series), 1979, 1980, 1982 (Second Series).

_____. Foreign Office. *Documents on German Foreign Policy, 1918–1945*. Vol. I. London: HMSO, 1949.

_____. Parliament. House of Commons. *Report on the Visit by an All Party Group of Members of Parliament to Spain*. London: Press Dept. of the Spanish Embassy, [1937?].

Greaves, H. R. G. *The Truth about Spain*. London: Gollancz, 1938.

Greenwall, Harry J. *Mediterranean Crisis*. London: Nicholson and Watson, 1939.

Gregory, Walter. *The Shallow Grave: A Memoir of the Spanish Civil War*. London: Gollancz, 1986.

Griffiths, Richard. *Fellow Travellers of the Right: British Enthusiasts for Nazi Germany, 1933–39*. London: Constable, 1980.

Grimau, Carmen. *El cartel republicano en la guerra civil*. Madrid: Cátedra, 1979.

Grisoni, Dominique, and Hertzog, Gilles. *Les brigades de la mer*. Paris: Grasset, 1979.

Gromyko, A. A., et al., eds. *Soviet Peace Efforts on the Eve of World War II*. Moscow: Progress, 1973.

Gros, José. *Abriendo Camino: Relatos de un guerrillero comunista español.* Pròlogo de Dolores Ibárruri. Paris: Globe, 1971.

Guadalajara. Madrid: Comisariado General de Guerra (Inspección Centro) Comisión de Propaganda, 1937.

Guardia Abella, Isidro. *Conversaciones sobre el movimiento obrero: Entrevistas con militantes de la CNT.* Madrid: La Piqueta, 1978.

Guarner, Vicente. *L'aixecament militar i la guerra civil a Catalunya, 1936–1939.* Montserrat: Toro, 1975.

———. *Las reformas militares de la república española.* Mexico City: España Nueva, 1947.

Guérin, Daniel. *L'anarchisme: De la doctrine à l'action.* Paris: Gallimard, 1965.

———. *Front populaire: Révolution manqúee, Témoignage militant.* Paris: Maspero, 1970.

———. *Ni dieu ni maître: Anthologie historique de mouvement anarchiste.* Paris: Delphes, [1967?].

Guerney, Jason. *Crusade in Spain.* London: Faber, 1974.

Guernica. London: Eyre and Spottiswoode, 1938.

La guerra de liberación nacional: Historia de la guerra. Vol. III. Zaragoza: Universidad de Zaragoza, 1961.

Guerra y revolución en España, 1936–1939. Vols. I, II, III, IV. Moscow: Progreso, 1967, 1966, 1971, 1977.

Guillén, Abraham. *El error militar de las "izquierdas."* Barcelona: Colectivo, 1980.

———. *Historia de la revolución española.* Buenos Aires: Coyoacan, 1961.

Guinea, José Luis. *Los movimientos obreros y sindicales en España de 1833 a 1978.* Madrid: Ibérico Europea de Ediciones, 1978.

Guixé, Juan. *Le vrai visage de la république espagnole.* Paris: Cooperative Étoile, 1938.

Gustavo, Soledad. *El sindicalismo y la anarquía: Política y sociología.* Paris: Tierra y Libertad, 1945.

Gutiérrez Molina, José Luis. *Colectividades libertarias en Castilla.* Madrid: Debate Libertario, 1977.

Gutiérrez-Ravé, José. *Las cortes errantes del frente popular.* Madrid: Editora Nacional, 1953.

———. *José Gil Robles, caudillo frustrado.* Madrid: Luyve, 1967.

Guttmann, Allen. *The Wound in the Heart: America and the Spanish Civil War.* New York: Free Press of Glencoe, 1962.

Guzmán, Eduardo de. *El año de la Victoria.* Madrid: Toro, 1974.

———. *Madrid, rojo y negro.* Barcelona: Tierra y Libertad, 1938.

———. *La muerte de la esperanza.* Madrid: Toro, 1973.

———. *Nosotros, los asesinos.* Madrid: Toro, 1976.

———. *La segunda república fue así.* Barcelona: Planeta, 1977.

Guzmán de Alfarache, J. *¡18 de julio! Historia del alzamiento glorioso de Sevilla.* Seville: F.E., 1937.

Györkei, Jenö. *Legenda, valóság, tragédia: A nemzetközí brigadok történetéböl.* Budapest: Zrinyi-Militärverlag, 1986.

Hacia una nueva revolución. Barcelona: Agrupación Amigos de Durruti, [1937]. See Balius, Jaime, *Towards a Fresh Revolution* (translation of *Hacia una nueva revolución*), and "Los Amigos de Durruti."

Hacia un mundo nuevo: Teoría y práctica del anarcosindicalismo. Valparaiso: Gutenberg, 1938.

Hager, Kurt. See Albin, Felix.

Haldane, Charlotte. *The Truth Will Out.* London: Right Book Club, 1949.

Halifax, Lord. *Fullness of Days.* New York: Dodd, Mead, 1957.

Hamilton, Ian. *Koestler: A Biography.* London: Secker and Warburg, 1982.

Hammond, Thomas T., ed. *The Anatomy of Communist Takeovers.* New Haven: Yale University Press, 1971.

Hanighen, Frank, ed. *Nothing But Danger: Thrilling Adventures of Ten Newspaper Correspondents in the Spanish Civil War.* New York: McBride, 1939.

Hargrave, John. *Montagu Norman.* New York: Greystone, 1942.

Harvey, John, ed. *The Diplomatic Diaries of Oliver Harvey, 1937–1940.* New York: St. Martin's, 1971.

Hayes, Paul. *The Twentieth Century, 1880–1939: Modern British Foreign Policy.* New York: St. Martin's, 1978.

Heine, Hartmut. *La oposición política al franquismo de 1939 a 1952.* Barcelona: Grijalbo, 1983.

Held, Walter. *Die spanische Revolution.* Paris: Jean Mekhler, [1938?].

Hellman, Lillian. *Three.* Boston: Little, Brown, 1979.

————. *An Unfinished Woman: A Memoir.* Boston: Little, Brown, 1969.

Hemingway, Ernest. *By-Line: Ernest Hemingway: Selected Articles and Dispatches of Four Decades.* New York: Scribner's Sons, 1967.

————. *The Fifth Column and Four Stories of the Spanish Civil War.* New York: Scribner's Sons, 1969.

Henderson, Sir Nevile. *Failure of a Mission.* London: Hodder and Stoughton, 1940.

Henríquez Caubín, Julián. *La Batalla del Ebro.* Mexico City: Unda y García, 1944.

Hericourt, Pierre. *Arms for Red Spain.* London: Burns Oates and Washbourne, [1937?].

————. *Pourquoi Franco a vaincu.* Paris: Baudinière, 1939.

————. *Pourquoi Franco vaincra.* Paris: Baudinière, 1936.

Hermet, Guy. *Los comunistas en España.* Paris: Ruedo Ibérico, 1972.

Hernández, Jesús. *A los intelectuales de España.* Valencia: Partido Comunista de España, Comisión Nacional de Agit-Prop, 1937.

————. *¡Atrás los invasores!* Barcelona: Partido Comunista de España, 1938.

*————. Correspondence with Burnett Bolloten.

————. *En el país de la gran mentira.* Madrid: Toro, 1974.

————. *Negro y rojo: Los anarquistas en la revolución española.* Mexico City: La España Contemporánea, 1946.

————. *El orgullo de sentirnos españoles.* Barcelona: S.G. de Publicaciones, [1938?].

————. *El partido comunista antes, durante y después de la crisis del gobierno Largo Caballero.* Valencia: Partido Comunista de España, 1937.

————. *Todo dentro del frente popular.* [Valencia?]: Partido Comunista de España, Comisión Nacional de Agit-Prop, 1937.

————. *Yo fui un ministro de Stalin.* Mexico City: Editorial America, 1953.

Hernández García, Antonio, *La represión en la rioja durante la guerra civil.* Vols. I, II, III. Logroño: Calahorra, 1984.

Hernández Zancajo, Carlos. *Tercera etapa de octubre.* Valencia: Meabe, 1937.

Herrick, William. *Hermanos!* Sag Harbor, N.Y.: Second Chance Press, 1969.

————. "A Memoir." Paper delivered at Siena College, 12 June 1938.

Herring, Hubert Clinton. *Spain, Battleground of Democracy.* New York: Pilgrim Press, 1937.

Heusser, Hans. *Der Kampf um Madrid.* Berne: Francke, [1937?].

*Hidalgo de Cisneros, Ignacio. Interview, notes taken by Burnett Bolloten.

————. *Memorias 2: La república y la guerra de España.* Paris: Librarie du Globe, 1964.

————. *Virage sur l'aile: Souvenirs.* Paris: Français Reunis, 1965.

Hidalgo Salazar, H. *La ayuda alemana a España, 1936–39: Legion Condor.* Madrid: San Martín, 1975.

Higuera y Velázquez, Alfonso G. de la. *Historia de la revolución española.* Madrid: Cervantes, 1940.

Hilger, Gustav, and Mayer, Alfred G. *The Incompatible Allies.* New York: Macmillan, 1953.

Hills, George. *Franco: The Man and His Nation.* New York: Macmillan, 1967.

————. *Monarquía, república y Franquismo, 1868–1974.* Madrid: San Martín, 1969.

Hinkel, John Vincent. *The Communistic Network.* New York: America Press, 1939.

Hiriartia, J. de. *El caso de los católicos vascos.* Buenos Aires: Egi-Alde, 1939.

Hispanicus [pseud.]. *Badajoz.* London: Friends of Spain, 1937.

————. *Foreign Intervention in Spain.* London: United Editorial, 1938.

Historia de la revolución nacional española. 2 vols. Paris: Sociedad Internacional de Ediciones y de Publicidad, 1940.

Historia del partido comunista de España. Paris: Ediciones Sociales, 1960.

Hitler, Adolf. *"Es spricht der Führer": 7 exemplarische Hitler Reden.* Gütersloh: Sigbert Mohn, 1966.

Hoare, Sir Samuel (Viscount Templewood). *Nine Troubled Years.* London: Collins, 1954.

Hoffman, Heinz. *Mannheim. Madrid. Moskau.* Berlin (VEB): Militärverlag der Deutschen Demokratischen Republik, 1981.

Hoggan, David L. *Der erzwungene Krieg.* Tübingen: Deutsche Hochschullehrer-Zeitung, 1961.

Homenaje a André Marty. Madrid: Comisariado de las Brigadas Internacionales, [1937?].

Homenaje del comité peninsular de la FAI a Buenaventura Durruti, 1896–1936. En el segundo aniversario de su muerte. Barcelona: n.p., 1938.

Hore, Charlie. *Spain, 1936: Popular Front or Workers' Power?* London: Bookmarks, 1986.

Hoskins, Katherine Bail. *Today the Struggle: Literature and Politics in England during the Spanish Civil War.* Austin and London: University of Texas Press, 1969.

How Mussolini Provoked the Spanish Civil War. London: United Editorial, [1938?].

How the German Fleet Shelled Almeria. London: Union of Democratic Control, [1937?].

Hoyos, Max. *Pedros y Pablos: Fliegen, Leben, Kämpfen in Spanien.* Munich: Druckmann, 1940.

*Hudson, Irene. Interview, notes taken by Burnett Bolloten.

I Accuse France. London: Spanish Press Services, [1937?].

Ibárruri, Dolores [La Pasionaria]. *Ejército popular unido, ejército de la victoria*. Madrid-Barcelona: Partido Comunista de España, 1938.

_____. *En la lucha: Palabras y hechos, 1936–1939*. Moscow: Progreso, 1968.

_____. *Es hora ya de crear el gran partido único del proletariado*. Madrid: Stajanov, 1937.

_____. *For the Independence of Spain, for Liberty, for the Republic, Union of All Spaniards*. Complete text of the Report to the Plenary Session of the Central Committee of the Communist Party of Spain, Madrid, May 23, 1938. Madrid: Communist Party of Spain, 1938.

_____. *Mémoires de La Pasionaria*. Paris: Julliard, 1964.

_____. *Memorias de Pasionaria, 1939–1977*. Barcelona: Planeta, 1984.

_____. *No hay mas posibilidad de gobernar que a través del frente popular*. Barcelona: Partido Comunista de España, 1938.

_____. *Un pleno histórico*. Valencia: Partido Comunista de España, Comisión Nacional de Agit-Prop, 1937.

_____. *Speeches and Articles, 1936–38*. London: Lawrence and Wishart, 1938.

_____. *They Shall Not Pass: The Autobiography of La Pasionaria*. New York: International Publishers, 1966.

_____. *El único camino*. Paris: Editions Sociales, 1962.

_____. *Unión de todos los españoles: Por la independencia de España. Por la libertad. Por la república*. Madrid-Barcelona: Partido Comunista de España, 1938.

Ibarzabal, Eugenio. *50 Años de nacionalismo vasco, 1928–1978*. Bilbao: Ediciones Vascas, 1978.

*Iglesias, Captain Ramón. Interview, notes taken by Burnett Bolloten.

Iglesias, Ignacio. See also Suárez, Andrés.

*_____. Correspondence with Burnett Bolloten.

_____. *La fase final de la guerra civil*. Barcelona: Planeta, 1977.

_____. *León Trotski y España, 1930–1939*. Madrid: Júcar, 1977.

_____. *Trotsky y la revolución española*. Madrid: Zero, 1976.

Iglesia y estado durante la segunda república española, 1931–1939. Barcelona: Monestir de Montserrat, 1977.

Informe sobre la guerra civil en el país vasco. Buenos Aires: Amorrortu, 1938.

Informe sobre la situación de las provincias vascongadas bajo el dominio rojo-separatista. Valladolid: Universidad de Valladolid, 1938.

Inglés, Martín. *Bajo las garras del SIM*. Barcelona: Librería Religiosa, 1940.

Iniesta, Juan de. *Escuchad, campesino*. Madrid: Comisión de Propaganda del Comité Regional del Centro, 1937.

In Spain with the International Brigade. London: Burns Oates and Washbourne, 1938.

Intellectuals and the Spanish Military Rebellion. London: Spanish Embassy, 1936.

International Committee of Coordination and Information to Aid Republican Spain. *Franco ami de la France?* Paris: Comité International de Coordination et d'information pour l'aide à l'Espagne républicaine, 1938.

International Military Tribunal. *The Trial of German Major War Criminals before the International Military Tribunal, Nuremberg*. Parts IX and X. London: HMSO, 1947.

International Telephone and Telegraph Co. Memoria, 1936–1940. Madrid, 1941.

Iribarren, José María. *Con el General Mola: Escenas y aspectos inéditos de la guerra civil.* Saragossa: Librería General, 1937.

———. *Mola.* Saragossa: Heraldo de Aragón, 1938.

Iribarren, Manuel. *Una perspectiva histórica de la guerra en España, 1936–1939.* Madrid: García Enciso, 1941.

*Irujo, Andrés María de. Correspondence with Burnett Bolloten.

*Irujo, Manuel de. "Datos Remitidos por el Señor Manuel de Irujo, Ministro Vasco en el Gobierno de la República Española." Memorandum sent by Irujo to the Basque Government-in-Exile. Hoover Institution, Bolloten Collection.

*———. "La guerra civil en Euzkadi antes del estatuto." Microfilm copy of this unpublished work loaned to Burnett Bolloten by Manuel de Irujo.

———. *Un vasco en el ministerio de justicia.* Vols. I, II. Buenos Aires: Vasca Ekin, 1976, 1978.

Irving, David. *Hitler's War.* New York: Viking Press, 1977.

———. *The War Path: Hitler's Germany, 1933–1939.* London: Joseph, 1978.

———, ed. *Breach of Security.* London: Kimber, 1968.

Istoriia vtoroi mirovoi voiny, 1939–1945. Moscow: Voennoe Izdatel'stvo, 1973–82. Vol. II (1974): "Nakanune voiny."

The Italian Air Force in Spain. London: United Editorial, n.d.

Italians in Spain. London: Friends of Democracy and Independence in Spain, [1937].

Iturralde, Juan de [Padre Juan Usabiaga]. *El catolicismo y la cruzada de Franco.* Vienne, France: Egi-Indarra, 1960.

Izaga, G. Arsenio de. *Los Presos de Madrid.* Madrid: Martosa, 1940.

Jackson, Gabriel. *A Concise History of the Spanish Civil War.* London: Thames and Hudson, 1974.

———. *Entre la reforma y la revolución, 1931–1939.* Barcelona: Grijalbo, 1980.

———. *The Spanish Republic and the Civil War, 1931–1939.* Princeton: Princeton University Press, 1965.

———, ed. *The Spanish Civil War.* Chicago: Quadrangle Books, 1972.

Jackson, Gabriel, and Centelles, Augustí. *Catalunya republicana i revolucionaria, 1931–1939.* Barcelona: Grijalbo, 1982.

Jalón, Cesar. *El cautiverio vasco.* Madrid: Ediciones Españolas, 1939.

James, Robert Rhodes, ed. *Winston S. Churchill: His Complete Speeches, 1897–1963.* Vol. VI. New York: Chelsea House, 1974.

Jean, André. *Transformation Economique en Catalogne.* Barcelona: Generalitat de Catalunya, [1936?].

Jellinek, Frank. *The Civil War in Spain.* London: Gollancz, 1938.

*Jiménez, Miguel. Correspondence with Burnett Bolloten.

Jiménez Campo, Javier. *El fascismo en la crisis de la II república española.* Madrid: Artifrafia, 1979.

Jiménez de Aberasturi, Luis María, and Jiménez de Aberasturi, Juan Carlos. *La guerra en Euskadi.* Esplugas de Llobregat: Plaza y Janés, 1978.

Jiménez de Asúa, Luis. *La constitución política de la democracia española.* Santiago de Chile: Ediciones Ercilla, 1942.

Joaniquet, Aurelio. *Calvo Sotelo.* Santander: Espasa-Calpe, 1939.

*Johnston, Verle B. "The International Brigades in the Spanish Civil War." Xerox copy of original manuscript published by Pennsylvania State University Press in conjunction with the Hoover Institution under the title of *Legions of Babel*. The manuscript contains a considerable amount of amplifying and qualifying material, which was eliminated from the published version.

————. *Legions of Babel: The International Brigades in the Spanish Civil War.* Hoover Institution Publications. University Park: The Pennsylvania State University Press, 1967.

Johnstone, Nancy. *Hotel in Spain.* London: Faber, 1937.

Joint Letter of the Spanish Bishops to the Bishops of the Whole World Concerning the War in Spain. London: Catholic Truth Society, 1937.

Joint Letter of the Spanish Bishops to the Bishops of the Whole World: The War in Spain. New York: America Press, 1937.

Joll, James. *The Anarchists.* London: Eyre and Spottiswoode, 1964.

Jones, Thomas. *A Diary of Letters.* Oxford: Oxford University Press, 1954.

Jong, Alberti de. See Schapiro, Alexander.

Jordan, Philip. *There Is No Return.* London: Cresset Press, 1938.

Joseph, Don. *Shop Talk on Spain.* New York: North American Committee to Aid Spanish Democracy, [1937?].

Jouve, Marguerite. *Vu en Espagne.* Paris: Flammarion, 1937.

Juliá, Santos. *La izquierda del PSOE, 1935–1936.* Madrid: Siglo XXI, 1977.

————. *Orígenes del frente popular en España, 1934–1936.* Madrid: Siglo XXI, 1979.

————, ed. *El socialismo en España: Desde la fundación del PSOE hasta 1975.* Madrid: Pablo Iglesias, 1986.

Junco, Alfonso. *Mexico y los refugiados.* Mexico City: Jus, 1959.

Juventud comunista ibérica. A los ocho meses de guerra civil. Barcelona: n.p., 1937.

Kaminski, H. E. *Ceux de Barcelone.* Paris: Denoël, 1937.

"Kandelaki Mission." Auswärtiges Amt. Film Serial 1907 H/429294-324. Washington, D.C.: National Archives.

Kantorowicz, Alfred. *Spanisches Kriegstagebuch.* Hamburg: Konkret-Literatur-Verlag, 1979.

Kaplan, Temma. *The Anarchists of Andalusia.* Princeton: Princeton University Press, 1977.

————. *Orígenes sociales del anarquismo en Andalucía.* Barcelona: Grijalbo, 1977.

Karaganda: La tragedia del antifascismo español. Toulouse: MLE-CNT, 1948.

Keding, Karl. *Feldgeistlicher bei Legion Condor.* Berlin: Ostwerk, [1938?].

Kemp, Peter. *Mine Were of Trouble.* London: Cassell, 1957.

Kennan, George F. *Russia and the West under Lenin and Stalin.* Boston: Little, Brown, 1960.

Kerillis, Henri de. *Français! Voici la guerre!* Paris: Bernard Grasset, 1936.

Khrushchev, Nikita. *Speech at a Session of the 20th Congress of the Communist Party of the Soviet Union on 25 February 1956.* Washington, D.C.: U.S. Department of State, 1956.

Kirkpatrick, Ivone. *Mussolini: A Study in Power.* New York: Hawthorn Books, 1964.

Kirkpatrick, Jeane J., ed. *The Strategy of Deception: A Study in World-Wide Communist Tactics*. New York: Farrar, Straus, 1963.

Klotz, Helmut. *Les leçons militaires de la guerre civile en Espagne*. Paris: Edité par l'Auteur, 1937.

Knickerbocker, H. R. *The Siege of Alcazar*. Philadelphia: McKay, 1936.

Knightly, Philip. *The First Casualty*. New York: Harcourt Brace Jovanovich, 1975.

Knoblaugh, H. Edward. *Correspondent in Spain*. New York: Sheed and Ward, 1937.

Koblyakov, I. K. *USSR for Peace against Aggression, 1933–1941*. Moscow: Progress, 1976.

Koestler, Arthur. *L'Espagne ensanglantée*. Paris: Carrefour, 1937.

————. *The Invisible Writing*. London: Collins with Hamish Hamilton, 1954.

————. *The Spanish Testament*. London: Gollancz, 1937.

Köhler, Klaus. *Kriegsfreiwilliger 1937*. Leipzig: Henig, 1939.

Koltzov, Mijail [Mikhail] E. *Diario de la guerra de España*. Paris: Ruedo Ibérico, 1963.

————. *Izbrannye proizvedeniia*. Vol. III. Moscow: Gosudarstvennoe Izdatelstvo Khudozhestvennoi Literatury, 1957.

Kommunisticheskii internatsional: Kratkii istoricheskii ocherk (Outline History of the Communist International). Moscow: Politzat Literatura, 1969.

Krehm, William. *Spain. Revolution and Counter-Revolution*. Toronto: League for a Revolutionary Workers' Party, [1937?].

Kristanov, Tsvetan. *Za svobodu Ispanii: Memuary bolgarskogo kommunista*. Moscow: Progress, 1969.

Krivitsky, Walter G. *In Stalin's Secret Service*. New York: Harper, 1939.

Kropp, Major A. *So kämpfen deutsche Soldaten*. Berlin: Wilhelm Limpert, 1939.

Kurzman, Dan. *Miracle of November*. New York: Putnam's Sons, 1980.

Kuznetsov, Nikolai G. *Na dalekom meridiane*. Moscow: Nauka, 1966.

Lacalle, Andrés García. *Mitos y verdades: La aviación de caza en la guerra española*. Mexico City: Oasis, 1973.

Lacouture, Jean. *Léon Blum*. Translated by George Holoch. New York: Holmes and Meier, 1982.

Lacruz, Francisco. *El alzamiento, la revolución y el terror en Barcelona*. Barcelona: Librería Arysel, 1943.

Lain, José. *Por un ejército regular disciplinado y fuerte: Conferencia nacional de juventudes, enero 1937*. Valencia: JSU, 1937.

Lamas Arroyo, Angel. *Unos . . . y . . . otros . . . .* Barcelona: Luis de Caralt, 1972.

Lambda [pseud.]. *The Truth about the Barcelona Events*. New York: Independent Communist League of New York, 1937.

Lamo de Espinosa, E. *Filosofía y política en Julián Besteiro*. Madrid: Edicusa, 1973.

Lamoneda, Ramón. *El camino de la unidad*. Madrid: n.p., 1937.

*————. Letter (carbon copy) sent in August 1939 to a member of the party, Paris, 1939.

————. *El partido socialista en la república española*. Mexico City: El Socialista, 1942.

Lamour, Philippe. *Sauvons la France en Espagne*. Paris: Baudinière, 1937.

*Landau, Katia. Correspondence with Burnett Bolloten.

———. *Le stalinisme en Espagne*. Paris: Spartacus, 1938.

Landis, Arthur H. *Spain: The Unfinished Revolution*. New York: International Publishers, 1972.

The Land of Socialism Today and Tomorrow: Reports and Speeches at the Eighteenth Congress of the Communist Party of the Soviet Union (Bolshevik), March 10– 21, 1939. Moscow: Foreign Languages Publishing House, 1939.

Langdon-Davies, John. *Behind the Spanish Barricades*. New York: Robert M. McBride, 1937.

———. *The Case for the Government*. New York: American Friends of Spanish Democracy, 1939.

———. *Gatherings from Catalonia*. London: Cassell, 1953.

———. *The Spanish Church and Politics*. New York: American Friends of Spanish Democracy, 1938.

Langhorne, Richard, ed. *Diplomacy and Intelligence during the Second World War*. Cambridge: Cambridge University Press, 1985.

Lapeyre, Aristide. *Le problème espagnol*. Paris: Edition "Ce qu'il faut dire," 1946.

Lapeyre, Paul. *Lueurs sur l'Espagne: Revolution et contre-revolution en Espagne republicaine*. Nimes: La Laborieuse, 1938.

———. *Révolution et contre-révolution en Espagne*. Paris: Spartacus, 1938.

Largo Caballero, Franciso. *Discurso pronunciado en Valencia el día 1 de febrero de 1937*. Valencia: Comisarido General de Guerra, 1937.

———. *Discursos a los trabajadores*. Madrid: Gráfica Socialista, 1934.

———. *Escritos de la república: Edición, estudio preliminar y notas de Santos Juliá*. Madrid: Pablo Iglesias, 1985.

———. *Largo Caballero denuncia*. Buenos Aires: Servicio de Propaganda España, 1937.

———. Letter to Diego Martínez Barrio, 26 Oct. 1937. International Institute of Social History, CNT-FAI Archives, Paquete 005, Caja 305, Dossier 66.

———. *Mis recuerdos: Cartas a un amigo*. Mexico City: Alianza, 1954. For information on these memoirs, see Chapter 45, n. 19.

———. "Notas Históricas sobre la Guerra de España." Manuscript. Fundación Pablo Iglesias, Madrid. For information on this manuscript, see Chapter 45, n. 19.

———. *Presente y futuro de la Unión General de Trabajadores de España*. Madrid: J. Morata Pedreño, [1925?].

———. *¿Qué se puede hacer?* Paris: n.p., 1940.

———. *La UGT y la guerra*. Valencia: Meabe, 1937.

Lario Sánchez, Juan. *Habla un aviador de la república*. Madrid: Toro, 1973.

Larios, José, Capitán de Aviación. *Combate sobre España: Memorias de un piloto de caza, 1936–1939*. Madrid: Aldus, 1966.

Larrañaga, Jesús. *¡Por la libertad de Euzkadi, dentro de las libertades de España!* Barcelona: Partido Comunista de España, 1937.

Last, Jef. *The Spanish Tragedy*. London: Routledge, 1939.

Lazareff, Pierre. *Deadline*. New York: Random House, 1942.

Lazarillo de Tormes [Benigno Bejarano]. *España, cuña de la libertad*. Valencia: "Ebro," [1937?].

————. *España, tumba del fascismo*. Valencia: Ediciones del Comité Nacional de la CNT, Sección Propaganda y Prensa, [1938?].

*————. "Les morts ne vous pardonnent pas." Photocopies of some of the pages of this unpublished work loaned to Burnett Bolloten by José Peirats are in the Hoover Institution.

Lazitch, Branko. *Los partidos comunistas de Europa, 1919–1955*. Madrid: Instituto de Estudio Políticos, 1961.

Lazitch, Branko, and Drachkovitch, Milorad M. *Biographical Dictionary of the Comintern*. Stanford: Hoover Institution, 1973.

League of American Writers, ed. *Writers Take Sides*. New York: League of American Writers, 1938.

Lefranc, Georges. *Histoire du front populaire*. Paris: Presses Universitaires de France, 1972.

The Legacy of Alexander Orlov. See U.S. Congress.

Lehning, Arthur. *Michel Bakounine et les autres*. Paris: Union Générale d'Editions, 1976.

Lenoir, P. *La finance internationale et la guerre d'Espagne*. Paris: Paix et Democratie, 1938.

Lent, Alfred. *Wir kämpften für Spanien*. Berlin: Gerhard Stalling, 1939.

Lera, Angel María de. *Angel Pestaña*. Barcelona: Argos, 1978.

Lerroux, Alejandro. *Mis memorias*. Madrid: Afrodisio Aguado, 1963.

————. *La pequeña historia*. Madrid: Afrodisio Aguado, [1963?].

Lerroux, Alejandro; Marañón, Gregorio; Unamuno, Miguel de; Baroja y Nessi, Pio. *Spanish Liberals Speak on the Counter-revolution in Spain*. Translated and edited by the Spanish Relief Committee. San Francisco: Spanish Relief Committee, 1937.

Lettre collective des évêques espagnols à ceux du monde entier à propos de la guerre en Espagne. Paris: n.p., 1937.

Leval, Gaston [Pierre Piller]. *L'anarchisme et la révolution espagnole*. Turin: Einaudi, 1971.

————. *Collectives in the Spanish Revolution*. Translated by Vernon Richards. London: Freedom Press, 1975.

————. *Le communisme*. Paris: Les Editions du Libertaire, n.d.

*————. Correspondence with Burnett Bolloten.

————. *Espagne libertaire, 1936–39: L'oeuvre constructive de la révolution espagnole*. Meuse: Editions du Cercle, 1971.

————. *L'indispensable révolution*. Paris: Editions du Libertaire, 1948.

————. *Marxisme et anarchisme*. Turin: Einaudi, 1971.

————. *Né Franco né Stalin: Le collettività anarchische spagnole nella lotta contro Franco e la reazione staliniana*. Milan: Istituto Editoriale Italiano, 1952.

————. *Nuestro programa de reconstrucción*. Barcelona: Oficinas de Propaganda, CNT-FAI, [1937?].

————. *Pour une renaissance du mouvement libertaire*. Turin: Einaudi, 1971.

————. *Social Reconstruction in Spain*. London: Spain and the World, 1938.

Leviatán: Antología. Selección y prólogo de Paul Preston. Madrid: Turner, 1976.

Levine, Isaac Don. *Eyewitness to History*. New York: Hawthorn Books, 1973.

————. *The Mind of an Assassin*. New York: Straus and Cudahy, 1959.

Lévy, Louis. *Vérités sur la France*. Harmondsworth, England: Editions Pingouin, 1941.

*Liarte, Ramón. Correspondence with Burnett Bolloten.

———. *Entre la revolución y la guerra*. Barcelona: Picazo, 1986.

Liddell Hart, Basil Henry. *Europe in Arms*. New York: Random House, 1937.

———. *The Memoirs of Captain Liddell Hart*. Vols. I, II. London: Cassell, 1965, 1967.

Liébana, José Manuel, and Orizana, G. *El movimiento nacional*. Valladolid: Vicente, [1937].

Linz, Juan. *The Party System of Spain: Past and Future*. New York: Free Press, 1967.

Líster, Enrique. *Así destruyó Carrillo el PCE*. Barcelona: Planeta, 1983.

———. *¡Basta!* n.p., [1971?].

———. *Memorias de un luchador*. Vol. I: *Los primeros combates*. Madrid: Toro, 1977.

———. *Nuestra guerra: Aportaciones para una historia de la guerra nacional revolucionaria del pueblo español, 1936–1939*. Paris: Librarie du Globe, 1966.

List of Ships Interfered with, Attacked or Sunk during the War in Spain, July 1936– June 1938. London: Press Dept. of the Spanish Embassy, [1938?].

Litvinov, Maxim. *Against Aggression*. London: Lawrence and Wishart, 1939.

Le livre blanc de l'intervention italienne en Espagne. Paris: Comité Franco-Espagnol, 1937.

Lizarra, A. de [Andrés María de Irujo]. *Los vascos y la república española*. Buenos Aires: Vasca Ekin, 1944. This book is based on the memoirs of Manuel de Irujo. (Andrés María was Manuel's brother and private secretary during the Civil War.)

Lizarza Iribarren, Antonio de. *Memorias de la conspiración 1931–1936*. Pamplona: Gómez, 1969.

Lizon Gadea, Adolfo. *Brigadas internacionales en España*. Madrid: Editora Nacional, 1940.

Lladó i Figueres, J. *El 19 de julio a Barcelona*. Barcelona: Biblioteca política de Catalunya, 1938.

Llarch, Joan. *La Batalla del Ebro*. Barcelona: Aura, 1972.

———. *Cipriano Mera: Un anarquista en la guerra civil española*. Barcelona: Producciones Editoriales, 1977.

———. *Los días rojinegros*. Barcelona: Ediciones 29, 1977.

———. *Morir en Madrid*. Barcelona: Producciones Editoriales, 1978.

———. *Le muerte de Durruti*. Barcelona: Plaza y Janés, 1976.

———. *Negrín: ¡Resistir es vencer!* Barcelona: Planeta, 1985.

———. *La tràgica mort de Companys*. Barcelona: Bruguera, 1979.

Llaugé, Félix. *El terror staliniano en la España republicana*. Barcelona: Aura, 1974.

Llorens, Carlos. *La guerra en Valencia y en el frente de Teruel*. Santander: Fernando Torres, 1978.

Llorens, Josep María. *La iglesia contra la república española*. Vieux, France: Galerie d'Art du Domaine de l'Espaliou, 1968.

Llovera, Fernando. *La columna Uribarry*. Valencia: Turia, [1937?].

Lloyd, Lord [George Ambrose]. *The British Case*. London: Eyre and Spottiswoode, 1939.

Lloyd George, David. *Spain and Britain*. New York: American Friends of Spanish Democracy, 1937.

Lluhí Vallescà, Joan. *Lluis Companys Jover, President de la Generalitat de Catalunya*. Mexico City: Imprenta Grafos, 1944.

Loewenstein, Prince Hubertus Friedrich of. *A Catholic in Republican Spain*. London: Gollancz, 1937.

Lojendio, Ignacio María de. *El derecho de revolucion*. Madrid: Revista de Derecho Privado, 1941.

Lojendio, Luis María de. *Operaciones militares de la guerra de España*. Barcelona: Montaner y Simón, 1940.

London, Arthur G. *L'aveu*. Paris: Gallimard, 1968.

_____. *Espagne*. Paris: Français Réunis, 1966.

Londonderry, K. G., The Marquess of. *Ourselves and Germany*. London: Hale, 1938.

_____. *Wings of Destiny*. London: Macmillan, 1943.

Longo, Luigi (Gallo). *Un anno di guerra in Spagna*. Paris: Coltúra Sociale, 1938.

_____. *Las brigadas internacionales en España*. Mexico City: Ediciones Era, 1966.

López, Juan. *Concepto del federalismo en la guerra y en la revolución*. [Barcelona?]: Oficinas de Propaganda CNT-FAI, n.d.

_____. *Una misión sin importancia: Memorias de un sindicalista*. Madrid: Editora Nacional, 1972.

López de Medrano, Luís. *986 días en el infierno*. Madrid: Asilo de Huérfanos del Sagrado Corazón de Jesús, 1939.

López Fernández, Captain Antonio. *Defensa de Madrid*. Mexico City: A.P. Márquez, 1945.

López-Muñiz, Lieutenant Colonel de E. M. *La batalla de Madrid*. Madrid: Gloria, 1943.

López Sevilla, Enrique. *El partido socialista obrero español en las cortes constituyentes de la segunda república*. Mexico City: Pablo Iglesias, 1969.

Lo que han hecho en Galicia. Paris: Editorial España, 1938.

Lorenzo, César M. *Les anarchistes espagnols et le pouvoir, 1868–1969*. Paris: Du Seuil, 1969. The author is the son of Horatio M. Prieto, onetime national secretary of the CNT.

Louzon, R. *La contrarevolución en España*. Buenos Aires: Imán, 1938.

Loveday, Arthur. *British Trade Interests and the Spanish War*. London: Spanish Press Services, [1937?].

_____. *World War in Spain*. London: Murray, 1939.

Lunn, Arnold. *Spain and the Christian Front: Ubi Crux Ibi Patria*. New York: Paulist Press, [1937?].

_____. *Spain: The Unpopular Front*. London: Catholic Truth Society, 1937.

_____. *Spanish Rehearsal*. London: Hutchinson, 1937.

Macarro Vera, José Manuel. *La utopía revolucionaria: Sevilla en la Segunda República*. Sevilla: Monte de Piedad, 1985.

McCabe, Joseph. *The Causes of the Civil War in Spain*. Kansas: Haldeman-Julius, 1937.

_____. *The Papacy in Politics Today*. London: Watts, 1937.

MacDonald, C. A. *The United States, Britain and Appeasement, 1936–1939.* London: Macmillan, 1981.

Macdonald, Nancy. *Homage to the Spanish Exiles.* New York: Insight Books, 1987.

MacDougall, Ian, ed. *Voices from the Spanish Civil War: Personal Recollections of Scottish Volunteers in Republican Spain, 1936–39.* Edinburgh: Polygon, 1986.

McGovern, John, M.P. *Terror in Spain.* London: Independent Labour Party, 1937.

_____. *Why Bishops Back Franco: Report of Visit of Investigation to Spain.* London: Independent Labour Party, [1936?].

McGraw-Hill Encyclopedia of Russia and the Soviet Union. New York: McGraw-Hill, [1961].

McLachlan, Donald. *In the Chair: Barrington-Ward of the Times, 1927–1948.* London: Weidenfeld and Nicolson, 1971.

Macleod, Iain. *Neville Chamberlain.* London: Muller, 1961.

MacMillan, Harold. *Winds of Change, 1914–1939.* New York: Harper and Row, 1966.

McMillan, Wayne. *This Is Our Concern.* New York: Social Workers Committee to Aid Spanish Democracy, 1937.

McNair, John. *Spanish Diary.* Manchester: Greater Manchester ILP Branch, [1937?].

McNeill-Moss, Geoffrey. *The Epic of the Alcázar.* London: Rich and Cowan, 1937.

_____. *The Legend of Badajoz.* London: Burns Oates and Washbourne, 1937.

Madariaga, Salvador de. *España.* Buenos Aires: Editorial Sudamericana, 1942.

_____. *Españoles de mi tiempo.* Barcelona: Planeta, 1974.

_____. *Memorias, 1921–1936.* Madrid: Espasa-Calpe, 1974.

_____. *Spain: A Modern History.* New York: Praeger, 1960. Second Printing.

Madrid Santos, Francisco. *Camillo Berneri, un anarchico italiano, 1897–1937: Rivoluzione e controrivoluzione in Europa, 1917–1937.* Pistoia: Archivo Famiglia Berneri, 1985.

Madrid: The "Military" Atrocities of the Rebels. London: Labour Party of Great Britain, 1937.

Maeztu, Ramiro de. *En vísperas de la tragedia.* Preface by José M. de Areilza. Madrid: Cultura Española, 1941.

Maidanik, K. L. *Ispanskii proletariat v natsionalno-revoliutsionnoi voine, 1936–1937.* Moscow: Akademiia Nauk, 1960.

Maisky, Ivan M. *Ispanskie Tetradi.* Moscow: Voennoe izdatel'stvo, 1962.

_____. *Iz istorii osvoboditelnoi borby ispanskogo naroda.* Moscow: Akademiia Nauk SSSR, 1959.

_____. *Memoirs of a Soviet Ambassador: The War, 1939–43.* London: Hutchinson, 1967.

_____. *Spanish Notebooks.* London: Hutchinson, 1966.

_____. *Who Helped Hitler?* London: Hutchinson, 1964.

Maitland, Frank. *Searchlight on the Duchess of Atholl.* Edinburgh, [1937?].

Maíz, B. Félix. *Mola, aquel hombre: Diario de la conspiración, 1936.* Barcelona: Planeta, 1976.

Majuelo Gil, Emilio. *La II república en Navarra: Conflictividad agraria en la Ribera Tudelana, 1931–1933.* Pamplona: Zarama, 1986.

Malaga Documents. International Institute of Social History, CNT-FAI Archives.

Paquete 63. D. Documentación General. I. Asuntos Especiales. Photocopies in Hoover Institution, Bolloten Collection.

Malefakis, Edward E. *Agrarian Reform and Peasant Revolution in Spain: Origins of the Civil War*. New Haven: Yale University Press, 1970.

Mallorca en guerra contra el marxismo. Palma de Mallorca: Sabater Mut, 1936.

Malraux, André. *The Fascist Threat to Culture*. Speech delivered March 8, 1937, Harvard University, Cambridge.

Maluquer i Wahal, Joan J. *L'aviació de Catalunya els primers mesos de la guerra civil*. Barcelona: Portic, 1978.

Manent i Segimon, Albert, and Raventós i Giralt, Josep. *L'Església clandestina a Catalunya durant la guerra civil, 1936–1939*. Montserrat: Abadia de Montserrat, 1984.

Manifesto of Catalan Intellectuals. Barcelona, 1936.

Manobens, E. *Crónicas de la guerra*. Valencia: Subsecretaria de Propaganda, 1937.

*Mansó, Juan José. Interview, notes taken by Burnett Bolloten.

Manuel, Frank E. *The Politics of Modern Spain*. New York: McGraw-Hill, 1938.

Manzanares, Alejandro. *Alzamiento nacional de España*. Logroño: Imprenta Moderna, 1937.

Marañon. Gregorio. *Liberalismo y comunismo*. Buenos Aires: OPYPRE, 1938.

————. *La revolución española*. n.p., 1938.

————. *Surveying the Spanish War: Liberalism and Communism*. New York, [1937?].

Marichal, Juan. See also Azaña, Manuel.

————. *La vocación de Manuel Azaña*. Madrid: Cuadernos para el Diálogo, 1971.

Marinello, Juan. *Cultura en la España Republicana*. New York: Spanish Information Bureau, 1937.

————. *Dos discursos al servicio de la causa popular*. Paris, 1937.

————. *Hombres de la España Leal*. Havana: Facetas, 1938.

Mario de Coca, Gabriel. *Anti-Caballero: Crítica marxista de la bolchevización del partido socialista, 1930–1936*. Madrid: Engels, 1936.

Maritain, Jacques. *Los rebeldes españoles no hacen una "guerra santa."* Madrid, 1937.

Márquez Tornero, A. C. *Testimonio de me tiempo: Memorias de un español republicano*. Madrid: Orígenes, 1979.

Marrast, Robert. *El teatre durant la guerra civil espanyola*. Barcelona: Edicions 62, 1978.

Marti-Ibañez, Félix. *Grandezas y miserias de la revolución social española*. Barcelona, [1937?].

Martin, Enrique. *Recuerdos de un militante de la CNT*. Barcelona: Picazo, 1979.

Martín, J. *La transformation politique et sociale de la Catalogne durant la révolution: 19 juillet–31 décembre, 1936*. Barcelona: Generalitat de Catalunya, 1938.

*Martín Blázquez, José. Correspondence with Burnett Bolloten.

————. *I Helped to Build an Army*. London: Secker and Warburg, 1939.

Martín i Ramos, Josep Lluís. *Els orígens del partit socialista unificat de Catalunya, 1930–1935*. Barcelona: Curial, 1977.

Martín Retortillo, Cirilo. *Huesca vencedora*. Huesca: Campo, 1938.

Martínez Abad, Julio. *¡17 de julio! La guarnición de Melilla inicia la salvación de*

España. Melilla: Artes Gráficas Postal Exprés, 1937.

Martínez Alier, Juan. *La estabilidad del latifundismo*. Paris: Ruedo Ibérico, 1968.

Martínez Amutio, Justo. *Chantage a un pueblo*. Madrid: Toro, 1974.

*————. Correspondence with Burnett Bolloten.

Martínez Bande, Colonel José Manuel. *Los asedios*. Madrid: San Martín, 1983.

————. *La batalla del Ebro*. Madrid: San Martín, 1978.

————. *La batalla de Teruel*. Madrid: Servicio Histórico Militar, 1974.

————. *La campaña de Andalucía*. Madrid: Servicio Histórico Militar, 1969.

————. *La campaña de Cataluña*. Madrid: San Martín, 1979.

————. *Los cien últimos días de la república*. Barcelona: Caralt, 1973.

————. *El final de la guerra civil*. Madrid: San Martín, 1985.

————. *El final del frente norte*. Madrid: San Martín, 1972.

————. *La gran ofensiva sobre Zaragoza*. Madrid: San Martín, 1973.

————. *La guerra en el norte*. Madrid: Servicio Histórico Militar, 1969.

————. *La intervención comunista en la guerra de España, 1936–1939*. Madrid: Servicio Informativo Español, 1965.

————. *La invasión de Aragón y el desembarco en Mallorca*. Madrid: Servicio Histórico Militar, 1970.

————. *La marcha sobre Madrid*. Madrid: Servicio Histórico Militar, 1968, rev. ed. 1982.

————. *La ofensiva sobre Segovia y la batalla de Brunete*. Madrid: San Martín, 1972.

————. *La ofensiva sobre Valencia*. Madrid: San Martín, 1977.

————. *Vizcaya*. Madrid: San Martín, 1971.

Martínez Barrio, Diego. *Memorias*. Barcelona: Planeta, 1983.

————. *Orígenes del frente popular español*. Buenos Aires: PHAC, 1943.

————. *Páginas para la historia del frente popular*. Madrid-Valencia: Ediciones Españolas, 1937.

*Martínez Cartón, Pedro. Interview, notes taken by Burnett Bolloten.

*Martínez Dasi, Salvador. Correspondence with Burnett Bolloten.

Martínez de Campos, Carlos. *Ayer, 1931–1953*. Madrid: Instituto de Estudios Políticos, 1970.

Martínez Leal, Comandante. *El asedio del Alcázar del Toledo*. Toledo: Editorial Católica Toledana, 1937.

Martínez Lorenzo, César. See Lorenzo, César M.

Martínez Prieto, Horacio. See Prieto, Horacio M.

Marty, André. *Douze mois sublimes*. Paris: Comité Populaire de Propagande, n.d.

————. *En Espagne . . . où se joue le destin de l'Europe*. Paris: Bureau d'Editions, 1937.

————. *L'Espagne, bastion avancé de la liberté et de la paix: Discours au Comité Central du PCF, 29 octobre, 1937*. Paris: La Brochure Populaire, 1937.

————. *Heroic Spain*. New York: Workers Library, 1937.

*Más, Valerio. Correspondence with Burnett Bolloten.

Massó i Escofet, C., and Gay de Montellá, R. *L'estatut de Catalunya*. Barcelona: Bosch, 1933.

Massot i Muntaner, Josep. *La guerra civil a Montserrat*. Montserrat: Abadia de Montserrat, 1984.

Mastny, Vojtech. *Russia's Road to the Cold War*. New York: Columbia University Press, 1979.

Mateu, Julio. *La obra de la federación campesina*. Barcelona: Partido Comunista de España, 1937.

Matthews, Herbert L. *The Education of a Correspondent*. New York: Harcourt, Brace, 1946.

_____. *Half of Spain Died: A Reappraisal of the Spanish Civil War*. New York: Scribner's Sons, 1973.

_____. *Return to Cuba*. Special issue of *Hispanic American Report*. Stanford: Institute of Hispanic American and Luzo-Brazilian Studies, 1964.

_____. *Two Wars and More to Come*. New York: Carrick and Evans, 1938.

_____. *The Yoke and the Arrows*. New York: Braziller, 1961.

Mattioli, Guido. *L'aviazione legionária in Spagna*. Rome: L'Aviazione, 1938.

Maura, Miguel. *Asi cayó Alfonso XIII*. Mexico City: Mañez, 1962.

Maurice, Jacques. *La reforma agraria en España en el siglo XX, 1900–1936*. Madrid: Siglo XXI, 1975.

Maurín, Jeanne. *Cómo se salvó Joaquín Maurín: Recuerdos y testimonios*. Madrid: Júcar, 1980.

Maurín, Joaquín. *En las prisiones de Franco*. Mexico City: Costa-Amic, 1974.

_____. Joaquín Maurín Archives. Hoover Institution.

_____. *Revolución y contrarevolución en España*. Paris: Ruedo Ibérico, 1966.

_____. *Révolution et contre-révolution en Espagne*. Paris: Rieder, 1937.

Meaker, Gerald H. *The Revolutionary Left in Spain, 1914–1923*. Stanford: Stanford University Press, 1974.

Medical Aid for Spain. London: Spanish Medical Aid Committee, 1937.

Medlicott, William N. *Britain and Germany: The Search for Agreement, 1930–37*. London: Athlone, 1969.

_____. *British Foreign Policy since Versailles, 1919-1963*. London: Methuen, 1968.

Medrano, Trifón. *Hombres nuevos y nuevos cuadros*. Valencia: JSU, 1937.

Melchor, Federico. *Organicemos la producción*. Valencia: JSU de España, 1937.

Meliani, Giovanni. *Barcelona sotto l'incubo del terrore rosso*. Milano: Buone Letture, 1938.

Meltzer, Albert, ed. *A New World in Our Hearts*. Orkney: Cienfuegos Press, 1978.

Méndez Luengo, E. *Tempestad al amanecer: La epopeya de Madrid*. Madrid: Toro, 1977.

*Menéndez, Alvaro. Interview, notes taken by Burnett Bolloten.

*Menéndez Beltrán, Leonor. Correspondence with Burnett Bolloten.

Mera, Cipriano. *Guerra, exilio y cárcel de un anarcosindicalista*. Paris: Ruedo Ibérico, 1976.

Mercier Vega, Luis. *Anarquismo, ayer y hoy*. Caracas: Monte Avila, 1970.

Meretskov, Kirill A. *Na sluzhbe narodu: Stranitsy vospominaniia*. Moscow: Politizdat, 1968.

Merin, Peter. *Spain between Death and Birth*. New York: Dodge, 1938.

Merkes, Manfred. *Die deutsche Politik gegenüber dem spanischen Bürgerkrieg, 1936–1939*. Bonn: Röhrscheid, 1961.

Merriman, Marion, and Lerude, Warren. *American Commander in Spain: Robert*

Hale Merriman and the Abraham Lincoln Brigade. Reno: University of Nevada Press, 1986.

Merry Del Val, Alfonso, The Marquis. *The Conflict in Spain*. London: Catholic Truth Society, 1937.

————. *Spain Is Fighting for Civilization*. New York, [1936?].

————. *Spanish Basques and Separatism*. London: Burns Oates and Washbourne, 1939.

Meshcheriakov, Marklin T. *Ispanskaya respublika i komintern: Natsional'no-revoliutsionnaia voina ispanskogo naroda i politika kommunisticheskogo internatsionala, 1936–1939 gg*. Moscow: Mysl, 1981.

Miaja, General José. Correspondence/documents. "Spain. Ejército. Estado Mayor, 1936–1939." Manuscript Division, Library of Congress.

*————. Interview, notes taken by Burnett Bolloten.

Micaud, Charles A. *The French Right and Nazi Germany, 1933–1939*. Durham, N.C.: Duke University Press, 1943.

Middlemas, Keith. *Diplomacy of Illusion*. London: Weidenfeld Nicolson, 1972.

Mieli, Renato. *Togliatti, 1937*. Milan: Rizzoli, 1964.

Mije, Antonio. *El papel de los sindicatos en los momentos actuales*. Madrid-Valencia: Partido Comunista de España, 1937.

————. *Por una potente industría de guerra*. Barcelona: Partido Comunista de España, 1937.

Mikusch, Dagobert von. *Franco befreit Spanien*. Leipzig: P. List, 1939.

Milicia Popular: Diario del 5º regimiento de milicias popularies. Preface by Vittorio Vidali. Milan: La Pietra, 1973.

Miller, John, ed. *Voices against Tyranny*. New York: Scribner's Sons, 1986.

*Milton, Harry. Copies of his correspondence with Léon Trotsky and George Kopp.

Minelli, Pablo M. *El pueblo español en armas*. Madrid-Valencia: Ediciones Españolas, 1937.

Mintz, Frank. *L'autogestion dans l'Espagne révolutionnaire*. Paris: Bélibaste, 1970.

Mintz, Frank, and Peciña, Miguel. *Los amigos de Durruti, los trotsquistas y los sucesos de mayo*. Madrid: Campo Abierto, 1978.

Mintz, Jerome R. *The Anarchists of Casas Viejas*. Chicago: University of Chicago Press, 1982.

Miralles Bravo, Rafael. *Españoles en Rusia*. Madrid: Publicaciones Españolas, 1947.

————. *¿Hacia dónde va Rusia?* Mexico City: Miralles, 1946.

————. *Memorias de un comandante rojo*. Madrid: San Martín, 1975.

Miravitlles, Juame. *El que jo he vist a Madrid: Conferencia donada pel comisari de propaganda*. Barcelona: Forja, 1938.

————. *Episodis de la guerra civil espanyola*. Barcelona: Pòrtic, 1972.

Mitchell, Mairin. *Storm over Spain*. London: Secker and Warburg, 1937.

Moch, Jules. *Rencontres avec . . . Léon Blum*. Paris: Plon, 1970.

Modesto, Juan. *Soy del quinto regimiento*. Presentación de Santiago Carrillo. Barcelona: Laia, 1978.

Mohr, E. *Wir im fernen Vaterland geboren . . . Die Centuria Thälmann*. Paris: Prométhée, 1938.

Molas, Isidre. *El sistema de partidos políticos en Cataluña, 1931–1936*. Barcelona: Península, 1974.

Mola Vidal, Emilio. *Obras completas.* Valladolid: Santarén, 1940.

_____. *El pasado, Azaña y el porvenir: Las tragedias de nuestras instituciones militares.* Madrid: Bergua, 1934.

*Molins i Fàbrega, Narcís. "Les Jornadas de Maig de Barcelona." Typewritten notes, Hoover Institution, Bolloten Collection.

Molodoi Leningrad. Leningrad: Molodaia Gvardiia, 1957.

Mommsen, Wolfgang J., and Kettenacker, Lothar, eds. *The Fascist Challenge and the Policy of Appeasement.* London: Allen and Unwin, 1983.

Monjo, Anna, and Vega, Carme. *Els treballadors i la guerra civil: Història d'une indústria catalana col·lectivitzada.* Barcelona: Empúries, 1986.

Monreal, Antoni. *El pensamiento político de Joaquín Maurín.* Barcelona: Edicions 62, 1984.

Montaldo, Jean. *Les finances du PCF.* Paris: Albin Michel, 1977.

_____. *Les secrets de la banque soviétique en France.* Paris: Albin Michel, 1979.

Montero, Antonio. *Historia de la persecución religiosa en España, 1936–1939.* Madrid: Biblioteca de Autores Cristianos, 1961.

Montero, José. *La CEDA.* Vols. I, II. Madrid: Revista del Trabajo, 1977.

_____. *El drama de la verdad en Manuel Azaña.* Sevilla: Universidad de Sevilla, [1979?].

Montiel, Francisco Félix. *Por qué he ingresado en el partido comunista.* Barcelona: Partido Comunista de España, Comisión Nacional de Agit-Prop, 1937.

Montseny, Federica. *La commune de Paris y la revolucion española. Conferencia pronunciada en el Cine Coliseum de Valencia el dia 14 de marzo de 1937.* Barcelona: Oficina de Información, Propaganda y Prensa del Comité Nacional CNT-FAI, 1937.

*_____. Correspondence with Burnett Bolloten.

_____. *María Silva: La libertaria.* Toulouse: Universo, 1951.

_____. *Seis años de mi vida, 1939–1945.* Barcelona: Galba, 1978.

Mora, Constancia de la. *In Place of Splendor.* New York: Harcourt Brace, 1939.

Morán, Gregorio. *Miseria y grandeza del Partido Comunista de España, 1939–1985.* Barcelona: Planeta, 1986.

Moreno, Admiral Franciso. *La guerra en el mar.* Barcelona: AHR, 1959.

Moreno, Enrique. *Catholicisme et Loyalisme.* Paris: Archives Espagnoles, [1937?].

Moreno Dávila, Julio. *Frente a Madrid.* Granada: Librería Prieto, 1937.

Moreno Gómez, Francisco. *La guerra civil en Córdoba, 1936–1939.* Madrid: Alpuerto, 1985.

Morgan-Witts, Max. *The Day Guernica Died.* London: Hodder and Stoughton, 1975.

Morón, Gabriel. *Política de ayer y política de mañana.* Mexico City: Talleres Linotipográficos Numancia, 1942.

Morrow, Felix. *The Civil War in Spain.* New York: Pioneer Publishers, 1938.

_____. *Revolution and Counter-Revolution in Spain.* New York: Pioneer Publishers, 1938.

Moscardó, General José. *Diario del Alcázar.* Preface by Joaquín Arrarás. Madrid: Ibiza, 1943.

Mosley, Leonard. *On Borrowed Time: How World War II Began.* New York: Random House, 1969.

El movimiento libertario español: Pasado, presente y futuro. Paris: Ruedo Ibérico, 1974.

Movimiento libertario y política. Prologue by Carlos Díaz. Madrid: Ediciones Júcar, 1978.

Mowat, Charles Loch. *Britain between the Wars, 1918–1940*. Boston: Beacon, 1971.

————. *Great Britain since 1914*. Ithaca, N.Y.: Cornell University Press, 1971.

Müehlen, Patrik v. zur. *Spanien war ihre Hoffnung: Die deutsche Linke im spanischen Bürgerkrieg, 1936–39*. Bonn: Neue Gesellschaft, 1983.

Muniesa, Bernat. *La burguesía catalana ante la II república española, 1931–1936*. Vols. I, II. Barcelona: Anthropos, 1985, 1986.

*Munis, G. [Manuel Fernández Grandizo]. Correspondence with Burnett Bolloten.

————. *Jalones de derrota: Promesa de victoria*. Mexico City: Lucha Obrera, 1948.

Muñoz, Máximo. *Dos conductas: Indalecio Prieto y yo*. Mexico City: n.p., 1952.

Muñoz Arconada, Felipe. *La juventud que defiende Madrid*. Valencia: JSU, 1937.

Muñoz Díez, Manuel. *Marianet*. Mexico City: Ediciones CNT, 1960.

*Muñoz Lopez, José. Interview, notes taken by Burnett Bolloten.

Muro Zegri, D. *La Epopeya del Alcázar*. Valladolid: Librería Santarén, 1937.

Namier, L. B. *Diplomatic Prelude, 1938–1939*. London: Macmillan, 1948.

————. *Europe in Decay, 1936–1940*. London: Macmillan, 1950.

Nash, Mary, ed. *"Mujeres Libres": España, 1936–1939*. Barcelona: Tusquets, 1976.

Nazi-Soviet Relations, 1939–1941. See U.S. Department of State.

Negre, Juan. *¿Qué es el colectivismo anarquista?* Barcelona: Agrupación Anarquista, Los de Ayer y Los de Hoy, 1937.

Negrín, Juan. *L'Adieu de Président Négrin aux Combattants Internationaux: Discours prononcé le 9 octobre, 1938*. Paris: Delegation de Propagande, 1938.

————. *Allocution prononcée le 24 décembre 1938*. Paris: Les Archives Espagnoles, 1938.

————. *Discours prononcé le 30 septembre, 1938*. Paris: Le Comité Franco-Espagnol, 1938.

————. *Un discurso*. Mexico City: Unión Democrática Española, 1942.

————. *Discurso pronunciado el día 26 de febrero de 1938*. Barcelona: Ediciones Españolas, 1938.

————. *Discurso pronunciado el 18 de junio de 1938*. Barcelona: Ediciones Españolas, 1938.

————. *L'Espagne en face de la situation internationale: Discours prononcé par S.E. le Dr. Juan Negrín à Barcelone, le 14 octobre 1938*. Paris: Delegation de Propagande, 1938.

————. *Three Speeches given at the League of Nations Assembly, September 1937*. Paris: Cooperative Etoile, 1937.

Negrín, Juan, and Martínez Barrio, Diego. *Documentos políticos para la historia de la república española*. Mexico City: Colección Malaga, 1945.

*Negrín, Juan, and Prieto, Indalecio. Carbon copies of letters exchanged between the two Socialist leaders in June 1939, given to Burnett Bolloten by Benigno Rodríguez.

Negrín's telegram to García Valdecasas, 22 Oct. 1938.

Negrín y Prieto, culpables de alta traicion. Buenos Aires: Servicio de Propaganda España, 1939.

Negro Castro, Juan. *Españoles en la URSS*. Madrid: Gráficos Escelicer, 1959.
*Nelken, Margarita. Interview, notes taken by Burnett Bolloten.
Nelson, Steve; Barrett, James R.; and Ruck, Rob. *Steve Nelson: American Radical*. Pittsburgh: University of Pittsburgh Press, 1981.
Nenni, Pietro. *España*. Madrid: Plaza y Janés, 1977.
————. *La guerre d'Espagne*. Paris: Maspero, 1960.
986 jours de lutte: La guerre nationale et révolutionnaire du peuple espagnol. Paris: Editions Sociales, 1962.
Neville, Edgar. *Frente de Madrid*. Madrid: Espasa-Calpe, 1941.
Newman, Simon. *March 1939: The British Guarantee to Poland*. Oxford: Clarendon, 1976.
Nicholson, Helen (Zglinitzki). *Death in the Morning*. London: Lovat Dickson, 1937.
Niclauss, Karlheinz. *Die Sowjetunion und Hitlers Machtergreifung*. Bonn: Ludwig Röhrscheid, 1966.
Nicolson, Harold. *Diaries and Letters, 1930–1939*. Vol. I. London: Collins, 1966.
————. *King George the Fifth: His Life and Reign*. London: Constable, 1952.
————. *The War Years: 1939–1945*. New York: Atheneum, 1967.
Nin, Andrés. *Els moviments d'emancipació nacional*. Paris: Edicions Catalanes, 1970.
————. *Las organizaciones obreras internacionales*. Madrid: Torre, 1977.
————. *Por la unificación marxista*. Madrid: Castellote, 1978.
————. *Los problemas de la revolución española*. Preface and compilation by Juan Andrade. Paris: Ruedo Ibérico, 1971.
————. *La revolución de octubre de 1934, la alianza obrera y el frente popular*. Preface by Juan Andrade. Paris: La Batalla, 1970.
————. *La revolución española, 1930–1937*. Barcelona: Fontamara, 1978.
Nino Nanetti. Paris: Coltúra Sociale, 1937.
Noja Ruiz, Higinio. *El arte en la revolución: conferencia pronunciada en el cine Coliseum de Barcelona, el día 21 de marzo de 1937*. Barcelona: Oficinas de Propaganda CNT-FAI, [1937?].
Nollau, Günther. *International Communism and World Revolution*. Foreword by Leonard Schapiro. New York: Praeger, 1961.
Norteamerica y la guerra de España. Valencia: Comisariado General de Guerra, 1937.
North, Joseph. *Men in the Ranks*. New York: Friends of the Abraham Lincoln Brigade, 1939.
————. *Why Spain Can Win*. New York: Workers Library, 1939.
Nuestra lucha por la unidad. Valencia: J.S.U., 1937.
Nuestra utopia: PSUC, cincuenta años de historia de Cataluña. Barcelona: Planeta, 1986.
Nuestro programa y el de la CNT. Valencia: Partido Comunista de España, Comisión Nacional de Agit-Prop, 1937.
Nunes, Leopoldo. *La guerra en España*. Granada: Prieto, 1938.
————. *Madrid trágico*. Cadiz: Cerón, 1938.
Nuñez Morgado, Aurelio. *Los sucesos de España vistos por un diplomático*. Buenos Aires: Rosso, 1941.
O'Duffy, Eoin. *Crusade in Spain*. London: Hale, 1938.

Oehler, Hugo. *Barricades in Barcelona*. New York: Demos Press, 1937.
O'Flanagan, Michael. *American Catholics and the War in Spain*. Verbatim speech given at Madison Square Garden. New York: n.p., 1938.
*Ogilvie-Forbes, Sir George. Correspondence with Burnett Bolloten.
Olaya, Francisco. *La comedia de la no intervención en la guerra civil española*. Madrid: Toro, 1976.
Oliveira, Mauricio de. *La tragedia española en el mar*. Vol. I: *Establecimientos Cerón*. Vol. II: *Las dos Españas en el mar*. Vol. III: *Marinos de España en guerra*. Vol. IV: *Aguas de España, zona de guerra*. Cádiz: Cerón, 1938–39.
Ollivier, Marcel. *La Guépéou en Espagne*. Paris: Librairie du Regionalisme, 1937.
──────. *Les journées sanglantes de Barcelone*. Paris: Spartacus, [1937?].
Olmedo Delgado, Antonio, and Cuesta Monereo, Lieutenant General José. *General Queipo de Llano*. Barcelona: AHR, 1958.
Oltra Picó, J. *El POUM i la col·lectivització d'industries i comerços*. Barcelona: Editorial Marxista, 1936.
──────. *Socialización de las fincas urbanas y municipalización de los servicios*. Barcelona: Editorial Marxista, 1937.
Orlov, Alexander. See also U.S. Congress. *The Legacy of Alexander Orlov*.
──────. "Answers to the Questionnaire of Professor Stanley G. Payne," 1 April 1968. A copy of this document given to Burnett Bolloten by Professor Payne is in the Hoover Institution.
──────. *Handbook of Intelligence and Guerrilla Warfare*. Ann Arbor: University of Michigan Press, 1963.
──────. *The Secret History of Stalin's Crimes*. New York: Random House, 1953.
d'Ormesson, Wladimir. *France*. London: Longmans, Green, 1939.
Ornitz, Lou. *Captured by Franco*. New York: Friends of the Abraham Lincoln Brigade, 1939.
Orr, Charles. "Some Facts on the Persecution of Foreign Revolutionaries in 'Republican' Spain." A copy of this typewritten document written by the editor of *The Spanish Revolution* is in the Hoover Institution.
Orr, Lois. See Cusick, Lois.
Ortiz de Villajos, C. G. *De Sevilla a Madrid*. Granada: Prieto, 1937.
Orwell, George. *Homage to Catalonia*. London: Secker and Warburg, 1938.
Ossorio y Gallardo, Angel. *Discursos pronunciados los días 25 de agosto y 6 de septiembre de 1936 respectivamente*. Madrid: Socorro Rojo Internacional, 1936.
──────. *Mis memorias*. Buenos Aires: Losada, 1946.
──────. *The Religious Problem in Spain*. Washington, D.C.: Bureau of Information, Spanish Embassy, 1937.
──────. *Spain's Future*. Speech made at the Maison de Chimie, Paris, Feb. 22, 1937. n.p., 1937.
──────. *Vida y sacrificio de Companys*. Buenos Aires: Losada, 1943.
Outline History of the Communist International. Moscow: Progress, 1971.
Ovendale, Ritchie. *Appeasement and the English Speaking World*. Cardiff: University of Wales Press, 1975.
Oyarzun, Roman. *Historia del Carlismo*. Bilbao: Ediciones FE, 1939.
Paassen, Pierre van. *Days of our Years*. New York: Hillman-Curl, 1939.
Pabón, Jesús. *Los virajes hacia la guerra, 1934–1939*. Madrid: Sucesores de Rivadeneyra, 1946.

Pacciardi, Randolfo. *Il battaglione Garibaldi.* Lugano: Nuove Edizioni di Capolago, 1938.

Padelford, Norman J. *International Law and Diplomacy in the Spanish Civil Strife.* New York: Macmillan, 1939.

Padilla Bolívar, Antonio. *El movimiento anarquista español.* Barcelona: Planeta, 1976.

Pagès, Pelai. *Andreu Nin: Su evolución política, 1911–1937.* Bilboa: Zero, 1975.

_____. *Historia del partido comunista de España.* Barcelona: Hacer, 1978.

_____. *El movimiento trotskista en España, 1930–1935: La izquierda comunista de España y las disidencias comunistas durante la segunda república.* Barcelona: Ediciones Península, 1977.

Palacín, Santiago. *La revolución y el campo.* Barcelona: Editorial Marxista, 1937.

Palacio, Léo. *1936: La maldonne espagnole. Ou la guerre d'Espagne comme répétition générale du 2ème conflit mondial.* Toulouse: Privat, 1986.

Palacio, Solano. *La tragedia del norte.* Barcelona: "Tierra y Libertad," 1938.

Palacio Atard, Vicente. *Cinco historias de la república y de la guerra.* Madrid: Editora Nacional, 1973.

_____, ed. *Cuadernos bibliográficos de la guerra de España, 1936–1939: Memorias.* Madrid: Universidad de Madrid, 1967.

Palacio Atard, Vicente, et al. *Aproximación histórica a la guerra española, 1936–1939.* Madrid: Universidad de Madrid, 1970.

Palencia, Isabel de. *I Must Have Liberty.* New York: Longmans, Green, 1940.

Pàmies, Teresa. *Una española llamada Dolores Ibárruri.* Mexico City: Roca, 1975.

Panés, Antonio. *Estampas de la revolución.* Madrid: Goya, 1941.

Paniagua, Xavier. *La sociedad libertaria: Agrarismo e industrialización en el anarquismo español, 1930–1939.* Barcelona: Grijalbo, 1982.

Pankrashova, M., and Sipols, V. *Why War Was Not Prevented.* Moscow: Novosti Press Agency, 1970.

Pantaloni-Ensegnat, Odette. *Segunda república y guerra civil.* Paris: Masson, 1970.

Para que el campesino tenga tierras, trabajo, libertad y bienestar. Barcelona: Ministerio de Agricultura, [1937?].

Parker, A. A. *The Catholic Church in Spain.* London: Catholic Truth Society, 1938.

Parliamentary Debates, Vol. 295, Fifth Series. London: HMSO.

Parti Communiste. Congrès National, 9th, Arles, 1937. *Le peuple de France aux côtes de l'Espagne républicaine: extraits des rapports et interventions. Discours de Camarade Delicado.* Paris: Comité populaire de propagande, 1938.

Partido Comunista de España. Comité Central. *Programa de acción común para la creación del partido unico del proletariado.* n.p., [1937?].

El partido comunista por la libertad y la independencia de España: Llamamientos y discursos. Valencia: Ediciones del P.C. de E., Comisión Nacional de Agitación y Propaganda, 1937.

El partido comunista y la unidad antifascista. Valencia: Sección de Prensa y Propaganda del Comité Peninsular de la FAI, 1937.

Pascual Cevallos, Fernando. *Luchas agrarias en Sevilla durante la segunda república.* Sevilla: Diputación Provincial de Sevilla, 1983.

La Pasionaria. See Ibárruri, Dolores.

Pastor Petit, D. *La cinquena columna a Catalunya, 1936-1939.* Barcelona: Galba, 1978.

_____. Los dossiers secretos de la guerra civil. Barcelona: Argos, 1978.

Paul, Elliot. The Life and Death of a Spanish Town. New York: Random House, 1937.

Paul Boncour, Joseph. Entre deux guerres: Sur les chemins de la defaite, 1935–1940. Vol. III. New York: Brentano's, 1946.

Payne, Robert. The Civil War in Spain, 1936–1939. New York: Putnam, 1962.

_____, ed. The Civil War in Spain, 1936–1939. London: Secker and Warburg, 1963.

Payne, Stanley G. Basque Nationalism. Reno: University of Nevada Press, 1975.

_____. Falange. Stanford: Stanford University Press, 1961.

_____. The Franco Regime, 1936–1975. Madison: University of Wisconsin Press, 1987.

_____. El nacionalismo vasco: De sus orígenes a la ETA. Barcelona: Dopesa, 1974.

_____. Politics and the Military in Modern Spain. Stanford: Stanford University Press, 1967.

_____. La revolución y la guerra civil española. Madrid: Júcar, 1976.

_____. The Spanish Revolution. New York: Norton, 1970.

_____, ed. Politics and Society in Twentieth-Century Spain. Introduction by Stanley G. Payne. New York: Franklin Watts, 1976.

Paz, Abel. Durruti en la revolución española. Barcelona: Laia, 1986.

_____. Durruti: Le peuple en armes. Paris: Tête de Feuilles, 1972.

Paz, Armando. Los servicios de espionaje en la guerra civil de España, 1936–1939. Madrid: San Martín, 1976.

PCE en sus documentos, 1920–1977. Madrid: Hoac, 1977.

*Pearson, Captain H. M. Correspondence with Burnett Bolloten.

Peers, E. Allison. Catalonia Infelix. London: Methuen, 1937.

_____. Spain, the Church and the Orders. London: Eyre and Spottiswoode, 1939.

_____. The Spanish Tragedy. New York: Oxford University Press, 1937.

Peirats, José (General Secretary of the Intercontinental Secretariat of the CNT in Exile). Los anarquistas en la crisis política española. Buenos Aires: Alfa, 1964.

_____. La CNT en la revolución española. Vols. I, II, III. Toulouse: C.N.Y., 1951, 1952, and 1953.

*_____. Correspondence with Burnett Bolloten.

_____. Examen crítico-constructivo del movimiento libertario español. Mexico City: Editores mexicanos unidos, 1967.

_____. Figuras del movimiento libertario español. Barcelona: Picazo, 1978.

Peiró, Juan. Pensamiento de J.P.: Trayectoria de la confederación nacional del trabajo; Ideas sobre sindicalismo y anarquismo; apuntes biográficos. Mexico City: CNT, 1959.

_____. Perill a la reraguarda. Mataró: Libertat, [1937?].

_____. Problemas del sindicalismo y del anarquismo. Toulouse: E.M.L.E., 1945.

_____. Problemas y cintarazos. Rennes: Imprimeries Réunies, 1946.

_____. Trayectoria de la CNT: Sindicalismo y anarquismo. Madrid: Júcar, 1979.

Penchienati, Carlo. Brigate internazionali in Spagna: Delitti della "Ceka" comunista. Milan: Echi del Secolo, 1950.

*Pérez, Emilio. Interview, notes taken by Burnett Bolloten.

Pérez, Manuel. *Cuatro meses de barbarie: Mallorca bajo el terror fascista.* Barcelona: Servicio de Información CNT-AIT, 1937.

Pérez-Baró, Albert. *Autogestió obrera i altres temes.* Barcelona: Pòrtic, 1974.

———. *Treinta meses de colectivismo en Cataluña, 1936–1939.* Barcelona: Ariel, 1974.

———. *30 mesos de col·lectivisme a Catalunya, 1936–1939.* Barcelona: Ariel, 1970.

Pérez de la Dehesa, Rafael, ed. *Joaquín Costa: Oligarquía y caciquismo. Colectivismo agrario y otros escritos.* Madrid: Alianza, 1979.

Pérez de Olaguer, Antonio. *El terror rojo en Andalucía.* Burgos: Ediciones Antisectarias, 1938.

———. *El terror rojo en Cataluña.* Burgos: Ediciones Antisectarias, 1937.

Pérez de Urbel, Justo. *Los mártires de la iglesia.* Barcelona: AHR, 1956.

Pérez Madrigal, Joaquín. *Aquí es la emisora de la flota republicana.* Avila: Sigirano Díaz, 1938.

———. *Augurios, estallido y episodios de la guerra civil.* Avila: Sigirano Díaz, 1938.

———. *Disparos a cero.* Madrid: Ediciones Españolas, 1939.

———. *Tipos y sombras de la tragedia.* Avila: Sigirano Díaz, 1937.

Pérez Ramírez, Antonio. *La gesta heroica de España: El movimiento patriótico en Aragón.* Zaragoza: Heraldo de Aragón, 1936.

*Pérez Salas, Colonel Jesús. Correspondence with Burnett Bolloten.

———. *Guerra en España, 1936–1939.* Preface by Colonel Mariano Salafranca. Mexico City: Imprenta Grafos, 1947.

Pérez Serrano, Nicolás. *La constitución española (9 dic. 1931): Antecedentes, texto, comentarios.* Madrid: Editorial Revista de Derecho Privado, 1932.

Pérez Solís, Oscar. *Sitio y defensa de Oviedo.* Valladolid-Palencia: Afrodisio Aguado, 1938.

La persécution religieuse en Espagne. Paris: Plon, 1937.

Pertinax. See Geraud, André.

Pétrement, Simone. *Simone Weil: A Life.* New York: Pantheon, 1976.

Pettifer, James, ed. *Cockburn in Spain: Despatches from the Spanish Civil War.* London: Lawrence and Wishart, 1986.

Le peuple de France aux côtés de l'Espagne républicaine. Paris: Comité Populaire de Propagande, 1937.

Piera, Dolores. *Informe presentado a la primera conferencia nacional del partido socialista unificado de cataluña (IC).* Barcelona: Agitación y Propaganda del PSUC, [1937?].

Pike, David Wingeate. *Conjecture, Propaganda, and Deceit and the Spanish Civil War.* Stanford: California Institute of International Studies, 1968.

———. *La crise espagnole de 1936 vue par la presse française.* Toulouse: Université de Toulouse, 1966.

———. *Les Français et la guerre d'Espagne, 1936–1939.* Paris: Presses Universitaires de France, 1975.

———. *Vae Victis! Los republicanos españoles refugiados en Francia, 1939–1944.* Paris: Ruedo Ibérico, 1969.

Pino, Francisco, *Asalto a la carcel modelo.* Madrid: Aguilar, 1939.

Pi Sunyer, Carles. *La república y la guerra: Memorias de un político catalan.* Mexico City: Oasis, 1975.
Pitcairn, Frank [Claud Cockburn]. *Reporter in Spain.* London: Lawrence and Wishart, 1936.
Pius XI. *Encyclical on Spain.* New York: America Press, 1937.
———. *The Spanish Terror.* London: Catholic Truth Society, 1936.
Plá, José. *Historia de la segunda república española.* Vols. I, II, III, IV. Barcelona: Destino, 1941.
Poblet, Josep M. *Els darrers temps de la Generalitat i la república.* Barcelona: Dopesa, 1978.
Pod znamenem ispanskoi respubliki, 1936–1939: Vospominaniia sovetskikh dobrovoltsev-uchastnikov. Moscow: Izdatel'stvo Nauka, 1965.
Política del frente popular en agricultura. Madrid-Valencia: Españolas, 1937.
La política financiera de la Generalidad durante la revolución y la guerra. Barcelona: Generalitat de Catalunya, 1936.
Pollitt, Harry. *Arms for Spain.* London: Communist Party of Great Britain, 1936.
———. *Pollitt Visits Spain: Harry Pollitt's Story of His Visit to Spain in December, 1937.* London: International Brigade Wounded and Dependents' Aid Fund, 1938.
———. *Save Spain from Fascism.* London, [1936?].
Ponamariova, L. V. *La formación del partit socialista unificat de Catalunya.* Barcelona: Icaria, 1977.
Ponce, Anibal. *Examen de la España actual.* Montevideo: Ediciones "Mundo," 1938.
Poncins, Léon de. *Histoire secrète de la révolution espagnole.* Paris: Beauchesne, 1938.
Ponomariov, B., ed. *Historia de la política exterior de la URSS, 1917–1945.* Moscow: Progreso, n.d.
Pons, Agustí. *Converses amb Frederica Montseny.* Barcelona: Laia, 1977.
Pons Prades, Eduardo. *Guerrillas españolas, 1936–1960.* Barcelona: Planeta, 1977.
Pool, James, and Pool, Suzanne. *Who Financed Hitler?.* New York: Dial, 1978.
Porcel, Baltasar. *Conversaciones con el honorable Tarradellas.* Barcelona: Plaza y Janés, 1977.
Poretsky, Elizabeth K. *Our Own People.* Ann Arbor: University of Michigan Press, 1969.
Por Euzkadi hacia la victoria. Madrid-Valencia: Ediciones Españolas, 1937.
Por la revolución agraria. Madrid: Federación Española de Trabajadores de la Tierra, UGT, 1937.
Portugal ante la guerra civil de España: Documentos y notas. Lisbon: SPN, n.d.
Portuondo, E. *La segunda república: Reforma, fascismo y revolución.* Madrid: Editorial Revolución, 1981.
Por una cooperativa en cada pueblo: Dentro del instituto de reforma agraria. Valencia: Ministerio de Agricultura, 1937.
Por una justicia popular, humana y democrática. Barcelona: Ministerio de Justicia, [1937?].
Possoni, Stefan Thomas. *A Century of Conflict: Communist Techniques of World Revolution.* Chicago: Regnery, 1953.
*Pou, Bernardo. Correspondence with Burnett Bolloten.

El POUM ante los problemas de la revolución española. Presentación de Wilebaldo Solano. Paris: La Batalla, 1972.

POUM. Hasta vencer o morir. Paris: Comité de Ayuda del POUM [1938?].

Pourquoi l'Italie fait la guerre à l'Espagne. Paris: Comité Franco-Espagnol, 1939.

Pous i Pagés, J. *Al marge de la revolució i de la guerra*. Barcelona: Casa de Cultura, 1937.

Powell, T. G. *Mexico and the Spanish Civil War*. Albuquerque: University of New Mexico Press, 1981.

*Pozas, General Sebastián. Interview, notes taken by Burnett Bolloten.

Pozharskaia, Svetlana Petrovna. *Sotsialisticheskaia rabochaia partiia Ispanii, 1931–1939*. Moscow: Nauka, 1966.

Prader, Jean. *Au secours de l'Espagne socialiste*. Paris: Spartacus, 1936.

Prado Moura, Angel de. *El movimiento obrero en Valladolid durante la II república, 1931–1936*. Valladolid: Junta de Castilla y León, 1985.

Prats, Alardo. *Vanguardia y retaguardia de Aragón*. Buenos Aires: Perseo, 1938.

Pratt, Lawrence R. *East of Malta, West of Suez: Britain's Mediterranean Crisis, 1936–1939*. Cambridge: Cambridge University Press, 1975.

The Premature Anti-Fascists: North American Volunteers in the Spanish Civil War, An Oral History. New York: Praeger, 1986.

Preston, Paul. *The Coming of the Spanish Civil War*. London: Macmillan, 1978.

_____. *Las derechas españoles en el siglo XX: Autoritarismo, fascismo y golpismo*. Madrid: Sistema, 1986.

_____. *La destrucción de la democracie en España*. Madrid: Turner, 1978.

_____. *The Spanish Civil War, 1936–1939*. London: Weidenfeld and Nicolson, 1986.

Prieto, Carlos. *Spanish Front*. London: Nelson, 1936.

Prieto, Horacio M. *El anarquismo español en la lucha política*. Paris: n.p., 1946.

_____. *Marxismo y socialismo libertario*. Paris: Ediciones Madrid, 1947.

_____. *El movimiento libertario español y sus necesidades urgentes*. Paris: Galería, n.d.

_____. *Posibilismo libertario*. Val-de-Marne, France: Gondoles, 1966.

Prieto, Indalecio. *Cómo y por qué salí del ministerio de defensa nacional*. Mexico City: Impresos y Papeles, 1940. Also French edition, Paris: Imprimerie Nouvelle, 1939.

_____. *Convulsiones de España*. Vols. I, II, III. Mexico City: Oasis, 1967.

*_____. Correspondence with Burnett Bolloten.

_____. *De mi vida*. Vol. I. Mexico City: Ediciones El Sitio, 1965.

_____. *Dentro y fuera del gobierno: Discursos parlamentarios*. Mexico City: Oasis, 1975.

_____. *Discursos fundamentales*. Preface by Edward Malefakis. Madrid: Turner, 1975.

_____. *Inauguración del círculo "Pablo Iglesias" de México*. Mexico City: n.p., 1940.

_____. *Palabras al viento*. Mexico City: Minerva, 1942.

_____. *Palabras de ayer y de hoy*. Santiago: Ercilla, 1938.

_____. "Reply to Jordi Arquer's Questionnaire." Hoover Institution, Bolloten Collection.

Prieto, Tomás. *Héroes y gestas de la cruzada: Datos para la historia*. Madrid: Tormes, 1942.

Primo de Rivera, José Antonio. *Discursos frente al parlamento*. Barcelona: F.E., 1939.

Programa de acción común para la creación del partido único del proletariado. Valencia: Partido Comunista de España, 1937.

Programa de unidad de acción entre UGT-CNT. Barcelona: Españolas, 1938.

Prominent Personalities in the USSR. Metuchen, N.J.: Scarecrow Press, 1968.

Propaganda y cultura en los frentes de guerra. Valencia: Ministerio de la Guerra, Comisariado General de Guerra, 1937.

Propagande culturelle. Valencia: Ministère de l'Instruction Publique, 1938.

"Proyecto que la Delegación Regional de Reforma Agraria Presenta para su Aprobación al Comité Regional del Frente Popular de Aragón." Archivo Histórico Nacional, Salamanca. Leg. 616/816-3.

Prudhommeaux, A., and Prudhommeaux, D. *Catalogne libertaire, 1936–1937: L'armement du peuple. Que sont la CNT et la FAI?* Paris: Spartacus, 1946.

PSOE en sus documentos, 1879–1977. Madrid: Hoac, 1977.

El PSU davant la situació actual. Barcelona: Agitació i Propaganda PSU, 1938.

Puente, Isaac. *El comunismo libertario: Apunte biográfico de Juan Ferrer*. Epílogo de Federica Montseny. Toulouse: Espoir, n.d.

———. *Finalidad de la CNT: El comunismo libertario*. Barcelona: Tierra y Libertad, 1936.

———. *Propaganda*. Barcelona: Tierra y Libertad, 1938.

Puig, Jaime J. *Historia de la Guardia Civil*. Barcelona: Editorial Mitre, 1984.

Puig Mora, E. [El Ciudadano Desconocido]. *La tragedia roja en Barcelona*. Saragossa: Librería General, 1937.

Puzzo, Dante A. *Spain and the Great Powers, 1936–1941*. New York: Columbia University Press, 1962.

Queipo de Llano, Rosario. *De la cheka de Atadell a la prisión de Alacuas*. Valladolid: Santarén, 1939.

Quintanilla, Luis. *Los rehenes del Alcázar de Toledo: Testimonios 2*. Paris: Ruedo Ibérico, 1967.

Rabasseire, Henri [Henry M. Pachter]. *Espagne: creuset politique*. Paris: Fustier, 1938.

Rama, Carlos M. *La crisis española del siglo XX*. Mexico City: Fondo de Cultura Económica, 1960.

———. *Fascismo y anarquismo en la España contemporánea*. Barcelona: Bruguera, 1979.

———, ed. *Camillo Berneri: Guerra de clases en España, 1936–1937*. Barcelona: Tusquets, 1977.

Ramirez Jiménez, Manuel. *Las reformas de la II república*. Madrid: Júcar, 1977.

Ramón Alonso, José. *Historia política del ejército español*. Madrid: Editora Nacional, 1974.

Ramón Jiménez, Juan. *Guerra en España*. Barcelona: Seix Barral, 1985.

Ramos, Vicente. *La guerra civil, 1936–1939, en la provincia de Alicante*. Vols. I, II, III. Alicante: Biblioteca Alicantina, 1972–74.

Ramos Oliveira, Antonio. *The Drama of Spain from the Proclamation of the Republic to the Civil War, 1931–1936*. London: National Council of Labour, [1936?].

———. *On the Eve of Civil War in Spain*. London: Friends of Spain, 1937.

_____. *Politics, Economics and Men of Modern Spain, 1808–1946*. London: Gollancz, 1946.

Ranzato, Gabriele. *Lucha de clases y lucha política en la guerra civil española*. Barcelona: Anagrama, 1979.

Ravines, Eudocio. *La gran estafa*. Mexico City: Libros y Revistas, 1952.

_____. *The Yenan Way* (translation of *La gran estafa*). New York: Scribner's Sons, 1951.

Raymundo, Francisco J. de. *Cómo se inició el glorioso movimiento nacional en Valladolid y la gesta heroica del Alto del León*. Valladolid: Imprenta Católica, 1936.

Read. Jan. *The Catalans*. London: Faber, 1978.

Redondo, General Luis, and Zavala, Comandante Juan de. *El Requeté: La Tradición no muere*. Barcelona: AHR, 1957.

La reforma agraria en España. Valencia: Instituto de Reforma Agraria, 1937.

La reforma agraria y los problemas del campo bajo la república española. Buenos Aires: Servicio Español de Información, Prensa Hispánica, [1938?].

*Regler, Gustav. Correspondence with Burnett Bolloten.

_____. *The Great Crusade*. New York: Longmans, Green, 1940.

_____. *The Owl of Minerva: The Autobiography of Gustav Regler*. London: Rupert Hart-Davis, 1959.

Reid, John T. *Modern Spain and Liberalism*. Stanford: Stanford University Press, 1937.

Relief Organizations. Reports and appeals by various relief organizations. Bound volume in Hoover Institution, Bolloten Collection.

Rello. Salvador. *La aviación en la guerra de España*. Madrid: San Martín, 1972.

*Renn, Ludwig. Interview, notes taken by Burnett Bolloten.

_____. *Der spanische Krieg*. Berlin: Aufbau, 1956.

Reparaz y Tresgallo de Souza, Captain Antonio. *Desde el cuartel general de Miaja al santuario de la Virgen de la Cabeza*. Valladolid: Afrodisio Aguado, 1937.

Report of a Religious Delegation to Spain, April 1937. London: Gollancz, 1937.

Reppard, Theodore. *The Spanish Revolt*. London: Gollancz, 1936.

Requeña Gallego, Manuel. *Los sucesos de Yeste*. Albacete: Instituto de Estudios Albacetenses, 1983.

"Reunión de la Comisión Agraria del Partido Comunista celebrada en Caspe el día 9 de Octubre de 1937." Archivo Histórico Nacional, Salamanca. Leg. 616/816-3.

La révolution espagnole, 1936–1939. Supplément à "Etudes Marxistes" No. 7–8. Paris: Etudes Marxistes, 1969.

Revolution und Gegenrevolution: Die Ereignisse des Mai 1937 in Katalonien. Barcelona: Asy, 1937.

Reynaud, Paul. *La France a sauvé l'Europe*. Vol. I. Paris: Flammarion, 1947.

Richards, Vernon. *Lessons of the Spanish Revolution, 1936–1939*. London: Freedom Press, 1953. Also revised and expanded editions published in 1972 and 1983.

Richardson, R. Dan. *Comintern Army: The International Brigades and the Spanish Civil War*. Lexington: University of Kentucky Press, 1982.

Rieger, Max. *Espionaje en España*. Preface by José Bergamín. Barcelona: Ediciones "Unidad," 1938.

Rienffer, Karl. *Comunistas españoles en América*. Madrid: Editora Nacional, 1953.

Rimblas, José. *España vence a la Internacional Comunista*. Barcelona: Sopena, 1939.

*Río, Ricardo del, director of the Febus news agency. Information on various important events written by Del Río and shorthand notes taken by Burnett Bolloten during conversations with him.

*_____. Unpublished report on the political and military situation in Catalonia during the last few months of the war.

Ríos, Fernando de los. *What Is Happening in Spain?* London: Spanish Embassy, 1937.

Ríos, Isabel. *Testimonio de la guerra civil*. Coruña: Castro, 1986.

Rio Tinto Company Limited: Report of the Transactions at the Sixty-Third Ordinary General Meeting. London: Río Tinto Company, 24 April 1936.

Risco, P. Alberto, S.J. *La epopeya del Alcázar de Toledo*. San Sebastian: Editorial Española, 1941.

Rivas, Fernando. *El frente popular*. Madrid: San Martín, 1976.

Rivas-Cherif, Cipriano. *Retrato de un desconocido: Vida de Manuel Azaña*. Mexico City: Oasis, 1961.

Rivero Sanchez, Manuel. *Odisea y gesta de Oviedo*. Las Palmas: Canaria, 1938.

Rivero Solozábal, Francisco. *Así fué . . . Santander: Revolución, 18 julio 1936–26 agosto 1937*. Santander: Alonso, n.d.

Robertson, Esmonde M., ed. *The Origins of the Second World War*. London: Macmillan, 1971.

Robinson, Richard A. H. *The Origins of Franco's Spain: The Right, the Republic and Revolution, 1931–1936*. Newton Abbott: David and Charles, 1970.

Robrieux, Philippe. *Histoire intérieure du parti communiste, 1920–1945*. Paris: Fayard, 1980.

Rock, William R. *British Appeasement in the 1930s*. New York: Norton, 1977.

Rocker Collection. Photocopies of several hundred pages of documents from the collection of Rudolph Rocker in the International Institute of Social History. Hoover Institution.

Rocker, Rudolf. *Anarcho-Syndicalism*. London: Secker and Warburg, 1938.

_____. *Extranjeros en España*. Buenos Aires: Imán, 1938.

_____. *The Tragedy of Spain*. New York: Freie Arbiter Stimme, 1937.

*Rodríguez, Benigno. Interview, notes taken by Burnett Bolloten.

Rodríguez de Cueto, José. *Epopeya del santuario de Santa María de la Cabeza*. San Sebastián: Editorial Española, 1939.

Rodríguez Salas, Eusebio. International Institute of Social History, Dossier, CNT-FAI Archives. Paquete 005, Caja 305. B. Informes. Dossier 90. Photocopies in Hoover Institution, Bolloten Collection.

Rodríguez Vega, José. *3er congres de la UGT a Catalunya: Discurs de José Rodríguez Vega, secretario general de la Union General de Trabajadores de España*. Barcelona: UGT, 1937.

Rojas, Carlos. *Azaña*. Barcelona: Planeta, 1973.

_____. *Los dos presidentes: Azaña—Companys*. Barcelona: Dirosa, 1977.

_____. *La guerra civil vista por los exiliados*. Barcelona: Planeta, 1975.

_____. *La guerra en Catalunya*. Barcelona: Plaza y Janés, 1979.

_____. *Por qué perdimos la guerra: Antología de testimonios de los vencidos en la contienda civil*. Barcelona: Nauta, 1970.

Rojo, General Vicente. *¡Alerta los pueblos! Estudio político-militar del período final de la guerra española*. Buenos Aires: López, 1939.

_____. *Así fué la defensa de Madrid*. Mexico City: Era, 1967.

_____. *España heroica*. Buenos Aires: Editorial Americalee, 1942.

Rolfe, Edwin. *The Lincoln Battalion*. New York: Random House, 1939.

Romano, Julio. *Sanjurjo*. Madrid: Imprenta de la Viuda de Juan Pueyo, 1940.

Romero, Colonel Luis. *Impresiones de un militar republicano*. Barcelona: Oficinas de Propaganda CNT-FAI, 1937.

Romero, Luis. *Cara y cruz de la república, 1931–1936*. Barcelona: Planet, 1980.

_____. *Desastre en Cartagena (marzo de 1939)*. Barcelona: Ariel, 1971.

_____. *El final de la guerra*. Barcelona: Ariel, 1976.

_____. *Por qué y cómo mataron a Calvo Sotelo*. Barcelona: Planet, 1982.

_____. *Tres días de julio: 18, 19 y 20 de 1936*. Barcelona: Ariel, 1967.

Romero Solano, Luis. *Vísperas de la guerra de España*. Mexico City: El Libro Perfecto, 1947.

Romilly, Esmond. *Boadilla*. London: Hamish Hamilton, 1937.

Ros, Félix. *Preventorio D*. Barcelona: Yunque, 1939.

Rosado, Antonio. *Tierra y libertad: Memorias de un campesino anarcosindicalista andaluz*. Barcelona: Grijalbo, 1979.

Rosal, Amaro del. *Los congresos internacionales en el siglo XX*. Barcelona: Grijalbo, 1975.

_____. *Historia de la UGT de España, 1901–1939*. Vol. II. Barcelona: Grijalbo, 1977.

_____. *El oro del Banco de España y la historia del Vita*. Barcelona: Grijalbo, 1977.

Rosselli, Carlo. *Oggi in Spagna, domani in Italia*. Paris: Edizioni di giustizia i libertà, 1938.

Das Rotbuch über Spanien. Berlin-Leipzig: Nibelungen, 1937.

Rothstein, Andrew. *The Munich Conspiracy*. London: Lawrence and Wishart, 1958.

Roux, Georges. *La guerre civile d'Espagne*. Paris: Fayard, 1963.

Roviri i Virgili, A. *Els darrers dies de la Catalunya republicana*. Buenos Aires: Edicions de la revista Cataluña, 1940.

Rowse, A. L. *All Souls*. London: Macmillan, 1961.

_____. *Appeasement*. New York: Norton, 1961.

Rubashkin, A. *Mikhail Koltsov*. Leningrad: Khudozhestvennaia Literatura, 1971.

Rubio, Javier. *Asilos y canjes durante la guerra civil española*. Barcelona: Planeta, 1979.

_____. *La emigración de la guerra civil de 1936–1939*. Vols. I, II, III. Madrid: San Martín, 1977.

_____. *La emigración española a Francia*. Barcelona: Ariel, 1974.

Rubio Cabeza, Manuel. *Las voces de la república*. Barcelona: Planeta, 1985.

Rubió i Tudurí, Mariano. *La justicia en Cataluña: 19 de julio de 1936–19 de febrero de 1937*. Paris: n.p., 1937.

Ruediger, Helmut. See also Dashar, M.

*_____. Correspondence with Burnett Bolloten.

————. *Ensayo crítico sobre la revolución española.* Buenos Aires: Imán, 1940.

————. *Informe para el congreso extraordinario de la AIT, el día 6 de diciembre de 1937. Paris, 1937.* (University of Michigan Library, Labadie Collection.)

————. Report to the AIT dated 8 May 1937. A copy of this report is in the Hoover Institution, Bolloten Collection.

Ruiz Vilaplana, Antonio. *Burgos Justice: A Year's Experience of Nationalist Spain.* New York: Knopf, 1938.

————. *Doy fe.* Buenos Aires: Perseo, 1938.

Russkie sovetskii pisateli-prozaiki. Vols. I, II, III, IV. Leningrad: Publichnaia Biblioteka, 1959–66.

Rust, William. *Britons in Spain.* London: Lawrence and Wishart, 1939.

————. *Spain Fights for Victory.* London: Communist Party of Great Britain, 1938.

Sabater, Jordi. *Anarquisme i catalanisme: La CNT i el fet nacional català durant la guerra civil.* Barcelona: Eds. 62, 1986.

Sabater, Miguel. *Estampas del cautiverio rojo: Memorias de un preso del SIM.* Barcelona: Librería Religiosa, 1942.

Saborit, Andrés. *Asturias y sus hombres.* Toulouse: Imprimerie Dulaurier, 1964.

*————. Correspondence with Burnett Bolloten.

————. *Julián Besteiro: Figuras del socialismo español.* Mexico City: Impresiones Modernas, 1961.

————. *El pensamiento político de Julián Besteiro.* Madrid: Seminarios y Ediciones, 1974.

Sáenz, Vicente. *España en sus gloriosas jornadas de julio y agosto de 1936.* San José, Costa Rica: La Tribuna, 1936.

————. *España heroica.* New York: Iberoamericana, 1938.

Sagardía, General. *Del Alto Ebro a las fuentes del Llobregat.* Barcelona: Editora Nacional, 1940.

Saíz Valdivielso, Alfonso Carlos. *Indalecio Prieto: Crónica de un corazón.* Barcelona: Planeta, 1984.

Salas Larrazábal, Jesús. *Intervención extranjera en la guerra de España.* Madrid: Editora Nacional, 1974.

Salas Larrazábal, Ramón. *Los datos exactos de la guerra civil.* Madrid: Dracena, 1980.

————. *Historia del ejército popular de la república.* Vols. I, II, III, IV. Madrid: Editora Nacional, 1973.

————. *Pérdidas de la guerra.* Barcelona: Planeta, 1977.

Salas Larrazábal, Ramón, and Salas Larrazábal, Jesús María. *Historia general de la guerra de España.* Madrid: Rialp, 1986.

Salaün, Serge. *La poesía de la guerra de España.* Madrid: Castalia, 1985.

Salazar, Ramón Hidalgo. *La ayuda alemana a España, 1936–1939.* Madrid: San Martín, 1975.

Sallés, Anna. *Quan Catalunya era d'Esquerra.* Barcelona: Eds. 62, 1986.

Salter, Cedric. *Try-Out in Spain.* New York: Harper, 1943.

*Saña, Heleno. Correspondence with Burnett Bolloten.

————. *La Internacional Comunista, 1919–1945.* Vols. I, II. Algorta (Vizcaya): Zero, 1972.

Sanabria, Fernando. *Madrid bajo las hordas.* Avila, SHADE, 1938.

Sánchez, José M. *The Spanish Civil War as a Religious Tragedy*. Notre Dame: University of Notre Dame Press, 1987.

Sánchez, Juan Lario. *Habla un aviador de la república*. Madrid: Toro, 1973.

Sánchez-Albornez, Claudio. *Anecdotario político*. Barcelona: Planeta, 1976.

_____. *Mi testamento histórico-político*. Barcelona: Planeta, 1975.

Sánchez del Arco, Manuel. *El sur de España en la reconquista de Madrid*. Seville: Sevillana, 1937.

Sánchez Guerra, Rafael. *Mes prisons: Mémoires d'un rouge*. Paris: Vigneau, 1947.

*Sánchez Román, Felipe. Interview, notes taken by Burnett Bolloten.

Sánchez y Rueda, Enrique. *De Sigüenza a Madrid pasando por Guadalajara*. Siguenza: Sánchez y Rueda, 1939.

Sandoval, José, and Azcárate, Manuel. *Spain, 1936–1939*. London: Lawrence and Wishart, 1963.

Sans, Ricard M. *Montserrat, 1936–1939: Episodis viscuts*. Montserrat: Abadia de Montserrat, 1984.

Sanz, Ricardo. *Buenaventura Durruti*. Toulouse: El Frente, 1945.

_____. *Los que fuimos a Madrid: Columna Durruti 26 Division*. Toulouse: Dulaurier, 1969.

_____. *El sindicalismo y la política: Los "solidarios" y "nostros."* Toulouse: Dulaurier, 1966.

Sanz y Díaz, José. *Por las rochas del Tajo*. Valladolid: Santarén, 1938.

Sardá, Rafael. *Las colectividades agrícolas*. Barcelona: Editorial Marxista, 1937.

Sartin, Max. *Berneri en Ispagna*. Newark, N.J.: Adunata dei Refrattari, [1938?].

Savich, Ovadii. *Dva goda v. Ispanii, 1937–1939*. Moscow: Sovetskii Pisatel', 1975.

Scanlon, Geraldine M. *La polémica feminista en la España contemporánea, 1868–1974*. Madrid: Siglo XXI, 1977.

Schapiro, Alexander, and Jong, Albert de. *Waarom verloren wij de revolutie?* Baarn: Archief, 1979.

Schapiro, Leonard B. *The Communist Party of the Soviet Union*. London: Eyre and Spottiswoode, 1960.

Schempp, Otto. *Das autoritäre Spanien*. Leipzig: Goldmann, 1939.

Schlayer, Felix. *Diplomat im roten Madrid*. Berlin: Herbig, 1938.

Schmid, Robert. *Das rot-schwartze Spanien: zur rolle des Anarchismus im Spanischen Bürgerkrieg*. Aachen: Rader, 1986.

Schmigalle, Günther. *André Malraux und der spanische Bürgerkrieg*. Bonn: Bouvier, 1980.

Schneider, Luis Mario. *II Congreso internacional de escritores antifascistas (1937)*. Vol. I: *Inteligencia y guerra civil en España*. Barcelona: Laia, 1978.

Schulz, Arno. *Seekriegsrechtliche Fragen im Spanischen Bürgerkrieg*. Würzburg-Aumühle: Triltsch, 1939.

Schwartz, Fernando. *La internacionalización de la guerra civil española, julio de 1936–marzo de 1937*. Barcelona: Ariel, 1971.

*Schwartzmann, Manuel. "L'Industrie de Guerre de la République Espagnole." Unpublished manuscript given to Burnett Bolloten by Schwartzmann.

*_____. "La Naissance et l'Activité de la D.E.C.A. en Espagne." Unpublished manuscript given to Burnett Bolloten by Schwartzmann, who worked under Soviet direction in the antiaircraft defense and war industries in the Republican zone.

Schweppenburg, Geyr von, and Franz, Leo Dietrich. *The Critical Years*. London: Wingate, 1952.

Scope of Soviet Activity in the United States. See U.S. Congress.

Seco Serrano, Carlos. *Historia de España: Gran historia general de los pueblos hispanos*. Vol. VI. Barcelona: Instituto Gallach de Librería y Ediciones, 1962.

Sedwick, Frank. *The Tragedy of Manuel Azaña and the Fate of the Spanish Republic*. Columbus: Ohio State University Press, 1963.

Segundo congreso del partido socialista obrero español en el exilio. Toulouse: PSOE, 1946.

*Seidman, Michael. "Work and Revolution: Workers' Control in Barcelona in the Spanish Civil War, 1936–38." Unpublished manuscript.

Semprún, Jorge. *Autobiografía de Federico Sánchez*. Barcelona: Planeta, 1977.

Semprún Gurrea, José María. *A Catholic Looks at Spain*. London: Labour Publications Dept., 1937.

Semprún Maura, Carlos. *Ni dios, ni amo, ni CNT*. Barcelona: Tusquets, 1978.

―――. *Révolution et contre-révolution en Catalogne*. Tours: Mame, 1974.

Sencourt, Robert. *Spain's Ordeal*. London: Longmans, Green, 1940.

Sender, Ramón. *Counter-Attack in Spain*. Boston: Houghton Mifflin, 1937.

―――. *Crónica del pueblo en armas*. Madrid-Valencia: Ediciones Españolas, 1936.

Serge, Victor. *Memoirs of a Revolutionary*. London: Oxford University Press, 1967.

*Serra Pàmies, Miguel. Interview, notes taken by Burnett Bolloten.

Serrano, Seundino. *La guerrilla antifranquista en Léon, 1936–1951*. Valladolid: Junta de Castilla y León, 1986.

Serrano Poncela, Segundo. *La conferencia nacional de juventudes*. Valencia: JSU de España, 1937.

Serrano Súñer, Ramón. *Entre Hendaya y Gibraltar: Frente a una leyenda*. Madrid: Ediciones y Publicaciones Españolas, 1947.

Servicio Español de Información. *Lo que los facciosos quieren que se olvide*. Madrid: Servicio Español de Información, 1936.

Servicio Histórico Militar. See also Martínez Bande, Colonel José Manuel.

―――. *Archivo de la Guerra de Liberación*. Documentación Roja. Madrid.

―――. *Partes oficiales de guerra, 1936–1939*. Vol. I: *El Ejército Nacional*. Vol. II: *El Ejército de la República*. Madrid: San Martín, 1977.

Seton-Watson, R. W. *Britain and the Dictators*. New York: Macmillan, 1938.

Sevilla Andrés, Diego. *Historia política de la zona roja*. Madrid: Rialp, 1963.

Sharkey, Paul. *The Friends of Durruti: A Chronology*. Tokyo: Editorial Crisol, 1984.

Shirer, William L. *The Rise and Fall of the Third Reich: A History of Nazi Germany*. New York: Simon and Schuster, 1960.

Shkarenkov, L. K. *Agoniia beloi emigratsii*. Moscow: Mysel, 1981.

Shubert, Adrian. *Hacia la revolución: Orígenes sociales del movimiento obrero en Asturias, 1860–1934*. Barcelona: Grijalbo, 1984.

Shubert, Adrian, and Esenwein, George. *The Spanish Civil War: War of Many Wars*. London: Longmans, 1988.

Sieberer, A. *Espagne contre Espagne*. Geneva: Jeheber, 1937.

Siete de octubre: Una nueva era en el campo. Madrid: Ministerio de Agricultura, 1936.

Sigüenza en 1936 bajo el dominio rojo. Siguenza: Sánchez y Rueda, 1937.

Silex, Karl. *Der Marsch auf Madrid.* Leipzig: Seemann, 1937.

Silva, José. *La revolución popular en el campo.* Valencia: Partido Comunista de España, 1937.

Simon, O. K. *Hitler en Espagne.* Paris: Denoël, 1938.

Simon, Sir John (Lord Templewood). *Retrospect.* London: Hutchinson, 1952.

Siqueiros, David Alfaro. *Me llamaban el coronelazo (memorias).* Mexico City: Biografías Gandesa, 1977.

Smith, Bradley F. *The American Road to Nuremberg: The Documentary Record, 1944–1945.* Stanford: Hoover Press, 1982.

———. *The Road to Nuremberg.* New York: Basic Books, 1981.

Smith, Lois Elwyn. *Mexico and the Spanish Republicans.* Berkeley: University of California Press, 1955.

Snellgrove, L. E. *Franco and the Spanish Civil War.* London: Longmans, Green, 1965.

Sobrequés i Callicó, Jaume, ed. *Història de Catalunya.* Vol. XII. Bilbao: Editorial La Gran Enciclopedia Vasca, 1982.

Sola, Victor María de, and Martel, Carlos. *Estelas gloriosas de la Escuadra Azul.* Cádiz: Ceron, 1937.

———. *Proa a España.* Cádiz: Ceron, 1937.

Solana, Fermin, ed. *Historia parlamentaria del socialismo: Julián Besteiro.* Vols. I, II. Madrid: Taurus, 1975.

*Solano, Wilebaldo. Correspondence with Burnett Bolloten.

*———. "Notas sobre el POUM en la Revolución de 1937: El Período de Clandestinidad." Copy of typescript.

———. *The Spanish Revolution: The Life of Andrés Nin.* London: Independent Labour Party, [1972?].

Soldevila, Ferran, and Bosch Gimpera, Pere. *Història de Catalunya.* Mexico City: Col·lecció Catalònia, 1946.

Solé i Sabaté, Josep M. *La repressió franquista a Catalunya, 1938–1953.* Barcelona: Edicions 62, 1985.

Soler, Juan M. *La guerra en el frente de Aragón.* Barcelona: Mi Revista, 1937.

Solé-Tura, Jordi. *Catalanismo y revolución burguesa.* Madrid: Cuadernos para el Diálogo, 1974.

Sommerfield, John. *Volunteer in Spain.* New York: Knopf, 1937.

Somoza Silva, Lázaro. *El General Miaja: Biografía de un héroe.* Mexico City: Tyris, 1944.

Sonadellas, Concepción. *Clase obrera y revolución social en España, 1936–1939.* Madrid: Zero, 1977.

Soria, Georges. *Guerra y revolución en España.* Vols. I, II, III, IV, V. Barcelona: Grijalbo, 1978.

———. *Trotskyism in the Service of Franco: A Documented Record of Treachery by the POUM in Spain.* London: Lawrence and Wishart, 1938.

Souchère, Eléna de la. *An Explanation of Spain.* New York: Random House, 1964.

Souchy, Agustín. *Anarcho-syndikalisten über Bürgerkrieg und Revolution in Spanien.* Darmstadt: März Verlag, 1969.

*———. Correspondence with Burnett Bolloten.

———. *Entre los campesinos de Aragón.* Barcelona: Tierra y Libertad, 1937.

*———. Interview, notes taken by Burnett Bolloten.

———. *Nacht über Spanien: Bürgerkrieg und Revolution in Spanien*. Darmstadt: Freie Gessellschaft, 1954.

———. *El socialismo libertario*. Havana: Editorial Estudios, 1950.

———. *Los sucesos de Barcelona*. Valencia: Ebro, 1937. (Although this booklet does not bear Souchy's name, it is undoubtedly the original Spanish text of *The Tragic Week in May*, whose title page does carry his name as author.)

———. *The Tragic Week in May*. Barcelona: Oficina de Información Exterior de la CNT-FAI, 1937. See *Los sucesos de Barcelona* for original Spanish text.)

———. *La verdad sobre los sucesos en la retaguardia leal*. Buenos Aires: F.A.C.A., 1937.

Souchy, Agustín, and Folgare, P. *Colectivizaciones: La obra constructiva de la revolución española*. Barcelona: Fontamara, 1977.

Southworth, Herbert R. *Antifalange*. Paris: Ruedo Ibérico, 1967.

———. *La destrucción de Guernica*. Paris: Ruedo Ibérico, 1975.

———. *El mito de la cruzada de Franco*. Barcelona: Plaza y Janés, 1986.

———. *El mito de la cruzada de Franco*. Paris: Ruedo Ibérico, 1963.

———. *Le mythe de la croisade de Franco*. Paris: Ruedo Ibérico, 1964. Revised edition of Spanish text.

Sovetskaia voennaia entsiklopediia. Moscow: Voennoe Izdatel'stva, 1978.

Sovetskie pisateli. Vol. I. Moscow: Gos. Izd-vo Khudozh, Lit-ry, 1959.

The Soviet Diplomatic Corps, 1917–1967. Compiled by the Institute for the Study of the USSR, Munich. Metuchen, N.J.: Scarecrow Press, 1970.

"Soviet newspapers." Translations by X. J. Eudin of articles in *Pravda* and *Izvestiia* (Hoover Institution, Bolloten Collection).

Los Soviets en España: La lucha por el poder, por la república obrera y campesina en España. Paris: Sudam, 1935.

Spain. Consejo nacional de educación premilitar física y cultural de la juventud. *Consejo nacional de educación premilitarfísica y cultural de la juventud*. Valencia: Alerta, 1937.

———. Ministerio de Agricultura. *7 de octubre: Una nueva era en el campo*. Madrid, 1936.

———. Ministerio fiscal. Tribunal Supremo. *Causa general: La dominación roja en España*. Madrid: Ministero de Justicia, 1943.

*———. Ministry of the National Defense: Documents on Battle for Teruel. Confidential reports on the progress of the republican offensive against Teruel, 31 December 1937–8 January 1938, by defense minister Indalecio Prieto. These copies were given to Burnett Bolloten by Francisco Giner de los Ríos, son of the minister of communications.

Spain. London: International Brigade Wounded and Dependents' Aid Committee, 1938.

Spain against the Invaders. London: United Editorial, 1938.

Spain: Catholic and Protestant Priests, Freemasons and Liberals Shot by the Rebels. London: Spanish Embassy, 1937.

Spain Defends Democracy. New York: Workers Library Publishers, 1936.

Spain Emergency Committee Deputations. Deputation to the Prime Minister, 7 Jan., 1939. Deputation to Mr. Atlee, Mr. Alfred Barnes, Sir Archibald Sinclair, 24 Jan., 1939. N.p., n.d.

Spain: Internal and Foreign Affairs, 1930–1939: Confidential U.S. State Department Central Files. Sixty-six microfilm reels. Frederick, Md.: University Publications of America, 1986.

Spain Organises for Victory. London: Communist Party of Great Britain, 1937.

Spain's Democracy Talks to America. New York: American League against War and Fascism, 1936.

Spain's War of Independence. Washington, D.C.: Spanish Embassy, 1938.

Spain's War of Independence: President Azaña, Premier Negrín, Defense Minister Prieto, Alvarez del Vayo, Martínez Barrio, and Portela Valladares Put the Case of the Spanish Republic before the World. Washington, D.C.: Spanish Embassy, 1937.

Spain: The Elections of February 16th, 1936. London: Press Department of the Spanish Embassy, 1936.

Spain: What Next? London: Communist Party of Great Britain, 1939.

"The Spanish Civil War." Six-part TV series, edited by Ronald Fraser, Hugh Thomas, and Javier Tusell. England: Granada Television.

Spanish Communists in the Kremlin and in the White House. n.p., n.d.

Spanish Gold. London: Times Publishing Company, 1937.

Spanish Information Bureau, New York. *American Democracy vs. the Spanish Hierarchy*. New York: Spanish Information Bureau, 1937.

Spender, Stephen. *The Thirties and After: Poetry, Politics, People, 1933–75*. New York: Random House, 1978.

Sperber, Murray A., ed. *And I Remember Spain*. New York: Macmillan, 1974.

SSSR i fashistskaia agressiia v Ispanii: Sbornik dokumentov. Moscow: Gosudarstvennoe Sotsial'no-Ekonomicheskoe Izdatelstvo, 1937.

Stache, Rud. *Armee mit geheimen Auftrag*. Bremen: Henry Burmester, n.d.

Stackelberg, Karl-George von. *Legion Condor: Deutsche Freiwillige in Spanien*. Berlin: Die Heimbücherei, 1939.

Stalin, Iosif. *Sochineniia*. Moscow: OGIZ, Gosdarstvennoe izdatel'stvo politischskoi literatury, 1946–1955. Vol. VII.

Stansky, Peter, and Abrahams, William. *Journey to the Frontier: Two Roads to the Spanish Civil War*. Boston: Little, Brown, 1966.

———. *Orwell: The Transformation*. New York: Knopf, 1980.

———. *The Unknown Orwell*. New York: Knopf, 1972.

Starobin, Joseph. *The Life and Death of an American Hero: The Story of Dave Doran*. New York: New Age, 1938.

Steer, G. L. *The Tree of Gernika*. London: Hodder and Stoughton, 1938.

Stefanov, Boris. "Las Causas de la Derrota de la República Española (en ruso)." Madrid: Archivo Histórico del Comité Central del PCE, Carpeta 58 (in Russian). A photocopy is in the Hoover Institution, Bolloten Collection.

Stimson, Henry L., and Bundy, McGeorge. *On Active Service in Peace and War*. New York: Harper and Bros., 1948.

The Story of the Abraham Lincoln Battalion. New York: Friends of the Abraham Lincoln Battalion, 1937.

Stoye, Johannes. *Spanien im Umbruch*. Berlin: Teubner, 1938.

Straight, Michael. *After Long Silence*. London: Collins, 1983.

Strong, Anna Louise. *Spain in Arms, 1937*. New York: Henry Holt, 1937.

The Struggle in Spain. New York: Fortune, 1937.

Suárez, Andrés [Ignacio Iglesias]. *El proceso contra el POUM.* Paris: Ruedo Ibérico, 1974.

Los sucesos de Barcelona. Valencia: Ebro, 1937. This was without doubt written by Agustín Souchy and is the original text of *The Tragic Week in May*, which bears his name as author.

Los sucesos de mayo en Barcelona. New York: Federación Local de Grupos Libertarios, n.d.

Sueiro, Daniel. *La flota es roja.* Barcelona: Argos Vergara, 1983.

Suero Roca, M. Teresa. *Militares republicanos de la guerra de España.* Barcelona: Península, 1981.

Suero Sánchez, Luciano. *Memorias de un campesino andaluz en la revolución española.* Madrid: Queimada, 1982.

Suñer, Enrique. *Los intelectuales y la tragedia española.* San Sebastian: Editorial Española, 1938.

Sutton, Antony C. *Wall Street and the Rise of Hitler.* Seal Beach, Calif.: '76 Press, 1976.

Symons, Julian. *The Thirties: A Dream Revolved.* London: Cresset, 1960.

Tabouis, Geneviève. *Blackmail or War.* England: Penguin Books, 1938.

———. *Ils l'ont appelée Cassandre.* New York: Editions de la Maison Française, 1942.

Tagüeña Lacorte, Manuel. *Testimonio de dos guerras.* Mexico City: Oasis, 1974.

Talón, Vicente. *Arde Guernica.* Madrid: Toro, 1973.

Tamames, Ramón. *España, 1931–1975: Una antología histórica.* Barcelona: Planeta, 1980.

Tamames, Ramón, et al. *La guerra civil española: Una reflexión moral 50 años después.* Barcelona: Planeta, 1986.

*Tarradellas, José. Correspondence with Burnett Bolloten.

Tarragona, Eduardo. *Las elecciones de 1936 en Cataluña.* Barcelona: Bruguera, 1977.

Tarrés i Claret, Pere. *Diari de guerra, 1938–1939.* Montserrat: Abadia, 1979.

Tasis i Marca, Rafael. *La revolución en los ayuntamientos.* Paris: Associación Hispanophile de France, 1937.

Taylor, A. J. P. *English History, 1914–1945.* New York: Oxford University Press, 1965.

———. *The Origins of the Second World War.* London: Hamilton, 1961.

Taylor, Foster Jay. *The United States and the Spanish Civil War.* New York: Bookman, 1956.

Tedeschi, Paolo. *Guadalajara.* Paris: Coltúra Sociale, 1937.

Templewood, Viscount. See Hoare, Sir Samuel.

Tercer avance del informe oficial sobre los asesinatos, violaciones, incendios y demás depredaciones y violencias cometidas en algunos pueblos del centro y mediodía de España por las hordas marxistas al servicio del llamada gobierno de Madrid. Seville: Estado Español, 1936.

Tercer congreso de la UGT a Catalunya. Informe de Josep del Barrio. Barcelona: Ediciones UGT, 1937.

Téry, Simone. *Front de la liberté.* Paris: Editions Sociales Internationales, 1938.

Thalmann, Clara, and Thalmann, Paul. *Revolution für die Freiheit*. Hamburg: Verlag GMBH, 1976.

Thomas, Hugh. *The Spanish Civil War*. London: Eyre and Spottiswoode, 1961.

_____. *The Spanish Civil War*. Rev. ed. Harmondsworth, England: Penguin Books, 1965.

_____. *The Spanish Civil War*. Rev. ed. New York: Harper and Row, 1977.

Thompson, Dorothy. *Let the Record Speak*. Boston: Houghton Mifflin, 1939.

Thompson, Neville. *The Anti-Appeasers: Conservative Opposition to Appeasement in the 1930s*. Oxford: Clarendon, 1971.

Thorning, Joseph F. *Professor De los Ríos Refutes Himself*. New York: Paulist Press, 1937.

Three Years of Struggle in Spain. London: Freedom Press, 1939.

Tijomírov, Mijaíl I. *El general Lukács: Novela*. Moscow: Progreso, [1953?].

The Times. *The History of the Times*. London: Office of the Times, 1935–1952.

Timmermans, Rodolphe. *Heroes of the Alcázar*. London: Eyre and Spottiswoode, 1937.

Togliatti. Díaz. Carrillo: Los comunistas y la revolución española. Barcelona: Bruguera, 1979.

Togliatti, Palmiro. *Escritos políticos*. Prologue by Adolfo Sánchez Vázquez. Mexico City: Era, 1971.

_____. *Escritos sobre la guerra de España*. Barcelona: Grijalbo, 1980.

Tökés, Rudolf L. *Béla Kun and the Hungarian Soviet Republic*. Stanford: Hoover Institution by F. A. Praeger, 1967.

Tomás, Pascual. *Discurso en el "Gran Prince" de Barcelona, el día 17 de enero de 1937*. Barcelona: Union General de Trabajadores, 1937.

Tommasini, Umberto. *L'anarchico triestino*. Milano: Antistato, 1984.

Torre Enciso, C., and Zegri, D. Muro. *La marcha sobre Barcelona*. Barcelona: Editora Nacional, 1939.

Torres, Estanislau. *La caiguda de Barcelona 1939*. Barcelona: Galba, 1978.

Torriente Brau, Pablo de la. *Peleando con los milicianos*. Mexico City: México Nuevo, 1938.

Toryho, Jacinto. *Del triunfo a la derrota*. Barcelona: Argos Vergara, 1978.

_____. *La independencia de España*. Barcelona: Tierra y Libertad, 1938.

_____. *No eramos tan malos*. Madrid: Toro, 1975.

_____. *La traición del Señor Azaña*. New York: Federación Libertaria, 1939.

Tosstorff, Reiner. "Dïe POUM während des Spanischen Bürgerkriegs, 1936–1939." Inauguraldissertation. (To be published in West Germany.) A copy of the dissertation is in the Hoover Institution, Bolloten Collection.

Toynbee, Arnold J. *The International Repercussions of the War in Spain, 1936–1937*. London: Oxford University Press, 1938.

_____. *Survey of International Affairs, 1936*. London: Oxford University Press, 1937.

Toynbee, Philip. *Friends Apart: A Memoir of Esmond Romilly and Jasper Ridley in the Thirties*. London: Macgibbon and Kee, 1954.

_____, ed. *The Distant Drum*. London: Sidgwick and Jackson, 1976.

Trade Union and Labour Party Members' Delegation to Spain. *Spain 1938: Report*. London: International Brigade Wounded and Dependents' Aid Committee, 1938.

Traina, Richard P. *American Diplomacy and the Spanish Civil War*. Bloomington: Indiana University Press, 1968.

Trautloft, Hannes. *Als Jagdflieger in Spanien*. Berlin: Nauch, n.d.

Trotsky, Leon. *The Case of Leon Trotsky*. New York: Harper and Brothers, 1937.

————. *Escritos sobre España*. Paris: Ruedo Ibérico, 1971.

————. *Leçon d'Espagne*. Paris: Pionniers, 1946.

————. *La révolution espagnole, 1930–40*. Textes recueillis et présentés par Pierre Broué. Paris: Minuit, 1975.

————. *The Spanish Revolution, 1931–39*. New York: Pathfinder, 1973.

Truth about Spain. London: Gollancz, 1938.

Tschapaiew: Das Bataillon der 21 Nationen. Madrid: Torrent, 1938.

Tuñon de Lara, Manuel. *La España del siglo XX, 1914–1939*. Paris: Librería Española, 1973.

————. *Historia de España*. Vol. IX: *La crisis del estado: Dictadura, república, guerra, 1923–1939*. Vol. XII: *Textos y documentos de historia moderna y contemporánea (siglos XVIII–XX)*. Barcelona: Editorial Labor, 1981.

————. *El movimiento obrero en la historia de España*. Madrid: Taurus, 1972.

————. *La II República*. Vols. I, II. Madrid: Siglo Veintiuno, 1976.

————, ed. *La crisis del estado española, 1898–1936*. Madrid: Edicusa, 1978.

————, ed. *La guerra civil española: 50 años después*. Barcelona: Editorial Labor, 1985.

Tusell Gómez, Javier. *Las elecciones del frente popular en España*. Vols. I, II. Madrid: Edicusa, 1974.

————. *Hijos de la sangre*. Madrid: Espsa-Calpe, 1986.

————. *Oligarquía y caciquismo en Andalucía, 1890–1923*. Barcelona: Planeta, 1976.

————, ed. See also Araquistáin, Luis. *Sobre la guerra y en la emigración*.

Tusell Gómez, Javier, et al. *Política y sociedad en la España del siglo XX*. Madrid: Akal, 1978.

*Ubach, Felipe. Interview, notes taken by Burnett Bolloten.

Udina, Ernest. *Josep Tarradellas: L'aventura d'una fidelitat*. Barcelona: Edicions 62, 1978.

UGT: Ple extraordinari del comité nacional, 27–30 octubre 1937, Valencia. Barcelona: UGT, 1937.

Uhse, Bodo. *Die erste Schlacht*. Strasbourg: Prométhée, 1938.

Uj Magyar Lexikon. Budapest: Akademiai Kaido [1959–1962]. Vol. III.

Ulam, Adam B. *Expansion and Coexistence: Soviet Foreign Policy, 1917–73*. New York: Praeger, 1974.

Ulmann, André. *Les darreres hores de la república espanyola*. Montpellier: Agit-Pro PSU, [1939?].

La Unió general de treballadors i la municipalització de serveis. Barcelona: UGT, 1937.

*"Unpublished Article by a Regular Army Corporal." Photostatic copy of original document loaned to Burnett Bolloten by Jordi Arquer.

Urales, Federico. *La anarquía al alcance de todos*. Barcelona: Revista Blanca, 1932.

Urban, Joan Barth. *Moscow and the Italian Communist Party: From Togliatti to Berlinguer*. Ithaca: Cornell University Press, 1987.

Uribarri, Manuel. *El SIM de la República*. Havana: n.p., 1943.

Uribarry Barutell, Manuel. *Sin contestar*. Valencia: Ruig, 1937.

Uribe, Vicente. *Los campesinos y la república*. Valencia: Partido Comunista de España, 1938.

―――. "Memorias" (typescript). Madrid: Archivo Histórico del Comité Central del PCE, Carpeta 60. Photocopy in Hoover Institution, Bolloten Collection.

―――. *Nuestra labor en el campo*. Barcelona: Partido Comunista de España, 1937.

―――. *Nuestros hermanos los campesinos*. Valencia: Partido Comunista de España, 1937.

―――. *La política agraria del partido comunista*. Valencia: Partido Comunista de España, 1937.

―――. *El problema de las nacionalidades en España a la luz de la guerra popular por la independencia de la república española*. n.p.: Ediciones del Partido Comunista de España, n.d.

Urra, Juan. *En las trincheras del frente de Madrid*. Madrid: Fermin Uriarte, 1966.

Usabiaga l'Abbé, Jean. Correspondence with Burnett Bolloten.

U.S. Congress. Senate. Committee on the Judiciary. *Hearing before the Subcommittee to Investigate the Administration of the Internal Security Act*. 83d Cong., 1st sess., 1953.

―――. *The Legacy of Alexander Orlov*. Prepared by the Subcommittee to Investigate the Administration of the Internal Security Act. 93d Cong., 1st sess., 1973. Washington, D.C.: U.S. Government Printing Office, 1973.

―――. *Scope of Soviet Activity in the United States: Hearings before the Subcommittee to Investigate the Administration of the Internal Security Act*. 85th Cong., 1st sess., 1957, 14 and 15 February 1957. Part 51. Washington, D.C.: U.S. Government Printing Office, 1957.

U.S. Department of State. *Documents on German Foreign Policy, 1918–1945*. Series C, Vols. IV, V, VI, and Series D, Vols. I, II, III, IV, V, VI. Washington, D.C.: U.S. Government Printing Office, 1949–83.

―――. *Foreign Relations of the United States: Diplomatic Papers, 1936 and 1937*. Vols. I, II. Washington, D.C.: U.S. Government Printing Office, 1954.

―――. *Nazi-Soviet Relations, 1939–1941: Documents from the Archives of the German Foreign Office*. Edited by Ramond James Sontag and James Stuart Biddie. Washington, D.C.: U.S. Government Printing Office, 1948.

―――. *[Spain:] Internal and Foreign Affairs, 1930–1939: Confidential U.S. State Department Central Files*. Sixty-six microfilm reels. Frederick, Md.: University Publications of America, 1986.

U.S. Office of the Attorney General. *Subversive Activities Control Board*. Docket No. 108-53. Herbert Brownell, Jr., Attorney General of the United States, Petitioner v. Veterans of the Abraham Lincoln Brigade, Respondent. Washington, D.C.: Subversive Activities Control Board, 1955.

Valdés, Miguel. *Informe presentado en la primera conferencia nacional del partido socialista unificado de cataluña, (I.C.) por el secretario de organizacion del c.c.* Barcelona: Agitación y Propaganda del PSUC, 1937.

Valdesoto, Fernando de. *Francisco Franco*. Madrid: Afrodisio Aguado, 1943.

Valera, Fernando. *La república es la revolución española: Discurso pronunciado a millares de ciudadanos el 11 de febrero de 1937 desde el local social de U.R., Valencia*. Valencia, [1937?].

Válgoma, Carlos de. *Mola: La vocación de servicio*. Madrid: Pace, n.d.

Vallescà, Lluhí. *Lluis Companys Jover*. Mexico City: Grafos, 1944.

Van Alstyne, R. W. *American Diplomacy in Action*. Stanford: Stanford University Press, 1944.

Vanni, Ettore. *Yo, comunista en Rusia*. Barcelona: Destino, 1950.

Vansittart, Lord. *The Mist Procession*. London: Hutchinson, 1958.

Varela Rendueles, José. *Rebelión en Sevilla: Memorias de su gobernador rebelde, 1936–1939*. Sevilla: Ayuntamiento, 1982.

Varga, Evgenii S. *Ispaniia v revoluitsii*. Moscow: Gos. Sots.-Ekon. Izd-vo, 1936.

Vaupshasov, Stanislav A. *Na trevozhnykh perekrestkakh: Zapiski chekista*. Moscow: Politizdat, 1971.

Vázquez, Mathilde, and Valero, Javier. *La guerra civil en Madrid*. Madrid: Giner, 1978.

Ventín Pereira, José Augusto. *La guerra de la radio, 1936–1939*. Barcelona: Mitre, 1986.

*Verbatim report of a meeting of political and military leaders on the Aragón front in September 1936 given to Burnett Bolloten by Colonel José Villalba.

Vereeken, Georges. *The GPU in the Trotskyist Movement*. New York: New Park Publications, 1976.

La víctoria exije el partido único del proletariado. Valencia: Partido Comunista de España, 1937.

Vidal, Miguel. "El Campo Español." Decrees of the Ministry of Agriculture and Comments. Unpublished typescript given to Burnett Bolloten by the author, who was an official in the ministry of agriculture during the Civil War.

Vidali, Vittorio. See also Contreras, Carlos J.

————. *La cadutta della repubblica*. Milan: Vangelista, 1979.

————. *Diary of the Twentieth Congress of the Communist Party of the Soviet Union*. Westport: Lawrence Hill, 1984.

*————. Interview, and conversations, notes taken by Burnett Bolloten.

————. *El quinto regimiento*. Mexico City: Grijalbo, 1977.

————. *Spagna lunga battaglia*. Milan: Vangelista, 1975.

Vidarte, Juan-Simeón. *El bienio negro y la insurrección de Asturias*. Barcelona: Grijalbo, 1978.

————. *Todos fuimos culpables*. Mexico City: Fondo de Cultura Económica, 1973.

Viereck, Peter. *Shame and Glory of the Intellectuals*. Boston: Beacon Press, 1953.

Vignaux, Paul. *Manuel de Irujo: Ministre de la république dans la guerre d'Espagne, 1936–1939*. Paris: Beauchesne, 1986.

Vigón, General Jorge. *General Mola: El conspirador*. Barcelona: AHR, 1957.

————. *Milicia y política*. Madrid: Instituto de Estudios Políticos, 1957.

Vilanova, Antonio. *La defensa del Alcázar de Toledo*. Mexico City: Mexicanos Unidos, 1963.

Vilar, Pierre. *La guerra civil española*. Barcelona: Crítica, 1986.

————. *Historia de España*. Barcelona: Grijalbo, 1979.

*Villalba, Colonel José. Report on the fall of Malaga to the Higher War Council, dated 12 February 1937. Typewritten copy of original document loaned to Burnett Bolloten by Colonel Villalba.

Villanueva, Francisco. *Azaña, el gobierno*. Mexico City: Moderna, 1941.

Villar, Manuel. *España en la ruta de la libertad*. Buenos Aires: Reconstruir, 1962.

Villarroya i Font, Joan. *Els bombardeigs de Barcelona durant la guerra civil, 1936–1939*. Montserrat: Abadia de Montserrat, 1981.

Viñas, Angel. *La Alemania nazi y el 18 de julio*. Madrid: Alianza, 1977.
*_____. Correspondence with Burnett Bolloten.
_____. *Guerra, Dinero, Dictadura*. Barcelona: Grijalbo, 1984.
_____. *El oro de Moscú*. Barcelona: Grijalbo, 1979.
_____. *El oro español en la guerra civil*. Madrid: Instituto de Estudios Fiscales. Ministerio de Hacienda, 1976.
Viñas, Ricard. *La formación de las juventudes socialistas unificadas, 1934–1936*. Madrid: Siglo XXI, 1978.
Vita, A. de. *Battaglione Garibaldi, ottobre 1936–aprile 1937*. Paris: Coltúra Sociale, 1937.
Vmeste s patriotami ispanii. Kiev: Politicheskaia Literatura, 1976.
The Voice of the Church in Spain. London: Burns Oates and Washbourne, 1937.
Volta, Sandro. *Spagna a ferro e fuoco*. Florence: Vallecchi, 1937.
Volunteer for Liberty. Edited by Ralph Bates, Edwin Rolfe, and John Tisa. New York: Veterans of the Abraham Lincoln Brigade, 1949. Organ of the English-speaking battalions of the International Brigades. Reproduction of complete collection from 24 May 1937 through 7 November 1938.
Vorobev, Evgenii. *Ia ne boius' ne byt': Dokumental'naia povest' o geroe Sovetskogo Soiuza Pole Armane*. Moscow: Politicheskaia Literatura, 1982.
Voros, Sandor. *American Commissar*. Philadelphia: Chilton, 1961.
Watson, Keith Scott. *Single in Spain*. London: Barker, 1937.
Weinberg, Gerhard L. *The Foreign Policy of Hitler's Germany: Diplomatic Revolution in Europe, 1933–1936*. Chicago: University of Chicago Press, 1970.
_____. *The Foreign Policy of Hitler's Germany, 1937–1939*. Chicago: University of Chicago Press, 1980.
_____. *Germany and the Soviet Union*. Leiden: Brill, 1954.
Weintraub, Stanley. *The Last Great Cause: The Intellectuals and the Spanish Civil War*. New York: Weybright and Talley, 1968.
Weizsäcker, Ernst von. *Memoirs of Ernst von Weizsäcker*. Chicago: Regnery, 1951.
Welles, Sumner. *The Time for Decision*. New York: Harper, 1944.
Wendt, Bernd Jürgen. *Economic Appeasement: Handel und Finanz in der britischen Deutschland-Politik, 1933–1939*. Düsseldorf: Bertelsmann Universität Verlag, 1971.
Werth, Alexander. *Which Way France?* New York: Harper, 1937.
We Saw in Spain. London: Labour Party, 1937.
Wheeler-Bennett, John W. *Munich: Prologue to Tragedy*. New York: Duell, Sloan and Pearce, 1948.
Who's Who in the Socialist Countries. New York and Munich: Saur, 1978.
Who Was Who in the USSR. Metuchen, N.J.: Scarecrow Press, 1972.
Who Was Who, 1961–1970. New York: St. Martin's, 1972.
Wintringham, Tom. *English Captain*. London: Faber and Faber, 1939.
Wojna narodoworewolucyjna Hiszpanii. Warsaw: Wydawnictwo ministerstwa brony Narodowej [1979].
Wolfe, Bertram D. *Civil War in Spain*. New York: Workers' Age, 1937.
_____. *Khrushchev and Stalin's Ghost*. New York: Praeger, 1957.
Wolfers, A. *Britain and France between Two Wars*. New York: Harcourt Brace, 1940.
Wood, Neal. *Communism and British Intellectuals*. New York: Columbia University Press, 1959.

Woodcock, George. *Anarchism: A History of Libertarian Ideas and Movements*. Cleveland: World Publishing Company, 1962.

Wrench, John Evelyn. *Geoffrey Dawson and Our Times*. Foreword by The Rt. Hon. Earl of Halifax. London: Hutchinson, 1955.

Wyden, Peter. *The Passionate War*. New York: Simon and Schuster, 1983.

Yagüe, María Eugenia. *Santiago Carrillo, perfil humano y político*. Madrid: Cambio 16, 1977.

Yakovlev, Alexander. *The Aim of a Lifetime*. Moscow: Progress, 1972.

Young, G. M. *Stanley Baldwin*. London: Rupert Hart-Davis, 1952.

Ypsilon [Julian Gumperz and Robert Rindl]. *Pattern for World Revolution*. Chicago-New York: Ziff Davis, 1947.

Zaculúa, Juan Antonio. *La resistencia socialista en Asturias, 1937*. Madrid: Fundación Pablo Iglesias, 1986.

Zahn, Michael. "Der spanische Anarchosyndikalismus." Dissertation. Self published, 1979. Copy at Stanford University.

Zamacois, Eduardo. *El asedio de Madrid*. Havana: Aurora, 1939.

———. *Crónicas de la guerra*. Valencia: Subsecretaria de Propaganda, 1937.

Zambrano, María. *Los intelectuales en el drama de España*. Santiago: Panorama, 1937.

Zaragoza, Cristóbal. *Ejército popular y militares de la república, 1936–1939*. Prólogo de Ramón Garriga. Barcelona: Planeta, 1983.

Zilliacus, Konni ("Vigilantes"). *Between Two Wars*. Harmondsworth, England: Penguin, 1939.

———. *Why We Are Losing the Peace*. London: Gollancz, 1939.

Zilmanovich, Dmitrii Iakovlevich. *Na orbite bolshoi zhizni: Dokumentalno-memuarnoe povestvovanie o dvazhdy geroe Sovetskogo Soiuza Ia. V. Smushkeviche*. Vilnius: Mintis, 1971.

Zugazagoitia, Julián. *Historia de la guerra en España*. Buenos Aires: La Vanguardia, 1940.

II. Newspapers and Periodicals

This list includes only those newspapers and periodicals that have been referred to in the text or notes. The material cited can be found in that section of the Bolloten Spanish Civil War Collection comprising bound newspapers, clippings, typewritten copies, photocopies, and microfilm housed in the library and archives of the Hoover Institution. See Section I for entries under Bolloten (clippings and microfilm).

ABC, Madrid.

ABC, Seville.

Acción Libertaria: Boletín Informativo sobre España, Buenos Aires.

Acción Socialista, Paris.

Acracia, Lérida.

L'Action Française, Paris.

Adelante, Alicante.

Adelante, Marseilles.

Adelante, Mexico City.

Adelante, Valencia.
El Adelanto, Salamanca.
L'Adunata dei Refrattari, New York.
Ahora, Madrid.
A.I.T. Servicio de Prensa, Stockholm.
The Alarm, San Francisco.
El Amigo del Pueblo, Barcelona.
Anarchist Review, Orkney.
Anarquía, Barcelona.
Antioch Review, Yellow Springs, Ohio.
Atlantic Monthly, Boston.
Avant, Barcelona.
La Batalla, Barcelona.
La Batalla, Paris.
BEIPI, Paris.
Boletín de Información (CNT National Committee), Valencia.
Boletín de Información, CNT-FAI, Barcelona.
Boletín de Información y Orientación Orgánica del Comité Peninsular de la Federación Anarquista Ibérica, Barcelona.
Boletín de Orientación Bibliográfica, Madrid.
Boletín Oficial del Estado, Burgos.
Butlletí del Partit Socialista Català, Mexico City.
Butlletí Oficial de la Generalitat de Catalunya, Barcelona.
Cahiers de l'Humanisme Libertaire, Paris.
Cahiers de l'I.S.E.A., La Rochelle.
Cahiers Leon Trotsky, Paris.
Cambio 16, Madrid.
Canadian Forum, Toronto (Public Library of Toronto).
Canarias, Las Palmas.
Candide, Paris.
Carta del Este, Madrid.
Castilla Libre, Madrid.
Catalunya, Barcelona.
Cenit, Toulouse.
Ce Soir, Paris.
Claridad, Madrid.
CNT, Madrid.
CNT, Paris.
CNT, Toulouse.
CNT-FAI-AIT Informationsdienst, Barcelona.
Colectivismo, Valencia.
Combat, Paris.
El Combatiente Rojo, Madrid.
Le Combat Syndicaliste, Paris.
Commonweal, New York.
The Communist International, London.
El Comunista, Madrid.
Congreso de los Diputados. Deputación Permanente, Valencia, Barcelona, Paris.

La Continental Obrera, Santiago, Chile.
Correo de Asturias, Buenos Aires.
La Correspondance Internationale, Paris.
La Correspondencia de Valencia, Valencia.
La Correspondencia Internacional, Paris.
Cuadernos para el Diálogo, Madrid.
Cuadernos Socialistas, Toulouse.
IV Internacional, Mexico City.
Cultura Proletaria, New York.
Cultura y Acción, Alcañiz.
Daily Express, London.
Daily Herald, London.
Daily Mail, London.
The Daily Telegraph, London.
Daily Worker, London.
Daily Worker, New York.
El Debate, Madrid.
Democracia, Madrid.
La Dépêche, Toulouse.
El Día Gráfico, Barcelona.
Dialéctica, Havana.
Diari de Barcelona, Barcelona.
Diario de Burgos, Burgos.
Diario de las Sesiones de Cortes, Madrid.
Diario de Sesiones de la Diputación Permanente de las Cortes, Madrid, Valencia, Barcelona, Paris.
Diari Oficial de la Generalitat de Catalunya, Barcelona.
Diario Oficial del Ministerio de Defensa Nacional, Valencia (later Barcelona).
Diario Oficial del Ministerio de la Guerra, Madrid (later Valencia).
Documentos Históricos de España, Buenos Aires.
Economies et Sociétés, Paris.
Encounter, London.
Enllà, Mexico City.
Ercilla, Santiago, Chile.
L'Ere Nouvelle, Paris.
Esfuerzo, Barcelona.
Espagne Antifasciste, Paris.
Espagne Nouvelle, Montpellier.
España Libre, New York.
España Libre, Paris.
España Libre, Toulouse.
España Nueva, Mexico City.
España Popular, Mexico City.
España Republicana, Buenos Aires.
Espoir, Toulouse.
European Studies Review, London.
Fight, London.
Foreign Affairs, New York.

Le Forze Armate, Rome.
IV International, Mexico.
Fragua Social, Valencia.
Frente Libertario, Madrid.
Frente Rojo, Valencia. [Published in Barcelona in November 1937, and in Figueras and Port Bou in February 1939.]
Frente y Retaguardia. [Place of publication not indicated.]
Full Català, Mexico City.
Gaceta de la República, Valencia, Barcelona.
Gaceta de Madrid, Madrid.
Il Grido del Populo, Paris.
Guerra di Classe, Barcelona.
Guión, Madrid.
Hansard, London.
Heraldo de Aragón, Saragossa.
Hispanic American Report, Stanford.
The Historian, London.
Historia 16, Madrid.
Historia y Vida, Barcelona.
Hoja Oficial del Lunes, Barcelona.
Hoy, Mexico City.
La Humanitat, Barcelona.
L'Humanité, Paris.
Ideal, Granada.
Ideas, Hospitalet.
Independent News, Paris.
Indice, Madrid.
Informaciones, Madrid.
Información Española, Madrid.
Information Bulletin (International Bureau for the Fourth International), New York.
Inquiétudes, Bordeaux.
Internacional, Paris.
International Labor and Working Class History, Yale.
International Press Correspondence.
L'Intransigeant, Paris.
Izvestiia, Moscow.
Le Jour, Paris.
Journal des Débats, Paris.
Journal of Contemporary History, London.
Journal of Modern History, London.
Justicia Social, Barcelona.
Juventud de España, Mexico City.
Juventud Libre, Madrid.
Komsomolskaya Pravda, Moscow.
The Labour Monthly, London.
Left News, London.
Left Review, London.
La Libertad, Madrid.

Le Libertaire, Paris.
Life, Chicago.
Linea de Fuego, Pueblo de Valverde.
Listener, London.
Llibertat, Mataró.
Lluita, Paris.
La Lutte Ouvrière, Paris.
Luz y Fuerza, Barcelona.
Man!, Los Angeles.
The Manchester Guardian, Manchester.
Mar y Tierra, Altea.
El Mercantil Valenciano, Valencia.
Milicia Popular, Madrid.
Modern Monthly, New York.
Mujeres Libres, Barcelona.
Mundo, Mexico City.
Mundo Obrero, Madrid.
Mundo Obrero, Paris.
Nada Cuadernos Internacionales, Barcelona.
The Nation, New York.
The National Review, London.
The New International, New York.
The New Leader, London.
New Masses, New York.
New Militant, New York.
The New Republic, New York.
The News Chronicle, London.
The News of Spain, New York.
The New Statesman and Nation, London.
The New York Herald Tribune, New York.
The New York Post, New York.
The New York Review of Books, New York.
The New York Times, New York.
La Noche, Barcelona.
El Norte de Castilla, Valladolid.
Nosotros, Valencia.
Las Noticias, Barcelona.
El Noticiero, Saragossa.
El Noticiero Universal, Barcelona.
La Nouvelle Espagne Antifasciste, Paris.
Novyi Mir, Moscow.
Nuestra Bandera, Barcelona.
Nuestra Bandera, Paris.
Nuestra España, Havana.
El Obrero de la Tierra, Madrid.
The Observer, London.
Orientaciones Nuevas, Granollers.
Orto, Barcelona.

L'Osservatore Romano, Vatican City.
El País, Madrid.
Pasaremos, Madrid.
El Pensamiento Navarro, Pamplona.
El Poble Català, Mexico City.
Política, Madrid.
Il Pòpolo d'Italia, Rome.
Pravda, Moscow.
La Publicitat, Barcelona.
Pueblo, Madrid.
El Pueblo, Valencia.
Quatrième Internationale, Paris.
Radio Liberty Research, Munich, New York.
Reader's Digest, Pleasantville.
Recerques, Esplugues de Llobregat.
Reconstruir, Buenos Aires.
Regeneración, Mexico City.
La République, Paris.
Le Reveil, Geneva.
The Review, Brussels.
The Review of Politics, Notre Dame, Indiana.
La Revista Blanca, Barcelona.
Revista del Occidente, Madrid.
Revista Histórica y Vida, Madrid.
La Révolution Prolétarienne, Paris.
Il Risveglio Anarchico, Geneva.
Rumbos Nuevos, Havana.
Ruta, Barcelona.
Saturday Evening Post, Philadelphia.
Saturday Review, New York.
Screen, London.
Service d'Information et de Presse por la Quatrième Internationale, Paris.
Slavic Review, Washington, D.C.
El Socialista, Algiers.
El Socialista, Madrid.
El Socialista, Paris.
El Socialista Español, Paris.
Socialist Appeal, New York.
Socialist Review, New York.
El Sol, Madrid.
Solidaridad Obrera, Barcelona.
Solidaridad Obrera, Mexico City.
Solidaridad Obrera, Paris.
Sotsialisticheskii Vestnik, Berlin, Paris, New York.
Soviet News, London.
Die Soziale Revolution, Barcelona.
Spain, London.
Spain and the World, London.

Spanish Labor Bulletin, Chicago.
Spanish Revolution, Barcelona.
Spanish Revolution, New York.
Spartacus, Alicante.
The Sunday Times, London.
Survey, London.
Le Temps, Paris.
Tiempo, Mexico City.
Tiempo de Historia, Madrid.
Tiempos Nuevos, Barcelona.
Tierra y Libertad, Barcelona.
Tierra y Libertad, Mexico City.
The Times, London.
The Times Literary Supplement, London.
Timón, Barcelona.
Timón, Buenos Aires.
Treball, Barcelona.
Tribuna, Mexico City.
Triunfo, Madrid.
Ultima Hora, Barcelona.
Umanità Nova, Rome.
Umbral, Barcelona.
Unión, Seville.
El Universal, Mexico City.
Universal Gráfico, Mexico City.
Universo, Toulouse.
Unser Wort, Brussels.
Vanguard, New York.
La Vanguardia, Barcelona.
Vanguardia, Mexico City.
Verdad, Valencia.
La Veu de Catalunya, Barcelona.
Vía Libre, New York.
Voelkischer Beobachter, Berlin.
Voenno-Istorischeskii Zhurnal, Moscow.
The Volunteer for Liberty, Madrid, Barcelona.
La Voz Lenista, Barcelona.
La Voz Valenciana, Valencia.
Vu, Paris.
Washington Post, Washington, D.C.
Die Wehrmacht, Berlin.
Workers' Age, New York.
World Affairs Report, Stanford.
Ya, Madrid.

Acknowledgments

Diego Abad de Santillán.
Martha Ackelsberg.
Francisco Aguiler.
José Antonio Aguirre.
Víctor Alba.
Marcos Alcón.
Jay Allen.
José Almudi.
Michael Alpert.
Jon Amsden.
Eustaquio Aparicio Bo ("Alfageme").
Luis Araquistáin.
Archivo Histórico del Comité Central del PCE, Madrid.
Archivo Histórico Nacional, Madrid.
Archivo Histórico Nacional, Salamanca.
Jordi Arquer.
General José Asensio.
Aymá, S.A.
Marjorie Bailey.
Jaime Balius.
Arturo Barea.
Ilsa Barea.
Lewis Bateman (see preface).
Ralph Bates.
Nicolás Bernal.
Linda Bernard.
Biblioteca Nacional, Madrid.
Biblioteca Universitaria de Barcelona.
Bibliothèque Nationale de Paris.
Roger Bland.
Betty F. Bolloten (see preface).
Gladys Bolloten (see preface).
Greg Bolloten (see preface).

Georges Borchardt, Inc.
Anna Bourquina.
Gerald Brenan.
The British Museum (Newspaper Library).
Ellen H. Brow.
Ronald Bulatoff.
José Bullejos.
Carmen de la Cal Mata.
Cambridge University Press.
Severino Campos.
Captain Aniceto Carbajal.
F. P. Carbajal.
Mariano Cardona Rosell.
Raymond Carr.
Wenceslao Carrillo.
Ralph H. Carruthers.
José Caruana y Gómez de Barreda.
Mariano Casasús Lacasta.
Enrique Castro.
Josefina Cedilla.
Centre International de Recherches sur l'Anarchisme, Geneva.
Pedro Checa.
Ricardo de la Cierva y de Hoces.
María Cifuentes.
José Clavería Prenafeta.
Montserrat Condomines Pereña.
Robert Conquest.
Larry Cott.
James Crafts.
Luis G. Cubero.
Curtis Brown.
Elena Danielson.
David and Charles (Holdings) Ltd. (Agents for Richard A. H. Robinson).
Midge Decter.
Moshe Decter.
Bernard Denham.
María Teresa Diez de los Ríos.
Milorad M. Drachkovitch.
Duell, Sloan and Pearce.
Thea Duijker.
José Duque.
Ediciones Oasis.
Les Editions Denoël.
Editorial Juventud.
Editorial La Vanguardia.
Editorial Losada.
Editorial Sudamericana.
Marianne Enckell.

Sylvia England.
John Erickson.
Robb Ernst.
Luis Escobar de la Serna.
Antonio Escribano.
George Esenwein (see preface).
Xenia J. Eudin.
Faber and Faber.
Febus news agency.
Ramón Fernández-Pousa Gil.
F. Ferrándiz Alborz.
Miguel Ferrer.
Gerritt E. Fielstra.
H. H. Fisher.
Manuel Fraga Iribarne.
Fundación Francisco Largo Caballero, Madrid.
Fundación Pablo Iglesias, Madrid.
Jesús de Galíndez.
Gabriel García Maroto.
Juan García Oliver.
J. García Pradas.
Alejandro García Val.
Antonio Garrigues Díaz-Cañabate.
Antoni Gilabert.
Francisco Giral.
José Giral.
Naida Glick.
Victor Gollancz, Ltd.
Colonel Juan B. Gómez.
F. González.
Efraín González Luna.
Antonio González Quintana.
Julián Gorkin.
Charles L. Grace.
Jorge Gracia.
Granada Publishing.
Pedro F. Grande (see preface).
Howard Green.
Rachel and Robert Green.
Isabel Guardiola.
Harcourt, Brace and Company.
Harper and Row.
Harvard College Library, Cambridge, Mass.
A. M. Heath and Company.
William Heinemann Ltd.
Hemeroteca Municipal de Madrid.
Hemeroteca Nacional, Madrid.
Luis Hernández.

Severiano Hernández.
General Ignacio Hidalgo de Cisneros.
Ronald Hilton (see preface).
Donald C. Holmes.
Henry Holt and Company.
Hoover Institution on War, Revolution, and Peace, Stanford University (Library and
    archives staff).
Editorial Hoy.
Ignacio Iglesias.
Ramón Iglesias.
Agnes Inglis.
Institut Municipal d'História, Barcelona.
International Institute of Social History, Amsterdam.
Andrés María de Irujo.
Manuel de Irujo.
Gabriel Jackson.
David Jaffe.
Miguel Jiménez.
Verle B. Johnston.
Rudolf de Jong.
Charles F. Keyser.
Kiepenheuer and Witsch.
Jaap Kloosterman.
Alfred A. Knopf.
Hilja Kukk (see preface).
Rosemary Kurpuis.
Katia Landau.
Pilar Leon Tello.
Gaston Leval.
Lena Lever.
Ramón Liarte.
Le Libertaire.
Librarie Plon.
The Library of Congress, Washington, D.C.
Francisca Linares de Vidarte.
Rudolfo Llopis.
El Marqués Juan Ignacio Luca de Tena.
Enrique Lumen.
Robert M. McBride and Company.
McGraw-Hill Book Company.
Philip T. McLean.
The Macmillan Press, London and Basingstoke.
Salvador de Madariaga.
Edward E. Malefakis.
Herbert Marshall.
J. Martín Blázquez.
Justo Martínez Amutio.
Colonel José Manuel Martínez Bande.

Pedro Martínez Cartón.
Salvador Martínez Dasi.
Aurelio Martín Nájera.
Valerio Más.
José Manuel Mata.
Alvaro Menéndez.
Leonora Menéndez Beltrán.
General José Miaja.
Harry Milton.
Ministerio de Cultura, Madrid.
Frank Mintz.
Federica Montseny.
Constancia de la Mora.
Felix Morrow.
William Morrow and Company.
Eusebio Mujal-Leon.
G. Munis (Manuel Grandizo Munis).
José Muñoz López.
Joaquím Nadal Farreras.
Luciano J. Navas (see preface).
Margarita Nelken.
New York Public Library.
Jack Norpel (Director of Research, U.S. Senate Security Subcommittee).
Paul North Rice (New York Public Library).
W. W. Norton and Company.
Ohio State University Press.
Eduardo Orozco y G. ("El Pintor").
Sonia Brownell Orwell.
Carlos Otero.
María Otero-Boisvert.
Oxford University Press.
Randolfo Pacciardi.
H. S. Parsons.
D. Pastor Petit.
Concha Patiño.
Arline B. Paul.
Stanley G. Payne (see preface).
José Peirats.
Pennsylvania State University Press.
Colonel Jesús Pérez Salas.
Arturo Perucho.
A. D. Peters and Company.
Agnes F. Peterson.
Melody Phillips.
D. Wingeate Pike (see preface).
Librairie Plon.
Luis Ponce de Leon.
Porrua Hermanos y Cia.

Eugene B. Power.
General Sebastián Pozas.
Javier Pradera (see preface).
Jacobo Prince.
Putnam and Company.
Alfonso Quintana y Pena.
Vicente Ramos.
A. Ramos Oliveira.
Reader's Digest.
Gustav Regler.
Ludwig Renn.
Reynal and Hitchcock.
Warner Rice.
Vernon Richards.
Ricardo del Río.
Miguel Robledo.
Benigno Rodríguez.
Helmut Ruediger.
Andrés Saborit.
María del Carmen Salas Larrazábal.
Heleno Saña.
Felipe Sánchez Román.
Editorial San Martín.
William T. Sayre-Smith.
Günther Schmigalle.
Stephen Schwartz (see preface).
Manuel Schwartzmann.
Charles Scribner's Sons.
Paul Seabury (see preface).
Martin Secker and Warburg.
Miguel Serra Pamies.
Servicio Histórico Militar, Madrid.
Mark Sharron.
Adrian Shubert.
Simon and Schuster.
David Alfaro Siqueiros.
Wilebaldo Solano.
Helen Solanum.
Agustín Souchy.
Stanford University Library.
Stanford University Press.
Luis Suárez.
Leopoldo Suárez del Real.
Alma Tapia.
José Tarradellas.
Clara Thalman.
Arne Thorne.
Carol Tonge.

Pauline B. Tooker (see preface).
Toronto Public Library.
Mathilda de la Torre.
Reiner Tosstorff.
Hugh Trevor-Roper, The Lord Dacre of Glanton.
Felipe Ubach.
Joan Connelly Ullman (see preface).
University of California Library, Berkeley.
University of California Library, San Diego.
University of Michigan Library, Ann Arbor.
University of Michigan Press.
University of North Carolina Press (editorial and administrative staff).
Cristina Usón.
Pilar Varela.
Margarita Vázquez de Parga.
Manuel Vidal.
Vittorio Vidali (Carlos Contreras).
The Viking Press.
José Villalba.
Antonio Villanueva.
Angel Viñas.
Pedro Voltes Bou.
Barbara I. Walker (see preface).
George Weller.
Bertram D. Wolfe.
Ella Wolfe (see preface).
Yale University Press.
Victor Zaragoza.

Index

See Author's Note (Proper Names), pp. xxii–xxiii.